Key to map symbols

Physical features

Elevation

- 6000m/19,686ft
- 4000m/13,124ft
- 3000m/9843ft
- 2000m/6562ft
- 1,000m/3281ft
- 500m/1640ft
- 250m/820ft
- 0
- Below sea level

△ Mountain

▽ Depression

⌂ Volcano

)(Pass/tunnel

Sandy desert

Drainage features

——— Major perennial river

——— Minor perennial river

– – – Seasonal river

——— Canal

| Waterfall

Perennial lake

Seasonal lake

Wetland

Ice features

Permanent ice cap/ice shelf

Winter limit of pack ice

Summer limit of pack ice

Borders

——— Full international border

– – – – Disputed de facto border

· · · · · Territorial claim border

×–×–× Cease-fire line

– – – Undefined boundary

——— Internal administrative boundary

Communications

——— Major road

——— Minor road

——— Rail

✈ International airport

Settlements

⊡ Above 500,000

⊙ 100,000 to 500,000

○ 50,000 to 100,000

○ Below 50,000

● National capital

● Internal administrative capital

Miscellaneous features

+ Site of interest

ⁿⁿⁿⁿⁿ Ancient wall

Graticule features

——— Line of latitude/longitude/ Equator

– – – Tropic/Polar circle

25° Degrees of latitude/ longitude

Names

Physical features

Andes	
Sahara	Landscape features
Ardennes	
Land's End	Headland
Mont Blanc 4,807m	Elevation/volcano/pass
Blue Nile	River/canal/waterfall
Ross Ice Shelf	Ice feature
PACIFIC OCEAN	
Sulu Sea	Sea features
Palk Strait	
Chile Rise	Undersea feature

Regions

FRANCE	Country
JERSEY (to UK)	Dependent territory
KANSAS	Administrative region
Dordogne	Cultural region

Settlements

PARIS	Capital city
SAN JUAN	Dependent territory capital city
Chicago	
Kettering	Other settlements
Burke	

Inset map symbols

Urban area

City

Park

■ Place of interest

□ Suburb/district

C O M P A C T
ATLAS
O F   T H E   W O R L D

Contents

The World Atlas

North &
Central America

South America

Africa

Europe

COMPACT ATLAS

OF THE WORLD

LONDON, NEW YORK, MELBOURNE, MUNICH, DELHI

LONDON, NEW YORK, MELBOURNE, MUNICH, DELHI

PUBLISHER
Jonathan Metcalf

ART DIRECTOR
Bryn Walls

MANAGING CARTOGRAPHER
David Roberts

SENIOR CARTOGRAPHIC EDITOR
Simon Mumford

PROJECT CARTOGRAPHER
Paul Eames

PROJECT DESIGN
Nimbus Design, Langworth, UK

SYSTEMS CO-ORDINATOR
Philip Rowles

PRODUCTION
Sophie Argyris

First published in Great Britain in 2001
by Dorling Kindersley Limited
80 Strand, London WC2R 0RL

A CIP catalogue record for this book is available from the British Library

ISBN 9-7814-0532-9033

Reprographics by MDP Ltd, Wiltshire, UK
Printed and bound by Star Standard, Singapore

see our complete catalogue at www.dk.com

North & West Asia

South & East Asia

Australasia & Oceania

Index – Gazetteer

The Political World

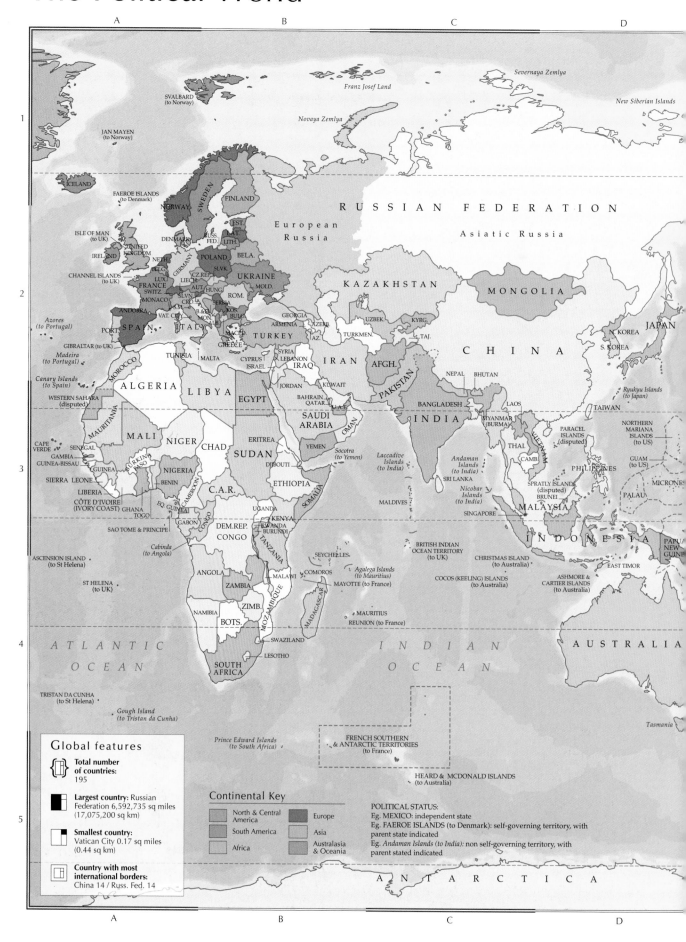

Global features

Total number of countries: 195

Largest country: Russian Federation 6,592,735 sq miles (17,075,200 sq km)

Smallest country: Vatican City 0.17 sq miles (0.44 sq km)

Country with most international borders: China 14 / Russ. Fed. 14

Continental Key

- North & Central America
- South America
- Africa
- Europe
- Asia
- Australasia & Oceania

POLITICAL STATUS:

Eg. MEXICO: independent state

Eg. FAEROE ISLANDS (to Denmark): self-governing territory, with parent state indicated

Eg. *Andaman Islands (to India)*: non self-governing territory, with parent stated indicated

The Physical World

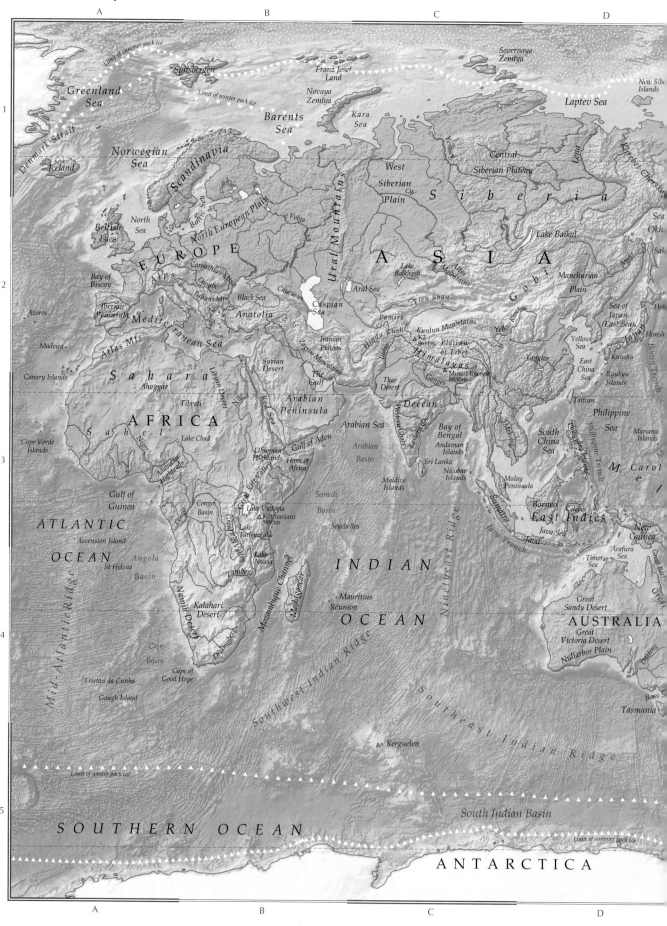

A   B   C   D

Limit of summer pack ice

Spitsbergen

Franz Josef Land

Severnaya Zemlya

Limit of winter pack ice

New Siberian Islands

1

Greenland Sea

Novaya Zemlya

Barents Sea

Kara Sea

Laptev Sea

Denmark Strait

Iceland

Norwegian Sea

Scandinavia

West Siberian Plain

Central Siberian Plateau

Lena

Kolyma

Ob

Yenisey

British Isles

North Sea

Baltic Sea

North European Plain

Volga

Ural Mountains

S i b e r i a

Lake Baikal

Sea of Okh

Sak

Bay of Biscay

Alps

Carpathian Mts

EUROPE

Danube

Balkans Mts

Black Sea

Caucasus

Caspian Sea

Aral Sea

A S I A

Lake Balkhash

Altai Mountains

Amur

Manchurian Plain

2

Azores

Iberian Peninsula

Anatolia

Pamirs

Tien Shan

Sea of Japan (East Sea)

Hok

Madeira

Atlas Mts

Mediterranean Sea

Iranian Plateau

Zagros Mountains

Hindu Kush

Kunlun Mountains

K2 8611m

Yellow River

Plateau of Tibet

Yangtze

Yellow Sea

Kyushu

Honshu

Ryukyu Islands

Canary Islands

S a h a r a

Ahaggar

Libyan Desert

Syrian Desert

The Gulf

Red Sea

Thar Desert

Ganges

Himalayas

Mount Everest 8850m

Deccan

East China Sea

Taiwan

Philippine Sea

Mariana Islands

3

Cape Verde Islands

S a h e l

Niger

Lake Chad

Nile

Arabian Peninsula

AFRICA

Tibesti

Adamawa Highlands

Ethiopian Highlands

Gulf of Aden

Horn of Africa

Arabian Sea

Arabian Basin

Western Ghats

Eastern Ghats

Bay of Bengal

Andaman Islands

Sri Lanka

Nicobar Islands

Maldive Islands

Mekong

South China Sea

Malay Peninsula

Philippine Islands

Philippine Trench

M Carol

Gulf of Guinea

Congo Basin

Congo

Great Rift Valley

Lake Victoria

Kilimanjaro 5895m

Somali Basin

Seychelles

Borneo

Celebes

East Indies

New Guinea

ATLANTIC

Ascension Island

St Helena

Angola Basin

Lake Tanganyika

Lake Nyasa

Zambezi

INDIAN

Sumatra

Java Sea

Java

Java Trench

Arafura Sea

Timor Sea

Great Bar

OCEAN

Mid-Atlantic Ridge

Namib Desert

Kalahari Desert

Okavango

Mozambique Channel

Madagascar

Mauritius

Réunion

OCEAN

Great Sandy Desert

AUSTRALIA

Great Victoria Desert

Nullarbor Plain

Darling

4

Cape Basin

Tristan da Cunha

Gough Island

Cape of Good Hope

Southwest Indian Ridge

Southeast Indian Ridge

Bass

Tasmania

Limit of winter pack ice

Kerguelen

5

South Indian Basin

SOUTHERN OCEAN

Limit of summer pack ice

ANTARCTICA

A   B   C   D

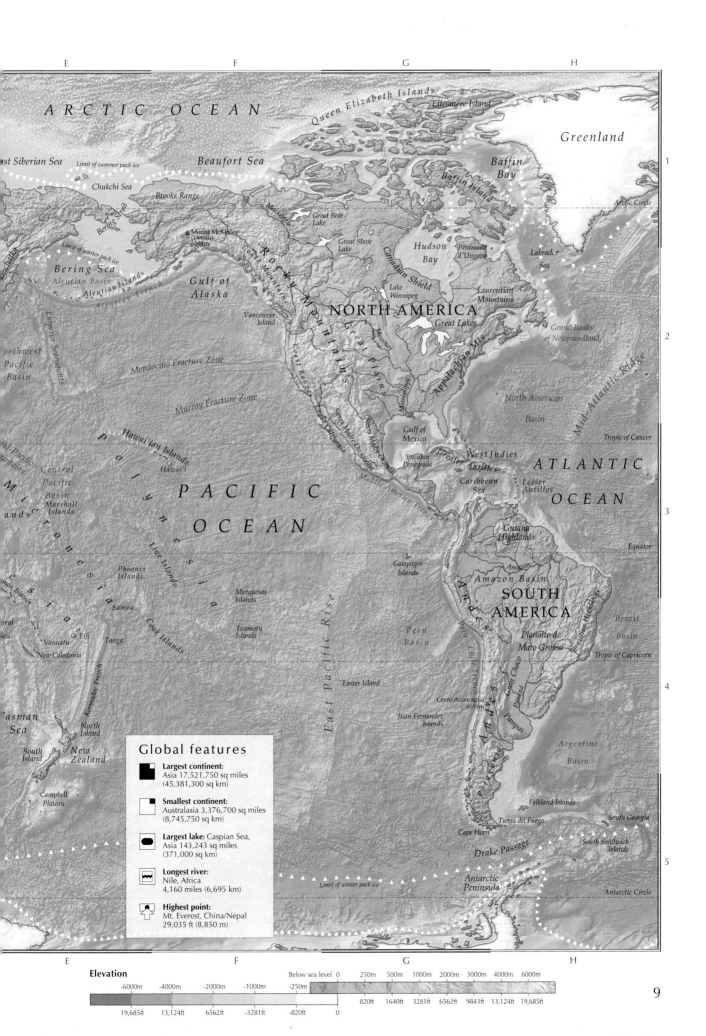

E   F   G   H

ARCTIC OCEAN

Queen Elizabeth Islands

Ellesmere Island

Greenland

st Siberian Sea

Limit of summer pack ice

Beaufort Sea

Baffin
Bay

Baffin Island

Arctic Circle

1

Chukchi Sea

Brooks Range

Mackenzie

Great Bear
Lake

Labrador
Sea

Bering Strait

Mount McKinley
(Denali)
6194m

Great Slave
Lake

Hudson
Bay

Péninsula
d'Ungava

Limit of winter pack ice

Bering Sea

Aleutian Basin

Gulf of
Alaska

Coast Mountains

Rocky Mountains

Canadian Shield

Lake
Winnipeg

Laurentian
Mountains

Aleutian Islands

Aleutian Trench

Vancouver
Island

NORTH AMERICA

2

orthwest
Pacific
Basin

Emperor Seamounts

Mendocino Fracture Zone

Coast Ranges

Great Plains

Missouri

Great Lakes

Grand Banks
of Newfoundland

Murray Fracture Zone

Sierra Nevada

North American
Basin

Mid-Atlantic Ridge

Hawai'ian Islands

Sierra Madre Occidental

Mississippi

Appalachian Mts

Tropic of Cancer

Central
Pacific
Basin

Hawai'i

Sierra Madre Oriental

Gulf of
Mexico

Greater
Antilles

West Indies

ATLANTIC

M
i
c
r
o
n
e
s
i
a

Marshall
Islands

PACIFIC

P
o
l
y
n
e
s
i
a

Yucatán
Peninsula

Middle America Trench

Caribbean
Sea

Lesser
Antilles

OCEAN

ands

OCEAN

Guiana
Highlands

3

mon Islands

Phoenix
Islands

Line Islands

Galápagos
Islands

Amazon

Equator

Marquesas
Islands

East Pacific Rise

Amazon Basin

SOUTH
AMERICA

Andes

Brazil
Basin

oral
ea

Samoa

Tuamotu
Islands

Peru
Basin

Peru-Chile Trench

Planalto de
Mato Grosso

Brazilian Highlands

Vanuatu

Fiji

Tonga

Cook Islands

Gran
Chaco

Tropic of Capricorn

New Caledonia

Easter Island

Paraná

asman
Sea

Kermadec Trench

North
Island

Juan Fernández
Islands

Cerro Aconcagua
6959m

Andes

Pampas

Argentine
Basin

4

South
Island

New
Zealand

Patagonia

Campbell
Plateau

Global features

■ **Largest continent:**
Asia 17,521,750 sq miles
(45,381,300 sq km)

□ **Smallest continent:**
Australasia 3,376,700 sq miles
(8,745,750 sq km)

● **Largest lake:** Caspian Sea,
Asia 143,243 sq miles
(371,000 sq km)

〰 **Longest river:**
Nile, Africa
4,160 miles (6,695 km)

⬆ **Highest point:**
Mt. Everest, China/Nepal
29,035 ft (8,850 m)

Falkland Islands

South Georgia

Tierra del Fuego

South Sandwich
Islands

Cape Horn

Drake Passage

5

Limit of winter pack ice

Antarctic
Peninsula

Antarctic Circle

E   F   G   H

Elevation

| | | | | | Below sea level 0 | 250m | 500m | 1000m | 2000m | 3000m | 4000m | 6000m |

-6000m   -4000m   -2000m   -1000m   -250m

820ft   1640ft   3281ft   6562ft   9843ft   13,124ft   19,685ft

19,685ft   13,124ft   6562ft   -3281ft   -820ft   0

Time zones

The numbers at the top of the map indicate how many hours each time zone is ahead or behind Coordinated Universal Time (UTC). The row of clocks indicate the time in each zone when it is 12:00 noon UTC.

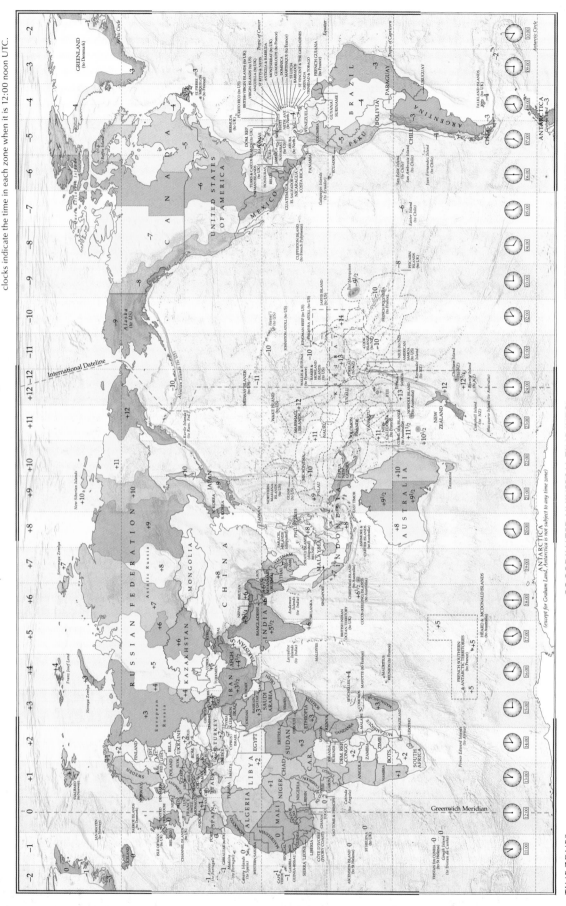

TIME ZONES

Because Earth is a rotating sphere, the Sun shines on only half of its surface at any one time. Thus, it is simultaneously morning, evening, and night time in different parts of the world. Because of these disparities, each country or part of a country adheres to a local time. A region of the Earth's surface within which a single local time is used is called a time zone.

COORDINATED UNIVERSAL TIME (UTC)

Coordinated Universal Time (UTC) is a reference by which the local time in each time zone is set. UTC is a successor to, and closely approximates, Greenwich Mean Time (GMT). However, UTC is based on an atomic clock, whereas GMT is determined by the Sun's position in the sky relative to the 0° longitudinal meridian, which runs through Greenwich, UK.

THE INTERNATIONAL DATELINE

The International Dateline is an imaginary line from pole to pole that roughly corresponds to the 180° longitudinal meridian. It is an arbitrary marker between calendar days. The dateline is needed because of the use of local times around the world rather than a single universal time.

The
WORLD
ATLAS

North & Central America

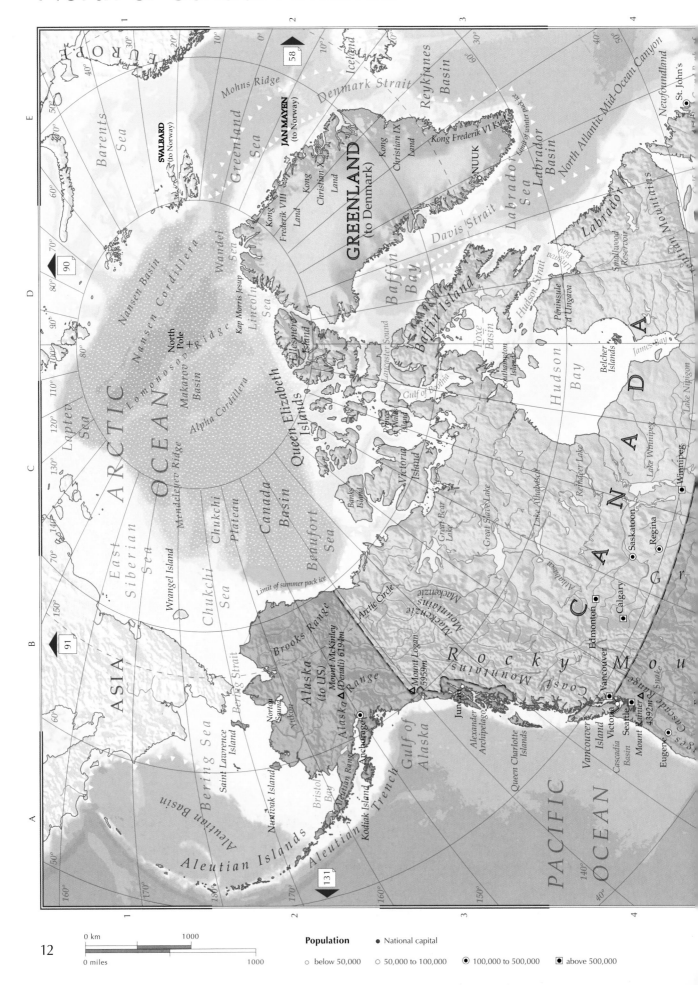

Population ● National capital

○ below 50,000   ○ 50,000 to 100,000   ◉ 100,000 to 500,000   ◼ above 500,000

0 km   1000

0 miles   1000

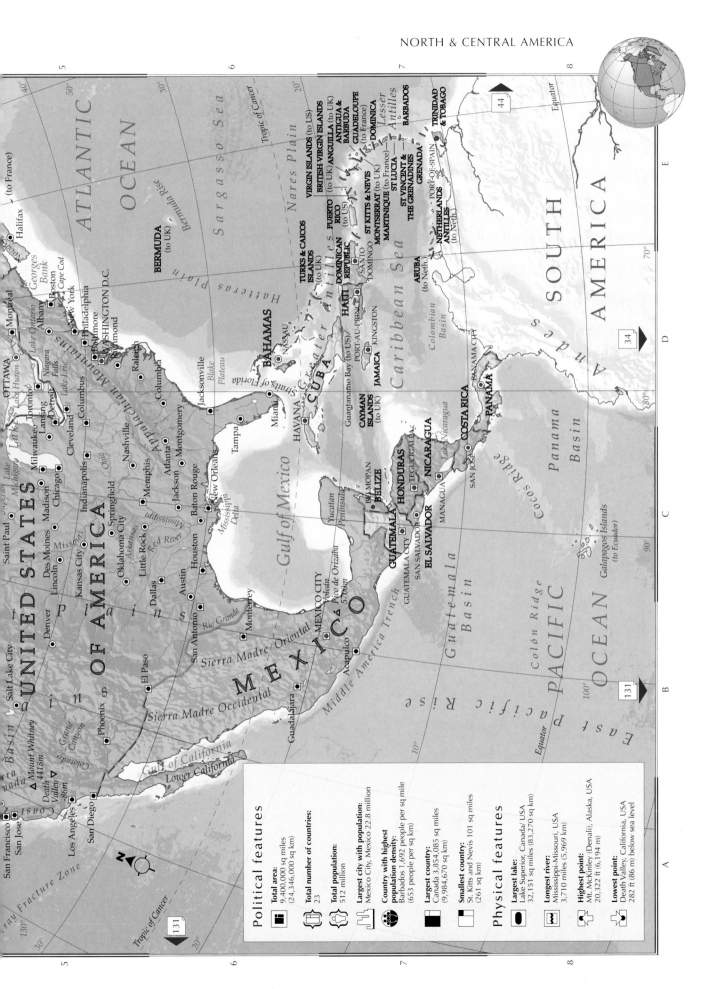

Political features

Total area:
9,400,000 sq miles
(24,346,000 sq km)

Total number of countries:
23

Total population:
512 million

Largest city with population:
Mexico City, Mexico 22.8 million

Country with highest population density:
Barbados 1,692 people per sq mile
(653 people per sq km)

Largest country:
Canada 3,854,085 sq miles
(9,984,670 sq km)

Smallest country:
St. Kitts and Nevis 101 sq miles
(261 sq km)

Physical features

Largest lake:
Lake Superior, Canada/ USA
32,151 sq miles (83,270 sq km)

Longest river:
Mississippi-Missouri, USA
3,710 miles (5,969 km)

Highest point:
Mt. McKinley (Denali), Alaska, USA
20,322 ft (6,194 m)

Lowest point:
Death Valley, California, USA
282 ft (86 m) below sea level

Western Canada & Alaska

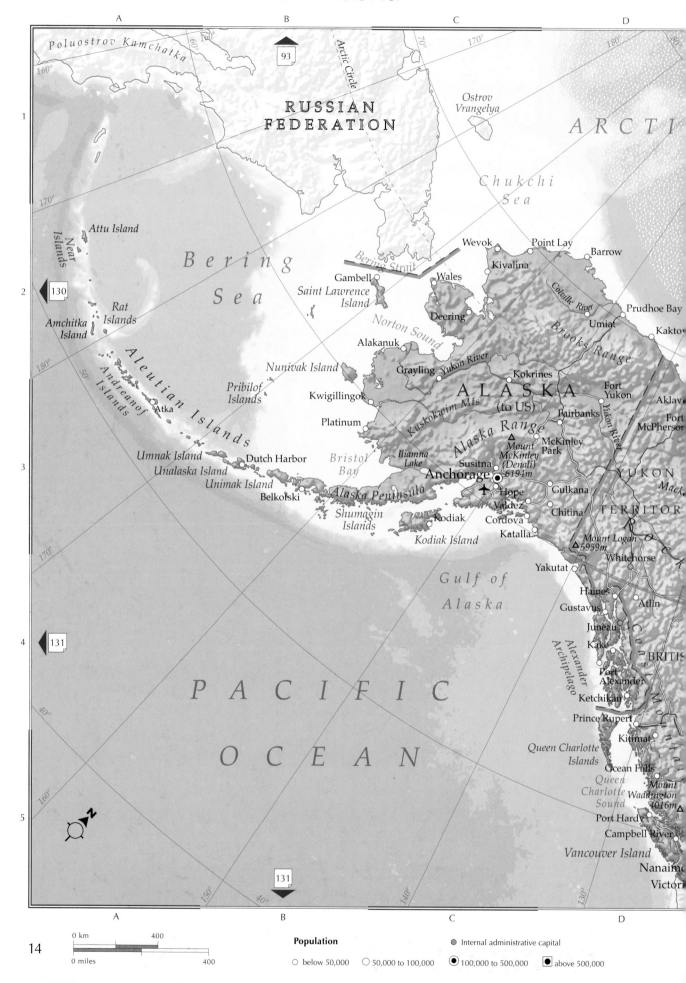

Poluostrov Kamchatka

RUSSIAN
FEDERATION

Arctic Circle

Ostrov
Vrangelya

ARCTI

Chukchi
Sea

Bering Strait

Wevok · Point Lay
Kivalina · Barrow
Coleville River
Prudhoe Bay
Umiat · Kaktov

Near
Islands

Attu Island

Bering
Sea

Gambell
Wales
Deering

Saint Lawrence
Island

Norton Sound

Brooks Range

130

Rat
Islands

Amchitka
Island

Alakanuk

Grayling   Yukon River   Kokrines

Fort
Yukon   Aklav

Nunivak Island

ALASKA
(to US)

Fairbanks

Fort
McPherson

Pribilof
Islands

Kwigillingok

Kuskokwim Mts

Aleutian Islands

Andreanof
Islands

Atka

Platinum

Mount
McKinley
(Denali)
6194m

Alaska Range

Mount
McKinley
Park

YUKON

Umnak Island

Dutch Harbor

Iliamna
Lake

Susitna

Anchorage

Hope   Gulkana

Mack

Unalaska Island

Bristol
Bay

Valdez

Chitina

TERRITOR

Unimak Island

Belkofski

Alaska Peninsula

Shumagin
Islands

Kodiak

Cordova
Katala

Mount Logan
5959m

Whitehorse

Kodiak Island

Yakutat

Haines   Atlin

Gulf of
Alaska

Gustavus

Juneau

Kake

131

Alexander
Archipelago

PACIFIC

Port
Alexander

Ketchikan

BRITIS

OCEAN

Prince Rupert

Kitimat

Queen Charlotte
Islands

Ocean Falls

Queen
Charlotte
Sound

Mount
Waddington
4016m

Port Hardy

Campbell River

Vancouver Island

Nanaimo

Victori

131

0 km   400

0 miles   400

Population

○ below 50,000   ○ 50,000 to 100,000   ◉ 100,000 to 500,000   ■ above 500,000

● Internal administrative capital

E   F   G   H

133

GREENLAND
(to Denmark)

Knud Rasmussen Land

Alert

Ellesmere Island

Axel Heiberg Island

Ellef Ringnes Island
Isachsen

Queen Elizabeth Islands

Amund Ringnes Island

Prince Patrick Island

Mould Bay

Bathurst Island
Cornwallis Island

Devon Island

Baffin Bay

Arctic Circle

60

Melville Island

Resolute
(Qausuittuq)

Lancaster Sound

Davis Strait

Banks Island

Viscount Melville Sound

Somerset Island

Brodeur Peninsula

Baffin Island

Cumberland Sound

OCEAN

aufort

Sea

chs Harbour
(Ikaahuk)

ktoyaktuk

ik

Paulatuk

Fort
Good Hope

Amundsen Gulf

Holman

McClintock Channel

Victoria Island

Prince of Wales Island

Boothia Peninsula

Gulf of Boothia

Igloolik

Melville Peninsula

Foxe Basin

Nettilling Lake

Amadjuak Lake

Iqaluit
(Frobisher Bay)

King William Island

Cambridge Bay
(Ikaluktutiak)

Gjoa Haven
(Uqsuqtuuq)

Kugaaruk
(Pelly Bay)

Kugluktuk
(Coppermine)

Great Bear Lake

Echo Bay

Burnside

Repulse Bay

Southampton Island

Hudson Strait

60

Back

Garry Lake

N U N A V U T

Coral Harbour

Mackenzie

Baker Lake

Rankin Inlet

Coats Island

Mansel Island

Péninsule d'Ungava

QUÉBEC

N O R T H W E S T
T E R R I T O R I E S

sten

Edzo   Yellowknife   Reliance

Whale Cove

Fort Simpson

Dubawnt

Arviat

Fort Providence

Great Slave Lake

Lutselk'e
(Snowdrift)

Hay River

Fort Liard

Fort Smith

Lake Athabasca

Churchill

*H u d s o n
B a y*

Belcher Islands

70

Fort Nelson

Reindeer Lake

Wollaston Lake

James Bay

LUMBIA

Fort Vermilion

Nelson

rince George

Fort St. John

Fort McMurray

Lynn Lake

Southern Indian Lake

C A N A D A

50

A L B E R T A

Grande Prairie

Buffalo Narrows

Thompson

Athabasca

SASKATCHEWAN

Flin Flon

O N T A R I O

Athabasca

North Saskatchewan

Saskatchewan

The Pas

Lake Winnipeg

Edmonton

Mount Robson 3954m

Leduc

Prince Albert

M A N I T O B A

Red Deer

Saskatoon

Kamloops

Calgary

Kindersley

Yorkton

Qu'Appelle

Lake Manitoba

Winnipeg

Lake of the Woods

Lake Superior

Kelowna

Regina

Brandon

Lake Huron

Cranbrook

Medicine Hat

Weyburn

Melita

ancouver

Lethbridge

Estevan

23

Lake Michigan

U N I T E D   S T A T E S   O F   A M E R I C A

16

E   F   G   H

Elevation

Below sea level 0   250m   500m 1000m 2000m 3000m 4000m 6000m

-8000m -6000m -4000m -2000m -1000m -500m   -250m

820ft 1640ft 3281ft 6562ft 9843ft 13,124ft 19,685ft

26,246ft 19,685ft 13,124ft 6562ft -3281ft -1640ft -820ft -100m/-328ft

Eastern Canada

NORTHWEST TERRITORIES

NUNAVUT

SASKATCHEWAN

MANITOBA

Churchill

Southern Indian Lake

Nelson

Hayes

Cedar Lake

Lake Winnipeg

Lake Winnipegosis

Lake Manitoba

C

Hudson Bay

Coats Island

Mansel Island

Ivujivik

Charles Island

Péninsule d' Ungava

Ottawa Islands

Inukjuak (Port Harrison)

Lac Minto

Bienv

Fort Severn

Belcher Islands

Peawanuk

Severn

Winisk

Sandy Lake

James Bay

Attawapiskat

Akimiski Island

QU

Eastmain

Rivière à Feuil

ONTARIO

Attawapiskat

Albany

Fort Albany

Moosonee

Moose

Harricana

Rivière de Rupert

Lac Mistassini

Chibougamau

A

N

A

Lac Seul

Armstrong

Hearst

Kapuskasing

Cochrane

Amos

Réservoir Gouin

Kenora

Dryden

Lake of the Woods

Lake Nipigon

Longlac

Timmins

Rouyn-Noranda

Val-d'Or

Fort Frances

Atikokan

Nipigon

Marathon

Tip Top Mountain △640m

Foleyet

Wawa

Kirkland Lake

Rainy Lake

NORTH DAKOTA

Red River

Thunder Bay

Lake Superior

Sault Ste.Marie

Sudbury

North Bay

Pembroke

Gatineau

Hull

OTTAWA

Law

MINNESOTA

MICHIGAN

Georgian Bay

Manitoulin Island

Lake Huron

Midland

Peterborough

Kingston

SOUTH DAKOTA

UNITED STATES

WISCONSIN

Lake Michigan

Brampton

Kitchener

Sarnia

Hamilton

Oshawa

Toronto

St.Catharines

London

Niagara Falls

Lake Ontari

OF AMERICA

IOWA

NEBRASKA

ILLINOIS

Windsor

Leamington

Lake Erie

NEW YORK

Mississippi River

INDIANA

OHIO

PENNSYLVANIA

| 0 km | 300 |
| 0 miles | 300 |

Population ● National capital ● Internal administrative capital
○ below 50,000 ○ 50,000 to 100,000 ◉ 100,000 to 500,000 ■ above 500,000

Labrador Sea

Baffin Island

Resolution Island

trait

• *Button Islands*

Ungava Bay

Akpatok Island

•Kuujjuaq

Rivière à la Baleine

•Nain

Caniapiscau

•Hopedale
•Makkovik

Cape Harrison

•Schefferville

N E W F O U N D L A N D

•Cartwright

Labrador

Réservoir de Caniapiscau

Smallwood Reservoir

Lake Melville

Churchill

E   C

D

& L A B R A D O R

•St.Anthony

•Gagnon

A

Réservoir Manicouagan

Laurentian Mountains

•Havre-St-Pierre

Strait of Belle Isle

+ •Gander
•Grand Falls

•Sept-Îles

Île d'Anticosti

•Corner Brook

Newfoundland

+ ◉ •St.John's

•Baie-Comeau

St. Lawrence

Gulf of St. Lawrence

Cape Race

Lac -Jean

•Chicoutimi

Péninsule de Gaspé

•Gaspé

•Channel-Port aux Basques

ST PIERRE & MIQUELON
(to France)

uière

•Matane

•Rimouski

Îles de la Madeleine

Cabot Strait

a Tuque

•Rivière-du-Loup

•Bathurst

PRINCE EDWARD ISLAND

•Glace Bay
•Sydney

•Edmundston

•Charlesbourg

NEW BRUNSWICK

•Charlottetown

Cape Breton Island

+ •Québec

•Moncton

•Amherst

•New Glasgow

Trois-Rivières
•St-Georges

•Oromocto

•Truro

NOVA SCOTIA

•Drummondville

•Fredericton

ntréal

•Sherbrooke

•Saint John

MAINE

Bay of Fundy

+ •Dartmouth
•Halifax

Sable Island

VERMONT

•Liverpool

NEW HAMPSHIRE

•Yarmouth

A T L A N T I C

MASSACHUSETTS

Cape Cod

O C E A N

CONNECTICUT

RHODE ISLAND

Elevation

| Below sea level | 0 | 250m | 500m | 1000m | 2000m | 3000m | 4000m | 6000m |

-8000m -6000m -4000m -2000m -1000m -500m -250m

820ft 1640ft 3281ft 6562ft 9843ft 13,124ft 19,685ft

26,246ft 19,685ft 13,124ft 6562ft -3281ft -1640ft -820ft -100m/-328ft

USA: The Northeast

Population
- National capital
- Internal administrative capital
- ○ below 50,000
- ○ 50,000 to 100,000
- ◉ 100,000 to 500,000
- ◼ above 500,000

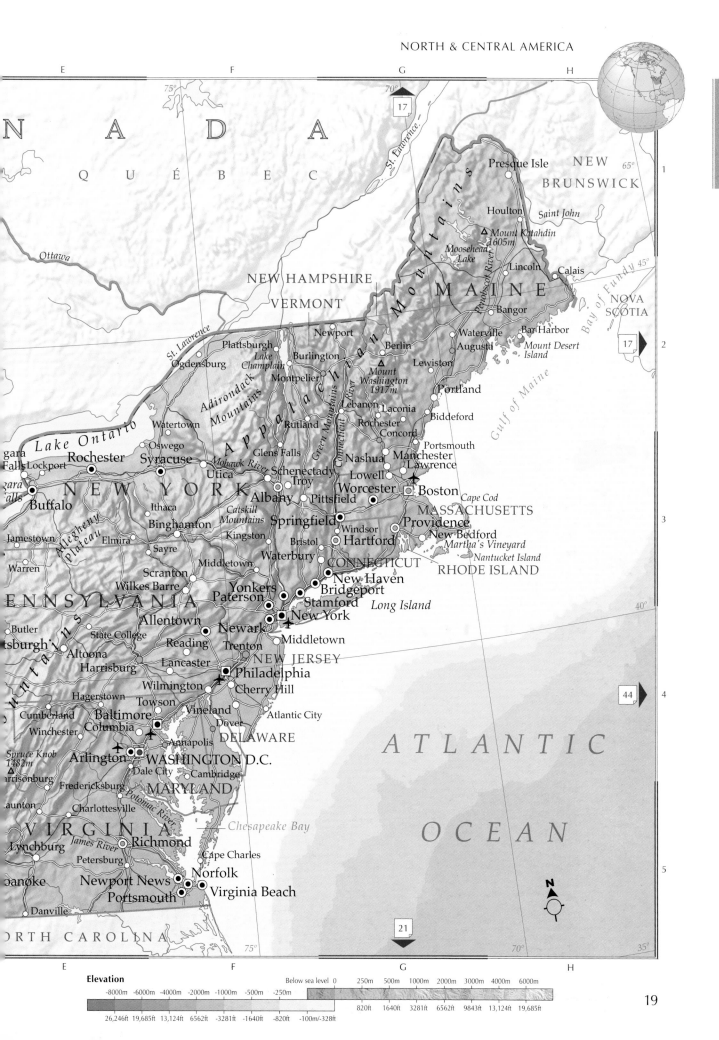

E   F   G   H

75°   70°   65°

NORTH & CENTRAL AMERICA

17

N A D A

Q U É B E C

1

NEW BRUNSWICK

Ottawa

Presque Isle

NEW

Houlton   Saint John

△ Mount Katahdin 1605m

Moosehead Lake

Appalachian Mountains

M A I N E

NEW HAMPSHIRE

VERMONT

Newport

Plattsburgh

St. Lawrence

Ogdensburg

Lake Champlain

Burlington

Montpelier

Berlin

Mount Washington 1917m

Lewiston

Waterville

Augusta

Lincoln   Calais

Bangor

Bar Harbor

Mount Desert Island

Gulf of Maine

Bay of Fundy

NOVA SCOTIA

17

2

Lebanon

Rutland

Green Mountains

Connecticut River

Laconia

Rochester

Concord

Portland

Biddeford

Portsmouth

Adirondack Mountains

Watertown

Lake Ontario

Oswego

gara Falls

Lockport   Rochester   Syracuse

gara alls

Buffalo

NEW YORK

Utica

Mohawk River

Glens Falls

Schenectady

Troy

Albany

Nashua   Manchester

Lowell   Lawrence

Worcester   Boston

Cape Cod

MASSACHUSETTS

Providence

3

Jamestown

Ithaca

Catskill Mountains

Binghamton

Pittsfield

Springfield

Windsor

New Bedford

Martha's Vineyard

Nantucket Island

RHODE ISLAND

Elmira

Allegheny Plateau

Warren

Kingston

Bristol

Hartford

Sayre

Waterbury

CONNECTICUT

Scranton

Middletown

New Haven

ENNSYLVANIA

Wilkes Barre

Yonkers   Bridgeport

Paterson   Stamford

Long Island

Butler

State College

Newark   New York

sburgh

Allentown

Reading

Middletown

4

Altoona

Lancaster

Trenton

Harrisburg

NEW JERSEY

Hagerstown

Wilmington

Philadelphia

Cherry Hill

44

Cumberland

Towson

Vineland

Atlantic City

Baltimore

Columbia

Dover

Winchester

Annapolis

DELAWARE

Spruce Knob 1482m △

Arlington   WASHINGTON D.C.

rrisonburg

Dale City   Cambridge

A T L A N T I C

Fredericksburg

MARYLAND

taunton

Charlottesville

Potomac River

Chesapeake Bay

O C E A N

V I R G I N I A

Lynchburg   James River   Richmond

Cape Charles

Petersburg

5

oanoke

Newport News   Norfolk

Danville

Portsmouth   Virginia Beach

N

RTH   CAROLINA

21

E   F   G   H

75°   70°   35°

Elevation

Below sea level 0   250m   500m   1000m   2000m   3000m   4000m   6000m

-8000m   -6000m   -4000m   -2000m   -1000m   -500m   -250m

820ft   1640ft   3281ft   6562ft   9843ft   13,124ft   19,685ft

26,246ft   19,685ft   13,124ft   6562ft   -3281ft   -1640ft   -820ft   -100m/-328ft

USA: The Southeast

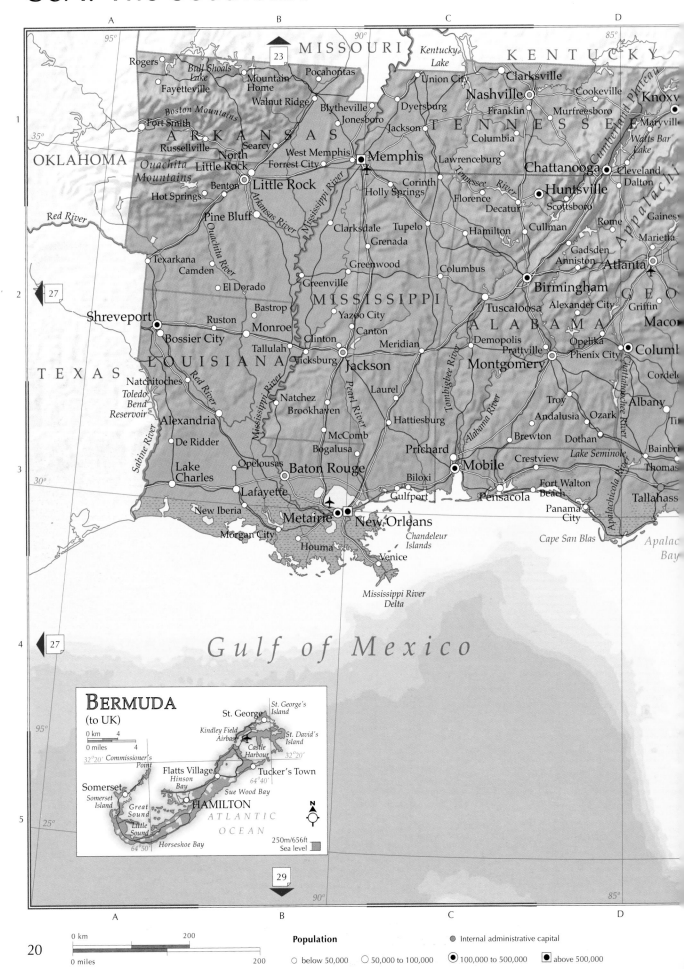

MISSOURI · Kentucky Lake · KENTUCKY

Rogers · Bull Shoals Lake · Mountain Home · Pocahontas · Union City · Clarksville · Cookeville · Knoxv
Fayetteville · Walnut Ridge · Blytheville · Dyersburg · Nashville · Franklin · Murfreesboro · Maryville
Boston Mountains · Jonesboro · Jackson · Columbia · TENNESSEE · Watts Bar Lake
Fort Smith · ARKANSAS · West Memphis · Memphis · Lawrenceburg · Chattanooga · Cleveland · Knoxv
Russellville · Searcy · Forrest City · Holly Springs · Corinth · Florence · Scottsboro · Huntsville · Dalton
OKLAHOMA · North Little Rock · Benton · Little Rock · Decatur · Cullman · Rome · Gaines
Ouachita Mountains · Hot Springs · Clarksdale · Tupelo · Hamilton · Gadsden · Anniston · Marietta
Red River · Pine Bluff · Grenada · Columbus · Atlanta · GEO
Texarkana · Camden · Greenwood · MISSISSIPPI · Birmingham · Alexander City · Griffin · Maco
El Dorado · Greenville · Tuscaloosa · ALABAMA · Colum
Shreveport · Bastrop · Ruston · Monroe · Yazoo City · Canton · Meridian · Demopolis · Opelika · Phenix City
Bossier City · Tallulah · Clinton · Montgomery · Prattville · Cordel
LOUISIANA · Vicksburg · Jackson · Laurel · Troy · Albany
Natchitoches · Red River · Natchez · Brookhaven · Hattiesburg · Andalusia · Ozark · Ti
Toledo Bend Reservoir · Alexandria · McComb · Brewton · Dothan · Bainbri
De Ridder · Bogalusa · Prichard · Crestview · Lake Seminole · Thomas
Lake Charles · Opelousas · Baton Rouge · Biloxi · Mobile · Fort Walton Beach · Pensacola · Tallahass
Lafayette · New Iberia · Metairie · Gulfport · Panama City · Cape San Blas · Apalac Bay
Morgan City · New Orleans · Houma · Chandeleur Islands · Venice · Mississippi River Delta

Gulf of Mexico

BERMUDA
(to UK)

0 km 4
0 miles 4

St. George's Island
St. George
Kindley Field Airbase
St. David's Island
Commissioner's Point
Castle Harbour
Flatts Village
Tucker's Town
Hinson Bay
Somerset · Sue Wood Bay
Somerset Island
HAMILTON
Great Sound
Little Sound
ATLANTIC OCEAN
Horseshoe Bay

250m/656ft
Sea level

0 km 200
0 miles 200

Population
○ below 50,000
○ 50,000 to 100,000
◉ 100,000 to 500,000
◼ above 500,000
⬤ Internal administrative capital

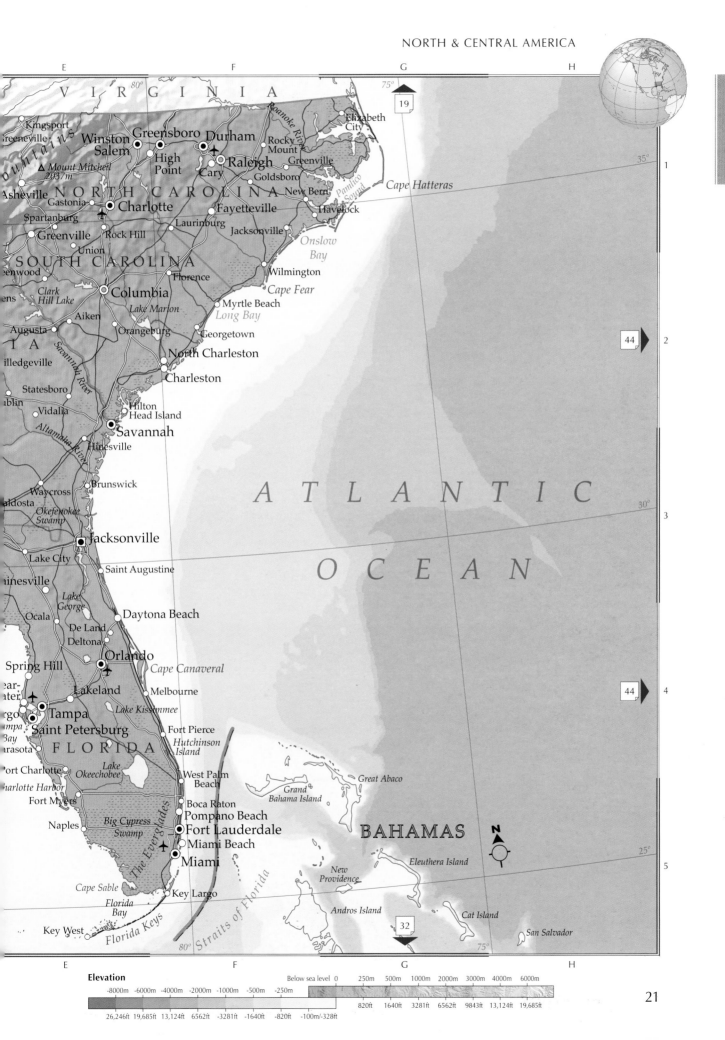

E   F   G   H

80°

75°

V I R G I N I A

19

Kingsport

Greenville

Blue Ridge Mountains

Winston Salem

Greensboro

Durham

Roanoke River

Elizabeth City

High Point

Raleigh

Rocky Mount

△ Mount Mitchell 2037m

Cary

Greenville

35° 1

Asheville

N O R T H   C A R O L I N A

Goldsboro

New Bern

Pamlico Sound

Cape Hatteras

Gastonia

Charlotte

Fayetteville

Havelock

Spartanburg

Laurinburg

Jacksonville

Onslow Bay

Greenville

Rock Hill

Union

S O U T H   C A R O L I N A

Florence

Wilmington

Cape Fear

Greenwood

Columbia

Myrtle Beach

Clark Hill Lake

Lake Marion

Long Bay

Aiken

Orangeburg

Georgetown

Augusta

North Charleston

44 2

Milledgeville

Charleston

Savannah River

Statesboro

Hilton Head Island

Dublin

Vidalia

Savannah

Altamaha River

Hinesville

Waycross

Brunswick

Valdosta

Okefenokee Swamp

A T L A N T I C

30° 3

Jacksonville

Lake City

O C E A N

Gainesville

Saint Augustine

Lake George

Ocala

Daytona Beach

De Land

Deltona

Spring Hill

Orlando

Cape Canaveral

Lakeland

Melbourne

44 4

Clearwater

Lake Kissimmee

Largo

Tampa

Fort Pierce

Tampa Bay

Saint Petersburg

Hutchinson Island

Sarasota

F L O R I D A

Port Charlotte

Lake Okeechobee

West Palm Beach

Charlotte Harbor

Fort Myers

Boca Raton

Great Abaco

Naples

Big Cypress Swamp

Pompano Beach

Grand Bahama Island

Fort Lauderdale

Miami Beach

BAHAMAS

N

Miami

Eleuthera Island

25° 5

Cape Sable

The Everglades

Key Largo

New Providence

Florida Bay

Straits of Florida

Andros Island

Cat Island

32

Key West

Florida Keys

San Salvador

80°

75°

E   F   G   H

Elevation

| Below sea level | 0 | 250m | 500m | 1000m | 2000m | 3000m | 4000m | 6000m |

-8000m -6000m -4000m -2000m -1000m -500m   -250m

820ft   1640ft   3281ft   6562ft   9843ft 13,124ft 19,685ft

26,246ft 19,685ft 13,124ft 6562ft -3281ft -1640ft -820ft -100m/-328ft

USA: Central States

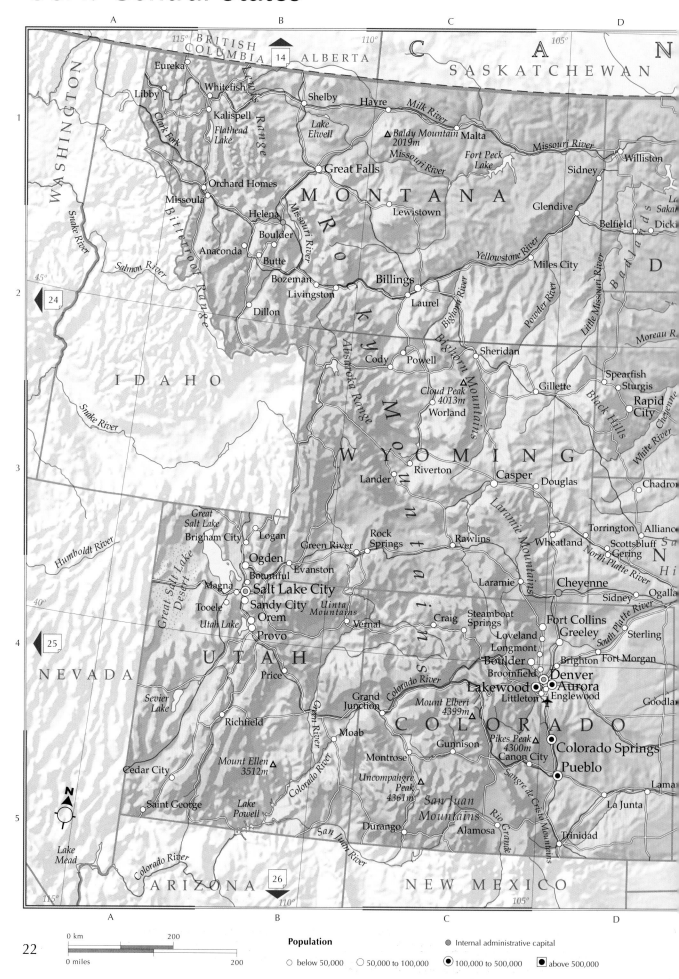

0 km   200

0 miles   200

Population

○ below 50,000   ○ 50,000 to 100,000   ◉ 100,000 to 500,000   ◼ above 500,000   ● Internal administrative capital

Elevation

Below sea level 0   250m   500m   1000m   2000m   3000m   4000m   6000m

-8000m -6000m -4000m -2000m -1000m -500m -250m

26,246ft 19,685ft 13,124ft 6562ft -3281ft -1640ft -820ft -100m/-328ft

820ft 1640ft 3281ft 6562ft 9843ft 13,124ft 19,685ft

USA: The West

LOS ANGELES

Places of interest
Regions/suburbs

Valencia
Santa Clarita
San Fernando
Burbank
Glendale
Pasadena
Universal Studios
Hollywood
Beverley Hills
Santa Monica
J. Paul Getty Museum
Venice
Torrance
Inglewood
Long Beach
Riverside
Buena Park
Anaheim
Disneyland
Santa Ana
Costa Mesa
Towney

San Gabriel Mountains
Santa Ana Mountains

20 km
20 miles

WYOMING

CANADA

ALBERTA

BRITISH COLUMBIA

MONTANA

IDAHO

WASHINGTON

OREGON

PACIFIC

Missouri River

Rexburg
Idaho Falls
Blackfoot
Pocatello
American Falls Reservoir
Bear Lake
Great Salt Lake
Burley
Twin Falls
Snake River Plain
Boise
Nampa
Caldwell
Owyhee River
Malheur Lake
Independence Mountains
Rocky Mountains

Pioneer Mountains
Lemhi Range
Salmon River Mountains
Bitterroot Mountains
Clearwater Mountains
Selway River
Salmon River
Snake River

Sandpoint
Lake Pend Oreille
Coeur d'Alene
Clark Fork
Saint Joe River
Franklin D. Roosevelt Lake
Columbia River
Spokane
Moscow
Lewiston
Pullman
Walla Walla
Pasco
Kennewick
Hermiston
Pendleton
La Grande
Baker
Blue Mountains
John Day River
Burns
Harney Basin
Columbia Plateau
Deschutes River
Bend
Goose Lake
Summer Lake
Klamath Falls
Upper Klamath Lake
Grants Pass
Roseburg
Medford
Ashland
Yreka
Klamath Mountains
Crescent City
Cape Blanco
Coos Bay
Coast
Eugene
Springfield
Lebanon
Albany
Corvallis
Salem
Woodburn
Oregon City
Gresham
Vancouver
The Dalles
Columbia River
Portland
Newberg
McMinnville
Cascades

Banks Lake
Wenatchee
Ellensburg
Yakima
Yakima River
Richland
Snake River
Cascades

Bellingham
Skagit River
Mount Vernon
Oak Harbor
Everett
Edmonds
Bellevue
Seattle
Auburn
Tacoma
Centralia
Kelso
Longview
Olympia
Bremerton
Puget Sound
Anacortes
Port Angeles
Olympic Mountains
Aberdeen

Strait of Georgia
Vancouver Island
Strait of Juan de Fuca

0 km   200
0 miles   200

Population

Internal administrative capital

○ below 50,000   ○ 50,000 to 100,000   ◉ 100,000 to 500,000   ◼ above 500,000

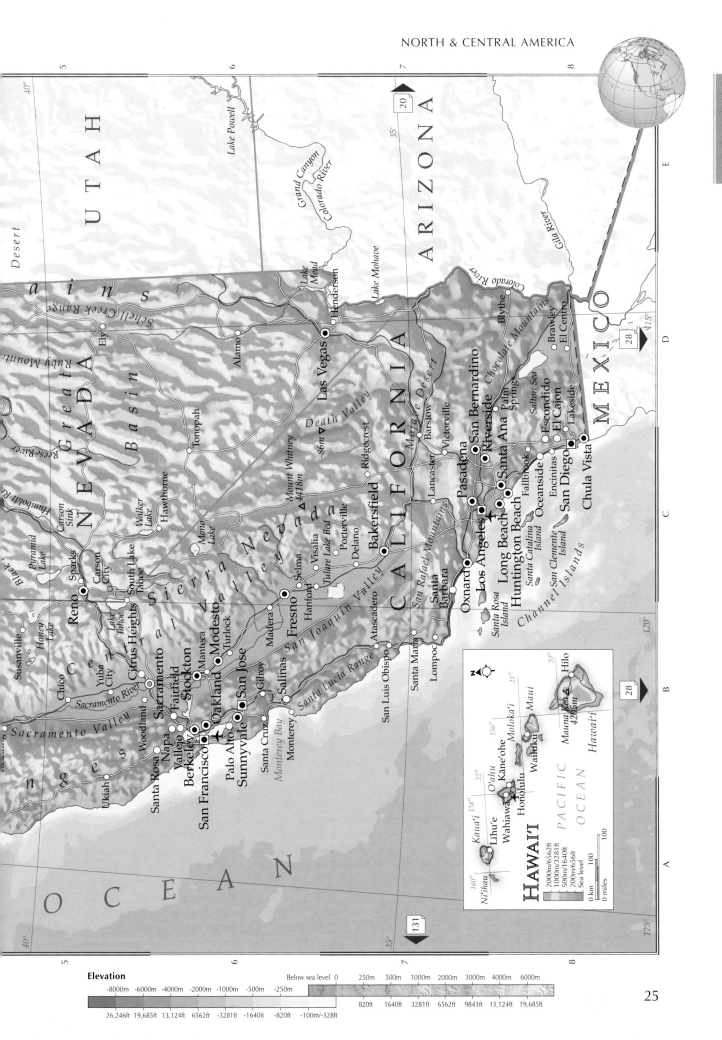

UTAH

Desert

Lake Powell

Grand Canyon

Colorado River

ARIZONA

a i n s

Schell Creek Range

Ruby Mount.

Lake Mead

Lake Mohave

Gila River

MEXICO

Henderson

NEVADA

Great Basin

Reese River

Humboldt R.

Ely

Alamo

Las Vegas

Death Valley
-86m ▽

Chocolate Mountains

Blythe

Brawley
El Centro

Salton Sea

Colorado River

Tonopah

Mount Whitney
△4418m

Ridgecrest

Barstow

Lancaster

Victorville

San Bernardino
Riverside
Santa Ana
Palm Springs
Escondido
Oceanside
Encinitas
Fallbrook
El Cajon
Lakeside
San Diego
Chula Vista

Hawthorne

Moho
Lake

Bakersfield

Mojave Desert

Pasadena
Los Angeles
Long Beach
Huntington Beach

Pyramid
Lake

Black R.

Carson Sink

Walker
Lake

Sierra Nevada

Porterville
Delano

Tulare Lake Bed

Visalia
Selma

Hanford

Fresno

CALIFORNIA

San Joaquin Valley

San Rafael Mountains

Lancaster

Santa Barbara

Oxnard

Santa Rosa
Island

Santa Cruz
Island

San Clemente
Island

San Catalina
Island

Channel Islands

Reno
Sparks
Carson City
South Lake
Tahoe
Lake
Tahoe
Cirrus Heights

Susanville

Honey
Lake

Chico

Yuba
City

Woodland

Sacramento River

Central Valley

Sacramento
Napa
Fairfield
Vallejo
Berkeley
Oakland
San Francisco
Palo Alto
Sunnyvale
San Jose

Stockton
Manteca
Modesto
Turlock

Gilroy
Salinas
Santa Cruz

Madera

Atascadero

Santa Lucia Range

San Luis Obispo

Santa Maria

Lompoc

Monterey Bay
Monterey

Sacramento Valley

Ukiah

n g e s

Santa Rosa

OCEAN

PACIFIC

HAWAI'I

Kaua'i
Ni'ihau
Lihu'e
Wahiawa
Honolulu
Waipahu
Kāne'ohe
O'ahu
Moloka'i
Maui
Wailuku
Mauna Kea △
4205m
Hilo
Hawai'i

PACIFIC OCEAN

Elevation			

Below sea level 0   250m   500m   1000m   2000m   3000m   4000m   6000m

-8000m -6000m -4000m -2000m -1000m -500m -250m

820ft   1640ft   3281ft   6562ft   9843ft   13,124ft   19,685ft

26,246ft 19,685ft 13,124ft 6562ft -3281ft -1640ft -820ft -100m/-328ft

25

USA: The Southwest

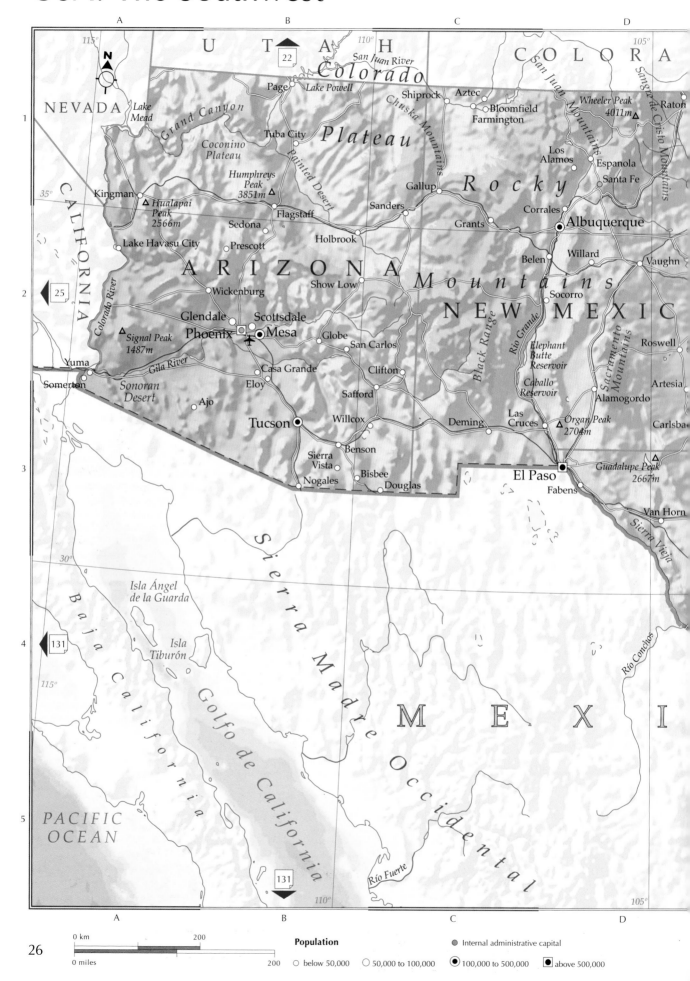

0 km   200
0 miles   200

Population

○ below 50,000   ○ 50,000 to 100,000   ◉ 100,000 to 500,000   ◼ above 500,000

● Internal administrative capital

E F G H

K A N S A S   MISSOURI

23

Miami
Table Rock
Lake

Boise City   Alva   Ponca City   Bartlesville   Vinita
                                                                  Claremore   Beaver
yton   Guymon   Woodward   Enid   Tulsa   Lake
        Perryton   Sand Springs   Broken Arrow
Dalhart   Clinton   Stillwater   Sapulpa   Tahlequah   1
        Dumas   The Village   Okmulgee   Muskogee
        Borger   El Reno Oklahoma City   Warner
Lake   Pampa   Moore   Eufaula
Meredith   Elk City   Norman   Shawnee   Lake
adian River   Chickasha   Ada   McAlester   35°
cumcari Amarillo   O K L A H O M A   Hugo   Idabel
         Canyon   Altus   Lawton   Duncan   2
Clovis   Hereford   Tulia   Red River   Ardmore   Lake   Durant
         Muleshoe   Childress   Vernon Burkburnett   Texoma   Paris   Texarkana
              Plainview   Wichita River   Denison   Atlanta
Littlefield   Lubbock   Wichita   Gainesville   Sherman   Sulphur Springs
Levelland   Falls   Denton   Greenville
Llano   Plano   Lake Tawakoni   Marshall
Estacado   Brownfield   Mineral Wells   Garland   Longview
obbs   Lamesa   Snyder   Fort Worth Dallas   Tyler
        Seminole   Sweetwater   Abilene   Cleburne Arlington   Henderson
Andrews   Big Spring   Colorado City   Stephenville   Ennis   Athens   Jacksonville
Midland   Ballinger   Coleman   Corsicana   Nacogdoches   Toledo Bend
Odessa   Brownwood   Waco   Trinity River   Lufkin   Reservoir   3
Monahans   San Angelo   T E X A S   Brazos River   Pineland
Pecos   McCamey   Brady   Killeen   Huntsville   Livingston   Neches River
Davis   Fort Stockton   Edwards Plateau   Copperas Cove Temple   Bryan   College Station   Conroe
Stockton   Pecos River   Lake   Belton   Taylor   Brenham   Beaumont   30°
Plateau   Buchanan   Houston   Baytown
pine   Kerrville   Lake Travis   Round Rock   Colorado River   Pasadena   Port Arthur
                                        Austin   San Marcos   Rosenberg Alvin   Texas City
Emory Peak   Amistad   New Braunfels   Seguin   Angleton   Galveston   4
2385m   Reservoir   Schertz   San Antonio   Hondo   El Campo   Bay   Lake Jackson
                     Del Rio   Uvalde   Guadalupe River   Edna   City   Freeport
                                        Pearsall   San Antonio River   Victoria   Port Lavaca
                     Eagle Pass   Kenedy   Port O'Connor
                              Rio Grande   Beeville
C   O   Robstown   Portland
                                    Alice   Corpus Christi
                     Laredo   Kingsville   5
                                        Laguna Madre   Gulf of
                                   Norias   Padre   Mexico
Sierra Madre Oriental   Edinburg   Island
                                   Mission   Harlingen
                              McAllen   San Benito
                              Brownsville
                                        29

E F G H

20

32

Elevation

Below sea level 0   250m   500m   1000m   2000m   3000m   4000m   6000m

-8000m -6000m -4000m -2000m -1000m -500m -250m

820ft 1640ft 3281ft 6562ft 9843ft 13,124ft 19,685ft

26,246ft 19,685ft 13,124ft 6562ft -3281ft -1640ft -820ft -100m/-328ft

Mexico

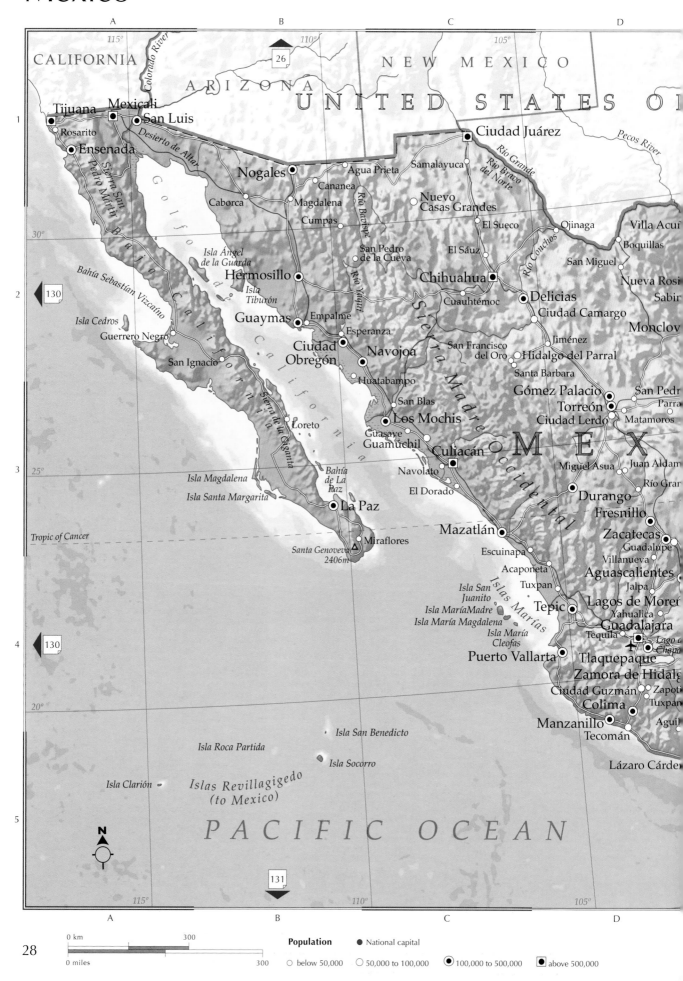

CALIFORNIA

UNITED STATES OF

ARIZONA

NEW MEXICO

Colorado River

Pecos River

26

Tijuana
Mexicali
San Luis
Rosarito
Ensenada

Desierto de Altar

Ciudad Juárez

Nogales
Agua Prieta
Samalayuca
Rio Grande
Rio Bravo del Norte

Sierra San Pedro Mártir

Cananea
Caborca
Magdalena
Cumpas

Nuevo Casas Grandes

El Sueco
Ojinaga
Villa Acuñ
Boquillas

Golfo

Bahía Sebastián Vizcaíno

Isla Ángel de la Guarda

San Pedro de la Cueva

San Miguel

Chihuahua
Cuauhtémoc

130

Isla Cedros

Hermosillo
Isla Tiburón

Nueva Rosi
Sabir

Delicias
Ciudad Camargo

Monclov

Guerrero Negro

Guaymas
Empalme
Esperanza

Rio Yaqui

San Francisco del Oro
Jiménez

San Ignacio

Ciudad Obregón
Navojoa

Hidalgo del Parral

Santa Barbara

Huatabampo

MEX

Gómez Palacio
Torreón
Ciudad Lerdo

San Pedr
Parra
Matamoros

San Blas

Baja California

Loreto

Sierra de la Giganta

Los Mochis
Guasave
Guamúchil
Culiacán
Navolato

Miguel Asua
Juan Aldam

Isla Magdalena
Isla Santa Margarita

Bahía de La Paz

El Dorado

Río Grar

Durango
Fresnillo

La Paz

Tropic of Cancer

Miraflores

Mazatlán

Zacatecas
Guadalupe

Santa Genoveva 2406m

Escuinapa

Villanueva
Aguascalientes
Jalpa

Acaponeta
Tuxpan

Isla San Juanito
Isla María Madre
Isla María Magdalena

Islas Marías

Lagos de Morer
Tepic
Yahualica

Isla María Cleofas

Guadalajara
Tequila
Lago d
Chapa

130

Puerto Vallarta

Tlaquepaque

Zamora de Hidalg

Ciudad Guzmán
Zapot

Colima
Tuxpan

Isla San Benedicto

Manzanillo
Tecomán

Aguil

Isla Roca Partida

Isla Socorro

Lázaro Cárde

Isla Clarión

Islas Revillagigedo
(to Mexico)

PACIFIC OCEAN

N

131

0 km   300

0 miles   300

Population ● National capital

○ below 50,000   ○ 50,000 to 100,000   ◉ 100,000 to 500,000   ■ above 500,000

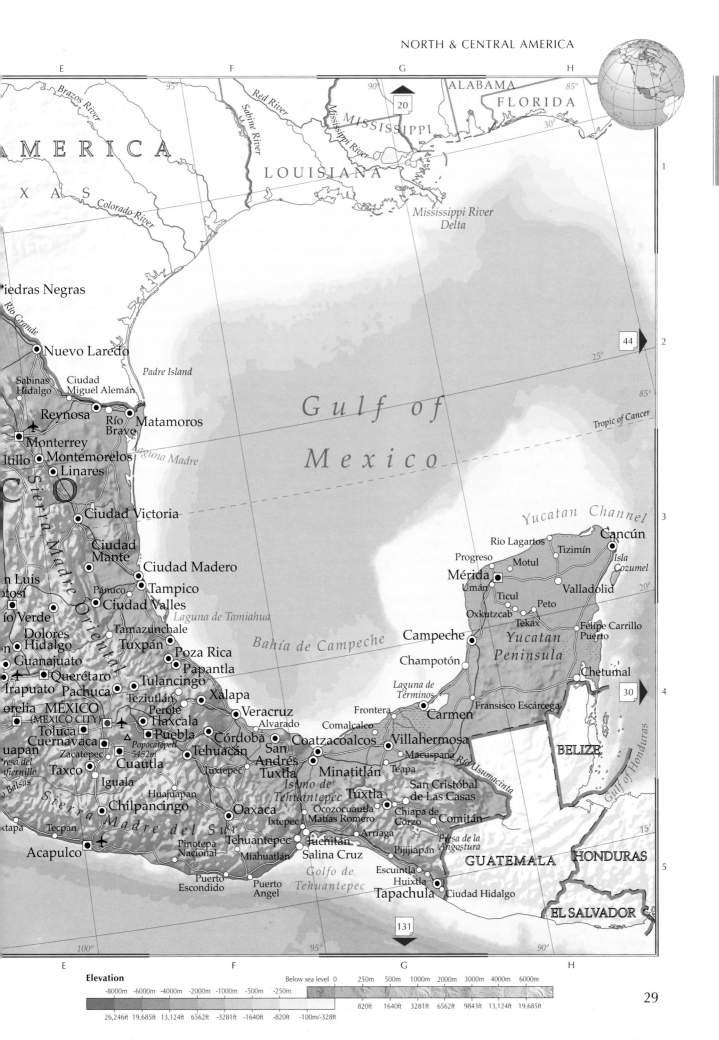

ALABAMA
FLORIDA

20

MISSISSIPPI
LOUISIANA

Mississippi River
Delta

A M E R I C A
X A S

Brazos River
Colorado River
Red River
Sabine River
Mississippi River

Piedras Negras

Rio Grande

Nuevo Laredo

44

Padre Island

Sabinas
Hidalgo
Ciudad
Miguel Alemán

Reynosa
Río
Bravo
Matamoros

Monterrey
Montemorelos
ltillo
Linares

Laguna Madre

*Gulf of
Mexico*

Tropic of Cancer

Ciudad Victoria

Ciudad
Mante

Ciudad Madero

n Luis
tosí

Pánuco
Tampico
Ciudad Valles

io Verde

Laguna de Tamiahua

Dolores
Hidalgo
Tamazunchale
Tuxpán

Guanajuato
Querétaro
rapuato
Pachuca
Poza Rica
Papantla
Tulancingo
Teziutlán
orelia
MEXICO
Perote
Xalapa
(MEXICO CITY)
Toluca
Tlaxcala
Veracruz
Cuernavaca
Puebla
Alvarado
uapan
Zacatepec
Popocatépetl
5452m
Córdoba
Cuautla
Tehuacán
San
Andrés
Coatzacoalcos
Taxco
Iguala
Tuxtepec
Tuxtla
Minatitlán

Bahía de Campeche

Campeche

Champotón

Laguna de
Términos

Frontera
Carmen

Comalcalco

Villahermosa

Macuspana
Teapa

Río Usumacinta

Fransisco Escárcega

Yucatan Channel

Rio Lagartos
Tizimín
Cancún

Progreso
Motul
Isla
Cozumel

Mérida
Umán
Valladolid

Ticul
Peto

Oxkutzcab
Tekax

Felipe Carrillo
Puerto

*Yucatan
Peninsula*

Chetumal

30

BELIZE

Chilpancingo
Oaxaca
Ocozocuautla
Matías Romero
Ixtepec
Arriaga
Tecpan
xtapa

Sierra Madre del Sur
Huajuapan
*Istmo de
Tehuantepec*
Tuxtla
San Cristóbal
de Las Casas
Chiapa de
Corzo
Comitán

Acapulco
Pinotepa
Nacional
Tehuantepec
Juchitán
Salina Cruz
Miahuatlán
Pijijiapán
Presa de la
Angostura

GUATEMALA
HONDURAS

Puerto
Escondido
Puerto
Angel

*Golfo de
Tehuantepec*

Escuintla
Huixtla
Tapachula
Ciudad Hidalgo

EL SALVADOR

131

Sierra Madre Oriental
esa del
fiernillo
Balsas

Elevation

Below sea level 0 250m 500m 1000m 2000m 3000m 4000m 6000m

-8000m -6000m -4000m -2000m -1000m -500m -250m

820ft 1640ft 3281ft 6562ft 9843ft 13,124ft 19,685ft

26,246ft 19,685ft 13,124ft 6562ft -3281ft -1640ft -820ft -100m/-328ft

Central America

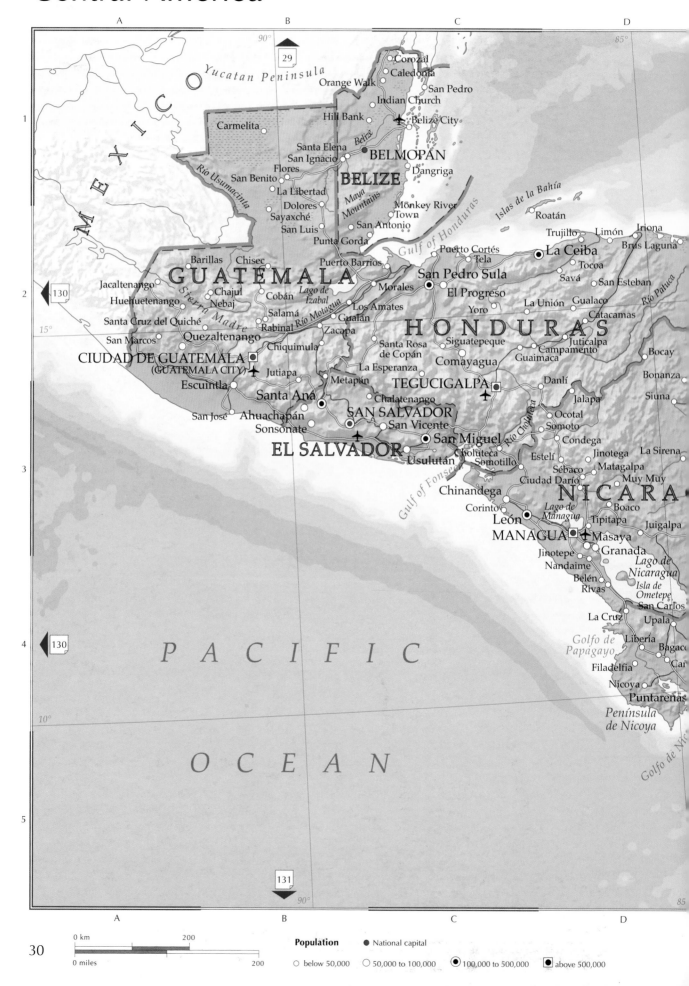

90°

MEXICO

Yucatan Peninsula

29

Corozal
Caledonia
Orange Walk
San Pedro
Indian Church
Hill Bank
Belize City

Carmelita

Santa Elena
San Ignacio
Flores
San Benito
La Libertad
Dolores
Sayaxché
San Luis

BELMOPAN

BELIZE

Dangriga

Río Usumacinta

Maya
Mountains

Monkey River
Town
San Antonio

Punta Gorda

Islas de la Bahía

Roatán

Trujillo   Limón   Iriona

Brus Laguna

Gulf of Honduras

Puerto Cortés
Tela

La Ceiba

Barillas   Chisec

GUATEMALA

Jacaltenango

Huehuetenango

Santa Cruz del Quiché

San Marcos

Chajul
Nebaj

Cobán

Salamá

Rabinal

Quezaltenango

Sierra Madre

Puerto Barrios

Lago de
Izabal

Morales

Los Amates
Gualán
Zacapa

Río Motagua

Chiquimula

Santa Rosa
de Copán

La Esperanza

Metapán

Tocoa
Savá

San Pedro Sula

El Progreso
Yoro

HONDURAS

Siguatepeque

Comayagua

San Esteban

La Unión   Gualaco

Catacamas

Guaimaca

Campamento

Juticalpa

Río Patuca

Bocay

Bonanza

Siuna

CIUDAD DE GUATEMALA
(GUATEMALA CITY)

Escuintla

Santa Ana

San José

Ahuachapán

Sonsonate

EL SALVADOR

Jutiapa

Chalatenango

SAN SALVADOR

San Vicente

Usulután

TEGUCIGALPA

Danlí

San Miguel

Choluteca
Somotillo

Gulf of Fonseca

Chinandega

Corinto

León

MANAGUA

Jinotepe

Nandaime

Belén
Rivas

La Cruz

Río Choluteca

Ocotal

Somoto

Condega

Estelí

Ciudad Darío

Sébaco

Jalapa

Jinotega

Matagalpa

La Sirena

Muy Muy

NICARA

Boaco

Tipitapa

Masaya

Granada

Juigalpa

Lago de
Managua

Lago de
Nicaragua

Isla de
Ometepe

San Carlos

Upala

Liberia

Bagace

Car

PACIFIC

OCEAN

Golfo de
Papagayo

Filadelfia

Nicoya

Puntarenas

Península
de Nicoya

Golfo de Nic

131

90°

0 km   200
0 miles   200

Population   ● National capital

○ below 50,000   ○ 50,000 to 100,000   ◉ 100,000 to 500,000   ◼ above 500,000

E   F   G   H

32

s Santilla
Honduras)

Bajo Nuevo
(to Colombia)

Cayo de Serranilla
(to Colombia)

15°

na de Caratasca

Puerto Lempira

Coco

33

75°

spam

Cayo de Serrana
(to Colombia)

Tuapi

Cayos Miskitos

Puerto Cabezas

ablis

C a r i b b e a n

Prinzapolka

Isla de Providencia
(to Colombia)

Barra de Río Grande

S e a

Mosquito Coast

Isla de San Andrés
(to Colombia)

Laguna de Perlas

Rama

Islas del Maíz

Bluefields

Punta Gorda

San Juan del Norte

an Juan
o
ejo

COSTA RICA

Istmo de Panamá

El Porvenir

Aligandí

Gulf of
Darien

esada

Siquirres

Portobelo

ela

Heredi

Limón

Colón

Cristóbal

Cordillera de San Blas

Lago Bayano

SAN JOSÉ

Guabito

Panama Canal

San Miguelito

Puerto Obaldía

Cartago

Almirante

Lago Gatún

PANAMÁ

Chimán

Cerro Chirripó

Cordillera de
Talamanca

Laguna
de Chiriquí

Golfo de los
Mosquitos

Balboa

(PANAMA CITY)

Grande
3819m
epos

Capira

La Palma

Yaviza

COLOMBIA

Buenos Aires

Volcán Barú 3475m

Penonomé

Archipiélago
de las Perlas

Isla
del Rey

El Real

Cortés

Palmar Sur

Boquete

Cordillera Central

P A N A M Á

Aguadulce

Garachiné

Bahía
Coronado

La Concepción

David

Santiago

Chitré

Golfo
de Panamá

nínsula de Osa

Golfo Dulce

Guarumal

Ocú

Las Tablas

Jaqué

Golfo
de Chiriquí

Península de
Azuero

Isla de Coiba

Isla
Cébaco

131

80°

E   F   G   H

Elevation

Below sea level   0   250m   500m   1000m   2000m   3000m   4000m   6000m

-8000m -6000m -4000m -2000m -1000m -500m -250m

820ft   1640ft   3281ft   6562ft   9843ft 13,124ft 19,685ft

26,246ft 19,685ft 13,124ft 6562ft -3281ft -1640ft -820ft -100m/-328ft

The Caribbean

UNITED STATES OF AMERICA

The Everglades

Gulf of Mexico

Florida Keys

Straits of Florida

Tropic of Cancer

Yucatan Channel

LA HABANA (HAVANA)
Artemisa
Guanabacoa
Pinar del Río
La Fé
Consolación del Sur
Matanzas
Cárdenas
Cienfuegos
Santa Clara
Sagua la Grande
Nueva Gerona
Isla de la Juventud
Placetas
Cayo Largo
Sancti Spíritus
Morón
Ciego de Ávila
Bahía de Cochinos
Archipiélago de los Canarreos
Archipiélago de los Jardines de la Reina
Camagüey
Nuevitas
Las Tunas
Holguín
Manzanillo
Bayamo
Palma Soriano
Guantánamo
Santiago de Cuba
Guantánamo Bay (to US)

CUBA

Grand Bahama Island
Freeport
Marsh Harbour
Great Abaco

Bimini Islands
Berry Islands
Nicholls Town
NASSAU
New Providence
Andros Town
Andros Island
Cay Sal
Anguilla Cays
Exuma Cays
George Town
Great Exuma Island
Ragged Island Range
Archipiélago de Camagüey

Northeast Providence Channel
Eleuthera Island
Rock Sound
Cat Island
Exuma Sound
San Salvador
Rum Cay
Long Island
Clarence Town
Crooked Island
Acklins Island
Mayaguana
Mayaguana Passage
Caicos Passage
Little Inagua
Lake Rosa
Matthew Town
Great Inag

BAHAMAS

Crooked Island Passage

CAYMAN ISLANDS (to UK)
Little Cayman
Cayman Brac
GEORGE TOWN
Grand Cayman

Montego Bay
Spanish Town
Portmore
KINGSTON
JAMAICA
Pedro Cays

NAVASSA ISLAND (to US)

Jamaica Channel

Windward Passage

Gonaïves
Île de la Gonâve
Jérémie
Cayes
Jacme
Cap
Haïtie
HAI
PORT-AU-PRINCE

HONDURAS

NICARAGUA

Caribbean

COSTA RICA

COLOMBIA

JAMAICA

Montego Bay
Lucea
Falmouth
Discovery Bay
St Ann's Bay
Ocho Rios
Annotto Bay
Buff Bay
Port Antonio
Cambridge
The Cockpit Country
Christiana
Ewarton
Savanna-La-Mar
Mandeville
Spanish Town
Blue Mountain Peak △2258m
Black River
May Pen
Old Harbour
KINGSTON
Portmore
Morant Bay
Portland Bight

Caribbean Sea

Caribbean Sea

0 km   20
0 miles 20

2000m/6562ft
1000m/3281ft
500m/1640ft
200m/656ft
Sea level

0 km   200
0 miles 200

Population   ● National capital

○ below 50,000   ○ 50,000 to 100,000   ◉ 100,000 to 500,000   ▣ above 500,000

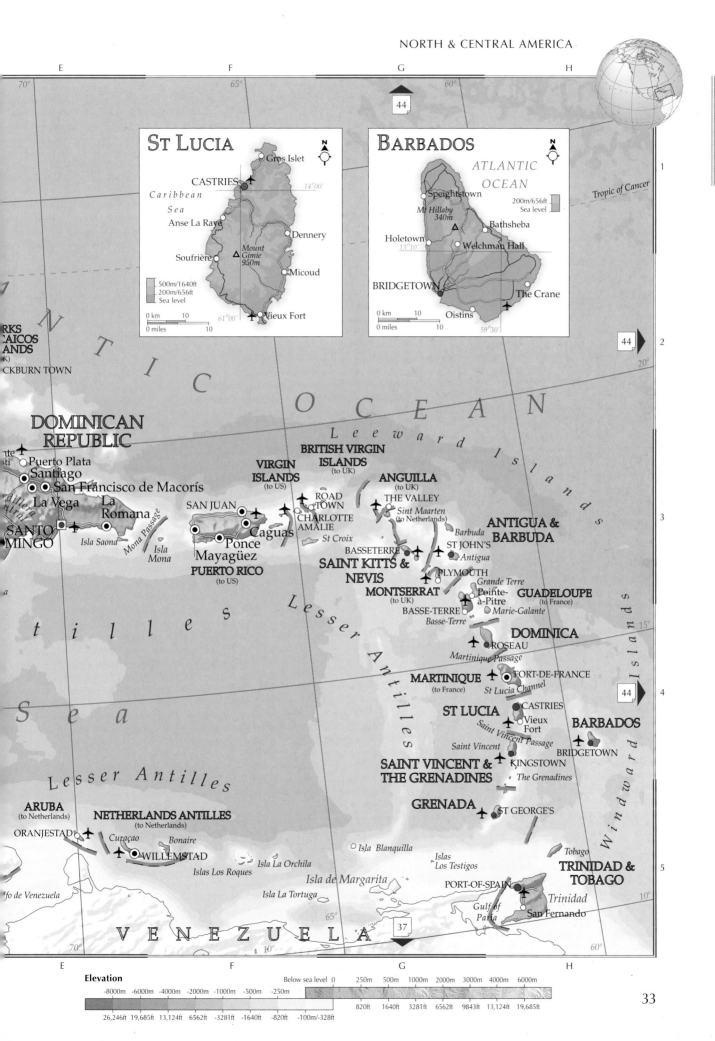

St Lucia

N

Gros Islet

CASTRIES

Caribbean
Sea

14°00'

Anse La Raye

Dennery

Soufrière

△ *Mount*
Gimie
950m

Micoud

500m/1640ft
200m/656ft
Sea level

0 km   10

0 miles   10

61°00'

Vieux Fort

Barbados

N

ATLANTIC
OCEAN

Speightstown

Mt Hillaby
340m

Bathsheba

△

Holetown

200m/656ft
Sea level

Welchman Hall

13°10'

BRIDGETOWN

The Crane

0 km   10

0 miles   10

Oistins

59°30'

Tropic of Cancer

20°

RKS
AICOS
ANDS
K)
CKBURN TOWN

A T L A N T I C   O C E A N

L e e w a r d   I s l a n d s

DOMINICAN
REPUBLIC

te

Puerto Plata

Santiago

San Francisco de Macorís

illera
ntral

La Vega

La
Romana

SANTO
MINGO

Isla Saona

Mona Passage

Isla
Mona

SAN JUAN

Caguas

Ponce

Mayagüez

PUERTO RICO
(to US)

VIRGIN
ISLANDS
(to US)

BRITISH VIRGIN
ISLANDS
(to UK)

ROAD
TOWN

CHARLOTTE
AMALIE

St Croix

ANGUILLA
(to UK)

THE VALLEY

Sint Maarten
(to Netherlands)

Barbuda

BASSETERRE

SAINT KITTS &
NEVIS

ST JOHN'S

Antigua

ANTIGUA &
BARBUDA

PLYMOUTH

MONTSERRAT
(to UK)

Grande Terre

Pointe-
à-Pitre

GUADELOUPE
(to France)

BASSE-TERRE

Basse-Terre

Marie-Galante

DOMINICA

ROSEAU

Martinique Passage

MARTINIQUE
(to France)

FORT-DE-FRANCE

St Lucia Channel

ST LUCIA

CASTRIES

Vieux
Fort

Saint Vincent Passage

Saint Vincent

SAINT VINCENT &
THE GRENADINES

KINGSTOWN

The Grenadines

BARBADOS

BRIDGETOWN

GRENADA

ST GEORGE'S

W i n d w a r d   I s l a n d s

a

n

t

i

l

l

e

s

Lesser Antilles

L e s s e r   A n t i l l e s

S e a

ARUBA
(to Netherlands)

ORANJESTAD

NETHERLANDS ANTILLES
(to Netherlands)

Curaçao

Bonaire

WILLEMSTAD

Islas Los Roques

Isla La Orchila

Isla Blanquilla

Islas
Los Testigos

Tobago

TRINIDAD &
TOBAGO

Isla de Margarita

Isla La Tortuga

PORT-OF-SPAIN

Trinidad

San Fernando

Gulf of
Paria

fo de Venezuela

V E N E Z U E L A

70°   10°   65°   10°   60°

15°

10°

44

44

44

37

E   65°   F   G   60°   H

Elevation

| Below sea level 0 | 250m | 500m | 1000m | 2000m | 3000m | 4000m | 6000m |

-8000m -6000m -4000m -2000m -1000m -500m -250m

820ft 1640ft 3281ft 6562ft 9843ft 13,124ft 19,685ft

26,246ft 19,685ft 13,124ft 6562ft -3281ft -1640ft -820ft -100m/-328ft

South America

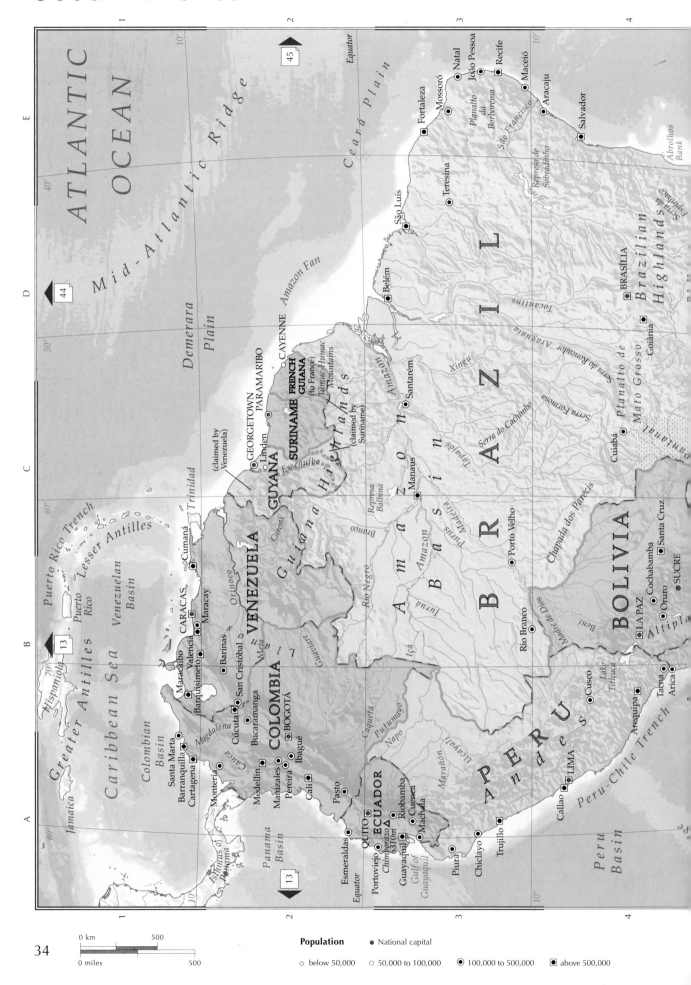

0 km   500

0 miles   500

Population   ● National capital

○ below 50,000   ◎ 50,000 to 100,000   ◉ 100,000 to 500,000   ◼ above 500,000

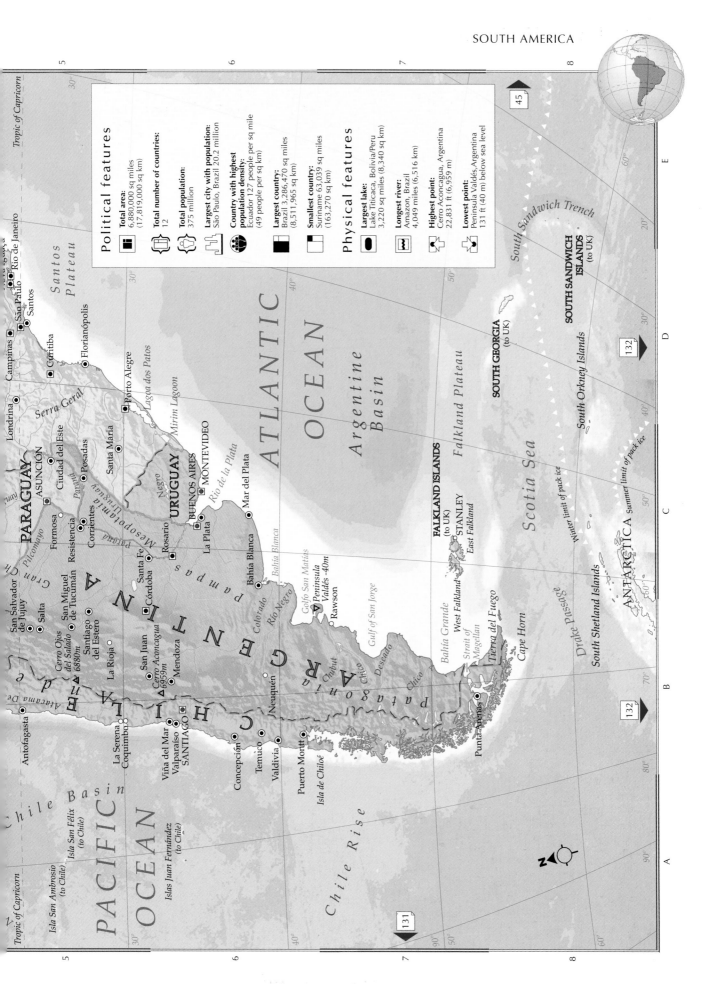

Political features

Total area:
6,880,000 sq miles
(17,819,000 sq km)

Total number of countries:
12

Total population:
375 million

Largest city with population:
São Paulo, Brazil 20.2 million

Country with highest population density:
Ecuador 127 people per sq mile
(49 people per sq km)

Largest country:
Brazil 3,286,470 sq miles
(8,511,965 sq km)

Smallest country:
Suriname 63,039 sq miles
(163,270 sq km)

Physical features

Largest lake:
Lake Titicaca, Bolivia/Peru
3,220 sq miles (8,340 sq km)

Longest river:
Amazon, Brazil
4,049 miles (6,516 km)

Highest point:
Cerro Aconcagua, Argentina
22,831 ft (6,959 m)

Lowest point:
Península Valdés, Argentina
131 ft (40 m) below sea level

Northern South America

Caribbean Sea

Lesser Ant

ARUBA
(to Netherlands)

Curaçao   Bonaire   NETHERLANDS
ANTILLES
(to Netherlands)

Isla
La Or

Islas
Los Roques

Península
de la
Guajira

Puerto López
Punto Fijo   Puerto
Coro   Cumarebo

Ríohacha
Maicao   Golfo de
Venezuela

Santa Marta   Dabajuro   Sabaneta

Barranquilla   Ciénaga   Maracaibo   San Felipe   Puerto
Cabello   CARACA

Soledad   Pico Cristóbal Colón
5775m   La Concepción   Cabimas   Carora   Barquisimeto   Valencia   Maracay

Cartagena   Sabanalarga   Machiques   Ciudad
Ojeda   San Juan
de los Mor

Valledupar   Carora   Valera   Acarigua

El Carmen
de Bolívar   San Carlos
del Zulia   Lago de
Maracaibo   Valle de
la Pasca

Sincelejo   Magangué   Mérida   Guanare   Calabozo

Montería   Cereté   El Vigía   Pico Bolívar
5007m   Barinas   Río Guanare   San Fernand

Planeta Rica   Ocaña   Cúcuta   San Cristóbal   Río Apure   L I a

Aguachica   Pamplona   Río Arauca   V E N

Caucasia   Bucaramanga

Dabeiba   Yarumal   Barrancabermeja   Arauca   Río Meta   Puerto Carreñ

Bello   Puerto Berrío   Puerto Ayacuc

Nuquí   Medellín   Sogamoso   Río Orinoco

Itagüí   Tunja   Yopal

Quibdó   Manizales   Zipaquirá   Río Meta

Pereira   BOGOTÁ

Armenia   Girardot   Villavicencio   Puerto Inírida
Río Guaviare

Buenaventura   Tuluá   Ibagué   Espinal

Buga   C O L O M B I A

Palmira   San José del
Guaviare

Cali   Neiva   Orinoquía- Amazonia

Popayán   Garzón

Tumaco   Pitalito   Mitú
Río Vaupés

Pasto   Mocoa   Florencia   Río Apaporis

Nevado de Cumbal
4764m

Ipiales   Orito   Río Japurá

Equator

E C U A D O R

Río Putumayo   Río Caquetá

Río Napo   Río Icá

P E R U   Amazon

PANAMA

Panama
Canal

Golfo de
Panamá

Gulf of
Darien

PACIFIC
OCEAN

0 km   200

0 miles   200

Population   ● National capital

○ below 50,000   ○ 50,000 to 100,000   ◉ 100,000 to 500,000   ■ above 500,000

60°   55°

33

SAINT VINCENT &
THE GRENADINES

BARBADOS

GRENADA

Isla Blanquilla

*Isla de
Margarita*

Islas Los Testigos

Tobago

A T L A N T I C

1

Portuga   La Asunción
Porlamar   Carúpano   TRINIDAD &
maná   Cariaco Guiria   TOBAGO
   Puerto La Cruz   *Gulf of*
                     Paria   *Trinidad*
Barcelona   *The Serpent's Mouth*
San Mateo   Maturín
  Anaco
raza Cantaura
        Tucupita

O C E A N

10°

El Tigre
        Río Orinoco
            Ciudad Guayana
                Upata

45

2

Ciudad
Bolívar

U E L A   *Embalse de Guri*

Matthews   Charity
Ridge

Spring Garden
El Callao   Parika   GEORGETOWN

El Dorado   *Cayuni River* Aurora   New
                                    Bartica   Amsterdam   PARAMARIBO
Río Paragua Peters Mine   Linden   Totness   Nieuw Amsterdam
                   Rockstone   St-Laurent-
Río Caura   Nieuw   du-Maroni Sinnamary
Salto   Kamarang   GUYANA   Nickerie   Kourou
Angel   Kaaimanston   5°
Río Caroní   Mount Roraima ▵   Orealla Apoera
                 2810m   *W. J. van*
                                                        Blommesteinmeer   CAYENNE
Pakaraima Mountains   *Montagnes*   Ouanary
Kurupukari   SURINAME   *de la Trinité* *Montagne*
                                                    ▵ *Juliana Top*   *Tortue*   St-Georges
(Venezuela claims all   1230m   Grand-   FRENCH
of Guyana west of   Santi   GUIANA
Essequibo River)   Lethem   (to France)   Camopi

Río Orinoco   *Essequibo River*   *Courantyne River*

G   Maroni River

u   *Tumuc-Humac Mountains*

y   Acarai Mountains   (claimed by
a   Suriname)
n   H i g h l a n d s   (claimed by
a   Suriname)

40

4

Rio Negro   Equator

B   R   A   Z   I   L

5

Amazon

z   o   n   B   a   s   i   n   *Amazon*

Amazon

Rio Purus   40

Rio Tapajós

60°   55°

E   F   G   H

Elevation

| -8000m | -6000m | -4000m | -2000m | -1000m | -500m | -250m | | Below sea level 0 | 250m | 500m | 1000m | 2000m | 3000m | 4000m | 6000m |

820ft   1640ft 3281ft 6562ft 9843ft 13,124ft 19,685ft

26,246ft 19,685ft 13,124ft 6562ft -3281ft -1640ft -820ft -100m/-328ft

Western South America

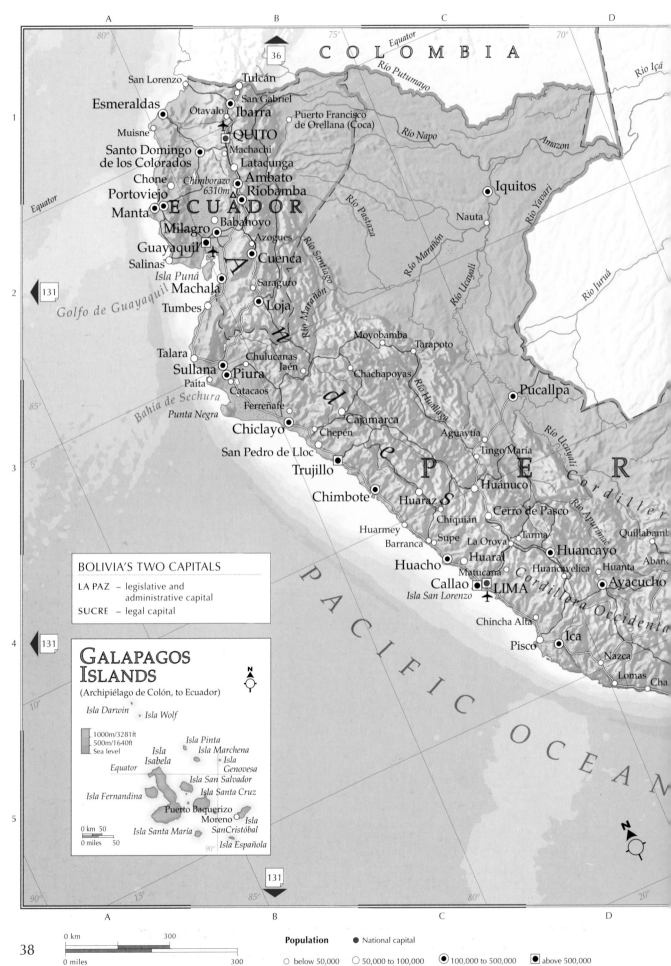

COLOMBIA

San Lorenzo
Tulcán
Esmeraldas
Otavalo · San Gabriel
Ibarra
Muisne
QUITO
Machachi
Santo Domingo
de los Colorados
Latacunga
Chone
Ambato
Chimborazo
6310m
Riobamba
Portoviejo
ECUADOR
Manta
Milagro · Babahoyo
Guayaquil
Azogues
Salinas
Cuenca
Isla Puná
Saraguto
Machala
Loja
Tumbes

Puerto Francisco
de Orellana (Coca)

Río Putumayo
Río Napo
Amazon
Iquitos
Nauta
Río Pastaza
Río Santiago
Río Marañón
Río Ucayali
Río Yavari
Río Juruá
Río Içá

Talara
Chulucanas
Jaén
Sullana
Piura
Paita
Catacaos
Ferreñafe
Punta Negra
Chiclayo
Chepén
San Pedro de Lloc
Trujillo
Chimbote
Huaraz
Chíquián
Huarmey
Supe
Barranca
Huacho
Callao
LIMA
Isla San Lorenzo

Moyobamba
Tarapoto
Chachapoyas
Río Huallaga
Cajamarca
Pucallpa
Aguaytía
Tingo María
Huánuco
Cerro de Pasco
Río Apurímac
La Oroya
Tarma
Huaral
Matucana
Huancayo
Huancavelica
Huanta
Ayacucho
Chincha Alta
Ica
Pisco
Nazca
Lomas

Quillabamb
Aband
Cha

PERU
Cordillera
Cordillera Occidental

Golfo de Guayaquil
Bahía de Sechura

PACIFIC OCEAN

BOLIVIA'S TWO CAPITALS

LA PAZ – legislative and
administrative capital
SUCRE – legal capital

GALAPAGOS ISLANDS

(Archipiélago de Colón, to Ecuador)

N

Isla Darwin · Isla Wolf

1000m/3281ft
500m/1640ft
Sea level

Isla Pinta
Isla Marchena
Isla
Isabela
Isla
Genovesa
Equator
Isla San Salvador
Isla Fernandina
Isla Santa Cruz
Puerto Baquerizo
Moreno
Isla
Isla Santa María
SanCristóbal
Isla Española

0 km   50
0 miles   50

N

0 km   300
0 miles   300

Population   ● National capital

○ below 50,000   ○ 50,000 to 100,000   ◉ 100,000 to 500,000   ◼ above 500,000

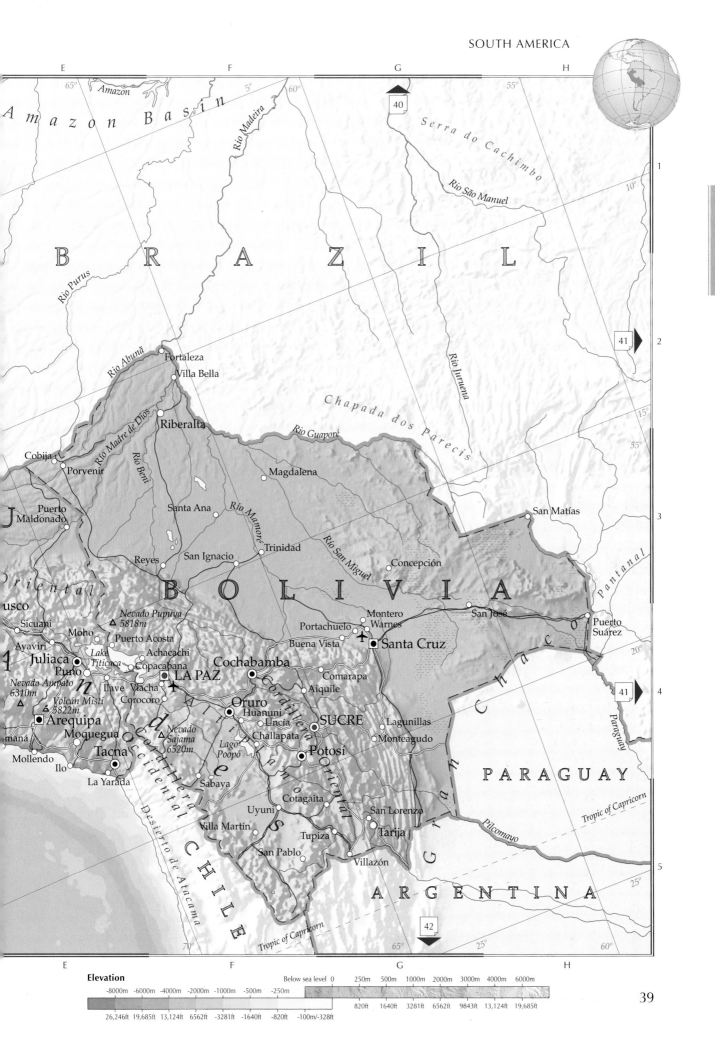

E   F   G   H

65° *Amazon* 5° 60° 55°

40

A m a z o n   B a s i n

Rio Madeira

Serra do Cachimbo

Rio São Manuel

1

10°

B   R   A   Z   I   L

Rio Purus

Rio Juruena

41

2

Fortaleza
Villa Bella
Rio Abunã

Chapada dos Parecis

15°

Rio Madre de Dios
Riberalta

Rio Guaporé

55°

Cobija
Rio Beni
Porvenir

Magdalena

San Matías

3

Puerto
Maldonado
Santa Ana

Rio Mamoré

San Ignacio
Reyes

Trinidad

Rio San Miguel
Concepción

Oriental

B   O   L   I   V   I   A

Pantanal

usco
Sicuani
Nevado Pupuya
△ *5818m*

San José
Puerto
Suárez

20°

Moho
Ayaviri
Puerto Acosta
Achacachi

Montero
Warnes
Portachuelo

Juliaca
Lake Titicaca
Copacabana
LA PAZ
Buena Vista

Santa Cruz

n

Puno
Ilave
Viacha
Cochabamba

Nevado Ampato
6310m
△
Corocoro

Comarapa
Aiquile

41

4

Volcán Misti
△ *5822m*
Arequipa
Oruro
Huanuni
Uncía

SUCRE
Lagunillas

Cordillera Oriental
Cordillera

Moquegua
Nevado Sajama
△ *6520m*
Challapata

Monteagudo

maná
Tacna
Lago Poopó
Potosí

Grand Chaco

Mollendo
Ilo
La Yarada
Sabaya

PARAGUAY

Occidental

Uyuni
Cotagaita
San Lorenzo

Tropic of Capricorn

Villa Martín
Tupiza
Tarija

5

25°

San Pablo
Villazón

Desierto de Atacama

C H I L E

A   R   G   E   N   T   I   N   A

Pilcomayo
Paraguay

42

Tropic of Capricorn
70° 65° 25° 60°

E   F   G   H

Elevation

Below sea level 0   250m   500m   1000m   2000m   3000m   4000m   6000m

-8000m   -6000m   -4000m   -2000m   -1000m   -500m   -250m

820ft   1640ft   3281ft   6562ft   9843ft   13,124ft   19,685ft

26,246ft   19,685ft   13,124ft   6562ft   -3281ft   -1640ft   -820ft   -100m/-328ft

39

Brazil

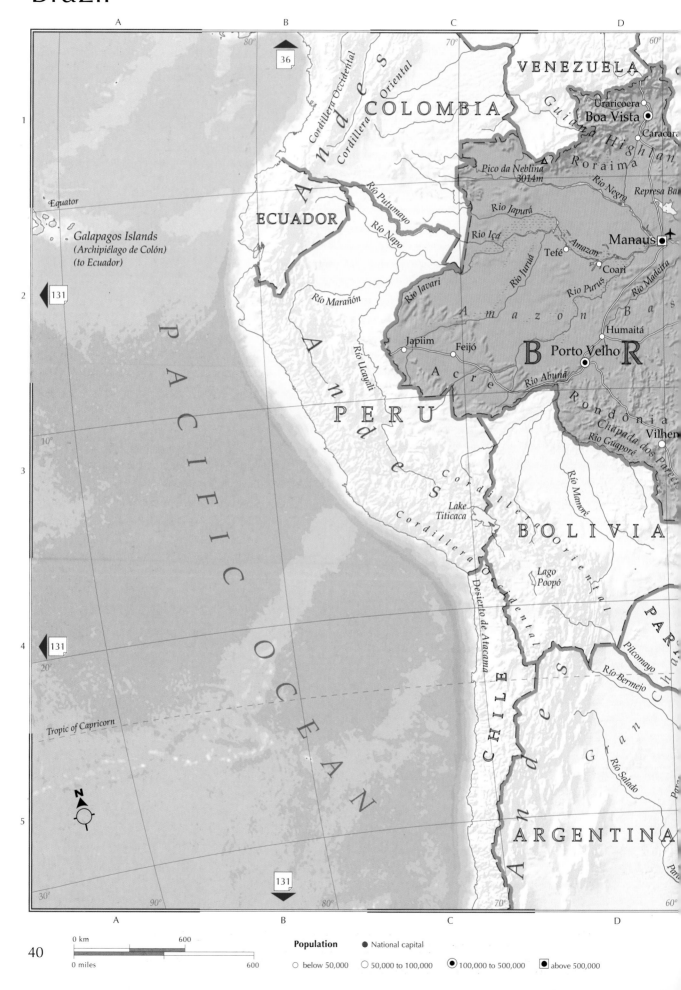

VENEZUELA

COLOMBIA

ECUADOR

PERU

BOLIVIA

ARGENTINA

CHILE

PACIFIC OCEAN

Galapagos Islands
(Archipiélago de Colón)
(to Ecuador)

Equator

Tropic of Capricorn

Cordillera Occidental

Cordillera Oriental

Río Putumayo

Río Napo

Río Marañón

Río Javari

Río Ucayali

Río Juruá

Río Içá

Río Japurá

Río Negro

Amazon

Rio Madeira

Rio Purus

Rio Abunã

Rio Guaporé

Rio Mamoré

Pilcomayo

Río Bermejo

Río Salado

Desierto de Atacama

Cordillera Oriental

Cordillera Occidental

A n d e s

Guiana Highlands

Roraima

Pico da Neblina
3014m

Represa Bal

Uraricoera

Boa Vista

Caracara

Manaus

Tefé

Coari

Humaitá

Porto Velho

Vilhen

Japiim

Feijó

Acre

Rondônia

Chapada dos Parec

B R

B a

Amazon

Lake
Titicaca

Lago
Poopó

G

Andes

PAR

N

36

131

131

131

Population   ● National capital

○ below 50,000   ○ 50,000 to 100,000   ◎ 100,000 to 500,000   ◼ above 500,000

0 km   600
0 miles   600

ATLANTIC OCEAN

SURINAME

FRENCH GUIANA (to France)

Tumuc-Humac Mountains

Mouths of the Amazon

Amapá

Macapá

Ilha Caviana de Fora

Baía de Marajó

Ilha de Marajó

Baía de São Marcos

Alenquer

Amazon

Belém

Santarém

Altamira

São Luís

Parnaíba

Camocim

Itaituba

Rio Xingu

Represa de Tucuruí

Bacabal

Piripiri

Fortaleza

Mossoró

Atol das Rocas

San Fernando de Noronha (to Brazil)

Maranhão

Teresina

Açu

Cabo de São Roque

Imperatriz

Ceará

Natal

Marabá

Rio Grande do Norte

Carolina

Floriano

Juazeiro do Norte

Paraíba

João Pessoa

Serra do Cachimbo

Balsas

Picos

Pernambuco

Campina Grande

A Z I L

Piauí

Recife

Rio Tocantins

Represa de Sobradinho

Alagoas

Maceió

Palmas do Tocantins

Rio São Francisco

Juazeiro

Aracaju

Tocantins

Chapada Diamantina

Estância

Rio Araguaia

Taguatinga

Feira de Santana

10°

Serra Formosa

Goiás

Salvador

Cuiabá

Planalto

Bahia

Baía de Todos os Santos

Mato Grosso

BRASÍLIA

Janaúba

Itabuna

ndonópolis

Anápolis

Central

Vitória da Conquista

Goiânia

Jataí

Montes Claros

Canavieiras

Minas

Araçuaí

Mato Grosso do Sul

Araguari

Gerais

Governador Valadares

antal

Uberlândia

Uberaba

Espírito Santo

Campo Grande

Belo Horizonte

Aquidauana

Ribeirão Preto

Divinópolis

Vitória

esidente Prudente

Marília

Juiz de Fora

Campos

20°

Londrina

São Paulo

Campinas

Nova

Maringá

Paraná

Iguaçu

Rio de Janeiro

São Paulo

Santos

Tropic of Capricorn

Represa de Itaipú

Ponta Grossa

Saltos do Rio Iguaçu

Curitiba

Iguaçu

Joinville

Paraná

Santa Catarina

Blumenau

Florianópolis

Rio Grande

Passo Fundo

nta Maria

do Sul

Canoas

RUGUAY

Bagé

Porto Alegre

Lagoa dos Patos

30°

Rio Negro

Rio Grande

Mirim Lagoon

ATLANTIC OCEAN

Equator

44

45

45

45

Elevation

| Below sea level | 0 | 250m | 500m | 1000m | 2000m | 3000m | 4000m | 6000m |

-8000m -6000m -4000m -2000m -1000m -500m -250m

26,246ft 19,685ft 13,124ft 6562ft -3281ft -1640ft -820ft -100m/-328ft

820ft 1640ft 3281ft 6562ft 9843ft 13,124ft 19,685ft

Southern South America

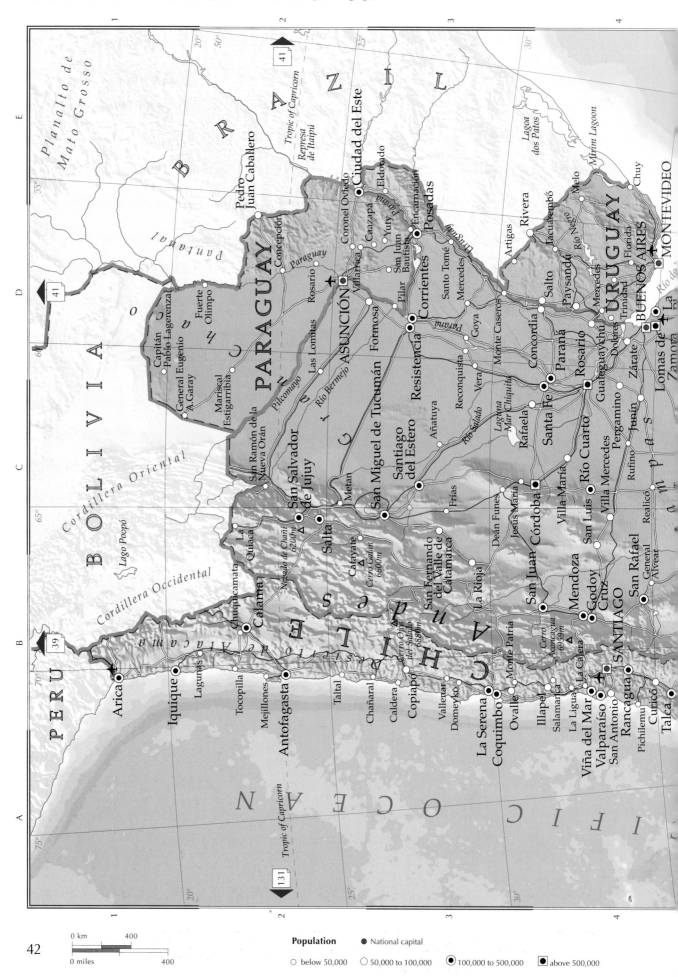

Planalto de Mato Grosso

BRAZIL

BOLIVIA

PERU

Cordillera Oriental

Cordillera Occidental

Lago Poopó

Pantanal

Pedro Juan Caballero

Tropic of Capricorn

Represa de Itaipú

Ciudad del Este

Eldorado

Encarnación

Posadas

Rivera

Lagoa dos Patos

Mirim Lagoon

Chuy

Melo

Tacuarembó

Río Negro

URUGUAY

Florida

Trinidad

MONTEVIDEO

BUENOS AIRES

Concepción

Paraguay

PARAGUAY

Coronel Oviedo

Caazapá

Yuty

San Juan Bautista

Villarrica

San Juan d

Artigas

Salto

Paysandú

Mercedes

La Plata

Capitán Pablo Lagerenza

Fuerte Olimpo

General Eugenio A.Garay

Mariscal Estigarribia

Rosario

Las Lomitas

ASUNCIÓN

Pilar

Formosa

Corrientes

Santo Tomé

Mercedes

Concordia

Paraná

Rosario

Zárate

Lomas de Zamora

Pilcomayo

Río Bermejo

Resistencia

Reconquista

Vera

Goya

Monte Caseros

Gualeguaychú

Dolores

Pergamino

Junín

San Ramón de la Nueva Orán

San Salvador de Jujuy

Metán

San Miguel de Tucumán

Santiago del Estero

Añatuya

Laguna Mar Chiquita

Río Salado

Rafaela

Santa Fe

Río Cuarto

Villa Mercedes

Rufino

Realicó

La Quiaca

Nevado de Chañi 6200m

Salta

Cafayate

Cerro Galán 6600m

Frías

Deán Funes

Jesús María

Córdoba

San Luis

San Fernando del Valle de Catamarca

La Rioja

CHILE

ARGENTINA

San Juan

Mendoza

Godoy Cruz

San Rafael

General Alvear

Chuquicamata

Calama

Cerro Ojos del Salado 6880m

Monte Patria

Cerro Aconcagua 6959m

Desierto de Atacama

Arica

Iquique

Lagunas

Tocopilla

Mejillones

Antofagasta

Taltal

Chañaral

Caldera

Copiapó

Vallenar

Domeyko

La Serena

Coquimbo

Ovalle

Illapel

Salamanca

La Ligua

La Calera

Viña del Mar

Valparaíso

San Antonio

Rancagua

Pichilemu

Curicó

Talca

Santiago

SANTIAGO

Tropic of Capricorn

PACIFIC OCEAN

0 km 400
0 miles 400

Population ● National capital

○ below 50,000 ○ 50,000 to 100,000 ◉ 100,000 to 500,000 ▣ above 500,000

ATLANTIC

OCEAN

ARGENTINA

Mar del Plata
Balcarce
Necochea
Coronel Dorrego
Tres Arroyos
Bahía Blanca
Punta Alta
Bahía Blanca
Choele Choel
Río Negro
San Antonio Oeste
Viedma
Golfo San Matías
Peninsula Valdés
Golfo Nuevo
Rawson

Cipolletti
Neuquén
Zapala
San Carlos de Bariloche
Lago Nahuel Huapi
Río Colorado
Río Chubut
Esquel
Paso de Indios
Trelew
Río Chico
Lago Musters
Sarmiento
Lago Buenos Aires
Comodoro Rivadavia
Golfo San Jorge
Caleta Olivia
Río Deseado
Puerto Deseado
Puerto San Julián

Concepción
Los Angeles
Lebu
Río Bío Bío
Temuco
Loncoche
Valdivia
Osorno
Puerto Varas
Puerto Montt
Ancud
Castro
Isla de Chiloé
Golfo Corcovado
Archipiélago de los Chonos
Golfo de Penas
Puerto Aisén
Coihaique
Chile Chico
Cochrane
Cerro San Valentín 4058m
Cerro Murallón Sur 3050m
Isla Wellington
Puerto Natales
Cerro Paine 2670m
El Calafate
Río Santa Cruz
Río Chico
Río Gallegos
Puerto Natales
Punta Arenas
Porvenir
Ushuaia
Tierra del Fuego
Strait of Magellan
Bahía Grande

CHILE

R E P U B L I C A

FALKLAND ISLANDS
(to UK)
West Falkland
STANLEY
East Falkland
Goose Green

Isla de los Estados
Beagle Channel
Cabo de Hornos
(Cape Horn)
D r a k e   P a s s a g e

Elevation

Below sea level 0   250m   500m   1000m   2000m   3000m   4000m   6000m

-8000m -6000m -4000m -2000m -1000m -500m -250m

820ft   1640ft   3281ft   6562ft   9843ft   13,124ft   19,685ft

26,246ft 19,685ft 13,124ft 6562ft -3281ft -1640ft -820ft
                                                    -100m/-328ft

The Atlantic Ocean

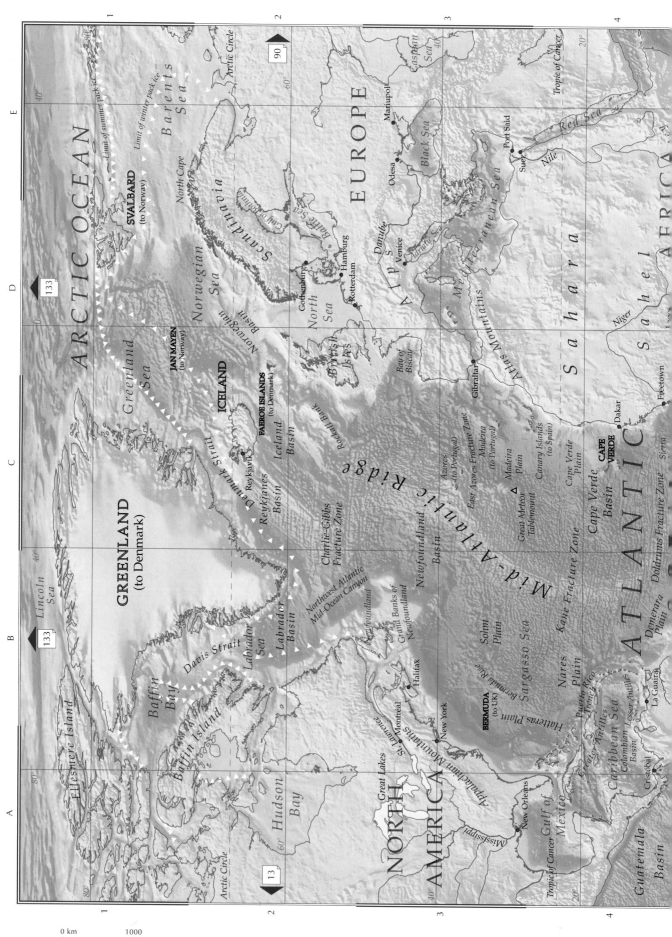

ARCTIC OCEAN

EUROPE

NORTH AMERICA

ATLANTIC

AFRICA

Lincoln Sea

Ellesmere Island

GREENLAND (to Denmark)

Baffin Bay

Baffin Island

Hudson Bay

Davis Strait

Labrador Sea

Labrador Basin

Denmark Strait

Greenland Sea

Barents Sea

Norwegian Sea

Norwegian Basin

Scandinavia

SVALBARD (to Norway)

North Cape

Limit of summer pack ice
Limit of winter pack ice

Arctic Circle

JAN MAYEN (to Norway)

ICELAND

Reykjavík

Reykjanes Basin

Iceland Basin

FAROE ISLANDS (to Denmark)

Rockall Bank

British Isles

Gulf of Bothnia

Baltic Sea

North Sea

Gothenburg

Hamburg

Rotterdam

Danube

Venice

Odesa

Mariupol'

Black Sea

Caspian Sea

Alps

Adriatic Sea

Mediterranean Sea

Atlas Mountains

Sahara

Sahel

Niger

Red Sea

Nile

Port Said

Suez

Gibraltar

Bay of Biscay

Azores (to Portugal)

East Azores Fracture Zone

Madeira (to Portugal)

Madeira Plain

Canary Islands (to Spain)

Great Meteor Tablemount

Cape Verde Plain

CAPE VERDE

Cape Verde Basin

Dakar

Freetown

Sierra

Doldrums Fracture Zone

Demerara Plain

Charlie-Gibbs Fracture Zone

Mid-Atlantic Ridge

Northwest Atlantic Mid-Ocean Canyon

Newfoundland Basin

Grand Banks of Newfoundland

Newfoundland

Solm Plain

Sargasso Sea

Bermuda Rise

BERMUDA (to UK)

Hatteras Plain

Nares Plain

Kane Fracture Zone

Puerto Rico Trench

Greater Antilles

Lesser Antilles

Caribbean Sea

Colombian Basin

La Guaira

Cristóbal

Guatemala Basin

Halifax

New York

Montréal

St. Lawrence

Great Lakes

Appalachian Mountains

Mississippi

New Orleans

Gulf of Mexico

Tropic of Cancer

Arctic Circle

• Major port

0 km   1000

0 miles   1000

44

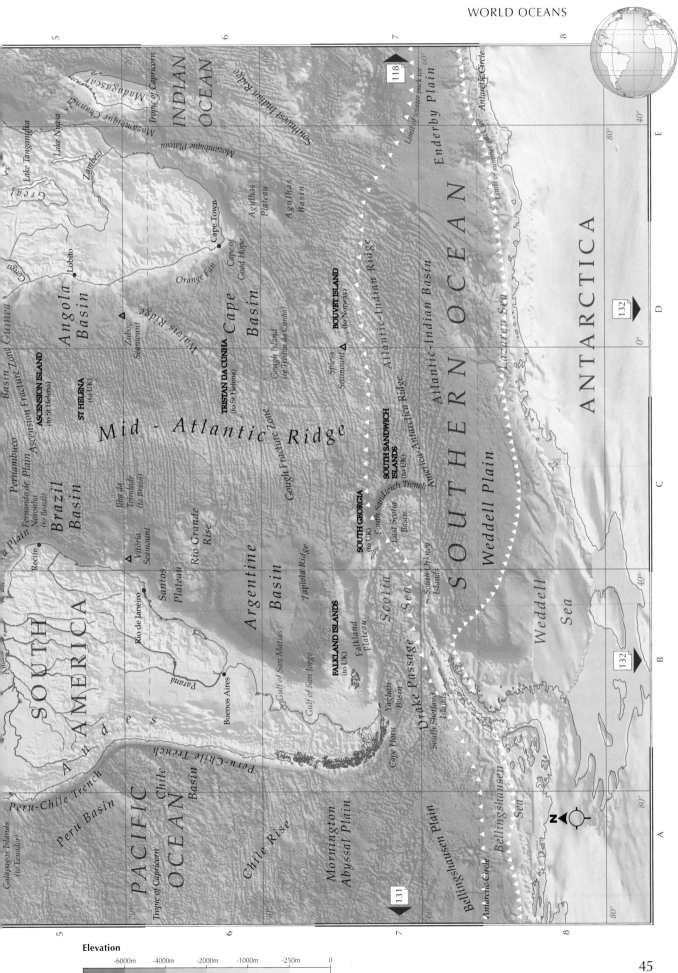

INDIAN OCEAN

Tropic of Capricorn

Madagascar

Mozambique Channel

Lake Tanganyika

Lake Nyasa

Zambezi

Great

Congo

Lobito

Mozambique Plateau

Southwest Indian Ridge

Cape Town

Agulhas Plateau

Agulhas Basin

Cape of Good Hope

Orange Fan

Enderby Plain

Limit of winter pack ice

Antarctic Circle

Angola Basin

Basin Zone

Ascension Fracture Zone

Zaïre Seamount

Walvis Ridge

Cape Basin

BOUVET ISLAND
(to Norway)

Atlantic-Indian Ridge

SOUTHERN OCEAN

ANTARCTICA

ASCENSION ISLAND
(to St Helena)

ST HELENA
(to UK)

TRISTAN DA CUNHA
(to St Helena)

Gough Island
(to Tristan da Cunha)

Spiess Seamount

Atlantic-Indian Basin

Lazarev Sea

Limit of summer pack ice

Pernambuco

Fernando de Noronha
(to Brazil)

Mid - Atlantic Ridge

Gough Fracture Zone

America-Antarctica Ridge

Weddell Plain

Brazil Basin

Ilha da Trindade
(to Brazil)

Rio Grande Rise

SOUTH SANDWICH ISLANDS
(to UK)

South Sandwich Trench

Recife

Vitória Seamount

Argentine Basin

SOUTH GEORGIA
(to UK)

East Scotia Basin

Santos Plateau

Zapiola Ridge

Scotia Sea

South Orkney Islands

Weddell Sea

SOUTH AMERICA

Rio de Janeiro

FALKLAND ISLANDS
(to UK)

Falkland Plateau

Andes

Paraná

Buenos Aires

Gulf of San Matias

Gulf of San Jorge

Yaghan Basin

Drake Passage

South Shetland Islands

Bellingshausen Plain

Galápagos Islands
(to Ecuador)

Cape Horn

Peru-Chile Trench

PACIFIC OCEAN

Chile Basin

Chile Rise

Mornington Abyssal Plain

Bellingshausen Sea

Antarctic Circle

Tropic of Capricorn

Peru Basin

Peru-Chile Trench

118

132

132

131

N

Elevation

-6000m	-4000m	-2000m	-1000m	-250m	0
19,685ft	13,124ft	6562ft	-3281ft	-820ft	0

Africa

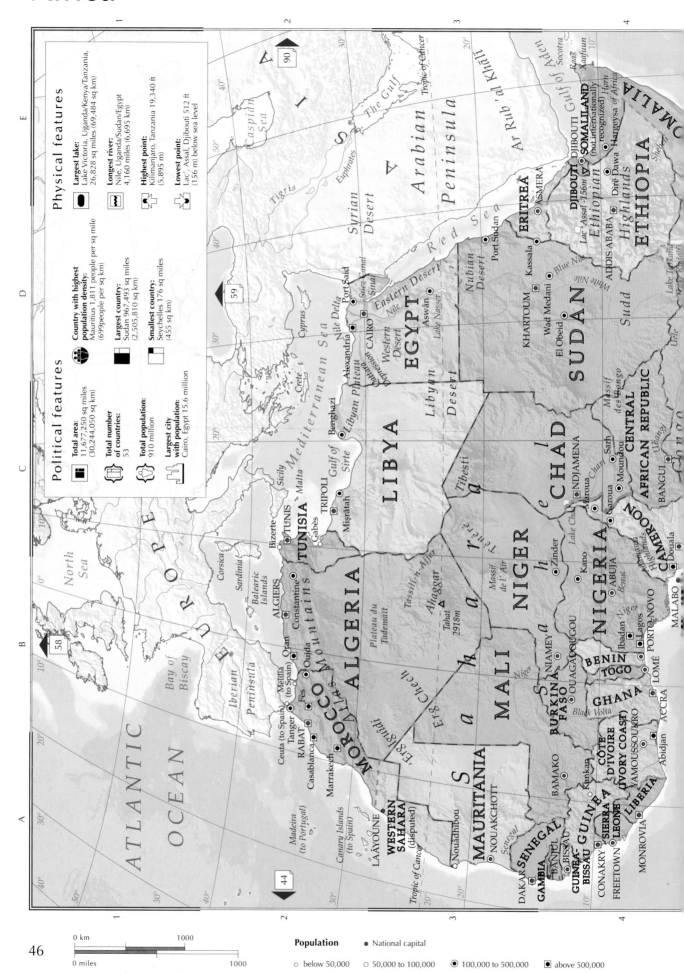

Political features

Total area:
11,677,250 sq miles
(30,244,050 sq km)

Total number of countries:
53

Total population:
910 million

Largest city with population:
Cairo, Egypt 15.6 million

Country with highest population density:
Mauritius 1,811 people per sq mile
(699people per sq km)

Largest country:
Sudan 967,493 sq miles
(2,505,810 sq km)

Smallest country:
Seychelles 176 sq miles
(455 sq km)

Physical features

Largest lake:
Lake Victoria, Uganda/Kenya/Tanzania,
26,828 sq miles (69,484 sq km)

Longest river:
Nile, Uganda/Sudan/Egypt
4,160 miles (6,695 km)

Highest point:
Kilimanjaro, Tanzania 19,340 ft
(5,895 m)

Lowest point:
Lac' Assal, Djibouti 512 ft
(156 m) below sea level

Population   • National capital

○ below 50,000   ○ 50,000 to 100,000   ◉ 100,000 to 500,000   ■ above 500,000

0 km   1000
0 miles   1000

ATLANTIC OCEAN

INDIAN OCEAN

Somali Basin

DEM. REP. CONGO
GABON
BRAZZAVILLE
Matadi
Cabinda (to Angola)
KINSHASA
Ilebo
Kasai
Kananga
LUANDA
Cuanza
Luvua
Lualaba
Cuango

Bukavu
BUJUMBURA
BURUNDI
RWANDA
NAIROBI
Kilimanjaro 5895m
Masai Steppe
Mombasa
Tanga
Pemba
Zanzibar
Dar es Salaam
TANZANIA
DODOMA
Lubumbashi
Lake Tanganyika
Lake Rukwa
Lake Mweru
Lake Nyasa
Kalemie

Aldabra Group

COMOROS
MORONI
MAYOTTE (to France)
Mahajanga
Nacala
Nampula
ANTANANARIVO
MADAGASCAR
Fianarantsoa
Toliara

Mozambique Channel

Madagascar Basin

INDIAN OCEAN

Great Rift Valley

MALAWI
LILONGWE
Blantyre
Ndola
Kitwe
ZAMBIA
LUSAKA
Victoria Falls
Lake Kariba
Lake Malawi
Ruvuma
Rungwe
Zambezi
MOZAMBIQUE
Beira

Madagascar Plateau

ANGOLA
Huambo
Môco 2619m
Lubango
Namibe
Bié Plateau
Cubango
Cunene
Cuando
Cuito
Zambezi
Okavango Delta
HARARE
ZIMBABWE
Bulawayo
Francistown
BOTSWANA
Kalahari Desert
GABORONE
Nossob
Zambezi
Limpopo
MAPUTO
MBABANE
SWAZILAND
TSHWANE/ PRETORIA
Johannesburg
Vaal
LESOTHO
MASERU
BLOEMFONTEIN
Durban
Maclear

Mozambique Plateau

NAMIBIA
WINDHOEK
Etosha Pan
Namib Desert
Orange River
SOUTH AFRICA
Great Karoo
Drakensberg
East London
Port Elizabeth
CAPE TOWN
Cape of Good Hope

Agulhas Plateau

Agulhas Basin

Orange Fan

Cape Basin

Angola Basin

ATLANTIC OCEAN

SAINT HELENA (to UK)
ASCENSION ISLAND (to Saint Helena)
Ascension Fracture Zone

Walvis Ridge

Southwest Indian Ridge

Crozet Plateau

Prince Edward Islands (to South Africa)

Mid-Atlantic Ridge

Atlantic-Indian Ridge

Tristan da Cunha (to Saint Helena)

Gough Island (to Tristan da Cunha)

Winter limit of pack ice

Tropic of Capricorn

M Basin

47

Northwest Africa

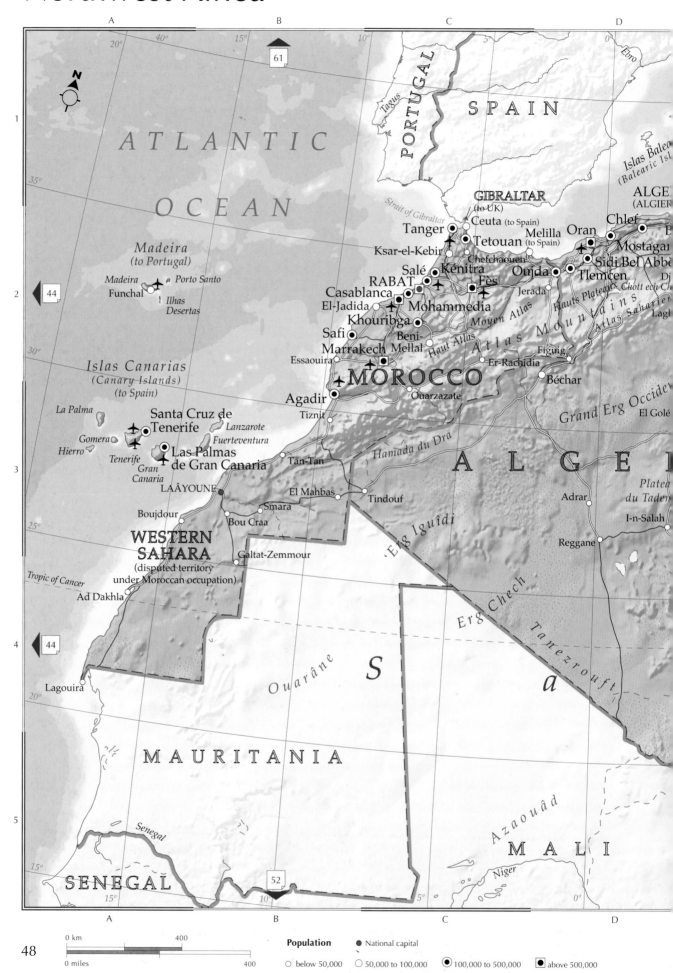

A   B   C   D

20°   40°   15°   10°   0°

ATLANTIC

OCEAN

PORTUGAL

SPAIN

Tagus

35°

Strait of Gibraltar

GIBRALTAR
(to UK)

Ceuta (to Spain)

Tanger
Tetouan
Melilla
(to Spain)

Ksar-el-Kebir
Chefchaouen

Oran
Mostaga
Sidi Bel Abb
Tlemcen

ALGE
(ALGIER)

Chlef

Islas Baleo
(Balearic Isl

Ebro

Madeira
(to Portugal)

Madeira   • *Porto Santo*

Funchal   *Ilhas*
Desertas

Salé
Kénitra
RABAT
Casablanca
El-Jadida   Mohammedia
Khouribga
Safi   Beni-
Marrakech   Mellal
Essaouira

Fès
Oujda
Jerada

Moyen Atlas
Haut Atlas

Hauts Plateaux   *Chott ech Ch*
Atlas Mountains
Atlas Saharien
Lagl

Figuig

30°

Islas Canarias
(Canary Islands)
(to Spain)

La Palma

Gomera   Santa Cruz de
Hierro   Tenerife

Lanzarote
Fuerteventura

Las Palmas
de Gran Canaria
Tenerife
Gran
Canaria

MOROCCO
Agadir
Ouarzazate
Tiznit

Er-Rachidia
Béchar

Grand Erg Occide   El Golé

A L G E
Plateo
du Tade

Adrar
I-n-Salah

Reggane

LAÂYOUNE

Hamada du Dra

Tan-Tan

El Mahbas
Smara   Tindouf
Bou Craa

25°

Boujdour

WESTERN
SAHARA
(disputed territory
under Moroccan occupation)

Galtat-Zemmour

Erg Iguîdi

Erg Chech

Tanezrouft

Tropic of Cancer

Ad Dakhla

20°

Lagouira

Ouarâne

S   a

MAURITANIA

15°

Senegal

Azaouâd

M A L I

Niger

SENEGAL

15°   10°   5°   0°

A   B   C   D

0 km   400

0 miles   400

Population   ● National capital

○ below 50,000   ○ 50,000 to 100,000   ◉ 100,000 to 500,000   ▣ above 500,000

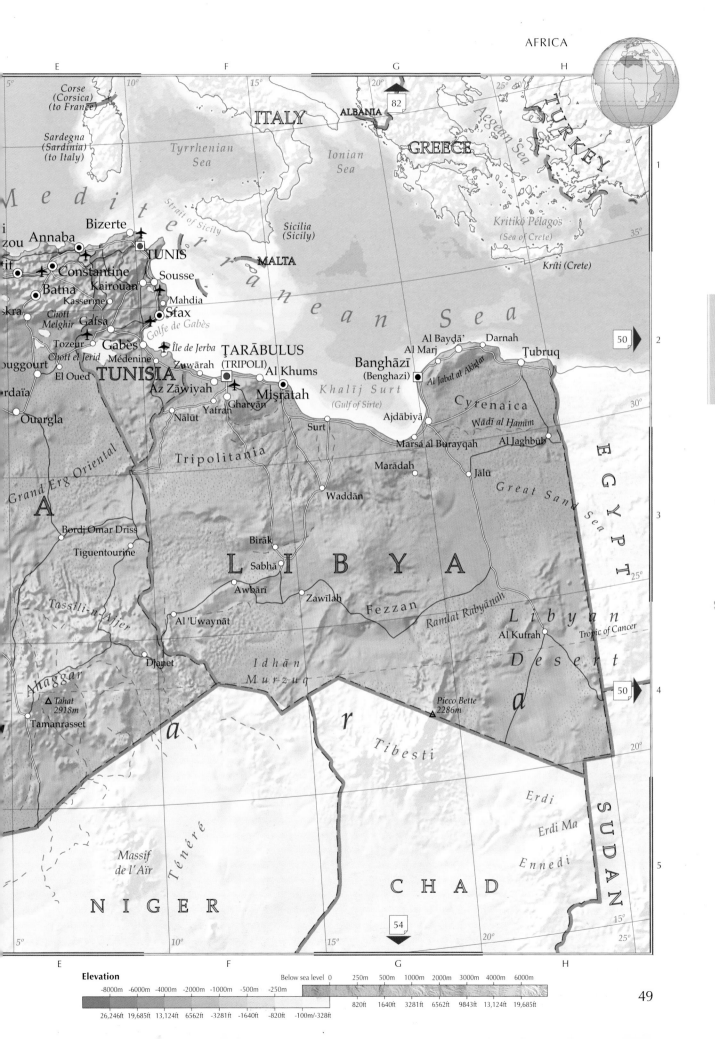

ITALY

ALBANIA

GREECE

TURKEY

Corse
(Corsica)
(to France)

Sardegna
(Sardinia)
(to Italy)

Tyrrhenian
Sea

Ionian
Sea

Aegean Sea

Kritikó Pélagos
(Sea of Crete)

M e d i t e r

Bizerte

Annaba

TUNIS

Constantine

Batna

Kasserine

Kairouan

Sousse

Mahdia

Sfax

Sicilia
(Sicily)

MALTA

Kríti (Crete)

r a n e a n   S e a

Gafsa

Chott
Melghir

Tozeur

Gabès

El Oued

Médenine

Golfe de Gabès

Strait of Sicily

Île de Jerba

Chott el Jerid

TUNISIA

Zuwārah

TҬARĀBULUS
(TRIPOLI)

Az Zāwiyah

Al Khums

Misҫrātah

Al Baydҫā'

Al Marj

Darnah

Tҫubruq

Banghāzī
(Benghazi)

Al Jabal al Akhdҫar

Cyrenaica

Ouargla

Nālūt

Yafran

Gharyān

Khalīj Surt
(Gulf of Sirte)

Ajdābiyā

Wādī al Hҫamīm

Marsá al Burayqah

Al Jaghbūb

Surt

Tripolitania

Grand Erg Oriental

Bordj Omar Driss

Tiguentourine

Birāk

Sabhā

Awbārī

Waddān

Marādah

Jālū

L   I   B   Y   A

Great Sand Sea

EGYPT

Al 'Uwaynāt

Zawīlah

Fezzan

Ramlat Rabyānah

Tassili-n-Ajjer

Libyan

Al Kufrah

Tropic of Cancer

Djanet

Idhān
Murzuq

Desert

Ahaggar

△ Tahat
2918m

Tamanrasset

Picco Bette
△ 2286m

Tibesti

Massif
de l'Aïr

Ténéré

Erdi

Erdi Ma

Ennedi

SUDAN

N   I   G   E   R

C   H   A   D

Northeast Africa

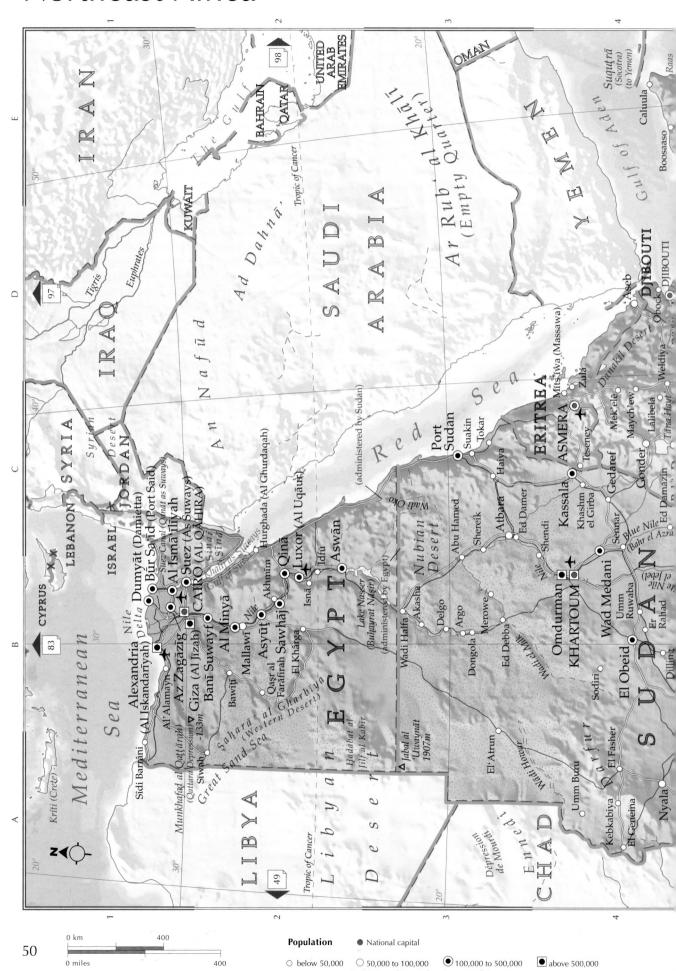

MEDITERRANEAN AREA NAMES (transcribed from map):

IRAN

SYRIA

LEBANON

ISRAEL

JORDAN

IRAQ

CYPRUS

KUWAIT

BAHRAIN

QATAR

UNITED ARAB EMIRATES

OMAN

SAUDI ARABIA

Ad Dahnā'

An Nafūd

Ar Rub' al Khālī
(Empty Quarter)

YEMEN

Suquṭrā
(Socotra)
(to Yemen)

Gulf of Aden

Calula

Boosaaso

DJIBOUTI

Aseb

Obock

DJIBOUTI

Weldiya

Raas

Danakil Desert

Mits'iwa (Massawa)

Zula

ERITREA

ASMERA

Mek'elē

Maych'ew

Lalibela

Lake Tana

Gonder

Ed Damazin

Teseney

Kassala

Gedaref

Khashm el Girba

Haiya

Sennar

Blue Nile
Bahr el Azraq

Suakin

Tokar

Port Sudan

Red Sea

Abu Hamed

Shereik

Atbara

Ed Damer

Shendi

Omdurman

KHARTOUM

Wad Medani

Umm Ruwaba

Er Rahad

El Obeid

Dilling

Nubian Desert

Akasha

Delgo

Argo

Merowe

Ed Debba

Dongola

Wadi Halfa

Wadi el Milk

Sodiri

Umm Buru

Kebkabiya

El Fasher

El Geneina

Nyala

Darfur

SUDAN

CHAD

Ennedi

Wadi Howar

Depression de Mourdi

El'Atrun

Jabal al 'Uwaynat
1907m

Hadabat al
Jilf al Kabir

Sahara' al Gharbīya
(Western Desert)

Great Sand Sea

Siwah

Munkhafad al Qattārah
(Qattara Depression) -133m

Al 'Alamayn

Sidi Barrani

Mediterranean Sea

Kríti (Crete)

Alexandria
(Al Iskandarīyah)

Nile Delta

Damietta (Dumyāṭ)

Būr Sa'īd (Port Said)

Al Ismā'īlīyah

Suez Canal (Qanāt as Suways)

Suez (As Suways)

Sinai Desert

CAIRO (AL QĀHIRA)

Giza (Al Jīzah)

Az Zaqāzīg

Banī Suwayf

Al Minyā

Bawīṭī

El Khārga

Qaṣr al Farāfirah

Mallawī

Asyūṭ

Sawhāj

Akhmīm

Qinā

Luxor (Al Uqṣur)

Isnā

Idfū

Aswān

Lake Nasser
(Buḥayrat Nāṣir)
(administered by Egypt)

Hurghada (Al Ghurdaqah)

Gulf of Suez (Khalīj as Suways)

Nile

Libyan Desert

LIBYA

EGYPT

Tropic of Cancer

Syrian Desert

Tigris

Euphrates

The Gulf

Wadi Oko

(administered by Sudan)

Blue Nile
The Nile (Bahr el Jebel)

50

Population
- ● National capital
- ○ below 50,000
- ◎ 50,000 to 100,000
- ◉ 100,000 to 500,000
- ■ above 500,000

0 km   400

0 miles   400

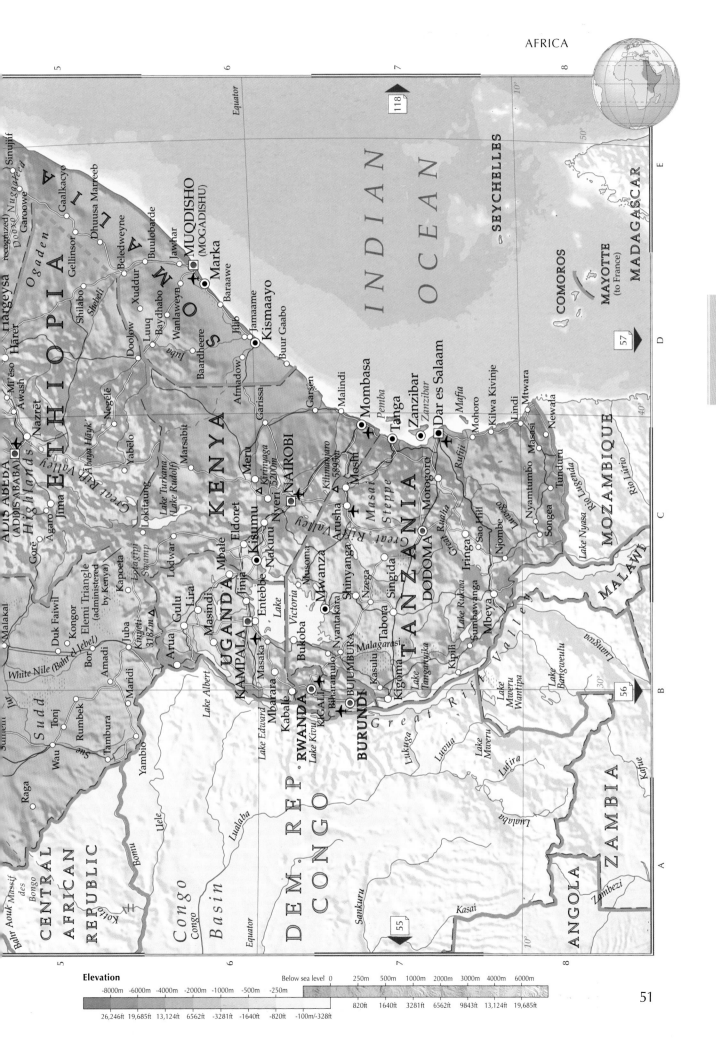

INDIAN

OCEAN

SEYCHELLES

COMOROS

MAYOTTE
(to France)

MADAGASCAR

ETHIOPIA

Ogaden

Danu Nugaaleed
(recognized)

Sinujiif
Garoowe
Gaalkacyo
Dhuusa Marreeb
Beledweyne
Buulobarde
Jawhar

MUQDISHO
(MOGADISHU)
Marka

Baraawe

Garsen

SOMALIA

Hargeysa
Härer
Mi'eso
Awash
Nazrēt
ADIS ABEBA
(ADDIS ABABA)

Goré
Agaro
Jima
Negēlē

Ethiopian Highlands

Lake Tana

Yabelo

Gellinsor
Xuddur
Baydhabo
Wanlaweyn

Luuq
Doolow
Baardheere
Jamaame
Kismaayo

Buur Gaabo
Jilib

Afmadow

Lake
Turkana
(Lake Rudolf)

Marsabit

Meru
Kirinyaga
5200m
Nyeri
Nakuru

KENYA

Eldoret
Kisumu

Lokitaung

Lodwar

Kapoeta

Sobat
Swamp

Kinyeti
3187m

Gulu
Lira
Masindi
Arua

UGANDA

Mbale
Jinja
KAMPALA
Entebbe

Masaka

Mbarara
Kabale

RWANDA
KIGALI

Biharamulo

BURUNDI
BUJUMBURA

Kasulu
Kigoma

Lake
Kivu

Lake
Tanganyika

Lukuga
Luvua
Lufira

Great Rift Valley

Lake
Mweru
Wantipa
Lake
Mweru

Lake
Bangweulu

ZAMBIA

ANGOLA

Zambezi
Kafue

Luapula

Malindi
Mombasa
Tanga
Zanzibar
Zanzibar
Dar es Salaam

Pemba

Mafia

Mohoro
Kilwa Kivinje
Lindi
Mtwara

Masasi
Newala

MOZAMBIQUE

Rio Lúrio

MALAWI

Lake
Nyasa
(Lake Malawi)

Songea
Tunduru
Nyamtumbo
Njombe
Sao Hill
Mbeya
Sumbawanga

TANZANIA

DODOMA
Morogoro
Iringa
Tabora
Singida
Nzega
Shinyanga
Nyantakara
Mwanza
Musoma

Masai
Steppe

Kilimanjaro
5895m
Moshi
Arusha

Great Rift Valley

NAIROBI

Bukoba

Lake
Victoria

Malagarasi

Lake
Rukwa

Kipili

Rukuga

Meru

Garissa

CENTRAL
AFRICAN
REPUBLIC

Bahr Aouk
des Bongo

Kotto

Raga
Malakal
Duk Faiwil
Kongor
Bor
Amadi
Maridi
Juba

White Nile (Bahr el Jebel)

Elemi Triangle
(administered
by Kenya)

Sudd

Sue

Jur

Sumen
Toni
Rumbek
Tambura
Wau
Yambio

DEM. REP.

CONGO

Congo

Congo
Basin

Uele
Bomu
Luluaba

Sankuru
Kasai

Lualaba

Equator

Shabelli
Shilabo

Gedo
Gori

Wabe
Shebele

Awash
Wabe Hayk'

West Africa

A   B   C   D

25°   20°   15°   10°

WESTERN SAHARA
(disputed territory
under Moroccan occupation)

'Aïn Ben Tili

Bîr Mogreïn

Tropic of Cancer

25°

Fdérik   Zouérat

Touâjîl

l'Erg   *Kâghet*   *El Hank*

Ouarâne

S

E

20°

Nouâdhibou

Choûm

Aṭâr

Chinguetti

Akjoujt

Oujeft

M A U R I T A N I A

El Mreyyé

Akchâr

CAPE VERDE

Ilhas de Barlavento

Santo Antão

Mindelo

São Vicente   Pedra Lume

São Nicolau   Sal

Boa Vista

NOUAKCHOTT   Idîni

Boutilimit

Rkîz

Magta' Lahjar

Tidjikja

Tîchît

Boûmdeïd

Aoukâr

'Ayoûn el 'Atroûs

Oualâta

Rosso

Aleg

Kiffa

Tâmchekket

Richard Toll   Dagana

Sénégal

Kaédi

Timbedgha

Néma

Saint Louis

Matam

Kobenni

Amourj

Santiago

Fogo   Maio

PRAIA

Ilhas de Sotavento

15°

Louga

Mékhé

SENEGAL

Sélibabi

Bassiko

DAKAR   Thiès   Mbaké

Nioro

S

Mbour   Diourbel

Kayes

Ténenko

Sokone   Kaolack

Toukoto

Kolokani

BANJUL   **GAMBIA**

Tambacounda

Ségou

25°

Bignona   Kolda

Gambia

Kita

Koulikoro

Ziguinchor

Sédhiou   Bafatá

Bafing

BAMAKO

BISSAU

Gaoual

Si

GUINEA-BISSAU

Boké   Labé   Pita

Dinguiraye

Tikinsso

Siguiri

Koul

10°

Mamou

Bagoé

Bougouni

Kindia   **G U I N E A**

Faranah

Kankan

CONAKRY

Tokounou

Odienné

Tengréla

Ferkessédo

Makeni   Kissidougou

Boundiali   Korl

SIERRA LEONE

Beyla

CÔTE D'IVOIRE

FREETOWN

Bo   Kenema

Katiola

(IVORY COAST)

Nzérékoré

Danané

Gbanga

YAMOUSSOUKRO

Tubmanburg

Harbel

Gagnoa

5°

MONROVIA

Zwedru

Divo

Buchanan   **LIBERIA**

Sassan

Harper

San-Pédro

5°

A T L A N T I C   O C E A N

N

44

44

45

45

20°   15°   10°

1

2

3

4

5

0 km   400

0 miles   400

Population   ● National capital

○ below 50,000   ○ 50,000 to 100,000   ◉ 100,000 to 500,000   ■ above 500,000

AFRICA

E   F   G   H

0°   5°   10°   15°

49

25° 1

L I B Y A

A L G E R I A

Tanezrouft

Tropic of Cancer

Taoudenni

Tassili-n-Ajjer

Ahaggar

Tibesti

54

Ténéré
du
Tafassâsset

Séguédine   20° 2

'Erg I-n-Sâkâne

Adrar des
Ifôghas

Tessalit

Assamakka   Iferouâne

Araouane

Azaouâd

Massif
de l'Aïr

M A L I

Monts Bagzane
2022m

Ténéré

Grand Erg de Bilma

aibine

Tombouctou

Agadez

Goundam   Gao

N I G E R   Ngourti   C H A D

Lac
Niangay   Ansongo   Ménaka

Dilia   15° 3

oti   Hombori   Ayorou   Tahoua   Keïta   Dakoro   Nguigmi   Lake Chad

Baudiagara   Tillabéri   Birnin
Konni   Zinder   Gouré

Ouahigouya   h   Dogondoutchi   Maradi   Tessaoua   Hadejia

URKINA   NIAMEY   e   Sokoto   Guidimouni   Nguru

udougou   Kaya   Jega   Katsina   Hadejia   Maiduguri

OUAGADOUGOU   Fada-
Ngourma   Gusau   Kano   Potiskum

FASO   Tenkodogo   Koko   Zaria   Gongola   Biu

bo-Dioulasso   Bawku   Yelwa   Kaduna   Bauchi   Kumo

Bolgatanga   Sansanné-
Mango   Natitingou   Kainji
Reservoir   Jos   Gombi

Wa   Kandi   Minna   Jos
Plateau   Yola   10° 4

Yendi   BENIN   N I G E R I A   54

Tamale   Parakou   Jebba   ABUJA   Lafia   Shebshi
Mountains

doukou   Sokodé   Ilorin   Niger   Benue   Adamawa Highlands

GHANA   Oyo   Ogbomosho   Wukari   Gotel
Mountains   C.A.R.

Wenchi   Ibadan   Ede   Lokoja   Makurdi

Sunyani   Lake
Volta   Abomey   PORTO-
NOVO   Owo   Benin
City   Enugu

engourou   Kumasi   Kpalimé   Lagos   Onitsha

Nsawam   LOMÉ   Cotonou   Sapele   Owerri   Calabar   5° 5

Asamankese   ACCRA   Warri   Aba   Uyo

Apoisso   Cape Coast   Bight of Benin   Port Harcourt   Uyo

idjan   Sekondi-Takoradi   Mouths of the Niger

Gulf of Guinea   Isla de Bioco   55

EQUATORIAL
GUINEA   C A M E R O O N

0°   5°   10°   15°

E   F   G   H

Elevation

Below sea level 0   250m 500m 1000m 2000m 3000m 4000m 6000m

-8000m -6000m -4000m -2000m -1000m -500m -250m

820ft 1640ft 3281ft 6562ft 9843ft 13,124ft 19,685ft

26,246ft 19,685ft 13,124ft 6562ft -3281ft -1640ft -820ft -100m/-328ft

Central Africa

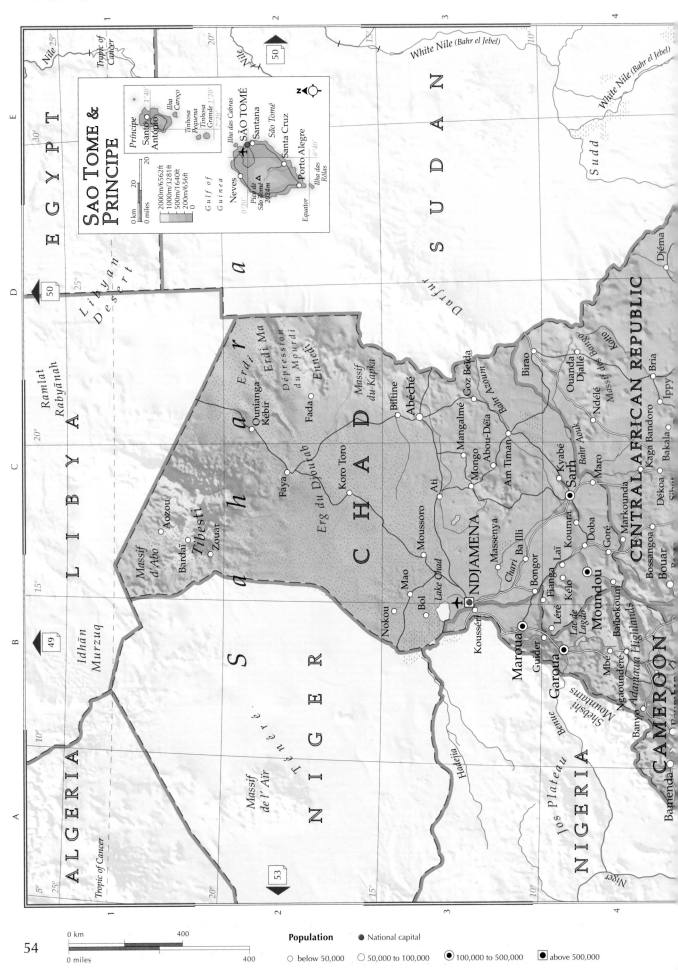

SÃO TOMÉ & PRINCIPE

Príncipe
Santo António
Ilha das Cabras
Ilha Caroço
Tinhosa Pequena
Tinhosa Grande

SÃO TOMÉ
Santana
São Tomé
Santa Cruz
Neves
Porto Alegre
Pico de São Tomé 2024m
Ilha das Rólas

Gulf of Guinea

0 km 20
0 miles 20

2000m/6562ft
1000m/3281ft
500m/1640ft
200m/656ft
0

EGYPT

Nile
Tropic of Cancer
Libyan Desert
Ramlat Rabyānah

LIBYA

Idhān Murzuq

ALGERIA

Tropic of Cancer

NIGER

Massif de l'Aïr

Ténéré

Sahara

Massif d'Abo
Aozou
Bardaï
Tibesti
Zouar

Erdi
Erdi Ma
Dépression du Mourdi
Ennedi

Ounianga Kébir
Fada
Faya
Erg du Djourab
Koro Toro

CHAD

Massif du Kapka
Biltine
Abéché

Ati
Moussoro
Mao
Bol
Lake Chad
Nokou

Goz Beïda
Mangalmé
Mongo
Abou-Déïa
Am Timan
Bahr Azoum

Birao
Ouanda Djallé
Ndélé
Massif des Bongo
Kotto
Bria
Ippy

NDJAMENA
Massenya
Chari
Bongor
Ba Illi

Kyabé
Sarh
Bahr Aouk
Maro
Koumra
Doba
Goré
Markounda
Kaga Bandoro
Dékoa
Sibut
Bossangoa
Bouar

CENTRAL AFRICAN REPUBLIC

Kousséri
Maroua
Guider
Garoua
Mbé
Ngaoundéré
Léré
Kélo
Lac de Léré
Fianga
Laï
Baïbokoum
Moundou

Bénoué
Shebshi Mountains
Banyo
Adamaua Highlands

CAMEROON

Jos Plateau
Hadejia

NIGERIA

Niger

Diéma

SUDAN

Darfur
Sudd

White Nile (Bahr el Jebel)
White Nile (Bahr el Jebel)

50

49

50

50

53

54

0 km 400
0 miles 400

Population

○ below 50,000
○ 50,000 to 100,000
◉ 100,000 to 500,000
■ above 500,000
● National capital

Elevation

| Below sea level | 0 | 250m | 500m | 1000m | 2000m | 3000m | 4000m | 6000m |

-8000m -6000m -4000m -2000m -1000m -500m -250m

820ft 1640ft 3281ft 6562ft 9843ft 13,124ft 19,685ft

26,246ft 19,685ft 13,124ft 6562ft -3281ft -1640ft -820ft -100m/-328ft

55

Southern Africa

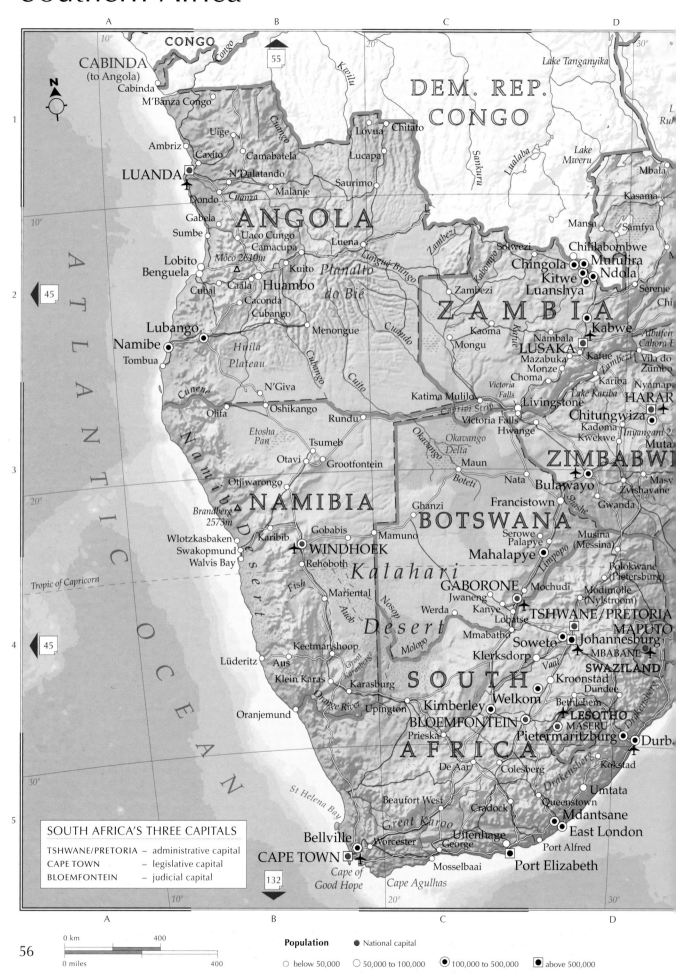

CONGO

CABINDA
(to Angola)
Cabinda
M'Banza Congo
Uíge
Ambriz
Caxito
Camabatela
LUANDA
N'Dalatando
Dondo
Cuanza
Gabela
Sumbe
Uaco Cungo
Camacupa
ANGOLA
Lobito
Benguela
Môco 2619m
Kuito
Cubal
Caála
Huambo
Caconda
Cubango
Lubango
Menongue
Namibe
Tombua
Huíla
Plateau
N'Giva
Cunene
Olifa
Oshikango
Rundu
Etosha
Pan
Tsumeb
Otavi
Grootfontein
Otjiwarongo
NAMIBIA
Brandberg
2573m
Karibib
Gobabis
Mamuno
Wlotzkasbaken
Swakopmund
WINDHOEK
Walvis Bay
Rehoboth
Tropic of Capricorn
Mariental
Fish
Auob
Kalahari
Nosop
Keetmanshoop
Lüderitz
Aus
Klein Karas
Karasburg
Molopo
Orange River
Oranjemund
Upington
Prieska
De Aar
Colesberg
Beaufort West
St Helena Bay
Great Karoo
Bellville
Worcester
George
CAPE TOWN
Cape of
Good Hope
Mosselbaai
Cape Agulhas

DEM. REP.
CONGO
Lake Tanganyika
Lovua
Chitato
Lucapa
Saurimo
Sankuru
Lualaba
Lake
Mweru
Mbala
Kasama
Mansa
Samfya
Luena
Lungué-Bungo
Zambezi
Solwezi
Chililabombwe
Chingola
Mufulira
Kitwe
Ndola
Serenje
Chi
ZAMBIA
Zambezi
Luanshya
Kaoma
Nambala
Kabwe
Mongu
LUSAKA
Mazabuka
Albufeira
Cahora
Monze
Kafue
Vila do
Choma
Zumbo
Kariba
Nyamap
Katima Mulilo
Victoria
Falls
Lake Kariba
HARAR
Capriri Strip
Livingstone
Chitungwiza
Victoria Falls
Hwange
Kadoma
Inyangani 2
Kwekwe
Muta
Okavango
Delta
Maun
ZIMBABWI
Boteti
Nata
Bulawayo
Masv
Ghanzi
Francistown
Shashe
Zvishavane
Gwanda
BOTSWANA
Serowe
Palapye
Musina
(Messina)
Mahalapye
Limpopo
Polokwane
(Pietersburg)
GABORONE
Mochudi
Modimolle
(Nylstroom)
Jwaneng
Kanye
TSHWANE/PRETORIA
Werda
Lobatse
MAPUTO
Mmabatho
Soweto
Johannesburg
MBABANE
Klerksdorp
SWAZILAND
SOUTH
Vaal
Kroonstad
Dundee
Welkom
Bethlehem
Kimberley
BLOEMFONTEIN
LESOTHO
MASERU
Pietermaritzburg
Durb
AFRICA
Kokstad
Cradock
Queenstown
Umtata
Mdantsane
East London
Uitenhage
Port Alfred
Port Elizabeth

ATLANTIC OCEAN

N

SOUTH AFRICA'S THREE CAPITALS
TSHWANE/PRETORIA – administrative capital
CAPE TOWN – legislative capital
BLOEMFONTEIN – judicial capital

0 km   400
0 miles   400

Population   ● National capital

○ below 50,000   ○ 50,000 to 100,000   ◉ 100,000 to 500,000   ■ above 500,000

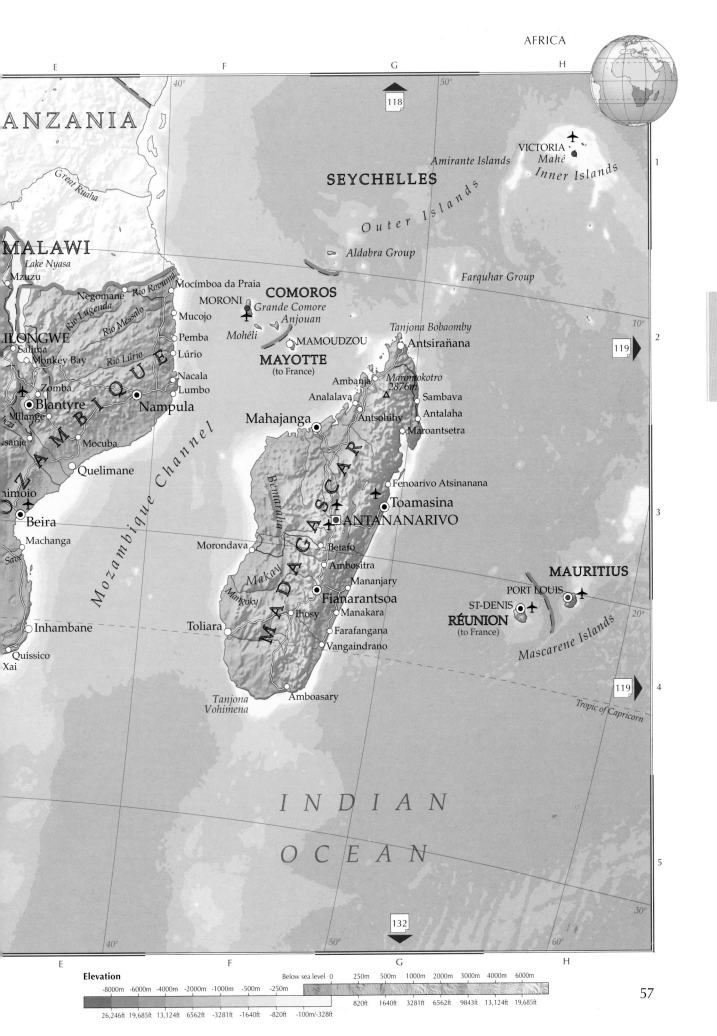

E   **F**   **G**   **H**

118

ANZANIA

TANZANIA

Great Ruaha

MALAWI

Lake Nyasa

Mzuzu

Negomane   *Rio Rovuma*   Mocímboa da Praia

Rio Lugenda   Mucojo

ILONGWE   *Rio Messalo*   Pemba

Salima   *Rio Lúrio*

Monkey Bay   Lúrio

Zomba   Nacala

Milange   Lumbo

Blantyre   Nampula

Isanje   Mocuba

MOZAMBIQUE

Quelimane

imoio

Beira

Machanga

Saex

Inhambane

Quissico

Xai

SEYCHELLES

Amirante Islands

VICTORIA   *Mahé*

Inner Islands

Outer Islands

Aldabra Group

Farquhar Group

COMOROS

MORONI   *Grande Comore*

Anjouan

Mohéli   MAMOUDZOU

MAYOTTE
(to France)

Ambanja

Analalava

Antsohihy

Mahajanga

Tanjona Bobaomby

Antsirañana

Maromokotro
2876m

Sambava

Antalaha

Maroantsetra

Mozambique Channel

MADAGASCAR

Betsiboka

Makay

Mangoky

Morondava

Betafo

Ambositra

Mananjary

Fianarantsoa

Ihosy   Manakara

Toliara   Farafangana

Vangaindrano

Fenoarivo Atsinanana

Toamasina

ANTANANARIVO

Tanjona
Vohimena

Amboasary

MAURITIUS

PORT LOUIS

ST-DENIS

RÉUNION
(to France)

Mascarene Islands

Tropic of Capricorn

119

119

I N D I A N

O C E A N

132

Elevation

Below sea level   0   250m   500m   1000m   2000m   3000m   4000m   6000m

-8000m -6000m -4000m -2000m -1000m -500m -250m

820ft   1640ft   3281ft   6562ft   9843ft   13,124ft   19,685ft

26,246ft 19,685ft 13,124ft 6562ft -3281ft -1640ft -820ft -100m/-328ft

Europe

133

Political features

Total area:
4,809,200 sq miles
(12,456,000 sq km)

Total number of countries:
44

Total population:
697 million

Largest city with population:
Moscow, European Russia 13.75 million

Country with highest population density:
Monaco 43,561 people per sq mile
(16,754 people per sq km)

Largest country:
European Russia 1,527,341 sq miles
(3,955,818 sq km)

Smallest country:
Vatican City, Italy 0.17 sq miles
(0.44 sq km)

Physical features

Largest lake:
Lake Lagoda, European Russia
7,100 sq miles (18,390 sq km)

Longest river:
Volga, European Russia
2,290 miles (3,688 km)

Highest point:
El'brus, Caucasus, European Russia
18,510ft (5,642 m)

Lowest point:
Volga Delta, Caspian Sea, European
Russia 92 ft (28m) below sea level

44
44
46

ICELAND
REYKJAVÍK
Vatnajökull
Arctic Circle
Limit of winter pack ice

Reykjanes Ridge
Iceland Basin
Hatton Ridge
Rockall Bank
Rockall Trough
Porcupine Plain
Biscay Plain

Norwegian Basin
Norwegian Sea
Faeroe-Iceland Ridge
FAEROE ISLANDS (to Denmark)
Faeroe-Shetland Trough
Shetland Islands
Outer Hebrides
Orkney Islands
Trondheim
Bergen
Stavanger
OSLO
Gothenburg
Aalborg
Jönköp
Jylland
DENMARK
Odense
COPENH
Malm

British Isles
Ireland
Glasgow
Edinburgh
Belfast
IRELAND ISLE OF MAN (to UK)
DUBLIN
Liverpool
Manchester
UNITED KINGDOM
Britain
Birmingham
Cardiff
LONDON
Celtic Sea
Celtic Shelf
English Channel
CHANNEL IS. (to UK)
le Havre
North Sea

NETHERLANDS
THE HAGUE AMSTERDAM
Rotterdam
BELGIUM
BRUSSELS
Liège
Bonn
LUXEMBOURG
LUXEMBOURG
Frankfurt am Main
GERMANY
Hamburg
Hannover
BERLIN
Elbe
Wrocł
PRA
CZECH REPUBLIC

ATLANTIC OCEAN
Azores-Biscay Rise
Charcot Seamounts
Iberian Plain
Galicia Bank
A Coruña
Bay of Biscay
Bordeaux
Bilbao
Cordillera Cantábrica
Duero
Rennes
PARIS
Nantes
Loire
Orléans
FRANCE
Strasbourg
Garonne
Lyon
Massif Central
Toulouse
Pyrenees
Rhône
Stuttgart
Munich
Zürich
BERN
SWITZERLAND
Mont Blanc 4807m
Innsbruck AUSTRIA
Salzburg
VIENNA
BRATI
LIECH.
Milan
Turin
Venice
Nice
ANDORRA
Marseille
MONACO
Pisa
Bologna
LJUBLJANA
SLOVENIA
Trieste
CROA
SAN MARINO
BO & H
Adriatic Sea

Horseshoe Seamounts
Tagus Plain
Madeira (to Portugal)
PORTUGAL
LISBON
Porto
Iberian Peninsula
Tagus
Zaragoza
MADRID
SPAIN
Ebro
Barcelona
Guadalquivir
Seville
Valencia
Palma
Balearic Islands
Corsica
Sardinia
VATICAN CITY
ROME
ITALY
Apennines
Naples
Bari
Tyrrhenian Sea
Algerian Basin
Cagliari
Cosenza
Palermo
Mount Etna 3340m
Sicily
Catania
Ion
Ba
MALTA
VALLETTA
Mediterranea
Sea

Málaga
GIBRALTAR (to UK)
Ceuta (to Spain)
Strait of Gibraltar
Melilla (to Spain)
Canary Islands (to Spain)
Atlas Mountains
AFRICA

0 km   500
0 miles   500

Population   ● National capital

○ below 50,000   ○ 50,000 to 100,000   ◉ 100,000 to 500,000   ▣ above 500,000

Barents Sea

North Cape

Murmansk

Kola Peninsula

Ostrov Kolguyev

White Sea

Arctic Circle

133

70°

80°

Ob'

Irtysh

80°

FINLAND

Archangel

Northern Dvina

Ural Mountains

R   U   S   S   I   A   N

60°

70°

Tampere

Lake Onega

Perm'

90

Turku   HELSINKI

Lake Ladoga

F   E   D   E   R   A   T   I   O   N

50°

70°

Saint Petersburg

Vologda

Ufa

psala

OCKHOLM   TALLINN

Kazan'

land

Yaroslavl'

ESTONIA

Nizhniy Novgorod

Orenburg

Ul'yanovsk

LATVIA

European Plain

MOSCOW

Samara

Ural

RĪGA

Volga Uplands

Aral Sea

Syr Darya

LITHUANIA

Kaunas

Vitsyebsk

Central Russian Upland

ngrad

VILNIUS

Volga

KALININGRAD
(to Russ.Fed).

MINSK

60°

oszcz

Babruysk

Ural

oss

WARSAW

BELARUS

Homyel'

Voronezh

Amu Darya

LAND

Brest

Pripet Marshes

Don

Volgograd

Dnieper Lowlands

40°

Kharkiv

Bug

Astrakhan'

Kraków

L'viv

Dniester

KIEV

Dnieper

*Volga Delta
-28m*

VAKIA

Carpathian Mountains

UKRAINE

Dnipropetrovs'k

Donets'k

60°

Chernivtsi

Rostov-na-Donu

Caspian Sea

APEST

MOLDOVA

CHIŞINĂU

Sea of Azov

Stavropol'

NGARY

Cluj-Napoca

Odesa

40°

ROMANIA

Crimea

90

BELGRADE

Braşov

C a u c a s u s

El'brus 5642m

Simferopol'

BUCHAREST

Danube

Constanţa

Black Sea

RBIA

KOSOVO
(disputed)

BULGARIA

Varna

Balkan Mountains

T.   PRISTINA

SOFIA

Burgas

GORICA

SKOPJE

MACED.

TURKEY

RANA

ANIA

Pindus Mountains

Aegean Sea

A n a t o l i a

GREECE

30°

ATHENS

96

Piraeus

Peloponnese

Irákleio

Cyprus

Tigris

Zágros Mountains

30°

e a

Crete

30°

40°

50°

Euphrates

The North Atlantic

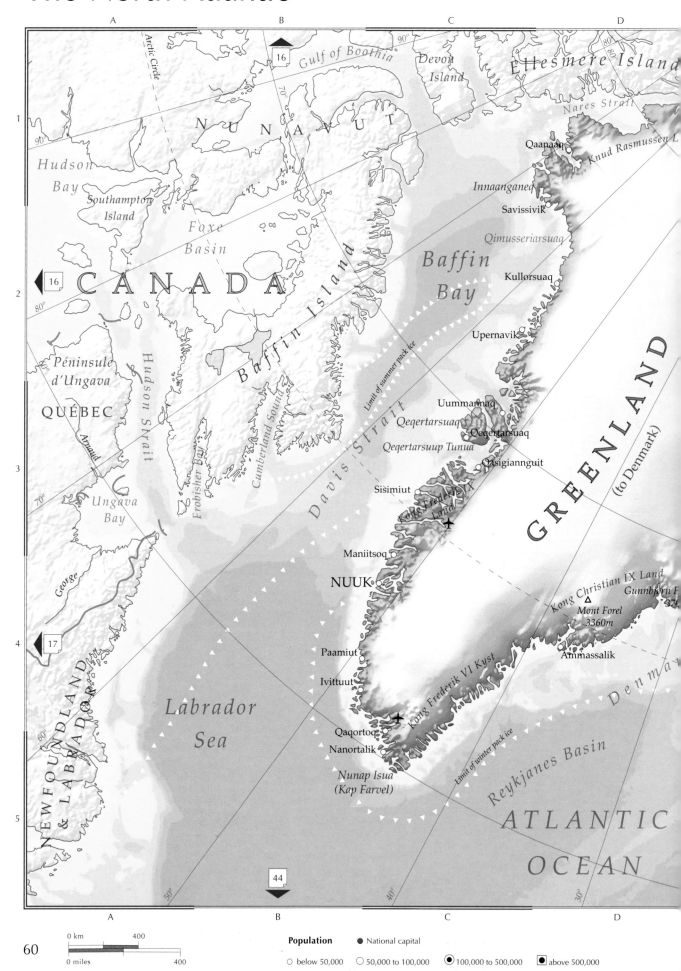

A B C D

Arctic Circle

16

Gulf of Boothia

Devon Island

Ellesmere Island

Nares Strait

90°

70°

NUNAVUT

Qaanaaq

Knud Rasmussen L.

Hudson Bay

Southampton Island

Foxe Basin

Innaanganeq

Savissivik

Qimusseriarsuaq

1

16

CANADA

Baffin Bay

Kullorsuaq

80°

Upernavik

Péninsule d'Ungava

Hudson Strait

Baffin Island

QUÉBEC

Arnaud

Cumberland Sound

Uummannaq

Qeqertarsuaq

Qeqertarsuup Tunua

Qeqertarsuaq

2

Frobisher Bay

Qasigiannguit

Davis Strait

Sisimiut

Kong Frederik IX Land

70°

Ungava Bay

Maniitsoq

GREENLAND

(to Denmark)

3

George

NUUK

Kong Christian IX Land

Gunnbjørn F.

370

Mont Forel
3360m

17

Paamiut

Ammassalik

Ivittuut

Kong Frederik VI Kyst

Denmar

60°

Labrador Sea

Qaqortoq

Nanortalik

Reykjanes Basin

NEWFOUNDLAND & LABRADOR

Nunap Isua
(Kap Farvel)

Limit of winter pack ice

4

5

ATLANTIC

OCEAN

50°

44

40°

30°

A B C D

0 km   400

0 miles   400

Population   ● National capital

60

○ below 50,000   ○ 50,000 to 100,000   ◉ 100,000 to 500,000   ◼ above 500,000

Limit of summer pack ice

*Lincoln
Sea*

Kap Morris Jesup

ARCTIC

OCEAN

*Wandel
Sea*

Independence Fjord

Nord

SVALBARD
(to Norway)

Spitsbergen

LONGYEARBYEN
Barentsburg

*Zemlya
Frantsa-Iosifa*

Kvitøya

Nordaustlandet

Kong Karls Land

Barentsøya

Edgeøya

Storfjorden

*Novaya
Zemlya*

Barents
Sea

Kong Frederik VIII Land

*Greenland
Sea*

Limit of winter pack ice

*Bjørnøya
(to Norway)*

*ng Christian X
Land*

Limit of summer pack ice

△ *Petermann Bjerg
2940m*

Daneborg

Kong Oscar Fjord

●Ittoqqortoormiit

Kangertittivaq

Kangikajik

Mohns Ridge

JAN MAYEN
(to Norway)

*Nordkapp
(North Cape)*

FINLAND

Arctic Circle

*Norwegian
Sea*

Vestfjorden

S
W
E
D
E
N

Norwegian Basin

trait

ICELAND

Bolungarvík
Siglufjördhur   Raufarhöfn
fjördhur
    Húsavík
    Akureyri
Stykkishólmur   Seydhisfjördhur
flói ●REYKJAVÍK   ○Neskaupstadhur
Selfoss   *Vatnajökull*
                ○Djúpivogur
horlákshöfn   △
    *Hvannadalshnúkur
    2119m*
Surtsey   Vestmannaeyjar

FAEROE ISLANDS
(to Denmark)

●TÓRSHAVN

N

*Shetland
Islands*

N O R W A Y

*Gulf
of
Bothnia*

133

88 ▶

62 ▶

63 ▼

Elevation

| Below sea level | 0 | 250m | 500m | 1000m | 2000m | 3000m | 4000m | 6000m |

-8000m -6000m -4000m -2000m -1000m -500m -250m

820ft 1640ft 3281ft 6562ft 9843ft 13,124ft 19,685ft

26,246ft 19,685ft 13,124ft 6562ft -3281ft -1640ft -820ft -100m/-328ft

Scandinavia & Finland

RUSSIAN FEDERATION

FINLAND

Barents Sea

ARCTIC OCEAN

Norwegian Sea

Lapland

Arctic Circle

Nordkapp
(North Cape)

Kirkenes
Varangerfjorden
Varangerhalvøya
Tana Bru
Deatnu
Magerøya
Porsangenfjorden
Lakselv
Alta
Talvik
Sørøya
Ringvassøya
Kvaløya
Tromsø
Senja
Andøya
Vesterålen
Lofoten
Vestfjorden
Bodø
Narvik
Harstad
Flatstad

Váljohka
Karigasniemi
Inarijärvi
Kaamanen
Ivalo
Saariselkä
Kautokeino
Enontekiö
Kaaresuvanto
Finnmarksvidda
Muonio
Muonionjoki
Kiruna
Tornetrask
Kebnekaise
2117 m
Malmberget
Gällivare
Skalka
Jokkmokk
Lulealven
Arvidsjaur
Fauske
Saltfjorden
Mo i Rana
Mosjøen
Vega
Namsos
Steinkjer
Kopparberg-
vattnet
Borgefjell
Dorotea
Vilhelmina
Storuman
Storuman
Hotagen
Angermana
Strömsund
Froøya
Froan

Sattanen
Sodankylä
Kittinen
Kittilä
Kolari
Rovaniemi
Kemijärvi
Kuusamo
Pudasjärvi
Suomussalmi
Kuhmo
Sotkamo
Kajaani
Oulujärvi
Oulu
Oulujoki
Kempele
Raahe
Haukoto
Hailuoto
Kokkola
(Karleby)
Umeå
Gulf of Bothnia

Ounasjoki
Kemijoki
Torniojoki
Tornio
Kemi
Haparanda
Kalix
Luleå
Piteå
Skellefteå
Skellefteälven
Lycksele
Umeelven
Boden

Visttasjohka

Population

● National capital

○ below 50,000
○ 50,000 to 100,000
◉ 100,000 to 500,000
◼ above 500,000

0 km   200
0 miles   200

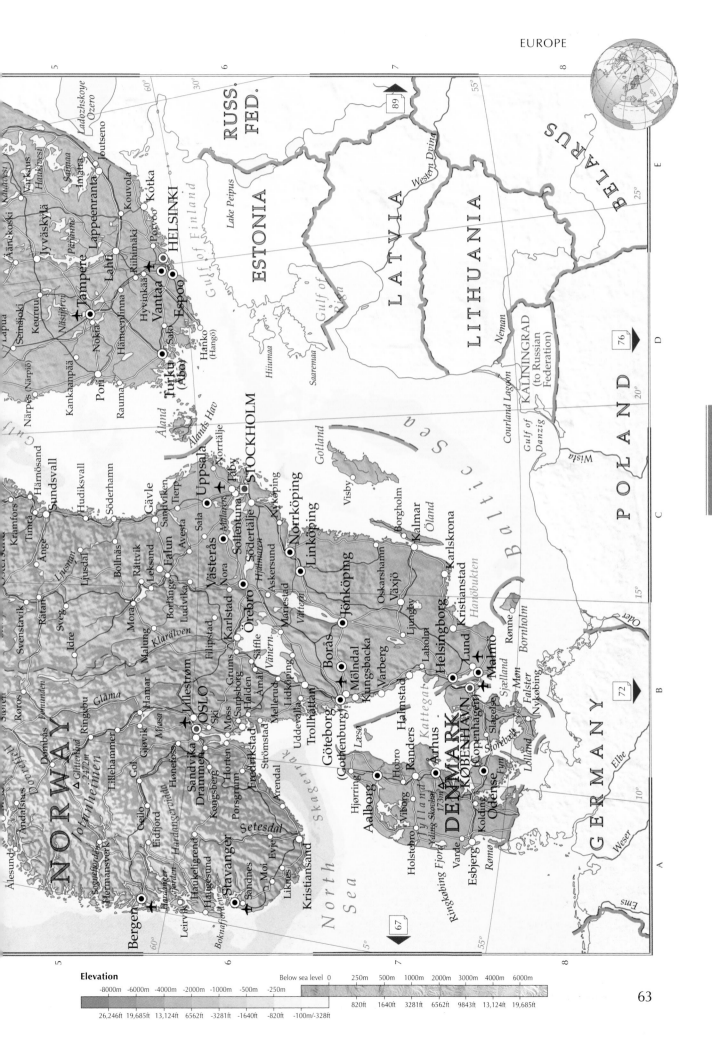

Elevation

| Below sea level | 0 | 250m | 500m | 1000m | 2000m | 3000m | 4000m | 6000m |

-8000m -6000m -4000m -2000m -1000m -500m -250m

-100m/-328ft

26,246ft 19,685ft 13,124ft 6562ft -3281ft -1640ft -820ft

820ft 1640ft 3281ft 6562ft 9843ft 13,124ft 19,685ft

The Low Countries

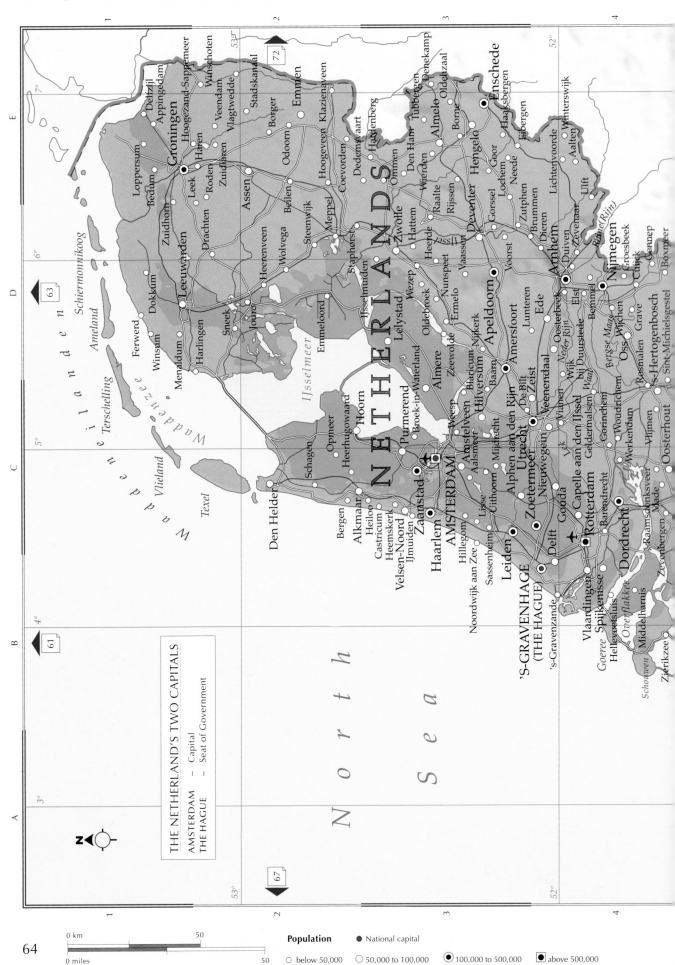

72
63
61
67

THE NETHERLAND'S TWO CAPITALS

AMSTERDAM – Capital
THE HAGUE – Seat of Government

Schiermonnikoog
Ameland
Terschelling
Vlieland
Texel

W a d d e n   e i l a n d e n

W a d d e n z e e

IJsselmeer

N o r t h   S e a

N E T H E R L A N D S

Loppersum
Deltzijl
Appingedam
Hoogezand-Sappemeer
Winschoten
Veendam
Stadskanaal
Vlagtwedde
Groningen
Haren
Leek
Roden
Zuidlaren
Emmen
Klazienaveen
Hoogeveen
Borger
Odoorn
Coevorden
Dedemsvaart
Hardenberg
Denekamp
Oldenzaal
Enschede
Haaksbergen
Eibergen
Lichtenvoorde
Aalten
Winterswijk
Ulft
Bedum
Zuidhorn
Assen
Beilen
Meppel
Staphorst
Hasselt
Zwolle
Hattem
Heerde
Ommen
Den Ham
Tubbergen
Almelo
Wierden
Raalte
Rijssen
Borne
Hengelo
Goor
Lochem
Neede
Zutphen
Brummen
Dieren
Zevenaar
Arnhem
Duiven
Nijmegen
Groesbeek
Cuijk
Boxmeer
Gennep
Zuidhorn
Leeuwarden
Dokkum
Ferwerd
Winsum
Menaldum
Harlingen
Sneek
Joure
Emmeloord
Drachten
Heerenveen
Wolvega
Steenwijk
IJsselmuiden
Genemuiden
Kampen
Vaassen
Voorst
Apeldoorn
Gorssel
Deventer
Elst
Bemmel
Wijchen
Grave
Oss
Rosmalen
's-Hertogenbosch
Sint-Michielsgestel
Den Helder
Bergen
Alkmaar
Heiloo
Castricum
Heemskerk
Velsen-Noord
IJmuiden
Schagen
Heerhugowaard
Opmeer
Hoorn
Purmerend
Broek-in-Waterland
Almere
Zeewolde
Harderwijk
Ermelo
Nunspeet
Wezep
Oldebroek
Nijkerk
Barneveld
Ede
Lunteren
Veenendaal
Wijk bij Duurstede
Tiel
Zaltbommel
Waal
Bergse Maas
Woudrichem
Gorinchem
Werkendam
Made
Raamsdonksveer
Zevenbergen
Heerhugowaard
Zaanstad
Haarlem
AMSTERDAM
Amstelveen
Aalsmeer
Uithoorn
Hilversum
Baarn
Amersfoort
Zeist
De Bilt
Utrecht
Nieuwegein
Vianen
IJsselstein
Gouda
Capelle aan den IJssel
Gelderhalsen
Hillegom
Noordwijk aan Zee
Lisse
Sassenheim
Leiden
Alphen aan den Rijn
Zoetermeer
'S-GRAVENHAGE
(THE HAGUE)
's-Gravenzande
Delft
Rotterdam
Barendrecht
Dordrecht
Vlaardingen
Spijkenisse
Goeree
Hellevoetsluis
Overflakkee
Middelharnis
Schouwen
Zierikzee
Oosterhout
Nieder Rijn
Rijn (Rijn)
Kanaal

Population

● National capital

○ below 50,000
○ 50,000 to 100,000
◉ 100,000 to 500,000
▣ above 500,000

0 km   50
0 miles   50

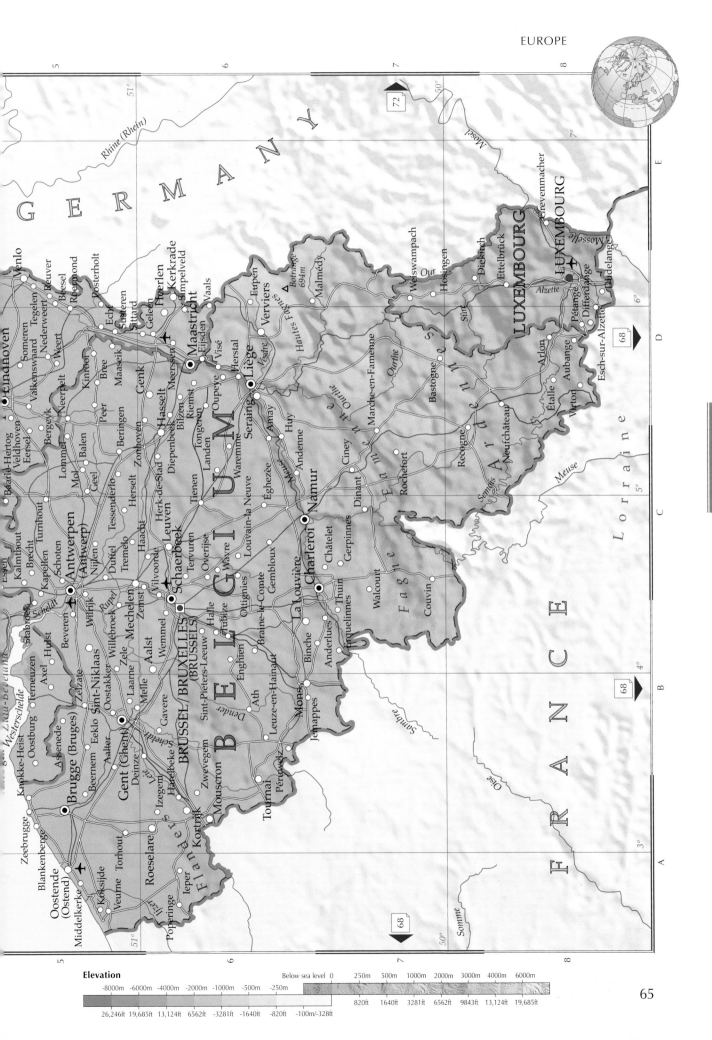

GERMANY

BELGIUM

LUXEMBOURG

FRANCE

Lorraine

Rhine (Rhein)

Mosel

Moselle

Zuid-Beveland

Westerschelde

Zeebrugge Knokke-Heist
Blankenberge
Oostende
(Ostend) Middelkerke
Koksijde
Veurne Torhout
Ieper Roeselare
Poperinge Izegem

Brugge (Bruges)
Oostburg Assenede Aalter
Beernem Eeklo Sint-Niklaas
Terneuzen Zelzate
Axel Hulst
Stabroek Beveren
Kallo

Flandre

Gistel Hadelbeke
Deinze Zwevegem
Kortrijk
Mouscron
Tournai

Gent (Ghent)
Gavere Melle
Laarne Oostakker
Sint-Pieters-Leeuw
Zwevegem

Scheldt
Leie
Dender

Zele
Aalst
Wemmel
Halle
Tubize

Menlo
Beesel Reuver Roermond Posterholt
Venlo Tegelen
Someren Nederweert
Veldhoven Weert Echt
Eindhoven Eersel Kinrooi Susteren
Bergeyk Neerpelt Bree Sittard
Baarle-Hertog Balen Maaseik Geleen
Lommel Mol Peer
Essen Brecht Geel Beringen Zonhoven
Kalmthout Turnhout Herselt Diepenbeek
Schoten Nijlen Herk-de-Stad Bilzen
Kapellen Duffel Tessenderlo Hasselt
Stabroek Tremelo Leuven
Wijnegem Mechelen Haacht Tervuren
Rupel Vilvoorde Overijse
Zemst
Willebroek

Heerlen Kerkrade
Simpelveld
Vaals
Maastricht
Eijsden Vaals
Visé Eupen
Oupeye Verviers
Herstal Botrange
Liège 694m
Seraing Amay
Huy
Waremme
Andenne
Louvain-la-Neuve Eghezée
Tienen Gembloux
Landen
Jodoigne
Namur

Genk
Meerssen
Riemst
Tongeren

Weiswampach
Our
Hosingen
Diekirch
Ettelbrück
Sûre
Arlon
Aubange
Virton
Étalle
Neufchâteau
Bastogne
Recogne
Rochefort
Dinant
Ciney
Marche-en-Famenne
Hautes Fagnes

Malmédy

GRENVENMACHER
LUXEMBOURG
Alzette
Pétange
Differdange
Esch-sur-Alzette
Dudelange

Ardenne

Ourthe

Semois

Meuse

Oise

Somme

Sambre

Fagne

Charleroi
Châtelet
Gerpinnes
Thuin
Walcourt
Couvin
Philippeville
Anderlues
Binche
Mons
Jemappes
Frameries
Péruwelz
Ath
Leuze-en-Hainaut
Enghien
Braine-le-Comte
La Louvière
Wavre
Ottignies
Schaerbeek
**BRUSSEL/BRUXELLES
(BRUSSELS)**

Elevation

-8000m	-6000m	-4000m	-2000m	-1000m	-500m	-250m
26,246ft	19,685ft	13,124ft	6562ft	-3281ft	-1640ft	-820ft	-100m/-328ft

Below sea level 0   250m   500m   1000m   2000m   3000m   4000m   6000m

820ft 1640ft 3281ft 6562ft 9843ft 13,124ft 19,685ft

The British Isles

Unst
Fetlar
Yell
Mainland
Lerwick
Shetland Islands

Fair Isle

Sanday
Kirkwall
Mainland
Hoy
John o'Groats
Orkney Islands

Thurso
Ben Hope
924m
North West Highlands
Ullapool
Inverness
Loch Ness
Aviemore
The Minch

Isle of Lewis
Stornoway
Harris
North Uist
South Uist
Barra
Outer Hebrides

St Kilda

Isle of Skye
Stromeferry
Mallaig
Eigg
Rhum
Coll
Tiree
Isle of Mull
Firth of Lorn
Jura
Islay
The Little Minch
Inner Hebrides

Fort William
Ben Nevis
1343m
Oban
Loch Lomond
Kintyre

Fraserburgh
Peterhead
Aberdeen
Elgin
Dee
Mountains
Spey
Montrose
Arbroath
Forfar
Dundee
St Andrews
Tay
Perth
Firth of Forth
Dunfermline
Forth
Stirling
Edinburgh
Glasgow
Hamilton
Paisley
Clyde
Greenock
East Kilbride
Kilmarnock
Prestwick
Isle of Arran
Ayr
S C O T L A N D
Grampian Mountains

Berwick-upon-Tweed
Galashiels
Hawick
Cheviot Hills
Newcastle upon Tyne
Southern Uplands

Coleraine
NORTHERN

North Sea

A T L A N T I C   O C E A N

Population

- National capital
- Internal administrative capital
- ○ below 50,000
- ○ 50,000 to 100,000
- ◉ 100,000 to 500,000
- ◼ above 500,000

0 km   100
0 miles   100

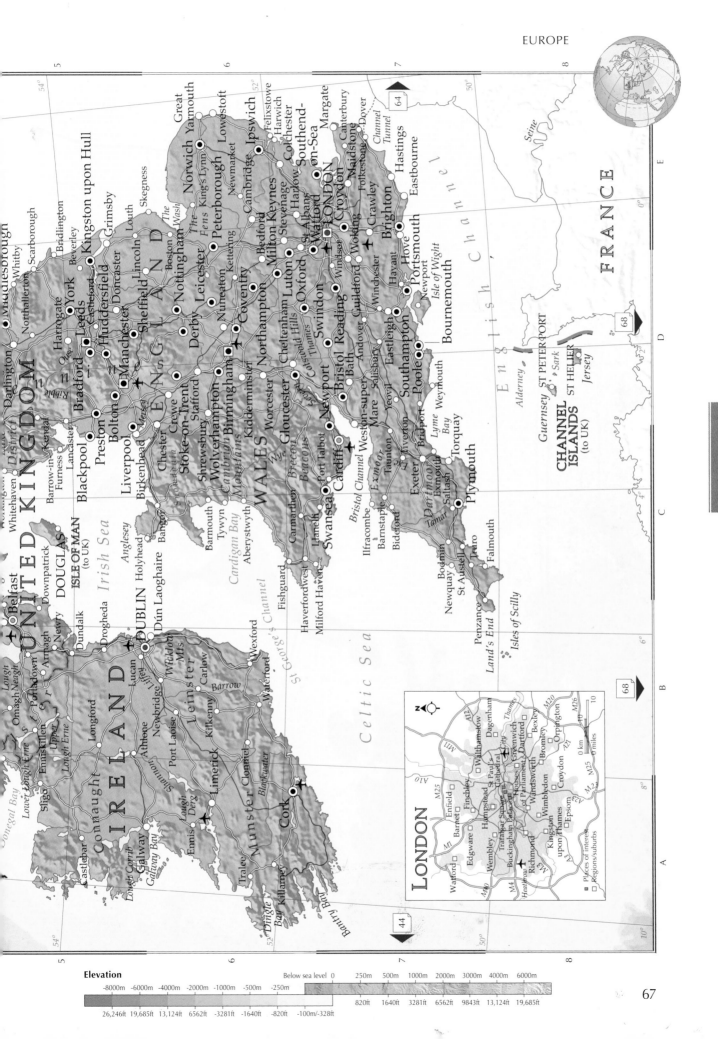

Elevation

| Below sea level | 0 | 250m | 500m | 1000m | 2000m | 3000m | 4000m | 6000m |

| -8000m | -6000m | -4000m | -2000m | -1000m | -500m | -250m |

| | | | 820ft | 1640ft | 3281ft | 6562ft | 9843ft | 13,124ft | 19,685ft |

| 26,246ft | 19,685ft | 13,124ft | 6562ft | -3281ft | -1640ft | -820ft | -100m/-328ft |

France, Andorra & Monaco

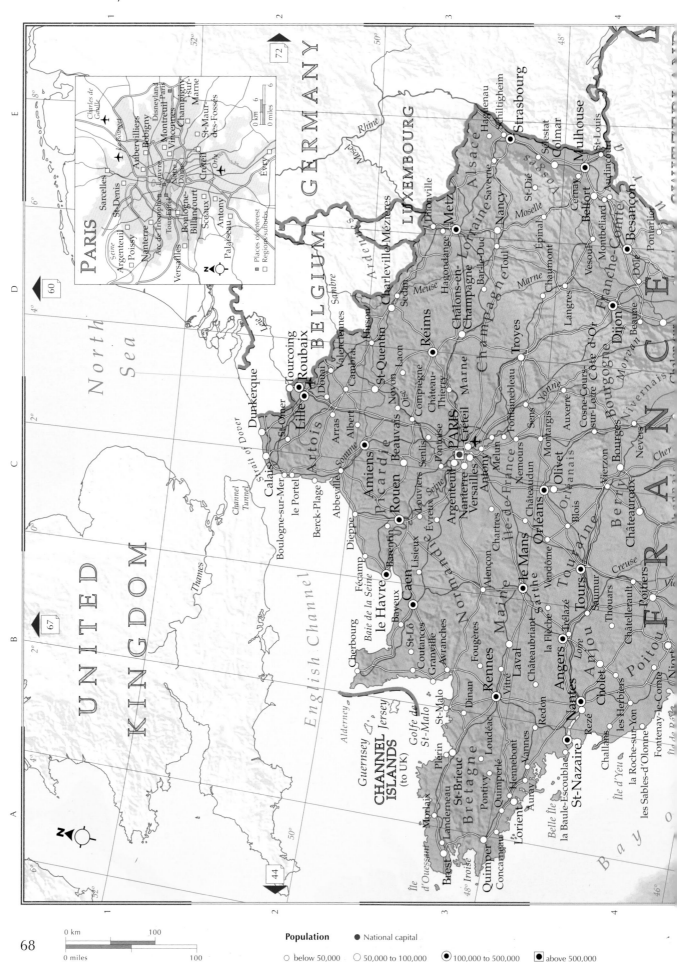

Population   ● National capital

○ below 50,000   ○ 50,000 to 100,000   ◉ 100,000 to 500,000   ◼ above 500,000

0 km   100

0 miles   100

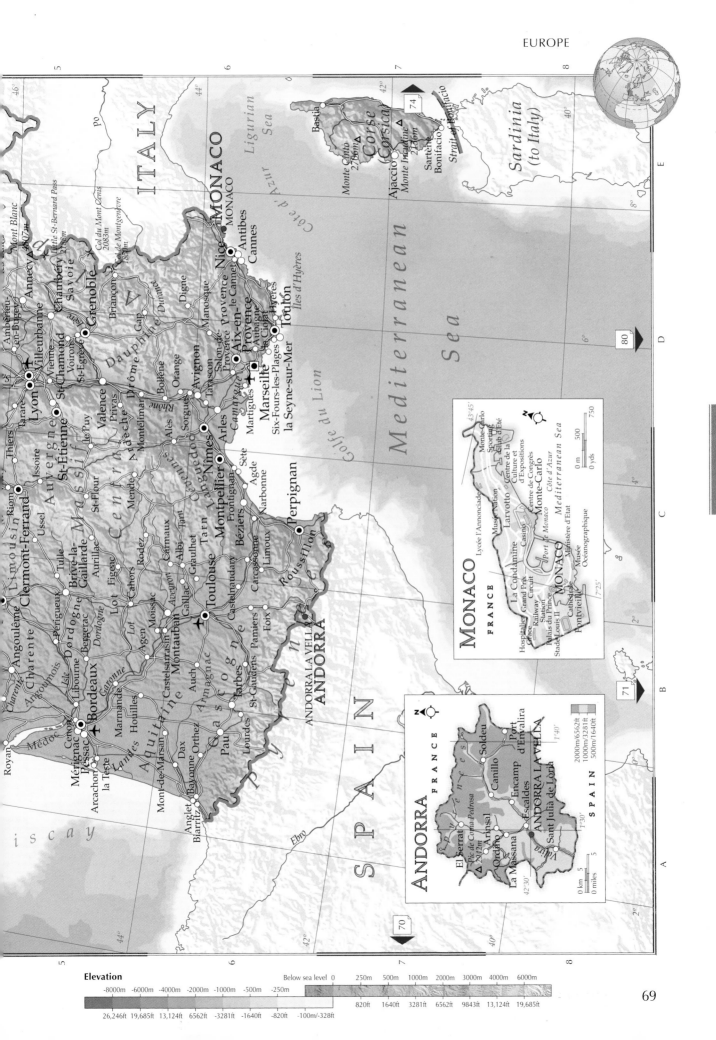

ITALY

MONACO

Ligurian Sea

Côte d'Azur

Corse (Corsica)

Strait of Bonifacio

Sardinia (to Italy)

Mediterranean Sea

Golfe du Lion

Mont Blanc 4807m
Col du Mont Cenis
Little St-Bernard Pass
Col de Montgenèvre

Annecy
Chambéry
Savoie
Grenoble
Amberieu-en-Bugey
Albertville
Villeurbanne
St-Chamond
Vienne
Voiron
St-Egrève
Gap
Briançon
Digne
Manosque
Durance
Drôme
Dauphiné
Aust
Lyon
Tarare
Thiers
St-Etienne
Le Puy
Privas
Ardèche
Valence
Montélimar
Bollène
Orange
Avignon
Sorgues
Tarascon
Arles
Camargue
Salon-de-Provence
Aix-en-Provence
Aubagne
Martigues
Marseille
Six-Fours-les-Plages
la Seyne-sur-Mer
St-Cloud
Toulon
Hyères
Îles d'Hyères
Provence
le Cannet
Antibes
Cannes
Nice
MONACO

Ussel
Tulle
Riom
Issoire
Clermont-Ferrand
Auvergne
St-Flour
Mende
Ardèche
Alès
Nîmes
Languedoc
Montpellier
Frontignan
Sète
Agde
Béziers
Narbonne
Perpignan
Roussillon
Limoux
Carcassonne
Castelnaudary
Pamiers
Foix
Tarn
Rodez
Millau
Carmaux
Albi
Gaillac
Graulhet
Castres
Toulouse
Montauban
Castelsarrasin
Moissac
Agen
Cahors
Figeac
Aveyron
Lot

Limousin
Angoulême
Périgueux
Tulle
Brive-la-Gaillarde
Bergerac
Dordogne
Libourne
Bordeaux
Pessac
Mérignac
Médoc
Cenon
Arcachon
la Teste
Royan
Charente
Angoubnois
Isle
Marmande
Ste
Landes
Mont-de-Marsan
Dax
Orthez
Pau
Lourdes
Tarbes
St-Gaudens
Auch
Gascogne
Armagnac
Aquitaine
Anglet
Bayonne
Biarritz
Pyrénées
Garonne
Lot
Dordogne

ANDORRA LA VELLA
ANDORRA

SPAIN

Ebro

iscay

74
80
71
70

MONACO

FRANCE

Monte-Carlo
Sporting Club d'Été
Centre de la Culture et d'Expositions
Larvotto
Casino
Musée National
Lycée l'Annonciade
La Condamine
Grand Prix Circuit
Port de Monaco
Railway Station
Hospitalier Grâce
Palais du Prince
Stade Louis II
MONACO
Centre de Congrès
Côte d'Azur
Ministère d'Etat
Cathédrale
Fontvieille
Musée Océanographique

Mediterranean Sea

0 m   500   750
0 yds

ANDORRA

FRANCE

SPAIN

Soldeu
Port d'Envalira
Encamp
Canillo
Escaldes
ANDORRA LA VELLA
Sant Julià de Lòria
Valira
Escalles
La Massana
Ordino
Arinsal
El Serrat
Pic de Coma Pedrosa 2942m
Pyrénées

2000m/6562ft
1000m/3281ft
500m/1640ft

0 km   5
0 miles   5

Elevation

| Below sea level | 0 | 250m | 500m | 1000m | 2000m | 3000m | 4000m | 6000m |

-8000m -6000m -4000m -2000m -1000m -500m -250m

820ft 1640ft 3281ft 6562ft 9843ft 13,124ft 19,685ft

26,246ft 19,685ft 13,124ft 6562ft -3281ft -1640ft -820ft -100m/-328ft

Spain & Portugal

ATLANTIC

OCEAN

PORTUGAL

Bay of Biscay
Costa Verde

A Coruña (La Coruña)
Ferrol
Laracha
Bétanzos
Luarca
Avilés
Gijon (Xixón)
Villaviciosa
Santander
Santa Comba
Cabo Fisterra
Outes
Muros
Ribeira
Pontevedra
Marín
Vigo
Santiago
Lalín
O Carballiño
Chantada
Monforte de Lemos
Ponferrada
León
Ponteareas
Ourense (Orense)
Xinzo de Limia
Astorga
Castilla-León
Burgos
Vilalba
Lugo
Tineo
Pravia
Pola de Lena
Mieres del Camino
Torrelavega
Llanes
Cantábrica
Reinosa
Cordillera Cantábrica
Oviedo
Cabañaquinta
Asturias
Galicia

Viana do Castelo
Póvoa de Varzim
Vila do Conde
Matosinhos
Porto (Oporto)
Vila Nova de Gaia
Ovar
Albergaria-a-Velha
Aveiro
Ílhavo
Coimbra
Figueira da Foz
Leiria
Peniche
Torres Vedras
Sintra
Cascais
LISBOA (LISBON)
Almada
Barreiro
Setúbal
Alcácer do Sal
Baía de Setúbal
Sines

Ponte da Barca
Braga
Guimarães
Vila Real
Lamego
São João da Madeira
Viseu
Alto da Torre 1993m
Serra da Estrela
Covilhã
Castelo Branco
Tomar
Abrantes
Entroncamento
Caldas da Rainha
Santarém
Coruche
Estremoz
Évora
Serra d'Ossa
Barragem do Alqueva

Bragança
Embalse de Ricobayo
Chaves
Douro
Minho
Ponteareas

Valladolid
Zamora
Toro
Duero
Medina del Campo
Salamanca
Segovia
Embalse de Almendra
Ciudad-Rodrigo
Guarda
Béjar
Sierra de Gredos
Ávila
Sistema Central
MADRID
Getafe
Plasencia
Coria
Talavera de la Reina
Aranjuez
Toledo
Cáceres
Embalse de Alcántara
Tagus
Embalse de Valdecañas
Trujillo
Herrera del Duque
Portalegre
Extremadura
Mérida
Villanueva de la Serena
Don Benito
Ciudad Real
Puertollano
Elvas
Badajoz
Almendralejo
Villafranca de los Barros
Castuera
Zafra
Pozoblanco
La Carolina
Azuaga
Jerez de los Caballeros
Guadiana
Sierra Morena
Montoro
Bailén
Córdoba
Beja
Cortegana
Nerva
Guadalquivir
Bujalance
Martos
Jaén
Alcaudete
Ourique
Valverde del Camino
La Algaba
Carmona
Écija
Lucena
Osuna
Andalucía
Sistema
Granada
Portimão
Lagos
Cabo de São Vicente
Algarve
Faro
Tavira
Olhão
Ayamonte
Lepe
Isla Cristina
Huelva
Sevilla (Seville)
Dos Hermanas
Las Cabezas de San Juan
Lebrija
Golfo de Cádiz
Antequera
Archidona
Olvera
Álora
Ronda
Málaga
Fuengirola
Marbella
Estepona
Costa del Sol
Sanlúcar de Barrameda
El Puerto de Santa María
Jerez de la Frontera
Ubrique
Cádiz
San Fernando
Vejer de la Frontera
Barbate de Franco
Costa de la Luz
Algeciras
Strait of Gibraltar
GIBRALTAR (to UK)
Ceuta (to Spain)
MOROCCO

AZORES (to Portugal)

Corvo
Flores
Graciosa
São Jorge
Terceira
Faial
Pico
São Miguel
Ponta Delgada
Santa Maria

0 km 100
0 miles 100

200m/656ft
Sea level

Population
National capital
○ below 50,000
○ 50,000 to 100,000
◉ 100,000 to 500,000
■ above 500,000

0 km 100
0 miles 100

70

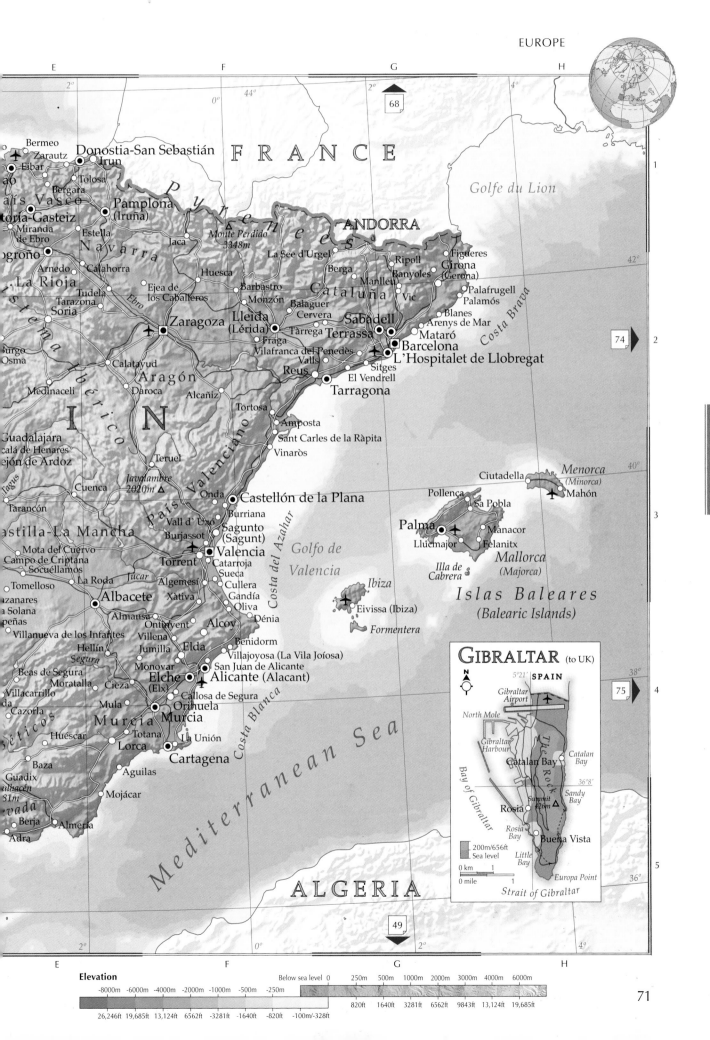

FRANCE

ANDORRA

Pyrenees

Monte Perdido
3348m

Cataluña

País Vasco

Navarra

La Rioja

Sistema Ibérico

Aragón

SPAIN

Castilla-La Mancha

País Valenciano

Golfe du Lion

Costa Brava

Golfo de
Valencia

Costa del Azahar

Ibiza

Formentera

Menorca
(Minorca)

Mallorca
(Majorca)

Illa de
Cabrera

Islas Baleares
(Balearic Islands)

Costa Blanca

Mediterranean Sea

ALGERIA

Bermeo
Zarautz
Eibar
Donostia-San Sebastián
Irun
Tolosa
Bergara
Pamplona
(Iruña)
Estella
Jaca
La Seo d'Urgel
Berga
Ripoll
Manlleu
Figueres
Girona
(Gerona)
Palafrugell
Palamós
Vic
Blanes
Arenys de Mar
Mataró
Barcelona
L'Hospitalet de Llobregat
Sabadell
Terrassa
Balaguer
Cervera
Tàrrega
Lleida
(Lérida)
Fraga
Vilafranca del Penedès
Valls
Sitges
El Vendrell
Reus
Tarragona
Miranda
de Ebro
Logroño
Vitoria-Gasteiz
Arnedo
Calahorra
Tudela
Tarazona
Soria
Ejea de
los Caballeros
Huesca
Barbastro
Monzón
Zaragoza
Medinaceli
Calatayud
Daroca
Alcañiz
Tortosa
Amposta
Sant Carles de la Ràpita
Vinaròs
Burgo de
Osma
Guadalajara
Alcalá de Henares
Torrejón de Ardoz
Tarancón
Teruel
Javalambre
2020m
Cuenca
Onda
Castellón de la Plana
Burriana
Vall d'Uxó
Sagunto
(Sagunt)
Burjassot
Torrent
Valencia
Catarroja
Sueca
Algemesí
Cullera
Gandía
Oliva
Dénia
Ciutadella
Pollença
Sa Pobla
Palma
Llucmajor
Manacor
Felanitx
Mahón
Eivissa (Ibiza)
Castilla-La Mancha
Mota del Cuervo
Campo de Criptana
Socuéllamos
La Roda
Tomelloso
Manzanares
La Solana
Valdepeñas
Villanueva de los Infantes
Albacete
Xàtiva
Ontinyent
Alcoy
Villena
Villajoyosa (La Vila Joíosa)
Benidorm
Hellín
Jumilla
Elda
Almansa
Beas de Segura
Moratalla
Monovar
Villacarrillo
Cazorla
Cieza
Mula
Elche
(Elx)
San Juan de Alicante
Alicante (Alacant)
Callosa de Segura
Orihuela
Murcia
Huéscar
Totana
Lorca
La Unión
Cartagena
Baza
Aguilas
Guadix
Mojácar
Mulhacén
3481m
Berja
Almería
Adra

Ebro

Segura

Júcar

Tajo

Sierra Nevada

Béticos

68
74
75
49

GIBRALTAR (to UK)

N

SPAIN

5°21'

Gibraltar
Airport

North Mole

Gibraltar
Harbour

Catalan Bay

The Rock

Catalan
Bay

Bay of Gibraltar

Rosia

Summit
420m

Sandy
Bay

Rosia
Bay

Buena Vista

Little
Bay

Europa Point

Strait of Gibraltar

36°8'

200m/656ft
Sea level

0 km   1
0 mile   1

Elevation

-8000m -6000m -4000m -2000m -1000m -500m -250m	Below sea level 0	250m 500m 1000m 2000m 3000m 4000m 6000m

26,246ft 19,685ft 13,124ft 6562ft -3281ft -1640ft -820ft -100m/-328ft

820ft 1640ft 3281ft 6562ft 9843ft 13,124ft 19,685ft

Germany & The Alpine States

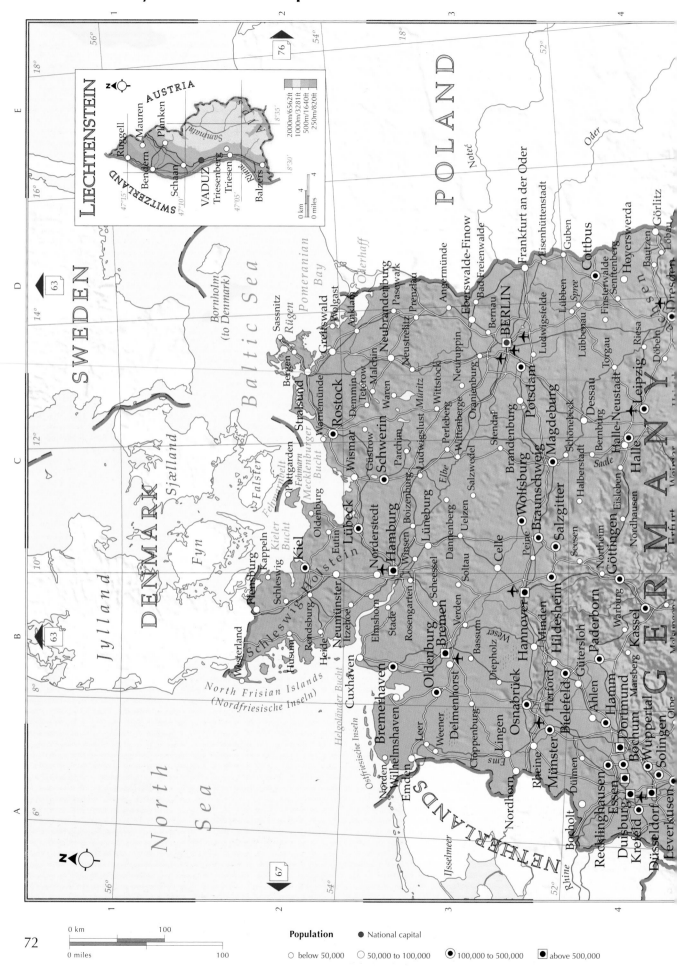

LIECHTENSTEIN

AUSTRIA

SWITZERLAND

Ruggell
Mauren
Planken
Bendern
Schaan
VADUZ
Triesenberg
Triesen
Balzers

Saminatal

2000m/6562ft
1000m/3281ft
500m/1640ft
250m/820ft

0 km   4
0 miles   4

SWEDEN

DENMARK

POLAND

NETHERLANDS

GERMANY

North Sea

Baltic Sea

Jylland
Sjælland
Fyn
Falster
Bornholm (to Denmark)

Pomeranian Bay

Oderhaff

Oder

Noteć

Places (selected labels)

Sassnitz
Rügen
Bergen
Stralsund
Warnemünde
Rostock
Greifswald
Wolgast
Usedom
Anklam
Pasewalk
Prenzlau
Neubrandenburg
Neustrelitz
Angermünde
Eberswalde-Finow
Bad Freienwalde
Frankfurt an der Oder
Eisenhüttenstadt
Guben
Cottbus
Hoyerswerda
Sentfenberg
Finsterwalde
Görlitz
Bautzen
Löbau
Dresden
Döbeln
Riesa
Torgau
Lübben
Lübbenau
Ludwigsfelde
Spree
Berlin
Potsdam
Bernau
Oranienburg
Neuruppin
Wittstock
Perleberg
Wittenberge
Müritz
Waren
Malchin
Demmin
Teterow
Güstrow
Schwerin
Wismar
Parchim
Ludwigslust
Boizenburg
Lüneburg
Dannenberg
Salzwedel
Stendal
Brandenburg
Magdeburg
Schönebeck
Bernburg
Halberstadt
Dessau
Halle-Neustadt
Leipzig
Halle
Eisleben
Nordhausen
Erfurt
Weimar
Wolfsburg
Braunschweig
Salzgitter
Peine
Seesen
Northeim
Göttingen
Warburg
Kassel
Marsberg
Celle
Soltau
Uelzen
Hannover
Hildesheim
Minden
Herford
Bielefeld
Gütersloh
Paderborn
Ahlen
Hamm
Dortmund
Bochum
Essen
Duisburg
Krefeld
Düsseldorf
Solingen
Wuppertal
Leverkusen
Recklinghausen
Münster
Rheine
Osnabrück
Nordhorn
Lingen
Meppen
Cloppenburg
Leer
Weener
Emden
Norden
Wilhelmshaven
Bremerhaven
Bremen
Delmenhorst
Oldenburg
Bassum
Diepholz
Verden
Rosengarten
Scheessel
Stade
Elmshorn
Cuxhaven
Hamburg
Norderstedt
Lübeck
Eutin
Oldenburg
Neumünster
Itzehoe
Heide
Husum
Westerland
Flensburg
Kappeln
Schleswig
Rendsburg
Kiel
Puttgarden
Fehmarn

Schleswig-Holstein
Mecklenburger Bucht
Kieler Bucht
Fehmarnbelt
Helgoländer Bucht
Ostfriesische Inseln
North Frisian Islands (Nordfriesische Inseln)
Ijsselmeer
Ems
Weser
Elbe
Saale
Rhine

Population

- ○ below 50,000
- ○ 50,000 to 100,000
- ◉ 100,000 to 500,000
- ◼ above 500,000
- ● National capital

0 km   100
0 miles   100

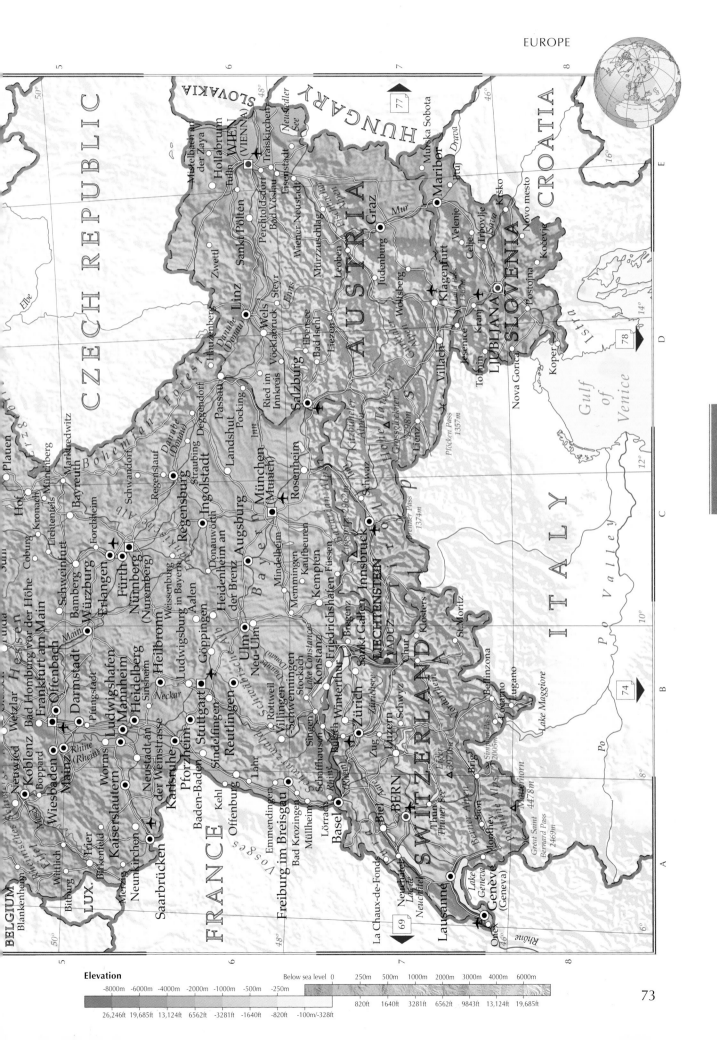

Elevation

| Below sea level | 0 | 250m | 500m | 1000m | 2000m | 3000m | 4000m | 6000m |

-8000m -6000m -4000m -2000m -1000m -500m -250m

26,246ft 19,685ft 13,124ft 6562ft -3281ft -1640ft -820ft -100m/-328ft

820ft 1640ft 3281ft 6562ft 9843ft 13,124ft 19,685ft

73

Italy

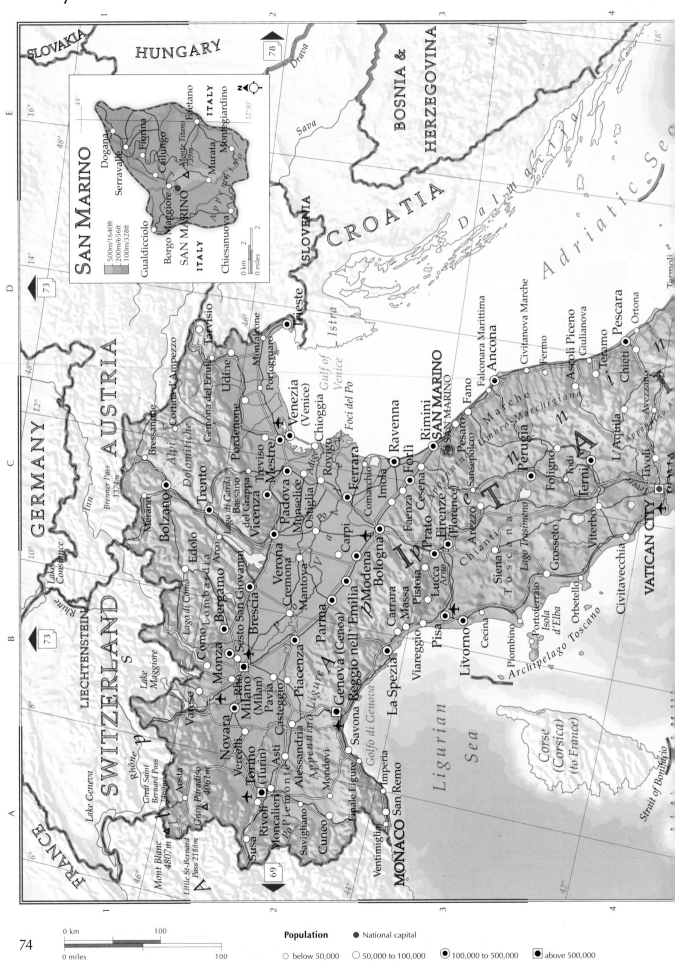

SLOVAKIA
HUNGARY
BOSNIA &
HERZEGOVINA
CROATIA
Drava
Sava
Dalmatia
Adriatic Sea

SAN MARINO

Dogana
Serravalle
Fiorina
Faetano
ITALY
Cailungo
Monte Titano 739m
Murata
Montegiardino
Borgo Maggiore
Gualdicciolo
SAN MARINO
ITALY
Chiesanuova
Appennino

500m/1640ft
200m/656ft
100m/328ft

0 km 2
0 miles 2

GERMANY
SWITZERLAND
LIECHTENSTEIN
AUSTRIA
FRANCE
SLOVENIA

Lake Constance
Lake Geneva
Rhône
Grand Saint Bernard Pass 2469m
Mont Blanc 4807m
Little St-Bernard Pass 2188m
Gran Paradiso 4061m
Brenner Pass 1374m
Inn
Rhine
Lake Maggiore

Istra
Trieste
Tarvisio
Monfalcone
Cortina d'Ampezzo
Bressanone
Merano
Bolzano
Dolomitiche
Alpi
Trento
Edolo
Arco
Lago di Garda
Bassano del Grappa
Gemona del Friuli
Udine
Pordenone
Treviso
Portogruaro
Mestre
Venezia (Venice)
Gulf of Venice
Chioggia
Foci del Po
Vicenza
Padova
Monselice
Ostiglia
Rovigo
Adige
Ferrara
Comacchio
Imola
Ravenna
Forlì
Cesena
Faenza

Lago di Como
Como
Lombardia
Bergamo
Brescia
Verona
Cremona
Mantova
Po
Carpi
Modena
Bologna
Emilia
Reggio nell'Emilia
Pistoia
Prato
Firenze (Florence)
Arezzo
Sansepolcro
Varese
Sesto San Giovanni
Monza
Milano (Milan)
Pavia
Piacenza
Parma
Appennino
Casteggio
Novara
Vercelli
Torino (Turin)
Asti
Alessandria
Piemonte
Savigliano
Cuneo
Susa
Rivoli
Moncalieri
Po

Carrara
Massa
Viareggio
Lucca
Pisa
Arno
Livorno
Cecina
Piombino
Portoferraio
Isola d'Elba
Archipelago Toscano
La Spezia
Savona
Finale Ligure
Golfo di Genova
Appennino Ligure
Genova (Genoa)
Reggio di Genova
Imperia
San Remo
Ventimiglia
MONACO

San Marino
Rimini
SAN MARINO
Fano
Pesaro
Falconara Marittima
Ancona
Civitanova Marche
Fermo
Ascoli Piceno
Giuliano
Teramo
Pescara
Ortona
Chieti
Avezzano
L'Aquila
Tivoli
VATICAN CITY
Civitavecchia
Orbetello
Grosseto
Lago Trasimeno
Siena
Chianti
Toscana
Perugia
Umbro-Marchigiano
Marche
Todi
Foligno
Terni
Viterbo

Corse (Corsica) (to France)
Ligurian Sea
Strait of Bonifacio

Population
● National capital
○ below 50,000
○ 50,000 to 100,000
◉ 100,000 to 500,000
■ above 500,000

0 km 100
0 miles 100

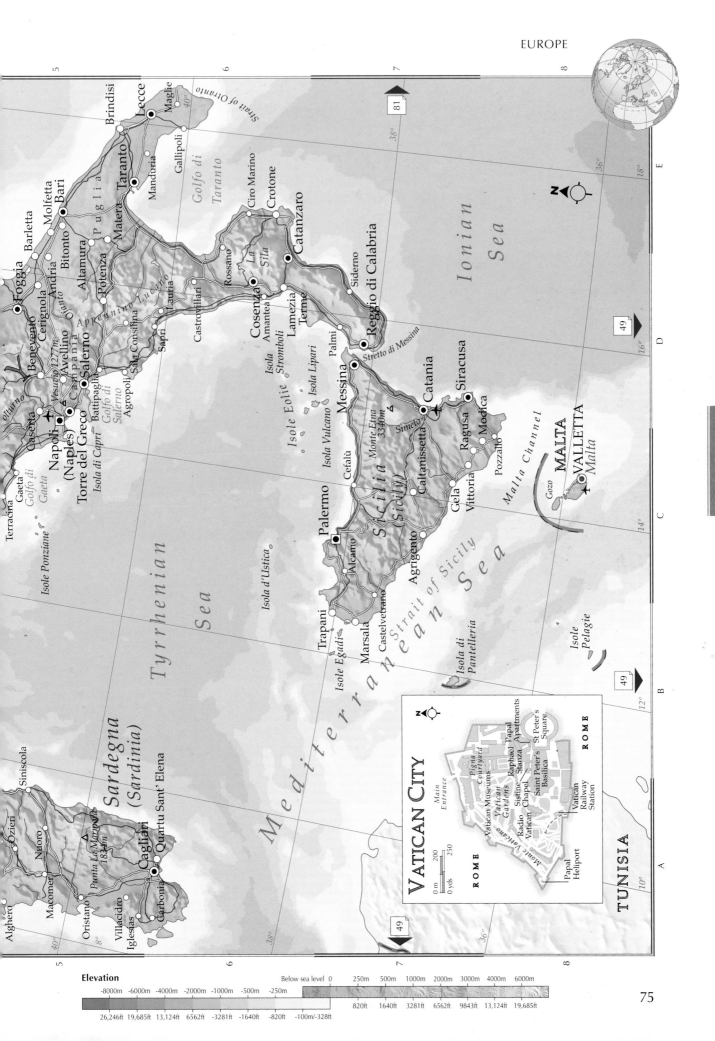

5

6

7

8

Brindisi
Lecce
Maglie
Taranto
Manduria
Gallipoli
Golfo di
Taranto
Strait of Otranto
Bari
Molfetta
Bitonto
Barletta
Andria
Altamura
Matera
Cerignola
Foggia
Benevento
Avellino
Cignola
Vesuvio 1277m
Caserta
Napoli
(Naples)
Torre del Greco
Salerno
Battipaglia
Golfo di
Salerno
Agropoli
Sala Consilina
Sapri
Lauria
Castrovillari
Potenza
Puglia
Appennino Lucano
Campania
Volturno
Ofanto
Agri
Ciro Marino
Crotone
Catanzaro
La
Sila
Rossano
Cosenza
Amantea
Lamezia
Terme
Palmi
Siderno
Reggio di Calabria
Stretto di Messina
Messina
Monte Etna
3340m
Simeto
Catania
Siracusa
Medica
Ragusa
Pozzallo
Caltanissetta
Agrigento
Gela
Vittoria
Cefalù
Sicilia
(Sicily)
Palermo
Alcamo
Castelvetrano
Marsala
Trapani
Isole Egadi
Isola d'Ustica
Isole Eolie
Isola Lipari
Isola Vulcano
Stromboli

Ionian
Sea

Tyrrhenian
Sea

Mediterranean
Sea

Strait of Sicily

Malta Channel
Gozo
MALTA
VALLETTA
Malta
Isole
Pelagie

Terracina
Gaeta
Golfo di
Gaeta
Isole Ponziane
Isola di Capri

Sardegna
(Sardinia)
Siniscola
Ozieri
Nuoro
Macomer
Oristano
Alghero
Villacido
Iglesias
Carbonia
Cagliari
Quartu Sant' Elena
Punta La Marmora
1834m

Isola di
Pantelleria

TUNISIA

40°

38°

36°

5°

6°

7°

8°

E
D
C
B
A

81

49

49

49

VATICAN CITY

Main
Entrance
Pigna
Courtyard
Vatican Museums
Vatican
Gardens
Raphael
Stanza
Sistine
Chapel
Papal
Apartments
Saint Peter's
Basilica
St Peter's
Square
Radio
Vatican
Monte Vaticano
Vatican
Railway
Station
Papal
Heliport

ROME
ROME
ROME

0 m   200
0 yds   250

Elevation

Below sea level 0   250m   500m   1000m   2000m   3000m   4000m   6000m

-8000m -6000m -4000m -2000m -1000m -500m -250m

26,246ft 19,685ft 13,124ft 6562ft -3281ft -1640ft -820ft -100m/-328ft

820ft 1640ft 3281ft 6562ft 9843ft 13,124ft 19,685ft

Central Europe

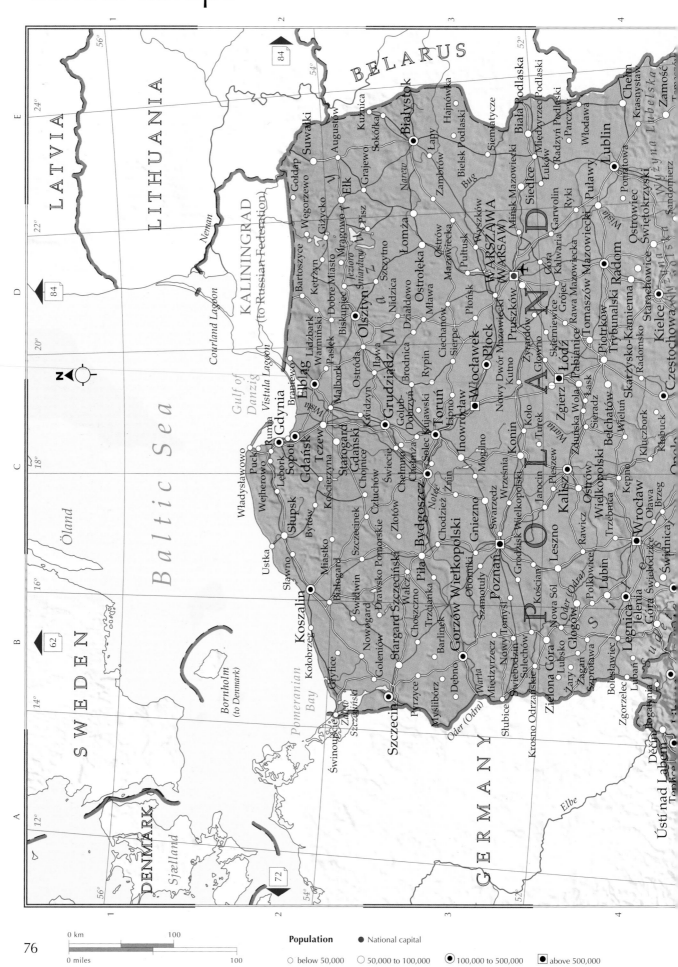

LATVIA

LITHUANIA

BELARUS

KALININGRAD
(to Russian Federation)

SWEDEN

DENMARK

GERMANY

Baltic Sea

Öland

*Bornholm
(to Denmark)*

*Pomeranian
Bay*

Sjælland

*Gulf of
Danzig*

Courland Lagoon

Vistula Lagoon

Neman

P O L A N D

WARSZAWA
(WARSAW)

Szczecin

Świnoujście

Koszalin
Kołobrzeg
Gryfice

Kołobrzeg

Słupsk
Ustka
Sławno
Białogard
Miastko
Szczecinek
Świdwin
Drawsko Pomorskie
Wałcz

Gdynia
Sopot
Gdańsk
Tczew
Puck
Władysławowo
Wejherowo
Lębork
Bytów
Kościerzyna

Rumia

Elbląg
Braniewo

Malbork
Starogard
Gdański
Kwidzyn
Chojnice
Czluchów
Złotów

Grudziądz
Golub-
Dobrzyń
Świecie
Chełmno
Chełmża

Toruń
Kujawski
Solec

Bydgoszcz
Nakło
Piła
Chodzież
Trzcianka

Inowrocław
Żnin
Mogilno
Gniezno

Włocławek
Lipno
Rypin

Płock

Ciechanów
Sierpc
Płońsk

Włocławek

Nowy Dwór Mazowiecki
Kutno
Koło
Turek
Konin
Września
Słupca
Pleszew

Poznań
Szamotuły
Oborniki
Swarzędz
Środa
Wielkopolski

Gorzów Wielkopolski
Barlinek
Dębno
Myślibórz

Kościan
Nowy
Tomyśl
Grodzisk Wielkopolski

Leszno
Nowa Sól
Polkowice
Rawicz

Zielona Góra
Lubsko
Żary
Żagań
Szprotawa
Głogów

Słubice
Krosno Odrzańskie
Sulechów
Świebodzin
Międzyrzecz

Bolesławiec
Zgorzelec
Lubań
Bogatynia

Jelenia
Góra
Świebodzice

Legnica
Świdnica
Lubin
Chojnów

Wrocław
Oława
Brzeg
Trzebnica
Oleśnica

Olsztyn
Lidzbark
Warmiński
Pasłek
Ostróda
Iława
Dobre Miasto
Biskupiec

Ketrzyn
Bartoszyce
Gołdap

Giżycko
Mrągowo
Węgorzewo
Suwałki
Augustów
Ełk
Pisz
Szczytno

Nidzica
Działdowo
Mława

Ostrołęka
Ostrów
Mazowiecka
Wyszków
Pułtusk

Łomża
Zambrów

Grajewo
Sokółka
Kuźnica

Białystok
Łapy
Hajnówka
Bielsk Podlaski
Siemiatycze

Biała Podlaska
Międzyrzec Podlaski
Radzyń Podlaski
Parczew
Łuków

Garwolin
Ryki
Puławy
Dęblin

Siedlce
Mińsk Mazowiecki

Łódź
Zgierz
Pabianice
Zduńska Wola
Sieradz
Łask
Wieluń
Wieruszów
Kępno
Ostrów
Wielkopolski
Ostrzeszów
Jarocin
Kalisz

Piotrków
Trybunalski
Tomaszów
Mazowiecki
Rawa Mazowiecka
Skierniewice
Głowno
Łowicz
Żyrardów
Sochaczew
Grójec

Radom
Kozienice
Pionki
Szydłowiec
Starachowice
Skarżysko-Kamienna
Radomsko
Bełchatów
Kluczbork
Kępno
Olesno

Kielce
Świętokrzyskie
Końskie
Ostrowiec
Świętokrzyski
Opatów

Lublin
Świdnik
Poniatowa
Kraśnik
Krasnystaw
Łęczna

Chełm
Zamość

Sandomierz

Częstochowa
Lubliniec

Ústí nad Labem
Děčín
Teplice

Elbe

Oder (Odra)

Warta

Noteć

Prosna

Warta

Oder (Odra)

Bóbr

Vistula

Wisła

Narew

Bug

Wisła

*Jezioro
Śniardwy*

Wyżyna Lubelska

Wyżyna Małopolska

0 km   100
0 miles   100

Population   ● National capital

○ below 50,000   ○ 50,000 to 100,000   ◉ 100,000 to 500,000   ■ above 500,000

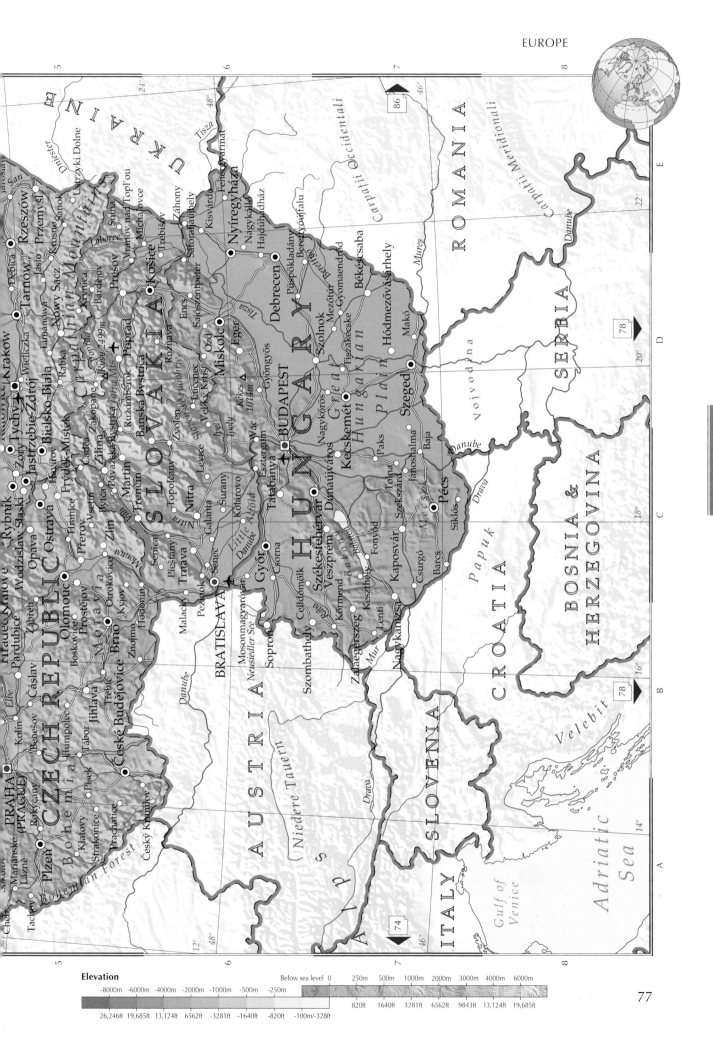

Elevation

| Below sea level | 0 | 250m | 500m | 1000m | 2000m | 3000m | 4000m | 6000m |

-8000m -6000m -4000m -2000m -1000m -500m -250m

26,246ft 19,685ft 13,124ft 6562ft -3281ft -1640ft -820ft -100m/-328ft

820ft 1640ft 3281ft 6562ft 9843ft 13,124ft 19,685ft

Southeast Europe

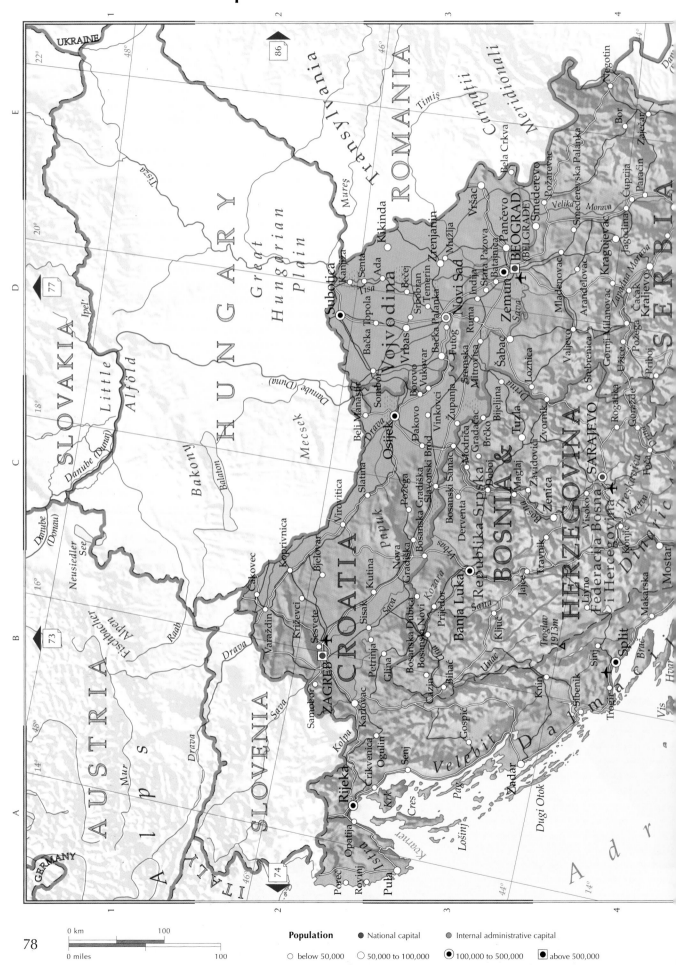

0 km   100

0 miles   100

Population   ● National capital   ● Internal administrative capital

○ below 50,000   ○ 50,000 to 100,000   ◉ 100,000 to 500,000   ■ above 500,000

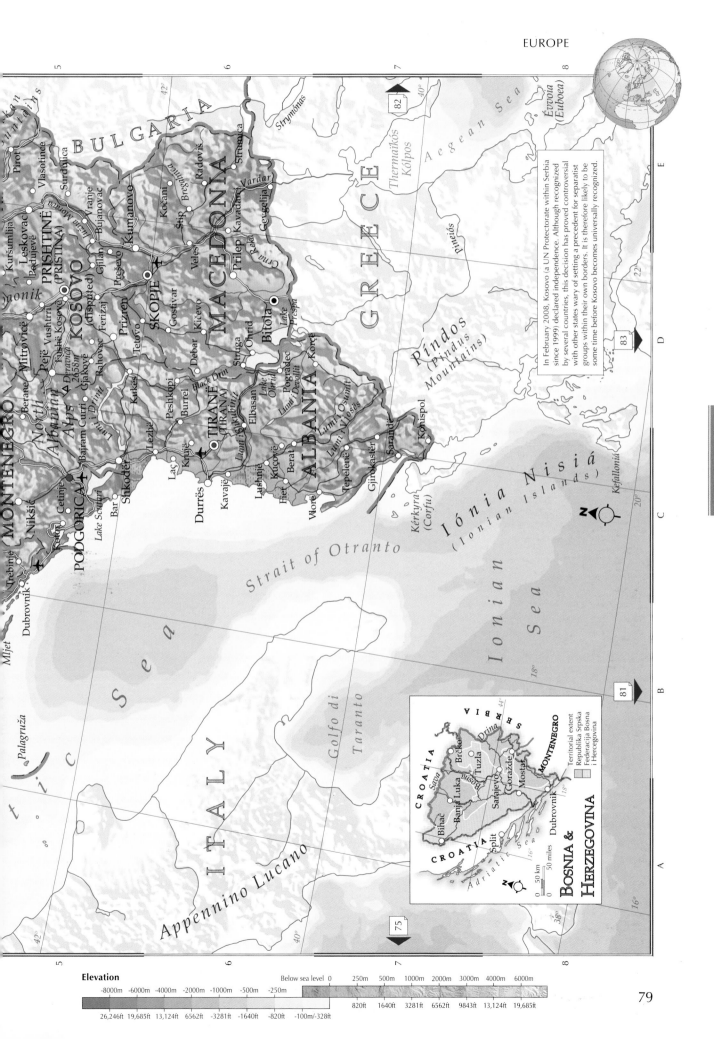

BULGARIA

MACEDONIA

GREECE

Aegean Sea

Thermaïkós Kólpos

Strymónas

Évvoia (Euboea)

Pirot
Vlasotince
Surdulica
Kursumlija
Leskovac
Padujevë
PRISHTINË (PRISTINA)
Vranje
Bujanovac
Kumanovo
KOSOVO (disputed)
Gilan
Preševo
Štip
Kočani
Bregalnica
Radoviš
Strumica
Gevgelija
Kavadar
Prilep
Vardar
Crna Reka
SKOPJE
Veles
Gostivar
Kičevo
Tetovo
Prizren
Ferizaj
Kahotec
Ohrid
Lake Ohrid
Bitola
Lake Prespa
Peshkopi
Debar
Struga
Pogradec
Korçë
Burrel
Lumi i Devollit
Lumi i Drini
Black Drin
Elbasan
Lumi i Shkumbinit
Berane
Mitrovicë
Pejë Vushtrri
Fushë Kosovë
Gjakovë
Daravica 2658m
North Albanian Alps
Bajram Curri
Lumi i Drini
Kukës
Lezhë
Krujë
Laç
Shkodër
Lake Scutari
Bar
Stkodër
Durrës
Kavajë
Lushnjë
Fier
Kuçovë
Berat
Vlorë
Lumi i Osumit
Lumi i Vjosës
Tepelenë
Gjirokastër
Sarandë
Konispol

Píndos (Pindus Mountains)

Pineiós

ALBANIA

TIRANË (TIRANA)

MONTENEGRO
PODGORICA
Nikšić
Cetinje
Kotor
Trebinje
Dubrovnik
Mljet

Píndos (Pindus Mountains)

Kérkyra (Corfu)
Iónia Nisiá (Ionian Islands)
Kefalloniá

Strait of Otranto

Golfo di Taranto

ITALY

Appennino Lucano

Ionian Sea

Palagruža

BOSNIA & HERZEGOVINA

CROATIA
SERBIA
MONTENEGRO
Bihać
Banja Luka
Brčko
Tuzla
Bosna
Sava
Drina
Sarajevo
Goražde
Mostar
Dubrovnik
Split
Visoko
Adriatic Sea

Territorial extent
Republika Srpska
Federacija Bosna i Hercegovina

0   50 km
0   50 miles

Elevation

| Below sea level | 0 | 250m | 500m | 1000m | 2000m | 3000m | 4000m | 6000m |

-8000m -6000m -4000m -2000m -1000m -500m -250m

820ft 1640ft 3281ft 6562ft 9843ft 13,124ft 19,685ft

26,246ft 19,685ft 13,124ft 6562ft -3281ft -1640ft -820ft -100m/-328ft

The Mediterranean

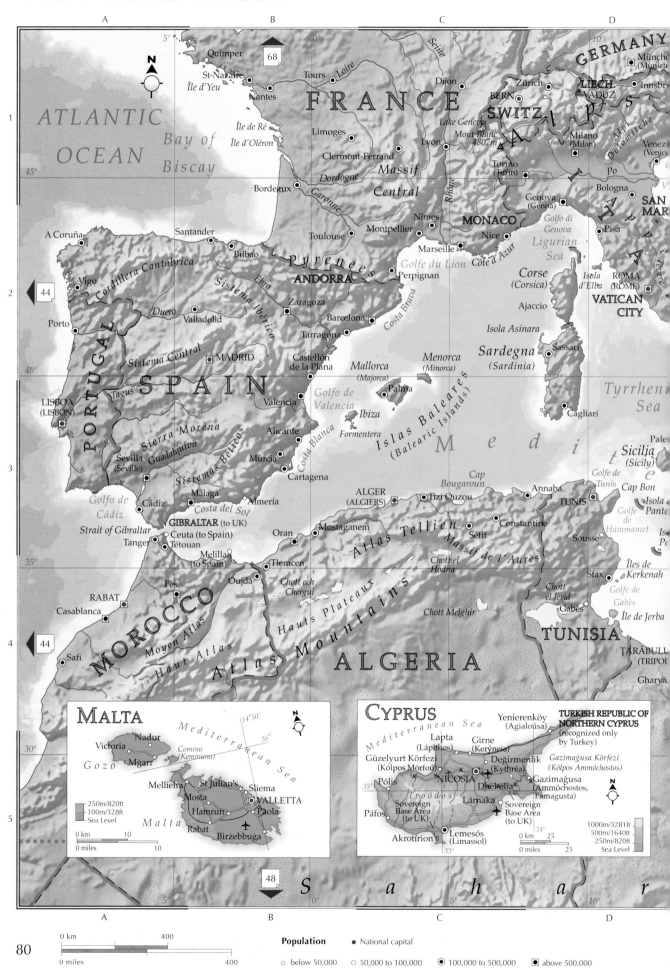

ATLANTIC OCEAN

Bay of Biscay

GERMANY

München (Munich)

LIECH.
VADUZ

Innsbr

FRANCE

Quimper

St-Nazaire
Île d'Yeu
Nantes

Tours
Loire

Dijon
Seine

Zürich
BERN

SWITZ

Limoges

Clermont-Ferrand

Lyon

Lake Geneva
Mont Blanc
4807m

Milano
(Milan)

Venez
(Venice)

Dordogne

Bordeaux

Garonne

Massif
Central

Rhône

Torino
(Turin)

Po

Bologna

Appe

A Coruña

Santander

Bilbao

Nîmes

Montpellier

MONACO

Nice
Côte d'Azur

Genova
(Genoa)

Golfo di
Genova

Ligurian
Sea

Pisa

SAN
MAR

Vigo

Cordillera Cantábrica

Ebro

PYRENEES

ANDORRA

Marseille

Golfe du Lion

Perpignan

Corse
(Corsica)

Isola
d'Elba

ROMA
(ROME)

Porto

Duero

Valladolid

Sistema Ibérico

Zaragoza

Barcelona

Costa Brava

Ajaccio

VATICAN
CITY

MADRID

SPAIN

PORTUGAL

Sistema Central

Tagus

Castellón
de la Plana

Tarragona

Mallorca
(Majorca)

Valencia

Golfo de
Valencia

Menorca
(Minorca)

Palma

Isola Asinara

Sardegna
(Sardinia)

Sassari

Tyrrheni
Sea

LISBOA
(LISBON)

Sierra Morena

Alicante

Ibiza

Islas Baleares
(Balearic Islands)

Cagliari

Sicilia
(Sicily)

Guadalquivir

Sevilla
(Seville)

Sistemas Béticos

Murcia

Formentera

Cartagena

Costa Blanca

Mediterranean

Cap
Bougaroun

Golfe de
Tunis

Cap Bon

Isola
Pante

Golfo de
Cádiz

Málaga

Costa del Sol

Almería

Cádiz

GIBRALTAR (to UK)

Strait of Gibraltar

Ceuta (to Spain)

Tanger

Tétouan

Melilla
(to Spain)

Oran

Mostaganem

ALGER
(ALGIERS)

Tizi Ouzou

Annaba

Sétif

Constantine

TUNIS

Golfe
de
Hammamet

Sousse

RABAT

Casablanca

Fes

Oujda

Chott ech
Chergui

MOROCCO

Tlemcen

Chott el
Hodna

Massif de l'Aurès

Chott
el Jerid

Sfax

Îles de
Kerkenah

Is
Pe

Safi

Moyen Atlas

Haut Atlas

Atlas Mountains

Hauts Plateaux

Atlas Tellien

Chott Melghir

Gabès

Golfe de
Gabès

Île de Jerba

ALGERIA

TUNISIA

ȚARĀBULL
(TRIPOI

Gharyā

MALTA

Mediterranean Sea

Nadur

Victoria

Gozo

Mġarr

Comino
(Kemmuna)

Mellieħa

Mosta

St Julian's

Sliema

VALLETTA

Hamrun

Paola

Malta

Rabat

Birżebbuġa

250m/820ft
100m/328ft
Sea Level

0 km   10
0 miles   10

CYPRUS

Mediterranean Sea

Lapta
(Lápithos)

Girne
(Kerýneia)

Yenierenköy
(Agialoúsa)

Güzelyurt Körfezi
(Kólpos Mórfou)

Pólis

NICOSIA

Değirmenlik
(Kythréa)

Dhekélia

TURKISH REPUBLIC OF
NORTHERN CYPRUS
(recognized only
by Turkey)

Gazimağusa Körfezi
(Kólpos Ammóchostos)

Gazimağusa
(Ammóchostos,
Famagusta)

Troódos

Sovereign
Base Area
(to UK)

Lárnaka

Páfos

Akrotírion

Lemesós
(Limassol)

Sovereign
Base Area
(to UK)

1000m/3281ft
500m/1640ft
250m/820ft
Sea Level

0 km   25
0 miles   25

Sahar

0 km   400
0 miles   400

Population   • National capital

○ below 50,000   ○ 50,000 to 100,000   ◉ 100,000 to 500,000   ◼ above 500,000

SLOVAKIA
WIEN
(VIENNA)
STRIA
Danube
BUDAPEST
HUNGARY
Great
Hungarian
Plain
UBLJANA
ZAGREB
CROATIA
Novi Sad
Sava
BOSNIA
& HERZ.
SARAJEVO
BEOGRAD
(BELGRADE)
SERBIA
MON.
PODGORICA
KOSOVO
(disputed)
SKOPJE
TIRANË
(TIRANA)
MACED.
oli (Naples)
Vesuvio 1277m
Lecce
Cosenza
Kérkyra
(Corfu)
Catanzaro
Ionian
Monte Etna
3340m
Catania
Kefallonia
GREECE
Siracusa
Zákynthos
ALLETTA
LTA
Kýthira

Carpathian Mountains
Satu Mare
ROMANIA
Târgu Mures
Carpaţii Meridonali
Tisza
BUCUREŞTI
(BUCHAREST)
Danube
BULGARIA
Balkan Mountains
PRISHTINË
(PRISTINA)
SOFIYA
(SOFIA)
Rhodope
Mountains
Thessaloníki
(Salonica)
Límnos
Pindós
(Pindus)
Mts
Lárisa
Aegean
Sea
Chíos
ATHÍNA
(ATHENS)
Mirtóo
Pelagos
Dodekánisa
(Dodecanese)
Sámos
Kykládes
(Cyclades)
Ionian
Sea
Kritikó Pélagos
(Sea of Crete)
Irakleio
Kríti
(Crete)
Ródos
(Rhodes)
Kárpathos

Bâlţi
MOLD.
CHIŞINĂU
UKRAINE
Kakhovs'ka
Vodoskhovyshche
Dniester
Odesa
Galaţi
Danube
Constanţa
Varna
Burgas
Edirne
İstanbul
Boğazı
(Bosporus)
İstanbul
Marmara
Denizi
Bursa
Balıkesir
İzmir

Dnieper
Berdyans'k
Sea of Azov
Kryms'kyy
Pivostrov
Kerch
RUSS.
FED.
Sevastopol'
Novorossiysk
Black Sea
Küre Dağları
Zonguldak
Samsun
Ordu
Kızıl Irmak
ANKARA
TURKEY
Tuz
Gölü
Kayseri
Toros Dağları
Antalya
Antalya
Körfezi
İskenderum Körfezi
Gaziantep
Adana
Halab
(Aleppo)
Euphrates
NICOSIA
CYPRUS
Lemesós
(Limassol)
Lárnaka
SYRIA
LEBANON
BEYROUTH
(BEIRUT)
DIMASHQ
(DAMASCUS)
Hefa
(Haifa)
ISRAEL
Tel Aviv-Yafo
JERUSALEM
Gaza
AMMĀN
Dead Sea
JORDAN
Al 'Aqabah
Elat
SAUDI
ARABIA

Mişrātah
Darnah
Khalīj Surt
(Gulf of Sirte)
Banghāzī
(Benghazi)
Surt
Ţubruq
Ajdābiyā
Waddān
LIBYA

Libyan
Plateau
Great Sand Sea
Libyan
Desert
EGYPT
Alexandria
(Al Iskandarīyah)
Munkhafad al Qaṭṭārah
(Qattara Depression)
CAIRO
(AL QĀHIRAH)
Giza
(Al Jīzah)
Nile
Nile
Delta
Bûr Sa'îd
(Port Said)
Suez
(As Suways)
Qanāt as Suways
(Suez Canal)
Sahara el Sharqiya
(Eastern Desert)
Khalīj as Suways
Sinai
(Sīnā)
Red
Sea

Elevation

Below sea level 0   250m   500m   1000m   2000m   3000m   4000m   6000m

-8000m -6000m -4000m -2000m -1000m -500m -250m

820ft   1640ft   3281ft   6562ft   9843ft 13,124ft 19,685ft

26,246ft 19,685ft 13,124ft 6562ft -3281ft -1640ft -820ft
                                   -100m/-328ft

Bulgaria & Greece

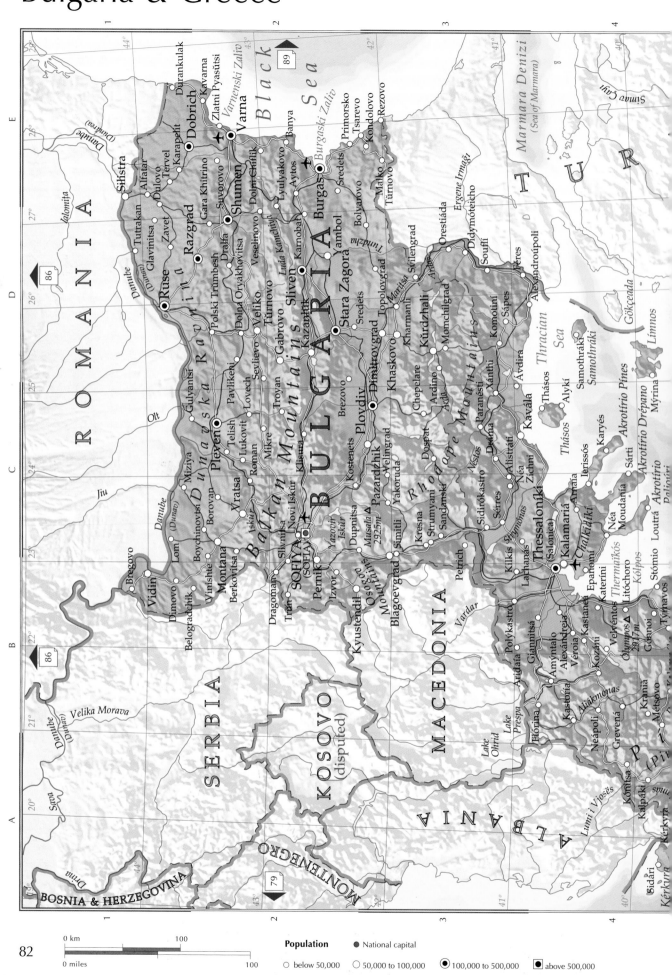

0 km   100

0 miles   100

Population   ● National capital

○ below 50,000   ○ 50,000 to 100,000   ◉ 100,000 to 500,000   ■ above 500,000

The Baltic States & Belarus

SWEDEN

FINLAND

RUSSIAN FEDERATION

ESTONIA

LATVIA

LITHUANIA

KALININGRAD
(to Russian Federation)

Gulf of Finland

Narva Bay

Narva Reservoir

Lake Peipus

Lake Pskov

Baltic Sea

Gulf of Riga

Gotland

Öland

Gotska Sandön

Ålands Hav

Skiftet

Hiiumaa

Saaremaa

Estonia cities and features:
Sillamäe, Narva, Kohtla-Järve, Kunda, Rakvere, Loksa, Maardu, Aegviidu, Raasiku, Tapa, Rakke, Palamuse, Kallaste, Räpina, Võnnu, Tartu, Otepää, Põlva, Võru, Puurmani, Viljandi, Mõisaküla, Rõngu, Tõrva, Valga, Paide, Rapla, Keila, TALLINN, Paldiski, Risti, Lihula, Haapsalu, Kärdla, Vormsi, Emmaste, Orissaare, Kuressaare, Sääre, Virtsu, Audru, Sindi, Pärnu, Pärnu-Jaagupi, Kilingi-Nõmme, Ainaži, Staicele, Rūjiena, Valka, Burtnieks, Aloja, Salacgrīva, Saulkrasti

Latvia cities and features:
Valmiera, Cēsis, Smiltene, Gulbene, Balvi, Viļaka, Aluksne, Ape, Jaunpiebalga, Rugāji, Balvi, Kārsava, Ludza, Rēzekne, Malta, DAUGAVPILS, Spoģi, Varakļāni, Līvāni, Jēkabpils, Madona, Lubāns, Pļaviņas, Grīziņkalns 311m, Viesīte, Nereta, Aizkraukle, Iecava, Bauska, Birži, Pasvalys, Subačius, Rokiškis, Jelgava, Jūrmala, RĪGA, Tukums, Engure, Mērsrags, Roja, Kolka, Kolkasrags, Ruhnu, Mazirbe, Ventspils, Ugāle, Talsi, Kandava, Engures Ezers, Broceni, Saldus, Kuldīga, Usmas Ezers, Pavilosta, Liepāja, Grobiņa, Durbe, Skuodas, Salantai, Mažeikiai, Papilē, Joniškis, Radviliškis, Pakruojis

Lithuania cities and features:
Šiauliai, PANEVĖŽYS, Naujamiestis, Dotnuva, Obeliai, Zarasai, Anykščiai, Utena, Telšiai, Plungė, Kelmė, Raseiniai, Skaudvilė, Šilalė, Kretinga, Gargždai, KLAIPĖDA, Priekulė, Šilutė, Tauragė, Jurbarkas, Neman, Nida, Neman, Žemaičių Aukštumas

Kaliningrad / Russia:
KALININGRAD, Zelenogradsk, Gvardeysk, Chernyakhovsk, Guse, Gusev, Nida, Courland Lagoon, Pionerskiy, Primorsk, Mamonovo, Bagrationovsk, Zheleznodorozhnyy

Gulf of Finland, Pärnu Laht, Suur Väin, Väinameri, Suur Munamägi 318m, Emajõgi, Gauja, Western Dvina, Venta

SCALE

0 km 100
0 miles 100

Population
● National capital
○ below 50,000
○ 50,000 to 100,000
◉ 100,000 to 500,000
▣ above 500,000

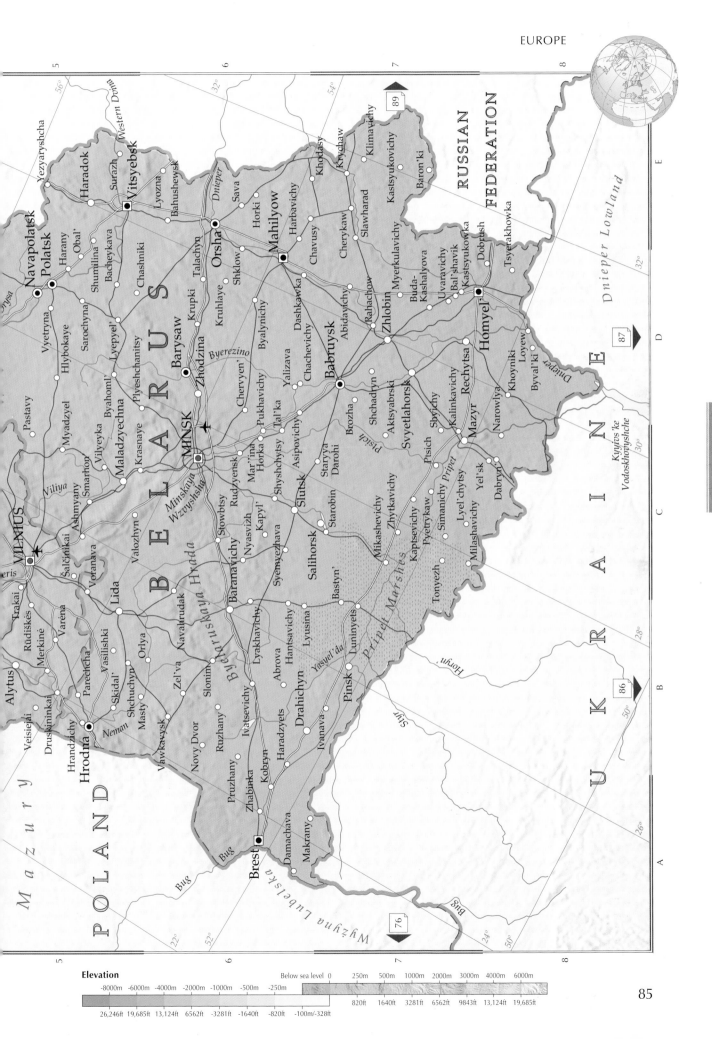

RUSSIAN

FEDERATION

POLAND

UKRAINE

BELARUS

Mazury

Dnieper Lowland

Pripet Marshes

Byelaruskaya Hrada

Minskaya Wzvyshsha

Wyżyna Lubelska

Navapolatsk
Polatsk
Haradok
Vitsyebsk
Surazh
Yezyarshcha
Harany
Obal'
Shumilina
Bacheykava
Chashniki
Lyozna
Bahushevsk
Talachyn
Orsha
Sava
Dnieper
Horki
Shklow
Mahilyow
Harbavichy
Chavusy
Cherykaw
Slawharad
Khodasy
Krychaw
Klimavichy
Kastsyukovichy
Baron'ki
Dobrush
Tsyerakhowka
Byval'ki
Loyew
Khoyniki
Homyel'
Rechytsa
Narowlya
Mazyr
Kalinkavichy
Svyetlahorsk
Aktsyabrski
Shchadryn
Babruysk
Zhlobin
Rahachow
Buda-Kashalyova
Uvaravichy
Bal'shavik
Kastsyukowka
Myerkulavichy
Abidavichy
Dashkawka
Krupki
Kruhlaye
Byalynichy
Yalizava
Chachevichy
Pukhavichy
Tal'ka
Chervyen'
Asipovichy
Staryya
Darohi
Brozha
Ptsich
Sveyshchy
Slychy
Pyetrykaw
Lyel'chytsy
Milashavichy
Yel'sk
Dabryn'
Tonyezh
Luninyets
Pinsk
Bastyn'
Starobin
Mikashevichy
Zhytkavichy
Zhkavichy
Kaptsevichy
Simanichy Pripet
Horyn'
Styr
Slut'
Bug

Navapolatsk
Polatsk
Vetryna
Hlybokaye
Lyepyel'
Sarochyna
Vilyeyka
Myadzyel
Pastavy
Smarhon
Ashmyany
Krasnaye
Maladzyechna
Vilnius
Šalčininkai
Voranava
Lida
Orlya
Zel'va
Navahrudak
Nyasvizh
Kapyl'
Stowbtsy
Baranavichy
Slonim
Ruzhany
Ivatsevichy
Lyakhavichy
Hantsavichy
Abrova
Lyusina
Drahichyn
Ivanava
Kobryn
Pruzhany
Zhabinka
Damachava
Makrany
Brest
Haradzyets
Novy Dvor
Vawkavysk
Masty
Shchuchyn
Skidal'
Hrodna
Neman
Herandzichy
Druskininkai
Veisiejai
Alytus
Merkinė
Varėna
Rūdiškės
Trakai
Šalčininkai
Vilyeyka
Valozhyn
Viliya
Vyetryna
Yalizava
Mar''ina
Horka
Rudzyensk
Svyslach
Shyshchytsy
Semyezhava
Svemyezhava
Hrozava
Kapyl'
Mar''ina
Minsk
Zhodzina
Barysaw
Lyepyel'
Byahoml'
Plyeshchanitsy
Pleshchanitsy
Bahoml'
Byerezino
Zhodzina

Vilnius
Neris
Rūdiškės
Paris

Minsk

Western Dvina

Orysa

Skidal'
Vasilishki
Parechcha
Merkinė

Elevation

Below sea level 0   250m   500m 1000m 2000m 3000m 4000m 6000m

-8000m -6000m -4000m -2000m -1000m -500m -250m

820ft 1640ft 3281ft 6562ft 9843ft 13,124ft 19,685ft

26,246ft 19,685ft 13,124ft 6562ft -3281ft -1640ft -820ft -100m/-328ft

Ukraine, Moldova & Romania

POLAND

Małopolska

Wyżyna Lubelska

Wisła

Carpathian Mountains

Tatra Mountains

SLOVAKIA

Slovenské Rudohorie

Tisza

HUNGARY

Great Hungarian Plain

BELARUS

Pripet

Pripet

Pripet Marshes

Styr

Kovel'
Sarny
Olevs'k
Ov

Volodymyr-Volyns'kyy
Novovolyns'k
Kivertsi
Luts'k
Rivne
Korosten'
Sluch

Sokal'
Dubno
Novohrad-Volyns'kyy
Malyn
Radomysh

Zhovkva
Chervonohrad
Slavuta
Kremenets'
Shepetivka
Polonne
Zhytomy
Berdych

Yavoriv
L'viv
Zolochiv
Izyaslav
Starokostyantyniv

Horodok
Zbarazh
Khmel'nyts'kyy
Koz

Sambir
Drohobych
Khodoriv
Berezhany
Ternopil'
U K R

Boryslav
Zhydachiv
Vinnytsya

Stryy
Kalush
Chortkiv
Zhmerynka
Lypove

Dolyna
Ivano-Frankivs'k
Podil's'ka Vysochina
Haysy

Uzhhorod
Nadvirna
Kam"yanets'-Podil's'kyy
Tul'ch

Mukacheve
Kolomyya
Mohyliv-Podil's'kyy
Dniester

Berehove
Chernivtsi

Vynohradiv
Khust
Hora Hoverla 2061m

Negreşti-Oaş
Darabani
Soroca

Satu Mare
Rădăuţi
Dorohoi
Bălţi
Ba

Carei
Baia Mare
Solca
Botoşani
Ribniţa

Marghita
Baia Sprie
Borşa
Suceava
MOLDOVA
Kot

Simleu Silvaniei
Zalău
Năsăud
Fălticeni
Paşcani
Călăraşi
Orhei

Oradea
Dej
Bistriţa
Toplita
Târgu-Neamţ
Iaşi
Ungheni
Străşeni
Du

Aleşd
Reghin
Bicaz
Roman
CHIŞINĂU
Tigh
(Bend

Salonta
Beiuş
Cluj-Napoca
Gheorgheni
Piatra-Neamţ
(KISHINEV)

Curtici
Ineu
T r a n s y l v a n i a
Ludus
Târgu Mureş
Bacău
Hînceşti
Tîraspol

Arad
Munţii
Turda
Cristuru
Secuiesc
Miercurea-Ciuc
Vaslui
Comrat
Basarabe

Sânnicolau Mare
Apuseni
Abrud
Aiud
Mediaş
Târgu Ocna
Bârlad
Ciadîr-Lun

Lipova
Alba Iulia
Rupea
Adjud
Taraclia
Artsyz

Jimbolia
Deva
R O M A N I A
Făgăraş
Târgu Secuiesc
Cahul
Bolhrad

Timişoara
Hunedoara
Sibiu
Codlea
Sfântu Gheorghe
Tecuci
Ozero Yalpuh
Kiliy

Lugoj
Cisnădie
Vârful Moldoveanu 2544m
Braşov
Focşani
Galaţi
Reni

Oţelu Roşu
Hateg
Câmpulung
Râşnov
Râmnicu Sărat
Izmayil

Bocşa
Carpaţii
Sinaia
Câmpina
Buzău
Măcin
Braila

Reşiţa
Petroşani
Meridionali
Curtea de Argeş
Tulcea

Oraviţa
Anina
Târgu Jiu
Moreni
Mizil
Isaccea
Babadag

Moldova Nouă
Călimăneşti
Pitesti
Târgovişte
Urziceni
Lacul Razim
Lacul Sinoie

Orşova
Râmnicu Vâlcea
Titu
Ploieşti
Ţăndărei
Hârşova

Drobeta-Turnu Severin
Motru
Streharia
Drăgăşani
Buftea
Slobozia

Filiaşi
Wallachia
Slatina
Ialomiţa
BUCUREŞTI
Feteşti
Medgidia

Craiova
Bals
Caracal
(BUCHAREST)
Călăraşi
Constanţa

Băileşti
Roşiori de Vede
Alexandria
Olteniţa

Calafat
Corabia
Turnu Măgurele
Giurgiu
Techirghiol
Eforie Sud

SERBIA
Danube (Dunărea)
Zimnicea
Dunavska Ravnina
Mangalia

Velika Morava
BULGARIA

Danube

Mureş
Timiş

Population
○ below 50,000
◎ 50,000 to 100,000
◉ 100,000 to 500,000
■ above 500,000
● National capital

86

0 km   100
0 miles   100

77
78
84
82

E　　　　　F　　　　　G　　　　　H

30°　　32°　　34°　　36°　　38°　　40°

52°

88

1

Dnieper
(Дняпро)

Horodnya

Shostka

Shchors

Hlukhiv

Chernihiv

Krolevets'

Konotop

RUSSIAN
FEDERATION

Desna

Nizhyn

Bakhmach

Romny

Sumy

Don

40°

Desna

Nosivka

Oster

jyivs'ke
khovyshche

Dnieper Lowland

Pryluky

Yahotyn

Pyryatyn

Okhtyrka

Zolochiv

Lebedyn

Psel

50°

88

XIV
(IV)

Brovary

Vasyl'kiv

tiv

arka

Kaniv s'ke
Vodoskhovyshche

Hrebinka

Lubny

Myrhorod

Lyubotyn

Derhachi

Kharkiv

Oskil

Kup"yans'k

Bila Tserkva

Kaniv

Merefa

Bohuslav

A

I

N

E

Hlobyne

Poltava

Donets

Izyum

Kreminna

Starobil's'k

Horodyshche

Zolotonosha

Cherkasy

Kremenchuts'ke
Vodoskhovyshche

Slov"yans'k

Rubizhne

Syeverodonets'k

venyhorodka

Smila

Chyhyryn

Kramators'k

Lysychans'k

Shpola

Kremenchuk

Zolote

Luhans'k

Tal'ne

Oleksandrivka

Svitlovods'k

Dniprodzerzhyns'ke
Vodoskhovyshche

Novomoskovs'k

Kostyantynivka

an'

Mala Vyska

Znam"yanka

Oleksandriya

Pavlohrad

Horlivka

Stakhanov

Holovanivs'k

Dniprodzerzhyns'k

Dnipropetrovs'k

Yenakiyeve

Krasnodon

Ulyanivka

Kirovohrad

Zhovti Vody

P"yatykhatky

Synel'nykove

Makiyivka

Krasnyy Luch

48°

3

Vil'shanka

Dolyns'ka

Pokrovs'ke

Donets'k

Torez

Pervomays'k

Bobrynets'

Kryvyy Rih

Amvrosiyivka

Kryve Ozero

Arbuzynka

Inhulets'

Zaporizhzhya

Orikhiv

Volnovakha

Dokuchayevs'k

Novyy Buh

Nikopol

Ordzhonikidze

Marhanets'

Dniprorudne

Polohy

Don

Voznesens'k

Kam"yanka-Dniprovs'ka

Tokmak

Mariupol'

Novoazovs'k

Kakhovs'ka
Vodoskhovyshche

Molochans'k

B

l

a

c

k

Mykolayiv

Dnieper
(Dnipro)

Melitopol'

Gulf of Taganrog

Yeya

Zhovtneve

Kakhovka

L

o

w

l

a

n

d

Prymors'ke

Berdyans'k

88

4

S

e

a

Kherson

Yakymivka

Ochakiv

Odesa

Hola Prystan'

Tsyurupyns'k

Chaplynka

Novotroyits'ke

Heniches'k

46°

Illichivs'k

Kalanchak

Armyans'k

Sea of Azov

Karkinits'ka Zatoka

Krasnoperekops'k

RUSSIAN
FEDERATION

Rozdol'ne

Dzhankoy

Kerch Strait

Chornomors'ke

Krasnohvardiys'ke

Zatoka
Syvash

Kerch

Kuban'

Nyzhn'ohirs'kyy

Lenine

Yevpatoriya

Kryms'kyy
Pivostriv

Saky

Simferopol'

Feodosiya

Sevastopol'

Bakhchysaray

Krymski Hory

Alushta

5

Yalta

44°

Alupka

B

l

a

c

k

S

e

a

94

E　　　　　F　　　　　G　　　　　H

32°　　34°　　36°　　38°　　40°

Elevation

Below sea level 0　250m　500m　1000m　2000m　3000m　4000m　6000m

-8000m　-6000m　-4000m　-2000m　-1000m　-500m　-250m

820ft　1640ft　3281ft　6562ft　9843ft　13,124ft　19,685ft

26,246ft　19,685ft　13,124ft　6562ft　-3281ft　-1640ft　-820ft　-100m/-328ft

European Russia

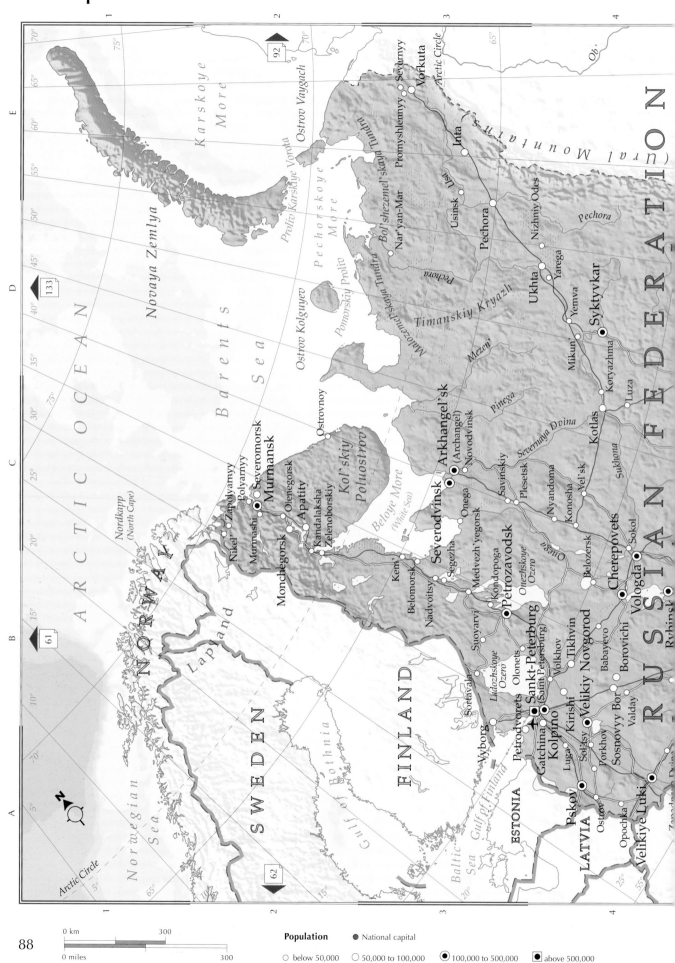

Karskoye More

Novaya Zemlya

Ostrov Vaygach

Proliv Karskiye Vorota

Severnyy
Vorkuta
Arctic Circle

Promyshlennyy
Inta

Usinsk   Usa
Ob'

Pechorskoye More

Ostrov Kolguyev

Bol'shezemel'skaya Tundra

Malozemel'skaya Tundra

Nar'yan-Mar

Pechora

Pechora

Nizhniy Odes

Pomorskiy Proliv

Pechora

Yarega

Ukhta

U r a l   M o u n t a i n s

R U S S I A N   F E D E R A T I O N

Timanskiy Kryazh

Mezen'

Mikun'   Yemva

Syktyvkar

Koryazhma
Luza

ARCTIC OCEAN

B a r e n t s   S e a

Ostrovnoy

Kol'skiy Poluostrov

Pinega

Kotlas

Sukhona

Vel'sk

Severnaya Dvina

Nordkapp
(North Cape)

Severomorsk
Polyarnyy
Zapolyarnyy

Murmansk

Olenegorsk
Apatity
Kandalaksha
Zelenoborskiy

Nikel' Murmashi

Monchegorsk

Arkhangel'sk
(Archangel)
Novodvinsk

Severodvinsk

Savinskiy

Plesetsk

Nyandoma

Konosha

Sokol

Vologda

Cherepovets

Belozersk

NORWAY

Lapland

Kem'
Belomorsk
Nadvoitsy

Segezha

Medvezh'yegorsk
Kondopoga

Onezhskoye Ozero

Onega

Beloye More
(White Sea)

Onega

Rybinsk

SWEDEN

Gulf of Bothnia

Suoyarvi

Sortavala

Lidozhskoye Ozero
Olonets

FINLAND

Petrozavodsk

Volkhov
Tikhvin

Babayevo
Borovichi

Valday

Norwegian Sea

Arctic Circle

Vyborg

Petrodvorets

Sankt-Peterburg
(Saint Petersburg)

Gatchina
Kolpino

Kirishi
Sol'tsy
Porkhov

Velikiy Novgorod

Sosnovyy Bor

Luga

Baltic Sea

Gulf of Finland

ESTONIA

LATVIA

Pskov

Ostrov
Opochka

Velikiye Luki

92
133
61
62

88

0 km   300
0 miles   300

Population   ● National capital

○ below 50,000   ◎ 50,000 to 100,000   ◉ 100,000 to 500,000   ◼ above 500,000

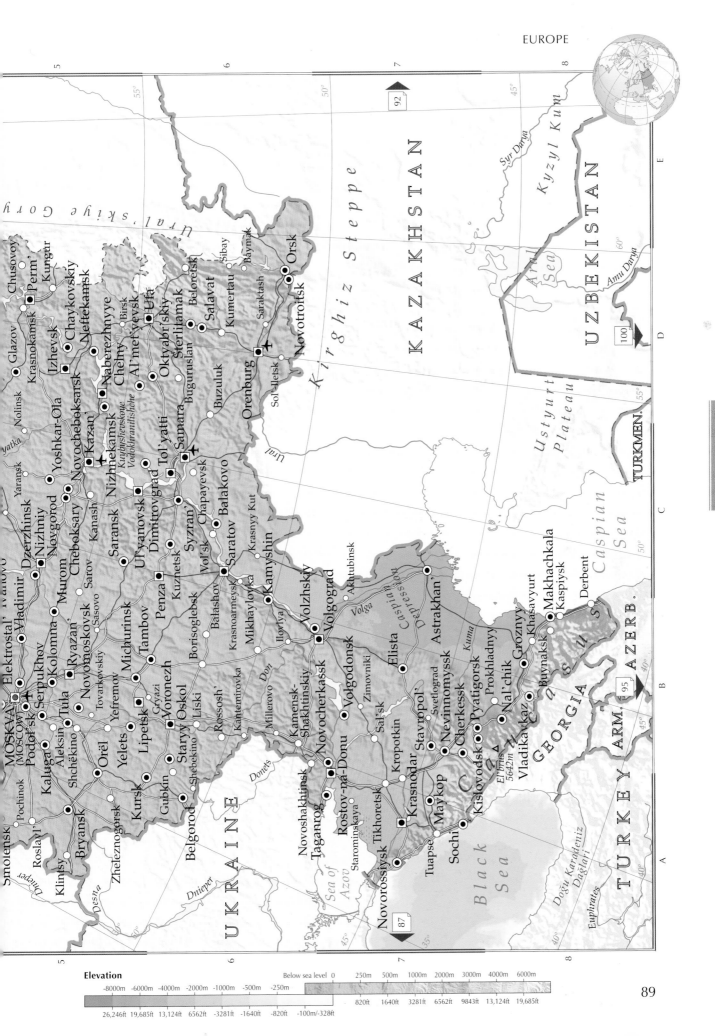

Elevation

| Below sea level | 0 | 250m | 500m | 1000m | 2000m | 3000m | 4000m | 6000m |

-8000m -6000m -4000m -2000m -1000m -500m -250m

820ft 1640ft 3281ft 6562ft 9843ft 13,124ft 19,685ft

26,246ft 19,685ft 13,124ft 6562ft -3281ft -1640ft -820ft -100m/-328ft

North & West Asia

A B C D

133

Franz Josef Land

A R C T I

Severnaya Ze

Ostrov Komsomolets

Ostrov Oktyabr'skoy Revolyutsii
Ostrov Bol'shevik

Novaya Zemlya

East Novaya Zemlya Trench

Kara Sea

Poluostrov Taymy

North Siber

Kheta

1

Norwegian Sea *North Cape*

Barents Sea

Ostrov Kolguyev

Poluostrov Yamal

● Noril'sk

Central Siberian Plateau

80°

Summer limit of pack ice

Winter limit of pack ice

70°

● Murmansk
Kola Peninsula

White Sea

R U S S I A N F

Kureyka

Ta

O

Arctic Circle

59

Gulf of Bothnia

● Archangel

Northern Dvina

Ob

West Siberian Plain

Lower Tunguska

Stony Tunguska

S I

2

60°

Lake Onega

Ural Mountains

Ob'

Yenisey

Angara

Baltic Sea

■ Saint Petersburg
■ Vologda
Yaroslavl'

Lake Ladoga

● MOSCOW

Nizhniy Novgorod

Perm' ■

● Yekaterinburg

Irtysh

Chulym

● Tomsk

■ Krasnoyarsk

Kaliningrad ■

Volga

Kazan' ■
Ufa ■

Chelyabinsk ●

Ishim

Irtysh

● Omsk

● Novosibirsk

■ Novokuznetsk

3

KALININGRAD
(to Russ. Fed.)

Central Russian Upland

Ul'yanovsk ●
■ Samara

Voronezh ●
Saratov ■

Orenburg ■

■ ASTANA

● Karaganda

Sayanskiy Khrebet

A S

Ir

50°

E U R O P E

Volgograd ■

Ural'sk ●

Kirghiz Steppe

Kazakh Uplands

Altai Mountains

● Rostov-na-Donu

Don

Volga

Ural

Aral'sk ○

KAZAKHSTAN

Ozero Zaysan

Astrakhan' ■

Danube

Stavropol' ●

El'brus 5642m

Caucasus

Caspian Sea

Aktau ●

Ustyurt Plateau

Aral Sea

Syr Darya

Lake Balkhash

Ili

● Almaty △ *Shan*

Black Sea

Istanbul ●

Küre Dağları

GEORGIA
T'BILISI ■
ARMENIA
YEREVAN ■ AZERB. ■ BAKU ●

Dasoguz ●

UZBEKISTAN

Kyzyl Kum

Taraz ●

Tien

△ Pik Pobedy 7443m

Kyzylorda ○

Amu Darya

BISHKEK ■

KYRGYZSTAN

4

81

Anatolia

ANKARA ■

Lake Van

TURKEY

Adana ●
Gaziantep ●
Aleppo ●

CYPRUS

SYRIA IRAQ ■
DAMASCUS
BEIRUT ■
LEBANON ■
BAGHDAD ■

Tabriz ●

Mosul ●

ASGABAT ■

TURKMENISTAN

Garagum

TASHKENT ■
DUSHANBE ■

TAJIKISTAN

Kunlun Mountains

40°

Qom ●
TEHRAN ■

Isfahan ●

IRAN

Iranian Plateau

Hindu Kush

KABUL ● Jlhalabad ●

Herat ●
AFGHANISTAN

Khyber Pass

Himalayas

ISRAEL ■
AMMAN ■
JERUSALEM ▽
Dead Sea -392m
JORDAN ■

Syrian Desert

Tigris
Euphrates

Basra ●

Zagros Mountains

KUWAIT ■
KUWAIT

Shiraz ●

The Gulf

Bandar-e 'Abbas ●

Zahedan ●

Thar Desert

Ganges

30°

An Nafud

MANAMA ●
BAHRAIN ● Dubai ●
RIYADH ■ DOHA ●
QATAR ● U.A.E. ●
SAUDI ARABIA ABU DHABI

Jedda ●

Gulf of Oman
MUSCAT ●
Sur ●

Indus Fan

Murray Ridge

Ganges Fan

Tropic of Cancer

20°

At Ta'if ●

Arabian Peninsula

Nile

Red Sea

Ar Rub' al Khali

OMAN

Bay of Bengal

A

AFRICA

5

N ▲

10°

SANA ●
Ta'izz ● Aden ●
YEMEN

Gulf of Aden

Socotra (to Yemen)

Arabian Sea

47

20° 40° 60° 80° 100°

A B C D

0 km   800

0 miles   800

Population ● National capital

○ below 50,000   ○ 50,000 to 100,000   ◉ 100,000 to 500,000   ■ above 500,000

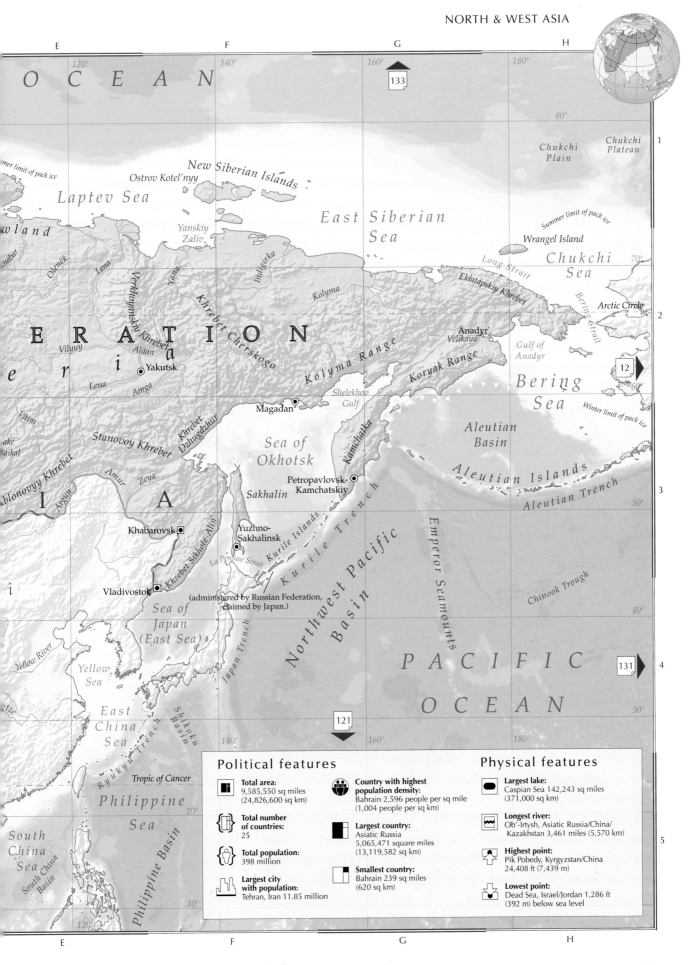

E   120°   F   140°   G   160°   H   180°

133

O C E A N

80°

Chukchi   Chukchi
Plain   Plateau

Summer limit of pack ice

New Siberian Islands

Ostrov Kotel'nyy

Laptev Sea

East Siberian
Sea

Summer limit of pack ice

Wrangel Island

Chukchi
Sea

nabar   Olenëk   Yanskiy
Zaliv

lowland

Lena

Verkhoyanskiy Khrebet

Yana

Indigirka

Khrebet Cherskogo

Kolyma

Long Strait

Ekiatapskiy Khrebet

Bering Strait

70°

Arctic Circle

E R A T I O N

Vilyuy   Aldan   a

Lena   Amga

Yakutsk

Kolyma Range

Koryak Range

Anadyr'
Velikaya

Gulf of
Anadyr

12

60°

Bering
Sea

Vitim

Amur   Zeya

Stanovoy Khrebet

Khrebet Dzhugdzhur

Magadan

Shelekhov
Gulf

Kamchatka

Winter limit of pack ice

Aleutian
Basin

ake
aikal

Sea of
Okhotsk

Petropavlovsk-
Kamchatskiy

Aleutian Islands

Aleutian Trench

50°

3

ablonovyy Khrebet

I   A

Argun   Amur

Sakhalin

Khabarovsk

Khrebet Sikhote-Alin'

Yuzhno-
Sakhalinsk

Kurile Islands

Kurile Trench

Northwest Pacific Basin

Emperor Seamounts

Chinook Trough

40°

i

Vladivostok

La Pérouse Strait

(administered by Russian Federation,
claimed by Japan.)

Sea of
Japan
(East Sea)

Japan Trench

P A C I F I C

131

4

Yellow River

Yellow
Sea

East
China
Sea

Ryukyu Trench

Shikoku Basin

O C E A N

30°

121

atze

140°   160°   180°

Tropic of Cancer

Philippine
Sea

20°

South
China
Sea

South China Basin

Philippine Basin

10°

120°

Political features

Total area:
9,585,550 sq miles
(24,826,600 sq km)

**Total number
of countries:**
25

Total population:
398 million

**Largest city
with population:**
Tehran, Iran 11.85 million

**Country with highest
population density:**
Bahrain 2,596 people per sq mile
(1,004 people per sq km)

Largest country:
Asiatic Russia
5,065,471 square miles
(13,119,582 sq km)

Smallest country:
Bahrain 239 sq miles
(620 sq km)

Physical features

Largest lake:
Caspian Sea 142,243 sq miles
(371,000 sq km)

Longest river:
Ob'-Irtysh, Asiatic Russia/China/
Kazakhstan 3,461 miles (5,570 km)

Highest point:
Pik Pobedy, Kyrgyzstan/China
24,408 ft (7,439 m)

Lowest point:
Dead Sea, Israel/Jordan 1,286 ft
(392 m) below sea level

E   F   G   H

Russia & Kazakhstan

0 km   600

0 miles   600

Population ● National capital

○ below 50,000   ○ 50,000 to 100,000   ◉ 100,000 to 500,000   ■ above 500,000

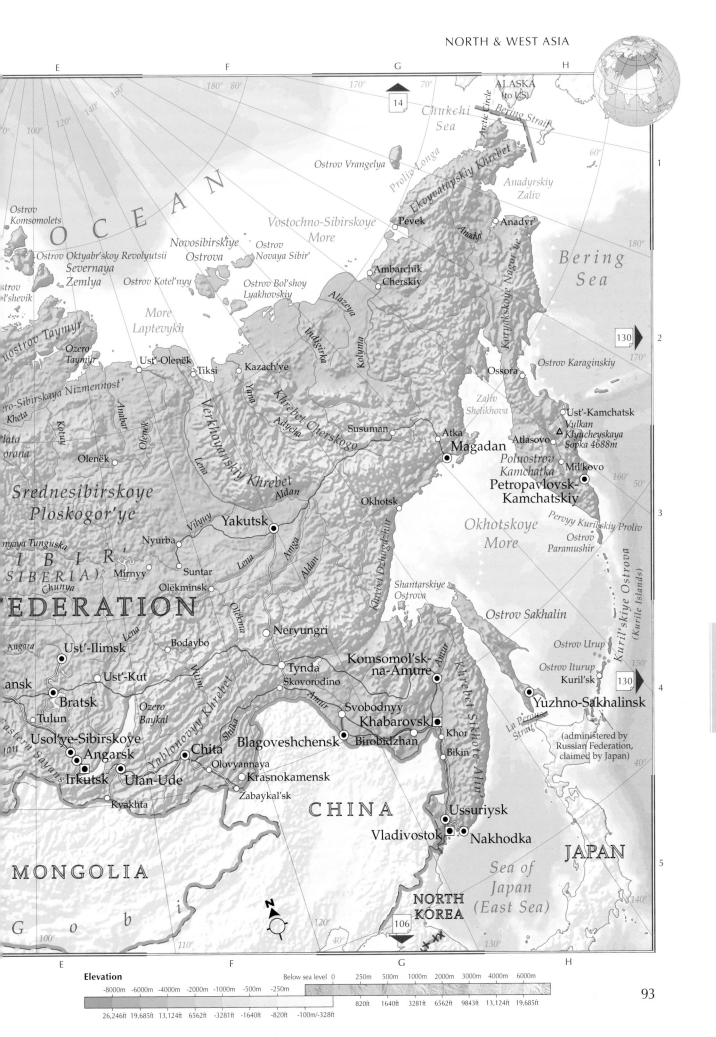

ALASKA
(to US)

Chukchi
Sea

Bering Strait

Arctic Circle

14

Ostrov Vrangelya

Ostrov
Komsomolets

O C E A N

Ekvyoatapyskiy Khrebet

Anadyrskiy
Zaliv

Pevek

Anadyr'

Anadys'

Bering
Sea

Ostrov Oktyabr'skoy Revolyutsii

Novosibirskiye
Ostrova

Vostochno-Sibirskoye
More

Ambarchik
Cherskiy

Ossora

180°

130

170°

Koryakskoye Nagor'ye

Ostrov
l'shevik

Ostrov
Novaya Sibir'

Severnaya
Zemlya

Ostrov Kotel'nyy

Ostrov Bol'shoy
Lyakhovskiy

Alazeya

Ostrov Karaginskiy

uostrov Taymyr

More
Laptevykh

Ust'-Olenëk

Tiksi

Kazach'ye

Indigirka

Kolyma

Susuman

Atka

Zaliv
Shelikhova

Ust'-Kamchatsk
Vulkan
Klyucheyskaya
Sopka 4688m

Ozero
Taymyr

ro-Sibirskaya Nizmennost'

Yana

Khrebet Cherskogo

Magadan

Atlasovo

Kheta

Verkhoyanskiy

Adycha

Okhotsk

Poluostrov
Kamchatka

Mil'kovo

160°

Kotuy

Anabar

Olenëk

Lena

Khrebet

Aldan

Petropavlovsk-
Kamchatskiy

50°

lato
orana

Olenëk

Srednesibirskoye
Ploskogor'ye

Vilyuy

Yakutsk

Okhotskoye
More

Pervyy Kuril'skiy Proliv

Ostrov
Paramushir

nyaya Tunguska

Nyurba

Lena

Amga

Khrebet Dzhugdzhur

3

IBIR'
(SIBERIA)

Chunya

Mirnyy

Suntar

Aldan

Shantarskiye
Ostrova

Ostrov Sakhalin

Olëkminsk

Kuril'skiye Ostrova
(Kurile Islands)

EDERATION

Lena

Olëkma

Bodaybo

Neryungri

Ostrov Urup

Ostrov Iturup

150°

Angara

Ust'-Ilimsk

Vitim

Tynda

Komsomol'sk-
na-Amure

Amur

Kuril'sk

130

4

ansk

Ust'-Kut

Skovorodino

Svobodnyy

Khrebet Sikhote Alin'

Yuzhno-Sakhalinsk

Bratsk

Ozero
Baykal

Amur

Khabarovsk

La Pérouse
Strait

Tulun

Yablonovyy Khrebet

Birobidzhan

Khor

(administered by
Russian Federation,
claimed by Japan)

Usol'ye-Sibirskoye

Shilka

Blagoveshchensk

Bikin

40°

Angarsk

Chita

astern Sayans

Irkutsk

Ulan-Ude

Olovyannaya

Krasnokamensk

CHINA

Ussuriysk

JAPAN

an

Kyakhta

Zabaykal'sk

Vladivostok

Nakhodka

5

MONGOLIA

Sea of
Japan
(East Sea)

G

o

b

i

N

NORTH
KOREA

120°

106

110°

40°

130°

140°

Elevation

Below sea level 0   250m   500m 1000m 2000m 3000m 4000m 6000m

-8000m -6000m -4000m -2000m -1000m -500m -250m

820ft 1640ft 3281ft 6562ft 9843ft 13,124ft 19,685ft

26,246ft 19,685ft 13,124ft 6562ft -3281ft -1640ft -820ft -100m/-328ft

Turkey & The Caucasus

ROMANIA

Iacul Sinoie

Danube

UKRAINE

Kryms'kyy
Pivostriv

86

BULGARIA

Varnenski
Zaliv

Burgaski
Zaliv

B l a c k   S e a

Maritsa

82

Kırklareli

Edirne

İnebolu

Sinop
Gerze

Cide

Ergene Çayi

Çorlu

Zonguldak

Bartın

K ü r e   D a ğ l a r ı

Kastamonu

Bafra

Tekirdağ

İstanbul

Devrek

Karabük

Kargı

Samsun

Marmara Denizi
(Sea of Marmara)

İzmit

Adapazarı

Çerkeş

Kastamonu

Merzifon

Üny

İstanbul Boğazı
(Bosporus)

Bandırma

Yalova

İznik Gölü

Bolu

Gerede

Çankırı

Kızıl Irmak

Çorum

Ord

Çanakkale

Bursa

Bilecik

ANKARA

Kalecik

Alaca

Tokat

Çanakkale
Boğazı
(Dardanelles)

Balıkesir

Bozüyük

Eskişehir

Polatlı

Kırıkkale

Sorgun

Yıldızeli

Edremit

Ayvalık

Kütahya

T U R K

Hirfanlı
Baraji

Şarkışla

Siva

Lésvos

Simav

Kulu

Boğazlıyan

Akhisar

Gediz

Tuz Gölü

Bünyan

Heki

Menemen

Manisa

Uşak

Afyon

Cihanbeyli

Nevşehir

İncesu

Gürün

İzmir

Gediz Nehri

Aksaray

Kayseri

Chíos

Alaşehir

Akşehir

A n a t o l i a

Sámos

Ödemiş

Nazilli

Dinar

Göksun

G ü

Aydın

Denizli

Beyşehir
Gölü

Konya

Niğde

Kahramanma

Söke

Büyükmenderes Nehri

Burdur

İsparta

Karaman

Gazian

Milas

Tavas

Burdur
Gölü

Suğla Gölü

Ereğli

Ceyhan

Osmaniye

Bodrum

Muğla

Karaman

Tarsus

Adana

83

T o r o s   D a ğ l a r ı

Mersin (İçel)

Kilis

Marmaris

Dalaman

Antalya

Manavgat

Mut

İskenderun

Kırıkhan

Doğekánisa
(Dodecánese)

Fethiye

Kaş

Alanya

Antakya

Ródos
(Rhodes)

Finike

Antalya
Körfezi

Silifke

Kárpathos

Anamur

CYPRUS

TURKISH REPUBLIC OF
NORTHERN CYPRUS
(recognized only by Turkey)

Orantes

LEBANON

M e d i t e r r a n e a n

S e a

50

0 km   200

0 miles   200

Population   National capital

below 50,000   50,000 to 100,000   100,000 to 500,000   above 500,000

RUSSIAN
FEDERATION

Caspian

Sea

Caucasus

Gagra
Gudaut'a
Ap'khazet'i
Sokhumi
Och'amch'ire
Mestia
Enguri
Kazbek
5047m △

K'ut'aisi
South
Ossetia
Samtredia
GEORGIA
Gori
P'ot'i
Tsalka
T'BILISI
Zaqatala
Xaçmaz
K'obulet'i
Akhalts'ikhe
Rust'avi
Quba
Siyäzän
Bat'umi
Achara
Hopa
Lesser
Şäki
100
Artvin
Caucasus
Kura
Gäncä
Mingäçevir
Märäzä
Sumqayıt
Trabzon
Rize
Pazar
Doğu Karadeniz Dağları
Gyumri
Vanadzor
Yevlax
BAKI
(BAKU)
Of
Çoruh Nehri
Artik
Sevan
AZERBAIJAN
Giresun
İspir
Kars
ARMENIA
Sevana Lich
Nagorno-
Karabakh
Imişli
Qazimämmäd
Äli-Bayramı
Doğu Karadeniz Dağları
Sarıkamış
YEREVAN
Xankändi
müşhane
Pasinler
Horasan
Artashat
Aras
Büyükağrı Dağı
(Mount Ararat) △
Aşkale
Goris
Biläsuvar
hiye
Erzincan
Tercan
Erzurum
Ağri
5137m
AZERBAIJAN
Kemah
Doğubayazıt
Naxçıvan
Länkäran
Patnos
Bingöl
Erciş
Muradiye
Aras
Elazığ
Keban
Barajı
Muş
Van
Gölü
Van
alatya
Tatvan
Reshteh-ye Kühhä-ye Alborz
(Elburz Mountains)
Toroslar
Bitlis
Silvan
Gevaş
Siirt
Daryācheh-ye
Orūmīyeh
IRAN
ılıyaman
Diyarbakır
Batman
Şırnak
Silverek
Mardin
Kurdistan
Viranşehir
Atatürk
Barajı
Nusaybin
Şanlıurfa
Ceylanpınar
98
Tigris
Al Jazīrah
Euphrates
Jabal Bishrī
hayrat
Āsad
IRAQ
Buhayrat
ath
Tharthār
98
RIA
Kühhä-ye Zagros
(Zagros Mountains)

Elevation

-8000m -6000m -4000m -2000m -1000m -500m -250m | Below sea level 0 250m 500m 1000m 2000m 3000m 4000m 6000m

26,246ft 19,685ft 13,124ft 6562ft -3281ft -1640ft -820ft | -100m/-328ft | 820ft 1640ft 3281ft 6562ft 9843ft 13,124ft 19,685ft

The Near East

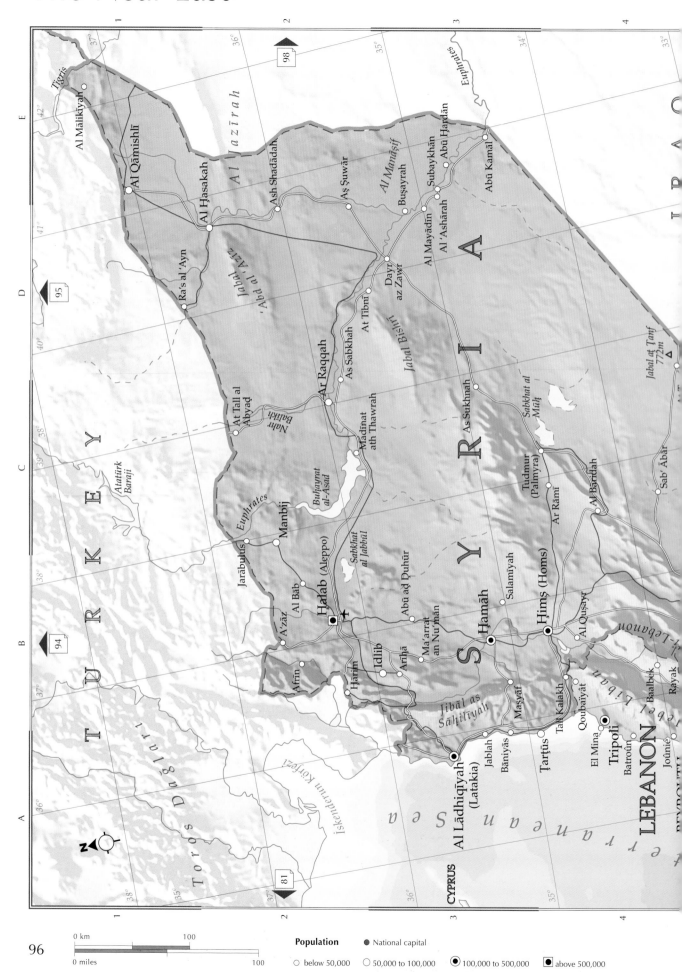

Population

● National capital

○ below 50,000　　○ 50,000 to 100,000　　◉ 100,000 to 500,000　　■ above 500,000

0 km　　　100

0 miles　　　100

WEST BANK

Jordan

Khirbet el 'Aujā et Tahtā
Jericho
Jenin
Jiftlik Post
Qabātiya
Nāblus
Nu'eima
Dead Sea
JORDAN
Ramallah
Bethlehem
Tülkarm
JERUSALEM
Qalqīlya
Hebron
Mas-hā

I S R A E L

Israeli settlement
Palestinian settlement
West Bank fence

Palestinian control
Mixed control
Israeli settlement block

0 km   20
0 miles   20

JORDAN

JERUSALEM (DAMASCUS)

Mount Hermon
2814m

Muqāt

Al Quṣayfrah

As Suwaydā'

Jabal ad Durūz
1798m

D e s e r t

As Ṣafāwī

As Suwaydā'

Dar'ā

Wāḥat al Azraq

Ar Ramthā
Az Zarqā'

Irbid

Al Mafraq

AMMAN (AMMAN)

Mādabā

As Salt

Ard as Ṣawwān

Bāyir

Al 'Umarī

Qā' al Jafr

Al Jafr

Al Hisā

Al Mudawwarah

S A U D I   A R A B I A

J O R D A N

Wādī as Sīr
Jericho
Al Mazra'ah
Al Karak
Al 'Aynā
Ash Shawbak
Ma'ān

Dar'ā

Dead Sea

Hebron

Aṭ Ṭafīlah
Sappir
Wādī Mūsā (Petra)

Ra's an Naqb

Al Quwayrah

Nahr el

Bent Jbail
Tsefat
Lake Tiberias
Tverya
Nazareth)
Natzrat

Golan Heights

Saïda
Soûr
En Nâqoûra
Nahariya
Hefa (Haifa)

Mitzpe Ramon

Be'er Menuha

Gharandal

Al 'Aqabah

Al Aqabah

Elat
Gulf of Aqaba

Jenin
Nāblus
WEST BANK
JERUSALEM
Bethlehem
'Arad
Be'er Sheva

Jordan

Petah Tikva
Holon
Rehovot

Tel Aviv-Yafo
Hadera
Netanya

Ashdod
Ashkelon
Gaza
GAZA STRIP
(under Palestinian administration)
Khān Yūnis
Rafah

I S R A E L

HaNegev
Wādī al 'Arabah

E G Y P T

S i n a i

M

Elevation

Below sea level 0   250m   500m   1000m   2000m   3000m   4000m   6000m

-8000m -6000m -4000m -2000m -1000m -500m -250m

820ft   1640ft   3281ft   6562ft   9843ft   13,124ft   19,685ft

26,246ft 19,685ft 13,124ft 6562ft -3281ft -1640ft -820ft -100m/-328ft

The Middle East

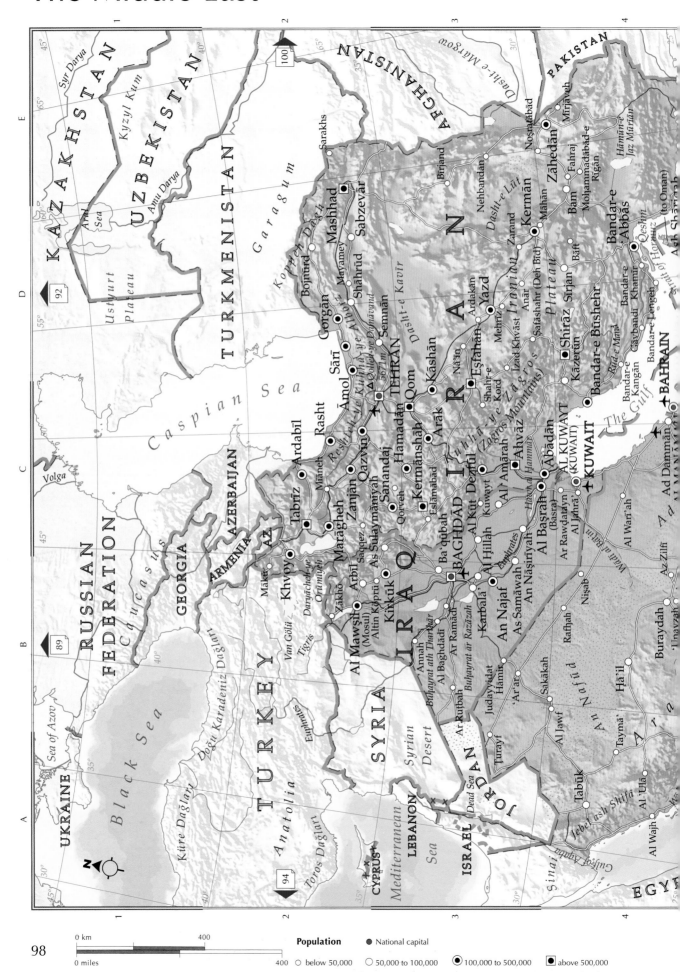

0 km 400

0 miles 400

Population ● National capital

○ below 50,000 ○ 50,000 to 100,000 ◉ 100,000 to 500,000 ■ above 500,000

KAZAKHSTAN

UZBEKISTAN

TURKMENISTAN

AFGHANISTAN

PAKISTAN

Dasht-e Mārgow

Sarakhs

Kyzyl Kum

Amu Darya

Sur Darya

Aral Sea

Ustyurt Plateau

Garagum

Koppeh Dāgh

Bojnūrd

Mashhad

Sabzevār

Gorgān

Birjand

Nehbandān

Nosratābād

Mirjāveh

Zāhedān

Fahraj

Hāmūn-e Jaz Mūriān

Mohammadābād-e Rīgān

Bam

Māhān

Kermān

Zarand

Anār

Iranian Plateau

Bandar-e Abbās

Qeshm

Strait of Hormūz

Ash Shāriqah

(to Oman)

Caspian Sea

Volga

Āmol

Sārī

Rasht

Qolleh-ye Damāvand 5671m

Reshteh-ye Kūhhā-ye Alborz

TEHRAN

Qom

Semnān

Mayāmey

Shāhrūd

Ardabīl

Kāshān

Nāṭanz

Ardakān

Yazd

Eṣfahān

Shahr-e Kord

Īzad Khvāst

Safāshahr (Deh Bīd)

Zagros Mountains

Kūhhā-ye Zāgros

Rūd-e Mand

Shīrāz

Sīrjān

Bāft

Kāzerūn

Bandar-e Būshehr

Bandar-e Khamīr

Bandar-e Lengeh

Bandar-e Kangān

Gāvbandī

RUSSIAN FEDERATION

Caucasus

AZERBAIJAN

ARMENIA

AZ

GEORGIA

Khvoy

Mākū

Darīācheh-ye Orūmīyeh

Tabrīz

Marāgheh

Mīāneh

Zanjān

Qazvīn

Sanandaj

Hamadān

Kermānshāh

Arāk

Qorveh

Saqqez

Eslāmābād

As Sulaymānīyah

Kuwayt

Al ʿAmārah

I R A Q

Ahvāz

Abādān

Al Başrah (Basra)

Hawr al Hammār

Al Jahrāʾ

AL KUWAYT (KUWAIT)

KUWAIT

The Gulf

BAHRAIN

MANAMA

Ad Dammām

UKRAINE

Black Sea

Sea of Azov

Küre Dağları

Doğu Karadeniz Dağları

TURKEY

Anatolia

Toros Dağları

Van Gölü

Tigris

Euphrates

Zākho

Altin Köprü

Arbīl

Kirkūk

Al Mawşil (Mosul)

ʿAnnah

Buḩayrat ath Tharthār

Al Baghdādī

Ar Ramādī

Bugayrat ar Razzāzah

BAGHDAD

Baʿqūbah

Al Kūt

Al Ḩillah

Karbalāʾ

An Najaf

As Samāwah

An Nāşirīyah

Ar Rawḑatayn

SYRIA

Syrian Desert

Ar Kūṭbah

LEBANON

CYPRUS

Mediterranean Sea

ISRAEL

Dead Sea

JORDAN

Buḩayrat ar Razzāzah

Judayyidat Ḩāmir

ʿArʿar

Turayf

Al Jawf

Taymāʾ

Tabūk

Al ʿUlā

Al Wajh

Sinai

Gulf of ʿAqaba

Jebel ash Shifāʾ

EGYPT

An Nafūd

Sakākah

Rafḩah

Nīşāb

Al Warīʿah

Az Zilfī

Burayḑah

ʿUnayzah

Ḩāʾil

Wādī al Bāṭin

Arabia

IRAN

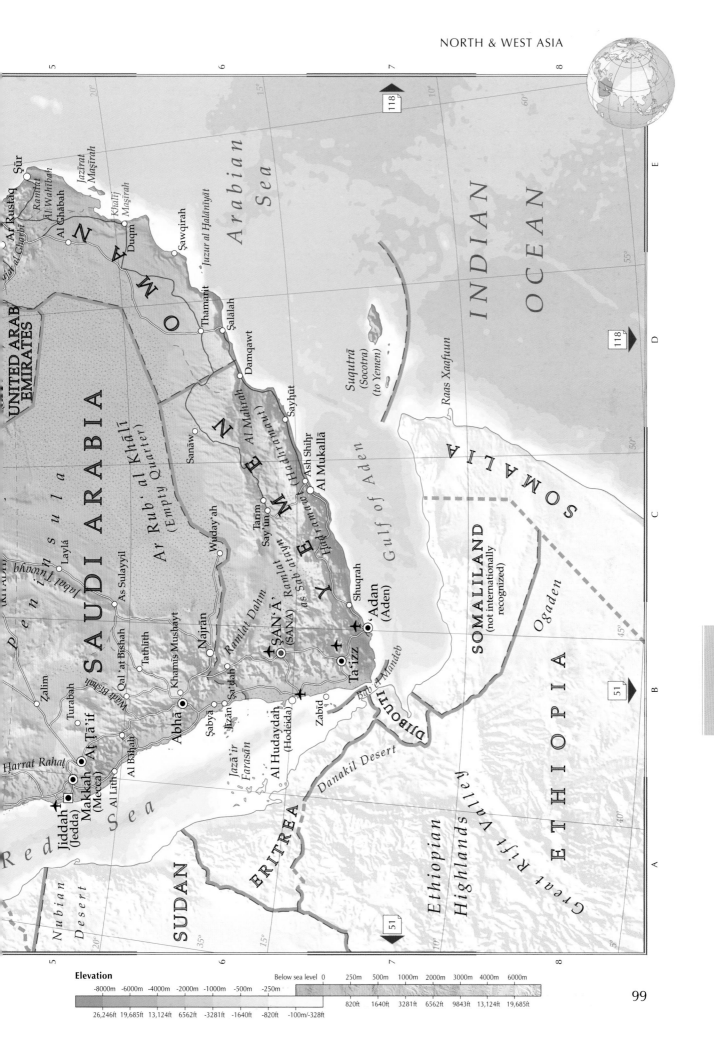

5

20°

15°

6

15°

7

10°

55°

8

60°

E

118

118

D

50°

C

45°

B

40°

A

5°

Arabian Sea

INDIAN OCEAN

Şūr

Ar Rustāq

Jazīrat Maşīrah

Ramlat Al Wahībah

Al Ghābah

Khalīj Maşīrah

Duqm

Şawqirah

Juzur al Halānīyāt

O M A N

Thamarīt

Damqawt

Salalah

Sayhūt

Suqutrā (Socotra) (to Yemen)

Raas Xaafuun

UNITED ARAB EMIRATES

Ar Rub' al Khālī (Empty Quarter)

Sanāw

Al Mahrah

Hadramawt (Hadhramaut)

Ash Shiḥr

Al Mukallā

SAUDI ARABIA

P e n i n s u l a

Jabal Tuwayq

Laylā

As Sulayyil

Wudayah

Tarīm

Say'ūn

Shuqrah

Adan (Aden)

Y E M E N

Ramlat as Sab'atayn

SOMALILAND (not internationally recognized)

SOMALIA

Ogaden

Zalim

Turabah

Ar Bishah

Qal 'at Bīshah

Najrān

Ramlat Dahm

ṢAN'Ā' (SANA)

Ta'izz

Khamis Mushayt

Saʻdah

DJIBOUTI

Aţ Ţā'if

Abhā

Al Bāḥah

Şabyā

Jīzān

Al Hudaydah (Hodeida)

Zabīd

Bāb el Mandeb

Makkah (Mecca)

Al Lith

Jazā'ir Farasān

ETHIOPIA

Ethiopian Highlands

Great Rift Valley

Ḥarrat Rahat

Jiddah (Jedda)

Red Sea

SUDAN

Danakil Desert

ERITREA

Nubian Desert

Tathlīth

Gulf of Aden

51

51

99

Elevation

Below sea level	0	250m	500m	1000m	2000m	3000m	4000m	6000m

-8000m -6000m -4000m -2000m -1000m -500m -250m

820ft 1640ft 3281ft 6562ft 9843ft 13,124ft 19,685ft

26,246ft 19,685ft 13,124ft 6562ft -3281ft -1640ft -820ft -100m/-328ft

Central Asia

RUSSIAN FEDERATION

GEORGIA

AZERBAIJAN

Caspian Sea

Ustyurt Plateau

Aral Sea

Mo'ynoq

Chimboy

Köneürgenç   Taxtako'pir

Taxiatosh   **Nukus**   *Kyzy*

Gurbansoltan Eje   Gubadag   Uchqudu

Daşoguz   **Urganch**

Garabogaz Aylagy   To'rtko'l   **UZBEK**

Xiva   Zarafsh

Gazojak   Lebap

Türkmenbaşy   * Üngüz*   Ga.

Türkmenbaşy Aylagy   Derweze   *Angyrsyndaky*   *Garagum*   G'ijd

Balkanabat   Bereket   *Garagum*   Buxo

Hazar

Türkmen Aylagy   **TURKMENISTAN**   Seýdi   **K**

Serdar   Galkynyş

Köpetdag Gershi   Baharly   *Garagum*   **Türkmenabat**

Magtymguly   Saýat

Abadan   *Garagum*   **K**

Esenguly   Gökdepe   **AŞGABAT**   Bayramaly   UZ

Gora Chapan 2889m   Tejen   **Mary**

Reshteh-ye Kūhhā-ye Alborz   Kaka   Murgap   And

Sarahs   *Garabil Belentligi*

Bālā Morghāb   Meyn

Kūhhā-ye Zāgros   Serhetabat   *Daryā ye Mo*

Towraghoudī   *Selseleh-ye Safīd Kūh*

Ghūrīān   **Herāt**

IRAN   **AFGHA**

Iranian   Shīndand

Plateau   *Farāh Rūd*

Farāh   Delārām

Dasht-e Khāsh   Gere

Hāmūn-e Şāberī   Lashkar Gāh

Chakhānsūr   Kūchn

Zaranj   *Dasht-e Mārgow*   Darw

Deh Shū

Daryā-ye Helmand   Rīg

Chāgai Hills

0 km   200

0 miles   200

Population   ● National capital

○ below 50,000   ○ 50,000 to 100,000   ◉ 100,000 to 500,000   ◼ above 500,000

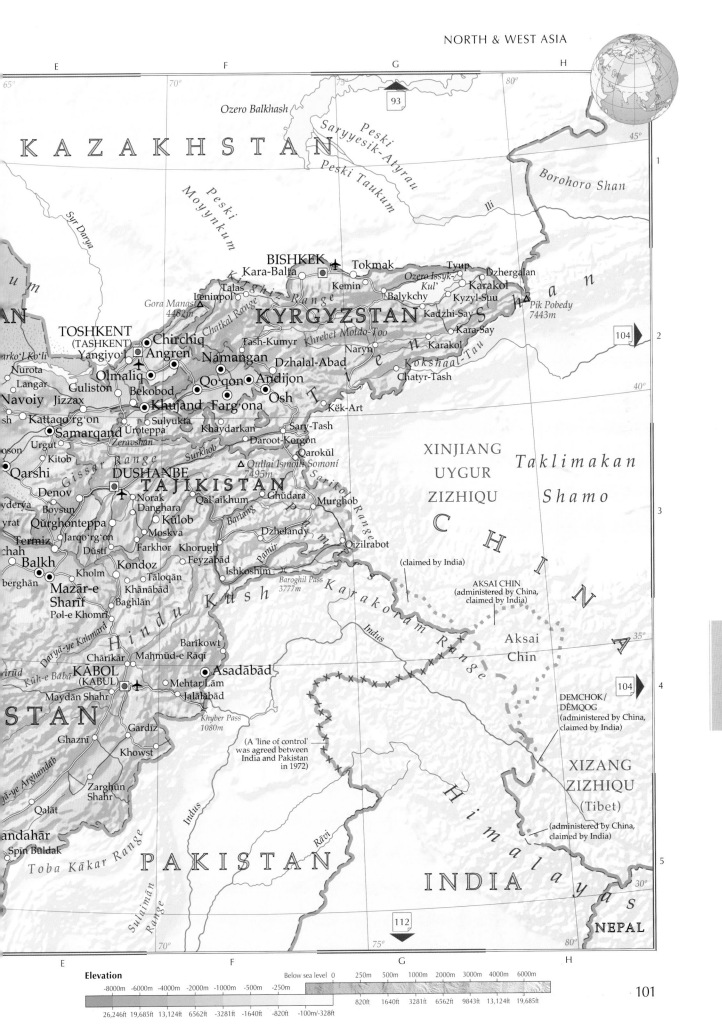

KAZAKHSTAN

Ozero Balkhash

Peski Saryyesik-Atyrau

Peski Taukum

93

Borohoro Shan

Peski Moyynkum

Syr Darya

BISHKEK
Kara-Balta • Tokmak • Tyup • Dzhergalan
Talas • Kemin • Karakol
Leninpol • *Ozero Issyk-Kul'* • Kyzyl-Suu
△ *Gora Manas* Balykchy • Karakol
4482m *Kirghiz Range* Kadzhi-Say • Pik Pobedy △
KYRGYZSTAN 7443m
Chatkal Range Tash-Kumyr *Khrebet Moldo-Too* • Kara-Say
TOSHKENT • Chirchiq Namangan Naryn • Karakol *Kokshaal-Tau*
(TASHKENT) Angren Dzhalal-Abad • Chatyr-Tash
Yangiyo'l *T i e n*
'arko'l Ko'li Olmaliq Qo'qon Andijon
Nurota Bekobod Farg'ona Osh Këk-Art
Langar Guliston
Navoiy Jizzax Khujand
sh Kattaqo'rg'on Sulyukta XINJIANG
oson Samarqand Ûroteppa Khaydarkan UYGUR
Urgut *Zeravshan* Sary-Tash ZIZHIQU *Taklimakan*
Kitob Daroot-Korgon
Range Qarokûl *Shamo*
Qarshi *Gissar* △ *Qullai Ismoili Somoni*
Denov DUSHANBE 7495m C H I N A
Surkhob Ghudara
yderya Norak Qai'aikhum Murghob
yrat Boysun Danghara *Bartang*
Qûrghonteppa Kûlob *Pamir* Dzhelandy (claimed by India)
Termiz Jarqo'rg'on Moskva *Range* Qizilrabot AKSAI CHIN
chah Dûsti Farkhor Khorugh (administered by China,
Balkh Kondoz Feyzâbâd *Sarikol* claimed by India)
berghān Kholm Tâloqân Ishkoshim Aksai
Mazâr-e Khânâbâd *Baroghil Pass* Chin
Sharif Baghlân *Hindu* 3777m *Karakoram Range*
Pol-e Khomri *Indus*
Kush DEMCHOK/
Barîkowt DÊMQOG
Chârîkâr Mahmûd-e Râqî (administered by China,
KABOL Asadâbâd claimed by India)
(KABUL) Mehtar Lâm XIZANG
Maydân Shahr Jalâlâbâd ZIZHIQU
STAN *Khyber Pass* (Tibet)
Ghaznî 1080m (administered by China,
Gardîz claimed by India)
Khowst (A 'line of control'
was agreed between *H* *Indus*
Zarghûn India and Pakistan *i*
Shahr in 1972) *m*
Qalât *a*
qā-ye Arghandāb *l*
andahār *Rāvi* *a*
Spîn Buldak *y*
Toba Kâkar Range P A K I S T A N *a*
Indus *s* NEPAL
INDIA
Sulaimān Range
112

Elevation

Below sea level 0   250m 500m 1000m 2000m 3000m 4000m 6000m

-8000m -6000m -4000m -2000m -1000m -500m -250m

820ft 1640ft 3281ft 6562ft 9843ft 13,124ft 19,685ft

26,246ft 19,685ft 13,124ft 6562ft -3281ft -1640ft -820ft -100m/-328ft

101

South & East Asia

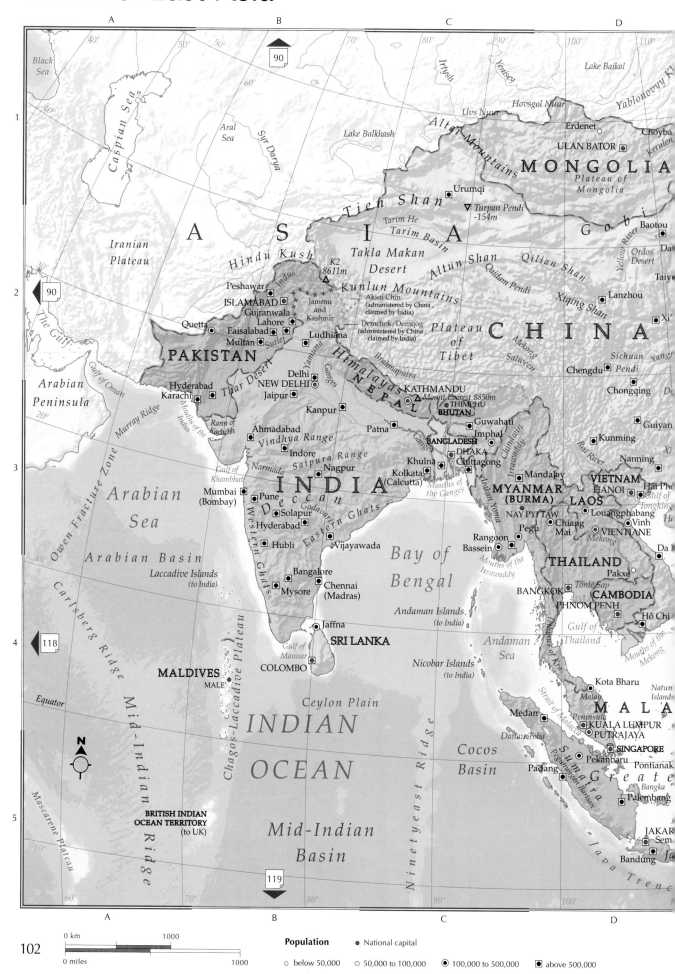

Black Sea
Caspian Sea
Aral Sea
Syr Darya
Lake Balkhash
Irtysh
Yenisey
Lake Baikal
Hovsgol Nuur
Uvs Nuur
Erdenet
Choyba
ULAN BATOR
Yablonovyy K
Kerulen

MONGOLIA
Plateau of Mongolia
Gobi
Baotou
Da

A S I A
Tien Shan
Urumqi
Turpan Pendi -154m
Tarim He
Tarim Basin
Takla Makan Desert
Altun Shan
Qilian Shan
Xiqing Shan
Ordos Desert
Yellow River
Taiy
Lanzhou
Xi'
Iranian Plateau
Hindu Kush
K2 8611m
Kunlun Mountains
Aksai Chin (administered by China, claimed by India)
Demchok/Demqog (administered by China, claimed by India)
Plateau of Tibet
Qaidam Pendi
Mekong
Salween
C H I N A
Sichuan Pendi
Chengdu
Chongqing
Guiyan

Peshawar
Indus
ISLAMABAD
Jammu and Kashmir
Gujranwala
Lahore
Quetta
Faisalabad
Multan
Sutlej
Ludhiana

PAKISTAN
Thar Desert
Yamuna
Ganges
Himalayas
NEPAL
KATHMANDU
Mount Everest 8850m
THIMPHU
BHUTAN
Brahmaputra
Guwahati
Imphal
Kunming
Nanning
Xi

The Gulf
Gulf of Oman
Arabian Peninsula
Hyderabad
Karachi
Rann of Kachchh
Mouths of the Indus
Delhi
NEW DELHI
Jaipur
Kanpur
Ahmadabad
Vindhya Range
Indore
Patna
Ganges
BANGLADESH
DHAKA
Khulna
Chittagong
Kolkata (Calcutta)
Mouths of the Ganges
Chindwin
Irrawaddy
Arakan Yoma
Mandalay
MYANMAR (BURMA)
VIETNAM
HANOI
Hai Pho
Gulf of Tongking

Murray Ridge
Narmada
Satpura Range
Nagpur
I N D I A
Mumbai (Bombay)
Pune
Deccan
Solapur
Godavari
Hyderabad
Hubli
Eastern Ghats
Western Ghats
Vijayawada
NAY PYI TAW
Pegu
Rangoon
Bassein
Chiang Mai
Louangphabang
Vinh
VIENTIANE
LAOS
Mekong
Da

Arabian Sea
Arabian Basin
Owen Fracture Zone
Laccadive Islands (to India)
Gulf of Khambhat
Bangalore
Mysore
Chennai (Madras)
Bay of Bengal
Andaman Islands (to India)
Mouths of the Irrawaddy
Andaman Sea
THAILAND
Pakxe
BANGKOK
Tonle Sap
CAMBODIA
PHNOM PENH
Hô Chi
Gulf of Thailand
Isthmus of Kra

Carlsberg Ridge
Chagos-Laccadive Plateau
Jaffna
Gulf of Mannar
SRI LANKA
COLOMBO
Nicobar Islands (to India)

Equator
MALDIVES
MALE
Ceylon Plain
INDIAN
OCEAN
Mid-Indian Basin
Mid-Indian Ridge
Ninetyeast Ridge
Cocos Basin
Kota Bharu
Natun Islands
Medan
Danau Toba
Malay Peninsula
M A L A
KUALA LUMPUR
PUTRAJAYA
SINGAPORE
Pekanbaru
Padang
Pegunungan Barisan
Strait of Malacca
Pontianak
Sumatra
Bangka
G r e a t e
Palembang

Mascarene Plateau
BRITISH INDIAN OCEAN TERRITORY (to UK)
JAKAR
Sem
Java Trench
Bandung
Ja

N

102

Population   ● National capital
○ below 50,000   ◎ 50,000 to 100,000   ◉ 100,000 to 500,000   ■ above 500,000

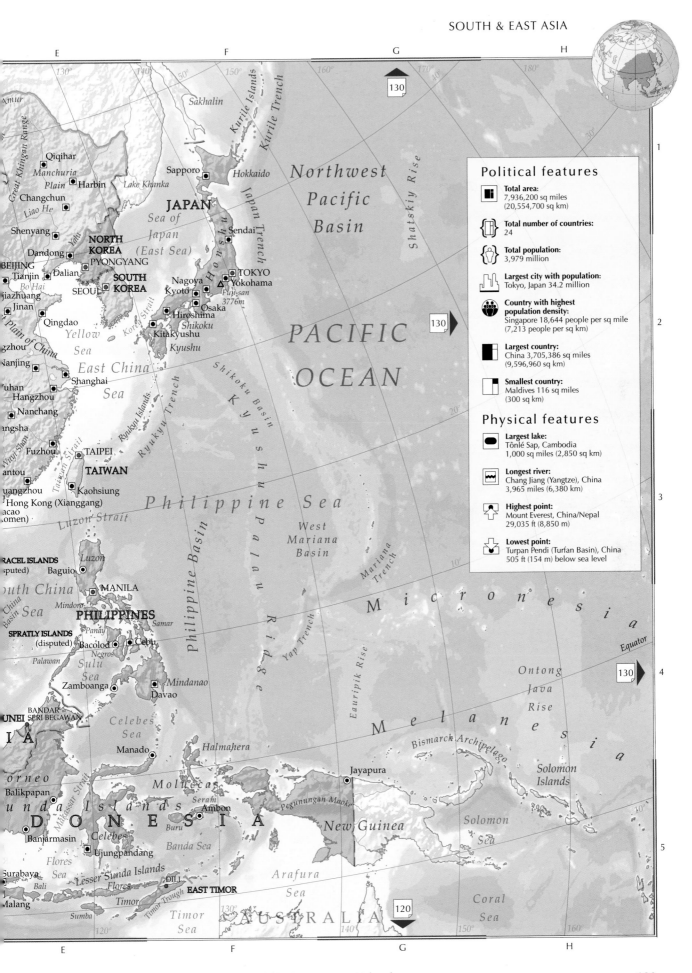

Political features

Total area:
7,936,200 sq miles
(20,554,700 sq km)

Total number of countries:
24

Total population:
3,979 million

Largest city with population:
Tokyo, Japan 34.2 million

Country with highest population density:
Singapore 18,644 people per sq mile
(7,213 people per sq km)

Largest country:
China 3,705,386 sq miles
(9,596,960 sq km)

Smallest country:
Maldives 116 sq miles
(300 sq km)

Physical features

Largest lake:
Tônlé Sap, Cambodia
1,000 sq miles (2,850 sq km)

Longest river:
Chang Jiang (Yangtze), China
3,965 miles (6,380 km)

Highest point:
Mount Everest, China/Nepal
29,035 ft (8,850 m)

Lowest point:
Turpan Pendi (Turfan Basin), China
505 ft (154 m) below sea level

Western China & Mongolia

RUSSIAN FE

KAZAKHSTAN

Kazakhskiy

Melkosopochnik

Kulunda Steppe

Zapadnyy Sayan

Yenisey

Höysgöl Nuur

Ozero Balkhash

Ozero Zaysan

Uvs Nuur

Ulaangom

Ölgiy

Mö

Altay

Hyargas Nuur

Tsetserleg

Har Us Nuur

Hovd

Har Nuur

M O N

Altay

Bayanhongor

Hangayn Nuru

Ulungur Hu

Karamay

Gurbantüngüt Shamo

Kuytun

Shihezi

Fukang

Jimsar

△ Aj Bogd Uul
3802m

Borohoro Shan

Yining

Ürümqi

Qitai

Atas Bogd
△ 2695m

Ozero Issyk-Kul'

KYRGYZSTAN

Tien Shan

Turpan

Turpan Pendi

Hami

G

Korla

Kuruktag

Bosten Hu

Xingxingxia

Dalian H

△ Tomür Feng
7443m

GANSU

Qilian Shan

Kashi

Tarim He

Tarim Basin

Lop Nur

Yengisar

Shache

XINJIANG UYGUR

TAJIKISTAN

AFGH.

Yecheng
(claimed by India)

Pishan

Moyu

ZIZHIQU

Ruoqiang

Altun Shan

Danghe Nanshan

Qilian Shan

Qinghai H

Taklimakan Shamo

Qaidam Pendi

Karakoram Range

K2
△ 8611m

Hotan

Qira

Kunlun Shan

Golmud

Burhan Budai Shan

Dulan

Kashmir

Indus

AKSAI CHIN

AKSAI CHIN
(administered by China, claimed by India)

C

QINGHAI

H

PAKISTAN

JAMMU AND KASHMIR

Rutog

Qingzang Gaoyuan
(Plateau of Tibet)

Tongtian He

Anyêmaqên

Bayan Har Sha

DEMCHOK/DÊMQOG
(administered by China, claimed by India)

Gar Xincun

XIZANG

Yushu

Mekong

Zanda

ZIZHIQU

Gozhê

Siling Co

Amdo

Tanggula Shan

Qamdo

Himalaya

Tangra Yumco

Nam Co

Nagqu

Salween

Brahmaputra

Gyaring Co

Ngangzê Co

Damxung

Nyainqêntanglha Shan

Jinsha Jiang

Hengduan Shan

(Tibet)

Yamuna

NEPAL

Lhazê

Xigazê

Maizhokunggar

ARUNACHAL PRADESH
(claimed by China)

Lhasa

Ganges

Gonggar

△ Mount Everest
8850m

Gyangzê

BHUTAN

INDIA

MYANMAR
(BURMA)

INDIA

0 km 400

0 miles 400

Population ● National capital ● Internal administrative capital

○ below 50,000 ○ 50,000 to 100,000 ◉ 100,000 to 500,000 ◼ above 500,000

RUSS. FED.

Ozero Baykal

Shilka

Ergun

Jagdaqi

Argun (Ergun He)

Amur (Heilong Jiang)

93

HEILONGJIANG

R A T I O N

Onon

Hulun Buir
(Hailar)

Manzhouli

Selenga

Sühbaatar

Hulun
Nur

Darhan

Onon Gol

Choybalsan

Lake
Khanka

Erdenet

ULAANBAATAR
(ULAN BATOR)

Menengiyn
Tal

Hulingol

Da Hinggan Ling

JILIN

gan

Dzuunmod

Öndörhaan

Baruun-Urt

O L I A

Kerulen

Tongliao

Sea of
Japan
(East Sea)

Xilinhot

Liao He

Saynshand

Erenhot

NEI MONGOL ZIZHIQU

Chifeng
(Ulanhad)

LIAONING

Dalandzadgad

(Inner Mongolia)

NORTH
KOREA

yn Nuruu

Ulan Qab (Jining)

Liaodong Wan

Korea
Bay

b i

Lang Shan

Hohhot

BEIJING

Bo Hai

SOUTH
KOREA

Baotou

Huang He
(Yellow River)

TIANJIN

JAPAN

Wuhai
(Haibowan)

Mu Us
Shadi

HEBEI

Yellow
Sea

Tengger
Shamo

SHANDONG

al Shan

Great Wall of China

NINGXIA

SHANXI

Huang He (Yellow River)

JIANGSU

108

ning

N

A

GANSU

HENAN

ANHUI

SHANGHAI SHI

East

SHAANXI

Han Shui

China

HUBEI

ZHEJIANG

Sea

SICHUAN

Chang Jiang (Yangtze)

CHONGQING

JIANGXI

Nansei-shotō
(to Japan)

HUNAN

FUJIAN

YUNNAN

107

Tropic of Cancer

GUIZHOU

TAIWAN

Elevation

| Below sea level 0 | 250m | 500m | 1000m | 2000m | 3000m | 4000m | 6000m |

-8000m -6000m -4000m -2000m -1000m -500m -250m

820ft 1640ft 3281ft 6562ft 9843ft 13,124ft 19,685ft

26,246ft 19,685ft 13,124ft 6562ft -3281ft -1640ft -820ft -100m/-328ft

Eastern China & Korea

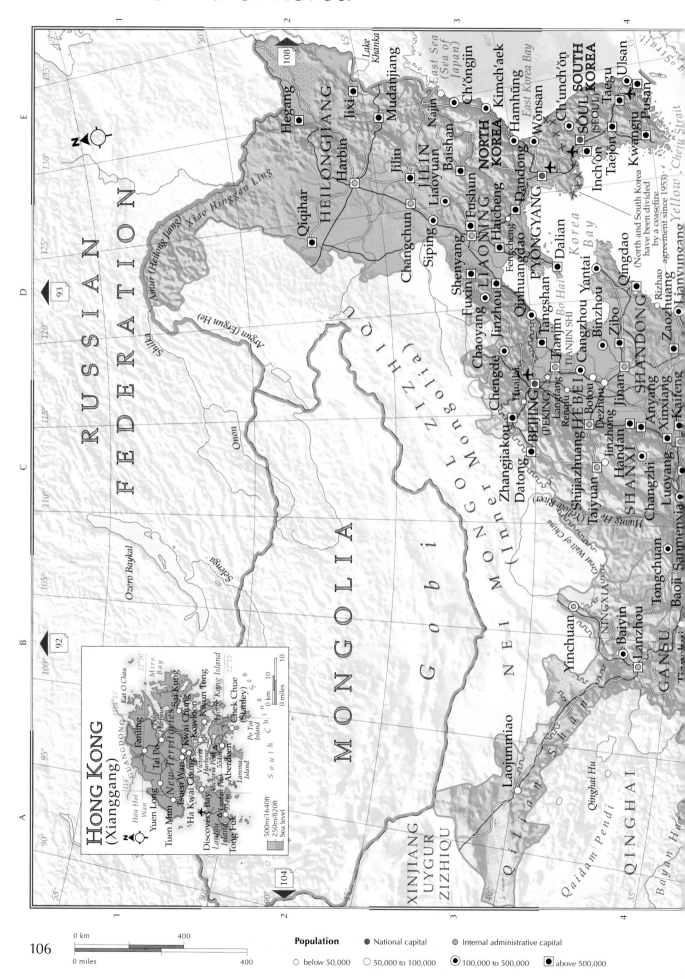

RUSSIAN FEDERATION

MONGOLIA

NEI MONGOL (Inner Mongolia)

HEILONGJIANG

JILIN

LIAONING

NORTH KOREA

SOUTH KOREA

HEBEI

SHANXI

SHANDONG

GANSU

QINGHAI

NINGXIA

XINJIANG UYGUR ZIZHIQU

Lake Khanka

East Sea (Sea of Japan)

East Korea Bay

Korea Bay

Bo Hai

Yellow Sea

Cheju Strait

South China Sea

Ozero Baykal

Selenga

Onon

Shilka

Amur (Heilong Jiang)

Argun (Ergun He)

Xiao Hinggan Ling

Gobi

Qilian Shan

Yin Shan

Huang He (Yellow River)

Great Wall of China

Qinghai Hu

Qaidam Pendi

Bayan Har

Hegang
Jixi
Mudanjiang
Najin
Ch'ŏngjin
Kimch'aek
Harbin
Qiqihar
Jilin
Liaoyuan
Baishan
Hamhŭng
Wŏnsan
Ch'unch'ŏn
Ulsan
Pusan
Taegu
Kwangju
SŎUL (SEOUL)
Inch'ŏn
Taejŏn
PYONGYANG
Dandong
Fengcheng
Haicheng
Fushun
Shenyang
Siping
Changchun
Fuxin
Chaoyang
Jinzhou
Qinhuangdao
Dalian
Yantai
Qingdao
Zibo
Jinan
Dezhou
Binzhou
Cangzhou
Tangshan
TIANJIN SHI
Tianjin
Langfang
Renqiu
Botou
Dongjing
Handan
Anyang
Xinxiang
Kaifeng
Luoyang
Zaozhuang
Rizhao
Lianyungang
Jinzhong
Changzhi
Taiyuan
Shijiazhuang
HEBEI
BEIJING (PEKING)
Chengde
Zhangjiakou
Datong
Huailai
Yinchuan
Baiyin
Lanzhou
Baoji
Sanmenxia
Tongchuan
Laojunmiao

108
93
92
104

HONG KONG (Xianggang)

GUANGDONG

Hau Hoi Wan

Mirs Bay

Kat O Chau

Sai Kung

Tai Po

Tsuen Wan

Kwai Chung

Kowloon

Kwun Tong

Chek Chue (Stanley)

Po Toi Island

Hong Kong Island

Lamma Island

Lantau Island

Aberdeen

Tong Fuk

Discovery Bay

Victoria Harbour

Victoria Peak 554m

Lantau Peak 934m

Tai O

Yuen Long

Tuen Mun

New Territories

Tolo Harbour

500m/1640ft
250m/820ft
Sea level

0 km   400
0 miles   400

Population

● National capital   ● Internal administrative capital

○ below 50,000   ○ 50,000 to 100,000   ◉ 100,000 to 500,000   ■ above 500,000

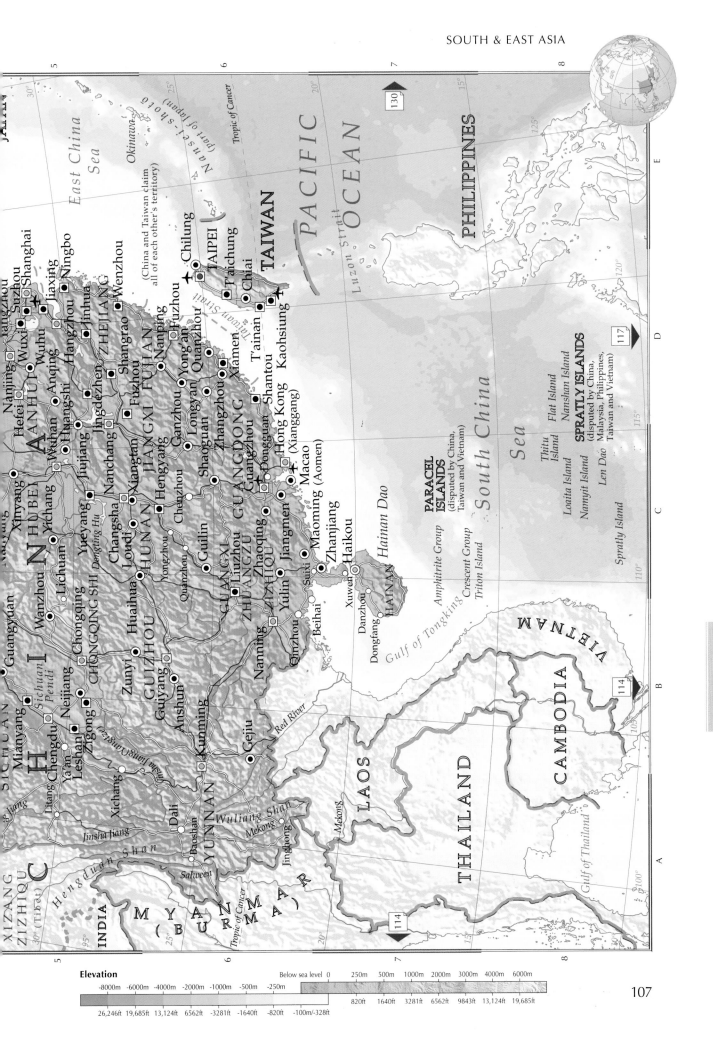

JAPAN

East China Sea

Okinawa

Tropic of Cancer

Nansei-shoto (part of Japan)

(China and Taiwan claim all of each other's territory)

Chilung
TAIPEI
Taichung
Chiai
TAIWAN

PACIFIC OCEAN

Luzon Strait

PHILIPPINES

Shanghai
Suzhou
Wuxi
Ningbo
Jiaxing
Wuhu
Wenzhou
Hangzhou
ZHEJIANG
ANHUI
Nanjing
Hefei
Anqing
Huangshi
Shangrao
Jingdezhen
Nanping
Fuzhou
Xiamen
T'ainan
Kaohsiung
Tainan
FUJIAN
JIANGXI
Ganzhou
Yong'an
Quanzhou
Shantou

South China Sea

PARACEL ISLANDS
(disputed by China, Taiwan and Vietnam)
Amphitrite Group
Crescent Group
Triton Island

SPRATLY ISLANDS
(disputed by China, Malaysia, Philippines, Taiwan and Vietnam)
Thitu Island
Flat Island
Nanshan Island
Loaita Island
Namyit Island
Len Dao
Spratly Island

HUBEI
Xinyang
Xiangyang
Xichang
Wuhan
Ezhou
Hangshi
Jiujiang
Nanchang
HUNAN
Changsha
Loudi
Yueyang
Hengyang
Chenzhou
Shaoguan
GUANGDONG
Guangzhou
Dongguan
Zhangzhou
Hong Kong (Xianggang)
Macao (Aomen)
Maoming
Zhanjiang
Haikou
Hainan Dao
HAINAN
Danzhou
Dongfang

Gulf of Tongking

VIETNAM

SICHUAN
Mianyang
Chengdu
Ya'an
Leshan
Zigong
Neijiang
Sichuan Pendi
CHONGQING SHI
Chongqing
Lichuan
Wanzhou
Guangyuan
Zunyi
GUIZHOU
Guiyang
Anshun
Huaihua
Lichuan
Jinsha Jiang (Yangtze)
Utang
Xichang
Dali
Baoshan
Wuliang Shan
YUNNAN
Kunming
Gejiu
Mekong
Salween
Jinghong
Hengduan Shan

XIZANG ZIZHIQU (Tibet)

INDIA

MYANMAR (BURMA)

Tropic of Cancer

Red River

LAOS

THAILAND

CAMBODIA

Gulf of Thailand

GUANGXI ZHUANGZU ZIZHIQU
Guilin
Yongzhou
Liuzhou
Zhaoqing
Jiangmen
Yulin
Qinzhou
Nanning
Beihai
Xuwen
Suixi

Mekong

Elevation

| -8000m | -6000m | -4000m | -2000m | -1000m | -500m | -250m |
| 26,246ft | 19,685ft | 13,124ft | 6562ft | -3281ft | -1640ft | -820ft | -100m/-328ft |

Below sea level 0 · 250m · 500m · 1000m · 2000m · 3000m · 4000m · 6000m

820ft · 1640ft · 3281ft · 6562ft · 9843ft · 13,124ft · 19,685ft

Japan

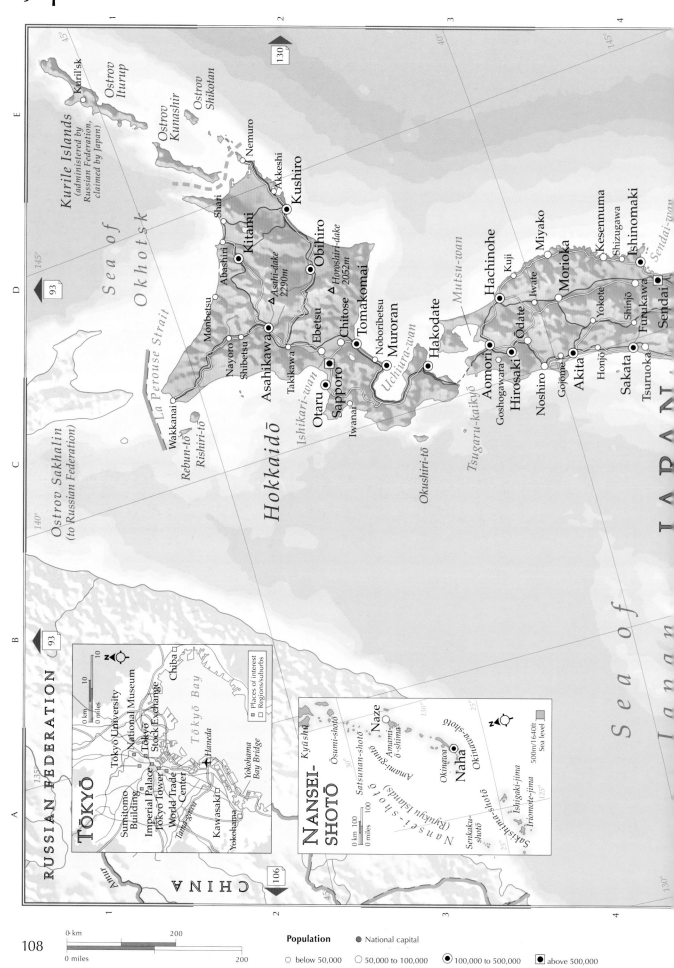

RUSSIAN FEDERATION

Amur

CHINA

Ostrov Sakhalin
(to Russian Federation)

Kurile Islands
(administered by
Russian Federation,
claimed by Japan)

Ostrov Iturup
Kuril'sk

Ostrov Kunashir

Ostrov Shikotan

Sea of Okhotsk

La Perouse Strait

Wakkanai
Rebun-tō
Rishiri-tō

Monbetsu

Nayoro
Shibetsu

Abashiri

Shari

Kitami

Asahi-dake
2290m

Nemuro

Akkeshi

Kushiro

Obihiro

Horoshiri-dake
2052m

Ebetsu
Chitose
Tomakomai

Takikawa

Asahikawa

Otaru
Sapporo
Iwanai

Hokkaidō

Ishikari-wan

Noboribetsu
Muroran

Uchiura-wan

Okushiri-tō

Okushiri-tō

Hakodate

Tsugaru-kaikyō

Mutsu-wan

Hachinohe

Kuji

Aomori
Goshogawara
Hirosaki

Noshiro

Gojome
Akita

Iwate

Odate

Honjō

Miyako

Morioka

Yokote

Shinjō
Furukawa

Sakata

Tsuruoka

Kesennuma
Shizugawa
Ishinomaki

Sendai

Sendai-wan

JAPAN

Sea of Japan

TŌKYŌ

Chiba

Tōkyō University
National Museum
Tōkyō Stock Exchange

Sumitomo Building
Imperial Palace
Tōkyō Tower
World Trade Center

Tama-gawa

Kawasaki

Yokohama

Tōkyō Bay

Haneda

Yokohama Bay Bridge

- Places of interest
- Regions/suburbs

NANSEI-SHOTŌ

Kyūshū

Ōsumi-shotō

Satsunan-shotō

Amami-guntō

Naze
Amami-ō-shima

Tokara-rettō

Okinawa
Naha

Okinawa-shotō

Senkaku-shotō

Ishigaki-jima
Iriomote-jima

Sakishima-shotō

500m/1640ft
Sea level

0 km   200
0 miles   200

Population   ● National capital

○ below 50,000   ○ 50,000 to 100,000   ◉ 100,000 to 500,000   ● above 500,000

(East Sea)

Honshū
Iwaki

Chōshi

Sukagawa
Iwaki
Hitachi
Utsunomiya
Mito
Oyama
Maebashi
Kawagoe
Chiba
Yokohama
TOKYO
Kawasaki
Fuji
Mikuni-sanmyaku
Nagaoka
Nagano
Matsumoto
Kōfu
Fuji-san
3776m △
Jōetsu
Toyama
Shizuoka
Toyota
Hamamatsu
Shinano-gawa
Itoigawa
Takaoka
Hida-
sanmyaku
Gifu
Nakatsugawa
Okazaki
Ise
Kanazawa
Komatsu
Ogaki
Nagoya
Ōtsu
Tsu
Owase
Fukui
Tsuruga
Kyōto
Shingū
Toyama-wan
Wakasa-wan
Biwa-ko
Kōbe
Gobō
Tanabe
Osaka
Wakayama
Chūgoku-sanchi
Tottori
Himeji
Akashi
Awaji-shima
Yonago
Matsue
Okayama
Kurashiki
Tokushima
Matsuyama
Kōchi
Oki-shotō
Dōgo
Dōzen
Liancourt Rocks
(claimed by Japan
& South Korea)
Gōtsu
Hamada
Masuda
Hiroshima
Iwakuni
Hōfu
Ube
Kure
Niihama
Shikoku
Tosa-wan
Nakamura
Sukumo
Shimonoseki
Yamaguchi
Nagato
Kitakyūshū
Fukuoka
Ōita
Nobeoka
Miyazaki
Miyakonojō
Kyūshū
Sasebo
Nagasaki
Kurume
Ōmuta
Kumamoto
Yatsushiro
Sendai
Kagoshima
Gotō-rettō
Koshikijima-rettō
Amakusa-
nada
Kagoshima-wan
Shibushi-wan
Tanega-shima
Yaku-shima
Ōsumi-shotō
Ōsumi-kaikyō
SOUTH
KOREA
Korea Strait
Tsushima
Iki
Kō-saki

PACIFIC OCEAN

Izu-shotō
Sagami-nada
Bōsō-hantō
Izu-hantō
Suruga-wan
Ise-wan
Kōzu-shima
Ō-shima
Nii-jima
Miyake-jima
Mikura-jima
Hachijō-jima
Kasumiga-ura

Kii-suidō
Harima-
nada
Bungo-suidō
Iyo-nada

East
China Sea

130
130
130
130
106

Elevation

-8000m	-6000m	-4000m	-2000m	-1000m	-500m	-250m			

Below sea level 0   250m   500m   1000m   2000m   3000m   4000m   6000m

820ft   1640ft   3281ft   6562ft   9843ft   13,124ft   19,685ft

26,246ft   19,685ft   13,124ft   6562ft   -3281ft   -1640ft   -820ft   -100m/-328ft

South India & Sri Lanka

Kalyān
Mumbai (Bombay)
112
Pune
Ahmadnagar
Nānded
Jagdalpu
Bārāmati
Nizāmābād
Karīmnagar
Vizianagaram
Solāpur
Sāngli
Secunderābād
Visākhapat
Kolhāpur
Gulbarga
Hyderābād
Rājahmur
Kākina
Belgaum
Karnātaka
Rāichūr
Krishna
Vijayawāda
Panaji
Gadag
Kurnool
Andhra
Machilīpatna
Hubli
Nandyāl
Pradesh
Chīrāla
Ongole
Tungabhadra Reservoir
Tādpatri
Kāvali
Dāvangere
Anantapur
Nellore
Shimoga
Cuddapah
Bhadrāvati
Udupi
Tumkūr
Chennai (Madras)
Mangalore
Bangalore
Vellore
Kānchīpuram
Kāsaragod
Mandya
Tiruppattūr
Krishnagiri
Kannur/Cannanore
Mysore
Salem
Pondicherry
Erode
Neyveli
Kozhikode/Calicut
Coimbatore
Tamil Nādu
Thrissur/Trichūr
Tiruchchirāppalli
Ernākulam
Dindigul
Madurai
Kochi/Cochin
Jaffna
Alappuzha/Alleppey
Rājapālaiyam
SRI LANK
Kollam/Quilon
Mannar
Vavuniya
Thiruvananthapuram/ Trivandrum
Tuticorin
Trincomalee
Nāgercoil
Puttalam
Anuradhapura
Gulf of Mannar
Batticaloa
Matale
Negombo
Kandy
COLOMBO
Sri Jayewardanapu
Kot
Kalutara
Ratnapura
Galle
Matara

Arabian
Sea
99
Amīndīvi Islands
Lakshadweep (Laccadive Islands) (to India)
Kavaratti Island
Kalpeni Island
Nine Degree Channel
Minicoy Island
Eight Degree Channel
Ihavandhippolhu Atoll
MALDIVES
Faadhippolhu Atoll
Horsburgh Atoll
51
Male' Atoll
Ari Atoll
MALE'
Felidhu Atoll
Mulakatholhu
Kolhumadulu
Hadhdhunmathi Atoll
North Huvadhu Atoll
South Huvadhu Atoll
Equator
Gan
118
Addu Atoll

Western Ghats
Eastern Ghats
Deccan
Kerala
Coromandel Coast
Palk Strait
Godāvari

I N D I A

I N D I A N

0 km   300
0 miles   300

Population   ● National capital

○ below 50,000   ○ 50,000 to 100,000   ◉ 100,000 to 500,000   ◼ above 500,000

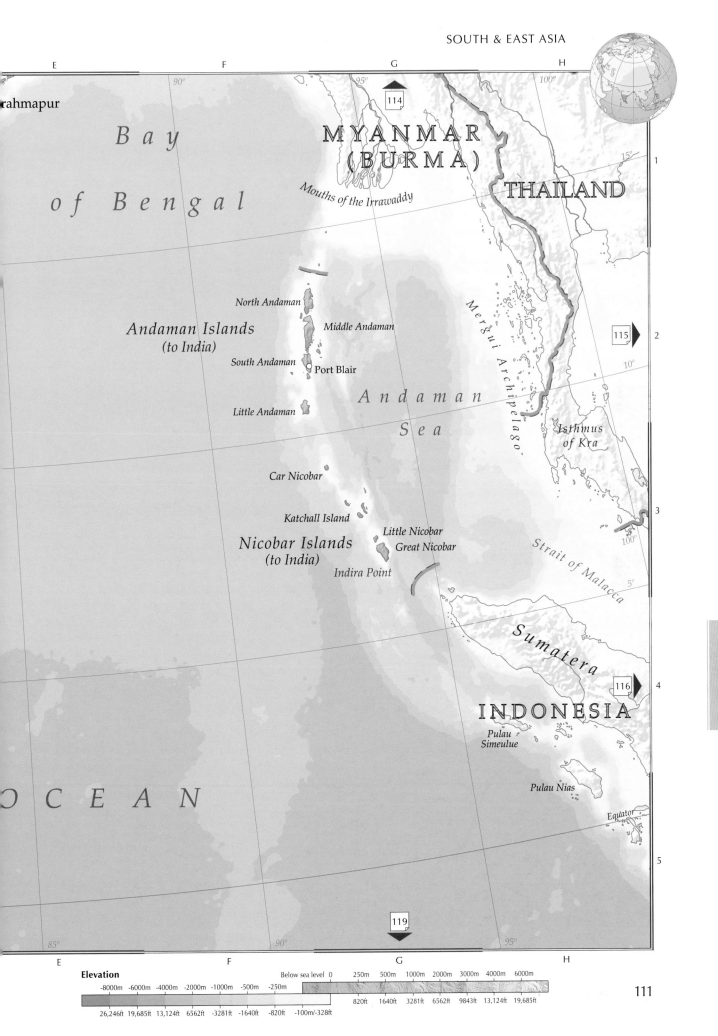

rahmapur

Bay

of Bengal

**MYANMAR
(BURMA)**

THAILAND

Mouths of the Irrawaddy

114

115

North Andaman

Middle Andaman

Andaman Islands
(to India)

South Andaman

Port Blair

Little Andaman

A n d a m a n

S e a

Mergui Archipelago

*Isthmus
of Kra*

Car Nicobar

Katchall Island

Nicobar Islands
(to India)

Little Nicobar

Great Nicobar

Indira Point

Strait of Malacca

116

Sumatera

INDONESIA

*Pulau
Simeulue*

Pulau Nias

Equator

OCEAN

119

Elevation

								Below sea level 0	250m	500m	1000m	2000m	3000m	4000m	6000m
-8000m	-6000m	-4000m	-2000m	-1000m	-500m	-250m									

| 26,246ft | 19,685ft | 13,124ft | 6562ft | -3281ft | -1640ft | -820ft | -100m/-328ft | | 820ft | 1640ft | 3281ft | 6562ft | 9843ft | 13,124ft | 19,685ft |

Northern India, Pakistan & Bangladesh

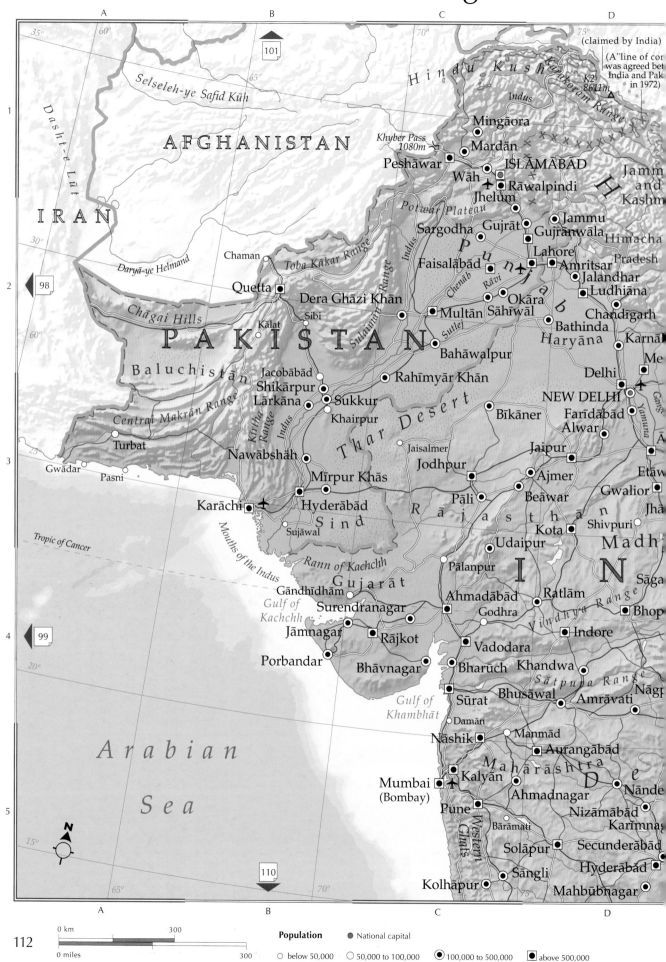

A | B | C | D

35° 60° 70° 75°

(claimed by India)

(A "line of con
was agreed bet
India and Pak
in 1972)

Selseleh-ye Safid Kūh

Hindu Kush

Karakoram Range

K2
8611m△

Indus

1

AFGHANISTAN

Dasht-e Lūt

Mingāora

Khyber Pass
1080m

Mardān

Peshāwar

Wāh ✈ ◉ ISLĀMĀBĀD

Jamm
and
Kashm

IRAN

30°

Jhelum ◉ Rāwalpindi

Potwar Plateau

Sargodha ◉ Gujrāt ◉ Gujrānwāla

Himacha
Pradesh

Chaman ◉

Daryā-ye Helmand

Toba Kākar Range

Faisalābād

Lahore ◼ ◉ Amritsar

Jalandhar

2

98

Quetta ◼

Dera Ghāzi Khān

Sulaimān Range

Indus

Chenāb

Rāvi

P u n j a b

Okāra Sāhīwal

Ludhiāna

Chandīgarh

Chāgai Hills

Kālat

Sibi

Multān

Sutlej

Bathinda

Haryāna

Karnāl

60°

P A K I S T A N

Bahāwalpur

Me

Baluchistān

Jacobābād

Shikārpur

Rahīmyār Khān

Delhi ◼ ◼ Me

Central Makrān Range

Lārkāna

Kirthā Range

Sukkur

Khairpur

Thar Desert

Bīkāner

NEW DELHI

Farīdābād

Yamuna

Alwar

25°

Turbat

Indus

Jaisalmer

Jaipur ◼

3

Gwādar ◉ Pasni

Nawābshāh

Jodhpur

Ajmer

Etāw

Mīrpur Khās

Pāli

Beāwar

Gwalior ◼

Jhā

Karāchi ◼ ✈

Hyderābād

S i n d

R ā j a s t h ā n

Kota ◼

Shivpuri

Tropic of Cancer

Sujāwal

Udaipur

Madh

20°

Rann of Kachchh

Pālanpur

I

N

Mouths of the Indus

G u j a r ā t

Gāndhīdhām

Ahmadābād

Ratlām

Sāga

*Gulf of
Kachchh*

Surendranagar

Godhra

Vindhya Range

◼ Bhop

4

99

Jāmnagar

Rājkot ◼

Vadodara

Indore ◼

Bhāvnagar

Bharūch

Khandwa

Satpura Range

Nāgr

Porbandar

Sūrat

Bhusāwal

Amrāvati

*Gulf of
Khambhāt*

Damān

Nāshik

Manmād

Aurangābād

D e

Nānde

A r a b i a n

Kalyān

M a h ā r ā s h t r a

S e a

Mumbai
(Bombay) ◼ ✈

Ahmadnagar

Nizāmābād

Karīmna

Pune ◼

Western Ghats

Bārāmati

Secunderābād

15°

N

Solāpur

Hyderābād

5

Sāngli

110

Kolhāpur

Mahbūbnagar

65° 70° 75°

A | B | C | D

0 km   300

0 miles   300

Population   ● National capital

○ below 50,000   ○ 50,000 to 100,000   ◉ 100,000 to 500,000   ◼ above 500,000

101

110

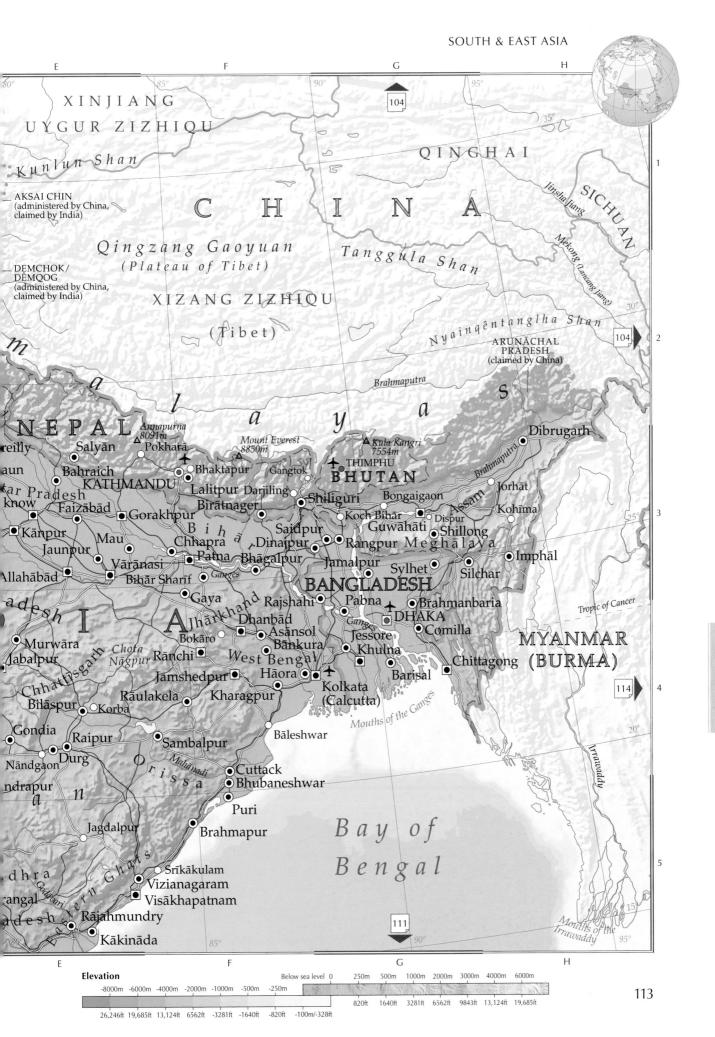

XINJIANG
UYGUR ZIZHIQU
Kunlun Shan
QINGHAI
SICHUAN
Jinsha Jiang
AKSAI CHIN
(administered by China,
claimed by India)
C H I N A
Qingzang Gaoyuan
(Plateau of Tibet)
Tanggula Shan
Mekong (Lancang Jiang)
DEMCHOK/
DÊMQOG
(administered by China,
claimed by India)
XIZANG ZIZHIQU
(Tibet)
Nyainqêntanglha Shan
ARUNĀCHAL
PRADESH
(claimed by China)
m
a
Brahmaputra
l
a
y
a
s
Dibrugarh
NEPAL
Annapurna
△ 8091m
Pokharā
Mount Everest
8850m
△ Kula Kangri
7554m
Brahmaputra
reilly
Salyān
Bhaktapur
Gangtok
THIMPHU
BHUTAN
Jorhat
aun
Bahraich
Lalitpur
Darjiling
Shiliguri
Bongaigaon
Assam
Kohīma
KATHMANDU
Birātnager
Koch Bihār
Dispur
Shillong
tar Pradesh
Faizābād
Gorakhpur
Saidpur
Guwāhāti
Meghālaya
know
B i h ā r
Dinajpur
Rangpur
Imphāl
Kānpur
Mau
Chhapra
Patna
Jamalpur
Silchar
Jaunpur
Vārānasi
Bhāgalpur
Sylhet
Allahābād
Bihār Sharīf
Ganges
BANGLADESH
adesh
Gaya
Jharkhand
Rajshahi
Pabna
Brahmanbaria
I N D I A
Dhanbād
DHAKA
Murwāra
Chota
Nāgpur
Bokāro
Asānsol
Bānkura
Ganges
Comilla
MYANMAR
(BURMA)
Jabalpur
Ranchi
West Bengal
Jessore
Khulna
Bilāspur
Chhattisgarh
Korba
Jamshedpur
Hāora
Barisal
Chittagong
Gondia
Rāulakela
Kharagpur
Kolkata
(Calcutta)
Tropic of Cancer
Raipur
Sambalpur
Bāleshwar
Mouths of the Ganges
Nāndgaon
Durg
O r i s s a
Mahānadi
Irrawaddy
ndrapur
a
n
Cuttack
Bhubaneshwar
Jagdalpur
Puri
Bay of
Bengal
Brahmapur
dhra
Srīkākulam
Eastern Ghats
Vizianagaram
Godāvari
Visākhapatnam
rangal
Rājahmundry
adesh
Kākināda
Mouths of the
Irrawaddy

Elevation

| | Below sea level | 0 | 250m | 500m | 1000m | 2000m | 3000m | 4000m | 6000m |

-8000m -6000m -4000m -2000m -1000m -500m -250m

820ft 1640ft 3281ft 6562ft 9843ft 13,124ft 19,685ft

26,246ft 19,685ft 13,124ft 6562ft -3281ft -1640ft -820ft -100m/-328ft

Mainland Southeast Asia

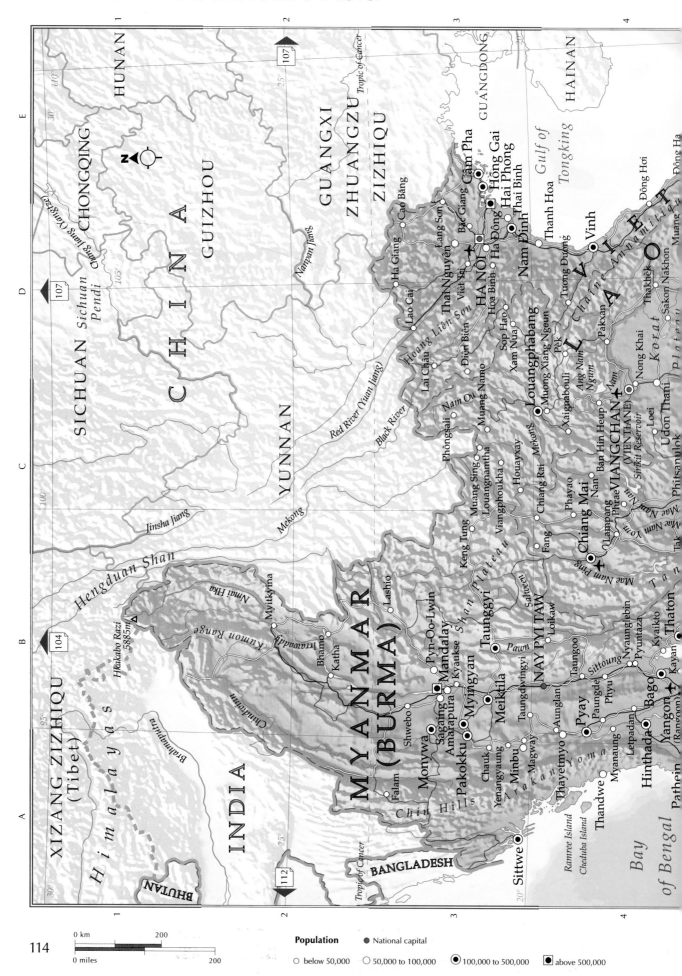

XIZANG ZIZHIQU (Tibet)

Himalayas

BHUTAN

Brahmaputra

INDIA

Chindwin

Hkakabo Razi 5885m

Kumon Range

Nmai Hka

Myitkyina

Bhamo

Katha

Hengduan Shan

Jinsha Jiang

Mekong

SICHUAN Sichuan Pendi

Chang Jiang (Yangtze)

CHONGQING

CHINA

GUIZHOU

YUNNAN

Nanpan Jiang

Red River (Yuan Jiang)

Black River

HUNAN

GUANGXI ZHUANGZU ZIZHIQU

GUANGDONG

HAINAN

Gulf of Tongking

Irrawaddy

MYANMAR (BURMA)

Shwebo

Monywa

Sagaing
Amarapura
Mandalay
Pyn-Oo-Lwin
Lashio

Kyaukse

Myingyan

Chauk

Meiktila

Pakokku

Yenangyaung

Minbu

Magway

Taungdwingyi

NAY PYI TAW

Pawn

Loikaw

Taungoo

Aunglan

Pyay

Paungde

Phyu

Sittoung

Falam

Chin Hills

Thayetmyo

Myanaung

Letpadan

Nyaunglebin

Pyuntaza

Kyaikto

Kayan

Thaton

Bago

Yangon (Rangoon)

Hinthada

Pathein

Ramree Island

Cheduba Island

Thandwe

Sittwe

BANGLADESH

Tropic of Cancer

Bay of Bengal

Arakan Yoma

Shan Plateau

Keng Tung

Muang Sing

Loungnamtha

Viangphoukha

Houayxay

Chiang Rai

Phayao

Fang

Chiang Mai

Lampang

Phrae

Nan

Mae Nam Ping

Tak

Mae Nam Yom

Mae Nam Nan

Phitsanulok

Tan

Salween

Phôngsali

Nam Ou

Muang Namo

Nam

Xam Nua

Sop Hao

LAOS

Louangphabang

Muong Xiang Ngeun

Pek

Xaigabouli

Ang Nam Ngum

VIANGCHAN (VIENTIANE)

Sirikit Reservoir

Loei

Udon Thani

Nong Khai

Ban Hin Heup

Pakxan

Thakhek

Sakon Nakhon

Korat Plateau

Muang

Ha Giang

Cao Bằng

Lao Cai

Lang Son

Hoang Liên Sơn

Thai Nguyên

Viêt Tri

Bắc Giang

Cam Pha

Hông Gai

Hai Phong

Hải Dương

HANOI

Hoa Binh

Nam Đinh

Thai Binh

Thanh Hoa

Tuong Đương

Vinh

Chaîne Annamitique

V I E T N A M

Đông Hơi

Đông Ha

Lai Châu

Điện Biên

L Chaîne Annamitique O

Population

● National capital

○ below 50,000   ○ 50,000 to 100,000   ◉ 100,000 to 500,000   ■ above 500,000

0 km   200
0 miles   200

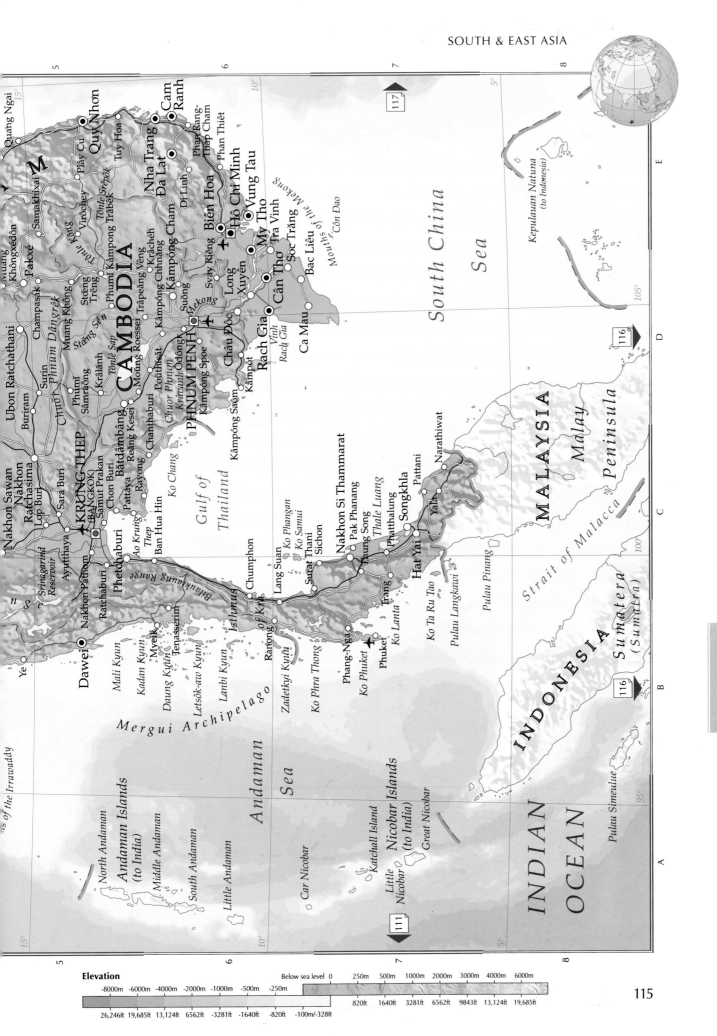

IM

Quang Ngai
Quy Nhon
Plây Cu
Cam Ranh
Khôngxédôn
Tuy Hoa
Samakhixai
Nha Trang
Pakxé
Virôchey
Đà Lạt
Tônlé Srêpôk
Di Linh
Phan Rang-Tháp Chàm
Champasak
St?êng Trêng
Phumi Kâmpóng Trabêk
Biên Hòa
Phan Thiết
Muang Không
Phnum Kâmpóng-Cham
Hồ Chí Minh
Ubon Ratchathani
Surin
Phumĭ Kâmpóng-Chhnăng
Krâchéh
My Tho
Vung Tau
Kraláñh
Trà Vinh
CAMBODIA
Moŭng Roessei
Tônlé Sap
Svay Riêng
Sóc Trăng
Stêng Sên
Phumi Sâmraông
Trâpeăng Vêng
Suông
Long Xuyên
Cần Thơ
Bạc Liêu
Buriram
Chuŏr Phnum Krâvanh Ŏdôngk
Bătdâmbâng
Reăng Kesei
Poŭthisăt
PHNUM PENH
Châu Đốc
Ca Mau
Nakhon Ratchasima
Kâmpóng Spœ
Ka Mpót
Rạch Gia
Lop Buri
Chanthaburi
Vinh Rạch Gia
Nakhon Sawan
Sara Buri
Chon Buri
Kâmpôt
Ayutthaya
KRUNG THEP
(BANGKOK)
Samut Prakan
Ko Chang
Kâmpóng Saôm
Nakhon Pathom
Pattaya
Rayong
Ratchaburi
Phetchaburi
Ao Krung Thep
Ban Hua Hin
Ko Phangan
Nakhon Si Thammarat
Ko Samui
Narathiwat
Chumphon
Surat Thani
Pak Phanang
Pattani
Lang Suan
Sichon
Thung Song
Yala
Songkhla
Dawei
Phatthalung
Hat Yai
Thale Luang
Mali Kyun
Isthmus of Kra
Trang
Kadan Kyun
Ranong
Phang-Nga
Ko Ta Ru Tao
Tenasserim
Daung Kyun
Myeik
Zadetkyi Kyun
Phuket
Pulau Pinang
Letsôk-aw Kyun
Ko Phra Thong
Ko Phuket
Ko Lanta
Lanbi Kyun
Pulau Langkawi
Mergui Archipelago
Pulau Pinang
MALAYSIA

South China Sea

Kepulauan Natuna
(to Indonesia)

Côn Đao
Mouths of the Mekong

Gulf of
Thailand

Bilauktaung Range

Andaman
Sea

INDONESIA

Sumatera
(Sumatra)

Malay Peninsula
Strait of Malacca

Andaman Islands
(to India)
North Andaman
Middle Andaman
South Andaman
Little Andaman

Little Nicobar
Nicobar Islands
(to India)
Car Nicobar
Katchall Island
Great Nicobar

INDIAN
OCEAN

Pulau Simeulue

of the Irrawaddy

Elevation

Below sea level 0   250m   500m   1000m   2000m   3000m   4000m   6000m

-8000m -6000m -4000m -2000m -1000m -500m   -250m

820ft   1640ft 3281ft 6562ft 9843ft 13,124ft 19,685ft

26,246ft 19,685ft 13,124ft 6562ft -3281ft -1640ft -820ft -100m/-328ft

Maritime Southeast Asia

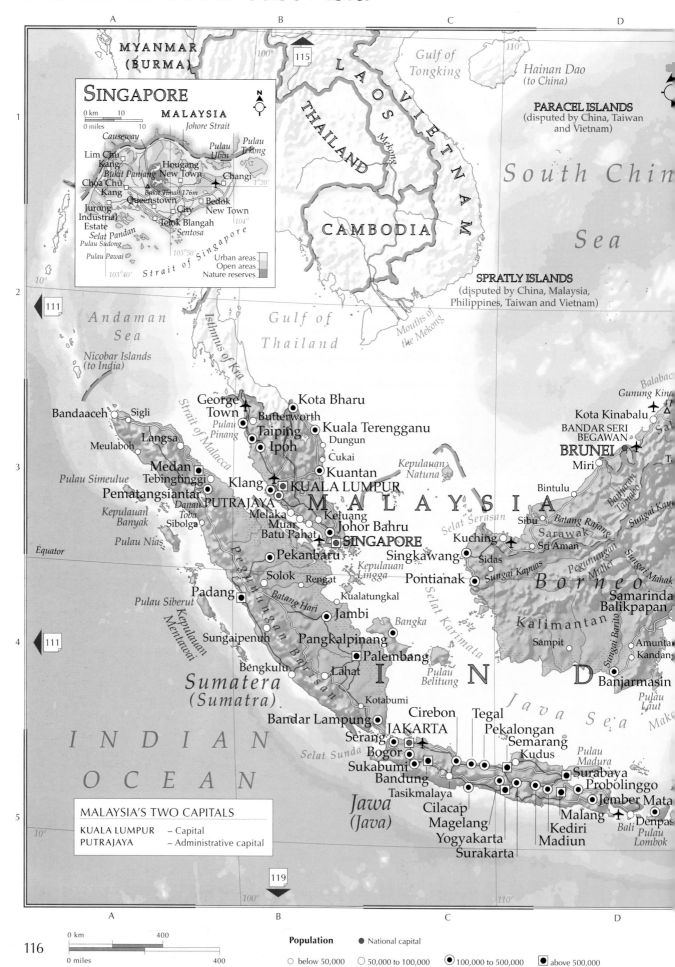

MYANMAR (BURMA)

SINGAPORE
MALAYSIA
Johore Strait
0 km   10
0 miles   10
Causeway
Lim Chu Kang
Pulau Ubin   *Pulau Tekong*
Hougang
Bukit Panjang   New Town
Choa Chu Kang
Changi
1°20'
Bukit Timah 176m
Queenstown
City   Bedok New Town
Jurong Industrial Estate
Telok Blangah
Selat Pandan   Sentosa
Pulau Sudong
103°50'
Pulau Pawai
103°40'
Strait of Singapore
104°
Urban areas
Open areas
Nature reserves
N

LAOS
VIETNAM
THAILAND
Mekong
CAMBODIA
Gulf of Tongking
110°
Hainan Dao (to China)

PARACEL ISLANDS
(disputed by China, Taiwan and Vietnam)

South China Sea

SPRATLY ISLANDS
(disputed by China, Malaysia, Philippines, Taiwan and Vietnam)

Andaman Sea
Nicobar Islands (to India)
Gulf of Thailand
Mouths of the Mekong

Isthmus of Kra
Bandaaceh   Sigli
Langsa
Meulaboh
George Town
Butterworth
Pulau Pinang   Taiping
Ipoh
Kota Bharu
Kuala Terengganu
Dungun
Cukai
Kepulauan Natuna
Balabac
Gunung Kina
Kota Kinabalu
BANDAR SERI BEGAWAN
BRUNEI
Miri

Medan
Tebingtinggi
Pulau Simeulue
Pematangsiantar
Klang
Kuantan
KUALA LUMPUR
PUTRAJAYA
M A L A Y S I A
Bintulu
Selat Serasan
Sibu
Batang Rajang
Banjarmasin/Tambabo
Sungai Kay

Strait of Malacca
Kepulauan Banyak
Danau Toba
Sibolga
Melaka
Keluang
Johor Bahru
Muar
Batu Pahat   **SINGAPORE**
Kuching
Sri Aman
Sarawak
Pegunungan Muller
B o r n e o
Samarinda
Balikpapan
Sungai Mahak
Pulau Nias
Pekanbaru
Singkawang
Sidas
Pontianak
Sungai Kapuas

Equator
Solok
Rengat
Kepulauan Lingga
Kalimantan
Sungai Barito
Padang
Pulau Siberut
Batang Hari
Kualatungkal
Bangka
Jambi
Sampit
Amunta
Kandan
Kepulauan Mentawai
Sungaipenuh
Pangkalpinang
Pegunungan Barisan
Palembang
Pulau Belitung
Banjarmasin
Pulau Laut
Bengkulu
Lahat
I N D
D

Sumatera (Sumatra)
Kotabumi
Java Sea
Make
Bandar Lampung
Cirebon   Tegal
Serang   **JAKARTA**
Pekalongan
Semarang
Kudus
Pulau Madura
Surabaya
Probolinggo
I N D I A N
O C E A N
Bogor
Sukabumi
Bandung
Tasikmalaya
Cilacap
Jawa (Java)
Magelang
Yogyakarta
Surakarta
Jember   Mata
Malang
Kediri
Madiun
Denpas
Bali
Pulau Lombok

MALAYSIA'S TWO CAPITALS
KUALA LUMPUR   – Capital
PUTRAJAYA   – Administrative capital

116

0 km   400
0 miles   400

Population   ● National capital
○ below 50,000   ○ 50,000 to 100,000   ◉ 100,000 to 500,000   ■ above 500,000

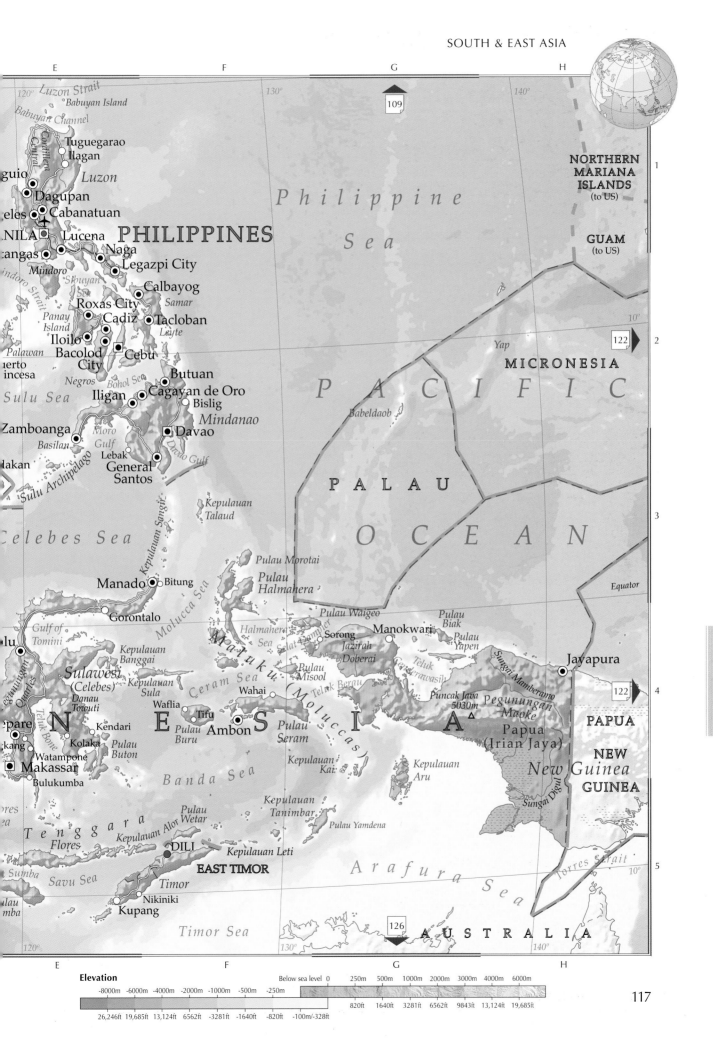

E   F   G   H

120°

Luzon Strait

°Babuyan Island

Babuyan Channel

109

NORTHERN
MARIANA
ISLANDS
(to US)

Cordillera Central

°Tuguegarao
°Ilagan

1

guio

Luzon

Dagupan
eles
NILA Cabanatuan
Lucena

PHILIPPINES

GUAM
(to US)

Philippine

Sea

angas
Naga
Legazpi City

Mindoro

Sibuyan Sea

Calbayog

Samar

Roxas City
Cadiz Tacloban

Leyte

Panay Island

Iloilo
Bacolod
City Cebu

Palawan

uerto
incesa

Sulu Sea

Negros

Bohol Sea

Butuan
Cagayan de Oro

Iligan Bislig

Mindanao

Zamboanga

Basilan

Moro Gulf

°Davao

Davao Gulf

Lebak
General
Santos

Sulu Archipelago

akan

130°

10°

122

2

MICRONESIA

Yap

P A C I F I C

Babeldaob

P A L A U

O C E A N

3

Kepulauan Talaud

Celebes Sea

Pulau Morotai

Pulau Halmahera

Manado Bitung

Gorontalo

Molucca Sea

Kepulauan Sangir

Gulf of Tomini

lu

Pulau Waigeo

Pulau Biak

Sorong *Jazirah Doberai* *Pulau Yapen*

Manokwari

Halmahera Sea

Selat Dampier

Teluk Cenderawasih

Sungai Mamberamo

Jayapura

Equator

140°

122

4

M a l u k u

Kepulauan
Banggai

Kepulauan
Sula

C e r a m S e a

Wahai

Waflia
Tifu

Pulau Buru

Ambon

Pulau Seram

(M o l u c c a s)

Teluk Berau

Pulau Misool

Kepulauan Kai

Kepulauan Aru

Puncak Jaya
5030m

Pegunungan Maoke

Papua
(Irian Jaya)

New Guinea

PAPUA

**NEW
GUINEA**

*Sulawesi
(Celebes)*

Danau Towuti

pare

N

E

S

I

A

Kendari

Kolaka

Pulau Buton

Watampone
Makassar

Bulukumba

B a n d a S e a

Kepulauan Tanimbar

Pulau Yamdena

Sungai Digul

Teluk Bone

Pegunungan Quarles

kang

Pulau Wetar

Kepulauan Alor

T e n g g a r a

Flores

DILI *Kepulauan Leti*

EAST TIMOR

Timor

Nikiniki

Kupang

Arafura Sea

Torres Strait

A U S T R A L I A

5

10°

ores
ea

Sumba

Savu Sea

Timor Sea

120°

lau
mba

130°

126

140°

E   F   G   H

Elevation

Below sea level 0   250m   500m   1000m   2000m   3000m   4000m   6000m

-8000m   -6000m   -4000m   -2000m   -1000m   -500m   -250m

820ft   1640ft   3281ft   6562ft   9843ft   13,124ft   19,685ft

26,246ft   19,685ft   13,124ft   6562ft   -3281ft   -1640ft   -820ft   -100m/-328ft

The Indian Ocean

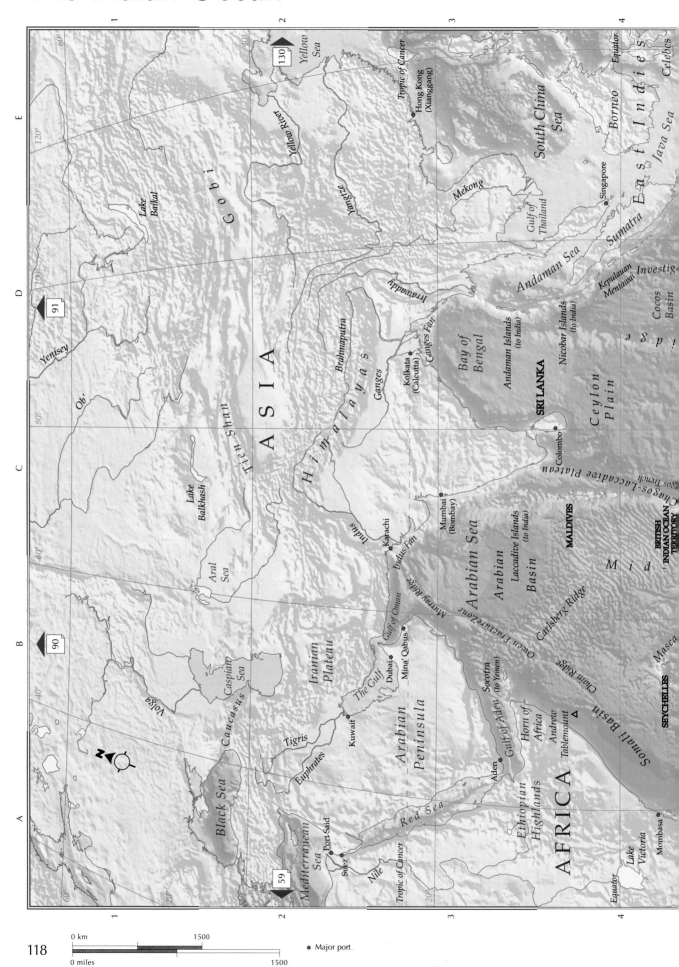

60°

130

91

90

59

E

D

C

B

A

120°

100°

80°

60°

40°

20°

Yellow
Sea

Yellow River

Lake
Baikal

Gobi

Yangtze

Tropic of Cancer

Hong Kong
(Xianggang)

South China
Sea

Borneo

East Indies

Equator

Celebes

Singapore

Sumatra

Java Sea

Mekong

Gulf of
Thailand

Andaman Sea

Kepulauan
Mentawai

Investig

Yenisey

Brahmaputra

Irrawaddy

Ganges Fan

Bay of
Bengal

Andaman Islands
(to India)

Nicobar Islands
(to India)

Cocos
Basin

Ob'

A S I A

Himalayas

Ganges

Kolkata
(Calcutta)

SRI LANKA

Ceylon
Plain

i d g e

Tien Shan

Aral
Sea

Lake
Balkhash

Indus

Karachi

Indus Fan

Mumbai
(Bombay)

Arabian Sea

Colombo

Chagos-Laccadive Plateau

ngos Trench

Mid

Caspian Sea

Iranian
Plateau

Gulf of Oman

Mina Qabus

Murray Ridge

Owen Fracture Zone

Arabian
Basin

Laccadive Islands
(to India)

MALDIVES

BRITISH
INDIAN OCEAN
TERRITORY

Volga

Black Sea

Caucasus

Tigris

The Gulf

Dubai

Kuwait

Arabian
Peninsula

Socotra
(to Yemen)

Horn of
Africa

Andrew
Tablemount

Gulf of Aden

Carlsberg Ridge

Chain Ridge

Somali Basin

SEYCHELLES

Masca

Euphrates

Aden

Ethiopian
Highlands

AFRICA

Equator

Lake
Victoria

Mombasa

Mediterranean
Sea

Port Said

Suez

Nile

Red Sea

Tropic of Cancer

0 km   1500

0 miles   1500

● Major port

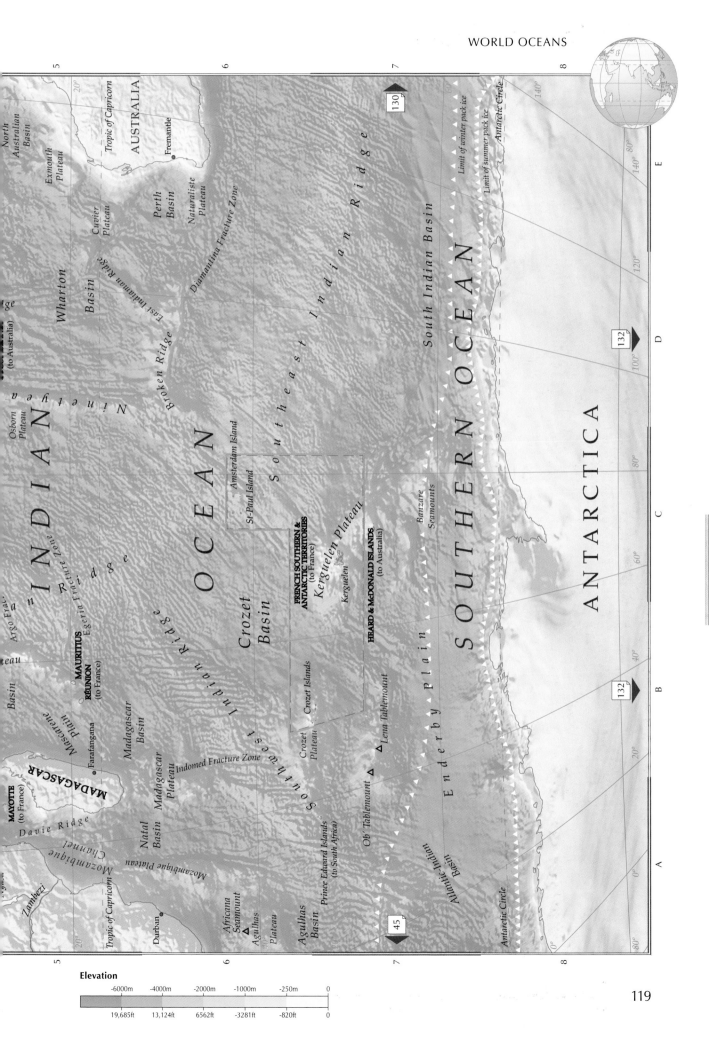

AUSTRALIA

Fremantle

Tropic of Capricorn

North Australian Basin

Exmouth Plateau

Cuvier Plateau

Perth Basin

Naturaliste Plateau

Diamantina Fracture Zone

Wharton Basin

East Indian Ridge

Broken Ridge

Ninetyeast

Southeast Indian Ridge

South Indian Basin

INDIAN

OCEAN

SOUTHERN OCEAN

ANTARCTICA

Osborn Plateau

Ridge

Rodriguez Fracture Zone

Egeria Fracture Zone

Argo Frac

Central Indian Ridge

Amsterdam Island

St-Paul Island

Limit of winter pack ice

Limit of summer pack ice

Antarctic Circle

MAURITIUS
RÉUNION
(to France)

MAYOTTE
(to France)

MADAGASCAR

Farafangana

Mascarene Plateau

Mascarene Plain

Madagascar Basin

Madagascar Plateau

Indomed Fracture Zone

Crozet Basin

Southwest Indian Ridge

FRENCH SOUTHERN &
ANTARCTIC TERRITORIES
(to France)
Kerguelen Plateau

Kerguelen

HEARD & McDONALD ISLANDS
(to Australia)

Crozet Plateau

Crozet Islands

Lena Tablemount

Banzare Seamounts

Enderby Plain

Davie Ridge

Natal Basin

Mozambique Plateau

Mozambique Channel

Zambezi

Tropic of Capricorn

Durban

Africana Seamount

Agulhas Plateau

Agulhas Basin

Prince Edward Islands
(to South Africa)

Ob' Tablemount

Atlantic-Indian Basin

Antarctic Circle

Elevation

-6000m	-4000m	-2000m	-1000m	-250m	0
19,685ft	13,124ft	6562ft	-3281ft	-820ft	0

Australasia & Oceania

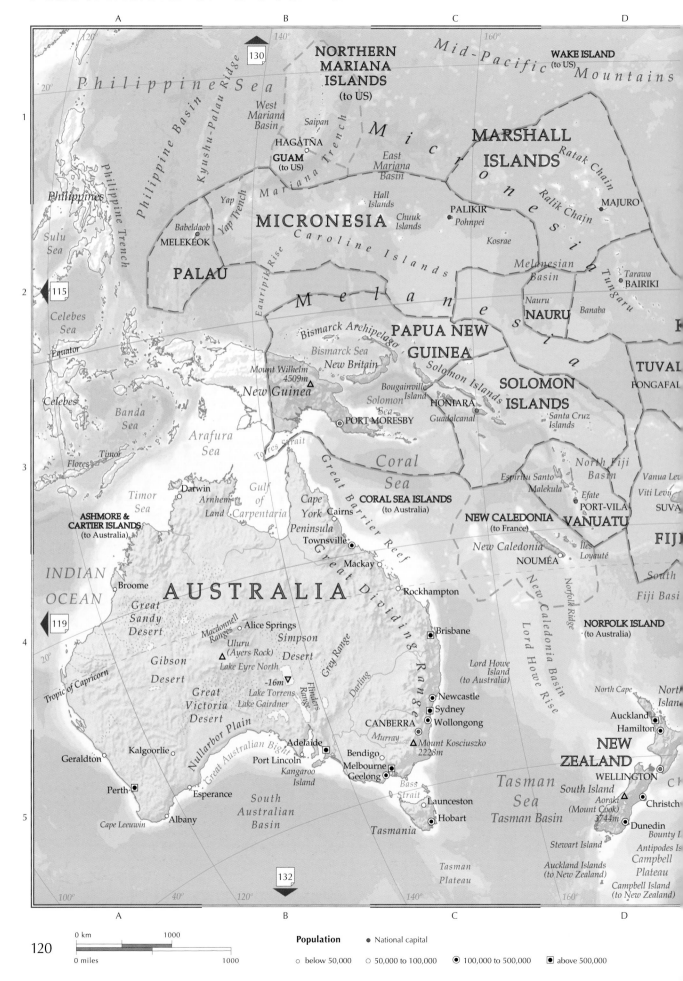

Philippine Sea

Mid-Pacific Mountains

NORTHERN MARIANA ISLANDS (to US)

WAKE ISLAND (to US)

West Mariana Basin

Saipan

Philippine Basin

Philippines

Philippine Trench

Kyushu-Palau Ridge

Yap

Yap Trench

Mariana Trench

HAGÅTÑA
GUAM (to US)

East Mariana Basin

Hall Islands

MARSHALL ISLANDS

Ratak Chain

MAJURO

Mi

c

r

o

n

e

s

i

a

PALIKIR
Pohnpei

Chuuk Islands

Ralik Chain

Babeldaob
MELEKEOK

MICRONESIA

PALAU

Caroline Islands

Eauripik Rise

Kosrae

Melanesian Basin

Tarawa
BAIRIKI

Tungaru

Sulu Sea

Celebes Sea

Equator

Celebes

Banda Sea

Timor

Flores

Timor Sea

ASHMORE & CARTIER ISLANDS (to Australia)

INDIAN OCEAN

Broome

M

e

l

a

n

Bismarck Archipelago

Bismarck Sea

New Britain

PAPUA NEW GUINEA

Mount Wilhelm 4509m

New Guinea

Solomon Islands

Bougainville Island

Solomon Sea

HONIARA

Guadalcanal

e

s

i

a

Nauru

Banaba

NAURU

SOLOMON ISLANDS

Santa Cruz Islands

TUVALU

FONGAFAL

Arafura Sea

Torres Strait

Gulf of Carpentaria

Darwin

Arnhem Land

Cape York

Coral Sea

CORAL SEA ISLANDS (to Australia)

North Fiji Basin

Espíritu Santo
Malekula

Efate
PORT-VILA

Vanua Lev

Viti Levu

SUVA

FIJI

Townsville

Cairns

Cape York Peninsula

Great Barrier Reef

NEW CALEDONIA (to France)

New Caledonia

Îles Loyauté

NOUMÉA

VANUATU

South Fiji Basi

Mackay

Rockhampton

Great Dividing Range

New Caledonia Ridge

Lord Howe Basin

Norfolk Ridge

AUSTRALIA

Great Sandy Desert

Gibson Desert

Great Victoria Desert

Macdonnell Ranges

Alice Springs

Uluru (Ayers Rock)

Simpson Desert

Lake Eyre North

-16m

Lake Torrens
Lake Gairdner

Flinders Range

Grey Range

Darling

Brisbane

Lord Howe Island (to Australia)

Newcastle
Sydney
Wollongong

CANBERRA

Murray

Mount Kosciuszko 2228m

NORFOLK ISLAND (to Australia)

North Cape

North Islan

Auckland

Hamilton

NEW ZEALAND

WELLINGTON

Tropic of Capricorn

Geraldton

Kalgoorlie

Nullarbor Plain

Adelaide

Great Australian Bight

Port Lincoln

Kangaroo Island

Bendigo

Melbourne
Geelong

Bass Strait

Tasman Sea

South Island

Aoraki (Mount Cook) 3744m

Christch

Ch

Perth

Esperance

South Australian Basin

Albany

Cape Leeuwin

Launceston

Hobart

Tasmania

Tasman Basin

Dunedin

Bounty I

Stewart Island

Antipodes Is

Campbell Plateau

Tasman Plateau

Auckland Islands (to New Zealand)

Campbell Island (to New Zealand)

130

115

119

132

0 km ___ 1000
0 miles ___ 1000

Population ● National capital

○ below 50,000 ○ 50,000 to 100,000 ◉ 100,000 to 500,000 ■ above 500,000

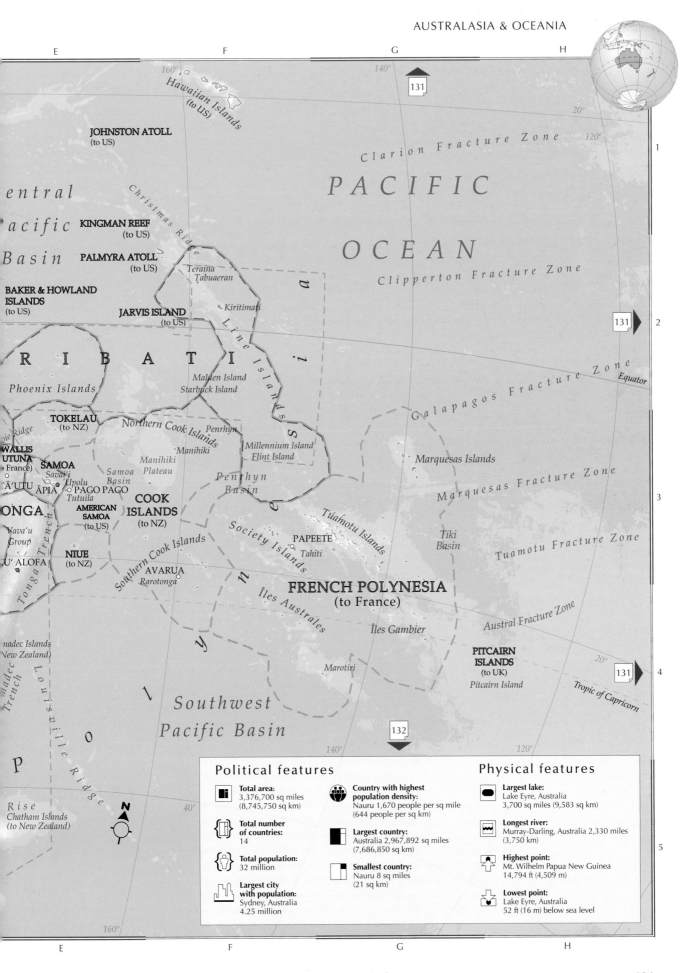

The Southwest Pacific

MARSHALL ISLANDS

NORTHERN MARIANA ISLANDS (to US)

Saipan
Tinian
Rota

GUAM (to US)
HAGÅTÑA

130

Enewetak Atoll
Bikini Atoll
Rongelap Atoll

Ailuk Atoll
Wotje Ato

Ujelang Atoll
Maloelap
Kwajalein Atoll
Majuro

Yap

MICRONESIA

Namu Atoll
Ailinglaplap Atoll
Jaluit Atoll

Mili Ato

Babeldaob
MELEKEOK

Chuuk Islands
PALIKIR
Pohnpei

Caroline Islands

Kosrae

Ebon Atoll

Mak

PALAU

117

Tara
BAIRIKI

Equator

Abeme
Non

NAURU

Banaba

Admiralty Islands
St.Matthias Group

Bismarck Archipelago

New Guinea

Bismarck Sea
New Ireland

INDONESIA

Madang

PAPUA NEW GUINEA

Central Range

△Mount Wilhelm
4509m   Lae

Owen Stanley Range

Bougainville Island

New Britain

Solomon Sea

New Georgia Islands

Choiseul

Santa Isabel

SOLOMON

Malaita

HONIARA
Guadalcanal

ISLANDS

Melanesia

Gulf of Papua

PORT MORESBY

D'Entrecasteaux Islands

San Cristobal
Rennell

Santa Cruz Islands

Torres Strait

Louisiade Archipelago

Arafura Sea

Arnhem Land

Groote Eylandt

Gulf of Carpentaria

Cape York Peninsula

Coral Sea

124

Barkly Tableland

Great Barrier Reef

CORAL SEA ISLANDS (to Australia)

Banks Islands

Espiritu Santo

Maéwo
Pentecost

Malekula
Ambrym
Epi

Efate
PORT-VILA

VANUATU

NEW CALEDONIA (to France)

Erromango
Tanna
Aneityum

NORTHERN

Great Dividing Range

Ouvéa
Lifou
Maré

New Caledonia

Iles Loyauté

TERRITORY

Tropic of Capricorn

Macdonnell

QUEENSLAND

NOUMÉA

Ranges

AUSTRALIA

127

0 km   750
0 miles   750

Population   ● National capital

○ below 50,000   ○ 50,000 to 100,000   ◉ 100,000 to 500,000   ◼ above 500,000

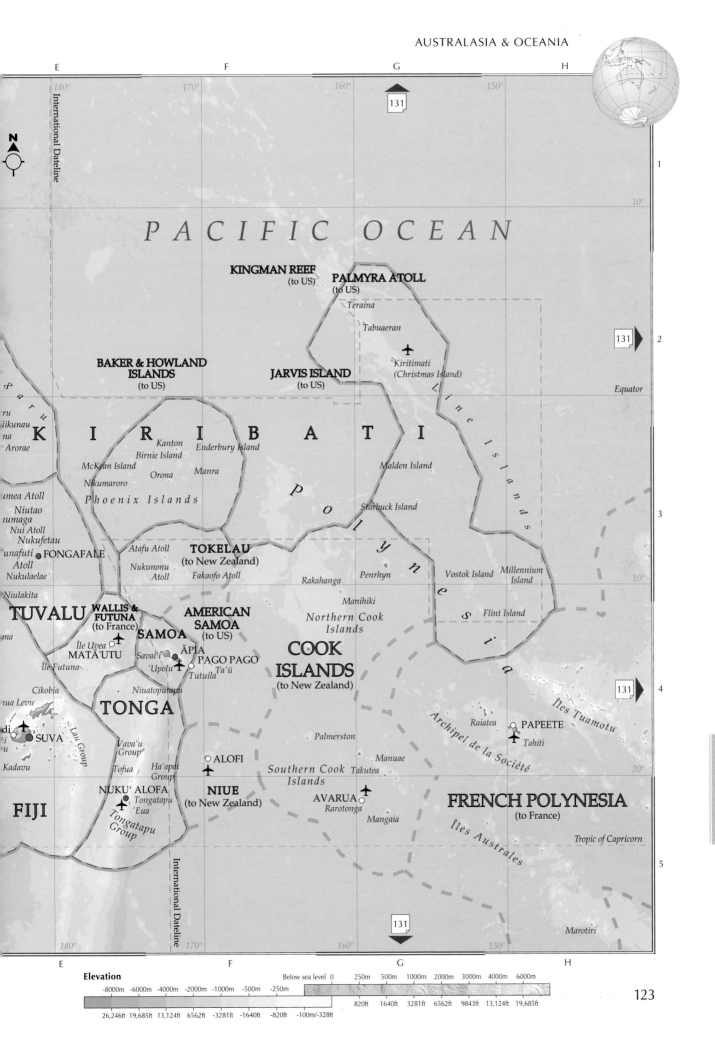

N

International Dateline

1

10°

P A C I F I C   O C E A N

KINGMAN REEF
(to US)

PALMYRA ATOLL
(to US)

Teraina

Tabuaeran

2

**BAKER & HOWLAND
ISLANDS**
(to US)

JARVIS ISLAND
(to US)

*Kiritimati
(Christmas Island)*

Equator

aru
likunau
na
Arorae

K   I   R   I   B   A   T   I

Kanton
Birnie Island
McKean Island
Nikumaroro

Enderbury Island

Orona

Manra

Malden Island

Phoenix Islands

umea Atoll
Niutao
oumaga
Nui Atoll
Nukufetau
unafuti ● **FONGAFALE**
Atoll
Nukulaelae

P
o
l
y
n
e
s
i
a

Starbuck Island

3

10°

Atafu Atoll

TOKELAU
(to New Zealand)

*Nukunonu
Atoll*

Fakaofo Atoll

Rakahanga

Penrhyn

Vostok Island

*Millennium
Island*

Line Islands

Niulakita

TUVALU

**WALLIS &
FUTUNA**
(to France)

**AMERICAN
SAMOA**
(to US)

SAMOA

Manihiki

*Northern Cook
Islands*

Flint Island

ma

Île Uvea
MATA'UTU

Île Futuna

Savai'i ● **ĀPIA**
'Upolu ○
Tutuila **PAGO PAGO**
Ta'ū

**COOK
ISLANDS**
(to New Zealand)

Cikobia
ua Levu

Niuatoputapu

TONGA

4

di ✈
○ **SUVA**

u
Kadavu

Lau Group

*Vava'u
Group*

Tofua

*Ha'apai
Group*

NUKU'ALOFA
Tongatapu
'Eua
*Tongatapu
Group*

○ **ALOFI**

NIUE
(to New Zealand)

Palmerston

Manuae

Takutea

*Southern Cook
Islands*

AVARUA ✈
Rarotonga

Mangaia

Archipel de la Société

Raiatea
○ **PAPEETE**
✈ *Tahiti*

Îles Tuamotu

FRENCH POLYNESIA
(to France)

FIJI

International Dateline

Îles Australes

Tropic of Capricorn

Marotiri

5

E   F   G   H

Elevation

| Below sea level | 0 | 250m | 500m | 1000m | 2000m | 3000m | 4000m | 6000m |

-8000m -6000m -4000m -2000m -1000m -500m -250m

820ft 1640ft 3281ft 6562ft 9843ft 13,124ft 19,685ft

26,246ft 19,685ft 13,124ft 6562ft -3281ft -1640ft -820ft -100m/-328ft

Western Australia

Arafura Sea

Arnhem Land

Croker Island
South Goulburn Island

Katherine

Daly Waters

Tennant Creek

Pine Creek

Top Springs Roadhouse

NORTHERN

Van Diemen Gulf

Darwin

Melville Island

Bathurst Island

Tanami Desert

TERRITORY

Macdonnell Ranges

Tropic of Capricorn

Timor Sea

Joseph Bonaparte Gulf

Victoria River

Wyndham
Kununurra

Halls Creek

Lake Mackay

EAST TIMOR

Timor

Cape Londonderry

Kimberley Plateau

Fitzroy Crossing

WESTERN

Great Sandy Desert

I N D O N E S I A

Bonaparte
Bigge Island
Archipelago
Heywood Islands

Fitzroy River

Percival Lakes

Flores

Tanimbar Kepulauan

King Sound

Broome

Marble Bar

Newman

Pulau Wetar

Pulau Sumba

Eighty Mile Beach

Hamersley Range

I N D I A N

Port Hedland

Bali

Pulau Lombok

Dampier

Fortescue River

Ashburton River

O C E A N

Barrow Island

Onslow

Barlee

Jawa

Exmouth

Exmouth Gulf

0 km   300
0 miles   300

Population

○ below 50,000   ○ 50,000 to 100,000   ◉ 100,000 to 500,000   ■ above 500,000

● Internal administrative capital

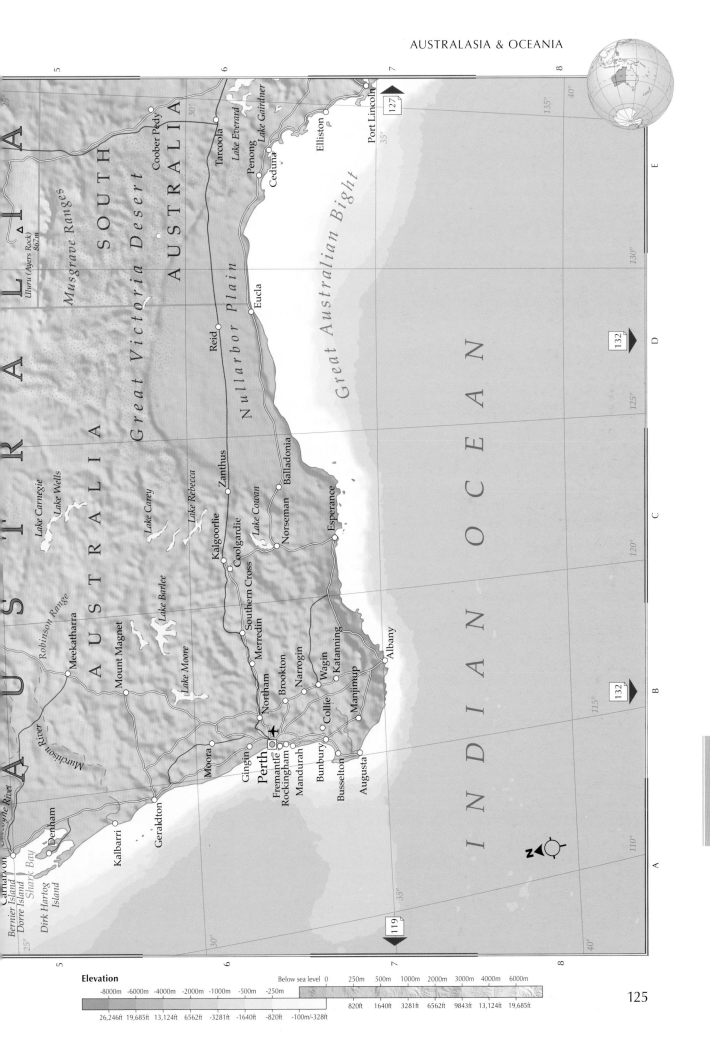

AUSTRALIA

SOUTH AUSTRALIA

Musgrave Ranges

Uluru (Ayers Rock)
862m

Great Victoria Desert

Coober Pedy

Tarcoola

Lake Everard
Lake Gairdner

Penong
Ceduna

Elliston

Port Lincoln

127

Nullarbor Plain

Eucla

Reid

Great Australian Bight

INDIAN OCEAN

132

Lake Carnegie
Lake Wells

Robinson Range

Meekatharra

Mount Magnet

Lake Carey

Lake Barlee

Lake Rebecca

Zanthus

Kalgoorlie
Coolgardie

Lake Cowan

Balladonia

Norseman

Esperance

Southern Cross
Merredin

Lake Moore

Brookton
Narrogin
Wagin
Katanning
Collie
Manjimup

Albany

132

Moora

Gingin
Perth
Fremantle
Rockingham
Mandurah
Bunbury
Busselton
Augusta

Northam

Murchison River
Gascoyne River

Carnarvon
Bernier Island
Dorre Island
Shark Bay
Denham
Dirk Hartog Island

Kalbarri

Geraldton

119

N

125

Elevation

Below sea level 0   250m   500m 1000m 2000m 3000m 4000m 6000m

-8000m -6000m -4000m -2000m -1000m -500m -250m

26,246ft 19,685ft 13,124ft 6562ft -3281ft -1640ft -820ft -100m/-328ft

820ft   1640ft   3281ft 6562ft 9843ft 13,124ft 19,685ft

Eastern Australia

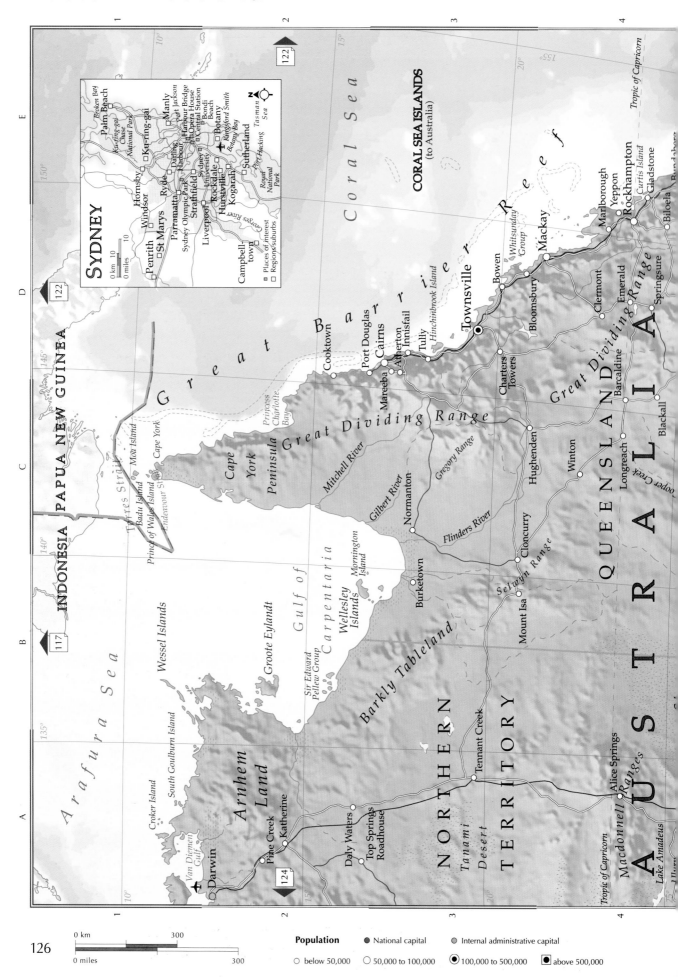

SYDNEY

Broken Bay
Palm Beach
Ku-ring-gai Chase National Park
Manly
Port Jackson
Ku-ring-gai
Harbour Bridge
Darling Harbour
Opera House
Central Station
Bondi
Botany
Kingsford Smith
Bondi Beach
Hornsby
Ryde
Sydney University
Botany Bay
Windsor
Parramatta
St Marys
Sydney Olympic Park
Strathfield
Rockdale
Sutherland
Penrith
Liverpool
Hurstville
Kogarah
Port Hacking
Royal National Park
Campbelltown
George's River
Tasman Sea

☐ Places of interest
☐ Regions/suburbs

0 km 10
0 miles 10

Coral Sea

CORAL SEA ISLANDS
(to Australia)

INDONESIA
PAPUA NEW GUINEA

Arafura Sea
Torres Strait
Moa Island
Badu Island
Prince of Wales Island
Endeavour Str
Cape York
Cape York Peninsula

Great Barrier Reef

Cooktown
Port Douglas
Cairns
Atherton
Mareeba
Innisfail
Tully
Hinchinbrook Island
Townsville
Bowen
Whitsunday Group
Mackay
Bloomsbury

Marlborough
Yeppon
Rockhampton
Curtis Island
Gladstone
Biloela
Tropic of Capricorn

Princess Charlotte Bay

Great Dividing Range

Mitchell River
Gilbert River
Normanton
Flinders River
Gregory Range

Charters Towers
Clermont
Emerald
Springsure
Barcaldine
Blackall

Hughenden
Winton
Longreach
Cooper Creek

QUEENSLAND

Gulf of Carpentaria

Mornington Island
Wellesley Islands
Burketown

Cloncurry
Selwyn Range
Mount Isa

Groote Eylandt
Sir Edward Pellew Group

Barkly Tableland

Wessel Islands
South Goulburn Island
Croker Island

Van Diemen Gulf
Darwin
Pine Creek
Katherine

Arnhem Land

NORTHERN TERRITORY

Daly Waters
Top Springs Roadhouse
Tennant Creek

Tanami Desert

Alice Springs
Macdonnell Ranges
Lake Amadeus
Tropic of Capricorn

AUSTRALIA

0 km   300
0 miles   300

Population

- National capital
- Internal administrative capital
- ○ below 50,000
- ○ 50,000 to 100,000
- ◉ 100,000 to 500,000
- ◼ above 500,000

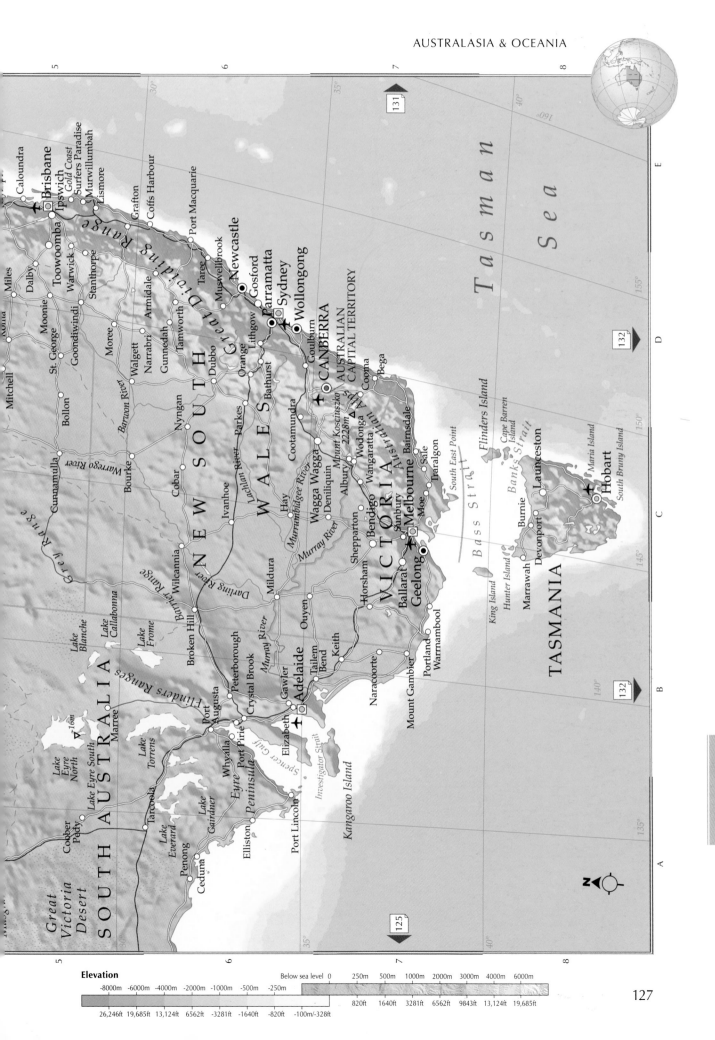

Elevation

| | | | | | | | | | | Below sea level | 0 | 250m | 500m | 1000m | 2000m | 3000m | 4000m | 6000m |

-8000m -6000m -4000m -2000m -1000m -500m -250m

26,246ft 19,685ft 13,124ft 6562ft -3281ft -1640ft -820ft -100m/-328ft

820ft 1640ft 3281ft 6562ft 9843ft 13,124ft 19,685ft

New Zealand

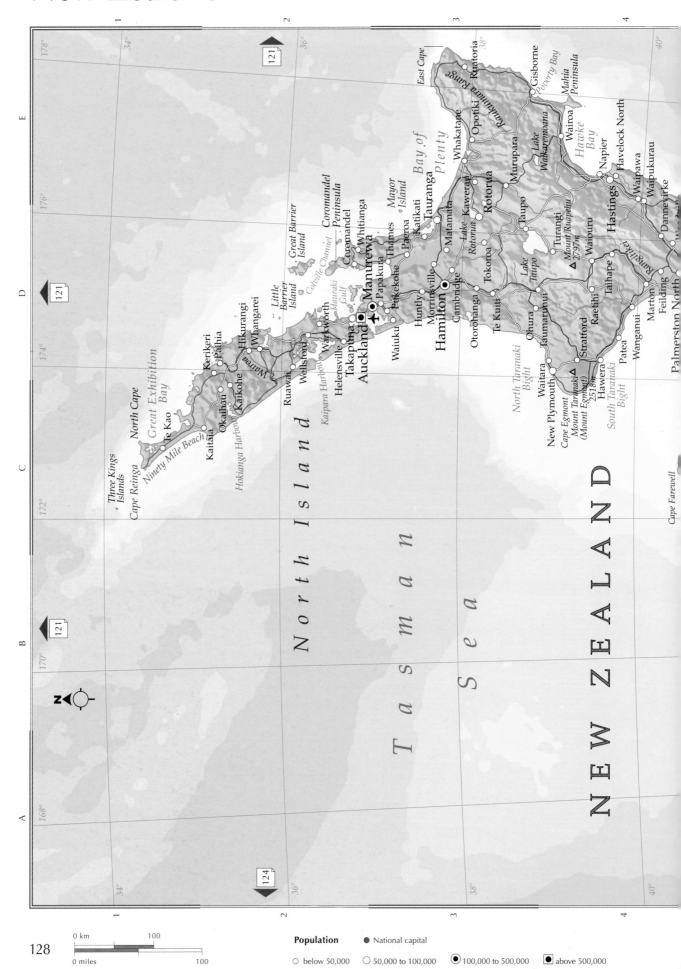

Population ● National capital

○ below 50,000 ○ 50,000 to 100,000 ◉ 100,000 to 500,000 ▣ above 500,000

0 km   100
0 miles   100

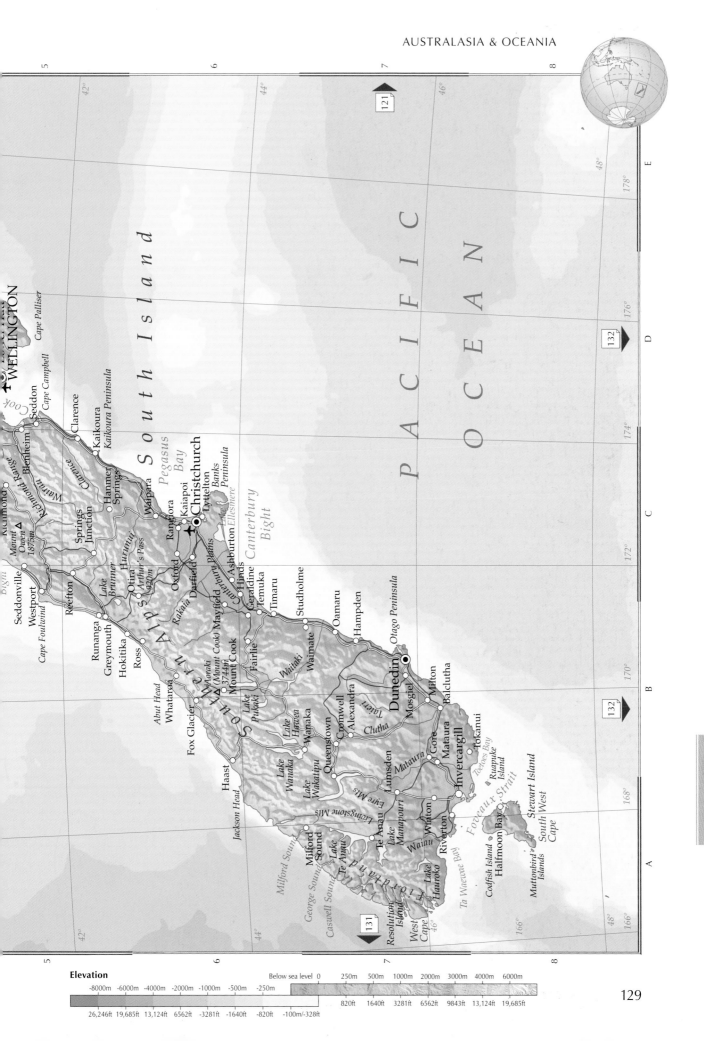

Elevation

Below sea level 0   250m   500m   1000m   2000m   3000m   4000m   6000m

-8000m -6000m -4000m -2000m -1000m -500m -250m

820ft   1640ft   3281ft   6562ft   9843ft   13,124ft   19,685ft

26,246ft 19,685ft 13,124ft 6562ft -3281ft -1640ft -820ft -100m/-328ft

The Pacific Ocean

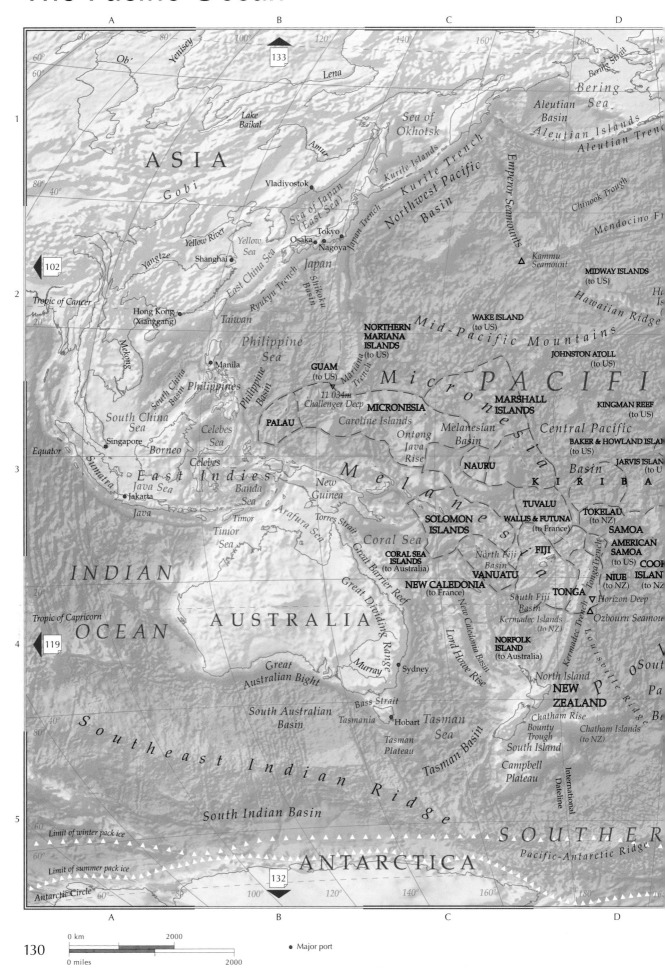

A B C D

133

ASIA

Ob'
Yenisey
Lena
Lake Baikal
Amur
Gobi
Vladivostok
Sea of Okhotsk
Kurile Islands
Kurile Trench
Northwest Pacific Basin
Emperor Seamounts
Aleutian Basin
Bering Sea
Aleutian Islands
Aleutian Trench
Chinook Trough
Mendocino Fr

102

Yellow River
Yangtze
Shanghai
Yellow Sea
Sea of Japan (East Sea)
Tokyo
Osaka
Nagoya
Japan
East China Sea
Japan Trench
Kammu Seamount
MIDWAY ISLANDS (to US)
Hawaiian Ridge
Ho

Tropic of Cancer
Hong Kong (Xianggang)
Taiwan
Ryukyu Trench
Shikoku Basin
Mid-Pacific Mountains
WAKE ISLAND (to US)
Philippine Sea
NORTHERN MARIANA ISLANDS (to US)
JOHNSTON ATOLL (to US)

Manila
Philippine Basin
GUAM (to US)
Mariana Trench
PACIFI
Mi cro
11 034m Challenger Deep
MICRONESIA
MARSHALL ISLANDS
KINGMAN REEF (to US)

South China Basin
Philippines
PALAU
Caroline Islands
Central Pacific
BAKER & HOWLAND ISLAN (to US)

South China Sea
Celebes Sea
Melanesian Basin
ne sia
JARVIS ISLAN (to U

Singapore
Borneo
Ontong Java Rise
NAURU
Basin

Equator
Celebes
M e l a
K I R I B A

Sumatra
Java Sea
East Indies
New Guinea
TUVALU
TOKELAU (to NZ)

Jakarta
Banda Sea
n e s
WALLIS & FUTUNA (to France)
SAMOA

Java
Timor
SOLOMON ISLANDS
FIJI
AMERICAN SAMOA (to US)

Timor Sea
Arafura Sea
Torres Strait
Coral Sea
CORAL SEA ISLANDS (to Australia)
North Fiji Basin
VANUATU
i a
NIUE (to NZ)
COO
ISLAN (to NZ

INDIAN
Great Barrier Reef
NEW CALEDONIA (to France)
New Caledonia Basin
South Fiji Basin
TONGA
Horizon Deep
Ozbourn Seamou

Tropic of Capricorn
Great Dividing Range
Lord Howe Rise
Kermadec Islands (to NZ)
NORFOLK ISLAND (to Australia)
North Island
P
Sout
Pa
Be

119
OCEAN
AUSTRALIA
Murray
Sydney
NEW ZEALAND

Great Australian Bight
South Australian Basin
Bass Strait
Tasmania
Hobart
Tasman Sea
Tasman Basin
Chatham Rise
Bounty Trough
Chatham Islands (to NZ)

Tasman Plateau
South Island
Campbell Plateau
International Dateline

S o u t h e a s t   I n d i a n   R i d g e

South Indian Basin

Limit of winter pack ice
SOUTHER
Pacific-Antarctic Ridge

Limit of summer pack ice
ANTARCTICA

Antarctic Circle
132

A B C D

0 km   2000
0 miles   2000

● Major port

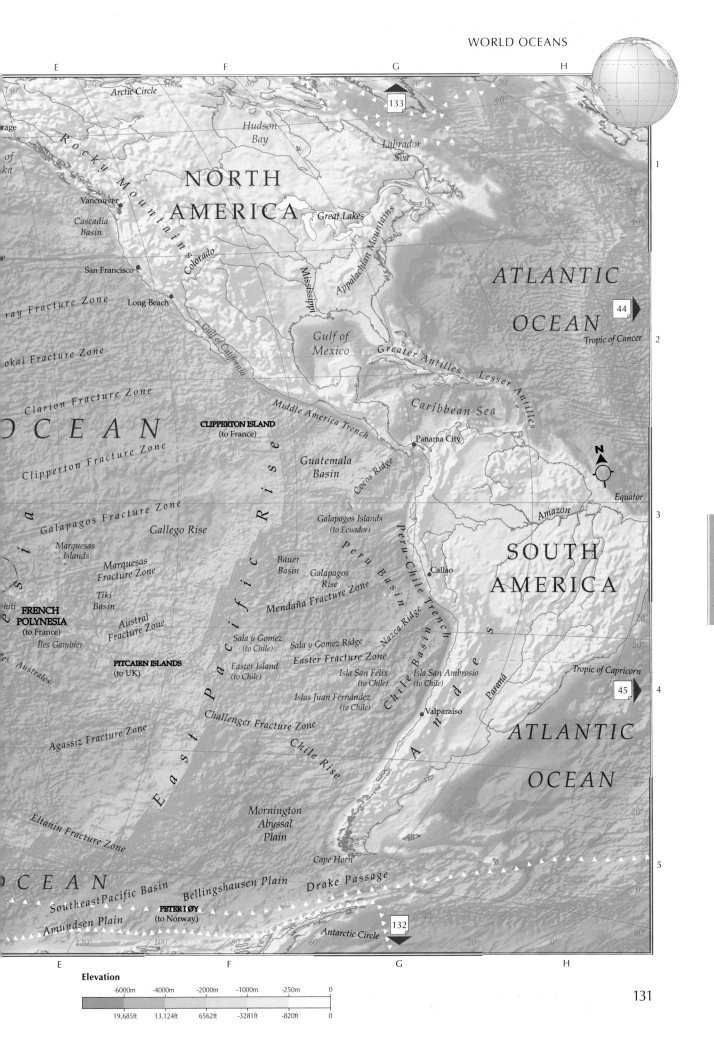

Arctic Circle

133

Rocky Mountains

Hudson Bay

NORTH AMERICA

Labrador Sea

Vancouver

Cascadia Basin

Great Lakes

Colorado

San Francisco

ATLANTIC

Long Beach

Gulf of California

Appalachian Mountains

OCEAN

44

Tropic of Cancer

Gulf of Mexico

Greater Antilles

Lesser Antilles

Caribbean Sea

Middle America Trench

CLIPPERTON ISLAND
(to France)

Guatemala Basin

Cocos Ridge

Panama City

OCEAN

Clarion Fracture Zone

Clipperton Fracture Zone

East Pacific Rise

Galapagos Islands
(to Ecuador)

N

Amazon

Equator

Galapagos Fracture Zone

Gallego Rise

Marquesas Islands

Bauer Basin

Galapagos Rise

Peru Basin

SOUTH AMERICA

Marquesas Fracture Zone

Callao

Peru-Chile Trench

Tiki Basin

Mendaña Fracture Zone

FRENCH POLYNESIA
(to France)

Austral Fracture Zone

Sala y Gomez
(to Chile)

Sala y Gomez Ridge

Nazca Ridge

Andes

Îles Gambier

Easter Fracture Zone

Chile Basin

Tropic of Capricorn

PITCAIRN ISLANDS
(to UK)

Easter Island
(to Chile)

Isla San Félix
(to Chile)

Isla San Ambrosio
(to Chile)

Paraná

45

Islas Juan Fernández
(to Chile)

Challenger Fracture Zone

Valparaiso

ATLANTIC

Agassiz Fracture Zone

Chile Rise

OCEAN

Eltanin Fracture Zone

Mornington Abyssal Plain

Cape Horn

OCEAN

Southeast Pacific Basin

Bellingshausen Plain

Drake Passage

132

PETER I ØY
(to Norway)

Amundsen Plain

Antarctic Circle

Elevation

-6000m	-4000m	-2000m	-1000m	-250m	0
19,685ft	13,124ft	6562ft	-3281ft	-820ft	0

Antarctica

ATLANTIC OCEAN

SOUTH GEORGIA (to UK)

SOUTH SANDWICH ISLANDS (to UK)

Scotia Sea

South Sandwich Trench

America–Antarctica Ridge

Atlantic-Indian Basin

SOUTHERN OCEAN

Antarctic Circle

Lazarev Sea

Enderby Plain

Weddell Plain

Orcadas (Argentina)

Signy (UK)

South Orkney Islands

South Shetland Islands

Drake Passage

Esperanza (Argentina)

Capitán Arturo Prat (Chile)

Palmer (US)

Rothera (UK)

San Martín (Argentina)

Antarctic Peninsula

Graham Land

Palmer Land

Alexander Island

Halley (UK)

Belgrano II (Argentina)

Berkner Island

Weddell Sea

Coats Land

Ronne Ice Shelf

Sanae (South Africa)

Georg von Neumayer (Germany)

Novolazarevskaya (Russian Federation)

Dronning Maud Land

Lützow Holmbukta

Syowa (Japan)

Molodezhnaya (Russian Federation)

Enderby Land

Mawson (Australia)

Cape Darnley

Mackenzie Bay

Prydz Bay

Princess Elizabeth Land

Davis (Australia)

Davis Sea

ANTARCTICA

Amundsen-Scott (US)

South Pole

East Antarctica

Mirny (Russian Federation)

Shackleton Ice Shelf

Vinson Massif 4897m

Bellingshausen Sea

PETER I ØY (to Norway)

Ellsworth Land

West Antarctica

Transantarctic Mountains

South Geomagnetic Pole

Vostok (Russian Federation)

Marie Byrd Land

Mount Kirkpatrick 4528m

Mount Markham 4351m

Ross Ice Shelf

Mount Sidley 4181m

Mount Siple 3100m

Amundsen Sea

Roosevelt Island

Scott Base (N.Z.)

McMurdo Base (US)

Mount Erebus 3794m

Victoria Land

Wilkes Land

Casey (Australia)

Cape Poinsett

Terre Adélie

Ross Sea

Amundsen Plain

SOUTHERN OCEAN

Cape Adare

Leningradskaya (Russian Federation)

George V Land

Dumont d'Urville (France)

South Indian Basin

Scott Island

Balleny Islands

Macquarie Ridge

Pacific-Antarctic Ridge

Udintsev Fracture Zone

Eltanin Fracture Zone

Limit of winter pack ice

Limit of summer pack ice

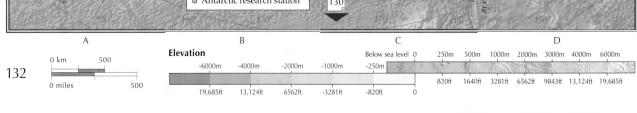

Elevation

Below sea level 0

−6000m −4000m −2000m −1000m −250m   250m 500m 1000m 2000m 3000m 4000m 6000m

19,685ft 13,124ft 6562ft −3281ft −820ft 0   820ft 1640ft 3281ft 6562ft 9843ft 13,124ft 19,685ft

◦ Antarctic research station

0 km 500

0 miles 500

Arctic Ocean

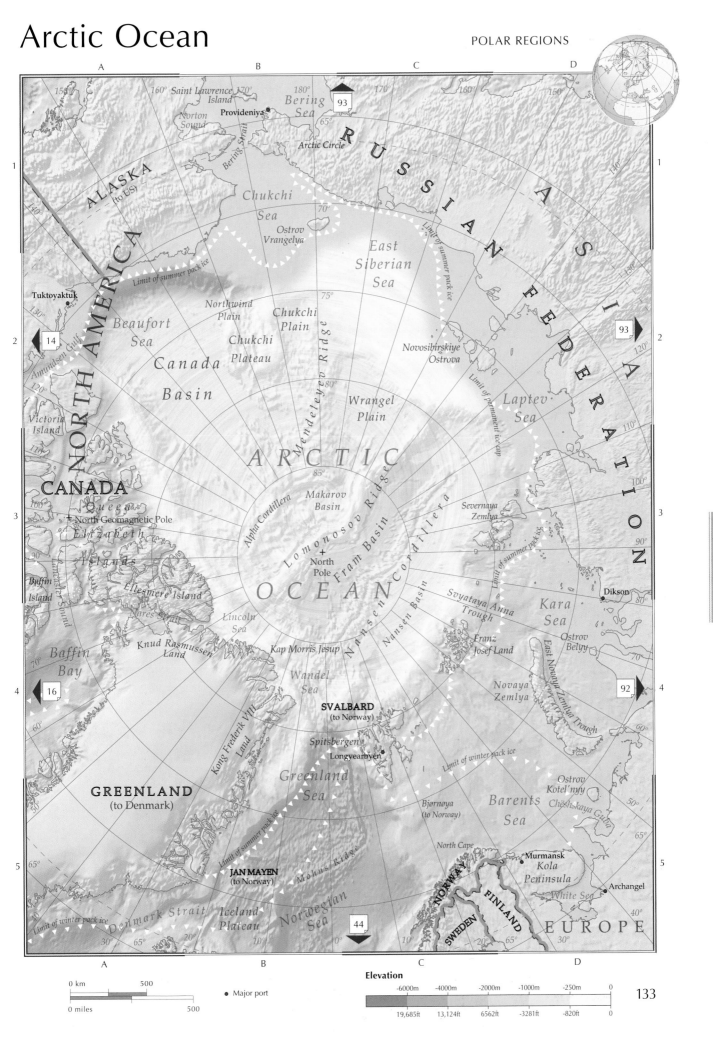

A B C D

150° 160° Saint Lawrence 170° 180° 93 170° 160° 150° 140°
Island
Norton ● Provideniya Bering 65°
Sound Sea
Arctic Circle R U S S I A N

1 ALASKA Chukchi 1
(to US) Sea 70°
Ostrov
Vrangelya East
Siberian
Limit of summer pack ice Sea Limit of summer pack ice
130°

Tuktoyaktuk Northwind 75° 130°
Plain Chukchi
Beaufort Chukchi Plain Novosibirskiye
2 14 Sea Plateau Ostrova 93 2
NORTH AMERICA Canada 80° Wrangel Laptev 120°
Basin Plain Sea

Victoria Mendeleyev Ridge Limit of permanent ice cap 110°
Island

CANADA 85° Severnaya F
North Geomagnetic Pole Alpha Cordillera Makarov Zemlya E
3 Queen Basin Limit of summer pack ice 90° 3
Elizabeth Lomonosov Ridge D Dikson 80°
Islands North E
Pole Fram Basin R
Baffin Ellesmere Island Svyataya Anna Kara A 70°
Island Nares Strait Lincoln O C E A N Trough Sea T
Sea Nansen Basin Franz Ostrov I
Knud Rasmussen Kap Morris Jesup Nansen Cordillera Josef Land Belyy O
Baffin Land Wandel N
4 Bay 16 Sea Novaya 92 4
Kong Frederik VIII SVALBARD Zemlya 60°
Land (to Norway) Ostrov
Kotel'nyy
Spitsbergen Chëshskaya Guba
Greenland Longyearbyen Limit of winter pack ice 50°
Sea Barents
GREENLAND Bjørnøya Sea 65°
(to Denmark) (to Norway)
North Cape Murmansk
5 JAN MAYEN Mohns Ridge Kola 5
(to Norway) Archangel
Limit of summer pack ice Norwegian NORWAY Peninsula
Iceland Sea FINLAND White Sea 40°
Plateau 44
Limit of winter pack ice Denmark Strait 20° 10° SWEDEN 20° 65° E U R O P E
30° 65° 65° 10° 30°

A B C D

Elevation

0 km 500
● Major port -6000m -4000m -2000m -1000m -250m 0
0 miles 500
19,685ft 13,124ft 6562ft -3281ft -820ft 0

Country Profiles

This Factfile is intended as a guide to a world that is continually changing as political fashions and personalities come and go. Nevertheless, all the material in these factfiles has been researched from the most up-to-date and authoritative sources to give an incisive portrait of the geographical, political, and social characteristics that make each country so unique.

There are currently 195 independent countries in the world - more than at any previous time - and 59 dependencies. Antarctica is the only land area on Earth that is not officially part of, and does not belong to, any single country.

Country profile key

Formation Date of independence / date current borders were established

Population Total population / population density – based on total *land* area / percentage of urban-based population

Languages An asterisk (*) denotes the official language(s)

Calorie consumption Average number of calories consumed daily per person

---

AFGHANISTAN
Central Asia

Page 100 D4

In 2001, following a US-led offensive, the hard-line Muslim taliban militia was replaced by a new interim government under Hamid Karazi

Official name The Islamic Republic of Afghanistan
Formation 1919 / 1919
Capital Kabul
Population 32.3 million / 128 people per sq mile (50 people per sq km) / 24%
Total area 250,000 sq. miles (647,500 sq. km)
Languages Pashtu*, Tajik, Dari*, Farsi, Uzbek, Turkmen
Religions Sunni Muslim 84%, Shi'a Muslim 15%, Other 1%
Ethnic mix Pashtun 38%, Tajik 25%, Hazara 19%, Uzbek and Turkmen 15%, Other 3%
Government Presidential system
Currency Afghani = 100 puls
Literacy rate 28%
Calorie consumption 1539 calories

ALBANIA
Southeast Europe

Page 79 C6

Lying at the southeastern end of the Adriatic Sea, Albania held its first multiparty elections in 1991, after nearly five decades of communism.

Official name Republic of Albania
Formation 1912 / 1921
Capital Tirana
Population 3.2 million / 302 people per sq mile (117 people per sq km) / 44%
Total area 11,100 sq. miles (28,748 sq. km)
Languages Albanian*, Greek
Religions Sunni Muslim 70%, Orthodox Christian 20%, Roman Catholic 10%
Ethnic mix Albanian 93%, Greek 5%, Other 2%
Government Parliamentary system
Currency Lek = 100 qindarka (qintars)
Literacy rate 99%
Calorie consumption 2848 calories

ALGERIA
North Africa

Page 48 C3

Algeria achieved independence from France in 1962. Today, its military-dominated government faces a severe challenge from Islamic extremists.

Official name People's Democratic Republic of Algeria
Formation 1962 / 1962
Capital Algiers
Population 33.9 million / 37 people per sq mile (14 people per sq km) / 59%
Total area 919,590 sq. miles (2,381,740 sq. km)
Languages Arabic*, Tamazight (Kabyle, Shawia, Tamashek), French
Religions Sunni Muslim 99%, Christian and Jewish 1%
Ethnic mix Arab 75%, Berber 24%, European and Jewish 1%
Government Presidential system
Currency Algerian dinar = 100 centimes
Literacy rate 70%
Calorie consumption 3022 calories

ANDORRA
Southwest Europe

Page 69 B6

A tiny landlocked principality, Andorra lies high in the eastern Pyrenees between France and Spain. It held its first full elections in 1993.

Official name Principality of Andorra
Formation 1278 / 1278
Capital Andorra la Vella
Population 71,822 / 399 people per sq mile (154 people per sq km) / 91%
Total area 181 sq. miles (468 sq. km)
Languages Spanish, Catalan*, French, Portuguese
Religions Roman Catholic 94%, Other 6%
Ethnic mix Spanish 46%, Andorran 28%, Other 18%, French 8%
Government Parliamentary system
Currency Euro = 100 cents
Literacy rate 99%
Calorie consumption Not available

ANGOLA
Southern Africa

Page 56 B2

Located in southwest Africa, Angola was in an almost constant state of civil war for nearly 30 years, until a peace deal was agreed in 2002.

Official name Republic of Angola
Formation 1975 / 1975
Capital Luanda
Population 16.9 million / 35 people per sq mile (14 people per sq km) / 36%
Total area 481,351 sq. miles (1,246,700 sq. km)
Languages Portuguese*, Umbundu, Kimbundu, Kikongo
Religions Roman Catholic 50%, Other 30%, Protestant 20%
Ethnic mix Ovimbundu 37%, Other 25%, Kimbundu 25%, Bakongo 13%
Government Presidential system
Currency Readjusted kwanza = 100 lwei
Literacy rate 67%
Calorie consumption 2083 calories

ANTIGUA & BARBUDA
West Indies

Page 33 H3

Lying on the Atlantic edge of the Leeward Islands, Antigua and Barbuda's area includes the uninhabited islet of Redonda.

Official name Antigua and Barbuda
Formation 1981 / 1981
Capital St. John's
Population 69,481 / 409 people per sq mile (158 people per sq km) / 38%
Total area 170 sq. miles (442 sq. km)
Languages English*, English patois
Religions Anglican 45%, Other Protestant 42%, Roman Catholic 10%, Other 2%, Rastafarian 1%
Ethnic mix Black African 95%, Other 5%
Government Parliamentary system
Currency Eastern Caribbean dollar = 100 cents
Literacy rate 86%
Calorie consumption 2349 calories

ARGENTINA
South America

Page 43 B5

Most of the southern half of South America is occupied by Argentina. The country returned to civilian rule in 1983 after a series of military coups.

Official name The Argentine Republic
Formation 1816 / 1816
Capital Buenos Aires
Population 39.5 million / 37 people per sq mile (14 people per sq km) / 90%
Total area 1,068,296 sq. miles (2,766,890 sq. km)
Languages Spanish*, Italian, Amerindian languages
Religions Roman Catholic 90%, Other 6%, Protestant 2%, Jewish 2%
Ethnic mix Indo-European 83%, Mestizo 14%, Jewish 2%, Amerindian 1%
Government Presidential system
Currency new Argentine peso = 100 centavos
Literacy rate 97%
Calorie consumption 2992 calories

ARMENIA
Southwest Asia

Page 95 F3

Smallest of the former USSR's republics, Armenia lies in the Lesser Caucasus mountains. Territorial war with Azerbaijan ended in a 1994 ceasefire.

Official name Republic of Armenia
Formation 1991 / 1991
Capital Yerevan
Population 3 million / 261 people per sq mile (101 people per sq km) / 64%
Total area 11,506 sq. miles (29,800 sq. km)
Languages Armenian*, Azeri, Russian
Religions Armenian Apostolic Church (Orthodox) 88%, Other 6%, Armenian Catholic Church 6%
Ethnic mix Armenian 98%, Other 1%, Yezidi 1%
Government Parliamentary system
Currency Dram = 100 luma
Literacy rate 99%
Calorie consumption 2268 calories

AUSTRALIA
Australasia & Oceania

Page 120 A4

An island continent located between the Indian and Pacific oceans, Australia was settled by Europeans 200 years ago, but now has many Asian immigrants.

Official name Commonwealth of Australia
Formation 1901 / 1901
Capital Canberra
Population 20.9 million / 7 people per sq mile (3 people per sq km) / 92%
Total area 2,967,893 sq. miles (7,686,850 sq. km)
Languages English*, Italian, Cantonese, Greek, Arabic, Vietnamese, Aboriginal languages
Religions Roman Catholic 26%, Protestant 38%, Other 23%, Nonreligious 13%,
Ethnic mix European 92%, Asian 5%, Aboriginal 2%, Other 1%
Government Parliamentary system
Currency Australian dollar = 100 cents
Literacy rate 99%
Calorie consumption 3054 calories

AUSTRIA
Central Europe

Page 73 D7

Bordering eight countries in the heart of Europe, Austria was created in 1920 after the collapse of the Austro-Hungarian Empire the previous year.

Official name Republic of Austria
Formation 1918 / 1919
Capital Vienna
Population 8.2 million / 257 people per sq mile (99 people per sq km) / 66%
Total area 32,378 sq. miles (83,858 sq. km)
Languages German*, Croatian, Slovenian, Hungarian (Magyar)
Religions Roman Catholic 78%, Other (including Jewish and Muslim) 17%, Protestant 5%
Ethnic mix Austrian 93%, Croat, Slovene, and Hungarian 6%, Other 1%
Government Parliamentary system
Currency Euro = 100 cents
Literacy rate 99%
Calorie consumption 3673 calories

AZERBAIJAN
Southwest Asia

Page 95 G2

Situated on the western coast of the Caspian Sea, Azerbaijan was the first Soviet republic to declare independence from Moscow in 1991.

Official name Republic of Azerbaijan
Formation 1991 / 1991
Capital Baku
Population 8.5 million / 254 people per sq mile (98 people per sq km) / 50%
Total area 33,436 sq. miles (86,600 sq. km)
Languages Azeri*, Russian
Religions Shi'a Muslim 68%, Sunni Muslim 26%, Russian Orthodox 3%, Armenian Apostolic Church (Orthodox) 2%, Other 1%
Ethnic mix Azeri 91%, Other 3%, Lazs 2%, Armenian 2%, Russian 2%
Government Presidential system
Currency New manat = 100 gopik
Literacy rate 99%
Calorie consumption 2575 calories

BAHAMAS
West Indies

Page 32 C1

Located in the western Atlantic, off the Florida coast, the Bahamas comprise some 700 islands and 2,400 cays, only 30 of which are inhabited.

Official name Commonwealth of the Bahamas
Formation 1973 / 1973
Capital Nassau
Population 305,655 / 79 people per sq mile (31 people per sq km) / 90%
Total area 5382 sq. miles (13,940 sq. km)
Languages English*, English Creole, French Creole
Religions Baptist 32%, Anglican 20%, Roman Catholic 19%, Other 17%, Methodist 6%, Church of God 6%
Ethnic mix Black African 85%, Other 15%
Government Parliamentary system
Currency Bahamian dollar = 100 cents
Literacy rate 96%
Calorie consumption 2755 calories

BAHRAIN
Southwest Asia

Page 98 C4

Bahrain is an archipelago of 33 islands between the Qatar peninsula and the Saudi Arabian mainland. Only three of these islands are inhabited.

Official name Kingdom of Bahrain
Formation 1971 / 1971
Capital Manama
Population 708,573 / 2596 people per sq mile (1004 people per sq km) / 90%
Total area 239 sq. miles (620 sq. km)
Languages Arabic
Religions Muslim (mainly Shi'a) 99%, Other 1%
Ethnic mix Bahraini 70%, Iranian, Indian, and Pakistani 24%, Other Arab 4%, European 2%
Government Mixed monarchical–parliamentary system
Currency Bahraini dinar = 1000 fils
Literacy rate 87%
Calorie consumption Not available

BANGLADESH
South Asia

Page 113 G3

Bangladesh lies at the north of the Bay of Bengal. It seceded from Pakistan in 1971 and, after much political instability, returned to democracy in 1991.

Official name People's Republic of Bangladesh
Formation 1971 / 1971
Capital Dhaka
Population 147 million / 2845 people per sq mile (1098 people per sq km) / 25%
Total area 55,598 sq. miles (144,000 sq. km)
Languages Bengali*, Urdu, Chakma, Marma (Magh), Garo, Khasi, Santhali, Tripuri, Mro
Religions Muslim (mainly Sunni) 87%, Hindu 12%, Other 1%
Ethnic mix Bengali 98%, Other 2%
Government Transitional regime
Currency Taka = 100 poisha
Literacy rate 41%
Calorie consumption 2205 calories

BARBADOS
West Indies

Page 33 H4

Barbados is the most easterly of the Caribbean Windward Islands. Under British rule for 339 years, it became fully independent in 1966.

Official name Barbados
Formation 1966 / 1966
Capital Bridgetown
Population 280,946 / 1692 people per sq mile (653 people per sq km) / 52%
Total area 166 sq. miles (430 sq. km)
Languages English*, Bajan (Barbadian English)
Religions Anglican 40%, Other 24%, Nonreligious 17%, Pentecostal 8%, Methodist 7%, Roman Catholic 4%
Ethnic mix Black African 92%, White 3%, Other 3%, Mixed race 2%
Government Parliamentary system
Currency Barbados dollar = 100 cents
Literacy rate 99%
Calorie consumption 3091 calories

BELARUS
Eastern Europe

Page 85 B6

Formerly known as White Russia, Belarus lies landlocked in eastern Europe. The country reluctantly became independent of the USSR in 1991.

Official name Republic of Belarus
Formation 1991 / 1991
Capital Minsk
Population 9.6 million / 120 people per sq mile (46 people per sq km) / 71%
Total area 80,154 sq. miles (207,600 sq. km)
Languages Belorussian*, Russian*
Religions Orthodox Christian 60%, Other 32%, Roman Catholic 8%
Ethnic mix Belorussian 81%, Russian 11%, Polish 4%, Other 2%, Ukrainian 2%
Government Presidential system
Currency Belorussian rouble = 100 kopeks
Literacy rate 99%
Calorie consumption 3000 calories

BELGIUM
Northwest Europe

Page 65 B6

Located in northwestern Europe, Belgium's history has been marked by the division between its Flemish- and French-speaking communities.

Official name Kingdom of Belgium
Formation 1830 / 1919
Capital Brussels
Population 10.5 million / 829 people per sq mile (320 people per sq km) / 97%
Total area 11,780 sq. miles (30,510 sq. km)
Languages Dutch*, French*, German*
Religions Roman Catholic 88%, Other 10%, Muslim 2%
Ethnic mix Fleming 58%, Walloon 33%, Other 6%, Italian 2%, Moroccan 1%
Government Parliamentary system
Currency Euro = 100 cents
Literacy rate 99%
Calorie consumption 3584 calories

BELIZE
Central America

Page 30 B1

The last Central American country to gain independence, this former British colony lies on the eastern shore of the Yucatan Peninsula.

Official name Belize
Formation 1981 / 1981
Capital Belmopan
Population 294,385 / 33 people per sq mile (13 people per sq km) / 48%
Total area 8867 sq. miles (22,966 sq. km)
Languages English*, English Creole, Spanish, Mayan, Garifuna (Carib)
Religions Roman Catholic 62%, Other 16%, Anglican 12%, Methodist 6%, Mennonite 4%,
Ethnic mix Mestizo 49%, Creole 25%, Maya 11%, Other 6%, Garifuna 6%, Asian Indian 3%
Government Parliamentary system
Currency Belizean dollar = 100 cents
Literacy rate 75%
Calorie consumption 2869 calories

BENIN
West Africa

Page 53 F4

Stretching north from the West African coast, Benin became one of the pioneers of African democratization in 1990, ending years of military rule.

Official name Republic of Benin
Formation 1960 / 1960
Capital Porto-Novo
Population 9 million / 211 people per sq mile (81 people per sq km) / 45%
Total area 43,483 sq. miles (112,620 sq. km)
Languages French*, Fon, Bariba, Yoruba, Adja, Houeda, Somba
Religions Voodoo 50%, Muslim 30%, Christian 20%
Ethnic mix Fon 41%, Other 21%, Adja 16%, Yoruba 12%, Bariba 10%
Government Presidential system
Currency CFA franc = 100 centimes
Literacy rate 35%
Calorie consumption 2548 calories

BHUTAN
South Asia

Page 113 G3

The landlocked Buddhist kingdom of Bhutan is perched in the eastern Himalayas between India and China. Gradual reforms protect its cultural identity.

Official name Kingdom of Bhutan
Formation 1656 / 1865
Capital Thimphu
Population 2.3 million / 127 people per sq mile (49 people per sq km) / 9%
Total area 18,147 sq. miles (47,000 sq. km)
Languages Dzongkha*, Nepali, Assamese
Religions Mahayana Buddhist 70%, Hindu 24%, Other 6%
Ethnic mix Bhute 50%, Other 25%, Nepalese 25%
Government Mixed monarchical–parliamentary system
Currency Ngultrum = 100 chetrum
Literacy rate 47%
Calorie consumption Not available

BOLIVIA
South America

Page 39 F3

Bolivia lies landlocked high in central South America. Mineral riches once made it the region's wealthiest state. Today, it is the poorest.

Official name Republic of Bolivia
Formation 1825 / 1938
Capital La Paz (administrative); Sucre (judicial)
Population 9.5 million / 23 people per sq mile (9 people per sq km) / 64%
Total area 424,162 sq. miles (1,098,580 sq. km)
Languages Aymara*, Quechua*, Spanish*
Religions Roman Catholic 93%, Other 7%
Ethnic mix Quechua 37%, Aymara 32%, Mixed race 13%, European 10%, Other 8%
Government Presidential system
Currency Boliviano = 100 centavos
Literacy rate 87%
Calorie consumption 2235 calories

BOSNIA & HERZEGOVINA
Southeast Europe

Page 78 B3

At the heart of the western Balkans, Bosnia and Herzegovina was the focus of the bitter conflict surrounding the breakup of the former Yugoslavia.

Official name Bosnia and Herzegovina
Formation 1992 / 1992
Capital Sarajevo
Population 3.9 million / 198 people per sq mile (76 people per sq km) / 45%
Total area 19,741 sq. miles (51,129 sq. km)
Languages Bosnian*, Croatian*, Serbian*
Religions Muslim (mainly Sunni) 40%, Orthodox Christian 31%, Roman Catholic 15%, Other 10%, Protestant 4%
Ethnic mix Bosniak 44%, Serb 31%, Croat 17%, Other 8%
Government Parliamentary system
Currency Marka = 100 pfeninga
Literacy rate 97%
Calorie consumption 2894 calories

BOTSWANA
Southern Africa

Page 56 C3

Once the British protectorate of Bechuanaland, Botswana lies landlocked in southern Africa. Diamonds provide it with a prosperous economy.

Official name Republic of Botswana
Formation 1966 / 1966
Capital Gaborone
Population 1.8 million / 8 people per sq mile (3 people per sq km) / 52%
Total area 231,803 sq. miles (600,370 sq. km)
Languages English*, Setswana, Shona, San, Khoikhoi, isiNdebele
Religions Traditional beliefs 50%, Christian (mainly Protestant) 30%, Other (including Muslim) 20%
Ethnic mix Tswana 98%, Other 2%
Government Presidential system
Currency Pula = 100 thebe
Literacy rate 81%
Calorie consumption 2151 calories

BRAZIL
South America

Page 40 C2

Brazil covers more than half of South America and is the site of the world's largest rain forest. The country has immense natural resources.

Official name Federative Republic of Brazil
Formation 1822 / 1828
Capital Brasília
Population 191 million / 59 people per sq mile (23 people per sq km) / 84%
Total area 3,286,470 sq. miles (8,511,965 sq. km)
Languages Portuguese*, German, Italian, Spanish, Polish, Japanese, Amerindian languages
Religions Roman Catholic 74%, Protestant 15%, Atheist 7%, Other 4%
Ethnic mix White 54%, Mixed race 38%, Black 6%, Other 2%
Government Presidential system
Currency Real = 100 centavos
Literacy rate 89%
Calorie consumption 3049 calories

BRUNEI
Southeast Asia

Page 116 D3

Lying on the northwestern coast of the island of Borneo, Brunei is surrounded and divided in two by the Malaysian state of Sarawak.

Official name Brunei Darussalam
Formation 1984 / 1984
Capital Bandar Seri Begawan
Population 374,577 / 184 people per sq mile (71 people per sq km) / 77%
Total area 2228 sq. miles (5770 sq. km)
Languages Malay*, English, Chinese
Religions Muslim (mainly Sunni) 66%, Buddhist 14%, Other 10%, Christian 10%
Ethnic mix Malay 67%, Chinese 16%, Other 11%, Indigenous 6%
Government Monarchy
Currency Brunei dollar = 100 cents
Literacy rate 93%
Calorie consumption 2855 calories

BULGARIA
Southeast Europe

Page 82 C2

Located in southeastern Europe, Bulgaria has made slow progress toward democracy since the fall of its communist regime in 1990.

Official name Republic of Bulgaria
Formation 1908 / 1947
Capital Sofia
Population 7.6 million / 178 people per sq mile (69 people per sq km) / 70%
Total area 42,822 sq. miles (110,910 sq. km)
Languages Bulgarian*, Turkish, Romani
Religions Orthodox Christian 83%, Muslim 12%, Other 4%, Roman Catholic 1%
Ethnic mix Bulgarian 84%, Turkish 9%, Roma 5%, Other 2%
Government Parliamentary system
Currency Lev = 100 stotinki
Literacy rate 98%
Calorie consumption 2848 calories

BURKINA FASO
West Africa

Page 53 E4

Known as Upper Volta until 1984, the West African state of Burkina Faso has been under military rule for most of its post-independence history.

Official name Burkina Faso
Formation 1960 / 1960
Capital Ouagadougou
Population 14 million / 132 people per sq mile (51 people per sq km) / 18%
Total area 105,869 sq. miles (274,200 sq. km)
Languages French*, Mossi, Fulani, Tuareg, Dyula, Songhai
Religions Muslim 55%, Traditional beliefs 35%, Roman Catholic 9%, Other Christian 1%
Ethnic mix Mossi 48%, Other 21%, Peul 10%, Lobi 7%, Bobo 7%, Mandé 7%
Government Presidential system
Currency CFA franc = 100 centimes
Literacy rate 22%
Calorie consumption 2462 calories

BURUNDI
Central Africa

Page 51 B7

Small, landlocked Burundi lies just south of the Equator, on the Nile-Congo watershed in Central Africa. Since 1993 it has been marked by violent ethnic conflict.

Official name Republic of Burundi
Formation 1962 / 1962
Capital Bujumbura
Population 8.1 million / 818 people per sq mile (316 people per sq km) / 10%
Total area 10,745 sq. miles (27,830 sq. km)
Languages Kirundi*, French*, Kiswahili
Religions Christian (mainly Roman Catholic) 60%, Traditional beliefs 39%, Muslim 1%
Ethnic mix Hutu 85%, Tutsi 14%, Twa 1%
Government Presidential system
Currency Burundian franc = 100 centimes
Literacy rate 59%
Calorie consumption 1649 calories

CAMBODIA
Southeast Asia

Page 115 D5

Located in mainland Southeast Asia, Cambodia has emerged from two decades of civil war and invasion from Vietnam.

Official name Kingdom of Cambodia
Formation 1953 / 1953
Capital Phnom Penh
Population 14.6 million / 214 people per sq mile (83 people per sq km) / 19%
Total area 69,900 sq. miles (181,040 sq. km)
Languages Khmer*, French, Chinese, Vietnamese, Cham
Religions Buddhist 93%, Muslim 6%, Christian 1%
Ethnic mix Khmer 90%, Other 5%, Vietnamese 4%, Chinese 1%
Government Parliamentary system
Currency Riel = 100 sen
Literacy rate 74%
Calorie consumption 2046 calories

CAMEROON
Central Africa

Page 54 A4

Situated on the central West African coast, Cameroon was effectively a one-party state for 30 years. Multiparty elections were held in 1992.

Official name Republic of Cameroon
Formation 1960 / 1961
Capital Yaoundé
Population 16.3 million / 94 people per sq mile (36 people per sq km) / 52%
Total area 183,567 sq. miles (475,400 sq. km)
Languages English*, French*, Bamileke, Fang, Fulani
Religions Roman Catholic 35%, Traditional beliefs 25%, Muslim 22%, Protestant 18%
Ethnic mix Cameroon highlanders 31%, Other 21%, Equatorial Bantu 19%, Kirdi 11%, Fulani 10%, Northwestern Bantu 8%
Government Presidential system
Currency CFA franc = 100 centimes
Literacy rate 68%
Calorie consumption 2273 calories

CANADA
North America

Page 15 E4

Canada extends from its US border north to the Arctic Ocean. In recent years, French-speaking Quebec has sought independence from the rest of the country.

Official name Canada
Formation 1867 / 1949
Capital Ottawa
Population 32.9 million / 9 people per sq mile (4 people per sq km) / 81%
Total area 3,854,085 sq. miles (9,984,670 sq. km)
Languages English*, French*, Chinese, Italian, German, Ukrainian, Portuguese, Inuktitut, Cree
Religions Roman Catholic 44%, Protestant 29%, Other and nonreligious 27%
Government Parliamentary system
Currency Canadian dollar = 100 cents
Literacy rate 99%
Calorie consumption 3589 calories

CAPE VERDE
Atlantic Ocean

Page 52 A2

Off the west coast of Africa, in the Atlantic Ocean, lies the group of islands that make up Cape Verde, a Portuguese colony until 1975.

Official name Republic of Cape Verde
Formation 1975 / 1975
Capital Praia
Population 423,613 / 272 people per sq mile (105 people per sq km) / 57%
Total area 1557 sq. miles (4033 sq. km)
Languages Portuguese*, Portuguese Creole
Religions Roman Catholic 97%, Other 2%, Protestant (Church of the Nazarene) 1%
Ethnic mix Mestiço 60%, African 30%, Other 10%
Government Mixed presidential–parliamentary system
Currency Cape Verde escudo = 100 centavos
Literacy rate 76%
Calorie consumption 3243 calories

CENTRAL AFRICAN REPUBLIC
Central Africa

Page 54 C4

This landlocked country lies between the basins of the Chad and Congo rivers. Its arid north sustains less than 2% of the population.

Official name Central African Republic
Formation 1960 / 1960
Capital Bangui
Population 4.2 million / 17 people per sq mile (7 people per sq km) / 43%
Total area 240,534 sq. miles (622,984 sq. km)
Languages French*, Sango, Banda, Gbaya
Religions Traditional beliefs 60%, Christian (mainly Roman Catholic) 35%, Muslim 5%
Ethnic mix Baya 34%, Banda 27%, Mandjia 21%, Sara 10%, Other 8%
Government Presidential system
Currency CFA franc = 100 centimes
Literacy rate 49%
Calorie consumption 1980 calories

CHAD
Central Africa

Page 54 C3

Landlocked in north central Africa, Chad has been torn by intermittent periods of civil war since it gained independence from France in 1960.

Official name Republic of Chad
Formation 1960 / 1960
Capital N'Djamena
Population 10.3 million / 21 people per sq mile (8 people per sq km) / 25%
Total area 495,752 sq. miles (1,284,000 sq. km)
Languages Arabic*, French*, Sara, Maba
Religions Muslim 55%, Traditional beliefs 35%, Christian 10%
Ethnic mix Other 30%, Sara 28%, Mayo-Kebbi 12%, Arab 12%, Ouaddai 9%, Kanem-Bornou 9%
Government Presidential system
Currency CFA franc = 100 centimes
Literacy rate 26%
Calorie consumption 2114 calories

CHILE
South America

Page 42 B3

Chile extends in a ribbon down the west coast of South America. It returned to democracy in 1989 after a referendum rejected its military dictator.

Official name Republic of Chile
Formation 1818 / 1883
Capital Santiago
Population 16.6 million / 57 people per sq mile (22 people per sq km) / 87%
Total area 292,258 sq. miles (756,950 sq. km)
Languages Spanish*, Amerindian languages
Religions Roman Catholic 80%, Other and nonreligious 20%
Ethnic mix Mixed race and European 90%, Other Amerindian 9%, Mapuche 1%
Government Presidential system
Currency Chilean peso = 100 centavos
Literacy rate 96%
Calorie consumption 2863 calories

CHINA
East Asia

Page 104 C4

This vast East Asian country was dominated by Mao Zedong for almost 30 years, but since the 1980's it has emerged as one of the world's major political and economic powers.

Official name People's Republic of China
Formation 960 / 1999
Capital Beijing
Population 1.33 billion / 370 people per sq mile (143 people per sq km) / 40%
Total area 3,705,386 sq. miles (9,596,960 sq. km)
Languages Mandarin*, Wu, Cantonese, Hsiang, Min, Hakka, Kan
Religions Nonreligious 59%, Traditional beliefs 20%, Other 13%, Buddhist 6%, Muslim 2%
Ethnic mix Han 92%, Other 4%, Hui 1%, Miao 1%, Manchu 1%, Zhuang 1%
Government One-party state
Currency Renminbi (known as yuan) = 10 jiao = 100 fen
Literacy rate 91%
Calorie consumption 2951 calories

COLOMBIA
South America

Page 36 B3

Lying in northwest South America, Colombia is one of the world's most violent countries, with powerful drugs cartels and guerrilla activity.

Official name Republic of Colombia
Formation 1819 / 1903
Capital Bogotá
Population 47 million / 117 people per sq mile (45 people per sq km) / 77%
Total area 439,733 sq. miles (1,138,910 sq. km)
Languages Spanish*, Wayuu, Páez, and other Amerindian languages
Religions Roman Catholic 95%, Other 5%
Ethnic mix Mestizo 58%, White 20%, European–African 14%, African 4%, African–Amerindian 3%, Amerindian 1%
Government Presidential system
Currency Colombian peso = 100 centavos
Literacy rate 93%
Calorie consumption 2585 calories

COMOROS
Indian Ocean

Page 57 F2

In the Indian Ocean, between Mozambique and Madagascar, lie the Comoros, comprising three main islands, and a number of smaller islets.

Official name Union of the Comoros
Formation 1975 / 1975
Capital Moroni
Population 711,417 / 826 people per sq mile (319 people per sq km) / 36%
Total area 838 sq. miles (2170 sq. km)
Languages Arabic*, Comoran*, French*
Religions Muslim (mainly Sunni) 98%, Other 1%, Roman Catholic 1%
Ethnic mix Comoran 97%, Other 3%
Government Presidential system
Currency Comoros franc = 100 centimes
Literacy rate 56%
Calorie consumption 1754 calories

CONGO
Central Africa

Page 55 B5

Astride the Equator in west central Africa, this former French colony emerged from 26 years of Marxist-Leninist rule in 1990.

Official name Republic of the Congo
Formation 1960 / 1960
Capital Brazzaville
Population 4.2 million / 32 people per sq mile (12 people per sq km) / 54%
Total area 132,046 sq. miles (342,000 sq. km)
Languages French*, Kongo, Teke, Lingala
Religions Traditional beliefs 50%, Roman Catholic 25%, Protestant 23%, Muslim 2%
Ethnic mix Bakongo 51%, Teke 17%, Other 16%, Mbochi 11%, Mbédé 5%
Government Presidential system
Currency CFA franc = 100 centimes
Literacy rate 83%
Calorie consumption 2162 calories

CONGO, DEM. REP.
Central Africa

Page 55 C6

Straddling the Equator in east central Africa, Dem. Rep. Congo is one of Africa's largest countries. It achieved independence from Belgium in 1960.

Official name Democratic Republic of the Congo
Formation 1960 / 1960
Capital Kinshasa
Population 61.2 million / 70 people per sq mile (27 people per sq km) / 33%
Total area 905,563 sq. miles (2,345,410 sq. km)
Languages French*, Kiswahili, Tshiluba, Kikongo, Lingala
Religions Roman Catholic 50%, Protestant 20%, Traditional beliefs and other 20%, Muslim 10%
Ethnic mix Other 55%, Mongo, Luba, Kongo, and Mangbetu-Azande 45%
Government Presidential system
Currency Congolese franc = 100 centimes
Literacy rate 67%
Calorie consumption 1599 calories

COSTA RICA
Central America

Page 31 E4

Costa Rica is the most stable country in Central America. Its neutrality in foreign affairs is long-standing, but it has very strong ties with the US.

Official name Republic of Costa Rica
Formation 1838 / 1838
Capital San José
Population 4.5 million / 228 people per sq mile (88 people per sq km) / 61%
Total area 19,730 sq. miles (51,100 sq. km)
Languages Spanish*, English Creole, Bribri, Cabecar
Religions Roman Catholic 76%, Other (including Protestant) 24%
Ethnic mix Mestizo and European 96%, Black 2%, Chinese 1%, Amerindian 1%
Government Presidential system
Currency Costa Rican colón = 100 céntimos
Literacy rate 95%
Calorie consumption 2876 calories

CÔTE D'IVOIRE
West Africa

Page 52 D4

One of the larger nations along the coast of West Africa, Côte d'Ivoire remains under the influence of its former colonial ruler, France.

Official name Republic of Côte d'Ivoire
Formation 1960 / 1960
Capital Yamoussoukro
Population 18.8 million / 153 people per sq mile (59 people per sq km) / 45%
Total area 124,502 sq. miles (322,460 sq. km)
Languages Akan, French*, Krou, Voltaique
Religions Muslim 38%, Traditional beliefs 25%, Roman Catholic 25%, Other 6%, Protestant 6%
Ethnic mix Akan 42%, Voltaique 18%, Mandé du Nord 17%, Krou 11%, Mandé du Sud 10%, Other 2%
Government Presidential system
Currency CFA franc = 100 centimes
Literacy rate 49%
Calorie consumption 2631 calories

CROATIA
Southeast Europe

Page 78 B2

Post-independence fighting in this former Yugoslav republic initially thwarted plans to capitalize on its location along the eastern Adriatic coast. A return to stability has resolved this situation.

Official name Republic of Croatia
Formation 1991 / 1991
Capital Zagreb
Population 4.6 million / 211 people per sq mile (81 people per sq km) / 59%
Total area 21,831 sq. miles (56,542 sq. km)
Languages Croatian*
Religions Roman Catholic 88%, Other 7%, Orthodox Christian 4%, Muslim 1%
Ethnic mix Croat 90%, Other 5%, Serb 5%
Government Parliamentary system
Currency Kuna = 100 lipa
Literacy rate 98%
Calorie consumption 2799 calories

CUBA
West Indies

Page 32 C2

Cuba is the largest island in the Caribbean and the only communist country in the Americas. It was led by Fidel Castro for almost 40 years until he stepped down in 2008.

Official name Republic of Cuba
Formation 1902 / 1902
Capital Havana
Population 11.3 million / 264 people per sq mile (102 people per sq km) / 76%
Total area 42,803 sq. miles (110,860 sq. km)
Languages Spanish
Religions Nonreligious 49%, Roman Catholic 40%, Atheist 6%, Other 4%, Protestant 1%
Ethnic mix White 66%, European–African 22%, Black 12%
Government One-party state
Currency Cuban peso = 100 centavos
Literacy rate 99%
Calorie consumption 3152 calories

CYPRUS
Southeast Europe

Page 80 C5

Cyprus lies in the eastern Mediterranean. Since 1974, it has been partitioned between the Turkish-occupied north and the Greek south (which joined the EU in 2004).

Official name Republic of Cyprus
Formation 1960 / 1960
Capital Nicosia
Population 788,457 / 221 people per sq mile (85 people per sq km) / 69%
Total area 3571 sq. miles (9250 sq. km)
Languages Greek*, Turkish*
Religions Orthodox Christian 78%, Muslim 18%, Other 4%
Ethnic mix Greek 81%, Turkish 11%, Other 8%
Government Presidential system
Currency Euro (Turkish lira in TRNC) = 100 cents (euro); 100 kurus (Turkish lira)
Literacy rate 97%
Calorie consumption 3255 calories

CZECH REPUBLIC
Central Europe

Page 77 A5

Once part of Czechoslovakia in eastern Europe, it became independent in 1993, after peacefully dissolving its federal union with Slovakia.

Official name Czech Republic
Formation 1993 / 1993
Capital Prague
Population 10.2 million / 335 people per sq mile (129 people per sq km) / 74%
Total area 30,450 sq. miles (78,866 sq. km)
Languages Czech*, Slovak, Hungarian (Magyar)
Religions Roman Catholic 39%, Atheist 38%, Other 18%, Protestant 3%, Hussite 2%
Ethnic mix Czech 90%, Other 4%, Moravian 4%, Slovak 2%
Government Parliamentary system
Currency Czech koruna = 100 haleru
Literacy rate 99%
Calorie consumption 3171 calories

DENMARK
Northern Europe

Page 63 A7

The country occupies the Jutland peninsula and over 400 islands in Scandinavia. Greenland and the Faeroe Islands are self-governing associated territories.

Official name Kingdom of Denmark
Formation 950 / 1944
Capital Copenhagen
Population 5.5 million / 336 people per sq mile (130 people per sq km) / 85%
Total area 16,639 sq. miles (43,094 sq. km)
Languages Danish
Religions Evangelical Lutheran 89%, Other 10%, Roman Catholic 1%
Ethnic mix Danish 96%, Other (including Scandinavian and Turkish) 3%, Faeroese and Inuit 1%
Government Parliamentary system
Currency Danish krone = 100 øre
Literacy rate 99%
Calorie consumption 3439 calories

DJIBOUTI
East Africa

Page 50 D4

A city state with a desert hinterland, Djibouti lies in northeast Africa. Once known as French Somaliland, its economy relies on its port.

Official name Republic of Djibouti
Formation 1977 / 1977
Capital Djibouti
Population 496,374 / 55 people per sq mile (21 people per sq km) / 84%
Total area 8494 sq. miles (22,000 sq. km)
Languages Arabic*, French*, Somali, Afar
Religions Muslim (mainly Sunni) 94%, Christian 6%
Ethnic mix Issa 60%, Afar 35%, Other 5%
Government Presidential system
Currency Djibouti franc = 100 centimes
Literacy rate 66%
Calorie consumption 2220 calories

DOMINICA
West Indies

Page 33 H4

The Caribbean island Dominica resisted European colonization until the 18th century, when it first came under the French, and then, the British

Official name Commonwealth of Dominica
Formation 1978 / 1978
Capital Roseau
Population 72,386 / 250 people per sq mile (97 people per sq km) / 72%
Total area 291 sq. miles (754 sq. km)
Languages English*, French Creole
Religions Roman Catholic 77%, Protestant 15%, Other 8%
Ethnic mix Black 87%, Mixed race 9%, Carib 3%, Other 1%
Government Parliamentary system
Currency Eastern Caribbean dollar = 100 cents
Literacy rate 88%
Calorie consumption 2763 calories

DOMINICAN REPUBLIC
West Indies

Page 33 E2

The republic occupies the eastern two-thirds of the island of Hispaniola in the Caribbean. Frequent coups and a strong US influence mark its recent past.

Official name Dominican Republic
Formation 1865 / 1865
Capital Santo Domingo
Population 9.1 million / 487 people per sq mile (188 people per sq km) / 60%
Total area 18,679 sq. miles (48,380 sq. km)
Languages Spanish*, French Creole
Religions Roman Catholic 92%, Other and nonreligious 8%
Ethnic mix Mixed race 75%, White 15%, Black 10%
Government Presidential system
Currency Dominican Republic peso = 100 centavos
Literacy rate 87%
Calorie consumption 2347 calories

EAST TIMOR
Southeast Asia

Page 116 F5

This new nation occupies the eastern half of the island of Timor. Invaded by Indonesiain 1975, it declared independence in 1999.

Official name Democratic Republic of Timor-Leste
Formation 2002 / 2002
Capital Dili
Population 1.1 million / 192 people per sq mile (74 people per sq km) / 8%
Total area 5756 sq. miles (14,874 sq. km)
Languages Tetum (Portuguese/Austronesian)*, Bahasa Indonesia, and Portuguese*
Religions Roman Catholic 95%, Other (including Muslim and Protestant) 5%
Government Parliamentary system
Currency US dollar = 100 cents
Literacy rate 59%
Calorie consumption 2806 calories

ECUADOR
South America

Page 38 A2

Ecuador sits high on South America's western coast. Once part of the Inca heartland, its territory includes the Galapagos Islands, to the west.

Official name Republic of Ecuador
Formation 1830 / 1942
Capital Quito
Population 13.6 million / 127 people per sq mile (49 people per sq km) / 62%
Total area 109,483 sq. miles (283,560 sq. km)
Languages Spanish*, Quechua, other Amerindian languages
Religions Roman Catholic 93%, Protestant, Jewish, and other 7%
Ethnic mix Mestizo 55%, Amerindian 25%, White 10%, Black 10%
Government Presidential system
Currency US dollar = 100 cents
Literacy rate 91%
Calorie consumption 2754 calories

EGYPT
North Africa

Page 50 B2

Egypt occupies the northeast corner of Africa. Its essentially pro-Western, military-backed regime is being challenged by Islamic fundamentalists.

Official name Arab Republic of Egypt
Formation 1936 / 1982
Capital Cairo
Population 76.9 million / 200 people per sq mile (77 people per sq km) / 42%
Total area 386,660 sq. miles (1,001,450 sq. km)
Languages Arabic*, French, English, Berber
Religions Muslim (mainly Sunni) 94%, Coptic Christian and other 6%
Ethnic mix Egyptian 99%, Nubian, Armenian, Greek, and Berber 1%
Government Presidential system
Currency Egyptian pound = 100 piastres
Literacy rate 71%
Calorie consumption 3338 calories

EL SALVADOR
Central America

Page 30 B3

El Salvador is Central America's smallest state. A 12-year war between US-backed government troops and left-wing guerrillas ended in 1992.

Official name Republic of El Salvador
Formation 1841 / 1841
Capital San Salvador
Population 7.1 million / 888 people per sq mile (343 people per sq km) / 60%
Total area 8124 sq. miles (21,040 sq. km)
Languages Spanish
Religions Roman Catholic 80%, Evangelical 18%, Other 2%
Ethnic mix Mestizo 94%, Amerindian 5%, White 1%
Government Presidential system
Currency Salvadorean colón & US dollar = 100 centavos (colón); 100 cents (US dollar)
Literacy rate 80%
Calorie consumption 2584 calories

EQUATORIAL GUINEA
Central Africa

Page 55 A5

The country comprises the Rio Muni mainland and five islands on the west coast of central Africa. Free elections were first held in 1988.

Official name Republic of Equatorial Guinea
Formation 1968 / 1968
Capital Malabo
Population 551,201 / 51 people per sq mile (20 people per sq km) / 49%
Total area 10,830 sq. miles (28,051 sq. km)
Languages French*, Spanish*, Fang, Bubi
Religions Roman Catholic 90%, Other 10%
Ethnic mix Fang 85%, Other 11%, Bubi 4%
Government Presidential system
Currency CFA franc = 100 centimes
Literacy rate 87%
Calorie consumption Not available

ERITREA
East Africa

Page 50 C3

Lying on the shores of the Red Sea, Eritrea effectively seceded from Ethiopia in 1993, following a 30-year war for independence.

Official name State of Eritrea
Formation 1993 / 2002
Capital Asmera
Population 4.7 million / 104 people per sq mile (40 people per sq km) / 20%
Total area 46,842 sq. miles (121,320 sq. km)
Languages Tigrinya*, English*, Tigre, Afar, Arabic*, Bilen, Kunama, Nara, Saho, Hadareb
Religions Christian 45%, Muslim 45%, Other 10%
Ethnic mix Tigray 50%, Tigray and Kunama 40%, Afar 4%, Other 3%, Saho 3%
Government Transitional regime
Currency Nakfa = 100 cents
Literacy rate 57%
Calorie consumption 1513 calories

ESTONIA
Northeast Europe

Page 84 D2

Estonia is the smallest and most developed of the three Baltic states. It has the highest standard of living of any of the former Soviet republics.

Official name Republic of Estonia
Formation 1991 / 1991
Capital Tallinn
Population 1.3 million / 75 people per sq mile (29 people per sq km) / 70%
Total area 17,462 sq. miles (45,226 sq. km)
Languages Estonian*, Russian
Religions Evangelical Lutheran 56%, Orthodox Christian 25%, Other 19%
Ethnic mix Estonian 68%, Russian 26%, Other 4%, Ukrainian 2%
Government Parliamentary system
Currency Kroon = 100 senti
Literacy rate 99%
Calorie consumption 3002 calories

ETHIOPIA
East Africa

Page 51 C5

Located in northeast Africa, Ethiopia was a Marxist regime from 1974–91. It has suffered a series of economic, civil, and natural crises.

Official name Federal Democratic Republic of Ethiopia
Formation 1896 / 2002
Capital Addis Ababa
Population 81.2 million / 189 people per sq mile (73 people per sq km) / 16%
Total area 435,184 sq. miles (1,127,127 sq. km)
Languages Amharic*, Tigrinya, Galla, Sidamo, Somali, English, Arabic
Religions Orthodox Christian 40%, Muslim 40%, Traditional beliefs 15%, Other 5%
Ethnic mix Oromo 32%, Amhara 30%, Other 38%
Government Parliamentary system
Currency Ethiopian birr = 100 cents
Literacy rate 42%
Calorie consumption 1857 calories

FIJI
Australasia & Oceania

Page 123 E5

A volcanic archipelago, Fiji comprises 882 islands in the southern Pacific Ocean. Ethnic Fijians and Indo-Fijians have been in conflict since 1987.

Official name Republic of the Fiji Islands
Formation 1970 / 1970
Capital Suva
Population 918,675 / 130 people per sq mile (50 people per sq km) / 52%
Total area 7054 sq. miles (18,270 sq. km)
Languages Fijian, English*, Hindi, Urdu, Tamil, Telugu
Religions Hindu 38%, Methodist 37%, Roman Catholic 9%, Other 8%, Muslim 8%
Ethnic mix Melanesian 51%, Indian 44%, Other 5%
Government Transitional regime
Currency Fiji dollar = 100 cents
Literacy rate 93%
Calorie consumption 2894 calories

FINLAND
Northern Europe

Page 62 D4

Finland's distinctive language and national identity have been influenced by both its Scandinavian and its Russian neighbors.

Official name Republic of Finland
Formation 1917 / 1947
Capital Helsinki
Population 5.3 million / 45 people per sq mile (17 people per sq km) / 61%
Total area 130,127 sq. miles (337,030 sq. km)
Languages Finnish*, Swedish*, Sámi
Religions Evangelical Lutheran 89%, Other 9%, Orthodox Christian 1%, Roman Catholic 1%
Ethnic mix Finnish 93%, Other (including Sámi) 7%
Government Parliamentary system
Currency Euro = 100 cents
Literacy rate 99%
Calorie consumption 3100 calories

FRANCE
Western Europe

Page 68 B4

Straddling Western Europe from the English Channel to the Mediterranean Sea, France, is one of the world's leading industrial powers.

Official name French Republic
Formation 987 / 1919
Capital Paris
Population 60.9 million / 287 people per sq mile (111 people per sq km) / 76%
Total area 211,208 sq. miles (547,030 sq. km)
Languages French*, Provençal, German, Breton, Catalan, Basque
Religions Roman Catholic 88%, Muslim 8%, Protestant 2%, Buddhist 1%, Jewish 1%
Ethnic mix French 90%, North African (mainly Algerian) 6%, German (Alsace) 2%, Other 2%
Government Mixed presidential–parliamentary system
Currency Euro = 100 cents
Literacy rate 99%
Calorie consumption 3654 calories

GABON
Central Africa

Page 55 A5

A former French colony straddling the Equator on Africa's west coast, it returned to multiparty politics in 1990, after 22 years of one-party rule.

Official name Gabonese Republic
Formation 1960 / 1960
Capital Libreville
Population 1.4 million / 14 people per sq mile (5 people per sq km) / 84%
Total area 103,346 sq. miles (267,667 sq. km)
Languages Fang, French*, Punu, Sira, Nzebi, Mpongwe
Religions Christian (mainly Roman Catholic) 55%, Traditional beliefs 40%, Other 4%, Muslim 1%
Ethnic mix Fang 26%, Shira-punu 24%, Other 16%, Foreign residents 15%, Nzabi-duma 11%, Mbédé-Teke 8%
Government Presidential system
Currency CFA franc = 100 centimes
Literacy rate 71%
Calorie consumption 2637 calories

GAMBIA
West Africa

Page 52 B3

A narrow state on the west coast of Africa, Gambia was renowned for its stability until its government was overthrown in a coup in 1994.

Official name Republic of the Gambia
Formation 1965 / 1965
Capital Banjul
Population 1.6 million / 414 people per sq mile (160 people per sq km) / 26%
Total area 4363 sq. miles (11,300 sq. km)
Languages English*, Mandinka, Fulani, Wolof, Jola, Soninke
Religions Sunni Muslim 90%, Christian 9%, Traditional beliefs 1%
Ethnic mix Mandinka 40%, Fulani 19%, Wolof 15%, Jola 11%, Serahuli 9%, Other 6%
Government Presidential system
Currency Dalasi = 100 butut
Literacy rate 38%
Calorie consumption 2273 calories

GEORGIA
Southwest Asia

Page 95 F2

Located on the eastern shore of the Black Sea, Georgia's northern provinces have been torn by civil war since independence from the USSR in 1991.

Official name Georgia
Formation 1991 / 1991
Capital Tbilisi
Population 4.4 million / 164 people per sq mile (63 people per sq km) / 52%
Total area 26,911 sq. miles (69,700 sq. km)
Languages Georgian*, Russian, Azeri, Armenian, Mingrelian, Ossetian, Abkhazian* (in Abkhazia)
Religions Georgian Orthodox 65%, Muslim 11%, Russian Orthodox 10%, Other 14%
Ethnic mix Georgian 84%, Armenian 6%, Azeri 6%, Russian 2%, Other 1%, Ossetian 1%
Government Presidential system
Currency Lari = 100 tetri
Literacy rate 99%
Calorie consumption 2354 calories

GERMANY
Northern Europe

Page 72 B4

Europe's strongest economic power, Germany's democratic west and Communist east were re-unified in 1990, after the fall of the east's regime.

Official name Federal Republic of Germany
Formation 1871 / 1990
Capital Berlin
Population 82.7 million / 613 people per sq mile (237 people per sq km) / 88%
Total area 137,846 sq. miles (357,021 sq. km)
Languages German*, Turkish
Religions Protestant 34%, Roman Catholic 33%, Other 30%, Muslim 3%
Ethnic mix German 92%, Other European 3%, Other 3%, Turkish 2%
Government Parliamentary system
Currency Euro = 100 cents
Literacy rate 99%
Calorie consumption 3496 calories

GHANA
West Africa

Page 53 E5

Once known as the Gold Coast, Ghana in West Africa has experienced intermittent periods of military rule since independence in 1957.

Official name Republic of Ghana
Formation 1957 / 1957
Capital Accra
Population 23 million / 259 people per sq mile (100 people per sq km) / 46%
Total area 92,100 sq. miles (238,540 sq. km)
Languages English*, Twi, Fanti, Ewe, Ga, Adangbe, Gurma, Dagomba (Dagbani)
Religions Christian 69%, Muslim 16%, Traditional beliefs 9%, Other 6%
Ethnic mix Akan 49%, Mole-Dagbani 17%, Ewe 13%, Other 9%, Ga and Ga-Adangbe 8%, Guan 4%
Government Presidential system
Currency Cedi = 100 pesewas
Literacy rate 58%
Calorie consumption 2667 calories

GREECE
Southeast Europe

Page 83 A5

Greece is the southernmost Balkan nation. Surrounded by the Mediterranean, Aegean, and Ionian Seas, it has a strong seafaring tradition.

Official name Hellenic Republic
Formation 1829 / 1947
Capital Athens
Population 11.2 million / 222 people per sq mile (86 people per sq km) / 61%
Total area 50,942 sq. miles (131,940 sq. km)
Languages Greek*, Turkish, Macedonian, Albanian
Religions Orthodox Christian 98%, Other 1%, Muslim 1%
Ethnic mix Greek 98%, Other 2%
Government Parliamentary system
Currency Euro = 100 cents
Literacy rate 96%
Calorie consumption 3721 calories

GRENADA
West Indies

Page 33 G5

The Windward island of Grenada became a focus of attention in 1983, when the US mounted an invasion to sever its growing links with Cuba.

Official name Grenada
Formation 1974 / 1974
Capital St. George's
Population 89,971 / 687 people per sq mile (265 people per sq km) / 41%
Total area 131 sq. miles (340 sq. km)
Languages English*, English Creole
Religions Roman Catholic 68%, Anglican 17%, Other 15%
Ethnic mix Black African 82%, Mulatto (mixed race) 13%, East Indian 3%, Other 2%
Government Parliamentary system
Currency Eastern Caribbean dollar = 100 cents
Literacy rate 96%
Calorie consumption 2932 calories

GUATEMALA
Central America

Page 30 A2

The largest state on the Central American isthmus, Guatemala returned to civilian rule in 1986, after 32 years of repressive military rule.

Official name Republic of Guatemala
Formation 1838 / 1838
Capital Guatemala City
Population 13.2 million / 315 people per sq mile (122 people per sq km) / 47%
Total area 42,042 sq. miles (108,890 sq. km)
Languages Spanish*, Quiché, Mam, Cakchiquel, Kekchí
Religions Roman Catholic 65%, Protestant 33%, Other and nonreligious 2%
Ethnic mix Amerindian 60%, Mestizo 30%, Other 10%
Government Presidential system
Currency Quetzal = 100 centavos
Literacy rate 69%
Calorie consumption 2219 calories

GUINEA
West Africa

Page 52 C4

Facing the Atlantic Ocean, on the west coast of Africa, Guinea became the first French colony in Africa to gain independence, in 1958.

Official name Republic of Guinea
Formation 1958 / 1958
Capital Conakry
Population 9.8 million / 103 people per sq mile (40 people per sq km) / 36%
Total area 94,925 sq. miles (245,857 sq. km)
Languages French*, Pulaar, Malinke, Soussou
Religions Muslim 65%, Traditional beliefs 33%, Christian 2%
Ethnic mix Peul 39%, Malinké 23%, Other 16%, Soussou 11%, Kissi 6%, Kpellé 5%
Government Presidential system
Currency Guinea franc = 100 centimes
Literacy rate 30%
Calorie consumption 2409 calories

GUINEA-BISSAU
West Africa

Page 52 B4

Known as Portuguese Guinea during its days as a colony, Guinea-Bissau is situated on Africa's west coast, bordered by Senegal and Guinea.

Official name Republic of Guinea-Bissau
Formation 1974 / 1974
Capital Bissau
Population 1.7 million / 157 people per sq mile (60 people per sq km) / 35%
Total area 13,946 sq. miles (36,120 sq. km)
Languages Portuguese*, Portuguese Creole, Balante, Fulani, Malinke
Religions Traditional beliefs 52%, Muslim 40%, Christian 8%
Ethnic mix Balante 30%, Fulani 20%, Other 17%, Mandyako 14%, Mandinka 12%, Papel 7%
Government Presidential system
Currency CFA franc = 100 centimes
Literacy rate 40%
Calorie consumption 2024 calories

GUYANA
South America

Page 37 F3

The only English-speaking country in South America, Guyana gained independence from Britain in 1966, and became a republic in 1970.

Official name The Co-operative Republic of Guyana
Formation 1966 / 1966
Capital Georgetown
Population 769,095 / 10 people per sq mile (4 people per sq km) / 38%
Total area 83,000 sq. miles (214,970 sq. km)
Languages English*, English Creole, Hindi, Tamil, Amerindian languages
Religions Christian 57%, Hindu 33%, Muslim 9%, Other 1%
Ethnic mix East Indian 43%, Black African 30%, Mixed race 17%, Amerindian 9%, Other 1%
Government Presidential system
Currency Guyanese dollar = 100 cents
Literacy rate 97%
Calorie consumption 2692 calories

HAITI
West Indies

Page 32 D3

Haiti shares the Caribbean island of Hispaniola with the Dominican Republic. At independence, in 1804, it became the world's first Black republic.

Official name Republic of Haiti
Formation 1804 / 1844
Capital Port-au-Prince
Population 8.8 million / 827 people per sq mile (319 people per sq km) / 38%
Total area 10,714 sq. miles (27,750 sq. km)
Languages French*, French Creole*
Religions Roman Catholic 80%, Protestant 16%, Other (including Voodoo) 3%, Nonreligious 1%
Ethnic mix Black African 95%, Mulatto (mixed race) and European 5%
Government Presidential system
Currency Gourde = 100 centimes
Literacy rate 52%
Calorie consumption 2086 calories

HONDURAS
Central America

Page 30 C2

Honduras straddles the Central American isthmus. The country returned to full democratic civilian rule in 1984, after a succession of military regimes.

Official name Republic of Honduras
Formation 1838 / 1838
Capital Tegucigalpa
Population 7.5 million / 174 people per sq mile (67 people per sq km) / 46%
Total area 43,278 sq. miles (112,090 sq. km)
Languages Spanish*, Garífuna (Carib), English Creole
Religions Roman Catholic 97%, Protestant 3%
Ethnic mix Mestizo 90%, Black African 5%, Amerindian 4%, White 1%
Government Presidential system
Currency Lempira = 100 centavos
Literacy rate 80%
Calorie consumption 2356 calories

HUNGARY
Central Europe

Page 77 C6

Hungary is bordered by seven states in Central Europe. It has changed its economic and political policies to develop closer ties with the EU.

Official name Republic of Hungary
Formation 1918 / 1947
Capital Budapest
Population 10 million / 280 people per sq mile (108 people per sq km) / 66%
Total area 35,919 sq. miles (93,030 sq. km)
Languages Hungarian (Magyar)*
Religions Roman Catholic 52%, Calvinist 16%, Other 15%, Nonreligious 14%, Lutheran 3%
Ethnic mix Magyar 94%, Other 5%, Roma 1%
Government Parliamentary system
Currency Forint = 100 fillér
Literacy rate 99%
Calorie consumption 3483 calories

ICELAND
Northwest Europe

Page 61 E4

Europe's westernmost country, Iceland lies in the North Atlantic, straddling the mid-Atlantic ridge. Its spectacular, volcanic landscape is largely uninhabited.

Official name Republic of Iceland
Formation 1944 / 1944
Capital Reykjavík
Population 301,931 / 8 people per sq mile (3 people per sq km) / 93%
Total area 39,768 sq. miles (103,000 sq. km)
Languages Icelandic*
Religions Evangelical Lutheran 93%, Nonreligious 6%, Other (mostly Christian) 1%
Ethnic mix Icelandic 94%, Other 5%, Danish 1%
Government Parliamentary system
Currency Icelandic króna = 100 aurar
Literacy rate 99%
Calorie consumption 3249 calories

INDIA
South Asia

Page 112 D4

Separated from the rest of Asia by the Himalayan mountain ranges, India forms a subcontinent. It is the world's second most populous country.

Official name Republic of India
Formation 1947 / 1947
Capital New Delhi
Population 1.14 billion / 989 people per sq mile (382 people per sq km) / 29%
Total area 1,269,338 sq. miles (3,287,590 sq. km)
Languages Hindi*, English*, Urdu, Bengali, Marathi, Telugu, Tamil, Bihari, Gujarati, Kanarese
Religions Hindu 81%, Muslim 13%, Christian 2%, Sikh 2%, Other 1%, Buddhist 1%
Ethnic mix Indo-Aryan 72%, Dravidian 25%, Mongoloid and other 3%
Government Parliamentary system
Currency Indian rupee = 100 paise
Literacy rate 61%
Calorie consumption 2459 calories

INDONESIA
Southeast Asia

Page 116 C4

Formerly the Dutch East Indies, Indonesia, the world's largest archipelago, stretches over 5,000 km (3,100 miles), from the Indian Ocean to the Pacific Ocean.

Official name Republic of Indonesia
Formation 1949 / 1999
Capital Jakarta
Population 228 million / 329 people per sq mile (127 people per sq km) / 47%
Total area 741,096 sq. miles (1,919,440 sq. km)
Languages Bahasa Indonesia*, Javanese, Sundanese, Madurese, Dutch
Religions Sunni Muslim 87%, Protestant 6%, Roman Catholic 3%, Hindu 2%, Other 1%, Buddhist 1%
Ethnic mix Javanese 42%, Sundanese 15%, Coastal Malays 12%, Madurese 3%, Other 28%
Government Presidential system
Currency Rupiah = 100 sen
Literacy rate 90%
Calorie consumption 2904 calories

IRAN
Southwest Asia

Page 98 B3

Since the 1979 revolution led by Ayatollah Khomeini, which sent Iran's Shah into exile, this Middle Eastern country has become the world's largest theocracy.

Official name Islamic Republic of Iran
Formation 1502 / 1990
Capital Tehran
Population 71.2 million / 113 people per sq mile (44 people per sq km) / 67%
Total area 636,293 sq. miles (1,648,000 sq. km)
Languages Farsi*, Azeri, Luri, Gilaki, Kurdish, Mazanderani, Turkmen, Arabic, Baluchi
Religions Shi'a Muslim 93%, Sunni Muslim 6%, Other 1%
Ethnic mix Persian 50%, Azari 24%, Other 10%, Kurdish 8%, Lur and Bakhtiari 8%
Government Islamic theocracy
Currency Iranian rial = 100 dinars
Literacy rate 77%
Calorie consumption 3085 calories

IRAQ
Southwest Asia

Page 98 B3

Oil-rich Iraq is situated in the central Middle East. A US-led invasion in 2003 toppled the regime of Saddam Hussein, prompting an insurgency that led to huge political and social turmoil.

Official name Republic of Iraq
Formation 1932 / 1990
Capital Baghdad
Population 30.3 million / 179 people per sq mile (69 people per sq km) / 67%
Total area 168,753 sq. miles (437,072 sq. km)
Languages Arabic*, Kurdish*, Turkic languages, Armenian, Assyrian
Religions Shi'a Muslim 60%, Sunni Muslim 35%, Other (including Christian) 5%
Ethnic mix Arab 80%, Kurdish 15%, Turkmen 3%, Other 2%
Government Parliamentary system
Currency New Iraqi dinar = 1000 fils
Literacy rate 74%
Calorie consumption 2197 calories

IRELAND
Northwest Europe

Page 67 A6

The Republic of Ireland occupies about 85% of the island of Ireland, with the remainder (Northern Ireland) being part of the United Kingdom.

Official name Ireland
Formation 1922 / 1922
Capital Dublin
Population 4.3 million / 162 people per sq mile (62 people per sq km) / 60%
Total area 27,135 sq. miles (70,280 sq. km)
Languages English*, Irish Gaelic*
Religions Roman Catholic 88%, Other and nonreligious 9%, Anglican 3%
Ethnic mix Irish 99%, Other 1%
Government Parliamentary system
Currency Euro = 100 cents
Literacy rate 99%
Calorie consumption 3656 calories

ISRAEL
Southwest Asia

Page 97 A7

Israel was created as a new state in 1948 on the east coast of the Mediterranean. Following wars with its Arab neighbors, it has extended its boundaries.

Official name State of Israel
Formation 1948 / 1994
Capital Jerusalem (not internationally recognized)
Population 7 million / 892 people per sq mile (344 people per sq km) / 92%
Total area 8019 sq. miles (20,770 sq. km)
Languages Hebrew*, Arabic*, Yiddish, German, Russian, Polish, Romanian, Persian
Religions Jewish 76%, Muslim (mainly Sunni) 16%, Other 4%, Druze 2%, Christian 2%
Ethnic mix Jewish 76%, Other (mostly Arab) 24%
Government Parliamentary system
Currency Shekel = 100 agorot
Literacy rate 97%
Calorie consumption 3666 calories

ITALY
Southern Europe

Page 74 B3

Projecting into the Mediterranean Sea in Southern Europe, Italy is an ancient land, but also one of the continent's newest unified states.

Official name Italian Republic
Formation 1861 / 1947
Capital Rome
Population 58.2 million / 513 people per sq mile (198 people per sq km) / 67%
Total area 116,305 sq. miles (301,230 sq. km)
Languages Italian*, German, French, Rhaeto-Romanic, Sardinian
Religions Roman Catholic 85%, Other and nonreligious 13%, Muslim 2%
Ethnic mix Italian 94%, Other 4%, Sardinian 2%
Government Parliamentary system
Currency Euro = 100 cents
Literacy rate 98%
Calorie consumption 3671 calories

JAMAICA
West Indies

Page 32 C3

First colonized by the Spanish and then, from 1655, by the English, Jamaica was the first of the Caribbean island nations to achieve independence, in 1962.

Official name Jamaica
Formation 1962 / 1962
Capital Kingston
Population 2.7 million / 646 people per sq mile (249 people per sq km) / 52%
Total area 4243 sq. miles (10,990 sq. km)
Languages English*, English Creole
Religions Other and nonreligious 45%, Other Protestant 20%, Church of God 18%, Baptist 10%, Anglican 7%
Ethnic mix Black African 92%, East Indian 1%, Mulatto (mixed race) 6%, Other 1%
Government Parliamentary system
Currency Jamaican dollar = 100 cents
Literacy rate 80%
Calorie consumption 2685 calories

JAPAN
East Asia

Page 108 C4

Japan comprises four principal islands and over 3,000 smaller ones. With the emperor as constitutional head, it is now one of the world's most powerful economies.

Official name Japan
Formation 1590 / 1972
Capital Tokyo
Population 128 million / 883 people per sq mile (341 people per sq km) / 66%
Total area 145,882 sq. miles (377,835 sq. km)
Languages Japanese*, Korean, Chinese
Religions Shinto and Buddhist 76%, Buddhist 16%, Other (including Christian) 8%
Ethnic mix Japanese 99%, Other (mainly Korean) 1%
Government Parliamentary system
Currency Yen = 100 sen
Literacy rate 99%
Calorie consumption 2761 calories

JORDAN
Southwest Asia

Page 97 B6

The kingdom of Jordan lies east of Israel. In 1993, King Hussein responded to calls for greater democracy by agreeing to multiparty elections.

Official name Hashemite Kingdom of Jordan
Formation 1946 / 1967
Capital Amman
Population 6 million / 175 people per sq mile (67 people per sq km) / 79%
Total area 35,637 sq. miles (92,300 sq. km)
Languages Arabic*
Religions Muslim (mainly Sunni) 92%, Other (mostly Christian) 8%
Ethnic mix Arab 98%, Circassian 1%, Armenian 1%
Government Monarchy
Currency Jordanian dinar = 1000 fils
Literacy rate 90%
Calorie consumption 2673 calories

KAZAKHSTAN
Central Asia

Page 92 B4

Second largest of the former Soviet republics, mineral-rich Kazakhstan has the potential to become the major Central Asian economic power.

Official name Republic of Kazakhstan
Formation 1991 / 1991
Capital Astana
Population 14.8 million / 14 people per sq mile (5 people per sq km) / 56%
Total area 1,049,150 sq. miles (2,717,300 sq. km)
Languages Kazakh*, Russian, Ukrainian, German, Uzbek, Tatar, Uighur
Religions Muslim (mainly Sunni) 47%, Orthodox Christian 44%, Other 9%
Ethnic mix Kazakh 57%, Russian 27%, Other 8%, Uzbek 3%, Ukrainian 3%, German 2%
Government Presidential system
Currency Tenge = 100 tiyn
Literacy rate 99%
Calorie consumption 2677 calories

KENYA
East Africa

Page 51 C6

Kenya became a multiparty democracy in 1992 and was led by President Daniel Moi from 1978 until 2002 when he was barred from re-election and Mwai Kibaki subsequently became president.

Official name Republic of Kenya
Formation 1963 / 1963
Capital Nairobi
Population 36 million / 164 people per sq mile (63 people per sq km) / 40%
Total area 224,961 sq. miles (582,650 sq. km)
Languages Kiswahili*, English*, Kikuyu, Luo, Kalenjin, Kamba
Religions Christian 60%, Traditional beliefs 25%, Other 9%, Muslim 6%
Ethnic mix Other 31%, Kikuyu 20%, Luhya 14%, Luo 13%, Kalenjin 11%, Kamba 11%
Government Mixed Presidential–Parliamentary system
Currency Kenya shilling = 100 cents
Literacy rate 74%
Calorie consumption 2090 calories

KIRIBATI
Australasia & Oceania

Page 123 F3

Part of the British colony of the Gilbert and Ellice Islands until independence in 1979, Kiribati comprises 33 islands in the mid-Pacific Ocean.

Official name Republic of Kiribati
Formation 1979 / 1979
Capital Bairiki (Tarawa Atoll)
Population 107,817 / 393 people per sq mile (152 people per sq km) / 49%
Total area 277 sq. miles (717 sq. km)
Languages English*, Kiribati
Religions Roman Catholic 53%, Kiribati Protestant Church 39%, Other 8%
Ethnic mix Micronesian 99%, Other 1%
Government Nonparty system
Currency Australian dollar = 100 cents
Literacy rate 99%
Calorie consumption 2859 calories

KOSOVO (not yet fully recognized)
Southeast Europe

Page 79 D5

In February 2008, Kosovo controversially declared independence from Serbia. It faces numerous economic and political challenges as it seeks to gain full international recognition.

Official name Republic of Kosovo
Formation 2008 / 2008
Capital Pristina
Population 2.1 million / 499 people per sq mile (193 people per sq km) / 40%
Total area 4212 sq miles (10,908 sq. km)
Languages Albanian*, Serbian*, Bosniak, Gorani, Roma, Turkish
Religions Muslim 92%, Roman Catholic 4%, Orthodox Christian 4%
Ethnic mix Albanian 92%, Serb 4%, Bosniak and Gorani 2%, Turkish 1%, Roma 1%
Government Parliamentary system
Currency Euro = 100 cents
Literacy rate 92%
Calorie consumption Not available

KUWAIT
Southwest Asia

Page 98 C4

Kuwait lies on the northwest extreme of the Persian Gulf. The state was a British protectorate from 1914 until 1961, when full independence was granted.

Official name State of Kuwait
Formation 1961 / 1961
Capital Kuwait City
Population 2.8 million / 407 people per sq mile (157 people per sq km) / 96%
Total area 6880 sq. miles (17,820 sq. km)
Languages Arabic*, English
Religions Sunni Muslim 45%, Shi'a Muslim 40%, Christian, Hindu, and other 15%
Ethnic mix Kuwaiti 45%, Other Arab 35%, South Asian 9%, Other 7%, Iranian 4%
Government Monarchy
Currency Kuwaiti dinar = 1000 fils
Literacy rate 93%
Calorie consumption 3010 calories

KYRGYZSTAN
Central Asia

Page 101 F2

A mountainous, landlocked state in Central Asia. The most rural of the ex-Soviet republics, it only gradually developed its own cultural nationalism.

Official name Kyrgyz Republic
Formation 1991 / 1991
Capital Bishkek
Population 5.4 million / 70 people per sq mile (27 people per sq km) / 34%
Total area 76,641 sq. miles (198,500 sq. km)
Languages Kyrgyz*, Russian*, Uzbek, Tatar, Ukrainian
Religions Muslim (mainly Sunni) 70%, Orthodox Christian 30%
Ethnic mix Kyrgyz 65%, Uzbek 14%, Russian 13%, Other 6%, Dungan 1%, Ukrainian 1%
Government Presidential system
Currency Som = 100 tyiyn
Literacy rate 99%
Calorie consumption 2999 calories

LAOS
Southeast Asia

Page 114 D4

A former French colony, independent in 1953, Laos lies landlocked in Southeast Asia. It has been under communist rule since 1975.

Official name Lao People's Democratic Republic
Formation 1953 / 1953
Capital Vientiane
Population 6.2 million / 70 people per sq mile (27 people per sq km) / 21%
Total area 91,428 sq. miles (236,800 sq. km)
Languages Lao*, Mon-Khmer, Yao, Vietnamese, Chinese, French
Religions Buddhist 85%, Other (including animist) 15%
Ethnic mix Lao Loum 66%, Lao Theung 30%, Other 2%, Lao Soung 2%
Government One-party state
Currency New kip = 100 at
Literacy rate 69%
Calorie consumption 2312 calories

LATVIA
Northeast Europe

Page 84 C3

Situated on the east coast of the Baltic Sea, Latvia, like its Baltic neighbors, became independent in 1991. It retains a large Russian population.

Official name Republic of Latvia
Formation 1991 / 1991
Capital Riga
Population 2.3 million / 92 people per sq mile (36 people per sq km) / 66%
Total area 24,938 sq. miles (64,589 sq. km)
Languages Latvian*, Russian
Religions Lutheran 55%, Roman Catholic 24%, Other 12%, Orthodox Christian 9%
Ethnic mix Latvian 59%, Russian 29%, Belorussian 4%, Polish 3%, Ukrainian 3%, Other 2%
Government Parliamentary system
Currency Lats = 100 santimi
Literacy rate 99%
Calorie consumption 2938 calories

LEBANON
Southwest Asia

Page 96 A4

Lebanon is dwarfed by its two powerful neighbors, Syria and Israel. The state started rebuilding in 1989, after 14 years of intense civil war.

Official name The Lebanese Republic
Formation 1941 / 1941
Capital Beirut
Population 3.7 million / 937 people per sq mile (362 people per sq km) / 88%
Total area 4015 sq. miles (10,400 sq. km)
Languages Arabic*, French, Armenian, Assyrian
Religions Muslim 70%, Christian 30%
Ethnic mix Arab 94%, Armenian 4%, Other 2%
Government Parliamentary system
Currency Lebanese pound = 100 piastres
Literacy rate 86%
Calorie consumption 3196 calories

LESOTHO
Southern Africa

Page 56 D4

The landlocked kingdom of Lesotho is entirely surrounded by South Africa, which provides all its land transportation links with the outside world.

Official name Kingdom of Lesotho
Formation 1966 / 1966
Capital Maseru
Population 1.8 million / 154 people per sq mile (59 people per sq km) / 18%
Total area 11,720 sq. miles (30,355 sq. km)
Languages English*, Sesotho*, isiZulu
Religions Christian 90%, Traditional beliefs 10%
Ethnic mix Sotho 97%, European and Asian 3%
Government Parliamentary system
Currency Loti = 100 lisente
Literacy rate 82%
Calorie consumption 2638 calories

LIBERIA
West Africa

Page 52 C5

Liberia faces the Atlantic Ocean in equatorial West Africa. Africa's oldest republic, it was established in 1847. Today, it is torn by civil war.

Official name Republic of Liberia
Formation 1847 / 1847
Capital Monrovia
Population 3.5 million / 94 people per sq mile (36 people per sq km) / 47%
Total area 43,000 sq. miles (111,370 sq. km)
Languages English*, Kpelle, Vai, Bassa, Kru, Grebo, Kissi, Gola, Loma
Religions Christian 68%, Traditional beliefs 18%, Muslim 14%
Ethnic mix Indigenous tribes (16 main groups) 95%, Americo-Liberians 5%
Government Presidential system
Currency Liberian dollar = 100 cents
Literacy rate 58%
Calorie consumption 1900 calories

LIBYA
North Africa

Page 49 F3

Libya has been under the leadership of Colonel Gaddafi since 1969. In recent years it has tried to shake off its political isolation and return to the international community.

Official name The Great Socialist People's Libyan Arab Jamahiriyah
Formation 1951 / 1951
Capital Tripoli
Population 6.1 million / 9 people per sq mile (3 people per sq km) / 87%
Total area 679,358 sq. miles (1,759,540 sq. km)
Languages Arabic*, Tuareg
Religions Muslim (mainly Sunni) 97%, Other 3%
Ethnic mix Arab and Berber 95%, Other 5%
Government One-party state
Currency Libyan dinar = 1000 dirhams
Literacy rate 82%
Calorie consumption 3320 calories

LIECHTENSTEIN
Central Europe

Page 73 B7

Tucked in the Alps between Switzerland and Austria, Liechtenstein became an independent principality of the Holy Roman Empire in 1719.

Official name Principality of Liechtenstein
Formation 1719 / 1719
Capital Vaduz
Population 34,247 / 552 people per sq mile (214 people per sq km) / 22%
Total area 62 sq. miles (160 sq. km)
Languages German*, Alemannish dialect, Italian
Religions Roman Catholic 81%, Other 12%, Protestant 7%
Ethnic mix Liechtensteiner 66%, Other 12%, Swiss 10%, Austrian 6%, German 3%, Italian 3%
Government Parliamentary system
Currency Swiss franc = 100 rappen/centimes
Literacy rate 99%
Calorie consumption Not available

LITHUANIA
Northeast Europe

Page 84 B4

The largest, most powerful and stable of the Baltic states, Lithuania was the first Baltic country to declare independence from Moscow, in 1991.

Official name Republic of Lithuania
Formation 1991 / 1991
Capital Vilnius
Population 3.4 million / 135 people per sq mile (52 people per sq km) / 67%
Total area 25,174 sq. miles (65,200 sq. km)
Languages Lithuanian*, Russian
Religions Roman Catholic 83%, Other 12%, Protestant 5%
Ethnic mix Lithuanian 83%, Polish 7%, Russian 6%, Other 3%, Belorussian 1%
Government Parliamentary system
Currency Litas = 100 centu
Literacy rate 99%
Calorie consumption 3324 calories

LUXEMBOURG
Northwest Europe

Page 65 D8

Making up part of the plateau of the Ardennes in Western Europe, Luxembourg is Europe's last independent duchy and one of its richest states.

Official name Grand Duchy of Luxembourg
Formation 1867 / 1867
Capital Luxembourg-Ville
Population 480,222 / 481 people per sq mile (186 people per sq km) / 92%
Total area 998 sq. miles (2586 sq. km)
Languages French*, German*, Luxembourgish*
Religions Roman Catholic 97%, Protestant, Orthodox Christian, and Jewish 3%
Ethnic mix Luxembourger 62%, Foreign residents 38%
Government Parliamentary system
Currency Euro = 100 cents
Literacy rate 99%
Calorie consumption 3701 calories

MACEDONIA
Southeast Europe

Page 79 D6

Landlocked in the southern Balkans, Macedonia has been affected by sanctions imposed on its northern trading partners and by Greek antagonism.

Official name Republic of Macedonia
Formation 1991 / 1991
Capital Skopje
Population 2 million / 201 people per sq mile (78 people per sq km) / 60%
Total area 9781 sq. miles (25,333 sq. km)
Languages Macedonian*, Albanian*, Turkish, Romani, Serbian
Religions Orthodox Christian 59%, Muslim 26%, Other 10%, Roman Catholic 4%, Protestant 1%
Ethnic mix Macedonian 64%, Albanian 25%, Turkish 4%, Roma 3%, Other 2%, Serb 2%
Government Mixed presidential–parliamentary system
Currency Macedonian denar = 100 deni
Literacy rate 96%
Calorie consumption 2655 calories

MADAGASCAR
Indian Ocean

Page 57 F4

Lying in the Indian Ocean, Madagascar is the world's fourth largest island. Free elections in 1993 ended 18 years of radical socialist government.

Official name Republic of Madagascar
Formation 1960 / 1960
Capital Antananarivo
Population 19.6 million / 87 people per sq mile (34 people per sq km) / 27%
Total area 226,656 sq. miles (587,040 sq. km)
Languages French*, Malagasy*, English*
Religions Traditional beliefs 52%, Christian (mainly Roman Catholic) 41%, Muslim 7%
Ethnic mix Other Malay 46%, Merina 26%, Betsimisaraka 15%, Betsileo 12%, Other 1%
Government Presidential system
Currency Ariary = 5 iraimbilanja
Literacy rate 71%
Calorie consumption 2005 calories

MALAWI
Southern Africa

Page 57 E1

A former British colony, Malawi lies landlocked in southeast Africa. Its name means "the land where the sun is reflected in the water like fire."

Official name Republic of Malawi
Formation 1964 / 1964
Capital Lilongwe
Population 13.5 million / 372 people per sq mile (143 people per sq km) / 17%
Total area 45,745 sq. miles (118,480 sq. km)
Languages English*, Chewa, Lomwe, Yao, Ngoni
Religions Protestant 55%, Roman Catholic 20%, Muslim 20%, Traditional beliefs 5%
Ethnic mix Bantu 99%, Other 1%
Government Presidential system
Currency Malawi kwacha = 100 tambala
Literacy rate 64%
Calorie consumption 2155 calories

MALAYSIA
Southeast Asia

Page 116 B3

Malaysia's three separate territories include Malaya, Sarawak, and Sabah. A financial crisis in 1997 ended a decade of spectacular financial growth.

Official name Malaysia
Formation 1963 / 1965
Capital Kuala Lumpur; Putrajaya (administrative)
Population 26.2 million / 207 people per sq mile (80 people per sq km) / 64%
Total area 127,316 sq. miles (329,750 sq. km)
Languages Bahasa Malaysia*, Malay, Chinese, Tamil, English
Religions Muslim (mainly Sunni) 53%, Other 9%, Buddhist 19%, Chinese faiths 12%, Christian 7%,
Ethnic mix Malay 50%, Chinese 25%, Indigenous tribes 11%, Other 7%, Indian 7%
Government Parliamentary system
Currency Ringgit = 100 sen
Literacy rate 89%
Calorie consumption 2881 calories

MALDIVES
Indian Ocean

Page 110 A4

Only 200 of the more than 1,000 Maldivian small coral islands in the Indian Ocean, are inhabited. Government rests in the hands of a few influential families.

Official name Republic of Maldives
Formation 1965 / 1965
Capital Male'
Population 369,031 / 3181 people per sq mile (1230 people per sq km) / 29%
Total area 116 sq. miles (300 sq. km)
Languages Dhivehi (Maldivian)*, Sinhala, Tamil, Arabic
Religions Sunni Muslim 100%
Ethnic mix Arab–Sinhalese–Malay 100%
Government Presidential system
Currency Rufiyaa = 100 laari
Literacy rate 96%
Calorie consumption 2548 calories

MALI
West Africa

Page 53 E2

Landlocked in the heart of West Africa, Mali held its first free elections in 1992, more than 30 years after it gained independence from France.

Official name Republic of Mali
Formation 1960 / 1960
Capital Bamako
Population 14.3 million / 30 people per sq mile (12 people per sq km) / 33%
Total area 478,764 sq. miles (1,240,000 sq. km)
Languages French*, Bambara, Fulani, Senufo, Soninke
Religions Muslim (mainly Sunni) 80%, Traditional beliefs 18%, Christian 1%, Other 1%
Ethnic mix Bambara 32%, Other 26%, Fulani 14%, Senufu 12%, Soninka 9%, Tuareg 7%
Government Presidential system
Currency CFA franc = 100 centimes
Literacy rate 19%
Calorie consumption 2174 calories

MALTA
Southern Europe

Page 80 A5

The Maltese archipelago lies off southern Sicily, midway between Europe and North Africa. The only inhabited islands are Malta, Gozo, and Kemmuna.

Official name Republic of Malta
Formation 1964 / 1964
Capital Valletta
Population 401,880 / 3241 people per sq mile (1256 people per sq km) / 92%
Total area 122 sq. miles (316 sq. km)
Languages Maltese*, English*
Religions Roman Catholic 98%, Other and nonreligious 2%
Ethnic mix Maltese 96%, Other 4%
Government Parliamentary system
Currency Euro = 100 cents
Literacy rate 88%
Calorie consumption 3587 calories

MARSHALL ISLANDS
Australasia & Oceania

Page 122 D1

A group of 34 atolls, the Marshall Islands were under US rule as part of the UN Trust Territory of the Pacific Islands until 1986. The economy depends on US aid.

Official name Republic of the Marshall Islands
Formation 1986 / 1986
Capital Majuro
Population 61,815 / 883 people per sq mile (342 people per sq km) / 67%
Total area 70 sq. miles (181 sq. km)
Languages Marshallese*, English*, Japanese, German
Religions Protestant 90%, Roman Catholic 8%, Other 2%
Ethnic mix Micronesian 97%, Other 3%
Government Presidential system
Currency US dollar = 100 cents
Literacy rate 91%
Calorie consumption Not available

MAURITANIA
West Africa

Page 52 C2

Situated in northwest Africa, two-thirds of Mauritania's territory is desert. A former French colony, it achieved independence in 1960.

Official name Islamic Republic of Mauritania
Formation 1960 / 1960
Capital Nouakchott
Population 3.2 million / 8 people per sq mile (3 people per sq km) / 63%
Total area 397,953 sq. miles (1,030,700 sq. km)
Languages Hassaniyah Arabic*, Wolof, French
Religions Sunni Muslim 100%
Ethnic mix Maure 81%, Wolof 7%, Tukolor 5%, Other 4%, Soninka 3%
Government Presidential system
Currency Ouguiya = 5 khoums
Literacy rate 51%
Calorie consumption 2772 calories

MAURITIUS
Indian Ocean

Page 57 H3

Located to the east of Madagascar in the Indian Ocean, Mauritius became a republic 25 years after it gained independence. Tourism is a mainstay of its economy.

Official name Republic of Mauritius
Formation 1968 / 1968
Capital Port Louis
Population 1.2 million / 1811 people per sq mile (699 people per sq km) / 44%
Total area 718 sq. miles (1860 sq. km)
Languages English*, French Creole, Hindi, Urdu, Tamil, Chinese, French
Religions Hindu 52%, Roman Catholic 26%, Muslim 17%, Other 3%, Protestant 2%
Ethnic mix Indo-Mauritian 68%, Creole 27%, Sino-Mauritian 3%, Franco-Mauritian 2%
Government Parliamentary system
Currency Mauritian rupee = 100 cents
Literacy rate 84%
Calorie consumption 2955 calories

MEXICO
North America

Page 28 D3

Located between the United States of America and the Central American states, Mexico was a Spanish colony for 300 years until 1836.

Official name United Mexican States
Formation 1836 / 1848
Capital Mexico City
Population 110 million / 149 people per sq mile (57 people per sq km) / 76%
Total area 761,602 sq. miles (1,972,550 sq. km)
Languages Spanish*, Nahuatl, Mayan, Zapotec, Mixtec, Otomi, Totonac, Tzotzil, Tzeltal
Religions Roman Catholic 88%, Other 7%, Protestant 5%
Ethnic mix Mestizo 60%, Amerindian 30%, European 9%, Other 1%
Government Presidential system
Currency Mexican peso = 100 centavos
Literacy rate 91%
Calorie consumption 3145 calories

MICRONESIA
Australasia & Oceania

Page 122 B1

The Federated States of Micronesia, situated in the western Pacific, comprise 607 islands and atolls grouped into four main island states.

Official name Federated States of Micronesia
Formation 1986 / 1986
Capital Palikir (Pohnpei Island)
Population 107,862 / 398 people per sq mile (154 people per sq km) / 30%
Total area 271 sq. miles (702 sq. km)
Languages English*, Trukese, Pohnpeian, Mortlockese, Kosraean
Religions Roman Catholic 50%, Protestant 48%, Other 2%
Ethnic mix Chuukese 49%, Pohnpeian 24%, Other 14%, Kosraean 6%, Yapese 5%, Asian 2%
Government Nonparty system
Currency US dollar = 100 cents
Literacy rate 81%
Calorie consumption Not available

MOLDOVA
Southeast Europe

Page 86 D3

The smallest and most densely populated of the ex-Soviet republics, Moldova has strong linguistic and cultural links with Romania to the west.

Official name Republic of Moldova
Formation 1991 / 1991
Capital Chisinau
Population 4.2 million / 323 people per sq mile (125 people per sq km) / 46%
Total area 13,067 sq. miles (33,843 sq. km)
Languages Moldovan*, Ukrainian, Russian
Religions Orthodox Christian 98%, Jewish 2%
Ethnic mix Moldovan 64%, Ukrainian 14%, Russian 13%, Gagauz 4%, Other 3%, Bulgarian 2%
Government Parliamentary system
Currency Moldovan leu = 100 bani
Literacy rate 98%
Calorie consumption 2806 calories

MONACO
Southern Europe

Page 69 E6

The smallest and most densely populated of the ex-Soviet republics, Moldova has strong linguistic and cultural links with Romania to the west.

Official name Principality of Monaco
Formation 1861 / 1861
Capital Monaco-Ville
Population 32,671 / 43,561 people per sq mile (16,754 people per sq km) / 100%
Total area 0.75 sq. miles (1.95 sq. km)
Languages French*, Italian, Monégasque, English
Religions Roman Catholic 89%, Protestant 6%, Other 5%
Ethnic mix French 32%, Other 29%, Italian 20%, Monégasque 19%
Government Mixed monarchical–parliamentary system
Currency Euro = 100 cents
Literacy rate 99%
Calorie consumption Not available

MONGOLIA
East Asia

Page 104 D2

Lying between Russia and China, Mongolia is a vast and isolated country with a small population. Over two-thirds of the country is desert.

Official name Mongolia
Formation 1924 / 1924
Capital Ulan Bator
Population 2.7 million / 4 people per sq mile (2 people per sq km) / 57%
Total area 604,247 sq. miles (1,565,000 sq. km)
Languages Khalkha Mongolian*, Kazakh, Chinese, Russian
Religions Tibetan Buddhist 96%, Muslim 4%
Ethnic mix Khalkh 82%, Other 9%, Kazakh 4%, Dorvod 3%, Bayad 2%
Government Mixed presidential–parliamentary system
Currency Tugrik (tögrög) = 100 möngö
Literacy rate 98%
Calorie consumption 2249 calories

MONTENEGRO
Southeast Europe

Page 79 C5

Montenegro voted to split from Serbia in 2006. Since then the country has developed politically and economically with a view towards eventual membership of the EU.

Official name Republic of Montenegro
Formation 2006 / 2006
Capital Podgorica
Population 684,736 / 128 people per sq mile (50 people per sq km) / 62%
Total area 5332 sq. miles (13,812 sq. km)
Languages Montenegrin*, Serbian, Albanian, Bosniak, Croatian
Religions Orthodox Christian 74%, Muslim 18%, Other 4%Roman Catholic 4%
Ethnic mix Montenegrin 43%, Serb 32%, Other 12%, Bosniak 8%, Albanian 5%
Government Parliamentary system
Currency Euro = 100 cents
Literacy rate 98%
Calorie consumption Not available

MOROCCO
North Africa

Page 48 C2

A former French colony in northwest Africa, independent in 1956, Morocco has occupied the disputed territory of Western Sahara since 1975.

Official name Kingdom of Morocco
Formation 1956 / 1969
Capital Rabat
Population 32.4 million / 188 people per sq mile (73 people per sq km) / 58%
Total area 172,316 sq. miles (446,300 sq. km)
Languages Arabic*, Tamazight (Berber), French, Spanish
Religions Muslim (mainly Sunni) 99%, Other (mostly Christian) 1%
Ethnic mix Arab 70%, Berber 29%, European 1%
Government Mixed monarchical–parliamentary system
Currency Moroccan dirham = 100 centimes
Literacy rate 52%
Calorie consumption 3052 calories

MOZAMBIQUE
Southern Africa

Page 57 E3

Mozambique lies on the southeast African coast. It was torn by a civil war between the Marxist government and a rebel group from 1977–1992.

Official name Republic of Mozambique
Formation 1975 / 1975
Capital Maputo
Population 20.5 million / 68 people per sq mile (26 people per sq km) / 37%
Total area 309,494 sq. miles (801,590 sq. km)
Languages Portuguese*, Makua, Xitsonga, Sena, Lomwe
Religions Traditional beliefs 56%, Christian 30%, Muslim 14%
Ethnic mix Makua Lomwe 47%, Tsonga 23%, Malawi 12%, Shona 11%, Yao 4%, Other 3%
Government Presidential system
Currency New metical = 100 centavos
Literacy rate 46%
Calorie consumption 2079 calories

MYANMAR (BURMA)
Southeast Asia

Page 114 A3

Myanmar forms the eastern shores of the Bay of Bengal and the Andaman Sea in Southeast Asia. Since 1988 it has been ruled by a repressive military regime.

Official name Union of Myanmar
Formation 1948 / 1948
Capital Nay Pyi Taw
Population 51.5 million / 203 people per sq mile (78 people per sq km) / 30%
Total area 261,969 sq. miles (678,500 sq. km)
Languages Burmese*, Shan, Karen, Rakhine, Chin, Yangbye, Kachin, Mon
Religions Buddhist 87%, Christian 6%, Muslim 4%, Other 2%, Hindu 1%
Ethnic mix Burman (Bamah) 68%, Other 13%, Shan 9%, Karen 6%, Rakhine 4%
Government Military-based regime
Currency Kyat = 100 pyas
Literacy rate 90%
Calorie consumption 2937 calories

NAMIBIA
Southern Africa

Page 56 B3

Located in southwestern Africa, Namibia became free of South African control in 1990, after years of uncertainty and guerrilla activity.

Official name Republic of Namibia
Formation 1990 / 1994
Capital Windhoek
Population 2.1 million / 7 people per sq mile (3 people per sq km) / 33%
Total area 318,694 sq. miles (825,418 sq. km)
Languages English*, Ovambo, Kavango, Bergdama, German, Afrikaans
Religions Christian 90%, Traditional beliefs 10%
Ethnic mix Ovambo 50%, Other tribes 24%, Kavango 9%, Damara 8%, Herero 8%, Other 1%
Government Presidential system
Currency Namibian dollar = 100 cents
Literacy rate 85%
Calorie consumption 2278 calories

NAURU
Australasia & Oceania

Page 122 D3

Nauru lies in the Pacific, 2,480 miles (4,000 km) northeast of Australia. For many years phosphate deposits provided great wealth but these are now virtually exhausted.

Official name Republic of Nauru
Formation 1968 / 1968
Capital None
Population 13,528 / 1670 people per sq mile (644 people per sq km) / 100%
Total area 8.1 sq. miles (21 sq. km)
Languages Nauruan*, Kiribati, Chinese, Tuvaluan, English
Religions Nauruan Congregational Church 60%, Roman Catholic 35%, Other 5%
Ethnic mix Nauruan 62%, Other Pacific islanders 27%, Asian 8%, European 3%
Government Nonparty system
Currency Australian dollar = 100 cents
Literacy rate 95%
Calorie consumption Not available

NEPAL
South Asia

Page 113 E3

Nepal lies between India and China, on the shoulder of the southern Himalayas. In 2008, after many years of unrest, Nepal was declared a republic and the monarchy was dissolved .

Official name Federal Democratic Republic of Nepal
Formation 1769 / 1769
Capital Kathmandu
Population 28.2 million / 534 people per sq mile (206 people per sq km) / 15%
Total area 54,363 sq. miles (140,800 sq. km)
Languages Nepali*, Maithili, Bhojpuri
Religions Hindu 90%, Buddhist 5%, Muslim 3%, Other (including Christian) 2%
Ethnic mix Other 52%, Chhetri 16%, Hill Brahman 13%, Tharu 7%, Magar 7%, Tamang 5%
Government Parliamentary system
Currency Nepalese rupee = 100 paisa
Literacy rate 49%
Calorie consumption 2453 calories

NETHERLANDS
Northwest Europe

Page 64 C3

Astride the delta of five major rivers in northwest Europe, the Netherlands has a long trading tradition. Rotterdam is the world's largest port.

Official name Kingdom of the Netherlands
Formation 1648 / 1839
Capital Amsterdam; The Hague (administrative)
Population 16.4 million / 1252 people per sq mile (483 people per sq km) / 66%
Total area 16,033 sq. miles (41,526 sq. km)
Languages Dutch*, Frisian
Religions Roman Catholic 36%, Other 34%, Protestant 27%, Muslim 3%
Ethnic mix Dutch 82%, Other 12%, Surinamese 2%, Turkish 2%, Moroccan 2%
Government Parliamentary system
Currency Euro = 100 cents
Literacy rate 99%
Calorie consumption 3362 calories

NEW ZEALAND
Australasia & Oceania

Page 128 A4

One of the Pacific Rim countries, New Zealand lies southeast of Australia, and comprises the North and South Islands, separated by the Cook Strait.

Official name New Zealand
Formation 1947 / 1947
Capital Wellington
Population 4.1 million / 40 people per sq mile (15 people per sq km) / 86%
Total area 103,737 sq. miles (268,680 sq. km)
Languages English*, Maori*
Religions Anglican 24%, Other 22%, Presbyterian 18%, Nonreligious 16%, Roman Catholic 15%, Methodist 5%
Ethnic mix European 75%, Maori 15%, Other 7%, Samoan 3%
Government Parliamentary system
Currency New Zealand dollar = 100 cents
Literacy rate 99%
Calorie consumption 3219 calories

NICARAGUA
Central America

Page 30 D3

Nicaragua lies at the heart of Central America. An 11-year war between left-wing Sandinistas and right-wing US-backed Contras ended in 1989.

Official name Republic of Nicaragua
Formation 1838 / 1838
Capital Managua
Population 5.7 million / 124 people per sq mile (48 people per sq km) / 58%
Total area 49,998 sq. miles (129,494 sq. km)
Languages Spanish*, English Creole, Miskito
Religions Roman Catholic 80%, Protestant Evangelical 17%, Other 3%
Ethnic mix Mestizo 69%, White 14%, Black 8%, Amerindian 5%, Zambo 4%
Government Presidential system
Currency Córdoba oro = 100 centavos
Literacy rate 77%
Calorie consumption 2298 calories

NIGER
West Africa

Page 53 F3

Niger lies landlocked in West Africa, but it is linked to the sea by the River Niger. Since 1973 it has suffered civil unrest and two major droughts.

Official name Republic of Niger
Formation 1960 / 1960
Capital Niamey
Population 14.9 million / 30 people per sq mile (12 people per sq km) / 23%
Total area 489,188 sq. miles (1,267,000 sq. km)
Languages French*, Hausa, Djerma, Fulani, Tuareg, Teda
Religions Muslim 85%, Traditional beliefs 14%, Other (including Christian) 1%
Ethnic mix Hausa 55%, Djerma and Songhai 21%, Peul 9%, Tuareg 9%, Other 6%
Government Presidential system
Currency CFA franc = 100 centimes
Literacy rate 29%
Calorie consumption 2130 calories

NIGERIA
West Africa

Page 53 F4

Africa's most populous state Nigeria, in West Africa, is a federation of 30 states. It adopted civilian rule in 1999 after 33 years of military government.

Official name Federal Republic of Nigeria
Formation 1960 / 1961
Capital Abuja
Population 137 million / 390 people per sq mile (151 people per sq km) / 47%
Total area 356,667 sq. miles (923,768 sq. km)
Languages English*, Hausa, Yoruba, Ibo
Religions Muslim 50%, Christian 40%, Traditional beliefs 10%
Ethnic mix Other 29%, Hausa 21%, Yoruba 21%, Ibo 18%, Fulani 11%
Government Presidential system
Currency Naira = 100 kobo
Literacy rate 67%
Calorie consumption 2726 calories

NORTH KOREA
East Asia

Page 106 E3

North Korea comprises the northern half of the Korean peninsula. A communist state since 1948, it is largely isolated from the outside world.

Official name Democratic People's Republic of Korea
Formation 1948 / 1953
Capital Pyongyang
Population 22.7 million / 488 people per sq mile (189 people per sq km) / 61%
Total area 46,540 sq. miles (120,540 sq. km)
Languages Korean*
Religions Atheist 100%
Ethnic mix Korean 100%
Government One-party state
Currency North Korean won = 100 chon
Literacy rate 98%
Calorie consumption 2142 calories

PAKISTAN
South Asia

Page 112 B2

Pakistan was created in 1947 as an independent Muslim state. Today, this nuclear armed country is struggling to deal with complex domestic and international tensions.

Official name Islamic Republic of Pakistan
Formation 1947 / 1971
Capital Islamabad
Population 165 million / 553 people per sq mile (214 people per sq km) / 34%
Total area 310,401 sq. miles (803,940 sq. km)
Languages Urdu*, Punjabi, Sindhi, Pashtu, Baluchi, Brahui
Religions Sunni Muslim 77%, Shi'a Muslim 20%, Hindu 2%, Christian 1%
Ethnic mix Punjabi 56%, Pathan (Pashtun) 15%, Sindhi 14%, Mohajir 7%, Other 4%, Baluchi 4%
Government Presidential system
Currency Pakistani rupee = 100 paisa
Literacy rate 50%
Calorie consumption 2419 calories

PAPUA NEW GUINEA
Australasia & Oceania

Page 122 B3

Achieving independence from Australia in 1975, PNG occupies the eastern section of the island of New Guinea and several other island groups.

Official name Independent State of Papua New Guinea
Formation 1975 / 1975
Capital Port Moresby
Population 6.1 million / 35 people per sq mile (13 people per sq km) / 13%
Total area 178,703 sq. miles (462,840 sq. km)
Languages English*, Pidgin English, Papuan, Motu, 750 (est.) native languages
Religions Protestant 60%, Roman Catholic 37%, Other 3%
Ethnic mix Melanesian and mixed race 100%
Government Parliamentary system
Currency Kina = 100 toea
Literacy rate 57%
Calorie consumption 2193 calories

PHILIPPINES
Southeast Asia

Page 117 E1

An archipelago of 7,107 islands between the South China Sea and the Pacific. After 21 years of dictatorship, democracy was restored in 1986.

Official name Republic of the Philippines
Formation 1946 / 1946
Capital Manila
Population 85.9 million / 746 people per sq mile (288 people per sq km) / 62%
Total area 115,830 sq. miles (300,000 sq. km)
Languages English*, Filipino*, Tagalog, Cebuano, Ilocano, Hiligaynon, many other local languages
Religions Roman Catholic 83%, Protestant 9%, Muslim 5%, Other (including Buddhist) 3%
Ethnic mix Other 34%, Tagalog 28%, Cebuano 13%, Ilocano 9%, Hiligaynon 8%, Bisaya 8%
Government Presidential system
Currency Philippine peso = 100 centavos
Literacy rate 93%
Calorie consumption 2379 calories

NORWAY
Northern Europe

Page 63 A5

The Kingdom of Norway traces the rugged western coast of Scandinavia. Settlements are largely restricted to southern and coastal areas.

Official name Kingdom of Norway
Formation 1905 / 1905
Capital Oslo
Population 4.7 million / 40 people per sq mile (15 people per sq km) / 80%
Total area 125,181 sq. miles (324,220 sq. km)
Languages Norwegian* (Bokmål "book language" and Nynorsk "new Norsk"), Sámi
Religions Evangelical Lutheran 89%, Other and nonreligious 10%, Roman Catholic 1%
Ethnic mix Norwegian 93%, Other 6%, Sámi 1%
Government Parliamentary system
Currency Norwegian krone = 100 øre
Literacy rate 99%
Calorie consumption 3484 calories

PALAU
Australasia & Oceania

Page 122 A2

The Palau archipelago, a group of over 200 islands, lies in the western Pacific Ocean. Since independence in 1994 it has prospered on a thriving tourist industry.

Official name Republic of Palau
Formation 1994 / 1994
Capital Melekeok
Population 20,842 / 106 people per sq mile (41 people per sq km) / 68%
Total area 177 sq. miles (458 sq. km)
Languages Palauan*, English*, Japanese, Angaur, Tobi, Sonsorolese
Religions Christian 66%, Modekngei 34%
Ethnic mix Palauan 74%, Filipino 16%, Other 6%, Chinese and other Asian 4%
Government Nonparty system
Currency US dollar = 100 cents
Literacy rate 98%
Calorie consumption Not available

PARAGUAY
South America

Page 42 D2

Landlocked in central South America. Its post-independence history has included periods of military rule. Free elections were held in 1993.

Official name Republic of Paraguay
Formation 1811 / 1938
Capital Asunción
Population 6.4 million / 42 people per sq mile (16 people per sq km) / 58%
Total area 157,046 sq. miles (406,750 sq. km)
Languages Spanish*, Guaraní, German
Religions Roman Catholic 96%, Protestant (including Mennonite) 4%
Ethnic mix Mestizo 91%, Other 7%, Amerindian 2%
Government Presidential system
Currency Guaraní = 100 céntimos
Literacy rate 93%
Calorie consumption 2565 calories

POLAND
Northern Europe

Page 76 B3

With its seven international borders and strategic location in the heart of Europe, Poland has always played an important role in European affairs.

Official name Republic of Poland
Formation 1918 / 1945
Capital Warsaw
Population 38.5 million / 328 people per sq mile (126 people per sq km) / 62%
Total area 120,728 sq. miles (312,685 sq. km)
Languages Polish*
Religions Roman Catholic 93%, Other and nonreligious 5%, Orthodox Christian 2%
Ethnic mix Polish 97%, Other 3%
Government Parliamentary system
Currency Zloty = 100 groszy
Literacy rate 99%
Calorie consumption 3374 calories

OMAN
Southwest Asia

Page 99 D6

Situated on the eastern coast of the Arabian Peninsula, Oman is the least developed of the Gulf states, despite modest oil exports.

Official name Sultanate of Oman
Formation 1951 / 1951
Capital Muscat
Population 2.7 million / 33 people per sq mile (13 people per sq km) / 78%
Total area 82,031 sq. miles (212,460 sq. km)
Languages Arabic*, Baluchi, Farsi, Hindi, Punjabi
Religions Ibadi Muslim 75%, Other Muslim and Hindu 25%
Ethnic mix Arab 88%, Baluchi 4%, Persian 3%, Indian and Pakistani 3%, African 2%
Government Monarchy
Currency Omani rial = 1000 baisa
Literacy rate 81%
Calorie consumption Not available

PANAMA
Central America

Page 31 F5

Southernmost of the Central American countries. The Panama Canal (returned to Panama from US control in 2000) links the Pacific and Atlantic oceans.

Official name Republic of Panama
Formation 1903 / 1903
Capital Panama City
Population 3.3 million / 112 people per sq mile (43 people per sq km) / 57%
Total area 30,193 sq. miles (78,200 sq. km)
Languages English Creole, Spanish*, Amerindian languages, Chibchan languages
Religions Roman Catholic 86%, Other 8%, Protestant 6%
Ethnic mix Mestizo 60%, White 14%, Black 12%, Amerindian 8%, Asian 4%, Other 2%
Government Presidential system
Currency Balboa = 100 centésimos
Literacy rate 92%
Calorie consumption 2272 calories

PERU
South America

Page 38 C3

Once the heart of the Inca empire, before the Spanish conquest in the 16th century, Peru lies on the Pacific coast of South America.

Official name Republic of Peru
Formation 1824 / 1941
Capital Lima
Population 28.8 million / 58 people per sq mile (22 people per sq km) / 74%
Total area 496,223 sq. miles (1,285,200 sq. km)
Languages Spanish*, Quechua*, Aymara
Religions Roman Catholic 95%, Other 5%
Ethnic mix Amerindian 50%, Mestizo 40%, White 7%, Other 3%
Government Presidential system
Currency New sol = 100 céntimos
Literacy rate 88%
Calorie consumption 2571 calories

PORTUGAL
Southwest Europe

Page 70 B3

Facing the Atlantic on the western side of the Iberian Peninsula, Portugal is the most westerly country on the European mainland.

Official name The Portuguese Republic
Formation 1139 / 1640
Capital Lisbon
Population 10.6 million / 299 people per sq mile (115 people per sq km) / 55%
Total area 35,672 sq. miles (92,391 sq. km)
Languages Portuguese*
Religions Roman Catholic 97%, Other 2%, Protestant 1%
Ethnic mix Portuguese 98%, African and other 2%
Government Parliamentary system
Currency Euro = 100 cents
Literacy rate 92%
Calorie consumption 3741 calories

QATAR
Southwest Asia

Page 98 C4

Projecting north from the Arabian Peninsula into the Persian Gulf, Qatar's reserves of oil and gas make it one of the region's wealthiest states.

Official name State of Qatar
Formation 1971 / 1971
Capital Doha
Population 907,229 / 214 people per sq mile (82 people per sq km) / 92%
Total area 4416 sq. miles (11,437 sq. km)
Languages Arabic*
Religions Muslim (mainly Sunni) 95%, Other 5%
Ethnic mix Arab 40%, Indian 18%, Pakistani 18%, Other 14%, Iranian 10%
Government Monarchy
Currency Qatar riyal = 100 dirhams
Literacy rate 89%
Calorie consumption Not available

ROMANIA
Southeast Europe

Page 86 B4

Romania lies on the Black Sea coast. Since the overthrow of its communist regime in 1989, it has been slowly converting to a free-market economy.

Official name Romania
Formation 1878 / 1947
Capital Bucharest
Population 21.5 million / 242 people per sq mile (93 people per sq km) / 55%
Total area 91,699 sq. miles (237,500 sq. km)
Languages Romanian*, Hungarian (Magyar), Romani, German
Religions Romanian Orthodox 87%, Roman Catholic 5%, Protestant 4%, Other 4%
Ethnic mix Romanian 89%, Magyar 7%, Roma 2%, Other 2%
Government Presidential system
Currency New Romanian leu = 100 bani
Literacy rate 97%
Calorie consumption 3455 calories

RUSSIAN FEDERATION
Europe / Asia

Page 92 D4

Still the world's largest state, despite the breakup of the USSR in 1991, the Russian Federation is a major power on the world stage, controlling vast mineral and energy reserves.

Official name Russian Federation
Formation 1480 / 1991
Capital Moscow
Population 142 million / 22 people per sq mile (8 people per sq km) / 73%
Total area 6,592,735 sq. miles (17,075,200 sq. km)
Languages Russian*, Tatar, Ukrainian, Chavash, various other national languages
Religions Orthodox Christian 75%, Muslim 14%, Other 11%
Ethnic mix Russian 80%, Other 12%, Tatar 4%, Ukrainian 2%, Bashkir 1%, Chavash 1%
Government Mixed Presidential–Parliamentary system
Currency Russian rouble = 100 kopeks
Literacy rate 99%
Calorie consumption 3072 calories

RWANDA
Central Africa

Page 51 B6

Rwanda lies just south of the Equator in east central Africa. Since independence from France in 1962, ethnic tensions have dominated politics.

Official name Republic of Rwanda
Formation 1962 / 1962
Capital Kigali
Population 9.4 million / 976 people per sq mile (377 people per sq km) / 20%
Total area 10,169 sq. miles (26,338 sq. km)
Languages Kinyarwanda*, French*, English*, Kiswahili
Religions Roman Catholic 56%, Traditional beliefs 25%, Muslim 10%, Protestant 9%
Ethnic mix Hutu 90%, Tutsi 9%, Other (including Twa) 1%
Government Presidential system
Currency Rwanda franc = 100 centimes
Literacy rate 65%
Calorie consumption 2084 calories

SAINT KITTS & NEVIS
West Indies

Page 33 G3

Separated by a channel, the two islands of Saint Kitts and Nevis are part of the Leeward Islands chain in the Caribbean. Nevis is the less developed of the two.

Official name Federation of Saint Christopher and Nevis
Formation 1983 / 1983
Capital Basseterre
Population 39,349 / 283 people per sq mile (109 people per sq km) / 32%
Total area 101 sq. miles (261 sq. km)
Languages English*, English Creole
Religions Anglican 33%, Methodist 29%, Other 22%, Moravian 9%, Roman Catholic 7%
Ethnic mix Black 95%, Mixed race 3%, White 1%, Other and Amerindian 1%
Government Parliamentary system
Currency Eastern Caribbean dollar = 100 cents
Literacy rate 98%
Calorie consumption 2609 calories

SAINT LUCIA
West Indies

Page 33 G4

Among the most beautiful of the Caribbean Windward Islands, Saint Lucia retains both French and British influences from its colonial history.

Official name Saint Lucia
Formation 1979 / 1979
Capital Castries
Population 170,649 / 723 people per sq mile (280 people per sq km) / 31%
Total area 239 sq. miles (620 sq. km)
Languages English*, French Creole
Religions Roman Catholic 90%, Other 10%
Ethnic mix Black 83%, Mulatto (mixed race) 13%, Asian 3%, Other 1%
Government Parliamentary system
Currency Eastern Caribbean dollar = 100 cents
Literacy rate 95%
Calorie consumption 2988 calories

ST. VINCENT & THE GRENADINES
West Indies

Page 33 G4

Formerly ruled by Britain, these volcanic islands form part of the Caribbean Windward Islands. Agriculture, notably banana production, dominates the economy.

Official name Saint Vincent and the Grenadines
Formation 1979 / 1979
Capital Kingstown
Population 118,149 / 902 people per sq mile (347 people per sq km) / 59%
Total area 150 sq. miles (389 sq. km)
Languages English*, English Creole
Religions Anglican 47%, Methodist 28%, Roman Catholic 13%, Other 12%
Ethnic mix Black 77%, Mulatto (mixed race) 16%, Other 3%, Carib 3%, Asian 1%
Government Parliamentary system
Currency Eastern Caribbean dollar = 100 cents
Literacy rate 88%
Calorie consumption 2599 calories

SAMOA
Australasia & Oceania

Page 123 F4

The southern Pacific islands of Samoa gained independence from New Zealand in 1962. Four of the nine islands are inhabited.

Official name Independent State of Samoa
Formation 1962 / 1962
Capital Apia
Population 214,265 / 196 people per sq mile (76 people per sq km) / 22%
Total area 1104 sq. miles (2860 sq. km)
Languages Samoan*, English*
Religions Christian 99%, Other 1%
Ethnic mix Polynesian 90%, Euronesian 9%, Other 1%
Government Parliamentary system
Currency Tala = 100 sene
Literacy rate 99%
Calorie consumption 2945 calories

SAN MARINO
Southern Europe

Page 74 C3

Perched on the slopes of Monte Titano in the Italian Appennino, San Marino has maintained its independence since the 4th century AD.

Official name Republic of San Marino
Formation 1631 / 1631
Capital San Marino
Population 29,615 / 1234 people per sq mile (485 people per sq km) / 89%
Total area 23.6 sq. miles (61 sq. km)
Languages Italian*
Religions Roman Catholic 93%, Other and nonreligious 7%
Ethnic mix Sammarinese 88%, Italian 10%, Other 2%
Government Parliamentary system
Currency Euro = 100 cents
Literacy rate 99%
Calorie consumption Not available

SÃO TOMÉ & PRÍNCIPE
West Africa

Page 55 A5

A former Portuguese colony off Africa's west coast, comprising two main islands and smaller islets. The 1991 elections ended 15 years of Marxism.

Official name The Democratic Republic of Sao Tome and Principe
Formation 1975 / 1975
Capital São Tomé
Population 199,579 / 538 people per sq mile (208 people per sq km) / 38%
Total area 386 sq. miles (1001 sq. km)
Languages Portuguese*, Portuguese Creole
Religions Roman Catholic 84%, Other 16%
Ethnic mix Black 90%, Portuguese and Creole 10%
Government Presidential system
Currency Dobra = 100 céntimos
Literacy rate 83%
Calorie consumption 2460 calories

SAUDI ARABIA
Southwest Asia

Page 99 B5

Occupying most of the Arabian Peninsula, the desert kingdom of Saudi Arabia, rich in oil and gas, covers an area the size of Western Europe.

Official name Kingdom of Saudi Arabia
Formation 1932 / 1932
Capital Riyadh
Population 25.8 million / 32 people per sq mile (12 people per sq km) / 88%
Total area 756,981 sq. miles (1,960,582 sq. km)
Languages Arabic*
Religions Sunni Muslim 85%, Shi'a Muslim 15%
Ethnic mix Arab 90%, Afro-Asian 10%
Government Monarchy
Currency Saudi riyal = 100 halalat
Literacy rate 79%
Calorie consumption 2844 calories

SENEGAL
West Africa

Page 52 B3

A former French colony, Senegal achieved independence in 1960. Its capital, Dakar, stands on the westernmost cape of Africa.

Official name Republic of Senegal
Formation 1960 / 1960
Capital Dakar
Population 12.2 million / 164 people per sq mile (63 people per sq km) / 50%
Total area 75,749 sq. miles (196,190 sq. km)
Languages French*, Wolof, Pulaar, Serer, Diola, Mandinka, Malinke, Soninke
Religions Sunni Muslim 90%, Christian (mainly Roman Catholic) 5%, Traditional beliefs 5%
Ethnic mix Wolof 43%, Serer 15%, Other 14%, Peul 14%, Toucouleur 9%, Diola 5%
Government Presidential system
Currency CFA franc = 100 centimes
Literacy rate 39%
Calorie consumption 2279 calories

SERBIA
Southeast Europe

Page 78 D4

One of seven states to emerge from the former Yugoslavia, Serbia has struggled to find stability amid ongoing ethnic and nationalist tensions.

Official name Republic of Serbia
Formation 2006 / 2008
Capital Belgrade
Population 8.1 million / 271 people per sq mile (105 people per sq km) / 52%
Total area 29,905 sq miles (77,453 sq km)
Languages Serbian*, Hungarian (Magyar)
Religions Orthodox Christian 85%, Other 6%, Roman Catholic 6%, Muslim 3%
Ethnic mix Serb 83%, Other 10%, Magyar 4%, Bosniak 2%, Roma 1%
Government Parliamentary system
Currency Dinar = 100 para
Literacy rate 96%
Calorie consumption 2678 calories

SINGAPORE
Southeast Asia

Page 116 A1

A city state linked to the southernmost tip of the Malay Peninsula by a causeway, Singapore is one of Asia's most important commercial centers.

Official name Republic of Singapore
Formation 1965 / 1965
Capital Singapore
Population 4.4 million / 18644 people per sq mile (7213 people per sq km) / 100%
Total area 250 sq. miles (648 sq. km)
Languages Mandarin*, Malay*, Tamil*, English*
Religions Buddhist 55%, Taoist 22%, Muslim 16%, Hindu, Christian, and Sikh 7%
Ethnic mix Chinese 77%, Malay 14%, Indian 8%, Other 1%
Government Parliamentary system
Currency Singapore dollar = 100 cents
Literacy rate 93%
Calorie consumption Not available

SOLOMON ISLANDS
Australasia & Oceania

Page 122 C3

The Solomon archipelago comprises several hundred islands scattered in the southwestern Pacific. Independence from Britain came in 1978.

Official name Solomon Islands
Formation 1978 / 1978
Capital Honiara
Population 566,842 / 52 people per sq mile (20 people per sq km) / 17%
Total area 10,985 sq. miles (28,450 sq. km)
Languages English*, Pidgin English, Melanesian Pidgin
Religions Church of Melanesia (Anglican) 34%, Roman Catholic 19%, South Seas Evangelical Church 17%, Methodist 11%, Other 19%
Ethnic mix Melanesian 94%, Polynesian 4%, Other 2%
Government Parliamentary system
Currency Solomon Islands dollar = 100 cents
Literacy rate 77%
Calorie consumption 2265 calories

SOUTH KOREA
East Asia

Page 106 E4

South Korea occupies the southern half of the Korean peninsula. It was separated from the communist North in 1948.

Official name Republic of Korea
Formation 1948 / 1953
Capital Seoul
Population 48.1 million / 1262 people per sq mile (487 people per sq km) / 81%
Total area 38,023 sq. miles (98,480 sq. km)
Languages Korean*
Religions Mahayana Buddhist 47%, Protestant 38%, Roman Catholic 11%, Confucianist 3%, Other 1%
Ethnic mix Korean 100%
Government Presidential system
Currency South Korean won = 100 chon
Literacy rate 98%
Calorie consumption 3058 calories

SEYCHELLES
Indian Ocean

Page 57 G1

A former British colony comprising 115 islands in the Indian Ocean. Under one-party rule for 16 years, it became a multiparty democracy in 1993.

Official name Republic of Seychelles
Formation 1976 / 1976
Capital Victoria
Population 81,895 / 787 people per sq mile (303 people per sq km) / 50%
Total area 176 sq. miles (455 sq. km)
Languages French Creole*, English*, French*
Religions Roman Catholic 90%, Anglican 8%, Other (including Muslim) 2%
Ethnic mix Creole 89%, Indian 5%, Other 4%, Chinese 2%
Government Presidential system
Currency Seychelles rupee = 100 cents
Literacy rate 92%
Calorie consumption 2465 calories

SLOVAKIA
Central Europe

Page 77 C6

Landlocked in Central Europe, Slovakia has been independent since 1993. It is the less developed half of the former Czechoslovakia.

Official name Slovak Republic
Formation 1993 / 1993
Capital Bratislava
Population 5.4 million / 285 people per sq mile (110 people per sq km) / 58%
Total area 18,859 sq. miles (48,845 sq. km)
Languages Slovak*, Hungarian (Magyar), Czech
Religions Roman Catholic 60%, Other 18%, Atheist 10%, Protestant 8%, Orthodox Christian 4%
Ethnic mix Slovak 86%, Magyar 10%, Roma 2%, Other 1%, Czech 1%
Government Parliamentary system
Currency Slovak koruna = 100 halierov
Literacy rate 99%
Calorie consumption 2889 calories

SOMALIA
East Africa

Page 51 E5

Italian and British Somaliland were united in 1960 to create this semiarid state occupying the horn of Africa. It has suffered years of civil war.

Official name The Somali Democratic Republic
Formation 1960 / 1960
Capital Mogadishu
Population 8.8 million / 36 people per sq mile (14 people per sq km) / 35%
Total area 246,199 sq. miles (637,657 sq. km)
Languages Somali*, Arabic*, English, Italian
Religions Sunni Muslim 98%, Christian 2%
Ethnic mix Somali 85%, Other 15%
Government Transitional regime
Currency Somali shilin = 100 senti
Literacy rate 24%
Calorie consumption 1628 calories

SPAIN
Southwest Europe

Page 70 D2

Lodged between mainland Europe and Africa, the Atlantic and the Mediterranean, Spain has occupied a pivotal position since it was united in 1492.

Official name Kingdom of Spain
Formation 1492 / 1713
Capital Madrid
Population 43.6 million / 226 people per sq mile (87 people per sq km) / 77%
Total area 194,896 sq. miles (504,782 sq. km)
Languages Spanish*, Catalan*, Galician*, Basque*
Religions Roman Catholic 96%, Other 4%
Ethnic mix Castilian Spanish 72%, Catalan 17%, Galician 6%, Basque 2%, Other 2%, Roma 1%
Government Parliamentary system
Currency Euro = 100 cents
Literacy rate 98%
Calorie consumption 3371 calories

SIERRA LEONE
West Africa

Page 52 C4

The West African state of Sierra Leone achieved independence from the British in 1961. Today, it is one of the world's poorest nations.

Official name Republic of Sierra Leone
Formation 1961 / 1961
Capital Freetown
Population 5.8 million / 210 people per sq mile (81 people per sq km) / 40%
Total area 27,698 sq. miles (71,740 sq. km)
Languages English*, Mende, Temne, Krio
Religions Muslim 30%, Traditional beliefs 30%, Other 30%, Christian 10%
Ethnic mix Mende 35%, Temne 32%, Other 21%, Limba 8%, Kuranko 4%
Government Presidential system
Currency Leone = 100 cents
Literacy rate 35%
Calorie consumption 1936 calories

SLOVENIA
Central Europe

Page 73 D8

Northernmost of the former Yugoslav republics, Slovenia has the closest links with Western Europe. In 1991, it gained independence with little violence.

Official name Republic of Slovenia
Formation 1991 / 1991
Capital Ljubljana
Population 2 million / 256 people per sq mile (99 people per sq km) / 51%
Total area 7820 sq. miles (20,253 sq. km)
Languages Slovenian*
Religions Roman Catholic 96%, Other 3%, Muslim 1%
Ethnic mix Slovene 83%, Other 12%, Serb 2%, Croat 2%, Bosniak 1%
Government Parliamentary system
Currency Euro = 100 cents
Literacy rate 99%
Calorie consumption 3001 calories

SOUTH AFRICA
Southern Africa

Page 56 C4

South Africa is the most southerly nation on the African continent. The multiracial elections of 1994 overturned 80 years of white minority rule.

Official name Republic of South Africa
Formation 1934 / 1994
Capital Pretoria; Cape Town; Bloemfontein
Population 47.7 million / 101 people per sq mile (39 people per sq km) / 57%
Total area 471,008 sq. miles (1,219,912 sq. km)
Languages English, isiZulu, isiXhosa, Afrikaans, Sepedi, Setswana, Sesotho, Xitsonga, siSwati, Tshivenda, isiNdebele
Religions Christian 68%, Traditional beliefs and animist 29%, Muslim 2%, Hindu 1%
Ethnic mix Black 79%, Colored 10%, White 9%, Asian 2%
Government Presidential system
Currency Rand = 100 cents
Literacy rate 82%
Calorie consumption 2956 calories

SRI LANKA
South Asia

Page 110 D3

The island republic of Sri Lanka is separated from India by the narrow Palk Strait. Since 1983, the Sinhalese and Tamil population have been in conflict.

Official name Democratic Socialist Republic of Sri Lanka
Formation 1948 / 1948
Capital Colombo
Population 21.1 million / 844 people per sq mile (326 people per sq km) / 21%
Total area 25,332 sq. miles (65,610 sq. km)
Languages Sinhala*, Tamil*, Sinhala-Tamil, English
Religions Buddhist 69%, Hindu 15%, Muslim 8%, Christian 8%
Ethnic mix Sinhalese 82%, Tamil 9%, Moor 8%, Other 1%
Government Mixed presidential–parliamentary system
Currency Sri Lanka rupee = 100 cents
Literacy rate 91%
Calorie consumption 2385 calories

SUDAN
East Africa

Page 50 B4

The largest country in Africa, part of Sudan borders the Red Sea. In 1989, an army coup installed a military Islamic fundamentalist regime.

Official name Republic of the Sudan
Formation 1956 / 1956
Capital Khartoum
Population 37.8 million / 39 people per sq mile (15 people per sq km) / 40%
Total area 967,493 sq. miles (2,505,810 sq. km)
Languages Arabic / Arabic, Dinka, Nuer, Nubian, Beja, Zande, Bari, Fur, Shilluk, Lotuko
Religions Muslim (mainly Sunni) 70%, Traditional beliefs 20%, Christian 9%, Other 1%
Ethnic mix Other Black 52%, Arab 40%, Dinka and Beja 7%, Other 1%
Government Presidential system
Currency new Sudanese pound or dinar = 100 piastres
Literacy rate 61%
Calorie consumption 2228 calories

SURINAME
South America

Page 37 G3

Suriname is a former Dutch colony on the north coast of South America. Democracy was restored in 1991, after almost 11 years of military rule.

Official name Republic of Suriname
Formation 1975 / 1975
Capital Paramaribo
Population 470,784 / 8 people per sq mile (3 people per sq km) / 77%
Total area 63,039 sq. miles (163,270 sq. km)
Languages Sranan (Creole), Dutch*, Javanese, Sarnami Hindi, Saramaccan, Chinese, Carib
Religions Hindu 27%, Protestant 25%, Roman Catholic 23%, Muslim 20%, Traditional beliefs 5%
Ethnic mix Creole 34%, South Asian 34%, Javanese 18%, Black 9%, Other 5%
Government Parliamentary system
Currency Surinamese dollar = 100 cents
Literacy rate 90%
Calorie consumption 2652 calories

SWAZILAND
Southern Africa

Page 56 D4

The tiny southern African kingdom of Swaziland gained independence from Britain in 1968. It is economically dependent on South Africa.

Official name Kingdom of Swaziland
Formation 1968 / 1968
Capital Mbabane
Population 1 million / 151 people per sq mile (58 people per sq km) / 24%
Total area 6704 sq. miles (17,363 sq. km)
Languages English*, siSwati*, isiZulu, Xitsonga
Religions Christian 60%, Traditional beliefs 40%
Ethnic mix Swazi 97%, Other 3%
Government Monarchy
Currency Lilangeni = 100 cents
Literacy rate 80%
Calorie consumption 2322 calories

SWEDEN
Northern Europe

Page 62 B4

The largest Scandinavian country in both population and area, Sweden's strong industrial base helps to fund its extensive welfare system.

Official name Kingdom of Sweden
Formation 1523 / 1921
Capital Stockholm
Population 9.1 million / 57 people per sq mile (22 people per sq km) / 83%
Total area 173,731 sq. miles (449,964 sq. km)
Languages Swedish*, Finnish, Sámi
Religions Evangelical Lutheran 82%, Other 13%, Roman Catholic 2%, Muslim 2%, Orthodox Christian 1%
Ethnic mix Swedish 86%, Foreign-born or first-generation immigrant 12%, Finnish and Sámi 2%
Government Parliamentary system
Currency Swedish krona = 100 öre
Literacy rate 99%
Calorie consumption 3185 calories

SWITZERLAND
Central Europe

Page 73 A7

One of the world's most prosperous countries, with a long tradition of neutrality in foreign affairs, it lies at the center of Western Europe.

Official name Swiss Confederation
Formation 1291 / 1857
Capital Bern
Population 7.3 million / 475 people per sq mile (184 people per sq km) / 68%
Total area 15,942 sq. miles (41,290 sq. km)
Languages German*, Swiss-German, French*, Italian*, Romansch
Religions Roman Catholic 42%, Protestant 35%, Other and nonreligious 19%, Muslim 4%
Ethnic mix German 64%, French 20%, Other 9%, Italian 6%, Romansch 1%
Government Parliamentary system
Currency Swiss franc = 100 rappen/centimes
Literacy rate 99%
Calorie consumption 3526 calories

SYRIA
Southwest Asia

Page 96 B3

Stretching from the eastern Mediterranean to the River Tigris, Syria's borders were created on its independence from France in 1946.

Official name Syrian Arab Republic
Formation 1941 / 1967
Capital Damascus
Population 20 million / 281 people per sq mile (109 people per sq km) / 50%
Total area 71,498 sq. miles (184,180 sq. km)
Languages Arabic*, French, Kurdish, Armenian, Circassian, Turkic languages, Assyrian, Aramaic
Religions Sunni Muslim 74%, Other Muslim 16%, Christian 10%
Ethnic mix Arab 89%, Kurdish 6%, Other 3%, Armenian, Turkmen, and Circassian 2%
Government One-party state
Currency Syrian pound = 100 piastres
Literacy rate 80%
Calorie consumption 3038 calories

TAIWAN
East Asia

Page 107 D6

The island republic of Taiwan lies 80 miles (130 km) off the southeast coast of mainland China. China considers it to be one of its provinces.

Official name Republic of China (ROC)
Formation 1949 / 1949
Capital Taipei
Population 22.9 million / 1835 people per sq mile (709 people per sq km) / 80%
Total area 13,892 sq. miles (35,980 sq. km)
Languages Amoy Chinese, Mandarin Chinese*, Hakka Chinese
Religions Buddhist, Confucianist, and Taoist 93%, Christian 5%, Other 2%
Ethnic mix Han (pre-20th-century migration) 84%, Han (20th-century migration) 14%, Aboriginal 2%
Government Presidential system
Currency Taiwan dollar = 100 cents
Literacy rate 97%
Calorie consumption Not available

TAJIKISTAN
Central Asia

Page 101 F3

Tajikistan lies landlocked on the western slopes of the Pamirs in Central Asia. The Tajiks' language and traditions are similar to those of Iran.

Official name Republic of Tajikistan
Formation 1991 / 1991
Capital Dushanbe
Population 6.7 million / 121 people per sq mile (47 people per sq km) / 25%
Total area 55,251 sq. miles (143,100 sq. km)
Languages Tajik*, Uzbek, Russian
Religions Sunni Muslim 80%, Other 15%, Shi'a Muslim 5%
Ethnic mix Tajik 80%, Uzbek 15%, Other 3%, Russian 1%, Kyrgyz 1%
Government Presidential system
Currency Somoni = 100 diram
Literacy rate 99%
Calorie consumption 1828 calories

TANZANIA
East Africa

Page 51 B7

The East African state of Tanzania was formed in 1964 by the union of Tanganyika and Zanzibar. A third of its area is game reserve or national park.

Official name United Republic of Tanzania
Formation 1964 / 1964
Capital Dodoma
Population 39.7 million / 116 people per sq mile (45 people per sq km) / 36%
Total area 364,898 sq. miles (945,087 sq. km)
Languages Kiswahili*, Sukuma, Chagga, Nyamwezi, Hehe, Makonde, Yao, Sandawe, English*
Religions Muslim 33%, Christian 33%, Traditional beliefs 30%, Other 4%
Ethnic mix Native African (over 120 tribes) 99%, European, Asian, and Arab 1%
Government Presidential system
Currency Tanzanian shilling = 100 cents
Literacy rate 69%
Calorie consumption 1975 calories

THAILAND
Southeast Asia

Page 115 C5

Thailand lies at the heart of mainland Southeast Asia. Continuing rapid industrialization has resulted in massive congestion in the capital.

Official name Kingdom of Thailand
Formation 1238 / 1907
Capital Bangkok
Population 68.3 million / 346 people per sq mile (134 people per sq km) / 32%
Total area 198,455 sq. miles (514,000 sq. km)
Languages Thai*, Chinese, Malay, Khmer, Mon, Karen, Miao
Religions Buddhist 95%, Muslim 4%, Other (including Christian) 1%
Ethnic mix Thai 83%, Chinese 12%, Malay 3%, Khmer and Other 2%
Government Parliamentary system
Currency Baht = 100 satang
Literacy rate 93%
Calorie consumption 2467 calories

TOGO
West Africa

Page 53 F4

Togo lies sandwiched between Ghana and Benin in West Africa. The 1993–94 presidential elections were the first since its independence in 1960.

Official name The Togolese Republic
Formation 1960 / 1960
Capital Lomé
Population 6.5 million / 310 people per sq mile (120 people per sq km) / 36%
Total area 21,924 sq. miles (56,785 sq. km)
Languages French*, Ewe, Kabye, Gurma
Religions Traditional beliefs 50%, Christian 35%, Muslim 15%
Ethnic mix Ewe 46%, Other African 41%, Kabye 12%, European 1%
Government Presidential system
Currency CFA franc = 100 centimes
Literacy rate 53%
Calorie consumption 2345 calories

TONGA
Australasia & Oceania

Page 123 E4

Northeast of New Zealand, in the South Pacific, Tonga is an archipelago of 170 islands, 45 of which are inhabited. Politics is effectively controlled by the king.

Official name Kingdom of Tonga
Formation 1970 / 1970
Capital Nuku'alofa
Population 116,921 / 421 people per sq mile (162 people per sq km) / 34%
Total area 289 sq. miles (748 sq. km)
Languages English*, Tongan*
Religions Free Wesleyan 41%, Other 17%, Roman Catholic 16%, Church of Jesus Christ of Latter-day Saints 14%, Free Church of Tonga 12%
Ethnic mix Tongan 98%, Other 2%
Government Monarchy
Currency Pa'anga (Tongan dollar) = 100 seniti
Literacy rate 99%
Calorie consumption Not available

TRINIDAD & TOBAGO
West Indies

Page 33 H5

The former British colony of Trinidad and Tobago is the most southerly of the West Indies, lying just 9 miles (15 km) off the coast of Venezuela.

Official name Republic of Trinidad and Tobago
Formation 1962 / 1962
Capital Port-of-Spain
Population 1.3 million / 656 people per sq mile (253 people per sq km) / 76%
Total area 1980 sq. miles (5128 sq. km)
Languages English Creole, English*, Hindi, French, Spanish
Religions Roman Catholic 32%, Hindu 24%, Protestant 14%, Anglican 14%, Other 9%, Muslim 7%
Ethnic mix East Indian 40%, Black 40%, Mixed race 18%, Other 1%, White and Chinese 1%
Government Parliamentary system
Currency Trinidad and Tobago dollar = 100 cents
Literacy rate 99%
Calorie consumption 2732 calories

TUNISIA
North Africa

Page 49 E2

Tunisia, in North Africa, has traditionally been one of the more liberal Arab states, but is now facing a challenge from Islamic fundamentalists.

Official name The Tunisian Republic
Formation 1956 / 1956
Capital Tunis
Population 10.3 million / 172 people per sq mile (66 people per sq km) / 64%
Total area 63,169 sq. miles (163,610 sq. km)
Languages Arabic*, French
Religions Muslim (mainly Sunni) 98%, Christian 1%, Jewish 1%
Ethnic mix Arab and Berber 98%, Jewish 1%, European 1%
Government Presidential system
Currency Tunisian dinar = 1000 millimes
Literacy rate 74%
Calorie consumption 3238 calories

TURKEY
Asia / Europe

Page 94 B3

Lying partly in Europe, but mostly in Asia, Turkey's position gives it significant influence in the Mediterranean, Black Sea, and Middle East.

Official name Republic of Turkey
Formation 1923 / 1939
Capital Ankara
Population 75.2 million / 253 people per sq mile (98 people per sq km) / 67%
Total area 301,382 sq. miles (780,580 sq. km)
Languages Turkish*, Kurdish, Arabic, Circassian, Armenian, Greek, Georgian, Ladino
Religions Muslim (mainly Sunni) 99%, Other 1%
Ethnic mix Turkish 70%, Kurdish 20%, Other 8%, Arab 2%
Government Parliamentary system
Currency new Turkish lira = 100 kurus
Literacy rate 98%
Calorie consumption 3357 calories

TURKMENISTAN
Central Asia

Page 100 B2

Stretching from the Caspian Sea into the deserts of Central Asia, the ex-Soviet state of Turkmenistan has adjusted better than most to independence.

Official name Turkmenistan
Formation 1991 / 1991
Capital Ashgabat
Population 5 million / 27 people per sq mile (10 people per sq km) / 46%
Total area 188,455 sq. miles (488,100 sq. km)
Languages Turkmen*, Uzbek, Russian, Kazakh, Tatar
Religions Sunni Muslim 87%, Orthodox Christian 11%, Other 2%
Ethnic mix Turkmen 77%, Uzbek 9%, Russian 7%, Other 4%, Kazakh 2%, Tatar 1%
Government One-party state
Currency Manat = 100 tenge
Literacy rate 99%
Calorie consumption 2742 calories

TUVALU
Australasia & Oceania

Page 123 E3

The former Ellice Islands, linked to the Gilbert Islands as a British colony until 1978, Tuvalu is an isolated chain of nine atolls in the Central Pacific.

Official name Tuvalu
Formation 1978 / 1978
Capital Fongafale, on Funafuti Atoll
Population 11,992 / 1199 people per sq mile (461 people per sq km) / 57%
Total area 10 sq. miles (26 sq. km)
Languages English*, Tuvaluan, Kiribati
Religions Church of Tuvalu 97%, Baha'i 1%, Seventh-day Adventist 1%, Other 1%
Ethnic mix Polynesian 92%, Other 6%, Kiribati 2%
Government Nonparty system
Currency Australian dollar and Tuvaluan dollar = 100 cents
Literacy rate 98%
Calorie consumption Not available

UGANDA
East Africa

Page 51 B6

Uganda lies landlocked in East Africa. It was ruled by one of Africa's more eccentric leaders, the dictator Idi Amin Dada, from 1971–1980.

Official name Republic of Uganda
Formation 1962 / 1962
Capital Kampala
Population 30.9 million / 401 people per sq mile (155 people per sq km) / 12%
Total area 91,135 sq. miles (236,040 sq. km)
Languages English*, Luganda, Nkole, Chiga, Lango, Acholi, Teso, Lugbara
Religions Roman Catholic 38%, Protestant 33%, Traditional beliefs 13%, Muslim 8%, Other 8%
Ethnic mix Other 50%, Baganda 17%, Banyakole 10%, Basoga 9%, Iteso 7%, Bakiga 7%
Government Presidential system
Currency New Uganda shilling = 100 cents
Literacy rate 67%
Calorie consumption 2410 calories

UKRAINE
Eastern Europe

Page 86 C2

Bordered by seven states, the former "breadbasket of the Soviet Union" balances assertive nationalism with concerns over its relations with Russia.

Official name Ukraine
Formation 1991 / 1991
Capital Kiev
Population 45.5 million / 195 people per sq mile (75 people per sq km) / 67%
Total area 233,089 sq. miles (603,700 sq. km)
Languages Ukrainian*, Russian, Tatar
Religions Christian (mainly Orthodox) 95%, Other 5%
Ethnic mix Ukrainian 78%, Russian 17%, Other 5%
Government Presidential system
Currency Hryvna = 100 kopiykas
Literacy rate 99%
Calorie consumption 3054 calories

UNITED ARAB EMIRATES
Southwest Asia

Page 99 D5

Bordering the Persian Gulf on the northern coast of the Arabian Peninsula, is the United Arab Emirates, a working federation of seven states.

Official name United Arab Emirates
Formation 1971 / 1972
Capital Abu Dhabi
Population 4.8 million / 149 people per sq mile (57 people per sq km) / 85%
Total area 32,000 sq. miles (82,880 sq. km)
Languages Arabic*, Farsi, Indian and Pakistani languages, English
Religions Muslim (mainly Sunni) 96%, Christian, Hindu, and other 4%
Ethnic mix Asian 60%, Emirian 25%, Other Arab 12%, European 3%
Government Monarchy
Currency UAE dirham = 100 fils
Literacy rate 77%
Calorie consumption 3225 calories

UNITED KINGDOM
Northwest Europe

Page 67 B5

Separated from continental Europe by the North Sea and the English Channel, the UK comprises England, Wales, Scotland, and Northern Ireland.

Official name United Kingdom of Great Britain and Northern Ireland
Formation 1707 / 1922
Capital London
Population 60 million / 643 people per sq mile (248 people per sq km) / 89%
Total area 94,525 sq. miles (244,820 sq. km)
Languages English*, Welsh* *(in Wales)*, Gaelic
Religions Anglican 45%, Roman Catholic 9%, Presbyterian 4%, Other 42%
Ethnic mix English 80%, Scottish 9%, West Indian, Asian, and other 5%, Northern Irish 3%, Welsh 3%
Government Parliamentary system
Currency Pound sterling = 100 pence
Literacy rate 99%
Calorie consumption 3412 calories

UNITED STATES
North America

Page 13 B5

Stretching across the most temperate part of North America, and with many natural resources, the USA is the sole truly global superpower.

Official name United States of America
Formation 1776 / 1959
Capital Washington D.C.
Population 304 million / 86 people per sq mile (33 people per sq km) / 80%
Total area 3,717,792 sq. miles (9,626,091 sq. km)
Languages English*, Spanish, Chinese, French, German, Tagalog, Vietnamese, Italian, Korean, Russian, Polish
Religions Protestant 52%, Roman Catholic 25%, Muslim 2%, Jewish 2%, Other 19%
Ethnic mix White 62%, Hispanic 13%, Black American/African 13%, Other 8%, Asian 4%
Government Presidential system
Currency US dollar = 100 cents
Literacy rate 99%
Calorie consumption 3774 calories

URUGUAY
South America

Page 42 D4

Uruguay is situated in southeastern South America. It returned to civilian government in 1985, after 12 years of military dictatorship.

Official name The Oriental Republic of Uruguay
Formation 1828 / 1828
Capital Montevideo
Population 3.5 million / 52 people per sq mile (20 people per sq km) / 93%
Total area 68,039 sq. miles (176,220 sq. km)
Languages Spanish*
Religions Roman Catholic 66%, Other and nonreligious 30%, Jewish 2%, Protestant 2%
Ethnic mix White 90%, Mestizo 6%, Black 4%
Government Presidential system
Currency Uruguayan peso = 100 centésimos
Literacy rate 98%
Calorie consumption 2828 calories

UZBEKISTAN
Central Asia

Page 100 D2

Sharing the Aral Sea coastline with its northern neighbor, Kazakhstan, Uzbekistan lies on the ancient Silk Road between Asia and Europe.

Official name Republic of Uzbekistan
Formation 1991 / 1991
Capital Tashkent
Population 27.4 million / 159 people per sq mile (61 people per sq km) / 37%
Total area 172,741 sq. miles (447,400 sq. km)
Languages Uzbek*, Russian, Tajik, Kazakh
Religions Sunni Muslim 88%, Orthodox Christian 9%, Other 3%
Ethnic mix Uzbek 80%, Other 6%, Russian 6%, Tajik 5%, Kazakh 3%
Government Presidential system
Currency Som = 100 tiyin
Literacy rate 99%
Calorie consumption 2241 calories

VANUATU
Australasia & Oceania

Page 122 D4

An archipelago of 82 islands and islets in the Pacific Ocean, it was ruled jointly by Britain and France from 1906 until independence in 1980.

Official name Republic of Vanuatu
Formation 1980 / 1980
Capital Port Vila
Population 211,971 / 45 people per sq mile (17 people per sq km) / 23%
Total area 4710 sq. miles (12,200 sq. km)
Languages Bislama* (Melanesian pidgin), English*, French*, other indigenous languages
Religions Presbyterian 37%, Other 19%, Anglican 15%, Roman Catholic 15%, Traditional beliefs 8%, Seventh-day Adventist 6%
Ethnic mix Melanesian 98%, Other 1%, European 1%
Government Parliamentary system
Currency Vatu = 100 centimes
Literacy rate 74%
Calorie consumption 2587 calories

VATICAN CITY
Southern Europe

Page 75 A8

The Vatican City, seat of the Roman Catholic Church, is a walled enclave in the city of Rome. It is the world's smallest fully independent state.

Official name The Vatican City
Formation 1929 / 1929
Capital Vatican City
Population 821 / 4829 people per sq mile (1866 people per sq km) / 100%
Total area 0.17 sq. miles (0.44 sq. km)
Languages Italian*, Latin*
Religions Roman Catholic 100%
Government Papal state
Currency Euro = 100 cents
Literacy rate 99%
Calorie consumption Not available

VENEZUELA
South America

Page 36 D2

Located on the north coast of South America, Venezuela has the continent's most urbanized society. Most people live in the northern cities.

Official name Bolivarian Republic of Venezuela
Formation 1830 / 1830
Capital Caracas
Population 27.7 million / 81 people per sq mile (31 people per sq km) / 88%
Total area 352,143 sq. miles (912,050 sq. km)
Languages Spanish*, Amerindian languages
Religions Roman Catholic 89%, Protestant and other 11%
Ethnic mix Mestizo 69%, White 20%, Black 9%, Amerindian 2%
Government Presidential system
Currency Bolívar = 100 céntimos
Literacy rate 93%
Calorie consumption 2336 calories

VIETNAM
Southeast Asia

Page 114 D4

Situated in the far east of mainland Southeast Asia, the country has made great progress towards recovery after the devastating 1962–75 Vietnam War.

Official name Socialist Republic of Vietnam
Formation 1976 / 1976
Capital Hanoi
Population 86.4 million / 688 people per sq mile (266 people per sq km) / 26%
Total area 127,243 sq. miles (329,560 sq. km)
Languages Vietnamese*, Chinese, Thai, Khmer, Muong, Nung, Miao, Yao, Jarai
Religions Nonreligious 81%, Buddhist 9%, Christian 7%, Other 3%
Ethnic mix Vietnamese 86%, Other 10%, Tay 2%Thai 2%
Government One-party state
Currency Dông = 10 hao = 100 xu
Literacy rate 90%
Calorie consumption 2566 calories

YEMEN
Southwest Asia

Page 99 C7

Located in southern Arabia, Yemen was formerly two countries – a socialist regime in the south, and a republic in the north. Both united in 1990.

Official name Republic of Yemen
Formation 1990 / 1990
Capital Sana
Population 22.3 million / 103 people per sq mile (40 people per sq km) / 26%
Total area 203,849 sq. miles (527,970 sq. km)
Languages Arabic*
Religions Sunni Muslim 55%, Shi'a Muslim 42%, Christian, Hindu, and Jewish 3%
Ethnic mix Arab 99%, Other 1%
Government Presidential system
Currency Yemeni rial = 100 fils
Literacy rate 49%
Calorie consumption 2038 calories

ZAMBIA
Southern Africa

Page 56 C2

Zambia lies landlocked at the heart of southern Africa. In 1991, it made a peaceful transition from single-party rule to multiparty democracy.

Official name Republic of Zambia
Formation 1964 / 1964
Capital Lusaka
Population 12.1 million / 42 people per sq mile (16 people per sq km) / 36%
Total area 290,584 sq. miles (752,614 sq. km)
Languages English*, Bemba, Tonga, Nyanja, Lozi, Lala-Bisa, Nsenga
Religions Christian 63%, Traditional beliefs 36%, Muslim and Hindu 1%
Ethnic mix Bemba 34%, Other African 26%, Tonga 16%, Nyanja 14%, Lozi 9%, European 1%
Government Presidential system
Currency Zambian kwacha = 100 ngwee
Literacy rate 68%
Calorie consumption 1927 calories

ZIMBABWE
Southern Africa

Page 56 D3

The former British colony of Southern Rhodesia became fully independent as Zimbabwe in 1980, after 15 years of troubled white minority rule.

Official name Republic of Zimbabwe
Formation 1980 / 1980
Capital Harare
Population 13.2 million / 88 people per sq mile (34 people per sq km) / 35%
Total area 150,803 sq. miles (390,580 sq. km)
Languages English*, Shona, isiNdebele
Religions Syncretic (Christian/traditional beliefs) 50%, Christian 25%, Traditional beliefs 24%, Other (including Muslim) 1%
Ethnic mix Shona 71%, Ndebele 16%, Other African 11%, White 1%, Asian 1%
Government Presidential system
Currency Zimbabwe dollar = 100 cents
Literacy rate 90%
Calorie consumption 1943 calories

Overseas Territories and Dependencies

Despite the rapid process of decolonization since the end of the Second World War, around 10 million people in more than 50 territories around the world continue to live under the protection of France, Australia, the Netherlands, Denmark, Norway, New Zealand, the United Kingdom or the USA. These remnants of former colonial empires may have persisted for economic, strategic or political reasons, and are administered in a variety of ways.

AUSTRALIA

ASHMORE & CARTIER ISLANDS
Indian Ocean
Claimed 1931
Capital not applicable
Area 2 sq miles (5.2 sq km)
Population None

CHRISTMAS ISLAND
Indian Ocean
Claimed 1958
Capital The Settlement
Area 52 sq miles (134.6 sq km)
Population 1,493

COCOS ISLANDS
Indian Ocean
Claimed 1955
Capital No official capital
Area 5.5 sq miles (14.24 sq km)
Population 574

CORAL SEA ISLANDS
Southwest Pacific
Claimed 1969
Capital None
Area Less than 1.16 sq miles (3 sq km)
Population below 10 (scientists)

HEARD & McDONALD ISLANDS
Indian Ocean
Claimed 1947
Capital not applicable
Area 161 sq miles (417 sq km)
Population None

NORFOLK ISLAND
Southwest Pacific
Claimed 1774
Capital Kingston
Area 13.3 sq miles (34 sq km)
Population 1,828

DENMARK

FAEROE ISLANDS
North Atlantic
Claimed 1380
Capital Tórshavn
Area 540 sq miles (1,399 sq km)
Population 47,246

GREENLAND
North Atlantic
Claimed 1380
Capital Nuuk
Area 840,000 sq miles (2,175,516 sq km)
Population 56,361

FRANCE

CLIPPERTON ISLAND
East Pacific
Claimed 1935
Capital not applicable
Area 2.7 sq miles (7 sq km)
Population None

FRENCH GUIANA
South America
Claimed 1817
Capital Cayenne
Area 35,135 sq miles (90,996 sq km)
Population 199,509

FRENCH POLYNESIA
South Pacific
Claimed 1843
Capital Papeete
Area 1,608 sq miles (4,165 sq km)
Population 260,000

GUADELOUPE
West Indies
Claimed 1635
Capital Basse-Terre
Area 687 sq miles (1,780 sq km)
Population 452,000

MARTINIQUE
West Indies
Claimed 1635
Capital Fort-de-France
Area 425 sq miles (1,100 sq km)
Population 397,000

MAYOTTE
Indian Ocean
Claimed 1843
Capital Mamoudzou
Area 144 sq miles (374 sq km)
Population 201,234

NEW CALEDONIA
Southwest Pacific
Claimed 1853
Capital Nouméa
Area 7,374 sq miles (19,103 sq km)
Population 241,000

RÉUNION
Indian Ocean
Claimed 1638
Capital Saint-Denis
Area 970 sq miles (2,512 sq km)
Population 796,000

ST. PIERRE & MIQUELON
North America
Claimed 1604
Capital Saint-Pierre
Area 93.4 sq miles (242 sq km)
Population 7,026

WALLIS & FUTUNA
South Pacific
Claimed 1842
Capital Matá'Utu
Area 106 sq miles (274 sq km)
Population 16,025

NETHERLANDS

ARUBA
West Indies
Claimed 1643
Capital Oranjestad
Area 75 sq miles (194 sq km)
Population 71,891

NETHERLANDS ANTILLES
West Indies
Claimed 1816
Capital Willemstad
Area 308 sq miles (800 sq km)
Population 184,000

NEW ZEALAND

COOK ISLANDS
South Pacific
Claimed 1901
Capital Avarua
Area 91 sq miles (235 sq km)
Population 21,388

NIUE
South Pacific
Claimed 1901
Capital Alofi
Area 102 sq miles (264 sq km)
Population 2,166

TOKELAU
South Pacific
Claimed 1926
Capital not applicable
Area 4 sq miles (10.4 sq km)
Population 1,392

NORWAY

BOUVET ISLAND
South Atlantic
Claimed 1928
Capital not applicable
Area 22 sq miles (58 sq km)
Population None

JAN MAYEN
North Atlantic
Claimed 1929
Capital not applicable
Area 147 sq miles (381 sq km)
Population None

PETER I ISLAND
Antarctica
Claimed 1931
Capital not applicable
Area 69 sq miles (180 sq km)
Population None

SVALBARD
Arctic Ocean
Claimed 1920
Capital Longyearbyen
Area 24,289 sq miles (62,906 sq km)
Population 2,701

UNITED KINGDOM

ANGUILLA
West Indies
Claimed 1650
Capital The Valley
Area 37 sq miles (96 sq km)
Population 13,477

ASCENSION ISLAND
South Atlantic
Claimed 1673
Capital Georgetown
Area 34 sq miles (88 sq km)
Population 1,177

BERMUDA
North Atlantic
Claimed 1612
Capital Hamilton
Area 20.5 sq miles (53 sq km)
Population 65,773

BRITISH INDIAN OCEAN TERRITORY
Indian Ocean
Claimed 1814
Capital Diego Garcia
Area 23 sq miles (60 sq km)
Population 4,000

BRITISH VIRGIN ISLANDS
West Indies
Claimed 1672
Capital Road Town
Area 59 sq miles (153 sq km)
Population 23,098

CAYMAN ISLANDS
West Indies
Claimed 1670
Capital George Town
Area 100 sq miles (259 sq km)
Population 45,436

FALKLAND ISLANDS
South Atlantic
Claimed 1832
Capital Stanley
Area 4,699 sq miles (12,173 sq km)
Population 2,967

GIBRALTAR
Southwest Europe
Claimed 1713
Capital Gibraltar
Area 2.5 sq miles (6.5 sq km)
Population 27,928

GUERNSEY
Northwest Europe
Claimed 1066
Capital St Peter Port
Area 25 sq miles (65 sq km)
Population 65,049

ISLE OF MAN
Northwest Europe
Claimed 1765
Capital Douglas
Area 221 sq miles (572 sq km)
Population 75,441

JERSEY
Northwest Europe
Claimed 1066
Capital St. Helier
Area 45 sq miles (116 sq km)
Population 90,084

MONTSERRAT
West Indies
Claimed 1632
Capital Plymouth (currently uninhabitable)
Area 40 sq miles (102 sq km)
Population 4,488

PITCAIRN ISLANDS
South Pacific
Claimed 1887
Capital Adamstown
Area 18 sq miles (47 sq km)
Population 45

ST. HELENA
South Atlantic
Claimed 1673
Capital Jamestown
Area 47 sq miles (122 sq km)
Population 4,299

SOUTH GEORGIA & THE SOUTH SANDWICH ISLANDS
South Atlantic
Capital not applicable
Claimed 1775
Area 1,387 sq miles (3,592 sq km)
Population None

TRISTAN DA CUNHA
South Atlantic
Claimed 1612
Capital Edinburgh
Area 38 sq miles (98 sq km)
Population 276

TURKS & CAICOS ISLANDS
West Indies
Claimed 1766
Capital Cockburn Town
Area 166 sq miles (430 sq km)
Population 21,152

UNITED STATES OF AMERICA

AMERICAN SAMOA
South Pacific
Claimed 1900
Capital Pago Pago
Area 75 sq miles (195 sq km)
Population 57,794

BAKER & HOWLAND ISLANDS
Central Pacific
Claimed 1856
Capital not applicable
Area 0.54 sq miles (1.4 sq km)
Population None

GUAM
West Pacific
Claimed 1898
Capital Hagåtña
Area 212 sq miles (549 sq km)
Population 172,000

JARVIS ISLAND
Central Pacific
Claimed 1856
Capital not applicable
Area 1.7 sq miles (4.5 sq km)
Population None

NORTHERN MARIANA ISLANDS
West Pacific
Claimed 1947
Capital Saipan
Area 177 sq miles (457 sq km)
Population 82,459

PALMYRA ATOLL
Central Pacific
Claimed 1898
Capital not applicable
Area 5 sq miles (12 sq km)
Population None

PUERTO RICO
West Indies
Claimed 1898
Capital San Juan
Area 3,515 sq miles (9,104 sq km)
Population 4.0 million

VIRGIN ISLANDS
West Indies
Claimed 1917
Capital Charlotte Amalie
Area 137 sq miles (355 sq km)
Population 108,605

WAKE ISLAND
Central Pacific
Claimed 1898
Capital not applicable
Area 2.5 sq miles (6.5 sq km)
Population 200

Geographical comparisons

Largest countries

Russ. Fed.	6,592,735 sq miles	(17,075,200 sq km)
Canada	3,854,085 sq miles	(9,984,670 sq km)
USA	3,717,792 sq miles	(9,629,091 sq km)
China	3,705,386 sq miles	(9,596,960 sq km)
Brazil	3,286,470 sq miles	(8,511,965 sq km)
Australia	2,967,893 sq miles	(7,686,850 sq km)
India	1,269,339 sq miles	(3,287,590 sq km)
Argentina	1,068,296 sq miles	(2,766,890 sq km)
Kazakhstan	1,049,150 sq miles	(2,717,300 sq km)
Sudan	967,493 sq miles	(2,505,810 sq km)

Smallest countries

Vatican City	0.17 sq miles	(0.44 sq km)
Monaco	0.75 sq miles	(1.95 sq km)
Nauru	8 sq miles	(21 sq km)
Tuvalu	10 sq miles	(26 sq km)
San Marino	24 sq miles	(61 sq km)
Liechtenstein	62 sq miles	(160 sq km)
Marshall Islands	70 sq miles	(181 sq km)
St. Kitts & Nevis	101 sq miles	(261 sq km)
Maldives	116 sq miles	(300 sq km)
Malta	124 sq miles	(320 sq km)

Largest islands

Greenland	849,400 sq miles (2,200,000 sq km)
New Guinea	312,000 sq miles (808,000 sq km)
Borneo	292,222 sq miles (757,050 sq km)
Madagascar	229,300 sq miles (594,000 sq km)
Sumatra	202,300 sq miles (524,000 sq km)
Baffin Island	183,800 sq miles (476,000 sq km)
Honshu	88,800 sq miles (230,000 sq km)
Britain	88,700 sq miles (229,800 sq km)
Victoria Island	81,900 sq miles (212,000 sq km)
Ellesmere Island	75,700 sq miles (196,000 sq km)

Richest countries (GNI per capita, in US$)

Luxembourg	65,630
Norway	59,590
Switzerland	54,930
Liechtenstein	50,000
Denmark	47,390
Iceland	46,320
USA	43,740
Sweden	41,060
Ireland	40,150
Japan	38,980

Poorest countries (GNI per capita, in US$)

Burundi	100
Somalia	120
Congo, Dem. Rep.	120
Liberia	130
Malawi	160
Ethiopia	160
Guinea-Bissau	180
Sierra Leone	220
Eritrea	220
Afghanistan	222

Most populous countries

China	1,331,400,000
India	1,135,600,000
USA	303,900,000
Indonesia	228,100,000
Brazil	191,300,000
Pakistan	164,600,000

Most populous countries *continued*

Bangladesh	147,100,000
Russian Federation	141,900,000
Nigeria	137,200,000
Japan	128,300,000

Least populous countries

Vatican City	821
Tuvalu	11,992
Nauru	13,528
Palau	20,842
San Marino	29,615
Monaco	32,671
Liechtenstein	34,247
St. Kitts & Nevis	39,349
Marshall Islands	61,815
Antigua & Barbuda	69,481

Most densely populated countries

Monaco	43,561 people per sq mile (16,754 per sq km)
Singapore	18,644 people per sq mile (7213 per sq km)
Vatican City	4829 people per sq mile (1866 per sq km)
Malta	3241 people per sq mile (1256 per sq km)
Maldives	3181 people per sq mile (1230 per sq km)
Bangladesh	2845 people per sq mile (1098 per sq km)
Bahrain	2596 people per sq mile (1004 per sq km)
Taiwan	1835 people per sq mile (709 per sq km)
Mauritius	1811 people per sq mile (699 per sq km)
Barbados	1692 people per sq mile (653 per sq km)

Most sparsely populated countries

Mongolia	4 people per sq mile	(2 per sq km)
Namibia	7 people per sq mile	(3 per sq km)
Australia	7 people per sq mile	(3 per sq km)
Iceland	8 people per sq mile	(3 per sq km)
Suriname	8 people per sq mile	(3 per sq km)
Botswana	8 people per sq mile	(3 per sq km)
Mauritania	8 people per sq mile	(3 per sq km)
Libya	9 people per sq mile	(4 per sq km)
Canada	9 people per sq mile	(4 per sq km)
Guyana	10 people per sq mile	(4 per sq km)

Most widely spoken languages

1. Chinese (Mandarin)	6. Arabic
2. English	7. Bengali
3. Hindi	8. Portuguese
4. Spanish	9. Malay-Indonesian
5. Russian	10. French

Largest conurbations

Tokyo	34,200,000
Mexico City	22,800,000
Seoul	22,300,000
New York	21,900,000
São Paulo	20,200,000
Mumbai	19,850,000
Delhi	19,700,000
Shanghai	18,150,000
Los Angeles	18,000,000
Osaka	16,800,000
Jakarta	16,550,000
Kolkata	15,650,000
Cairo	15,600,000
Manila	14,950,000
Karachi	14,300,000
Moscow	13,750,000
Buenos Aires	13,450,000
Dacca	13,250,000

Largest conurbations *continued*

Rio de Janeiro	12,150,000
Beijing	12,100,000
London	12,000,000
Tehran	11,850,000
Istanbul	11,500,000
Lagos	11,100,000
Shenzhen	10,700,000

Longest rivers

Nile (NE Africa)	4160 miles	(6695 km)
Amazon (South America)	4049 miles	(6516 km)
Yangtze (China)	3915 miles	(6299 km)
Mississippi/Missouri (US)	3710 miles	(5969 km)
Ob'-Irtysh (Russ. Fed.)	3461 miles	(5570 km)
Yellow River (China)	3395 miles	(5464 km)
Congo (Central Africa)	2900 miles	(4667 km)
Mekong (Southeast Asia)	2749 miles	(4425 km)
Lena (Russian Federation)	2734 miles	(4400 km)
Mackenzie (Canada)	2640 miles	(4250 km)
Yenisey (Russ. Federation)	2541 miles	(4090 km)

Highest mountains

(Height above sea level)

Everest	29,035 ft	(8850 m)
K2	28,253 ft	(8611 m)
Kanchenjunga I	28,210 ft	(8598 m)
Makalu I	27,767 ft	(8463 m)
Cho Oyu	26,907 ft	(8201 m)
Dhaulagiri I	26,796 ft	(8167 m)
Manaslu I	26,783 ft	(8163 m)
Nanga Parbat I	26,661 ft	(8126 m)
Annapurna I	26,547 ft	(8091 m)
Gasherbrum I	26,471 ft	(8068 m)

Largest bodies of inland water

(Area & depth)

Caspian Sea	143,243 sq miles (371,000 sq km)	3215 ft (980 m)
Lake Superior	32,151 sq miles (83,270 sq km)	1289 ft (393 m)
Lake Victoria	26,560 sq miles (68,880 sq km)	328 ft (100 m)
Lake Huron	23,436 sq miles (60,700 sq km)	751 ft (229 m)
Lake Michigan	22,402 sq miles (58,020 sq km)	922 ft (281 m)
Lake Tanganyika	12,703 sq miles (32,900 sq km)	4700 ft (1435 m)
Great Bear Lake	12,274 sq miles (31,790 sq km)	1047 ft (319 m)
Lake Baikal	11,776 sq miles (30,500 sq km)	5712 ft (1741 m)
Great Slave Lake	10,981 sq miles (28,440 sq km)	459 ft (140 m)
Lake Erie	9915 sq miles (25,680 sq km)	197 ft (60 m)

Deepest ocean features

Challenger Deep, Mariana Trench (Pacific)	36,201 ft (11,034 m)
Vityaz III Depth, Tonga Trench (Pacific)	35,704 ft (10,882 m)
Vityaz Depth, Kurile-Kamchatka Trench (Pacific)	34,588 ft (10,542 m)
Cape Johnson Deep, Philippine Trench (Pacific)	34,441 ft (10,497 m)
Kermadec Trench (Pacific)	32,964 ft (10,047 m)
Ramapo Deep, Japan Trench (Pacific)	32,758 ft (9984 m)
Milwaukee Deep, Puerto Rico Trench (Atlantic)	30,185 ft (9200 m)
Argo Deep, Torres Trench (Pacific)	30,070 ft (9165 m)
Meteor Depth, South Sandwich Trench (Atlantic)	30,000 ft (9144 m)
Planet Deep, New Britain Trench (Pacific)	29,988 ft (9140 m)

Greatest waterfalls

(Mean flow of water)

Boyoma (Congo, Dem. Rep.)	600,400 cu. ft/sec (17,000 cu.m/sec)
Khône (Laos/Cambodia)	410,000 cu. ft/sec (11,600 cu.m/sec)
Niagara (USA/Canada)	195,000 cu. ft/sec (5500 cu.m/sec)
Grande (Uruguay)	160,000 cu. ft/sec (4500 cu.m/sec)
Paulo Afonso (Brazil)	100,000 cu. ft/sec (2800 cu.m/sec)
Urubupunga (Brazil)	97,000 cu. ft/sec (2750 cu.m/sec)
Iguaçu (Argentina/Brazil)	62,000 cu. ft/sec (1700 cu.m/sec)
Maribondo (Brazil)	53,000 cu. ft/sec (1500 cu.m/sec)
Victoria (Zimbabwe)	39,000 cu. ft/sec (1100 cu.m/sec)

Greatest waterfalls *continued*

Kabalega (Uganda)	42,000 cu. ft/sec (1200 cu.m/sec)
Churchill (Canada)	35,000 cu. ft/sec (1000 cu.m/sec)
Cauvery (India)	33,000 cu. ft/sec (900 cu.m/sec)

Highest waterfalls

Angel (Venezuela)	3212 ft	(979 m)
Tugela (South Africa)	3110 ft	(948 m)
Utigard (Norway)	2625 ft	(800 m)
Mongefossen (Norway)	2539 ft	(774 m)
Mtarazi (Zimbabwe)	2500 ft	(762 m)
Yosemite (USA)	2425 ft	(739 m)
Ostre Mardola Foss (Norway)	2156 ft	(657 m)
Tyssestrengane (Norway)	2119 ft	(646 m)
*Cuquenan (Venezuela)	2001 ft	(610 m)
Sutherland (New Zealand)	1903 ft	(580 m)
*Kjellfossen (Norway)	1841 ft	(561 m)

* indicates that the total height is a single leap

Largest deserts

Sahara	3,450,000 sq miles (9,065,000 sq km)
Gobi	500,000 sq miles (1,295,000 sq km)
Ar Rub al Khali	289,600 sq miles (750,000 sq km)
Great Victorian	249,800 sq miles (647,000 sq km)
Sonoran	120,000 sq miles (311,000 sq km)
Kalahari	120,000 sq miles (310,800 sq km)
Garagum	115,800 sq miles (300,000 sq km)
Takla Makan	100,400 sq miles (260,000 sq km)
Namib	52,100 sq miles (135,000 sq km)
Thar	33,670 sq miles (130,000 sq km)

NB – Most of Antarctica is a polar desert, with only 2 inches (50 mm) of precipitation annually

Hottest inhabited places

Djibouti (Djibouti)	86.0°F	(30.0°C)
Timbouctou (Mali)	84.7°F	(29.3°C)
Tirunelveli (India)	84.7°F	(29.3°C)
Tuticorin (India)	84.7°F	(29.3°C)
Nellore (India)	84.5°F	(29.2°C)
Santa Marta (Colombia)	84.5°F	(29.2°C)
Aden (Yemen)	84.0°F	(29.0°C)
Madurai (India)	84.0°F	(29.0°C)
Niamey (Niger)	84.0°F	(29.0°C)

Driest inhabited places

Aswân (Egypt)	0.02 in	(0.5 mm)
Luxor (Egypt)	0.03 in	(0.7 mm)
Arica (Chile)	0.04 in	(1.1 mm)
Ica (Peru)	0.10 in	(2.3 mm)
Antofagasta (Chile)	0.20 in	(4.9 mm)
El Minya (Egypt)	0.20 in	(5.1 mm)
Asyût (Egypt)	0.20 in	(5.2 mm)
Callao (Peru)	0.50 in	(12.0 mm)
Trujillo (Peru)	0.55 in	(14.0 mm)
El Faiyûm (Egypt)	0.80 in	(19.0 mm)

Wettest inhabited places

Buenaventura (Colombia)	265 in	(6743 mm)
Monrovia (Liberia)	202 in	(5131 mm)
Pago Pago (American Samoa)	196 in	(4990 mm)
Moulmein (Myanmar)	191 in	(4852 mm)
Lae (Papua New Guinea)	183 in	(4645 mm)
Baguio (Luzon I., Philippines)	180 in	(4573 mm)
Sylhet (Bangladesh)	176 in	(4457 mm)
Padang (Sumatra, Indonesia)	166 in	(4225 mm)
Bogor (Java, Indonesia)	166 in	(4225 mm)
Conakry (Guinea)	171 in	(4341 mm)

Aa – Al Minyā

A

Aa *see* Gauja
Aachen 72 A4 *Dut.* Aken, *Fr.* Aix-la-Chapelle; *anc.* Aquae Grani, Aquisgranum. Nordrhein-Westfalen, W Germany
Aaiún *see* Laâyoune
Aalborg 63 B7 *var.* Ålborg, Ålborg-Nørresundby; *anc.* Alburgum. Nordjylland, N Denmark
Aalen 73 B6 Baden-Württemberg, S Germany
Aalsmeer 64 C3 Noord-Holland, C Netherlands
Aalst 65 B6 Oost-Vlaanderen, C Belgium
Aalten 64 E4 Gelderland, E Netherlands
Aalter 65 B5 Oost-Vlaanderen, NW Belgium
Aanaarjärvi *see* Inarijärvi
Äänekoski 63 D5 Länsi-Suomi, W Finland
Aar *see* Aare
Aare 73 A7 *var.* Aar. *river* W Switzerland
Aarhus *see* Århus
Aarlen *see* Arlon
Aat *see* Ath
Aba 55 E5 Orientale, NE Dem. Rep. Congo
Aba 53 G5 Abia, S Nigeria
Abā as Su'ūd *see* Najrān
Abaco Island *see* Great Abaco, N Bahamas
Ābādān 98 C4 Khūzestān, SW Iran
Abadan 100 C3 *prev.* Bezmein, Büzmeýin, *Rus.* Byuzmeyin. Ahal Welaýaty, C Turkmenistan
Abai *see* Blue Nile
Abakan 92 D4 Respublika Khakasiya, S Russian Federation
Abancay 38 D4 Apurímac, SE Peru
Abariringa *see* Kanton
Abashiri 108 D2 *var.* Abasiri. Hokkaidō, NE Japan
Abasiri *see* Abashiri
Ābay Wenz *see* Blue Nile
Abbaia *see* Ābaya Hāyk'
Abbatis Villa *see* Abbeville
Abbazia *see* Opatija
Abbeville 68 C2 *anc.* Abbatis Villa. Somme, N France
'Abd al 'Azīz, Jabal 96 D2 *mountain range* NE Syria
Abéché 54 C3 *var.* Abécher, Abeshr. Ouaddaï, SE Chad
Abécher *see* Abéché
Abela *see* Ávila
Abellinum *see* Avellino
Abemama 122 D2 *var.* Apamama; *prev.* Roger Simpson Island. *atoll* Tungaru, W Kiribati
Abengourou 53 E5 E Ivory Coast
Aberbrothock *see* Arbroath
Abercorn *see* Mbala
Aberdeen 66 D3 *anc.* Devana. NE Scotland, United Kingdom
Aberdeen 23 E2 South Dakota, N USA
Aberdeen 24 B2 Washington, NW USA
Abergwaun *see* Fishguard
Abertawe *see* Swansea
Aberystwyth 67 C6 W Wales, United Kingdom
Abeshr *see* Abéché
Abhā 99 B6 'Asīr, SW Saudi Arabia
Abidavichy 85 D7 *Rus.* Obidovichi. Mahilyowskaya Voblasts', E Belarus
Abidjan 53 E5 S Ivory Coast
Abilene 27 F3 Texas, SW USA
Abingdon *see* Pinta, Isla
Abkhazia *see* Ap'khazet'i
Åbo *see* Turku
Aboisso 53 E5 SE Ivory Coast
Abo, Massif d' 54 B1 *mountain range* NW Chad
Abomey 53 F5 S Benin
Abou-Déïa 54 C3 Salamat, SE Chad
Aboudouhour *see* Abū aḑ Ḑuhūr
Abou Kémal *see* Abū Kamāl
Abrantes 70 B3 *var.* Abrántes. Santarém, C Portugal
Abrashlare *see* Brezovo
Abrolhos Bank 34 E4 *undersea bank* W Atlantic Ocean
Abrova 85 B6 *Rus.* Obrovo. Brestskaya Voblasts', SW Belarus
Abrud 86 B4 *Ger.* Gross-Schlatten, *Hung.* Abrudbánya. Alba, SW Romania
Abrudbánya *see* Abrud
Abruzzese, Appennino 74 C4 *mountain range* C Italy
Absaroka Range 22 B2 *mountain range* Montana/Wyoming, NW USA
Abū aḑ Ḑuhūr 96 B3 *Fr.* Aboudouhour. Idlib, NW Syria
Abu Dhabi *see* Abū Ẓaby
Abu Hamed 50 C3 River Nile, N Sudan
Abū Ḩardān 96 E3 *var.* Hajîne. Dayr az Zawr, E Syria
Abuja 53 G4 *country capital* Federal Capital District, C Nigeria
Abū Kamāl 96 E3 *Fr.* Abou Kémal. Dayr az Zawr, E Syria
Abula *see* Ávila
Abunã, Rio 40 C2 *var.* Río Abuná. *river* Bolivia/Brazil
Abut Head 129 B6 *headland* South Island, New Zealand
Abuye Meda 50 D4 *mountain* C Ethiopia
Abū Ẓabī *see* Abū Ẓaby
Abū Ẓaby 99 C5 *var.* Abū Ẓabī, *Eng.* Abu Dhabi. *country capital* Abū Ẓaby, C United Arab Emirates
Abyaḑ, Al Baḩr al *see* White Nile
Abyla *see* Ávila
Abyssinia *see* Ethiopia
Acalayong 55 A5 SW Equatorial Guinea
Acaponeta 28 D4 Nayarit, C Mexico
Acapulco 29 E5 *var.* Acapulco de Juárez. Guerrero, S Mexico
Acapulco de Juárez *see* Acapulco
Acarai Mountains 37 F4 *Sp.* Serra Acaraí. *mountain range* Brazil/Guyana
Acaraí, Serra *see* Acarai Mountains
Acarigua 36 D2 Portuguesa, N Venezuela
Accra 53 E5 *country capital* SE Ghana
Achacachi 39 E4 La Paz, W Bolivia
Achara 95 F2 *var.* Ajaria. *autonomous republic* SW Georgia
Acklins Island 32 C2 *island* SE Bahamas
Aconcagua, Cerro 42 B4 *mountain* W Argentina
Açores/Açores, Arquipélago dos/Açores, Ilhas dos *see* Azores
A Coruña 70 B1 *Cast.* La Coruña, *Eng.* Corunna; *anc.* Caronium. Galicia, NW Spain
Acre 40 C2 *off.* Estado do Acre. *region* W Brazil
Acre 40 C2 *off.* Estado do Acre. *state* W Brazil
Açu 41 G2 *var.* Assu. Rio Grande do Norte, E Brazil
Acunum Acusio *see* Montélimar
Ada 78 D3 Vojvodina, N Serbia
Ada 27 G2 Oklahoma, C USA
Ada Bazar *see* Adapazarı
Adalia *see* Antalya
Adalia, Gulf of *see* Antalya Körfezi
Adama *see* Nazrēt
'Adan 99 B7 *Eng.* Aden. SW Yemen
Adana 94 D4 *var.* Seyhan. Adana, S Turkey
Adâncata *see* Horlivka
Adapazarı 94 B2 *prev.* Ada Bazar. Sakarya, NW Turkey
Adare, Cape 132 B4 *cape* Antarctica
Ad Dahna 98 C4 *desert* E Saudi Arabia
Ad Dakhla 48 A4 *var.* Dakhla. SW Western Sahara
Ad Dalanj *see* Dilling
Ad Damar *see* Ed Damer
Ad Damazīn *see* Ed Damazin
Ad Dāmir *see* Ed Damer
Ad Dammān 98 C4 *var.* Dammām. Ash Sharqīyah, NE Saudi Arabia
Ad Dāmūr *see* Damoûr
Ad Dawḩah 98 C4 *Eng.* Doha. *country capital* C Qatar
Aḑ Ḑiffah *see* Libyan Plateau
Addis Ababa *see* Ādīs Ābeba
Addoo Atoll *see* Addu Atoll
Addu Atoll 110 A5 *var.* Addoo Atoll, Seenu Atoll. *atoll* S Maldives
Adelaide 127 B6 *state capital* South Australia
Adelsberg *see* Postojna
Aden *see* 'Adan
Aden, Gulf of 99 C7 *gulf* SW Arabian Sea
Adige 74 C2 *Ger.* Etsch. *river* N Italy
Adirondack Mountains 19 F2 *mountain range* New York, NE USA
Ādīs Ābeba 51 C5 *Eng.* Addis Ababa. *country capital* Ādīs Ābeba, C Ethiopia
Adıyaman 95 E4 Adıyaman, SE Turkey
Adjud 86 C4 Vrancea, E Romania
Admiralty Islands 122 B3 *island group* N Papua New Guinea
Adra 71 E5 Andalucía, S Spain
Adrar 48 D3 C Algeria
Adrian 18 C3 Michigan, N USA
Adrianople/Adrianopolis *see* Edirne
Adriatico, Mare *see* Adriatic Sea
Adriatic Sea 81 E2 *Alb.* Deti Adriatik, *It.* Mare Adriatico, *SCr.* Jadransko More, *Slvn.* Jadransko Morje. *sea* N Mediterranean Sea
Adriatik, Deti *see* Adriatic Sea
Adycha 93 F2 *river* NE Russian Federation
Aegean Sea 83 C5 *Gk.* Aigaíon Pelagos, Aigaío Pélagos, *Turk.* Ege Denizi. *sea* NE Mediterranean Sea
Aegviidu 84 D2 *Ger.* Charlottenhof. Harjumaa, NW Estonia
Aegyptus *see* Egypt
Aelana *see* Al 'Aqabah
Aelok *see* Ailuk Atoll
Aelōnlaplap *see* Ailinglaplap Atoll
Aemona *see* Ljubljana
Aeolian Islands 75 C6 *var.* Isole Lipari, *Eng.* Aeolian Islands, Lipari Islands. *island group* S Italy
Aeolian Islands *see* Eolie, Isole
Æsernia *see* Isernia
Afar Depression *see* Danakil Desert
Afars et des Issas, Territoire Français des *see* Djibouti
Afghānestān, Dowlat-e Eslāmī-ye *see* Afghanistan
Afghanistan 100 C4 *off.* Islamic Republic of Afghanistan, *Per.* Dowlat-e Eslāmī-ye Afghānestān; *prev.* Republic of Afghanistan. *country* C Asia
Afmadow 51 D6 Jubbada Hoose, S Somalia
Africa 46 *continent*
Africa, Horn of 46 E4 *physical region* Ethiopia/Somalia
Africana Seamount 119 A6 *seamount* SW Indian Ocean
'Afrīn 96 B2 Ḩalab, N Syria
Afyon 94 B3 *prev.* Afyonkarahisar. Afyon, W Turkey
Agadès *see* Agadez
Agadez 53 G3 *prev.* Agadès. Agadez, C Niger
Agadir 48 B3 SW Morocco
Agana/Agaña *see* Hagåtña
Āgaro 51 C5 Oromīya, C Ethiopia
Agassiz Fracture Zone 121 G5 *fracture zone* S Pacific Ocean
Agatha *see* Agde
Agathónisi 83 D6 *island* Dodekánisa, Greece, Aegean Sea
Agde 69 C6 *anc.* Agatha. Hérault, S France
Agedabia *see* Ajdābiyā
Agen 69 B5 *anc.* Aginnum. Lot-et-Garonne, SW France
Agendicum *see* Sens
Aghri Dagh *see* Büyükağrı Dağı
Agiá 82 B4 *var.* Ayiá. Thessalía, C Greece
Agialoúsa *see* Yenierenköy
Agía Marína 83 E6 Léros, Dodekánisa, Greece, Aegean Sea
Aginnum *see* Agen
Ágios Efstrátios 82 D4 *var.* Áyios Evstrátios, Hagios Evstrátios. *island* E Greece
Ágios Nikólaos 83 D8 *var.* Áyios Nikólaos. Kríti, Greece, E Mediterranean Sea
Āgra 112 D3 Uttar Pradesh, N India
Agra and Oudh, United Provinces of *see* Uttar Pradesh
Agram *see* Zagreb
Ağrı 95 F3 *var.* Karaköse; *prev.* Karakılısse. Ağrı, NE Turkey
Agri Dagi *see* Büyükağrı Dağı
Agrigento 75 C7 *Gk.* Akragas; *prev.* Girgenti. Sicilia, Italy, C Mediterranean Sea
Agriovótano 83 C5 Évvoia, C Greece
Agropoli 75 D5 Campania, S Italy
Aguachica 36 B2 Cesar, N Colombia
Aguadulce 31 F5 Coclé, S Panama
Agua Prieta 28 B1 Sonora, NW Mexico
Aguascalientes 28 D4 Aguascalientes, C Mexico
Aguaytía 38 C3 Ucayali, C Peru
Aguilas 71 E4 Murcia, SE Spain
Aguililla 28 D4 Michoacán de Ocampo, SW Mexico
Agulhas Basin 47 D8 *undersea basin* SW Indian Ocean
Agulhas Plateau 45 D6 *undersea plateau* SW Indian Ocean
Ahaggar 53 F2 *high plateau region* SE Algeria
Ahlen 72 B4 Nordrhein-Westfalen, W Germany
Ahmadābād 112 C4 *var.* Ahmedabad. Gujarāt, W India
Ahmadnagar 112 C5 *var.* Ahmednagar. Mahārāshtra, W India
Ahmedabad *see* Ahmadābād
Ahmednagar *see* Ahmadnagar
Ahuachapán 30 B3 Ahuachapán, W El Salvador
Ahvāz 98 C3 *var.* Ahwāz; *prev.* Nāsiri. Khūzestān, SW Iran
Ahvenanmaa *see* Åland
Ahwāz *see* Ahvāz
Aigaíon Pelagos/Aigaío Pélagos *see* Aegean Sea
Aígina 83 C6 *var.* Aíyina, Egina. Aígina, C Greece
Aígio 83 B5 *var.* Egio; *prev.* Aíyion. Dytikí Ellás, S Greece
Aiken 21 E2 South Carolina, SE USA
Ailinglaplap Atoll 122 D2 *var.* Aelōnlaplap. *atoll* Ralik Chain, S Marshall Islands
Ailuk Atoll 122 D1 *var.* Aelok. *atoll* Ratak Chain, NE Marshall Islands
Ainaži 84 D3 *Est.* Heinaste, *Ger.* Hainasch. Limbaži, N Latvia
'Aïn Ben Tili 52 D1 Tiris Zemmour, N Mauritania
Aintab *see* Gaziantep
Aïoun el Atrous/Aïoun el Atroûss *see* 'Ayoûn el 'Atroûs
Aiquile 39 F4 Cochabamba, C Bolivia
Aïr *see* Aïr, Massif de l'
Air du Azbine *see* Aïr, Massif de l'
Aïr, Massif de l' 53 G2 *var.* Aïr, Air du Azbine, Asben. *mountain range* NC Niger
Aiud 86 B4 *Ger.* Strassburg, *Hung.* Nagyenyed; *prev.* Engeten. Alba, SW Romania
Aix *see* Aix-en-Provence
Aix-en-Provence 69 D6 *var.* Aix; *anc.* Aquae Sextiae. Bouches-du-Rhône, SE France
Aix-la-Chapelle *see* Aachen
Aíyina *see* Aígina
Aíyion *see* Aígio
Aizkraukle 84 C4 Aizkraukle, S Latvia
Ajaccio 69 E7 Corse, France, C Mediterranean Sea
Ajaria *see* Achara
Ajastan *see* Armenia
Aj Bogd Uul 104 D2 *mountain* SW Mongolia
Ajdābiyā 49 G2 *var.* Agedabia, Ajdābiyah. NE Libya
Ajdābiyah *see* Ajdābiyā
Ajjinena *see* El Geneina
Ajmer 112 D3 *var.* Ajmere. Rājasthān, N India
Ajo 26 A3 Arizona, SW USA
Akaba *see* Al 'Aqabah
Akamagaseki *see* Shimonoseki
Akasha 50 B3 Northern, N Sudan
Akchâr 52 C2 *desert* W Mauritania
Aken *see* Aachen
Akermanceaster *see* Bath
Akhalts'ikhe 95 F2 SW Georgia
Akhisar 94 A3 Manisa, W Turkey
Akhmīm 50 B2 *var.* Akhmîm; *anc.* Panopolis. C Egypt
Akhtubinsk 89 C7 Astrakhanskaya Oblast', SW Russian Federation
Akhtyrka *see* Okhtyrka
Akimiski Island 16 C3 *island* Nunavut, C Canada
Akinovka 87 F4 Zaporiz'ka Oblast', S Ukraine
Akita 108 D4 Akita, Honshū, C Japan
Akjoujt 52 C2 *prev.* Fort-Repoux. Inchiri, W Mauritania
Akkeshi 108 E2 Hokkaidō, NE Japan
Aklavik 14 D3 Northwest Territories, NW Canada
Akmola *see* Astana
Akmolinsk *see* Astana
Aknavásár *see* Târgu Ocna
Akpatok Island 17 E1 *island* Nunavut, E Canada
Akragas *see* Agrigento
Akron 18 D4 Ohio, N USA
Akrotiri *see* Akrotírion
Akrotírion 80 C5 *var.* Akrotiri. *UK air base* S Cyprus
Aksai Chin 102 B2 *Chin.* Aksayqin. *disputed region* China/India
Aksaray 94 C4 Aksaray, C Turkey
Aksayqin *see* Aksai Chin
Akşehir 94 B4 Konya, W Turkey
Aktash *see* Oqtosh
Aktau 92 A4 *Kaz.* Aqtaū; *prev.* Shevchenko. Mangistau, W Kazakhstan
Aktjubinsk/Aktyubinsk *see* Aktobe
Aktobe 92 B4 *Kaz.* Aqtöbe; *prev.* Aktjubinsk, Aktyubinsk. Aktyubinsk, NW Kazakhstan
Aktsyabrski 85 C7 *Rus.* Oktyabr'skiy; *prev.* Karpilovka. Homyel'skaya Voblasts', SE Belarus
Aktyubinsk *see* Aktobe
Akula 55 C5 Equateur, NW Dem. Rep. Congo
Akureyri 61 E4 Nordhurland Eystra, N Iceland
Akyab *see* Sittwe
Alabama 20 C2 *off.* State of Alabama, *also known as* Camellia State, Heart of Dixie, The Cotton State, Yellowhammer State. *state* S USA
Alabama River 20 C3 *river* Alabama, S USA
Alaca 94 C3 Çorum, N Turkey
Alacant *see* Alicante
Alagoas 41 G2 *off.* Estado de Alagoas. *state* E Brazil
Alagoas 41 G2 *off.* Estado de Alagoas. *region* E Brazil
Alais *see* Alès
Alajuela 31 E4 Alajuela, C Costa Rica
Alakanuk 14 C2 Alaska, USA
Al 'Alamayn 50 B1 *var.* El 'Alamein. N Egypt
Al 'Amārah 98 C3 *var.* Amara. Maysān, E Iraq
Alamo 25 D6 Nevada, W USA
Alamogordo 26 D3 New Mexico, SW USA
Alamosa 22 C5 Colorado, C USA
Aland Islands 63 C6 *var.* Aland Islands, *Fin.* Ahvenanmaa. *island group* SW Finland
Aland Islands *see* Åland
Aland Sea 63 C6 *var.* Aland Sea. *strait* Baltic Sea/Gulf of Bothnia
Aland Sea *see* Ålands Hav
Alanya 94 C4 Antalya, S Turkey
Al 'Aqabah 97 B8 *var.* Akaba, Aqaba, 'Aqaba; *anc.* Aelana, Elath. Al 'Aqabah, SW Jordan
Al 'Arabīyah as Su'ūdīyah *see* Saudi Arabia
Alasca, Golfo de *see* Alaska, Gulf of
Alaşehir 94 A4 Manisa, W Turkey
Al 'Ashārah 96 E3 *var.* Ashara. Dayr az Zawr, E Syria
Alaska 14 C3 *off.* State of Alaska, *also known as* Land of the Midnight Sun, The Last Frontier, Seward's Folly; *prev.* Russian America. *state* NW USA
Alaska, Gulf of 14 C4 *var.* Golfo de Alasca. *gulf* Canada/USA
Alaska Peninsula 14 C3 *peninsula* Alaska, USA
Alaska Range 12 B2 *mountain range* Alaska, USA
Al-Asnam *see* Chlef
Alattio *see* Alta
Al Awaynāt *see* Al 'Uwaynāt
Alaykel'/Alay-Kuu *see* Këk-Art
Al 'Aynā 97 B7 Al Karak, W Jordan
Alazeya 93 G2 *river* NE Russian Federation
Al Bāb 96 B2 Ḩalab, N Syria
Albacete 71 E3 Castilla-La Mancha, C Spain
Al Baghdādī 98 B3 *var.* Khān al Baghdādī. Al Anbār, SW Iraq
Al Bāha *see* Al Bāḩah
Al Bāḩah 99 B5 *var.* Al Bāha. Al BāḨah, SW Saudi Arabia
Al Baḩrayn *see* Bahrain
Alba Iulia 86 B4 *Ger.* Weissenburg, *Hung.* Gyulafehérvár; *prev.* Bălgrad, Karlsburg, Károly-Fehérvár. Alba, W Romania
Albania 79 C7 *off.* Republic of Albania, *Alb.* Republika e Shqipqërisë, Shqipëria; *prev.* People's Socialist Republic of Albania. *country* SE Europe
Albania *see* Aubagne
Albany 125 B7 Western Australia
Albany 20 D3 Georgia, SE USA
Albany 19 F3 *state capital* New York, NE USA
Albany 24 B3 Oregon, NW USA
Albany 16 C3 *river* Ontario, S Canada
Alba Regia *see* Székesfehérvár
Al Bāridah 96 C4 *var.* Bāridah. Ḩimş, C Syria
Al Başrah 98 C3 *Eng.* Basra, *hist.* Busra, Bussora. Al Başrah, SE Iraq
Al Batrūn *see* Batroûn
Al Bayḑā' 49 G2 *var.* Beida. NE Libya
Albemarle Island *see* Isabela, Isla
Albemarle Sound 21 G1 *inlet* W Atlantic Ocean
Albergaria-a-Velha 70 B2 Aveiro, N Portugal
Albert 68 C3 Somme, N France
Alberta 15 E4 *province* SW Canada
Albert Edward Nyanza *see* Edward, Lake
Albert, Lake 51 B6 *var.* Albert Nyanza, Lac Mobutu Sese Seko. *lake* Uganda/Dem. Rep. Congo
Albert Lea 23 F3 Minnesota, N USA
Albert Nyanza *see* Albert, Lake
Albertville *see* Kalemie
Albi 69 C6 *anc.* Albiga. Tarn, S France
Albiga *see* Albi
Ålborg *see* Aalborg
Ålborg-Nørresundby *see* Aalborg
Albuquerque 26 D2 New Mexico, SW USA
Al Burayqah *see* Marsá al Burayqah
Alburgum *see* Aalborg
Albury 127 C7 New South Wales, SE Australia
Alcácer do Sal 70 B4 Setúbal, W Portugal
Alcalá de Henares 71 E3 *Ar.* Alkal'a; *anc.* Complutum. Madrid, C Spain
Alcamo 75 C7 Sicilia, Italy, C Mediterranean Sea
Alcañiz 71 F2 Aragón, NE Spain
Alcántara, Embalse de 70 C3 *reservoir* W Spain
Alcaudete 70 D4 Andalucía, S Spain
Alcázar *see* Ksar-el-Kebir
Alcazarquivir *see* Ksar-el-Kebir
Alcoi *see* Alcoy
Alcoy 71 F4 *Cat.* Alcoi. País Valenciano, E Spain
Aldabra Group 57 G2 *island group* SW Seychelles
Aldan 93 F3 *river* NE Russian Federation
al Dar al Baida *see* Rabat
Alderney 68 A2 *island* Channel Islands
Aleg 52 C3 Brakna, SW Mauritania
Aleksandriya *see* Oleksandriya
Aleksandropol' *see* Gyumri
Aleksandrovka *see* Oleksandrivka
Aleksandrovsk *see* Zaporizhzhya
Aleksin 89 B5 Tul'skaya Oblast', W Russian Federation
Aleksinac 78 E4 Serbia, SE Serbia
Alençon 68 B3 Orne, N France
Alenquer 41 E2 Pará, NE Brazil
Alep/Aleppo *see* Ḩalab
Alert 15 F1 Ellesmere Island, Nunavut, N Canada
Alès 69 C6 *prev.* Alais. Gard, S France
Aleşd 86 B3 *Hung.* Élesd. Bihor, SW Romania
Alessandria 74 B2 *Fr.* Alexandrie. Piemonte, N Italy
Ålesund 63 A5 Møre og Romsdal, S Norway
Aleutian Basin 91 G3 *undersea basin* Bering Sea
Aleutian Islands 14 A3 *island group* Alaska, USA
Aleutian Range 12 A2 *mountain range* Alaska, USA
Aleutian Trench 91 H3 *trench* S Bering Sea
Alexander Archipelago 14 D4 *island group* Alaska, USA
Alexander City 20 D2 Alabama, S USA
Alexander Island 132 A3 *island* Antarctica
Alexander Range *see* Kirghiz Range
Alexandra 129 B7 Otago, South Island, New Zealand
Alexándreia 82 B4 *var.* Alexándria. Kentrikí Makedonía, N Greece
Alexandretta *see* İskenderun
Alexandretta, Gulf of *see* İskenderun Körfezi
Alexandria 50 B1 *Ar.* Al Iskandarīyah. N Egypt
Alexandria 86 C5 Teleorman, S Romania
Alexandria 20 B3 Louisiana, S USA
Alexandria 23 F2 Minnesota, N USA
Alexándria *see* Alexándreia
Alexandrie *see* Alessandria
Alexandroúpoli 82 D3 *var.* Alexandroúpolis, *Turk.* Dedeagaç, Dedeagach. Anatolikí Makedonía kai Thráki, NE Greece
Alexandroúpolis *see* Alexandroúpoli
Al Fāshir *see* El Fasher
Alfatar 82 E1 Silistra, NE Bulgaria
Alfeiós 83 B6 *prev.* Alfiós; *anc.* Alpheius, Alpheus. *river* S Greece
Alfiós *see* Alfeiós
Alföld *see* Great Hungarian Plain
Al-Furāt *see* Euphrates
Alga 92 B4 *Kaz.* Algha. Aktyubinsk, NW Kazakhstan
Algarve 70 B4 *cultural region* S Portugal
Algeciras 70 C5 Andalucía, SW Spain
Algemesí 71 F3 País Valenciano, E Spain
Al-Genain *see* El Geneina
Alger 49 E1 *var.* Algiers, El Djazaïr, Al Jazair. *country capital* N Algeria
Algeria 48 C3 *off.* Democratic and Popular Republic of Algeria. *country* N Africa
Algeria, Democratic and Popular Republic of *see* Algeria
Algerian Basin 58 C5 *var.* Balearic Plain. *undersea basin* W Mediterranean Sea
Algha *see* Alga
Al Ghābah 99 E5 *var.* Ghaba. C Oman
Alghero 75 A5 Sardegna, Italy, C Mediterranean Sea
Al Ghurdaqah *see* Hurghada
Algiers *see* Alger
Al Golea *see* El Goléa
Algona 23 F3 Iowa, C USA
Al Hajar al Gharbi 99 D5 *mountain range* N Oman
Al Hamad *see* Syrian Desert
Al Ḩasakah 96 D2 *var.* Al Hasijah, El Haseke, *Fr.* Hassetché. Al Ḩasakah, NE Syria
Al Hasijah *see* Al Ḩasakah
Al Ḩillah 98 B3 *var.* Hilla. Bābil, C Iraq
Al Ḩisā 97 B7 Aţ Ţafīlah, W Jordan
Al Ḩudaydah 99 B6 *Eng.* Hodeida. W Yemen
Al Hufūf 98 C4 *var.* Hofuf. Ash Sharqīyah, NE Saudi Arabia
Aliákmon *see* Aliákmonas
Aliákmonas 82 B4 *prev.* Aliákmon; *anc.* Haliacmon. *river* N Greece
Alíartos 83 C5 Stereá Ellás, C Greece
Alicante 71 F4 *Cat.* Alacant, *Lat.* Lucentum. País Valenciano, SE Spain
Alice 27 G5 Texas, SW USA
Alice Springs 126 A4 Northern Territory, C Australia
Alifu Atoll *see* Ari Atoll
Aligandí 31 G4 Kuna Yala, NE Panama
Aliki *see* Alykí
Alima 55 B6 *river* C Congo
Al Imārāt al 'Arabīyahal Muttaḩidah *see* United Arab Emirates
Alindao 54 C4 Basse-Kotto, S Central African Republic
Aliquippa 18 D4 Pennsylvania, NE USA
Al Iskandarīyah *see* Alexandria
Alistráti 82 C3 Kentrikí Makedonía, NE Greece
Alivéri 83 C5 *var.* Alivérion. Évvoia, C Greece
Alivérion *see* Alivéri
Al Jabal al Akhḑar 49 G2 *mountain range* NE Libya
Al Jafr 97 B7 Ma'ān, S Jordan
Al Jaghbūb 49 H3 NE Libya
Al Jahrā' 98 C4 *var.* Al Jahrah, Jahra. C Kuwait
Al Jahrah *see* Al Jahrā'
Al Jamāhīrīyah al 'Arabīyah al Lībīyah ash Sha'bīyah al Ishtirākīy *see* Libya
Al Jawf 98 B4 *off.* Jauf. Al Jawf, NW Saudi Arabia
Al Jawlān *see* Golan Heights
Al Jazair *see* Alger
Al Jazirah 96 E2 *physical region* Iraq/Syria
Al Jīzah *see* Giza
Al Junaynah *see* El Geneina
Alkal'a *see* Alcalá de Henares
Al Karak 97 B7 *var.* El Kerak, Karak, Kerak; *anc.* Kir Moab, Kir of Moab. Al Karak, W Jordan
Al-Kasr al-Kebir *see* Ksar-el-Kebir
Al Khalīl *see* Hebron
Al Khārijah 50 B2 *var.* El Khârga. C Egypt
Al Khums 49 F2 *var.* Homs, Khoms, Khums. NW Libya
Alkmaar 64 C2 Noord-Holland, NW Netherlands
Al Kufrah 49 H4 SE Libya
Al Kūt 98 C3 *var.* Kūt al 'Amārah, Kut al Imara. Wāsiţ, E Iraq
Al-Kuwait *see* Al Kuwayt
Al Kuwayt 98 C4 *var.* Al-Kuwait, *Eng.* Kuwait, Kuwait City; *prev.* Qurein. *country capital* E Kuwait
Al Lādhiqīyah 96 A3 *Eng.* Latakia, *Fr.* Lattaquié; *anc.* Laodicea, Laodicea ad Mare. Al Lādhiqīyah, W Syria
Allahābād 113 E3 Uttar Pradesh, N India
Allanmyo *see* Aunglan
Allegheny Plateau 19 E3 *mountain range* New York/Pennsylvania, NE USA
Allenstein *see* Olsztyn
Allentown 19 F4 Pennsylvania, NE USA
Alleppey 110 C3 *var.* Alappuzha. Kerala, SW India
Alliance 22 D3 Nebraska, C USA
Al Līth 99 B5 Makkah, SW Saudi Arabia
Al Lubnān *see* Lebanon
Alma-Ata *see* Almaty
Almada 70 B4 Setúbal, W Portugal
Al Madīnah 99 A5 *Eng.* Medina. Al Madīnah, W Saudi Arabia
Al Mafraq 97 B6 *var.* Mafraq. Al Mafraq, N Jordan
Al Mahdīyah *see* Mahdia
Al Mahrah 99 C6 *mountain range* E Yemen
Al Majma'ah 98 B4 Ar Riyāḑ, C Saudi Arabia
Al Mālikīyah 96 E1 *var.* Malkiye. Al Ḩasakah, N Syria
Almalyk *see* Olmaliq
Al Mamlakah *see* Morocco
Al Mamlaka al Urdunīya al Hashemīyah *see* Jordan
Al Manāmah 98 C4 *Eng.* Manama. *country capital* N Bahrain
Al Manāşif 96 E3 *mountain range* E Syria
Almansa 71 F4 Castilla-La Mancha, C Spain
Al-Mariyya *see* Almería
Al Marj 49 G2 *var.* Barka, *It.* Barce. NE Libya
Almaty 92 C5 *var.* Alma-Ata. Almaty, SE Kazakhstan
Al Mawşil 98 B2 *Eng.* Mosul. Nīnawá, N Iraq
Al Mayādīn 96 D3 *var.* Mayadin, *Fr.* Meyadine. Dayr az Zawr, E Syria
Al Mazra' *see* Al Mazra'ah
Al Mazra'ah 97 B6 *var.* Al Mazra', Mazra'a. Al Karak, W Jordan
Almelo 64 E3 Overijssel, E Netherlands
Almendra, Embalse de 70 C2 *reservoir* Castilla-León, NW Spain
Almendralejo 70 C4 Extremadura, W Spain
Almere 64 C3 *var.* Almere-stad. Flevoland, C Netherlands
Almere-stad *see* Almere
Almería 71 E5 *Ar.* Al-Mariyya; *anc.* Unci, *Lat.* Portus Magnus. Andalucía, S Spain
Al'met'yevsk 89 D5 Respublika Tatarstan, W Russian Federation
Al Mīnā' *see* El Mina
Al Minyā 50 B2 *var.* El Minya, Minya. C Egypt

Almirante – Arkansas

Almirante *31 E4* Bocas del Toro, NW Panama
Al Mudawwarah *97 B8* Ma'ān, SW Jordan
Al Mukallā *99 C6* *var.* Mukalla. SE Yemen
Al Obayyid *see* El Obeid
Alofi *123 F4* *dependent territory capital* W Niue
Aloha State *see* Hawai'i
Aloja *84 D3* Limbaži, N Latvia
Alónnisos *83 C5* *island* Vóreies Sporádes, Greece, Aegean Sea
Álora *70 D5* Andalucía, S Spain
Alor, Kepulauan *117 E5* *island group* E Indonesia
Al Oued *see* El Oued
Alpen *see* Alps
Alpena *18 D2* Michigan, N USA
Alpes *see* Alps
Alpha Cordillera *133 B3* *var.* Alpha Ridge. *seamount range* Arctic Ocean
Alpha Ridge *see* Alpha Cordillera
Alpheius *see* Alfeiós
Alphen *see* Alphen aan den Rijn
Alphen aan den Rijn *64 C3* *var.* Alphen. Zuid-Holland, C Netherlands
Alpheus *see* Alfeiós
Alpi *see* Alps
Alpine *27 E4* Texas, SW USA
Alps *80 C1* *Fr.* Alpes, *Ger.* Alpen, *It.* Alpi. *mountain range* C Europe
Al Qaḍārif *see* Gedaref
Al Qāhirah *see* Cairo
Al Qāmishlī *96 E1* *var.* Kamishli, Qamishly. Al Ḥasakah, NE Syria
Al Qaşrayn *see* Kasserine
Al Qayrawān *see* Kairouan
Al-Qsar al-Kbir *see* Ksar-el-Kebir
Al Qubayyāt *see* Qoubaïyât
Al Quds/Al Quds ash Sharīf *see* Jerusalem
Alqueva, Barragem do *70 C4* *reservoir* Portugal/Spain
Al Qunayṭirah *97 B5* *var.* El Kuneitra, El Quneitra, Kuneitra, Qunaytra. Al Qunayṭirah, SW Syria
Al Quşayr *96 B4* *var.* El Quseir, Quşayr, *Fr.* Kousseir. Ḥimş, W Syria
Al Quwayrah *97 B8* *var.* El Quweira. Al 'Aqabah, SW Jordan
Alsace *68 E3* *Ger.* Elsass; *anc.* Alsatia. *cultural region* NE France
Alsatia *see* Alsace
Alsdorf *72 A4* Nordrhein-Westfalen, W Germany
Alt *see* Olt
Alta *62 D2* *Fin.* Alattio. Finnmark, N Norway
Altai *see* Altai Mountains
Altai Mountains *104 C2* *var.* Altai, *Chin.* Altay Shan, *Rus.* Altay. *mountain range* Asia/Europe
Altamaha River *21 E3* *river* Georgia, SE USA
Altamira *41 E2* Pará, NE Brazil
Altamura *75 E5* *anc.* Lupatia. Puglia, SE Italy
Altar, Desierto de *28 A1* *var.* Sonoran Desert. *desert* Mexico/USA
Altar, Desierto de *see* Sonoran Desert
Altay *104 C2* Xinjiang Uygur Zizhiqu, NW China
Altay *104 D2* *prev.* Yösönbulag. Govĭ-Altay, W Mongolia
Altay Altai Mountains, Asia/Europe
Altay Shan *see* Altai Mountains
Altbetsche *see* Bečej
Altenburg *see* Bucureşti, Romania
Altin Köprü *98 B3* *var.* Altun Kupri. At Ta'mīn, N Iraq
Altiplano *39 F4* *physical region* W South America
Altkanischa *see* Kanjiža
Alton *18 B5* Illinois, N USA
Alton *18 B4* Missouri, C USA
Altoona *19 E4* Pennsylvania, NE USA
Alto Paraná *see* Paraná
Altpasua *see* Stara Pazova
Alt-Schwanenburg *see* Gulbene
Altsohl *see* Zvolen
Altun Kupri *see* Altin Köprü
Altun Shan *104 C3* *var.* Altyn Tagh. *mountain range* NW China
Altus *27 F2* Oklahoma, C USA
Altyn Tagh *see* Altun Shan
Al Ubayyiḍ *see* El Obeid
Alūksne *84 D3* *Ger.* Marienburg. Alūksne, NE Latvia
Al 'Ulā *98 A4* Al Madīnah, NW Saudi Arabia
Al 'Umarī *97 C6* 'Ammān, E Jordan
Alupka *87 F5* Respublika Krym, S Ukraine
Al Uqşur *see* Luxor
Al Urdunn *see* Jordan
Alushta *87 F5* Respublika Krym, S Ukraine
Al 'Uwaynāt *49 F4* *var.* Al Awaynāt. SW Libya
Alva *27 F1* Oklahoma, C USA
Alvarado *29 F4* Veracruz-Llave, E Mexico
Alvin *27 H4* Texas, SW USA
Al Wajh *98 A4* Tabūk, NW Saudi Arabia
Alwar *112 D3* Rājasthān, N India
Al Warī'ah *98 C4* Ash Sharqīyah, N Saudi Arabia
Al Yaman *see* Yemen
Alykí *82 C4* *var.* Aliki. Thásos, N Greece
Alytus *85 B5* *Pol.* Olita. Alytus, S Lithuania
Alzette *65 D8* *river* S Luxembourg
Amadeus, Lake *125 D5* *seasonal lake* Northern Territory, C Australia
Amadi *51 B5* Western Equatoria, SW Sudan
Amadjuak Lake *15 G3* *lake* Baffin Island, Nunavut, N Canada
Amakusa-nada *109 A7* *gulf* SW Japan
Åmål *63 B6* Västra Götaland, S Sweden
Amami-gunto *108 A3* *island group* SW Japan
Amami-o-shim *108 A3* *island* S Japan
Amantea *75 D6* Calabria, SW Italy
Amapá *41 E1* *off.* Estado de Amapá; *prev.* Território de Amapá. *region* NE Brazil
Amapá *41 E1* *off.* Estado de Amapá; *prev.* Território de Amapá. *state* NE Brazil
Amapá, Estado de *see* Amapá
Amapá, Território de *see* Amapá
Amara *see* Al 'Amārah
Amarapura *114 B3* Mandalay, C Myanmar (Burma)
Amarillo *27 E2* Texas, SW USA
Amay *65 C6* Liège, E Belgium
Amazon *41 E1* *Sp.* Amazonas. *river* Brazil/Peru
Amazonas *see* Amazon
Amazon Basin *40 D2* *basin* N South America
Amazon, Mouths of the *41 F1* *delta* NE Brazil
Ambam *55 B5* Sud, S Cameroon
Ambanja *57 G2* Antsirañana, N Madagascar
Ambarchik *93 G2* Respublika Sakha (Yakutiya), NE Russian Federation
Ambato *38 B1* Tungurahua, C Ecuador
Ambérieu-en-Bugey *69 D5* Ain, E France
Ambianum *see* Amiens
Amboasary *57 F4* Toliara, S Madagascar
Amboina *see* Ambon
Ambon *117 F4* *prev.* Amboina, Amboyna. Pulau Ambon, E Indonesia
Ambositra *57 G3* Fianarantsoa, SE Madagascar
Amboyna *see* Ambon
Ambracia *see* Árta
Ambre, Cap d' *see* Bobaomby, Tanjona
Ambrim *see* Ambrym
Ambriz *56 A1* Bengo, NW Angola
Ambrym *122 D4* *var.* Ambrim. *island* C Vanuatu
Amchitka Island *14 A2* *island* Aleutian Islands, Alaska, USA
Amdo *104 C5* Xizang Zizhiqu, W China
Ameland *64 D1* *Fris.* It Amelân. *island* Waddeneilanden, N Netherlands
Amelân, It *see* Ameland
America *see* United States of America
America-Antarctica Ridge *45 C7* *undersea ridge* S Atlantic Ocean
America in Miniature *see* Maryland
American Falls Reservoir *24 E4* *reservoir* Idaho, NW USA
American Samoa *123 E4* *US unincorporated territory* W Polynesia
Amersfoort *64 D3* Utrecht, C Netherlands
Ames *23 F3* Iowa, C USA
Amfilochía *83 A5* *var.* Amfilokhía. Dytikí Ellás, C Greece
Amfilokhía *see* Amfilochía
Amga *93 F3* *river* NE Russian Federation
Amherst *17 F4* Nova Scotia, SE Canada
Amherst *see* Kyaikkami
Amida *see* Diyarbakır
Amiens *68 C3* *anc.* Ambianum, Samarobriva. Somme, N France
Amíndaion/Amindeo *see* Amýntaio
Amindivi Islands *110 A2* *island group* Lakshadweep, India, N Indian Ocean
Amirante Islands *57 G1* *var.* Amirantes Group. *island group* C Seychelles
Amirantes Group *see* Amirante Islands
Amistad, Presa de la *see* Amistad Reservoir
Amistad Reservoir *27 F4* *var.* Presa de la Amistad. *reservoir* Mexico/USA
Amisus *see* Samsun
Ammaia *see* Portalegre
'Ammān *97 B6* *var.* Amman; *anc.* Philadelphia, *Bibl.* Rabbah Ammon, Rabbath Ammon. *country capital* 'Ammān, NW Jordan
Ammassalik *60 D4* *var.* Angmagssalik. Tunu, S Greenland
Ammóchostos *see* Gazimağusa
Ammóchostos, Kólpos *see* Gazimağusa Körfezi
Amnok-kang *see* Yalu
Amoea *see* Portalegre
Amoentai *see* Amuntai
Āmol *98 D2* *var.* Amul. Māzandarān, N Iran
Amorgós *83 D6* Amorgós, Kykládes, Greece, Aegean Sea
Amorgós *83 D6* *island* Kykládes, Greece, Aegean Sea
Amos *16 D4* Québec, SE Canada
Amourj *52 D3* Hodh ech Chargui, SE Mauritania
Amoy *see* Xiamen
Ampato, Nevado *39 E4* *mountain* S Peru
Amposta *71 F2* Cataluña, NE Spain
Amraoti *see* Amrāvati
Amrāvati *112 D4* *prev.* Amraoti. Mahārāshtra, C India
Amritsar *112 D2* Punjab, N India
Amstelveen *64 C3* Noord-Holland, C Netherlands
Amsterdam *64 C3* *country capital* Noord-Holland, C Netherlands
Amsterdam Island *119 C6* *island* NE French Southern and Antarctic Territories
Am Timan *54 C3* Salamat, SE Chad
Amu Darya *100 D2* *Rus.* Amudar'ya, *Taj.* Dar"yoi Amu, *Turkm.* Amyderya, *Uzb.* Amudaryo; *anc.* Oxus. *river* C Asia
Amu-Dar'ya *see* Amyderýa
Amudar'ya/Amudaryo/Amu, Dar"yoi *see* Amu Darya
Amul *see* Āmol
Amund Ringnes Island *15 F2* *Island* Nunavut, N Canada
Amundsen Basin *see* Fram Basin
Amundsen Gulf *15 E2* *gulf* Northwest Territories, N Canada
Amundsen Plain *132 A4* *abyssal plain* S Pacific Ocean
Amundsen-Scott *132 B3* *US research station* Antarctica
Amundsen Sea *132 A4* *sea* S Pacific Ocean
Amuntai *116 D4* *prev.* Amoentai. Borneo, C Indonesia
Amur *93 G4* *Chin.* Heilong Jiang. *river* China/Russian Federation
Amvrosiyevka *see* Amvrosiyivka
Amvrosiyivka *87 H3* *Rus.* Amvrosiyevka. Donets'ka Oblast', SE Ukraine
Amyderýa *101 E3* *Rus.* Amu-Dar'ya. Lebap Welaýaty, NE Turkmenistan
Amyderya *see* Amu Darya
Amýntaio *82 B4* *var.* Amindeo; *prev.* Amíndaion. Dytikí Makedonía, N Greece
Anabar *93 E2* *river* NE Russian Federation
An Abhainn Mhór *see* Blackwater
Anaco *37 E2* Anzoátegui, NE Venezuela
Anaconda *22 B2* Montana, NW USA
Anacortes *24 B1* Washington, NW USA
Anadolu Dağları *see* Doğu Karadeniz Dağları
Anadyr' *93 H1* Chukotskiy Avtonomnyy Okrug, NE Russian Federation
Anadyr' *93 G1* *river* NE Russian Federation
Anadyr, Gulf of *93 H1* *Eng.* Gulf of Anadyr. *gulf* NE Russian Federation
Anadyr, Gulf of *see* Anadyrskiy Zaliv
Anáfi *83 D7* *anc.* Anaphe. *island* Kykládes, Greece, Aegean Sea
'Ānah *see* 'Annah
Anaheim *24 E2* California, W USA
Anaiza *see* 'Unayzah
Analalava *57 G2* Mahajanga, NW Madagascar
Anamur *94 C5* İçel, S Turkey
Anantapur *110 C2* Andhra Pradesh, S India
Anaphe *see* Anáfi
Anápolis *41 F3* Goiás, C Brazil
Anār *98 D3* Kermān, C Iran
Anatolia *94 C4* *plateau* C Turkey
Anatom *see* Aneityum
Añatuya *42 C3* Santiago del Estero, N Argentina
An Bhearú *see* Barrow
Anchorage *14 C3* Alaska, USA
Ancona *74 C3* Marche, C Italy
Ancud *43 B6* *prev.* San Carlos de Ancud. Los Lagos, S Chile
Ancyra *see* Ankara
Åndalsnes *63 A5* Møre og Romsdal, S Norway
Andalucía *70 D4* *cultural region* S Spain
Andalusia *20 C3* Alabama, S USA
Andaman Islands *102 B4* *island group* India, NE Indian Ocean
Andaman Sea *102 C4* *sea* NE Indian Ocean
Andenne *65 C6* Namur, SE Belgium
Anderlues *65 B7* Hainaut, S Belgium
Anderson *18 C4* Indiana, N USA
Andes *42 B3* *mountain range* W South America
Andhra Pradesh *113 E5* *cultural region* E India
Andijon *101 F2* *Rus.* Andizhan. Andijon Viloyati, E Uzbekistan
Andikíthira *see* Antikýthira
Andipaxi *see* Antípaxoi
Andípsara *see* Antípsara
Ándissa *see* Ántissa
Andizhan *see* Andijon
Andkhvoy *100 D3* Fāryāb, N Afghanistan
Andorra *69 A7* *off.* Principality of Andorra, *Cat.* Valls d'Andorra, *Fr.* Vallée d'Andorre. *country* SW Europe
Andorra *see* Andorra la Vella
Andorra la Vella *69 A8* *var.* Andorra, *Fr.* Andorre la Vielle, *Sp.* Andorra la Vieja. *country capital* C Andorra
Andorra la Vieja *see* Andorra la Vella
Andorra, Principality of *see* Andorra
Andorra, Valls d'/Andorra, Vallée d' *see* Andorra
Andorre la Vielle *see* Andorra la Vella
Andover *67 D7* S England, United Kingdom
Andøya *62 C2* *island* C Norway
Andreanof Islands *14 A3* *island group* Aleutian Islands, Alaska, USA
Andrews *27 E3* Texas, SW USA
Andrew Tablemount *118 A4* *var.* Gora Andryu. *seamount* W Indian Ocean
Andria *75 D5* Puglia, SE Italy
An Droichead Nua *see* Newbridge
Andropov *see* Rybinsk
Ándros *83 D6* Ándros, Kykládes, Greece, Aegean Sea
Ándros *83 C6* *island* Kykládes, Greece, Aegean Sea
Andros Island *32 B2* *island* NW Bahamas
Andros Town *32 C1* Andros Island, NW Bahamas
Andryu, Gora *see* Andrew Tablemount
Aneityum *122 D5* *var.* Anatom; *prev.* Kéamu. *island* S Vanuatu
Ānewetak *see* Enewetak Atoll
Angara *93 E4* *river* C Russian Federation
Angarsk *93 E4* Irkutskaya Oblast', S Russian Federation
Ånge *63 C5* Västernorrland, C Sweden
Ángel de la Guarda, Isla *28 B2* *island* NW Mexico
Angeles *117 E1* *off.* Angeles City. Luzon, N Philippines
Angeles City *see* Angeles
Angel Falls *see* Ángel, Salto
Ángel, Salto *37 E3* *Eng.* Angel Falls. *waterfall* E Venezuela
Angerburg *see* Węgorzewo
Ångermanälven *62 C4* *river* N Sweden
Angermünde *72 D3* Brandenburg, NE Germany
Angers *68 B4* *anc.* Juliomagus. Maine-et-Loire, NW France
Anglesey *67 C5* *island* NW Wales, United Kingdom
Anglet *69 A6* Pyrénées-Atlantiques, SW France
Angleton *27 H4* Texas, SW USA
Anglia *see* England
Anglo-Egyptian Sudan *see* Sudan
Angmagssalik *see* Ammassalik
Ang Nam Ngum *114 C4* *lake* C Laos
Angola *56 B2* *off.* Republic of Angola; *prev.* People's Republic of Angola, Portuguese West Africa. *country* SW Africa
Angola Basin *47 B5* *undersea basin* E Atlantic Ocean
Angola, People's Republic of *see* Angola
Angola, Republic of *see* Angola
Angora *see* Ankara
Angostura *see* Ciudad Bolívar
Angostura, Presa de la *29 G5* *reservoir* SE Mexico
Angoulême *69 B5* *anc.* Iculisma. Charente, W France
Angoumois *69 B5* *cultural region* W France
Angra Pequena *see* Lüderitz
Angren *101 F2* Toshkent Viloyati, E Uzbekistan
Anguilla *33 G3* *UK dependent territory* E West Indies
Anguilla Cays *32 B2* *islets* SW Bahamas
Anhui *106 C5* *var.* Anhui Sheng, Anhwei, Wan. *province* E China
AnhuiSheng/Anhwei Wan *see* Anhui
Anicium *see* le Puy
Anina *86 A4* *Ger.* Steierdorf, *Hung.* Stájerlakanina; *prev.* Staierdorf-Anina, Steierdorf-Anina, Steyerlak-Anina. Caraş-Severin, SW Romania
Anjou *68 B4* *cultural region* NW France
Anjouan *57 F2* *var.* Ndzouani, Nzwani. *island* SE Comoros
Ankara *94 C3* *prev.* Angora; *anc.* Ancyra. *country capital* Ankara, C Turkey
Ankeny *23 F3* Iowa, C USA
Anklam *72 D2* Mecklenburg-Vorpommern, NE Germany
An Mhuir Cheilteach *see* Celtic Sea
Annaba *49 E1* *prev.* Bône. NE Algeria
An Nafud *98 B4* *desert* NW Saudi Arabia
'Annah *98 B3* *var.* 'Ānah. Al Anbār, NW Iraq
An Najaf *98 B3* *var.* Najaf. An Najaf, S Iraq
Annamitique, Chaîne *114 D4* *mountain range* C Laos
Annapolis *19 F4* *state capital* Maryland, NE USA
Annapurṇa *113 E3* *mountain* C Nepal
An Nāqūrah *see* En Nâqoûra
Ann Arbor *18 C3* Michigan, N USA
An Nāşirīyah *98 C3* *var.* Nasiriya. Dhī Qār, SE Iraq
Anneciacum *see* Annecy
Annecy *69 D5* *anc.* Anneciacum. Haute-Savoie, E France
An Nīl al Abyaḍ *see* White Nile
An Nīl al Azraq *see* Blue Nile
Anniston *20 D2* Alabama, S USA
Annotto Bay *32 B4* C Jamaica
An Ómaigh *see* Omagh
Anqing *106 D5* Anhui, E China
Anse La Raye *33 F1* NW Saint Lucia
Anshun *106 B6* Guizhou, S China
Ansongo *53 E3* Gao, E Mali
An Srath Bán *see* Strabane
Antakya *94 D4* *anc.* Antioch, Antiochia. Hatay, S Turkey
Antalaha *57 G2* Antsirañana, NE Madagascar
Antalya *94 B4* *prev.* Adalia; *anc.* Attaleia, *Bibl.* Attalia. Antalya, SW Turkey
Antalya, Gulf of *94 B4* *var.* Gulf of Adalia, *Eng.* Gulf of Antalya. *gulf* SW Turkey
Antalya, Gulf of *see* Antalya Körfezi
Antananarivo *57 G3* *prev.* Tananarive. *country capital* Antananarivo, C Madagascar
Antarctica *132 B3* *continent*
Antarctic Peninsula *132 A2* *peninsula* Antarctica
Antep *see* Gaziantep
Antequera *70 D5* *anc.* Anticaria, Antiquaria. Andalucía, S Spain
Antequera *see* Oaxaca
Antibes *69 D6* *anc.* Antipolis. Alpes-Maritimes, SE France
Anticaria *see* Antequera
Anticosti, Île d' *17 F3* *Eng.* Anticosti Island. *island* Québec, E Canada
Anticosti Island *see* Anticosti, Île d'
Antigua *33 G3* *island* S Antigua and Barbuda, Leeward Islands
Antigua and Barbuda *33 G3* *country* E West Indies
Antikythira *83 B7* *var.* Andikíthira. *island* S Greece
Anti-Lebanon *96 B4* *var.* Jebel esh Sharqi, *Ar.* Al Jabal ash Sharqī, *Fr.* Anti-Liban. *mountain range* Lebanon/Syria
Anti-Liban *see* Anti-Lebanon
Antioch *see* Antakya
Antiochia *see* Antakya
Antípaxoi *83 A5* *var.* Andipaxi. *island* Iónia Nísiá, Greece, C Mediterranean Sea
Antipodes Islands *120 D5* *island group* S New Zealand
Antipolis *see* Antibes
Antípsara *83 D5* *var.* Andípsara. *island* E Greece
Antiquaria *see* Antequera
Ántissa *83 D5* *var.* Ándissa. Lésvos, E Greece
An tIúr *see* Newry
Antivari *see* Bar
Antofagasta *42 B2* Antofagasta, N Chile
Antony *68 E2* Hauts-de-Seine, N France
An tSionainn *see* Shannon
Antsirañana *57 G2* *province* N Madagascar
Antsohihy *57 G2* Mahajanga, NW Madagascar
An-tung *see* Dandong
Antwerpen *65 C5* *Eng.* Antwerp, *Fr.* Anvers. Antwerpen, N Belgium
Anuradhapura *110 D3* North Central Province, C Sri Lanka
Anvers *see* Antwerpen
Anyang *106 C4* Henan, C China
A'nyêmaqên Shan *104 D4* *mountain range* C China
Anykščiai *84 C4* Utena, E Lithuania
Anzio *75 C5* Lazio, C Italy
Aomen *see* Macao
Aomori *108 D3* Aomori, Honshū, C Japan
Aóos *see* Vjosës, Lumi i
Aoraki *129 B6* *prev.* Aorangi, Mount Cook. *mountain* South Island, New Zealand
Aorangi *see* Aoraki
Aosta *74 A1* *anc.* Augusta Praetoria. Valle d'Aosta, NW Italy
Aoukâr *52 D3* *var.* Aouker. *plateau* C Mauritania
Aouk, Bahr *54 C4* *river* Central African Republic/Chad
Aouker *see* Aoukâr
Aozou *54 C1* Borkou-Ennedi-Tibesti, N Chad
Apalachee Bay *20 D3* *bay* Florida, SE USA
Apalachicola River *20 D3* *river* Florida, SE USA
Apamama *see* Abemama
Apaporis, Río *36 C4* *river* Brazil/Colombia
Apatity *88 C2* Murmanskaya Oblast', NW Russian Federation
Ape *84 D3* Alūksne, NE Latvia
Apeldoorn *64 D3* Gelderland, E Netherlands
Apennines *74 E2* *Eng.* Apennines. *mountain range* Italy/San Marino
Apennines *see* Appennino
Āpia *123 F4* *country capital* Upolu, SE Samoa
Ap'khazet'i *95 E1* *var.* Abkhazia. *autonomous republic* NW Georgia
Apoera *37 G3* Sipaliwini, NW Suriname
Apostle Islands *18 B1* *island group* Wisconsin, N USA
Appalachian Mountains *13 D5* *mountain range* E USA
Appingedam *64 E1* Groningen, NE Netherlands
Appleton *18 B2* Wisconsin, N USA
Apulia *see* Puglia
Apure, Río *36 C2* *river* W Venezuela
Apurímac, Río *38 D3* *river* S Peru
Apuseni, Munții *86 A4* *mountain range* W Romania
Aqaba/'Aqaba *see* Al 'Aqabah
Aqaba, Gulf of *98 A4* *var.* Gulf of Elat, *Ar.* Khalīj al 'Aqabah; *anc.* Sinus Aelaniticus. *gulf* NE Red Sea
'Aqabah, Khalīj al *see* Aqaba, Gulf of
Āqchah *101 E3* *var.* Āqcheh. Jowzjān, N Afghanistan
Āqcheh *see* Āqchah
Aqmola *see* Astana
Aqtöbe *see* Aktobe
Aquae Augustae *see* Dax
Aquae Calidae *see* Bath
Aquae Flaviae *see* Chaves
Aquae Grani *see* Aachen
Aquae Sextiae *see* Aix-en-Provence
Aquae Solis *see* Bath
Aquae Tarbelicae *see* Dax
Aquidauana *41 E4* Mato Grosso do Sul, S Brazil
Aquila/Aquila degli Abruzzi *see* L'Aquila
Aquisgranum *see* Aachen
Aquitaine *69 B6* *cultural region* SW France
'Arabah, Wadi al *97 B7* *Heb.* Ha'Arava. *dry watercourse* Israel/Jordan
Arabian Basin *102 A4* *undersea basin* N Arabian Sea
Arabian Desert *see* Sahara el Sharqîya
Arabian Peninsula *99 B5* *peninsula* SW Asia
Arabian Sea *102 A3* *sea* NW Indian Ocean
Arabicus, Sinus *see* Red Sea
'Arabī, Khalīj al *see* Gulf, The
'Arabīyah as Su'ūdīyah, Al Mamlakah al *see* Saudi Arabia
'Arabīyah Jumhūrīyah, Mişr al *see* Egypt
Arab Republic of Egypt *see* Egypt
Aracaju *41 G3* *state capital* Sergipe, E Brazil
Araçuai *41 F3* Minas Gerais, SE Brazil
Arad *97 B7* Southern, S Israel
Arad *86 A4* Arad, W Romania
Arafura Sea *120 A3* *Ind.* Laut Arafuru. *sea* W Pacific Ocean
Arafuru, Laut *see* Arafura Sea
Aragón *71 E2* *autonomous community* E Spain
Araguaia, Río *41 E3* *var.* Araguaya. *river* C Brazil
Araguari *41 F3* Minas Gerais, SE Brazil
Araguaya *see* Araguaia, Río
Ara Jovis *see* Aranjuez
Arāk *98 C3* *prev.* Sultānābād. Markazī, W Iran
Arakan Yoma *114 A3* *mountain range* W Myanmar (Burma)
Araks/Arak's *see* Aras
Aral *see* Aralsk, Kazakhstan
Aral Sea *100 C1* *Kaz.* Aral Tengizi, *Rus.* Aral'skoye More, *Uzb.* Orol Dengizi. *inland sea* Kazakhstan/Uzbekistan
Aral'sk *92 B4* *Kaz.* Aral. Kzylorda, SW Kazakhstan
Aral'skoye More/Aral Tengizi *see* Aral Sea
\randa de Duero *70 D2* Castilla-León, N Spain
Aranđelovac *78 D4* *prev.* Arandjelovac. Serbia, C Serbia
Arandjelovac *see* Aranđelovac
Aranjuez *70 D3* *anc.* Ara Jovis. Madrid, C Spain
Araouane *53 E2* Tombouctou, N Mali
'Ar'ar *98 B3* Al Ḥudūd ash Shamālīyah, NW Saudi Arabia
Mount Ararat *95 F3* *var.* Aghri Dagh, Agri Dagi, Koh I Noh, Masis, *Eng.* Great Ararat, Mount Ararat. *mountain* E Turkey
Ararat, Mount *see* Büyükağrı Dağı
Aras *95 G3* *Arm.* Arak's, *Az.* Araz Nehri, *Per.* Rūd-e Aras, *Rus.* Araks; *prev.* Araxes. *river* SW Asia
Aras, Rūd-e *see* Aras
Arauca *36 C2* Arauca, NE Colombia
Arauca, Río *36 C2* *river* Colombia/Venezuela
Arausio *see* Orange
Araxes *see* Aras
Araz Nehri *see* Aras
Arbela *see* Arbīl
Arbīl *98 B2* *var.* Erbil, Irbīl, *Kurd.* Hawlēr; *anc.* Arbela. Arbīl, N Iraq
Arbroath *66 D3* *anc.* Aberbrothock. E Scotland, United Kingdom
Arbuzinka *see* Arbuzynka
Arbuzynka *87 E3* *Rus.* Arbuzinka. Mykolayivs'ka Oblast', S Ukraine
Arcachon *69 B5* Gironde, SW France
Arcae Remorum *see* Châlons-en-Champagne
Arcata *24 A4* California, W USA
Archangel *see* Arkhangel'sk
Archangel Bay *see* Chëshskaya Guba
Archidona *70 D5* Andalucía, S Spain
Arco *74 C2* Trentino-Alto Adige, N Italy
Arctic Mid Oceanic Ridge *see* Nansen Cordillera
Arctic Ocean *133 B3* *ocean*
Arda *82 C3* *var.* Ardhas, *Gk.* Ardas. *river* Bulgaria/Greece
Ardabīl *98 C2* *var.* Ardebil. Ardabīl, NW Iran
Ardakān *98 D3* Yazd, C Iran
Ardas *82 D3* *var.* Ardhas, *Bul.* Arda. *river* Bulgaria/Greece
Arḍ aş Şawwān *97 C7* *var.* Ardh es Suwwān. *plain* S Jordan
Ardeal *see* Transylvania
Ardebil *see* Ardabīl
Ardèche *69 C5* *cultural region* E France
Ardennes *65 C8* *physical region* Belgium/France
Ardhas *see* Arda/Ardas
Ardh es Suwwān *see* Arḍ aş Şawwān
Ardino *82 D3* Kŭrdzhali, S Bulgaria
Ard Mhacha *see* Armagh
Ardmore *27 G2* Oklahoma, C USA
Arel *see* Arlon
Arelas/Arelate *see* Arles
Arendal *63 A6* Aust-Agder, S Norway
Arensburg *see* Kuressaare
Arenys de Mar *71 G2* Cataluña, NE Spain
Areópoli *83 B7* *prev.* Areópolis. Pelopónnisos, S Greece
Areópolis *see* Areópoli
Arequipa *39 E4* Arequipa, SE Peru
Arezzo *74 C3* *anc.* Arretium. Toscana, C Italy
Argalastí *83 C5* Thessalía, C Greece
Argenteuil *68 D1* Val-d'Oise, N France
Argentina *43 B5* *off.* Argentine Republic. *country* S South America
Argentina Basin *see* Argentine Basin
Argentine Basin *35 C7* *var.* Argentina Basin. *undersea basin* SW Atlantic Ocean
Argentine Republic *see* Argentina
Argentine Rise *see* Falkland Plateau
Argentoratum *see* Strasbourg
Darya-ye Arghandab *101 E5* *river* SE Afghanistan
Argirocastro *see* Gjirokastër
Argo *50 B3* Northern, N Sudan
Argo Fracture Zone *119 C5* *tectonic Feature* C Indian Ocean
Árgos *83 B6* Pelopónnisos, S Greece
Argostóli *83 A5* *var.* Argostólion. Kefallonía, Iónia Nísiá, Greece, C Mediterranean Sea
Argostólion *see* Argostóli
Argun *103 E1* *Chin.* Ergun He, *Rus.* Argun'. *river* China/Russian Federation
Argyrokastron *see* Gjirokastër
Århus *63 B7* *var.* Aarhus. Århus, C Denmark
Aria *see* Herāt
Ari Atoll *110 A4* *var.* Alifu Atoll. *atoll* C Maldives
Arica *42 B1* *hist.* San Marcos de Arica. Tarapacá, N Chile
Aridaía *82 B3* *var.* Aridea, Aridhaía. Dytikí Makedonía, N Greece
Aridea *see* Aridaía
Aridhaía *see* Aridaía
Arīhā *96 B3* Al Karak, W Jordan
Arīḥā *see* Jericho
Ariminum *see* Rimini
Arinsal *69 A7* NW Andorra Europe
Arizona *26 A2* *off.* State of Arizona, *also known as* Copper State, Grand Canyon State. *state* SW USA
Arkansas *20 A1* *off.* State of Arkansas, *also known as* The Land of Opportunity. *state* S USA

Arkansas City – Balıkesir

Arkansas City 23 F5 Kansas, C USA
Arkansas River 27 G1 river C USA
Arkhangel'sk 92 B2 Eng. Archangel. Arkhangel'skaya Oblast', NW Russian Federation
Arkoí 83 E6 island Dodekánisa, Greece, Aegean Sea
Arles 69 D6 var. Arles-sur-Rhône; anc. Arelas, Arelate. Bouches-du-Rhône, SE France
Arles-sur-Rhône see Arles
Arlington 27 G2 Texas, SW USA
Arlington 19 E4 Virginia, NE USA
Arlon 65 D8 Dut. Aarlen, Ger. Arel, Lat. Orolaunum. Luxembourg, SE Belgium
Armagh 67 B5 Ir. Ard Mhacha. S Northern Ireland, United Kingdom
Armagnac 69 B6 cultural region S France
Armenia 36 B3 Quindío, W Colombia
Armenia 95 F3 off. Republic of Armenia, var. Ajastan, Arm. Hayastani Hanrapetut'yun; prev. Armenian Soviet Socialist Republic. country SW Asia
Armenian Soviet Socialist Republic see Armenia
Armenia, Republic of see Armenia
Armidale 127 D6 New South Wales, SE Australia
Armstrong 16 B3 Ontario, S Canada
Armyans'k 87 F4 Rus. Armyansk. Respublika Krym, S Ukraine
Arnaía 82 C4 Cont. Arnea. Kentrikí Makedonía, N Greece
Arnaud 60 A3 river Québec, E Canada
Arnea see Arnaía
Arnedo 71 E2 La Rioja, N Spain
Arnhem 64 D4 Gelderland, SE Netherlands
Arnhem Land 126 A2 physical region Northern Territory, N Australia
Arno 74 B3 river C Italy
Arnold 23 G4 Missouri, C USA
Arnswalde see Choszczno
Aroe Islands see Aru, Kepulauan
Arorae 123 E3 atoll Tungaru, W Kiribati
Arrabona see Győr
Ar Rahad see Er Rahad
Ar Ramādī 98 B3 var. Ramadi, Rumadiya. Al Anbār, SW Iraq
Ar Rāmī 96 C4 Ḩimş, C Syria
Ar Ramthā 97 B5 var. Ramtha. Irbid, N Jordan
Arran, Isle of 66 C4 island SW Scotland, United Kingdom
Ar Raqqah 96 C2 var. Rakka; anc. Nicephorium. Ar Raqqah, N Syria
Arras 68 C2 anc. Nemetocenna. Pas-de-Calais, N France
Ar Rawḑatayn 98 C4 var. Raudhatain. N Kuwait
Arretium see Arezzo
Arriaca see Guadalajara
Arriaga 29 G5 Chiapas, SE Mexico
Ar Riyāḑ 99 C5 Eng. Riyadh. country capital Ar Riyāḑ, C Saudi Arabia
Ar Rub 'al Khali 99 C6 Eng. Empty Quarter, Great Sandy Desert. desert SW Asia
Ar Rustāq 99 E5 var. Rostak, Rustaq. N Oman
Ar Ruţbah 98 B3 var. Rutba. Al Anbār, SW Iraq
Árta 83 A5 anc. Ambracia. Ípeiros, W Greece
Artashat 95 F3 S Armenia
Artemisa 32 B2 La Habana, W Cuba
Artesia 26 D3 New Mexico, SW USA
Arthur's Pass 129 C6 pass South Island, New Zealand
Artigas 42 D3 prev. San Eugenio, San Eugenio del Cuareim. Artigas, N Uruguay
Art'ik 95 F2 W Armenia
Artois 68 C2 cultural region N France
Artsiz see Artsyz
Artsyz 86 D4 Rus. Artsiz. Odes'ka Oblast', SW Ukraine
Artvin 95 F2 Artvin, NE Turkey
Arua 51 B6 NW Uganda
Aruba 36 C1 var. Oruba. Dutch autonomous region S West Indies
Aru Islands see Aru, Kepulauan
Aru, Kepulauan 117 G4 Eng. Aru Islands; prev. Aroe Islands. island group E Indonesia
Arunāchal Pradesh 113 G3 prev. North East Frontier Agency, North East Frontier Agency of Assam. cultural region NE India
Arusha 51 C7 Arusha, N Tanzania
Arviat 15 G4 prev. Eskimo Point. Nunavut, C Canada
Arvidsjaur 62 C4 Norrbotten, N Sweden
Arys' 92 B5 Kaz. Arys. Yuzhnyy Kazakhstan, S Kazakhstan
Arys see Arys'
Asadābād 101 F4 var. Asadābād; prev. Chaghasarāy. Konar, E Afghanistan
Asadābād see Asadābād
Asahi-dake 108 D2 mountain Hokkaidō, N Japan
Asahikawa 108 D2 Hokkaidō, N Japan
Asamankese 53 E5 SE Ghana
Āsānsol 113 F4 West Bengal, NE India
Asben see Aïr, Massif de l'
Ascension Fracture Zone 47 A5 tectonic Feature C Atlantic Ocean
Ascension Island 45 C5 dependency of St.Helena C Atlantic Ocean
Ascoli Piceno 74 C4 anc. Asculum Picenum. Marche, C Italy
Asculum Picenum see Ascoli Piceno
'Aseb 50 D4 var. Assab, Amh. Āseb. SE Eritrea
Aşgabat 100 C3 prev. Ashgabat, Ashkhabad, Poltoratsk. country capital Ahal Welaýaty, C Turkmenistan
Ashara see Al 'Ashārah
Ashburton 129 C6 Canterbury, South Island, New Zealand
Ashburton River 124 A4 river Western Australia
Ashdod 97 A6 anc. Azotos, Lat. Azotus. Central, W Israel
Asheville 21 E1 North Carolina, SE USA
Ashgabat see Aşgabat
Ashkelon 97 A6 prev. Ashqelon. Southern, C Israel
Ashkhabad see Aşgabat
Ashland 24 B4 Oregon, NW USA
Ashland 18 B1 Wisconsin, N USA
Ashmore and Cartier Islands 120 A3 Australian external territory E Indian Ocean
Ashmyany 85 C5 Rus. Oshmyany. Hrodzyenskaya Voblasts', W Belarus
Ashqelon see Ashkelon
Ash Shadādah 96 D2 var. Ash Shaddādah, Jisr ash Shadadi, Shaddādī, Shedadi, Tell Shedadi. Al Ḩasakah, NE Syria
Ash Shaddādah see Ash Shadādah
Ash Sharah 97 B7 var. Esh Sharā. mountain range W Jordan
Ash Shāriqah 98 D4 Eng. Sharjah. Ash Shāriqah, NE United Arab Emirates
Ash Shawbak 97 B7 Ma'ān, W Jordan
Ash Shiḩr 99 C6 SE Yemen
Asia 90 continent
Asinara 74 A4 island W Italy
Asipovichy 85 D6 Rus. Osipovichi. Mahilyowskaya Voblasts', C Belarus
Aşkale 95 E3 Erzurum, NE Turkey
Askersund 63 C6 Örebro, C Sweden
Asmara see Asmera
Asmera 50 C4 var. Asmara. country capital C Eritrea
Aspadana see Eşfahān
Asphaltites, Lacus see Dead Sea
Aspinwall see Colón
Assab see 'Aseb
As Sabkhah 96 D2 var. Sabkha. Ar Raqqah, NE Syria
Assad, Lake 96 C2 Eng. Lake Assad. lake N Syria
Assad, Lake see Asad, Buḩayrat al
Aş Şafāwī 97 C6 Al Mafraq, N Jordan
Aş Şaḩrā' ash Sharqīyah see Sahara el Sharqîya
As Salamīyah see Salamīyah
'Assal, Lac 46 E4 lake C Djibouti
As Salţ 97 B6 var. Salt. Al Balqā', NW Jordan
Assamaka see Assamakka
Assamakka 53 F2 var. Assamaka. Agadez, NW Niger
As Samāwah 98 B3 var. Samawa. Al Muthannā, S Iraq
Assen 64 E2 Drenthe, NE Netherlands
Assenede 65 B5 Oost-Vlaanderen, NW Belgium
Assiout see Asyūţ
Assiut see Asyūţ
Assling see Jesenice
Assouan see Aswân
Assu see Açu
Assuan see Aswân
As Sukhnah 96 C3 var. Sukhne, Fr. Soukhné. Ḩimş, C Syria
As Sulaymānīyah 98 C3 var. Sulaimaniya, Kurd. Slēmānī. As Sulaymānīyah, NE Iraq
As Sulayyil 99 B5 Ar Riyāḑ, S Saudi Arabia
Aş Şuwar 96 D2 var. Şuwār. Dayr az Zawr, E Syria
As Suwaydā' 97 B5 var. El Suweida, Es Suweida, Suweida, Fr. Soueida. As Suwaydā', SW Syria
As Suways see Suez
Asta Colonia see Asti
Astacus see İzmit
Astana 92 C4 prev. Akmola, Akmolinsk, Tselinograd, Aqmola. country capital Akmola, N Kazakhstan
Asta Pompeia see Asti
Astarabad see Gorgān
Asterābād see Gorgān
Asti 74 A2 anc. Asta Colonia, Asta Pompeia, Hasta Colonia, Hasta Pompeia. Piemonte, NW Italy
Astigi see Ecija
Astipálaia see Astypálaia
Astorga 70 C1 anc. Asturica Augusta. Castilla-León, N Spain
Astrabad see Gorgān
Astrakhan' 89 C7 Astrakhanskaya Oblast', SW Russian Federation
Asturias 70 C1 autonomous community NW Spain
Asturias see Oviedo
Asturica Augusta see Astorga
Astypálaia 83 D7 var. Astipálaia, It. Stampalia. island Kykládes, Greece, Aegean Sea
Asunción 42 D2 country capital Central, S Paraguay
Aswân 50 B2 var. Assouan, Assuan, Aswān; anc. Syene. SE Egypt
Aswān see Aswân
Asyūţ 50 B2 var. Assiout, Assiut, Asyût, Siut; anc. Lycopolis. C Egypt
Asyût see Asyūţ
Atacama Desert 42 B2 Eng. Atacama Desert. desert N Chile
Atacama Desert see Atacama, Desierto de
Atafu Atoll 123 E3 island NW Tokelau
Atamyrat 100 D3 prev. Kerki. Lebap Welaýaty, E Turkmenistan
Atâr 52 C2 Adrar, W Mauritania
Atas Bogd 104 D3 mountain SW Mongolia
Atascadero 25 B7 California, W USA
Atatürk Barajı 95 E4 reservoir S Turkey
Atbara 50 C3 var. 'Aṭbārah. River Nile, NE Sudan
'Aṭbārah/'Aṭbarah, Nahr see Atbara
Atbasar 92 C4 Akmola, N Kazakhstan
Atchison 23 F4 Kansas, C USA
Aternum see Pescara
Ath 65 B6 var. Aat. Hainaut, SW Belgium
Athabasca 15 E5 Alberta, SW Canada
Athabasca 15 E5 var. Athabaska. river Alberta, SW Canada
Athabasca, Lake 15 F4 lake Alberta/Saskatchewan, SW Canada
Athabaska see Athabasca
Athenae see Athína
Athens 21 E2 Georgia, SE USA
Athens 18 D4 Ohio, N USA
Athens 27 G3 Texas, SW USA
Athens see Athína
Atherton 126 D3 Queensland, NE Australia
Athína 83 C6 Eng. Athens, prev. Athínai; anc. Athenae. country capital Attikí, C Greece
Athínai see Athína
Athlone 67 B5 Ir. Baile Átha Luain. C Ireland
Ath Thawrah see Madīnat ath Thawrah
Ati 54 C3 Batha, C Chad
Atikokan 16 B4 Ontario, S Canada
Atka 93 G3 Magadanskaya Oblast', E Russian Federation
Atka 14 A3 Atka Island, Alaska, USA
Atlanta 20 D2 state capital Georgia, SE USA
Atlanta 27 H2 Texas, SW USA
Atlantic City 19 F4 New Jersey, NE USA
Atlantic-Indian Basin 45 D7 undersea basin SW Indian Ocean
Atlantic-Indian Ridge 47 B8 undersea ridge SW Indian Ocean
Atlantic Ocean 44 B4 ocean
Atlas Mountains 48 C2 mountain range NW Africa
Atlasovo 93 H3 Kamchatskaya Oblast', E Russian Federation
Atlas, Tell 80 C3 Eng. Tell Atlas. mountain range N Algeria
Atlas, Tell see Atlas Tellien
Atlin 14 D4 British Columbia, W Canada
Aţ Ţafīlah 97 B7 var. Et Tafila, Tafila. Aţ Ţafīlah, W Jordan
Aţ Ţā'if 99 B5 Makkah, W Saudi Arabia
Attaleia/Attalia see Antalya
At Tall al Abyaḑ 96 C2 var. Tall al Abyaḑ, Tell Abyad, Fr. Tell Abiad. Ar Raqqah, N Syria
Aţ Ţanf 96 D4 Ḩimş, S Syria
Attapu see Samakhixai
Attawapiskat 16 C3 Ontario, C Canada
Attawapiskat 16 C3 river Ontario, S Canada
At Tibnī 96 D2 var. Tibnī. Dayr az Zawr, NE Syria
Attopeu see Samakhixai
Attu Island 14 A2 island Aleutian Islands, Alaska, USA
Atyrau 92 B4 prev. Gur'yev. Atyrau, W Kazakhstan
Aubagne 69 D6 anc. Albania. Bouches-du-Rhône, SE France
Aubange 65 D8 Luxembourg, SE Belgium
Aubervilliers 68 E1 Seine-St-Denis, Île-de-France, N France Europe
Auburn 24 B2 Washington, NW USA
Auch 69 B6 Lat. Augusta Auscorum, Elimberrum. Gers, S France
Auckland 128 D2 Auckland, North Island, New Zealand
Auckland Islands 120 C5 island group S New Zealand
Audern see Audru
Audincourt 68 E4 Doubs, E France
Audru 84 D2 Ger. Audern. Pärnumaa, SW Estonia
Augathella 127 D5 Queensland, E Australia
Augsbourg see Augsburg
Augsburg 73 C6 Fr. Augsbourg; anc. Augusta Vindelicorum. Bayern, S Germany
Augusta 125 A7 Western Australia
Augusta 21 E2 Georgia, SE USA
Augusta 19 G2 state capital Maine, NE USA
Augusta see London
Augusta Auscorum see Auch
Augusta Emerita see Mérida
Augusta Praetoria see Aosta
Augusta Trajana see Stara Zagora
Augusta Treverorum see Trier
Augusta Vangionum see Worms
Augusta Vindelicorum see Augsburg
Augustobona Tricassium see Troyes
Augustodurum see Bayeux
Augustoritum Lemovicensium see Limoges
Augustów 76 E2 Rus. Avgustov. Podlaskie, NE Poland
Aulie Ata/Auliye-Ata see Taraz
Aunglan 114 B4 var. Allanmyo, Myaydo. Magway, C Myanmar (Burma)
Auob 56 B4 var. Oup. river Namibia/South Africa
Aurangābād 112 D5 Mahārāshtra, C India
Auray 68 A3 Morbihan, NW France
Aurelia Aquensis see Baden-Baden
Aurelianum see Orléans
Aurès, Massif de l' 80 C4 mountain range NE Algeria
Aurillac 69 C5 Cantal, C France
Aurium see Ourense
Aurora 37 F2 NW Guyana
Aurora 22 D4 Colorado, C USA
Aurora 18 B3 Illinois, N USA
Aurora 23 G5 Missouri, C USA
Aurora see Maéwo, Vanuatu
Aus 56 B4 Karas, SW Namibia
Ausa see Vic
Aussig see Ústí nad Labem
Austin 23 G3 Minnesota, N USA
Austin 27 G3 state capital Texas, SW USA
Australes, Archipel des see Australes, Îles
Australes et Antarctiques Françaises, Terres see French Southern and Antarctic Territories
Australes, Îles 121 F4 var. Archipel des Australes, Îles Tubuai, Tubuai Islands, Eng. Austral Islands. island group SW French Polynesia
Austral Fracture Zone 121 H4 tectonic feature S Pacific Ocean
Australia 120 A4 off. Commonwealth of Australia. country
Australia, Commonwealth of see Australia
Australian Alps 127 C7 mountain range SE Australia
Australian Capital Territory 127 D7 prev. Federal Capital Territory. territory SE Australia
Australie, Bassin Nord de l' see North Australian Basin
Austral Islands see Australes, Îles
Austrava see Ostrov
Austria 73 D7 off. Republic of Austria, Ger. Österreich. country C Europe
Austria, Republic of see Austria
Autesiodorum see Auxerre
Autissiodorum see Auxerre
Autricum see Chartres
Auvergne 69 C5 cultural region C France
Auxerre 68 C4 anc. Autesiodorum, Autissiodorum. Yonne, C France
Avaricum see Bourges
Avarua 123 G5 dependent territory capital Rarotonga, S Cook Islands
Avasfelsőfalu see Negrești-Oaș
Ávdira 82 C3 Anatolikí Makedonía kai Thráki, NE Greece
Aveiro 70 B2 anc. Talabriga. Aveiro, W Portugal
Avela see Ávila
Avellino 75 D5 anc. Abellinum. Campania, S Italy
Avenio see Avignon
Avesta 63 C6 Dalarna, C Sweden
Aveyron 69 C6 river S France
Avezzano 74 C4 Abruzzo, C Italy
Avgustov see Augustów
Aviemore 66 C3 N Scotland, United Kingdom
Avignon 69 D6 anc. Avenio. Vaucluse, SE France
Ávila 70 D3 var. Avila; anc. Abela, Abula, Abyla, Avela. Castilla-León, C Spain
Avilés 70 C1 Asturias, NW Spain
Avranches 68 B3 Manche, N France
Avveel see Ivalo, Finland
Avvil see Ivalo
Awaji-shima 109 C6 island SW Japan
Āwash 51 D5 Āfar, NE Ethiopia
Awbārī 49 F3 SW Libya
Ax see Dax
Axel 65 B5 Zeeland, SW Netherlands
Axel Heiberg Island 15 E1 var. Axel Heiburg. island Nunavut, N Canada
Axel Heiburg see Axel Heiberg Island
Axiós see Vardar
Ayacucho 38 D4 Ayacucho, S Peru
Ayagoz 92 C5 var. Ayaguz, Kaz. Ayakoz. river E Kazakhstan
Ayamonte 70 C4 Andalucía, S Spain
Ayaviri 39 E4 Puno, S Peru
Aydarko'l Ko'li 101 E2 Rus. Ozero Aydarkul'. lake C Uzbekistan
Aydarkul', Ozero see Aydarko'l Ko'li
Aydın 94 A4 var. Aïdin; anc. Tralles Aydin. Aydın, SW Turkey
Ayers Rock see Uluru
Ayeyarwady see Irrawaddy
Ayiá see Agiá
Áyios Evstrátios see Ágios Efstrátios
Áyios Nikólaos see Ágios Nikólaos
Ayorou 53 E3 Tillabéri, W Niger
'Ayoûn el 'Atroûs 52 D3 var. Aïoun el Atrous, Aïoun el Atroûss. Hodh el Gharbi, SE Mauritania
Ayr 66 C4 W Scotland, United Kingdom
Ayteke Bi 92 B4 Kaz. Zhangaqazaly; prev. Novokazalinsk. Kzylorda, SW Kazakhstan
Aytos 82 E2 Burgas, E Bulgaria
Ayutthaya 115 C5 var. Phra Nakhon Si Ayutthaya. Phra Nakhon Si Ayutthaya, C Thailand
Ayvalık 94 A3 Balıkesir, W Turkey
Azahar, Costa del 71 F3 coastal region E Spain
Azaouâd 53 E3 desert C Mali
Azärbaycan/Azärbaycan Respublikasī see Azerbaijan
A'zāz 96 B2 Ḩalab, NW Syria
Azerbaijan 95 G2 off. Azerbaijani Republic, Az. Azärbaycan, Azärbaycan Respublikası; prev. Azerbaijan SSR. country SE Asia
Azerbaijani Republic see Azerbaijan
Azerbaijan SSR see Azerbaijan
Azimabad see Patna
Azizie see Telish
Azogues 38 B2 Cañar, S Ecuador
Azores 70 A4 var. Açores, Ilhas dos Açores, Port. Arquipélago dos Açores. island group Portugal, NE Atlantic Ocean
Azores-Biscay Rise 58 A3 undersea rise E Atlantic Ocean
Azotos/Azotus see Ashdod
Azoum, Bahr 54 C3 seasonal river SE Chad
Azov, Sea of 81 H1 Rus. Azovskoye More, Ukr. Azovs'ke More. sea NE Black Sea
Azovs'ke More/Azovskoye More see Azov, Sea of
Azraq, Wāḩat al 97 C6 oasis N Jordan
Aztec 26 C1 New Mexico, SW USA
Azuaga 70 C4 Extremadura, W Spain
Azuero, Península de 31 F5 peninsula S Panama
Azul 43 D5 Buenos Aires, E Argentina
Azur, Côte d' 69 E6 coastal region SE France
'Azza see Gaza
Az Zaqāzīq 50 B1 var. Zagazig var. Az Zaqāzīq. N Egypt
Az Zaqāzīq see Az Zaqāzīq
Az Zarqā' 97 B6 var. Zarqa. Az Zarqā', NW Jordan
Az Zāwiyah 49 F2 var. Zawia. NW Libya
Az Zilfī 98 B4 Ar Riyāḑ, N Saudi Arabia

B

Baalbek 96 B4 var. Ba'labakk; anc. Heliopolis. E Lebanon
Baardheere 51 D6 var. Bardere, It. Bardera. Gedo, SW Somalia
Baarle-Hertog 65 C5 Antwerpen, N Belgium
Baarn 64 C3 Utrecht, C Netherlands
Babadag 86 D5 Tulcea, SE Romania
Babahoyo 38 B2 prev. Bodegas. Los Ríos, C Ecuador
Bābā, Kūh-e 101 E4 mountain range C Afghanistan
Babayevo 88 B4 Vologodskaya Oblast', NW Russian Federation
Babeldaob 122 A1 var. Babeldaop, Babelthuap. island N Palau
Babeldaop see Babeldaob
Bab el Mandeb 99 B7 strait Gulf of Aden/Red Sea
Babelthuap see Babeldaob
Babian Jiang see Black River
Babruysk 85 D7 Rus. Bobruysk. Mahilyowskaya Voblasts', E Belarus
Babuyan Channel 117 E1 channel N Philippines
Babuyan Island 117 E1 island N Philippines
Bacabal 41 F2 Maranhão, E Brazil
Bacău 86 C4 Hung. Bákó. Bacău, NE Romania
Băc Bô, Vinh see Tongking, Gulf of
Băc Giang 114 D3 Ha Băc, N Vietnam
Bacheykava 85 D5 Rus. Bocheykovo. Vitsyebskaya Voblasts', N Belarus
Back 15 F3 river Nunavut, N Canada
Bačka Palanka 78 D3 prev. Palanka. Serbia, NW Serbia
Bačka Topola 78 D3 Hung. Topolya; prev. Hung. Bácstopolya. Vojvodina, N Serbia
Bac Liêu 115 D6 var. Vinh Loi. Minh Hai, S Vietnam
Bacolod 103 E4 off. Bacolod City. Negros, C Philippines
Bacolod City see Bacolod
Bácsszenttamás see Srbobran
Bácstopolya see Bačka Topola
Bactra see Balkh
Badajoz 70 C4 anc. Pax Augusta. Extremadura, W Spain
Baden-Baden 73 B6 anc. Aurelia Aquensis. Baden-Württemberg, SW Germany
Bad Freienwalde 72 D3 Brandenburg, NE Germany
Badger State see Wisconsin
Bad Hersfeld 72 B4 Hessen, C Germany
Bad Homburg see Bad Homburg vor der Höhe
Bad Homburg vor der Höhe 73 B5 var. Bad Homburg. Hessen, W Germany
Bad Ischl 73 D7 Oberösterreich, N Austria
Bad Krozingen 73 A6 Baden-Württemberg, SW Germany
Badlands 22 D2 physical region North Dakota/South Dakota, N USA
Badu Island 126 C1 island Queensland, NE Australia
Bad Vöslau 73 E6 Niederösterreich, NE Austria
Baeterrae/Baeterrae Septimanorum see Béziers
Baetic Cordillera/Baetic Mountains see Béticos, Sistemas
Bafatá 52 C4 C Guinea-Bissau
Baffin Bay 15 G2 bay Canada/Greenland
Baffin Island 15 G2 island Nunavut, NE Canada
Bafing 52 C3 river W Africa
Bafoussam 54 A4 Ouest, W Cameroon
Bafra 94 D2 Samsun, N Turkey
Bāft 98 D4 Kermān, S Iran
Bagaces 30 D4 Guanacaste, NW Costa Rica
Bagdad see Baghdād
Bagé 41 E5 Rio Grande do Sul, S Brazil
Baghdād 98 B3 var. Bagdad, Eng. Baghdad. country capital Baghdād, C Iraq
Baghdad see Baghdād
Baghlān 101 E3 Baghlān, NE Afghanistan
Bago 114 B4 var. Pegu. Bago, SW Myanmar (Burma)
Bagoé 52 D4 river Ivory Coast/Mali
Bagrationovsk 84 A4 Ger. Preussisch Eylau. Kaliningradskaya Oblast', W Russian Federation
Bagrax Hu see Bosten Hu
Baguio 117 E1 off. Baguio City. Luzon, N Philippines
Baguio City see Baguio
Bagzane, Monts 53 F3 mountain N Niger
Bahama Islands see Bahamas
Bahamas 32 C2 off. Commonwealth of the Bahamas. country N West Indies
Bahamas 13 D6 var. Bahama Islands. island group N West Indies
Bahamas, Commonwealth of the see Bahamas
Baharly 100 C3 var. Bäherden, Rus. Bakharden; prev. Bakherden. Ahal Welaýaty, C Turkmenistan
Bahāwalpur 112 C2 Punjab, E Pakistan
Bäherden see Baharly
Bahia 41 F3 off. Estado da Bahia. region E Brazil
Bahia 41 F3 off. Estado da Bahia. state E Brazil
Bahía Blanca 43 C5 Buenos Aires, E Argentina
Bahia, Estado da see Bahia
Bahir Dar 50 C4 var. Bahr Dar, Bahrdar Giyorgis. Āmara, N Ethiopia
Bahraich 113 E3 Uttar Pradesh, N India
Bahrain 98 C4 off. State of Bahrain, Dawlat al Bahrayn, Ar. Al Baḩrayn, prev. Bahrein; anc. Tylos, Tyros. country SW Asia
Bahrain, State of see Bahrain
Bahrayn, Dawlat al see Bahrain
Bahr Dar/Bahrdar Giyorgis see Bahir Dar
Bahrein see Bahrain
Bahr el, Azraq see Blue Nile
Bahr Tabariya, Sea of see Tiberias, Lake
Bahushewsk 85 E6 Rus. Bogushëvsk. Vitsyebskaya Voblasts', NE Belarus
Baia Mare 86 B3 Ger. Frauenbach, Hung. Nagybánya; prev. Neustadt. Maramureș, NW Romania
Baia Sprie 86 B3 Ger. Mittelstadt, Hung. Felsőbánya. Maramureș, NW Romania
Baïbokoum 54 B4 Logone-Oriental, SW Chad
Baidoa see Baydhabo
Baie-Comeau 17 E3 Québec, SE Canada
Baikal, Lake 93 E4 Eng. Lake Baikal. lake S Russian Federation
Baikal, Lake see Baykal, Ozero
Baile Átha Cliath see Dublin
Baile Átha Luain see Athlone
Bailén 70 D4 Andalucía, S Spain
Baile na Mainistreach see Newtownabbey
Băilești 86 B5 Dolj, SW Romania
Ba Illi 54 B3 Chari-Baguirmi, SW Chad
Bainbridge 20 D3 Georgia, SE USA
Bā'ir see Bāyir
Baireuth see Bayreuth
Bairiki 122 D2 country capital Tarawa, NW Kiribati
Bairnsdale 127 C7 Victoria, SE Australia
Baishan 107 E3 prev. Hunjiang. Jilin, NE China
Baiyin 106 B4 Gansu, C China
Baja 77 C7 Bács-Kiskun, S Hungary
Baja California 28 B2 state NW Mexico
Bajo Boquete see Boquete
Bajram Curri 79 D5 Kukës, N Albania
Bakala 54 C4 Ouaka, C Central African Republic
Bakan see Shimonoseki
Baker 24 C3 Oregon, NW USA
Baker and Howland Islands 123 E2 US unincorporated territory W Polynesia
Baker Lake 15 F3 Nunavut, N Canada
Bakersfield 25 C7 California, W USA
Bakharden see Baharly
Bakhchisaray see Bakhchysaray
Bakhchysaray 87 F5 Rus. Bakhchisaray. Respublika Krym, S Ukraine
Bakherden see Baharly
Bakhmach 87 F1 Chernihivs'ka Oblast', N Ukraine
Bākhtarān see Kermānshāh
Bakı 95 H2 Eng. Baku. country capital E Azerbaijan
Bákó see Bacău
Bakony 77 C7 Eng. Bakony Mountains, Ger. Bakonywald. mountain range W Hungary
Bakony Mountains/Bakonywald see Bakony
Baku see Bakı
Bakwanga see Mbuji-Mayi
Balabac Island 107 C8 island W Philippines
Balabac, Selat see Balabac Strait
Balabac Strait 116 D2 var. Selat Balabac. strait Malaysia/Philippines
Ba'labakk see Baalbek
Balaguer 71 F2 Cataluña, NE Spain
Balakovo 89 C6 Saratovskaya Oblast', W Russian Federation
Bālā Morghāb 100 D4 Laghmān, NW Afghanistan
Balashov 89 B6 Saratovskaya Oblast', W Russian Federation
Balasore see Bāleshwar
Balaton, Lake 77 C7 var. Lake Balaton, Ger. Plattensee. lake W Hungary
Balaton, Lake see Balaton
Balbina, Represa 40 D1 reservoir NW Brazil
Balboa 31 G4 Panamá, C Panama
Balcarce 43 D5 Buenos Aires, E Argentina
Balclutha 129 B7 Otago, South Island, New Zealand
Baldy Mountain 22 C1 mountain Montana, NW USA
Bâle see Basel
Balearic Plain see Algerian Basin
Baleares Major see Mallorca
Balearic Islands 71 G3 Eng. Balearic Islands. island group Spain, W Mediterranean Sea
Balearic Islands see Baleares, Islas
Balearis Minor see Menorca
Baleine, Rivière à la 17 E2 river Québec, E Canada
Balen 65 C5 Antwerpen, N Belgium
Bāleshwar 113 F4 prev. Balasore. Orissa, E India
Bālgrad see Alba Iulia
Bali 116 D5 island C Indonesia
Balıkesir 94 A3 Balıkesir, W Turkey

Balīkh, Nahr – Bermeo

Balīkh, Nahr 96 C2 river N Syria
Balikpapan 116 D4 Borneo, C Indonesia
Balkanabat 100 B2 Rus. Nebitdag. Balkan Welaýaty, W Turkmenistan
Balkan Mountains 82 C2 Bul./SCr. Stara Planina. mountain range Bulgaria/Serbia
Balkh 101 E3 anc. Bactra. Balkh, N Afghanistan
Balkhash 92 C5 Kaz. Balqash. Karaganda, SE Kazakhstan
Lake Balkhash 92 C5 Eng. Lake Balkhash, Kaz. Balqash. lake SE Kazakhstan
Balkhash, Lake see Balkhash, Ozero
Balladonia 125 C6 Western Australia
Ballarat 127 C7 Victoria, SE Australia
Balleny Islands 132 B5 island group Antarctica
Ballinger 27 F3 Texas, SW USA
Balochistān see Baluchistān
Balqash see Balkhash/Balkhash, Ozero
Balş 86 B5 Olt, S Romania
Balsas 41 F2 Maranhão, E Brazil
Balsas, Río 29 E5 var. Río Mexcala. river S Mexico
Bal'shavik 85 D7 Rus. Bol'shevik. Homyel'skaya Voblasts', SE Belarus
Balta 86 D3 Odes'ka Oblast', SW Ukraine
Bălţi 86 D3 Rus. Bel'tsy. N Moldova
Baltic Port see Paldiski
Baltic Sea 63 C7 Ger. Ostee, Rus. Baltiskoye More. sea N Europe
Baltimore 19 F4 Maryland, NE USA
Baltischport/Baltiski see Paldiski
Baltiskoye More see Baltic Sea
Baltkrievija see Belarus
Baluchistān 112 B3 var. Balochistān, Beluchistan. province SW Pakistan
Balvi 84 D4 Balvi, NE Latvia
Balykchy 101 G2 Kir. Ysyk-Köl; prev. Issyk-Kul', Rybach'ye. Issyk-Kul'skaya Oblast', NE Kyrgyzstan
Balzers 72 E2 S Liechtenstein
Bam 98 E4 Kermān, SE Iran
Bamako 52 D4 country capital Capital District, SW Mali
Bambari 54 C4 Ouaka, C Central African Republic
Bamberg 73 C5 Bayern, SE Germany
Bamenda 54 A4 Nord-Ouest, W Cameroon
Banaba 122 D2 var. Ocean Island. island Tungaru, W Kiribati
Banaras see Vārānasi
Bandaaceh 116 A3 var. Banda Atjeh; prev. Koetaradja, Kutaradja, Kutaraja. Sumatera, W Indonesia
Banda Atjeh see Bandaaceh
Banda, Laut see Banda Sea
Bandama 52 D5 var. Bandama Fleuve. river S Ivory Coast
Bandama Fleuve see Bandama
Bandar 'Abbās see Bandar-e 'Abbās
Bandarbeyla 51 E5 var. Bender Beila, Bender Beyla. Bari, NE Somalia
Bandar-e 'Abbās 98 D4 var. Bandar 'Abbās; prev. Gombroon. Hormozgān, S Iran
Bandar-e Būshehr 98 C4 var. Būshehr, Eng. Bushire. Būshehr, S Iran
Bandar-e Kangān 98 D4 var. Kangān. Būshehr, S Iran
Bandar-e Khamīr 98 D4 Hormozgān, S Iran
Bandar-e Langeh see Bandar-e Lengeh
Bandar-e Lengeh 98 D4 var. Bandar-e Langeh, Lingeh. Hormozgān, S Iran
Bandar Kassim see Boosaaso
Bandar Lampung 116 C4 var. Bandarlampung, Tanjungkarang-Telukbetung; prev. Tandjoengkarang, Tanjungkarang, Teloekbetoeng, Telukbetung. Sumatera, W Indonesia
Bandarlampung see Bandar Lampung
Bandar Maharani see Muar
Bandar Masulipatnam see Machilīpatnam
Bandar Penggaram see Batu Pahat
Bandar Seri Begawan 116 D3 prev. Brunei Town. country capital N Brunei
Banda Sea 117 F5 var. Laut Banda. sea E Indonesia
Bandiagara 53 E3 Mopti, C Mali
Bandırma 94 A3 var. Penderma. Balıkesir, NW Turkey
Bandjarmasin see Banjarmasin
Bandoeng see Bandung
Bandundu 55 C6 prev. Banningville. Bandundu, W Dem. Rep. Congo
Bandung 116 C5 prev. Bandoeng. Jawa, C Indonesia
Bangalore 110 C2 var. Bengalooru. state capital Karnātaka, S India
Bangassou 54 D4 Mbomou, SE Central African Republic
Banggai, Kepulauan 117 E4 island group C Indonesia
Banghāzī 49 G2 Eng. Bengazi, Benghazi, It. Bengasi. NE Libya
Bangka, Pulau 116 C4 island W Indonesia
Bangkok see Krung Thep
Bangkok, Bight of see Krung Thep, Ao
Bangladesh 113 G3 off. People's Republic of Bangladesh; prev. East Pakistan. country S Asia
Bangladesh, People's Republic of see Bangladesh
Bangor 67 C6 NW Wales, United Kingdom
Bangor 67 B5 Ir. Beannchar. E Northern Ireland, United Kingdom
Bangor 19 G2 Maine, NE USA
Bang Pla Soi see Chon Buri
Bangui 55 B5 country capital Ombella-Mpoko, SW Central African Republic
Bangweulu, Lake 51 B8 var. Lake Bengweulu. lake N Zambia
Ban Hat Yai see Hat Yai
Ban Hin Heup 114 C4 Viangchan, C Laos
Ban Houayxay/Ban Houei Sai see Houayxay
Ban Hua Hin 115 C6 var. Hua Hin. Prachuap Khiri Khan, SW Thailand
Bani 52 D3 river S Mali
Banias see Bāniyās
Banijska Palanka see Glina
Banī Suwayf 50 B2 var. Beni Suef. N Egypt
Bāniyās 96 B3 var. Banias, Baniyas, Paneas. Ţarţūs, W Syria
Banjak, Kepulauan see Banyak, Kepulauan
Banja Luka 78 B3 Republika Srpska, NW Bosnia and Herzegovina
Banjarmasin 116 D4 prev. Bandjarmasin. Borneo, C Indonesia
Banjul 52 B3 prev. Bathurst. country capital W Gambia
Banks, Îles see Banks Islands
Banks Island 15 E2 island Northwest Territories, NW Canada
Banks Islands 122 D4 Fr. Îles Banks. island group N Vanuatu
Banks Lake 24 B1 reservoir Washington, NW USA
Banks Peninsula 129 C6 peninsula South Island, New Zealand
Banks Strait 127 C8 strait SW Tasman Sea
Bānkura 113 F4 West Bengal, NE India
Ban Mak Khaeng see Udon Thani
Banmo see Bhamo
Banningville see Bandundu
Bañolas see Banyoles
Ban Pak Phanang see Pak Phanang
Ban Sichon see Sichon
Banská Bystrica 77 C6 Ger. Neusohl, Hung. Besztercebánya. Banskobystricky Kraj, C Slovakia
Bantry Bay 67 A7 Ir. Bá Bheanntraí. bay SW Ireland
Banya 82 E2 Burgas, E Bulgaria
Banyak, Kepulauan 116 A3 prev. Kepulauan Banjak. island group NW Indonesia
Banyo 54 B4 Adamaoua, NW Cameroon
Banyoles 71 G2 var. Bañolas. Cataluña, NE Spain
Banzare Seamounts 119 C7 seamount range S Indian Ocean
Banzart see Bizerte
Baoji 106 B4 var. Pao-chi, Paoki. Shaanxi, C China
Baoro 54 B4 Nana-Mambéré, W Central African Republic
Baoshan 106 A6 var. Pao-shan. Yunnan, SW China
Baotou 105 F3 var. Pao-t'ou, Paotow. Nei Mongol Zizhiqu, N China
Ba'qūbah 98 B3 var. Qubba. Diyālá, C Iraq
Baquerizo Moreno see Puerto Baquerizo Moreno
Bar 79 C5 It. Antivari. S Montenegro
Baraawe 51 D6 It. Brava. Shabeellaha Hoose, S Somalia
Bārāmati 112 C5 Mahārāshtra, W India
Baranavichy 85 B6 Pol. Baranowicze, Rus. Baranovichi. Brestskaya Voblasts', SW Belarus
Baranovichi/Baranowicze see Baranavichy
Barbados 33 G1 country SE West Indies
Barbastro 71 F2 Aragón, NE Spain
Barbate de Franco 70 C5 Andalucía, S Spain
Barbuda 33 G3 island N Antigua and Barbuda
Barcaldine 126 C4 Queensland, E Australia
Barcarozsnyó see Râşnov
Barcău see Berettyó
Barce see Al Marj
Barcelona 71 G2 anc. Barcino, Barcinona. Cataluña, E Spain
Barcelona 37 E2 Anzoátegui, NE Venezuela
Barcino/Barcinona see Barcelona
Barcoo see Cooper Creek
Barcs 77 C7 Somogy, SW Hungary
Bardaï 54 C1 Borkou-Ennedi-Tibesti, N Chad
Bardejov 77 D5 Ger. Bartfeld, Hung. Bártfa. Presovský Kraj, E Slovakia
Bardera/Bardere see Baardheere
Barduli see Barletta
Bareilly 113 E3 var. Bareli. Uttar Pradesh, N India
Bareli see Bareilly
Barendrecht 64 C4 Zuid-Holland, SW Netherlands
Barentin 68 C3 Seine-Maritime, N France
Barentsburg 61 G2 Spitsbergen, W Svalbard
Barentsevo More/Barents Havet see Barents Sea
Barentsøya 61 G2 island E Svalbard
Barents Sea 88 C2 Nor. Barents Havet, Rus. Barentsevo More. sea Arctic Ocean
Bar Harbor 19 H2 Mount Desert Island, Maine, NE USA
Bari 75 E5 var. Bari delle Puglie; anc. Barium. Puglia, SE Italy
Bāridah see Al Bāridah
Bari delle Puglie see Bari
Barikot see Barīkowţ
Barīkowţ 101 F4 var. Barikot. Konar, NE Afghanistan
Barillas 30 A2 var. Santa Cruz Barillas. Huehuetenango, NW Guatemala
Barinas 36 C2 Barinas, W Venezuela
Barisal 113 G4 Barisal, S Bangladesh
Barisan, Pegunungan 116 B4 mountain range Sumatera, W Indonesia
Barito, Sungai 116 D4 river Borneo, C Indonesia
Barium see Bari
Barka see Al Marj
Barkly Tableland 126 B3 plateau Northern Territory/Queensland, N Australia
Bârlad 86 D4 prev. Bîrlad. Vaslui, E Romania
Barlavento, Ilhas de 52 A2 var. Windward Islands. island group N Cape Verde
Bar-le-Duc 68 D3 var. Bar-sur-Ornain. Meuse, NE France
Barlee, Lake 125 B6 lake Western Australia
Barlee Range 124 A4 mountain range Western Australia
Barletta 75 D5 anc. Barduli. Puglia, SE Italy
Barlinek 76 B3 Ger. Berlinchen. Zachodnio-pomorskie, NW Poland
Barmen-Elberfeld see Wuppertal
Barmouth 67 C6 NW Wales, United Kingdom
Barnaul 92 D4 Altayskiy Kray, C Russian Federation
Barnet 67 A7 United Kingdom
Barnstaple 67 C7 SW England, United Kingdom
Baroda see Vadodara
Baroghil Pass 101 F3 var. Kowtal-e Barowghīl. pass Afghanistan/Pakistan
Baron'ki 85 E7 Rus. Boron'ki. Mahilyowskaya Voblasts', E Belarus
Barowghīl, Kowtal-e see Baroghil Pass
Barquisimeto 36 C2 Lara, NW Venezuela
Barra 66 B3 island NW Scotland, United Kingdom
Barra de Río Grande 31 E3 Región Autónoma Atlántico Sur, E Nicaragua
Barranca 38 C3 Lima, W Peru
Barrancabermeja 36 B2 Santander, N Colombia
Barranquilla 36 B1 Atlántico, N Colombia
Barreiro 70 B4 Setúbal, W Portugal
Barrier Range 127 C6 hill range New South Wales, SE Australia
Barrow 14 D2 Alaska, USA
Barrow 67 B6 Ir. An Bhearú. river SE Ireland
Barrow-in-Furness 67 C5 NW England, United Kingdom
Barrow Island 124 A4 island Western Australia
Barstow 25 C7 California, W USA
Bar-sur-Ornain see Bar-le-Duc
Bartang 101 F3 river SE Tajikistan
Bartenstein see Bartoszyce
Bártfa/Bartfeld see Bardejov
Bartica 37 F3 N Guyana
Bartın 94 C2 Bartın, NW Turkey
Bartlesville 27 G1 Oklahoma, C USA
Bartoszyce 76 D2 Ger. Bartenstein. Warmińsko-mazurskie, NE Poland
Baruun-Urt 105 F2 Sühbaatar, E Mongolia
Barú, Volcán 31 E5 var. Volcán de Chiriquí. volcano W Panama
Barwon River 127 D5 river New South Wales, SE Australia
Barysaw 85 D6 Rus. Borisov. Minskaya Voblasts', NE Belarus
Basarabeasca 86 D4 Rus. Bessarabka. SE Moldova
Basel 73 A7 Eng. Basle, Fr. Bâle. Basel-Stadt, NW Switzerland
Basilan 117 E3 island Mindanao, SW Philippines Asia Celebes Sea/Sulu Sea Pacific Ocean
Basle see Basel
Basra see Al Başrah
Bassano del Grappa 74 C2 Veneto, NE Italy
Bassein see Pathein
Basseterre 33 G4 country capital Saint Kitts, Saint Kitts and Nevis
Basse-Terre 33 G3 dependent territory capital Basse Terre, SW Guadeloupe
Basse Terre 33 G4 island W Guadeloupe
Bassikounou 52 D3 Hodh ech Chargui, SE Mauritania
Bass, Îlots de see Marotiri
Bass Strait 127 C7 strait SE Australia
Bassum 72 B3 Niedersachsen, NW Germany
Bastia 69 E7 Corse, France, C Mediterranean Sea
Bastogne 65 D7 Luxembourg, SE Belgium
Bastrop 20 B2 Louisiana, S USA
Bastyn' 85 B7 Rus. Bostyn'. Brestskaya Voblasts', SW Belarus
Basuo see Dongfang
Basutoland see Lesotho
Bata 55 A5 NW Equatorial Guinea
Batae Coritanorum see Leicester
Batajnica 78 D3 Vojvodina, N Serbia
Batangas 117 E2 off. Batangas City. Luzon, N Philippines
Batangas City see Batangas
Batavia see Jakarta
Bătdâmbâng 115 C5 prev. Battambang. Bătdâmbâng, NW Cambodia
Batéké, Plateaux 55 B6 plateau S Congo
Bath 67 D7 hist. Akermanceaster; anc. Aquae Calidae, Aquae Solis. SW England, United Kingdom
Bathinda 112 D2 Punjab, NW India
Bathsheba 33 G1 E Barbados
Bathurst 127 D6 New South Wales, SE Australia
Bathurst 17 F4 New Brunswick, SE Canada
Bathurst see Banjul
Bathurst Island 124 D2 island Northern Territory, N Australia
Bathurst Island 15 F2 island Parry Islands, Nunavut, N Canada
Wadi al Batin 98 C4 dry watercourse SW Asia
Batman 95 E4 var. İluh. Batman, SE Turkey
Batna 49 E2 NE Algeria
Baton Rouge 20 B3 state capital Louisiana, S USA
Batroûn 96 A4 var. Al Batrūn. N Lebanon
Battambang see Bătdâmbâng
Batticaloa 110 D3 Eastern Province, E Sri Lanka
Battipaglia 75 D5 Campania, S Italy
Battle Born State see Nevada
Bat'umi 95 F2 W Georgia
Batu Pahat 116 B3 prev. Bandar Penggaram. Johor, Peninsular Malaysia
Bauchi 53 G4 Bauchi, NE Nigeria
Bauer Basin 131 F3 undersea basin E Pacific Ocean
Bauska 84 C3 Ger. Bauske. Bauska, S Latvia
Bauske see Bauska
Bautzen 72 D4 Lus. Budyšin. Sachsen, E Germany
Bauzanum see Bolzano
Bavaria see Bayern
Bavarian Alps 73 C7 Ger. Bayrische Alpen. mountain range Austria/Germany
Bavière see Bayern
Bavispe, Río 28 C2 river NW Mexico
Bawīţī 50 B2 var. Bawîţi. N Egypt
Bawîţi see Bawīţī
Bawku 53 E4 N Ghana
Bayamo 32 C3 Granma, E Cuba
Bayan Har Shan 104 D4 var. Bayan Khar. mountain range C China
Bayanhongor 104 D2 Bayanhongor, C Mongolia
Bayan Khar see Bayan Har Shan
Bayano, Lago 31 G4 lake E Panama
Bay City 18 C3 Michigan, N USA
Bay City 27 G4 Texas, SW USA
Baydhabo 51 D6 var. Baydhowa, Isha Baydhabo, It. Baidoa. Bay, SW Somalia
Baydhowa see Baydhabo
Bayern 73 C6 Eng. Bavaria, Fr. Bavière. state SE Germany
Bayeux 68 B3 anc. Augustodurum. Calvados, N France
Bāyir 97 C7 var. Bā'ir. Ma'ān, S Jordan
Bay Islands 30 C1 Eng. Bay Islands. island group N Honduras
Bay Islands see Bahía, Islas de la
Baymak 89 D6 Respublika Bashkortostan, W Russian Federation
Bayonne 69 A6 anc. Lapurdum. Pyrénées-Atlantiques, SW France
Bayou State see Mississippi
Bayram-Ali see Baýramaly
Baýramaly 100 D3 var. Bayramaly; prev. Bayram-Ali. Mary Welaýaty, S Turkmenistan
Bayreuth 73 C5 var. Baireuth. Bayern, SE Germany
Bayrische Alpen see Bavarian Alps
Bayrūt see Beyrouth
Bay State see Massachusetts
Baysun see Boysun
Bayt Laḩm see Bethlehem
Baytown 27 H4 Texas, SW USA
Baza 71 E4 Andalucía, S Spain
Bazargic see Dobrich
Bazin see Pezinok
Beagle Channel 43 C8 channel Argentina/Chile
Béal Feirste see Belfast
Beannchar see Bangor, Northern Ireland, UK
Bear Island see Bjørnøya
Bear Lake 24 E4 lake Idaho/Utah, NW USA
Beas de Segura 71 E4 Andalucía, S Spain
Beata, Isla 33 E3 island SW Dominican Republic
Beatrice 23 F4 Nebraska, C USA
Beaufort Sea 14 D2 sea Arctic Ocean
Beaufort-Wes see Beaufort West
Beaufort West 56 C5 Afr. Beaufort-Wes. Western Cape, SW South Africa
Beaumont 27 H3 Texas, SW USA
Beaune 68 D4 Côte d'Or, C France
Beauvais 68 C3 anc. Bellovacum, Caesaromagus. Oise, N France
Beaver Island 18 C2 island Michigan, N USA
Beaver Lake 27 H1 reservoir Arkansas, C USA
Beaver River 27 F1 river Oklahoma, C USA
Beaver State see Oregon
Beāwar 112 C3 Rājasthān, N India
Bečej 78 D3 Ger. Altbetsche, Hung. Óbecse, Rácz-Becse; prev. Magyar-Becse, Stari Bečej. Vojvodina, N Serbia
Béchar 48 D2 prev. Colomb-Béchar. W Algeria
Beckley 18 D5 West Virginia, NE USA
Bécs see Wien
Bedford 67 D6 E England, United Kingdom
Bedum 64 E1 Groningen, NE Netherlands
Beehive State see Utah
Be'er Menuha 97 B7 prev. Be'ér Menuẖa. Southern, S Israel
Be'ér Menuẖa see Be'er Menuha
Beernem 65 A5 West-Vlaanderen, NW Belgium
Beersheba see Be'er Sheva
Be'er Sheva 97 A7 var. Beersheba, Ar. Bir es Saba; prev. Be'ér Sheva'. Southern, S Israel
Be'ér Sheva' see Be'er Sheva
Beesel 65 D5 Limburg, SE Netherlands
Beeville 27 G4 Texas, SW USA
Bega 127 D7 New South Wales, SE Australia
Begoml' see Byahoml'
Begovat see Bekobod
Behagle see Laï
Behar see Bihār
Beibu Wan see Tongking, Gulf of
Beida see Al Bayḑā'
Beihai 106 B6 Guangxi Zhuangzu Zizhiqu, S China
Beijing 106 C3 var. Pei-ching, Eng. Peking; prev. Pei-p'ing. country capital Beijing Shi, E China
Beilen 64 E2 Drenthe, NE Netherlands
Beira 57 E3 Sofala, C Mozambique
Beirut see Beyrouth
Beiuş 86 B3 Hung. Belényes. Bihor, NW Romania
Beja 70 B4 anc. Pax Julia. Beja, SE Portugal
Béjar 70 C3 Castilla-León, N Spain
Bejraburi see Phetchaburi
Bekabad see Bekobod
Békás see Bicaz
Bek-Budi see Qarshi
Békéscsaba 77 D7 Rom. Bichiş-Ciaba. Békés, SE Hungary
Bekobod 101 E2 Rus. Bekabad; prev. Begovat. Toshkent Viloyati, E Uzbekistan
Bela Crkva 78 E3 Ger. Weisskirchen, Hung. Fehértemplom. Vojvodina, W Serbia
Belarus 85 B6 off. Republic of Belarus, var. Belorussia, Latv. Baltkrievija; prev. Belorussian SSR, Rus. Belorusskaya SSR. country E Europe
Belarus, Republic of see Belarus
Belau see Palau
Belaya Tserkov' see Bila Tserkva
Bełchatów 76 C4 var. Belchatow. Łódzski, C Poland
Belchatow see Bełchatów
Belcher, Îles see Belcher Islands
Belcher Islands 16 C2 Fr. Îles Belcher. island group Nunavut, SE Canada
Beledweyne 51 D5 var. Belet Huen, It. Belet Uen. Hiiraan, C Somalia
Belém 41 F1 var. Pará. state capital Pará, N Brazil
Belén 30 D4 Rivas, SW Nicaragua
Belen 26 D2 New Mexico, SW USA
Belényes see Beiuş
Belet Huen/Belet Uen see Beledweyne
Belfast 67 B5 Ir. Béal Feirste. national capital E Northern Ireland, United Kingdom
Belfield 22 D2 North Dakota, N USA
Belfort 68 E4 Territoire-de-Belfort, E France
Belgard see Białogard
Belgaum 110 B1 Karnātaka, W India
Belgian Congo see Congo (Democratic Republic of)
België/Belgique see Belgium
Belgium 65 B6 off. Kingdom of Belgium, Dut. België, Fr. Belgique. country NW Europe
Belgium, Kingdom of see Belgium
Belgorod 89 A6 Belgorodskaya Oblast', W Russian Federation
Belgrano II 132 A2 Argentinian research station Antarctica
Belice see Belize/Belize City
Beligrad see Berat
Beli Manastir 78 C3 Hung. Pélmonostor; prev. Monostor. Osijek-Baranja, NE Croatia
Bélinga 55 B5 Ogooué-Ivindo, NE Gabon
Belitung, Pulau 116 C4 island W Indonesia
Belize 30 B1 Sp. Belice; prev. British Honduras, Colony of Belize. country Central America
Belize 30 B1 river Belize/Guatemala
Belize see Belize City
Belize City 30 C1 var. Belize, Sp. Belice. Belize, NE Belize
Belize, Colony of see Belize
Beljak see Villach
Belkofski 14 B3 Alaska, USA
Belle Île 68 A4 island NW France
Belle Isle, Strait of 17 G3 strait Newfoundland and Labrador, E Canada
Bellenz see Bellinzona
Belleville 18 B4 Illinois, N USA
Bellevue 23 F4 Iowa, C USA
Bellevue 24 B2 Washington, NW USA
Bellingham 24 B1 Washington, NW USA
Belling Hausen Mulde see Southeast Pacific Basin
Bellingshausen Abyssal Plain see Bellingshausen Plain
Bellingshausen Plain 131 F5 var. Bellingshausen Abyssal Plain. abyssal plain SE Pacific Ocean
Bellingshausen Sea 132 A3 sea Antarctica
Bellinzona 73 B8 Ger. Bellenz. Ticino, S Switzerland
Bello 36 B2 Antioquia, W Colombia
Bello Horizonte see Belo Horizonte
Bellovacum see Beauvais
Bellville 56 B5 Western Cape, SW South Africa
Belmopan 30 C1 country capital Cayo, C Belize
Belogradchik 82 B1 Vidin, NW Bulgaria
Belo Horizonte 41 F4 prev. Bello Horizonte. state capital Minas Gerais, SE Brazil
Belomorsk 88 B3 Respublika Kareliya, NW Russian Federation
Beloretsk 89 D6 Respublika Bashkortostan, W Russian Federation
Belorussia/Belorussian SSR see Belarus
Belorusskaya Gryada see Byelaruskaya Hrada
Belorusskaya SSR see Belarus
Beloshchel'ye see Nar'yan-Mar
Belostok see Białystok
Belovár see Bjelovar
Belozërsk 88 B4 Vologodskaya Oblast', NW Russian Federation
Belton 27 G3 Texas, SW USA
Bel'tsy see Bălţi
Beluchistan see Baluchistān
Belukha, Gora 92 D5 mountain Kazakhstan/ Russian Federation
Belynichi see Byalynichy
Belyy, Ostrov 92 D2 island N Russian Federation
Bemaraha 57 F3 var. Plateau du Bemaraha. mountain range W Madagascar
Bemaraha, Plateau du see Bemaraha
Bemidji 23 F1 Minnesota, N USA
Bemmel 64 D4 Gelderland, SE Netherlands
Benaco see Garda, Lago di
Benares see Vārānasi
Benavente 70 D2 Castilla-León, N Spain
Bend 24 B3 Oregon, NW USA
Bender see Tighina
Bender Beila/Bender Beyla see Bandarbeyla
Bender Cassim/Bender Qaasim see Boosaaso
Bendern 72 E1 NW Liechtenstein Europe
Bendery see Tighina
Bendigo 127 C7 Victoria, SE Australia
Beneschau see Benešov
Beneški Zaliv see Venice, Gulf of
Benešov 77 B5 Ger. Beneschau. Středočeský Kraj, W Czech Republic
Benevento 75 D5 anc. Beneventum, Malventum. Campania, S Italy
Beneventum see Benevento
Bengal, Bay of 102 C4 bay N Indian Ocean
Bengalooru see Bangalore
Bengasi see Banghāzī
Bengazi see Banghāzī
Bengbu 106 D5 var. Peng-pu. Anhui, E China
Benghazi see Banghāzī
Bengkulu 116 B4 prev. Bengkoeloe, Benkoelen, Benkulen. Sumatera, W Indonesia
Benguela 56 A2 var. Benguella. Benguela, W Angola
Benguella see Benguela
Bengweulu, Lake see Bangweulu, Lake
Ben Hope 66 B2 mountain N Scotland, United Kingdom
Beni 55 E5 Nord-Kivu, NE Dem. Rep. Congo
Benidorm 71 F4 País Valenciano, SE Spain
Beni-Mellal 48 C2 C Morocco
Benin 53 F4 off. Republic of Benin; prev. Dahomey. country W Africa
Benin, Bight of 53 F5 gulf W Africa
Benin City 53 F5 Edo, SW Nigeria
Benin, Republic of see Benin
Beni, Río 39 E3 river N Bolivia
Beni Suef see Banī Suwayf
Ben Nevis 66 C3 mountain N Scotland, United Kingdom
Bénoué see Benue
Benson 26 B3 Arizona, SW USA
Bent Jbaïl 97 A5 var. Bint Jubayl. S Lebanon
Benton 20 B1 Arkansas, C USA
Benue 54 B4 Fr. Bénoué. river Cameroon/ Nigeria
Beograd 78 D3 Eng. Belgrade. Serbia, N Serbia
Berane 79 D5 prev. Ivangrad. E Montenegro
Berat 79 C6 var. Berati, SCr. Beligrad. Berat, C Albania
Berătău see Berettyó
Berati see Berat
Berau, Teluk 117 G4 var. MacCluer Gulf. bay Papua, E Indonesia
Berbera 50 D4 Sahil, NW Somalia
Berbérati 55 B5 Mambéré-Kadéï, SW Central African Republic
Berck-Plage 68 C2 Pas-de-Calais, N France
Berdichev see Berdychiv
Berdyans'k 87 G4 Rus. Berdyansk; prev. Osipenko. Zaporiz'ka Oblast', SE Ukraine
Berdychiv 86 D2 Rus. Berdichev. Zhytomyrs'ka Oblast', N Ukraine
Beregovo/Beregszász see Berehove
Berehove 86 B3 Cz. Berehovo, Hung. Beregszász, Rus. Beregovo. Zakarpats'ka Oblast', W Ukraine
Berehovo see Berehove
Bereket 100 B2 prev. Rus. Gazandzhyk, Kazandzhik, Turkm. Gazanjyk. Balkan Welaýaty, W Turkmenistan
Beretău see Berettyó
Berettyó 77 D7 Rom. Barcău; prev. Berătău, Beretău. river Hungary/Romania
Berettyóújfalu 77 D6 Hajdú-Bihar, E Hungary
Berezhany 86 C2 Pol. Brzeżany. Ternopil's'ka Oblast', W Ukraine
Berezina see Byerezino
Berezniki 89 D5 Permskaya Oblast', NW Russian Federation
Berga 71 G2 Cataluña, NE Spain
Bergamo 74 B2 anc. Bergomum. Lombardia, N Italy
Bergara 71 E1 País Vasco, N Spain
Bergen 72 D2 Mecklenburg-Vorpommern, NE Germany
Bergen 64 C2 Noord-Holland, NW Netherlands
Bergen 63 A5 Hordaland, S Norway
Bergen see Mons
Bergerac 69 B5 Dordogne, SW France
Bergeyk 65 C5 Noord-Brabant, S Netherlands
Bergomum see Bergamo
Bergse Maas 64 D4 river S Netherlands
Beringen 65 C5 Limburg, NE Belgium
Beringov Proliv see Bering Strait
Bering Sea 14 A2 sea N Pacific Ocean
Bering Strait 14 C2 Rus. Beringov Proliv. strait Bering Sea/Chukchi Sea
Berja 71 E5 Andalucía, S Spain
Berkeley 25 B6 California, W USA
Berkner Island 132 A2 island Antarctica
Berkovitsa 82 C2 Montana, NW Bulgaria
Berlin 72 D3 country capital Berlin, NE Germany
Berlin 19 G2 New Hampshire, NE USA
Berlinchen see Barlinek
Bermejo, Río 42 C2 river N Argentina
Bermeo 71 E1 País Vasco, N Spain

Bermuda – Bravo, Río

Bermuda 13 D6 var. Bermuda Islands, Bermudas; prev. Somers Islands. UK crown colony NW Atlantic Ocean
Bermuda Islands see Bermuda
Bermuda Rise 13 E6 undersea rise C Sargasso Sea
Bermudas see Bermuda
Bern 73 A7 Fr. Berne. country capital Bern, W Switzerland
Bernau 72 D3 Brandenburg, NE Germany
Bernburg 72 C4 Sachsen-Anhalt, C Germany
Berne see Bern
Berner Alpen 73 A7 var. Berner Oberland, Eng. Bernese Oberland. mountain range SW Switzerland
Berner Oberland/Bernese Oberland see Berner Alpen
Bernier Island 125 A5 island Western Australia
Beroea see Ḩalab
Berry 68 C4 cultural region C France
Berry Islands 32 C1 island group N Bahamas
Bertoua 55 B5 Est, E Cameroon
Beru 123 E2 var. Peru. atoll Tungaru, W Kiribati
Berwick-upon-Tweed 66 D4 N England, United Kingdom
Berytus see Beyrouth
Besançon 68 D4 anc. Besontium, Vesontio. Doubs, E France
Beskra see Biskra
Besontium see Besançon
Bessarabka see Basarabeasca
Beszterce see Bistriţa
Besztercebánya see Banská Bystrica
Betafo 57 G3 Antananarivo, C Madagascar
Betanzos 70 B1 Galicia, NW Spain
Bethlehem 56 D4 Free State, C South Africa
Bethlehem 97 B6 Ar. Bayt Laḩm, Heb. Bet Leḩem. C West Bank
Béticos, Sistemas 70 D4 var. Sistema Penibético, Eng. Baetic Cordillera, Baetic Mountains. mountain range S Spain
Bet Leḩem see Bethlehem
Bétou 55 C5 Likouala, N Congo
Bette, Picco 49 G4 var. Bikkū Bīttī, It. Picco Bette. mountain S Libya
Bette, Picco see Bette, Picco
Beulah 18 C2 Michigan, N USA
Beuthen see Bytom
Beveren 65 B5 Oost-Vlaanderen, N Belgium
Beverley 67 D5 E England, United Kingdom
Bexley 67 B8 Bexley, SE England, United Kingdom
Beyla 52 D4 SE Guinea
Beyrouth 96 A4 var. Bayrūt, Eng. Beirut; anc. Berytus. country capital W Lebanon
Beyşehir 94 B4 Konya, SW Turkey
Beyşehir Gölü 94 B4 lake C Turkey
Béziers 69 C6 anc. Baeterrae, Baeterrae Septimanorum, Julia Beterrae. Hérault, S France
Bezmein see Abadan
Bezwada see Vijayawāda
Bhadrāvati 110 C2 Karnātaka, SW India
Bhāgalpur 113 F3 Bihār, NE India
Bhaktapur 113 F3 Central, C Nepal
Bhamo 114 B2 var. Banmo. Kachin State, N Myanmar (Burma)
Bhārat see India
Bharūch 112 C4 Gujarāt, W India
Bhaunagar see Bhāvnagar
Bhāvnagar 112 C4 prev. Bhaunagar. Gujarāt, W India
Bheanntraí, Bá see Bantry Bay
Bhopāl 112 D4 state capital Madhya Pradesh, C India
Bhubaneshwar 113 F5 prev. Bhubaneswar, Bhuvaneshwar. state capital Orissa, E India
Bhubaneswar see Bhubaneshwar
Bhuket see Phuket
Bhusaval see Bhusāwal
Bhusāwal 112 D4 prev. Bhusaval. Mahārāshtra, C India
Bhutan 113 G3 off. Kingdom of Bhutan, var. Druk-yul. country S Asia
Bhutan, Kingdom of see Bhutan
Bhuvaneshwar see Bhubaneshwar
Biak, Pulau 117 G4 island E Indonesia
Biała Podlaska 76 E3 Lubelskie, E Poland
Białogard 76 B2 Ger. Belgard. Zachodnio-pomorskie, NW Poland
Białystok 76 E3 Rus. Belostok, Bielostok. Podlaskie, NE Poland
Bianco, Monte see Blanc, Mont
Biarritz 69 A6 Pyrénées-Atlantiques, SW France
Bicaz 86 C3 Hung. Békás. Neamţ, NE Romania
Bichiş-Ciaba see Békéscsaba
Biddeford 19 G2 Maine, NE USA
Bideford 67 C7 SW England, United Kingdom
Biel 73 A7 Fr. Bienne. Bern, W Switzerland
Bielefeld 72 B4 Nordrhein-Westfalen, NW Germany
Bielitz/Bielitz-Biala see Bielsko-Biała
Bielostok see Białystok
Bielsko-Biała 77 C5 Ger. Bielitz, Bielitz-Biala. Śląskie, S Poland
Bielsk Podlaski 76 E3 Białystok, E Poland
Bien Bien see Điên Biên
Biên Đông see South China Sea
Biên Hoa 115 E6 Đông Nai, S Vietnam
Bienne see Biel
Bienville, Lac 16 D2 lake Québec, C Canada
Bié Plateau 56 B2 var. Bié Plateau. plateau C Angola
Bié Plateau see Bié, Planalto do
Big Cypress Swamp 21 E5 wetland Florida, SE USA
Bigge Island 124 C2 island Western Australia
Bighorn Mountains 22 C2 mountain range Wyoming, C USA
Bighorn River 22 C2 river Montana/Wyoming, NW USA
Bignona 52 B3 SW Senegal
Bigorra see Tarbes
Bigosovo see Bihosava
Big Sioux River 23 E2 river Iowa/South Dakota, N USA
Big Spring 27 E3 Texas, SW USA
Bihać 78 B3 Federacija Bosna I Hercegovina, NW Bosnia and Herzegovina
Bihār 113 F3 prev. Behar. cultural region N India
Bihār see Bihār Sharīf
Biharamulo 51 B7 Kagera, NW Tanzania
Bihār Sharīf 113 F3 var. Bihār. Bihār, N India
Bihosava 85 D5 Rus. Bigosovo. Vitsyebskaya Voblasts', NW Belarus
Bijeljina 78 C3 Republika Srpska, NE Bosnia and Herzegovina
Bijelo Polje 79 D5 E Montenegro
Bikāner 112 C3 Rājasthān, NW India
Bikin 93 G4 Khabarovskiy Kray, SE Russian Federation
Bikini Atoll 122 C1 var. Pikinni. atoll Ralik Chain, NW Marshall Islands
Bikkū Bīttī see Bette, Picco
Bilāspur 113 E4 Chhattīsgarh, C India
Biläsuvar 95 H3 Rus. Bilyasuvar; prev. Pushkino. SE Azerbaijan
Bila Tserkva 87 E2 Rus. Belaya Tserkov'. Kyyivs'ka Oblast', N Ukraine
Bilauktaung Range 115 C6 var. Thanintari Taungdan. mountain range Myanmar (Burma)/ Thailand
Bilbao 71 E1 Basq. Bilbo. País Vasco, N Spain
Bilbo see Bilbao
Bilecik 94 B3 Bilecik, NW Turkey
Billings 22 C2 Montana, NW USA
Bilma, Grand Erg de 53 H3 desert NE Niger
Biloela 126 D4 Queensland, E Australia
Biloxi 20 C3 Mississippi, S USA
Biltine 54 C3 Biltine, E Chad
Bilwi see Puerto Cabezas
Bilyasuvar see Biläsuvar
Bilzen 65 D6 Limburg, NE Belgium
Bimini Islands 32 C1 island group W Bahamas
Binche 65 B7 Hainaut, S Belgium
Bindloe Island see Marchena, Isla
Bin Ghalfān, Jazā'ir see Ḩalāniyāt, Juzur al
Binghamton 19 F3 New York, NE USA
Bingöl 95 E3 Bingöl, E Turkey
Bint Jubayl see Bent Jbaïl
Bintulu 116 D3 Sarawak, East Malaysia
Binzhou 106 D4 Shandong, E China
Bío Bío, Río 43 B5 river C Chile
Bioco, Isla de 55 A5 var. Bioko, Eng. Fernando Po, Sp. Fernando Póo; prev. Macías Nguema Biyogo. island NW Equatorial Guinea
Bioko see Bioco, Isla de
Birāk 49 F3 var. Brak. C Libya
Birao 54 D3 Vakaga, NE Central African Republic
Birātnagar 113 F3 Eastern, SE Nepal
Bir es Saba see Be'er Sheva
Birjand 98 E3 Khorāsān-e Janūbī, E Iran
Birkenfeld 73 A5 Rheinland-Pfalz, SW Germany
Birkenhead 67 C5 NW England, United Kingdom
Birlad see Bârlad
Birmingham 67 C6 C England, United Kingdom
Birmingham 20 C2 Alabama, S USA
Bir Moghrein see Bîr Mogreïn
Bîr Mogreïn 52 C1 var. Bir Moghrein; prev. Fort-Trinquet. Tiris Zemmour, N Mauritania
Birnie Island 123 E3 atoll Phoenix Islands, C Kiribati
Birnin Konni 53 F3 var. Birni-Nkonni. Tahoua, SW Niger
Birni-Nkonni see Birnin Konni
Birobidzhan 93 G4 Yevreyskaya Avtonomnaya Oblast', SE Russian Federation
Birsen see Biržai
Birsk 89 D5 Respublika Bashkortostan, W Russian Federation
Biržai 84 C4 Ger. Birsen. Panevėžys, NE Lithuania
Birżebbuġa 80 B5 SE Malta
Bisanthe see Tekirdağ
Bisbee 26 B3 Arizona, SW USA
Biscaia, Baía de see Biscay, Bay of
Biscay, Bay of 58 B4 Sp. Golfo de Vizcaya, Port. Baía de Biscaia. bay France/Spain
Biscay Plain 58 B3 abyssal plain SE Bay of Biscay
Bischofsburg see Biskupiec
Bishah, Wadi 99 B5 dry watercourse C Saudi Arabia
Bishkek 101 G2 var. Pishpek; prev. Frunze. country capital Chuyskaya Oblast', N Kyrgyzstan
Bishop's Lynn see King's Lynn
Bishrī, Jabal 96 D3 mountain range E Syria
Biskara see Biskra
Biskra 49 E2 var. Beskra, Biskara. NE Algeria
Biskupiec 76 D2 Ger. Bischofsburg. Warmińsko-Mazurskie, NE Poland
Bislig 117 F2 Mindanao, S Philippines
Bismarck 23 E2 state capital North Dakota, N USA
Bismarck Archipelago 122 B3 island group NE Papua New Guinea
Bismarck Sea 122 B3 sea W Pacific Ocean
Bisnulok see Phitsanulok
Bissau 52 B4 country capital W Guinea-Bissau
Bistriţa 86 B3 Ger. Bistritz, Hung. Beszterce; prev. Nösen. Bistriţa-Năsăud, N Romania
Bistritz see Bistriţa
Bitam 55 B5 Woleu-Ntem, N Gabon
Bitburg 73 A5 Rheinland-Pfalz, SW Germany
Bitlis 95 F3 Bitlis, SE Turkey
Bitoeng see Bitung
Bitola 79 D6 Turk. Monastir; prev. Bitolj. S FYR Macedonia
Bitolj see Bitola
Bitonto 75 D5 anc. Butuntum. Puglia, SE Italy
Bitterroot Range 24 D2 mountain range Idaho/ Montana, NW USA
Bitung 117 F3 prev. Bitoeng. Sulawesi, C Indonesia
Biu 53 H4 Borno, E Nigeria
Biwa-ko 109 C6 lake Honshū, SW Japan
Bizerta see Bizerte
Bizerte 49 E1 Ar. Banzart, Eng. Bizerta. N Tunisia
Bjelovar 78 B2 Hung. Belovár. Bjelovar-Bilogora, N Croatia
Bjeshkët e Namuna see North Albanian Alps
Björneborg see Pori
Bjørnøya 61 F3 Eng. Bear Island. island N Norway
Blackall 126 C4 Queensland, E Australia
Black Drin 79 D6 Alb. Lumi i Drinit të Zi, SCr. Crni Drim. river Albania/FYR Macedonia
Blackfoot 24 E4 Idaho, NW USA
Black Forest 73 B6 Eng. Black Forest. mountain range SW Germany
Black Forest see Schwarzwald
Black Hills 22 D3 mountain range South Dakota/ Wyoming, N USA
Blackpool 67 C5 NW England, United Kingdom
Black Range 26 C2 mountain range New Mexico, SW USA
Black River 32 A5 W Jamaica
Black River 114 C3 Chin. Babian Jiang, Lixian Jiang, Fr. Rivière Noire, Vtn. Sông Đa. river China/Vietnam
Black Rock Desert 25 C5 desert Nevada, W USA
Black Sand Desert see Garagum
Black Sea 94 B1 var. Euxine Sea, Bul. Cherno More, Rom. Marea Neagră, Rus. Chernoye More, Turk. Karadeniz, Ukr. Chorne More. sea Asia/Europe
Black Sea Lowland 87 E4 Ukr. Prychornomor'ska Nyzovyna. depression SE Europe
Black Volta 53 E4 var. Borongo, Mouhoun, Moun Hou, Fr. Volta Noire. river W Africa
Blackwater 67 A6 Ir. An Abhainn Mhór. river S Ireland
Blackwater State see Nebraska
Blagoevgrad 82 C3 prev. Gorna Dzhumaya. Blagoevgrad, W Bulgaria
Blagoveshchensk 93 G4 Amurskaya Oblast', SE Russian Federation
Blake Plateau 13 D6 var. Blake Terrace. undersea plateau W Atlantic Ocean
Blake Terrace see Blake Plateau
Blanca, Bahía 43 C5 bay E Argentina
Blanca, Costa 71 F4 physical region SE Spain
Blanche, Lake 127 B5 lake South Australia
Blanc, Mont 69 D5 It. Monte Bianco. mountain France/Italy
Blanco, Cape 24 A4 headland Oregon, NW USA
Blanes 71 G2 Cataluña, NE Spain
Blankenberge 65 A5 West-Vlaanderen, NW Belgium
Blankenheim 73 A5 Nordrhein-Westfalen, W Germany
Blanquilla, Isla 37 E1 var. La Blanquilla. island N Venezuela
Blanquilla, La see Blanquilla, Isla
Blantyre 57 E2 var. Blantyre-Limbe. Southern, S Malawi
Blantyre-Limbe see Blantyre
Blaricum 64 C3 Noord-Holland, C Netherlands
Blatnitsa see Durankulak
Blenheim 129 C5 Marlborough, South Island, New Zealand
Blesae see Blois
Blida 48 D2 var. El Boulaida, El Boulaïda. N Algeria
Bloemfontein 56 C4 var. Mangaung. country capital Free State, C South Africa
Blois 68 C4 anc. Blesae. Loir-et-Cher, C France
Bloomfield 26 C1 New Mexico, SW USA
Bloomington 18 B4 Illinois, N USA
Bloomington 18 C4 Indiana, N USA
Bloomington 23 F2 Minnesota, N USA
Bloomsbury 126 D3 Queensland, NE Australia
Bluefield 18 D5 West Virginia, NE USA
Bluefields 31 E3 Región Autónoma Atlántico Sur, SE Nicaragua
Bluegrass State see Kentucky
Blue Hen State see Delaware
Blue Law State see Connecticut
Blue Mountain Peak 32 B5 mountain E Jamaica
Blue Mountains 24 C3 mountain range Oregon/ Washington, NW USA
Blue Nile 50 C4 var. Abai, Bahr el, Azraq, Amh. Ābay Wenz, Ar. An Nīl al Azraq. river Ethiopia/ Sudan
Blumenau 41 E5 Santa Catarina, S Brazil
Blythe 25 D8 California, W USA
Blytheville 20 C1 Arkansas, C USA
Bo 52 C4 S Sierra Leone
Boaco 30 D3 Boaco, S Nicaragua
Boa Vista 40 D1 state capital Roraima, NW Brazil
Boa Vista 52 A3 island Ilhas de Barlavento, E Cape Verde
Bobaomby, Tanjona 57 G2 Fr. Cap d'Ambre. headland N Madagascar
Bobigny 68 E1 Seine-St-Denis, N France
Bobo-Dioulasso 52 D4 SW Burkina
Bobrinets see Bobrynets'
Bobruysk see Babruysk
Bobrynets' 87 E3 Rus. Bobrinets. Kirovohrads'ka Oblast', C Ukraine
Boca Raton 21 F5 Florida, SE USA
Bocay 30 D2 Jinotega, N Nicaragua
Bocheykovo see Bacheykava
Bocholt 72 A4 Nordrhein-Westfalen, W Germany
Bochum 72 A4 Nordrhein-Westfalen, W Germany
Bocşa 86 A4 Ger. Bokschen, Hung. Boksánbánya. Caraş-Severin, SW Romania
Bodaybo 93 F4 Irkutskaya Oblast', E Russian Federation
Bodegas see Babahoyo
Boden 62 D4 Norrbotten, N Sweden
Bodensee see Constance, Lake, C Europe
Bodmin 67 C7 SW England, United Kingdom
Bodø 62 C3 Nordland, C Norway
Bodrum 94 A4 Muğla, SW Turkey
Boeloekoemba see Bulukumba
Boende 55 C5 Equateur, C Dem. Rep. Congo
Boeroe see Buru, Pulau
Boetoeng see Buton, Pulau
Bogale 114 B4 Ayeyarwady, SW Myanmar (Burma)
Bogalusa 20 B3 Louisiana, S USA
Bogatynia 76 B4 Ger. Reichenau. Dolnośląskie, SW Poland
Boğazlıyan 94 D3 Yozgat, C Turkey
Bogendorf see Łuków
Bogor 116 C5 Dut. Buitenzorg. Jawa, C Indonesia
Bogotá 36 B3 prev. Santa Fe, Santa Fe de Bogotá. country capital Cundinamarca, C Colombia
Bogushëvsk see Bahushewsk
Boguslav see Bohuslav
Bo Hai 106 D4 var. Gulf of Chihli. gulf NE China
Bohemia 77 A5 Cz. Čechy, Ger. Böhmen. W Czech Republic
Bohemian Forest 73 C5 Cz. Český Les, Šumava, Ger. Böhmerwald. mountain range C Europe
Böhmen see Bohemia
Böhmerwald see Bohemian Forest
Böhmisch-Krumau see Český Krumlov
Bohol Sea 117 E2 var. Mindanao Sea. sea S Philippines
Bohuslav 87 E2 Rus. Boguslav. Kyyivs'ka Oblast', N Ukraine
Boise 24 D3 var. Boise City. state capital Idaho, NW USA
Boise City 27 E1 Oklahoma, C USA
Boise City see Boise
Bois, Lac des see Woods, Lake of the
Bois-le-Duc see 's-Hertogenbosch
Boizenburg 72 C3 Mecklenburg-Vorpommern, N Germany
Bojador see Boujdour
Bojnūrd 98 D2 var. Bujnurd. Khorāsān-e Shemālī, N Iran
Bokāro 113 F4 Jhārkhand, N India
Boké 52 C4 W Guinea
Bokhara see Buxoro
Boknafjorden 63 A6 fjord S Norway
Boksánbánya/Bokschen see Bocşa
Bol 54 B3 Lac, W Chad
Bolgatanga 53 E4 N Ghana
Bolgrad see Bolhrad
Bolhrad 86 D4 Rus. Bolgrad. Odes'ka Oblast', SW Ukraine
Bolívar, Pico 36 C2 mountain W Venezuela
Bolivia 39 F3 off. Republic of Bolivia. country W South America
Bolivia, Republic of see Bolivia
Bollène 69 D6 Vaucluse, SE France
Bollnäs 63 C5 Gävleborg, C Sweden
Bollon 127 D5 Queensland, C Australia
Bologna 74 C3 Emilia-Romagna, N Italy
Bol'shevik see Bal'shavik
Bol'shevik, Ostrov 93 E2 island Severnaya Zemlya, N Russian Federation
Bol'shezemel'skaya Tundra 88 E3 physical region NW Russian Federation
Bol'shoy Lyakhovskiy, Ostrov 93 F2 island NE Russian Federation
Bolton 67 D5 prev. Bolton-le-Moors. NW England, United Kingdom
Bolton-le-Moors see Bolton
Bolu 94 B3 Bolu, NW Turkey
Bolungarvík 61 E4 Vestfirdhir, NW Iceland
Bolyarovo 82 D3 prev. Pashkeni. Yambol, E Bulgaria
Bolzano 74 C1 Ger. Bozen; anc. Bauzanum. Trentino-Alto Adige, N Italy
Boma 55 B6 Bas-Congo, W Dem. Rep. Congo
Bombay see Mumbai
Bomu 54 D4 var. Mbomou, Mbomu, M'Bomu. river Central African Republic/Dem. Rep. Congo
Bonaire 33 F5 island E Netherlands Antilles
Bonanza 30 D2 Región Autónoma Atlántico Norte, NE Nicaragua
Bonaparte Archipelago 124 C2 island group Western Australia
Bon, Cap 80 D3 headland N Tunisia
Bonda 55 B6 Ogooué-Lolo, C Gabon
Bondoukou 53 E4 E Ivory Coast
Bône see Annaba, Algeria
Bone see Watampone, Indonesia
Bone, Teluk 117 E4 bay Sulawesi, C Indonesia
Bongaigaon 113 G3 Assam, NE India
Bongo, Massif des 54 D4 var. Chaîne des Mongos. mountain range NE Central African Republic
Bongor 54 B3 Mayo-Kébbi, SW Chad
Bonifacio 69 E7 Corse, France, C Mediterranean Sea
Bonifacio, Bocche de/Bonifacio, Bouches de see Bonifacio, Strait of
Bonifacio, Strait of 74 A4 Fr. Bouches de Bonifacio, It. Bocche di Bonifacio. strait C Mediterranean Sea
Bonn 73 A5 Nordrhein-Westfalen, W Germany
Bononia see Vidin, Bulgaria
Bononia see Boulogne-sur-Mer, France
Boosaaso 50 E4 var. Bandar Kassim, Bender Qaasim, Bosaso, It. Bender Cassim. Bari, N Somalia
Boothia Felix see Boothia Peninsula
Boothia, Gulf of 15 F2 gulf Nunavut, NE Canada
Boothia Peninsula 15 F2 prev. Boothia Felix. peninsula Nunavut, NE Canada
Boppard 73 A5 Rheinland-Pfalz, W Germany
Boquete 31 E5 var. Bajo Boquete. Chiriquí, W Panama
Boquillas 28 D2 var. Boquillas del Carmen. Coahuila de Zaragoza, NE Mexico
Boquillas del Carmen see Boquillas
Bor 78 E4 Serbia, E Serbia
Bor 51 B5 Jonglei, S Sudan
Borås 63 B7 Västra Götaland, S Sweden
Borbetomagus see Worms
Borborema, Planalto da 34 E3 plateau NE Brazil
Bordeaux 69 B5 anc. Burdigala. Gironde, SW France
Bordj Omar Driss 49 E3 E Algeria
Borgå see Porvoo
Børgefjelt 62 C4 mountain range C Norway
Borger 64 E2 Drenthe, NE Netherlands
Borger 27 E1 Texas, SW USA
Borgholm 63 C7 Kalmar, S Sweden
Borgo Maggiore 74 E1 NW San Marino
Borislav see Boryslav
Borisoglebsk 89 B6 Voronezhskaya Oblast', W Russian Federation
Borisov see Barysaw
Borlänge 63 C6 Dalarna, C Sweden
Borne 64 E3 Overijssel, E Netherlands
Borneo 116 C4 island Brunei/Indonesia/Malaysia
Bornholm 63 B8 island E Denmark
Borohoro Shan 104 B2 mountain range NW China
Borongo see Black Volta
Boron'ki see Baron'ki
Borosjenő see Ineu
Borovan 82 C2 Vratsa, NW Bulgaria
Borovichi 88 B4 Novgorodskaya Oblast', W Russian Federation
Borovo 78 C3 Vukovar-Srijem, NE Croatia
Borşa 86 C3 Hung. Borsa. Maramureş, N Romania
Boryslav 86 B2 Pol. Borysław, Rus. Borislav. L'vivs'ka Oblast', NW Ukraine
Borysław see Boryslav
Bosanska Dubica 78 B3 var. Kozarska Dubica. Republika Srpska, NW Bosnia and Herzegovina
Bosanska Gradiška 78 B3 var. Gradiška. Republika Srpska, N Bosnia and Herzegovina
Bosanski Novi 78 B3 var. Novi Grad. Republika Srpska, NW Bosnia and Herzegovina
Bosanski Šamac 78 C3 var. Šamac. Republika Srpska, N Bosnia and Herzegovina
Bosaso see Boosaaso
Bösing see Pezinok
Boskovice 77 B5 Ger. Boskowitz. Jihomoravský Kraj, SE Czech Republic
Boskowitz see Boskovice
Bosna 78 C4 river N Bosnia and Herzegovina
Bosnia and Herzegovina 78 B3 off. Republic of Bosnia and Herzegovina. country SE Europe
Bosnia and Herzegovina, Republic of see Bosnia and Herzegovina
Boso-hanto 109 D6 peninsula Honshū, S Japan
Bosphorus/Bosporus see İstanbul Boğazı
Bosporus 94 B2 var. Bosporus Thracius, Eng. Bosphorus, Bosporus, Turk. Karadeniz Boğazi. strait NW Turkey
Bosporus Cimmerius see Kerch Strait
Bosporus Thracius see İstanbul Boğazı
Bossangoa 54 C4 Ouham, C Central African Republic
Bossembélé 54 C4 Ombella-Mpoko, C Central African Republic
Bossier City 20 A2 Louisiana, S USA
Bosten Hu 104 C3 var. Bagrax Hu. lake NW China
Boston 67 E6 prev. St.Botolph's Town. E England, United Kingdom
Boston 19 G3 state capital Massachusetts, NE USA
Boston Mountains 20 B1 mountain range Arkansas, C USA
Bostyn' see Bastyn'
Botany 126 E2 New South Wales, E Australia
Botany Bay 126 E2 inlet New South Wales, SE Australia
Boteti 56 C3 var. Botletle. river N Botswana
Bothnia, Gulf of 63 D5 Fin. Pohjanlahti, Swe. Bottniska Viken. gulf N Baltic Sea
Botletle see Boteti
Botoşani 86 C3 Hung. Botosány. Botoşani, NE Romania
Botosány see Botoşani
Botou 106 C4 prev. Bozhen. Hebei, E China
Botrange 65 D6 mountain E Belgium
Botswana 56 C3 off. Republic of Botswana. country S Africa
Botswana, Republic of see Botswana
Bottniska Viken see Bothnia, Gulf of
Bouar 54 B4 Nana-Mambéré, W Central African Republic
Bou Craa 48 B3 var. Bu Craa. NW Western Sahara
Bougainville Island 120 B3 island NE Papua New Guinea
Bougaroun, Cap 80 C3 headland NE Algeria
Bougouni 52 D4 Sikasso, SW Mali
Boujdour 48 A3 var. Bojador. W Western Sahara
Boulder 22 C4 Colorado, C USA
Boulder 22 B2 Montana, NW USA
Boulogne see Boulogne-sur-Mer
Boulogne-Billancourt 68 D1 Hauts-de-Seine, Île-de-France, N France Europe
Boulogne-sur-Mer 68 C2 var. Boulogne; anc. Bononia, Gesoriacum, Gessoriacum. Pas-de-Calais, N France
Boûmdeïd 52 C3 var. Boumdeït. Assaba, S Mauritania
Boumdeït see Boûmdeïd
Boundiali 52 D4 N Ivory Coast
Bountiful 22 B4 Utah, W USA
Bounty Basin see Bounty Trough
Bounty Islands 120 D5 island group S New Zealand
Bounty Trough 130 C5 var. Bounty Basin. trough S Pacific Ocean
Bourbonnais 68 C4 cultural region C France
Bourbon Vendée see la Roche-sur-Yon
Bourg see Bourg-en-Bresse
Bourgas see Burgas
Bourge-en-Bresse see Bourg-en-Bresse
Bourg-en-Bresse 69 D5 var. Bourg, Bourge-en-Bresse. Ain, E France
Bourges 68 C4 anc. Avaricum. Cher, C France
Bourgogne 68 C4 Eng. Burgundy. cultural region E France
Bourke 127 C5 New South Wales, SE Australia
Bournemouth 67 D7 S England, United Kingdom
Boutilimit 52 C3 Trarza, SW Mauritania
Bouvet Island 45 D7 Norwegian dependency S Atlantic Ocean
Bowen 126 D3 Queensland, NE Australia
Bowling Green 18 B5 Kentucky, S USA
Bowling Green 18 C3 Ohio, N USA
Boxmeer 64 D4 Noord-Brabant, SE Netherlands
Boyarka 87 E2 Kyyivs'ka Oblast', N Ukraine
Boysun 101 E3 Rus. Baysun. Surkhondaryo Viloyati, S Uzbekistan
Bozeman 22 B2 Montana, NW USA
Bozen see Bolzano
Bozhen see Botou
Bozüyük 94 B3 Bilecik, NW Turkey
Brač 78 B4 var. Brach, It. Brazza; anc. Brattia. island S Croatia
Bracara Augusta see Braga
Brach see Brač
Bradford 67 D5 N England, United Kingdom
Brady 27 F3 Texas, SW USA
Braga 70 B2 anc. Bracara Augusta. Braga, NW Portugal
Bragança 70 C2 Eng. Braganza; anc. Julio Briga. Bragança, NE Portugal
Braganza see Bragança
Brahestad see Raahe
Brahmanbaria 113 G4 Chittagong, E Bangladesh
Brahmapur 113 F5 Orissa, E India
Brahmaputra 113 H3 var. Padma, Tsangpo, Ben. Jamuna, Chin. Yarlung Zangbo Jiang, Ind. Bramaputra, Dihang, Siang. river S Asia
Brăila 86 D4 Brăila, E Romania
Braine-le-Comte 65 B6 Hainaut, SW Belgium
Brainerd 23 F2 Minnesota, N USA
Brak see Birāk
Bramaputra see Brahmaputra
Brampton 16 D5 Ontario, S Canada
Branco, Rio 34 C3 river N Brazil
Brandberg 56 A3 mountain NW Namibia
Brandenburg 72 C3 var. Brandenburg an der Havel. Brandenburg, NE Germany
Brandenburg an der Havel see Brandenburg
Brandon 15 F5 Manitoba, S Canada
Braniewo 76 D2 Ger. Braunsberg. Warmińsko-mazurskie, N Poland
Brasil see Brazil
Brasília 41 F3 country capital Distrito Federal, C Brazil
Brasil, República Federativa do see Brazil
Braşov 86 C4 Ger. Kronstadt, Hung. Brassó; prev. Oraşul Stalin. Braşov, C Romania
Brassó see Braşov
Bratislava 77 C6 Ger. Pressburg, Hung. Pozsony. country capital Bratislavský Kraj, W Slovakia
Bratsk 93 E4 Irkutskaya Oblast', C Russian Federation
Brattia see Brač
Braunsberg see Braniewo
Braunschweig 72 C4 Eng./Fr. Brunswick. Niedersachsen, N Germany
Brava see Baraawe
Brava, Costa 71 H2 coastal region NE Spain
Bravo del Norte, Río/Bravo, Río see Grande, Rio
Bravo, Río 28 C1 river Mexico/USA North America

Brawley – Cardigan Bay

Brawley 25 D8 California, W USA
Brazil 40 C2 off. Federative Republic of Brazil, Port. República Federativa do Brasil, Sp. Brasil; prev. United States of Brazil. country South America
Brazil Basin 45 C5 var. Brazilian Basin, Brazil'skaya Kotlovina. undersea basin W Atlantic Ocean
Brazil, Federative Republic of see Brazil
Brazilian Basin see Brazil Basin
Brazilian Highlands 41 F3 var. Brazilian Highlands. mountain range E Brazil
Brazilian Highlands see Central, Planalto
Brazil'skaya Kotlovina see Brazil Basin
Brazil, United States of see Brazil
Brazos River 27 G3 river Texas, SW USA
Brazza see Brač
Brazzaville 55 B6 country capital Capital District, S Congo
Brčko 78 C3 Republika Srpska, NE Bosnia and Herzegovina
Brecht 65 C5 Antwerpen, N Belgium
Brecon Beacons 67 C6 mountain range S Wales, United Kingdom
Breda 64 C4 Noord-Brabant, S Netherlands
Bree 65 D5 Limburg, NE Belgium
Bregalnica 79 E6 river E FYR Macedonia
Bregenz 35 B7 anc. Brigantium. Vorarlberg, W Austria
Bregovo 82 B1 Vidin, NW Bulgaria
Bremen 72 B3 Fr. Brême. Bremen, NW Germany
Bremerhaven 72 B3 Bremen, NW Germany
Bremerton 24 B2 Washington, NW USA
Brenham 27 G3 Texas, SW USA
Brenner, Col du/Brennero, Passo del see Brenner Pass
Brenner Pass 74 C1 var. Brenner Sattel, Fr. Col du Brenner, Ger. Brennerpass, It. Passo del Brennero. pass Austria/Italy
Brennerpass see Brenner Pass
Brenner Sattel see Brenner Pass
Brescia 74 B2 anc. Brixia. Lombardia, N Italy
Breslau see Wrocław
Bressanone 74 C1 Ger. Brixen. Trentino-Alto Adige, N Italy
Brest 85 A6 Pol. Brześć nad Bugiem, Rus. Brest-Litovsk; prev. Brześć Litewski. Brestskaya Voblasts', SW Belarus
Brest 68 A3 Finistère, NW France
Brest-Litovsk see Brest
Bretagne 68 A3 Eng. Brittany, Lat. Britannia Minor. cultural region NW France
Brewster, Kap see Kangikajik
Brewton 20 C3 Alabama, S USA
Brezhnev see Naberezhnyye Chelny
Brezovo 82 D2 prev. Abrashlare. Plovdiv, C Bulgaria
Bria 54 D4 Haute-Kotto, C Central African Republic
Briançon 69 D5 anc. Brigantio. Hautes-Alpes, SE France
Bricgstow see Bristol
Bridgeport 19 F3 Connecticut, NE USA
Bridgetown 33 G2 country capital SW Barbados
Bridlington 67 D5 E England, United Kingdom
Bridport 67 D7 S England, United Kingdom
Brieg see Brzeg
Brig 73 A7 Fr. Brigue, It. Briga. Valais, SW Switzerland
Briga see Brig
Brigantio see Briançon
Brigantium see Bregenz
Brigham City 22 B3 Utah, W USA
Brighton 67 E7 SE England, United Kingdom
Brighton 22 D4 Colorado, C USA
Brigue see Brig
Brindisi 75 E5 anc. Brundisium, Brundusium. Puglia, SE Italy
Briovera see St-Lô
Brisbane 127 E5 state capital Queensland, E Australia
Bristol 67 D7 anc. Bricgstow. SW England, United Kingdom
Bristol 19 F3 Connecticut, NE USA
Bristol 18 D5 Tennessee, S USA
Bristol Bay 14 B3 bay Alaska, USA
Bristol Channel 67 C7 inlet England/Wales, United Kingdom
Britain 58 C3 var. Great Britain. island United Kingdom
Britannia Minor see Bretagne
British Columbia 14 D4 Fr. Colombie-Britannique. province SW Canada
British Guiana see Guyana
British Honduras see Belize
British Indian Ocean Territory 119 B5 UK dependent territory C Indian Ocean
British Isles 67 island group NW Europe
British North Borneo see Sabah
British Solomon Islands Protectorate see Solomon Islands
British Virgin Islands 33 F3 var. Virgin Islands. UK dependent territory E West Indies
Brittany see Bretagne
Briva Curretia see Brive-la-Gaillarde
Briva Isarae see Pontoise
Brive see Brive-la-Gaillarde
Brive-la-Gaillarde 69 C5 prev. Brive; anc. Briva Curretia. Corrèze, C France
Brixen see Bressanone
Brixia see Brescia
Brno 77 B5 Ger. Brünn. Jihomoravský Kraj, SE Czech Republic
Broceni 84 B3 Saldus, SW Latvia
Brod/Bród see Slavonski Brod
Brodeur Peninsula 15 F2 peninsula Baffin Island, Nunavut, NE Canada
Brod na Savi see Slavonski Brod
Brodnica 76 C3 Ger. Buddenbrock. Kujawski-pomorskie, C Poland
Broek-in-Waterland 64 C3 Noord-Holland, C Netherlands
Broken Arrow 27 G1 Oklahoma, C USA
Broken Bay 126 E1 bay New South Wales, SE Australia
Broken Hill 127 B6 New South Wales, SE Australia
Broken Ridge 119 D6 undersea plateau S Indian Ocean
Bromberg see Bydgoszcz
Bromley 67 B8 United Kingdom
Brookhaven 20 B3 Mississippi, S USA
Brookings 23 F3 South Dakota, N USA
Brooks Range 14 D2 mountain range Alaska, USA
Brookton 125 B6 Western Australia
Broome 124 B3 Western Australia
Broomfield 22 D4 Colorado, C USA
Broucsella see Brussel/Bruxelles
Brovary 87 E2 Kyyivs'ka Oblast', N Ukraine
Brownfield 27 E2 Texas, SW USA
Brownsville 27 G5 Texas, SW USA
Brownwood 27 F3 Texas, SW USA
Brozha 85 D7 Mahilyowskaya Voblasts', E Belarus
Bruges see Brugge
Brugge 65 A5 Fr. Bruges. West-Vlaanderen, NW Belgium
Brummen 64 D3 Gelderland, E Netherlands
Brundisium/Brundusium see Brindisi
Brunei 116 D3 off. Brunei Darussalam, Mal. Negara Brunei Darussalam. country SE Asia
Brunei Darussalam see Brunei
Brunei Town see Bandar Seri Begawan
Brünn see Brno
Brunner, Lake 129 C5 lake South Island, New Zealand
Brunswick 21 E3 Georgia, SE USA
Brunswick see Braunschweig
Brusa see Bursa
Brus Laguna 30 D2 Gracias a Dios, E Honduras
Brussa see Bursa
Brussel 65 C6 var. Brussels, Fr. Bruxelles, Ger. Brüssel; anc. Broucsella. country capital Brussels, C Belgium
Brüssel/Brussels see Brussel/Bruxelles
Brüx see Most
Bruxelles see Brussel
Bryan 27 G3 Texas, SW USA
Bryansk 89 A5 Bryanskaya Oblast', W Russian Federation
Brzeg 76 C4 Ger. Brieg; anc. Civitas Altae Ripae. Opolskie, S Poland
Brześć Litewski/Brześć nad Bugiem see Brest
Brzeżany see Berezhany
Bucaramanga 36 B2 Santander, N Colombia
Buchanan 52 C5 prev. Grand Bassa. SW Liberia
Buchanan, Lake 27 F3 reservoir Texas, SW USA
Bucharest see București
Buckeye State see Ohio
Bu Craa see Bou Craa
București 86 C5 Eng. Bucharest, Ger. Bukarest, prev. Altenburg; anc. Cetatea Damboviței. country capital București, S Romania
Buda-Kashalyova 85 D7 Rus. Buda-Koshelëvo. Homyel'skaya Voblasts', SE Belarus
Buda-Koshelëvo see Buda-Kashalyova
Budapest 77 C6 off. Budapest Főváros, SCr. Budimpešta. country capital Pest, N Hungary
Budapest Főváros see Budapest
Budaun 112 D3 Uttar Pradesh, N India
Buddenbrock see Brodnica
Budimpešta see Budapest
Budweis see České Budějovice
Budyšin see Bautzen
Buena Park 24 E2 California, W USA North America
Buenaventura 36 A3 Valle del Cauca, W Colombia
Buena Vista 39 G4 Santa Cruz, C Bolivia
Buena Vista 71 H5 S Gibraltar Europe
Buena Vista 71 H5 S Gibraltar Europe
Buenavista 71 H5 Baja California Sur, W Mexico
Buenavista 71 H5 Sonora, NW Mexico
Buena Vista 71 H5 Cerro Largo, Uruguay
Buena Vista 71 H5 Colorado, C USA
Buena Vista 71 H5 Georgia, SE USA
Buena Vista 71 H5 Virginia, NE USA
Buenos Aires 42 D4 hist. Santa Maria del Buen Aire. country capital Buenos Aires, E Argentina
Buenos Aires 31 E5 Puntarenas, SE Costa Rica
Buenos Aires, Lago 43 B6 var. Lago General Carrera. lake Argentina/Chile
Buffalo 19 E3 New York, NE USA
Buffalo Narrows 15 F4 Saskatchewan, C Canada
Buff Bay 32 B5 E Jamaica
Buftea 86 C5 Ilfov, S Romania
Bug 59 E3 Bel. Zakhodni Buh, Eng. Western Bug, Rus. Zapadnyy Bug, Ukr. Zakhidnyy Buh. river E Europe
Buga 36 B3 Valle del Cauca, W Colombia
Bughotu see Santa Isabel
Buguruslan 89 D6 Orenburgskaya Oblast', W Russian Federation
Buitenzorg see Bogor
Bujalance 70 D4 Andalucía, S Spain
Bujanovac 79 E5 Kosovo, SE Serbia
Bujnurd see Bojnūrd
Bujumbura 51 B7 prev. Usumbura. country capital W Burundi
Bukarest see București
Bukavu 55 E6 prev. Costermansville. Sud-Kivu, E Dem. Rep. Congo
Bukhara see Buxoro
Bukoba 51 B6 Kagera, NW Tanzania
Bülach 73 B7 Zürich, NW Switzerland
Bulawayo 56 D3 Matabeleland North, SW Zimbabwe
Bulgan 105 E2 Bulgan, N Mongolia
Bulgaria 82 C2 off. Republic of Bulgaria, Bul. Bŭlgariya; prev. People's Republic of Bulgaria. country SE Europe
Bulgaria, People's Republic of see Bulgaria
Bulgaria, Republic of see Bulgaria
Bŭlgariya see Bulgaria
Bullion State see Missouri
Bull Shoals Lake 20 B1 reservoir Arkansas/Missouri, C USA
Bulukumba 117 E4 prev. Boeloekoemba. Sulawesi, C Indonesia
Bumba 55 D5 Equateur, N Dem. Rep. Congo
Bunbury 125 A7 Western Australia
Bundaberg 126 E4 Queensland, E Australia
Bungo-suido 109 B7 strait SW Japan
Bunia 55 E5 Orientale, NE Dem. Rep. Congo
Bünyan 94 D3 Kayseri, C Turkey
Buraida see Buraydah
Buraydah 98 B4 var. Buraida. Al Qaşīm, N Saudi Arabia
Burdigala see Bordeaux
Burdur 94 B4 var. Buldur. Burdur, SW Turkey
Burdur Gölü 94 B4 salt lake SW Turkey
Burē 50 C4 Āmara, N Ethiopia
Burgas 82 E2 var. Bourgas. Burgas, E Bulgaria
Burgaski Zaliv 82 E2 gulf E Bulgaria
Burgos 70 D2 Castilla-León, N Spain
Burgundy see Bourgogne
Burhan Budai Shan 104 D4 mountain range C China
Buriram 115 D5 var. Buri Ram, Puriramya. Buri Ram, E Thailand
Buri Ram see Buriram
Burjassot 71 F3 País Valenciano, E Spain
Burkburnett 27 F2 Texas, SW USA
Burketown 126 B3 Queensland, NE Australia
Burkina 53 E4 off. Burkina Faso; prev. Upper Volta. country W Africa
Burkina see Burkina
Burkina Faso see Burkina
Burley 24 D4 Idaho, NW USA
Burlington 23 G4 Iowa, C USA
Burlington 19 F2 Vermont, NE USA
Burma 114 A3 off. Union of Myanmar. country SE Asia
Burnie 127 C8 Tasmania, SE Australia
Burns 24 C3 Oregon, NW USA
Burnside 15 F3 river Nunavut, NW Canada
Burnsville 23 F2 Minnesota, N USA
Burrel 79 D6 var. Burreli. Dibër, C Albania
Burreli see Burrel
Burriana 71 F3 País Valenciano, E Spain
Bursa 94 B3 var. Brussa, prev. Brusa; anc. Prusa. Bursa, NW Turkey
Būr Sa'īd 50 B1 var. Port Said. N Egypt
Burtnieks 84 C3 var. Burtnieks Ezers. lake N Latvia
Burtnieks Ezers see Burtnieks
Burundi 51 B7 off. Republic of Burundi; prev. Kingdom of Burundi, Urundi. country C Africa
Burundi, Kingdom of see Burundi
Burundi, Republic of see Burundi
Buru, Pulau 117 F4 prev. Boeroe. island E Indonesia
Busan see Pusan
Buşayrah 96 D3 Dayr az Zawr, E Syria
Būshehr/Bushire see Bandar-e Būshehr
Busra see Al Başrah, Iraq
Busselton 125 A7 Western Australia
Bussora see Al Başrah
Buta 55 D5 Orientale, N Dem. Rep. Congo
Butembo 55 E5 Nord-Kivu, NE Dem. Rep. Congo
Butler 19 E4 Pennsylvania, NE USA
Buton, Pulau 117 E4 var. Pulau Butung; prev. Boetoeng. island C Indonesia
Bütow see Bytów
Butte 22 B2 Montana, NW USA
Butterworth 116 B3 Pinang, Peninsular Malaysia
Button Islands 17 E1 island group Nunavut, NE Canada
Butuan 117 F2 off. Butuan City. Mindanao, S Philippines
Butuan City see Butuan
Butung, Pulau see Buton, Pulau
Butuntum see Bitonto
Buulobarde 51 D5 var. Buulo Berde. Hiiraan, C Somalia
Buulo Berde see Buulobarde
Buur Gaabo 51 D6 Jubbada Hoose, S Somalia
Buxoro 100 D2 var. Bokhara, Rus. Bukhara. Buxoro Viloyati, C Uzbekistan
Buynaksk 89 B8 Respublika Dagestan, SW Russian Federation
Büyükmenderes Nehri 94 A4 river SW Turkey
Buzău 86 C4 Buzău, SE Romania
Büzmeýin see Abadan
Buzuluk 89 D6 Orenburgskaya Oblast', W Russian Federation
Byahoml' 85 D5 Rus. Begoml'. Vitsyebskaya Voblasts', N Belarus
Byalynichy 85 D6 Rus. Belynichi. Mahilyowskaya Voblasts', E Belarus
Byan Tumen see Choybalsan
Bydgoszcz 76 C3 Ger. Bromberg. Kujawski-pomorskie, C Poland
Byelaruskaya Hrada 85 B6 Rus. Belorusskaya Gryada. ridge N Belarus
Byerezino 85 D6 Rus. Berezina. river C Belarus
Byron Island see Nikunau
Bystrovka see Kemin
Bytča 77 C5 Žilinský Kraj, N Slovakia
Bytom 77 C5 Ger. Beuthen. Śląskie, S Poland
Bytów 76 C2 Ger. Bütow. Pomorskie, N Poland
Byuzmeyin see Abadan
Byval'ki 85 D8 Homyel'skaya Voblasts', SE Belarus
Byzantium see İstanbul

C

Caála 56 B2 var. Kaala, Robert Williams, Port. Vila Robert Williams. Huambo, C Angola
Caazapá 42 D3 Caazapá, S Paraguay
Caballo Reservoir 26 C3 reservoir New Mexico, SW USA
Cabañaquinta 70 D1 Asturias, N Spain
Cabanatuan 117 E1 off. Cabanatuan City. Luzon, N Philippines
Cabanatuan City see Cabanatuan
Cabillonum see Chalon-sur-Saône
Cabimas 36 C1 Zulia, NW Venezuela
Cabinda 56 A1 var. Kabinda. Cabinda, NW Angola
Cabinda 56 A1 var. Kabinda. province NW Angola
Lake Cabora Bassa 56 D2 var. Lake Cabora Bassa. reservoir NW Mozambique
Cabora Bassa, Lake see Cahora Bassa, Albufeira de
Caborca 28 B1 Sonora, NW Mexico
Cabot Strait 17 G4 strait E Canada
Cabo Verde, Ilhas do see Cape Verde
Cabras, Ilha das 54 E2 island S Sao Tome and Principe, Africa, E Atlantic Ocean
Cabrera 71 G3 river NW Spain
Cáceres 70 C3 Ar. Qazris. Extremadura, W Spain
Cachimbo, Serra do 41 E2 mountain range C Brazil
Caconda 56 B2 Huíla, C Angola
Čadca 77 C5 Hung. Csaca. Žilinský Kraj, N Slovakia
Cadillac 18 C2 Michigan, N USA
Cadiz 117 E2 off. Cadiz City. Negros, C Philippines
Cádiz 70 C5 anc. Gades, Gadier, Gadir, Gadire. Andalucía, SW Spain
Cadiz City see Cadiz
Gulf of Cadiz 70 B5 Eng. Gulf of Cadiz. gulf Portugal/Spain
Cadiz, Gulf of see Cádiz, Golfo de
Cadurcum see Cahors
Caen 68 B3 Calvados, N France
Caene/Caenepolis see Qinā
Caerdydd see Cardiff
Caer Glou see Gloucester
Caer Gybi see Holyhead
Caerleon see Chester
Caer Luel see Carlisle
Caesaraugusta see Zaragoza
Caesarea Mazaca see Kayseri
Caesarobriga see Talavera de la Reina
Caesarodunum see Tours
Caesaromagus see Beauvais
Caesena see Cesena
Cafayate 42 C2 Salta, N Argentina
Cagayan de Oro 117 E2 off. Cagayan de Oro City. Mindanao, S Philippines
Cagayan de Oro City see Cagayan de Oro
Cagliari 75 A6 anc. Caralis. Sardegna, Italy, C Mediterranean Sea
Caguas 33 F3 E Puerto Rico
Cahors 69 C5 anc. Cadurcum. Lot, S France
Cahul 86 D4 Rus. Kagul. S Moldova
Caicos Passage 32 D2 strait Bahamas/Turks and Caicos Islands
Caiffa see Hefa
Cailungo 74 E1 N San Marino
Caiphas see Hefa
Cairns 126 D3 Queensland, NE Australia
Cairo 50 B2 var. El Qâhira, Ar. Al Qāhirah. country capital N Egypt
Caisleán an Bharraigh see Castlebar
Cajamarca 38 B3 prev. Caxamarca. Cajamarca, NW Peru
Čakovec 78 B2 Ger. Csakathurn, Hung. Csáktornya; prev. Ger. Tschakathurn. Medimurje, N Croatia
Calabar 53 G5 Cross River, S Nigeria
Calabozo 36 D2 Guárico, C Venezuela
Calafat 86 B5 Dolj, SW Romania
Calafate see El Calafate
Calahorra 71 E2 La Rioja, N Spain
Calais 68 C2 Pas-de-Calais, N France
Calais 19 H2 Maine, NE USA
Calais, Pas de see Dover, Strait of
Calama 42 B2 Antofagasta, N Chile
Călăras see Călărași
Călărași 86 D3 var. Călăras, Rus. Kalarash. C Moldova
Călărași 86 C5 Călărași, SE Romania
Calatayud 71 E2 Aragón, NE Spain
Calbayog 117 E2 off. Calbayog City. Samar, C Philippines
Calbayog City see Calbayog
Calcutta 113 G4 West Bengal, N India
Caldas da Rainha 70 B3 Leiria, W Portugal
Caldera 42 B3 Atacama, N Chile
Caldwell 24 C3 Idaho, NW USA
Caledonia 30 C1 Corozal, N Belize
Caleta Olivia 43 B6 Santa Cruz, SE Argentina
Calgary 15 E5 Alberta, SW Canada
Cali 36 B3 Valle del Cauca, W Colombia
Calicut 110 C2 var. Kozhikode. Kerala, SW India
California 25 B7 off. State of California, also known as El Dorado, The Golden State. state W USA
Gulf of California 28 B2 Eng. Gulf of California; prev. Sea of Cortez. gulf W Mexico
California, Gulf of see California, Golfo de
Călimănești 86 B4 Vâlcea, SW Romania
Calisia see Kalisz
Callabonna, Lake 127 B5 lake South Australia
Callao 38 C4 Callao, W Peru
Callatis see Mangalia
Callosa de Segura 71 F4 País Valenciano, E Spain
Calmar see Kalmar
Caloundra 127 E5 Queensland, E Australia
Caltanissetta 75 C7 Sicilia, Italy, C Mediterranean Sea
Caluula 50 E4 Bari, NE Somalia
Camabatela 56 B1 Cuanza Norte, NW Angola
Camacupa 56 B2 var. General Machado, Port. Vila General Machado. Bié, C Angola
Camagüey 32 C2 prev. Puerto Príncipe. Camagüey, C Cuba
Camagüey, Archipiélago de 32 C2 island group C Cuba
Camana 39 E4 var. Camaná. Arequipa, SW Peru
Camargue 69 D6 physical region SE France
Ca Mau 115 D6 var. Quan Long. Minh Hai, S Vietnam
Cambay, Gulf of see Khambhāt, Gulf of
Camberia see Chambéry
Cambodia 115 D5 off. Kingdom of Cambodia, var. Democratic Kampuchea, Roat Kampuchea, Cam. Kampuchea; prev. People's Democratic Republic of Kampuchea. country SE Asia
Cambodia, Kingdom of see Cambodia
Cambrai 68 C2 Flem. Kameryk, prev. Cambray; anc. Cameracum. Nord, N France
Cambray see Cambrai
Cambrian Mountains 67 C6 mountain range C Wales, United Kingdom
Cambridge 32 A4 W Jamaica
Cambridge 128 D3 Waikato, North Island, New Zealand
Cambridge 67 E6 Lat. Cantabrigia. E England, United Kingdom
Cambridge 19 F4 Maryland, NE USA
Cambridge 18 D4 Ohio, NE USA
Cambridge Bay 15 F3 var. Ikaluktutiak. Victoria Island, Nunavut, NW Canada
Camden 20 B2 Arkansas, C USA
Camellia State see Alabama
Cameracum see Cambrai
Cameroon 54 A4 off. Republic of Cameroon, Fr. Cameroun. country W Africa
Cameroon, Republic of see Cameroon
Cameroun see Cameroon
Camocim 41 F2 Ceará, E Brazil
Camopi 37 H3 E French Guiana
Campamento 30 C2 Olancho, C Honduras
Campania 75 D5 Eng. Champagne. region S Italy
Campbell, Cape 129 D5 headland South Island, New Zealand
Campbell Island 120 D5 island S New Zealand
Campbell Plateau 120 D5 undersea plateau SW Pacific Ocean
Campbell River 14 D5 Vancouver Island, British Columbia, SW Canada
Campeche 29 G4 Campeche, SE Mexico
Bay of Campeche 29 F4 Eng. Bay of Campeche. bay E Mexico
Campeche, Bay of see Campeche, Bahía de
Câm Pha 114 E3 Quang Ninh, N Vietnam
Câmpina 86 C4 prev. Cîmpina. Prahova, SE Romania
Campina Grande 41 G2 Paraíba, E Brazil
Campinas 41 F4 São Paulo, S Brazil
Campobasso 75 D5 Molise, C Italy
Campo Criptana see Campo de Criptana
Campo de Criptana 71 E3 var. Campo Criptana. Castilla-La Mancha, C Spain
Campo dos Goitacazes see Campos
Campo Grande 41 E4 state capital Mato Grosso do Sul, SW Brazil
Campos 41 F4 var. Campo dos Goitacazes. Rio de Janeiro, SE Brazil
Câmpulung 86 B4 prev. Câmpulung-Mușcel, Cîmpulung. Argeș, S Romania
Câmpulung-Mușcel see Câmpulung
Campus Stellae see Santiago
Cam Ranh 115 E6 Khanh Hoa, S Vietnam
Canada 12 B4 country N North America
Canada Basin 12 C2 undersea basin Arctic Ocean
Canadian River 27 E2 river SW USA
Çanakkale 94 A3 var. Dardanelli; prev. Chanak, Kale Sultanie. Çanakkale, W Turkey
Cananea 28 B1 Sonora, NW Mexico
Canarreos, Archipiélago de los 32 B2 island group W Cuba
Canary Islands 48 A2 Eng. Canary Islands. island group Spain, NE Atlantic Ocean
Canary Islands see Canarias, Islas
Cañas 30 D4 Guanacaste, NW Costa Rica
Canaveral, Cape 21 E4 headland Florida, SE USA
Canavieiras 41 G3 Bahia, E Brazil
Canberra 120 C4 country capital Australian Capital Territory, SE Australia
Cancún 29 H3 Quintana Roo, SE Mexico
Candia see Irákleio
Canea see Chaniá
Cangzhou 106 D4 Hebei, E China
Caniapiscau 17 E2 river Québec, E Canada
Caniapiscau, Réservoir de 16 D3 reservoir Québec, C Canada
Canik Dağları 94 D2 mountain range N Turkey
Canillo 69 A7 Canillo, C Andorra Europe
Çankırı 94 C3 var. Chankiri; anc. Gangra, Germanicopolis. Çankın, N Turkey
Cannanore 110 B2 var. Kannur. Kerala, SW India
Cannes 69 D6 Alpes-Maritimes, SE France
Canoas 41 E5 Rio Grande do Sul, S Brazil
Canon City 22 C5 Colorado, C USA
Cantabria 70 D1 autonomous community N Spain
Cantábrica, Cordillera 70 C1 mountain range N Spain
Cantabrigia see Cambridge
Cantaura 37 E2 Anzoátegui, NE Venezuela
Canterbury 67 E7 hist. Cantwaraburh; anc. Durovernum, Lat. Cantuaria. SE England, United Kingdom
Canterbury Bight 129 C6 bight South Island, New Zealand
Canterbury Plains 129 C6 plain South Island, New Zealand
Cân Thơ 115 E6 Cân Thơ, S Vietnam
Canton 20 B2 Mississippi, S USA
Canton 18 D4 Ohio, N USA
Canton see Guangzhou
Canton Island see Kanton
Cantuaria/Cantwaraburh see Canterbury
Canyon 27 E2 Texas, SW USA
Cao Bǎng 114 D3 var. Caobang. Cao Bǎng, N Vietnam
Caobang see Cao Bǎng
Cap-Breton, Île du see Cape Breton Island
Cape Barren Island 127 C8 island Furneaux Group, Tasmania, SE Australia
Cape Basin 47 B7 undersea basin S Atlantic Ocean
Cape Breton Island 17 G4 Fr. Île du Cap-Breton. island Nova Scotia, SE Canada
Cape Charles 19 F5 Virginia, NE USA
Cape Coast 53 E5 prev. Cape Coast Castle. S Ghana
Cape Coast Castle see Cape Coast
Cape Girardeau 23 H5 Missouri, C USA
Capelle aan den IJssel 64 C4 Zuid-Holland, SW Netherlands
Cape Palmas see Harper
Cape Saint Jacques see Vung Tau
Cape Town 56 B5 var. Ekapa, Afr. Kaapstad, Kapstad. country capital Western Cape, SW South Africa
Cape Verde 52 A2 off. Republic of Cape Verde, Port. Cabo Verde, Ilhas do Cabo Verde. country E Atlantic Ocean
Cape Verde Basin 44 C4 undersea basin E Atlantic Ocean
Cape Verde Plain 44 C4 abyssal plain E Atlantic Ocean
Cape Verde, Republic of see Cape Verde
Cape York Peninsula 126 C2 peninsula Queensland, N Australia
Cap-Haïtien 32 D3 var. Le Cap. N Haiti
Capira 31 G5 Panamá, C Panama
Capitán Arturo Prat 132 A2 Chilean research station South Shetland Islands, Antarctica
Capitán Pablo Lagerenza 42 D1 var. Mayor Pablo Lagerenza. Chaco, N Paraguay
Capodistria see Koper
Capri 75 C5 island S Italy
Caprivi Concession see Caprivi Strip
Caprivi Strip 56 C3 Ger. Caprivizipfel; prev. Caprivi Concession. cultural region NE Namibia
Caprivizipfel see Caprivi Strip
Cap Saint-Jacques see Vung Tau
Caquetá, Río 36 C5 var. Rio Japurá, Yapurá. river Brazil/Colombia
Caquetá, Río see Japurá, Rio
CAR see Central African Republic
Caracal 86 B5 Olt, S Romania
Caracaraí 40 D1 Rondônia, W Brazil
Caracas 36 D1 country capital Distrito Federal, N Venezuela
Caralis see Cagliari
Caratasca, Laguna de 31 E2 lagoon NE Honduras
Carballiño see O Carballiño
Carbondale 18 B5 Illinois, N USA
Carbonia 75 A6 var. Carbonia Centro. Sardegna, Italy, C Mediterranean Sea
Carbonia Centro see Carbonia
Carcaso see Carcassonne
Carcassonne 69 C6 anc. Carcaso. Aude, S France
Cardamomes, Chaîne des see Krâvanh, Chuŏr Phnum
Cardamom Mountains see Krâvanh, Chuŏr Phnum
Cárdenas 32 B2 Matanzas, W Cuba
Cardiff 67 C7 Wel. Caerdydd. national capital S Wales, United Kingdom
Cardigan Bay 67 C6 bay W Wales, United Kingdom

Carei - Chisholm

Carei 86 B3 Ger. Gross-Karol, Karol, Hung. Nagykároly; prev. Careii-Mari. Satu Mare, NW Romania
Careii-Mari see Carei
Carey, Lake 125 B6 lake Western Australia
Cariaco 37 E1 Sucre, NE Venezuela
Caribbean Sea 32 C4 sea W Atlantic Ocean
Caribrod see Dimitrovgrad
Carlisle 66 C4 anc. Caer Luel, Luguvallium, Luguvallum. NW England, United Kingdom
Carlow 67 B6 Ir. Ceatharlach. SE Ireland
Carlsbad 26 D3 New Mexico, SW USA
Carlsbad see Karlovy Vary
Carlsberg Ridge 118 B4 undersea ridge S Arabian Sea
Carlsruhe see Karlsruhe
Carmana/Carmania see Kermān
Carmarthen 67 C6 SW Wales, United Kingdom
Carmaux 69 C6 Tarn, S France
Carmel 18 C4 Indiana, N USA
Carmelita 30 B1 Petén, N Guatemala
Carmen 29 G4 var. Ciudad del Carmen. Campeche, SE Mexico
Carmona 70 C4 Andalucía, S Spain
Carmona see Uíge
Carnaro see Kvarner
Carnarvon 125 A5 Western Australia
Carnegie, Lake 125 B5 salt lake Western Australia
Car Nicobar 111 F3 island Nicobar Islands, India, NE Indian Ocean
Caroço, Ilha 54 E1 island N Sao Tome and Principe, Africa, E Atlantic Ocean
Carolina 41 F2 Maranhão, E Brazil
Caroline Island see Millennium Island
Caroline Islands 122 B2 island group C Micronesia
Carolopois see Châlons-en-Champagne
Caroní, Río 37 E3 river E Venezuela
Caronium see A Coruña
Carora 36 C1 Lara, N Venezuela
Carpathian Mountains 59 E4 var. Carpathians, Cz./Pol. Karpaty, Ger. Karpaten. mountain range E Europe
Carpathians see Carpathian Mountains
Carpathos/Carpathus see Kárpathos
Carpații Sudici see Carpații Meridionali
Carpentaria, Gulf of 126 B2 gulf N Australia
Carpi 74 C2 Emilia-Romagna, N Italy
Carrara 74 B3 Toscana, C Italy
Carson City 25 C5 state capital Nevada, W USA
Carson Sink 25 C5 salt flat Nevada, W USA
Carstensz, Puntjak see Jaya, Puncak
Cartagena 36 B1 var. Cartagena de los Indes. Bolívar, NW Colombia
Cartagena 71 F4 anc. Carthago Nova. Murcia, SE Spain
Cartagena de los Indes see Cartagena
Cartago 31 E4 Cartago, C Costa Rica
Carthage 23 F5 Missouri, C USA
Carthago Nova see Cartagena
Cartwright 17 F2 Newfoundland and Labrador, E Canada
Carúpano 37 E1 Sucre, NE Venezuela
Carusbur see Cherbourg
Caruthersville 23 H5 Missouri, C USA
Cary 21 F1 North Carolina, SE USA
Casablanca 48 C2 Ar. Dar-el-Beida. NW Morocco
Casa Grande 26 B2 Arizona, SW USA
Cascade Range 24 B3 mountain range Oregon/ Washington, NW USA
Cascadia Basin 12 A4 undersea basin NE Pacific Ocean
Cascais 70 B4 Lisboa, C Portugal
Caserta 75 D5 Campania, S Italy
Casey 132 D4 Australian research station Antarctica
Čáslav 77 B5 Ger. Tschaslau. Střední Čechy, C Czech Republic
Casper 22 C3 Wyoming, C USA
Caspian Depression 89 B7 Kaz. Kaspiy Mangy Oypaty, Rus. Prikaspiyskaya Nizmennost'. depression Kazakhstan/Russian Federation
Caspian Sea 92 A4 Az. Xäzär Dänizi, Kaz. Kaspiy Tengizi, Per. Baḩr-e Khazar, Daryā-ye Khazar, Rus. Kaspiyskoye More. inland sea Asia/Europe
Cassai see Kasai
Cassel see Kassel
Castamoni see Kastamonu
Casteggio 74 B2 Lombardia, N Italy
Castelló de la Plana see Castellón de la Plana
Castellón see Castellón de la Plana
Castellón de la Plana 71 F3 var. Castellón, Cat. Castelló de la Plana. País Valenciano, E Spain
Castelnaudary 69 C6 Aude, S France
Castelo Branco 70 C3 Castelo Branco, C Portugal
Castelsarrasin 69 B6 Tarn-et-Garonne, S France
Castelvetrano 75 C7 Sicilia, Italy, C Mediterranean Sea
Castilla-La Mancha 71 E3 autonomous community NE Spain
Castilla-León 70 C2 var. Castillia y Leon. autonomous community NW Spain
Castilla y Leon see Castilla-León
Castlebar 67 A5 Ir. Caisleán an Bharraigh. W Ireland
Castleford 67 D5 N England, United Kingdom
Castle Harbour 20 B5 inlet Bermuda, NW Atlantic Ocean
Castra Regina see Regensburg
Castricum 64 C3 Noord-Holland, W Netherlands
Castries 33 F1 country capital N Saint Lucia
Castro 43 B6 Los Lagos, W Chile
Castrovillari 75 D6 Calabria, SW Italy
Castuera 70 D4 Extremadura, W Spain
Caswell Sound 129 A7 sound South Island, New Zealand
Catacamas 30 D2 Olancho, C Honduras
Catacaos 38 B3 Piura, NW Peru
Catalan Bay 71 H4 bay E Gibraltar, Mediterranean Sea
Cataluña 71 G2 N Spain
Catamarca see San Fernando del Valle de Catamarca
Catania 75 D7 Sicilia, Italy, C Mediterranean Sea
Catanzaro 75 D6 Calabria, SW Italy
Catarroja 71 F3 País Valenciano, E Spain
Cat Island 32 C1 island C Bahamas
Catskill Mountains 19 F3 mountain range New York, NE USA
Cattaro see Kotor
Cauca, Río 36 B2 river N Colombia
Caucasia 36 B2 Antioquia, NW Colombia
Caucasus 59 G4 Rus. Kavkaz. mountain range Georgia/Russian Federation
Caura, Río 37 E3 river C Venezuela
Cavaia see Kavajë
Cavalla 52 D5 var. Cavally, Cavally Fleuve. river Ivory Coast/Liberia
Cavally/Cavally Fleuve see Cavalla
Caviana de Fora, Ilha 41 E1 var. Ilha Caviana. island N Brazil
Caviana, Ilha see Caviana de Fora, Ilha
Cawnpore see Kānpur
Caxamarca see Cajamarca
Caxito 56 B1 Bengo, NW Angola
Cayenne 37 H3 dependent territory/ arrondissement capital NE French Guiana
Cayes 32 D3 var. Les Cayes. SW Haiti
Cayman Brac 32 B3 island E Cayman Islands
Cayman Islands 32 B3 UK dependent territory W West Indies
Cayo see San Ignacio
Cay Sal 32 B2 islet SW Bahamas
Cazin 78 B3 Federacija Bosna I Hercegovina, NW Bosnia and Herzegovina
Cazorla 71 E4 Andalucía, S Spain
Ceadâr-Lunga see Ciadîr-Lunga
Ceará 41 F2 off. Estado do Ceará. state C Brazil
Ceará 41 F2 off. Estado do Ceará. region C Brazil
Ceará see Fortaleza
Ceara Abyssal Plain see Ceará Plain
Ceará, Estado do see Ceará
Ceará Plain 34 E3 var. Ceara Abyssal Plain. abyssal plain W Atlantic Ocean
Ceatharlach see Carlow
Cébaco, Isla 31 F5 island SW Panama
Cebu 117 E2 off. Cebu City. Cebu, C Philippines
Cebu City see Cebu
Čechy see Bohemia
Cecina 74 B3 Toscana, C Italy
Cedar City 22 A5 Utah, W USA
Cedar Falls 23 G3 Iowa, C USA
Cedar Lake 16 A2 lake Manitoba, C Canada
Cedar Rapids 23 G3 Iowa, C USA
Cedros, Isla 28 A2 island W Mexico
Ceduna 127 A6 South Australia
Cefalù 75 C7 anc. Cephaloedium. Sicilia, Italy, C Mediterranean Sea
Celebes 117 E4 Eng. Celebes. island C Indonesia
Celebes see Sulawesi
Celebes Sea 117 E3 Ind. Laut Sulawesi. sea Indonesia/Philippines
Celje 73 E7 Ger. Cilli. C Slovenia
Celldömölk 77 C6 Vas, W Hungary
Celle 72 B3 var. Zelle. Niedersachsen, N Germany
Celovec see Klagenfurt
Celtic Sea 67 B7 Ir. An Mhuir Cheilteach. sea SW British Isles
Celtic Shelf 58 B3 continental shelf E Atlantic Ocean
Cenderawasih, Teluk 117 G4 var. Teluk Irian, Teluk Sarera. bay W Pacific Ocean
Cenon 69 B5 Gironde, SW France
Centennial State see Colorado
Centrafricaine, République see Central African Republic
Central African Republic 54 C4 var. République Centrafricaine, abbrev. CAR; prev. Ubangi-Shari, Oubangui-Chari, Territoire de l'Oubangui-Chari. country C Africa
Central, Cordillera 36 B3 mountain range W Colombia
Cordillera Central 33 E3 mountain range C Dominican Republic
Cordillera Central 31 F5 mountain range C Panama
Central, Cordillera 117 E1 mountain range Luzon, N Philippines
Central Group see Inner Islands
Centralia 24 B2 Washington, NW USA
Central Indian Ridge see Mid-Indian Ridge
Central Makran Range 112 A3 mountain range W Pakistan
Central Pacific Basin 120 D1 undersea basin C Pacific Ocean
Central Provinces and Berar see Madhya Pradesh
Central Range 122 B3 mountain range NW Papua New Guinea
Central Russian Upland 87 G1 Eng. Central Russian Upland. mountain range W Russian Federation
Central Russian Upland see Srednerusskaya Vozvyshennost'
Central Siberian Plateau 92 D3 var. Central Siberian Uplands, Eng. Central Siberian Plateau. mountain range N Russian Federation
Central Siberian Plateau/Central Siberian Uplands see Srednesibirskoye Ploskogor'ye
Central, Sistema 70 D3 mountain range C Spain
Central Valley 25 B6 valley California, W USA
Centum Cellae see Civitavecchia
Ceos see Tziá
Cephaloedium see Cefalù
Ceram see Seram, Pulau
Ceram Sea 117 F4 Ind. Laut Seram. sea E Indonesia
Cerasus see Giresun
Cereté 36 B2 Córdoba, NW Colombia
Cergy-Pontoise see Pontoise
Cerignola 75 D5 Puglia, SE Italy
Çerkes 94 C2 Çankırı, N Turkey
Cernăuți see Chernivtsi
Cernay 68 E4 Haut-Rhin, NE France
Cerro de Pasco 38 C3 Pasco, C Peru
Cervera 71 F2 Cataluña, NE Spain
Cervino, Monte see Matterhorn
Cesena 74 C3 anc. Caesena. Emilia-Romagna, N Italy
Cēsis 84 D3 Ger. Wenden. Cēsis, C Latvia
Česká Republika see Czech Republic
České Budějovice 77 B5 Ger. Budweis. Jihočeský Kraj, S Czech Republic
Český Krumlov 77 A5 var. Böhmisch-Krumau, Ger. Krummau. Jihočeský Kraj, S Czech Republic
Ceský Les see Bohemian Forest
Cetatea Damboviței see București
Cetinje 79 C5 It. Cettigne. S Montenegro
Cette see Sète
Cettigne see Cetinje
Ceuta 48 C2 enclave Spain, N Africa
Cévennes 69 C6 mountain range S France
Ceyhan 94 D4 Adana, S Turkey
Ceylanpınar 95 E4 Şanlıurfa, SE Turkey
Ceylon see Sri Lanka
Ceylon Plain 102 B4 abyssal plain N Indian Ocean
Ceyre to the Caribs see Marie-Galante
Chachapoyas 38 B2 Amazonas, NW Peru
Chachevichy 85 D6 Rus. Chechevichi. Mahilyowskaya Voblasts', E Belarus
Chaco see Gran Chaco
Chad 54 C3 off. Republic of Chad, Fr. Tchad. country C Africa
Chad, Lake 54 B3 Fr. Lac Tchad. lake C Africa
Chad, Republic of see Chad
Chadron 22 D3 Nebraska, C USA
Chadyr-Lunga see Ciadîr-Lunga
Chagai Hills 112 A2 var. Chāh Gay. mountain range Afghanistan/Pakistan
Chaghasarāy see Asadābād
Chagos-Laccadive Plateau 102 B4 undersea plateau N Indian Ocean
Chagos Trench 119 C5 trench N Indian Ocean
Chāh Gay see Chāgai Hills
Chaillu, Massif du 55 B6 mountain range C Gabon
Chain Ridge 118 B4 undersea ridge W Indian Ocean
Chajul 30 B2 Quiché, W Guatemala
Chakhānsūr 100 D5 Nīmrūz, SW Afghanistan
Chala 38 D4 Arequipa, SW Peru
Chalatenango 30 C3 Chalatenango, N El Salvador
Chalcidice see Chalkidikí
Chalcis see Chalkída
Chalki 83 E7 island Dodekánisa, Greece, Aegean Sea
Chalkída 83 C5 var. Halkida, prev. Khalkís; anc. Chalcis. Evvoia, E Greece
Chalkidikí 82 C4 var. Khalkidhikí; anc. Chalcidice. peninsula NE Greece
Challans 68 B4 Vendée, NW France
Challapata 39 F4 Oruro, SW Bolivia
Challenger Deep 130 B3 trench W Pacific Ocean
Challenger Deep see Mariana Trench
Challenger Fracture Zone 131 F4 tectonic feature SE Pacific Ocean
Châlons-en-Champagne 68 D3 prev. Châlons-sur-Marne, hist. Arcae Remorum; anc. Carolopois. Marne, NE France
Châlons-sur-Marne see Châlons-en-Champagne
Chalon-sur-Saône 68 D4 anc. Cabillonum. Saône-et-Loire, C France
Cha Mai see Thung Song
Chaman 112 B2 Baluchistān, SW Pakistan
Chambéry 69 D5 anc. Camberia. Savoie, E France
Champagne 68 D3 cultural region N France
Champagne see Campania
Champaign 18 B4 Illinois, N USA
Champasak 115 D5 Champasak, S Laos
Champlain, Lake 19 F2 lake Canada/USA
Champotón 29 G4 Campeche, SE Mexico
Chanak see Çanakkale
Chañaral 42 B3 Atacama, N Chile
Chan-chiang/Chanchiang see Zhanjiang
Chandeleur Islands 20 C3 island group Louisiana, S USA
Chandīgarh 112 D2 state capital Punjab, N India
Chandrapur 113 E5 Mahārāshtra, C India
Changan see Xi'an, Shaanxi, C China
Changane 57 E3 river S Mozambique
Changchun 106 D3 var. Ch'angch'un, Ch'ang-ch'un; prev. Hsinking. province capital Jilin, NE China
Ch'angch'un/Ch'ang-ch'un see Changchun
Changkiakow see Zhangjiakou
Chang, Ko 115 C6 island S Thailand
Changsha 106 C5 var. Ch'angsha, Ch'ang-sha. province capital Hunan, S China
Ch'angsha/Ch'ang-sha see Changsha
Changzhi 106 C4 Shanxi, C China
Chaniá 83 C7 var. Hania, Khaniá, Eng. Canea; anc. Cydonia. Kríti, Greece, E Mediterranean Sea
Chañi, Nevado de 42 B2 mountain NW Argentina
Chankiri see Çankırı
Channel Islands 67 C8 Fr. Iles Normandes. island group S English Channel
Channel Islands 25 B8 island group California, W USA
Channel-Port aux Basques 17 G4 Newfoundland and Labrador, SE Canada
Channel, The see English Channel
Channel Tunnel 68 C2 tunnel France/United Kingdom
Chantabun/Chantaburi see Chanthaburi
Chantada 70 C1 Galicia, NW Spain
Chanthaburi 115 C6 var. Chantabun, Chantaburi. Chantaburi, S Thailand
Chanute 23 F5 Kansas, C USA
Chaouèn see Chefchaouen
Chaoyang 106 D3 Liaoning, NE China
Chapala, Lago de 28 D4 lake C Mexico
Chapan, Gora 100 B3 mountain C Turkmenistan
Chapayevsk 89 C6 Samarskaya Oblast', W Russian Federation
Chaplynka 87 F4 Khersons'ka Oblast', S Ukraine
Chapra see Chhapra
Charcot Seamounts 58 B3 seamount range E Atlantic Ocean
Chardzhev see Türkmenabat
Chardzhou/Chardzhui see Türkmenabat
Charente 69 B5 cultural region W France
Charente 69 B5 river W France
Chari 54 B3 var. Shari. river Central African Republic/Chad
Chārīkār 101 E4 Parvān, NE Afghanistan
Charity 37 F2 NW Guyana
Chärjew see Türkmenabat
Charkhlik/Charkhliq see Ruoqiang
Charleroi 65 C7 Hainaut, S Belgium
Charlesbourg 17 E4 Québec, SE Canada
Charles de Gaulle 68 E1 international airport Seine-et-Marne, N France
Charles Island 16 D1 island Nunavut, NE Canada
Charles Island see Santa María, Isla
Charleston 21 F2 South Carolina, SE USA
Charleston 18 D5 state capital West Virginia, NE USA
Charleville 127 D5 Queensland, E Australia
Charleville-Mézières 68 D3 Ardennes, N France
Charlie-Gibbs Fracture Zone 44 C2 tectonic feature N Atlantic Ocean
Charlotte 21 E1 North Carolina, SE USA
Charlotte Amalie 33 F3 prev. Saint Thomas. dependent territory capital Saint Thomas, N Virgin Islands (US)
Charlotte Harbor 21 E5 inlet Florida, SE USA
Charlottenhof see Aegviidu
Charlottesville 19 E5 Virginia, NE USA
Charlottetown 17 F4 province capital Prince Edward Island, Prince Edward Island, SE Canada
Charlotte Town see Roseau, Dominica
Charsk see Shar
Charters Towers 126 D3 Queensland, NE Australia
Chartres 68 C3 anc. Autricum, Civitas Carnutum. Eure-et-Loir, C France
Chashniki 85 D5 Vitsyebskaya Voblasts', N Belarus
Châteaubriant 68 B4 Loire-Atlantique, NW France
Châteaudun 68 C3 Eure-et-Loir, C France
Châteauroux 68 C4 prev. Indreville. Indre, C France
Château-Thierry 68 C3 Aisne, N France
Châtelet 65 C7 Hainaut, S Belgium
Châtelherault see Châtellerault
Châtellerault 68 B4 var. Châtelherault. Vienne, W France
Chatham Island see San Cristóbal, Isla
Chatham Island Rise see Chatham Rise
Chatham Islands 121 E5 island group New Zealand, SW Pacific Ocean
Chatham Rise 120 D5 var. Chatham Island Rise. undersea rise S Pacific Ocean
Chatkal Range 101 F2 Rus. Chatkal'skiy Khrebet. mountain range Kyrgyzstan/Uzbekistan
Chatkal'skiy Khrebet see Chatkal Range
Chāttagām see Chittagong
Chattahoochee River 20 D3 river SE USA
Chattanooga 20 D1 Tennessee, S USA
Chatyr-Tash 101 G2 Narynskaya Oblast', C Kyrgyzstan
Châu Đôc 115 D6 var. Chauphu, Chau Phu. An Giang, S Vietnam
Chauk 114 A3 Magway, W Myanmar (Burma)
Chaumont 68 D4 prev. Chaumont-en-Bassigny. Haute-Marne, N France
Chaumont-en-Bassigny see Chaumont
Chau Phu see Châu Đôc
Chausy see Chavusy
Chaves 70 C2 anc. Aquae Flaviae. Vila Real, N Portugal
Chávez, Isla see Santa Cruz, Isla
Chavusy 85 E6 Rus. Chausy. Mahilyowskaya Voblasts', E Belarus
Chaykovskiy 89 D5 Permskaya Oblast', NW Russian Federation
Cheb 77 A5 Ger. Eger. Karlovarský Kraj, W Czech Republic
Cheboksary 89 C5 Chuvashskaya Respublika, W Russian Federation
Cheboygan 18 C2 Michigan, N USA
Chechaouèn see Chefchaouen
Chech, Erg 52 D1 desert Algeria/Mali
Chechevichi see Chachevichy
Che-chiang see Zhejiang
Cheduba Island 114 A4 island W Myanmar (Burma)
Chefchaouen 48 C2 var. Chaouèn, Chechaouèn, Sp. Xauen. N Morocco
Chefoo see Yantai
Cheju-do 107 E4 Jap. Saishū; prev. Quelpart. island S South Korea
Cheju Strait 107 E4 Eng. Cheju Strait. strait S South Korea
Cheju Strait see Cheju-haehyŏp
Chekiang see Zhejiang
Cheleken see Hazar
Chelkar see Shalkar
Chełm 76 E4 Rus. Kholm. Lubelskie, SE Poland
Chełmno 76 C3 Ger. Culm, Kulm. Kujawski-pomorskie, C Poland
Chełmża 76 C3 Ger. Culmsee, Kulmsee. Kujawski-pomorskie, C Poland
Cheltenham 67 D6 C England, United Kingdom
Chelyabinsk 92 C3 Chelyabinskaya Oblast', C Russian Federation
Chemnitz 72 D4 prev. Karl-Marx-Stadt. Sachsen, E Germany
Chemulpo see Inch'ŏn
Chenāb 112 C2 river India/Pakistan
Chengchiatun see Liaoyuan
Ch'eng-chou/Chengchow see Zhengzhou
Chengde 106 D3 var. Jehol. Hebei, E China
Chengdu 106 B5 var. Chengtu, Ch'eng-tu. province capital Sichuan, C China
Chenghsien see Zhengzhou
Chengtu/Ch'eng-tu see Chengdu
Chennai 110 D2 prev. Madras. state capital Tamil Nādu, S India
Chenstokhov see Częstochowa
Chen Xian/Chenxian/Chen Xiang see Chenzhou
Chenzhou 106 C6 var. Chenxian, Chen Xian, Chen Xiang. Hunan, S China
Chepelare 82 C3 Smolyan, S Bulgaria
Chepén 38 B3 La Libertad, C Peru
Cher 68 C4 river C France
Cherbourg 68 B3 anc. Carusbur. Manche, N France
Cherepovets 88 B4 Vologodskaya Oblast', NW Russian Federation
Chergui, Chott ech 48 D2 salt lake NW Algeria
Cherikov see Cherykaw
Cherkassy see Cherkasy
Cherkasy 87 E2 Rus. Cherkassy. Cherkas'ka Oblast', C Ukraine
Cherkessk 89 B7 Karachayevo-Cherkesskaya Respublika, SW Russian Federation
Chernigov see Chernihiv
Chernihiv 87 E1 Rus. Chernigov. Chernihivs'ka Oblast', NE Ukraine
Chernivtsi 86 C3 Ger. Czernowitz, Rom. Cernăuți, Rus. Chernovtsy. Chernivets'ka Oblast', W Ukraine
Cherno More see Black Sea
Chernomorskoye see Chornomors'ke
Chernovtsy see Chernivtsi
Chernoye More see Black Sea
Chernyakhovsk 84 A4 Ger. Insterburg. Kaliningradskaya Oblast', W Russian Federation
Cherry Hill 19 F4 New Jersey, NE USA
Cherski Range see Cherskogo, Khrebet
Cherskiy 93 G2 Respublika Sakha (Yakutiya), NE Russian Federation
Cherskogo, Khrebet 93 F2 var. Cherski Range. mountain range NE Russian Federation
Cherso see Cres
Cherven' see Chervyen'
Chervonograd see Chervonohrad
Chervonohrad 86 C2 Rus. Chervonograd. L'vivs'ka Oblast', NW Ukraine
Chervyen' 85 D6 Rus. Cherven'. Minskaya Voblasts', C Belarus
Cherykaw 85 E7 Rus. Cherikov. Mahilyowskaya Voblasts', E Belarus
Chesapeake Bay 19 F5 inlet NE USA
Chesha Bay see Chëshskaya Guba
Chëshskaya Guba 133 D5 var. Archangel Bay, Chesha Bay, Dvina Bay. bay NW Russian Federation
Chester 67 C6 Wel. Caerleon, hist. Legaceaster, Lat. Deva, Devana Castra. C England, United Kingdom
Chetumal 29 H4 var. Payo Obispo. Quintana Roo, SE Mexico
Cheviot Hills 66 D4 hill range England/Scotland, United Kingdom
Cheyenne 22 D4 state capital Wyoming, C USA
Cheyenne River 22 D3 river South Dakota/ Wyoming, N USA
Chezdi-Oşorheiu see Târgu Secuiesc
Chhapra 113 F3 prev. Chapra. Bihār, N India
Chhattīsgarh 113 E4 cultural region E India
Chiai 106 D6 var. Chia-i, Chiayi, Kiayi, Jiayi, Jap. Kagi. C Taiwan
Chia-i see Chiai
Chiang-hsi see Jiangxi
Chiang Mai 114 B4 var. Chiangmai, Chiengmai, Kiangmai. Chiang Mai, NW Thailand
Chiangmai see Chiang Mai
Chiang Rai 114 C3 var. Chianpai, Chienrai, Muang Chiang Rai. Chiang Rai, NW Thailand
Chiang-su see Jiangsu
Chianning/Chian-ning see Nanjing
Chianpai see Chiang Rai
Chianti 74 C3 cultural region C Italy
Chiapa see Chiapa de Corzo
Chiapa de Corzo 29 G5 var. Chiapa. Chiapas, SE Mexico
Chiayi see Chiai
Chiba 108 B1 var. Tiba. Chiba, Honshū, S Japan
Chibougamau 16 D3 Québec, SE Canada
Chicago 18 B3 Illinois, N USA
Ch'i-ch'i-ha-erh see Qiqihar
Chickasha 27 G2 Oklahoma, C USA
Chiclayo 38 B3 Lambayeque, NW Peru
Chico 25 B5 California, W USA
Chico, Río 43 B7 river SE Argentina
Chico, Río 43 B6 river S Argentina
Chicoutimi 17 E4 Québec, SE Canada
Chiengmai see Chiang Mai
Chienrai see Chiang Rai
Chiesanuova 74 D2 SW San Marino
Chieti 74 D4 var. Teate. Abruzzo, C Italy
Chifeng 105 G2 var. Ulanhad. Nei Mongol Zizhiqu, N China
Chigirin see Chyhyryn
Chih-fu see Yantai
Chihli see Hebei
Chihli, Gulf of see Bo Hai
Chihuahua 28 C2 Chihuahua, NW Mexico
Childress 27 F2 Texas, SW USA
Chile 42 B3 off. Republic of Chile. country SW South America
Chile Basin 35 A5 undersea basin E Pacific Ocean
Chile Chico 43 B6 Aisén, W Chile
Chile, Republic of see Chile
Chile Rise 35 A7 undersea rise SE Pacific Ocean
Chilia-Nouă see Kiliya
Chililabombwe 56 D2 Copperbelt, C Zambia
Chi-lin see Jilin
Chillán 43 B5 Bío Bío, C Chile
Chillicothe 18 D4 Ohio, N USA
Chill Mhantáin, Sléibhte see Wicklow Mountains
Chiloé, Isla de 43 A6 var. Isla Grande de Chiloé. island W Chile
Chilpancingo 29 E5 var. Chilpancingo de los Bravos. Guerrero, S Mexico
Chilpancingo de los Bravos see Chilpancingo
Chilung 106 D6 var. Keelung, Jap. Kirun, Kirun'; prev. Sp. Santissima Trinidad. N Taiwan
Chimán 31 G5 Panamá, E Panama
Chimbay see Chimboy
Chimborazo 38 A1 volcano C Ecuador
Chimbote 38 C3 Ancash, W Peru
Chimboy 100 D1 Rus. Chimbay. Qoraqalpog'iston Respublikasi, NW Uzbekistan
Chimkent see Shymkent
Chimoio 57 E3 Manica, C Mozambique
China 102 C2 off. People's Republic of China, Chin. Chung-hua Jen-min Kung-ho-kuo, Zhonghua Renmin Gongheguo; prev. Chinese Empire. country E Asia
Chi-nan/Chinan see Jinan
Chinandega 30 C3 Chinandega, NW Nicaragua
China, People's Republic of see China
China, Republic of see Taiwan
Chincha Alta 38 D4 Ica, SW Peru
Chin-chiang see Quanzhou
Chin-chou/Chinchow see Jinzhou
Chindwin see Chindwinn
Chindwinn 114 B2 var. Chindwin. river N Myanmar (Burma)
Chinese Empire see China
Chinghai see Qinghai
Ch'ing Hai see Qinghai Hu, China
Chingola 56 D2 Copperbelt, C Zambia
Ching-Tao/Ch'ing-tao see Qingdao
Chinguețți 52 C2 var. Chinguetti. Adrar, C Mauritania
Chin Hills 114 A3 mountain range W Myanmar (Burma)
Chinhsien see Jinzhou
Chinnereth see Tiberias, Lake
Chinook Trough 91 H4 trough N Pacific Ocean
Chioggia 74 C2 anc. Fossa Claudia. Veneto, NE Italy
Chíos 83 D5 var. Hios, Khíos, It. Scio, Turk. Sakiz-Adasi. Chíos, E Greece
Chíos 83 D5 var. Khíos. island E Greece
Chipata 56 D2 prev. Fort Jameson. Eastern, E Zambia
Chiquián 38 C3 Ancash, W Peru
Chiquimula 30 B2 Chiquimula, SE Guatemala
Chīrāla 110 D1 Andhra Pradesh, E India
Chirchik see Chirchiq
Chirchiq 101 E2 Rus. Chirchik. Toshkent Viloyati, E Uzbekistan
Chiriqui Gulf 31 E5 Eng. Chiriqui Gulf. gulf SW Panama
Chiriqui Gulf see Chiriquí, Golfo de
Chiriquí, Laguna de 31 E5 lagoon NW Panama
Chiriquí, Volcán de see Barú, Volcán
Chirripó, Cerro see Chirripó Grande, Cerro
Chirripó Grande, Cerro 30 D4 var. Cerro Chirripó. mountain SE Costa Rica
Chisec 30 B2 Alta Verapaz, C Guatemala
Chisholm 23 F1 Minnesota, N USA

Chisimaio/Chisimayu – Crooked Island

Chisimaio/Chisimayu see Kismaayo
Chişinău 86 D4 Rus. Kishinev. country capital C Moldova
Chita 93 F4 Chitinskaya Oblast', S Russian Federation
Chitangwiza see Chitungwiza
Chitato 56 C1 Lunda Norte, NE Angola
Chitina 14 D3 Alaska, USA
Chitose 108 D2 var. Titose. Hokkaidō, NE Japan
Chitré 31 F5 Herrera, S Panama
Chittagong 113 G4 Ben. Châttagâm. Chittagong, SE Bangladesh
Chitungwiza 56 D3 prev. Chitangwiza. Mashonaland East, NE Zimbabwe
Chkalov see Orenburg
Chlef 48 D2 var. Ech Cheliff, Ech Chleff; prev. Al-Asnam, El Asnam, Orléansville. NW Algeria
Chocolate Mountains 25 D8 mountain range California, W USA
Chodorów see Khodoriv
Chodzież 76 C3 Wielkopolskie, C Poland
Choele Choel 43 C5 Río Negro, C Argentina
Choiseul 122 C3 var. Lauru. island NW Solomon Islands
Chojnice 76 C2 Ger. Konitz. Pomorskie, N Poland
Ch'ok'ē 50 C4 var. Choke Mountains. mountain range NW Ethiopia
Choke Mountains see Ch'ok'ē
Cholet 68 B4 Maine-et-Loire, NW France
Choluteca 30 C3 Choluteca, S Honduras
Choluteca, Río 30 C3 river SW Honduras
Choma 56 D2 Southern, S Zambia
Chomutov 76 A4 Ger. Komotau. Ústecký Kraj, NW Czech Republic
Chona 91 E2 river C Russian Federation
Chon Buri 115 C5 prev. Bang Pla Soi. Chon Buri, S Thailand
Chone 38 A1 Manabí, W Ecuador
Ch'ŏngjin 107 E3 NE North Korea
Chongqing 106 B5 var. Ch'ung-ching, Ch'ung-ch'ing, Chungking, Pahsien, Tchongking, Yuzhou. Chongqing Shi, C China
Chonnacht see Connaught
Chonos, Archipiélago de los 43 A6 island group S Chile
Chóra Sfakíon 83 C8 var. Sfákia. Kríti, Greece, E Mediterranean Sea
Chorne More see Black Sea
Chornomors'ke 87 E4 Rus. Chernomorskoye. Respublika Krym, S Ukraine
Chorokh/Chorokhi see Çoruh Nehri
Chortkiv 86 C2 Rus. Chortkov. Ternopil's'ka Oblast', W Ukraine
Chortkov see Chortkiv
Chorzów 77 C5 Ger. Königshütte; prev. Królewska Huta. Śląskie, S Poland
Chośebuz see Cottbus
Chōsen-kaikyō see Korea Strait
Chōshi 109 D5 var. Tyôsi. Chiba, Honshū, S Japan
Chosŏn-minjujuŭi-inmin-kanghwaguk see North Korea
Choszczno 76 B3 Ger. Arnswalde. Zachodnio-pomorskie, NW Poland
Chota Nagpur 113 E4 plateau N India
Choûm 52 C2 Adrar, C Mauritania
Choybalsan 105 F2 prev. Byan Tumen. Dornod, E Mongolia
Christchurch 129 C6 Canterbury, South Island, New Zealand
Christiana 32 B5 C Jamaica
Christiania see Oslo
Christiansand see Kristiansand
Christianshåb see Qasigiannguit
Christiansund see Kristiansund
Christmas Island 119 D5 Australian external territory E Indian Ocean
Christmas Island see Kiritimati
Christmas Ridge 121 E1 undersea ridge C Pacific Ocean
Chuan see Sichuan
Ch'uan-chou see Quanzhou
Chubek see Moskva
Chubut, Río 43 B6 river SE Argentina
Ch'u-chiang see Shaoguan
Chudskoye Ozero see Peipus, Lake
Chugoku-sanchi 109 B6 mountain range Honshū, SW Japan
Chuí see Chuy
Chukai see Cukai
Chukchi Plain 133 B2 abyssal plain Arctic Ocean
Chukchi Plateau 12 C2 undersea plateau Arctic Ocean
Chukchi Sea 12 B2 Rus. Chukotskoye More. sea Arctic Ocean
Chukotskoye More see Chukchi Sea
Chula Vista 25 C8 California, W USA
Chulucanas 38 B2 Piura, NW Peru
Chulym 92 D4 river C Russian Federation
Chumphon 115 C6 var. Jumporn. Chumphon, SW Thailand
Ch'unch'ŏn 107 E4 Jap. Shunsen. N South Korea
Ch'ung-ch'ing/Ch'ung-ching see Chongqing
Chung-hua Jen-min Kung-ho-kuo see China
Chungking see Chongqing
Chunya 93 E3 river C Russian Federation
Chuquicamata 42 B2 Antofagasta, N Chile
Chuquisaca see Sucre
Chur 73 B7 Fr. Coire, It. Coira, Rmsch. Cuera, Quera; anc. Curia Rhaetorum. Graubünden, E Switzerland
Churchill 15 G4 Manitoba, C Canada
Churchill 16 B2 river Manitoba/Saskatchewan, C Canada
Churchill 17 F2 river Newfoundland and Labrador, E Canada
Chuska Mountains 26 C1 mountain range Arizona/New Mexico, SW USA
Chusovoy 89 D5 Permskaya Oblast', NW Russian Federation
Chust see Khust
Chuuk Islands 122 B2 var. Hogoley Islands; prev. Truk Islands. island group Caroline Islands, C Micronesia
Chuy 42 E4 var. Chuí. Rocha, E Uruguay
Chyhyryn 87 E2 Rus. Chigirin. Cherkas'ka Oblast', N Ukraine
Ciadîr-Lunga 86 D4 var. Ceadâr-Lunga, Rus. Chadyr-Lunga. S Moldova
Cide 94 C2 Kastamonu, N Turkey
Ciechanów 76 D3 prev. Zichenau. Mazowieckie, C Poland
Ciego de Ávila 32 C2 Ciego de Ávila, C Cuba
Ciénaga 36 B1 Magdalena, N Colombia
Cienfuegos 32 B2 Cienfuegos, C Cuba
Cieza 71 E4 Murcia, SE Spain
Cihanbeyli 94 C3 Konya, C Turkey
Cikobia 123 E4 prev. Thikombia. island N Fiji
Cilacap 116 C5 prev. Tjilatjap. Jawa, C Indonesia
Cill Airne see Killarney
Cill Chainnigh see Kilkenny
Cilli see Celje
Cill Mhantáin see Wicklow
Cîmpina see Câmpina
Cîmpulung see Câmpulung
Cina Selatan, Laut see South China Sea
Cincinnati 18 C4 Ohio, N USA
Ciney 65 C7 Namur, SE Belgium
Cinto, Monte 69 E7 mountain Corse, France, C Mediterranean Sea
Cintra see Sintra
Cipolletti 43 B5 Río Negro, C Argentina
Cirebon 116 C4 prev. Tjirebon. Jawa, S Indonesia
Cirkvenica see Crikvenica
Ciro Marina 75 E6 Calabria, S Italy
Cirquenizza see Crikvenica
Cisnădie 86 B4 Ger. Heltau, Hung. Nagydisznód. Sibiu, SW Romania
Citharista see la Ciotat
Citlaltépetl see Orizaba, Volcán Pico de
Citrus Heights 25 B5 California, W USA
Ciudad Acuña see Villa Acuña
Ciudad Bolívar 37 E2 prev. Angostura. Bolívar, E Venezuela
Ciudad Camargo 28 D2 Chihuahua, N Mexico
Ciudad Cortés see Cortés
Ciudad Darío 30 D3 var. Dario. Matagalpa, W Nicaragua
Ciudad de Dolores Hidalgo see Dolores Hidalgo
Ciudad de Guatemala 30 B2 Eng. Guatemala City; prev. Santiago de los Caballeros. country capital Guatemala, C Guatemala
Ciudad del Carmen see Carmen
Ciudad del Este 42 E2 prev. Ciudad Presidente Stroessner, Presidente Stroessner, Puerto Presidente Stroessner. Alto Paraná, SE Paraguay
Ciudad Delicias see Delicias
Ciudad de México see México
Ciudad de Panama see Panamá
Ciudad Guayana 37 E2 prev. San Tomé de Guayana, Santo Tomé de Guayana. Bolívar, NE Venezuela
Ciudad Guzmán 28 D4 Jalisco, SW Mexico
Ciudad Hidalgo 29 G5 Chiapas, SE Mexico
Ciudad Juárez 28 C1 Chihuahua, N Mexico
Ciudad Lerdo 28 D3 Durango, C Mexico
Ciudad Madero 29 E3 var. Villa Cecilia. Tamaulipas, C Mexico
Ciudad Mante 29 E3 Tamaulipas, C Mexico
Ciudad Miguel Alemán 29 E2 Tamaulipas, C Mexico
Ciudad Obregón 28 B2 Sonora, NW Mexico
Ciudad Ojeda 36 C1 Zulia, NW Venezuela
Ciudad Porfirio Díaz see Piedras Negras
Ciudad Presidente Stroessner see Ciudad del Este
Ciudad Quesada see Quesada
Ciudad Real 70 D3 Castilla-La Mancha, C Spain
Ciudad-Rodrigo 70 C3 Castilla-León, N Spain
Ciudad Trujillo see Santo Domingo
Ciudad Valles 29 E3 San Luis Potosí, C Mexico
Ciudad Victoria 29 E3 Tamaulipas, C Mexico
Ciutadella 71 H3 var. Ciutadela de Menorca. Menorca, Spain, W Mediterranean Sea
Ciutadela Ciutadella de Menorca see Ciutadella
Civitanova Marche 74 D3 Marche, C Italy
Civitas Altae Ripae see Brzeg
Civitas Carnutum see Chartres
Civitas Eburovicum see Évreux
Civitavecchia 74 C4 anc. Centum Cellae, Trajani Portus. Lazio, C Italy
Claremore 27 G1 Oklahoma, C USA
Clarence 129 C5 Canterbury, South Island, New Zealand
Clarence 129 C5 river South Island, New Zealand
Clarence Town 32 D2 Long Island, C Bahamas
Clarinda 23 F4 Iowa, C USA
Clarion Fracture Zone 131 E2 tectonic feature NE Pacific Ocean
Clarión, Isla 28 A5 island W Mexico
Clark Fork 22 A1 river Idaho/Montana, NW USA
Clark Hill Lake 21 E2 var. J.Storm Thurmond Reservoir. reservoir Georgia/South Carolina, SE USA
Clarksburg 18 D4 West Virginia, NE USA
Clarksdale 20 B2 Mississippi, S USA
Clarksville 20 C1 Tennessee, S USA
Clausentum see Southampton
Clayton 27 E1 New Mexico, SW USA
Clearwater 21 E4 Florida, SE USA
Clearwater Mountains 24 D2 mountain range Idaho, NW USA
Cleburne 27 G3 Texas, SW USA
Clermont 126 D4 Queensland, E Australia
Clermont-Ferrand 69 C5 Puy-de-Dôme, C France
Cleveland 18 D3 Ohio, N USA
Cleveland 20 D1 Tennessee, S USA
Clifton 26 C2 Arizona, SW USA
Clinton 20 B2 Mississippi, S USA
Clinton 27 F1 Oklahoma, C USA
Clipperton Fracture Zone 131 E3 tectonic feature E Pacific Ocean
Clipperton Island 13 A7 French dependency of French Polynesia E Pacific Ocean
Cloncurry 126 B3 Queensland, C Australia
Clonmel 67 B6 Ir. Cluain Meala. S Ireland
Cloppenburg 72 B3 Niedersachsen, NW Germany
Cloquet 23 G2 Minnesota, N USA
Cloud Peak 22 C3 mountain Wyoming, C USA
Clovis 27 E2 New Mexico, SW USA
Cluain Meala see Clonmel
Cluj see Cluj-Napoca
Cluj-Napoca 86 B3 Ger. Klausenburg, Hung. Kolozsvár; prev. Cluj. Cluj, NW Romania
Clutha 129 B7 river South Island, New Zealand
Clyde 66 C4 river W Scotland, United Kingdom
Coari 40 D2 Amazonas, N Brazil
Coast Mountains 14 D4 Fr. Chaîne Côtière. mountain range Canada/USA
Coast Ranges 24 A4 mountain range W USA
Coats Island 15 G3 island Nunavut, NE Canada
Coats Land 132 B2 physical region Antarctica
Coatzacoalcos 29 G4 var. Quetzalcoalco; prev. Puerto México. Veracruz-Llave, E Mexico
Cobán 30 B2 Alta Verapaz, C Guatemala
Cobar 127 C6 New South Wales, SE Australia
Cobija 39 E3 Pando, NW Bolivia
Coblence/Coblenz see Koblenz
Coburg 73 C5 Bayern, SE Germany
Coca see Puerto Francisco de Orellana
Cocanada see Kākināda
Cochabamba 39 F4 hist. Oropeza. Cochabamba, C Bolivia
Cochin 110 C3 var. Kochchi, Kochi. Kerala, SW India
Cochrane 16 C4 Ontario, S Canada
Cochrane 43 B7 Aisén, S Chile
Cocibolca see Nicaragua, Lago de
Cockade State see Maryland
Cockburn Town 33 E2 San Salvador, E Bahamas
Cockpit Country, The 32 A4 physical region W Jamaica
Cocobeach 55 A5 Estuaire, NW Gabon
Coconino Plateau 26 B1 plain Arizona, SW USA
Coco, Río 31 E2 var. Río Wanki, Segoviao Wangkí. river Honduras/Nicaragua
Cocos Basin 102 C5 undersea basin E Indian Ocean
Cocos Island Ridge see Cocos Ridge
Cocos Islands 119 D5 island group E Indian Ocean
Cocos Ridge 13 C8 var. Cocos Island Ridge. undersea ridge E Pacific Ocean
Cod, Cape 19 G3 headland Massachusetts, NE USA
Codfish Island 129 A8 island SW New Zealand
Codlea 86 C4 Ger. Zeiden, Hung. Feketehalom. Braşov, C Romania
Cody 22 C2 Wyoming, C USA
Coeur d'Alene 24 C2 Idaho, NW USA
Coevorden 64 E2 Drenthe, NE Netherlands
Coffs Harbour 127 E6 New South Wales, SE Australia
Cognac 69 B5 anc. Compniacum. Charente, W France
Cohalm see Rupea
Coiba, Isla de 31 E5 island SW Panama
Coihaique 43 B6 var. Coyhaique. Aisén, S Chile
Coimbatore 110 C3 Tamil Nādu, S India
Coimbra 70 B3 anc. Conimbria, Conimbriga. Coimbra, W Portugal
Coín 70 D5 Andalucía, S Spain
Coira/Coire see Chur
Coirib, Loch see Corrib, Lough
Colby 23 E4 Kansas, C USA
Colchester 67 E6 Connecticut, NE USA
Coleman 27 F3 Texas, SW USA
Coleraine 66 B4 Ir. Cúil Raithin. N Northern Ireland, United Kingdom
Colesberg 56 C5 Northern Cape, C South Africa
Colima 28 D4 Colima, S Mexico
Coll 66 B3 island W Scotland, United Kingdom
College Station 27 G3 Texas, SW USA
Collie 125 A7 Western Australia
Collipo see Leiria
Colmar 68 E4 Ger. Kolmar. Haut-Rhin, NE France
Cöln see Köln
Cologne see Köln
Colomb-Béchar see Béchar
Colombia 36 B3 off. Republic of Colombia. country N South America
Colombian Basin 34 A1 undersea basin SW Caribbean Sea
Colombia, Republic of see Colombia
Colombie-Britannique see British Columbia
Colombo 110 C4 country capital Western Province, W Sri Lanka
Colón 31 G4 prev. Aspinwall. Colón, C Panama
Colonia Agrippina see Köln
Colón Ridge 13 B8 undersea ridge E Pacific Ocean
Colorado 22 C4 off. State of Colorado, also known as Centennial State, Silver State. state C USA
Colorado City 27 F3 Texas, SW USA
Colorado Plateau 26 B1 plateau W USA
Colorado, Río 43 C5 river E Argentina
Colorado, Río see Colorado River
Colorado River 13 B5 var. Río Colorado. river Mexico/USA
Colorado River 27 G4 river Texas, SW USA
Colorado Springs 22 D5 Colorado, C USA
Columbia 19 E4 Maryland, NE USA
Columbia 23 G4 Missouri, C USA
Columbia 21 E2 state capital South Carolina, SE USA
Columbia 20 C1 Tennessee, S USA
Columbia River 24 B3 river Canada/USA
Columbia Plateau 24 C3 plateau Idaho/Oregon, NW USA
Columbus 20 D2 Georgia, SE USA
Columbus 18 C4 Indiana, N USA
Columbus 20 C2 Mississippi, S USA
Columbus 23 F4 Nebraska, C USA
Columbus 18 D4 state capital Ohio, N USA
Colville Channel 128 D2 channel North Island, New Zealand
Colville River 14 D2 river Alaska, USA
Comacchio 74 C3 var. Commachio; anc. Comactium. Emilia-Romagna, N Italy
Comactium see Comacchio
Comalcalco 29 G4 Tabasco, SE Mexico
Coma Pedrosa, Pic de 69 A7 mountain NW Andorra
Comarapa 39 F4 Santa Cruz, C Bolivia
Comayagua 30 C2 Comayagua, W Honduras
Comer See see Como, Lago di
Comilla 113 G4 Ben. Kumillā. Chittagong, E Bangladesh
Comino 80 A5 Malt. Kemmuna. island C Malta
Comitán 29 G5 var. Comitán de Domínguez. Chiapas, SE Mexico
Comitán de Domínguez see Comitán
Commachio see Comacchio
Commissioner's Point 20 A5 headland W Bermuda
Communism Peak 101 F3 prev. Qullai Kommunizm. mountain E Tajikistan
Como 74 B2 anc. Comum. Lombardia, N Italy
Comodoro Rivadavia 43 B6 Chubut, SE Argentina
Como, Lake 74 B2 var. Lario, Eng. Lake Como, Ger. Comer See. lake N Italy
Como, Lake see Como, Lago di
Comores, République Fédérale Islamique des see Comoros
Comoros 57 F2 off. Federal Islamic Republic of the Comoros, Fr. République Fédérale Islamique des Comores. country W Indian Ocean
Comoros, Federal Islamic Republic of the see Comoros
Compiègne 68 C3 Oise, N France
Complutum see Alcalá de Henares
Compniacum see Cognac
Compostella see Santiago
Comrat 86 D4 Rus. Komrat. S Moldova
Comum see Como
Conakry 52 C4 country capital SW Guinea
Conca see Cuenca
Concarneau 68 A3 Finistère, NW France
Concepción 39 G3 Santa Cruz, E Bolivia
Concepción 43 B5 Bío Bío, C Chile
Concepción 42 D2 var. Villa Concepción. Concepción, C Paraguay
Concepción see La Concepción
Concepción de la Vega see La Vega
Conchos, Río 26 D4 river NW Mexico
Conchos, Río 28 D2 river C Mexico
Concord 19 G3 state capital New Hampshire, NE USA
Concordia 42 D4 Entre Ríos, E Argentina
Concordia 23 E4 Kansas, C USA
Côn Đao 115 E7 var. Con Son. island S Vietnam
Condate see Rennes, Ille-et-Vilaine, France
Condate see St-Claude, Jura, France
Condega 30 D3 Estelí, NW Nicaragua
Condivincum see Nantes
Confluentes see Koblenz
Công Hoa Xa Hôi Chu Nghia Viêt Nam see Vietnam
Congo 55 D5 off. Republic of the Congo, Fr. Moyen-Congo; prev. Middle Congo. country C Africa
Congo 55 C6 off. Democratic Republic of Congo; prev. Zaire, Belgian Congo, Congo (Kinshasa). country C Africa
Congo 55 C6 var. Kongo, Fr. Zaire. river C Africa
Congo Basin 55 C6 drainage basin W Dem. Rep. Congo
Congo/Congo (Kinshasa) see Congo (Democratic Republic of)
Coni see Cuneo
Conimbria/Conimbriga see Coimbra
Conjeeveram see Kānchipuram
Connacht see Connaught
Connaught 67 A5 var. Connacht, Ir. Chonnacht, Cúige. province W Ireland
Connecticut 19 F3 off. State of Connecticut, also known as Blue Law State, Constitution State, Land of Steady Habits, Nutmeg State. state NE USA
Connecticut 19 G3 river Canada/USA
Conroe 27 G3 Texas, SW USA
Consentia see Cosenza
Consolación del Sur 32 A2 Pinar del Río, W Cuba
Con Son see Côn Đao
Constance see Konstanz
Constance, Lake 73 B7 Ger. Bodensee. lake C Europe
Constanţa 86 D5 var. Küstendje, Eng. Constanza, Ger. Konstanza, Turk. Küstence. Constanţa, SE Romania
Constantia see Coutances
Constantia see Konstanz
Constantine 49 E2 var. Qacentina, Ar. Qoussantina. NE Algeria
Constantinople see İstanbul
Constantiola see Olteniţa
Constanz see Konstanz
Constanza see Constanţa
Constitution State see Connecticut
Coo see Kos
Coober Pedy 127 A5 South Australia
Cookeville 20 D1 Tennessee, S USA
Cook Islands 123 F4 territory in free association with New Zealand S Pacific Ocean
Cook, Mount see Aoraki
Cook Strait 129 D5 var. Raukawa. strait New Zealand
Cooktown 126 D2 Queensland, NE Australia
Coolgardie 125 B6 Western Australia
Cooma 127 D7 New South Wales, SE Australia
Coomassie see Kumasi
Coon Rapids 23 F2 Minnesota, N USA
Cooper Creek 126 C4 var. Barcoo, Cooper's Creek. seasonal river Queensland/South Australia
Cooper's Creek see Cooper Creek
Coos Bay 24 A3 Oregon, NW USA
Cootamundra 127 D6 New South Wales, SE Australia
Copacabana 39 E4 La Paz, W Bolivia
Copenhagen see København
Copiapó 42 B3 Atacama, N Chile
Copperas Cove 27 G3 Texas, SW USA
Coppermine see Kugluktuk
Copper State see Arizona
Coquilhatville see Mbandaka
Coquimbo 42 B3 Coquimbo, N Chile
Corabia 86 B5 Olt, S Romania
Coral Harbour 15 G3 Southampton Island, Nunavut, NE Canada
Coral Sea 120 B3 sea SW Pacific Ocean
Coral Sea Islands 122 B4 Australian external territory SW Pacific Ocean
Corantijn Rivier see Courantyne River
Corcovado, Golfo 43 B6 gulf S Chile
Corcyra Nigra see Korčula
Cordele 20 D3 Georgia, SE USA
Córdoba 42 C3 Córdoba, C Argentina
Córdoba 29 F4 Veracruz-Llave, E Mexico
Córdoba 70 D4 var. Cordoba, Eng. Cordova; anc. Corduba. Andalucía, SW Spain
Cordova 14 C3 Alaska, USA
Cordova/Cordoba see Córdoba
Corduba see Córdoba
Corentyne River see Courantyne River
Corfu 82 A4 var. Kérkira, Eng. Corfu. island Iónia Nisiá, Greece, C Mediterranean Sea
Corfu see Kérkyra
Coria 70 C3 Extremadura, W Spain
Corinth 20 C1 Mississippi, S USA
Corinth see Kórinthos
Corinth, Gulf of 83 B5 Eng. Gulf of Corinth; anc. Corinthiacus Sinus. gulf C Greece
Corinth, Gulf of/Corinthiacus Sinus see Korinthiakós Kólpos
Corinthus see Kórinthos
Corinto 30 C3 Chinandega, NW Nicaragua
Cork 67 A6 Ir. Corcaigh. S Ireland
Çorlu 94 A2 Tekirdağ, NW Turkey
Corner Brook 17 G3 Newfoundland, Newfoundland and Labrador, E Canada
Cornhusker State see Nebraska
Corn Islands 31 E3 var. Corn Islands. island group SE Nicaragua
Corn Islands see Maíz, Islas del
Cornwallis Island 15 F2 Island Nunavut, N Canada
Coro 36 C1 prev. Santa Ana de Coro. Falcón, NW Venezuela
Corocoro 39 F4 La Paz, W Bolivia
Coromandel 128 D2 Waikato, North Island, New Zealand
Coromandel Coast 110 D2 coast E India
Coromandel Peninsula 128 D2 peninsula North Island, New Zealand
Coronado, Bahía de 30 D5 bay S Costa Rica
Coronel Dorrego 43 C5 Buenos Aires, E Argentina
Coronel Oviedo 42 D2 Caaguazú, SE Paraguay
Corozal 30 C1 Corozal, N Belize
Corpus Christi 27 G4 Texas, SW USA
Corrales 26 D2 New Mexico, SW USA
Corrib, Lough 67 A5 Ir. Loch Coirib. lake W Ireland
Corrientes 42 D3 Corrientes, NE Argentina
Corriza see Korçë
Corsica 69 E7 Eng. Corsica. island France, C Mediterranean Sea
Corsica see Corse
Corsicana 27 G3 Texas, SW USA
Cortegana 70 C4 Andalucía, S Spain
Cortés 31 E5 var. Ciudad Cortés. Puntarenas, SE Costa Rica
Cortez, Sea of see California, Golfo de
Cortina d'Ampezzo 74 C1 Veneto, NE Italy
Coruche 70 B3 Santarém, C Portugal
Çoruh Nehri 95 E3 Geor. Chorokh, Rus. Chorokhi. river Georgia/Turkey
Çorum 94 D3 var. Chorum. Çorum, N Turkey
Corunna see A Coruña
Corvallis 24 B3 Oregon, NW USA
Corvo 70 A5 var. Ilha do Corvo. island Azores, Portugal, NE Atlantic Ocean
Corvo, Ilha do see Corvo
Cos see Kos
Cosenza 75 D6 anc. Consentia. Calabria, SW Italy
Cosne-Cours-sur-Loire 68 C4 Nièvre, Bourgogne, C France Europe
Costa Mesa 24 D2 California, W USA North America
Costa Rica 31 E4 off. Republic of Costa Rica. country Central America
Costa Rica, Republic of see Costa Rica
Costermansville see Bukavu
Cotagaita 39 F5 Potosí, S Bolivia
Côte d'Ivoire see Ivory Coast
Côte d'Ivoire, République de la see Ivory Coast
Côte d'Or 68 D4 cultural region C France
Côte Française des Somalis see Djibouti
Côtière, Chaîne see Coast Mountains
Cotonou 53 F5 var. Kotonu. S Benin
Cotrone see Crotone
Cotswold Hills 67 D6 var. Cotswolds. hill range S England, United Kingdom
Cotswolds see Cotswold Hills
Cottbus 72 D4 Lus. Chośebuz; prev. Kottbus. Brandenburg, E Germany
Cotton State, The see Alabama
Cotyora see Ordu
Couentrey see Coventry
Council Bluffs 23 F4 Iowa, C USA
Courantyne River 37 G4 var. Corantijn Rivier, Corentyne River. river Guyana/Suriname
Courland Lagoon 84 A4 Ger. Kurisches Haff, Rus. Kurskiy Zaliv. lagoon Lithuania/Russian Federation
Courtrai see Kortrijk
Coutances 68 B3 anc. Constantia. Manche, N France
Couvin 65 C7 Namur, S Belgium
Coventry 67 D6 anc. Couentrey. C England, United Kingdom
Covilhã 70 C3 Castelo Branco, E Portugal
Cowan, Lake 125 B6 lake Western Australia
Coxen Hole see Roatán
Coxin Hole see Roatán
Coyhaique see Coihaique
Coyote State, The see South Dakota
Cozhê 104 C5 Xizang Zizhiqu, W China
Cozumel, Isla 29 H3 island SE Mexico
Cracovia/Cracow see Kraków
Cradock 56 C5 Eastern Cape, S South Africa
Craig 22 C4 Colorado, C USA
Craiova 86 B5 Dolj, SW Romania
Cranbrook 15 E5 British Columbia, SW Canada
Crane see The Crane
Cranz see Zelenogradsk
Crawley 67 E7 SE England, United Kingdom
Cremona 74 B2 Lombardia, N Italy
Creole State see Louisiana
Cres 78 A3 It. Cherso; anc. Crexa. island W Croatia
Crescent City 24 A4 California, W USA
Crescent Group 106 C7 island group C Paracel Islands
Creston 23 F4 Iowa, C USA
Crestview 20 D3 Florida, SE USA
Crete 83 C7 Eng. Crete. island Greece, Aegean Sea
Créteil 68 E2 Val-de-Marne, N France
Sea of Crete 83 D7 var. Kretikon Delagos, Eng. Sea of Crete; anc. Mare Creticum. sea Greece, Aegean Sea
Crete, Sea of/Creticum, Mare see Kritikó Pélagos
Creuse 68 B4 river C France
Crewe 67 D6 C England, United Kingdom
Crexa see Cres
Crikvenica 78 A3 It. Cirquenizza; prev. Cirkvenica, Crjkvenica. Primorje-Gorski Kotar, NW Croatia
Crimea 59 F4 peninsula SE Ukraine Europe
Cristóbal 31 G4 Colón, C Panama
Cristóbal Colón, Pico 36 B1 mountain N Colombia
Cristur/Cristuru Săcuiesc see Cristuru Secuiesc
Cristuru Secuiesc 86 C4 prev. Cristur, Cristuru Săcuiesc, Sitaş Cristuru, Ger. Kreutz, Hung. Székelykeresztúr, Szitás-Keresztúr. Harghita, C Romania
Crjkvenica see Crikvenica
Crna Gora see Montenegro
Crna Reka 79 D6 river S FYR Macedonia
Crni Drim see Black Drin
Croatia 78 B3 off. Republic of Croatia, Ger. Kroatien, SCr. Hrvatska. country SE Europe
Croatia, Republic of see Croatia
Crocodile see Limpopo
Croia see Krujë
Croker Island 124 E2 island Northern Territory, N Australia
Cromwell 129 B7 Otago, South Island, New Zealand
Crooked Island 32 D2 island SE Bahamas

Crooked Island Passage – Doberai Peninsula

Crooked Island Passage *32 D2 channel* SE Bahamas
Crookston *23 F1* Minnesota, N USA
Crossen *see* Krosno Odrzańskie
Croton/Crotona *see* Crotone
Crotone *75 E6 var.* Cotrone; *anc.* Croton, Crotona. Calabria, SW Italy
Croydon *67 A8* SE England, United Kingdom
Crozet Basin *119 B6 undersea basin* S Indian Ocean
Crozet Islands *119 B7 island group* French Southern and Antarctic Territories
Crozet Plateau *119 B7 var.* Crozet Plateaus. *undersea plateau* SW Indian Ocean
Crozet Plateaus *see* Crozet Plateau
Crystal Brook *127 B6* South Australia
Csaca *see* Čadca
Csakathurn/Csáktornya *see* Čakovec
Csíkszereda *see* Miercurea-Ciuc
Csorna *77 C6* Győr-Moson-Sopron, NW Hungary
Csurgó *77 C7* Somogy, SW Hungary
Cuando *56 C2 var.* Kwando. *river* S Africa
Cuango *56 B1 var.* Kwango. *river* Angola/Dem. Rep. Congo
Cuango *see* Kwango
Cuanza *56 B1 var.* Kwanza. *river* C Angola
Cuauhtémoc *28 C2* Chihuahua, N Mexico
Cuautla *29 E4* Morelos, S Mexico
Cuba *32 B2 off.* Republic of Cuba. *country* W West Indies
Cubal *56 B2* Benguela, W Angola
Cubango *56 B2 var.* Kuvango, *Port.* Vila Artur de Paiva, Vila da Ponte. Huíla, SW Angola
Cubango *56 B2 var.* Kavango, Kavengo, Kubango, Okavango, Okavanggo. *river* S Africa
Cuba, Republic of *see* Cuba
Cúcuta *36 C2 var.* San José de Cúcuta. Norte de Santander, N Colombia
Cuddapah *110 C2* Andhra Pradesh, S India
Cuenca *38 B2* Azuay, S Ecuador
Cuenca *71 E3 anc.* Conca. Castilla-La Mancha, C Spain
Cuera *see* Chur
Cuernavaca *29 E4* Morelos, S Mexico
Cuiabá *41 E3 prev.* Cuyabá. *state capital* Mato Grosso, SW Brazil
Cúige *see* Connaught
Cúige Laighean *see* Leinster
Cúige Mumhan *see* Munster
Cuijck *64 D4* Noord-Brabant, SE Netherlands
Cúil Raithin *see* Coleraine
Cuito *56 B2 var.* Kwito. *river* SE Angola
Cukai *116 B3 var.* Chukai, Kemaman. Terengganu, Peninsular Malaysia
Cularo *see* Grenoble
Culiacán *28 C3 var.* Culiacán Rosales, Culiacán-Rosales. Sinaloa, C Mexico
Culiacán-Rosales/Culiacán Rosales *see* Culiacán
Cullera *71 F3* País Valenciano, E Spain
Cullman *20 C2* Alabama, S USA
Culm *see* Chełmno
Culmsee *see* Chełmża
Cumaná *37 E1* Sucre, NE Venezuela
Cumbal, Nevado de *36 A4 elevation* S Colombia
Cumberland *19 E4* Maryland, NE USA
Cumberland Plateau *20 D1 plateau* E USA
Cumberland Sound *15 H3 inlet* Baffin Island, Nunavut, NE Canada
Cumpas *28 B2* Sonora, NW Mexico
Cuneo *74 A2 Fr.* Coni. Piemonte, NW Italy
Cunnamulla *127 C5* Queensland, E Australia
Ćuprija *78 E4* Serbia, E Serbia
Curaçao *33 E5 island* Netherlands Antilles
Curia Rhaetorum *see* Chur
Curicó *42 B4* Maule, C Chile
Curieta *see* Krk
Curitiba *41 E4 prev.* Curytiba. *state capital* Paraná, S Brazil
Curtbunar *see* Tervel
Curtea de Argeș *86 C4 var.* Curtea-de-Arges. Argeș, S Romania
Curtea-de-Arges *see* Curtea de Argeș
Curtici *86 A4 Ger.* Kurtitsch, *Hung.* Kürtös. Arad, W Romania
Curtis Island *126 E4 island* Queensland, SE Australia
Curytiba *see* Curitiba
Curzola *see* Korčula
Cusco *39 E4 var.* Cuzco. Cusco, C Peru
Cusset *69 C5* Allier, C France
Cutch, Gulf of *see* Kachchh, Gulf of
Cuttack *113 F4* Orissa, E India
Cuvier Plateau *119 E6 undersea plateau* E Indian Ocean
Cuxhaven *72 B2* Niedersachsen, NW Germany
Cuyabá *see* Cuiabá
Cuyuni, Río *see* Cuyuni River
Cuyuni River *37 F3 var.* Río Cuyuni. *river* Guyana/Venezuela
Cuzco *see* Cusco
Cyclades *83 D6 var.* Kikládhes, *Eng.* Cyclades. *island group* SE Greece
Cyclades *see* Kykládes
Cydonia *see* Chaniá
Cymru *see* Wales
Cyprus *80 C4 off.* Republic of Cyprus, *Gk.* Kypros, *Turk.* Kıbrıs, Kıbrıs Cumhuriyeti. *country* E Mediterranean Sea
Cyprus, Republic of *see* Cyprus
Cythnos *see* Kýthnos
Czech Republic *77 A5 Cz.* Česká Republika. *country* C Europe
Czenstochau *see* Częstochowa
Czernowitz *see* Chernivtsi
Częstochowa *76 C4 Ger.* Czenstochau, Tschenstochau, *Rus.* Chenstokhov. Śląskie, S Poland
Człuchów *76 C3 Ger.* Schlochau. Pomorskie, NW Poland

D

Dabajuro *36 C1* Falcón, NW Venezuela
Dabeiba *36 B2* Antioquia, NW Colombia
Dąbrowa Tarnowska *77 D5* Małopolskie, S Poland
Dabryn' *85 C8 Rus.* Dobryn'. Homyel'skaya Voblasts', SE Belarus
Dacca *see* Dhaka
Daegu *see* Taegu
Dagana *52 B3* N Senegal
Dagda *84 D4* Krāslava, SE Latvia
Dagden *see* Hiiumaa
Dagenham *67 B8* United Kingdom
Dağliq Quarabağ *see* Nagorno-Karabakh
Dagö *see* Hiiumaa
Dagupan *117 E1 off.* Dagupan City. Luzon, N Philippines
Dagupan City *see* Dagupan
Dahm, Ramlat *99 B6 desert* NW Yemen
Dahomey *see* Benin
Daihoku *see* T'aipei
Daimiel *70 D3* Castilla-La Mancha, C Spain
Daimoniá *83 B7* Pelopónnisos, S Greece
Dainan *see* T'ainan
Daingin, Bá an *see* Dingle Bay
Dairen *see* Dalian
Dakar *52 B3 country capital* W Senegal
Dakhla *see* Ad Dakhla
Dakoro *53 G3* Maradi, S Niger
Đakovica *see* Gjakovë
Đakovo *78 C3 var.* Djakovo, *Hung.* Diakovár. Osijek-Baranja, E Croatia
Dakshin *see* Deccan
Dalain Hob *104 D3 var.* Ejin Qi. Nei Mongol Zizhiqu, N China
Dalai Nor *see* Hulun Nur
Dalaman *94 A4* Muğla, SW Turkey
Dalandzadgad *105 E3* Ömnögovĭ, S Mongolia
Đa Lat *115 E6* Lâm Đông, S Vietnam
Dalby *127 D5* Queensland, E Australia
Dale City *19 E4* Virginia, NE USA
Dalhart *27 E1* Texas, SW USA
Dali *106 A6 var.* Xiaguan. Yunnan, SW China
Dalian *106 D4 var.* Dairen, Dalien, Jay Dairen, Lüda, Ta-lien, *Rus.* Dalny. Liaoning, NE China
Dalien *see* Dalian
Dallas *27 G2* Texas, SW USA
Dalmacija *78 B4 Eng.* Dalmatia, *Ger.* Dalmatien, *It.* Dalmazia. *cultural region* S Croatia
Dalmatia/Dalmatien/Dalmazia *see* Dalmacija
Dalny *see* Dalian
Dalton *20 D1* Georgia, SE USA
Dálvvadis *see* Jokkmokk
Daly Waters *126 A2* Northern Territory, N Australia
Damachava *85 A6 var.* Damachova, *Pol.* Domaczewo, *Rus.* Domachëvo. Brestskaya Voblasts', SW Belarus
Damachova *see* Damachava
Damān *112 C4* Damān and Diu, W India
Damara *54 C4* Ombella-Mpoko, S Central African Republic
Damas *see* Dimashq
Damasco *see* Dimashq
Damascus *see* Dimashq
Qolleh-ye Damavand *98 D3 mountain* N Iran
Damietta *see* Dumyāt
Dammām *see* Ad Dammān
Damoûr *97 A5 var.* Ad Dāmūr. W Lebanon
Dampier *124 A4* Western Australia
Dampier, Selat *117 F4 strait* Papua, E Indonesia
Damqawt *99 D6 var.* Damqut. E Yemen
Damqut *see* Damqawt
Damxung *104 C5 var.* Gongtang. Xizang Zizhiqu, W China
Danakil Desert *50 D4 var.* Afar Depression, Danakil Plain. *desert* E Africa
Danakil Plain *see* Danakil Desert
Danané *52 D5* W Ivory Coast
Đă Nâng *115 E5 prev.* Tourane. Quang Nam-Đa Nâng, C Vietnam
Danborg *see* Daneborg
Dandong *106 D3 var.* Tan-tung; *prev.* An-tung. Liaoning, NE China
Daneborg *61 E3 var.* Danborg. Tunu, N Greenland
Dänew *see* Galkynyş
Dangara *see* Danghara
Dangerous Archipelago *see* Tuamotu, Îles
Danghara *101 E3 Rus.* Dangara. SW Tajikistan
Danghe Nanshan *104 D3 mountain range* W China
Dang Raek, Phanom/Dangrek, Chaîne des *see* Dângrêk, Chuŏr Phnum
Chuor Phnum Dangrek *115 D5 var.* Phanom Dang Raek, Phanom Dong Rak, *Fr.* Chaîne des Dangrek. *mountain range* Cambodia/Thailand
Dangriga *30 C1 prev.* Stann Creek. Stann Creek, E Belize
Danish West Indies *see* Virgin Islands (US)
Danlí *30 D2* El Paraíso, S Honduras
Danmark *see* Denmark
Danmarksstraedet *see* Denmark Strait
Dannenberg *72 C3* Niedersachsen, N Germany
Dannevirke *128 D4* Manawatu-Wanganui, North Island, New Zealand
Dantzig *see* Gdańsk
Danube *59 E4 Bul.* Dunav, *Cz.* Dunaj, *Ger.* Donau, *Hung.* Duna, *Rom.* Dunărea. *river* C Europe
Danubian Plain *82 C2 Eng.* Danubian Plain. *lowlands* N Bulgaria
Danubian Plain *see* Dunavska Ravnina
Danum *see* Doncaster
Danville *19 E5* Virginia, NE USA
Danxian/Dan Xian *see* Danzhou
Danzhou *106 C7 prev.* Danxian, Dan Xian, Nada. Hainan, S China
Danzig *see* Gdańsk
Danziger Bucht *see* Danzig, Gulf of
Danzig, Gulf of *76 C2 var.* Gulf of Gdańsk, *Ger.* Danziger Bucht, *Pol.* Zakota Gdańska, *Rus.* Gdan'skaya Bukhta. *gulf* N Poland
Daqm *see* Duqm
Dar'ā *97 B5 var.* Der'a, *Fr.* Déraa. Dar'ā, SW Syria
Darabani *86 C3* Botoșani, NW Romania
Daraut-Kurgan *see* Daroot-Korgon
Dardanelles *94 A2 Eng.* Dardanelles. *strait* NW Turkey
Dardanelles *see* Çanakkale Boğazı
Dardanelli *see* Çanakkale
Dar-el-Beida *see* Casablanca
Dar es Salaam *51 C7* Dar es Salaam, E Tanzania
Darfield *129 C6* Canterbury, South Island, New Zealand
Darfur *50 A4 var.* Darfur Massif. *cultural region* W Sudan
Darfur Massif *see* Darfur
Darhan *105 E2* Darhan Uul, N Mongolia
Darién, Golfo del *see* Darien, Gulf of
Darien, Gulf of *36 A2 Sp.* Golfo del Darién. *gulf* S Caribbean Sea
Darien, Isthmus of *see* Panama, Istmo de
Darién, Serranía del *31 H5 mountain range* Colombia/Panama
Dario *see* Ciudad Darío
Dariorigum *see* Vannes
Darjeeling *see* Dārjiling
Dārjiling *113 F3 prev.* Darjeeling. West Bengal, NE India
Darling River *127 C6 river* New South Wales, SE Australia
Darlington *67 D5* N England, United Kingdom
Darmstadt *73 B5* Hessen, SW Germany
Darnah *49 G2 var.* Dérna. NE Libya
Darnley, Cape *132 D2 cape* Antarctica
Daroca *71 E2* Aragón, NE Spain
Daroot-Korgon *101 F3 var.* Daraut-Kurgan. Oshskaya Oblast', SW Kyrgyzstan
Dartford *67 B8* SE England, United Kingdom
Dartmoor *67 C7 moorland* SW England, United Kingdom
Dartmouth *17 F4* Nova Scotia, SE Canada
Darvaza *see* Derweze, Turkmenistan
Darwin *124 D2 prev.* Palmerston, Port Darwin. *territory capital* Northern Territory, N Australia
Darwin, Isla *38 A4 island* Galápagos, Galapagos Islands, W Ecuador
Dashhowuz *see* Daşoguz
Dashkawka *85 D6 Rus.* Dashkovka. Mahilyowskaya Voblasts', E Belarus
Dashkovka *see* Dashkawka
Daşoguz *100 C2 Rus.* Dashkhovuz, *Turkm.* Dashhowuz; *prev.* Tashauz. Daşoguz Welaýaty, N Turkmenistan
Đa, Sông *see* Black River
Datong *106 C3 var.* Tatung, Ta-t'ung. Shanxi, C China
Daugava *see* Western Dvina
Daugavpils *84 D4 Ger.* Dünaburg; *prev. Rus.* Dvinsk. Daugvapils, SE Latvia
Daung Kyun *115 B6 island* S Myanmar (Burma)
Dauphiné *69 D5 cultural region* E France
Dāvangere *110 C2* Karnātaka, W India
Davao *117 F3 off.* Davao City. Mindanao, S Philippines
Davao City *see* Davao
Davao Gulf *117 F3 gulf* Mindanao, S Philippines
Davenport *23 G3* Iowa, C USA
David *31 E5* Chiriquí, W Panama
Davie Ridge *119 A5 undersea ridge* W Indian Ocean
Davis *132 D3 Australian research station* Antarctica
Davis Sea *132 D3 sea* Antarctica
Davis Strait *60 B3 strait* Baffin Bay/Labrador Sea
Dawei *115 B5 var.* Tavoy, Htawei. Tanintharyi, S Myanmar (Burma)
Dawlat Qaṭar *see* Qatar
Dax *69 B6 var.* Ax; *anc.* Aquae Augustae, Aquae Tarbelicae. Landes, SW France
Dayr az Zawr *96 D3 var.* Deir ez Zor. Dayr az Zawr, E Syria
Dayton *18 C4* Ohio, N USA
Daytona Beach *21 E4* Florida, SE USA
De Aar *56 C5* Northern Cape, C South Africa
Dead Sea *97 B6 var.* Bahret Lut, Lacus Asphaltites, *Ar.* Al Baḥr al Mayyit, Baḥrat Lūt, *Heb.* Yam HaMelaḥ. *salt lake* Israel/Jordan
Deán Funes *42 C3* Córdoba, C Argentina
Death Valley *25 C7 valley* California, W USA
Deatnu *62 D2 Fin.* Tenojoki, *Nor.* Tana. *river* Finland/Norway
Debar *79 D6 Ger.* Dibra, *Turk.* Debre. W FYR Macedonia
De Behagle *see* Laï
Dębica *77 D5* Podkarpackie, SE Poland
De Bildt *see* De Bilt
De Bilt *64 C3 var.* De Bildt. Utrecht, C Netherlands
Dębno *76 B3* Zachodnio-pomorskie, NW Poland
Debre *see* Debar
Debrecen *77 D6 Ger.* Debreczin, *Rom.* Debrețin; *prev.* Debreczen. Hajdú-Bihar, E Hungary
Debreczen/Debreczin *see* Debrecen
Debrețin *see* Debrecen
Decatur *20 C1* Alabama, S USA
Decatur *18 B4* Illinois, N USA
Deccan *112 D5 Hind.* Dakshin. *plateau* C India
Děčín *76 B4 Ger.* Tetschen. Ústecký Kraj, NW Czech Republic
Dedeagaç/Dedeagach *see* Alexandroúpoli
Dedemsvaart *64 E3* Overijssel, E Netherlands
Dee *66 C3 river* NE Scotland, United Kingdom
Deering *14 C2* Alaska, USA
Deés *see* Dej
Deggendorf *73 D6* Bayern, SE Germany
Değirmenlik *80 C5 Gk.* Kythréa. N Cyprus
Deh Bīd *see* Şafāshahr
Dehli *see* Delhi
Deh Shū *100 D5 var.* Deshu. Helmand, S Afghanistan
Deinze *65 B5* Oost-Vlaanderen, NW Belgium
Deir ez Zor *see* Dayr az Zawr
Deirgeirt, Loch *see* Derg, Lough
Dej *86 B3 Hung.* Dés; *prev.* Deés. Cluj, NW Romania
De Jouwer *see* Joure
Dekéleia *see* Dhekélia
Dékoa *54 C4* Kémo, C Central African Republic
De Land *21 E4* Florida, SE USA
Delano *25 C7* California, W USA
Delārām *100 D5* Nīmrūz, SW Afghanistan
Delaware *18 D4* Ohio, N USA
Delaware *19 F4 off.* State of Delaware, *also known as* Blue Hen State, Diamond State, First State. *state* NE USA
Delft *64 B4* Zuid-Holland, W Netherlands
Delfzijl *64 E1* Groningen, NE Netherlands
Delgo *50 B3* Northern, N Sudan
Delhi *112 D3 var.* Dehli, *Hind.* Dilli, *hist.* Shahjahanabad. *union territory capital* Delhi, N India
Delicias *28 D2 var.* Ciudad Delicias. Chihuahua, N Mexico
Déli-Kárpátok *see* Carpații Meridionali
Delmenhorst *72 B3* Niedersachsen, NW Germany
Del Rio *27 F4* Texas, SW USA
Deltona *21 E4* Florida, SE USA
Demba *55 D6* Kasai-Occidental, C Dem. Rep. Congo
Dembia *54 D4* Mbomou, SE Central African Republic
Demchok *104 A5 var.* Dèmqog. *disputed region* China/India
Demerara Plain *34 C2 abyssal plain* W Atlantic Ocean
Deming *26 C3* New Mexico, SW USA
Demmin *72 C2* Mecklenburg-Vorpommern, NE Germany
Demopolis *20 C2* Alabama, S USA
Dèmqog *104 A5 var.* Demchok. China/India
Denali *see* McKinley, Mount
Denau *see* Denow
Dender *65 B6 Fr.* Dendre. *river* W Belgium
Dendre *see* Dender
Denekamp *64 E3* Overijssel, E Netherlands
Den Haag *see* 's-Gravenhage
Denham *125 A5* Western Australia
Den Ham *64 E3* Overijssel, E Netherlands
Den Helder *64 C2* Noord-Holland, NW Netherlands
Dénia *71 F4* País Valenciano, E Spain
Deniliquin *127 C7* New South Wales, SE Australia
Denison *23 F3* Iowa, C USA
Denison *27 G2* Texas, SW USA
Denizli *94 B4* Denizli, SW Turkey
Denmark *63 A7 off.* Kingdom of Denmark, *Dan.* Danmark; *anc.* Hafnia. *country* N Europe
Denmark, Kingdom of *see* Denmark
Denmark Strait *60 D4 var.* Danmarksstraedet. *strait* Greenland/Iceland
Dennery *33 F1* E Saint Lucia
Denow *101 E3 Rus.* Denau. Surkhondaryo Viloyati, S Uzbekistan
Denpasar *116 D5 prev.* Paloe. Bali, C Indonesia
Denton *27 G2* Texas, SW USA
D'Entrecasteaux Islands *122 B3 island group* SE Papua New Guinea
Denver *22 D4 state capital* Colorado, C USA
Der'a/Derá/Déraa *see* Dar'ā
Dera Ghāzi Khān *112 C2 var.* Dera Ghāzikhān. Punjab, C Pakistan
Dera Ghāzikhān *see* Dera Ghāzi Khān
Deravica *79 D5 mountain* S Serbia
Derbent *89 B8* Respublika Dagestan, SW Russian Federation
Derby *67 D6* C England, United Kingdom
Dereli *see* Gónnoi
Dergachi *see* Derhachi
Derg, Lough *67 A6 Ir.* Loch Deirgeirt. *lake* W Ireland
Derhachi *87 G2 Rus.* Dergachi. Kharkivs'ka Oblast', E Ukraine
De Ridder *20 A3* Louisiana, S USA
Dérna *see* Darnah
Derry *see* Londonderry
Dertosa *see* Tortosa
Derventa *78 B3* Republika Srpska, N Bosnia and Herzegovina
Derweze *100 C2 Rus.* Darvaza. Ahal Welaýaty, C Turkmenistan
Dés *see* Dej
Deschutes River *24 B3 river* Oregon, NW USA
Desē *50 C4 var.* Desse, *It.* Dessie. Āmara, N Ethiopia
Deseado, Río *43 B7 river* S Argentina
Desertas, Ilhas *48 A2 island group* Madeira, Portugal, NE Atlantic Ocean
Deshu *see* Deh Shū
Des Moines *23 F3 state capital* Iowa, C USA
Desna *87 E2 river* Russian Federation/Ukraine
Dessau *72 C4* Sachsen-Anhalt, E Germany
Desse *see* Desē
Dessie *see* Desē
Destêrro *see* Florianópolis
Detroit *18 D3* Michigan, N USA
Detroit Lakes *23 F2* Minnesota, N USA
Deurne *65 D5* Noord-Brabant, SE Netherlands
Deutschendorf *see* Poprad
Deutsch-Eylau *see* Iława
Deutsch Krone *see* Wałcz
Deutschland/Deutschland, Bundesrepublik *see* Germany
Deutsch-Südwestafrika *see* Namibia
Deva *86 B4 Ger.* Diemrich, *Hung.* Déva. Hunedoara, W Romania
Déva *see* Deva
Deva *see* Chester
Devana *see* Aberdeen
Devana Castra *see* Chester
Devdelija *see* Gevgelija
Deventer *64 D3* Overijssel, E Netherlands
Devils Lake *23 E1* North Dakota, N USA
Devoll *see* Devollit, Lumi i
Devollit, Lumi i *79 D6 var.* Devoll. *river* SE Albania
Devon Island *15 F2 prev.* North Devon Island. *island* Parry Islands, Nunavut, NE Canada
Devonport *127 C8* Tasmania, SE Australia
Devrek *94 C2* Zonguldak, N Turkey
Dexter *23 H5* Missouri, C USA
Deynau *see* Galkynyş
Dezfūl *98 C3 var.* Dizful. Khūzestān, SW Iran
Dezhou *106 D4* Shandong, E China
Dhaka *113 G4 prev.* Dacca. *country capital* Dhaka, C Bangladesh
Dhanbād *113 F4* Jhārkhand, NE India
Dhekélia *80 C5 Eng.* Dhekelia, *Gk.* Dekéleia. *UK air base* SE Cyprus
see Dhekélia
Dhidhimótikhon *see* Didymóteicho
Dhíkti Ori *see* Díkti
Dhodhekánisos *see* Dodekánisa
Dhomokós *see* Domokós
Dhráma *see* Dráma
Dhrepanon, Akrotírio *see* Drépano, Akrotirio
Dhún na nGall, Bá *see* Donegal Bay
Dhuusa Marreeb *51 E5 var.* Dusa Marreb, *It.* Dusa Mareb. Galguduud, C Somalia
Diakovár *see* Đakovo
Diamantina, Chapada *41 F3 mountain range* E Brazil
Diamantina Fracture Zone *119 E6 tectonic feature* E Indian Ocean
Diamond State *see* Delaware
Diarbekr *see* Diyarbakır
Dibio *see* Dijon
Dibra *see* Debar
Dibrugarh *113 H3* Assam, NE India
Dickinson *22 D2* North Dakota, N USA
Dicle *see* Tigris
Didimotiho *see* Didymóteicho
Didymóteicho *82 D3 var.* Dhidhimótikhon, Didimotiho. Anatolikí Makedonía kai Thráki, NE Greece
Diedenhofen *see* Thionville
Diekirch *65 D7* Diekirch, C Luxembourg
Diemrich *see* Deva
Điên Biên *114 D3 var.* Bien Bien, Dien Bien Phu. Lai Châu, N Vietnam
Dien Bien Phu *see* Điên Biên
Diepenbeek *65 D6* Limburg, NE Belgium
Diepholz *72 B3* Niedersachsen, NW Germany
Dieppe *68 C2* Seine-Maritime, N France
Dieren *64 D4* Gelderland, E Netherlands
Differdange *65 D8* Luxembourg, SW Luxembourg
Digne *69 D6 var.* Digne-les-Bains. Alpes-de-Haute-Provence, SE France
Digne-les-Bains *see* Digne
Digoel *see* Digul, Sungai
Digoin *68 C4* Saône-et-Loire, C France
Digul, Sungai *117 H5 prev.* Digoel. *river* Papua, E Indonesia
Dihang *see* Brahmaputra
Dijlah *see* Tigris
Dijon *68 D4 anc.* Dibio. Côte d'Or, C France
Dikhil *50 D4* SW Djibouti
Dikson *92 D2* Taymyrskiy (Dolgano-Nenetskiy) Avtonomnyy Okrug, N Russian Federation
Díkti *83 D8 var.* Dhíkti Ori. *mountain range* Kríti, Greece, E Mediterranean Sea
Dili *117 F5 var.* Dilli, Dilly. *country capital* N East Timor
Dilia *53 G3 var.* Dillia. *river* SE Niger
Di Linh *115 E6* Lâm Đông, S Vietnam
Dilli *see* Dili, East Timor
Dilli *see* Delhi, India
Dillia *see* Dilia
Dilling *50 B4 var.* Ad Dalanj. Southern Kordofan, C Sudan
Dillon *22 B2* Montana, NW USA
Dilly *see* Dili
Dilolo *55 D7* Katanga, S Dem. Rep. Congo
Dimashq *97 B5 var.* Ash Shām, Esh Sham, *Eng.* Damascus, *Fr.* Damas, *It.* Damasco. *country capital* Dimashq, SW Syria
Dimitrovgrad *82 D3* Khaskovo, S Bulgaria
Dimitrovgrad *89 C6 prev.* Caribrod. Serbia, SE Serbia
Dimitrovo *see* Pernik
Dimovo *82 B1* Vidin, NW Bulgaria
Dinajpur *113 F3* Rajshahi, NW Bangladesh
Dinan *68 B3* Côtes d'Armor, NW France
Dinant *65 C7* Namur, S Belgium
Dinar *94 B4* Afyon, SW Turkey
Dinara *see* Dinaric Alps
Dinaric Alps *78 C4 var.* Dinara. *mountain range* Bosnia and Herzegovina/Croatia
Dindigul *110 C3* Tamil Nādu, SE India
Dingle Bay *67 A6 Ir.* Bá an Daingin. *bay* SW Ireland
Dinguiraye *52 C4* N Guinea
Diourbel *52 B3* W Senegal
Dirē Dawa *51 D5* Dirē Dawa, E Ethiopia
Dirk Hartog Island *125 A5 island* Western Australia
Dirschau *see* Tczew
Disappointment, Lake *124 C4 salt lake* Western Australia
Discovery Bay *32 B4* Middlesex, Jamaica, Greater Antilles, C Jamaica Caribbean Sea
Disko Bugt *see* Qeqertarsuup Tunua
Dispur *113 G3 state capital* Assam, NE India
Divinópolis *41 F4* Minas Gerais, SE Brazil
Divo *52 D5* S Ivory Coast
Divodurum Mediomatricum *see* Metz
Diyarbakır *95 E4 var.* Diarbekr; *anc.* Amida. Diyarbakır, SE Turkey
Dizful *see* Dezfūl
Djailolo *see* Halmahera, Pulau
Djajapura *see* Jayapura
Djakarta *see* Jakarta
Djakovo *see* Đakovo
Djambala *55 B6* Plateaux, C Congo
Djambi *see* Hari, Batang
Djambi *see* Jambi
Djanet *49 E4 prev.* Fort Charlet. SE Algeria
Djéblé *see* Jablah
Djelfa *48 D2 var.* El Djelfa. N Algeria
Djéma *54 D4* Haut-Mbomou, E Central African Republic
Djember *see* Jember
Djérablous *see* Jarābulus
Djerba *49 F2 var.* Djerba, Jazīrat Jarbah. *island* E Tunisia
Djerba *see* Jerba, Île de
Djérem *54 B4 river* C Cameroon
Djevdjelija *see* Gevgelija
Djibouti *50 D4 var.* Jibuti. *country capital* E Djibouti
Djibouti *50 D4 off.* Republic of Djibouti, *var.* Jibuti; *prev.* French Somaliland, French Territory of the Afars and Issas, *Fr.* Côte Française des Somalis, Territoire Français des Afars et des Issas. *country* E Africa
Djibouti, Republic of *see* Djibouti
Djokjakarta *see* Yogyakarta
Djourab, Erg du *54 C2 desert* N Chad
Djúpivogur *61 E5* Austurland, SE Iceland
Dmitriyevsk *see* Makiyivka
Dnepr *see* Dnieper
Dneprodzerzhinsk *see* Romaniv
Dneprodzerzhinskoye Vodokhranilishche *see* Dniprodzerzhyns'ke Vodoskhovyshche
Dnepropetrovsk *see* Dnipropetrovs'k
Dneprorudnoye *see* Dniprorudne
Dnestr *see* Dniester
Dnieper *59 F4 Bel.* Dnyapro, *Rus.* Dnepr, *Ukr.* Dnipro. *river* E Europe
Dnieper Lowland *87 E2 Bel.* Prydnyaprowskaya Nizina, *Ukr.* Prydniprovs'ka Nyzovyna. *lowlands* Belarus/Ukraine
Dniester *59 E4 Rom.* Nistru, *Rus.* Dnestr, *Ukr.* Dnister; *anc.* Tyras. *river* Moldova/Ukraine
Dnipro *see* Dnieper
Dniprodzerzhyns'k *see* Romaniv
Dniprodzerzhyns'ke Vodoskhovyshche *87 F3 Rus.* Dneprodzerzhinskoye Vodokhranilishche. *reservoir* C Ukraine
Dnipropetrovs'k *87 F3 Rus.* Dnepropetrovsk; *prev.* Yekaterinoslav. Dnipropetrovs'ka Oblast', E Ukraine
Dniprorudne *87 F3 Rus.* Dneprorudnoye. Zaporiz'ka Oblast', SE Ukraine
Dnister *see* Dniester
Dnyapro *see* Dnieper
Doba *54 C4* Logone-Oriental, S Chad
Döbeln *72 D4* Sachsen, E Germany
Doberai Peninsula *117 G4 Dut.* Vogelkop. *peninsula* Papua, E Indonesia

Doboj – El Vendrell

Doboj *78 C3* Republiks Srpska, N Bosnia and Herzegovina
Dobre Miasto *76 D2 Ger.* Guttstadt. Warmińsko-mazurskie, NE Poland
Dobrich *82 E1 Rom.* Bazargic; *prev.* Tolbukhin. Dobrich, NE Bulgaria
Dobrush *85 D7* Homyel'skaya Voblasts', SE Belarus
Dobryn' *see* Dabryn'
Dodecanese *83 D6 var.* Nóties Sporádes, *Eng.* Dodecanese; *prev.* Dhodhekánisos, Dodekanisos. *island group* SE Greece
Dodecanese *see* Dodekánisa
Dodekanisos *see* Dodekánisa
Dodge City *23 E5* Kansas, C USA
Dodoma *47 D5 country capital* Dodoma, C Tanzania
Dogana *74 E1* NE San Marino Europe
Dogo *109 B6 island* Oki-shotō, SW Japan
Dogondoutchi *53 F3* Dosso, SW Niger
Dogrular *see* Pravda
Doğubayazıt *95 F3* Ağrı, E Turkey
Doğu Karadeniz Dağları *95 E3 var.* Anadolu Dağları. *mountain range* NE Turkey
Doha *see* Ad Dawḩah
Doire *see* Londonderry
Dokkum *64 D1* Friesland, N Netherlands
Dokuchayevs'k *87 G3 var.* Dokuchayevsk. Donets'ka Oblast', SE Ukraine
Dokuchayevsk *see* Dokuchayevs'k
Doldrums Fracture Zone *44 C4 fracture zone* W Atlantic Ocean
Dôle *68 D4* Jura, E France
Dolina *see* Dolyna
Dolinskaya *see* Dolyns'ka
Dolisie *55 B6 prev.* Loubomo. Niari, S Congo
Dolomites *74 C1 var.* Dolomiti, *Eng.* Dolomites. *mountain range* NE Italy
Dolomites/Dolomiti *see* Dolomitiche, Alpi
Dolores *42 D4* Buenos Aires, E Argentina
Dolores *30 B1* Petén, N Guatemala
Dolores *42 D4* Soriano, SW Uruguay
Dolores Hidalgo *29 E4 var.* Ciudad de Dolores Hidalgo. Guanajuato, C Mexico
Dolyna *86 B2 Rus.* Dolina. Ivano-Frankivs'ka Oblast', W Ukraine
Dolyns'ka *87 F3 Rus.* Dolinskaya. Kirovohrads'ka Oblast', S Ukraine
Domachëvo/Domaczewo *see* Damachava
Dombås *63 B5* Oppland, S Norway
Domel Island *see* Letsôk-aw Kyun
Domesnes, Cape *see* Kolkasrags
Domeyko *42 B3* Atacama, N Chile
Dominica *33 H4 off.* Commonwealth of Dominica. *country* E West Indies
Dominica Channel *see* Martinique Passage
Dominica, Commonwealth of *see* Dominica
Dominican Republic *33 E2 country* C West Indies
Domokós *83 B5 var.* Dhomokós. Stereá Ellás, C Greece
Don *89 B6 var.* Duna, Tanais. *river* SW Russian Federation
Donau *see* Danube
Donauwörth *73 C6* Bayern, S Germany
Don Benito *70 C3* Extremadura, W Spain
Doncaster *67 D5 anc.* Danum. N England, United Kingdom
Dondo *56 B1* Cuanza Norte, NW Angola
Donegal *67 B5 Ir.* Dún na nGall. Donegal, NW Ireland
Donegal Bay *67 A5 Ir.* Bá Dhún na nGall. *bay* NW Ireland
Donets *87 G2 river* Russian Federation/Ukraine
Donets'k *87 G3 Rus.* Donetsk; *prev.* Stalino. Donets'ka Oblast', E Ukraine
Dongfang *106 B7 var.* Basuo. Hainan, S China
Dongguan *106 C6* Guangdong, S China
Đông Hà *114 E4* Quang Tri, C Vietnam
Dong Hai *see* East China Sea
Đông Hơi *114 D4* Quang Binh, C Vietnam
Dongliao *see* Liaoyuan
Dongola *50 B3 var.* Donqola, Dunqulah. Northern, N Sudan
Dongou *55 C5* Likouala, NE Congo
Dong Rak, Phanom *see* Dângrêk, Chuŏr Phnum
Dongting Hu *106 C5 var.* Tung-t'ing Hu. *lake* S China
Donostia-San Sebastián *71 E1* País Vasco, N Spain
Donqola *see* Dongola
Doolow *51 D5* Sumalē, E Ethiopia
Doornik *see* Tournai
Door Peninsula *18 C2 peninsula* Wisconsin, N USA
Dooxo Nugaaleed *51 E5 var.* Nogal Valley. *valley* E Somalia
Dordogne *69 B5 cultural region* SW France
Dordogne *69 B5 river* W France
Dordrecht *64 C4 var.* Dordt, Dort. Zuid-Holland, SW Netherlands
Dordt *see* Dordrecht
Dorohoi *86 C3* Botoşani, NE Romania
Dorotea *62 C4* Västerbotten, N Sweden
Dorpat *see* Tartu
Dorre Island *125 A5 island* Western Australia
Dort *see* Dordrecht
Dortmund *72 A4* Nordrhein-Westfalen, W Germany
Dos Hermanas *70 C4* Andalucía, S Spain
Dospad Dagh *see* Rhodope Mountains
Dospat *82 C3* Smolyan, S Bulgaria
Dothan *20 D3* Alabama, S USA
Dotnuva *84 B4* Kaunas, C Lithuania
Douai *68 C2 prev.* Douay; *anc.* Duacum. Nord, N France
Douala *55 A5 var.* Duala. Littoral, W Cameroon
Douay *see* Douai
Douglas *67 C5 dependent territory capital* E Isle of Man
Douglas *26 C3* Arizona, SW USA
Douglas *22 D3* Wyoming, C USA
Douma *see* Dūmā
Douro *see* Duero
Douvres *see* Dover
Dover *67 E7 Fr.* Douvres, *Lat.* Dubris Portus. SE England, United Kingdom
Dover *19 F4 state capital* Delaware, NE USA
Dover, Strait of *68 C2 var.* Straits of Dover, *Fr.* Pas de Calais. *strait* England, United Kingdom/ France
Dover, Straits of *see* Dover, Strait of
Dovrefjell *63 B5 plateau* S Norway
Downpatrick *67 B5 Ir.* Dún Pádraig. SE Northern Ireland, United Kingdom
Dozen *109 B6 island* Oki-shotō, SW Japan
Drâa, Hammada du *see* Dra, Hamada du
Drač/Draç *see* Durrës
Drachten *64 D2* Friesland, N Netherlands
Drăgăşani *86 B5* Vâlcea, SW Romania
Dragoman *82 B2* Sofiya, W Bulgaria
Dra, Hamada du *48 C3 var.* Hammada du Drâa, Haut Plateau du Dra. *plateau* W Algeria
Dra, Haut Plateau du *see* Dra, Hamada du
Drahichyn *85 B6 Pol.* Drohiczyn Poleski, *Rus.* Drogichin. Brestskaya Voblasts', SW Belarus
Drakensberg *56 D5 mountain range* Lesotho/ South Africa
Drake Passage *35 B8 passage* Atlantic Ocean/ Pacific Ocean
Dralfa *82 D2* Tŭrgovishte, N Bulgaria
Dráma *82 C3 var.* Dhráma. Anatolikí Makedonía kai Thráki, NE Greece
Dramburg *see* Drawsko Pomorskie
Drammen *63 B6* Buskerud, S Norway
Drau *see* Drava
Drava *78 C3 var.* Drau, *Eng.* Drave, *Hung.* Dráva. *river* C Europe
Dráva/Drave *see* Drau/Drava
Drawsko Pomorskie *76 B3 Ger.* Dramburg. Zachodnio-pomorskie, NW Poland
Drépano, Akrotírio *82 C4 var.* Akrotírio Dhrepanon. *headland* N Greece
Drepanum *see* Trapani
Dresden *72 D4* Sachsen, E Germany
Drin *see* Drinit, Lumi
Drina *78 C3 river* Bosnia and Herzegovina/Serbia
Drinit, Lumi *79 D5 var.* Drin. *river* NW Albania
Drinit të Zi, Lumi i *see* Black Drin
Drissa *see* Drysa
Drobeta-Turnu Severin *86 B5 prev.* Turnu Severin. Mehedinţi, SW Romania
Drogheda *67 B5 Ir.* Droichead Átha. NE Ireland
Drogichin *see* Drahichyn
Drogobych *see* Drohobych
Drohiczyn Poleski *see* Drahichyn
Drohobych *86 B2 Pol.* Drohobycz, *Rus.* Drogobych. L'vivs'ka Oblast', NW Ukraine
Drohobycz *see* Drohobych
Droichead Átha *see* Drogheda
Drôme *69 D5 cultural region* E France
Dronning Maud Land *132 B2 physical region* Antarctica
Drontheim *see* Trondheim
Drug *see* Durg
Druk-yul *see* Bhutan
Drummondville *17 E4* Québec, SE Canada
Druskieniki *see* Druskininkai
Druskininkai *85 B5 Pol.* Druskienniki. Alytus, S Lithuania
Dryden *16 B3* Ontario, C Canada
Drysa *85 D5 Rus.* Drissa. *river* N Belarus
Duacum *see* Douai
Duala *see* Douala
Dubai *see* Dubayy
Dubăsari *86 D3 Rus.* Dubossary. NE Moldova
Dubawnt *15 F4 river* Nunavut, NW Canada
Dubayy *98 D4 Eng.* Dubai. Dubayy, NE United Arab Emirates
Dubbo *127 D6* New South Wales, SE Australia
Dublin *67 B5 Ir.* Baile Átha Cliath; *anc.* Eblana. *country capital* Dublin, E Ireland
Dublin *21 E2* Georgia, SE USA
Dubno *86 C2* Rivnens'ka Oblast', NW Ukraine
Dubossary *see* Dubăsari
Dubris Portus *see* Dover
Dubrovnik *79 B5 It.* Ragusa. Dubrovnik-Neretva, SE Croatia
Dubuque *23 G3* Iowa, C USA
Dudelange *65 D8 var.* Forge du Sud, *Ger.* Dudelingen. Luxembourg, S Luxembourg
Dudelingen *see* Dudelange
Duero *70 D2 Port.* Douro. *river* Portugal/Spain
Duero *70 B2 Port.* Douro. *river* Portugal/Spain
Duesseldorf *see* Düsseldorf
Duffel *65 C5* Antwerpen, C Belgium
Dugi Otok *78 A4 var.* Isola Grossa, *It.* Isola Lunga. *island* W Croatia
Duinekerke *see* Dunkerque
Duisburg *72 A4 prev.* Duisburg-Hamborn. Nordrhein-Westfalen, W Germany
Duisburg-Hamborn *see* Duisburg
Duiven *64 D4* Gelderland, E Netherlands
Duk Faiwil *51 B5* Jonglei, SE Sudan
Dulan *104 D4 var.* Qagan Us. Qinghai, C China
Dulce, Golfo *31 E5 gulf* S Costa Rica
Dulce, Golfo *see* Izabal, Lago de
Dülmen *72 A4* Nordrhein-Westfalen, W Germany
Dulovo *82 E1* Silistra, NE Bulgaria
Duluth *23 G2* Minnesota, N USA
Dūmā *97 B5 Fr.* Douma. Dimashq, SW Syria
Dumas *27 E1* Texas, SW USA
Dumfries *66 C4* S Scotland, United Kingdom
Dumont d'Urville *132 C4 French research station* Antarctica
Dumyāṭ *50 B1 var.* Dumyât, *Eng.* Damietta. N Egypt
Duna *see* Danube, C Europe
Düna *see* Western Dvina
Duna *see* Don, Russian Federation
Dünaburg *see* Daugavpils
Dunaj *see* Wien, Austria
Dunaj *see* Danube, C Europe
Dunapentele *see* Dunaújváros
Dunărea *see* Danube
Dunaújváros *77 C7 prev.* Dunapentele, Sztálinváros. Fejér, C Hungary
Dunav *see* Danube
Duncan *27 G2* Oklahoma, C USA
Dundalk *67 B5 Ir.* Dún Dealgan. Louth, NE Ireland
Dún Dealgan *see* Dundalk
Dundee *56 D4* KwaZulu/Natal, E South Africa
Dundee *66 C4* E Scotland, United Kingdom
Dunedin *129 B7* Otago, South Island, New Zealand
Dunfermline *66 C4* C Scotland, United Kingdom
Dungu *55 E5* Orientale, NE Dem. Rep. Congo
Dungun *116 B3 var.* Kuala Dungun. Terengganu, Peninsular Malaysia
Dunholme *see* Durham
Dunkerque *68 C2 Eng.* Dunkirk, *Flem.* Duinekerke; *prev.* Dunquerque. Nord, N France
Dunkirk *see* Dunkerque
Dún Laoghaire *67 B6 Eng.* Dunleary; *prev.* Kingstown. E Ireland
Dunleary *see* Dún Laoghaire
Dún Pádraig *see* Downpatrick
Dunquerque *see* Dunkerque
Dunqulah *see* Dongola
Dupnitsa *82 C2 prev.* Marek, Stanke Dimitrov. Kyustendil, W Bulgaria
Duqm *99 E5 var.* Daqm. E Oman
Durance *69 D6 river* SE France
Durango *28 D3 var.* Victoria de Durango. Durango, W Mexico
Durango *22 C5* Colorado, C USA
Durankulak *82 E1 Rom.* Răcari; *prev.* Blatnitsa, Duranulac. Dobrich, NE Bulgaria
Durant *27 G2* Oklahoma, C USA
Duranulac *see* Durankulak
Durazzo *see* Durrës
Durban *56 D4 var.* Port Natal. KwaZulu/Natal, E South Africa
Durbe *84 B3 Ger.* Durben. Liepāja, W Latvia
Durben *see* Durbe
Durg *113 E4 prev.* Drug. Chhattīsgarh, C India
Durham *67 D5 hist.* Dunholme. N England, United Kingdom
Durham *21 F1* North Carolina, SE USA
Durocortorum *see* Reims
Durostorum *see* Silistra
Durovernum *see* Canterbury
Durrës *79 C6 var.* Durrësi, Dursi, *It.* Durazzo, *SCr.* Drač, *Turk.* Draç. Durrës, W Albania
Durrësi *see* Durrës
Dursi *see* Durrës
Durūz, Jabal ad *97 C5 mountain* SW Syria
D'Urville Island *128 C4 island* C New Zealand
Dusa Mareb/Dusa Marreb *see* Dhuusa Marreeb
Dushanbe *101 E3 var.* Dyushambe; *prev.* Stalinabad, *Taj.* Stalinobod. *country capital* W Tajikistan
Düsseldorf *72 A4 var.* Duesseldorf. Nordrhein-Westfalen, W Germany
Dŭsti *101 E3 Rus.* Dusti. SW Tajikistan
Dutch East Indies *see* Indonesia
Dutch Guiana *see* Suriname
Dutch Harbor *14 B3* Unalaska Island, Alaska, USA
Dutch New Guinea *see* Papua
Dutch West Indies *see* Netherlands Antilles
Duzdab *see* Zāhedān
Dvina Bay *see* Chëshskaya Guba
Dvinsk *see* Daugavpils
Dyanev *see* Galkynyş
Dyersburg *20 C1* Tennessee, S USA
Dyushambe *see* Dushanbe
Dza Chu *see* Mekong
Dzaudzhikau *see* Vladikavkaz
Dzerzhinsk *89 C5* Nizhegorodskaya Oblast', W Russian Federation
Dzerzhinskiy *see* Nar'yan-Mar
Dzhalal-Abad *101 F2 Kir.* Jalal-Abad. Dzhalal-Abadskaya Oblast', W Kyrgyzstan
Dzhambul *see* Taraz
Dzhankoy *87 F4* Respublika Krym, S Ukraine
Dzharkurgan *see* Jarqo'rg'on
Dzhelandy *101 F3* SE Tajikistan
Dzhergalan *101 G2 Kir.* Jyrgalan. Issyk-Kul'skaya Oblast', NE Kyrgyzstan
Dzhezkazgan *see* Zhezkazgan
Dzhizak *see* Jizzax
Dzhugdzhur, Khrebet *93 G3 mountain range* E Russian Federation
Dzhusaly *92 B4 Kaz.* Zhosaly. Kzylorda, SW Kazakhstan
Działdowo *76 D3* Warmińsko-Mazurskie, C Poland
Dzuunmod *105 E2* Töv, C Mongolia
Dzüün Soyonī Nuruu *see* Eastern Sayans
Dzvina *see* Western Dvina

E

Eagle Pass *27 F4* Texas, SW USA
East Açores Fracture Zone *see* East Azores Fracture Zone
East Antarctica *132 C3 var.* Greater Antarctica. *physical region* Antarctica
East Australian Basin *see* Tasman Basin
East Azores Fracture Zone *44 C3 var.* East Açores Fracture Zone. *tectonic feature* E Atlantic Ocean
Eastbourne *67 E7* SE England, United Kingdom
East Cape *128 E3 headland* North Island, New Zealand
East China Sea *103 E2 Chin.* Dong Hai. *sea* W Pacific Ocean
Easter Fracture Zone *131 G4 tectonic feature* E Pacific Ocean
Easter Island *131 F4 var.* Rapa Nui, Easter Island. *island* E Pacific Ocean
Easter Island *see* Pascua, Isla de
Eastern Desert *46 D3 var.* Aş Şaḩrā' ash Sharqīyah, *Eng.* Arabian Desert, Eastern Desert. *desert* E Egypt
Eastern Desert *see* Sahara el Sharqîya
Eastern Ghats *102 B3 mountain range* SE India
Eastern Sayans *93 E4 Mong.* Dzüün Soyonī Nuruu, *Rus.* Vostochnyy Sayan. *mountain range* Mongolia/Russian Federation
Eastern Sierra Madre *see* Madre Oriental, Sierra
East Falkland *43 D8 var.* Isla Soledad. *island* E Falkland Islands
East Frisian Islands *72 A3 Eng.* East Frisian Islands. *island group* NW Germany
East Frisian Islands *see* Ostfriesische Inseln
East Grand Forks *23 E1* Minnesota, N USA
East Indiaman Ridge *119 D6 undersea ridge* E Indian Ocean
East Indies *130 A3 island group* SE Asia
East Kilbride *66 C4* S Scotland, United Kingdom
East Korea Bay *107 E3 bay* E North Korea
Eastleigh *67 D7* S England, United Kingdom
East London *56 D5 Afr.* Oos-Londen; *prev.* Emonti, Port Rex. Eastern Cape, S South Africa
Eastmain *16 D3 river* Québec, C Canada
East Mariana Basin *120 B1 undersea basin* W Pacific Ocean
East Novaya Zemlya Trough *90 C1 var.* Novaya Zemlya Trough. *trough* W Kara Sea
East Pacific Rise *131 F4 undersea rise* E Pacific Ocean
East Pakistan *see* Bangladesh
East Saint Louis *18 B4* Illinois, N USA
East Scotia Basin *45 C7 undersea basin* SE Scotia Sea
East Sea *108 A4 var.* Sea of Japan, *Rus.* Yapanskoye More. *Sea* NW Pacific Ocean
East Siberian Sea *93 F1 Eng.* East Siberian Sea. *sea* Arctic Ocean
East Siberian Sea *see* Vostochno-Sibirskoye More
East Timor *117 F5 var.* Loro Sae; *prev.* Portuguese Timor, Timor Timur. *country* S Indonesia
Eau Claire *18 A2* Wisconsin, N USA
Eau Claire, Lac à L' *see* St. Clair, Lake
Eauripik Rise *120 B2 undersea rise* W Pacific Ocean
Ebensee *73 D6* Oberösterreich, N Austria
Eberswalde-Finow *72 D3* Brandenburg, E Germany
Ebetsu *108 D2 var.* Ebetu. Hokkaidō, NE Japan
Ebetu *see* Ebetsu
Eblana *see* Dublin
Ebolowa *55 A5* Sud, S Cameroon
Ebon Atoll *122 D2 var.* Epoon. *atoll* Ralik Chain, S Marshall Islands
Ebora *see* Évora
Eboracum *see* York
Ebro *71 E2 river* NE Spain
Eburacum *see* York
Ebusus *see* Eivissa
Ebusus *see* Eivissa
Ebusus *see* Eivissa
Ecbatana *see* Hamadān
Ech Cheliff/Ech Chleff *see* Chlef
Echo Bay *15 E3* Northwest Territories, NW Canada
Echt *65 D5* Limburg, SE Netherlands
Ecija *70 D4 anc.* Astigi. Andalucía, SW Spain
Eckengraf *see* Viesīte
Ecuador *38 B1 off.* Republic of Ecuador. *country* NW South America
Ecuador, Republic of *see* Ecuador
Ed Da'ein *50 A4* Southern Darfur, W Sudan
Ed Damazin *50 C4 var.* Ad Damazīn. Blue Nile, E Sudan
Ed Damer *50 C3 var.* Ad Dāmir, Ad Damar. River Nile, NE Sudan
Ed Debba *50 B3* Northern, N Sudan
Ede *64 D4* Gelderland, C Netherlands
Ede *53 F5* Osun, SW Nigeria
Edéa *55 A5* Littoral, SW Cameroon
Edessa *see* Şanlıurfa
Edfu *see* Idfū
Edgeøya *61 G2 island* S Svalbard
Edgware *67 A7* Harrow, SE England, United Kingdom
Edinburg *27 G5* Texas, SW USA
Edinburgh *66 C4 national capital* S Scotland, United Kingdom
Edingen *see* Enghien
Edirne *94 A2 Eng.* Adrianople; *anc.* Adrianopolis, Hadrianopolis. Edirne, NW Turkey
Edmonds *24 B2* Washington, NW USA
Edmonton *15 E5 province capital* Alberta, SW Canada
Edmundston *17 E4* New Brunswick, SE Canada
Edna *27 G4* Texas, SW USA
Edolo *74 B1* Lombardia, N Italy
Edremit *94 A3* Balıkesir, NW Turkey
Edward, Lake *55 E5 var.* Albert Edward Nyanza, Edward Nyanza, Lac Idi Amin, Lake Rutanzige. *lake* Uganda/Dem. Rep. Congo
Edward Nyanza *see* Edward, Lake
Edwards Plateau *27 F3 plain* Texas, SW USA
Edzo *31 E4 prev.* Rae-Edzo. Northwest Territories, NW Canada
Eeklo *65 B5 var.* Eekloo. Oost-Vlaanderen, NW Belgium
Eekloo *see* Eeklo
Eems *see* Ems
Eersel *65 C5* Noord-Brabant, S Netherlands
Eesti Vabariik *see* Estonia
Efate *122 D4 var.* Efate, *Fr.* Vaté; *prev.* Sandwich Island. *island* C Vanuatu
Efate *see* Éfaté
Effingham *18 B4* Illinois, N USA
Eforie Sud *86 D5* Constanţa, E Romania
Egadi Is. *75 B7 island group* S Italy
Ege Denizi *see* Aegean Sea
Eger *77 D6 Ger.* Erlau. Heves, NE Hungary
Eger *see* Cheb, Czech Republic
Egeria Fracture Zone *119 C5 tectonic feature* W Indian Ocean
Éghezée *65 C6* Namur, C Belgium
Egina *see* Aígina
Egio *see* Aígio
Egmont *see* Taranaki, Mount
Egmont, Cape *128 C4 headland* North Island, New Zealand
Egoli *see* Johannesburg
Egypt *50 B2 off.* Arab Republic of Egypt, *Ar.* Jumhūrīyah Mişr al 'Arabīyah, *prev.* United Arab Republic; *anc.* Aegyptus. *country* NE Africa
Eibar *71 E1* País Vasco, N Spain
Eibergen *64 E3* Gelderland, E Netherlands
Eidfjord *63 A5* Hordaland, S Norway
Eifer-Berg *see* Suur Munamägi
Eifel *73 A5 plateau* W Germany
Eiger *73 B7 mountain* C Switzerland
Eigg *66 B3 island* W Scotland, United Kingdom
Eight Degree Channel *110 B3 channel* India/ Maldives
Eighty Mile Beach *124 B4 beach* Western Australia
Eijsden *65 D6* Limburg, SE Netherlands
Eilat *see* Elat
Eindhoven *65 D5* Noord-Brabant, S Netherlands
Eipel *see* Ipel'
Éire *see* Ireland
Éireann, Muir *see* Irish Sea
Eisenhüttenstadt *72 D4* Brandenburg, E Germany
Eisenmarkt *see* Hunedoara
Eisenstadt *73 E6* Burgenland, E Austria
Eisleben *72 C4* Sachsen-Anhalt, C Germany
Eivissa *71 G3 var.* Iviza, *Cast.* Ibiza; *anc.* Ebusus. Ibiza, Spain, W Mediterranean Sea
Eivissa *71 G3 var.* Iviza, *Cast.* Ibiza; *anc.* Ebusus. Ibiza, Spain, W Mediterranean Sea
Eivissa *71 G3 var.* Iviza, *Cast.* Ibiza; *anc.* Ebusus. Ibiza, Spain, W Mediterranean Sea
Ejea de los Caballeros *71 E2* Aragón, NE Spain
Ejin Qi *see* Dalain Hob
Ekapa *see* Cape Town
Ekaterinodar *see* Krasnodar
Ekvyvatapskiy Khrebet *93 G1 mountain range* NE Russian Federation
El 'Alamein *see* Al 'Alamayn
El Asnam *see* Chlef
Elat *97 B8 var.* Eilat, Elath. Southern, S Israel
Elat, Gulf of *see* Aqaba, Gulf of
Elath *see* Elat, Israel
Elath *see* Al 'Aqabah, Jordan
El'Atrun *50 B3* Northern Darfur, NW Sudan
Elâzığ *95 E3 var.* Elâziğ, Elâziz. Elâzığ, E Turkey
Elba *74 B4 island* Archipelago Toscano, C Italy
Elbasan *79 D6 var.* Elbasani. Elbasan, C Albania
Elbasani *see* Elbasan
Elbe *58 D3 Cz.* Labe. *river* Czech Republic/ Germany
Elbert, Mount *22 C4 mountain* Colorado, C USA
Elbing *see* Elbląg
Elbląg *76 C2 var.* Elblag, *Ger.* Elbing. Warmińsko-Mazurskie, NE Poland
El Boulaida/El Boulaïda *see* Blida
El'brus *89 A8 var.* Gora El'brus. *mountain* SW Russian Federation
El'brus, Gora *see* El'brus
El Burgo de Osma *71 E2* Castilla-León, C Spain
Elburz Mountains *98 C2 Eng.* Elburz Mountains. *mountain range* N Iran
Elburz Mountains *see* Alborz, Reshteh-ye Kūhhā-ye
El Cajon *25 C8* California, W USA
El Calafate *43 B7 var.* Calafate. Santa Cruz, S Argentina
El Callao *37 E2* Bolívar, E Venezuela
El Campo *27 G4* Texas, SW USA
El Carmen de Bolívar *36 B2* Bolívar, NW Colombia
El Cayo *see* San Ignacio
El Centro *25 D8* California, W USA
Elche *71 F4 Cat.* Elx; *anc.* Ilici, *Lat.* Illicis. País Valenciano, E Spain
Elda *71 F4* País Valenciano, E Spain
El Djazaïr *see* Alger
El Djelfa *see* Djelfa
Eldorado *42 E3* Misiones, NE Argentina
El Dorado *28 C3* Sinaloa, C Mexico
El Dorado *20 B2* Arkansas, C USA
El Dorado *23 F5* Kansas, C USA
El Dorado *37 F2* Bolívar, E Venezuela
El Dorado *see* California
Eldoret *51 C6* Rift Valley, W Kenya
Elektrostal' *89 B5* Moskovskaya Oblast', W Russian Federation
Elemi Triangle *51 B5 disputed region* Kenya/Sudan
Elephant Butte Reservoir *26 C2 reservoir* New Mexico, SW USA
Élesd *see* Aleşd
Eleuthera Island *32 C1 island* N Bahamas
El Fasher *50 A4 var.* Al Fāshir. Northern Darfur, W Sudan
El Ferrol/El Ferrol del Caudillo *see* Ferrol
El Gedaref *see* Gedaref
El Geneina *50 A4 var.* Ajjinena, Al-Genain, Al Junaynah. Western Darfur, W Sudan
Elgin *66 C3* NE Scotland, United Kingdom
Elgin *18 B3* Illinois, N USA
El Gîza *see* Giza
El Goléa *48 D3 var.* Al Golea. C Algeria
El Hank *52 D1 cliff* N Mauritania
El Haseke *see* Al Ḩasakah
Elimberrum *see* Auch
Eliocroca *see* Lorca
Élisabethville *see* Lubumbashi
Elista *89 B7* Respublika Kalmykiya, SW Russian Federation
Elizabeth *127 B6* South Australia
Elizabeth City *21 G1* North Carolina, SE USA
Elizabethtown *18 C5* Kentucky, S USA
El-Jadida *48 C2 prev.* Mazagan. W Morocco
Ełk *76 E2 Ger.* Lyck. Warmińsko-mazurskie, NE Poland
Elk City *27 F1* Oklahoma, C USA
El Khalil *see* Hebron
El Khârga *see* Al Khārijah
Elkhart *18 C3* Indiana, N USA
El Khartûm *see* Khartoum
Elk River *23 F2* Minnesota, N USA
El Kuneitra *see* Al Qunayţirah
Ellás *see* Greece
Ellef Ringnes Island *15 E1 island* Nunavut, N Canada
Ellen, Mount *22 B5 mountain* Utah, W USA
Ellensburg *24 B2* Washington, NW USA
Ellesmere Island *15 F1 island* Queen Elizabeth Islands, Nunavut, N Canada
Ellesmere, Lake *129 C6 lake* South Island, New Zealand
Ellice Islands *see* Tuvalu
Elliston *127 A6* South Australia
Ellsworth Land *132 A3 physical region* Antarctica
El Mahbas *48 B3 var.* Mahbés. SW Western Sahara
El Mina *96 B4 var.* Al Mīnā'. N Lebanon
El Minya *see* Al Minyā
Elmira *19 E3* New York, NE USA
El Mreyyé *52 D2 desert* E Mauritania
Elmshorn *72 B3* Schleswig-Holstein, N Germany
El Muglad *50 B4* Western Kordofan, C Sudan
El Obeid *50 B4 var.* Al Obayyid, Al Ubayyiḑ. Northern Kordofan, C Sudan
El Ouâdi *see* El Oued
El Oued *49 E2 var.* Al Oued, El Ouâdi, El Wad. NE Algeria
Eloy *26 B2* Arizona, SW USA
El Paso *26 D3* Texas, SW USA
El Porvenir *31 G4* Kuna Yala, N Panama
El Progreso *30 C2* Yoro, NW Honduras
El Puerto de Santa María *70 C5* Andalucía, S Spain
El Qâhira *see* Cairo
El Quneitra *see* Al Qunayţirah
El Quseir *see* Al Quşayr
El Quweira *see* Al Quwayrah
El Rama *31 E3* Región Autónoma Atlántico Sur, SE Nicaragua
El Real *31 H5 var.* El Real de Santa María. Darién, SE Panama
El Real de Santa María *see* El Real
El Reno *27 F1* Oklahoma, C USA
El Salvador *30 B3 off.* Republica de El Salvador. *country* Central America
El Salvador, Republica de *see* El Salvador
Elsass *see* Alsace
El Sáuz *28 C2* Chihuahua, N Mexico
El Serrat *69 A7* N Andorra Europe
Elst *64 D4* Gelderland, E Netherlands
El Sueco *28 C2* Chihuahua, N Mexico
El Suweida *see* As Suwaydā'
El Suweis *see* Suez
Eltanin Fracture Zone *131 E5 tectonic feature* SE Pacific Ocean
El Tigre *37 E2* Anzoátegui, NE Venezuela
Elvas *70 C4* Portalegre, C Portugal
El Vendrell *71 G2* Cataluña, NE Spain

Fort Providence – Gobi

Fort Providence 15 E4 var. Providence. Northwest Territories, W Canada
Fort-Repoux see Akjoujt
Fort Rosebery see Mansa
Fort Rousset see Owando
Fort-Royal see Fort-de-France
Fort St. John 15 E4 British Columbia, W Canada
Fort Scott 23 F5 Kansas, C USA
Fort Severn 16 C2 Ontario, C Canada
Fort-Shevchenko 92 A4 Mangistau, W Kazakhstan
Fort-Sibut see Sibut
Fort Simpson 15 E4 var. Simpson. Northwest Territories, W Canada
Fort Smith 15 E4 Northwest Territories, W Canada
Fort Smith 20 B1 Arkansas, C USA
Fort Stockton 27 E3 Texas, SW USA
Fort-Trinquet see Bîr Mogreïn
Fort Vermilion 15 E4 Alberta, W Canada
Fort Victoria see Masvingo
Fort Walton Beach 20 C3 Florida, SE USA
Fort Wayne 18 C4 Indiana, N USA
Fort William 66 C3 N Scotland, United Kingdom
Fort Worth 27 G2 Texas, SW USA
Fort Yukon 14 D3 Alaska, USA
Forum Alieni see Ferrara
Forum Livii see Forlì
Fossa Claudia see Chioggia
Fougamou 55 A6 Ngounié, C Gabon
Fougères 68 B3 Ille-et-Vilaine, NW France
Fou-hsin see Fuxin
Foulwind, Cape 129 B5 headland South Island, New Zealand
Foumban 54 A4 Ouest, NW Cameroon
Fou-shan see Fushun
Foveaux Strait 129 A8 strait S New Zealand
Foxe Basin 15 G3 sea Nunavut, N Canada
Fox Glacier 129 B6 West Coast, South Island, New Zealand
Fraga 71 F2 Aragón, NE Spain
Fram Basin 133 C3 var. Amundsen Basin. undersea basin Arctic Ocean
France 68 B4 off. French Republic, It./Sp. Francia; prev. Gaul, Gaule, Lat. Gallia. country W Europe
Franceville 55 B6 var. Massoukou, Masuku. Haut-Ogooué, E Gabon
Francfort see Frankfurt am Main
Franche-Comté 68 D4 cultural region E France
Francia see France
Francis Case, Lake 23 E3 reservoir South Dakota, N USA
Francisco Escárcega 29 G4 Campeche, SE Mexico
Francistown 56 D3 North East, NE Botswana
Franconian Jura see Fränkische Alb
Frankenalb see Fränkische Alb
Frankenstein/Frankenstein in Schlesien see Ząbkowice Śląskie
Frankfort 18 C5 state capital Kentucky, S USA
Frankfort on the Main see Frankfurt am Main
Frankfurt see Frankfurt am Main, Germany
Frankfurt see Słubice, Poland
Frankfurt am Main 73 B5 var. Frankfurt, Fr. Francfort; prev. Eng. Frankfort on the Main. Hessen, SW Germany
Frankfurt an der Oder 72 D3 Brandenburg, E Germany
Fränkische Alb 73 C6 var. Frankenalb, Eng. Franconian Jura. mountain range S Germany
Franklin 20 C1 Tennessee, S USA
Franklin D. Roosevelt Lake 24 C1 reservoir Washington, NW USA
Franz Josef Land 92 D1 Eng. Franz Josef Land. island group N Russian Federation
Franz Josef Land see Frantsa-Iosifa, Zemlya
Fraserburgh 66 D3 NE Scotland, United Kingdom
Fraser Island 126 E4 var. Great Sandy Island. island Queensland, E Australia
Frauenbach see Baia Mare
Frauenburg see Saldus, Latvia
Fredericksburg 19 E5 Virginia, NE USA
Fredericton 17 F4 province capital New Brunswick, SE Canada
Frederikshåb see Paamiut
Fredrikshald see Halden
Fredrikstad 63 B6 Østfold, S Norway
Freeport 32 C1 Grand Bahama Island, N Bahamas
Freeport 27 H4 Texas, SW USA
Free State see Maryland
Freetown 52 C4 country capital W Sierra Leone
Freiburg see Freiburg im Breisgau, Germany
Freiburg im Breisgau 73 A6 var. Freiburg, Fr. Fribourg-en-Brisgau. Baden-Württemberg, SW Germany
Freiburg in Schlesien see Świebodzice
Fremantle 125 A6 Western Australia
Fremont 23 F4 Nebraska, C USA
French Guiana 37 H3 var. Guiana, Guyane. French overseas department N South America
French Guinea see Guinea
French Polynesia 121 F4 French overseas territory S Pacific Ocean
French Republic see France
French Somaliland see Djibouti
French Southern and Antarctic Territories 119 B7 Fr. Terres Australes et Antarctiques Françaises. French overseas territory S Indian Ocean
French Sudan see Mali
French Territory of the Afars and Issas see Djibouti
French Togoland see Togo
Fresnillo 28 D3 var. Fresnillo de González Echeverría. Zacatecas, C Mexico
Fresnillo de González Echeverría see Fresnillo
Fresno 25 C6 California, W USA
Frías 42 C3 Catamarca, N Argentina
Fribourg-en-Brisgau see Freiburg im Breisgau
Friedek-Mistek see Frýdek-Místek
Friedrichshafen 73 B7 Baden-Württemberg, S Germany
Friendly Islands see Tonga
Frisches Haff see Vistula Lagoon
Frobisher Bay 60 B3 inlet Baffin Island, Nunavut, NE Canada
Frobisher Bay see Iqaluit
Frohavet 62 B4 sound C Norway
Frome, Lake 127 B6 salt lake South Australia
Frontera 29 G4 Tabasco, SE Mexico
Frontignan 69 C6 Hérault, S France
Frostviken see Kvarnbergsvattnet
Frøya 62 A4 island W Norway
Frumentum see Formentera
Frunze see Bishkek
Frýdek-Místek 77 C5 Ger. Friedek-Mistek. Moravskoslezský Kraj, E Czech Republic
Fu-chien see Fujian
Fu-chou see Fuzhou
Fu-chou see Fuzhou
Fuengirola 70 D5 Andalucía, S Spain
Fuerte Olimpo 42 D2 var. Olimpo. Alto Paraguay, NE Paraguay
Fuerte, Río 26 C5 river C Mexico
Fuerteventura 48 B3 island Islas Canarias, Spain, NE Atlantic Ocean
Fuhkien see Fujian
Fu-hsin see Fuxin
Fuji 109 D6 var. Huzi. Shizuoka, Honshū, S Japan
Fujian 106 D6 var. Fu-chien, Fuhkien, Fukien, Min, Fujian Sheng. province SE China
Fujian Sheng see Fujian
Mount Fuji 109 C6 var. Fujiyama, Eng. Mount Fuji. mountain Honshū, SE Japan
Fuji, Mount/Fujiyama see Fuji-san
Fukang 104 C2 Xinjiang Uygur Zizhiqu, W China
Fukien see Fujian
Fukui 109 C6 var. Hukui. Fukui, Honshū, SW Japan
Fukuoka 109 A7 var. Hukuoka, hist. Najima. Fukuoka, Kyūshū, SW Japan
Fukushima 108 D4 var. Hukusima. Fukushima, Honshū, C Japan
Fulda 73 B5 Hessen, C Germany
Funafuti see Fongafale
Funafuti Atoll 123 E3 atoll C Tuvalu
Funchal 48 A2 Madeira, Portugal, NE Atlantic Ocean
Fundy, Bay of 17 F5 bay Canada/USA
Fünen see Fyn
Fünfkirchen see Pécs
Furnes see Veurne
Fürth 73 C5 Bayern, S Germany
Furukawa 108 D4 var. Hurukawa, Ōsaki. Miyagi, Honshū, C Japan
Fusan see Pusan
Fushë Kosovë 79 D5 Serb. Kosovo Polje. C Kosovo
Fushun 106 D3 var. Fou-shan, Fu-shun. Liaoning, NE China
Fu-shun see Fushun
Fusin see Fuxin
Füssen 73 C7 Bayern, S Germany
Futog 78 D3 Vojvodina, NW Serbia
Futuna, Île 123 E4 island S Wallis and Futuna
Fuxin 106 D3 var. Fou-hsin, Fu-hsin, Fusin. Liaoning, NE China
Fuzhou 106 D6 var. Foochow, Fu-chou. province capital Fujian, SE China
Fuzhou 106 D5 var. Foochow, Fu-chou. province capital Fujian, SE China
Fyn 63 B8 Ger. Fünen. island C Denmark
FYR Macedonia/FYROM see Macedonia, FYR
Fyzabad see Feyzābād

G

Gaafu Alifu Atoll see North Huvadhu Atoll
Gaalkacyo 51 E5 var. Galka'yo, It. Galcaio. Mudug, C Somalia
Gabela 56 B2 Cuanza Sul, W Angola
Gaberones see Gaborone
Gabès 49 E2 var. Qābis. E Tunisia
Gabès, Golfe de 49 F2 Ar. Khalīj Qābis. gulf E Tunisia
Gabon 55 B6 off. Gabonese Republic. country C Africa
Gabonese Republic see Gabon
Gaborone 56 C4 prev. Gaberones. country capital South East, SE Botswana
Gabrovo 82 D2 Gabrovo, N Bulgaria
Gadag 110 C1 Karnātaka, W India
Gades/Gadier/Gadir/Gadire see Cádiz
Gadsden 20 D2 Alabama, S USA
Gaeta 75 C5 Lazio, C Italy
Gaeta, Gulf of 75 C5 var. Gulf of Gaeta. gulf C Italy
Gaeta, Gulf of see Gaeta, Golfo di
Gäfle see Gävle
Gafsa 49 E2 var. Qafṣah. W Tunisia
Gagnoa 52 D5 C Ivory Coast
Gagra 95 E1 NW Georgia
Gaillac 69 C6 var. Gaillac-sur-Tarn. Tarn, S France
Gaillac-sur-Tarn see Gaillac
Gaillimh see Galway
Gaillimhe, Cuan na see Galway Bay
Gainesville 21 E3 Florida, SE USA
Gainesville 20 D2 Georgia, SE USA
Gainesville 27 G2 Texas, SW USA
Lake Gairdner 127 A6 salt lake South Australia
Gaizina Kalns see Gaiziņakalns
Gaiziņakalns 84 C3 var. Gaizina Kalns. mountain E Latvia
Galán, Cerro 42 B3 mountain NW Argentina
Galanta 77 C6 Hung. Galánta. Trnavský Kraj, W Slovakia
Galapagos Fracture Zone 131 E3 tectonic feature E Pacific Ocean
Galapagos Islands 131 F3 var. Islas de los Galápagos, Eng. Galapagos Islands, Tortoise Islands. island group Ecuador, E Pacific Ocean
Galapagos Islands see Colón, Archipiélago de
Galápagos, Islas de los see Colón, Archipiélago de
Galapagos Rise 131 F3 undersea rise E Pacific Ocean
Galashiels 66 C4 SE Scotland, United Kingdom
Galați 86 D4 Ger. Galatz. Galați, E Romania
Galatz see Galați
Galcaio see Gaalkacyo
Galesburg 18 B3 Illinois, N USA
Galicia 70 B1 anc. Gallaecia. autonomous community NW Spain
Galicia Bank 58 B4 undersea bank E Atlantic Ocean
Galilee, Sea of see Tiberias, Lake
Galka'yo see Gaalkacyo
Galkynyş 100 D3 prev. Rus. Deynau, Dyanev, Turkm. Dänew. Lebap Welaýaty, NE Turkmenistan
Gallaecia see Galicia
Galle 110 D4 prev. Point de Galle. Southern Province, SW Sri Lanka
Gallego Rise 131 F3 undersea rise E Pacific Ocean
Gallegos see Río Gallegos
Gallia see France
Gallipoli 75 E6 Puglia, SE Italy
Gällivare 62 C3 Lapp. Váhtjer. Norrbotten, N Sweden
Gallup 26 C1 New Mexico, SW USA
Galtat-Zemmour 48 B3 C Western Sahara
Galveston 27 H4 Texas, SW USA
Galway 67 A5 Ir. Gaillimh. W Ireland
Galway Bay 67 A6 Ir. Cuan na Gaillimhe. bay W Ireland
Gámas see Kaamanen
Gambell 14 C2 Saint Lawrence Island, Alaska, USA
Gambia 52 B3 off. Republic of The Gambia, The Gambia. country W Africa
Gambia 52 C3 Fr. Gambie. river W Africa
Gambia, Republic of The see Gambia
Gambia, The see Gambia
Gambie see Gambia
Gambier, Îles 121 G4 island group E French Polynesia
Gamboma 55 B6 Plateaux, E Congo
Gamlakarleby see Kokkola
Gan 110 B5 Addu Atoll, C Maldives
Gan see Gansu, China
Gan see Jiangxi, China
Ganaane see Juba
Gäncä 95 G2 Rus. Gyandzha; prev. Kirovabad, Yelisavetpol. W Azerbaijan
Gand see Gent
Gandajika 55 D7 Kasai-Oriental, S Dem. Rep. Congo
Gander 17 G3 Newfoundland and Labrador, SE Canada
Gāndhīdhām 112 C4 Gujarāt, W India
Gandía 71 F3 País Valenciano, E Spain
Ganges 113 F3 Ben. Padma. river Bangladesh/India
Ganges Cone see Ganges Fan
Ganges Fan 118 D3 var. Ganges Cone. undersea fan N Bay of Bengal
Ganges, Mouths of the 113 G4 delta Bangladesh/India
Gangra see Çankırı
Gangtok 113 F3 state capital Sikkim, N India
Gansos, Lago dos see Goose Lake
Gansu 106 B4 var. Gan, Gansu Sheng, Kansu. province N China
Gansu Sheng see Gansu
Gantsevichi see Hantsavichy
Ganzhou 106 D6 Jiangxi, S China
Gao 53 E3 Gao, E Mali
Gaocheng see Litang
Gaoual 52 C4 N Guinea
Gaoxiong see Kaohsiung
Gap 69 D5 anc. Vapincum. Hautes-Alpes, SE France
Gaplaňgyr Platosy 100 C2 Rus. Plato Kaplangky. ridge Turkmenistan/Uzbekistan
Gar see Gar Xincun
Garabil Belentligi 100 D3 Rus. Vozvyshennost' Karabil'. mountain range S Turkmenistan
Garabogaz Aylagy 100 B2 Rus. Zaliv Kara-Bogaz-Gol. bay NW Turkmenistan
Garachiné 31 G5 Darién, SE Panama
Garagum 100 C3 var. Garagumy, Qara Qum, Eng. Black Sand Desert, Kara Kum; prev. Peski Karakumy. desert C Turkmenistan
Garagum Canal 100 D3 var. Kara Kum Canal, Rus. Karagumskiy Kanal, Karakumskiy Kanal. canal C Turkmenistan
Garagumy see Garagum
Gara Khitrino 82 D2 Shumen, NE Bulgaria
Gárassavon see Kaaresuvanto
Garda, Lake 74 C2 var. Benaco, Eng. Lake Garda, Ger. Gardasee. lake NE Italy
Garda, Lake see Garda, Lago di
Gardasee see Garda, Lago di
Garden City 23 E5 Kansas, C USA
Garden State, The see New Jersey
Gardner Island see Nikumaroro
Garegegasnjárga see Karigasniemi
Gargždai 84 B3 Klaipėda, W Lithuania
Garissa 51 D6 Coast, E Kenya
Garland 27 G2 Texas, SW USA
Garoe see Garoowe
Garonne 69 B5 anc. Garumna. river S France
Garoowe 51 E5 var. Garoe. Nugaal, N Somalia
Garoua 54 B4 var. Garua. Nord, N Cameroon
Garry Lake 15 F3 lake Nunavut, N Canada
Garsen 51 D6 Coast, S Kenya
Garua see Garoua
Garumna see Garonne
Garwolin 76 D4 Mazowieckie, E Poland
Gar Xincun 104 A4 prev. Gar. Xizang Zizhiqu, W China
Gary 18 B3 Indiana, N USA
Garzón 36 B4 Huila, S Colombia
Gasan-Kuli see Esenguly
Gascogne 69 B6 Eng. Gascony. cultural region S France
Gascony see Gascogne
Gascoyne River 125 A5 river Western Australia
Gaspé 17 F3 Québec, SE Canada
Gaspé, Péninsule de 17 E4 var. Péninsule de la Gaspésie. peninsula Québec, SE Canada
Gaspésie, Péninsule de la see Gaspé, Péninsule de
Gastonia 21 E1 North Carolina, SE USA
Gastoúni 83 B6 Dytikí Ellás, S Greece
Gatchina 88 B4 Leningradskaya Oblast', NW Russian Federation
Gatineau 16 D4 Québec, SE Canada
Gatooma see Kadoma
Gatún, Lake 31 F4 reservoir C Panama
Gauhāti see Guwāhāti
Gauja 84 D3 Ger. Aa. river Estonia/Latvia
Gaul/Gaule see France
Gauteng see Johannesburg, South Africa
Gāvbandī 98 D4 Hormozgān, S Iran
Gávdos 83 C8 island SE Greece
Gavere 65 B6 Oost-Vlaanderen, NW Belgium
Gävle 63 C6 var. Gäfle; prev. Gefle. Gävleborg, C Sweden
Gawler 127 B6 South Australia
Gaya 113 F3 Bihār, N India
Gaya see Kyjov
Gayndah 127 E5 Queensland, E Australia
Gaysin see Haysyn
Gaza 97 A6 Ar. Ghazzah, Heb. 'Azza. NE Gaza Strip
Gaz-Achak see Gazojak
Gazandzhyk/Gazanjyk see Bereket
Gaza Strip 97 A7 Ar. Qita Ghazzah. disputed region SW Asia
Gaziantep 94 D4 var. Gazi Antep; prev. Aintab, Antep. Gaziantep, S Turkey
Gazi Antep see Gaziantep
Gazimağusa 80 D5 var. Famagusta, Gk. Ammóchostos. E Cyprus
Gazli 100 D2 Buxoro Viloyati, C Uzbekistan
Gazojak 100 D2 Rus. Gaz-Achak. Lebap Welaýaty, NE Turkmenistan
Gbanga 52 D5 var. Gbarnga. N Liberia
Gbarnga see Gbanga
Gdańsk 76 C2 Fr. Dantzig, Ger. Danzig. Pomorskie, N Poland
Gdan'skaya Bukhta/Gdańsk, Gulf of see Danzig, Gulf of
Gdańska, Zakota see Danzig, Gulf of
Gdingen see Gdynia
Gdynia 76 C2 Ger. Gdingen. Pomorskie, N Poland
Gedaref 50 C4 var. Al Qaḍārif, El Gedaref. Gedaref, E Sudan
Gediz 94 B3 Kütahya, W Turkey
Gediz Nehri 94 A3 river W Turkey
Geel 65 C5 var. Gheel. Antwerpen, N Belgium
Geelong 127 C7 Victoria, SE Australia
Ge'e'mu see Golmud
Gefle see Gävle
Geilo 63 A5 Buskerud, S Norway
Gejiu 106 B6 var. Kochiu. Yunnan, S China
Gëkdepe see Gökdepe
Gela 75 C7 prev. Terranova di Sicilia. Sicilia, Italy, C Mediterranean Sea
Geldermalsen 64 C4 Gelderland, C Netherlands
Geleen 65 D6 Limburg, SE Netherlands
Gelib see Jilib
Gellinsor 51 E5 Mudug, C Somalia
Gembloux 65 C6 Namur, Belgium
Gemena 55 C5 Equateur, NW Dem. Rep. Congo
Gem of the Mountains see Idaho
Gemona del Friuli 74 D2 Friuli-Venezia Giulia, NE Italy
Gem State see Idaho
Genalē Wenz see Juba
Genck see Genk
General Alvear 42 B4 Mendoza, W Argentina
General Carrera, Lago see Buenos Aires, Lago
General Eugenio A. Garay 42 C1 var. Fortín General Eugenio Garay; prev. Yrendagüé. Nueva Asunción, NW Paraguay
General José F.Uriburu see Zárate
General Machado see Camacupa
General Santos 117 F3 off. General Santos City. Mindanao, S Philippines
General Santos City see General Santos
Gênes see Genova
Geneva see Genève
Geneva, Lake 73 A7 Fr. Lac de Genève, Lac Léman, le Léman, Ger. Genfer See. lake France/Switzerland
Genève 73 A7 Eng. Geneva, Ger. Genf, It. Ginevra. Genève, SW Switzerland
Genève, Lac de see Geneva, Lake
Genf see Genève
Genfer See see Geneva, Lake
Genichesk see Heniches'k
Genk 65 D6 var. Genck. Limburg, NE Belgium
Gennep 64 D4 Limburg, SE Netherlands
Genoa see Genova
Genoa, Gulf of 74 A3 Eng. Gulf of Genoa. gulf NW Italy
Genoa, Gulf of see Genova, Golfo di
Genova 80 D1 Eng. Genoa; anc. Genua, Fr. Gênes. Liguria, NW Italy
Genovesa, Isla 38 B5 var. Tower Island. island Galapagos Islands, Ecuador, E Pacific Ocean
Gent 65 B5 Eng. Ghent, Fr. Gand. Oost-Vlaanderen, NW Belgium
Genua see Genova
Geok-Tepe see Gökdepe
George 56 C5 Western Cape, S South Africa
George 60 A4 river Newfoundland and Labrador/Québec, E Canada
George, Lake 21 E3 lake Florida, SE USA
Georgenburg see Jurbarkas
Georges Bank 13 D5 undersea bank W Atlantic Ocean
George Sound 129 A7 sound South Island, New Zealand
Georges River 126 D2 river New South Wales, E Australia
Georgetown 37 F2 country capital N Guyana
George Town 32 C2 Great Exuma Island, C Bahamas
George Town 32 B3 var. Georgetown. dependent territory capital Grand Cayman, SW Cayman Islands
George Town 116 B3 var. Penang, Pinang. Pinang, Peninsular Malaysia
Georgetown 21 F2 South Carolina, SE USA
Georgetown see George Town
George V Land 132 C4 physical region Antarctica
Georgia 95 F2 off. Republic of Georgia, Geor. Sak'art'velo, Rus. Gruzinskaya SSR, Gruziya. country SW Asia
Georgia 20 D2 off. State of Georgia, also known as Empire State of the South, Peach State. state SE USA
Georgian Bay 18 D2 lake bay Ontario, S Canada
Georgia, Republic of see Georgia
Georgia, Strait of 24 A1 strait British Columbia, W Canada
Georgi Dimitrov see Kostenets
Georgiu-Dezh see Liski
Georg von Neumayer 132 A2 German research station Antarctica
Gera 72 C4 Thüringen, E Germany
Geráki 83 B6 Pelopónnisos, S Greece
Geraldine 129 B6 Canterbury, South Island, New Zealand
Geraldton 125 A6 Western Australia
Geral, Serra 35 D5 mountain range S Brazil
Gerede 94 C2 Bolu, N Turkey
Gereshk 100 D5 Helmand, SW Afghanistan
Gering 22 D3 Nebraska, C USA
German East Africa see Tanzania
Germanicopolis see Çankırı
Germanicum, Mare/German Ocean see North Sea
German Southwest Africa see Namibia
Germany 72 B4 off. Federal Republic of Germany, Bundesrepublik Deutschland, Ger. Deutschland. country N Europe
Germany, Federal Republic of see Germany
Geroliménas 83 B7 Pelopónnisos, S Greece
Gerona see Girona
Gerpinnes 65 C7 Hainaut, S Belgium
Gerunda see Girona
Gerze 94 D2 Sinop, N Turkey
Gesoriacum see Boulogne-sur-Mer
Gessoriacum see Boulogne-sur-Mer
Getafe 70 D3 Madrid, C Spain
Gevaş 95 F3 Van, SE Turkey
Gevgeli see Gevgelija
Gevgelija 79 E6 var. Đevđelija, Djevdjelija, Turk. Gevgeli. SE Macedonia
Ghaba see Al Ghābah
Ghana 53 E5 off. Republic of Ghana. country W Africa
Ghanzi 56 C3 var. Khanzi. Ghanzi, W Botswana
Gharandal 97 B7 Al 'Aqabah, SW Jordan
Gharbt, Jabal al see Liban, Jebel
Ghardaïa 48 D2 N Algeria
Gharvān see Gharyān
Gharyān 49 F2 var. Gharvān. NW Libya
Ghawdex see Gozo
Ghaznī 101 E4 var. Ghazni. Ghaznī, E Afghanistan
Ghazzah see Gaza
Gheel see Geel
Ghent see Gent
Gheorgheni 86 C4 prev. Gheorghieni, Sîn-Miclăuș, Ger. Niklasmarkt, Hung. Gyergyószentmiklós. Harghita, C Romania
Gheorghieni see Gheorgheni
Ghūdara 101 F3 var. Gudara, Rus. Kudara. SE Tajikistan
Ghurdaqah see Hurghada
Ghūriān 100 D4 Herāt, W Afghanistan
Giamame see Jamaame
Giannitsá 82 B4 var. Yiannitsá. Kentrikí Makedonía, N Greece
Gibraltar 71 G4 UK dependent territory SW Europe
Gibraltar, Bay of 71 G5 bay Gibraltar/Spain Europe Mediterranean Sea Atlantic Ocean
Gibraltar, Détroit de/Gibraltar, Estrecho de see Gibraltar, Strait of
Gibraltar, Strait of 70 C5 Fr. Détroit de Gibraltar, Sp. Estrecho de Gibraltar. strait Atlantic Ocean/Mediterranean Sea
Gibson Desert 125 B5 desert Western Australia
Giedraičiai 85 C5 Utena, E Lithuania
Giessen 73 B5 Hessen, W Germany
Gifu 109 C6 var. Gihu. Gifu, Honshū, SW Japan
Giganta, Sierra de la 28 B3 mountain range W Mexico
Gihu see Gifu
G'ijduvon 100 D2 Rus. Gizhduvon. Buxoro Viloyati, C Uzbekistan
Gijón 70 D1 var. Xixón. Asturias, NW Spain
Gila River 26 A2 river Arizona, SW USA
Gilbert Islands see Tungaru
Gilbert River 126 C3 river Queensland, NE Australia
Gilf Kebir Plateau see Haḍabat al Jilf al Kabīr
Gillette 22 D3 Wyoming, C USA
Gilolo see Halmahera, Pulau
Gilroy 25 B6 California, W USA
Gimie, Mount 33 F1 mountain C Saint Lucia
Gimma see Jīma
Ginevra see Genève
Gingin 125 A6 Western Australia
Giohar see Jawhar
Gipeswic see Ipswich
Girardot 36 B3 Cundinamarca, C Colombia
Giresun 95 E2 var. Kerasunt; anc. Cerasus, Pharnacia. Giresun, NE Turkey
Girgenti see Agrigento
Girin see Jilin
Girne 80 C5 Gk. Kerýneia, Kyrenia. N Cyprus
Giron see Kiruna
Girona 71 G2 var. Gerona; anc. Gerunda. Cataluña, NE Spain
Gisborne 128 E3 Gisborne, North Island, New Zealand
Gissar Range 101 E3 Rus. Gissarskiy Khrebet. mountain range Tajikistan/Uzbekistan
Gissarskiy Khrebet see Gissar Range
Githio see Gýtheio
Giulianova 74 D4 Abruzzi, C Italy
Giumri see Gyumri
Giurgiu 86 C5 Giurgiu, S Romania
Giza 50 B1 var. Al Jīzah, El Giza, Gizeh. N Egypt
Gizhduvon see G'ijduvon
Giżycko 76 D2 Ger. Lötzen. Warmińsko-Mazurskie, NE Poland
Gjakovë 79 D5 Serb. Đakovica. W Kosovo
Gjilan 79 D5 Serb. Gnjilane. E Kosovo
Gjinokastër see Gjirokastër
Gjirokastër 79 C7 var. Gjirokastra; prev. Gjinokastër, Gk. Argyrokastron, It. Argirocastro. Gjirokastër, S Albania
Gjirokastra see Gjirokastër
Gjoa Haven 15 F3 var. Uqsuqtuuq. King William Island, Nunavut, NW Canada
Gjøvik 63 B5 Oppland, S Norway
Glace Bay 17 G4 Cape Breton Island, Nova Scotia, SE Canada
Gladstone 126 E4 Queensland, E Australia
Glåma 63 B5 var. Glommen. river S Norway
Glasgow 66 C4 S Scotland, United Kingdom
Glavn'a Morava see Velika Morava
Glazov 89 D5 Udmurtskaya Respublika, NW Russian Federation
Gleiwitz see Gliwice
Glendale 26 B2 Arizona, SW USA
Glendive 22 D2 Montana, NW USA
Glens Falls 19 F3 New York, NE USA
Glevum see Gloucester
Glina 78 B3 var. Banijska Palanka. Sisak-Moslavina, NE Croatia
Glittertind 63 A5 mountain S Norway
Gliwice 77 C5 Ger. Gleiwitz. Śląskie, S Poland
Globe 26 B2 Arizona, SW USA
Globino see Hlobyne
Glogau see Głogów
Głogów 76 B4 Ger. Glogau, Glogow. Dolnośląskie, SW Poland
Glogow see Głogów
Glomma see Glåma
Glommen see Glåma
Gloucester 67 D6 hist. Caer Glou, Lat. Glevum. C England, United Kingdom
Glowno 76 D4 Łódź, C Poland
Glubokoye see Hlybokaye
Glukhov see Hlukhiv
Gnesen see Gniezno
Gniezno 76 C3 Ger. Gnesen. Weilkopolskie, C Poland
Gnjilane see Gjilan
Gobabis 56 B3 Omaheke, E Namibia
Gobi 104 D3 desert China/Mongolia

Gobō – Haines

Gobō 109 C6 Wakayama, Honshū, SW Japan
Godavari 102 B3 var. Godavari. river C India
Godavari see Godāvari
Godhavn see Qeqertarsuaq
Godhra 112 C4 Gujarāt, W India
Göding see Hodonín
Godoy Cruz 42 B4 Mendoza, W Argentina
Godthaab/Godthåb see Nuuk
Godwin Austen, Mount see K2
Goede Hoop, Kaap de see Good Hope, Cape of
Goeie Hoop, Kaap die see Good Hope, Cape of
Goeree 64 B4 island SW Netherlands
Goes 65 B5 Zeeland, SW Netherlands
Goettingen see Göttingen
Gogebic Range 18 B1 hill range Michigan/Wisconsin, N USA
Goiânia 41 E3 prev. Goyania. state capital Goiás, C Brazil
Goiás 41 E3 off. Estado de Goiás; prev. Goiaz, Goyaz. state C Brazil
Goiás 41 E3 off. Estado de Goiás; prev. Goiaz, Goyaz. region C Brazil
Goiás, Estado de see Goiás
Goiaz see Goiás
Goidhoo Atoll see Horsburgh Atoll
Gojōme 108 D4 Akita, Honshū, NW Japan
Gökçeada 82 D4 var. Imroz Adasī, Gk. Imbros. island NW Turkey
Gökdepe 100 C3 Rus. Gëkdepe, Geok-Tepe. Ahal Welaýaty, C Turkmenistan
Göksun 94 D4 Kahramanmaraş, C Turkey
Gol 63 A5 Buskerud, S Norway
Golan Heights 97 B5 Ar. Al Jawlān, Heb. HaGolan. mountain range SW Syria
Golaya Pristan see Hola Prystan'
Gołdap 76 E2 Ger. Goldap. Warmińsko-Mazurskie, NE Poland
Gold Coast 127 E5 cultural region Queensland, E Australia
Golden Bay 128 C4 bay South Island, New Zealand
Golden State, The see California
Goldingen see Kuldīga
Goldsboro 21 F1 North Carolina, SE USA
Goleniów 76 B3 Ger. Gollnow. Zachodnio-pomorskie, NW Poland
Gollnow see Goleniów
Golmo see Golmud
Golmud 104 D4 var. Ge'e'mu, Golmo, Chin. Ko-erh-mu. Qinghai, C China
Golovanevsk see Holovanivs'k
Golub-Dobrzyń 76 C3 Kujawski-pomorskie, C Poland
Goma 55 E6 Nord-Kivu, NE Dem. Rep. Congo
Gombi 53 H4 Adamawa, E Nigeria
Gombroon see Bandar-e 'Abbās
Gomel' see Homyel'
Gomera 48 A3 island Islas Canarias, Spain, NE Atlantic Ocean
Gómez Palacio 28 D3 Durango, C Mexico
Gonaïves 32 D3 var. Les Gonaïves. N Haiti
Gonâve, Île de la 32 D3 island C Haiti
Gondar see Gonder
Gonder 50 C4 var. Gondar. Āmara, NW Ethiopia
Gondia 113 E4 Mahārāshtra, C India
Gonggar 104 C5 var. Gyixong. Xizang Zizhiqu, W China
Gongola 53 G4 river E Nigeria
Gongtang see Damxung
Gonni/Gónnos see Gónnoi
Gónnoi 82 B4 var. Gonni, Gónnos; prev. Derelí. Thessalía, C Greece
Good Hope, Cape of 56 B5 Afr. Kaap de Goede Hoop, Kaap die Goeie Hoop. headland SW South Africa
Goodland 22 D4 Kansas, C USA
Goondiwindi 127 D5 Queensland, E Australia
Goor 64 E3 Overijssel, E Netherlands
Goose Green 43 D7 var. Prado del Ganso. East Falkland, Falkland Islands
Goose Lake 24 B4 var. Lago dos Gansos. lake California/Oregon, W USA
Gopher State see Minnesota
Göppingen 73 B6 Baden-Württemberg, SW Germany
Góra Kalwaria 92 D4 Mazowieckie, C Poland
Gorakhpur 113 E3 Uttar Pradesh, N India
Gorany see Harany
Goražde 78 C4 Federacija Bosna I Hercegovina, SE Bosnia and Herzegovina
Gorbovichi see Harbavichy
Goré 54 C4 Logone-Oriental, S Chad
Gorē 51 C5 Oromīya, C Ethiopia
Gore 129 B7 Southland, South Island, New Zealand
Gorgān 98 D2 var. Astarabad, Astrabad, Gurgan, prev. Asterābād; anc. Hyrcania. Golestān, N Iran
Gori 95 F2 C Georgia
Gorinchem 64 C4 var. Gorkum. Zuid-Holland, C Netherlands
Goris 95 G3 SE Armenia
Gorki see Horki
Gor'kiy see Nizhniy Novgorod
Gorkum see Gorinchem
Görlitz 72 D4 Sachsen, E Germany
Görlitz see Zgorzelec
Gorlovka see Horlivka
Gorna Dzhumaya see Blagoevgrad
Gornja Mužlja see Mužlja
Gornji Milanovac 78 C4 Serbia, C Serbia
Gorodets see Haradzyets
Gorodishche see Horodyshche
Gorodnya see Horodnya
Gorodok see Haradok
Gorodok/Gorodok Yagellonski see Horodok
Gorontalo 117 E4 Sulawesi, C Indonesia
Gorontalo, Teluk see Tomini, Gulf of
Gorssel 64 D3 Gelderland, E Netherlands
Goryn see Horyn'
Gorzów Wielkopolski 76 B3 Ger. Landsberg, Landsberg an der Warthe. Lubuskie, W Poland
Gosford 127 D6 New South Wales, SE Australia
Goshogawara 108 D3 var. Gosyogawara. Aomori, Honshū, C Japan
Gospić 78 A3 Lika-Senj, C Croatia
Gostivar 79 D6 W FYR Macedonia
Gosyogawara see Goshogawara
Göteborg 63 B7 Eng. Gothenburg. Västra Götaland, S Sweden
Gotel Mountains 53 G5 mountain range E Nigeria
Gotha 72 C4 Thüringen, C Germany
Gothenburg see Göteborg
Gotland 63 C7 island SE Sweden
Goto-retto 109 A7 island group SW Japan
Gotska Sandön 84 B1 island SE Sweden
Gōtsu 109 B6 var. Gôtu. Shimane, Honshū, SW Japan
Göttingen 72 B4 var. Goettingen. Niedersachsen, C Germany
Gottschee see Kočevje
Gottwaldov see Zlín
Gôtu see Gōtsu
Gouda 64 C4 Zuid-Holland, C Netherlands
Gough Fracture Zone 45 C6 tectonic feature S Atlantic Ocean
Gough Island 47 B8 island Tristan da Cunha, S Atlantic Ocean
Gouin, Réservoir 16 D4 reservoir Québec, SE Canada
Goulburn 127 D6 New South Wales, SE Australia
Goundam 53 E3 Tombouctou, NW Mali
Gouré 53 G3 Zinder, SE Niger
Goverla, Gora see Hoverla, Hora
Governador Valadares 41 F4 Minas Gerais, SE Brazil
Govi Altayn Nuruu 105 E3 mountain range S Mongolia
Goya 42 D3 Corrientes, NE Argentina
Goyania see Goiânia
Goyaz see Goiás
Goz Beïda 54 C3 Ouaddaï, SE Chad
Gozo 75 C8 var. Ghawdex. island N Malta
Graciosa 70 A5 var. Ilha Graciosa. island Azores, Portugal, NE Atlantic Ocean
Graciosa, Ilha see Graciosa
Gradačac 78 C3 Federacija Bosna I Hercegovina, N Bosnia and Herzegovina
Gradaús, Serra dos 41 E3 mountain range C Brazil
Gradiška see Bosanska Gradiška
Grafton 127 E5 New South Wales, SE Australia
Grafton 23 E1 North Dakota, N USA
Graham Land 132 A2 physical region Antarctica
Grajewo 76 E3 Podlaskie, NE Poland
Grampian Mountains 66 C3 mountain range C Scotland, United Kingdom
Gran see Esztergom, Hungary
Granada 30 D3 Granada, SW Nicaragua
Granada 70 D5 Andalucía, S Spain
Gran Canaria 48 A3 var. Grand Canary. island Islas Canarias, Spain, NE Atlantic Ocean
Gran Chaco 42 D2 var. Chaco. lowland plain South America
Grand Bahama Island 32 B1 island N Bahamas
Grand Banks of Newfoundland 12 E4 undersea basin NW Atlantic Ocean
Grand Bassa see Buchanan
Grand Canary see Gran Canaria
Grand Canyon 26 A1 canyon Arizona, SW USA
Grand Canyon State see Arizona
Grand Cayman 32 B3 island SW Cayman Islands
Grand Duchy of Luxembourg see Luxembourg
Grande, Bahía 43 B7 bay S Argentina
Grande-Comore see Ngazidja
Grande de Chiloé, Isla see Chiloé, Isla de
Grande Prairie 15 E4 Alberta, W Canada
Grand Erg Occidental 48 D3 desert W Algeria
Grand Erg Oriental 49 E3 desert Algeria/Tunisia
Rio Grande 29 E2 var. Río Bravo, Sp. Río Bravo del Norte, Bravo del Norte. river Mexico/USA
Grande Terre 33 G3 island E West Indies
Grand Falls 17 G3 Newfoundland, Newfoundland and Labrador, SE Canada
Grand Forks 23 E1 North Dakota, N USA
Grandichi see Hrandzichy
Grand Island 23 E4 Nebraska, C USA
Grand Junction 22 C4 Colorado, C USA
Grand Paradis see Gran Paradiso
Grand Rapids 18 C3 Michigan, N USA
Grand Rapids 23 F1 Minnesota, N USA
Grand-Saint-Bernard, Col du see Great Saint Bernard Pass
Grand-Santi 37 G3 W French Guiana
Granite State see New Hampshire
Gran Lago see Nicaragua, Lago de
Gran Malvina see West Falkland
Gran Paradiso 74 A2 Fr. Grand Paradis. mountain NW Italy
Gran San Bernardo, Passo di see Great Saint Bernard Pass
Gran Santiago see Santiago
Grants 26 C2 New Mexico, SW USA
Grants Pass 24 B4 Oregon, NW USA
Granville 68 B3 Manche, N France
Gratianopolis see Grenoble
Gratz see Graz
Graudenz see Grudziądz
Graulhet 69 C6 Tarn, S France
Grave 64 D4 Noord-Brabant, SE Netherlands
Grayling 14 C2 Alaska, USA
Graz 73 E7 prev. Gratz. Steiermark, SE Austria
Great Abaco 32 C1 var. Abaco Island. island N Bahamas
Great Alfold see Great Hungarian Plain
Great Ararat see Büyükağrı Dağı
Great Australian Bight 125 D7 bight S Australia
Great Barrier Island 128 D2 island N New Zealand
Great Barrier Reef 126 D2 reef Queensland, NE Australia
Great Basin 25 C5 basin W USA
Great Bear Lake 15 E3 Fr. Grand Lac de l'Ours. lake Northwest Territories, NW Canada
Great Belt 63 B8 var. Store Bælt, Eng. Great Belt, Storebelt. channel Baltic Sea/Kattegat
Great Belt see Storebælt
Great Bend 23 E5 Kansas, C USA
Great Britain see Britain
Great Dividing Range 126 D4 mountain range NE Australia
Greater Antilles 32 D3 island group West Indies
Greater Caucasus 95 G2 mountain range Azerbaijan/Georgia/Russian Federation Asia/Europe
Greater Sunda Islands 102 D5 var. Sunda Islands. island group Indonesia
Great Exhibition Bay 128 C1 inlet North Island, New Zealand
Great Exuma Island 32 C2 island C Bahamas
Great Falls 22 B1 Montana, NW USA
Great Grimsby see Grimsby
Great Hungarian Plain 77 C7 var. Great Alfold, Plain of Hungary, Hung. Alföld. plain SE Europe
Great Inagua 32 D2 var. Inagua Islands. island S Bahamas
Great Indian Desert see Thar Desert
Great Khingan Range 105 G1 Eng. Great Khingan Range. mountain range NE China
Great Khingan Range see Da Hinggan Ling
Great Lake see Tônlé Sap
Great Lakes 13 C5 lakes Ontario, Canada/USA
Great Lakes State see Michigan
Great Meteor Seamount see Great Meteor Tablemount
Great Meteor Tablemount 44 B3 var. Great Meteor Seamount. seamount E Atlantic Ocean
Great Nicobar 111 G3 island Nicobar Islands, India, NE Indian Ocean
Great Plain of China 103 E2 plain E China
Great Plains 23 E3 var. High Plains. plains Canada/USA
Great Rift Valley 51 C5 var. Rift Valley. depression Asia/Africa
Great Ruaha 51 C7 river S Tanzania
Great Saint Bernard Pass 74 A1 Fr. Col du Grand-Saint-Bernard, It. Passo del Gran San Bernardo. pass Italy/Switzerland
Great Salt Desert see Kavīr, Dasht-e
Great Salt Lake 22 A3 salt lake Utah, W USA
Great Salt Lake Desert 22 A4 plain Utah, W USA
Great Sand Sea 49 H3 desert Egypt/Libya
Great Sandy Desert 124 C4 desert Western Australia
Great Sandy Desert see Ar Rub 'al Khālī
Great Sandy Island see Fraser Island
Great Slave Lake 15 E4 Fr. Grand Lac des Esclaves. lake Northwest Territories, NW Canada
Great Socialist People's Libyan Arab Jamahiriya see Libya
Great Sound 20 A5 sound Bermuda, NW Atlantic Ocean
Great Victoria Desert 125 C5 desert South Australia/Western Australia
Great Wall of China 106 C4 ancient monument N China Asia
Great Yarmouth 67 E6 var. Yarmouth. E England, United Kingdom
Grebenka see Hrebinka
Gredos, Sierra de 70 D3 mountain range W Spain
Greece 83 A5 off. Hellenic Republic, Gk. Ellás; anc. Hellas. country SE Europe
Greeley 22 D4 Colorado, C USA
Green Bay 18 B2 Wisconsin, N USA
Green Bay 18 B2 lake bay Michigan/Wisconsin, N USA
Greeneville 21 E1 Tennessee, S USA
Greenland 60 D3 Dan. Grønland, Inuit Kalaallit Nunaat. Danish external territory NE North America
Greenland Sea 61 F2 sea Arctic Ocean
Green Mountains 19 G2 mountain range Vermont, NE USA
Green Mountain State see Vermont
Greenock 66 C4 W Scotland, United Kingdom
Green River 22 B3 Wyoming, C USA
Green River 18 C5 river Kentucky, C USA
Green River 22 B4 river Utah, W USA
Greensboro 21 F1 North Carolina, SE USA
Greenville 20 B2 Mississippi, S USA
Greenville 21 F1 North Carolina, SE USA
Greenville 21 E1 South Carolina, SE USA
Greenville 27 G2 Texas, SW USA
Greenwich 67 B8 United Kingdom
Greenwood 20 B2 Mississippi, S USA
Greenwood 21 E2 South Carolina, SE USA
Gregory Range 126 C3 mountain range Queensland, E Australia
Greifenberg/Greifenberg in Pommern see Gryfice
Greifswald 72 D2 Mecklenburg-Vorpommern, NE Germany
Grenada 20 C2 Mississippi, S USA
Grenada 33 G5 country SE West Indies
Grenadines, The 33 H4 island group Grenada/St Vincent and the Grenadines
Grenoble 69 D5 anc. Cularo, Gratianopolis. Isère, E France
Gresham 24 B3 Oregon, NW USA
Grevená 82 B4 Dytikí Makedonía, N Greece
Grevenmacher 65 E8 Grevenmacher, E Luxembourg
Greymouth 129 B5 West Coast, South Island, New Zealand
Grey Range 127 C5 mountain range New South Wales/Queensland, E Australia
Greytown see San Juan del Norte
Griffin 20 D2 Georgia, SE USA
Grimari 54 C4 Ouaka, C Central African Republic
Grimsby 67 E5 prev. Great Grimsby. E England, United Kingdom
Grobin see Grobiņa
Grobiņa 84 B3 Ger. Grobin. Liepāja, W Latvia
Gródek Jagielloński see Horodok
Grodno see Hrodna
Grodzisk Wielkopolski 76 B3 Wielkopolskie, C Poland
Groesbeek 64 D4 Gelderland, SE Netherlands
Grójec 76 D4 Mazowieckie, C Poland
Groningen 64 E1 Groningen, NE Netherlands
Grønland see Greenland
Groote Eylandt 126 B2 island Northern Territory, N Australia
Grootfontein 56 B3 Otjozondjupa, N Namibia
Groot Karasberge 56 B4 mountain range S Namibia
Gros Islet 33 F1 N Saint Lucia
Grossa, Isola see Dugi Otok
Grossbetschkerek see Zrenjanin
Grosse Morava see Velika Morava
Grosser Sund see Suur Väin
Grosseto 74 B4 Toscana, C Italy
Grossglockner 73 C7 mountain W Austria
Grosskanizsa see Nagykanizsa
Gross-Karol see Carei
Grosskikinda see Kikinda
Grossmichel see Michalovce
Gross-Schlatten see Abrud
Grosswardein see Oradea
Groznyy 89 B8 Chechenskaya Respublika, SW Russian Federation
Grudovo see Sredets
Grudziądz 76 C3 Ger. Graudenz. Kujawsko-pomorskie, C Poland
Grums 63 B6 Värmland, C Sweden
Grünberg/Grünberg in Schlesien see Zielona Góra
Grüneberg see Zielona Góra
Gruzinskaya SSR/Gruziya see Georgia
Gryazi 89 B6 Lipetskaya Oblast', W Russian Federation
Gryfice 76 B2 Ger. Greifenberg, Greifenberg in Pommern. Zachodnio-pomorskie, NW Poland
Guabito 31 E4 Bocas del Toro, NW Panama
Guadalajara 28 D4 Jalisco, C Mexico
Guadalajara 71 E3 Ar. Wad Al-Hajarah; anc. Arriaca. Castilla-La Mancha, C Spain
Guadalcanal 122 C3 island C Solomon Islands
Guadalquivir 70 D4 river W Spain
Guadalupe 28 D3 Zacatecas, C Mexico
Guadalupe Peak 26 D3 mountain Texas, SW USA
Guadalupe River 27 G4 river SW USA
Guadarrama, Sierra de 71 E2 mountain range C Spain
Guadeloupe 33 H3 French overseas department E West Indies
Guadiana 70 C4 river Portugal/Spain
Guadix 71 E4 Andalucía, S Spain
Guaimaca 30 C2 Francisco Morazán, C Honduras
Guajira, Península de la 36 B1 peninsula N Colombia
Gualaco 30 D2 Olancho, C Honduras
Gualán 30 B2 Zacapa, C Guatemala
Gualdicciolo 74 D1 NW San Marino
Gualeguaychú 42 D4 Entre Ríos, E Argentina
Guam 122 B1 US unincorporated territory W Pacific Ocean
Guamúchil 28 C3 Sinaloa, C Mexico
Guanabacoa 32 B2 La Habana, W Cuba
Guanajuato 29 E4 Guanajuato, C Mexico
Guanare 36 C2 Portuguesa, N Venezuela
Guanare, Río 36 D2 river W Venezuela
Guangdong 106 C6 var. Guangdong Sheng, Kuang-tung, Kwangtung, Yue. province S China
Guangdong Sheng see Guangdong
Guangju see Kwangju
Guangxi see Guangxi Zhuangzu Zizhiqu
Guangxi Zhuangzu Zizhiqu 106 C6 var. Guangxi, Gui, Kuang-hsi, Kwangsi, Eng. Kwangsi Chuang Autonomous Region. autonomous region S China
Guangyuan 106 B5 var. Kuang-yuan, Kwangyuan. Sichuan, C China
Guangzhou 106 C6 var. Kuang-chou, Kwangchow, Eng. Canton. province capital Guangdong, S China
Guantánamo 32 D3 Guantánamo, SE Cuba
Guantánamo, Bahía de 32 D3 Eng. Guantanamo Bay. US military base SE Cuba
Guantanamo Bay see Guantánamo, Bahía de
Guaporé, Rio 40 D3 var. Río Iténez. river Bolivia/Brazil
Guarda 70 C3 Guarda, N Portugal
Guarumal 31 F5 Veraguas, S Panama
Guasave 28 C3 Sinaloa, C Mexico
Guatemala 30 A2 off. Republic of Guatemala. country Central America
Guatemala Basin 13 B7 undersea basin E Pacific Ocean
Guatemala City see Ciudad de Guatemala
Guatemala, Republic of see Guatemala
Guaviare 34 B2 off. Comisaría Guaviare. province S Colombia
Guaviare, Comisaría see Guaviare
Guaviare, Río 36 D3 river E Colombia
Guayanas, Macizo de las see Guiana Highlands
Guayaquil 38 A2 var. Santiago de Guayaquil. Guayas, SW Ecuador
Guayaquil, Gulf of 38 A2 var. Gulf of Guayaquil. gulf SW Ecuador
Guayaquil, Gulf of see Guayaquil, Golfo de
Guaymas 28 B2 Sonora, NW Mexico
Gubadag 100 C2 Turkm. Tel'man; prev. Tel'mansk. Daşoguz Welaýaty, N Turkmenistan
Guben 72 D4 var. Wilhelm-Pieck-Stadt. Brandenburg, E Germany
Gudara see Ghŭdara
Gudaut'a 95 E1 NW Georgia
Guéret 68 C4 Creuse, C France
Guernsey 67 D8 island Channel Islands, NW Europe
Guerrero Negro 28 A2 Baja California Sur, NW Mexico
Gui see Guangxi Zhuangzu Zizhiqu
Guiana see French Guiana
Guiana Highlands 40 D1 var. Macizo de las Guayanas. mountain range N South America
Guiba see Juba
Guidder see Guider
Guider 54 B4 var. Guidder. Nord, N Cameroon
Guidimouni 53 G3 Zinder, S Niger
Guildford 67 D7 SE England, United Kingdom
Guilin 106 C6 var. Kuei-lin, Kweilin. Guangxi Zhuangzu Zizhiqu, S China
Guimarães 70 B2 var. Guimaráes. Braga, N Portugal
Guimaráes see Guimarães
Guinea 52 C4 off. Republic of Guinea, var. Guinée; prev. French Guinea, People's Revolutionary Republic of Guinea. country W Africa
Guinea Basin 47 A5 undersea basin E Atlantic Ocean
Guinea-Bissau 52 B4 off. Republic of Guinea-Bissau, Fr. Guinée-Bissau, Port. Guiné-Bissau; prev. Portuguese Guinea. country W Africa
Guinea-Bissau, Republic of see Guinea-Bissau
Guinea, Gulf of 46 B4 Fr. Golfe de Guinée. gulf E Atlantic Ocean
Guinea, People's Revolutionary Republic of see Guinea
Guinea, Republic of see Guinea
Guiné-Bissau see Guinea-Bissau
Guinée see Guinea
Guinée-Bissau see Guinea-Bissau
Guinée, Golfe de see Guinea, Gulf of
Güiria 37 E1 Sucre, NE Venezuela
Guiyang 106 B6 var. Kuei-yang, Kuei-yang, Kueyang, Kweiyang; prev. Kweichu. province capital Guizhou, S China
Guizhou 106 B6 China
Gujarāt 112 C4 var. Gujerat. cultural region W India
Gujerat see Gujarāt
Gujrānwāla 112 D2 Punjab, NE Pakistan
Gujrāt 112 D2 Punjab, E Pakistan
Gulbarga 110 C1 Karnātaka, C India
Gulbene 84 D3 Ger. Alt-Schwanenburg. Gulbene, NE Latvia
Gulf of Liaotung see Liaodong Wan
Gulfport 20 C3 Mississippi, S USA
Gulf, The 98 C4 var. Persian Gulf, Ar. Khalīj al 'Arabī, Per. Khalīj-e Fars. gulf SW Asia
Gulistan see Guliston
Guliston 101 E2 Rus. Gulistan. Sirdaryo Viloyati, E Uzbekistan
Gulja see Yining
Gulkana 14 D3 Alaska, USA
Gulu 51 B6 N Uganda
Gulyantsi 82 C1 Pleven, N Bulgaria
Guma see Pishan
Gumbinnen see Gusev
Gumpolds see Humpolec
Gümülcine/Gümüljina see Komotiní
Gümüşane see Gümüşhane
Gümüşhane 95 E3 var. Gümüşane, Gumushkhane. Gümüşhane, NE Turkey
Gumushkhane see Gümüşhane
Güney Doğu Toroslar 95 E4 mountain range SE Turkey
Gunnbjørn Fjeld 60 D4 var. Gunnbjörns Bjerge. mountain C Greenland
Gunnbjörns Bjerge see Gunnbjørn Fjeld
Gunnedah 127 D6 New South Wales, SE Australia
Gunnison 22 C5 Colorado, C USA
Gurbansoltan Eje 100 C2 prev. Ýylanly, Rus. Il'yaly. Daşoguz Welaýaty, N Turkmenistan
Gurbantünggüt Shamo 104 B2 desert W China
Gurgan see Gorgān
Guri, Embalse de 37 E2 reservoir E Venezuela
Gurkfeld see Krško
Gurktaler Alpen 73 D7 mountain range S Austria
Gürün 94 D3 Sivas, C Turkey
Gur'yev/Gur'yevskaya Oblast' see Atyrau
Gusau 53 G4 Zamfara, NW Nigeria
Gusev 84 B4 Ger. Gumbinnen. Kaliningradskaya Oblast', W Russian Federation
Gustavus 14 D4 Alaska, USA
Güstrow 72 C3 Mecklenburg-Vorpommern, NE Germany
Guta/Gúta see Kolárovo
Gütersloh 72 B4 Nordrhein-Westfalen, W Germany
Gutta see Kolárovo
Guttstadt see Dobre Miasto
Guwāhāti 113 G3 prev. Gauhāti. Assam, NE India
Guyana 37 F3 off. Co-operative Republic of Guyana; prev. British Guiana. country N South America
Guyana, Co-operative Republic of see Guyana
Guyane see French Guiana
Guymon 27 E1 Oklahoma, C USA
Güzelyurt 80 C5 Gk. Kólpos Mórfu, Morphou. W Cyprus
Gvardeysk 84 A4 Ger. Tapaiu. Kaliningradskaya Oblast', W Russian Federation
Gwādar 112 A3 var. Gwadur. Baluchistān, SW Pakistan
Gwadur see Gwādar
Gwalior 112 D3 Madhya Pradesh, C India
Gwanda 56 D3 Matabeleland South, SW Zimbabwe
Gwy see Wye
Gyandzha see Gäncä
Gyangzê 104 C5 Xizang Zizhiqu, W China
Gyaring Co 104 C5 lake W China
Gyêgu see Yushu
Gyergyószentmiklós see Gheorgheni
Gyixong see Gonggar
Gympie 127 E5 Queensland, E Australia
Gyomaendrőd 77 D7 Békés, SE Hungary
Gyöngyös 77 D6 Heves, NE Hungary
Győr 77 C6 Ger. Raab, Lat. Arrabona. Győr-Moson-Sopron, NW Hungary
Gýtheio 83 B6 var. Githio; prev. Ýíthion. Pelopónnisos, S Greece
Gyulafehérvár see Alba Iulia
Gyumri 95 F2 var. Giumri, Rus. Kumayri; prev. Aleksandropol', Leninakan. W Armenia
Gyzyrlabat see Serdar

H

Haabai see Ha'apai Group
Haacht 65 C6 Vlaams Brabant, C Belgium
Haaksbergen 64 E3 Overijssel, E Netherlands
Ha'apai Group 123 F4 var. Haabai. island group C Tonga
Haapsalu 84 D2 Ger. Hapsal. Läänemaa, W Estonia
Ha'Arava see 'Arabah, Wādī al
Haarlem 64 C3 prev. Harlem. Noord-Holland, W Netherlands
Haast 129 B6 West Coast, South Island, New Zealand
Hachijo-jima 109 D6 island Izu-shotō, SE Japan
Hachinohe 108 D3 Aomori, Honshū, C Japan
Haḍabat al Jilf al Kabīr 50 A2 var. Gilf Kebir Plateau. plateau SW Egypt
Hadama see Nazrēt
Hadejia 53 G4 Jigawa, N Nigeria
Hadejia 53 G3 river N Nigeria
Hadera 97 A6 var. Khadera; prev. Ḩadera. Haifa, C Israel
Ḩadera see Hadera
Hadhdhunmathi Atoll 110 A5 atoll S Maldives
Ha Đông 114 D3 var. Hadong. Ha Tây, N Vietnam
Hadong see Ha Đông
Hadramaut 99 C6 Eng. Hadramaut. mountain range S Yemen
Hadramaut see Ḩaḑramawt
Hadrianopolis see Edirne
Haerbin/Haerhpin/Ha-erh-pin see Harbin
Hafnia see Denmark
Hafnia see København
Hafren see Severn
Hafun, Ras see Xaafuun, Raas
Hagåtña 122 B1, var. Agaña. dependent territory capital NW Guam
Hagerstown 19 E4 Maryland, NE USA
Ha Giang 114 D3 Ha Giang, N Vietnam
Hagios Evstrátios see Ágios Efstrátios
HaGolan see Golan Heights
Hagondange 68 D3 Moselle, NE France
Haguenau 68 E3 Bas-Rhin, NE France
Haibowan see Wuhai
Haicheng 106 D3 Liaoning, NE China
Haidarabad see Hyderābād
Haifa see Hefa
Haifa, Bay of see Mifrats Hefa
Haifong see Hai Phong
Haikou 106 C7 var. Hai-k'ou, Hoihow, Fr. Hoï-Hao. province capital Hainan, S China
Hai-k'ou see Haikou
Ḩā'il 98 B4 Ḩā'il, NW Saudi Arabia
Hailuoto 62 D4 Swe. Karlö. island W Finland
Hainan 106 B7 var. Hainan Sheng, Qiong. province S China
Hainan Dao 106 C7 island S China
Hainan Sheng see Hainan
Hainasch see Ainaži
Haines 14 D4 Alaska, USA

Hainichen – Huailai

Hainichen *72 D4* Sachsen, E Germany
Hai Phong *114 D3 var.* Haifong, Haiphong. N Vietnam
Haiphong *see* Hai Phong
Haiti *32 D3 off.* Republic of Haiti. *country* C West Indies
Haiti, Republic of *see* Haiti
Haiya *50 C3* Red Sea, NE Sudan
Hajdúhadház *77 D6* Hajdú-Bihar, E Hungary
Hajîne *see* Abū Ḩardān
Hajnówka *76 E3 Ger.* Hermhausen. Podlaskie, NE Poland
Hakodate *108 D3* Hokkaidō, NE Japan
Hal *see* Halle
Ḩalab *96 B2 Eng.* Aleppo, *Fr.* Alep; *anc.* Beroea. Ḩalab, NW Syria
Ḩalāniyāt, Juzur al *99 D6 var.* Jazā'ir Bin Ghalfān, *Eng.* Kuria Muria Islands. *island group* S Oman
Halberstadt *72 C4* Sachsen-Anhalt, C Germany
Halden *63 B6 prev.* Fredrikshald. Østfold, S Norway
Halfmoon Bay *129 A8 var.* Oban. Stewart Island, Southland, New Zealand
Haliacmon *see* Aliákmonas
Halifax *17 F4 province capital* Nova Scotia, SE Canada
Halkida *see* Chalkída
Halle *65 B6 Fr.* Hal. Vlaams Brabant, C Belgium
Halle *72 C4 var.* Halle an der Saale. Sachsen-Anhalt, C Germany
Halle an der Saale *see* Halle
Halle-Neustadt *72 C4* Sachsen-Anhalt, C Germany
Halley *132 B2 UK research station* Antarctica
Hall Islands *120 B2 island group* C Micronesia
Halls Creek *124 C3* Western Australia
Halmahera, Laut *see* Halmahera Sea
Halmahera, Pulau *117 F3 prev.* Djailolo, Gilolo, Jailolo. *island* E Indonesia
Halmahera Sea *117 F4 Ind.* Laut Halmahera. *sea* E Indonesia
Halmstad *63 B7* Halland, S Sweden
Hälsingborg *see* Helsingborg
Hamada *109 B6* Shimane, Honshū, SW Japan
Hamadān *98 C3 anc.* Ecbatana. Hamadān, W Iran
Ḩamāh *96 B3 var.* Hama; *anc.* Epiphania, *Bibl.* Hamath. Ḩamāh, W Syria
Hamamatsu *109 D6 var.* Hamamatu. Shizuoka, Honshū, S Japan
Hamamatu *see* Hamamatsu
Hamar *63 B5 prev.* Storhammer. Hedmark, S Norway
Hamath *see* Ḩamāh
Hamburg *72 B3* Hamburg, N Germany
Hamd, Wadi al *98 A4 dry watercourse* W Saudi Arabia
Hämeenlinna *63 D5 Swe.* Tavastehus. Etelä-Suomi, S Finland
HaMela h, Yam *see* Dead Sea
Hamersley Range *124 A4 mountain range* Western Australia
Hamhŭng *107 E3* C North Korea
Hami *104 C3 var.* Ha-mi, *Uigh.* Kumul, Qomul. Xinjiang Uygur Zizhiqu, NW China
Ha-mi *see* Hami
Hamilton *20 A5 dependent territory capital* C Bermuda
Hamilton *16 D5* Ontario, S Canada
Hamilton *128 D3* Waikato, North Island, New Zealand
Hamilton *66 C4* S Scotland, United Kingdom
Hamilton *20 C2* Alabama, S USA
Hamim, Wadi al *49 G2 river* NE Libya
Hamïs Musait *see* Khamīs Mushayt
Hamm *72 B4 var.* Hamm in Westfalen. Nordrhein-Westfalen, W Germany
Ḩammāmāt, Khalīj al *see* Hammamet, Golfe de
Ḩammamet, Golfe de *80 D3 Ar.* Khalīj al Ḩammāmāt. *gulf* NE Tunisia
Hammar, Hawr al *98 C3 lake* SE Iraq
Hamm in Westfalen *see* Hamm
Hampden *129 B7* Otago, South Island, New Zealand
Hampstead *67 A7* Maryland, USA
Ħamrun *80 B5* C Malta
Hāmūn, Daryācheh-ye *see* Şāberī, Hāmūn-e/ Sīstān, Daryācheh-ye
Hamwih *see* Southampton
Hânceşti *see* Hînceşti
Hancewicze *see* Hantsavichy
Handan *106 C4 var.* Han-tan. Hebei, E China
Haneda *108 A2* international airport Tōkyō, Honshū, S Japan
Hanford *25 C6* California, W USA
Hangayn Nuruu *104 D2 mountain range* C Mongolia
Hang-chou/Hangchow *see* Hangzhou
Hangö *see* Hanko
Hangzhou *106 D5 var.* Hang-chou, Hangchow. *province capital* Zhejiang, SE China
Hania *see* Chaniá
Hanka, Lake *see* Khanka, Lake
Hanko *63 D6 Swe.* Hangö. Etelä-Suomi, SW Finland
Han-kou/Han-k'ou/Hankow *see* Wuhan
Hanmer Springs *129 C5* Canterbury, South Island, New Zealand
Hannibal *23 G4* Missouri, C USA
Hannover *72 B3 Eng.* Hanover. Niedersachsen, NW Germany
Hanöbukten *63 B7 bay* S Sweden
Ha Nôi *114 D3 Eng.* Hanoi, *Fr.* Hanoï. *country capital* N Vietnam
Hanover *see* Hannover
Han Shui *105 E4 river* C China
Han-tan *see* Handan
Hantsavichy *85 B6 Pol.* Hancewicze, *Rus.* Gantsevichi. Brestskaya Voblasts', SW Belarus
Hanyang *see* Wuhan
Hanzhong *106 B5* Shaanxi, C China
Hāora *113 F4 prev.* Howrah. West Bengal, NE India
Haparanda *62 D4* Norrbotten, N Sweden
Hapsal *see* Haapsalu
Haradok *85 E5 Rus.* Gorodok. Vitsyebskaya Voblasts', N Belarus
Haradzyets *85 B6 Rus.* Gorodets. Brestskaya Voblasts', SW Belarus
Haramachi *108 D4* Fukushima, Honshū, E Japan
Harany *85 D5 Rus.* Gorany. Vitsyebskaya Voblasts', N Belarus
Harare *56 D3 prev.* Salisbury. *country capital* Mashonaland East, NE Zimbabwe
Harbavichy *85 E6 Rus.* Gorbovichi. Mahilyowskaya Voblasts', E Belarus
Harbel *52 C5* W Liberia
Harbin *107 E2 var.* Haerbin, Ha-erh-pin, Kharbin; *prev.* Haerhpin, Pingkiang, Pinkiang. *province capital* Heilongjiang, NE China
Hardangerfjorden *63 A6 fjord* S Norway
Hardangervidda *63 A6 plateau* S Norway
Hardenberg *64 E3* Overijssel, E Netherlands
Harelbeke *65 A6 var.* Harlebeke. West-Vlaanderen, W Belgium
Harem *see* Ḩārim
Haren *64 E2* Groningen, NE Netherlands
Hārer *51 D5* E Ethiopia
Hargeisa *see* Hargeysa
Hargeysa *51 D5 var.* Hargeisa. Woqooyi Galbeed, NW Somalia
Hariana *see* Haryāna
Hari, Batang *116 B4 prev.* Djambi. *river* Sumatera, W Indonesia
Ḩārim *96 B2 var.* Harem. Idlib, W Syria
Harima-nada *109 B6 sea* S Japan
Harirud *101 E4 var.* Tedzhen, *Turkm.* Tejen. *river* Afghanistan/Iran
Harlan *23 F3* Iowa, C USA
Harlebeke *see* Harelbeke
Harlem *see* Haarlem
Harlingen *64 D2 Fris.* Harns. Friesland, N Netherlands
Harlingen *27 G5* Texas, SW USA
Harlow *67 E6* E England, United Kingdom
Harney Basin *24 B4 basin* Oregon, NW USA
Härnösand *63 C5 var.* Hernösand. Västernorrland, C Sweden
Harns *see* Harlingen
Harper *52 D5 var.* Cape Palmas. NE Liberia
Harricana *16 D3 river* Québec, SE Canada
Harris *66 B3 physical region* NW Scotland, United Kingdom
Harrisburg *19 E4 state capital* Pennsylvania, NE USA
Harrisonburg *19 E4* Virginia, NE USA
Harrison, Cape *17 F2 headland* Newfoundland and Labrador, E Canada
Harris Ridge *see* Lomonosov Ridge
Harrogate *67 D5* N England, United Kingdom
Hârşova *86 D5 prev.* Hîrşova. Constanţa, SE Romania
Harstad *62 C2* Troms, N Norway
Hartford *19 G3 state capital* Connecticut, NE USA
Hartlepool *67 D5* N England, United Kingdom
Harunabad *see* Eslāmābād
Har Us Gol *104 C2 lake* Hovd, W Mongolia
Har Us Nuur *104 C2 lake* NW Mongolia
Harwich *67 E6* E England, United Kingdom
Haryāna *112 D2 var.* Hariana. *cultural region* N India
Hashemite Kingdom of Jordan *see* Jordan
Hasselt *65 C6* Limburg, NE Belgium
Hassetché *see* Al Ḩasakah
Hasta Colonia/Hasta Pompeia *see* Asti
Hastings *128 E4* Hawke's Bay, North Island, New Zealand
Hastings *67 E7* SE England, United Kingdom
Hastings *23 E4* Nebraska, C USA
Haţeg *86 B4 Ger.* Wallenthal, *Hung.* Hátszeg; *prev.* Hatzeg, Hötzing. Hunedoara, SW Romania
Hátszeg *see* Haţeg
Hattem *64 D3* Gelderland, E Netherlands
Hatteras, Cape *21 G1 headland* North Carolina, SE USA
Hatteras Plain *13 D6 abyssal plain* W Atlantic Ocean
Hattiesburg *20 C3* Mississippi, S USA
Hatton Bank *see* Hatton Ridge
Hatton Ridge *58 B2 var.* Hatton Bank. *undersea ridge* N Atlantic Ocean
Hat Yai *115 C7 var.* Ban Hat Yai. Songkhla, SW Thailand
Hatzeg *see* Haţeg
Hatzfeld *see* Jimbolia
Haugesund *63 A6* Rogaland, S Norway
Haukeligrend *63 A6* Telemark, S Norway
Haukivesi *63 E5 lake* SE Finland
Hauraki Gulf *128 D2 gulf* North Island, N New Zealand
Hauroko, Lake *129 A7 lake* South Island, New Zealand
Hautes Fagnes *65 D6 Ger.* Hohes Venn. *mountain range* E Belgium
Hauts Plateaux *48 D2 plateau* Algeria/Morocco
Hauzenberg *73 D6* Bayern, SE Germany
Havana *13 D6* Illinois, N USA
Havana *see* La Habana
Havant *67 D7* S England, United Kingdom
Havelock *21 F1* North Carolina, SE USA
Havelock North *128 E4* Hawke's Bay, North Island, New Zealand
Haverfordwest *67 C6* SW Wales, United Kingdom
Havířov *77 C5* Moravskoslezský Kraj, E Czech Republic
Havre *22 C1* Montana, NW USA
Havre *see* le Havre
Havre-St-Pierre *17 F3* Québec, E Canada
Hawai'i *25 A8 off.* State of Hawai'i, *also known as* Aloha State, Paradise of the Pacific, *var.* Hawaii. *state* USA, C Pacific Ocean
Hawai'i *25 B8 var.* Hawaii. *island* Hawaiian Islands, USA, C Pacific Ocean
Hawaiian Islands *130 D2 prev.* Sandwich Islands. *island group* Hawaii, USA
Hawaiian Ridge *130 H4 undersea ridge* N Pacific Ocean
Hawea, Lake *129 B6 lake* South Island, New Zealand
Hawera *128 D4* Taranaki, North Island, New Zealand
Hawick *66 C4* SE Scotland, United Kingdom
Hawke Bay *128 E4 bay* North Island, New Zealand
Hawkeye State *see* Iowa
Hawlēr *see* Arbil
Hawthorne *25 C6* Nevada, W USA
Hay *127 C6* New South Wales, SE Australia
HaYarden *see* Jordan
Hayastani Hanrapetut'yun *see* Armenia
Hayes *16 B2 river* Manitoba, C Canada
Hay River *15 E4* Northwest Territories, W Canada
Hays *23 E5* Kansas, C USA
Haysyn *86 D3 Rus.* Gaysin. Vinnyts'ka Oblast', C Ukraine
Hazar *100 B2 prev. Rus.* Cheleken. Balkan Welaýaty, W Turkmenistan
Heard and McDonald Islands *119 B7 Australian external territory* S Indian Ocean
Hearst *16 C4* Ontario, S Canada
Heart of Dixie *see* Alabama
Heathrow *67 A8 international airport* SE England, United Kingdom
Hebei *106 C4 var.* Hebei Sheng, Hopeh, Hopei, Ji; *prev.* Chihli. *province* E China
Hebei Sheng *see* Hebei
Hebron *97 A6 var.* Al Khalīl, El Khalil, *Heb.* Hevron; *anc.* Kiriath-Arba. S West Bank
Heemskerk *64 C3* Noord-Holland, W Netherlands
Heerde *64 D3* Gelderland, E Netherlands
Heerenveen *64 D2 Fris.* It Hearrenfean. Friesland, N Netherlands
Heerhugowaard *64 C2* Noord-Holland, NW Netherlands
Heerlen *65 D6* Limburg, SE Netherlands
Heerwegen *see* Polkowice
Hefa *97 A5 var.* Haifa, *hist.* Caiffa, Caiphas; *anc.* Sycaminum. Haifa, N Israel
Ḩefa, Mifraẓ *see* Mifrats Hefa
Hefei *106 D5 var.* Hofei, *hist.* Luchow. *province capital* Anhui, E China
Hegang *107 E2* Heilongjiang, NE China
Hei *see* Heilongjiang
Heide *72 B2* Schleswig-Holstein, N Germany
Heidelberg *73 B5* Baden-Württemberg, SW Germany
Heidenheim *see* Heidenheim an der Brenz
Heidenheim an der Brenz *73 B6 var.* Heidenheim. Baden-Württemberg, S Germany
Hei-ho *see* Nagqu
Heilbronn *73 B6* Baden-Württemberg, SW Germany
Heiligenbeil *see* Mamonovo
Heilongjiang *106 D2 var.* Hei, Heilongjiang Sheng, Hei-lung-chiang, Heilungkiang. *province* NE China
Heilong Jiang *see* Amur
Heilongjiang Sheng *see* Heilongjiang
Heiloo *64 C3* Noord-Holland, NW Netherlands
Heilsberg *see* Lidzbark Warmiński
Hei-lung-chiang/Heilungkiang *see* Heilongjiang
Heimdal *63 B5* Sør-Trøndelag, S Norway
Heinaste *see* Ainaži
Hekimhan *94 D3* Malatya, C Turkey
Helena *22 B2 state capital* Montana, NW USA
Helensville *128 D2* Auckland, North Island, New Zealand
Helgoland Bay *see* Helgoländer Bucht
Helgoländer Bucht *72 A2 var.* Helgoland Bay, Heligoland Bight. *bay* NW Germany
Heligoland Bight *see* Helgoländer Bucht
Heliopolis *see* Baalbek
Hellas *see* Greece
Hellenic Republic *see* Greece
Hellevoetsluis *64 B4* Zuid-Holland, SW Netherlands
Hellín *71 E4* Castilla-La Mancha, C Spain
Darya-ye Helmand *100 D5 var.* Rūd-e Hīrmand. *river* Afghanistan/Iran
Helmantica *see* Salamanca
Helmond *65 D5* Noord-Brabant, S Netherlands
Helsingborg *63 B7 prev.* Hälsingborg. Skåne, S Sweden
Helsingfors *see* Helsinki
Helsinki *63 D6 Swe.* Helsingfors. *country capital* Etelä-Suomi, S Finland
Heltau *see* Cisnădie
Helvetia *see* Switzerland
Henan *106 C5 var.* Henan Sheng, Honan, Yu. *province* C China
Henderson *18 B5* Kentucky, S USA
Henderson *25 D7* Nevada, W USA
Henderson *27 H3* Texas, SW USA
Hendū Kosh *see* Hindu Kush
Hengchow *see* Hengyang
Hengduan Shan *106 A5 mountain range* SW China
Hengelo *64 E3* Overijssel, E Netherlands
Hengnan *see* Hengyang
Hengyang *106 C6 var.* Hengnan, Heng-yang; *prev.* Hengchow. Hunan, S China
Heng-yang *see* Hengyang
Heniches'k *87 F4 Rus.* Genichesk. Khersons'ka Oblast', S Ukraine
Hennebont *68 A3* Morbihan, NW France
Henrique de Carvalho *see* Saurimo
Henzada *see* Hinthada
Herakleion *see* Irákleio
Herāt *100 D4 var.* Herat; *anc.* Aria. Herāt, W Afghanistan
Heredia *31 E4* Heredia, C Costa Rica
Hereford *27 E2* Texas, SW USA
Herford *72 B4* Nordrhein-Westfalen, NW Germany
Hérristal *see* Herstal
Herk-de-Stad *65 C6* Limburg, NE Belgium
Herlen Gol/Herlen He *see* Kerulen
Hermannstadt *see* Sibiu
Hermansverk *63 A5* Sogn Og Fjordane, S Norway
Hermhausen *see* Hajnówka
Hermiston *24 C2* Oregon, NW USA
Hermon, Mount *97 B5 Ar.* Jabal ash Shaykh. *mountain* S Syria
Hermosillo *28 B2* Sonora, NW Mexico
Hermoupolis *see* Ermoúpoli
Hernösand *see* Härnösand
Herrera del Duque *70 D3* Extremadura, W Spain
Herselt *65 C5* Antwerpen, C Belgium
Herstal *65 D6 Fr.* Héristal. Liège, E Belgium
Herzogenbusch *see* 's-Hertogenbosch
Hesse *see* Hessen
Hessen *73 B5 Eng./Fr.* Hesse. *state* C Germany
Hevron *see* Hebron
Heydebrech *see* Kędzierzyn-Kozle
Heydekrug *see* Šilutė
Heywood Islands *124 C3 island group* Western Australia
Hibbing *23 F1* Minnesota, N USA
Hibernia *see* Ireland
Hidalgo del Parral *28 C2 var.* Parral. Chihuahua, N Mexico
Hida-sanmyaku *109 C5 mountain range* Honshū, S Japan
Hierosolyma *see* Jerusalem
Hierro *48 A3 var.* Ferro. *island* Islas Canarias, Spain, NE Atlantic Ocean
High Atlas *48 C2 Eng.* High Atlas. *mountain range* C Morocco
High Atlas *see* Haut Atlas
High Plains *see* Great Plains
High Point *21 E1* North Carolina, SE USA
Hiiumaa *84 C2 Ger.* Dagden, *Swe.* Dagö. *island* W Estonia
Hikurangi *128 D2* Northland, North Island, New Zealand
Hildesheim *72 B4* Niedersachsen, N Germany
Hilla *see* Al Ḩillah
Hillaby, Mount *33 G1 mountain* N Barbados
Hill Bank *30 C1* Orange Walk, N Belize
Hillegom *64 C3* Zuid-Holland, W Netherlands
Hilo *25 B8* Hawaii, USA, C Pacific Ocean
Hilton Head Island *21 E2* South Carolina, SE USA
Hilversum *64 C3* Noord-Holland, C Netherlands
Himalaya/Himalaya Shan *see* Himalayas
Himalayas *113 E2 var.* Himalaya, *Chin.* Himalaya Shan. *mountain range* S Asia
Himeji *109 C6 var.* Himezi. Hyōgo, Honshū, SW Japan
Himezi *see* Himeji
Ḩimş *96 B4 var.* Homs; *anc.* Emesa. Ḩimş, C Syria
Hînceşti *86 D4 var.* Hânceşti; *prev.* Kotovsk. C Moldova
Hinchinbrook Island *126 D3 island* Queensland, NE Australia
Hinds *129 C6* Canterbury, South Island, New Zealand
Hindu Kush *101 F4 Per.* Hendū Kosh. *mountain range* Afghanistan/Pakistan
Hinesville *21 E3* Georgia, SE USA
Hinnøya *62 C3 Lapp.* Iinnasuolu. *island* C Norway
Hinson Bay *20 A5 bay* W Bermuda W Atlantic Ocean
Hinthada *114 B4 var.* Henzada. Ayeyarwady, SW Myanmar (Burma)
Hios *see* Chíos
Hirfanlı Barajı *94 C3 reservoir* C Turkey
Hīrmand, Rūd-e *see* Helmand, Daryā-ye
Hirosaki *108 D3* Aomori, Honshū, C Japan
Hiroshima *109 B6 var.* Hirosima. Hiroshima, Honshū, SW Japan
Hirschberg/Hirschberg im Riesengebirge/ Hirschberg in Schlesien *see* Jelenia Góra
Hirson *68 D3* Aisne, N France
Hîrşova *see* Hârşova
Hispalis *see* Sevilla
Hispana/Hispania *see* Spain
Hispaniola *34 B1 island* Dominion Republic/Haiti
Hitachi *109 D5 var.* Hitati. Ibaraki, Honshū, S Japan
Hitati *see* Hitachi
Hitra *62 A4 prev.* Hitteren. *island* S Norway
Hitteren *see* Hitra
Hjälmaren *63 C6 Eng.* Lake Hjalmar. *lake* C Sweden
Hjalmar, Lake *see* Hjälmaren
Hjørring *63 B7* Nordjylland, N Denmark
Hkakabo Razi *114 B1 mountain* Myanmar (Burma)/China
Hlobyne *87 F2 Rus.* Globino. Poltavs'ka Oblast', NE Ukraine
Hlukhiv *87 F1 Rus.* Glukhov. Sums'ka Oblast', NE Ukraine
Hlybokaye *85 D5 Rus.* Glubokoye. Vitsyebskaya Voblasts', N Belarus
Hoa Binh *114 D3* Hoa Binh, N Vietnam
Hoang Lien Son *114 D3 mountain range* N Vietnam
Hobart *127 C8 prev.* Hobarton, Hobart Town. *state capital* Tasmania, SE Australia
Hobarton/Hobart Town *see* Hobart
Hobbs *27 E3* New Mexico, SW USA
Hobro *63 A7* Nordjylland, N Denmark
Hô Chi Minh *115 E6 var.* Ho Chi Minh City; *prev.* Saigon. S Vietnam
Ho Chi Minh City *see* Hô Chi Minh
Hodeida *see* Al Ḩudaydah
Hódmezővásárhely *77 D7* Csongrád, SE Hungary
Hodna, Chott El *80 C4 var.* Chott el-Hodna, *Ar.* Shatt al-Hodna. *salt lake* N Algeria
Hodna, Chott el-/Hodna, Shatt al- *see* Hodna, Chott El
Hodonín *77 C5 Ger.* Göding. Jihomoravský Kraj, SE Czech Republic
Hoei *see* Huy
Hoey *see* Huy
Hof *73 C5* Bayern, SE Germany
Hofei *see* Hefei
Hōfu *109 B7* Yamaguchi, Honshū, SW Japan
Hofuf *see* Al Hufūf
Hogoley Islands *see* Chuuk Islands
Hohensalza *see* Inowrocław
Hohenstadt *see* Zábřeh
Hohes Venn *see* Hautes Fagnes
Hohe Tauern *73 C7 mountain range* W Austria
Hohhot *105 F3 var.* Huhehot, Huhohaote, *Mong.* Kukukhoto; *prev.* Kweisui, Kwesui. Nei Mongol Zizhiqu, N China
Hôi An *115 E5 prev.* Faifo. Quang Nam-Đa Nång, C Vietnam
Hoï-Hao/Hoihow *see* Haikou
Hokianga Harbour *128 C2 inlet* SE Tasman Sea
Hokitika *129 B5* West Coast, South Island, New Zealand
Hokkaido *108 C2 prev.* Ezo, Yeso, Yezo. *island* NE Japan
Hola Prystan' *87 E4 Rus.* Golaya Pristan. Khersons'ka Oblast', S Ukraine
Holbrook *26 B2* Arizona, SW USA
Holetown *33 G1 prev.* Jamestown. W Barbados
Holguín *32 C2* Holguín, SE Cuba
Hollabrunn *73 E6* Niederösterreich, NE Austria
Holland *see* Netherlands
Hollandia *see* Jayapura
Holly Springs *20 C1* Mississippi, S USA
Holman *15 E3* Victoria Island, Northwest Territories, N Canada
Holmsund *62 D4* Västerbotten, N Sweden
Holon *97 A6 var.* Kholon; *prev.* Ḩolon. Tel Aviv, C Israel
Ḩolon *see* Holon
Holovanivs'k *87 E3 Rus.* Golovanevsk. Kirovohrads'ka Oblast', C Ukraine
Holstebro *63 A7* Ringkøbing, W Denmark
Holsteinborg/Holsteinsborg/Holstenborg/ Holstensborg *see* Sisimiut
Holyhead *67 C5 Wel.* Caer Gybi. NW Wales, United Kingdom
Hombori *53 E3* Mopti, S Mali
Homs *see* Al Khums, Libya
Homs *see* Ḩimş
Homyel' *85 D7 Rus.* Gomel'. Homyel'skaya Voblasts', SE Belarus
Honan *see* Luoyang, China
Honan *see* Henan, China
Hondo *27 F4* Texas, SW USA
Hondo *see* Honshū
Honduras *30 C2 off.* Republic of Honduras. *country* Central America
Honduras, Golfo de *see* Honduras, Gulf of
Honduras, Gulf of *30 C2 Sp.* Golfo de Honduras. *gulf* W Caribbean Sea
Honduras, Republic of *see* Honduras
Hønefoss *63 B6* Buskerud, S Norway
Honey Lake *25 B5 lake* California, W USA
Hon Gai *see* Hông Gai
Hongay *see* Hông Gai
Hông Gai *114 E3 var.* Hon Gai, Hongay. Quang Ninh, N Vietnam
Hông Hà, Sông *see* Red River
Hong Kong *106 A1 Chin.* Xianggang. Hong Kong, S China
Hong Kong Island *106 B2 island* S China Asia
Honiara *122 C3 country capital* Guadalcanal, C Solomon Islands
Honjō *108 D4 var.* Honzyô, Yurihonjō. Akita, Honshū, C Japan
Honolulu *25 A8 state capital* O'ahu, Hawaii, USA, C Pacific Ocean
Honshu *109 E5 var.* Hondo, Honsyû. *island* SW Japan
Honsyû *see* Honshū
Honte *see* Westerschelde
Honzyô *see* Honjō
Hoogeveen *64 E2* Drenthe, NE Netherlands
Hoogezand-Sappemeer *64 E2* Groningen, NE Netherlands
Hoorn *64 C2* Noord-Holland, NW Netherlands
Hoosier State *see* Indiana
Hopa *95 E2* Artvin, NE Turkey
Hope *14 C3* British Columbia, SW Canada
Hopedale *17 F2* Newfoundland and Labrador, NE Canada
Hopeh/Hopei *see* Hebei
Hopkinsville *18 B5* Kentucky, S USA
Horasan *95 F3* Erzurum, NE Turkey
Horizon Deep *130 D4 trench* W Pacific Ocean
Horki *85 E6 Rus.* Gorki. Mahilyowskaya Voblasts', E Belarus
Horlivka *87 G3 Rom.* Adâncata, *Rus.* Gorlovka. Donets'ka Oblast', E Ukraine
Hormoz, Tangeh-ye *see* Hormuz, Strait of
Hormuz, Strait of *98 D4 var.* Strait of Ormuz, *Per.* Tangeh-ye Hormoz. *strait* Iran/Oman
Cape Horn *43 C8 Eng.* Cape Horn. *headland* S Chile
Horn, Cape *see* Hornos, Cabo de
Hornsby *126 E1* New South Wales, SE Australia
Horodnya *87 E1 Rus.* Gorodnya. Chernihivs'ka Oblast', NE Ukraine
Horodok *86 B2 Pol.* Gródek Jagielloński, *Rus.* Gorodok, Gorodok Yagellonski. L'vivs'ka Oblast', NW Ukraine
Horodyshche *87 E2 Rus.* Gorodishche. Cherkas'ka Oblast', C Ukraine
Horoshiri-dake *108 D2 var.* Horosiri Dake. *mountain* Hokkaidō, N Japan
Horosiri Dake *see* Horoshiri-dake
Horsburgh Atoll *110 A4 var.* Goidhoo Atoll. *atoll* N Maldives
Horseshoe Bay *20 A5 bay* W Bermuda W Atlantic Ocean
Horseshoe Seamounts *58 A4 seamount range* E Atlantic Ocean
Horsham *127 B7* Victoria, SE Australia
Horst *65 D5* Limburg, SE Netherlands
Horten *63 B6* Vestfold, S Norway
Horyn' *85 B7 Rus.* Goryn. *river* NW Ukraine
Hosingen *65 D7* Diekirch, NE Luxembourg
Hospitalet *see* L'Hospitalet de Llobregat
Hotan *104 B4 var.* Khotan, *Chin.* Ho-t'ien. Xinjiang Uygur Zizhiqu, NW China
Ho-t'ien *see* Hotan
Hoting *62 C4* Jämtland, C Sweden
Hot Springs *20 B1* Arkansas, C USA
Hötzing *see* Haţeg
Houayxay *114 C3 var.* Ban Houayxay. Bokèo, N Laos
Houghton *18 B1* Michigan, N USA
Houilles *69 B5* Yvelines, Île-de-France, N France Europe
Houlton *19 H1* Maine, NE USA
Houma *20 B3* Louisiana, S USA
Houston *27 H4* Texas, SW USA
Hovd *104 C2 var.* Khovd, Kobdo; *prev.* Jirgalanta. Hovd, W Mongolia
Hove *67 E7* SE England, United Kingdom
Hoverla, Hora *86 C3 Rus.* Gora Goverla. *mountain* W Ukraine
Hovsgol, Lake *see* Hövsgöl Nuur
Hövsgöl Nuur *104 D1 var.* Lake Hovsgol. *lake* N Mongolia
Howa, Ouadi *see* Howar, Wādi
Howar, Wadi *50 A3 var.* Ouadi Howa. *river* Chad/Sudan
Howrah *see* Hāora
Hoy *66 C2 island* N Scotland, United Kingdom
Hoyerswerda *72 D4 Lus.* Wojerecy. Sachsen, E Germany
Hpa-an *114 B4 var.* Pa-an. Kayin State, S Myanmar (Burma)
Hpyu *see* Phyu
Hradec Králové *77 B5 Ger.* Königgrätz. Královéhradecký Kraj, N Czech Republic
Hrandzichy *85 B5 Rus.* Grandichi. Hrodzyenskaya Voblasts', W Belarus
Hranice *77 C5 Ger.* Mährisch-Weisskirchen. Olomoucký Kraj, E Czech Republic
Hrebinka *87 E2 Rus.* Grebenka. Poltavs'ka Oblast', NE Ukraine
Hrodna *85 B5 Pol.* Grodno. Hrodzyenskaya Voblasts', W Belarus
Hrvatska *see* Croatia
Hsia-men *see* Xiamen
Hsiang-t'an *see* Xiangtan
Hsi Chiang *see* Xi Jiang
Hsing-K'ai Hu *see* Khanka, Lake
Hsi-ning/Hsining *see* Xining
Hsinking *see* Changchun
Hsin-yang *see* Xinyang
Hsu-chou *see* Xuzhou
Htawei *see* Dawei
Huacho *38 C4* Lima, W Peru
Hua Hin *see* Ban Hua Hin
Huaihua *106 C5* Hunan, S China
Huailai *106 C3 var.* Shacheng. Hebei, E China

Huainan – Jamdena

Huainan 106 D5 var. Huai-nan, Hwainan. Anhui, E China
Huai-nan see Huainan
Huajuapan 29 F5 var. Huajuapan de León. Oaxaca, SE Mexico
Huajuapan de León see Huajuapan
Hualapai Peak 26 A2 mountain Arizona, SW USA
Huallaga, Río 38 C3 river N Peru
Huambo 56 B2 Port. Nova Lisboa. Huambo, C Angola
Huancavelica 38 D4 Huancavelica, SW Peru
Huancayo 38 D3 Junín, C Peru
Huang Hai see Yellow Sea
Huangshi 106 C5 var. Huang-shih, Hwangshih. Hubei, C China
Huang-shih see Huangshi
Huanta 38 D4 Ayacucho, C Peru
Huánuco 38 C3 Huánuco, C Peru
Huanuni 39 F4 Oruro, W Bolivia
Huaral 38 C4 Lima, W Peru
Huarás see Huaraz
Huaraz 38 C3 var. Huarás. Ancash, W Peru
Huarmey 38 C3 Ancash, W Peru
Huatabampo 28 C2 Sonora, NW Mexico
Hubli 102 B3 Karnātaka, SW India
Huddersfield 67 D5 N England, United Kingdom
Hudiksvall 63 C5 Gävleborg, C Sweden
Hudson Bay 15 G4 bay NE Canada
Hudson, Détroit d' see Hudson Strait
Hudson Strait 15 H3 Fr. Détroit d'Hudson. strait Northwest Territories/Québec, NE Canada
Hudur see Xuddur
Huê 114 E4 Th,a Thiên-Huê, C Vietnam
Huehuetenango 30 A2 Huehuetenango, W Guatemala
Huelva 70 C4 anc. Onuba. Andalucía, SW Spain
Huesca 71 F2 anc. Osca. Aragón, NE Spain
Huéscar 71 E4 Andalucía, S Spain
Hughenden 126 C3 Queensland, NE Australia
Hugo 27 G2 Oklahoma, C USA
Huhehot/Huhohaote see Hohhot
Huíla Plateau 56 B2 plateau S Angola
Huixtla 29 G5 Chiapas, SE Mexico
Hulingol 105 G2 prev. Huolin Gol. Nei Mongol Zizhiqu, N China
Hull 16 D4 Québec, SE Canada
Hull see Kingston upon Hull
Hull Island see Orona
Hulst 65 B5 Zeeland, SW Netherlands
Hulun see Hulun Buir
Hulun Buir 105 F1 var. Hailar; prev. Hulun. Nei Mongol Zizhiqu, N China
Hu-lun Ch'ih see Hulun Nur
Hulun Nur 105 F1 var. Hu-lun Ch'ih; prev. Dalai Nor. lake NE China
Humaitá 40 D2 Amazonas, N Brazil
Humboldt River 25 C5 river Nevada, W USA
Humphreys Peak 26 B1 mountain Arizona, SW USA
Humpolec 77 B5 Ger. Gumpolds, Humpoletz. Vysočina, C Czech Republic
Humpoletz see Humpolec
Hunan 106 C6 var. Hunan Sheng, Xiang. province S China
Hunan Sheng see Hunan
Hunedoara 86 B4 Ger. Eisenmarkt, Hung. Vajdahunyad. Hunedoara, SW Romania
Hünfeld 73 B5 Hessen, C Germany
Hungarian People's Republic see Hungary
Hungary 77 C6 off. Republic of Hungary, Ger. Ungarn, Hung. Magyarország, Rom. Ungaria, SCr. Mađarska, Ukr. Uhorshchyna; prev. Hungarian People's Republic. country C Europe
Hungary, Plain of see Great Hungarian Plain
Hungary, Republic of see Hungary
Hunjiang see Baishan
Hunter Island 127 B8 island Tasmania, SE Australia
Huntington 18 D4 West Virginia, NE USA
Huntington Beach 25 B8 California, W USA
Huntly 128 D3 Waikato, North Island, New Zealand
Huntsville 20 D1 Alabama, S USA
Huntsville 27 G3 Texas, SW USA
Huolin Gol see Hulingol
Hurghada 50 C2 var. Al Ghurdaqah, Ghurdaqah. E Egypt
Huron 23 E3 South Dakota, N USA
Huron, Lake 18 D2 lake Canada/USA
Hurukawa see Furukawa
Hurunui 129 C5 river South Island, New Zealand
Húsavík 61 E4 Nordhurland Eystra, NE Iceland
Husté see Khust
Husum 72 B2 Schleswig-Holstein, N Germany
Huszt see Khust
Hutchinson 23 E5 Kansas, C USA
Hutchinson Island 21 F4 island Florida, SE USA
Huy 65 C6 Dut. Hoei, Hoey. Liège, E Belgium
Huzi see Fuji
Hvannadalshnúkur 61 E5 volcano S Iceland
Hvar 78 B4 It. Lesina; anc. Pharus. island S Croatia
Hwainan see Huainan
Hwange 56 D3 prev. Wankie. Matabeleland North, W Zimbabwe
Hwang-Hae see Yellow Sea
Hwangshih see Huangshi
Hyargas Nuur 104 C2 lake NW Mongolia
Hyderābād 112 D5 var. Haidarabad. state capital Andhra Pradesh, C India
Hyderābād 112 B3 var. Haidarabad. Sind, SE Pakistan
Hyères 69 D6 Var, SE France
Hyères, Îles d' 69 D6 island group S France
Hypanis see Kuban'
Hyrcania see Gorgān
Hyvinge see Hyvinkää
Hyvinkää 63 D5 Swe. Hyvinge. Etelä-Suomi, S Finland

I

Iader see Zadar
Ialomiţa 86 C5 river SE Romania
Iaşi 86 D3 Ger. Jassy. Iaşi, NE Romania
Ibadan 53 F5 Oyo, SW Nigeria
Ibagué 36 B3 Tolima, C Colombia
Ibar 78 D4 Alb. Ibër. river C Serbia
Ibarra 38 B1 var. San Miguel de Ibarra. Imbabura, N Ecuador
Ibër see Ibar
Iberia see Spain
Iberian Mountains see Ibérico, Sistema
Iberian Peninsula 58 B4 physical region Portugal/Spain
Iberian Plain 58 B4 abyssal plain E Atlantic Ocean
Ibérica, Cordillera see Ibérico, Sistema
Ibérico, Sistema 71 E2 var. Cordillera Ibérica, Eng. Iberian Mountains. mountain range NE Spain
Ibiza see Eivissa
Ibiza see Eivissa
Ibiza see Eivissa
Ibo see Sassandra
Ica 38 D4 Ica, SW Peru
Icaria see Ikaría
Içá, Rio 40 C2 var. Río Putumayo. river NW South America
Içá, Rio see Putumayo, Río
İçel see Mersin
Iceland 61 E4 off. Republic of Iceland, Dan. Island, Icel. Ísland. country N Atlantic Ocean
Iceland Basin 58 B1 undersea basin N Atlantic Ocean
Icelandic Plateau see Iceland Plateau
Iceland Plateau 133 B6 var. Icelandic Plateau. undersea plateau S Greenland Sea
Iceland, Republic of see Iceland
Iconium see Konya
Iculisma see Angoulême
Idabel 27 H2 Oklahoma, C USA
Idaho 24 D3 off. State of Idaho, also known as Gem of the Mountains, Gem State. state NW USA
Idaho Falls 24 E3 Idaho, NW USA
Idensalmi see Iisalmi
Idfu 50 B2 var. Edfu. SE Egypt
Idi Amin, Lac see Edward, Lake
Idîni 52 B2 Trarza, W Mauritania
Idlib 96 B3 Idlib, NW Syria
Idre 63 B5 Dalarna, C Sweden
Iecava 84 C3 Bauska, S Latvia
Ieper 65 A6 Fr. Ypres. West-Vlaanderen, W Belgium
Ierápetra 83 D8 Kríti, Greece, E Mediterranean Sea
Ierisós see Ierissós
Ierissós 82 C4 var. Ierisós. Kentrikí Makedonía, N Greece
Iferouâne 53 G2 Agadez, N Niger
Ifôghas, Adrar des 53 E2 var. Adrar des Iforas. mountain range NE Mali
Iforas, Adrar des see Ifôghas, Adrar des
Igarka 92 D3 Krasnoyarskiy Kray, N Russian Federation
Igaunija see Estonia
Iglau/Iglawa/Igława see Jihlava
Iglesias 75 A5 Sardegna, Italy, C Mediterranean Sea
Igloolik 15 G2 Nunavut, N Canada
Igoumenítsa 82 A4 Ípeiros, W Greece
Iguaçu, Rio 41 E4 Sp. Río Iguazú. river Argentina/Brazil
Iguaçu, Salto do 41 E4 Sp. Cataratas del Iguazú; prev. Victoria Falls. waterfall Argentina/Brazil
Iguala 29 E4 var. Iguala de la Independencia. Guerrero, S Mexico
Iguala de la Independencia see Iguala
Iguazú, Cataratas del see Iguaçu, Salto do
Iguazú, Río see Iguaçu, Rio
Iguid, Erg see Iguidi, 'Erg
Iguidi, 'Erg 48 C3 var. Erg Iguid. desert Algeria/Mauritania
Ihavandhippolhu Atoll 110 A3 var. Ihavandiffulu Atoll. atoll N Maldives
Ihavandiffulu Atoll see Ihavandhippolhu Atoll
Ihosy 57 F4 Fianarantsoa, S Madagascar
Iinnasuolu see Hinnøya
Iisalmi 62 E4 var. Idensalmi. Itä-Suomi, C Finland
IJmuiden 64 C3 Noord-Holland, W Netherlands
IJssel 64 D3 var. Yssel. river Netherlands
IJsselmeer 64 C2 prev. Zuider Zee. lake N Netherlands
IJsselmuiden 64 D3 Overijssel, E Netherlands
Ijzer 65 A6 river W Belgium
Ikaahuk see Sachs Harbour
Ikaluktutiak see Cambridge Bay
Ikaría 83 D6 var. Kariot, Nicaria, Nikaria; anc. Icaria. island Dodekánisa, Greece, Aegean Sea
Ikela 55 D6 Equateur, C Dem. Rep. Congo
Iki 109 A7 island SW Japan
Ilagan 117 E1 Luzon, N Philippines
Ilave 39 E4 Puno, S Peru
Iława 76 D3 Ger. Deutsch-Eylau. Warmińsko-Mazurskie, NE Poland
Ilebo 55 C6 prev. Port-Francqui. Kasai-Occidental, W Dem. Rep. Congo
Île-de-France 68 C3 cultural region N France
Ilerda see Lleida
Ilfracombe 67 C7 SW England, United Kingdom
Ílhavo 70 B2 Aveiro, N Portugal
Iliamna Lake 14 C3 lake Alaska, USA
Il'ichevsk see Illichivs'k, Ukraine
Ilici see Elche
Iligan 117 E2 off. Iligan City. Mindanao, S Philippines
Iligan City see Iligan
Illapel 42 B4 Coquimbo, C Chile
Illichivs'k 87 E4 Rus. Il'ichevsk. Odes'ka Oblast', SW Ukraine
Illicis see Elche
Illinois 18 A4 off. State of Illinois, also known as Prairie State, Sucker State. state C USA
Illinois River 18 B4 river Illinois, N USA
Illuro see Mataró
Ilo 39 E4 Moquegua, SW Peru
Iloilo 117 E2 off. Iloilo City. Panay Island, C Philippines
Iloilo City see Iloilo
Ilorin 53 F4 Kwara, W Nigeria
Ilovlya 89 B6 Volgogradskaya Oblast', SW Russian Federation
Iluh see Batman
Il'yaly see Gurbansoltan Eje
Imatra 63 E5 Etelä-Suomi, SE Finland
Imbros see Gökçeada
Imishli see İmişli
İmişli 95 H3 Rus. Imishli. C Azerbaijan
Imola 74 C3 Emilia-Romagna, N Italy
Imperatriz 41 F2 Maranhão, NE Brazil
Imperia 74 A3 Liguria, NW Italy
Impfondo 55 C5 Likouala, NE Congo
Imphāl 113 H3 state capital Manipur, NE India
Imroz Adası see Gökçeada
Inagua Islands see Little Inagua
Inagua Islands see Great Inagua
Inarijärvi 62 D2 Lapp. Aanaarjävri, Swe. Enareträsk. lake N Finland
Inău see Ineu
Inawashiro-ko 109 D5 var. Inawasiro Ko. lake Honshū, C Japan
Inawasiro Ko see Inawashiro-ko
İncesu 94 D3 Kayseri, Turkey Asia
Inch'ŏn 107 E4 off. Inch'ŏn-gwangyŏksi, Jap. Jinsen; prev. Chemulpo. NW South Korea
Inch'ŏn-gwangyŏksi see Inch'ŏn
Incudine, Monte 69 E7 mountain Corse, France, C Mediterranean Sea
Indefatigable Island see Santa Cruz, Isla
Independence 23 F4 Missouri, C USA
Independence Fjord 61 E1 fjord N Greenland
Independence Island see Malden Island
Independence Mountains 24 C4 mountain range Nevada, USA
India 102 B3 off. Republic of India, var. Indian Union, Union of India, Hind. Bhārat. country S Asia
India see Inđija
Indiana 18 B4 off. State of Indiana, also known as Hoosier State. state N USA
Indianapolis 18 C4 state capital Indiana, N USA
Indian Church 30 C1 Orange Walk, N Belize
Indian Desert see Thar Desert
Indianola 23 F4 Iowa, C USA
Indian Union see India
India, Republic of see India
India, Union of see India
Indigirka 93 F2 river NE Russian Federation
Inđija 78 D3 Hung. India; prev. Indjija. Vojvodina, N Serbia
Indira Point 110 G3 headland Andaman and Nicobar Island, India, NE Indian Ocean
Indjija see Inđija
Indomed Fracture Zone 119 B6 tectonic feature SW Indian Ocean
Indonesia 116 B4 off. Republic of Indonesia, Ind. Republik Indonesia; prev. Dutch East Indies, Netherlands East Indies, United States of Indonesia. country SE Asia
Indonesian Borneo see Kalimantan
Indonesia, Republic of see Indonesia
Indonesia, Republik see Indonesia
Indonesia, United States of see Indonesia
Indore 112 D4 Madhya Pradesh, C India
Indreville see Châteauroux
Indus 112 C2 Chin. Yindu He; prev. Yin-tu Ho. river S Asia
Indus Cone see Indus Fan
Indus Fan 90 C5 var. Indus Cone. undersea fan N Arabian Sea
Indus, Mouths of the 112 B4 delta S Pakistan
İnebolu 94 C2 Kastamonu, N Turkey
Ineu 86 A4 Hung. Borosjenő; prev. Inău. Arad, W Romania
Infiernillo, Presa del 29 E4 reservoir S Mexico
Inglewood 24 D2 California, W USA
Ingolstadt 73 C6 Bayern, S Germany
Ingulets see Inhulets'
Inguri see Enguri
Inhambane 57 E4 Inhambane, SE Mozambique
Inhulets' 87 F3 Rus. Ingulets. Dnipropetrovs'ka Oblast', E Ukraine
I-ning see Yining
Inis see Ennis
Inis Ceithleann see Enniskillen
Inn 73 C6 river C Europe
Innaanganeq 60 C1 var. Kap York. headland NW Greenland
Inner Hebrides 66 B4 island group W Scotland, United Kingdom
Inner Islands 57 H1 var. Central Group. island group NE Seychelles
Innisfail 126 D3 Queensland, NE Australia
Inniskilling see Enniskillen
Innsbruch see Innsbruck
Innsbruck 73 C7 var. Innsbruch. Tirol, W Austria
Inoucdjouac see Inukjuak
Inowrazlaw see Inowrocław
Inowrocław 76 C3 Ger. Hohensalza; prev. Inowrazlaw. Kujawski-pomorskie, C Poland
I-n-Sakane, 'Erg 53 E2 desert N Mali
I-n-Salah 48 D3 var. In Salah. C Algeria
Insterburg see Chernyakhovsk
Insula see Lille
Inta 88 E3 Respublika Komi, NW Russian Federation
Interamna see Teramo
Interamna Nahars see Terni
International Falls 23 F1 Minnesota, N USA
Inukjuak 16 D2 var. Inoucdjouac; prev. Port Harrison. Québec, NE Canada
Inuuvik see Inuvik
Inuvik 14 D3 var. Inuuvik. Northwest Territories, NW Canada
Invercargill 129 A7 Southland, South Island, New Zealand
Inverness 66 C3 N Scotland, United Kingdom
Investigator Ridge 119 D5 undersea ridge E Indian Ocean
Investigator Strait 127 B7 strait South Australia
Inyangani 56 D3 mountain NE Zimbabwe
Ioánnina 82 A4 var. Janina, Yannina. Ípeiros, W Greece
Iola 23 F5 Kansas, C USA
Ionia Basin see Ionian Basin
Ionian Basin 58 D5 var. Ionia Basin. undersea basin Ionian Sea, C Mediterranean Sea
Ionian Sea 81 E3 Gk. Iónio Pélagos, It. Mar Ionio. sea C Mediterranean Sea
Iónioi Nísoi 83 A5 Eng. Ionian Islands. region W Greece
Ionio, Mar/Iónio Pélagos see Ionian Sea
Íos 83 D6 var. Nio. island Kykládes, Greece, Aegean Sea
Íos 83 D6 var. Nio. island Kykládes, Greece, Aegean Sea
Íos 83 D6 var. Nio. island Kykládes, Greece, Aegean Sea
Ioulís 83 C6 prev. Kéa. Tziá, Kykládes, Greece, Aegean Sea
Iowa 23 F3 off. State of Iowa, also known as Hawkeye State. state C USA
Iowa City 23 G3 Iowa, C USA
Iowa Falls 23 G3 Iowa, C USA
Ipel' 77 C6 var. Ipoly, Ger. Eipel. river Hungary/Slovakia
Ipiales 36 A4 Nariño, SW Colombia
Ipoh 116 B3 Perak, Peninsular Malaysia
Ipoly see Ipel'
Ippy 54 C4 Ouaka, C Central African Republic
Ipswich 127 E5 Queensland, E Australia
Ipswich 67 E6 hist. Gipeswic. E England, United Kingdom
Iqaluit 15 H3 prev. Frobisher Bay. province capital Baffin Island, Nunavut, NE Canada
Iquique 42 B1 Tarapacá, N Chile
Iquitos 38 C1 Loreto, N Peru
Irákleio 83 D7 var. Herakleion, Eng. Candia; prev. Iráklion. Kríti, Greece, E Mediterranean Sea
Iráklion see Irákleio
Iran 98 C3 off. Islamic Republic of Iran; prev. Persia. country SW Asia
Iranian Plateau 98 D3 var. Plateau of Iran. plateau N Iran
Iran, Islamic Republic of see Iran
Iran, Plateau of see Iranian Plateau
Irapuato 29 E4 Guanajuato, C Mexico
Iraq 98 B3 off. Republic of Iraq, Ar. 'Irāq. country SW Asia
'Irāq see Iraq
Iraq, Republic of see Iraq
Irbid 97 B5 Irbid, N Jordan
Irbil see Arbil
Ireland 67 A5 off. Republic of Ireland, Ir. Éire. country NW Europe
Ireland 58 C3 Lat. Hibernia. island Ireland/United Kingdom
Ireland, Republic of see Ireland
Irian see New Guinea
Irian Barat see Papua
Irian Jaya see Papua
Irian, Teluk see Cenderawasih, Teluk
Iringa 51 C7 Iringa, C Tanzania
Iriomote-jima 108 A4 island Sakishima-shotō, SW Japan
Iriona 30 D2 Colón, NE Honduras
Irish Sea 67 C5 Ir. Muir Éireann. sea C British Isles
Irkutsk 93 E4 Irkutskaya Oblast', S Russian Federation
Irminger Basin see Reykjanes Basin
Iroise 68 A3 sea NW France
Iron Mountain 18 B2 Michigan, N USA
Ironwood 18 B1 Michigan, N USA
Irrawaddy 114 B2 var. Ayeyarwady. river W Myanmar (Burma)
Irrawaddy, Mouths of the 115 A5 delta SW Myanmar (Burma)
Irtish see Irtysh
Irtysh 92 C4 var. Irtish, Kaz. Ertis. river C Asia
Irun 71 E1 Cast. Irún. País Vasco, N Spain
Irún see Irun
Iruña see Pamplona
Isabela, Isla 38 A5 var. Albemarle Island. island Galapagos Islands, Ecuador, E Pacific Ocean
Isaccea 86 D4 Tulcea, E Romania
Isachsen 15 F1 Ellef Ringnes Island, Nunavut, N Canada
Ísafjördhur 61 E4 Vestfirdhir, NW Iceland
Isbarta see Isparta
Isca Damnoniorum see Exeter
Ise 109 C6 Mie, Honshū, SW Japan
Iseghem see Izegem
Isère 69 D5 river E France
Isernia 75 D5 var. Æsernia. Molise, C Italy
Ise-wan 109 C6 bay S Japan
Isfahan see Eşfahān
Isha Baydhabo see Baydhabo
Ishigaki-jima 108 A4 island Sakishima-shotō, SW Japan
Ishikari-wan 108 C2 bay Hokkaidō, NE Japan
Ishim 92 C4 Tyumenskaya Oblast', C Russian Federation
Ishim 92 C4 Kaz. Esil. river Kazakhstan/Russian Federation
Ishinomaki 108 D4 var. Isinomaki. Miyagi, Honshū, C Japan
Ishkashim see Ishkoshim
Ishkoshim 101 F3 Rus. Ishkashim. S Tajikistan
Isinomaki see Ishinomaki
Isiro 55 E5 Orientale, NE Dem. Rep. Congo
Iskăr see Iskŭr
İskenderun 94 D4 Eng. Alexandretta. Hatay, S Turkey
İskenderun Körfezi 96 A2 Eng. Gulf of Alexandretta. gulf S Turkey
Iskur 82 C2 var. Iskăr. river NW Bulgaria
Yazovir Iskur 82 B2 prev. Yazovir Stalin. reservoir W Bulgaria
Isla Cristina 70 C4 Andalucía, S Spain
Isla de León see San Fernando
Islāmābād 112 C1 country capital Federal Capital Territory Islāmābād, NE Pakistan
Island/Ísland see Iceland
Islay 66 B4 island SW Scotland, United Kingdom
Isle 69 B5 river W France
Isle of Man 67 B5 UK crown dependency NW Europe
Isles of Scilly 67 B8 island group SW England, United Kingdom
Ismailia see Al Ismā'īlīya
Al Ismā'īlīya 50 B1 var. Ismailia, Ismâ'ilîya. N Egypt
Ismâ'ilîya see Al Ismā'īlīya
Ismid see İzmit
Isnā 50 B2 var. Esna. SE Egypt
Isoka 56 D1 Northern, NE Zambia
Isparta 94 B4 var. Isbarta. Isparta, SW Turkey
Ispir 95 E3 Erzurum, NE Turkey
Israel 97 A7 off. State of Israel, var. Medinat Israel, Heb. Yisrael, Yisra'el. country SW Asia
Israel, State of see Israel
Issa see Vis
Issiq Köl see Issyk-Kul', Ozero
Issoire 69 C5 Puy-de-Dôme, C France
Issyk-Kul' see Balykchy
Issyk-Kul', Ozero 101 G2 var. Issiq Köl, Kir. Ysyk-Köl. lake E Kyrgyzstan
İstanbul 94 B2 Bul. Tsarigrad, Eng. Istanbul, prev. Constantinople; anc. Byzantium. Istanbul, NW Turkey
Istarska Županija see Istra
Istra 78 A3 off. Istarska Županija. province NW Croatia
Istra 78 A3 Eng. Istria, Ger. Istrien. cultural region NW Croatia
Istria/Istrien see Istra
Itabuna 41 G3 Bahia, E Brazil
Itagüí 36 B3 Antioquia, W Colombia
Itaipú, Represa de 41 E4 reservoir Brazil/Paraguay
Itaituba 41 E2 Pará, NE Brazil
Italia/Italiana, Republica/Italian Republic, The see Italy
Italian Somaliland see Somalia
Italy 74 C3 off. The Italian Republic, It. Italia, Repubblica Italiana. country S Europe
Iténez, Río see Guaporé, Rio
Ithaca 19 E3 New York, NE USA
It Hearrenfean see Heerenveen
Itoigawa 109 C5 Niigata, Honshū, C Japan
Itseqqortoormiit see Ittoqqortoormiit
Ittoqqortoormiit 61 E3 var. Itseqqortoormiit, Dan. Scoresbysund, Eng. Scoresby Sound. Tunu, C Greenland
Iturup, Ostrov 108 E1 island Kuril'skiye Ostrova, SE Russian Federation
Itzehoe 72 B2 Schleswig-Holstein, N Germany
Ivalo 62 D2 Lapp. Avveel, Avvil. Lappi, N Finland
Ivanava 85 B7 Pol. Janów, Janów Poleski, Rus. Ivanovo. Brestskaya Voblasts', SW Belarus
Ivangrad see Berane
Ivanhoe 127 C6 New South Wales, SE Australia
Ivano-Frankivs'k 86 C2 Ger. Stanislau, Pol. Stanisławów, Rus. Ivano-Frankovsk; prev. Stanislav. Ivano-Frankivs'ka Oblast', W Ukraine
Ivano-Frankovsk see Ivano-Frankivs'k
Ivanovo 89 B5 Ivanovskaya Oblast', W Russian Federation
Ivanovo see Ivanava
Ivantsevichi/Ivatsevichi see Ivatsevichy
Ivatsevichy 85 B6 Pol. Iwacewicze, Rus. Ivantsevichi, Ivatsevichi. Brestskaya Voblasts', SW Belarus
Ivigtut see Ivittuut
Ivittuut 60 B4 var. Ivigtut. Kitaa, S Greenland
Iviza see Eivissa/Ibiza
Iviza see Eivissa/Ibiza
Iviza see Eivissa/Ibiza
Ivory Coast 52 D4 off. Republic of the Ivory Coast, Fr. Côte d'Ivoire, République de la Côte d'Ivoire. country W Africa
Ivory Coast, Republic of the see Ivory Coast
Ivujivik 16 D1 Québec, NE Canada
Iwacewicze see Ivatsevichy
Iwaki 109 D5 Fukushima, Honshū, N Japan
Iwakuni 109 B7 Yamaguchi, Honshū, SW Japan
Iwanai 108 C2 Hokkaidō, NE Japan
Iwate 108 D3 Iwate, Honshū, N Japan
Ixtapa 29 E5 Guerrero, S Mexico
Ixtepec 29 F5 Oaxaca, SE Mexico
Iyo-nada 109 B7 sea S Japan
Izabal, Lago de 30 B2 prev. Golfo Dulce. lake E Guatemala
Īzad Khvāst 98 D3 Fārs, C Iran
Izegem 65 A6 prev. Iseghem. West-Vlaanderen, W Belgium
Izhevsk 89 D5 prev. Ustinov. Udmurtskaya Respublika, NW Russian Federation
Izmail see Izmayil
Izmayil 86 D4 Rus. Izmail. Odes'ka Oblast', SW Ukraine
İzmir 94 A3 prev. Smyrna. Izmir, W Turkey
İzmit 94 B2 var. Ismid; anc. Astacus. Kocaeli, NW Turkey
İznik Gölü 94 B3 lake NW Turkey
Izu-hantō 109 D6 peninsula Honshū, S Japan
Izu Shichito see Izu-shotō
Izu-shotō 109 D6 var. Izu Shichito. island group S Japan
Izvor 82 B2 Pernik, W Bulgaria
Izyaslav 86 C2 Khmel'nyts'ka Oblast', W Ukraine
Izyum 87 G2 Kharkivs'ka Oblast', E Ukraine

J

Jabal ash Shifā 98 A4 desert NW Saudi Arabia
Jabalpur 113 E4 prev. Jubbulpore. Madhya Pradesh, C India
Jabbūl, Sabkhat al 96 B2 sabkha NW Syria
Jablah 96 A3 var. Jeble, Fr. Djéblé. Al Lādhiqīyah, W Syria
Jaca 71 F1 Aragón, NE Spain
Jacaltenango 30 A2 Huehuetenango, W Guatemala
Jackson 20 B2 state capital Mississippi, S USA
Jackson 23 H5 Missouri, C USA
Jackson 20 C1 Tennessee, S USA
Jackson Head 129 A6 headland South Island, New Zealand
Jacksonville 21 E3 Florida, SE USA
Jacksonville 18 B4 Illinois, N USA
Jacksonville 21 F1 North Carolina, SE USA
Jacksonville 27 G3 Texas, SW USA
Jacmel 32 D3 var. Jaquemel. S Haiti
Jacob see Nkayi
Jacobābād 112 B3 Sind, SE Pakistan
Jadotville see Likasi
Jadransko More/Jadransko Morje see Adriatic Sea
Jaén 38 B2 Cajamarca, N Peru
Jaén 70 D4 Andalucía, SW Spain
Jaffna 110 D3 Northern Province, N Sri Lanka
Jagannath see Puri
Jagdalpur 113 E5 Chhattīsgarh, C India
Jagdaqi 105 G1 Nei Mongol Zizhiqu, N China
Jagodina 78 D4 prev. Svetozarevo. Serbia, C Serbia
Jahra see Al Jahrā'
Jailolo see Halmahera, Pulau
Jaipur 112 D3 prev. Jeypore. state capital Rājasthān, N India
Jaisalmer 112 C3 Rājasthān, NW India
Jajce 78 B3 Federacija Bosna I Hercegovina, W Bosnia and Herzegovina
Jakarta 116 C5 prev. Djakarta, Dut. Batavia. country capital Jawa, C Indonesia
Jakobstad 62 D4 Fin. Pietarsaari. Länsi-Suomi, W Finland
Jakobstadt see Jēkabpils
Jalālābād 101 F4 var. Jalalabad, Jelalabad. Nangarhār, E Afghanistan
Jalal-Abad see Dzhalal-Abad, Dzhalal-Abadskaya Oblast', Kyrgyzstan
Jalandhar 112 D2 prev. Jullundur. Punjab, N India
Jalapa 30 D3 Nueva Segovia, NW Nicaragua
Jalpa 28 D4 Zacatecas, C Mexico
Jālū 49 G3 var. Jūlā. NE Libya
Jaluit Atoll 122 D2 var. Jālwōj. atoll Ralik Chain, S Marshall Islands
Jālwōj see Jaluit Atoll
Jamaame 51 D6 It. Giamame; prev. Margherita. Jubbada Hoose, S Somalia
Jamaica 32 A4 country W West Indies
Jamaica 34 A1 island W West Indies
Jamaica Channel 32 D3 channel Haiti/Jamaica
Jamālpur 113 F3 Bihār, NE India
Jambi 116 B4 var. Telanaipura; prev. Djambi. Sumatera, W Indonesia
Jamdena see Yamdena, Pulau

K

Karkinits'ka Zatoka – Klintsy

Karkinits'ka Zatoka 87 E4 Rus. Karkinitskiy Zaliv. gulf S Ukraine
Karkinitskiy Zaliv see Karkinits'ka Zatoka
Karkūk see Kirkūk
Karleby see Kokkola
Karl-Marx-Stadt see Chemnitz
Karlö see Hailuoto
Karlovac 78 B3 Ger. Karlstadt, Hung. Károlyváros. Karlovac, C Croatia
Karlovy Vary 77 A5 Ger. Karlsbad; prev. Eng. Carlsbad. Karlovarský Kraj, W Czech Republic
Karlsbad see Karlovy Vary
Karlsburg see Alba Iulia
Karlskrona 63 C7 Blekinge, S Sweden
Karlsruhe 73 B6 var. Carlsruhe. Baden-Württemberg, SW Germany
Karlstad 63 B6 Värmland, C Sweden
Karlstadt see Karlovac
Karnāl 112 D2 Haryāna, N India
Karnātaka 110 C1 var. Kanara; prev. Maisur, Mysore. cultural region W India
Karnobat 82 D2 Burgas, E Bulgaria
Karnul see Kurnool
Karol see Carei
Károly-Fehérvár see Alba Iulia
Károlyváros see Karlovac
Karpaten see Carpathian Mountains
Kárpathos 83 E7 Kárpathos, SE Greece
Kárpathos 83 E7 It. Scarpanto; anc. Carpathos, Carpathus. island SE Greece
Karpaty see Carpathian Mountains
Karpenísi 83 B5 prev. Karpenísion. Stereá Ellás, C Greece
Karpenísion see Karpenísi
Karpilovka see Aktsyabrski
Kars 95 F2 var. Qars. Kars, NE Turkey
Karsau see Kārsava
Kārsava 84 D4 Ger. Karsau; prev. Rus. Korsovka. Ludza, E Latvia
Karshi see Qarshi, Uzbekistan
Karyés 82 C4 var. Karies. Ágion Óros, N Greece
Kárystos 83 C6 var. Káristos. Évvoia, C Greece
Kasai 55 C6 var. Cassai, Kassai. river Angola/Dem. Rep. Congo
Kasaji 55 D7 Katanga, S Dem. Rep. Congo
Kasama 56 D1 Northern, N Zambia
Kasan see Koson
Kāsaragod 110 B2 Kerala, SW India
Kaschau see Košice
Kāshān 98 C3 Eşfahān, C Iran
Kashgar see Kashi
Kashi 104 A3 Chin. Kaxgar, K'o-shih, Uigh. Kashgar. Xinjiang Uygur Zizhiqu, NW China
Kasi see Vārānasi
Kasongo 55 D6 Maniema, E Dem. Rep. Congo
Kasongo-Lunda 55 C7 Bandundu, SW Dem. Rep. Congo
Kásos 83 D7 island S Greece
Kaspiy Mangy Oypaty see Caspian Depression
Kaspiysk 89 B8 Respublika Dagestan, SW Russian Federation
Kaspiyskoye More/Kaspiy Tengizi see Caspian Sea
Kassa see Košice
Kassai see Kasai
Kassala 50 C4 Kassala, E Sudan
Kassel 72 B4 prev. Cassel. Hessen, C Germany
Kasserine 49 E2 var. Al Qaşrayn. W Tunisia
Kastamonu 94 C2 var. Castamoni, Kastamuni. Kastamonu, N Turkey
Kastamuni see Kastamonu
Kastaneá 82 B4 Kentrikí Makedonía, N Greece
Kastélli see Kíssamos
Kastoría 82 B4 Dytikí Makedonía, N Greece
Kástro 83 C6 Sífnos, Kykládes, Greece, Aegean Sea
Kastsyukovichy 85 E7 Rus. Kostyukovichi. Mahilyowskaya Voblasts', E Belarus
Kastsyukowka 85 D7 Rus. Kostyukovka. Homyel'skaya Voblasts', SE Belarus
Kasulu 51 B7 Kigoma, W Tanzania
Kasumiga-ura 109 D5 lake Honshū, S Japan
Katahdin, Mount 19 G1 mountain Maine, NE USA
Katalla 14 C3 Alaska, USA
Katana see Qaţanā
Katanning 125 B7 Western Australia
Katawaz see Zarghūn Shahr
Katchall Island 111 F3 island Nicobar Islands, India, NE Indian Ocean
Kateríni 82 B4 Kentrikí Makedonía, N Greece
Katha 114 B2 Sagaing, N Myanmar (Burma)
Katherine 126 A2 Northern Territory, N Australia
Kathmandu 102 C3 prev. Kantipur. country capital Central, C Nepal
Katikati 128 D3 Bay of Plenty, North Island, New Zealand
Katima Mulilo 56 C3 Caprivi, NE Namibia
Katiola 52 D4 C Ivory Coast
Káto Achaïa 83 B5 var. Kato Ahaia, Káto Akhaía. Dytikí Ellás, S Greece
Kato Ahaia/Káto Akhaía see Káto Achaïa
Katoúna 83 A5 Dytikí Ellás, C Greece
Katowice 77 C5 Ger. Kattowitz. Śląskie, S Poland
Katsina 53 G3 Katsina, N Nigeria
Kattakurgan see Kattaqo'rg'on
Kattaqo'rg'on 101 E2 Rus. Kattakurgan. Samarqand Viloyati, C Uzbekistan
Kattavía 83 E7 Ródos, Dodekánisa, Greece, Aegean Sea
Kattegat 63 B7 Dan. Kattegatt. strait N Europe
Kattegatt see Kattegat
Kattowitz see Katowice
Kaua'i 25 A7 var. Kauai. island Hawaiian Islands, Hawai'i, USA, C Pacific Ocean
Kauai see Kaua'i
Kauen see Kaunas
Kaufbeuren 73 C6 Bayern, S Germany
Kaunas 84 B4 Ger. Kauen, Pol. Kowno; prev. Rus. Kovno. Kaunas, C Lithuania
Kavadar see Kavadarci
Kavadarci 79 E6 Turk. Kavadar. C Macedonia
Kavaja see Kavajë
Kavajë 79 C6 It. Cavaia, Kavaja. Tiranë, W Albania
Kavakli see Topolovgrad
Kavála 82 C3 prev. Kaválla. Anatolikí Makedonía kai Thráki, NE Greece
Kāvali 110 D2 Andhra Pradesh, E India
Kaválla see Kavála
Kavango see Cubango/Okavango
Kavaratti Island 110 A3 island Lakshadweep, Lakshadweep, SW India Asia N Indian Ocean
Kavarna 82 E2 Dobrich, NE Bulgaria
Kavengo see Cubango/Okavango
Kavir, Dasht-e 98 D3 var. Great Salt Desert. salt pan N Iran
Kavkaz see Caucasus
Kawagoe 109 D5 Saitama, Honshū, S Japan
Kawasaki 108 A2 Kanagawa, Honshū, S Japan
Kawerau 128 E3 Bay of Plenty, North Island, New Zealand
Kaxgar see Kashi
Kaya 53 E3 C Burkina
Kayan 114 B4 Yangon, SW Myanmar (Burma)
Kayan, Sungai 116 D3 prev. Kajan. river Borneo, C Indonesia
Kayes 52 C3 Kayes, W Mali
Kayseri 94 D3 var. Kaisaria; anc. Caesarea Mazaca, Mazaca. Kayseri, C Turkey
Kazach'ye 93 F2 Respublika Sakha (Yakutiya), NE Russian Federation
Kazakhskaya SSR/Kazakh Soviet Socialist Republic see Kazakhstan
Kazakhstan 92 B4 off. Republic of Kazakhstan, var. Kazakstan, Kaz. Qazaqstan, Qazaqstan Respublikasy; prev. Kazakh Soviet Socialist Republic, Rus. Kazakhskaya SSR. country C Asia
Kazakhstan, Republic of see Kazakhstan
Kazakh Uplands 92 C4 Eng. Kazakh Uplands, Kirghiz Steppe, Kaz. Saryarqa. uplands C Kazakhstan
Kazakh Uplands see Kazakhskiy Melkosopochnik
Kazakstan see Kazakhstan
Kazan' 89 C5 Respublika Tatarstan, W Russian Federation
Kazandzhik see Bereket
Kazanlik see Kazanlŭk
Kazanlŭk 82 D2 prev. Kazanlik. Stara Zagora, C Bulgaria
Kazatin see Kozyatyn
Kazbegi see Kazbek
Kazbek 95 F1 var. Kazbegi, Geor. Mqinvartsveri. mountain N Georgia
Kāzerūn 98 D4 Fārs, S Iran
Kazi Magomed see Qazimämmäd
Kazvin see Qazvīn
Kéa see Tziá
Kéa see Ioulís
Kea, Mauna 25 B8 mountain Hawai'i, USA
Kéamu see Aneityum
Kearney 23 E4 Nebraska, C USA
Keban Barajı 95 E3 reservoir C Turkey
Kebkabiya 50 A4 Northern Darfur, W Sudan
Kebnekaise 62 C3 mountain N Sweden
Kecskemét 77 D7 Bács-Kiskun, C Hungary
Kediri 116 D5 Jawa, C Indonesia
Kędzierzyn-Koźle 77 C5 Ger. Heydebrech. Opolskie, S Poland
Keelung see Chilung
Keetmanshoop 56 B4 Karas, S Namibia
Kefallinía see Kefallonía
Kefallonía 83 A5 var. Kefallinía. island Iónia Nisiá, Greece, C Mediterranean Sea
Kefe see Feodosiya
Kegel see Keila
Kehl 73 A6 Baden-Württemberg, SW Germany
Kei Islands see Kai, Kepulauan
Keijō see Sŏul
Keila 84 D2 Ger. Kegel. Harjumaa, NW Estonia
Keïta 53 F3 Tahoua, C Niger
Keith 127 B7 South Australia
Kĕk-Art 101 G2 prev. Alaykel', Alay-Kuu. Oshskaya Oblast', SW Kyrgyzstan
Kékes 77 C6 mountain N Hungary
Kelamayi see Karamay
Kelang see Klang
Kelat see Kalāt
Kelifskiy Uzboy see Kelif Uzboýy
Kelif Uzboýy 100 D3 Rus. Kelifskiy Uzboy. salt marsh E Turkmenistan
Kelkit Çayı 95 E3 river N Turkey
Kelmė 84 B4 Šiaulai, C Lithuania
Kélo 54 B4 Tandjilé, SW Chad
Kelowna 15 E5 British Columbia, SW Canada
Kelso 24 B2 Washington, NW USA
Keltsy see Kielce
Keluang 116 B3 var. Kluang. Johor, Peninsular Malaysia
Kem' 88 B3 Respublika Kareliya, NW Russian Federation
Kemah 95 E3 Erzincan, E Turkey
Kemaman see Cukai
Kemerovo 92 D4 prev. Shcheglovsk. Kemerovskaya Oblast', C Russian Federation
Kemi 62 D4 Lappi, NW Finland
Kemijärvi 62 D3 Swe. Kemiträsk. Lappi, N Finland
Kemijoki 62 D3 river NW Finland
Kemin 101 G2 prev. Bystrovka. Chuyskaya Oblast', N Kyrgyzstan
Kemins Island see Nikumaroro
Kemiträsk see Kemijärvi
Kemmuna see Comino
Kempele 62 D4 Oulu, C Finland
Kempten 73 B7 Bayern, S Germany
Kendal 67 D5 NW England, United Kingdom
Kendari 117 E4 Sulawesi, C Indonesia
Kenedy 27 G4 Texas, SW USA
Kenema 52 C4 SE Sierra Leone
Këneurgench see Köneurgench
Kenge 55 C6 Bandundu, SW Dem. Rep. Congo
Keng Tung 114 C3 var. Kentung. Shan State, E Myanmar (Burma)
Kénitra 48 C2 prev. Port-Lyautey. NW Morocco
Kennett 23 H5 Missouri, C USA
Kennewick 24 C2 Washington, NW USA
Kenora 16 A3 Ontario, S Canada
Kenosha 18 B3 Wisconsin, N USA
Kentau 92 B5 Yuzhnyy Kazakhstan, S Kazakhstan
Kentucky 18 C5 off. Commonwealth of Kentucky, also known as Bluegrass State. state C USA
Kentucky Lake 18 B5 reservoir Kentucky/Tennessee, S USA
Kentung see Keng Tung
Kenya 51 C6 off. Republic of Kenya. country E Africa
Kenya, Mount see Kirinyaga
Kenya, Republic of see Kenya
Keokuk 23 G4 Iowa, C USA
Kéos see Tziá
Kępno 76 C4 Wielkopolskie, C Poland
Keppel Island see Niuatoputapu
Kerak see Al Karak
Kerala 110 C2 cultural region S India
Kerasunt see Giresun
Keratéa 83 C6 var. Keratea. Attikí, C Greece
Keratea see Keratéa
Kerbala/Kerbela see Karbalā'
Kerch 87 G5 Rus. Kerch'. Respublika Krym, SE Ukraine
Kerch' see Kerch
Kerchens'ka Protska/Kerchenskiy Proliv see Kerch Strait
Kerch Strait 87 G4 var. Bosporus Cimmerius, Enikale Strait, Rus. Kerchenskiy Proliv, Ukr. Kerchens'ka Protska. strait Black Sea/Sea of Azov
Keremitlik see Lyulyakovo
Kerguelen 119 C7 island C French Southern and Antarctic Territories
Kerguelen Plateau 119 C7 undersea plateau S Indian Ocean
Kerí 83 A6 Zákynthos, Iónia Nisiá, Greece, C Mediterranean Sea
Kerikeri 128 D2 Northland, North Island, New Zealand
Kerkenah, Îles de 80 D4 var. Kerkenna Islands, Ar. Juzur Qarqannah. island group E Tunisia
Kerkenna Islands see Kerkenah, Îles de
Kerki see Atamyrat
Kérkira see Kérkyra
Kerkrade 65 D6 Limburg, SE Netherlands
Kerkuk see Kirkūk
Kérkyra 82 A4 var. Kérkira, Eng. Corfu. Kérkyra, Iónia Nisiá, Greece, C Mediterranean Sea
Kermadec Islands 130 C4 island group New Zealand, SW Pacific Ocean
Kermadec Trench 121 E4 trench SW Pacific Ocean
Kermān 98 D3 var. Kirman; anc. Carmana. Kermān, C Iran
Kermānshāh 98 C3 var. Qahremānshahr; prev. Bākhtarān. Kermānshāhān, W Iran
Kerrville 27 F4 Texas, SW USA
Kertel see Kärdla
Kerulen 105 E2 Chin. Herlen He, Mong. Herlen Gol. river China/Mongolia
Keryneia see Girne
Kesennuma 108 D4 Miyagi, Honshū, C Japan
Keszthely 77 C7 Zala, SW Hungary
Ketchikan 14 D4 Revillagigedo Island, Alaska, USA
Kętrzyn 76 D2 Ger. Rastenburg. Warmińsko-Mazurskie, NE Poland
Kettering 67 D6 C England, United Kingdom
Kettering 18 C4 Ohio, N USA
Keupriya see Primorsko
Keuruu 63 D5 Länsi-Suomi, C Finland
Keweenaw Peninsula 18 B1 peninsula Michigan, N USA
Key Largo 21 F5 Key Largo, Florida, SE USA
Keystone State see Pennsylvania
Key West 21 E5 Florida Keys, Florida, SE USA
Kezdivásárhely see Târgu Secuiesc
Khabarovsk 93 G4 Khabarovskiy Kray, SE Russian Federation
Khachmas see Xaçmaz
Khadera see Hadera
Khairpur 112 B3 Sind, SE Pakistan
Khalīj as Suways 50 B2 var. Suez, Gulf of. gulf NE Egypt
Khalkidhikí see Chalkidikí
Khalkís see Chalkída
Gulf of Khambhat 112 C4 Eng. Gulf of Cambay. gulf W India
Khamīs Mushayt 99 B6 var. Hamīs Musait. 'Asīr, SW Saudi Arabia
Khānābād 101 E3 Kunduz, NE Afghanistan
Khān al Baghdādī see Al Baghdādī
Khandwa 112 D4 Madhya Pradesh, C India
Khanh Hung see Soc Trăng
Khaniá see Chaniá
Khanka, Lake 107 E2 var. Hsing-K'ai Hu, Lake Hanka, Chin. Xingkai Hu, Rus. Ozero Khanka. lake China/Russian Federation
Khanka, Ozero see Khanka, Lake
Khankendi see Xankändi
Khanthabouli 114 D4 prev. Savannakhét. Savannakhét, S Laos
Khanty-Mansiysk 92 C3 prev. Ostyako-Voguls'k. Khanty-Mansiyskiy Avtonomnyy Okrug-Yugra, C Russian Federation
Khān Yūnis 97 A7 var. Khān Yūnus. S Gaza Strip
Khān Yūnus see Khān Yūnis
Khanzi see Ghanzi
Kharagpur 113 F4 West Bengal, NE India
Kharbin see Harbin
Kharkiv 87 G2 Rus. Khar'kov. Kharkivs'ka Oblast', NE Ukraine
Khar'kov see Kharkiv
Kharmanli 82 D3 Khaskovo, S Bulgaria
Khartoum 50 B4 var. El Khartûm, Khartum. country capital Khartoum, C Sudan
Khartum see Khartoum
Khasavyurt 89 B8 Respublika Dagestan, SW Russian Federation
Khash, Dasht-e 100 D5 Eng. Khash Desert. desert SW Afghanistan
Khash Desert see Khāsh, Dasht-e
Khashim Al Qirba/Khashm al Qirbah see Khashm el Girba
Khashm el Girba 50 C4 var. Khashim Al Qirba, Khashm al Qirbah. Kassala, E Sudan
Khaskovo 82 D3 Khaskovo, S Bulgaria
Khaybar, Kowtal-e see Khyber Pass
Khaydarkan 101 F2 var. Khaydarken. Batkenskaya Oblast', SW Kyrgyzstan
Khaydarken see Khaydarkan
Khazar, Baḥr-e/Khazar, Daryā-ye see Caspian Sea
Khelat see Kalāt
Kherson 87 E4 Khersons'ka Oblast', S Ukraine
Kheta 93 E2 river N Russian Federation
Khíos see Chíos
Khirbet el 'Aujā et Taḥtā 97 E7 E West Bank Asia
Khiva/Khiwa see Xiva
Khmel'nitskiy see Khmel 'nyts'kyy
Khmel 'nyts'kyy 86 C2 Rus. Khmel'nitskiy; prev. Proskurov. Khmel'nyts'ka Oblast', W Ukraine
Khodasy 85 E6 Rus. Khodosy. Mahilyowskaya Voblasts', E Belarus
Khodoriv 86 C2 Pol. Chodorów, Rus. Khodorov. L'vivs'ka Oblast', NW Ukraine
Khodorov see Khodoriv
Khodosy see Khodasy
Khodzhent see Khujand
Khoi see Khvoy
Khojend see Khujand
Khokand see Qo'qon
Kholm 101 E3 var. Tashqurghan, Pash. Khulm. Balkh, N Afghanistan
Kholm see Chełm
Kholon see Holon
Khoms see Al Khums
Khong Sedone see Muang Khôngxédôn
Khon Kaen 114 D4 var. Muang Khon Kaen. Khon Kaen, E Thailand
Khor 93 G4 Khabarovskiy Kray, SE Russian Federation
Khorat see Nakhon Ratchasima
Khorog see Khorugh
Khorugh 101 F3 Rus. Khorog. S Tajikistan
Khotan see Hotan
Khouribga 48 B2 C Morocco
Khovd see Hovd
Khowst 101 F4 Khowst, E Afghanistan
Khoy see Khvoy
Khoyniki 85 D8 Homyel'skaya Voblasts', SE Belarus
Khudzhand see Khujand
Khujand 101 E2 var. Khodzhent, Khojend, Rus. Khudzhand; prev. Leninabad, Taj. Leninobod. N Tajikistan
Khulm see Kholm
Khulna 113 G4 Khulna, SW Bangladesh
Khums see Al Khums
Khust 86 B3 var. Husté, Cz. Chust, Hung. Huszt. Zakarpats'ka Oblast', W Ukraine
Khvoy 98 C2 var. Khoi, Khoy. Āžarbāyjān-e Bākhtarī, NW Iran
Khyber Pass 112 C1 var. Kowtal-e Khaybar. pass Afghanistan/Pakistan
Kiangmai see Chiang Mai
Kiang-ning see Nanjing
Kiangsi see Jiangxi
Kiangsu see Jiangsu
Kiáto 83 B6 prev. Kiáton. Pelopónnisos, S Greece
Kiáton see Kiáto
Kiayi see Chiai
Kibangou 55 B6 Niari, SW Congo
Kibombo 55 D6 Maniema, E Dem. Rep. Congo
Kıbrıs/Kıbrıs Cumhuriyeti see Cyprus
Kičevo 79 D6 SW FYR Macedonia
Kidderminster 67 D6 C England, United Kingdom
Kiel 72 B2 Schleswig-Holstein, N Germany
Kielce 76 D4 Rus. Keltsy. Świętokrzyskie, C Poland
Kieler Bucht 72 B2 bay N Germany
Kiev see Kyyiv
Kiev Reservoir 87 E1 Eng. Kiev Reservoir, Rus. Kiyevskoye Vodokhranilishche. reservoir N Ukraine
Kiev Reservoir see Kyyivs'ke Vodoskhovyshche
Kiffa 52 C3 Assaba, S Mauritania
Kigali 51 B6 country capital C Rwanda
Kigoma 51 B7 Kigoma, W Tanzania
Kihnu 84 C2 var. Kihnu Saar, Ger. Kühnö. island SW Estonia
Kihnu Saar see Kihnu
Kii-suido 109 C7 strait S Japan
Kikinda 78 D3 Ger. Grosskikinda, Hung. Nagykikinda; prev. Velika Kikinda. Vojvodina, N Serbia
Kikládhes see Kykládes
Kikwit 55 C6 Bandundu, W Dem. Rep. Congo
Kilien Mountains see Qilian Shan
Kilimane see Quelimane
Kilimanjaro 47 E5 region E Tanzania
Kilimanjaro 51 C7 var. Uhuru Peak. volcano NE Tanzania
Kilingi-Nõmme 84 D3 Ger. Kurkund. Pärnumaa, SW Estonia
Kilis 94 D4 Kilis, S Turkey
Kiliya 86 D4 Rom. Chilia-Nouă. Odes'ka Oblast', SW Ukraine
Kilkenny 67 B6 Ir. Cill Chainnigh. Kilkenny, S Ireland
Kilkís 82 B3 Kentrikí Makedonía, N Greece
Killarney 67 A6 Ir. Cill Airne. Kerry, SW Ireland
Killeen 27 G3 Texas, SW USA
Kilmain see Quelimane
Kilmarnock 66 C4 W Scotland, United Kingdom
Kilwa see Kilwa Kivinje
Kilwa Kivinje 51 C7 var. Kilwa. Lindi, SE Tanzania
Kimberley 56 C4 Northern Cape, C South Africa
Kimberley Plateau 124 C3 plateau Western Australia
Kimch'aek 107 E3 prev. Sŏngjin. E North Korea
Kími see Kými
Kinabalu, Gunung 116 D3 mountain East Malaysia
Kindersley 15 F5 Saskatchewan, S Canada
Kindia 52 C4 Guinée-Maritime, SW Guinea
Kindley Field 20 A4 air base E Bermuda
Kindu 55 D6 prev. Kindu-Port-Empain. Maniema, C Dem. Rep. Congo
Kindu-Port-Empain see Kindu
Kineshma 89 C5 Ivanovskaya Oblast', W Russian Federation
King Charles Islands see Kong Karls Land
King Christian IX Land see Kong Christian IX Land
King Frederik VI Coast see Kong Frederik VI Kyst
King Frederik VIII Land see Kong Frederik VIII Land
King Island 127 B8 island Tasmania, SE Australia
King Island see Kadan Kyun
Kingissepp see Kuressaare
Kingman 26 A1 Arizona, SW USA
Kingman Reef 123 E2 US territory C Pacific Ocean
Kingsford Smith 126 E2 international airport New South Wales, SE Australia
King's Lynn 67 E6 var. Bishop's Lynn, Kings Lynn, Lynn, Lynn Regis. E England, United Kingdom
Kings Lynn see King's Lynn
King Sound 124 B3 sound Western Australia
Kingsport 21 E1 Tennessee, S USA
Kingston 32 B5 country capital E Jamaica
Kingston 16 D5 Ontario, SE Canada
Kingston 19 F3 New York, NE USA
Kingston upon Hull 67 D5 var. Hull. E England, United Kingdom
Kingston upon Thames 67 A8 SE England, United Kingdom
Kingstown 33 H4 country capital Saint Vincent, Saint Vincent and the Grenadines
Kingstown see Dún Laoghaire
Kingsville 27 G5 Texas, SW USA
King William Island 15 F3 island Nunavut, N Canada
Kinneret, Yam see Tiberias, Lake
Kinrooi 65 D5 Limburg, NE Belgium
Kinshasa 55 B6 prev. Léopoldville. country capital Kinshasa, W Dem. Rep. Congo
Kintyre 66 B4 peninsula W Scotland, United Kingdom
Kinyeti 51 B5 mountain S Sudan
Kiparissía see Kyparissía
Kipili 51 B7 Rukwa, W Tanzania
Kipushi 55 D8 Katanga, SE Dem. Rep. Congo
Kirdzhali see Kŭrdzhali
Kirghizia see Kyrgyzstan
Kirghiz Range 101 F2 Rus. Kirgizskiy Khrebet; prev. Alexander Range. mountain range Kazakhstan/Kyrgyzstan
Kirghiz SSR see Kyrgyzstan
Kirghiz Steppe see Kazakhskiy Melkosopochnik
Kirgizskaya SSR see Kyrgyzstan
Kirgizskiy Khrebet see Kirghiz Range
Kiriath-Arba see Hebron
Kiribati 123 F2 off. Republic of Kiribati. country C Pacific Ocean
Kiribati, Republic of see Kiribati
Kırıkhan 94 D4 Hatay, S Turkey
Kırıkkale 94 C3 province C Turkey
Kirin see Jilin
Kirinyaga 51 C6 prev. Mount Kenya. volcano C Kenya
Kirishi 88 B4 var. Kirisi. Leningradskaya Oblast', NW Russian Federation
Kirisi see Kirishi
Kiritimati 123 G2 prev. Christmas Island. atoll Line Islands, E Kiribati
Kirkenes 62 E2 Fin. Kirkkoniemi. Finnmark, N Norway
Kirk-Kilissa see Kırklareli
Kirkkoniemi see Kirkenes
Kirkland Lake 16 D4 Ontario, S Canada
Kırklareli 94 A2 prev. Kirk-Kilissa. Kırklareli, NW Turkey
Kirkpatrick, Mount 132 B3 mountain Antarctica
Kirksville 23 G4 Missouri, C USA
Kirkūk 98 B3 var. Karkūk, Kerkuk. At Ta'mīn, N Iraq
Kirkwall 66 C2 NE Scotland, United Kingdom
Kirkwood 23 G4 Missouri, C USA
Kir Moab/Kir of Moab see Al Karak
Kirov 89 C5 prev. Vyatka. Kirovskaya Oblast', NW Russian Federation
Kirovabad see Gäncä
Kirovakan see Vanadzor
Kirovo-Chepetsk 89 D5 Kirovskaya Oblast', NW Russian Federation
Kirovohrad 87 E3 Rus. Kirovograd; prev. Kirovo, Yelizavetgrad, Zinov'yevsk. Kirovohrads'ka Oblast', C Ukraine
Kirovo/Kirovograd see Kirovohrad
Kirthar Range 112 B3 mountain range S Pakistan
Kiruna 62 C3 Lapp. Giron. Norrbotten, N Sweden
Kirun/Kirun' see Chilung
Kisalföld see Little Alföld
Kisangani 55 D5 prev. Stanleyville. Orientale, NE Dem. Rep. Congo
Kishinev see Chişinău
Kislovodsk 89 B7 Stavropol'skiy Kray, SW Russian Federation
Kismaayo 51 D6 var. Chisimayu, Kismayu, It. Chisimaio. Jubbada Hoose, S Somalia
Kismayu see Kismaayo
Kíssamos 83 C7 prev. Kastélli. Kríti, Greece, E Mediterranean Sea
Kissidougou 52 C4 Guinée-Forestière, S Guinea
Kissimmee, Lake 21 E4 lake Florida, SE USA
Kistna see Krishna
Kisumu 51 C6 prev. Port Florence. Nyanza, W Kenya
Kisvárda 77 E6 Ger. Kleinwardein. Szabolcs-Szatmár-Bereg, E Hungary
Kita 52 D3 Kayes, W Mali
Kitab see Kitob
Kitakyūshū 109 A7 var. Kitakyûsyû. Fukuoka, Kyūshū, SW Japan
Kitakyûsyû see Kitakyūshū
Kitami 108 D2 Hokkaidō, NE Japan
Kitchener 16 C5 Ontario, S Canada
Kíthnos see Kýthnos
Kitimat 14 D4 British Columbia, SW Canada
Kitinen 62 D3 river N Finland
Kitob 101 E3 Rus. Kitab. Qashqadaryo Viloyati, S Uzbekistan
Kitwe 56 D2 var. Kitwe-Nkana. Copperbelt, C Zambia
Kitwe-Nkana see Kitwe
Kitzbüheler Alpen 73 C7 mountain range W Austria
Kivalina 14 C2 Alaska, USA
Kivalo 62 D3 ridge C Finland
Kivertsi 86 C1 Pol. Kiwerce, Rus. Kivertsy. Volyns'ka Oblast', NW Ukraine
Kivertsy see Kivertsi
Kivu, Lac see Kivu, Lake
Kivu, Lake 55 E6 Fr. Lac Kivu. lake Rwanda/Dem. Rep. Congo
Kiwerce see Kivertsi
Kiyev see Kyyiv
Kiyevskoye Vodokhranilishche see Kyyivs'ke Vodoskhovyshche
Kızıl Irmak 94 C3 river C Turkey
Kizil Kum see Kyzyl Kum
Kizyl-Arvat see Serdar
Kjølen see Kölen
Kladno 77 A5 Středočeský, NW Czech Republic
Klagenfurt 73 D7 Slvn. Celovec. Kärnten, S Austria
Klaipėda 84 B3 Ger. Memel. Klaipeda, NW Lithuania
Klamath Falls 24 B4 Oregon, NW USA
Klamath Mountains 24 A4 mountain range California/Oregon, W USA
Klang 116 B3 var. Kelang; prev. Port Swettenham. Selangor, Peninsular Malaysia
Klarälven 63 B6 river Norway/Sweden
Klatovy 77 A5 Ger. Klattau. Plzeňský Kraj, W Czech Republic
Klattau see Klatovy
Klausenburg see Cluj-Napoca
Klazienaveen 64 E2 Drenthe, NE Netherlands
Kleines Ungarisches Tiefland see Little Alföld
Klein Karas 56 B4 Karas, S Namibia
Kleinwardein see Kisvárda
Kleisoúra 83 A5 Ípeiros, W Greece
Klerksdorp 56 D4 North-West, N South Africa
Klimavichy 85 E7 Rus. Klimovichi. Mahilyowskaya Voblasts', E Belarus
Klimovichi see Klimavichy
Klintsy 89 A5 Bryanskaya Oblast', W Russian Federation

Klisura – Kuzi

Klisura 82 C2 Plovdiv, C Bulgaria
Ključ 78 B3 Federacija Bosna I Hercegovina, NW Bosnia and Herzegovina
Kłobuck 76 C4 Śląskie, S Poland
Klosters 73 B7 Graubünden, SE Switzerland
Kluang see Keluang
Kluczbork 76 C4 Ger. Kreuzburg, Kreuzburg in Oberschlesien. Opolskie, S Poland
Klyuchevskaya Sopka, Vulkan 93 H3 volcano E Russian Federation
Knin 78 B4 Šibenik-Knin, S Croatia
Knjaževac 78 E4 Serbia, E Serbia
Knokke-Heist 65 A5 West-Vlaanderen, NW Belgium
Knoxville 20 D1 Tennessee, S USA
Knud Rasmussen Land 60 D1 physical region N Greenland
Kobdo see Hovd
Kōbe 109 C6 Hyōgo, Honshū, SW Japan
København 63 B7 Eng. Copenhagen; anc. Hafnia. country capital Sjælland, København, E Denmark
Kobenni 52 D3 Hodh el Gharbi, S Mauritania
Koblenz 73 A5 prev. Coblenz, Fr. Coblence; anc. Confluentes. Rheinland-Pfalz, W Germany
Kobrin see Kobryn
Kobryn 85 A6 Rus. Kobrin. Brestskaya Voblasts', SW Belarus
K'obulet'i 95 F2 W Georgia
Kočani 79 E6 NE FYR Macedonia
Kočevje 73 D8 Ger. Gottschee. S Slovenia
Koch Bihār 113 G3 West Bengal, NE India
Kochchi Cochin/Kochi
Kōchi 109 B7 var. Kôti. Kōchi, Shikoku, SW Japan
Kochiu see Gejiu
Kodiak 14 C3 Kodiak Island, Alaska, USA
Kodiak Island 14 C3 island Alaska, USA
Koedoes see Kudus
Koeln see Köln
Koepang see Kupang
Ko-erh-mu see Golmud
Koetai see Mahakam, Sungai
Koetaradja see Bandaaceh
Kōfu 109 D5 var. Kôhu. Yamanashi, Honshū, S Japan
Kogarah 126 E2 New South Wales, E Australia
Kogon 100 D2 Rus. Kagan. Buxoro Viloyati, C Uzbekistan
Kőhalom see Rupea
Kohīma 113 H3 state capital Nāgāland, E India
Koh I Noh see Büyükağrı Dağı
Kohtla-Järve 84 E2 Ida-Virumaa, NE Estonia
Kôhu see Kōfu
Kokand see Qo'qon
Kokchetav see Kokshetau
Kokkola 62 D4 Swe. Karleby; prev. Swe. Gamlakarleby. Länsi-Suomi, W Finland
Koko 53 F4 Kebbi, W Nigeria
Kokomo 18 C4 Indiana, N USA
Koko Nor see Qinghai, China
Koko Nor see Qinghai Hu, China
Kokrines 14 C2 Alaska, USA
Kokshaal-Tau 101 G2 Rus. Khrebet Kakshaal-Too. mountain range China/Kyrgyzstan
Kokshetau 92 C4 Kaz. Kökshetaū; prev. Kokchetav. Kokshetau, N Kazakhstan
Kökshetaū see Kokshetau
Koksijde 65 A5 West-Vlaanderen, W Belgium
Koksoak 16 D2 river Québec, E Canada
Kokstad 56 D5 KwaZulu/Natal, E South Africa
Kolaka 117 E4 Sulawesi, C Indonesia
K'o-la-ma-i see Karamay
Kola Peninsula 88 C2 Eng. Kola Peninsula. peninsula NW Russian Federation
Kola Peninsula see Kol'skiy Poluostrov
Kolari 62 D3 Lappi, NW Finland
Kolárovo 77 C7 Ger. Gutta; prev. Guta, Hung. Gúta. Nitriansky Kraj, SW Slovakia
Kolberg see Kołobrzeg
Kolda 52 C3 S Senegal
Kolding 63 A7 Vejle, C Denmark
Kölen 59 E1 Nor. Kjølen. mountain range Norway/Sweden
Kolguyev, Ostrov 88 C2 island NW Russian Federation
Kolhāpur 110 B1 Mahārāshtra, SW India
Kolhumadulu 110 A5 var. Thaa Atoll. atoll S Maldives
Kolín 77 B5 Ger. Kolin. Střední Čechy, C Czech Republic
Kolka 84 C2 Talsi, NW Latvia
Kolkasrags 84 C2 prev. Eng. Cape Domesnes. headland NW Latvia
Kolmar see Colmar
Köln 72 A4 var. Koeln, Eng./Fr. Cologne, prev. Cöln; anc. Colonia Agrippina, Oppidum Ubiorum. Nordrhein-Westfalen, W Germany
Koło 76 C3 Wielkopolskie, C Poland
Kołobrzeg 76 B2 Ger. Kolberg. Zachodnio-pomorskie, NW Poland
Kolokani 52 D3 Koulikoro, W Mali
Kolomea see Kolomyya
Kolomna 89 B5 Moskovskaya Oblast', W Russian Federation
Kolomyya 86 C3 Ger. Kolomea. Ivano-Frankivs'ka Oblast', W Ukraine
Kolosjoki see Nikel'
Kolozsvár see Cluj-Napoca
Kolpa 78 A2 Ger. Kulpa, SCr. Kupa. river Croatia/Slovenia
Kolpino 88 B4 Leningradskaya Oblast', NW Russian Federation
Kólpos Mórfu see Güzelyurt
Kolwezi 55 D7 Katanga, S Dem. Rep. Congo
Kolyma 93 G2 river NE Russian Federation
Komatsu 109 C5 var. Komatu. Ishikawa, Honshū, SW Japan
Komatu see Komatsu
Kommunizm, Qullai see Ismoili Somoní, Qullai
Komoé 53 E4 var. Komoé Fleuve. river E Ivory Coast
Komoé Fleuve see Komoé
Komotau see Chomutov
Komotiní 82 D3 var. Gümüljina, Turk. Gümülcine. Anatolikí Makedonía kai Thráki, NE Greece
Kompong see Kâmpóng Chhnăng
Kompong Cham see Kâmpóng Cham
Kompong Som see Kâmpóng Saôm
Kompong Speu see Kâmpóng Spoe
Komrat see Comrat
Komsomolets, Ostrov 93 E1 island Severnaya Zemlya, N Russian Federation
Komsomol'sk-na-Amure 93 G4 Khabarovskiy Kray, SE Russian Federation
Kondolovo 82 E3 Burgas, E Bulgaria
Kondopoga 88 B3 Respublika Kareliya, NW Russian Federation
Kondoz 101 E3 Pash. Kunduz. province NE Afghanistan
Köneurgench 100 C2 var. Köneürgench, Rus. Këneurgench; prev. Kunya-Urgench. Daşoguz Welaýaty, N Turkmenistan
Kong Christian IX Land 60 D4 Eng. King Christian IX Land. physical region SE Greenland
Kong Frederik IX Land 60 C3 physical region SW Greenland
Kong Frederik VIII Land 61 E2 Eng. King Frederik VIII Land. physical region NE Greenland
Kong Frederik VI Kyst 60 C4 Eng. King Frederik VI Coast. physical region SE Greenland
Kong Karls Land 61 G2 Eng. King Charles Islands. island group SE Svalbard
Kongo see Congo (river)
Kongolo 55 D6 Katanga, E Dem. Rep. Congo
Kongor 51 B5 Jonglei, SE Sudan
Kong Oscar Fjord 61 E3 fjord E Greenland
Kongsberg 63 B6 Buskerud, S Norway
Kông, Tônle 115 E5 var. Xê Kong. river Cambodia/Laos
Kong, Xê see Kông, Tônle
Königgrätz see Hradec Králové
Königshütte see Chorzów
Konin 76 C3 Ger. Kuhnau. Weilkopolskie, C Poland
Koninkrijk der Nederlanden see Netherlands
Konispol 79 C7 var. Konispoli. Vlorë, S Albania
Konispoli see Konispol
Kónitsa 82 A4 Ípeiros, W Greece
Konitz see Chojnice
Konjic 78 C4 Federacija Bosna I Hercegovina, S Bosnia and Herzegovina
Konosha 88 C4 Arkhangel'skaya Oblast', NW Russian Federation
Konotop 87 F1 Sums'ka Oblast', NE Ukraine
Konstantinovka see Kostyantynivka
Konstanz 73 B7 var. Constanz, Eng. Constance, hist. Kostnitz; anc. Constantia. Baden-Württemberg, S Germany
Konstanza see Constanța
Konya 94 C4 var. Konieh, prev. Konia; anc. Iconium. Konya, C Turkey
Kopaonik 79 D5 mountain range S Serbia
Kopar see Koper
Koper 73 D8 It. Capodistria; prev. Kopar. SW Slovenia
Köpetdag Gershi 100 C3 mountain range Iran/Turkmenistan
Köpetdag Gershi/Kopetdag, Khrebet see Koppeh Dāgh
Koppeh Dāgh 98 D2 Rus. Khrebet Kopetdag, Turkm. Köpetdag Gershi. mountain range Iran/Turkmenistan
Kopreinitz see Koprivnica
Koprivnica 78 B2 Ger. Kopreinitz, Hung. Kaproncza. Koprivnica-Kri»zevci, N Croatia
Köprülü see Veles
Koptsevichi see Kaptsevichy
Kopyl' see Kapyl'
Korat see Nakhon Ratchasima
Korat Plateau 114 D4 plateau E Thailand
Korba 113 E4 Chhattīsgarh, C India
Korça see Korçë
Korçë 79 D6 var. Korça, Gk. Korytsa, It. Corriza; prev. Koritsa. Korçë, SE Albania
Korčula 78 B4 It. Curzola; anc. Corcyra Nigra. island S Croatia
Korea Bay 105 G3 bay China/North Korea
Korea, Democratic People's Republic of see North Korea
Korea, Republic of see South Korea
Korea Strait 109 A7 Jap. Chōsen-kaikyō, Kor. Taehan-haehyŏp. channel Japan/South Korea
Korhogo 52 D4 N Ivory Coast
Kórinthos 83 B6 anc. Corinthus Eng. Corinth. Pelopónnisos, S Greece
Koritsa see Korçë
Kōriyama 109 D5 Fukushima, Honshū, C Japan
Korla 104 C3 Chin. K'u-erh-lo. Xinjiang Uygur Zizhiqu, NW China
Körmend 77 B7 Vas, W Hungary
Koróni 83 B6 Pelopónnisos, S Greece
Koror 122 A2 var. Oreor. Oreor, N Palau
Kőrös see Križevci
Korosten' 86 D1 Zhytomyrs'ka Oblast', NW Ukraine
Koro Toro 54 C2 Borkou-Ennedi-Tibesti, N Chad
Korsovka see Kārsava
Kortrijk 65 A6 Fr. Courtrai. West-Vlaanderen, W Belgium
Koryak Range 93 H2 var. Koryakskiy Khrebet, Eng. Koryak Range. mountain range NE Russian Federation
Koryak Range see Koryakskoye Nagor'ye
Koryakskiy Khrebet see Koryakskoye Nagor'ye
Koryazhma 88 C4 Arkhangel'skaya Oblast', NW Russian Federation
Korytsa see Korçë
Kos 83 E6 Kos, Dodekánisa, Greece, Aegean Sea
Kos 83 E6 It. Coo; anc. Cos. island Dodekánisa, Greece, Aegean Sea
Ko-saki 109 A7 headland Nagasaki, Tsushima, SW Japan
Kościan 76 B4 Ger. Kosten. Wielkopolskie, C Poland
Kościerzyna 76 C2 Pomorskie, NW Poland
Kosciusko, Mount see Kosciuszko, Mount
Kosciuszko, Mount 127 C7 prev. Mount Kosciusko. mountain New South Wales, SE Australia
K'o-shih see Kashi
Koshikijima-retto 109 A8 var. Kosikizima Rettô. island group SW Japan
Kōshū see Kwangju
Košice 77 D6 Ger. Kaschau, Hung. Kassa. Košický Kraj, E Slovakia
Kosikizima Rettô see Koshikijima-rettō
Köslin see Koszalin
Koson 101 E3 Rus. Kasan. Qashqadaryo Viloyati, S Uzbekistan
Kosovo 79 D5 prev. Autonomous Province of Kosovo and Metohija. country SE Europe
Kosovo and Metohija, Autonomous Province of see Kosovo
Kosovo Polje see Fushë Kosovë
Kosovska Mitrovica see Mitrovicë
Kosrae 122 C2 prev. Kusaie. island Caroline Islands, E Micronesia
Kossou, Lac de 52 D5 lake C Ivory Coast
Kostanay 92 C4 var. Kustanay, Kaz. Qostanay. Kostanay, N Kazakhstan
Kosten see Kościan
Kostenets 82 C2 prev. Georgi Dimitrov. Sofiya, W Bulgaria
Kostnitz see Konstanz
Kostroma 88 B4 Kostromskaya Oblast', NW Russian Federation
Kostyantynivka 87 G3 Rus. Konstantinovka. Donets'ka Oblast', SE Ukraine
Kostyukovichi see Kastsyukovichy
Kostyukovka see Kastsyukowka
Koszalin 76 B2 Ger. Köslin. Zachodnio-pomorskie, NW Poland
Kota 112 D3 prev. Kotah. Rājasthān, N India
Kota Baharu see Kota Bharu
Kota Bahru see Kota Bharu
Kotabaru see Jayapura
Kota Bharu 116 B3 var. Kota Baharu, Kota Bahru. Kelantan, Peninsular Malaysia
Kotaboemi see Kotabumi
Kotabumi 116 B4 prev. Kotaboemi. Sumatera, W Indonesia
Kotah see Kota
Kota Kinabalu 116 D3 prev. Jesselton. Sabah, East Malaysia
Kotel'nyy, Ostrov 93 E2 island Novosibirskiye Ostrova, N Russian Federation
Kotka 63 E5 Etelä-Suomi, S Finland
Kotlas 88 C4 Arkhangel'skaya Oblast', NW Russian Federation
Kotonu see Cotonou
Kotor 79 C5 It. Cattaro. SW Montenegro
Kotovs'k 86 D3 Rus. Kotovsk. Odes'ka Oblast', SW Ukraine
Kotovsk see Hîncești
Kottbus see Cottbus
Kotto 54 D4 river Central African Republic/Dem. Rep. Congo
Kotuy 93 E2 river N Russian Federation
Koudougou 53 E4 C Burkina
Koulamoutou 55 B6 Ogooué-Lolo, C Gabon
Koulikoro 52 D3 Koulikoro, SW Mali
Koumra 54 C4 Moyen-Chari, S Chad
Kourou 37 H3 N French Guiana
Kousseir see Al Quṣayr
Kousséri 54 B3 prev. Fort-Foureau. Extrême-Nord, NE Cameroon
Koutiala 52 D4 Sikasso, S Mali
Kouvola 63 E5 Etelä-Suomi, S Finland
Kovel' 86 C1 Pol. Kowel. Volyns'ka Oblast', NW Ukraine
Kovno see Kaunas
Koweit see Kuwait
Kowel see Kovel'
Kowloon 106 A2 Hong Kong, S China
Kowno see Kaunas
Kozáni 82 B4 Dytikí Makedonía, N Greece
Kozara 78 B3 mountain range NW Bosnia and Herzegovina
Kozarska Dubica see Bosanska Dubica
Kozu-shima 109 D6 island E Japan
Kozyatyn 86 D2 Rus. Kazatin. Vinnyts'ka Oblast', C Ukraine
Kpalimé 53 E5 var. Palimé. SW Togo
Krâchéh 115 D6 prev. Kratie. Krâchéh, E Cambodia
Kragujevac 78 D4 Serbia, C Serbia
Krainburg see Kranj
Kra, Isthmus of 115 B6 isthmus Malaysia/Thailand
Krakau see Kraków
Kraków 77 D5 Eng. Cracow, Ger. Krakau; anc. Cracovia. Małopolskie, S Poland
Krâlănh 115 D5 Siĕmréab, NW Cambodia
Kraljevo 78 D4 prev. Rankovićevo. Serbia, C Serbia
Kramators'k 87 G3 Rus. Kramatorsk. Donets'ka Oblast', SE Ukraine
Kramatorsk see Kramators'k
Kramfors 63 C5 Västernorrland, C Sweden
Kranéa see Kraniá
Kraniá 82 B4 var. Kranéa. Dytikí Makedonía, N Greece
Kranj 73 D7 Ger. Krainburg. NW Slovenia
Kranz see Zelenogradsk
Krāslava 84 D4 Krāslava, SE Latvia
Krasnaye 85 C5 Rus. Krasnoye. Minskaya Voblasts', C Belarus
Krasnoarmeysk 89 C6 Saratovskaya Oblast', W Russian Federation
Krasnodar 89 A7 prev. Ekaterinodar, Yekaterinodar. Krasnodarskiy Kray, SW Russian Federation
Krasnodon 87 H3 Luhans'ka Oblast', E Ukraine
Krasnogor see Kallaste
Krasnogvardeyskoye see Krasnohvardiys'ke
Krasnohvardiys'ke 87 F4 Rus. Krasnogvardeyskoye. Respublika Krym, S Ukraine
Krasnokamensk 93 F4 Chitinskaya Oblast', S Russian Federation
Krasnokamsk 89 D5 Permskaya Oblast', W Russian Federation
Krasnoperekops'k 87 F4 Rus. Krasnoperekopsk. Respublika Krym, S Ukraine
Krasnoperekopsk see Krasnoperekops'k
Krasnostav see Krasnystaw
Krasnovodsk see Türkmenbaşy
Krasnovodskiy Zaliv see Türkmenbasy Aylagy
Krasnowodsk Aylagy see Türkmenbasy Aylagy
Krasnoyarsk 92 D4 Krasnoyarskiy Kray, S Russian Federation
Krasnoye see Krasnaye
Krasnystaw 76 E4 Rus. Krasnostav. Lubelskie, SE Poland
Krasnyy Kut 89 C6 Saratovskaya Oblast', W Russian Federation
Krasnyy Luch 87 H3 prev. Krindachevka. Luhans'ka Oblast', E Ukraine
Kratie see Krâchéh
Krâvanh, Chuŏr Phnum 115 C6 Eng. Cardamom Mountains, Fr. Chaîne des Cardamomes. mountain range W Cambodia
Krefeld 72 A4 Nordrhein-Westfalen, W Germany
Kreisstadt see Krosno Odrzańskie
Kremenchug see Kremenchuk
Kremenchugskoye Vodokhranilishche/ Kremenchuk Reservoir see Kremenchuts'ke Vodoskhovyshche
Kremenchuk 87 F2 Rus. Kremenchug. Poltavs'ka Oblast', NE Ukraine
Kremenchuk Reservoir 87 F2 Eng. Kremenchuk Reservoir, Rus. Kremenchugskoye Vodokhranilishche. reservoir C Ukraine
Kremenets' 86 C2 Pol. Krzemieniec, Rus. Kremenets. Ternopil's'ka Oblast', W Ukraine
Kremennaya see Kreminna
Kreminna 87 G2 Rus. Kremennaya. Luhans'ka Oblast', E Ukraine
Kresena see Kresna
Kresna 82 C3 var. Kresena. Blagoevgrad, SW Bulgaria
Kretikon Delagos see Kritikó Pélagos
Kretinga 84 B3 Ger. Krottingen. Klaipėda, NW Lithuania
Kreutz see Cristuru Secuiesc
Kreuz see Križevci, Croatia
Kreuz see Risti, Estonia
Kreuzburg/Kreuzburg in Oberschlesien see Kluczbork
Krichëv see Krychaw
Krievija see Russian Federation
Krindachevka see Krasnyy Luch
Krishna 110 C1 prev. Kistna. river C India
Krishnagiri 110 C2 Tamil Nādu, SE India
Kristiania see Oslo
Kristiansand 63 A6 var. Christiansand. Vest-Agder, S Norway
Kristianstad 63 B7 Skåne, S Sweden
Kristiansund 62 A4 var. Christiansund. Møre og Romsdal, S Norway
Krivoy Rog see Kryvyy Rih
Križevci 78 B2 Ger. Kreuz, Hung. Kőrös. Varaždin, NE Croatia
Krk 78 A3 It. Veglia; anc. Curieta. island NW Croatia
Kroatien see Croatia
Krolevets' 87 F1 Rus. Krolevets. Sums'ka Oblast', NE Ukraine
Krolevets see Krolevets'
Królewska Huta see Chorzów
Kronach 73 C5 Bayern, E Germany
Kronstadt see Brașov
Kroonstad 56 D4 Free State, C South Africa
Kropotkin 89 A7 Krasnodarskiy Kray, SW Russian Federation
Krosno 77 D5 Ger. Krossen. Podkarpackie, SE Poland
Krosno Odrzańskie 76 B3 Ger. Crossen, Kreisstadt. Lubuskie, W Poland
Krossen see Krosno
Krottingen see Kretinga
Krško 73 E8 Ger. Gurkfeld; prev. Videm-Krško. E Slovenia
Krugloye see Kruhlaye
Kruhlaye 85 D6 Rus. Krugloye. Mahilyowskaya Voblasts', E Belarus
Kruja see Krujë
Krujë 79 C6 var. Kruja, It. Croia. Durrës, C Albania
Krummau see Český Krumlov
Krung Thep 115 C5 var. Krung Thep Mahanakhon, Eng. Bangkok. country capital Bangkok, C Thailand
Krung Thep, Ao 115 C5 var. Bight of Bangkok. bay S Thailand
Krung Thep Mahanakhon see Krung Thep
Krupki 85 D6 Minskaya Voblasts', C Belarus
Krušné Hory see Erzgebirge
Krychaw 85 E7 Rus. Krichëv. Mahilyowskaya Voblasts', E Belarus
Kryms'ki Hory 87 F5 mountain range S Ukraine
Kryms'kyy Pivostriv 87 F5 peninsula S Ukraine
Krynica 77 D5 Ger. Tannenhof. Małopolskie, S Poland
Kryve Ozero 87 E3 Odes'ka Oblast', SW Ukraine
Kryvyy Rih 87 F3 Rus. Krivoy Rog. Dnipropetrovs'ka Oblast', SE Ukraine
Krzemieniec see Kremenets'
Ksar al Kabir see Ksar-el-Kebir
Ksar al Soule see Er-Rachidia
Ksar-el-Kebir 48 C2 var. Alcázar, Ksar al Kabir, Ksar-el-Kébir, Ar. Al-Kasr al-Kebir, Al-Qsar al-Kbir, Sp. Alcazarquivir. NW Morocco
Ksar-el-Kébir see Ksar-el-Kebir
Kuala Dungun see Dungun
Kuala Lumpur 116 B3 country capital Kuala Lumpur, Peninsular Malaysia
Kuala Terengganu 116 B3 var. Kuala Trengganu. Terengganu, Peninsular Malaysia
Kualatungkal 116 B4 Sumatera, W Indonesia
Kuang-chou see Guangzhou
Kuang-hsi see Guangxi Zhuangzu Zizhiqu
Kuang-tung see Guangdong
Kuang-yuan see Guangyuan
Kuantan 116 B3 Pahang, Peninsular Malaysia
Kuba see Quba
Kuban' 87 G5 var. Hypanis. river SW Russian Federation
Kubango see Cubango/Okavango
Kuching 116 C3 prev. Sarawak. Sarawak, East Malaysia
Kūchnay Darweyshān 100 D5 Helmand, S Afghanistan
Kuçova see Kuçovë
Kuçovë 79 C6 var. Kuçova; prev. Qyteti Stalin. Berat, C Albania
Kudara see Ghŭdara
Kudus 116 C5 prev. Koedoes. Jawa, C Indonesia
Kuei-lin see Guilin
Kuei-Yang/Kuei-yang see Guiyang
K'u-erh-lo see Korla
Kueyang see Guiyang
Kugaaruk 15 G3 prev. Pelly Bay. Nunavut, N Canada
Kugluktuk 31 E3 var. Qurlurtuuq; prev. Coppermine. Nunavut, NW Canada
Kuhmo 62 E4 Oulu, E Finland
Kuhnau see Konin
Kühnö see Kihnu
Kuibyshev see Kuybyshevskoye Vodokhranilishche
Kuito 56 B2 Port. Silva Porto. Bié, C Angola
Kuji 108 D3 var. Kuzi. Iwate, Honshū, C Japan
Kukës 79 D5 var. Kukësi. Kukës, NE Albania
Kukësi see Kukës
Kukong see Shaoguan
Kukukhoto see Hohhot
Kula Kangri 113 G3 var. Kulhakangri. mountain Bhutan/China
Kuldīga 84 B3 Ger. Goldingen. Kuldīga, W Latvia
Kuldja see Yining
Kulhakangri see Kula Kangri
Kullorsuaq 60 D2 var. Kuvdlorssuak. Kitaa, C Greenland
Kulm see Chełmno
Kulmsee see Chełmża
Kŭlob 101 F3 Rus. Kulyab. SW Tajikistan
Kulpa see Kolpa
Kulu 94 C3 Konya, W Turkey
Kulunda Steppe 92 C4 Kaz. Qulyndy Zhazyghy, Rus. Kulundinskaya Ravnina. grassland Kazakhstan/Russian Federation
Kulundinskaya Ravnina see Kulunda Steppe
Kulyab see Kŭlob
Kum see Qom
Kuma 89 B7 river SW Russian Federation
Kumamoto 109 A7 Kumamoto, Kyūshū, SW Japan
Kumanova see Kumanovo
Kumanovo 79 E5 Turk. Kumanova. N Macedonia
Kumasi 53 E5 prev. Coomassie. C Ghana
Kumayri see Gyumri
Kumba 55 A5 Sud-Ouest, W Cameroon
Kumertau 89 D6 Respublika Bashkortostan, W Russian Federation
Kumillā see Comilla
Kumo 53 G4 Gombe, E Nigeria
Kumon Range 114 B2 mountain range N Myanmar (Burma)
Kumul see Hami
Kunashiri see Kunashir, Ostrov
Kunashir, Ostrov 108 E1 var. Kunashiri. island Kuril'skiye Ostrova, SE Russian Federation
Kunda 84 E2 Lääne-Virumaa, NE Estonia
Kunduz see Kondoz
Kunene 47 C6 var. Kunene. river Angola/Namibia
Kunene see Cunene
Kungsbacka 63 B7 Halland, S Sweden
Kungur 89 D5 Permskaya Oblast', NW Russian Federation
Kunlun Mountains see Kunlun Shan
Kunlun Shan 104 B4 Eng. Kunlun Mountains. mountain range NW China
Kunming 106 B6 var. K'un-ming; prev. Yunnan. province capital Yunnan, SW China
K'un-ming see Kunming
Kununurra 124 D3 Western Australia
Kunya-Urgench see Köneurgench
Kuopio 63 E5 Itä-Suomi, C Finland
Kupa see Kolpa
Kupang 117 E5 prev. Koepang. Timor, C Indonesia
Kup"yans'k 87 G2 Rus. Kupyansk. Kharkivs'ka Oblast', E Ukraine
Kupyansk see Kup"yans'k
Kür see Kura
Kura 95 H3 Az. Kür, Geor. Mtkvari, Turk. Kura Nehri. river SW Asia
Kura Nehri see Kura
Kurashiki 109 B6 var. Kurasiki. Okayama, Honshū, SW Japan
Kurasiki see Kurashiki
Kurdistan 95 F4 cultural region SW Asia
Kŭrdzhali 82 D3 var. Kirdzhali. Kŭrdzhali, S Bulgaria
Kure 109 B7 Hiroshima, Honshū, SW Japan
Küre Dağları 94 C2 mountain range N Turkey
Kuressaare 84 C2 Ger. Arensburg; prev. Kingissepp. Saaremaa, W Estonia
Kureyka 90 D2 river N Russian Federation
Kurgan-Tyube see Qŭrghonteppa
Kuria Muria Islands see Ḥalāniyāt, Juzur al
Kurile Islands 93 H4 Eng. Kurile Islands. island group SE Russian Federation
Kurile Islands see Kuril'skiye Ostrova
Kurile-Kamchatka Depression see Kurile Trench
Kurile Trench 91 F3 var. Kurile-Kamchatka Depression. trench NW Pacific Ocean
Kuril'sk 108 E1 Jap. Shana. Kuril'skiye Ostrova, Sakhalinskaya Oblats', SE Russian Federation
Ku-ring-gai 126 E1 New South Wales, E Australia
Kurisches Haff see Courland Lagoon
Kurkund see Kilingi-Nõmme
Kurnool 110 C1 var. Karnul. Andhra Pradesh, S India
Kursk 89 A6 Kurskaya Oblast', W Russian Federation
Kurskiy Zaliv see Courland Lagoon
Kuršumlija 79 D5 Serbia, S Serbia
Kurtbunar see Tervel
Kurtitsch/Kürtös see Curtici
Kuruktag 104 C3 mountain range NW China
Kurume 109 A7 Fukuoka, Kyūshū, SW Japan
Kurupukari 37 F3 C Guyana
Kusaie see Kosrae
Kushiro 108 D2 var. Kusiro. Hokkaidō, NE Japan
Kushka see Serhetabat
Kusiro see Kushiro
Kuskokwim Mountains 14 C3 mountain range Alaska, USA
Kustanay see Kostanay
Küstence/Küstendje see Constanța
Kütahya 94 B3 prev. Kutaia. Kütahya, W Turkey
Kutai see Mahakam, Sungai
K'ut'aisi 95 F2 W Georgia
Kūt al 'Amārah see Al Kūt
Kut al Imara see Al Kūt
Kutaradja/Kutaraja see Bandaaceh
Kutch, Gulf of see Kachchh, Gulf of
Kutch, Rann of see Kachchh, Rann of
Kutina 78 B3 Sisak-Moslavina, NE Croatia
Kutno 76 C3 Łódzkie, C Poland
Kuujjuaq 17 E2 prev. Fort-Chimo. Québec, E Canada
Kuusamo 62 E3 Oulu, E Finland
Kuvango see Cubango
Kuvdlorssuak see Kullorsuaq
Kuwait 98 C4 off. State of Kuwait, var. Dawlat al Kuwait, Koweit, Kuweit. country SW Asia
Kuwait see Al Kuwayt
Kuwait City see Al Kuwayt
Kuwait, Dawlat al see Kuwait
Kuwait, State of see Kuwait
Kuwajleen see Kwajalein Atoll
Kuwayt 98 C3 Maysān, E Iraq
Kuweit see Kuwait
Kuybyshev see Samara
Kuybyshev Reservoir 89 C5 var. Kuibyshev, Eng. Kuybyshev Reservoir. reservoir W Russian Federation
Kuybyshev Reservoir see Kuybyshevskoye Vodokhranilishche
Kuytun 104 B2 Xinjiang Uygur Zizhiqu, NW China
Kuzi see Kuji

Kuznetsk – Lichtenvoorde

Kuznetsk 89 B6 Penzenskaya Oblast', W Russian Federation
Kuźnica 76 E2 Białystok, NE Poland Europe
Kvaløya 62 C2 island N Norway
Kvarnbergsvattnet 62 B4 var. Frostviken. lake N Sweden
Kvarner 78 A3 var. Carnaro, It. Quarnero. gulf W Croatia
Kvitøya 61 G1 island NE Svalbard
Kwajalein Atoll 122 C1 var. Kuwajleen. atoll Ralik Chain, C Marshall Islands
Kwando see Cuando
Kwangchow see Guangzhou
Kwangchu see Kwangju
Kwangju 107 E4 off. Kwangju-gwangyŏksi, var. Guangju, Kwangchu, Jap. Kōshū. SW South Korea
Kwangju-gwangyŏksi see Kwangju
Kwango 55 C7 Port. Cuango. river Angola/Dem. Rep. Congo
Kwango see Cuango
Kwangsi/Kwangsi Chuang Autonomous Region see Guangxi Zhuangzu Zizhiqu
Kwangtung see Guangdong
Kwangyuan see Guangyuan
Kwanza see Cuanza
Kweichu see Guiyang
Kweilin see Guilin
Kweisui see Hohhot
Kweiyang see Guiyang
Kwekwe 56 D3 prev. Que Que. Midlands, C Zimbabwe
Kwesui see Hohhot
Kwidzyń 76 C2 Ger. Marienwerder. Pomorskie, N Poland
Kwigillingok 14 C3 Alaska, USA
Kwilu 55 C6 river W Dem. Rep. Congo
Kwito see Cuito
Kyabé 54 C4 Moyen-Chari, S Chad
Kyaikkami 115 B5 prev. Amherst. Mon State, S Myanmar (Burma)
Kyaiklat 114 B4 Ayeyarwady, SW Myanmar (Burma)
Kyaikto 114 B4 Mon State, S Myanmar (Burma)
Kyakhta 93 E5 Respublika Buryatiya, S Russian Federation
Kyaukse 114 B3 Mandalay, C Myanmar (Burma)
Kyjov 77 C5 Ger. Gaya. Jihomoravský Kraj, SE Czech Republic
Kými 83 C5 prev. Kími. Évvoia, C Greece
Kyŏngsŏng see Sŏul
Kyōto 109 C6 Kyōto, Honshū, SW Japan
Kyparissía 83 B6 var. Kiparissía. Pelopónnisos, S Greece
Kypros see Cyprus
Kyrá Panagía 83 C5 island Vóreies Sporádes, Greece, Aegean Sea
Kyrenia see Girne
Kyrgyz Republic see Kyrgyzstan
Kyrgyzstan 101 F2 off. Kyrgyz Republic, var. Kirghizia; prev. Kirgizskaya SSR, Kirghiz SSR, Republic of Kyrgyzstan. country C Asia
Kyrgyzstan, Republic of see Kyrgyzstan
Kythira 83 C7 var. Kíthira, It. Cerigo, Lat. Cythera. island S Greece
Kýthnos 83 C6 Kńythnos, Kykládes, Greece, Aegean Sea
Kythnos 83 C6 var. Kíthnos, Thermiá, It. Termia; anc. Cythnos. island Kykládes, Greece, Aegean Sea
Kythréa see Değirmenlik
Kyushu 109 B7 var. Kyûsyû. island SW Japan
Kyushu-Palau Ridge 103 F3 var. Kyusyu-Palau Ridge. undersea ridge W Pacific Ocean
Kyustendil 82 B2 anc. Pautalia. Kyustendil, W Bulgaria
Kyûsyû see Kyūshū
Kyusyu-Palau Ridge see Kyushu-Palau Ridge
Kyyiv 87 E2 Eng. Kiev, Rus. Kiyev. country capital Kyyivs'ka Oblast', N Ukraine
Kyzyl 92 D4 Respublika Tyva, C Russian Federation
Kyzyl Kum 100 D2 var. Kizil Kum, Qizil Qum, Uzb. Qizilqum. desert Kazakhstan/Uzbekistan
Kyzylorda 92 B5 var. Kzyl-Orda, Qizil Orda, Qyzylorda; prev. Perovsk. Kyzylorda, S Kazakhstan
Kyzylrabot see Qizilrabot
Kyzyl-Suu 101 G2 prev. Pokrovka. Issyk-Kul'skaya Oblast', NE Kyrgyzstan
Kzyl-Orda see Kyzylorda

L

Laaland see Lolland
La Algaba 70 C4 Andalucía, S Spain
Laarne 65 B5 Oost-Vlaanderen, NW Belgium
La Asunción 37 E1 Nueva Esparta, NE Venezuela
Laatokka see Ladozhskoye, Ozero
Laâyoune 48 B3 var. Aaiún. country capital NW Western Sahara
La Banda Oriental see Uruguay
la Baule-Escoublac 68 A4 Loire-Atlantique, NW France
Labé 52 C4 NW Guinea
Labe see Elbe
Laborca see Laborec
Laborec 77 E5 Hung. Laborca. river E Slovakia
Labrador 17 F2 cultural region Newfoundland and Labrador, SW Canada
Labrador Basin 12 E3 var. Labrador Sea Basin. undersea basin Labrador Sea
Labrador Sea 60 A4 sea NW Atlantic Ocean
Labrador Sea Basin see Labrador Basin
Labudalin see Ergun
Labutta 115 A5 Ayeyarwady, SW Myanmar (Burma)
Laç 79 C6 var. Laci. Lezhë, C Albania
La Calera 42 B4 Valparaíso, C Chile
La Carolina 70 D4 Andalucía, S Spain
Laccadive Islands 110 A3 Eng. Laccadive Islands. island group India, N Indian Ocean
Laccadive Islands/Laccadive Minicoy and Amindivi Islands, the see Lakshadweep
La Ceiba 30 D2 Atlántida, N Honduras
Lachanás 82 B3 Kentrikí Makedonía, N Greece
La Chaux-de-Fonds 73 A7 Neuchâtel, W Switzerland
Lachlan River 127 C6 river New South Wales, SE Australia
Laci see Laç
la Ciotat 69 D6 anc. Citharista. Bouches-du-Rhône, SE France
Lacobriga see Lagos
La Concepción 31 E5 var. Concepción. Chiriquí, W Panama
La Concepción 36 C1 Zulia, NW Venezuela
La Condamine 69 C8 W Monaco
Laconia 19 G2 New Hampshire, NE USA
La Crosse 18 A2 Wisconsin, N USA
La Cruz 30 D4 Guanacaste, NW Costa Rica
Lake Ladoga 88 B3 Eng. Lake Ladoga, Fin. Laatokka. lake NW Russian Federation
Ladoga, Lake see Ladozhskoye, Ozero
Ladysmith 18 B2 Wisconsin, N USA
Lae 122 B3 Morobe, W Papua New Guinea
Læsø 63 B7 island N Denmark
La Esperanza 30 C2 Intibucá, SW Honduras
Lafayette 18 C4 Indiana, N USA
Lafayette 20 B3 Louisiana, S USA
La Fé 32 A2 Pinar del Río, W Cuba
Lafia 53 G4 Nassarawa, C Nigeria
la Flèche 68 B4 Sarthe, NW France
Lagdo, Lac de 54 B4 lake N Cameroon
Laghouat 48 D2 N Algeria
Lagos 53 F5 Lagos, SW Nigeria
Lagos 70 B5 anc. Lacobriga. Faro, S Portugal
Lagos de Moreno 29 E4 Jalisco, SW Mexico
Lagouira 48 A4 SW Western Sahara
La Grande 24 C3 Oregon, NW USA
La Guaira 44 B4 Distrito Federal, N Venezuela
Lagunas 42 B1 Tarapacá, N Chile
Lagunillas 39 G4 Santa Cruz, SE Bolivia
La Habana 32 B2 var. Havana. country capital Ciudad de La Habana, W Cuba
Lahat 116 B4 Sumatera, W Indonesia
La Haye see 's-Gravenhage
Laholm 63 B7 Halland, S Sweden
Lahore 112 D2 Punjab, NE Pakistan
Lahr 73 A6 Baden-Württemberg, S Germany
Lahti 63 D5 Swe. Lahtis. Etelä-Suomi, S Finland
Lahtis see Lahti
Laï 54 B4 prev. Behagle, De Behagle. Tandjilé, S Chad
Laibach see Ljubljana
Lai Châu 114 D3 Lai Châu, N Vietnam
Laila see Laylā
La Junta 22 D5 Colorado, C USA
Lake Charles 20 A3 Louisiana, S USA
Lake City 21 E3 Florida, SE USA
Lake District 67 C5 physical region NW England, United Kingdom
Lake Havasu City 26 A2 Arizona, SW USA
Lake Jackson 27 H4 Texas, SW USA
Lakeland 21 E4 Florida, SE USA
Lakeside 25 C8 California, W USA
Lake State see Michigan
Lakewood 22 D4 Colorado, C USA
Lakhnau see Lucknow
Lakonikós Kólpos 83 B7 gulf S Greece
Lakselv 62 D2 Lapp. Leavdnja. Finnmark, N Norway
la Laon see Laon
Lalibela 50 C4 Āmara, Ethiopia
La Libertad 30 B1 Petén, N Guatemala
La Ligua 42 B4 Valparaíso, C Chile
Lalín 70 C1 Galicia, NW Spain
Lalitpur 113 F3 Central, C Nepal
La Louvière 65 B6 Hainaut, S Belgium
la Maddalena 74 A4 Sardegna, Italy, C Mediterranean Sea
la Manche see English Channel
Lamar 22 D5 Colorado, C USA
La Marmora, Punta 75 A5 mountain Sardegna, Italy, C Mediterranean Sea
La Massana 69 A8 La Massana, W Andorra Europe
Lambaréné 55 A6 Moyen-Ogooué, W Gabon
Lamego 70 C2 Viseu, N Portugal
Lamesa 27 E3 Texas, SW USA
Lamezia Terme 75 D6 Calabria, SE Italy
Lamía 83 B5 Stereá Ellás, C Greece
Lamoni 23 F4 Iowa, C USA
Lampang 114 C4 var. Muang Lampang. Lampang, NW Thailand
Lámpeia 83 B6 Dytikí Ellás, S Greece
Lanbi Kyun 115 B6 prev. Sullivan Island. island Mergui Archipelago, S Myanmar (Burma)
Lancang Jiang see Mekong
Lancaster 67 D5 NW England, United Kingdom
Lancaster 25 C7 California, W USA
Lancaster 19 F4 Pennsylvania, NE USA
Lancaster Sound 15 F2 sound Nunavut, N Canada
Lan-chou/Lan-chow/Lanchow see Lanzhou
Landao see Lantau Island
Landen 65 C6 Vlaams Brabant, C Belgium
Lander 22 C3 Wyoming, C USA
Landerneau 68 A3 Finistère, NW France
Landes 69 B5 cultural region SW France
Land of Enchantment see New Mexico
The Land of Opportunity see Arkansas
Land of Steady Habits see Connecticut
Land of the Midnight Sun see Alaska
Landsberg see Gorzów Wielkopolski, Lubuskie, Poland
Landsberg an der Warthe see Gorzów Wielkopolski
Land's End 67 B8 headland SW England, United Kingdom
Landshut 73 C6 Bayern, SE Germany
Langar 101 E2 Rus. Lyangar. Navoiy Viloyati, C Uzbekistan
Langfang 106 D4 Hebei, E China
Langkawi, Pulau 115 B7 island Peninsular Malaysia
Langres 68 D4 Haute-Marne, N France
Langsa 116 A3 Sumatera, W Indonesia
Lang Shan 105 E3 mountain range N China
Lang Sơn 114 D3 var. Langson. Lang Sơn, N Vietnam
Langson see Lang Sơn
Lang Suan 115 B6 Chumphon, SW Thailand
Languedoc 69 C6 cultural region S France
Länkäran 95 H3 Rus. Lenkoran'. S Azerbaijan
Lansing 18 C3 state capital Michigan, N USA
Lanta, Ko 115 B7 island S Thailand
Lantau Island 106 A2 Cant. Tai Yue Shan, Chin. Landao. island Hong Kong, S China
Lan-ts'ang Chiang see Mekong
Lantung, Gulf of see Liaodong Wan
Lanzarote 48 B3 island Islas Canarias, Spain, NE Atlantic Ocean
Lanzhou 106 B4 var. Lan-chou, Lanchow, Lan-chow; prev. Kaolan. province capital Gansu, C China
Lao Cai 114 D3 Lao Cai, N Vietnam
Laodicea/Laodicea ad Mare see Al Lādhiqīyah
Laoet see Laut, Pulau
Laojunmiao 106 A3 prev. Yumen. Gansu, N China
Laon 68 D3 var. la Laon; anc. Laudunum. Aisne, N France
Lao People's Democratic Republic see Laos
La Orchila, Isla 36 D1 island N Venezuela
La Oroya 38 C3 Junín, C Peru
Laos 114 D4 off. Lao People's Democratic Republic. country SE Asia
La Palma 31 G5 Darién, SE Panama
La Palma 48 A3 island Islas Canarias, Spain, NE Atlantic Ocean
La Paz 39 F4 var. La Paz de Ayacucho. country capital La Paz, W Bolivia
La Paz 28 B3 Baja California Sur, NW Mexico
La Paz, Bahía de 28 B3 bay W Mexico
La Paz de Ayacucho see La Paz
La Perouse Strait 108 D1 Jap. Sōya-kaikyō, Rus. Proliv Laperuza. strait Japan/Russian Federation
Laperuza, Proliv see La Perouse Strait
Lápithos see Lapta
Lapland 62 D3 Fin. Lappi, Swe. Lappland. cultural region N Europe
La Plata 42 D4 Buenos Aires, E Argentina
La Plata see Sucre
Lappeenranta 63 E5 Swe. Villmanstrand. Etelä-Suomi, SE Finland
Lappi/Lappland see Lapland
Lappo see Lapua
Lapta 80 C5 Gk. Lápithos. NW Cyprus
Laptev Sea 93 E2 Eng. Laptev Sea. sea Arctic Ocean
Laptev Sea see Laptevykh, More
Lapua 63 D5 Swe. Lappo. Länsi-Suomi, W Finland
Lapurdum see Bayonne
Łapy 76 E3 Podlaskie, NE Poland
La Quiaca 42 C2 Jujuy, N Argentina
L'Aquila 74 C4 var. Aquila, Aquila degli Abruzzi. Abruzzo, C Italy
Laracha 70 B1 Galicia, NW Spain
Laramie 22 C4 Wyoming, C USA
Laramie Mountains 22 C3 mountain range Wyoming, C USA
Laredo 71 E1 Cantabria, N Spain
Laredo 27 F5 Texas, SW USA
La Réunion see Réunion
Largeau see Faya
Largo 21 E4 Florida, SE USA
Largo, Cayo 32 B2 island W Cuba
Lario see Como, Lago di
La Rioja 42 C3 La Rioja, NW Argentina
La Rioja 71 E2 autonomous community N Spain
Lárisa 82 B4 var. Larissa. Thessalía, C Greece
Larissa see Lárisa
Lārkāna 112 B3 var. Larkhana. Sind, SE Pakistan
Larkhana see Lārkāna
Larnaca see Lárnaka
Lárnaka 80 C5 var. Larnaca, Larnax. SE Cyprus
Larnax see Lárnaka
la Rochelle 68 B4 anc. Rupella. Charente-Maritime, W France
la Roche-sur-Yon 68 B4 prev. Bourbon Vendée, Napoléon-Vendée. Vendée, NW France
La Roda 71 E3 Castilla-La Mancha, C Spain
La Romana 33 E3 E Dominican Republic
Larvotto 69 C8 N Monaco Europe
La-sa see Lhasa
Las Cabezas de San Juan 70 C5 Andalucía, S Spain
Las Cruces 26 D3 New Mexico, SW USA
La See d'Urgel 71 G1 var. La Seu d'Urgell, Seo de Urgel. Cataluña, NE Spain
La Serena 42 B3 Coquimbo, C Chile
La Seu d'Urgell see La See d'Urgel
la Seyne-sur-Mer 69 D6 Var, SE France
Lashio 114 B3 Shan State, E Myanmar (Burma)
Lashkar Gāh 100 D5 var. Lash-Kar-Gar'. Helmand, S Afghanistan
Lash-Kar-Gar' see Lashkar Gāh
La Sila 75 D6 mountain range SW Italy
La Sirena 30 D3 Región Autónoma Atlántico Sur, E Nicaragua
Łask 76 C4 Łódzkie, C Poland
Las Lomitas 42 D2 Formosa, N Argentina
La Solana 71 E4 Castilla-La Mancha, C Spain
Las Palmas 48 A3 var. Las Palmas de Gran Canaria. Gran Canaria, Islas Canarias, Spain, NE Atlantic Ocean
Las Palmas de Gran Canaria see Las Palmas
La Spezia 74 B3 Liguria, NW Italy
Lassa see Lhasa
Las Tablas 31 F5 Los Santos, S Panama
Last Frontier, The see Alaska
Las Tunas 32 C2 var. Victoria de las Tunas. Las Tunas, E Cuba
La Suisse see Switzerland
Las Vegas 25 D7 Nevada, W USA
Latacunga 38 B1 Cotopaxi, C Ecuador
la Teste 69 B5 Gironde, SW France
Latina 75 C5 prev. Littoria. Lazio, C Italy
La Tortuga, Isla 37 E1 var. Isla Tortuga. island N Venezuela
La Tuque 17 E4 Québec, SE Canada
Latvia 84 C3 off. Republic of Latvia, Ger. Lettland, Latv. Latvija, Latvijas Republika; prev. Latvian SSR, Rus. Latviyskaya SSR. country NE Europe
Latvian SSR/Latvija/Latvijas Republika/Latviyskaya SSR see Latvia
Latvia, Republic of see Latvia
Laudunum see Laon
Laudus see St-Lô
Lauenburg/Lauenburg in Pommern see Lębork
Lau Group 123 E4 island group E Fiji
Lauis see Lugano
Launceston 127 C8 Tasmania, SE Australia
La Unión 30 C2 Olancho, C Honduras
La Unión 71 F4 Murcia, SE Spain
Laurel 20 C3 Mississippi, S USA
Laurel 22 C2 Montana, NW USA
Laurentian Highlands see Laurentian Mountains
Laurentian Mountains 17 E3 var. Laurentian Highlands, Fr. Les Laurentides. plateau Newfoundland and Labrador/Québec, Canada
Laurentides, Les see Laurentian Mountains
Lauria 75 D6 Basilicata, S Italy
Laurinburg 21 F1 North Carolina, SE USA
Lauru see Choiseul
Lausanne 73 A7 It. Losanna. Vaud, SW Switzerland
Laut, Pulau 116 D4 prev. Laoet. island Borneo, C Indonesia
Laval 16 D4 Québec, SE Canada
Laval 68 B3 Mayenne, NW France
La Vall D'Uixó 71 F3 var. Vall D'Uxó. País Valenciano, E Spain
La Vega 33 E3 var. Concepción de la Vega. C Dominican Republic
La Vila Joíosa see Villajoyosa
Lávrio 83 C6 prev. Lávrion. Attikí, C Greece
Lávrion see Lávrio
Lawrence 19 G3 Massachusetts, NE USA
Lawrenceburg 20 C1 Tennessee, S USA
Lawton 27 F2 Oklahoma, C USA
La Yarada 39 E4 Tacna, SW Peru
Laylā 99 C5 var. Laila. Ar Riyāḍ, C Saudi Arabia
Lazarev Sea 132 B1 sea Antarctica
Lázaro Cárdenas 29 E5 Michoacán de Ocampo, SW Mexico
Leal see Lihula
Leamhcán see Lucan
Leamington 16 C5 Ontario, S Canada
Leavdnja see Lakselv
Lebak 117 E3 Mindanao, S Philippines
Lebanese Republic see Lebanon
Lebanon 23 G5 Missouri, C USA
Lebanon 19 G2 New Hampshire, NE USA
Lebanon 24 B3 Oregon, NW USA
Lebanon 96 A4 off. Lebanese Republic, Ar. Al Lubnān, Fr. Liban. country SW Asia
Lebanon, Mount see Liban, Jebel
Lebap 100 D2 Lebapskiy Velayat, NE Turkmenistan
Lebedin see Lebedyn
Lebedyn 87 F2 Rus. Lebedin. Sums'ka Oblast', NE Ukraine
Lębork 76 C2 var. Lębórk, Ger. Lauenburg, Lauenburg in Pommern. Pomorskie, N Poland
Lebrija 70 C5 Andalucía, S Spain
Lebu 43 A5 Bío Bío, C Chile
le Cannet 69 D6 Alpes-Maritimes, SE France
Le Cap see Cap-Haïtien
Lecce 75 E6 Puglia, SE Italy
Lechainá 83 B6 var. Lehena, Lekhainá. Dytikí Ellás, S Greece
Ledo Salinarius see Lons-le-Saunier
Leduc 15 E5 Alberta, SW Canada
Leech Lake 23 F2 lake Minnesota, N USA
Leeds 67 D5 N England, United Kingdom
Leek 64 E2 Groningen, NE Netherlands
Leer 72 A3 Niedersachsen, NW Germany
Leeuwarden 64 D1 Fris. Ljouwert. Friesland, N Netherlands
Leeuwin, Cape 120 A5 headland Western Australia
Leeward Islands 33 G3 island group E West Indies
Leeward Islands see Sotavento, Ilhas de
Lefkáda 83 A5 prev. Levkás. Lefkáda, Iónia Nisiá, Greece, C Mediterranean Sea
Lefkáda 83 A5 It. Santa Maura, prev. Levkás; anc. Leucas. island Iónia Nisiá, Greece, C Mediterranean Sea
Lefká Óri 83 C7 mountain range Kríti, Greece, E Mediterranean Sea
Lefkímmi 83 A5 var. Levkímmi. Kérkyra, Iónia Nisiá, Greece, C Mediterranean Sea
Lefkosia/Lefkoşa see Nicosia
Legaceaster see Chester
Legaspi see Legazpi City
Leghorn see Livorno
Legnica 76 B4 Ger. Liegnitz. Dolnośląskie, SW Poland
le Havre 68 B3 Eng. Havre; prev. le Havre-de-Grâce. Seine-Maritime, N France
le Havre-de-Grâce see le Havre
Lehena see Lechainá
Leicester 67 D6 Lat. Batae Coritanorum. C England, United Kingdom
Leiden 64 B3 prev. Leyden; anc. Lugdunum Batavorum. Zuid-Holland, W Netherlands
Leie 68 D2 Fr. Lys. river Belgium/France
Leinster 67 B6 Ir. Cúige Laighean. cultural region E Ireland
Leipsic see Leipzig
Leipsoí 83 E6 island Dodekánisa, Greece, Aegean Sea
Leipzig 72 C4 Pol. Lipsk, hist. Leipsic; anc. Lipsia. Sachsen, E Germany
Leiria 70 B3 anc. Collipo. Leiria, C Portugal
Leirvik 63 A6 Hordaland, S Norway
Lek 64 C4 river SW Netherlands
Lekhainá see Lechainá
Lekhchevo 82 C2 Montana, NW Bulgaria
Leksand 63 C5 Dalarna, C Sweden
Lel'chitsy see Lyel'chytsy
le Léman see Geneva, Lake
Lelystad 64 D3 Flevoland, C Netherlands
Léman, Lac see Geneva, Lake
le Mans 68 B3 Sarthe, NW France
Lemberg see L'viv
Lemesós 80 C5 var. Limassol. SW Cyprus
Lemhi Range 24 D3 mountain range Idaho, C USA North America
Lemnos see Límnos
Lemovices see Limoges
Lena 93 F3 river NE Russian Federation
Lena Tablemount 119 B7 seamount S Indian Ocean
Len Dao 106 C8 island S Spratly Islands
Lengshuitan see Yongzhou
Leninabad see Khujand
Leninakan see Gyumri
Lenine 87 G5 Rus. Lenino. Respublika Krym, S Ukraine
Leningor see Ridder
Leningrad see Sankt-Peterburg
Leningradskaya 132 B4 Russian research station Antarctica
Lenino see Lenine, Ukraine
Leninobod see Khujand
Leninpol' 101 F2 Talasskaya Oblast', NW Kyrgyzstan
Lenin-Turkmenski see Türkmenabat
Lenkoran' see Länkäran
Lenti 77 B7 Zala, SW Hungary
Lentia see Linz
Leoben 73 E7 Steiermark, C Austria
León 29 E4 var. León de los Aldamas. Guanajuato, C Mexico
León 30 C3 León, NW Nicaragua
León 70 D1 Castilla-León, NW Spain
León de los Aldamas see León
Leonídio 83 B6 var. Leonídi. Pelopónnisos, S Greece
Leonídi see Leonídio
Léopold II, Lac see Mai-Ndombe, Lac
Léopoldville see Kinshasa
Lepe 70 C4 Andalucía, S Spain
Lepel' see Lyepyel'
le Portel 68 C2 Pas-de-Calais, N France
Le Puglie see Puglia
le Puy 69 C5 prev. le Puy-en-Velay, hist. Anicium, Podium Anicensis. Haute-Loire, C France
le Puy-en-Velay see le Puy
Léré 54 B4 Mayo-Kébbi, SW Chad
Lérida see Lleida
Lerma 70 D2 Castilla-León, N Spain
Leros 83 D6 island Dodekánisa, Greece, Aegean Sea
Lerrnayin Gharabakh see Nagorno-Karabakh
Lerwick 66 D1 NE Scotland, United Kingdom
Lesbos 94 A3 anc. Lesbos. island E Greece
Lesbos see Lésvos
Les Cayes see Cayes
Les Gonaïves see Gonaïves
Leshan 106 B5 Sichuan, C China
les Herbiers 68 B4 Vendée, NW France
Lesh/Leshi see Lezhë
Lesina see Hvar
Leskovac 79 E5 Serbia, SE Serbia
Lesnoy 92 C3 Sverdlovskaya Oblast', C Russian Federation
Lesotho 56 D4 off. Kingdom of Lesotho; prev. Basutoland. country S Africa
Lesotho, Kingdom of see Lesotho
les Sables-d'Olonne 68 B4 Vendée, NW France
Lesser Antarctica see West Antarctica
Lesser Antilles 33 G4 island group E West Indies
Lesser Caucasus 95 F2 Rus. Malyy Kavkaz. mountain range SW Asia
Lesser Khingan Range see Xiao Hinggan Ling
Lesser Sunda Islands 117 E5 Eng. Lesser Sunda Islands. island group C Indonesia
Lesser Sunda Islands see Nusa Tenggara
Leszno 76 B4 Ger. Lissa. Wielkopolskie, C Poland
Lethbridge 15 E5 Alberta, SW Canada
Lethem 37 F3 S Guyana
Leti, Kepulauan 117 F5 island group E Indonesia
Letpadan 114 B4 Bago, SW Myanmar (Burma)
Letsôk-aw Kyun 115 B6 var. Letsutan Island; prev. Domel Island. island Mergui Archipelago, S Myanmar (Burma)
Letsutan Island see Letsôk-aw Kyun
Lettland see Latvia
Lëtzebuerg see Luxembourg
Leucas see Lefkáda
Leuven 65 C6 Fr. Louvain, Ger. Löwen. Vlaams Brabant, C Belgium
Leuze see Leuze-en-Hainaut
Leuze-en-Hainaut 65 B6 var. Leuze. Hainaut, SW Belgium
Léva see Levice
Levanger 62 B4 Nord-Trøndelag, C Norway
Levelland 27 E2 Texas, SW USA
Leverkusen 72 A4 Nordrhein-Westfalen, W Germany
Levice 77 C6 Ger. Lewentz, Hung. Léva, Lewenz. Nitriansky Kraj, SW Slovakia
Levin 128 D4 Manawatu-Wanganui, North Island, New Zealand
Levkás see Lefkáda
Levkímmi see Lefkímmi
Lewentz/Lewenz see Levice
Lewis, Isle of 66 B2 island NW Scotland, United Kingdom
Lewis Range 22 B1 mountain range Montana, NW USA
Lewiston 24 C2 Idaho, NW USA
Lewiston 19 G2 Maine, NE USA
Lewistown 22 C1 Montana, NW USA
Lexington 18 C5 Kentucky, S USA
Lexington 23 E4 Nebraska, C USA
Leyden see Leiden
Leyte 117 F2 island C Philippines
Leżajsk 77 E5 Podkarpackie, SE Poland
Lezha see Lezhë
Lezhë 79 C6 var. Lezha; prev. Lesh, Leshi. Lezhë, NW Albania
Lhasa 104 C5 var. La-sa, Lassa. Xizang Zizhiqu, W China
Lhaviyani Atoll see Faadhippolhu Atoll
Lhazê 104 C5 var. Quxar. Xizang Zizhiqu, China E Asia
L'Hospitalet de Llobregat 71 G2 var. Hospitalet. Cataluña, NE Spain
Liancourt Rocks 109 A5 island group Japan/South Korea
Lianyungang 106 D4 var. Xinpu. Jiangsu, E China
Liao see Liaoning
Liaodong Wan 105 G3 Eng. Gulf of Lantung, Gulf of Liaotung. gulf NE China
Liao He 103 E1 river NE China
Liaoning 106 D3 var. Liao, Liaoning Sheng, Shengking, hist. Fengtien, Shenking. province NE China
Liaoning Sheng see Liaoning
Liaoyuan 107 E3 var. Dongliao, Shuang-liao, Jap. Chengchiatun. Jilin, NE China
Liard see Fort Liard
Liban see Lebanon
Liban, Jebel 96 B4 Ar. Jabal al Gharbt, Jabal Lubnān, Eng. Mount Lebanon. mountain range C Lebanon
Libau see Liepāja
Libby 22 A1 Montana, NW USA
Liberal 23 E5 Kansas, C USA
Liberalitas Julia see Évora
Liberec 76 B4 Ger. Reichenberg. Liberecký Kraj, N Czech Republic
Liberia 30 D4 Guanacaste, NW Costa Rica
Liberia 52 C5 off. Republic of Liberia. country W Africa
Liberia, Republic of see Liberia
Libian Desert see Libyan Desert
Lībīyah, Aş Şahrā' al see Libyan Desert
Libourne 69 B5 Gironde, SW France
Libreville 55 A5 country capital Estuaire, NW Gabon
Libya 49 F3 off. Great Socialist People's Libyan Arab Jamahiriya, Ar. Al Jamāhīrīyah al 'Arabīyah al Lībīyah ash Sha'bīyah al Ishtirākīy; prev. Libyan Arab Republic. country N Africa
Libyan Arab Republic see Libya
Libyan Desert 49 H4 var. Libian Desert, Ar. Aş Şahrā' al Lībīyah. desert N Africa
Libyan Plateau 81 F4 var. Aḍ Diffah. plateau Egypt/Libya
Lichtenfels 73 C5 Bayern, SE Germany
Lichtenvoorde 64 E4 Gelderland, E Netherlands

Lichuan – Ma'dabā

Lichuan 106 C5 Hubei, C China
Lida 85 B5 Hrodzyenskaya Voblasts', W Belarus
Lidhorikíon see Lidoríki
Lidköping 63 B6 Västra Götaland, S Sweden
Lidokhorikion see Lidoríki
Lidoríki 83 B5 prev. Lidhorikíon, Lidokhorikion. Stereá Ellás, C Greece
Lidzbark Warmiński 76 D2 Ger. Heilsberg. Olsztyn, N Poland
Liechtenstein 72 D1 off. Principality of Liechtenstein. country C Europe
Liechtenstein, Principality of see Liechtenstein
Liège 65 D6 Dut. Luik, Ger. Lüttich. Liège, E Belgium
Liegnitz see Legnica
Lienz 73 D7 Tirol, W Austria
Liepāja 84 B3 Ger. Libau. Liepāja, W Latvia
Lietuva see Lithuania
Lievenhof see Līvāni
Liezen 73 D7 Steiermark, C Austria
Liffey 67 B6 river Ireland
Lifou 122 D5 island Îles Loyauté, E New Caledonia
Liger see Loire
Ligure, Appennino 74 A2 Eng. Ligurian Mountains. mountain range NW Italy
Ligure, Mar see Ligurian Sea
Ligurian Mountains see Ligure, Appennino
Ligurian Sea 74 A3 Fr. Mer Ligurienne, It. Mar Ligure. sea N Mediterranean Sea
Ligurienne, Mer see Ligurian Sea
Lihu'e 25 A7 var. Lihue. Kaua'i, Hawaii, USA
Lihue see Lihu'e
Lihula 84 D2 Ger. Leal. Läänemaa, W Estonia
Liivi Laht see Riga, Gulf of
Likasi 55 D7 prev. Jadotville. Shaba, SE Dem. Rep. Congo
Liknes 63 A6 Vest-Agder, S Norway
Lille 68 C2 var. l'Isle, Dut. Rijssel, Flem. Ryssel, prev. Lisle; anc. Insula. Nord, N France
Lillehammer 63 B5 Oppland, S Norway
Lillestrøm 63 B6 Akershus, S Norway
Lilongwe 57 E2 country capital Central , W Malawi
Lilybaeum see Marsala
Lima 38 C4 country capital Lima, W Peru
Limanowa 77 D5 Małopolskie, S Poland
Limassol see Lemesós
Limerick 67 A6 Ir. Luimneach. Limerick, SW Ireland
Limín Vathéos see Sámos
Límnos 81 F3 anc. Lemnos. island E Greece
Limoges 69 C5 anc. Augustoritum Lemovicensium, Lemovices. Haute-Vienne, C France
Limón 31 E4 var. Puerto Limón. Limón, E Costa Rica
Limón 30 D2 Colón, NE Honduras
Limonum see Poitiers
Limousin 69 C5 cultural region C France
Limoux 69 C6 Aude, S France
Limpopo 56 D3 var. Crocodile. river S Africa
Linares 42 B4 Maule, C Chile
Linares 29 E3 Nuevo León, NE Mexico
Linares 70 D4 Andalucía, S Spain
Lincoln 67 D5 anc. Lindum, Lindum Colonia. E England, United Kingdom
Lincoln 19 H2 Maine, NE USA
Lincoln 23 F4 state capital Nebraska, C USA
Lincoln Sea 12 D2 sea Arctic Ocean
Linden 37 F3 E Guyana
Líndhos see Líndos
Lindi 51 D8 Lindi, SE Tanzania
Líndos 83 E7 var. Líndhos. Ródos, Dodekánisa, Greece, Aegean Sea
Lindum/Lindum Colonia see Lincoln
Line Islands 123 G3 island group E Kiribati
Lingeh see Bandar-e Lengeh
Lingen 72 A3 var. Lingen an der Ems. Niedersachsen, NW Germany
Lingen an der Ems see Lingen
Lingga, Kepulauan 116 B4 island group W Indonesia
Linköping 63 C6 Östergötland, S Sweden
Linz 73 D6 anc. Lentia. Oberösterreich, N Austria
Lion, Gulf of 69 C7 Eng. Gulf of Lion, Gulf of Lions; anc. Sinus Gallicus. gulf S France
Lion, Gulf of/Lions, Gulf of see Lion, Golfe du
Liozno see Lyozna
Lipari 75 D6 island Isole Eolie, S Italy
Lipari Islands/Lipari, Isole see Eolie, Isole
Lipetsk 89 B5 Lipetskaya Oblast', W Russian Federation
Lipno 76 C3 Kujawsko-pomorskie, C Poland
Lipova 86 A4 Hung. Lippa. Arad, W Romania
Lipovets see Lypovets'
Lippa see Lipova
Lipsia/Lipsk see Leipzig
Lira 51 B6 N Uganda
Lisala 55 C5 Equateur, N Dem. Rep. Congo
Lisboa 70 B4 Eng. Lisbon; anc. Felicitas Julia, Olisipo. country capital Lisboa, W Portugal
Lisbon see Lisboa
Lisichansk see Lysychans'k
Lisieux 68 B3 anc. Noviomagus. Calvados, N France
Liski 89 B6 prev. Georgiu-Dezh. Voronezhskaya Oblast', W Russian Federation
Lisle/l'Isle see Lille
Lismore 127 E5 New South Wales, SE Australia
Lissa see Vis, Croatia
Lissa see Leszno, Poland
Lisse 64 C3 Zuid-Holland, W Netherlands
Litang 106 A5 var. Gaocheng. Sichuan, C China
Lītani, Nahr el 97 B5 var. Nahr al Litant. river C Lebanon
Litant, Nahr al see Lītani, Nahr el
Litauen see Lithuania
Lithgow 127 D6 New South Wales, SE Australia
Lithuania 84 B4 off. Republic of Lithuania, Ger. Litauen, Lith. Lietuva, Pol. Litwa, Rus. Litva; prev. Lithuanian SSR, Rus. Litovskaya SSR. country NE Europe
Lithuanian SSR see Lithuania
Lithuania, Republic of see Lithuania
Litóchoro 82 B4 var. Litohoro, Litókhoron. Kentrikí Makedonía, N Greece
Litohoro/Litókhoron see Litóchoro
Litovskaya SSR see Lithuania
Little Alföld 77 C6 Ger. Kleines Ungarisches Tiefland, Hung. Kisalföld, Slvk. Podunajská Rovina. plain Hungary/Slovakia
Little Andaman 111 F2 island Andaman Islands, India, NE Indian Ocean
Little Barrier Island 128 D2 island N New Zealand
Little Bay 71 H5 bay Alboran Sea, Mediterranean Sea
Little Cayman 32 B3 island E Cayman Islands
Little Falls 23 F2 Minnesota, N USA
Littlefield 27 E2 Texas, SW USA
Little Inagua 32 D2 var. Inagua Islands. island S Bahamas
Little Minch, The 66 B3 strait NW Scotland, United Kingdom
Little Missouri River 22 D2 river NW USA
Little Nicobar 111 G3 island Nicobar Islands, India, NE Indian Ocean
Little Rhody see Rhode Island
Little Rock 20 B1 state capital Arkansas, C USA
Little Saint Bernard Pass 69 D5 Fr. Col du Petit St-Bernard, It. Colle del Piccolo San Bernardo. pass France/Italy
Little Sound 20 A5 bay Bermuda, NW Atlantic Ocean
Littleton 22 D4 Colorado, C USA
Littoria see Latina
Litva/Litwa see Lithuania
Liu-chou/Liuchow see Liuzhou
Liuzhou 106 C6 var. Liu-chou, Liuchow. Guangxi Zhuangzu Zizhiqu, S China
Livanátai see Livanátes
Livanátes 83 B5 prev. Livanátai. Stereá Ellás, C Greece
Līvāni 84 D4 Ger. Lievenhof. Preiļi, SE Latvia
Liverpool 17 F5 Nova Scotia, SE Canada
Liverpool 67 C5 NW England, United Kingdom
Livingston 22 B2 Montana, NW USA
Livingston 27 H3 Texas, SW USA
Livingstone 56 C3 var. Maramba. Southern, S Zambia
Livingstone 27 H3 var. Maramba. Southern, S Zambia
Livingstone Mountains 129 A7 mountain range South Island, New Zealand
Livno 78 B4 Federicija Bosna I Hercegovina, SW Bosnia and Herzegovina
Livojoki 62 D4 river C Finland
Livonia 18 D3 Michigan, N USA
Livorno 74 B3 Eng. Leghorn. Toscana, C Italy
Lixian Jiang see Black River
Lixoúri 83 A5 prev. Lixoúrion. Kefallinía, Iónia Nisiá, Greece, C Mediterranean Sea
Lixoúrion see Lixoúri
Lizarra see Estella
Ljouwert see Leeuwarden
Ljubelj see Loibl Pass
Ljubljana 73 D7 Ger. Laibach, It. Lubiana; anc. Aemona, Emona. country capital C Slovenia
Ljungby 63 B7 Kronoberg, S Sweden
Ljusdal 63 C5 Gävleborg, C Sweden
Ljusnan 63 C5 river C Sweden
Llanelli 67 C6 prev. Llanelly. SW Wales, United Kingdom
Llanelly see Llanelli
Llanes 70 D1 Asturias, N Spain
Llanos 36 D2 physical region Colombia/Venezuela
Lleida 71 F2 Cast. Lérida; anc. Ilerda. Cataluña, NE Spain
Llucmajor 71 G3 Mallorca, Spain, W Mediterranean Sea
Loaita Island 106 C8 island W Spratly Islands
Loanda see Luanda
Lobatse 56 C4 var. Lobatsi. Kgatleng, SE Botswana
Lobatsi see Lobatse
Löbau 72 D4 Sachsen, E Germany
Lobito 56 B2 Benguela, W Angola
Lob Nor see Lop Nur
Lobositz see Lovosice
Loburi see Lop Buri
Locarno 73 B8 Ger. Luggarus. Ticino, S Switzerland
Lochem 64 E3 Gelderland, E Netherlands
Lockport 19 E3 New York, NE USA
Lodja 55 D6 Kasai-Oriental, C Dem. Rep. Congo
Lodwar 51 C6 Rift Valley, NW Kenya
Łódź 76 D4 Rus. Lodz. Łódź, C Poland
Loei 114 C4 var. Loey, Muang Loei. Loei, C Thailand
Loey see Loei
Lofoten 62 B3 var. Lofoten Islands. island group C Norway
Lofoten Islands see Lofoten
Logan 22 B3 Utah, W USA
Logan, Mount 14 D3 mountain Yukon Territory, W Canada
Logroño 71 E1 anc. Vareia, Lat. Juliobriga. La Rioja, N Spain
Loibl Pass 73 D7 Ger. Loiblpass, Slvn. Ljubelj. pass Austria/Slovenia
Loiblpass see Loibl Pass
Loikaw 114 B4 Kayah State, C Myanmar (Burma)
Loire 68 B4 var. Liger. river C France
Loja 38 B2 Loja, S Ecuador
Lokitaung 51 C5 Rift Valley, NW Kenya
Lokoja 53 G4 Kogi, C Nigeria
Loksa 84 E2 Ger. Loxa. Harjumaa, NW Estonia
Lolland 63 B8 prev. Laaland. island S Denmark
Lom 82 C1 prev. Lom-Palanka. Montana, NW Bulgaria
Lomami 55 D6 river C Dem. Rep. Congo
Lomas 38 D4 Arequipa, SW Peru
Lomas de Zamora 42 D4 Buenos Aires, E Argentina
Lombardia 74 B2 Eng. Lombardy. region N Italy
Lombardy see Lombardia
Lombok, Pulau 116 D5 island Nusa Tenggara, C Indonesia
Lomé 53 F5 country capital S Togo
Lomela 55 D6 Kasai-Oriental, C Dem. Rep. Congo
Lommel 65 C5 Limburg, N Belgium
Lomond, Loch 66 B4 lake C Scotland, United Kingdom
Lomonosov Ridge 133 B3 var. Harris Ridge, Rus. Khrebet Homonsova. undersea ridge Arctic Ocean
Lomonsova, Khrebet see Lomonosov Ridge
Lom-Palanka see Lom
Lompoc 25 B7 California, W USA
Lom Sak 114 C4 var. Muang Lom Sak. Phetchabun, C Thailand
Łomża 76 D3 Rus. Lomzha. Podlaskie, NE Poland
Lomzha see Łomża
Loncoche 43 B5 Araucanía, C Chile
Londinium see London
London 67 A7 anc. Augusta, Lat. Londinium. country capital SE England, United Kingdom
London 16 C5 Ontario, S Canada
London 18 C5 Kentucky, S USA
Londonderry 66 B4 var. Derry, Ir. Doire. NW Northern Ireland, United Kingdom
Londonderry, Cape 124 C2 cape Western Australia
Londrina 41 E4 Paraná, S Brazil
Lone Star State see Texas
Long Bay 21 F2 bay W Jamaica
Long Beach 25 C7 California, W USA
Longford 67 B5 Ir. An Longfort. Longford, C Ireland
Long Island 32 D2 island C Bahamas
Long Island 19 G4 island New York, NE USA
Longlac 16 C3 Ontario, S Canada
Longmont 22 D4 Colorado, C USA
Longreach 126 C4 Queensland, E Australia
Long Strait 93 G1 Eng. Long Strait. strait NE Russian Federation
Long Strait see Longa, Proliv
Longview 27 H3 Texas, SW USA
Longview 24 B2 Washington, NW USA
Long Xuyên 115 D6 var. Longxuyen. An Giang, S Vietnam
Longxuyen see Long Xuyên
Longyan 106 D6 Fujian, SE China
Longyearbyen 61 G2 dependent territory capital Spitsbergen, W Svalbard
Lons-le-Saunier 68 D4 anc. Ledo Salinarius. Jura, E France
Lop Buri 115 C5 var. Loburi. Lop Buri, C Thailand
Lop Nor see Lop Nur
Lop Nur 104 C3 var. Lob Nor, Lop Nor, Lo-pu Po. seasonal lake NW China
Loppersum 64 E1 Groningen, NE Netherlands
Lo-pu Po see Lop Nur
Lorca 71 E4 Ar. Lurka; anc. Eliocroca, Lat. Illurco. Murcia, S Spain
Lord Howe Island 120 C4 island E Australia
Lord Howe Rise 120 C4 undersea rise SW Pacific Ocean
Loreto 28 B3 Baja California Sur, W Mexico
Lorient 68 A3 prev. l'Orient. Morbihan, NW France
l'Orient see Lorient
Lorn, Firth of 66 B4 inlet W Scotland, United Kingdom
Loro Sae see East Timor
Lörrach 73 A7 Baden-Württemberg, S Germany
Lorraine 68 D3 cultural region NE France
Los Alamos 26 C1 New Mexico, SW USA
Los Amates 30 B2 Izabal, E Guatemala
Los Ángeles 43 B5 Bío Bío, C Chile
Los Angeles 25 C7 California, W USA
Losanna see Lausanne
Lošinj 78 A3 Ger. Lussin, It. Lussino. island W Croatia
Loslau see Wodzisław Śląski
Los Mochis 28 C3 Sinaloa, C Mexico
Losonc/Losontz see Lučenec
Los Roques, Islas 36 D1 island group N Venezuela
Lot 69 B5 cultural region S France
Lot 69 B5 river S France
Lotagipi Swamp 51 C5 wetland Kenya/Sudan
Lötzen see Giżycko
Loualaba see Lualaba
Louangnamtha 114 C3 var. Luong Nam Tha. Louang Namtha, N Laos
Louangphabang 102 D3 var. Louangphrabang, Luang Prabang. Louangphabang, N Laos
Louangphrabang see Louangphabang
Loubomo see Dolisie
Loudéac 68 A3 Côtes d'Armor, NW France
Loudi 106 C5 Hunan, S China
Louga 52 B3 NW Senegal
Louisiade Archipelago 122 B4 island group SE Papua New Guinea
Louisiana 20 A2 off. State of Louisiana, also known as Creole State, Pelican State. state S USA
Louisville 18 C5 Kentucky, S USA
Louisville Ridge 121 E4 undersea ridge S Pacific Ocean
Loup River 23 E4 river Nebraska, C USA
Lourdes 69 B6 Hautes-Pyrénées, S France
Lourenço Marques see Maputo
Louth 67 E5 E England, United Kingdom
Loutrá 82 C4 Kentrikí Makedonía, N Greece
Louvain see Leuven
Louvain-la Neuve 65 C6 Walloon Brabant, C Belgium
Louviers 68 C3 Eure, N France
Lovech 82 C2 Lovech, N Bulgaria
Loveland 22 D4 Colorado, C USA
Lovosice 76 A4 Ger. Lobositz. Ústecký Kraj, NW Czech Republic
Lóvua 56 C1 Moxico, E Angola
Lowell 19 G3 Massachusetts, NE USA
Löwen see Leuven
Lower California 26 A4 Eng. Lower California. peninsula NW Mexico
Lower California see Baja California
Lower Hutt 129 D5 Wellington, North Island, New Zealand
Lower Lough Erne 67 A5 lake SW Northern Ireland, United Kingdom
Lower Red Lake 23 F1 lake Minnesota, N USA
Lower Rhine see Neder Rijn
Lower Tunguska 93 E3 Eng. Lower Tunguska. river N Russian Federation
Lower Tunguska see Nizhnyaya Tunguska
Lowestoft 67 E6 E England, United Kingdom
Loxa see Loksa
Lo-yang see Luoyang
Loyauté, Îles 122 D5 island group S New Caledonia
Loyev see Loyew
Loyew 85 D8 Rus. Loyev. Homyel'skaya Voblasts', SE Belarus
Loznica 78 C3 Serbia, W Serbia
Lu see Shandong, China
Lualaba 55 D6 Fr. Loualaba. river SE Dem. Rep. Congo
Luanda 56 A1 var. Loanda, Port. São Paulo de Loanda. country capital Luanda, NW Angola
Luang Prabang see Louangphabang
Luang, Thale 115 C7 lagoon S Thailand
Luangua, Rio see Luangwa
Luangwa 51 B8 var. Aruângua, Rio Luangua. river Mozambique/Zambia
Luanshya 56 D2 Copperbelt, C Zambia
Luarca 70 C1 Asturias, N Spain
Lubaczów 77 E5 var. Lubaczów. Podkarpackie, SE Poland
L'uban' 76 B4 Leningradskaya Oblast', Russian Federation
Lubānas Ezers see Lubāns
Lubango 56 B2 Port. Sá da Bandeira. Huíla, SW Angola
Lubāns 84 D4 var. Lubānas Ezers. lake E Latvia
Lubao 55 D6 Kasai-Oriental, C Dem. Rep. Congo
Lübben 72 D4 Brandenburg, E Germany
Lübbenau 72 D4 Brandenburg, E Germany
Lubbock 27 E2 Texas, SW USA
Lübeck 72 C2 Schleswig-Holstein, N Germany
Lubelska, Wyżyna 76 E4 plateau SE Poland
Lüben see Lubin
Lubiana see Ljubljana
Lubin 76 B4 Ger. Lüben. Dolnośląskie, SW Poland
Lublin 76 E4 Rus. Lyublin. Lubelskie, E Poland
Lubliniec 76 C4 Śląskie, S Poland
Lubnān, Jabal see Liban, Jebel
Lubny 87 F2 Poltavs'ka Oblast', NE Ukraine
Lubsko 76 B4 Ger. Sommerfeld. Lubuskie, W Poland
Lubumbashi 55 E8 prev. Élisabethville. Shaba, SE Dem. Rep. Congo
Lubutu 55 D6 Maniema, E Dem. Rep. Congo
Luca see Lucca
Lucan 67 B5 Ir. Leamhcán. Dublin, E Ireland
Lucanian Mountains see Lucano, Appennino
Lucano, Appennino 75 D5 Eng. Lucanian Mountains. mountain range S Italy
Lucapa 56 C1 var. Lukapa. Lunda Norte, NE Angola
Lucca 74 B3 anc. Luca. Toscana, C Italy
Lucea 32 A4 W Jamaica
Lucena 117 E1 off. Lucena City. Luzon, N Philippines
Lucena 70 D4 Andalucía, S Spain
Lucena City see Lucena
Lučenec 77 D6 Ger. Losontz, Hung. Losonc. Banskobystrický Kraj, C Slovakia
Lucentum see Alicante
Lucerna/Lucerne see Luzern
Luchow see Hefei
Łuck see Luts'k
Lucknow 113 E3 var. Lakhnau. state capital Uttar Pradesh, N India
Lüda see Dalian
Luda Kamchiya 82 D2 river E Bulgaria
Ludasch see Luduş
Lüderitz 56 B4 prev. Angra Pequena. Karas, SW Namibia
Ludhiāna 112 D2 Punjab, N India
Ludington 18 C2 Michigan, N USA
Ludsan see Ludza
Luduş 86 B4 Ger. Ludasch, Hung. Marosludas. Mureş, C Romania
Ludvika 63 C6 Dalarna, C Sweden
Ludwigsburg 73 B6 Baden-Württemberg, SW Germany
Ludwigsfelde 72 D3 Brandenburg, NE Germany
Ludwigshafen 73 B5 var. Ludwigshafen am Rhein. Rheinland-Pfalz, W Germany
Ludwigshafen am Rhein see Ludwigshafen
Ludwigslust 72 C3 Mecklenburg-Vorpommern, N Germany
Ludza 84 D4 Ger. Ludsan. Ludza, E Latvia
Luebo 55 C6 Kasai-Occidental, SW Dem. Rep. Congo
Luena 56 C2 var. Lwena, Port. Luso. Moxico, E Angola
Lufira 55 E7 river SE Dem. Rep. Congo
Lufkin 27 H3 Texas, SW USA
Luga 88 A4 Leningradskaya Oblast', NW Russian Federation
Lugano 73 B8 Ger. Lauis. Ticino, S Switzerland
Lugansk see Luhans'k
Lugdunum see Lyon
Lugdunum Batavorum see Leiden
Lugenda, Rio 57 E2 river N Mozambique
Luggarus see Locarno
Lugh Ganana see Luuq
Lugo 70 C1 anc. Lugus Augusti. Galicia, NW Spain
Lugoj 86 A4 Ger. Lugosch, Hung. Lugos. Timiş, W Romania
Lugos/Lugosch see Lugoj
Lugus Augusti see Lugo
Luguvallium/Luguvallum see Carlisle
Luhans'k 87 H3 Rus. Lugansk; prev. Voroshilovgrad. Luhans'ka Oblast', E Ukraine
Luimneach see Limerick
Lukapa see Lucapa
Lukenie 55 C6 river C Dem. Rep. Congo
Lukovit 82 C2 Lovech, N Bulgaria
Łuków 76 E4 Ger. Bogendorf. Lubelskie, E Poland
Lukuga 55 D7 river SE Dem. Rep. Congo
Luleå 62 D4 Norrbotten, N Sweden
Luleälven 62 C3 river N Sweden
Lulonga 55 C5 river NW Dem. Rep. Congo
Lulua 55 D7 river S Dem. Rep. Congo
Luluabourg see Kananga
Lumber State see Maine
Lumbo 57 F2 Nampula, NE Mozambique
Lumsden 129 A7 Southland, South Island, New Zealand
Lund 63 B7 Skåne, S Sweden
Lüneburg 72 C3 Niedersachsen, N Germany
Lunga, Isola see Dugi Otok
Lungkiang see Qiqihar
Lungué-Bungo 56 C2 var. Lungwebungu. river Angola/Zambia
Lungwebungu see Lungué-Bungo
Luninets see Luninyets
Łuniniec see Luninyets
Luninyets 85 B7 Pol. Łuniniec, Rus. Luninets. Brestskaya Voblasts', SW Belarus
Lunteren 64 D4 Gelderland, C Netherlands
Luong Nam Tha see Louangnamtha
Luoyang 106 C4 var. Honan, Lo-yang. Henan, C China
Lupatia see Altamura
Lúrio 57 F2 Nampula, NE Mozambique
Lúrio, Rio 57 E2 river NE Mozambique
Lurka see Lorca
Lusaka 56 D2 country capital Lusaka, SE Zambia
Lushnja see Lushnjë
Lushnjë 79 C6 var. Lushnja. Fier, C Albania
Luso see Luena
Lussin/Lussino see Lošinj
Lūt, Baḩrat/Lut, Bahret see Dead Sea
Lut, Dasht-e 98 D3 var. Kavīr-e Lūt. desert E Iran
Lutetia/Lutetia Parisiorum see Paris
Lūt, Kavīr-e see Lūt, Dasht-e
Luton 67 D6 E England, United Kingdom
Łutselk'e 15 F4 prev. Snowdrift. Northwest Territories, W Canada
Luts'k 86 C1 Pol. Łuck, Rus. Lutsk. Volyns'ka Oblast', NW Ukraine
Lutsk see Luts'k
Lüttich see Liège
Lutzow-Holm Bay 132 C2 var. Lutzow-Holm Bay. bay Antarctica
Lutzow-Holm Bay see Lützow Holmbukta
Luuq 51 D6 It. Lugh Ganana. Gedo, SW Somalia
Luvua 55 D7 river SE Dem. Rep. Congo
Luwego 51 C8 river S Tanzania
Luxembourg 65 D8 country capital Luxembourg, S Luxembourg
Luxembourg 65 D8 off. Grand Duchy of Luxembourg, var. Lëtzebuerg, Luxemburg. country NW Europe
Luxemburg see Luxembourg
Luxor 50 B2 Ar. Al Uqşur. E Egypt
Luza 88 C4 Kirovskaya Oblast', NW Russian Federation
Luz, Costa de la 70 C5 coastal region SW Spain
Luzern 73 B7 Fr. Lucerne, It. Lucerna. Luzern, C Switzerland
Luzon 117 E1 island N Philippines
Luzon Strait 103 E3 strait Philippines/Taiwan
L'viv 86 B2 Ger. Lemberg, Pol. Lwów, Rus. L'vov. L'vivs'ka Oblast', W Ukraine
L'vov see L'viv
Lwena see Luena
Lwów see L'viv
Lyakhavichy 85 B6 Rus. Lyakhovichi. Brestskaya Voblasts', SW Belarus
Lyakhovichi see Lyakhavichy
Lyallpur see Faisalābād
Lyangar see Langar
Lyck see Ełk
Lycksele 62 C4 Västerbotten, N Sweden
Lycopolis see Asyūţ
Lyel'chytsy 85 C7 Rus. Lel'chitsy. Homyel'skaya Voblasts', SE Belarus
Lyepyel' 85 D5 Rus. Lepel'. Vitsyebskaya Voblasts', N Belarus
Lyme Bay 67 C7 bay S England, United Kingdom
Lynchburg 19 E5 Virginia, NE USA
Lynn see King's Lynn
Lynn Lake 15 F4 Manitoba, C Canada
Lynn Regis see King's Lynn
Lyon 69 D5 Eng. Lyons; anc. Lugdunum. Rhône, E France
Lyons see Lyon
Lyozna 85 E6 Rus. Liozno. Vitsyebskaya Voblasts', NE Belarus
Lypovets' 86 D2 Rus. Lipovets. Vinnyts'ka Oblast', C Ukraine
Lys see Leie
Lysychans'k 87 H3 Rus. Lisichansk. Luhans'ka Oblast', E Ukraine
Lyttelton 129 C6 South Island, New Zealand
Lyublin see Lublin
Lyubotin see Lyubotyn
Lyubotyn 87 G2 Rus. Lyubotin. Kharkivs'ka Oblast', E Ukraine
Lyulyakovo 82 E2 prev. Keremitlik. Burgas, E Bulgaria
Lyusina 85 B6 Rus. Lyusino. Brestskaya Voblasts', SW Belarus
Lyusino see Lyusina

M

Maale see Male'
Ma'ān 97 B7 Ma'ān, SW Jordan
Maardu 84 D2 Ger. Maart. Harjumaa, NW Estonia
Ma'aret-en-Nu'man see Ma'arrat an Nu'mān
Ma'arrat an Nu'mān 96 B3 var. Ma'aret-en-Nu'man, Fr. Maarret enn Naamâne. Idlib, NW Syria
Maarret enn Naamâne see Ma'arrat an Nu'mān
Maart see Maardu
Maas see Meuse
Maaseik 65 D5 prev. Maeseyck. Limburg, NE Belgium
Maastricht 65 D6 var. Maestricht; anc. Traiectum ad Mosam, Traiectum Tungorum. Limburg, SE Netherlands
Macao 107 C6 Chin. Aomen, Port. Macau. E Asia
Macapá 41 E1 state capital Amapá, N Brazil
Macarsca see Makarska
Macassar see Makassar
Macău see Makó, Hungary
Macau see Macao
MacCluer Gulf see Berau, Teluk
Macdonnell Ranges 124 D4 mountain range Northern Territory, C Australia
Macedonia see Macedonia, FYR
Macedonia, FYR 79 D6 off. the Former Yugoslav Republic of Macedonia, var. Macedonia, Mac. Makedonija, abbrev. FYR Macedonia, FYROM. country SE Europe
Macedonia, the Former Yugoslav Republic of see Macedonia, FYR
Maceió 41 G3 state capital Alagoas, E Brazil
Machachi 38 B1 Pichincha, C Ecuador
Machala 38 B2 El Oro, SW Ecuador
Machanga 57 E3 Sofala, E Mozambique
Machilīpatnam 110 D1 var. Bandar Masulipatnam. Andhra Pradesh, E India
Machiques 36 C2 Zulia, NW Venezuela
Macías Nguema Biyogo see Bioco, Isla de
Măcin 86 D5 Tulcea, SE Romania
Mackay 126 D4 Queensland, NE Australia
Mackay, Lake 124 C4 salt lake Northern Territory/Western Australia
Mackenzie 15 E3 river Northwest Territories, NW Canada
Mackenzie Bay 132 D3 bay Antarctica
Mackenzie Mountains 14 D3 mountain range Northwest Territories, NW Canada
Macleod, Lake 124 A4 lake Western Australia
Macomb 18 A4 Illinois, N USA
Macomer 75 A5 Sardegna, Italy, C Mediterranean Sea
Mâcon 69 D5 anc. Matisco, Matisco Ædourum. Saône-et-Loire, C France
Macon 20 D2 Georgia, SE USA
Macon 23 G4 Missouri, C USA
Macquarie Ridge 132 C5 undersea ridge SW Pacific Ocean
Macuspana 29 G4 Tabasco, SE Mexico
Ma'dabā 97 B6 var. Mādabā, Madeba; anc. Medeba. Ma'dabā, NW Jordan

Mādabā – Masuku

Mādabā see Ma'dabā
Madagascar 57 F3 off. Democratic Republic of Madagascar, Malg. Madagasikara; prev. Malagasy Republic. country W Indian Ocean
Madagascar 57 F3 island W Indian Ocean
Madagascar Basin 47 E7 undersea basin W Indian Ocean
Madagascar, Democratic Republic of see Madagascar
Madagascar Plateau 47 E7 var. Madagascar Ridge, Madagascar Rise, Rus. Madagaskarskiy Khrebet. undersea plateau W Indian Ocean
Madagascar Rise/Madagascar Ridge see Madagascar Plateau
Madagasikara see Madagascar
Madagaskarskiy Khrebet see Madagascar Plateau
Madang 122 B3 Madang, N Papua New Guinea
Madanīyīn see Médenine
Madarska see Hungary
Made 64 C4 Noord-Brabant, S Netherlands
Madeba see Ma'dabā
Madeira 48 A2 var. Ilha de Madeira. island Madeira, Portugal, NE Atlantic Ocean
Madeira, Ilha de see Madeira
Madeira Plain 44 C3 abyssal plain E Atlantic Ocean
Madeira, Rio 40 D2 var. Río Madera. river Bolivia/Brazil
Madeleine, Îles de la 17 F4 Eng. Magdalen Islands. island group Québec, E Canada
Madera 25 B6 California, W USA
Madera, Río see Madeira, Rio
Madhya Pradesh 113 E4 prev. Central Provinces and Berar. cultural region C India
Madīnat ath Thawrah 96 C2 var. Ath Thawrah. Ar Raqqah, N Syria
Madioen see Madiun
Madison 23 F3 South Dakota, N USA
Madison 18 B3 state capital Wisconsin, N USA
Madiun 116 D5 prev. Madioen. Jawa, C Indonesia
Madoera see Madura, Pulau
Madona 84 D4 Ger. Modohn. Madona, E Latvia
Madras see Chennai
Madras see Tamil Nādu
Madre de Dios, Río 39 E3 river Bolivia/Peru
Madre del Sur, Sierra 29 E5 mountain range S Mexico
Madre, Laguna 29 F3 lagoon NE Mexico
Madre, Laguna 27 G5 lagoon Texas, SW USA
Madre Occidental, Sierra 28 C3 var. Western Sierra Madre. mountain range C Mexico
Madre Oriental, Sierra 29 E3 var. Eastern Sierra Madre. mountain range C Mexico
Madrid 70 D3 country capital Madrid, C Spain
Madura see Madurai
Madurai 110 C3 prev. Madura, Mathurai. Tamil Nādu, S India
Madura, Pulau 116 D5 prev. Madoera. island C Indonesia
Maebashi 109 D5 var. Maebasi, Mayebashi. Gunma, Honshū, S Japan
Maebasi see Maebashi
Mae Nam Khong see Mekong
Mae Nam Nan 114 C4 river NW Thailand
Mae Nam Yom 114 C4 river W Thailand
Maeseyck see Maaseik
Maestricht see Maastricht
Maéwo 122 D4 prev. Aurora. island C Vanuatu
Mafia 51 D7 island E Tanzania
Mafraq/Muḥāfaẓat al Mafraq see Al Mafraq
Magadan 93 G3 Magadanskaya Oblast', E Russian Federation
Magallanes see Punta Arenas
Magallanes, Estrecho de see Magellan, Strait of
Magangué 36 B2 Bolívar, N Colombia
Magdalena 39 F3 Beni, N Bolivia
Magdalena 28 B1 Sonora, NW Mexico
Isla Magdalena 28 B3 island W Mexico
Magdalena, Río 36 B2 river C Colombia
Magdalen Islands see Madeleine, Îles de la
Magdeburg 72 C4 Sachsen-Anhalt, C Germany
Magelang 116 C5 Jawa, C Indonesia
Magellan, Strait of 43 B8 Sp. Estrecho de Magallanes. strait Argentina/Chile
Magerøy see Magerøya
Magerøya 62 D1 var. Magerøy, Lapp. Máhkarávju. island N Norway
Maggiore, Lago see Maggiore, Lake
Maggiore, Lake 74 B1 It. Lago Maggiore. lake Italy/Switzerland
Maglaj 78 C3 Federacija Bosna I Hercegovina, N Bosnia and Herzegovina
Maglie 75 E6 Puglia, SE Italy
Magna 22 B4 Utah, W USA
Magnesia see Manisa
Magnitogorsk 92 B4 Chelyabinskaya Oblast', C Russian Federation
Magnolia State see Mississippi
Magta' Lahjar 52 C3 var. Magta Lahjar, Magta' Lahjar, Magtá Lahjar. Brakna, SW Mauritania
Magway 114 A3 var. Magwe. Magway, W Myanmar (Burma)
Magyar-Becse see Bečej
Magyarkanizsa see Kanjiža
Magyarország see Hungary
Mahajanga 57 F2 var. Majunga. Mahajanga, NW Madagascar
Mahakam, Sungai 116 D4 var. Koetai, Kutai. river Borneo, C Indonesia
Mahalapye 56 D3 var. Mahalatswe. Central, SE Botswana
Mahalatswe see Mahalapye
Māhān 98 D3 Kermān, E Iran
Mahanādi 113 F4 river E India
Mahārāshtra 112 D5 cultural region W India
Mahbés see El Mahbas
Mahbūbnagar 112 D5 Andhra Pradesh, C India
Mahdia 49 F2 var. Al Mahdīyah, Mehdia. NE Tunisia
Mahé 57 H1 island Inner Islands, NE Seychelles
Mahia Peninsula 128 E4 peninsula North Island, New Zealand
Mahilyow 85 D6 Rus. Mogilëv. Mahilyowskaya Voblasts', E Belarus
Máhkarávju see Magerøya
Mahmūd-e 'Erāqī see Maḥmūd-e Rāqī
Maḥmūd-e Rāqī 101 E4 var. Mahmūd-e 'Erāqī. Kāpīsā, NE Afghanistan
Mahón 71 H3 Cat. Maó, Eng. Port Mahon; anc. Portus Magonis. Menorca, Spain, W Mediterranean Sea
Mähren see Moravia
Mährisch-Weisskirchen see Hranice
Maicao 36 C1 La Guajira, N Colombia
Mai Ceu/Mai Chio see Maych'ew
Maidstone 67 E7 SE England, United Kingdom
Maiduguri 53 H4 Borno, NE Nigeria
Mailand see Milano
Maimāna see Meymaneh
Main 73 B5 river C Germany
Mai-Ndombe, Lac 55 C6 prev. Lac Léopold II. lake W Dem. Rep. Congo
Maine 19 G2 off. State of Maine, also known as Lumber State, Pine Tree State. state NE USA
Maine 68 B3 cultural region NW France
Maine, Gulf of 19 H2 gulf NE USA
Mainland 66 C2 island N Scotland, United Kingdom
Mainland 66 D1 island NE Scotland, United Kingdom
Mainz 73 B5 Fr. Mayence. Rheinland-Pfalz, SW Germany
Maio 52 A3 var. Mayo. island Ilhas de Sotavento, SE Cape Verde
Maisur see Mysore, India
Maisur see Karnātaka, India
Maizhokunggar 104 C5 Xizang Zizhiqu, W China
Majorca 71 G3 Eng. Majorca; anc. Baleares Major. island Islas Baleares, Spain, W Mediterranean Sea
Majorca see Mallorca
Mājro see Majuro Atoll
Majunga see Mahajanga
Majuro Atoll 122 D2 var. Mājro. atoll Ratak Chain, SE Marshall Islands
Makale see Mek'elē
Makarov Basin 133 B3 undersea basin Arctic Ocean
Makarska 78 B4 It. Macarsca. Split-Dalmacija, SE Croatia
Makasar see Makassar
Makasar, Selat see Makassar Straits
Makassar 117 E4 var. Macassar, Makasar; prev. Ujungpandang. Sulawesi, C Indonesia
Makassar Straits 116 D4 Ind. Makasar Selat. strait C Indonesia
Makay 57 F3 var. Massif du Makay. mountain range SW Madagascar
Makay, Massif du see Makay
Makedonija see Macedonia, FYR
Makeni 52 C4 C Sierra Leone
Makeyevka see Makiyivka
Makhachkala 92 A4 prev. Petrovsk-Port. Respublika Dagestan, SW Russian Federation
Makin 122 D2 prev. Pitt Island. atoll Tungaru, W Kiribati
Makira see San Cristobal
Makiyivka 87 G3 Rus. Makeyevka; prev. Dmitriyevsk. Donets'ka Oblast', E Ukraine
Makkah 99 A5 Eng. Mecca. Makkah, W Saudi Arabia
Makkovik 17 F2 Newfoundland and Labrador, NE Canada
Makó 77 D7 Rom. Macău. Csongrád, SE Hungary
Makoua 55 B5 Cuvette, C Congo
Makran Coast 98 E4 coastal region SE Iran
Makrany 85 A6 Rus. Mokrany. Brestskaya Voblasts', SW Belarus
Mākū 98 B2 Āzarbāyjān-e Gharbī, NW Iran
Makurdi 53 G4 Benue, C Nigeria
Mala see Malaita, Solomon Islands
Malabār Coast 110 B3 coast SW India
Malabo 55 A5 prev. Santa Isabel. country capital Isla de Bioco, NW Equatorial Guinea
Malaca see Málaga
Malacca, Strait of 116 B3 Ind. Selat Malaka. strait Indonesia/Malaysia
Malacka see Malacky
Malacky 77 C6 Hung. Malacka. Bratislavský Kraj, W Slovakia
Maladzyechna 85 C5 Pol. Molodeczno, Rus. Molodechno. Minskaya Voblasts', C Belarus
Málaga 70 D5 anc. Malaca. Andalucía, S Spain
Malagarasi River 51 B7 river W Tanzania Africa
Malagasy Republic see Madagascar
Malaita 122 C3 var. Mala. island N Solomon Islands
Malakal 51 B5 Upper Nile, S Sudan
Malakula see Malekula
Malang 116 D5 Jawa, C Indonesia
Malange see Malanje
Malanje 56 B1 var. Malange. Malanje, NW Angola
Mälaren 63 C6 lake C Sweden
Malatya 95 E4 anc. Melitene. Malatya, SE Turkey
Mala Vyska 87 E3 Rus. Malaya Viska. Kirovohrads'ka Oblast', S Ukraine
Malawi 57 E1 off. Republic of Malaŵi; prev. Nyasaland, Nyasaland Protectorate. country S Africa
Malawi, Lake see Nyasa, Lake
Malaŵi, Republic of see Malawi
Malaya Viska see Mala Vyska
Malay Peninsula 102 D4 peninsula Malaysia/Thailand
Malaysia 116 B3 off. Malaysia, var. Federation of Malaysia; prev. the separate territories of Federation of Malaya, Sarawak and Sabah (North Borneo) and Singapore. country SE Asia
Malaysia, Federation of see Malaysia
Malbork 76 C2 Ger. Marienburg, Marienburg in Westpreussen. Pomorskie, N Poland
Malchin 72 C3 Mecklenburg-Vorpommern, N Germany
Malden 23 H5 Missouri, C USA
Malden Island 123 G3 prev. Independence Island. atoll E Kiribati
Maldives 110 A4 off. Maldivian Divehi, Republic of Maldives. country N Indian Ocean
Maldives, Republic of see Maldives
Maldivian Divehi see Maldives
Male' 110 B4 Div. Maale. country capital Male' Atoll, C Maldives
Male' Atoll 110 B4 var. Kaafu Atoll. atoll C Maldives
Malekula 122 D4 var. Malakula; prev. Mallicolo. island W Vanuatu
Malesína 83 C5 Stereá Ellás, E Greece
Malheur Lake 24 C3 lake Oregon, NW USA
Mali 53 E3 off. Republic of Mali, Fr. République du Mali; prev. French Sudan, Sudanese Republic. country W Africa
Malik, Wadi al see Milk, Wadi el
Mali Kyun 115 B5 var. Tavoy Island. island Mergui Archipelago, S Myanmar (Burma)
Malin see Malyn
Malindi 51 D7 Coast, SE Kenya
Malines see Mechelen
Mali, Republic of see Mali
Mali, République du see Mali
Malkiye see Al Mālikīyah
Malko Tŭrnovo 82 E3 Burgas, E Bulgaria
Mallaig 66 B3 N Scotland, United Kingdom
Mallawī 50 B2 var. Mallawi. C Egypt
Mallawi see Mallawī
Mallicolo see Malekula
Malmberget 62 C3 Lapp. Malmivaara. Norrbotten, N Sweden
Malmédy 65 D6 Liège, E Belgium
Malmivaara see Malmberget
Malmö 63 B7 Skåne, S Sweden
Maloelap see Maloelap Atoll
Maloelap Atoll 122 D1 var. Maloelap. atoll E Marshall Islands
Małopolska, Wyżyna 76 D4 plateau S Poland
Malozemel'skaya Tundra 88 D3 physical region NW Russian Federation
Malta 84 D4 Rēzekne, SE Latvia
Malta 22 C1 Montana, NW USA
Malta 75 C8 off. Republic of Malta. country C Mediterranean Sea
Malta 75 C8 island Malta, C Mediterranean Sea
Malta, Canale di see Malta Channel
Malta Channel 75 C8 It. Canale di Malta. strait Italy/Malta
Malta, Republic of see Malta
Maluku, Laut see Molucca Sea
Malung 63 B6 Dalarna, C Sweden
Malventum see Benevento
Malvina, Isla Gran see West Falkland
Malvinas, Islas see Falkland Islands
Malyn 86 D2 Rus. Malin. Zhytomyrs'ka Oblast', N Ukraine
Malyy Kavkaz see Lesser Caucasus
Mamberamo, Sungai 117 H4 river Papua, E Indonesia
Mambij see Manbij
Mamonovo 84 A4 Ger. Heiligenbeil. Kaliningradskaya Oblast', W Russian Federation
Mamoré, Rio 39 F3 river Bolivia/Brazil
Mamou 52 C4 W Guinea
Mamoudzou 57 F2 dependent territory capital C Mayotte
Mamuno 56 C3 Ghanzi, W Botswana
Manacor 71 G3 Mallorca, Spain, W Mediterranean Sea
Manado 117 F3 prev. Menado. Sulawesi, C Indonesia
Managua 30 D3 country capital Managua, W Nicaragua
Managua, Lake 30 C3 var. Xolotlán. lake W Nicaragua
Manakara 57 G4 Fianarantsoa, SE Madagascar
Manama see Al Manāmah
Mananjary 57 G3 Fianarantsoa, SE Madagascar
Manáos see Manaus
Manapouri, Lake 129 A7 lake South Island, New Zealand
Manar see Mannar
Manas, Gora 101 E2 mountain Kyrgyzstan/Uzbekistan
Manaus 40 D2 prev. Manáos. state capital Amazonas, NW Brazil
Manavgat 94 B4 Antalya, SW Turkey
Manbij 96 C2 var. Mambij, Fr. Membidj. Ḥalab, N Syria
Manchester 67 D5 Lat. Mancunium. NW England, United Kingdom
Manchester 19 G3 New Hampshire, NE USA
Man-chou-li see Manzhouli
Manchurian Plain 103 E1 plain NE China
Máncio Lima see Japiim
Mancunium see Manchester
Mand see Mand, Rūd-e
Mandalay 114 B3 Mandalay, C Myanmar (Burma)
Mandan 23 E2 North Dakota, N USA
Mandeville 32 B5 C Jamaica
Mándra 83 C6 Attikí, C Greece
Rud-e Mand 98 D4 var. Mand. river S Iran
Mandurah 125 A6 Western Australia
Manduria 75 E5 Puglia, SE Italy
Mandya 110 C2 Karnātaka, C India
Manfredonia 75 D5 Puglia, SE Italy
Mangai 55 C6 Bandundu, W Dem. Rep. Congo
Mangaia 123 G5 island group S Cook Islands
Mangalia 86 D5 anc. Callatis. Constanța, SE Romania
Mangalmé 54 C3 Guéra, SE Chad
Mangalore 110 B2 Karnātaka, W India
Mangaung see Bloemfontein
Mango see Sansanné-Mango, Togo
Mangoky 57 F3 river W Madagascar
Manhattan 23 F4 Kansas, C USA
Manicouagan, Réservoir 16 D3 lake Québec, E Canada
Manihiki 123 G4 atoll N Cook Islands
Manihiki Plateau 121 E3 undersea plateau C Pacific Ocean
Maniitsoq 60 C3 var. Manitsoq, Dan. Sukkertoppen. Kitaa, S Greenland
Manila 117 E1 off. City of Manila. country capital Luzon, N Philippines
Manila, City of see Manila
Manisa 94 A3 var. Manissa, prev. Saruhan; anc. Magnesia. Manisa, W Turkey
Manissa see Manisa
Manitoba 15 F5 province S Canada
Manitoba, Lake 15 F5 lake Manitoba, S Canada
Manitoulin Island 16 C4 island Ontario, S Canada
Manītsoq see Maniitsoq
Manizales 36 B3 Caldas, W Colombia
Manjimup 125 A7 Western Australia
Mankato 23 F3 Minnesota, N USA
Manlleu 71 G2 Cataluña, NE Spain
Manly 126 E1 Iowa, C USA
Manmād 112 C5 Mahārāshtra, W India
Mannar 110 C3 var. Manar. Northern Province, NW Sri Lanka
Mannar, Gulf of 110 C3 gulf India/Sri Lanka
Mannheim 73 B5 Baden-Württemberg, SW Germany
Manono 55 E7 Shaba, SE Dem. Rep. Congo
Manosque 69 D6 Alpes-de-Haute-Provence, SE France
Manra 123 F3 prev. Sydney Island. atoll Phoenix Islands, C Kiribati
Mansa 56 D2 prev. Fort Rosebery. Luapula, N Zambia
Mansel Island 15 G3 island Nunavut, NE Canada
Mansfield 18 D4 Ohio, N USA
Manta 38 A2 Manabí, W Ecuador
Manteca 25 B6 California, W USA
Mantoue see Mantova
Mantova 74 B2 Eng. Mantua, Fr. Mantoue. Lombardia, NW Italy
Mantua see Mantova
Manuae 123 G4 island S Cook Islands
Manukau see Manurewa
Manurewa 128 D3 var. Manukau. Auckland, North Island, New Zealand
Manzanares 71 E3 Castilla-La Mancha, C Spain
Manzanillo 32 C3 Granma, E Cuba
Manzanillo 28 D4 Colima, SW Mexico
Manzhouli 105 F1 var. Man-chou-li. Nei Mongol Zizhiqu, N China
Mao 54 B3 Kanem, W Chad
Maó see Mahón
Maoke, Pegunungan 117 H4 Dut. Sneeuw-gebergte, Eng. Snow Mountains. mountain range Papua, E Indonesia
Maoming 106 C6 Guangdong, S China
Mapmaker Seamounts 103 H2 seamount range N Pacific Ocean
Maputo 56 D4 prev. Lourenço Marques. country capital Maputo, S Mozambique
Marabá 41 F2 Pará, NE Brazil
Maracaibo 36 C1 Zulia, NW Venezuela
Maracaibo, Gulf of see Venezuela, Golfo de
Maracaibo, Lake 36 C2 var. Lake Maracaibo. inlet NW Venezuela
Maracaibo, Lake see Maracaibo, Lago de
Maracay 36 D2 Aragua, N Venezuela
Marada see Marādah
Marādah 49 G3 var. Marada. N Libya
Maradi 53 G3 Maradi, S Niger
Maragha see Marāgheh
Marāgheh 98 C2 var. Maragha. Āzarbāyjān-e Khāvarī, NW Iran
Marajó, Baía de 41 F1 bay N Brazil
Marajó, Ilha de 41 E1 island N Brazil
Marakesh see Marrakech
Maramba see Livingstone
Maramba see Livingstone
Maranhão 41 F2 off. Estado do Maranhão. state E Brazil
Maranhão 41 F2 off. Estado do Maranhão. region E Brazil
Maranhão, Estado do see Maranhão
Marañón, Río 38 B2 river N Peru
Marathon 16 C4 Ontario, S Canada
Marathón see Marathónas
Marathónas 83 C5 prev. Marathón. Attikí, C Greece
Märäzä 95 H2 Rus. Maraza. E Azerbaijan
Maraza see Märäzä
Marbella 70 D5 Andalucía, S Spain
Marble Bar 124 B4 Western Australia
Marburg see Marburg an der Lahn, Germany
Marburg see Maribor, Slovenia
Marburg an der Lahn 72 B4 hist. Marburg. Hessen, W Germany
March see Morava
Marche 74 C3 Eng. Marches. region C Italy
Marche 69 C5 cultural region C France
Marche-en-Famenne 65 C7 Luxembourg, SE Belgium
Marchena, Isla 38 B5 var. Bindloe Island. island Galapagos Islands, Ecuador, E Pacific Ocean
Marches see Marche
Mar Chiquita, Laguna 42 C3 lake C Argentina
Marcounda see Markounda
Mardān 112 C1 North-West Frontier Province, N Pakistan
Mar del Plata 43 D5 Buenos Aires, E Argentina
Mardin 95 E4 Mardin, SE Turkey
Maré 122 D5 island Îles Loyauté, E New Caledonia
Marea Neagră see Black Sea
Mareeba 126 D3 Queensland, NE Australia
Marek see Dupnitsa
Marganets see Marhanets'
Margarita, Isla de 37 E1 island N Venezuela
Margate 67 E7 prev. Mergate. SE England, United Kingdom
Margherita see Jamaame
Margherita, Lake 51 C5 Eng. Lake Margherita, It. Abbaia. lake SW Ethiopia
Margherita, Lake see Ābaya Hāyk'
Marghita 86 B3 Hung. Margitta. Bihor, NW Romania
Margitta see Marghita
Marhanets' 87 F3 Rus. Marganets. Dnipropetrovs'ka Oblast', E Ukraine
María Cleofas, Isla 28 C4 island C Mexico
Maria Island 127 C8 island Tasmania, SE Australia
María Madre, Isla 28 C4 island C Mexico
María Magdalena, Isla 28 C4 island C Mexico
Mariana Trench 103 G4 var. Challenger Deep. trench W Pacific Ocean
Mariánské Lázně 77 A5 Ger. Marienbad. Karlovarský Kraj, W Czech Republic
Marías, Islas 28 C4 island group C Mexico
Maria-Theresiopel see Subotica
Maribor 73 E7 Ger. Marburg. NE Slovenia
Marica see Maritsa
Maridi 51 B5 Western Equatoria, SW Sudan
Marie Byrd Land 132 A3 physical region Antarctica
Marie-Galante 33 G4 var. Ceyre to the Caribs. island SE Guadeloupe
Marienbad see Mariánské Lázně
Marienburg see Alūksne, Latvia
Marienburg see Malbork, Poland
Marienburg in Westpreussen see Malbork
Marienhausen see Viļaka
Mariental 56 B4 Hardap, SW Namibia
Marienwerder see Kwidzyń
Mariestad 63 B6 Västra Götaland, S Sweden
Marietta 20 D2 Georgia, SE USA
Marijampolė 84 B4 prev. Kapsukas. Marijampolė, S Lithuania
Marília 41 E4 São Paulo, S Brazil
Marín 70 B1 Galicia, NW Spain
Mar'ina Gorka see Mar"ina Horka
Mar"ina Horka 85 C6 Rus. Mar'ina Gorka. Minskaya Voblasts', C Belarus
Maringá 41 E4 Paraná, S Brazil
Marion 23 G3 Iowa, C USA
Marion 18 D4 Ohio, N USA
Marion, Lake 21 E2 reservoir South Carolina, SE USA
Mariscal Estigarribia 42 D2 Boquerón, NW Paraguay
Maritsa 82 D3 var. Marica, Gk. Évros, Turk. Meriç; anc. Hebrus. river SW Europe
Maritzburg see Pietermaritzburg
Mariupol' 87 G4 prev. Zhdanov. Donets'ka Oblast', SE Ukraine
Marka 51 D6 var. Merca. Shabeellaha Hoose, S Somalia
Markham, Mount 132 B4 mountain Antarctica
Markounda 54 C4 var. Marcounda. Ouham, NW Central African Republic
Marktredwitz 73 C5 Bayern, E Germany
Marlborough 126 D4 Queensland, E Australia
Marmanda see Marmande
Marmande 69 B5 anc. Marmanda. Lot-et-Garonne, SW France
Sea of Marmara 94 A2 Eng. Sea of Marmara. sea NW Turkey
Marmara, Sea of see Marmara Denizi
Marmaris 94 A4 Muğla, SW Turkey
Marne 68 C3 cultural region N France
Marne 68 D3 river N France
Maro 54 C4 Moyen-Chari, S Chad
Maroantsetra 57 G2 Toamasina, NE Madagascar
Maromokotro 57 G2 mountain N Madagascar
Maroni 37 G3 Dut. Marowijne. river French Guiana/Suriname
Maroshevíz see Toplița
Marosludas see Luduș
Marosvásárhely see Târgu Mureș
Marotiri 121 F4 var. Îlots de Bass, Morotiri. island group Îles Australes, SW French Polynesia
Maroua 54 B3 Extrême-Nord, N Cameroon
Marowijne see Maroni
Marquesas Fracture Zone 131 E3 fracture zone E Pacific Ocean
Marquette 18 B1 Michigan, N USA
Marrakech 48 C2 var. Marakesh, Eng. Marrakesh; prev. Morocco. W Morocco
Marrakesh see Marrakech
Marrawah 127 C8 Tasmania, SE Australia
Marree 127 B5 South Australia
Marsá al Burayqah 49 G3 var. Al Burayqah. N Libya
Marsabit 51 C6 Eastern, N Kenya
Marsala 75 B7 anc. Lilybaeum. Sicilia, Italy, C Mediterranean Sea
Marsberg 72 B4 Nordrhein-Westfalen, W Germany
Marseille 69 D6 Eng. Marseilles; anc. Massilia. Bouches-du-Rhône, SE France
Marseilles see Marseille
Marshall 23 F2 Minnesota, N USA
Marshall 27 H2 Texas, SW USA
Marshall Islands 122 C1 off. Republic of the Marshall Islands. country W Pacific Ocean
Marshall Islands, Republic of the see Marshall Islands
Marshall Seamounts 103 H3 seamount range SW Pacific Ocean
Marsh Harbour 32 C1 Great Abaco, W Bahamas
Martaban 114 B4 var. Moktama. Mon State, S Myanmar (Burma)
Martha's Vineyard 19 G3 island Massachusetts, NE USA
Martigues 69 D6 Bouches-du-Rhône, SE France
Martin 77 C5 Ger. Sankt Martin, Hung. Turócszentmárton; prev. Turčianský Svätý Martin. Žilinský Kraj, N Slovakia
Martinique 33 G4 French overseas department E West Indies
Martinique Channel see Martinique Passage
Martinique Passage 33 G4 var. Dominica Channel, Martinique Channel. channel Dominica/Martinique
Marton 128 D4 Manawatu-Wanganui, North Island, New Zealand
Martos 70 D4 Andalucía, S Spain
Marungu 55 E7 mountain range SE Dem. Rep. Congo
Mary 100 D3 prev. Merv. Mary Welaýaty, S Turkmenistan
Maryborough 127 D4 Queensland, E Australia
Maryborough see Port Laoise
Mary Island see Kanton
Maryland 19 E5 off. State of Maryland, also known as America in Miniature, Cockade State, Free State, Old Line State. state NE USA
Maryland, State of see Maryland
Maryville 23 F4 Missouri, C USA
Maryville 20 D1 Tennessee, S USA
Masai Steppe 51 C7 grassland NW Tanzania
Masaka 51 B6 SW Uganda
Masallı 95 H3 Rus. Masally. S Azerbaijan
Masally see Masallı
Masasi 51 C8 Mtwara, SE Tanzania
Masawa/Massawa see Mits'iwa
Masaya 30 D3 Masaya, W Nicaragua
Mascarene Basin 119 B5 undersea basin W Indian Ocean
Mascarene Islands 57 H4 island group W Indian Ocean
Mascarene Plain 119 B5 abyssal plain W Indian Ocean
Mascarene Plateau 119 B5 undersea plateau W Indian Ocean
Maseru 56 D4 country capital W Lesotho
Mas-ha 97 D7 W West Bank Asia
Mashhad 98 E2 var. Meshed. Khorāsān-Razavī, NE Iran
Masindi 51 B6 W Uganda
Masīra see Maṣīrah, Jazīrat
Masira, Gulf of 99 E5 var. Gulf of Masira. bay E Oman
Masira, Gulf of see Maṣīrah, Khalīj
Maṣīrah, Jazīrat 99 E5 var. Masīra. island E Oman
Masis see Büyükağrı Dağı
Maskat see Masqaṭ
Mason City 23 F3 Iowa, C USA
Masqaṭ 99 E5 var. Maskat, Eng. Muscat. country capital NE Oman
Massa 74 B3 Toscana, C Italy
Massachusetts 19 G3 off. Commonwealth of Massachusetts, also known as Bay State, Old Bay State, Old Colony State. state NE USA
Massenya 54 B3 Chari-Baguirmi, SW Chad
Massif Central 69 C5 plateau C France
Massilia see Marseille
Massoukou see Franceville
Mastanli see Momchilgrad
Masterton 129 D5 Wellington, North Island, New Zealand
Masty 85 B5 Rus. Mosty. Hrodzyenskaya Voblasts', W Belarus
Masuda 109 B6 Shimane, Honshū, SW Japan
Masuku see Franceville

Masvingo – Mocuba

Masvingo *56 D3 prev.* Fort Victoria, Nyanda, Victoria. Masvingo, SE Zimbabwe
Maşyāf *96 B3 Fr.* Misiaf. Ḩamāh, C Syria
Matadi *55 B6* Bas-Congo, W Dem. Rep. Congo
Matagalpa *30 D3* Matagalpa, C Nicaragua
Matale *110 D3* Central Province, C Sri Lanka
Matam *52 C3* NE Senegal
Matamata *128 D3* Waikato, North Island, New Zealand
Matamoros *28 D3* Coahuila de Zaragoza, NE Mexico
Matamoros *29 E2* Tamaulipas, C Mexico
Matane *17 E4* Québec, SE Canada
Matanzas *32 B2* Matanzas, NW Cuba
Matara *110 D4* Southern Province, S Sri Lanka
Mataram *116 D5* Pulau Lombok, C Indonesia
Mataró *71 G2 anc.* Illuro. Cataluña, E Spain
Mataura *129 B7* Southland, South Island, New Zealand
Mataura *129 B7 river* South Island, New Zealand
Mata Uta *see* Matā'utu
Matā'utu *123 E4 var.* Mata Uta. *dependent territory capital* Île Uvea, Wallis and Futuna
Matera *75 E5* Basilicata, S Italy
Mathurai *see* Madurai
Matianus *see* Orūmīyeh, Daryācheh-ye
Matías Romero *29 F5* Oaxaca, SE Mexico
Matisco/Matisco Ædourum *see* Mâcon
Mato Grosso *41 E3 off.* Estado de Mato Grosso; *prev.* Matto Grosso. *state* W Brazil
Mato Grosso *41 E3 off.* Estado de Mato Grosso; *prev.* Matto Grosso. *region* W Brazil
Mato Grosso do Sul *41 E4 off.* Estado de Mato Grosso do Sul. *state* S Brazil
Mato Grosso do Sul *41 E4 off.* Estado de Mato Grosso do Sul. *region* S Brazil
Mato Grosso do Sul, Estado de *see* Mato Grosso do Sul
Mato Grosso, Estado de *see* Mato Grosso
Mato Grosso, Planalto de *34 C4 plateau* C Brazil
Matosinhos *70 B2 prev.* Matozinhos. Porto, NW Portugal
Matozinhos *see* Matosinhos
Matsue *109 B6 var.* Matsuye, Matue. Shimane, Honshū, SW Japan
Matsumoto *109 C5 var.* Matumoto. Nagano, Honshū, S Japan
Matsuyama *109 B7 var.* Matuyama. Ehime, Shikoku, SW Japan
Matsuye *see* Matsue
Matterhorn *73 A8 It.* Monte Cervino. *mountain* Italy/Switzerland
Matthews Ridge *37 F2* N Guyana
Matthew Town *32 D2* Great Inagua, S Bahamas
Matto Grosso *see* Mato Grosso
Matucana *38 C4* Lima, W Peru
Matue *see* Matsue
Matumoto *see* Matsumoto
Maturín *37 E2* Monagas, NE Venezuela
Matuyama *see* Matsuyama
Mau *113 E3 var.* Maunāth Bhanjan. Uttar Pradesh, N India
Maui *25 B8 island* Hawai'i, USA, C Pacific Ocean
Maun *56 C3* North-West, C Botswana
Maunāth Bhanjan *see* Mau
Mauren *72 E1* NE Liechtenstein Europe
Maurice *see* Mauritius
Mauritania *52 C2 off.* Islamic Republic of Mauritania, *Ar.* Mūrītānīyah. *country* W Africa
Mauritania, Islamic Republic of *see* Mauritania
Mauritius *57 H3 off.* Republic of Mauritius, *Fr.* Maurice. *country* W Indian Ocean
Mauritius *119 B5 island* W Indian Ocean
Mauritius, Republic of *see* Mauritius
Mawlamyaing *see* Mawlamyine
Mawlamyine *114 B4 var.* Mawlamyaing, Moulmein. Mon State, S Myanmar (Burma)
Mawson *132 D2 Australian research station* Antarctica
Mayadin *see* Al Mayādīn
Mayaguana *32 D2 island* SE Bahamas
Mayaguana Passage *32 D2 passage* SE Bahamas
Mayagüez *33 F3* W Puerto Rico
Mayamey *98 D2* Semnān, N Iran
Maya Mountains *30 B2 Sp.* Montañas Mayas. *mountain range* Belize/Guatemala
Mayas, Montañas *see* Maya Mountains
Maych'ew *50 C4 var.* Mai Chio, *It.* Mai Ceu. Tigray, N Ethiopia
Maydān Shahr *see* Meydān Shahr
Mayebashi *see* Maebashi
Mayence *see* Mainz
Mayfield *129 B6* Canterbury, South Island, New Zealand
Maykop *89 A7* Respublika Adygeya, SW Russian Federation
Maymana *see* Meymaneh
Maymyo *see* Pyin-Oo-Lwin
Mayo *see* Maio
Mayor Island *128 D3 island* NE New Zealand
Mayor Pablo Lagerenza *see* Capitán Pablo Lagerenza
Mayotte *57 F2 French territorial collectivity* E Africa
May Pen *32 B5* C Jamaica
Mayyit, Al Baḩr al *see* Dead Sea
Mazabuka *56 D2* Southern, S Zambia
Mazaca *see* Kayseri
Mazagan *see* El-Jadida
Mazār-e Sharīf *101 E3 var.* Mazār-i Sharif. Balkh, N Afghanistan
Mazār-i Sharif *see* Mazār-e Sharīf
Mazatlán *28 C3* Sinaloa, C Mexico
Mažeikiai *84 B3* Telšiai, NW Lithuania
Mazirbe *84 C2* Talsi, NW Latvia
Mazra'a *see* Al Mazra'ah
Mazury *76 D3 physical region* NE Poland
Mazyr *85 C7 Rus.* Mozyr'. Homyel'skaya Voblasts', SE Belarus
Mbabane *56 D4 country capital* NW Swaziland
Mbacké *see* Mbaké
Mbaïki *55 C5 var.* M'Baiki. Lobaye, SW Central African Republic
M'Baiki *see* Mbaïki
Mbaké *52 B3 var.* Mbacké. W Senegal
Mbala *56 D1 prev.* Abercorn. Northern, NE Zambia
Mbale *51 C6* E Uganda
Mbandaka *55 C5 prev.* Coquilhatville. Equateur, NW Dem. Rep. Congo
M'Banza Congo *56 B1 var.* Mbanza Congo; *prev.* São Salvador, São Salvador do Congo. Dem. Rep. Congo, NW Angola
Mbanza-Ngungu *55 B6* Bas-Congo, W Dem. Rep. Congo
Mbarara *51 B6* SW Uganda
Mbé *54 B4* Nord, N Cameroon
Mbeya *51 C7* Mbeya, SW Tanzania
Mbomou/M'Bomu/Mbomu *see* Bomu
Mbour *52 B3* W Senegal
Mbuji-Mayi *55 D7 prev.* Bakwanga. Kasai-Oriental, S Dem. Rep. Congo
McAlester *27 G2* Oklahoma, C USA
McAllen *27 G5* Texas, SW USA
McCamey *27 E3* Texas, SW USA
McClintock Channel *15 F2 channel* Nunavut, N Canada
McComb *20 B3* Mississippi, S USA
McCook *23 E4* Nebraska, C USA
McKean Island *123 E3 island* Phoenix Islands, C Kiribati
Mount McKinley *14 C3 var.* Denali. *mountain* Alaska, USA
McKinley Park *14 C3* Alaska, USA
McMinnville *24 B3* Oregon, NW USA
McMurdo *132 B4 US research station* Antarctica
McPherson *23 E5* Kansas, C USA
McPherson *see* Fort McPherson
Mdantsane *56 D5* Eastern Cape, SE South Africa
Mead, Lake *25 D6 reservoir* Arizona/Nevada, W USA
Mecca *see* Makkah
Mechelen *65 C5 Eng.* Mechlin, *Fr.* Malines. Antwerpen, C Belgium
Mechlin *see* Mechelen
Mecklenburger Bucht *72 C2 bay* N Germany
Mecsek *77 C7 mountain range* SW Hungary
Medan *116 B3* Sumatera, E Indonesia
Medeba *see* Ma'dabā
Medellín *36 B3* Antioquia, NW Colombia
Médenine *49 F2 var.* Madanīyīn. SE Tunisia
Medeshamstede *see* Peterborough
Medford *24 B4* Oregon, NW USA
Medgidia *86 D5* Constanța, SE Romania
Medgyes *see* Mediaş
Mediaş *86 B4 Ger.* Mediasch, *Hung.* Medgyes. Sibiu, C Romania
Mediasch *see* Mediaş
Medicine Hat *15 F5* Alberta, SW Canada
Medina *see* Al Madīnah
Medinaceli *71 E2* Castilla-León, N Spain
Medina del Campo *70 D2* Castilla-León, N Spain
Medinat Israel *see* Israel
Mediolanum *see* Saintes, France
Mediolanum *see* Milano, Italy
Mediomatrica *see* Metz
Mediterranean Sea *80 D3 Fr.* Mer Méditerranée. *sea* Africa/Asia/Europe
Méditerranée, Mer *see* Mediterranean Sea
Médoc *69 B5 cultural region* SW France
Medvezh'yegorsk *88 B3* Respublika Kareliya, NW Russian Federation
Meekatharra *125 B5* Western Australia
Meemu Atoll *see* Mulakatholhu
Meerssen *65 D6 var.* Mersen. Limburg, SE Netherlands
Meerut *112 D2* Uttar Pradesh, N India
Megáli Préspa, Límni *see* Prespa, Lake
Meghālaya *91 G3 cultural region* NE India
Mehdia *see* Mahdia
Meheso *see* Mī'ēso
Me Hka *see* Nmai Hka
Mehrīz *98 D3* Yazd, C Iran
Mehtar Lām *101 F4 var.* Mehtarlām, Meterlam, Methariam, Metharlam. Laghmān, E Afghanistan
Mehtarlām *see* Mehtar Lām
Meiktila *114 B3* Mandalay, C Myanmar (Burma)
Méjico *see* Mexico
Mejillones *42 B2* Antofagasta, N Chile
Mek'elē *50 C4 var.* Makale. Tigray, N Ethiopia
Mékhé *52 B3* NW Senegal
Mekong *102 D3 var.* Lan-ts'ang Chiang, *Cam.* Mékôngk, *Chin.* Lancang Jiang, *Lao.* Mènam Khong, *Th.* Mae Nam Khong, *Tib.* Dza Chu, *Vtn.* Sông Tiên Giang. *river* SE Asia
Mékôngk *see* Mekong
Mekong, Mouths of the *115 E6 delta* S Vietnam
Melaka *116 B3 var.* Malacca. Melaka, Peninsular Malaysia
Melaka, Selat *see* Malacca, Strait of
Melanesia *122 D3 island group* W Pacific Ocean
Melanesian Basin *120 C2 undersea basin* W Pacific Ocean
Melbourne *127 C7 state capital* Victoria, SE Australia
Melbourne *21 E4* Florida, SE USA
Meleda *see* Mljet
Melghir, Chott *49 E2 var.* Chott Melrhir. *salt lake* E Algeria
Melilla *58 B5 anc.* Rusaddir, Russadir. Melilla, Spain, N Africa
Melilla *48 D2 enclave* Spain, N Africa
Melita *15 F5* Manitoba, S Canada
Melita *see* Mljet
Melitene *see* Malatya
Melitopol' *87 F4* Zaporiz'ka Oblast', SE Ukraine
Melle *65 B5* Oost-Vlaanderen, NW Belgium
Mellerud *63 B6* Västra Götaland, S Sweden
Mellieħa *80 B5* E Malta
Mellizo Sur, Cerro *43 A7 mountain* S Chile
Melo *42 E4* Cerro Largo, NE Uruguay
Melodunum *see* Melun
Melrhir, Chott *see* Melghir, Chott
Melsungen *72 B4* Hessen, C Germany
Melun *68 C3 anc.* Melodunum. Seine-et-Marne, N France
Melville Bay/Melville Bugt *see* Qimusseriarsuaq
Melville Island *124 D2 island* Northern Territory, N Australia
Melville Island *15 E2 island* Parry Islands, Northwest Territories, NW Canada
Melville, Lake *17 F2 lake* Newfoundland and Labrador, E Canada
Melville Peninsula *15 G3 peninsula* Nunavut, NE Canada
Melville Sound *see* Viscount Melville Sound
Membidj *see* Manbij
Memel *see* Neman, NE Europe
Memel *see* Klaipeda, Lithuania
Memmingen *73 B6* Bayern, S Germany
Memphis *20 C1* Tennessee, S USA
Menaam *see* Menaldum
Menado *see* Manado
Ménaka *53 F3* Goa, E Mali
Menaldum *64 D1 Fris.* Menaam. Friesland, N Netherlands
Mènam Khong *see* Mekong
Mendaña Fracture Zone *131 F4 fracture zone* E Pacific Ocean
Mende *69 C5 anc.* Mimatum. Lozère, S France
Mendeleyev Ridge *133 B2 undersea ridge* Arctic Ocean
Mendocino Fracture Zone *130 D2 fracture zone* NE Pacific Ocean
Mendoza *42 B4* Mendoza, W Argentina
Menemen *94 A3* İzmir, W Turkey
Menengiyn Tal *105 F2 plain* E Mongolia
Menongue *56 B2 var.* Vila Serpa Pinto, *Port.* Serpa Pinto. Cuando Cubango, C Angola
Mentawai, Kepulauan *116 A4 island group* W Indonesia
Meppel *64 D2* Drenthe, NE Netherlands
Meran *see* Merano
Merano *74 C1 Ger.* Meran. Trentino-Alto Adige, N Italy
Merca *see* Marka
Mercedes *42 D3* Corrientes, NE Argentina
Mercedes *42 D4* Soriano, SW Uruguay
Meredith, Lake *27 E1 reservoir* Texas, SW USA
Merefa *87 G2* Kharkivs'ka Oblast', E Ukraine
Mergate *see* Margate
Mergui *see* Myeik
Mergui Archipelago *115 B6 island group* S Myanmar (Burma)
Mérida *29 H3* Yucatán, SW Mexico
Mérida *70 C4 anc.* Augusta Emerita. Extremadura, W Spain
Mérida *36 C2* Mérida, W Venezuela
Meridian *20 C2* Mississippi, S USA
Mérignac *69 B5* Gironde, SW France
Merín, Laguna *see* Mirim Lagoon
Merkulovichi *see* Myerkulavichy
Merowe *50 B3* Northern, N Sudan
Merredin *125 B6* Western Australia
Mersen *see* Meerssen
Mersey *67 D5 river* NW England, United Kingdom
Mersin *94 C4 var.* İçel. İçel, S Turkey
Mērsrags *84 C3* Talsi, NW Latvia
Meru *51 C6* Eastern, C Kenya
Merv *see* Mary
Merzifon *94 D2* Amasya, N Turkey
Merzig *73 A5* Saarland, SW Germany
Mesa *26 B2* Arizona, SW USA
Meseritz *see* Międzyrzecz
Meshed *see* Mashhad
Mesopotamia *35 C5 var.* Mesopotamia Argentina. *physical region* NE Argentina
Mesopotamia Argentina *see* Mesopotamia
Messalo, Rio *57 E2 var.* Mualo. *river* NE Mozambique
Messana/Messene *see* Messina
Messina *75 D7 var.* Messana, Messene; *anc.* Zancle. Sicilia, Italy, C Mediterranean Sea
Messina *see* Musina
Messina, Strait of *75 D7 Eng.* Strait of Messina. *strait* SW Italy
Messina, Strait of *see* Messina, Stretto di
Messíni *83 B6* Pelopónnisos, S Greece
Mesta *see* Néstos
Mestghanem *see* Mostaganem
Mestia *95 F1 var.* Mestiya. N Georgia
Mestiya *see* Mestia
Mestre *74 C2* Veneto, NE Italy
Metairie *20 B3* Louisiana, S USA
Metán *42 C2* Salta, N Argentina
Metapán *30 B2* Santa Ana, NW El Salvador
Meta, Río *36 D3 river* Colombia/Venezuela
Meterlam *see* Mehtar Lām
Methariam/Metharlam *see* Mehtar Lām
Metis *see* Metz
Metković *78 B4* Dubrovnik-Neretva, SE Croatia
Métsovo *82 B4 prev.* Métsovon. Ípeiros, C Greece
Métsovon *see* Métsovo
Metz *68 D3 anc.* Divodurum Mediomatricum, Mediomatrica, Metis. Moselle, NE France
Meulaboh *116 A3* Sumatera, W Indonesia
Meuse *65 C6 Dut.* Maas. *river* W Europe
Mexcala, Río *see* Balsas, Río
Mexicali *28 A1* Baja California, NW Mexico
Mexicanos, Estados Unidos *see* Mexico
México *29 E4 var.* Ciudad de México, *Eng.* Mexico City. *country capital* México, C Mexico
Mexico *23 G4* Missouri, C USA
Mexico *28 C3 off.* United Mexican States, *var.* Méjico, México, *Sp.* Estados Unidos Mexicanos. *country* N Central America
México *see* Mexico
Mexico City *see* México
México, Golfo de *see* Mexico, Gulf of
Mexico, Gulf of *29 F2 Sp.* Golfo de México. *gulf* W Atlantic Ocean
Meyadine *see* Al Mayādīn
Meydān Shahr *101 E4 var.* Maydān Shahr. Vardak, E Afghanistan
Meymaneh *100 D3 var.* Maimāna, Maymana. Fāryāb, NW Afghanistan
Mezen' *88 D3 river* NW Russian Federation
Mezőtúr *77 D7* Jász-Nagykun-Szolnok, E Hungary
Mġarr *80 A5* Gozo, N Malta
Miadzioł Nowy *see* Myadzyel
Miahuatlán *29 F5 var.* Miahuatlán de Porfirio Díaz. Oaxaca, SE Mexico
Miahuatlán de Porfirio Díaz *see* Miahuatlán
Miami *21 F5* Florida, SE USA
Miami *27 G1* Oklahoma, C USA
Miami Beach *21 F5* Florida, SE USA
Mīāneh *98 C2 var.* Miyāneh. Āžarbāyjān-e Sharqī, NW Iran
Mianyang *106 B5* Sichuan, C China
Miastko *76 C2 Ger.* Rummelsburg in Pommern. Pomorskie, N Poland
Mi Chai *see* Nong Khai
Michalovce *77 E5 Ger.* Grossmichel, *Hung.* Nagymihály. Košický Kraj, E Slovakia
Michigan *18 C1 off.* State of Michigan, *also known as* Great Lakes State, Lake State, Wolverine State. *state* N USA
Michigan, Lake *18 C2 lake* N USA
Michurin *see* Tsarevo
Michurinsk *89 B5* Tambovskaya Oblast', W Russian Federation
Micoud *33 F2* SE Saint Lucia
Micronesia *122 B1 off.* Federated States of Micronesia. *country* W Pacific Ocean
Micronesia *122 C1 island group* W Pacific Ocean
Micronesia, Federated States of *see* Micronesia
Mid-Atlantic Cordillera *see* Mid-Atlantic Ridge
Mid-Atlantic Ridge *44 C3 var.* Mid-Atlantic Cordillera, Mid-Atlantic Rise, Mid-Atlantic Swell. *undersea ridge* Atlantic Ocean
Mid-Atlantic Rise/Mid-Atlantic Swell *see* Mid-Atlantic Ridge
Middelburg *65 B5* Zeeland, SW Netherlands
Middelharnis *64 B4* Zuid-Holland, SW Netherlands
Middelkerke *65 A5* West-Vlaanderen, W Belgium
Middle America Trench *13 B7 trench* E Pacific Ocean
Middle Andaman *111 F2 island* Andaman Islands, India, NE Indian Ocean
Middle Atlas *48 C2 Eng.* Middle Atlas. *mountain range* N Morocco
Middle Atlas *see* Moyen Atlas
Middleburg Island *see* 'Eua
Middle Congo *see* Congo (Republic of)
Middlesboro *18 C5* Kentucky, S USA
Middlesbrough *67 D5* N England, United Kingdom
Middletown *19 F4* New Jersey, NE USA
Middletown *19 F3* New York, NE USA
Mid-Indian Basin *119 C5 undersea basin* N Indian Ocean
Mid-Indian Ridge *119 C5 var.* Central Indian Ridge. *undersea ridge* C Indian Ocean
Midland *16 D5* Ontario, S Canada
Midland *18 C3* Michigan, N USA
Midland *27 E3* Texas, SW USA
Mid-Pacific Mountains *130 C2 var.* Mid-Pacific Seamounts. *seamount range* NW Pacific Ocean
Mid-Pacific Seamounts *see* Mid-Pacific Mountains
Midway Islands *130 D2 US territory* C Pacific Ocean
Miechów *77 D5* Małopolskie, S Poland
Międzyrzec Podlaski *76 E3* Lubelskie, E Poland
Międzyrzecz *76 B3 Ger.* Meseritz. Lubuskie, W Poland
Mielec *77 D5* Podkarpackie, SE Poland
Miercurea-Ciuc *86 C4 Ger.* Szeklerburg, *Hung.* Csíkszereda. Harghita, C Romania
Mieres del Camín *see* Mieres del Camino
Mieres del Camino *70 D1 var.* Mieres del Camín. Asturias, NW Spain
Mī'ēso *51 D5 var.* Meheso, Miesso. Oromīya, C Ethiopia
Miesso *see* Mī'ēso
Mifrats Hefa *97 A5 Eng.* Bay of Haifa; *prev.* MifrazḤefa. *bay* N Israel
Miguel Asua *28 D3 var.* Miguel Auza. Zacatecas, C Mexico
Miguel Auza *see* Miguel Asua
Mijdrecht *64 C3* Utrecht, C Netherlands
Mikashevichi *see* Mikashevichy
Mikashevichy *85 C7 Pol.* Mikaszewicze, *Rus.* Mikashevichi. Brestskaya Voblasts', SW Belarus
Mikaszewicze *see* Mikashevichy
Mikhaylovgrad *see* Montana
Mikhaylovka *89 B6* Volgogradskaya Oblast', SW Russian Federation
Míkonos *see* Mýkonos
Mikre *82 C2* Lovech, N Bulgaria
Mikun' *88 D4* Respublika Komi, NW Russian Federation
Mikuni-sanmyaku *109 D5 mountain range* Honshū, N Japan Asia
Mikura-jima *109 D6 island* E Japan
Milagro *38 B2* Guayas, SW Ecuador
Milan *see* Milano
Milange *57 E2* Zambézia, NE Mozambique
Milano *74 B2 Eng.* Milan, *Ger.* Mailand; *anc.* Mediolanum. Lombardia, N Italy
Milas *94 A4* Muğla, SW Turkey
Milashavichy *85 C7 Rus.* Milashevichi. Homyel'skaya Voblasts', SE Belarus
Milashevichi *see* Milashavichy
Mildura *127 C6* Victoria, SE Australia
Mile *see* Mili Atoll
Miles *127 D5* Queensland, E Australia
Miles City *22 C2* Montana, NW USA
Milford *see* Milford Haven
Milford Haven *67 C6 prev.* Milford. SW Wales, United Kingdom
Milford Sound *129 A6* Southland, South Island, New Zealand
Milford Sound *129 A6 inlet* South Island, New Zealand
Milh, Baḩr al *see* Razāzah, Buḩayrat ar
Mili Atoll *122 D2 var.* Mile. *atoll* Ratak Chain, SE Marshall Islands
Mil'kovo *93 H3* Kamchatskaya Oblast', E Russian Federation
Milk River *15 E5* Alberta, SW Canada
Milk River *22 C1 river* Montana, NW USA
Milk, Wadi el *66 B4 var.* Wadi al Malik. *river* C Sudan
Milledgeville *21 E2* Georgia, SE USA
Mille Lacs Lake *23 F2 lake* Minnesota, N USA
Millennium Island *121 F3 prev.* Caroline Island, Thornton Island. *atoll* Line Islands, E Kiribati
Millerovo *89 B6* Rostovskaya Oblast', SW Russian Federation
Mílos *83 C6 island* Kykládes, Greece, Aegean Sea
Mílos *83 C6 island* Kykládes, Greece, Aegean Sea
Mílos *83 C7 island* Kykládes, Greece, Aegean Sea
Milton *129 B7* Otago, South Island, New Zealand
Milton Keynes *67 D6* SE England, United Kingdom
Milwaukee *18 B3* Wisconsin, N USA
Mimatum *see* Mende
Min *see* Fujian
Mīnā' Qābūs *118 B3* NE Oman
Minas Gerais *41 F3 off.* Estado de Minas Gerais. *state* E Brazil
Minas Gerais *41 F3 off.* Estado de Minas Gerais. *region* E Brazil
Minas Gerais, Estado de *see* Minas Gerais
Minatitlán *29 F4* Veracruz-Llave, E Mexico
Minbu *114 A3* Magway, W Myanmar (Burma)
Minch, The *66 B3 var.* North Minch. *strait* NW Scotland, United Kingdom
Mindanao *117 F2 island* S Philippines
Mindanao Sea *see* Bohol Sea
Mindelheim *73 C6* Bayern, S Germany
Mindello *see* Mindelo
Mindelo *52 A2 var.* Mindello; *prev.* Porto Grande. São Vicente, N Cape Verde
Minden *72 B4 anc.* Minthun. Nordrhein-Westfalen, NW Germany
Mindoro *117 E2 island* N Philippines
Mindoro Strait *117 E2 strait* W Philippines
Mineral Wells *27 F2* Texas, SW USA
Mingäçevir *95 G2 Rus.* Mingechaur, Mingechevir. C Azerbaijan
Mingechaur/Mingechevir *see* Mingäçevir
Mingora *see* Saidu Sharif
Minho *70 B2 former province* N Portugal
Minho *70 B2 Sp.* Miño. *river* Portugal/Spain
Minho, Rio *see* Miño
Minicoy Island *110 B3 island* SW India
Minius *see* Miño
Minna *53 G4* Niger, C Nigeria
Minneapolis *23 F2* Minnesota, N USA
Minnesota *23 F2 off.* State of Minnesota, *also known as* Gopher State, New England of the West, North Star State. *state* N USA
Miño *70 B2 var.* Mino, Minius, *Port.* Rio Minho. *river* Portugal/Spain
Miño *see* Minho, Rio
Minorca *71 H3 Eng.* Minorca; *anc.* Balearis Minor. *island* Islas Baleares, Spain, W Mediterranean Sea
Minorca *see* Menorca
Minot *23 E1* North Dakota, N USA
Minsk *85 C6 country capital* Minskaya Voblasts', C Belarus
Minskaya Wzvyshsha *85 C6 mountain range* C Belarus
Mińsk Mazowiecki *76 D3 var.* Nowo-Minsk. Mazowieckie, C Poland
Minthun *see* Minden
Minto, Lac *16 D2 lake* Québec, C Canada
Minya *see* Al Minyā
Miraflores *28 C3* Baja California Sur, W Mexico
Miranda de Ebro *71 E1* La Rioja, N Spain
Mirgorod *see* Myrhorod
Miri *116 D3* Sarawak, East Malaysia
Mirim Lagoon *41 E5 var.* Lake Mirim, *Sp.* Laguna Merín. *lagoon* Brazil/Uruguay
Mirim, Lake *see* Mirim Lagoon
Mírina *see* Mýrina
Mīrjāveh *98 E4* Sīstān va Balūchestān, SE Iran
Mirny *132 C3 Russian research station* Antarctica
Mirnyy *93 F3* Respublika Sakha (Yakutiya), NE Russian Federation
Mīrpur Khās *112 B3* Sind, SE Pakistan
Mirtoan Sea *83 C6 Eng.* Mirtoan Sea; *anc.* Myrtoum Mare. *sea* S Greece
Mirtoan Sea *see* Mirtóo Pélagos
Misiaf *see* Maşyāf
Miskito Coast *see* La Mosquitia
Miskitos, Cayos *31 E2 island group* NE Nicaragua
Miskolc *77 D6* Borsod-Abaúj-Zemplén, NE Hungary
Misool, Pulau *117 F4 island* Maluku, E Indonesia
Mişrātah *49 F2 var.* Misurata. NW Libya
Mission *27 G5* Texas, SW USA
Mississippi *20 B2 off.* State of Mississippi, *also known as* Bayou State, Magnolia State. *state* SE USA
Mississippi Delta *20 B4 delta* Louisiana, S USA
Mississippi River *13 C6 river* C USA
Missoula *22 B1* Montana, NW USA
Missouri *23 F5 off.* State of Missouri, *also known as* Bullion State, Show Me State. *state* C USA
Missouri River *23 E3 river* C USA
Mistassini, Lac *16 D3 lake* Québec, SE Canada
Mistelbach an der Zaya *73 E6* Niederösterreich, NE Austria
Misti, Volcán *39 E4 volcano* S Peru
Misurata *see* Mişrātah
Mitau *see* Jelgava
Mitchell *127 D5* Queensland, E Australia
Mitchell *23 E3* South Dakota, N USA
Mitchell, Mount *21 E1 mountain* North Carolina, SE USA
Mitchell River *126 C2 river* Queensland, NE Australia
Mi Tho *see* My Tho
Mitilíni *see* Mytilíni
Mito *109 D5* Ibaraki, Honshū, S Japan
Mitrovica/Mitrovicë *see* Kosovska Mitrovica, Serbia
Mitrovica/Mitrowitz *see* Sremska Mitrovica, Serbia
Mitrovicë *79 D5 Serb.* Mitrovica, Kosovska Mitrovica, Titova Mitrovica. N Kosovo
Mits'iwa *50 C4 var.* Masawa, Massawa. E Eritrea
Mitspe Ramon *97 A7 prev.* Mizpe Ramon. Southern, S Israel
Mittelstadt *see* Baia Sprie
Mitú *36 C4* Vaupés, SE Colombia
Mitumba, Chaîne des/Mitumba Range *see* Mitumba, Monts
Mitumba Range *55 E7 var.* Chaîne des Mitumba, Mitumba Range. *mountain range* E Dem. Rep. Congo
Miueru Wantipa, Lake *55 E7 lake* N Zambia
Miyake-jima *109 D6 island* Sakishima-shotō, SW Japan
Miyako *108 D4* Iwate, Honshū, C Japan
Miyakonojō *109 B8 var.* Miyakonzyô. Miyazaki, Kyūshū, SW Japan
Miyakonzyô *see* Miyakonojō
Miyāneh *see* Mīāneh
Miyazaki *109 B8* Miyazaki, Kyūshū, SW Japan
Mizil *86 C5* Prahova, SE Romania
Miziya *82 C1* Vratsa, NW Bulgaria
Mizpe Ramon *see* Mitspe Ramon
Mjøsa *63 B6 var.* Mjøsen. *lake* S Norway
Mjøsen *see* Mjøsa
Mladenovac *78 D4* Serbia, C Serbia
Mława *76 D3* Mazowieckie, C Poland
Mljet *79 B5 It.* Meleda; *anc.* Melita. *island* S Croatia
Mmabatho *56 C4* North-West, N South Africa
Moab *22 B5* Utah, W USA
Moa Island *126 C1 island* Queensland, NE Australia
Moanda *55 B6 var.* Mouanda. Haut-Ogooué, SE Gabon
Moba *55 E7* Katanga, E Dem. Rep. Congo
Mobay *see* Montego Bay
Mobaye *55 C5* Basse-Kotto, S Central African Republic
Moberly *23 G4* Missouri, C USA
Mobile *20 C3* Alabama, S USA
Mobutu Sese Seko, Lac *see* Albert, Lake
Moçâmedes *see* Namibe
Mochudi *56 C4* Kgatleng, SE Botswana
Mocímboa da Praia *57 F2 var.* Vila de Mocímboa da Praia. Cabo Delgado, N Mozambique
Môco *56 B2 var.* Morro de Môco. *mountain* W Angola
Mocoa *36 A4* Putumayo, SW Colombia
Môco, Morro de *see* Môco
Mocuba *57 E3* Zambézia, NE Mozambique

Modena – Nagyvárad

Modena *74 B3 anc.* Mutina. Emilia-Romagna, N Italy
Modesto *25 B6* California, W USA
Modica *75 C7 anc.* Motyca. Sicilia, Italy, C Mediterranean Sea
Modimolle *56 D4 prev.* Nylstroom. Limpopo, NE South Africa
Modohn *see* Madona
Modriča *78 C3* Republika Srpska, N Bosnia and Herzegovina
Moe *127 C7* Victoria, SE Australia
Möen *see* Møn, Denmark
Moero, Lac *see* Mweru, Lake
Moeskroen *see* Mouscron
Mogadiscio/Mogadishu *see* Muqdisho
Mogador *see* Essaouira
Mogilëv *see* Mahilyow
Mogilev-Podol'skiy *see* Mohyliv-Podil's'kyy
Mogilno *76 C3* Kujawsko-pomorskie, C Poland
Moḩammadābād-e Rīgān *98 E4* Kermān, SE Iran
Mohammedia *48 C2 prev.* Fédala. NW Morocco
Mohave, Lake *25 D7 reservoir* Arizona/Nevada, W USA
Mohawk River *19 F3 river* New York, NE USA
Mohéli *see* Mwali
Mohns Ridge *61 F3 undersea ridge* Greenland Sea/Norwegian Sea
Moho *39 E4* Puno, SE Peru
Mohoro *51 C7* Pwani, E Tanzania
Mohyliv-Podil's'kyy *86 D3 Rus.* Mogilev-Podol'skiy. Vinnyts'ka Oblast', C Ukraine
Moi *63 A6* Rogaland, S Norway
Moili *see* Mwali
Mo i Rana *62 C3* Nordland, C Norway
Mõisaküla *84 D3 Ger.* Moiseküll. Viljandimaa, S Estonia
Moiseküll *see* Mõisaküla
Moissac *69 B6* Tarn-et-Garonne, S France
Mojácar *71 E5* Andalucía, S Spain
Mojave Desert *25 D7 plain* California, W USA
Mokrany *see* Makrany
Moktama *see* Martaban
Mol *65 C5 prev.* Moll. Antwerpen, N Belgium
Moldavia *see* Moldova
Moldavian SSR/Moldavskaya SSR *see* Moldova
Molde *63 A5* Møre og Romsdal, S Norway
Moldotau, Khrebet *see* Moldo-Too, Khrebet
Moldo-Too, Khrebet *101 G2 prev.* Khrebet Moldotau. *mountain range* C Kyrgyzstan
Moldova *86 D3 off.* Republic of Moldova, *var.* Moldavia; *prev.* Moldavian SSR, *Rus.* Moldavskaya SSR. *country* SE Europe
Moldova Nouă *86 A4 Ger.* Neumoldowa, *Hung.* Újmoldova. Caraș-Severin, SW Romania
Moldova, Republic of *see* Moldova
Moldoveanul *see* Vârful Moldoveanu
Molfetta *75 E5* Puglia, SE Italy
Moll *see* Mol
Mollendo *39 E4* Arequipa, SW Peru
Mölndal *63 B7* Västra Götaland, S Sweden
Molochans'k *87 G4 Rus.* Molochansk. Zaporiz'ka Oblast', SE Ukraine
Molodechno/Molodeczno *see* Maladzyechna
Molodezhnaya *132 C2 Russian research station* Antarctica
Moloka'i *25 B8 var.* Molokai. *island* Hawaiian Islands, Hawai'i, USA
Molokai Fracture Zone *131 E2 tectonic feature* NE Pacific Ocean
Molopo *56 C4 seasonal river* Botswana/South Africa
Mólos *83 B5* Stereá Ellás, C Greece
Molotov *see* Severodvinsk, Arkhangel'skaya Oblast', Russian Federation
Molotov *see* Perm', Permskaya Oblast', Russian Federation
Moluccas *117 F4 Dut.* Molukken, *Eng.* Moluccas; *prev.* Spice Islands. *island group* E Indonesia
Moluccas *see* Maluku
Molucca Sea *117 F4 Ind.* Laut Maluku. *sea* E Indonesia
Molukken *see* Maluku
Mombasa *51 D7* Coast, SE Kenya
Mombetsu *see* Monbetsu
Momchilgrad *82 D3 prev.* Mastanli. Kŭrdzhali, S Bulgaria
Møn *63 B8 prev.* Möen. *island* SE Denmark
Mona, Canal de la *see* Mona Passage
Monaco *69 C7 var.* Monaco-Ville; *anc.* Monoecus. *country capital* S Monaco
Monaco *69 E6 off.* Principality of Monaco. *country* W Europe
Monaco *see* München
Monaco, Port de *69 C8 bay* S Monaco W Mediterranean Sea
Monaco, Principality of *see* Monaco
Monaco-Ville *see* Monaco
Monahans *27 E3* Texas, SW USA
Mona, Isla *33 E3 island* W Puerto Rico
Mona Passage *33 E3 Sp.* Canal de la Mona. *channel* Dominican Republic/Puerto Rico
Monastir *see* Bitola
Monbetsu *108 D2 var.* Mombetsu, Monbetu. Hokkaidō, NE Japan
Monbetu *see* Monbetsu
Moncalieri *74 A2* Piemonte, NW Italy
Monchegorsk *88 C2* Murmanskaya Oblast', NW Russian Federation
Monclova *28 D2* Coahuila de Zaragoza, NE Mexico
Moncton *17 F4* New Brunswick, SE Canada
Mondovì *74 A2* Piemonte, NW Italy
Monfalcone *74 D2* Friuli-Venezia Giulia, NE Italy
Monforte de Lemos *70 C1* Galicia, NW Spain
Mongo *54 C3* Guéra, C Chad
Mongolia *104 C2 Mong.* Mongol Uls. *country* E Asia
Mongolia, Plateau of *102 D1 plateau* E Mongolia
Mongol Uls *see* Mongolia
Mongora *see* Saidu Sharif
Mongos, Chaîne des *see* Bongo, Massif des
Mongu *56 C2* Western, W Zambia
Monkchester *see* Newcastle upon Tyne
Monkey Bay *57 E2* Southern, SE Malawi
Monkey River *see* Monkey River Town
Monkey River Town *30 C2 var.* Monkey River. Toledo, SE Belize
Monoecus *see* Monaco
Mono Lake *25 C6 lake* California, W USA
Monostor *see* Beli Manastir
Monovar *71 F4 Cat.* Monover. País Valenciano, E Spain
Monover *see* Monovar
Monroe *20 B2* Louisiana, S USA
Monrovia *52 C5 country capital* W Liberia
Mons *65 B6 Dut.* Bergen. Hainaut, S Belgium
Monselice *74 C2* Veneto, NE Italy
Montana *82 C2 prev.* Ferdinand, Mikhaylovgrad. Montana, NW Bulgaria
Montana *22 B1 off.* State of Montana, *also known as* Mountain State, Treasure State. *state* NW USA
Montargis *68 C4* Loiret, C France
Montauban *69 B6* Tarn-et-Garonne, S France
Montbéliard *68 D4* Doubs, E France
Mont Cenis, Col du *69 D5 pass* E France
Mont-de-Marsan *69 B6* Landes, SW France
Monteagudo *39 G4* Chuquisaca, S Bolivia
Montecarlo *69 C8* Misiones, NE Argentina
Monte Caseros *42 D3* Corrientes, NE Argentina
Monte Cristi *32 D3 var.* San Fernando de Monte Cristi. NW Dominican Republic
Monte Croce Carnico, Passo di *see* Plöcken Pass
Montegiardino *74 E2* SE San Marino
Montego Bay *32 A4 var.* Mobay. W Jamaica
Montélimar *69 D5 anc.* Acunum Acusio, Montilium Adhemari. Drôme, E France
Montemorelos *29 E3* Nuevo León, NE Mexico
Montenegro *79 C5 Serb.* Crna Gora. *country* SW Europe
Monte Patria *42 B3* Coquimbo, N Chile
Monterey *25 B6* California, W USA
Monterey *see* Monterrey
Monterey Bay *25 A6 bay* California, W USA
Montería *36 B2* Córdoba, NW Colombia
Montero *39 G4* Santa Cruz, C Bolivia
Monterrey *29 E3 var.* Monterey. Nuevo León, NE Mexico
Montes Claros *41 F3* Minas Gerais, SE Brazil
Montevideo *42 D4 country capital* Montevideo, S Uruguay
Montevideo *23 F2* Minnesota, N USA
Montgenèvre, Col de *69 D5 pass* France/Italy
Montgomery *20 D2 state capital* Alabama, S USA
Montgomery *see* Sāhīwāl
Monthey *73 A7* Valais, SW Switzerland
Montilium Adhemari *see* Montélimar
Montluçon *68 C4* Allier, C France
Montoro *70 D4* Andalucía, S Spain
Montpelier *19 G2 state capital* Vermont, NE USA
Montpellier *69 C6* Hérault, S France
Montréal *17 E4 Eng.* Montreal. Québec, SE Canada
Montrose *66 D3* E Scotland, United Kingdom
Montrose *22 C5* Colorado, C USA
Montserrat *33 G3 var.* Emerald Isle. *UK dependent territory* E West Indies
Monywa *114 B3* Sagaing, C Myanmar (Burma)
Monza *74 B2* Lombardia, N Italy
Monze *56 D2* Southern, S Zambia
Monzón *71 F2* Aragón, NE Spain
Moonie *127 D5* Queensland, E Australia
Moon-Sund *see* Väinameri
Moora *125 A6* Western Australia
Moore *27 G1* Oklahoma, C USA
Moore, Lake *125 B6 lake* Western Australia
Moorhead *23 F2* Minnesota, N USA
Moose *16 C3 river* Ontario, S Canada
Moosehead Lake *19 G1 lake* Maine, NE USA
Moosonee *16 C3* Ontario, SE Canada
Mopti *53 E3* Mopti, C Mali
Moquegua *39 E4* Moquegua, SE Peru
Mora *63 C5* Dalarna, C Sweden
Morales *30 C2* Izabal, E Guatemala
Morant Bay *32 B5* E Jamaica
Moratalla *71 E4* Murcia, SE Spain
Morava *77 C5 var.* March. *river* C Europe
Morava *see* Moravia, Czech Republic
Morava *see* Velika Morava, Serbia
Moravia *77 B5 Cz.* Morava, *Ger.* Mähren. *cultural region* E Czech Republic
Moray Firth *66 C3 inlet* N Scotland, United Kingdom
Morea *see* Pelopónnisos
Moreau River *22 D2 river* South Dakota, N USA
Moree *127 D5* New South Wales, SE Australia
Morelia *29 E4* Michoacán de Ocampo, S Mexico
Morena, Sierra *70 C4 mountain range* S Spain
Moreni *86 C5* Dâmbovița, S Romania
Morgan City *20 B3* Louisiana, S USA
Darya-ye Morghab *100 D3 Rus.* Murgab, Murghab, *Turkm.* Murgap, Murgap Deryasy. *river* Afghanistan/Turkmenistan
Darya-ye Morghab *100 D3 Rus.* Murgab, Murghab, *Turkm.* Murgap, Murgap Deryasy. *river* Afghanistan/Turkmenistan
Morghāb, Daryā-ye *see* Murgap
Morioka *108 D4* Iwate, Honshū, C Japan
Morlaix *68 A3* Finistère, NW France
Mormon State *see* Utah
Mornington Abyssal Plain *45 A7 abyssal plain* SE Pacific Ocean
Mornington Island *126 B2 island* Wellesley Islands, Queensland, N Australia
Morocco *48 B3 off.* Kingdom of Morocco, *Ar.* Al Mamlakah. *country* N Africa
Morocco *see* Marrakech
Morocco, Kingdom of *see* Morocco
Morogoro *51 C7* Morogoro, E Tanzania
Moro Gulf *117 E3 gulf* S Philippines
Morón *32 C2* Ciego de Ávila, C Cuba
Mörön *104 D2* Hövsgöl, N Mongolia
Morondava *57 F3* Toliara, W Madagascar
Moroni *57 F2 country capital* Grande Comore, NW Comoros
Morotai, Pulau *117 F3 island* Maluku, E Indonesia
Morotiri *see* Marotiri
Morphou *see* Güzelyurt
Morrinsville *128 D3* Waikato, North Island, New Zealand
Morris *23 F2* Minnesota, N USA
Morris Jesup, Kap *61 E1 headland* N Greenland
Morvan *68 D4 physical region* C France
Moscow *24 C2* Idaho, NW USA
Moscow *see* Moskva
Mosel *73 A5 Fr.* Moselle. *river* W Europe
Mosel *see* Moselle
Moselle *65 E8 Ger.* Mosel. *river* W Europe
Moselle *see* Mosel
Mosgiel *129 B7* Otago, South Island, New Zealand
Moshi *51 C7* Kilimanjaro, NE Tanzania
Mosjøen *62 B4* Nordland, C Norway
Moskovskiy *see* Moskva
Moskva *89 B5 Eng.* Moscow. *country capital* Gorod Moskva, W Russian Federation
Moskva *101 E3 Rus.* Moskovskiy; *prev.* Chubek. SW Tajikistan
Moson and Magyaróvár *see* Mosonmagyaróvár
Mosonmagyaróvár *77 C6 Ger.* Wieselburg-Ungarisch-Altenburg; *prev.* Moson and Magyaróvár, *Ger.* Wieselburg and Ungarisch-Altenburg. Győr-Moson-Sopron, NW Hungary
Mosquito Coast *31 E3 var.* Miskito Coast, *Eng.* Mosquito Coast. *coastal region* E Nicaragua
Mosquito Coast *see* La Mosquitia
Mosquito Gulf *31 F4 Eng.* Mosquito Gulf. *gulf* N Panama
Mosquito Gulf *see* Mosquitos, Golfo de los
Moss *63 B6* Østfold, S Norway
Mossâmedes *see* Namibe
Mosselbaai *56 C5 var.* Mosselbai, *Eng.* Mossel Bay. Western Cape, SW South Africa
Mosselbai/Mossel Bay *see* Mosselbaai
Mossendjo *55 B6* Niari, SW Congo
Mossoró *41 G2* Rio Grande do Norte, NE Brazil
Most *76 A4 Ger.* Brüx. Ústecký Kraj, NW Czech Republic
Mosta *80 B5 var.* Musta. C Malta
Mostaganem *48 D2 var.* Mestghanem. NW Algeria
Mostar *78 C4* Federacija Bosna I Hercegovina, S Bosnia and Herzegovina
Mosty *see* Masty
Mosul *see* Al Mawṣil
Mota del Cuervo *71 E3* Castilla-La Mancha, C Spain
Motagua, Río *30 B2 river* Guatemala/Honduras
Mother of Presidents/Mother of States *see* Virginia
Motril *70 D5* Andalucía, S Spain
Motru *86 B4* Gorj, SW Romania
Motueka *129 C5* Tasman, South Island, New Zealand
Motul *29 H3 var.* Motul de Felipe Carrillo Puerto. Yucatán, SE Mexico
Motul de Felipe Carrillo Puerto *see* Motul
Motyca *see* Modica
Mouanda *see* Moanda
Mouhoun *see* Black Volta
Mouila *55 A6* Ngounié, C Gabon
Moukden *see* Shenyang
Mould Bay *15 E2* Prince Patrick Island, Northwest Territories, N Canada
Moulins *68 C4* Allier, C France
Moulmein *see* Mawlamyine
Moundou *54 B4* Logone-Occidental, SW Chad
Moŭng Roessei *115 D5* Bătdâmbâng, W Cambodia
Moun Hou *see* Black Volta
Mountain Home *20 B1* Arkansas, C USA
Mountain State *see* Montana
Mountain State *see* West Virginia
Mount Cook *129 B6* Canterbury, South Island, New Zealand
Mount Desert Island *19 H2 island* Maine, NE USA
Mount Gambier *127 B7* South Australia
Mount Isa *126 B3* Queensland, C Australia
Mount Magnet *125 B5* Western Australia
Mount Pleasant *23 G4* Iowa, C USA
Mount Pleasant *18 C3* Michigan, N USA
Mount Vernon *18 B5* Illinois, N USA
Mount Vernon *24 B1* Washington, NW USA
Mourdi, Dépression du *54 C2 desert lowland* Chad/Sudan
Mouscron *65 A6 Dut.* Moeskroen. Hainaut, W Belgium
Mouse River *see* Souris River
Moussoro *54 B3* Kanem, W Chad
Moyen-Congo *see* Congo (Republic of)
Mo'ynoq *100 C1 Rus.* Muynak. Qoraqalpog'iston Respublikasi, NW Uzbekistan
Moyobamba *38 B2* San Martín, NW Peru
Moyu *104 B3 var.* Karakax. Xinjiang Uygur Zizhiqu, NW China
Moyynkum, Peski *101 F1 Kaz.* Moyynqum. *desert* S Kazakhstan
Moyynqum *see* Moyynkum, Peski
Mozambika, Lakandranon' i *see* Mozambique Channel
Mozambique *57 E3 off.* Republic of Mozambique; *prev.* People's Republic of Mozambique, Portuguese East Africa. *country* S Africa
Mozambique Basin *see* Natal Basin
Mozambique, Canal de *see* Mozambique Channel
Mozambique Channel *57 E3 Fr.* Canal de Mozambique, *Mal.* Lakandranon' i Mozambika. *strait* W Indian Ocean
Mozambique, People's Republic of *see* Mozambique
Mozambique Plateau *47 D7 var.* Mozambique Rise. *undersea plateau* SW Indian Ocean
Mozambique, Republic of *see* Mozambique
Mozambique Rise *see* Mozambique Plateau
Mozyr' *see* Mazyr
Mpama *55 B6 river* C Congo
Mpika *56 D2* Northern, NE Zambia
Mqinvartsveri *see* Kazbek
Mrągowo *76 D2 Ger.* Sensburg. Warmińsko-Mazurskie, NE Poland
Mtkvari *see* Kura
Mtwara *51 D8* Mtwara, SE Tanzania
Mualo *see* Messalo, Rio
Muang Chiang Rai *see* Chiang Rai
Muang Kalasin *see* Kalasin
Muang Khammouan *see* Thakhèk
Muang Không *115 D5* Champasak, S Laos
Muang Khôngxédôn *115 D5 var.* Khong Sedone. Salavan, S Laos
Muang Khon Kaen *see* Khon Kaen
Muang Lampang *see* Lampang
Muang Loei *see* Loei
Muang Lom Sak *see* Lom Sak
Muang Nakhon Sawan *see* Nakhon Sawan
Muang Namo *114 C3* Oudômxai, N Laos
Muang Nan *see* Nan
Muang Phalan *114 D4 var.* Muang Phalane. Savannakhét, S Laos
Muang Phalane *see* Muang Phalan
Muang Phayao *see* Phayao
Muang Phitsanulok *see* Phitsanulok
Muang Phrae *see* Phrae
Muang Roi Et *see* Roi Et
Muang Sakon Nakhon *see* Sakon Nakhon
Muang Samut Prakan *see* Samut Prakan
Muang Sing *114 C3* Louang Namtha, N Laos
Muang Ubon *see* Ubon Ratchathani
Muang Xaignabouri *see* Xaignabouli
Muar *116 B3 var.* Bandar Maharani. Johor, Peninsular Malaysia
Mucojo *57 F2* Cabo Delgado, N Mozambique
Mudanjiang *107 E3 var.* Mu-tan-chiang. Heilongjiang, NE China
Mudon *115 B5* Mon State, S Myanmar (Burma)
Muenchen *see* München
Muenster *see* Münster
Mufulira *56 D2* Copperbelt, C Zambia
Mughla *see* Muğla
Muğla *94 A4 var.* Mughla. Muğla, SW Turkey
Mūḩ, Sabkhat al *96 C3 lake* C Syria
Muhu Väin *see* Väinameri
Muisne *38 A1* Esmeraldas, NW Ecuador
Mukacheve *86 B3 Hung.* Munkács, *Rus.* Mukachevo. Zakarpats'ka Oblast', W Ukraine
Mukachevo *see* Mukacheve
Mukalla *see* Al Mukallā
Mukden *see* Shenyang
Mula *71 E4* Murcia, SE Spain
Mulakatholhu *110 B4 var.* Meemu Atoll, Mulaku Atoll. *atoll* C Maldives
Mulaku Atoll *see* Mulakatholhu
Muleshoe *27 E2* Texas, SW USA
Mulhacén *71 E5 var.* Cerro de Mulhacén. *mountain* S Spain
Mulhacén, Cerro de *see* Mulhacén
Mülhausen *see* Mulhouse
Mülheim *73 A6 var.* Mulheim an der Ruhr. Nordrhein-Westfalen, W Germany
Mulheim an der Ruhr *see* Mülheim
Mulhouse *68 E4 Ger.* Mülhausen. Haut-Rhin, NE France
Müller-gerbergte *see* Muller, Pegunungan
Muller, Pegunungan *116 D4 Dut.* Müller-gerbergte. *mountain range* Borneo, C Indonesia
Mull, Isle of *66 B4 island* W Scotland, United Kingdom
Mulongo *55 D7* Katanga, SE Dem. Rep. Congo
Multān *112 C2* Punjab, E Pakistan
Mumbai *112 C5 prev.* Bombay. *state capital* Mahārāshtra, W India
Munamägi *see* Suur Munamägi
Münchberg *73 C5* Bayern, E Germany
München *73 C6 var.* Muenchen, *Eng.* Munich, *It.* Monaco. Bayern, SE Germany
Muncie *18 C4* Indiana, N USA
Mungbere *55 E5* Orientale, NE Dem. Rep. Congo
Mu Nggava *see* Rennell
Munich *see* München
Munkács *see* Mukacheve
Münster *72 A4 var.* Muenster, Münster in Westfalen. Nordrhein-Westfalen, W Germany
Munster *67 A6 Ir.* Cúige Mumhan. *cultural region* S Ireland
Münster in Westfalen *see* Münster
Muong Xiang Ngeun *114 C4 var.* Xieng Ngeun. Louangphabang, N Laos
Muonio *62 D3* Lappi, N Finland
Muonioälv/Muoniojoki *see* Muonionjoki
Muonionjoki *62 D3 var.* Muoniojoki, *Swe.* Muonioälv. *river* Finland/Sweden
Muqāṭ *97 C5* Al Mafraq, E Jordan
Muqdisho *51 D6 Eng.* Mogadishu, *It.* Mogadiscio. *country capital* Banaadir, S Somalia
Mur *73 E7 SCr.* Mura. *river* C Europe
Mura *see* Mur
Muradiye *95 F3* Van, E Turkey
Murapara *see* Murupara
Murata *74 E2* S San Marino
Murchison River *125 A5 river* Western Australia
Murcia *71 F4* Murcia, SE Spain
Murcia *71 E4 autonomous community* SE Spain
Mureș *86 A4 river* Hungary/Romania
Murfreesboro *20 D1* Tennessee, S USA
Murgab *see* Morghāb, Daryā-ye/Murgap/Murghob
Murgab *see* Morghāb, Daryā-ye/Murgap/Murghob
Murgab *see* Murghob
Murgap *100 D3* Mary Welaýaty, S Turkmenistan
Murgap *100 D3 var.* Deryasy Murgap, Murghab, *Pash.* Daryā-ye Morghāb, *Rus.* Murgab. *river* Afghanistan/Turkmenistan
Murgap *see* Morghāb, Daryā-ye
Murgap *see* Morghāb, Daryā-ye
Murgap Deryasy *see* Morghāb, Daryā-ye
Murgap Deryasy *see* Morghāb, Daryā-ye
Murghab *see* Morghāb, Daryā-ye
Murghab *see* Morghāb, Daryā-ye
Murghob *101 F3 Rus.* Murgab. SE Tajikistan
Murgon *127 E5* Queensland, E Australia
Mūrītānīyah *see* Mauritania
Müritz *72 C3 var.* Müritzee. *lake* NE Germany
Müritzee *see* Müritz
Murmansk *88 C2* Murmanskaya Oblast', NW Russian Federation
Murmashi *88 C2* Murmanskaya Oblast', NW Russian Federation
Murom *89 B5* Vladimirskaya Oblast', W Russian Federation
Muroran *108 D3* Hokkaidō, NE Japan
Muros *70 B1* Galicia, NW Spain
Murray Fracture Zone *131 E2 fracture zone* NE Pacific Ocean
Murray Range *see* Murray Ridge
Murray Ridge *90 C5 var.* Murray Range. *undersea ridge* N Arabian Sea
Murray River *127 B6 river* SE Australia
Murrumbidgee River *127 C6 river* New South Wales, SE Australia
Murska Sobota *73 E7 Ger.* Olsnitz. NE Slovenia
Murupara *128 E3 var.* Murapara. Bay of Plenty, North Island, New Zealand
Murviedro *see* Sagunto
Murwāra *113 E4* Madhya Pradesh, N India
Murwillumbah *127 E5* New South Wales, SE Australia
Murzuq, Edeyin *see* Murzuq, Idhān
Murzuq, Idhan *49 F4 var.* Edeyin Murzuq. *desert* SW Libya
Mürzzuschlag *73 E7* Steiermark, E Austria
Muş *95 F3 var.* Mush. Muş, E Turkey
Musa, Gebel *50 C2 var.* Gebel Mûsa. *mountain* NE Egypt
Mûsa, Gebel *see* Mūsá, Jabal
Musala *82 B3 mountain* W Bulgaria
Muscat *see* Masqaṭ
Muscat and Oman *see* Oman
Muscatine *23 G3* Iowa, C USA
Musgrave Ranges *125 D5 mountain range* South Australia
Musina *56 D3 prev.* Messina. Limpopo, NE South Africa
Muskegon *18 C3* Michigan, N USA
Muskogean *see* Tallahassee
Muskogee *27 G1* Oklahoma, C USA
Musoma *51 C6* Mara, N Tanzania
Musta *see* Mosta
Mustafa-Pasha *see* Svilengrad
Musters, Lago *43 B6 lake* S Argentina
Muswellbrook *127 D6* New South Wales, SE Australia
Mut *94 C4* İçel, S Turkey
Mu-tan-chiang *see* Mudanjiang
Mutare *56 D3 var.* Mutari; *prev.* Umtali. Manicaland, E Zimbabwe
Mutari *see* Mutare
Mutina *see* Modena
Mutsu-wan *108 D3 bay* N Japan
Muttonbird Islands *129 A8 island group* SW New Zealand
Mu Us Shadi *105 E3 var.* Ordos Desert; *prev.* Mu Us Shamo. *desert* N China
Mu Us Shamo *see* Mu Us Shadi
Muy Muy *30 D3* Matagalpa, C Nicaragua
Muynak *see* Mo'ynoq
Mužlja *78 D3 Hung.* Felsőmuzslya; *prev.* Gornja Mužlja. Vojvodina, N Serbia
Mwali *57 F2 var.* Moili, *Fr.* Mohéli. *island* S Comoros
Mwanza *51 B6* Mwanza, NW Tanzania
Mweka *55 C6* Kasai-Occidental, C Dem. Rep. Congo
Mwene-Ditu *55 D7* Kasai-Oriental, S Dem. Rep. Congo
Mweru, Lake *55 D7 var.* Lac Moero. *lake* Dem. Rep. Congo/Zambia
Myadel' *see* Myadzyel
Myadzyel *85 C5 Pol.* Miadzioł Nowy, *Rus.* Myadel'. Minskaya Voblasts', N Belarus
Myanaung *114 B4* Ayeyarwady, SW Myanmar (Burma)
Myaungmya *114 A4* Ayeyarwady, SW Myanmar (Burma)
Myaydo *see* Aunglan
Myeik *115 B6 var.* Mergui. Tanintharyi, S Myanmar (Burma)
Myerkulavichy *85 D7 Rus.* Merkulovichi. Homyel'skaya Voblasts', SE Belarus
Myingyan *114 B3* Mandalay, C Myanmar (Burma)
Myitkyina *114 B2* Kachin State, N Myanmar (Burma)
Mykolayiv *87 E4 Rus.* Nikolayev. Mykolayivs'ka Oblast', S Ukraine
Mykonos *83 D6 var.* Míkonos. *island* Kykládes, Greece, Aegean Sea
Myrhorod *87 F2 Rus.* Mirgorod. Poltavs'ka Oblast', NE Ukraine
Mýrina *82 D4 var.* Mírina. Límnos, SE Greece
Myrtle Beach *21 F2* South Carolina, SE USA
Mýrtos *83 D8* Kríti, Greece, E Mediterranean Sea
Myrtoum Mare *see* Mirtóo Pélagos
Myślibórz *76 B3* Zachodnio-pomorskie, NW Poland
Mysore *110 C2 var.* Maisur. Karnātaka, W India
Mysore *see* Karnātaka
My Tho *115 E6 var.* Mi Tho. Tiền Giang, S Vietnam
Mytilene *see* Mytilíni
Mytilíni *83 D5 var.* Mitilíni; *anc.* Mytilene. Lésvos, E Greece
Mzuzu *57 E2* Northern, N Malawi

N

Naberezhnyye Chelny *89 D5 prev.* Brezhnev. Respublika Tatarstan, W Russian Federation
Nablus *97 A6 var.* Nābulus, *Heb.* Shekhem; *anc.* Neapolis, *Bibl.* Shechem. N West Bank
Nābulus *see* Nablus
Nacala *57 F2* Nampula, NE Mozambique
Na-Ch'ii *see* Nagqu
Nada *see* Danzhou
Nadi *123 E4 prev.* Nandi. Viti Levu, W Fiji
Nadur *80 A5* Gozo, N Malta
Nadvirna *86 C3 Pol.* Nadwórna, *Rus.* Nadvornaya. Ivano-Frankivs'ka Oblast', W Ukraine
Nadvoitsy *88 B3* Respublika Kareliya, NW Russian Federation
Nadvornaya/Nadwórna *see* Nadvirna
Nadym *92 C3* Yamalo-Nenetskiy Avtonomnyy Okrug, N Russian Federation
Náfpaktos *83 B5 var.* Návpaktos. Dytikí Ellás, C Greece
Náfplio *83 B6 prev.* Návplion. Pelopónnisos, S Greece
Naga *117 E2 off.* Naga City; *prev.* Nueva Caceres. Luzon, N Philippines
Naga City *see* Naga
Nagano *109 C5* Nagano, Honshū, S Japan
Nagaoka *109 D5* Niigata, Honshū, C Japan
Nagara Pathom *see* Nakhon Pathom
Nagara Sridharmaraj *see* Nakhon Si Thammarat
Nagara Svarga *see* Nakhon Sawan
Nagasaki *109 A7* Nagasaki, Kyūshū, SW Japan
Nagato *109 A7* Yamaguchi, Honshū, SW Japan
Nāgercoil *110 C3* Tamil Nādu, SE India
Nagorno-Karabakh *95 G3 var.* Nagorno-Karabakhskaya Avtonomnaya Oblast, *Arm.* Lerrnayin Gharabakh, *Az.* Dağliq Quarabağ, *Rus.* Nagornyy Karabakh. *former autonomous region* SW Azerbaijan
Nagorno- Karabakhskaya Avtonomnaya Oblast *see* Nagorno-Karabakh
Nagornyy Karabakh *see* Nagorno-Karabakh
Nagoya *109 C6* Aichi, Honshū, SW Japan
Nāgpur *112 D4* Mahārāshtra, C India
Nagqu *104 C5 Chin.* Na-Ch'ii; *prev.* Hei-ho. Xizang Zizhiqu, W China
Nagybánya *see* Baia Mare
Nagybecskerek *see* Zrenjanin
Nagydisznód *see* Cisnădie
Nagyenyed *see* Aiud
Nagykálló *77 E6* Szabolcs-Szatmár-Bereg, E Hungary
Nagykanizsa *77 C7 Ger.* Grosskanizsa. Zala, SW Hungary
Nagykároly *see* Carei
Nagykikinda *see* Kikinda
Nagykőrös *77 D7* Pest, C Hungary
Nagymihály *see* Michalovce
Nagysurány *see* Šurany
Nagyszalonta *see* Salonta
Nagyszeben *see* Sibiu
Nagyszentmiklós *see* Sânnicolau Mare
Nagyszöllös *see* Vynohradiv
Nagyszombat *see* Trnava
Nagytapolcsány *see* Topoľčany
Nagyvárad *see* Oradea

Naha – Nizhyn

Naha 108 A3 Okinawa, Okinawa, SW Japan
Nahariya 97 A5 prev. Nahariyya. Northern, N Israel
Nahariyya see Nahariya
Nahuel Huapí, Lago 43 B5 lake W Argentina
Nain 17 F2 Newfoundland and Labrador, NE Canada
Nā'īn 98 D3 Eşfahān, C Iran
Nairobi 47 E5 country capital Nairobi Area, S Kenya
Nairobi 51 C6 Nairobi Area, S Kenya
Naissus see Niš
Najaf see An Najaf
Najima see Fukuoka
Najin 107 E3 NE North Korea
Najrān 99 B6 var. Abā as Su'ūd. Najrān, S Saudi Arabia
Nakambé see White Volta
Nakamura 109 B7 var. Shimanto. Kôchi, Shikoku, SW Japan
Nakatsugawa 109 C6 var. Nakatugawa. Gifu, Honshū, SW Japan
Nakatugawa see Nakatsugawa
Nakhichevan' see Naxçıvan
Nakhodka 93 G5 Primorskiy Kray, SE Russian Federation
Nakhon Pathom 115 C5 var. Nagara Pathom, Nakorn Pathom. Nakhon Pathom, W Thailand
Nakhon Ratchasima 115 C5 var. Khorat, Korat. Nakhon Ratchasima, E Thailand
Nakhon Sawan 115 C5 var. Muang Nakhon Sawan, Nagara Svarga. Nakhon Sawan, W Thailand
Nakhon Si Thammarat 115 C7 var. Nagara Sridharmaraj, Nakhon Sithamnaraj. Nakhon Si Thammarat, SW Thailand
Nakhon Sithamnaraj see Nakhon Si Thammarat
Nakorn Pathom see Nakhon Pathom
Nakuru 51 C6 Rift Valley, SW Kenya
Nal'chik 89 B8 Kabardino-Balkarskaya Respublika, SW Russian Federation
Nālūt 49 F2 NW Libya
Namakan Lake 18 A1 lake Canada/USA
Namangan 101 F2 Namangan Viloyati, E Uzbekistan
Nambala 56 D2 Central, C Zambia
Nam Co 104 C5 lake W China
Nam Định 114 D3 Nam Ha, N Vietnam
Namib Desert 56 B3 desert W Namibia
Namibe 56 A2 Port. Moçâmedes, Mossâmedes. Namibe, SW Angola
Namibia 56 B3 off. Republic of Namibia, var. South West Africa, Afr. Suidwes-Afrika, Ger. Deutsch-Südwestafrika; prev. German Southwest Africa, South-West Africa. country S Africa
Namibia, Republic of see Namibia
Namnetes see Nantes
Namo see Namu Atoll
Nam Ou 114 C3 river N Laos
Nampa 24 D3 Idaho, NW USA
Nampula 57 E2 Nampula, NE Mozambique
Namsos 62 B4 Nord-Trøndelag, C Norway
Nam Tha 114 C4 river N Laos
Namu Atoll 122 D2 var. Namo. atoll Ralik Chain, C Marshall Islands
Namur 65 C6 Dut. Namen. Namur, SE Belgium
Namyit Island 106 C8 island S Spratly Islands
Nan 114 C4 var. Muang Nan. Nan, NW Thailand
Nanaimo 14 D5 Vancouver Island, British Columbia, SW Canada
Nanchang 106 C5 var. Nan-ch'ang, Nanch'ang-hsien. province capital Jiangxi, S China
Nan-ch'ang see Nanchang
Nanch'ang-hsien see Nanchang
Nan-ching see Nanjing
Nancy 68 D3 Meurthe-et-Moselle, NE France
Nandaime 30 D3 Granada, SW Nicaragua
Nānded 112 D5 Mahārāshtra, C India
Nandi see Nadi
Nándorhgy see Oţelu Roşu
Nandyāl 110 C1 Andhra Pradesh, E India
Nan Hai see South China Sea
Naniwa see Ōsaka
Nanjing 106 D5 var. Nan-ching, Nanking; prev. Chianning, Chian-ning, Kiang-ning, Jiangsu. province capital Jiangsu, E China
Nanking see Nanjing
Nanning 106 B6 var. Nan-ning; prev. Yung-ning. Guangxi Zhuangzu Zizhiqu, S China
Nan-ning see Nanning
Nanortalik 60 C5 Kitaa, S Greenland
Nanpan Jiang 114 D2 river S China
Nanping 106 D6 var. Nan-p'ing; prev. Yenping. Fujian, SE China
Nan-p'ing see Nanping
Nansei Syotō Trench see Ryukyu Trench
Nansen Basin 133 C4 undersea basin Arctic Ocean
Nansen Cordillera 133 B3 var. Arctic Mid Oceanic Ridge, Nansen Ridge. seamount range Arctic Ocean
Nansen Ridge see Nansen Cordillera
Nansha Qundao see Spratly Islands
Nanterre 68 D1 Hauts-de-Seine, N France
Nantes 68 B4 Bret. Naoned; anc. Condivincum, Namnetes. Loire-Atlantique, NW France
Nantucket Island 19 G3 island Massachusetts, NE USA
Nanumaga 123 E3 var. Nanumanga. atoll NW Tuvalu
Nanumanga see Nanumaga
Nanumea Atoll 123 E3 atoll NW Tuvalu
Nanyang 106 C5 var. Nan-yang. Henan, C China
Nan-yang see Nanyang
Naoned see Nantes
Napa 25 B6 California, W USA
Napier 128 E4 Hawke's Bay, North Island, New Zealand
Naples 21 E5 Florida, SE USA
Naples see Napoli
Napo 34 A3 province NE Ecuador
Napoléon-Vendée see la Roche-sur-Yon
Napoli 75 C5 Eng. Naples, Ger. Neapel; anc. Neapolis. Campania, S Italy
Napo, Río 38 C1 river Ecuador/Peru
Naracoorte 127 B7 South Australia
Naradhivas see Narathiwat
Narathiwat 115 C7 var. Naradhivas. Narathiwat, SW Thailand
Narbada see Narmada
Narbo Martius see Narbonne
Narbonne 69 C6 anc. Narbo Martius. Aude, S France
Narborough Island see Fernandina, Isla
Nares Abyssal Plain see Nares Plain
Nares Plain 13 E6 var. Nares Abyssal Plain. abyssal plain NW Atlantic Ocean
Nares Stræde see Nares Strait
Nares Strait 60 D1 Dan. Nares Stræde. strait Canada/Greenland
Narew 76 E3 river E Poland
Narmada 102 B3 var. Narbada. river C India
Narova see Narva
Narovlya see Narowlya
Narowlya 85 C8 Rus. Narovlya. Homyel'skaya Voblasts', SE Belarus
Närpes 63 D5 Fin. Närpiö. Länsi-Suomi, W Finland
Närpiö see Närpes
Narrabri 127 D6 New South Wales, SE Australia
Narrogin 125 B6 Western Australia
Narva 84 E2 Ida-Virumaa, NE Estonia
Narva 84 E2 prev. Narova. river Estonia/Russian Federation
Narva Bay 84 E2 Est. Narva Laht, Ger. Narwa-Bucht, Rus. Narvskiy Zaliv. bay Estonia/Russian Federation
Narva Laht see Narva Bay
Narva Reservoir 84 E2 Est. Narva Veehoidla, Rus. Narvskoye Vodokhranilishche. reservoir Estonia/Russian Federation
Narva Veehoidla see Narva Reservoir
Narvik 62 C3 Nordland, C Norway
Narvskiy Zaliv see Narva Bay
Narvskoye Vodokhranilishche see Narva Reservoir
Narwa-Bucht see Narva Bay
Nar'yan-Mar 88 D3 prev. Beloshchel'ye, Dzerzhinskiy. Nenetskiy Avtonomnyy Okrug, NW Russian Federation
Naryn 101 G2 Narynskaya Oblast', C Kyrgyzstan
Năsăud 86 B3 Ger. Nussdorf, Hung. Naszód. Bistriţa-Năsăud, N Romania
Nase see Naze
Nāshik 112 C5 prev. Nāsik. Mahārāshtra, W India
Nashua 19 G3 New Hampshire, NE USA
Nashville 20 C1 state capital Tennessee, S USA
Näsijärvi 63 D5 lake SW Finland
Nāsik see Nāshik
Nasir, Buhayrat/Nâşir,Buḩeiret see Nasser, Lake
Nāsiri see Ahvāz
Nasiriya see An Nāşirīyah
Nassau 32 C1 country capital New Providence, N Bahamas
Nasser, Lake 50 B3 var. Buhayrat Nasir, Buḩayrat Nāşir, Buheiret Nâsir. lake Egypt/Sudan
Naszód see Năsăud
Nata 56 C3 Central, NE Botswana
Natal 41 G2 state capital Rio Grande do Norte, E Brazil
Natal Basin 119 A6 var. Mozambique Basin. undersea basin W Indian Ocean
Natanya see Netanya
Natchez 20 B3 Mississippi, S USA
Natchitoches 20 A2 Louisiana, S USA
Nathanya see Netanya
Natitingou 53 F4 NW Benin
Natsrat see Natzrat
Natuna Islands see Natuna, Kepulauan
Natuna, Kepulauan 102 D4 var. Natuna Islands. island group W Indonesia
Naturaliste Plateau 119 E6 undersea plateau E Indian Ocean
Natzrat 97 A5 var. Natsrat, Ar. En Nazira, Eng. Nazareth; prev. Nazerat. Northern, N Israel
Naugard see Nowogard
Naujamiestis 84 C4 Panevėžys, C Lithuania
Nauru 122 D2 off. Republic of Nauru; prev. Pleasant Island. country W Pacific Ocean
Nauru, Republic of see Nauru
Nauta 38 C2 Loreto, N Peru
Navahrudak 85 C6 Pol. Nowogródek, Rus. Novogrudok. Hrodzyenskaya Voblasts', W Belarus
Navanagar see Jāmnagar
Navapolatsk 85 D5 Rus. Novopolotsk. Vitsyebskaya Voblasts', N Belarus
Navarra 71 E2 Eng./Fr. Navarre. autonomous community N Spain
Navarre see Navarra
Navassa Island 32 C3 US unincorporated territory C West Indies
Navoi see Navoiy
Navoiy 101 E2 Rus. Navoi. Navoiy Viloyati, C Uzbekistan
Navojoa 28 C2 Sonora, NW Mexico
Navolat see Navolato
Navolato 28 C3 var. Navolat. Sinaloa, C Mexico
Návpaktos see Náfpaktos
Návplion see Náfplio
Nawabashah see Nawābshāh
Nawābshāh 112 B3 var. Nawabashah. Sind, S Pakistan
Naxçıvan 95 G3 Rus. Nakhichevan'. SW Azerbaijan
Náxos 83 D6 var. Naxos. Náxos, Kykládes, Greece, Aegean Sea
Náxos 83 D6 island Kykládes, Greece, Aegean Sea
Nayoro 108 D2 Hokkaidō, NE Japan
Nay Pyi Taw 114 B4 country capital Mandalay, C Myanmar (Burma)
Nazareth see Natzrat
Nazca 38 D4 Ica, S Peru
Nazca Ridge 35 A5 undersea ridge E Pacific Ocean
Naze 108 B3 var. Nase. Kagoshima, Amami-ōshima, SW Japan
Nazerat see Natzrat
Nazilli 94 A4 Aydın, SW Turkey
Nazrēt 51 C5 var. Adama, Hadama. Oromīya, C Ethiopia
N'Dalatando 56 B1 Port. Salazar, Vila Salazar. Cuanza Norte, NW Angola
Ndélé 54 C4 Bamingui-Bangoran, N Central African Republic
Ndendé 55 B6 Ngounié, S Gabon
Ndindi 55 A6 Nyanga, S Gabon
Ndjamena 54 B3 var. N'Djamena; prev. Fort-Lamy. country capital Chari-Baguirmi, W Chad
N'Djamena see Ndjamena
Ndjolé 55 A5 Moyen-Ogooué, W Gabon
Ndola 56 D2 Copperbelt, C Zambia
Ndzouani see Anjouan
Neagh, Lough 67 B5 lake E Northern Ireland, United Kingdom
Néa Moudania 82 C4 var. Néa Moudhaniá. Kentrikí Makedonía, N Greece
Néa Moudhaniá see Néa Moudanía
Neapel see Napoli
Neápoli 82 B4 prev. Neápolis. Dytikí Makedonía, N Greece
Neápoli 83 D8 Kríti, Greece, E Mediterranean Sea
Neápoli 83 C7 Pelopónnisos, S Greece
Neápolis see Neápoli, Greece
Neapolis see Napoli, Italy
Neapolis see Nablus, West Bank
Near Islands 14 A2 island group Aleutian Islands, Alaska, USA
Néa Zíchni 82 C3 var. Néa Zíkhni; prev. Néa Zíkhna. Kentrikí Makedonía, NE Greece
Néa Zíkhna/Néa Zíkhni see Néa Zíchni
Nebaj 30 B2 Quiché, W Guatemala
Nebitdag see Balkanabat
Neblina, Pico da 40 C1 mountain NW Brazil
Nebraska 22 D4 off. State of Nebraska, also known as Blackwater State, Cornhusker State, Tree Planters State. state C USA
Nebraska City 23 F4 Nebraska, C USA
Neches River 27 H3 river Texas, SW USA
Neckar 73 B6 river SW Germany
Necochea 43 D5 Buenos Aires, E Argentina
Nederland see Netherlands
Neder Rijn 64 D4 Eng. Lower Rhine. river C Netherlands
Nederweert 65 D5 Limburg, SE Netherlands
Neede 64 E3 Gelderland, E Netherlands
Neerpelt 65 D5 Limburg, NE Belgium
Neftekamsk 89 D5 Respublika Bashkortostan, W Russian Federation
Neftezavodsk see Seýdi
Negara Brunei Darussalam see Brunei
Negēlē 51 D5 var. Negelli, It. Neghelli. Oromīya, C Ethiopia
Negelli see Negēlē
Negev 97 A7 Eng. Negev. desert S Israel
Negev see HaNegev
Neghelli see Negēlē
Negomane 57 E2 var. Negomano. Cabo Delgado, N Mozambique
Negomano see Negomane
Negombo 110 C3 Western Province, SW Sri Lanka
Negotin 78 E4 Serbia, E Serbia
Negra, Punta 38 A3 headland NW Peru
Negreşti see Negreşti-Oaş
Negreşti-Oaş 86 B3 Hung. Avasfelsőfalu; prev. Negreşti. Satu Mare, NE Romania
Negro, Río 43 C5 river E Argentina
Negro, Río 40 D1 river N South America
Negro, Río 42 D4 river Brazil/Uruguay
Negros 117 E2 island C Philippines
Nehbandān 98 E3 Khorāsān, E Iran
Neijiang 106 B5 Sichuan, C China
Neiva 36 B3 Huila, S Colombia
Nellore 110 D2 Andhra Pradesh, E India
Nelson 129 C5 Nelson, South Island, New Zealand
Nelson 15 G4 river Manitoba, C Canada
Néma 52 D3 Hodh ech Chargui, SE Mauritania
Neman 84 B4 Ger. Ragnit. Kaliningradskaya Oblast', W Russian Federation
Neman 84 A4 Bel. Nyoman, Ger. Memel, Lith. Nemunas, Pol. Niemen. river NE Europe
Nemausus see Nîmes
Neméa 83 B6 Pelopónnisos, S Greece
Nemetocenna see Arras
Nemours 68 C3 Seine-et-Marne, N France
Nemunas see Neman
Nemuro 108 E2 Hokkaidō, NE Japan
Neochóri 83 B5 Dytikí Ellás, C Greece
Nepal 113 E3 off. Nepal. country S Asia
Nepal see Nepal
Nereta 84 C4 Aizkraukle, S Latvia
Neretva 78 C4 river Bosnia and Herzegovina/Croatia
Neris 85 C5 Bel. Viliya, Pol. Wilia; prev. Pol. Wilja. river Belarus/Lithuania
Neris see Viliya
Nerva 70 C4 Andalucía, S Spain
Neryungri 93 F4 Respublika Sakha (Yakutiya), NE Russian Federation
Neskaupstadhur 61 E5 Austurland, E Iceland
Ness, Loch 66 C3 lake N Scotland, United Kingdom
Nesterov see Zhovkva
Néstos 82 C3 Bul. Mesta, Turk. Kara Su. river Bulgaria/Greece
Nesvizh see Nyasvizh
Netanya 97 A6 var. Natanya, Nathanya. Central, C Israel
Netherlands 64 C3 off. Kingdom of the Netherlands, var. Holland, Dut. Koninkrijk der Nederlanden, Nederland. country NW Europe
Netherlands Antilles 33 E5 prev. Dutch West Indies. Dutch autonomous region S Caribbean Sea
Netherlands East Indies see Indonesia
Netherlands Guiana see Suriname
Netherlands, Kingdom of the see Netherlands
Netherlands New Guinea see Papua
Nettilling Lake 15 G3 lake Baffin Island, Nunavut, N Canada
Netze see Noteć
Neu Amerika see Puławy
Neubrandenburg 72 D3 Mecklenburg-Vorpommern, NE Germany
Neuchâtel 73 A7 Ger. Neuenburg. Neuchâtel, W Switzerland
Neuchâtel, Lac de 73 A7 Ger. Neuenburger See. lake W Switzerland
Neuenburger See see Neuchâtel, Lac de
Neufchâteau 65 D8 Luxembourg, SE Belgium
Neugradisk see Nova Gradiška
Neuhof see Zgierz
Neukuhren see Pionerskiy
Neumarkt see Târgu Secuiesc, Covasna, Romania
Neumarkt see Târgu Mureş
Neumoldowa see Moldova Nouă
Neumünster 72 B2 Schleswig-Holstein, N Germany
Neunkirchen 73 A5 Saarland, SW Germany
Neuquén 43 B5 Neuquén, SE Argentina
Neuruppin 72 C3 Brandenburg, NE Germany
Neusalz an der Oder see Nowa Sól
Neu Sandec see Nowy Sącz
Neusatz see Novi Sad
Neusiedler See 73 E6 Hung. Fertő. lake Austria/Hungary
Neusohl see Banská Bystrica
Neustadt see Baia Mare, Maramureş, Romania
Neustadt an der Haardt see Neustadt an der Weinstrasse
Neustadt an der Weinstrasse 73 B5 prev. Neustadt an der Haardt, hist. Niewenstat; anc. Nova Civitas. Rheinland-Pfalz, SW Germany
Neustadtl see Novo mesto
Neustettin see Szczecinek
Neustrelitz 72 D3 Mecklenburg-Vorpommern, NE Germany
Neutra see Nitra
Neu-Ulm 73 B6 Bayern, S Germany
Neuwied 73 A5 Rheinland-Pfalz, W Germany
Neuzen see Terneuzen
Nevada 25 C5 off. State of Nevada, also known as Battle Born State, Sagebrush State, Silver State. state W USA
Nevers 68 C4 anc. Noviodunum. Nièvre, C France
Neves 54 E2 São Tomé, S Sao Tome and Principe, Africa
Nevinnomyssk 89 B7 Stavropol'skiy Kray, SW Russian Federation
Nevşehir 94 C3 var. Nevshehr. Nevşehir, C Turkey
Newala 51 C8 Mtwara, SE Tanzania
New Albany 18 C5 Indiana, N USA
New Amsterdam 37 G3 E Guyana
Newark 19 F4 New Jersey, NE USA
New Bedford 19 G3 Massachusetts, NE USA
Newberg 24 B3 Oregon, NW USA
New Bern 21 F1 North Carolina, SE USA
New Braunfels 27 G4 Texas, SW USA
Newbridge 67 B6 Ir. An Droichead Nua. Kildare, C Ireland
New Britain 122 B3 island E Papua New Guinea
New Brunswick 17 E4 Fr. Nouveau-Brunswick. province SE Canada
New Caledonia 122 D4 var. Kanaky, Fr. Nouvelle-Calédonie. French overseas territory SW Pacific Ocean
New Caledonia 122 C5 island SW Pacific Ocean
New Caledonia Basin 120 C4 undersea basin W Pacific Ocean
Newcastle 127 D6 New South Wales, SE Australia
Newcastle see Newcastle upon Tyne
Newcastle upon Tyne 66 D4 var. Newcastle, hist. Monkchester, Lat. Pons Aelii. NE England, United Kingdom
New Delhi 112 D3 country capital Delhi, N India
New England of the West see Minnesota
Newfoundland 17 G3 Fr. Terre-Neuve. island Newfoundland and Labrador, SE Canada
Newfoundland and Labrador 17 F2 Fr. Terre Neuve. province E Canada
Newfoundland Basin 44 B3 undersea feature NW Atlantic Ocean
New Georgia Islands 122 C3 island group NW Solomon Islands
New Glasgow 17 F4 Nova Scotia, SE Canada
New Goa see Panaji
New Guinea 122 A3 Dut. Nieuw Guinea, Ind. Irian. island Indonesia/Papua New Guinea
New Hampshire 19 F2 off. State of New Hampshire, also known as Granite State. state NE USA
New Haven 19 G3 Connecticut, NE USA
New Hebrides see Vanuatu
New Iberia 20 B3 Louisiana, S USA
New Ireland 122 C3 island NE Papua New Guinea
New Jersey 19 F4 off. State of New Jersey, also known as The Garden State. state NE USA
Newman 124 B4 Western Australia
Newmarket 67 E6 E England, United Kingdom
New Mexico 26 C2 off. State of New Mexico, also known as Land of Enchantment, Sunshine State. state SW USA
New Orleans 20 B3 Louisiana, S USA
New Plymouth 128 C4 Taranaki, North Island, New Zealand
Newport 67 D7 S England, United Kingdom
Newport 67 C7 SE Wales, United Kingdom
Newport 18 C4 Kentucky, S USA
Newport 19 G2 Vermont, NE USA
Newport News 19 F5 Virginia, NE USA
New Providence 32 C1 island N Bahamas
Newquay 67 C7 SW England, United Kingdom
Newry 67 B5 Ir. An tIúr. SE Northern Ireland, United Kingdom
New Sarum see Salisbury
New Siberian Islands 93 F1 Eng. New Siberian Islands. island group N Russian Federation
New Siberian Islands see Novosibirskiye Ostrova
New South Wales 127 C6 state SE Australia
Newton 23 G3 Iowa, C USA
Newton 23 F5 Kansas, C USA
Newtownabbey 67 B5 Ir. Baile na Mainistreach. E Northern Ireland, United Kingdom
New Ulm 23 F2 Minnesota, N USA
New York 19 F4 New York, NE USA
New York 19 F3 state NE USA
New Zealand 128 A4 country SW Pacific Ocean
Neyveli 110 C2 Tamil Nādu, SE India
Nezhin see Nizhyn
Ngangze Co 104 B5 lake W China
Ngaoundéré 54 B4 var. N'Gaoundéré. Adamaoua, N Cameroon
N'Gaoundéré see Ngaoundéré
Ngazidja 57 F2 Fr. Grande-Comore. island NW Comoros
N'Giva 56 B3 var. Ondjiva, Port. Vila Pereira de Eça. Cunene, S Angola
Ngo 55 B6 Plateaux, SE Congo
Ngoko 55 B5 river Cameroon/Congo
Ngourti 53 H3 Diffa, E Niger
Nguigmi 53 H3 var. N'Guigmi. Diffa, SE Niger
N'Guigmi see Nguigmi
N'Gunza see Sumbe
Nguru 53 G3 Yobe, NE Nigeria
Nha Trang 115 E6 Khanh Hoa, S Vietnam
Niagara Falls 16 D5 Ontario, S Canada
Niagara Falls 19 E3 New York, NE USA
Niagara Falls 18 D3 waterfall Canada/USA
Niamey 53 F3 country capital Niamey, SW Niger
Niangay, Lac 53 E3 lake E Mali
Nia-Nia 55 E5 Orientale, NE Dem. Rep. Congo
Nias, Pulau 116 A3 island W Indonesia
Nicaea see Nice
Nicaragua 30 D3 off. Republic of Nicaragua. country Central America
Lake Nicaragua 30 D4 var. Cocibolca, Gran Lago, Eng. Lake Nicaragua. lake S Nicaragua
Nicaragua, Lake see Nicaragua, Lago de
Nicaragua, Republic of see Nicaragua
Nicaria see Ikaría
Nice 69 D6 It. Nizza; anc. Nicaea. Alpes-Maritimes, SE France
Nicephorium see Ar Raqqah
Nicholas II Land see Severnaya Zemlya
Nicholls Town 32 C1 Andros Island, NW Bahamas
Nicobar Islands 102 B4 island group India, E Indian Ocean
Nicosia 80 C5 Gk. Lefkosía, Turk. Lefkoşa. country capital C Cyprus
Nicoya 30 D4 Guanacaste, W Costa Rica
Nicoya, Golfo de 30 D5 gulf W Costa Rica
Nicoya, Península de 30 D4 peninsula NW Costa Rica
Nida 84 A3 Ger. Nidden. Klaipėda, SW Lithuania
Nidaros see Trondheim
Nidden see Nida
Nidzica 76 D3 Ger. Niedenburg. Warmińsko-Mazurskie, NE Poland
Niedenburg see Nidzica
Niedere Tauern 77 A6 mountain range C Austria
Niemen see Neman
Nieśwież see Nyasvizh
Nieuw Amsterdam 37 G3 Commewijne, NE Suriname
Nieuw-Bergen 64 D4 Limburg, SE Netherlands
Nieuwegein 64 C4 Utrecht, C Netherlands
Nieuw Guinea see New Guinea
Nieuw Nickerie 37 G3 Nickerie, NW Suriname
Niewenstat see Neustadt an der Weinstrasse
Niğde 94 C4 Niğde, C Turkey
Niger 53 F3 off. Republic of Niger. country W Africa
Niger 53 F4 river W Africa
Nigeria 53 F4 off. Federal Republic of Nigeria. country W Africa
Nigeria, Federal Republic of see Nigeria
Niger, Mouths of the 53 F5 delta S Nigeria
Niger, Republic of see Niger
Nihon see Japan
Niigata 109 D5 Niigata, Honshū, C Japan
Niihama 109 B7 Ehime, Shikoku, SW Japan
Ni'ihau 25 A7 var. Niihau. island Hawai'i, USA, C Pacific Ocean
Nii-jima 109 D6 island E Japan
Nijkerk 64 D3 Gelderland, C Netherlands
Nijlen 65 C5 Antwerpen, N Belgium
Nijmegen 64 D4 Ger. Nimwegen; anc. Noviomagus. Gelderland, SE Netherlands
Nikaria see Ikaría
Nikel' 88 C2 Finn. Kolosjoki. Murmanskaya Oblast', NW Russian Federation
Nikiniki 117 E5 Timor, S Indonesia
Niklasmarkt see Gheorgheni
Nikolainkaupunki see Vaasa
Nikolayev see Mykolayiv
Nikol'sk see Ussuriysk
Nikol'sk-Ussuriyskiy see Ussuriysk
Nikopol' 87 F3 Dnipropetrovs'ka Oblast', SE Ukraine
Nikšić 79 C5 C Montenegro
Nikumaroro 123 E3; prev. Gardner Island. atoll Phoenix Islands, C Kiribati
Nikunau 123 E3 var. Nukunau; prev. Byron Island. atoll Tungaru, W Kiribati
Nile 50 B2 former province NW Uganda
Nile 46 D3 Ar. Nahr an Nīl. river N Africa
Nile Delta 50 B1 delta N Egypt
Nīl, Nahr an see Nile
Nîmes 69 C6 anc. Nemausus, Nismes. Gard, S France
Nimwegen see Nijmegen
Nine Degree Channel 110 B3 channel India/Maldives
Ninetyeast Ridge 119 D5 undersea feature E Indian Ocean
Ninety Mile Beach 128 C1 beach North Island, New Zealand
Ningbo 106 D5 var. Ning-po, Yin-hsien; prev. Ninghsien. Zhejiang, SE China
Ning-hsia see Ningxia
Ninghsien see Ningbo
Ning-po see Ningbo
Ningsia/Ningsia Hui/Ningsia Hui Autonomous Region see Ningxia
Ningxia 106 B4 off. Ningxia Huizu Zizhiqu, var. Ning-hsia, Ningsia, Eng. Ningsia Hui, Ningsia Hui Autonomous Region. autonomous region N China
Ningxia Huizu Zizhiqu see Ningxia
Nio see Íos
Nio see Íos
Nio see Íos
Niobrara River 23 E3 river Nebraska/Wyoming, C USA
Nioro 52 D3 var. Nioro du Sahel. Kayes, W Mali
Nioro du Sahel see Nioro
Niort 68 B4 Deux-Sèvres, W France
Nipigon 16 B4 Ontario, S Canada
Nipigon, Lake 16 B3 lake Ontario, S Canada
Nippon see Japan
Niš 79 E5 Eng. Nish, Ger. Nisch; anc. Naissus. Serbia, SE Serbia
Nişab 98 B4 Al Ḩudūd ash Shamālīyah, N Saudi Arabia
Nisch/Nish see Niš
Nisibin see Nusaybin
Nisiros see Nísyros
Nisko 76 E4 Podkrapackie, SE Poland
Nismes see Nîmes
Nistru see Dniester
Nísyros 83 E7 var. Nisiros. island Dodekánisa, Greece, Aegean Sea
Nitra 77 C6 Ger. Neutra, Hung. Nyitra. Nitriansky Kraj, SW Slovakia
Nitra 77 C6 Ger. Neutra, Hung. Nyitra. river W Slovakia
Niuatobutabu see Niuatoputapu
Niuatoputapu 123 E4 var. Niuatobutabu; prev. Keppel Island. island N Tonga
Niue 123 F4 self-governing territory in free association with New Zealand S Pacific Ocean
Niulakita 123 E3 var. Nurakita. atoll S Tuvalu
Niutao 123 E3 atoll NW Tuvalu
Nivernais 68 C4 cultural region C France
Nizāmābād 112 D5 Andhra Pradesh, C India
Nizhnegorskiy see Nyzhn'ohirs'kyy
Nizhnekamsk 89 C5 Respublika Tatarstan, W Russian Federation
Nizhnevartovsk 92 D3 Khanty-Mansiyskiy Avtonomnyy Okrug-Yugra, C Russian Federation
Nizhniy Novgorod 89 C5 prev. Gor'kiy. Nizhegorodskaya Oblast', W Russian Federation
Nizhniy Odes 88 D4 Respublika Komi, NW Russian Federation
Nizhyn 87 E1 Rus. Nezhin. Chernihivs'ka Oblast', NE Ukraine

Oppidum Ubiorum – Pátra

Oppidum Ubiorum see Köln
Oqtosh 101 E2 Rus. Aktash. Samarqand Viloyati, C Uzbekistan
Oradea 86 B3 prev. Oradea Mare, Ger. Grosswardein, Hung. Nagyvárad. Bihor, NW Romania
Oradea Mare see Oradea
Orahovac see Rahovec
Oral see Ural'sk
Oran 48 D2 var. Ouahran, Wahran. NW Algeria
Orange 127 D6 New South Wales, SE Australia
Orange 69 D6 anc. Arausio. Vaucluse, SE France
Orangeburg 21 E2 South Carolina, SE USA
Orange Cone see Orange Fan
Orange Fan 47 C7 var. Orange Cone. undersea feature SW Indian Ocean
Orange Mouth/Orangemund see Oranjemund
Orange River 56 B4 Afr. Oranjerivier. river S Africa
Orange Walk 30 C1 Orange Walk, N Belize
Oranienburg 72 D3 Brandenburg, NE Germany
Oranjemund 56 B4 var. Orangemund; prev. Orange Mouth. Karas, SW Namibia
Oranjerivier see Orange River
Oranjestad 33 E5 dependent territory capital W Aruba
Orany see Varėna
Orașul Stalin see Brașov
Oravicabánya see Oravița
Oravița 86 A4 Ger. Orawitza, Hung. Oravicabánya. Caraș-Severin, SW Romania
Orawitza see Oravița
Orbetello 74 B4 Toscana, C Italy
Orcadas 132 A1 Argentinian research station South Orkney Islands, Antarctica
Orchard Homes 22 B1 Montana, NW USA
Ordino 69 A8 Ordino, NW Andorra Europe
Ordos Desert see Mu Us Shadi
Ordu 94 D2 anc. Cotyora. Ordu, N Turkey
Ordzhonikidze 87 F3 Dnipropetrovs'ka Oblast', E Ukraine
Ordzhonikidze see Vladikavkaz, Russian Federation
Ordzhonikidze see Yenakiyeve, Ukraine
Orealla 37 G3 E Guyana
Örebro 63 C6 Örebro, C Sweden
Oregon 24 B3 off. State of Oregon, also known as Beaver State, Sunset State, Valentine State, Webfoot State. state NW USA
Oregon City 24 B3 Oregon, NW USA
Oregon, State of see Oregon
Orekhov see Orikhiv
Orël 89 B5 Orlovskaya Oblast', W Russian Federation
Orem 22 B4 Utah, W USA
Ore Mountains 73 C5 Cz. Krušné Hory, Eng. Ore Mountains. mountain range Czech Republic/ Germany
Ore Mountains see Erzgebirge/Krušné Hory
Orenburg 89 D6 prev. Chkalov. Orenburgskaya Oblast', W Russian Federation
Orense see Ourense
Oreor see Koror
Orestiáda 82 D3 prev. Orestiás. Anatolikí Makedonía kai Thráki, NE Greece
Orestiás see Orestiáda
Organ Peak 26 D3 mountain New Mexico, SW USA
Orgeyev see Orhei
Orhei 86 D3 var. Orheiu, Rus. Orgeyev. N Moldova
Orheiu see Orhei
Oriental, Cordillera 38 D3 mountain range Bolivia/Peru
Oriental, Cordillera 36 B3 mountain range C Colombia
Orihuela 71 F4 País Valenciano, E Spain
Orikhiv 87 G3 Rus. Orekhov. Zaporiz'ka Oblast', SE Ukraine
Orinoco, Río 37 E2 river Colombia/Venezuela
Orissa 113 F4 cultural region NE India
Orissaar see Orissaare
Orissaare 84 C2 Ger. Orissaar. Saaremaa, W Estonia
Oristano 75 A5 Sardegna, Italy, C Mediterranean Sea
Orito 36 A4 Putumayo, SW Colombia
Orizaba, Volcán Pico de 13 C7 var. Citlaltépetl. mountain S Mexico
Orkney see Orkney Islands
Orkney Islands 66 C2 var. Orkney, Orkneys. island group N Scotland, United Kingdom
Orkneys see Orkney Islands
Orlando 21 E4 Florida, SE USA
Orléanais 68 C4 cultural region C France
Orléans 68 C4 anc. Aurelianum. Loiret, C France
Orléansville see Chlef
Orly 68 E2 international airport Essonne, N France
Orlya 85 B6 Hrodzyenskaya Voblasts', W Belarus
Ormsö see Vormsi
Ormuz, Strait of see Hormuz, Strait of
Örnsköldsvik 63 C5 Västernorrland, C Sweden
Orolaunum see Arlon
Orol Dengizi see Aral Sea
Oromocto 17 F4 New Brunswick, SE Canada
Orona 123 F3 prev. Hull Island. atoll Phoenix Islands, C Kiribati
Oropeza see Cochabamba
Orosirá Rodhópis see Rhodope Mountains
Orpington 67 B8 United Kingdom
Orschowa see Orșova
Orsha 85 E6 Vitsyebskaya Voblasts', NE Belarus
Orsk 92 B4 Orenburgskaya Oblast', W Russian Federation
Orșova 86 A4 Ger. Orschowa, Hung. Orsova. Mehedinți, SW Romania
Ortelsburg see Szczytno
Orthez 69 B6 Pyrénées-Atlantiques, SW France
Ortona 74 D4 Abruzzo, C Italy
Oruba see Aruba
Oruro 39 F4 Oruro, W Bolivia
Oryokko see Yalu
Ōsaka 109 C6 hist. Naniwa. Ōsaka, Honshū, SW Japan
Ōsaki see Furukawa
Osa, Península de 31 E5 peninsula S Costa Rica
Osborn Plateau 119 D5 undersea feature E Indian Ocean
Osca see Huesca
Ösel see Saaremaa
Osh 101 F2 Oshskaya Oblast', SW Kyrgyzstan
Oshawa 16 D5 Ontario, SE Canada
Oshikango 56 B3 Ohangwena, N Namibia
O-shima 109 D6 island S Japan
Oshkosh 18 B2 Wisconsin, N USA
Oshmyany see Ashmyany
Osiek see Osijek
Osijek 78 C3 prev. Osiek, Osjek, Ger. Esseg, Hung. Eszék. Osijek-Baranja, E Croatia
Osipenko see Berdyans'k
Osipovichi see Asipovichy
Osjek see Osijek
Oskaloosa 23 G4 Iowa, C USA
Oskarshamn 63 C7 Kalmar, S Sweden
Öskemen see Ust'-Kamenogorsk
Oskil 87 G2 Rus. Oskil. river Russian Federation/ Ukraine
Oskil see Oskil
Oslo 63 B6 prev. Christiania, Kristiania. country capital Oslo, S Norway
Osmaniye 94 D4 Osmaniye, S Turkey
Osnabrück 72 A3 Niedersachsen, NW Germany
Osogov Mountains 82 B3 var. Osogovske Planine, Osogovski Planina, Mac. Osogovski Planini. mountain range Bulgaria/FYR Macedonia
Osogovske Planine/Osogovski Planina/ Osogovski Planini see Osogov Mountains
Oșorhei see Târgu Mureș
Osorno 43 B5 Los Lagos, C Chile
Oss 64 D4 Noord-Brabant, S Netherlands
Ossa, Serra d' 70 C4 mountain range SE Portugal
Ossora 93 H2 Koryakskiy Avtonomnyy Okrug, E Russian Federation
Ostee see Baltic Sea
Ostend/Ostende see Oostende
Oster 87 E1 Chernihivs'ka Oblast', N Ukraine
Östermyra see Seinäjoki
Osterode/Osterode in Ostpreussen see Ostróda
Österreich see Austria
Östersund 63 C5 Jämtland, C Sweden
Ostia Aterni see Pescara
Ostiglia 74 C2 Lombardia, N Italy
Ostrava 77 C5 Moravskoslezský Kraj, E Czech Republic
Ostróda 76 D3 Ger. Osterode, Osterode in Ostpreussen. Warmińsko-Mazurskie, NE Poland
Ostrołęka 76 D3 Ger. Wiesenhof, Rus. Ostrolenka. Mazowieckie, C Poland
Ostrolenka see Ostrołęka
Ostrov 88 A4 Latv. Austrava. Pskovskaya Oblast', W Russian Federation
Ostrovets see Ostrowiec Świętokrzyski
Ostrovnoy 88 C2 Murmanskaya Oblast', NW Russian Federation
Ostrów see Ostrów Wielkopolski
Ostrowiec see Ostrowiec Świętokrzyski
Ostrowiec Świętokrzyski 76 D4 var. Ostrowiec, Rus. Ostrovets. Świętokrzyskie, C Poland
Ostrów Mazowiecka 76 D3 var. Ostrów Mazowiecki. Mazowieckie, NE Poland
Ostrów Mazowiecki see Ostrów Mazowiecka
Ostrowo see Ostrów Wielkopolski
Ostrów Wielkopolski 76 C4 var. Ostrów, Ger. Ostrowo. Wielkopolskie, C Poland
Ostyako-Voguls'k see Khanty-Mansiysk
Osum see Osumit, Lumi i
Ōsumi-shotō 109 A8 island group Kagoshima, Nansei-shotō, SW Japan Asia East China Sea Pacific Ocean
Osumit, Lumi i 79 D7 var. Osum. river SE Albania
Osuna 70 D4 Andalucía, S Spain
Oswego 19 F2 New York, NE USA
Otago Peninsula 129 B7 peninsula South Island, New Zealand
Otaki 128 D4 Wellington, North Island, New Zealand
Otaru 108 C2 Hokkaidō, NE Japan
Otavalo 38 B1 Imbabura, N Ecuador
Otavi 56 B3 Otjozondjupa, N Namibia
Oțelu Roșu 86 B4 Ger. Ferdinandsberg, Hung. Nándorhgy. Caraș-Severin, SW Romania
Otepää 84 D3 Ger. Odenpäh. Valgamaa, SE Estonia
Oti 53 E4 river N Togo
Otira 129 C6 West Coast, South Island, New Zealand
Otjiwarongo 56 B3 Otjozondjupa, N Namibia
Otorohanga 128 D3 Waikato, North Island, New Zealand
Otranto, Canale d' see Otranto, Strait of
Otranto, Strait of 79 C6 It. Canale d'Otranto. strait Albania/Italy
Otrokovice 77 C5 Ger. Otrokowitz. Zlínský Kraj, E Czech Republic
Otrokowitz see Otrokovice
Ōtsu 109 C6 var. Ōtu. Shiga, Honshū, SW Japan
Ottawa 16 D5 country capital Ontario, SE Canada
Ottawa 18 B3 Illinois, N USA
Ottawa 23 F5 Kansas, C USA
Ottawa 19 E2 Fr. Outaouais. river Ontario/ Québec, SE Canada
Ottawa Islands 16 C1 island group Nunavut, C Canada
Ottignies 65 C6 Wallon Brabant, C Belgium
Ottumwa 23 G4 Iowa, C USA
Ōtu see Ōtsu
Ouachita Mountains 20 A1 mountain range Arkansas/Oklahoma, C USA
Ouachita River 20 B2 river Arkansas/Louisiana, C USA
Ouagadougou 53 E4 var. Wagadugu. country capital C Burkina
Ouahigouya 53 E3 NW Burkina
Ouahran see Oran
Oualâta 52 D3 var. Oualata. Hodh ech Chargui, SE Mauritania
Ouanary 37 H3 E French Guiana
Ouanda Djallé 54 D4 Vakaga, NE Central African Republic
Ouarâne 52 D2 desert C Mauritania
Ouargla 49 E2 var. Wargla. NE Algeria
Ouarzazate 48 C3 S Morocco
Oubangui 55 C5 Fr. Oubangui. river C Africa
Oubangui see Ubangi
Oubangui-Chari see Central African Republic
Oubangui-Chari, Territoire de l' see Central African Republic
Oudjda see Oujda
Ouessant, Île d' 68 A3 Eng. Ushant. island NW France
Ouésso 55 B5 Sangha, NW Congo
Oujda 48 D2 Ar. Oudjda, Ujda. NE Morocco
Oujeft 52 C2 Adrar, C Mauritania
Oulu 62 D4 Swe. Uleåborg. Oulu, C Finland
Oulujärvi 62 D4 Swe. Uleträsk. lake C Finland
Oulujoki 62 D4 Swe. Uleälv. river C Finland
Ounasjoki 62 D3 river N Finland
Ounianga Kébir 54 C2 Borkou-Ennedi-Tibesti, N Chad
Oup see Auob
Oupeye 65 D6 Liège, E Belgium
Our 65 D6 river NW Europe
Ourense 70 C1 Cast. Orense, Lat. Aurium. Galicia, NW Spain
Ourique 70 B4 Beja, S Portugal
Ours, Grand Lac de l' see Great Bear Lake
Ourthe 65 D7 river E Belgium
Ouse 67 D5 river N England, United Kingdom
Outaouais see Ottawa
Outer Hebrides 66 B3 var. Western Isles. island group NW Scotland, United Kingdom
Outer Islands 57 G1 island group SW Seychelles Africa W Indian Ocean
Outes 70 B1 Galicia, NW Spain
Ouvéa 122 D5 island Îles Loyauté, NE New Caledonia
Ouyen 127 C6 Victoria, SE Australia
Ovalle 42 B3 Coquimbo, N Chile
Ovar 70 B2 Aveiro, N Portugal
Overflakkee 64 B4 island SW Netherlands
Overijse 65 C6 Vlaams Brabant, C Belgium
Oviedo 70 C1 anc. Asturias. Asturias, NW Spain
Ovilava see Wels
Ovruch 86 D1 Zhytomyrs'ka Oblast', N Ukraine
Owando 55 B5 prev. Fort Rousset. Cuvette, C Congo
Owase 109 C6 Mie, Honshū, SW Japan
Owatonna 23 F3 Minnesota, N USA
Owen Fracture Zone 118 B4 tectonic feature W Arabian Sea
Owen, Mount 129 C5 mountain South Island, New Zealand
Owensboro 18 B5 Kentucky, S USA
Owen Stanley Range 122 B3 mountain range S Papua New Guinea
Owerri 53 G5 Imo, S Nigeria
Owo 53 F5 Ondo, SW Nigeria
Owyhee River 24 C4 river Idaho/Oregon, NW USA
Oxford 129 C6 Canterbury, South Island, New Zealand
Oxford 67 D6 Lat. Oxonia. S England, United Kingdom
Oxkutzcab 29 H4 Yucatán, SE Mexico
Oxnard 25 B7 California, W USA
Oxonia see Oxford
Oxus see Amu Darya
Oyama 109 D5 Tochigi, Honshū, S Japan
Oyem 55 B5 Woleu-Ntem, N Gabon
Oyo 55 B6 Cuvette, C Congo
Oyo 53 F4 Oyo, W Nigeria
Ozark 20 D3 Alabama, S USA
Ozark Plateau 23 G5 plain Arkansas/Missouri, C USA
Ozarks, Lake of the 23 F5 reservoir Missouri, C USA
Ozbourn Seamount 130 D4 undersea feature W Pacific Ocean
Ózd 77 D6 Borsod-Abaúj-Zemplén, NE Hungary
Ozieri 75 A5 Sardegna, Italy, C Mediterranean Sea

P

Paamiut 60 B4 var. Pâmiut, Dan. Frederikshåb. S Greenland
Pa-an see Hpa-an
Pabianice 76 C4 Łódzski, Poland
Pabna 113 G4 Rajshahi, W Bangladesh
Pacaraima, Sierra/Pacaraim, Serra see Pakaraima Mountains
Pachuca 29 E4 var. Pachuca de Soto. Hidalgo, C Mexico
Pachuca de Soto see Pachuca
Pacific-Antarctic Ridge 132 B5 undersea feature S Pacific Ocean
Pacific Ocean 130 D3 ocean
Padalung see Phatthalung
Padang 116 B4 Sumatera, W Indonesia
Paderborn 72 B4 Nordrhein-Westfalen, NW Germany
Padma see Brahmaputra
Padma see Ganges
Padova 74 C2 Eng. Padua; anc. Patavium. Veneto, NE Italy
Padre Island 27 G5 island Texas, SW USA
Padua see Padova
Paducah 18 B5 Kentucky, S USA
Paeroa 128 D3 Waikato, North Island, New Zealand
Páfos 80 C5 var. Paphos. W Cyprus
Pag 78 A3 It. Pago. island Zadar, C Croatia
Page 26 B1 Arizona, SW USA
Pago see Pag
Pago Pago 123 F4 dependent territory capital Tutuila, W American Samoa
Pahiatua 128 D4 Manawatu-Wanganui, North Island, New Zealand
Pahsien see Chongqing
Paide 84 D2 Ger. Weissenstein. Järvamaa, N Estonia
Paihia 128 D2 Northland, North Island, New Zealand
Päijänne 63 D5 lake S Finland
Paine, Cerro 43 A7 mountain S Chile
Painted Desert 26 B1 desert Arizona, SW USA
Paisance see Piacenza
Paisley 66 C4 W Scotland, United Kingdom
País Valenciano 71 F3 var. Valencia, Cat. València; anc. Valentia. autonomous community NE Spain
País Vasco 71 E1 cultural region N Spain
Paita 38 B3 Piura, NW Peru
Pakanbaru see Pekanbaru
Pakaraima Mountains 37 E3 var. Serra Pacaraim, Sierra Pacaraima. mountain range N South America
Pakistan 112 A2 off. Islamic Republic of Pakistan, var. Islami Jamhuriya e Pakistan. country S Asia
Pakistan, Islamic Republic of see Pakistan
Pakistan, Islami Jamhuriya e see Pakistan
Paknam see Samut Prakan
Pakokku 114 A3 Magway, C Myanmar (Burma)
Pak Phanang 115 C7 var. Ban Pak Phanang. Nakhon Si Thammarat, SW Thailand
Pakruojis 84 C4 Šiaulai, N Lithuania
Paks 77 C7 Tolna, S Hungary
Paksé see Pakxé
Pakxé 115 D5 var. Paksé. Champasak, S Laos
Palafrugell 71 G2 Cataluña, NE Spain
Palagruža 79 B5 It. Pelagosa. island SW Croatia
Palaiá Epídavros 83 C6 Pelopónnisos, S Greece
Palaiseau 68 D2 Essonne, N France
Palamós 71 G2 Cataluña, NE Spain
Palamuse 84 E2 Ger. Sankt-Bartholomäi. Jõgevamaa, E Estonia
Palanka see Bačka Palanka
Pālanpur 112 C4 Gujarāt, W India
Palantia see Palencia
Palapye 56 D3 Central, SE Botswana
Palau 122 A2 var. Belau. country W Pacific Ocean
Palawan 117 E2 island W Philippines
Palawan Passage 116 D2 passage W Philippines
Paldiski 84 D2 prev. Baltiski, Eng. Baltic Port, Ger. Baltischport. Harjumaa, NW Estonia
Palembang 116 B4 Sumatera, W Indonesia
Palencia 70 D2 anc. Palantia, Pallantia. Castilla-León, NW Spain
Palerme see Palermo
Palermo 75 C7 Fr. Palerme; anc. Panhormus, Panormus. Sicilia, Italy, C Mediterranean Sea
Pāli 112 C3 Rājasthān, N India
Palikir 122 C2 country capital Pohnpei, E Micronesia
Palimé see Kpalimé
Palioúri, Akrotírio 82 C4 var. Akrotirio Kanestron. headland N Greece
Palk Strait 110 C3 strait India/Sri Lanka
Pallantia see Palencia
Palliser, Cape 129 D5 headland North Island, New Zealand
Palma 71 G3 var. Palma de Mallorca. Mallorca, Spain, W Mediterranean Sea
Palma del Río 70 D4 Andalucía, S Spain
Palma de Mallorca see Palma
Palmar Sur 31 E5 Puntarenas, SE Costa Rica
Palma Soriano 32 C3 Santiago de Cuba, E Cuba
Palm Beach 126 E1 New South Wales, E Australia
Palmer 132 A2 US research station Antarctica
Palmer Land 132 A3 physical region Antarctica
Palmerston 123 F4 island S Cook Islands
Palmerston see Darwin
Palmerston North 128 D4 Manawatu-Wanganui, North Island, New Zealand
The Palmetto State see South Carolina
Palmi 75 D7 Calabria, SW Italy
Palmira 36 B3 Valle del Cauca, W Colombia
Palm Springs 25 D7 California, W USA
Palmyra see Tudmur
Palmyra Atoll 123 G2 US privately owned unincorporated territory C Pacific Ocean
Palo Alto 25 B6 California, W USA
Paloe see Denpasar, Bali, C Indonesia
Paloe see Palu
Palu 117 E4 prev. Paloe. Sulawesi, C Indonesia
Pamiers 69 B6 Ariège, S France
Pamir 101 F3 var. Daryā-ye Pāmīr, Taj. Dar"yoi Pomir. river Afghanistan/Tajikistan
Pāmīr, Daryā-ye see Pamir
Pamir/Pāmīr, Daryā-ye see Pamirs
Pamirs 101 F3 Pash. Daryā-ye Pāmīr, Rus. Pamir. mountain range C Asia
Pâmiut see Paamiut
Pamlico Sound 21 G1 sound North Carolina, SE USA
Pampa 27 E1 Texas, SW USA
Pampa Aullagas, Lago see Poopó, Lago
Pampas 42 C4 plain C Argentina
Pampeluna see Pamplona
Pamplona 36 C2 Norte de Santander, N Colombia
Pamplona 71 E1 Basq. Iruña, prev. Pampeluna; anc. Pompaelo. Navarra, N Spain
Panaji 110 B1 var. Pangim, Panjim, New Goa. state capital Goa, W India
Panamá 31 G4 var. Ciudad de Panama, Eng. Panama City. country capital Panamá, C Panama
Panama 31 G5 off. Republic of Panama. country Central America
Panama Basin 13 C8 undersea feature E Pacific Ocean
Panama Canal 31 F4 canal E Panama
Panama City 20 D3 Florida, SE USA
Panama City see Panamá
Gulf of Panama 31 G5 var. Gulf of Panamá. gulf S Panama
Panama, Gulf of see Panamá, Golfo de
Isthmus of Panama 31 G4 Eng. Isthmus of Panama; prev. Isthmus of Darien. isthmus E Panama
Panama, Isthmus of see Panama, Istmo de
Panama, Republic of see Panama
Panay Island 117 E2 island C Philippines
Pančevo 78 D3 Ger. Pantschowa, Hung. Pancsova. Vojvodina, N Serbia
Pancsova see Pančevo
Paneas see Bāniyās
Panevėžys 84 C4 Panevėžys, C Lithuania
Pangim see Panaji
Pangkalpinang 116 C4 Pulau Bangka, W Indonesia
Pang-Nga see Phang-Nga
Panhormus see Palermo
Panjim see Panaji
Panopolis see Akhmīm
Pánormos 83 C7 Kríti, Greece, E Mediterranean Sea
Panormus see Palermo
Pantanal 41 E3 var. Pantanalmato-Grossense. swamp SW Brazil
Pantanalmato-Grossense see Pantanal
Pantelleria, Isola di 75 B7 island SW Italy
Pantschowa see Pančevo
Pánuco 29 E3 Veracruz-Llave, E Mexico
Pao-chi/Paoki see Baoji
Paola 80 B5 E Malta
Pao-shan see Baoshan
Pao-t'ou/Paotow see Baotou
Papagayo, Golfo de 30 C4 gulf NW Costa Rica
Papakura 128 D3 Auckland, North Island, New Zealand
Papantla 29 F4 var. Papantla de Olarte. Veracruz-Llave, E Mexico
Papantla de Olarte see Papantla
Papeete 123 H4 dependent territory capital Tahiti, W French Polynesia
Paphos see Páfos
Papile 84 B3 Šiaulai, NW Lithuania
Papillion 23 F4 Nebraska, C USA
Papua 117 H4 var. Irian Barat, West Irian, West New Guinea, West Papua; prev. Dutch New Guinea, Irian Jaya, Netherlands New Guinea. province E Indonesia
Papua and New Guinea, Territory of see Papua New Guinea
Papua, Gulf of 122 B3 gulf S Papua New Guinea
Papua New Guinea 122 B3 off. Independent State of Papua New Guinea; prev. Territory of Papua and New Guinea. country NW Melanesia
Papua New Guinea, Independent State of see Papua New Guinea
Papuk 78 C3 mountain range NE Croatia
Pará 41 E2 off. Estado do Pará. state NE Brazil
Pará 41 E2 off. Estado do Pará. region NE Brazil
Pará see Belém
Paracel Islands 103 E3 disputed territory SE Asia
Paraćin 78 D4 Serbia, C Serbia
Paradise of the Pacific see Hawai'i
Pará, Estado do see Pará
Paragua, Río 37 E3 river SE Venezuela
Paraguay 42 C2 country C South America
Paraguay 42 D2 var. Río Paraguay. river C South America
Paraguay, Río see Paraguay
Parahiba/Parahyba see Paraíba
Paraíba 41 G2 off. Estado da Paraíba; prev. Parahiba, Parahyba. state E Brazil
Paraíba 41 G2 off. Estado da Paraíba; prev. Parahiba, Parahyba. region E Brazil
Paraíba see João Pessoa
Paraíba, Estado da see Paraíba
Parakou 53 F4 C Benin
Paramaribo 37 G3 country capital Paramaribo, N Suriname
Paramushir, Ostrov 93 H3 island SE Russian Federation
Paraná 41 E4 Entre Ríos, E Argentina
Paraná 41 E5 off. Estado do Paraná. region S Brazil
Paraná 41 E5 off. Estado do Paraná. state S Brazil
Paraná 35 C5 var. Alto Paraná. river C South America
Paraná, Estado do see Paraná
Paranésti 82 C3 var. Paranestio. Anatolikí Makedonía kai Thráki, NE Greece
Paranestio see Paranésti
Paraparaumu 129 D5 Wellington, North Island, New Zealand
Parchim 72 C3 Mecklenburg-Vorpommern, N Germany
Parczew 76 E4 Lubelskie, E Poland
Pardubice 77 B5 Ger. Pardubitz. Pardubický Kraj, C Czech Republic
Pardubitz see Pardubice
Parechcha 85 B5 Pol. Porzecze, Rus. Porech'ye. Hrodzyenskaya Voblasts', W Belarus
Parecis, Chapada dos 40 D3 var. Serra dos Parecis. mountain range W Brazil
Parecis, Serra dos see Parecis, Chapada dos
Parenzo see Poreč
Parepare 117 E4 Sulawesi, C Indonesia
Párga 83 A5 Ípeiros, W Greece
Paria, Golfo de see Paria, Gulf of
Paria, Gulf of 37 E1 var. Golfo de Paria. gulf Trinidad and Tobago/Venezuela
Parika 37 F2 NE Guyana
Paris 68 D1 anc. Lutetia, Lutetia Parisiorum, Parisii. country capital Paris, N France
Paris 27 G2 Texas, SW USA
Parisii see Paris
Parkersburg 18 D4 West Virginia, NE USA
Parkes 127 D6 New South Wales, SE Australia
Parkhar see Farkhor
Parma 74 B2 Emilia-Romagna, N Italy
Parnahyba see Parnaíba
Parnaíba 41 F2 var. Parnahyba. Piauí, E Brazil
Pärnu 84 D2 Ger. Pernau, Latv. Pērnava; prev. Rus. Pernov. Pärnumaa, SW Estonia
Pärnu 84 D2 var. Parnu Jõgi, Ger. Pernau. river SW Estonia
Pärnu-Jaagupi 84 D2 Ger. Sankt-Jakobi. Pärnumaa, SW Estonia
Parnu Jõgi see Pärnu
Pärnu Laht 84 D2 Ger. Pernauer Bucht. bay SW Estonia
Paropamisus Range see Sefid Kūh, Selseleh-ye
Páros 83 D6 island Kykládes, Greece, Aegean Sea
Páros 83 D6 island Kykládes, Greece, Aegean Sea
Páros 83 C6 island Kykládes, Greece, Aegean Sea
Parral 42 B4 Maule, C Chile
Parral see Hidalgo del Parral
Parramatta 126 D1 New South Wales, SE Australia
Parras 28 D3 var. Parras de la Fuente. Coahuila de Zaragoza, NE Mexico
Parras de la Fuente see Parras
Parsons 23 F5 Kansas, C USA
Pasadena 25 C7 California, W USA
Pasadena 27 H4 Texas, SW USA
Pașcani 86 C3 Hung. Páskán. Iași, NE Romania
Pasco 24 C2 Washington, NW USA
Pasewalk 72 D3 Mecklenburg-Vorpommern, NE Germany
Pashkeni see Bolyarovo
Pasinler 95 F3 Erzurum, NE Turkey
Páskán see Pașcani
Pasłęk 76 D2 Ger. Preußisch Holland. Warmińsko-Mazurskie, NE Poland
Pasni 112 A3 Baluchistān, SW Pakistan
Paso de Indios 43 B6 Chubut, S Argentina
Passarowitz see Požarevac
Passau 73 D6 Bayern, SE Germany
Passo Fundo 41 E5 Rio Grande do Sul, S Brazil
Pastavy 85 C5 Pol. Postawy, Rus. Postavy. Vitsyebskaya Voblasts', NW Belarus
Pastaza, Río 38 B2 river Ecuador/Peru
Pasto 36 A4 Nariño, SW Colombia
Pasvalys 84 C4 Panevėžys, N Lithuania
Patagonia 35 B7 physical region Argentina/Chile
Patalung see Phatthalung
Patani see Pattani
Patavium see Padova
Patea 128 D4 Taranaki, North Island, New Zealand
Paterson 19 F3 New Jersey, NE USA
Pathein 114 A4 var. Bassein. Ayeyarwady, SW Myanmar (Burma)
Pátmos 83 D6 island Dodekánisa, Greece, Aegean Sea
Patna 113 F3 var. Azimabad. state capital Bihār, N India
Patnos 95 F3 Ağrı, E Turkey
Patos, Lagoa dos 41 E5 lagoon S Brazil
Pátra 83 B5 Eng. Patras; prev. Pátrai. Dytikí Ellás, S Greece

Pátrai/Patras – Port An Dúnáin

Pátrai/Patras see Pátra
Pattani 115 C7 var. Patani. Pattani, SW Thailand
Pattaya 115 C5 Chon Buri, S Thailand
Patuca, Río 30 D2 river E Honduras
Pau 69 B6 Pyrénées-Atlantiques, SW France
Paulatuk 15 E3 Northwest Territories, NW Canada
Paungde 114 B4 Bago, C Myanmar (Burma)
Pautalia see Kyustendil
Pavia 74 B2 anc. Ticinum. Lombardia, N Italy
Pāvilosta 84 B3 Liepāja, W Latvia
Pavlikeni 82 D2 Veliko Tŭrnovo, N Bulgaria
Pavlodar 92 C4 Pavlodar, NE Kazakhstan
Pavlograd see Pavlohrad
Pavlohrad 87 G3 Rus. Pavlograd. Dnipropetrovs'ka Oblast', E Ukraine
Pawai, Pulau 116 A2 island SW Singapore Asia
Pawn 114 B3 river C Myanmar (Burma)
Pax Augusta see Badajoz
Pax Julia see Beja
Paxoí 83 A5 island Iónia Nisiá, Greece, C Mediterranean Sea
Payo Obispo see Chetumal
Paysandú 42 D4 Paysandú, W Uruguay
Pazar 95 E2 Rize, NE Turkey
Pazardzhik 82 C3 prev. Tatar Pazardzhik. Pazardzhik, SW Bulgaria
Peace Garden State see North Dakota
Peach State see Georgia
Pearl Islands 31 G5 Eng. Pearl Islands. island group SE Panama
Pearl Islands see Perlas, Archipiélago de las
Pearl Lagoon 31 E3 Eng. Pearl Lagoon. lagoon E Nicaragua
Pearl Lagoon see Perlas, Laguna de
Pearl River 20 B3 river Louisiana/Mississippi, S USA
Pearsall 27 F4 Texas, SW USA
Peawanuk 16 C2 prev. Winisk. Ontario, C Canada
Peawanuk 16 C2 river Ontario, S Canada
Peć see Pejë
Pechora 88 D3 Respublika Komi, NW Russian Federation
Pechora 88 D3 river NW Russian Federation
Pechora Sea 88 D2 Eng. Pechora Sea. sea NW Russian Federation
Pechora Sea see Pechorskoye More
Pecos 27 E3 Texas, SW USA
Pecos River 27 E3 river New Mexico/Texas, SW USA
Pécs 77 C7 Ger. Fünfkirchen, Lat. Sopianae. Baranya, SW Hungary
Pedra Lume 52 A3 Sal, NE Cape Verde
Pedro Cays 32 C3 island group Greater Antilles, S Jamaica North America N Caribbean Sea W Atlantic Ocean
Pedro Juan Caballero 42 D2 Amambay, E Paraguay
Peer 65 D5 Limburg, NE Belgium
Pegasus Bay 129 C6 bay South Island, New Zealand
Pegu see Bago
Pehuajó 42 C4 Buenos Aires, E Argentina
Pei-ching see Beijing/Beijing Shi
Peine 72 B3 Niedersachsen, C Germany
Pei-p'ing see Beijing/Beijing Shi
Peipsi Järv/Peipus-See see Peipus, Lake
Peipus, Lake 84 E3 Est. Peipsi Järv, Ger. Peipus-See, Rus. Chudskoye Ozero. lake Estonia/Russian Federation
Peiraías 83 C6 prev. Piraiévs, Eng. Piraeus. Attikí, C Greece
Pejë 79 D5 Serb. Peć. W Kosovo
Pèk 114 D4 var. Xieng Khouang; prev. Xiangkhoang. Xiangkhoang, N Laos
Pekalongan 116 C4 Jawa, C Indonesia
Pekanbaru 116 B3 var. Pakanbaru. Sumatera, W Indonesia
Pekin 18 B4 Illinois, N USA
Peking see Beijing/Beijing Shi
Pelagie 75 B8 island group SW Italy
Pelagosa see Palagruža
Pelican State see Louisiana
Pelly Bay see Kugaaruk
Pélmonostor see Beli Manastir
Peloponnese 83 B6 var. Morea, Eng. Peloponnese; anc. Peloponnesus. peninsula S Greece
Peloponnese/Peloponnesus see Pelopónnisos
Pematangsiantar 116 B3 Sumatera, W Indonesia
Pemba 57 F2 prev. Port Amelia, Porto Amélia. Cabo Delgado, NE Mozambique
Pemba 51 D7 island E Tanzania
Pembroke 16 D4 Ontario, SE Canada
Penang see George Town
Penang see Pinang, Pulau, Peninsular Malaysia
Penas, Golfo de 43 A7 gulf S Chile
Penderma see Bandırma
Pendleton 24 C3 Oregon, NW USA
Pend Oreille, Lake 24 D2 lake Idaho, NW USA
Peneius see Pineiós
Peng-pu see Bengbu
Penibético, Sistema see Béticos, Sistemas
Peniche 70 B3 Leiria, W Portugal
Peninsular State see Florida
Penninae, Alpes/Pennine, Alpi see Pennine Alps
Pennine Alps 73 A8 Fr. Alpes Pennines, It. Alpi Pennine, Lat. Alpes Penninae. mountain range Italy/Switzerland
Pennine Chain see Pennines
Pennines 67 D5 var. Pennine Chain. mountain range N England, United Kingdom
Pennines, Alpes see Pennine Alps
Pennsylvania 19 E4 off. Commonwealth of Pennsylvania, also known as Keystone State. state NE USA
Penobscot River 19 G2 river Maine, NE USA
Penong 127 A6 South Australia
Penonomé 31 F5 Coclé, C Panama
Penrhyn 123 G3 atoll N Cook Islands
Penrhyn Basin 121 F3 undersea feature C Pacific Ocean
Penrith 126 D1 New South Wales, SE Australia
Penrith 67 D5 NW England, United Kingdom
Pensacola 20 C3 Florida, SE USA
Pentecost 122 D4 Fr. Pentecôte. island C Vanuatu
Pentecôte see Pentecost
Penza 89 C6 Penzenskaya Oblast', W Russian Federation
Penzance 67 C7 SW England, United Kingdom
Peoria 18 B4 Illinois, N USA
Perchtoldsdorf 73 E6 Niederösterreich, NE Austria
Percival Lakes 124 C4 lakes Western Australia
Perdido, Monte 71 F1 mountain NE Spain
Perece Vela Basin see West Mariana Basin
Pereira 36 B3 Risaralda, W Colombia
Peremyshl see Przemyśl
Pergamino 42 C4 Buenos Aires, E Argentina
Périgueux 69 C5 anc. Vesuna. Dordogne, SW France
Perito Moreno 43 B6 Santa Cruz, S Argentina
Perleberg 72 C3 Brandenburg, N Germany
Perlepe see Prilep
Perm' 92 C3 prev. Molotov. Permskaya Oblast', NW Russian Federation
Pernambuco 41 G2 off. Estado de Pernambuco. region E Brazil
Pernambuco 41 G2 off. Estado de Pernambuco. state E Brazil
Pernambuco see Recife
Pernambuco Abyssal Plain see Pernambuco Plain
Pernambuco, Estado de see Pernambuco
Pernambuco Plain 45 C5 var. Pernambuco Abyssal Plain. undersea feature E Atlantic Ocean
Pernau see Pärnu
Pernauer Bucht see Pärnu Laht
Pērnava see Pärnu
Pernik 82 B2 prev. Dimitrovo. Pernik, W Bulgaria
Pernov see Pärnu
Perote 29 F4 Veracruz-Llave, E Mexico
Pérouse see Perugia
Perovsk see Kyzylorda
Perpignan 69 C6 Pyrénées-Orientales, S France
Perryton 27 F1 Texas, SW USA
Perryville 23 H5 Missouri, C USA
Persia see Iran
Perth 125 A6 state capital Western Australia
Perth 66 C4 C Scotland, United Kingdom
Perth Basin 119 E6 undersea feature SE Indian Ocean
Peru 38 C3 off. Republic of Peru. country W South America
Peru see Beru
Peru Basin 45 A5 undersea feature E Pacific Ocean
Peru-Chile Trench 34 A4 undersea feature E Pacific Ocean
Perugia 74 C4 Fr. Pérouse; anc. Perusia. Umbria, C Italy
Perugia, Lake of see Trasimeno, Lago
Peru, Republic of see Peru
Perusia see Perugia
Péruwelz 65 B6 Hainaut, SW Belgium
Pervomays'k 87 E3 prev. Ol'viopol'. Mykolayivs'ka Oblast', S Ukraine
Pervyy Kuril'skiy Proliv 93 H3 strait E Russian Federation
Pesaro 74 C3 anc. Pisaurum. Marche, C Italy
Pescara 74 D4 anc. Aternum, Ostia Aterni. Abruzzo, C Italy
Peshāwar 112 C1 North-West Frontier Province, N Pakistan
Peshkopi 79 C6 var. Peshkopia, Peshkopija. Dibër, NE Albania
Peshkopia/Peshkopija see Peshkopi
Pessac 69 B5 Gironde, SW France
Petach-Tikva see Petah Tikva
Petah Tikva 97 A6 var. Petach-Tikva, Petah Tiqva, Petakh Tikva; prev. Petaḥ Tiqwa. Tel Aviv, C Israel
Petaḥ Tiqwa see Petah Tikva
Petakh Tikva/Petah Tiqva see Petah Tikva
Pétange 65 D8 Luxembourg, SW Luxembourg
Petchaburi see Phetchaburi
Peterborough 127 B6 South Australia
Peterborough 16 D5 Ontario, SE Canada
Peterborough 67 E6 prev. Medeshamstede. E England, United Kingdom
Peterhead 66 D3 NE Scotland, United Kingdom
Peter I Øy 132 A3 Norwegian dependency Antarctica
Petermann Bjerg 61 E3 mountain C Greenland
Petersburg 19 E5 Virginia, NE USA
Peters Mine 37 F3 var. Peter's Mine. N Guyana
Petit St-Bernard, Col du see Little Saint Bernard Pass
Peto 29 H4 Yucatán, SE Mexico
Petoskey 18 C2 Michigan, N USA
Petra see Wādī Mūsā
Petrich 82 C3 Blagoevgrad, SW Bulgaria
Petrikau see Piotrków Trybunalski
Petrikov see Pyetrykaw
Petrinja 78 B3 Sisak-Moslavina, C Croatia
Petroaleksandrovsk see To'rtkok'l
Petrodvorets 88 A4 Fin. Pietarhovi. Leningradskaya Oblast', NW Russian Federation
Petrograd see Sankt-Peterburg
Petrokov see Piotrków Trybunalski
Petropavl see Petropavlovsk
Petropavlovsk 92 C4 Kaz. Petropavl. Severnyy Kazakhstan, N Kazakhstan
Petropavlovsk-Kamchatskiy 93 H3 Kamchatskaya Oblast', E Russian Federation
Petroșani 86 B4 var. Petroșeni, Ger. Petroschen, Hung. Petrozsény. Hunedoara, W Romania
Petroschen/Petroșeni see Petroșani
Petroskoi see Petrozavodsk
Petrovgrad see Zrenjanin
Petrovsk-Port see Makhachkala
Petrozavodsk 92 B2 Fin. Petroskoi. Respublika Kareliya, NW Russian Federation
Petrozsény see Petroșani
Pettau see Ptuj
Pevek 93 G1 Chukotskiy Avtonomnyy Okrug, NE Russian Federation
Pezinok 77 C6 Ger. Bösing, Hung. Bazin. Bratislavský Kraj, W Slovakia
Pforzheim 73 B6 Baden-Württemberg, SW Germany
Pfungstadt 73 B5 Hessen, W Germany
Phangan, Ko 115 C6 island SW Thailand
Phang-Nga 115 B7 var. Pang-Nga, Phangnga. Phangnga, SW Thailand
Phangnga see Phang-Nga
Phan Rang/Phanrang see Phan Rang-Thap Cham
Phan Rang-Thap Cham 115 E6 var. Phanrang, Phan Rang, Phan Rang Thap Cham. Ninh Thuân, S Vietnam
Phan Thiêt 115 E6 Binh Thuân, S Vietnam
Pharnacia see Giresun
Pharus see Hvar
Phatthalung 115 C7 var. Padalung, Patalung. Phatthalung, SW Thailand
Phayao 114 C4 var. Muang Phayao. Phayao, NW Thailand
Phenix City 20 D2 Alabama, S USA
Phet Buri see Phetchaburi
Phetchaburi 115 C5 var. Bejraburi, Petchaburi, Phet Buri. Phetchaburi, SW Thailand
Philadelphia 19 F4 Pennsylvania, NE USA
Philadelphia see 'Ammān
Philippine Basin 103 F3 undersea feature W Pacific Ocean
Philippine Islands 117 E1 island group W Pacific Ocean
Philippines 117 E1 off. Republic of the Philippines. country SE Asia
Philippine Sea 103 F3 sea W Pacific Ocean
Philippines, Republic of the see Philippines
Philippine Trench 120 A1 undersea feature W Philippine Sea
Philippopolis see Plovdiv
Phitsanulok 114 C4 var. Bisnulok, Muang Phitsanulok, Pitsanulok. Phitsanulok, C Thailand
Phlórina see Flórina
Phnom Penh see Phnum Penh
Phnum Penh 115 D6 var. Phnom Penh. country capital Phnum Penh, S Cambodia
Phoenix 26 B2 state capital Arizona, SW USA
Phoenix Islands 123 E3 island group C Kiribati
Phôngsali 114 C3 var. Phong Saly. Phôngsali, N Laos
Phong Saly see Phôngsali
Phrae 114 C4 var. Muang Phrae, Prae. Phrae, NW Thailand
Phra Nakhon Si Ayutthaya see Ayutthaya
Phra Thong, Ko 115 B6 island SW Thailand
Phuket 115 B7 var. Bhuket, Puket, Mal. Ujung Salang; prev. Junkseylon, Salang. Phuket, SW Thailand
Phuket, Ko 115 B7 island SW Thailand
Phumĭ Kâmpóng Trâbêk 115 D5 prev. Phum Kompong Trabek. Kâmpóng Thum, C Cambodia
Phumĭ Sâmraông 115 D5 prev. Phum Samrong. Siĕmréab, NW Cambodia
Phum Kompong Trabek see Phumĭ Kâmpóng Trâbêk
Phum Samrong see Phumĭ Sâmraông
Phu Vinh see Tra Vinh
Phyu 114 B4 var. Hpyu, Pyu. Bago, C Myanmar (Burma)
Piacenza 74 B2 Fr. Paisance; anc. Placentia. Emilia-Romagna, N Italy
Piatra-Neamț 86 C4 Hung. Karácsonkő. Neamț, NE Romania
Piauhy see Piauí
Piauí 41 F2 off. Estado do Piauí; prev. Piauhy. state E Brazil
Piauí 41 F2 off. Estado do Piauí; prev. Piauhy. region E Brazil
Piauí, Estado do see Piauí
Picardie 68 C3 Eng. Picardy. cultural region N France
Picardy see Picardie
Piccolo San Bernardo, Colle di see Little Saint Bernard Pass
Pichilemu 42 B4 Libertador, C Chile
Pico 70 A5 var. Ilha do Pico. island Azores, Portugal, NE Atlantic Ocean
Pico, Ilha do see Pico
Picos 41 F2 Piauí, E Brazil
Picton 129 C5 Marlborough, South Island, New Zealand
Piedmont see Piemonte
Piedras Negras 29 E2 var. Ciudad Porfirio Díaz. Coahuila de Zaragoza, NE Mexico
Pielavesi 62 D4 lake C Finland
Pielinen 62 E4 var. Pielisjärvi. lake E Finland
Pielisjärvi see Pielinen
Piemonte 74 A2 Eng. Piedmont. region NW Italy
Pierre 23 E3 state capital South Dakota, N USA
Piešťany 77 C6 Ger. Pistyan, Hung. Pöstyén. Tranavský Kraj, W Slovakia
Pietarhovi see Petrodvorets
Pietari see Sankt-Peterburg
Pietarsaari see Jakobstad
Pietermaritzburg 56 C5 var. Maritzburg. KwaZulu/Natal, E South Africa
Pietersburg see Polokwane
Bay of Pigs 32 B2 Eng. Bay of Pigs. bay SE Cuba
Pigs, Bay of see Cochinos, Bahía de
Pihkva Järv see Pskov, Lake
Pijijiapán 29 G5 Chiapas, SE Mexico
Pikes Peak 22 C5 mountain Colorado, C USA
Pikeville 18 D5 Kentucky, S USA
Pikinni see Bikini Atoll
Piła 76 B3 Ger. Schneidemühl. Wielkopolskie, C Poland
Pilar 42 D3 var. Villa del Pilar. Ñeembucú, S Paraguay
Pilcomayo, Rio 35 C5 river C South America
Pilos see Pýlos
Pilsen see Plzeň
Pilzno see Plzeň
Pinang see Pinang, Pulau, Peninsular Malaysia
Pinang see George Town
Pinang, Pulau 116 B3 var. Penang, Pinang; prev. Prince of Wales Island. island Peninsular Malaysia
Pinar del Río 32 A2 Pinar del Río, W Cuba
Píndhos/Píndhos Óros see Píndos
Pindus Mountains 82 A4 var. Píndhos Óros, Eng. Pindus Mountains; prev. Píndhos. mountain range C Greece
Pindus Mountains see Píndos
Pine Bluff 20 B2 Arkansas, C USA
Pine Creek 124 D2 Northern Territory, N Australia
Pinega 88 C3 river NW Russian Federation
Pineiós 82 B4 var. Piniós; anc. Peneius. river C Greece
Pineland 27 H3 Texas, SW USA
Pínes, Akrotírio 82 C4 var. Akrotírio Pínnes. headland N Greece
Pines, The Isle of the see Juventud, Isla de la
Pine Tree State see Maine
Pingdingshan 106 C4 Henan, C China
Pingkiang see Harbin
Ping, Mae Nam 114 B4 river W Thailand
Piniós see Pineiós
Pinkiang see Harbin
Pínnes, Akrotírio see Pínes, Akrotírio
Pinos, Isla de see Juventud, Isla de la
Pinotepa Nacional 29 F5 var. Santiago Pinotepa Nacional. Oaxaca, SE Mexico
Pinsk 85 B7 Pol. Pińsk. Brestskaya Voblasts', SW Belarus
Pinta, Isla 38 A5 var. Abingdon. island Galapagos Islands, Ecuador, E Pacific Ocean
Piombino 74 B3 Toscana, C Italy
Pioneer Mountains 24 D3 mountain range Montana, N USA North America
Pionerskiy 84 A4 Ger. Neukuhren. Kaliningradskaya Oblast', W Russian Federation
Piotrków Trybunalski 76 D4 Ger. Petrikau, Rus. Petrokov. Łodzkie, C Poland
Piraeus/Piraiévs see Peiraías
Pírgos see Pýrgos
Pirineos see Pyrenees
Piripiri 41 F2 Piauí, E Brazil
Pirna 72 D4 Sachsen, E Germany
Pirot 79 E5 Serbia, SE Serbia
Piryatin see Pyryatyn
Pisa 74 B3 var. Pisae. Toscana, C Italy
Pisae see Pisa
Pisaurum see Pesaro
Pisco 38 D4 Ica, SW Peru
Písek 77 A5 Budĕjovický Kraj, S Czech Republic
Pishan 104 A3 var. Guma. Xinjiang Uygur Zizhiqu, NW China
Pishpek see Bishkek
Pistoia 74 B3 anc. Pistoria, Pistoriæ. Toscana, C Italy
Pistoria/Pistoriæ see Pistoia
Pistyan see Piešťany
Pisz 76 D3 Ger. Johannisburg. Warmińsko-Mazurskie, NE Poland
Pita 52 C4 NW Guinea
Pitalito 36 B4 Huila, S Colombia
Pitcairn Island 121 G4 island S Pitcairn Islands
Pitcairn Islands 121 G4 UK dependent territory C Pacific Ocean
Piteå 62 D4 Norrbotten, N Sweden
Pitești 86 B5 Argeș, S Romania
Pitsanulok see Phitsanulok
Pitt Island see Makin
Pittsburg 23 F5 Kansas, C USA
Pittsburgh 19 E4 Pennsylvania, NE USA
Pittsfield 19 F3 Massachusetts, NE USA
Piura 38 B2 Piura, NW Peru
Pivdennyy Buh 87 E3 Rus. Yuzhnyy Bug. river S Ukraine
Placentia see Piacenza
Placetas 32 B2 Villa Clara, C Cuba
Plainview 27 E2 Texas, SW USA
Planeta Rica 36 B2 Córdoba, NW Colombia
Planken 72 E1 C Liechtenstein Europe
Plano 27 G2 Texas, SW USA
Plasencia 70 C3 Extremadura, W Spain
Plate, River 42 D4 var. River Plate. estuary Argentina/Uruguay
Plate, River see Plata, Río de la
Platinum 14 C3 Alaska, USA
Plattensee see Balaton
Platte River 23 E4 river Nebraska, C USA
Plattsburgh 19 F2 New York, NE USA
Plauen 73 C5 var. Plauen im Vogtland. Sachsen, E Germany
Plauen im Vogtland see Plauen
Pļaviņas 84 D4 Ger. Stockmannshof. Aizkraukle, S Latvia
Plây Cu 115 E5 var. Pleiku. Gia Lai, C Vietnam
Pleasant Island see Nauru
Pleiku see Plây Cu
Plenty, Bay of 128 E3 bay North Island, New Zealand
Plérin 68 A3 Côtes d'Armor, NW France
Plesetsk 88 C3 Arkhangel'skaya Oblast', NW Russian Federation
Pleshchenitsy see Plyeshchanitsy
Pleskau see Pskov
Pleskauer See see Pskov, Lake
Pleskava see Pskov
Pleszew 76 C4 Wielkopolskie, C Poland
Pleven 82 C2 prev. Plevna. Pleven, N Bulgaria
Plevlja/Plevlje see Pljevlja
Plevna see Pleven
Pljevlja 78 C4 prev. Plevlja, Plevlje. N Montenegro
Plocce see Ploče
Ploče 78 B4 It. Plocce; prev. Kardeljevo. Dubrovnik-Neretva, SE Croatia
Płock 76 D3 Ger. Plozk. Mazowieckie, C Poland
Plöcken Pass 73 C7 Ger. Plöckenpass, It. Passo di Monte Croce Carnico. pass SW Austria
Plöckenpass see Plöcken Pass
Ploești see Ploiești
Ploiești 86 C5 prev. Ploești. Prahova, SE Romania
Plomári 83 D5 prev. Plomárion. Lésvos, E Greece
Plomárion see Plomári
Płońsk 76 D3 Mazowieckie, C Poland
Plovdiv 82 C3 prev. Eumolpias; anc. Evmolpia, Philippopolis, Lat. Trimontium. Plovdiv, C Bulgaria
Plozk see Płock
Plungė 84 B3 Telšiai, W Lithuania
Plyeshchanitsy 85 D5 Rus. Pleshchenitsy. Minskaya Voblasts', N Belarus
Plymouth 33 G3 dependent territory capital SW Montserrat
Plymouth 67 C7 SW England, United Kingdom
Plzeň 77 A5 Ger. Pilsen, Pol. Pilzno. Plzeňský Kraj, W Czech Republic
Po 58 D4 river N Italy
Pobedy, Pik 104 B3 Chin. Tomür Feng. mountain China/Kyrgyzstan
Po, Bocche del see Po, Foci del
Pocahontas 20 B1 Arkansas, C USA
Pocatello 24 E4 Idaho, NW USA
Pochinok 89 A5 Smolenskaya Oblast', W Russian Federation
Pocking 73 D6 Bayern, SE Germany
Poděbrady 77 B5 Ger. Podiebrad. Středočeský Kraj, C Czech Republic
Podgorica 79 C5 prev. Titograd. country capital S Montenegro
Podiebrad see Poděbrady
Podil's'ka Vysochina 86 D3 plateau W Ukraine
Podium Anicensis see le Puy
Podol'sk 89 B5 Moskovskaya Oblast', W Russian Federation
Podravska Slatina see Slatina
Podujevë 79 D5 Serb. Podujevo. N Kosovo
Podujevo see Podujevë
Podunajská Rovina see Little Alföld
Poetovio see Ptuj
Pogradec 79 D6 var. Pogradeci. Korçë, SE Albania
Pogradeci see Pogradec
Pohjanlahti see Bothnia, Gulf of
Pohnpei 122 C2 prev. Ponape Ascension Island. island E Micronesia
Poictiers see Poitiers
Poinsett, Cape 132 D4 headland Antarctica
Point de Galle see Galle
Pointe-à-Pitre 33 G3 Grande Terre, C Guadeloupe
Pointe-Noire 55 B6 Kouilou, S Congo
Point Lay 14 C2 Alaska, USA
Poitiers 68 B4 prev. Poictiers; anc. Limonum. Vienne, W France
Poitou 68 B4 cultural region W France
Pokharā 113 E3 Western, C Nepal
Pokrovka see Kyzyl-Suu
Pokrovs'ke 87 G3 Rus. Pokrovskoye. Dnipropetrovs'ka Oblast', E Ukraine
Pokrovskoye see Pokrovs'ke
Pola see Pula
Pola de Lena 70 D1 Asturias, N Spain
Poland 76 B4 off. Republic of Poland, var. Polish Republic, Pol. Polska, Rzeczpospolita Polska; prev. Pol. Polska Rzeczpospolita Ludowa, The Polish People's Republic. country C Europe
Poland, Republic of see Poland
Polatlı 94 C3 Ankara, C Turkey
Polatsk 85 D5 Rus. Polotsk. Vitsyebskaya Voblasts', N Belarus
Pol-e Khomrī 101 E4 var. Pul-i-Khumri. Baghlān, NE Afghanistan
Poli see Pólis
Polikastro/Políkastron see Polýkastro
Polikrayshte 82 D2 Veliko Tŭrnovo, N Bulgaria
Pólis 80 C5 var. Poli. W Cyprus
Polish People's Republic, The see Poland
Polish Republic see Poland
Polkowice 76 B4 Ger. Heerwegen. Dolnośląskie, W Poland
Pollença 71 G3 Mallorca, Spain, W Mediterranean Sea
Pologi see Polohy
Polohy 87 G3 Rus. Pologi. Zaporiz'ka Oblast', SE Ukraine
Polokwane 56 D4 prev. Pietersburg. Limpopo, NE South Africa
Polonne 86 D2 Rus. Polonnoye. Khmel'nyts'ka Oblast', NW Ukraine
Polonnoye see Polonne
Polotsk see Polatsk
Polska/Polska, Rzeczpospolita/Polska Rzeczpospolita Ludowa see Poland
Polsko Kosovo 82 D2 Ruse, N Bulgaria
Poltava 87 F2 Poltavs'ka Oblast', NE Ukraine
Poltoratsk see Aşgabat
Põlva 84 E3 Ger. Pölwe. Põlvamaa, SE Estonia
Pölwe see Põlva
Polyarnyy 88 C2 Murmanskaya Oblast', NW Russian Federation
Polýkastro 82 B3 var. Polikastro; prev. Políkastron. Kentrikí Makedonía, N Greece
Polynesia 121 F4 island group C Pacific Ocean
Pomeranian Bay 72 D2 Ger. Pommersche Bucht, Pol. Zatoka Pomorska. bay Germany/Poland
Pomir, Dar"yoi see Pamir/Pāmīr, Daryā-ye
Pommersche Bucht see Pomeranian Bay
Pomorska, Zatoka see Pomeranian Bay
Pomorskiy Proliv 88 D2 strait NW Russian Federation
Po, Mouth of the 74 C2 var. Bocche del Po. river NE Italy
Pompaelo see Pamplona
Pompano Beach 21 F5 Florida, SE USA
Ponape Ascension Island see Pohnpei
Ponca City 27 G1 Oklahoma, C USA
Ponce 33 F3 C Puerto Rico
Pondicherry 110 C2 var. Puduchcheri, Fr. Pondichéry. Pondicherry, SE India
Ponferrada 70 C1 Castilla-León, NW Spain
Poniatowa 76 E4 Lubelskie, E Poland
Pons Aelii see Newcastle upon Tyne
Pons Vetus see Pontevedra
Ponta Delgada 70 B5 São Miguel, Azores, Portugal, NE Atlantic Ocean
Ponta Grossa 41 E4 Paraná, S Brazil
Pontarlier 68 D4 Doubs, E France
Ponteareas 70 B2 Galicia, NW Spain
Ponte da Barca 70 B2 Viana do Castelo, N Portugal
Pontevedra 70 B1 anc. Pons Vetus. Galicia, NW Spain
Pontiac 18 D3 Michigan, N USA
Pontianak 116 C4 Borneo, C Indonesia
Pontisarae see Pontoise
Pontivy 68 A3 Morbihan, NW France
Pontoise 68 C3 anc. Briva Isarae, Cergy-Pontoise, Pontisarae. Val-d'Oise, N France
Ponziane Island 75 C5 island C Italy
Poole 67 D7 S England, United Kingdom
Poona see Pune
Poopó, Lago 39 F4 var. Lago Pampa Aullagas. lake W Bolivia
Popayán 36 B4 Cauca, SW Colombia
Poperinge 65 A6 West-Vlaanderen, W Belgium
Poplar Bluff 23 G5 Missouri, C USA
Popocatépetl 29 E4 volcano S Mexico
Popper see Poprad
Poprad 77 D5 Ger. Deutschendorf, Hung. Poprád. Prešovský Kraj, E Slovakia
Poprád 77 D5 Ger. Popper, Hung. Poprád. river Poland/Slovakia
Porbandar 112 B4 Gujarāt, W India
Porcupine Plain 58 B3 undersea feature E Atlantic Ocean
Pordenone 74 C2 anc. Portenau. Friuli-Venezia Giulia, NE Italy
Poreč 78 A2 It. Parenzo. Istra, NW Croatia
Porech'ye see Parechcha
Pori 63 D5 Swe. Björneborg. Länsi-Suomi, SW Finland
Porirua 129 D5 Wellington, North Island, New Zealand
Porkhov 88 A4 Pskovskaya Oblast', W Russian Federation
Porlamar 37 E1 Nueva Esparta, NE Venezuela
Póros 83 C6 Póros, S Greece
Póros 83 A5 Kefallinía, Iónia Nisiá, Greece, C Mediterranean Sea
Pors see Porsangenfjorden
Porsangenfjorden 62 D2 Lapp. Pors. fjord N Norway
Porsgrunn 63 B6 Telemark, S Norway
Portachuelo 39 G4 Santa Cruz, C Bolivia
Portadown 67 B5 Ir. Port An Dúnáin. S Northern Ireland, United Kingdom
Portalegre 70 C3 anc. Ammaia, Amoea. Portalegre, E Portugal
Port Alexander 14 D4 Baranof Island, Alaska, USA
Port Alfred 56 D5 Eastern Cape, S South Africa
Port Amelia see Pemba
Port An Dúnáin see Portadown

Port Angeles – Răcari

Port Angeles *24 B1* Washington, NW USA
Port Antonio *32 B5* NE Jamaica
Port Arthur *27 H4* Texas, SW USA
Port Augusta *127 B6* South Australia
Port-au-Prince *32 D3 country capital* C Haiti
Port Blair *111 F2* Andaman and Nicobar Islands, SE India
Port Charlotte *21 E4* Florida, SE USA
Port Darwin *see* Darwin
Port d'Envalira *69 B8* E Andorra Europe
Port Douglas *126 D3* Queensland, NE Australia
Port Elizabeth *56 C5* Eastern Cape, S South Africa
Portenau *see* Pordenone
Porterville *25 C7* California, W USA
Port-Étienne *see* Nouâdhibou
Port Florence *see* Kisumu
Port-Francqui *see* Ilebo
Port-Gentil *55 A6* Ogooué-Maritime, W Gabon
Port Harcourt *53 G5* Rivers, S Nigeria
Port Hardy *14 D5* Vancouver Island, British Columbia, SW Canada
Port Harrison *see* Inukjuak
Port Hedland *124 B4* Western Australia
Port Huron *18 D3* Michigan, N USA
Portimão *70 B4 var.* Vila Nova de Portimão. Faro, S Portugal
Port Jackson *126 E1 harbour* New South Wales, E Australia
Portland *127 B7* Victoria, SE Australia
Portland *19 G2* Maine, NE USA
Portland *24 B3* Oregon, NW USA
Portland *27 G4* Texas, SW USA
Portland Bight *32 B5 bay* S Jamaica
Portlaoighise *see* Port Laoise
Port Laoise *67 B6 var.* Portlaoise, *Ir.* Portlaoighise; *prev.* Maryborough. C Ireland
Portlaoise *see* Port Laoise
Port Lavaca *27 G4* Texas, SW USA
Port Lincoln *127 A6* South Australia
Port Louis *57 H3 country capital* NW Mauritius
Port-Lyautey *see* Kénitra
Port Macquarie *127 E6* New South Wales, SE Australia
Port Mahon *see* Mahón
Portmore *32 B5* C Jamaica
Port Moresby *122 B3 country capital* Central/National Capital District, SW Papua New Guinea
Port Natal *see* Durban
Porto *70 B2 Eng.* Oporto; *anc.* Portus Cale. Porto, NW Portugal
Porto Alegre *41 E5 var.* Pôrto Alegre. *state capital* Rio Grande do Sul, S Brazil
Porto Alegre *54 E2* São Tomé, S Sao Tome and Principe, Africa
Porto Alegre *54 E2* São Tomé, S Sao Tome and Principe, Africa
Porto Alexandre *see* Tombua
Porto Amélia *see* Pemba
Porto Bello *see* Portobelo
Portobelo *31 G4 var.* Porto Bello, Puerto Bello. Colón, N Panama
Port O'Connor *27 G4* Texas, SW USA
Porto Edda *see* Sarandë
Portoferraio *74 B4* Toscana, C Italy
Port-of-Spain *33 H5 country capital* Trinidad, Trinidad and Tobago
Porto Grande *see* Mindelo
Portogruaro *74 C2* Veneto, NE Italy
Porto-Novo *53 F5 country capital* S Benin
Porto Rico *see* Puerto Rico
Porto Santo *48 A2 var.* Ilha do Porto Santo. *island* Madeira, Portugal, NE Atlantic Ocean
Porto Santo, Ilha do *see* Porto Santo
Porto Torres *75 A5* Sardegna, Italy, C Mediterranean Sea
Porto Velho *40 D2 var.* Velho. *state capital* Rondônia, W Brazil
Portoviejo *38 A2 var.* Puertoviejo. Manabí, W Ecuador
Port Pirie *127 B6* South Australia
Port Rex *see* East London
Port Said *see* Būr Saʿīd
Portsmouth *67 D7* S England, United Kingdom
Portsmouth *19 G3* New Hampshire, NE USA
Portsmouth *18 D4* Ohio, N USA
Portsmouth *19 F5* Virginia, NE USA
Port Stanley *see* Stanley
Port Sudan *50 C3* Red Sea, NE Sudan
Port Swettenham *see* Klang/Pelabuhan Klang
Port Talbot *67 C7* S Wales, United Kingdom
Portugal *70 B3 off.* Portuguese Republic. *country* SW Europe
Portuguese East Africa *see* Mozambique
Portuguese Guinea *see* Guinea-Bissau
Portuguese Republic *see* Portugal
Portuguese Timor *see* East Timor
Portuguese West Africa *see* Angola
Portus Cale *see* Porto
Portus Magnus *see* Almería
Portus Magonis *see* Mahón
Port-Vila *122 D4 var.* Vila. *country capital* Éfaté, C Vanuatu
Porvenir *39 E3* Pando, NW Bolivia
Porvenir *43 B8* Magallanes, S Chile
Porvoo *63 E6 Swe.* Borgå. Etelä-Suomi, S Finland
Porzecze *see* Parechcha
Posadas *42 D3* Misiones, NE Argentina
Poschega *see* Požega
Posen *see* Poznań
Posnania *see* Poznań
Postavy/Postawy *see* Pastavy
Posterholt *65 D5* Limburg, SE Netherlands
Postojna *73 D8 Ger.* Adelsberg, *It.* Postumia. SW Slovenia
Postumia *see* Postojna
Pöstyén *see* Piešťany
Potamós *83 C7* Antikýthira, S Greece
Potentia *see* Potenza
Potenza *75 D5 anc.* Potentia. Basilicata, S Italy
P'ot'i *95 F2* W Georgia
Potiskum *53 G4* Yobe, NE Nigeria
Potomac River *19 E5 river* NE USA
Potosí *39 F4* Potosí, S Bolivia
Potsdam *72 D3* Brandenburg, NE Germany
Potwar Plateau *112 C2 plateau* NE Pakistan
Poŭthĭsăt *115 D6 prev.* Pursat. Poŭthĭsăt, W Cambodia
Po, Valle del *see* Po Valley
Po Valley *74 C2 It.* Valle del Po. *valley* N Italy
Považská Bystrica *77 C5 Ger.* Waagbistritz, *Hung.* Vágbeszterce. Trenčiansky Kraj, W Slovakia
Poverty Bay *128 E4 inlet* North Island, New Zealand
Póvoa de Varzim *70 B2* Porto, NW Portugal
Powder River *22 D2 river* Montana/Wyoming, NW USA
Powell *22 C2* Wyoming, C USA
Powell, Lake *22 B5 lake* Utah, W USA
Požarevac *78 D4 Ger.* Passarowitz. Serbia, NE Serbia
Poza Rica *29 F4 var.* Poza Rica de Hidalgo. Veracruz-Llave, E Mexico
Poza Rica de Hidalgo *see* Poza Rica
Požega *78 D4 prev.* Slavonska Požega, *Ger.* Poschega, *Hung.* Pozsega. Požega-Slavonija, NE Croatia
Požega *78 D4* Serbia
Poznań *76 C3 Ger.* Posen, Posnania. Wielkolpolskie, C Poland
Pozoblanco *70 D4* Andalucía, S Spain
Pozsega *see* Požega
Pozsony *see* Bratislava
Pozzallo *75 C8* Sicilia, Italy, C Mediterranean Sea
Prachatice *77 A5 Ger.* Prachatitz. Jihočeský Kraj, S Czech Republic
Prachatitz *see* Prachatice
Prado del Ganso *see* Goose Green
Prae *see* Phrae
Prag/Praga/Prague *see* Praha
Praha *77 A5 Eng.* Prague, *Ger.* Prag, *Pol.* Praga. *country capital* Středočeský Kraj, NW Czech Republic
Praia *52 A3 country capital* Santiago, S Cape Verde
Prairie State *see* Illinois
Prathet Thai *see* Thailand
Prato *74 B3* Toscana, C Italy
Pratt *23 E5* Kansas, C USA
Prattville *20 D2* Alabama, S USA
Pravda *82 D1 prev.* Dogrular. Silistra, NE Bulgaria
Pravia *70 C1* Asturias, N Spain
Preny *see* Prienai
Prenzlau *72 D3* Brandenburg, NE Germany
Prerau *see* Přerov
Přerov *77 C5 Ger.* Prerau. Olomoucký Kraj, E Czech Republic
Preschau *see* Prešov
Prescott *26 B2* Arizona, SW USA
Preševo *79 D5* Serbia, SE Serbia
Presidente Epitácio *41 E4* São Paulo, S Brazil
Presidente Stroessner *see* Ciudad del Este
Prešov *77 D5 var.* Preschau, *Ger.* Eperies, *Hung.* Eperjes. Prešovský Kraj, E Slovakia
Prespa, Lake *79 D6 Alb.* Liqen i Prespës, *Gk.* Límni Megáli Préspa, Límni Prespa, *Mac.* Prespansko Ezero, *Serb.* Prespansko Jezero. *lake* SE Europe
Prespa, Limni/Prespansko Ezero/Prespansko Jezero/Prespës, Liqen i *see* Prespa, Lake
Presque Isle *19 H1* Maine, NE USA
Pressburg *see* Bratislava
Preston *67 D5* NW England, United Kingdom
Prestwick *66 C4* W Scotland, United Kingdom
Preussisch Eylau *see* Bagrationovsk
Preußisch Holland *see* Pasłęk
Preussisch-Stargard *see* Starogard Gdański
Préveza *83 A5* Ípeiros, W Greece
Pribilof Islands *14 A3 island group* Alaska, USA
Priboj *78 C4* Serbia, W Serbia
Price *22 B4* Utah, W USA
Prichard *20 C3* Alabama, S USA
Priekulė *84 B3 Ger.* Prökuls. Klaipėda, W Lithuania
Prienai *85 B5 Pol.* Preny. Kaunas, S Lithuania
Prieska *56 C4* Northern Cape, C South Africa
Prijedor *78 B3* Republika Srpska, NW Bosnia and Herzegovina
Prijepolje *78 D4* Serbia, W Serbia
Prikaspiyskaya Nizmennost' *see* Caspian Depression
Prilep *79 D6 Turk.* Perlepe. S FYR Macedonia
Priluki *see* Pryluky
Primorsk *84 A4 Ger.* Fischhausen. Kaliningradskaya Oblast', W Russian Federation
Primorsko *82 E2 prev.* Keupriya. Burgas, E Bulgaria
Primorsk/Primorskoye *see* Prymors'k
Prince Albert *15 F5* Saskatchewan, S Canada
Prince Edward Island *17 F4 Fr.* Île-du Prince-Édouard. *province* SE Canada
Prince Edward Islands *47 E8 island group* S South Africa
Prince George *15 E5* British Columbia, SW Canada
Prince of Wales Island *126 B1 island* Queensland, E Australia
Prince of Wales Island *15 F2 island* Queen Elizabeth Islands, Nunavut, NW Canada
Prince of Wales Island *see* Pinang, Pulau
Prince Patrick Island *15 E2 island* Parry Islands, Northwest Territories, NW Canada
Prince Rupert *14 D4* British Columbia, SW Canada
Prince's Island *see* Príncipe
Princess Charlotte Bay *126 C2 bay* Queensland, NE Australia
Princess Elizabeth Land *132 C3 physical region* Antarctica
Príncipe *55 A5 var.* Príncipe Island, *Eng.* Prince's Island. *island* N Sao Tome and Principe
Príncipe Island *see* Príncipe
Prinzapolka *31 E3* Región Autónoma Atlántico Norte, NE Nicaragua
Pripet *85 C7 Bel.* Prypyats', *Ukr.* Pryp"yat'. *river* Belarus/Ukraine
Pripet Marshes *85 B7 wetland* Belarus/Ukraine
Prishtinë *79 D5 Eng.* Pristina, *Serb.* Priština. C Kosovo
Pristina *see* Prishtinë
Priština *see* Prishtinë
Privas *69 D5* Ardèche, E France
Prizren *79 D5* S Kosovo
Probolinggo *116 D5* Jawa, C Indonesia
Probstberg *see* Wyszków
Progreso *29 H3* Yucatán, SE Mexico
Prokhladnyy *89 B8* Kabardino-Balkarskaya Respublika, SW Russian Federation
Prokletije *see* North Albanian Alps
Prökuls *see* Priekulė
Prokuplje *79 D5* Serbia, SE Serbia
Prome *see* Pyay
Promyshlennyy *88 E3* Respublika Komi, NW Russian Federation
Prościejów *see* Prostějov
Proskurov *see* Khmel 'nyts'kyy
Prossnitz *see* Prostějov
Prostějov *77 C5 Ger.* Prossnitz, *Pol.* Prościejów. Olomoucký Kraj, E Czech Republic
Provence *69 D6 cultural region* SE France
Providence *19 G3 state capital* Rhode Island, NE USA
Providence *see* Fort Providence
Providencia, Isla de *31 F3 island* NW Colombia, Caribbean Sea
Provideniya *133 B1* Chukotskiy Avtonomnyy Okrug, NE Russian Federation
Provo *22 B4* Utah, W USA
Prudhoe Bay *14 D2* Alaska, USA
Prusa *see* Bursa
Pruszków *76 D3 Ger.* Kaltdorf. Mazowieckie, C Poland
Prut *86 D4 Ger.* Pruth. *river* E Europe
Pruth *see* Prut
Pružana *see* Pruzhany
Pruzhany *85 B6 Pol.* Prużana. Brestskaya Voblasts', SW Belarus
Prychornomor'ska Nyzovyna *see* Black Sea Lowland
Prydniprovs'ka Nyzovyna/Prydnyaprowskaya Nizina *see* Dnieper Lowland
Prydz Bay *132 D3 bay* Antarctica
Pryluky *87 E2 Rus.* Priluki. Chernihivs'ka Oblast', NE Ukraine
Prymors'k *87 G4 Rus.* Primorsk; *prev.* Primorskoye. Zaporiz'ka Oblast', SE Ukraine
Pryp"yat'/Prypyats' *see* Pripet
Przemyśl *77 E5 Rus.* Peremyshl. Podkarpackie, C Poland
Przheval'sk *see* Karakol
Psará *83 D5 island* E Greece
Psel *87 F2 Rus.* Psël. *river* Russian Federation/Ukraine
Psël *see* Psel
Pskov *92 B2 Ger.* Pleskau, *Latv.* Pleskava. Pskovskaya Oblast', W Russian Federation
Pskov, Lake *84 E3 Est.* Pihkva Järv, *Ger.* Pleskauer See, *Rus.* Pskovskoye Ozero. *lake* Estonia/Russian Federation
Pskovskoye Ozero *see* Pskov, Lake
Ptich' *see* Ptsich
Ptsich *85 C7 Rus.* Ptich'. Homyel'skaya Voblasts', SE Belarus
Ptsich *85 C7 Rus.* Ptich'. *river* SE Belarus
Ptuj *73 E7 Ger.* Pettau; *anc.* Poetovio. NE Slovenia
Pucallpa *38 C3* Ucayali, C Peru
Puck *76 C2* Pomorskie, N Poland
Pudasjärvi *62 D4* Oulu, C Finland
Puebla *29 F4 var.* Puebla de Zaragoza. Puebla, S Mexico
Puebla de Zaragoza *see* Puebla
Pueblo *22 D5* Colorado, C USA
Puerto Acosta *39 E4* La Paz, W Bolivia
Puerto Aisén *43 B6* Aisén, S Chile
Puerto Ángel *29 F5* Oaxaca, SE Mexico
Puerto Argentino *see* Stanley
Puerto Ayacucho *36 D3* Amazonas, SW Venezuela
Puerto Baquerizo Moreno *38 B5 var.* Baquerizo Moreno. Galapagos Islands, Ecuador, E Pacific Ocean
Puerto Barrios *30 C2* Izabal, E Guatemala
Puerto Bello *see* Portobelo
Puerto Berrío *36 B2* Antioquia, C Colombia
Puerto Cabello *36 D1* Carabobo, N Venezuela
Puerto Cabezas *31 E2 var.* Bilwi. Región Autónoma Atlántico Norte, NE Nicaragua
Puerto Carreño *36 D3* Vichada, E Colombia
Puerto Cortés *30 C2* Cortés, NW Honduras
Puerto Cumarebo *36 C1* Falcón, N Venezuela
Puerto Deseado *43 C7* Santa Cruz, SE Argentina
Puerto Escondido *29 F5* Oaxaca, SE Mexico
Puerto Francisco de Orellana *38 B1 var.* Coca. Orellana, N Ecuador
Puerto Gallegos *see* Río Gallegos
Puerto Inírida *36 D3 var.* Obando. Guainía, E Colombia
Puerto La Cruz *37 E1* Anzoátegui, NE Venezuela
Puerto Lempira *31 E2* Gracias a Dios, E Honduras
Puerto Limón *see* Limón
Puertollano *70 D4* Castilla-La Mancha, C Spain
Puerto López *36 C1* La Guajira, N Colombia
Puerto Maldonado *39 E3* Madre de Dios, E Peru
Puerto México *see* Coatzacoalcos
Puerto Montt *43 B5* Los Lagos, C Chile
Puerto Natales *43 B7* Magallanes, S Chile
Puerto Obaldía *31 H5* Kuna Yala, NE Panama
Puerto Plata *33 E3 var.* San Felipe de Puerto Plata. N Dominican Republic
Puerto Presidente Stroessner *see* Ciudad del Este
Puerto Princesa *117 E2 off.* Puerto Princesa City. Palawan, W Philippines
Puerto Princesa City *see* Puerto Princesa
Puerto Príncipe *see* Camagüey
Puerto Rico *33 F3 off.* Commonwealth of Puerto Rico; *prev.* Porto Rico. *US commonwealth territory* C West Indies
Puerto Rico *34 B1 island* C West Indies
Puerto Rico, Commonwealth of *see* Puerto Rico
Puerto Rico Trench *34 B1 trench* NE Caribbean Sea
Puerto San José *see* San José
Puerto San Julián *43 B7 var.* San Julián. Santa Cruz, SE Argentina
Puerto Suárez *39 H4* Santa Cruz, E Bolivia
Puerto Vallarta *28 D4* Jalisco, SW Mexico
Puerto Varas *43 B5* Los Lagos, C Chile
Puerto Viejo *31 E4* Heredia, NE Costa Rica
Puertoviejo *see* Portoviejo
Puget Sound *24 B1 sound* Washington, NW USA
Puglia *75 E5 var.* Le Puglie, *Eng.* Apulia. *region* SE Italy
Pukaki, Lake *129 B6 lake* South Island, New Zealand
Pukekohe *128 D3* Auckland, North Island, New Zealand
Puket *see* Phuket
Pukhavichy *85 C6 Rus.* Pukhovichi. Minskaya Voblasts', C Belarus
Pukhovichi *see* Pukhavichy
Pula *78 A3 It.* Pola; *prev.* Pulj. Istra, NW Croatia
Pulaski *18 D5* Virginia, NE USA
Puławy *76 D4 Ger.* Neu Amerika. Lubelskie, E Poland
Pul-i-Khumri *see* Pol-e Khomrī
Pulj *see* Pula
Pullman *24 C2* Washington, NW USA
Pułtusk *76 D3* Mazowieckie, C Poland
Puná, Isla *38 A2 island* SW Ecuador
Pune *112 C5 prev.* Poona. Mahārāshtra, W India
Punjab *112 C2 prev.* West Punjab, Western Punjab. *province* E Pakistan
Puno *39 E4* Puno, SE Peru
Punta Alta *43 C5* Buenos Aires, E Argentina
Punta Arenas *43 B8 prev.* Magallanes. Magallanes, S Chile
Punta Gorda *30 C2* Toledo, SE Belize
Punta Gorda *31 E4* Región Autónoma Atlántico Sur, SE Nicaragua
Puntarenas *30 D4* Puntarenas, W Costa Rica
Punto Fijo *36 C1* Falcón, N Venezuela
Pupuya, Nevado *39 E4 mountain* W Bolivia
Puri *113 F5 var.* Jagannath. Orissa, E India
Puriramya *see* Buriram
Purmerend *64 C3* Noord-Holland, C Netherlands
Pursat *see* Poŭthĭsăt, Poŭthĭsăt, W Cambodia
Purus, Rio *40 C2 var.* Río Purús. *river* Brazil/Peru
Pusan *107 E4 off.* Pusan-gwangyŏksi, *var.* Busan, *Jap.* Fusan. SE South Korea
Pusan-gwangyŏksi *see* Pusan
Pushkino *see* Biläsuvar
Püspökladány *77 D6* Hajdú-Bihar, E Hungary
Putorana, Gory/Putorana Mountains *see* Putorana, Plato
Putorana Mountains *93 E3 var.* Gory Putorana, *Eng.* Putorana Mountains. *mountain range* N Russian Federation
Putrajaya *116 B3 country capital* Kuala Lumpur, Peninsular Malaysia
Puttalam *110 C3* North Western Province, W Sri Lanka
Puttgarden *72 C2* Schleswig-Holstein, N Germany
Putumayo, Río *36 B5 var.* Içá, Rio. *river* NW South America
Putumayo, Río *see* Içá, Rio
Puurmani *84 D2 Ger.* Talkhof. Jõgevamaa, E Estonia
Pyatigorsk *89 B7* Stavropol'skiy Kray, SW Russian Federation
Pyatikhatki *see* P"yatykhatky
P"yatykhatky *87 F3 Rus.* Pyatikhatki. Dnipropetrovs'ka Oblast', E Ukraine
Pyay *114 B4 var.* Prome, Pye. Bago, C Myanmar (Burma)
Pye *see* Pyay
Pyetrykaw *85 C7 Rus.* Petrikov. Homyel'skaya Voblasts', SE Belarus
Pyinmana *114 B4* Mandalay, C Myanmar (Burma)
Pyin-Oo-Lwin *114 B3 var.* Maymyo. Mandalay, C Myanmar (Burma)
Pýlos *83 B6* Pelopónnisos, S Greece
P'yŏngyang *107 E3 var.* P'yŏngyang-si, *Eng.* Pyongyang. *country capital* SW North Korea
P'yŏngyang-si *see* P'yŏngyang
Pyramid Lake *25 C5 lake* Nevada, W USA
Pyrenaei Montes *see* Pyrenees
Pyrenees *80 B2 Fr.* Pyrénées, *Sp.* Pirineos; *anc.* Pyrenaei Montes. *mountain range* SW Europe
Pýrgos *83 B6 var.* Pírgos. Dytikí Ellás, S Greece
Pyritz *see* Pyrzyce
Pyryatyn *87 E2 Rus.* Piryatin. Poltavs'ka Oblast', NE Ukraine
Pyrzyce *76 B3 Ger.* Pyritz. Zachodnio-pomorskie, NW Poland
Pyu *see* Phyu
Pyuntaza *114 B4* Bago, SW Myanmar (Burma)

Q

Qāʿ al Jafr *97 C7 lake* S Jordan
Qaanaaq *60 D1 var.* Qânâq, *Dan.* Thule. Avannaarsua, N Greenland
Qabātiya *97 E6* N West Bank Asia
Qābis *see* Gabès
Qābis, Khalīj *see* Gabès, Golfe de
Qacentina *see* Constantine
Qafṣah *see* Gafsa
Qagan Us *see* Dulan
Qahremānshahr *see* Kermānshāh
Qaidam Pendi *104 C4 basin* C China
Qal'aikhum *101 F3 Rus.* Kalaikhum. S Tajikistan
Qalāt *101 E5 Per.* Kalāt. Zābol, S Afghanistan
Qalʿat Bīshah *99 B5* ʿAsīr, SW Saudi Arabia
Qalqīlya *97 D6* Central, W West Bank Asia
Qamdo *104 D5* Xizang Zizhiqu, W China
Qamishly *see* Al Qāmishlī
Qânâq *see* Qaanaaq
Qaqortoq *60 C4 Dan.* Julianehåb. Kitaa, S Greenland
Qaraghandy/Qaraghandy Oblysy *see* Karaganda
Qara Qum *see* Garagum
Qarataū *see* Karatau, Zhambyl, Kazakhstan
Qarkilik *see* Ruoqiang
Qarokŭl *101 F3 Rus.* Karakul'. E Tajikistan
Qarqannah, Juzur *see* Kerkenah, Îles de
Qars *see* Kars
Qarshi *101 E3 Rus.* Karshi; *prev.* Bek-Budi. Qashqadaryo Viloyati, S Uzbekistan
Qasigianguit *see* Qasigiannguit
Qasigiannguit *60 C3 var.* Qasigianguit, *Dan.* Christianshåb. Kitaa, C Greenland
Qaṣr al Farāfirah *50 B2 var.* Qasr Farâfra. W Egypt
Qasr Farâfra *see* Qaṣr al Farāfirah
Qaṭanā *97 B5 var.* Katana. Dimashq, S Syria
Qatar *98 C4 off.* State of Qatar, *Ar.* Dawlat Qaṭar. *country* SW Asia
Qatar, State of *see* Qatar
Qattara Depression *50 A1 var.* Munkhafaḍ al Qaṭṭārah *var.* Monkhafad el Qaṭṭâra, *Eng.* Qattara Depression. *desert* NW Egypt
Qattara Depression/Qaṭṭārah, Munkhafaḍ al *see* Qaṭṭâra, Monkhafad el
Qaṭṭâra, Monkhafad el *see* Qaṭṭārah, Munkhafaḍ al
Qausuittuq *see* Resolute
Qazaqstan/Qazaqstan Respublikasy *see* Kazakhstan
Qazimämmäd *95 H3 Rus.* Kazi Magomed. SE Azerbaijan
Qazris *see* Cáceres
Qazvīn *98 C2 var.* Kazvin. Qazvīn, N Iran
Qena *see* Qinā
Qeqertarssuaq *see* Qeqertarsuaq
Qeqertarsuaq *60 C3 var.* Qeqertarssuaq, *Dan.* Godhavn. Kitaa, S Greenland
Qeqertarsuaq *60 C3 island* W Greenland
Qeqertarsuup Tunua *60 C3 Dan.* Disko Bugt. *inlet* W Greenland
Qerveh *see* Qorveh
Qeshm *98 D4 var.* Jazīreh-ye Qeshm, Qeshm Island. *island* S Iran
Qeshm Island/Qeshm, Jazīreh-ye *see* Qeshm
Qilian Shan *104 D3 var.* Kilien Mountains. *mountain range* N China
Qimusseriarsuaq *60 C2 Dan.* Melville Bugt, *Eng.* Melville Bay. *bay* NW Greenland
Qinā *50 B2 var.* Qena; *anc.* Caene, Caenepolis. E Egypt
Qing *see* Qinghai
Qingdao *106 D4 var.* Ching-Tao, Ch'ing-tao, Tsingtao, Tsintao, *Ger.* Tsingtau. Shandong, E China
Qinghai *104 C4 var.* Chinghai, Koko Nor, Qing, Qinghai Sheng, Tsinghai. *province* C China
Qinghai Hu *104 D4 var.* Ch'ing Hai, Tsing Hai, *Mong.* Koko Nor. *lake* C China
Qinghai Sheng *see* Qinghai
Qinhuangdao *106 D3* Hebei, E China
Qinzhou *106 B6* Guangxi Zhuangzu Zizhiqu, S China
Qiong *see* Hainan
Qiqihar *106 D2 var.* Ch'i-ch'i-ha-erh, Tsitsihar; *prev.* Lungkiang. Heilongjiang, NE China
Qira *104 B4* Xinjiang Uygur Zizhiqu, NW China
Qita Ghazzah *see* Gaza Strip
Qitai *104 C3* Xinjiang Uygur Zizhiqu, NW China
Qīzān *see* Jīzān
Qizil Orda *see* Kyzylorda
Qizil Qum/Qizilqum *see* Kyzyl Kum
Qizilrabot *101 G3 Rus.* Kyzylrabot. SE Tajikistan
Qogir Feng *see* K2
Qom *98 C3 var.* Kum, Qum. Qom, N Iran
Qomolangma Feng *see* Everest, Mount
Qomul *see* Hami
Qo'qon *101 F2 var.* Khokand, *Rus.* Kokand. Farg'ona Viloyati, E Uzbekistan
Qorveh *98 C3 var.* Qerveh, Qurveh. Kordestān, W Iran
Qostanay/Qostanay Oblysy *see* Kostanay
Qoubaïyât *96 B4 var.* Al Qubayyāt. N Lebanon
Qoussantina *see* Constantine
Quang Ngai *115 E5 var.* Quangngai, Quang Nghia. Quang Ngai, C Vietnam
Quangngai *see* Quang Ngai
Quang Nghia *see* Quang Ngai
Quan Long *see* Ca Mau
Quanzhou *106 D6 var.* Ch'uan-chou, Tsinkiang; *prev.* Chin-chiang. Fujian, SE China
Quanzhou *106 C6* Guangxi Zhuangzu Zizhiqu, S China
Qu'Appelle *15 F5 river* Saskatchewan, S Canada
Quarles, Pegunungan *117 E4 mountain range* Sulawesi, C Indonesia
Quarnero *see* Kvarner
Quartu Sant' Elena *75 A6* Sardegna, Italy, C Mediterranean Sea
Quba *95 H2 Rus.* Kuba. N Azerbaijan
Qubba *see* Baʿqūbah
Québec *17 E4 var.* Quebec. *province capital* Québec, SE Canada
Québec *16 D3 var.* Quebec. *province* SE Canada
Queen Charlotte Islands *14 C5 Fr.* Îles de la Reine-Charlotte. *island group* British Columbia, SW Canada
Queen Charlotte Sound *14 C5 sea area* British Columbia, W Canada
Queen Elizabeth Islands *15 E1 Fr.* Îles de la Reine-Élisabeth. *island group* Nunavut, N Canada
Queensland *126 B4 state* N Australia
Queenstown *129 B7* Otago, South Island, New Zealand
Queenstown *56 D5* Eastern Cape, S South Africa
Quelimane *57 E3 var.* Kilimane, Kilmain, Quilimane. Zambézia, NE Mozambique
Quelpart *see* Cheju-do
Quepos *31 E4* Puntarenas, S Costa Rica
Que Que *see* Kwekwe
Quera *see* Chur
Querétaro *29 E4* Querétaro de Arteaga, C Mexico
Quesada *31 E4 var.* Ciudad Quesada, San Carlos. Alajuela, N Costa Rica
Quetta *112 B2* Baluchistān, SW Pakistan
Quetzalcoalco *see* Coatzacoalcos
Quezaltenango *30 A2 var.* Quetzaltenango. Quezaltenango, W Guatemala
Quibdó *36 A3* Chocó, W Colombia
Quilimane *see* Quelimane
Quillabamba *38 D3* Cusco, C Peru
Quilon *110 C3 var.* Kollam. Kerala, SW India
Quimper *68 A3 anc.* Quimper Corentin. Finistère, NW France
Quimper Corentin *see* Quimper
Quimperlé *68 A3* Finistère, NW France
Quincy *18 A4* Illinois, N USA
Qui Nhon/Quinhon *see* Quy Nhơn
Quissico *57 E4* Inhambane, S Mozambique
Quito *38 B1 country capital* Pichincha, N Ecuador
Qulyndy Zhazyghy *see* Kulunda Steppe
Qum *see* Qom
Qurein *see* Al Kuwayt
Qŭrghonteppa *101 E3 Rus.* Kurgan-Tyube. SW Tajikistan
Qurlurtuuq *see* Kugluktuk
Qurveh *see* Qorveh
Quṣayr *see* Al Quṣayr
Quxar *see* Lhazê
Quy Nhơn *115 E5 var.* Quinhon, Qui Nhon. Binh Định, C Vietnam
Qyteti Stalin *see* Kuçovë
Qyzylorda *see* Kyzylorda

R

Raab *78 B1 Hung.* Rába. *river* Austria/Hungary
Raab *see* Rába
Raab *see* Győr
Raahe *62 D4 Swe.* Brahestad. Oulu, W Finland
Raalte *64 D3* Overijssel, E Netherlands
Raamsdonksveer *64 C4* Noord-Brabant, S Netherlands
Raasiku *84 D2 Ger.* Rasik. Harjumaa, NW Estonia
Rába *77 B7 Ger.* Raab. *river* Austria/Hungary
Rába *see* Raab
Rabat *48 C2 var.* al Dar al Baida. *country capital* NW Morocco
Rabat *80 B5* W Malta
Rabat *see* Victoria
Rabbah Ammon/Rabbath Ammon *see* ʿAmmān
Rabinal *30 B2* Baja Verapaz, C Guatemala
Rabka *77 D5* Małopolskie, S Poland
Râbniţa *see* Rîbniţa
Rabyanah Ramlat *49 G4 var.* Rebiana Sand Sea, Ṣaḥrāʾ Rabyānah. *desert* SE Libya
Rabyānah, Ṣaḥrāʾ *see* Rabyānah, Ramlat
Răcari *see* Durankulak

Rudzyensk – San Marino

Rudzyensk 85 C6 Rus. Rudensk. Minskaya Voblasts', C Belarus
Rufiji 51 C7 river E Tanzania
Rufino 42 C4 Santa Fe, C Argentina
Rugāji 84 D4 Balvi, E Latvia
Rügen 72 D2 headland NE Germany
Ruggell 72 E1 N Liechtenstein Europe
Ruhja see Rūjiena
Ruhnu 84 C2 var. Ruhnu Saar, Swe. Runö. island SW Estonia
Ruhnu Saar see Ruhnu
Rujen see Rūjiena
Rūjiena 84 D3 Est. Ruhja, Ger. Rujen. Valmiera, N Latvia
Rukwa, Lake 51 B7 lake SE Tanzania
Rum see Rhum
Ruma 78 D3 Vojvodina, N Serbia
Rumadiya see Ar Ramādī
Rumania/Rumänien see Romania
Rumbek 51 B5 El Buhayrat, S Sudan
Rum Cay 32 D2 island C Bahamas
Rumia 76 C2 Pomorskie, N Poland
Rummah, Wādī ar see Rimah, Wādī ar
Rummelsburg in Pommern see Miastko
Rumuniya/Rumŭniya/Rumunjska see Romania
Runanga 129 B5 West Coast, South Island, New Zealand
Rundu 56 C3 var. Runtu. Okavango, NE Namibia
Runö see Ruhnu
Runtu see Rundu
Ruoqiang 104 C3 var. Jo-ch'iang, Uigh. Charkhlik, Charkhliq, Qarkilik. Xinjiang Uygur Zizhiqu, NW China
Rupea 86 C4 Ger. Reps, Hung. Kőhalom; prev. Cohalm. Braşov, C Romania
Rupel 65 B5 river N Belgium
Rupella see la Rochelle
Rupert, Rivière de 16 D3 river Québec, C Canada
Rusaddir see Melilla
Ruschuk/Rusçuk see Ruse
Ruse 82 D1 var. Ruschuk, Rustchuk, Turk. Rusçuk. Ruse, N Bulgaria
Russadir see Melilla
Russellville 20 A1 Arkansas, C USA
Russia see Russian Federation
Russian America see Alaska
Russian Federation 90 D2 off. Russian Federation, var. Russia, Latv. Krievija, Rus. Rossiyskaya Federatsiya. country Asia/Europe
Russian Federation see Russian Federation
Rustaq see Ar Rustāq
Rust'avi 95 G2 SE Georgia
Rustchuk see Ruse
Ruston 20 B2 Louisiana, S USA
Rutanzige, Lake see Edward, Lake
Rutba see Ar Ruṭbah
Rutlam see Ratlām
Rutland 19 F2 Vermont, NE USA
Rutog 104 A4 var. Rutög, Rutok. Xizang Zizhiqu, W China
Rutok see Rutog
Ruvuma 47 E5 var. Rio Rovuma. river Mozambique/Tanzania
Ruvuma see Rovuma, Rio
Ruwenzori 55 E5 mountain range Dem. Rep. Congo/Uganda
Ruzhany 85 B6 Brestskaya Voblasts', SW Belarus
Ružomberok 77 C5 Ger. Rosenberg, Hung. Rózsahegy. Žilinský Kraj, N Slovakia
Rwanda 51 B6 off. Rwandese Republic; prev. Ruanda. country C Africa
Rwandese Republic see Rwanda
Ryazan' 89 B5 Ryazanskaya Oblast', W Russian Federation
Rybach'ye see Balykchy
Rybinsk 88 B4 prev. Andropov. Yaroslavskaya Oblast', W Russian Federation
Rybnik 77 C5 Śląskie, S Poland
Rybnitsa see Rîbniţa
Ryde 126 E1 United Kingdom
Ryki 76 D4 Lubelskie, E Poland
Rykovo see Yenakiyeve
Rypin 76 C3 Kujawsko-pomorskie, C Poland
Ryssel see Lille
Rysy 77 C5 mountain S Poland
Ryukyu Islands 103 E3 Eng. Ryukyu Islands. island group SW Japan
Ryukyu Islands 108 A2 Eng. Ryukyu Islands. island group SW Japan
Ryukyu Islands see Nansei-shotō
Ryukyu Islands see Nansei-shotō
Ryukyu Trench 103 F3 var. Nansei Syotō Trench. trench S East China Sea
Rzeszów 77 E5 Podkarpackie, SE Poland
Rzhev 88 B4 Tverskaya Oblast', W Russian Federation

S

Saale 72 C4 river C Germany
Saalfeld 73 C5 var. Saalfeld an der Saale. Thüringen, C Germany
Saalfeld an der Saale see Saalfeld
Saarbrücken 73 A6 Fr. Sarrebruck. Saarland, SW Germany
Sääre 84 C2 var. Sjar. Saaremaa, W Estonia
Saare see Saaremaa
Saaremaa 84 C2 Ger. Oesel, Ösel; prev. Saare. island W Estonia
Saariselkä 62 D2 Lapp. Suoločielgi. Lappi, N Finland
Sab' Ābār 96 C4 var. Sab'a Biyar, Sa'b Bi'ār. Ḥimṣ, C Syria
Sab'a Biyar see Sab' Ābār
Šabac 78 D3 Serbia, W Serbia
Sabadell 71 G2 Cataluña, E Spain
Sabah 116 D3 prev. British North Borneo, North Borneo. state East Malaysia
Sabanalarga 36 B1 Atlántico, N Colombia
Sabaneta 36 C1 Falcón, N Venezuela
Sabaria see Szombathely
Sab'atayn, Ramlat as 99 C6 desert C Yemen
Sabaya 39 F4 Oruro, S Bolivia
Sa'b Bi'ār see Sab' Ābār
Saberi, Hamun-e 100 C5 var. Daryācheh-ye Hāmun, Daryācheh-ye Sīstān. lake Afghanistan/Iran
Sabhā 49 F3 C Libya
Sabi see Save
Sabinas 29 E2 Coahuila de Zaragoza, NE Mexico
Sabinas Hidalgo 29 E2 Nuevo León, NE Mexico
Sabine River 27 H3 river Louisiana/Texas, SW USA
Sabkha see As Sabkhah
Sable, Cape 21 E5 headland Florida, SE USA
Sable Island 17 G4 island Nova Scotia, SE Canada
Şabyā 99 B6 Jīzān, SW Saudi Arabia
Sabzawar see Sabzevār
Sabzevār 98 D2 var. Sabzawar. Khorāsān-Razavī, NE Iran
Sachsen 72 D4 Eng. Saxony, Fr. Saxe. state E Germany
Sachs Harbour 15 E2 var. Ikaahuk. Banks Island, Northwest Territories, N Canada
Sächsisch-Reen/Sächsisch-Regen see Reghin
Sacramento 25 B5 state capital California, W USA
Sacramento Mountains 26 D2 mountain range New Mexico, SW USA
Sacramento River 25 B5 river California, W USA
Sacramento Valley 25 B5 valley California, W USA
Sá da Bandeira see Lubango
Şa'dah 99 B6 NW Yemen
Sado 109 C5 var. Sadoga-shima. island C Japan
Sadoga-shima see Sado
Saena Julia see Siena
Safad see Tsefat
Şafāqis see Sfax
Şafāshahr 98 D3 var. Deh Bīd. Fārs, C Iran
Safed see Tsefat
Säffle 63 B6 Värmland, C Sweden
Safford 26 C3 Arizona, SW USA
Safi 48 B2 W Morocco
Selseleh-ye Safīd Kuh 100 D4 Eng. Paropamisus Range. mountain range W Afghanistan
Sagaing 114 B3 Sagaing, C Myanmar (Burma)
Sagami-nada 109 D6 inlet SW Japan
Sagan see Żagań
Sāgar 112 D4 prev. Saugor. Madhya Pradesh, C India
Sagarmāthā see Everest, Mount
Sagebrush State see Nevada
Saghez see Saqqez
Saginaw 18 C3 Michigan, N USA
Saginaw Bay 18 D2 lake bay Michigan, N USA
Sagua la Grande 32 B2 Villa Clara, C Cuba
Sagunto 71 F3 Cat. Sagunt, Ar. Murviedro; anc. Saguntum. País Valenciano, E Spain
Sagunt/Saguntum see Sagunto
Sahara 46 B3 desert Libya/Algeria
Sahara el Gharbîya see Şaḩrā' al Gharbīyah
Saharan Atlas 48 D2 var. Saharan Atlas. mountain range Algeria/Morocco
Saharan Atlas see Atlas Saharien
Sahel 52 D3 physical region C Africa
Sāḩilīyah, Jibāl as 96 B3 mountain range NW Syria
Sāhīwāl 112 C2 prev. Montgomery. Punjab, E Pakistan
Saïda 97 A5 var. Şaydā, Sayida; anc. Sidon. W Lebanon
Sa'īdābād see Sīrjān
Saidpur 113 G3 var. Syedpur. Rajshahi, NW Bangladesh
Saidu Sharif 112 C1 var. Mingora, Mongora. North-West Frontier Province, N Pakistan
Saigon see Hô Chi Minh
Saimaa 63 E5 lake SE Finland
St Albans 67 E6 anc. Verulamium. E England, United Kingdom
Saint Albans 18 D5 West Virginia, NE USA
St Andrews 66 C4 E Scotland, United Kingdom
Saint Anna Trough see Svyataya Anna Trough
St. Ann's Bay 32 B4 C Jamaica
St. Anthony 17 G3 Newfoundland and Labrador, SE Canada
Saint Augustine 21 E3 Florida, SE USA
St Austell 67 C7 SW England, United Kingdom
St.Botolph's Town see Boston
St-Brieuc 68 A3 Côtes d'Armor, NW France
St. Catharines 16 D5 Ontario, S Canada
St-Chamond 69 D5 Loire, E France
Saint Christopher and Nevis, Federation of see Saint Kitts and Nevis
Saint Christopher-Nevis see Saint Kitts and Nevis
Saint Clair, Lake 18 D3 var. Lac à L'Eau Claire. lake Canada/USA
St-Claude 69 D5 anc. Condate. Jura, E France
Saint Cloud 23 F2 Minnesota, N USA
Saint Croix 33 F3 island S Virgin Islands (US)
Saint Croix River 18 A2 river Minnesota/Wisconsin, N USA
St David's Island 20 B5 island E Bermuda
St-Denis 57 G4 dependent territory capital NW Réunion
St-Dié 68 E4 Vosges, NE France
St-Egrève 69 D5 Isère, E France
Sainte Marie, Cap see Vohimena, Tanjona
Saintes 69 B5 anc. Mediolanum. Charente-Maritime, W France
St-Étienne 69 D5 Loire, E France
St-Flour 69 C5 Cantal, C France
St-Gall/Saint Gall/St. Gallen see Sankt Gallen
St-Gaudens 69 B6 Haute-Garonne, S France
Saint George 127 D5 Queensland, E Australia
St George 20 B4 N Bermuda
Saint George 22 A5 Utah, W USA
St. George's 33 G5 country capital SW Grenada
St-Georges 17 E4 Québec, SE Canada
St-Georges 37 H3 E French Guiana
Saint George's Channel 67 B6 channel Ireland/Wales, United Kingdom
St George's Island 20 B4 island E Bermuda
Saint Helena 47 B6 UK dependent territory C Atlantic Ocean
St. Helena Bay 56 B5 bay SW South Africa
St Helier 67 D8 dependent territory capital S Jersey, Channel Islands
St.Iago de la Vega see Spanish Town
Saint Ignace 18 C2 Michigan, N USA
St-Jean, Lac 17 E4 lake Québec, SE Canada
Saint Joe River 24 D2 river Idaho, NW USA North America
St. John 17 F4 New Brunswick, SE Canada
Saint-John see Saint John
Saint John River 19 H1 Fr. Saint-John. river Canada/USA
St John's 33 G3 country capital Antigua, Antigua and Barbuda
St. John's 17 H3 province capital Newfoundland and Labrador, E Canada
Saint Joseph 23 F4 Missouri, C USA
St Julian's 80 B5 N Malta
St Kilda 66 A3 island NW Scotland, United Kingdom
Saint Kitts and Nevis 33 F3 off. Federation of Saint Christopher and Nevis, var. Saint Christopher-Nevis. country E West Indies
St-Laurent see St-Laurent-du-Maroni
St-Laurent-du-Maroni 37 H3 var. St-Laurent. NW French Guiana
St-Laurent, Fleuve see St. Lawrence
St. Lawrence 17 E4 Fr. Fleuve St-Laurent. river Canada/USA
St. Lawrence, Gulf of 17 F3 gulf NW Atlantic Ocean
Saint Lawrence Island 14 B2 island Alaska, USA
St-Lô 68 B3 anc. Briovera, Laudus. Manche, N France
St-Louis 68 E4 Haut-Rhin, NE France
Saint Louis 52 B3 NW Senegal
Saint Louis 23 G4 Missouri, C USA
Saint Lucia 33 E1 country SE West Indies
Saint Lucia Channel 33 H4 channel Martinique/Saint Lucia
St-Malo 68 B3 Ille-et-Vilaine, NW France
St-Malo, Golfe de 68 A3 gulf NW France
Saint Martin see Sint Maarten
St.Matthew's Island see Zadetkyi Kyun
St. Matthias Group 122 B3 island group NE Papua New Guinea
St-Maur-des-Fossés 68 E2 Val-de-Marne, Île-de-France, N France Europe
St. Moritz 73 B7 Ger. Sankt Moritz, Rmsch. San Murezzan. Graubünden, SE Switzerland
St-Nazaire 68 A4 Loire-Atlantique, NW France
Saint Nicholas see São Nicolau
Saint-Nicolas see Sint-Niklaas
St-Omer 68 C2 Pas-de-Calais, N France
Saint Paul 23 F2 state capital Minnesota, N USA
St-Paul, Île 119 C6 island Île St-Paul, NE French Southern and Antarctic Territories Antarctica Indian Ocea
St Peter Port 67 D8 dependent territory capital C Guernsey, Channel Islands
Saint Petersburg 21 E4 Florida, SE USA
Saint Petersburg see Sankt-Peterburg
St-Pierre and Miquelon 17 G4 Fr. Îles St-Pierre et Miquelon. French territorial collectivity NE North America
St-Quentin 68 C3 Aisne, N France
Saint Thomas see São Tomé, Sao Tome and Principe
Saint Thomas see Charlotte Amalie, Virgin Islands (US)
Saint Ubes see Setúbal
Saint Vincent 33 G4 island N Saint Vincent and the Grenadines
Saint Vincent see São Vicente
Saint Vincent and the Grenadines 33 H4 country SE West Indies
Saint Vincent, Cape see São Vicente, Cabo de
Saint Vincent Passage 33 H4 passage Saint Lucia/Saint Vincent and the Grenadines
Saint Yves see Setúbal
Saipan 120 B1 island/country capital S Northern Mariana Islands
Saishū see Cheju-do
Sajama, Nevado 39 F4 mountain W Bolivia
Sajószentpéter 77 D6 Borsod-Abaúj-Zemplén, NE Hungary
Sakākah 98 B4 Al Jawf, NW Saudi Arabia
Sakakawea, Lake 22 D1 reservoir North Dakota, N USA
Sak'art'velo see Georgia
Sakata 108 D4 Yamagata, Honshū, C Japan
Sakhalin 93 G4 var. Sakhalin. island SE Russian Federation
Sakhalin see Sakhalin, Ostrov
Sakhon Nakhon see Sakon Nakhon
Şäki 95 G2 Rus. Sheki; prev. Nukha. NW Azerbaijan
Saki see Saky
Sakishima-shoto 108 A3 var. Sakisima Syotô. island group SW Japan
Sakisima Syotô see Sakishima-shotō
Sakiz see Saqqez
Sakiz-Adasi see Chíos
Sakon Nakhon 114 D4 var. Muang Sakon Nakhon, Sakhon Nakhon. Sakon Nakhon, E Thailand
Saky 87 F5 Rus. Saki. Respublika Krym, S Ukraine
Sal 52 A3 island Ilhas de Barlavento, NE Cape Verde
Sala 63 C6 Västmanland, C Sweden
Salacgrīva 84 C3 Est. Salatsi. Limbaži, N Latvia
Sala Consilina 75 D5 Campania, S Italy
Salado, Río 40 D5 river E Argentina
Salado, Río 42 C3 river C Argentina
Şalālah 99 D6 SW Oman
Salamá 30 B2 Baja Verapaz, C Guatemala
Salamanca 42 B4 Coquimbo, C Chile
Salamanca 70 D2 anc. Helmantica, Salmantica. Castilla-León, NW Spain
Salamīyah 96 B3 var. As Salamīyah. Ḩamāh, W Syria
Salang see Phuket
Salantai 84 B3 Klaipėda, NW Lithuania
Salatsi see Salacgrīva
Salavan 115 D5 var. Saravan, Saravane. Salavan, S Laos
Salavat 89 D6 Respublika Bashkortostan, W Russian Federation
Sala y Gomez 131 F4 island Chile, E Pacific Ocean
Sala y Gomez Fracture Zone see Sala y Gomez Ridge
Sala y Gomez Ridge 131 G4 var. Sala y Gomez Fracture Zone. fracture zone SE Pacific Ocean
Salazar see N'Dalatando
Šalčininkai 85 C5 Vilnius, SE Lithuania
Salduba see Zaragoza
Saldus 84 B3 Ger. Frauenburg. Saldus, W Latvia
Sale 127 C7 Victoria, SE Australia
Salé 48 C2 NW Morocco
Salekhard 92 D3 prev. Obdorsk. Yamalo-Nenetskiy Avtonomnyy Okrug, N Russian Federation
Salem 110 C2 Tamil Nādu, SE India
Salem 24 B3 state capital Oregon, NW USA
Salerno 75 D5 anc. Salernum. Campania, S Italy
Salerno, Gulf of 75 C5 Eng. Gulf of Salerno. gulf S Italy
Salerno, Gulf of see Salerno, Golfo di
Salernum see Salerno
Salihorsk 85 C7 Rus. Soligorsk. Minskaya Voblasts', S Belarus
Salima 57 E2 Central, C Malawi
Salina 23 E5 Kansas, C USA
Salina Cruz 29 F5 Oaxaca, SE Mexico
Salinas 38 A2 Guayas, W Ecuador
Salinas 25 B6 California, W USA
Salisbury 67 D7 var. New Sarum. S England, United Kingdom
Salisbury see Harare
Sállan see Sørøya
Sallyana see Şalyan
Salmantica see Salamanca
Salmon River 24 D3 river Idaho, NW USA
Salmon River Mountains 24 D3 mountain range Idaho, NW USA
Salo 63 D6 Länsi-Suomi, SW Finland
Salon-de-Provence 69 D6 Bouches-du-Rhône, SE France
Salonica/Salonika see Thessaloníki
Salonta 86 A3 Hung. Nagyszalonta. Bihor, W Romania
Sal'sk 89 B7 Rostovskaya Oblast', SW Russian Federation
Salt see As Salṭ
Salta 42 C2 Salta, NW Argentina
Saltash 67 C7 SW England, United Kingdom
Saltillo 29 E3 Coahuila de Zaragoza, NE Mexico
Salt Lake City 22 B4 state capital Utah, W USA
Salto 42 D4 Salto, N Uruguay
Salton Sea 25 D8 lake California, W USA
Salvador 41 G3 prev. São Salvador. state capital Bahia, E Brazil
Salween 102 C2 Bur. Thanlwin, Chin. Nu Chiang, Nu Jiang. river SE Asia
Şalyan 113 E3 var. Sallyana. Mid Western, W Nepal
Salzburg 73 D6 anc. Juvavum. Salzburg, N Austria
Salzgitter 72 C4 prev. Watenstedt-Salzgitter. Niedersachsen, C Germany
Salzwedel 72 C3 Sachsen-Anhalt, N Germany
Šamac see Bosanski Šamac
Samakhixai 115 E5 var. Attapu, Attopeu. Attapu, S Laos
Samalayuca 28 C1 Chihuahua, N Mexico
Samar 117 F2 island C Philippines
Samara 92 B3 prev. Kuybyshev. Samarskaya Oblast', W Russian Federation
Samarang see Semarang
Samarinda 116 D4 Borneo, C Indonesia
Samarkand see Samarqand
Samarkandski/Samarkandskoye see Temirtau
Samarobriva see Amiens
Samarqand 101 E2 Rus. Samarkand. Samarqand Viloyati, C Uzbekistan
Samawa see As Samāwah
Sambalpur 113 F4 Orissa, E India
Sambava 57 G2 Antsiranana, NE Madagascar
Sambir 86 B2 Rus. Sambor. L'vivs'ka Oblast', NW Ukraine
Sambor see Sambir
Sambre 68 D2 river Belgium/France
Samfya 56 D2 Luapula, N Zambia
Saminatal 72 E2 valley Austria/Liechtenstein Europe
Samnān see Semnān
Sam Neua see Xam Nua
Samoa 123 E4 off. Independent State of Western Samoa, var. Sāmoa; prev. Western Samoa. country W Polynesia
Sāmoa see Samoa
Samoa Basin 121 E3 undersea basin W Pacific Ocean
Samobor 78 A2 Zagreb, N Croatia
Sámos 83 E6 prev. Limín Vathéos. Sámos, Dodekánisa, Greece, Aegean Sea
Sámos 83 D6 island Dodekánisa, Greece, Aegean Sea
Samothrace see Samothráki
Samothráki 82 D4 Samothráki, NE Greece
Samothráki 82 C4 anc. Samothrace. island NE Greece
Sampit 116 C4 Borneo, C Indonesia
Samsun 94 D2 anc. Amisus. Samsun, N Turkey
Samtredia 95 F2 W Georgia
Samui, Ko 115 C6 island SW Thailand
Samut Prakan 115 C5 var. Muang Samut Prakan, Paknam. Samut Prakan, C Thailand
San 52 D3 Ségou, C Mali
San 77 E5 river SE Poland
Şan'ā' 99 B6 Eng. Sana. country capital W Yemen
Sana 78 B3 river NW Bosnia and Herzegovina
Sanae 132 B2 South African research station Antarctica
Sanaga 55 B5 river C Cameroon
San Ambrosio, Isla 35 A5 Eng. San Ambrosio Island. island W Chile
San Ambrosio Island see San Ambrosio, Isla
Sanandaj 98 C3 prev. Sinneh. Kordestān, W Iran
San Andrés, Isla de 31 F3 island NW Colombia, Caribbean Sea
San Andrés Tuxtla 29 F4 var. Tuxtla. Veracruz-Llave, E Mexico
San Angelo 27 F3 Texas, SW USA
San Antonio 30 B2 Toledo, S Belize
San Antonio 42 B4 Valparaíso, C Chile
San Antonio 27 F4 Texas, SW USA
San Antonio Oeste 43 C5 Río Negro, E Argentina
San Antonio River 27 G4 river Texas, SW USA
Sanāw 99 C6 var. Sanaw. NE Yemen
San Benedicto, Isla 28 B4 island W Mexico
San Benito 30 B1 Petén, N Guatemala
San Benito 27 G5 Texas, SW USA
San Bernardino 25 C7 California, W USA
San Blas 28 C3 Sinaloa, C Mexico
San Blas, Cape 20 D3 headland Florida, SE USA
San Blas, Cordillera de 31 G4 mountain range NE Panama
San Carlos 30 D4 Río San Juan, S Nicaragua
San Carlos 26 B2 Arizona, SW USA
San Carlos see Quesada, Costa Rica
San Carlos de Ancud see Ancud
San Carlos de Bariloche 43 B5 Río Negro, SW Argentina
San Carlos del Zulia 36 C2 Zulia, W Venezuela
San Clemente Island 25 B8 island Channel Islands, California, W USA
San Cristóbal 36 C2 Táchira, W Venezuela
San Cristobal 122 C4 var. Makira. island SE Solomon Islands
San Cristóbal see San Cristóbal de Las Casas
San Cristóbal de Las Casas 29 G5 var. San Cristóbal. Chiapas, SE Mexico
San Cristóbal, Isla 38 B5 var. Chatham Island. island Galapagos Islands, Ecuador, E Pacific Ocean
Sancti Spíritus 32 B2 Sancti Spíritus, C Cuba
Sandakan 116 D3 Sabah, East Malaysia
Sandalwood Island see Sumba, Pulau
Sandanski 82 C3 prev. Sveti Vrach. Blagoevgrad, SW Bulgaria
Sanday 66 D2 island NE Scotland, United Kingdom
Sanders 26 C2 Arizona, SW USA
Sand Hills 22 D3 mountain range Nebraska, C USA
San Diego 25 C8 California, W USA
Sandnes 63 A6 Rogaland, S Norway
Sandomierz 76 D4 Rus. Sandomir. Świętokrzyskie, C Poland
Sandomir see Sandomierz
Sandoway see Thandwe
Sandpoint 24 C1 Idaho, NW USA
Sand Springs 27 G1 Oklahoma, C USA
Sandusky 18 D3 Ohio, N USA
Sandvika 63 A6 Akershus, S Norway
Sandviken 63 C6 Gävleborg, C Sweden
Sandwich Island see Éfaté
Sandwich Islands see Hawaiian Islands
Sandy Bay 71 H5 Saskatchewan, C Canada
Sandy City 22 B4 Utah, W USA
Sandy Lake 16 B3 lake Ontario, C Canada
San Esteban 30 D2 Olancho, C Honduras
San Eugenio/San Eugenio del Cuareim see Artigas
San Felipe 36 D1 Yaracuy, NW Venezuela
San Felipe de Puerto Plata see Puerto Plata
San Félix, Isla 35 A5 Eng. San Felix Island. island W Chile
San Felix Island see San Félix, Isla
San Fernando 70 C5 prev. Isla de León. Andalucía, S Spain
San Fernando 33 H5 Trinidad, Trinidad and Tobago
San Fernando 24 D1 California, W USA
San Fernando 36 D2 var. San Fernando de Apure. Apure, C Venezuela
San Fernando de Apure see San Fernando
San Fernando del Valle de Catamarca 42 C3 var. Catamarca. Catamarca, NW Argentina
San Fernando de Monte Cristi see Monte Cristi
San Francisco 25 B6 California, W USA
San Francisco del Oro 28 C2 Chihuahua, N Mexico
San Francisco de Macorís 33 E3 C Dominican Republic
San Fructuoso see Tacuarembó
San Gabriel 38 B1 Carchi, N Ecuador
San Gabriel Mountains 24 E1 mountain range California, USA
Sangihe, Kepulauan see Sangir, Kepulauan
Sangir, Kepulauan 117 F3 var. Kepulauan Sangihe. island group N Indonesia
Sāngli 110 B1 Mahārāshtra, W India
Sangmélima 55 B5 Sud, S Cameroon
Sangre de Cristo Mountains 26 D1 mountain range Colorado/New Mexico, C USA
San Ignacio 30 B1 prev. Cayo, El Cayo. Cayo, W Belize
San Ignacio 39 F3 Beni, N Bolivia
San Ignacio 28 B2 Baja California Sur, W Mexico
San Joaquin Valley 25 B7 valley California, W USA
San Jorge, Gulf of 43 C6 var. Gulf of San Jorge. gulf S Argentina
San Jorge, Gulf of see San Jorge, Golfo
San José 31 E4 country capital San José, C Costa Rica
San José 39 G3 var. San José de Chiquitos. Santa Cruz, E Bolivia
San José 30 B3 var. Puerto San José. Escuintla, S Guatemala
San Jose 25 B6 California, W USA
San José see San José del Guaviare, Colombia
San José de Chiquitos see San José
San José de Cúcuta see Cúcuta
San José del Guaviare 36 C4 var. San José. Guaviare, S Colombia
San Juan 42 B4 San Juan, W Argentina
San Juan 33 F3 dependent territory capital NE Puerto Rico
San Juan see San Juan de los Morros
San Juan Bautista 42 D3 Misiones, S Paraguay
San Juan Bautista see Villahermosa
San Juan Bautista Tuxtepec see Tuxtepec
San Juan de Alicante 71 F4 País Valenciano, E Spain
San Juan del Norte 31 E4 var. Greytown. Río San Juan, SE Nicaragua
San Juan de los Morros 36 D2 var. San Juan. Guárico, N Venezuela
San Juanito, Isla 28 C4 island C Mexico
San Juan Mountains 26 D1 mountain range Colorado, C USA
San Juan, Río 31 E4 river Costa Rica/Nicaragua
San Juan River 26 C1 river Colorado/Utah, W USA
San Julián see Puerto San Julián
Sankt-Bartholomäi see Palamuse
Sankt Gallen 73 B7 var. St. Gallen, Eng. Saint Gall, Fr. St-Gall. Sankt Gallen, NE Switzerland
Sankt-Georgen see Sfântu Gheorghe
Sankt-Jakobi see Pärnu-Jaagupi, Pärnumaa, Estonia
Sankt Martin see Martin
Sankt Moritz see St. Moritz
Sankt-Peterburg 88 B4 prev. Leningrad, Petrograd, Eng. Saint Petersburg, Fin. Pietari. Leningradskaya Oblast', NW Russian Federation
Sankt Pölten 73 E6 Niederösterreich, N Austria
Sankt Veit am Flaum see Rijeka
Sankuru 55 D6 river C Dem. Rep. Congo
Şanlıurfa 95 E4 prev. Sanli Urfa, Urfa; anc. Edessa. şanlıurfa, S Turkey
Sanli Urfa see Şanlıurfa
San Lorenzo 39 G5 Tarija, S Bolivia
San Lorenzo 38 A1 Esmeraldas, N Ecuador
San Lorenzo, Isla 38 C4 island W Peru
Sanlúcar de Barrameda 70 C5 Andalucía, S Spain
San Luis 42 C4 San Luis, C Argentina
San Luis 30 B2 Petén, NE Guatemala
San Luis 28 A1 var. San Luis Río Colorado. Sonora, NW Mexico
San Luis Obispo 25 B7 California, W USA
San Luis Potosí 29 E3 San Luis Potosí, C Mexico
San Luis Río Colorado see San Luis
San Marcos 30 A2 San Marcos, W Guatemala
San Marcos 27 G4 Texas, SW USA
San Marino 74 E1 country capital C San Marino

San Marino – Shaddādī

San Marino *74 D1 off.* Republic of San Marino. *country* S Europe
San Marino, Republic of *see* San Marino
San Martín *132 A2 Argentinian research station* Antarctica
San Mateo *37 E2* Anzoátegui, NE Venezuela
San Matías *39 H3* Santa Cruz, E Bolivia
San Matías, Gulf of *43 C5 var.* Gulf of San Matías. *gulf* E Argentina
San Matías, Gulf of *see* San Matías, Golfo
Sanmenxia *106 C4 var.* Shan Xian. Henan, C China
Sânmiclăuș Mare *see* Sânnicolau Mare
San Miguel *30 C3* San Miguel, SE El Salvador
San Miguel *28 D2* Coahuila de Zaragoza, N Mexico
San Miguel de Ibarra *see* Ibarra
San Miguel de Tucumán *42 C3 var.* Tucumán. Tucumán, N Argentina
San Miguelito *31 G4* Panamá, C Panama
San Miguel, Río *39 G3 river* E Bolivia
San Murezzan *see* St. Moritz
Sannâr *see* Sennar
Sânnicolaul-Mare *see* Sânnicolau Mare
Sânnicolau Mare *86 A4 var.* Sânnicolaul-Mare, *Hung.* Nagyszentmiklós; *prev.* Sânmiclăuș Mare, Sînnicolau Mare. Timiș, W Romania
Sanok *77 E5* Podkarpackie, SE Poland
San Pablo *39 F5* Potosí, S Bolivia
San Pedro *30 C1* Corozal, NE Belize
San-Pédro *52 D5* S Ivory Coast
San Pedro *28 D3 var.* San Pedro de las Colonias. Coahuila de Zaragoza, NE Mexico
San Pedro de la Cueva *28 C2* Sonora, NW Mexico
San Pedro de las Colonias *see* San Pedro
San Pedro de Lloc *38 B3* La Libertad, NW Peru
San Pedro Mártir, Sierra *28 A1 mountain range* NW Mexico
San Pedro Sula *30 C2* Cortés, NW Honduras
San Rafael *42 B4* Mendoza, W Argentina
San Rafael Mountains *25 C7 mountain range* California, W USA
San Ramón de la Nueva Orán *42 C2* Salta, N Argentina
San Remo *74 A3* Liguria, NW Italy
San Salvador *30 B3 country capital* San Salvador, SW El Salvador
San Salvador *32 D2 prev.* Watlings Island. *island* E Bahamas
San Salvador de Jujuy *42 C2 var.* Jujuy. Jujuy, N Argentina
San Salvador, Isla *38 A4 island* Ecuador
Sansanné-Mango *53 E4 var.* Mango. N Togo
Sansepolcro *74 C3* Toscana, C Italy
San Severo *75 D5* Puglia, SE Italy
Santa Ana *39 F3* Beni, N Bolivia
Santa Ana *30 B3* Santa Ana, NW El Salvador
Santa Ana *24 D2* California, W USA
Santa Ana de Coro *see* Coro
Santa Ana Mountains *24 E2 mountain range* California, W USA
Santa Barbara *28 C2* Chihuahua, N Mexico
Santa Barbara *25 C7* California, W USA
Santa Catalina Island *25 B8 island* Channel Islands, California, W USA
Santa Catarina *41 E5 off.* Estado de Santa Catarina. *state* S Brazil
Santa Catarina *41 E5 off.* Estado de Santa Catarina. *region* S Brazil
Santa Catarina, Estado de *see* Santa Catarina
Santa Clara *32 B2* Villa Clara, C Cuba
Santa Clarita *24 D1* California, USA
Santa Comba *70 B1* Galicia, NW Spain
Santa Cruz *54 E2* São Tomé, S Sao Tome and Principe, Africa
Santa Cruz *25 B6* California, W USA
Santa Cruz *39 G4 department* E Bolivia
Santa Cruz Barillas *see* Barillas
Santa Cruz del Quiché *30 B2* Quiché, W Guatemala
Santa Cruz de Tenerife *48 A3* Tenerife, Islas Canarias, Spain, NE Atlantic Ocean
Santa Cruz, Isla *38 B5 var.* Indefatigable Island, Isla Chávez. *island* Galapagos Islands, Ecuador, E Pacific Ocean
Santa Cruz Islands *122 D3 island group* E Solomon Islands
Santa Cruz, Río *43 B7 river* S Argentina
Santa Elena *30 B1* Cayo, W Belize
Santa Fe *42 C4* Santa Fe, C Argentina
Santa Fe *26 D1 state capital* New Mexico, SW USA
Santa Fe *see* Bogotá
Santa Fe de Bogotá *see* Bogotá
Santa Genoveva *28 B3 mountain* W Mexico
Santa Isabel *122 C3 var.* Bughotu. *island* N Solomon Islands
Santa Isabel *see* Malabo
Santa Lucia Range *25 B7 mountain range* California, W USA
Santa Margarita, Isla *28 B3 island* W Mexico
Santa Maria *41 E5* Rio Grande do Sul, S Brazil
Santa Maria *25 B7* California, USA
Santa Maria *70 A5 island* Azores, Portugal, NE Atlantic Ocean
Santa María del Buen Aire *see* Buenos Aires
Santa María, Isla *38 A5 var.* Isla Floreana, Charles Island. *island* Galapagos Islands, Ecuador, E Pacific Ocean
Santa Marta *36 B1* Magdalena, N Colombia
Santa Maura *see* Lefkáda
Santa Monica *24 D1* California, W USA
Santana *54 E2* São Tomé, C Sao Tome and Principe, Africa
Santander *70 D1* Cantabria, N Spain
Santarém *41 E2* Pará, N Brazil
Santarém *70 B3 anc.* Scalabis. Santarém, W Portugal
Santa Rosa *42 C4* La Pampa, C Argentina
Santa Rosa *see* Santa Rosa de Copán
Santa Rosa de Copán *30 C2 var.* Santa Rosa. Copán, W Honduras
Santa Rosa Island *25 B8 island* California, W USA
Sant Carles de la Rápida *see* Sant Carles de la Ràpita
Sant Carles de la Ràpita *71 F3 var.* Sant Carles de la Rápida. Cataluña, NE Spain
Santiago *42 B4 var.* Gran Santiago. *country capital* Santiago, C Chile
Santiago *33 E3 var.* Santiago de los Caballeros. N Dominican Republic
Santiago *31 F5* Veraguas, S Panama
Santiago *70 B1 var.* Santiago de Compostela, *Eng.* Compostella; *anc.* Campus Stellae. Galicia, NW Spain
Santiago *52 A3 var.* São Tiago. *island* Ilhas de Sotavento, S Cape Verde
Santiago *see* Santiago de Cuba, Cuba
Santiago de Compostela *see* Santiago
Santiago de Cuba *32 C3 var.* Santiago. Santiago de Cuba, E Cuba
Santiago de Guayaquil *see* Guayaquil
Santiago del Estero *42 C3* Santiago del Estero, C Argentina
Santiago de los Caballeros *see* Santiago, Dominican Republic
Santiago de los Caballeros *see* Ciudad de Guatemala, Guatemala
Santiago Pinotepa Nacional *see* Pinotepa Nacional
Santiago, Río *38 B2 river* N Peru
Santi Quaranta *see* Sarandë
Santissima Trinidad *see* Chilung
Sant Julià de Lòria *69 A8* Sant Julià de Lòria, SW Andorra Europe
Santo *see* Espiritu Santo
Santo Antão *52 A2 island* Ilhas de Barlavento, N Cape Verde
Santo António *54 E1* Príncipe, N Sao Tome and Principe, Africa
Santo Domingo *33 D3 prev.* Ciudad Trujillo. *country capital* SE Dominican Republic
Santo Domingo de los Colorados *38 B1* Pichincha, NW Ecuador
Santo Domingo Tehuantepec *see* Tehuantepec
San Tomé de Guayana *see* Ciudad Guayana
Santos *41 F4* São Paulo, S Brazil
Santos Plateau *35 D5 undersea plateau* SW Atlantic Ocean
Santo Tomé *42 D3* Corrientes, NE Argentina
Santo Tomé de Guayana *see* Ciudad Guayana
San Valentín, Cerro *43 A6 mountain* S Chile
San Vicente *30 C3* San Vicente, C El Salvador
São Francisco, Rio *41 F3 river* E Brazil
Sao Hill *51 C7* Iringa, S Tanzania
São João da Madeira *70 B2* Aveiro, N Portugal
São Jorge *70 A5 island* Azores, Portugal, NE Atlantic Ocean
São Luís *41 F2 state capital* Maranhão, NE Brazil
São Mandol *see* São Manuel, Rio
São Manuel, Rio *41 E3 var.* São Mandol, Teles Pirés. *river* C Brazil
São Marcos, Baía de *41 F1 bay* N Brazil
São Miguel *70 A5 island* Azores, Portugal, NE Atlantic Ocean
Saona, Isla *33 E3 island* SE Dominican Republic
Saône *69 D5 river* E France
São Nicolau *52 A3 Eng.* Saint Nicholas. *island* Ilhas de Barlavento, N Cape Verde
São Paulo *41 E4 state capital* São Paulo, S Brazil
São Paulo *41 E4 off.* Estado de São Paulo. *state* S Brazil
São Paulo *41 E4 off.* Estado de São Paulo. *region* S Brazil
São Paulo de Loanda *see* Luanda
São Paulo, Estado de *see* São Paulo
São Pedro do Rio Grande do Sul *see* Rio Grande
São Roque, Cabo de *41 G2 headland* E Brazil
São Salvador *see* Salvador, Brazil
São Salvador/São Salvador do Congo *see* M'Banza Congo, Angola
São Tiago *see* Santiago
São Tomé *55 A5 country capital* São Tomé, S Sao Tome and Principe
São Tomé *54 E2 Eng.* Saint Thomas. *island* S Sao Tome and Principe
Sao Tome and Principe *54 D1 off.* Democratic Republic of Sao Tome and Principe. *country* E Atlantic Ocean
Sao Tome and Principe, Democratic Republic of *see* Sao Tome and Principe
São Tomé, Pico de *54 D2 mountain* São Tomé, C Sao Tome and Principe, Africa
São Vicente *52 A3 Eng.* Saint Vincent. *island* Ilhas de Barlavento, N Cape Verde
São Vicente, Cabo de *70 B5 Eng.* Cape Saint Vincent, *Port.* Cabode São Vicente. *cape* S Portugal
São Vicente, Cabo de *see* São Vicente, Cabo de
Sápai *see* Sápes
Sapele *53 F5* Delta, S Nigeria
Sápes *82 D3 var.* Sápai. Anatolikí Makedonía kai Thráki, NE Greece
Sapir *97 B7 prev.* Sappir. Southern, S Israel
Sa Pobla *71 G3* Mallorca, Spain, W Mediterranean Sea
Sappir *see* Sapir
Sapporo *108 D2* Hokkaidō, NE Japan
Sapri *75 D6* Campania, S Italy
Sapulpa *27 G1* Oklahoma, C USA
Saqqez *98 C2 var.* Saghez, Sakiz, Saqqiz. Kordestān, NW Iran
Saqqiz *see* Saqqez
Sara Buri *115 C5 var.* Saraburi. Saraburi, C Thailand
Saraburi *see* Sara Buri
Saragossa *see* Zaragoza
Saragt *see* Sarahs
Saraguro *38 B2* Loja, S Ecuador
Sarahs *100 D3 var.* Saragt, *Rus.* Serakhs. Ahal Welaýaty, S Turkmenistan
Sarajevo *78 C4 country capital* Federacija Bosna I Hercegovina, SE Bosnia and Herzegovina
Sarakhs *98 E2* Khorāsān-Razavī, NE Iran
Saraktash *89 D6* Orenburgskaya Oblast', W Russian Federation
Saran' *92 C4 Kaz.* Saran. Karaganda, C Kazakhstan
Saranda *see* Sarandë
Sarandë *79 C7 var.* Saranda, *It.* Porto Edda; *prev.* Santi Quaranta. Vlorë, S Albania
Saransk *89 C5* Respublika Mordoviya, W Russian Federation
Sarasota *21 E4* Florida, SE USA
Saratov *92 B3* Saratovskaya Oblast', W Russian Federation
Saravan/Saravane *see* Salavan
Sarawak *116 D3 state* East Malaysia
Sarawak *see* Kuching
Sarcelles *68 D1* Val-d'Oise, Île-de-France, N France Europe
Sardinia *75 A5 Eng.* Sardinia. *island* Italy, C Mediterranean Sea
Sardinia *see* Sardegna
Sarera, Teluk *see* Cenderawasih, Teluk
Sargasso Sea *44 B4 sea* W Atlantic Ocean
Sargodha *112 C2* Punjab, NE Pakistan
Sarh *54 C4 prev.* Fort-Archambault. Moyen-Chari, S Chad
Sārī *98 D2 var.* Sari, Sāri. Māzandarān, N Iran
Saría *83 E7 island* SE Greece
Sarıkamış *95 F3* Kars, NE Turkey
Sarikol Range *101 G3 Rus.* Sarykol'skiy Khrebet. *mountain range* China/Tajikistan
Sark *67 D8 Fr.* Sercq. *island* Channel Islands
Şarkışla *94 D3* Sivas, C Turkey
Sarmiento *43 B6* Chubut, S Argentina
Sarnia *16 C5* Ontario, S Canada
Sarny *86 C1* Rivnens'ka Oblast', NW Ukraine
Sarochyna *85 D5 Rus.* Sorochino. Vitsyebskaya Voblasts', N Belarus
Sarov *89 C5 prev.* Sarova. Respublika Mordoviya, SW Russian Federation
Sarova *see* Sarov
Sarpsborg *63 B6* Østfold, S Norway
Sarrebruck *see* Saarbrücken
Sartène *69 E7* Corse, France, C Mediterranean Sea
Sarthe *68 B4 river* N France
Sárti *82 C4* Kentrikí Makedonía, N Greece
Saruhan *see* Manisa
Saryarqa *see* Kazakhskiy Melkosopochnik
Sarykol'skiy Khrebet *see* Sarikol Range
Sary-Tash *101 F2* Oshskaya Oblast', SW Kyrgyzstan
Saryyesik-Atyrau, Peski *101 G1 desert* E Kazakhstan
Sasebo *109 A7* Nagasaki, Kyūshū, SW Japan
Saskatchewan *15 F5 province* SW Canada
Saskatchewan *15 F5 river* Manitoba/ Saskatchewan, C Canada
Saskatoon *15 F5* Saskatchewan, S Canada
Sasovo *89 B5* Ryazanskaya Oblast', W Russian Federation
Sassandra *52 D5* S Ivory Coast
Sassandra *52 D5 var.* Ibo, Sassandra Fleuve. *river* S Ivory Coast
Sassandra Fleuve *see* Sassandra
Sassari *75 A5* Sardegna, Italy, C Mediterranean Sea
Sassenheim *64 C3* Zuid-Holland, W Netherlands
Sassnitz *72 D2* Mecklenburg-Vorpommern, NE Germany
Sathmar *see* Satu Mare
Sátoraljaújhely *77 D6* Borsod-Abaúj-Zemplén, NE Hungary
Satpura Range *112 D4 mountain range* C India
Satsuma-Sendai *see* Sendai
Satsunan-shoto *108 A3 island group* Nansei-shotō, SW Japan Asia
Sattanen *62 D3* Lappi, NE Finland
Satu Mare *86 B3 Ger.* Sathmar, *Hung.* Szatmárrnémeti. Satu Mare, NW Romania
Sau *see* Sava
Saudi Arabia *99 B5 off.* Kingdom of Saudi Arabia, Al 'Arabīyah as Su'ūdīyah, *Ar.* Al Mamlakah al 'Arabīyah as Su'ūdīyah. *country* SW Asia
Saudi Arabia, Kingdom of *see* Saudi Arabia
Sauer *see* Sûre
Saugor *see* Sāgar
Saulkrasti *84 C3* Rīga, C Latvia
Sault Sainte Marie *18 C1* Michigan, N USA
Sault Sainte Marie *16 C4* Michigan, N USA
Sault Ste. Marie *16 C4* Ontario, S Canada
Saumur *68 B4* Maine-et-Loire, NW France
Saurimo *56 C1 Port.* Henrique de Carvalho, Vila Henrique de Carvalho. Lunda Sul, NE Angola
Sava *85 E6* Mahilyowskaya Voblasts', E Belarus
Savá *30 D2* Colón, N Honduras
Savai'i *123 E4 island* NW Samoa
Savannah *21 E2* Georgia, SE USA
Savannah River *21 E2 river* Georgia/South Carolina, SE USA
Savannakhét *see* Khanthabouli
Savanna-La-Mar *32 A5* W Jamaica
Savaria *see* Szombathely
Save *78 B3 Eng.* Save, *Ger.* Sau, *Hung.* Száva. *river* SE Europe
Save *see* Sava
Save, Rio *57 E3 var.* Sabi. *river* Mozambique/ Zimbabwe
Saverne *68 E3 var.* Zabern; *anc.* Tres Tabernae. Bas-Rhin, NE France
Savigliano *74 A2* Piemonte, NW Italy
Savigsivik *see* Savissivik
Savinski *see* Savinskiy
Savinskiy *88 C3 var.* Savinski. Arkhangel'skaya Oblast', NW Russian Federation
Savissivik *60 D1 var.* Savigsivik. Avannaarsua, N Greenland
Savoie *69 D5 cultural region* E France
Savona *74 A2* Liguria, NW Italy
Savu Sea *117 E5 Ind.* Laut Sawu. *sea* S Indonesia
Sawakin *see* Suakin
Sawdirī *see* Sodiri
Sawhāj *50 B2 var.* Sawhāj *var.* Sohâg, Suliag. C Egypt
Sawhāj *see* Sawhāj
Şawqirah *99 D6 var.* Suqrah. S Oman
Sawu, Laut *see* Savu Sea
Saxe *see* Sachsen
Saxony *see* Sachsen
Sayabouty *see* Xaignabouli
Sayanskiy Khrebet *90 D3 mountain range* S Russian Federation
Saýat *100 D3 Rus.* Sayat. Lebap Welaýaty, E Turkmenistan
Sayaxché *30 B2* Petén, N Guatemala
Şaydā/Sayida *see* Saïda
Sayḥūt *99 D6* E Yemen
Saynshand *105 E2* Dornogovĭ, SE Mongolia
Sayre *19 E3* Pennsylvania, NE USA
Say'ūn *99 C6 var.* Saywūn. C Yemen
Saywūn *see* Say'ūn
Scalabis *see* Santarém
Scandinavia *44 D2 geophysical region* NW Europe
Scarborough *67 D5* N England, United Kingdom
Scarpanto *see* Kárpathos
Scebeli *see* Shebeli
Schaan *72 E1* W Liechtenstein Europe
Schaerbeek *65 C6* Brussels, C Belgium
Schaffhausen *73 B7 Fr.* Schaffhouse. Schaffhausen, N Switzerland
Schaffhouse *see* Schaffhausen
Schagen *64 C2* Noord-Holland, NW Netherlands
Schaulen *see* Šiauliai
Schebschi Mountains *see* Shebshi Mountains
Scheessel *72 B3* Niedersachsen, NW Germany
Schefferville *17 E2* Québec, E Canada
Schelde *see* Scheldt
Scheldt *65 B5 Dut.* Schelde, *Fr.* Escaut. *river* W Europe
Schell Creek Range *25 D5 mountain range* Nevada, W USA
Schenectady *19 F3* New York, NE USA
Schertz *27 G4* Texas, SW USA
Schiermonnikoog *64 D1 Fris.* Skiermûntseach. *island* Waddeneilanden, N Netherlands
Schijndel *64 D4* Noord-Brabant, S Netherlands
Schil *see* Jiu
Schiltigheim *68 E3* Bas-Rhin, NE France
Schivelbein *see* Świdwin
Schleswig *72 B2* Schleswig-Holstein, N Germany
Schleswig-Holstein *72 B2 state* N Germany
Schlettstadt *see* Sélestat
Schlochau *see* Człuchów
Schneekoppe *see* Sněžka
Schneidemühl *see* Piła
Schoden *see* Skuodas
Schönebeck *72 C4* Sachsen-Anhalt, C Germany
Schönlanke *see* Trzcianka
Schooten *see* Schoten
Schoten *65 C5 var.* Schooten. Antwerpen, N Belgium
Schouwen *64 B4 island* SW Netherlands
Schwabenalb *see* Schwäbische Alb
Schwäbische Alb *73 B6 var.* Schwabenalb, *Eng.* Swabian Jura. *mountain range* S Germany
Schwandorf *73 C5* Bayern, SE Germany
Schwaz *73 C7* Tirol, W Austria
Schweidnitz *see* Świdnica
Schweinfurt *73 B5* Bayern, SE Germany
Schweiz *see* Switzerland
Schwerin *72 C3* Mecklenburg-Vorpommern, N Germany
Schwertberg *see* Świecie
Schwiebus *see* Świebodzin
Schwyz *73 B7 var.* Schwiz. Schwyz, C Switzerland
Schyl *see* Jiu
Scio *see* Chíos
Scoresby Sound/Scoresbysund *see* Ittoqqortoormiit
Scoresby Sund *see* Kangertittivaq
Scotia Sea *35 C8 sea* SW Atlantic Ocean
Scotland *66 C3 cultural region* Scotland, U K
Scott Base *132 B4 NZ research station* Antarctica
Scott Island *132 B5 island* Antarctica
Scottsbluff *22 D3* Nebraska, C USA
Scottsboro *20 D1* Alabama, S USA
Scottsdale *26 B2* Arizona, SW USA
Scranton *19 F3* Pennsylvania, NE USA
Scrobesbyrig' *see* Shrewsbury
Scupi *see* Skopje
Scutari *see* Shkodër
Scutari, Lake *79 C5 Alb.* Liqeni i Shkodrës, *SCr.* Skadarsko Jezero. *lake* Albania/Montenegro
Scyros *see* Skýros
Searcy *20 B1* Arkansas, C USA
Seattle *24 B2* Washington, NW USA
Sébaco *30 D3* Matagalpa, W Nicaragua
Sebaste/Sebastia *see* Sivas
Sebastián Vizcaíno, Bahía *28 A2 bay* NW Mexico
Sebastopol *see* Sevastopol'
Sebenico *see* Šibenik
Sechura, Bahía de *38 A3 bay* NW Peru
Secunderābād *112 D5 var.* Sikandarabad. Andhra Pradesh, C India
Sedan *68 D3* Ardennes, N France
Seddon *129 D5* Marlborough, South Island, New Zealand
Seddonville *129 C5* West Coast, South Island, New Zealand
Sédhiou *52 B3* SW Senegal
Sedlez *see* Siedlce
Sedona *26 B2* Arizona, SW USA
Sedunum *see* Sion
Seeland *see* Sjælland
Seenu Atoll *see* Addu Atoll
Seesen *72 B4* Niedersachsen, C Germany
Segestica *see* Sisak
Segezha *88 B3* Respublika Kareliya, NW Russian Federation
Seghedin *see* Szeged
Segna *see* Senj
Segodunum *see* Rodez
Ségou *52 D3 var.* Segu. Ségou, C Mali
Segovia *70 D2* Castilla-León, C Spain
Segoviao Wangkí *see* Coco, Río
Segu *see* Ségou
Séguédine *53 H2* Agadez, NE Niger
Seguin *27 G4* Texas, SW USA
Segura *71 E4 river* S Spain
Seinäjoki *63 D5 Swe.* Östermyra. Länsi-Suomi, W Finland
Seine *68 D1 river* N France
Seine, Baie de la *68 B3 bay* N France
Sekondi *see* Sekondi-Takoradi
Sekondi-Takoradi *53 E5 var.* Sekondi. S Ghana
Selânik *see* Thessaloníki
Selenga *105 E1 Mong.* Selenge Mörön. *river* Mongolia/Russian Federation
Selenge Mörön *see* Selenga
Sélestat *68 E4 Ger.* Schlettstadt. Bas-Rhin, NE France
Seleucia *see* Silifke
Selfoss *61 E5* Sudhurland, SW Iceland
Sélibabi *52 C3 var.* Sélibaby. Guidimaka, S Mauritania
Sélibaby *see* Sélibabi
Selma *25 C6* California, W USA
Selway River *24 D2 river* Idaho, NW USA North America
Selwyn Range *126 B3 mountain range* Queensland, C Australia
Selzaete *see* Zelzate
Semarang *116 C5 var.* Samarang. Jawa, C Indonesia
Sembé *55 B5* Sangha, NW Congo
Semendria *see* Smederevo
Semey *see* Semipalatinsk
Semezhevo *see* Syemyezhava
Seminole *27 E3* Texas, SW USA
Seminole, Lake *20 D3 reservoir* Florida/Georgia, SE USA
Semipalatinsk *92 D4 Kaz.* Semey. Vostochnyy Kazakhstan, E Kazakhstan
Semnān *98 D3 var.* Samnān. Semnān, N Iran
Semois *65 C8 river* SE Belgium
Sendai *109 A8 var.* Satsuma-Sendai. Kagoshima, Kyūshū, SW Japan
Sendai *108 D4* Miyagi, Honshū, C Japan
Sendai-wan *108 D4 bay* E Japan
Senec *77 C6 Ger.* Wartberg, *Hung.* Szenc; *prev.* Szempcz. Bratislavský Kraj, W Slovakia
Senegal *52 B3 off.* Republic of Senegal, *Fr.* Sénégal. *country* W Africa
Senegal *52 C3 Fr.* Sénégal. *river* W Africa
Senegal, Republic of *see* Senegal
Senftenberg *72 D4* Brandenburg, E Germany
Senia *see* Senj
Senica *77 C6 Ger.* Senitz, *Hung.* Szenice. Trnavský Kraj, W Slovakia
Seniça *see* Sjenica
Senitz *see* Senica
Senj *78 A3 Ger.* Zengg, *It.* Segna; *anc.* Senia. Lika-Senj, NW Croatia
Senja *62 C2 prev.* Senjen. *island* N Norway
Senjen *see* Senja
Senkaku-shoto *108 A3 island group* SW Japan
Senlis *68 C3* Oise, N France
Sennar *50 C4 var.* Sannār. Sinnar, C Sudan
Senones *see* Sens
Sens *68 C3 anc.* Agendicum, Senones. Yonne, C France
Sensburg *see* Mrągowo
Sên, Stœng *115 D5 river* C Cambodia
Senta *78 D3 Hung.* Zenta. Vojvodina, N Serbia
Seo de Urgel *see* La See d'Urgel
Seoul *see* Sŏul
Şepși-Sângeorz/Sepsiszentgyőrgy *see* Sfântu Gheorghe
Sept-Îles *17 E3* Québec, SE Canada
Seraing *65 D6* Liège, E Belgium
Serakhs *see* Sarahs
Seram, Laut *see* Ceram Sea
Pulau Seram *117 F4 var.* Serang, *Eng.* Ceram. *island* Maluku, E Indonesia
Serang *116 C5* Jawa, C Indonesia
Serang *see* Seram, Pulau
Serasan, Selat *116 C3 strait* Indonesia/Malaysia
Serbia *78 D4 off.* Federal Republic of Serbia; *prev.* Yugoslavia, *SCr.* Jugoslavija. *country* SE Europe
Serbia, Federal Republic of *see* Serbia
Sercq *see* Sark
Serdar *100 C2 prev. Rus.* Gyzyrlabat, Kizyl-Arvat. Balkan Welaýaty, W Turkmenistan
Serdica *see* Sofiya
Serdobol' *see* Sortavala
Serenje *56 D2* Central, E Zambia
Seres *see* Sérres
Seret/Sereth *see* Siret
Serhetabat *100 D4 prev. Rus.* Gushgy, Kushka. Mary Welaýaty, S Turkmenistan
Sérifos *83 C6 anc.* Seriphos. *island* Kykládes, Greece, Aegean Sea
Seriphos *see* Sérifos
Serov *92 C3* Sverdlovskaya Oblast', C Russian Federation
Serowe *56 D3* Central, SE Botswana
Serpa Pinto *see* Menongue
Serpent's Mouth, The *37 F2 Sp.* Boca de la Serpiente. *strait* Trinidad and Tobago/Venezuela
Serpiente, Boca de la *see* Serpent's Mouth, The
Serpukhov *89 B5* Moskovskaya Oblast', W Russian Federation
Sérrai *see* Sérres
Serrana, Cayo de *31 F2 island group* NW Colombia South America
Serranilla, Cayo de *31 F2 island group* NW Colombia South America Caribbean Sea
Serravalle *74 E1* N San Marino
Sérres *82 C3 var.* Seres; *prev.* Sérrai. Kentrikí Makedonía, NE Greece
Sesdlets *see* Siedlce
Sesto San Giovanni *74 B2* Lombardia, N Italy
Sesvete *78 B2* Zagreb, N Croatia
Setabis *see* Xàtiva
Sète *69 C6 prev.* Cette. Hérault, S France
Setesdal *63 A6 valley* S Norway
Sétif *49 E2 var.* Stif. N Algeria
Setté Cama *55 A6* Ogooué-Maritime, SW Gabon
Setúbal *70 B4 Eng.* Saint Ubes, Saint Yves. Setúbal, W Portugal
Setúbal, Baía de *70 B4 bay* W Portugal
Seul, Lac *16 B3 lake* Ontario, S Canada
Sevan *95 G2* C Armenia
Sevan, Lake *95 G3 Eng.* Lake Sevan, *Rus.* Ozero Sevan. *lake* E Armenia
Sevan, Lake/Sevan, Ozero *see* Sevana Lich
Sevastopol' *87 F5 Eng.* Sebastopol. Respublika Krym, S Ukraine
Severn *16 B2 river* Ontario, S Canada
Severn *67 D6 Wel.* Hafren. *river* England/Wales, United Kingdom
Severnaya Zemlya *93 E2 var.* Nicholas II Land. *island group* N Russian Federation
Severnyy *88 E3* Respublika Komi, NW Russian Federation
Severodonetsk *see* Syeverodonets'k
Severodvinsk *88 C3 prev.* Molotov, Sudostroy. Arkhangel'skaya Oblast', NW Russian Federation
Severomorsk *88 C2* Murmanskaya Oblast', NW Russian Federation
Seversk *92 D4* Tomskaya Oblast', C Russian Federation
Sevier Lake *22 A4 lake* Utah, W USA
Sevilla *70 C4 Eng.* Seville; *anc.* Hispalis. Andalucía, SW Spain
Seville *see* Sevilla
Sevlievo *82 D2* Gabrovo, N Bulgaria
Sevluš/Sevlyush *see* Vynohradiv
Seward's Folly *see* Alaska
Seychelles *57 G1 off.* Republic of Seychelles. *country* W Indian Ocean
Seychelles, Republic of *see* Seychelles
Seydhisfjördhur *61 E5* Austurland, E Iceland
Seýdi *100 D2 Rus.* Seydi; *prev.* Neftezavodsk. Lebap Welaýaty, E Turkmenistan
Seyhan *see* Adana
Sfákia *see* Chóra Sfakíon
Sfântu Gheorghe *86 C4 Ger.* Sankt-Georgen, *Hung.* Sepsiszentgyőrgy; *prev.* Şepși-Sângeorz, Sfintu Gheorghe. Covasna, C Romania
Sfax *49 F2 Ar.* Şafāqis. E Tunisia
Sfintu Gheorghe *see* Sfântu Gheorghe
's-Gravenhage *64 B4 var.* Den Haag, *Eng.* The Hague, *Fr.* La Haye. *country capital* Zuid-Holland, W Netherlands
's-Gravenzande *64 B4* Zuid-Holland, W Netherlands
Shaan/Shaanxi Sheng *see* Shaanxi
Shaanxi *106 B5 var.* Shaan, Shaanxi Sheng, Shan-hsi, Shenshi, Shensi. *province* C China
Shabani *see* Zvishavane
Shabeelle, Webi *see* Shebeli
Shache *104 A3 var.* Yarkant. Xinjiang Uygur Zizhiqu, NW China
Shacheng *see* Huailai
Shackleton Ice Shelf *132 D3 ice shelf* Antarctica
Shaddādī *see* Ash Shadādah

Shāhābād – Soltau

Shāhābād see Eslāmābād
Sha Hi see Orūmīyeh, Daryācheh-ye
Shahjahanabad see Delhi
Shahr-e Kord 98 C3 var. Shahr Kord. Chahār Maḩall va Bakhtīārī, C Iran
Shahr Kord see Shahr-e Kord
Shāhrūd 98 D2 prev. Emāmrūd, Emāmshahr. Semnān, N Iran
Shalkar 92 B4 var. Chelkar. Aktyubinsk, W Kazakhstan
Shām, Bādiyat ash see Syrian Desert
Shana see Kuril'sk
Shandi see Shendi
Shandong 106 D4 var. Lu, Shandong Sheng, Shantung. province E China
Shandong Sheng see Shandong
Shanghai 106 D5 var. Shang-hai. Shanghai Shi, E China
Shangrao 106 D5 Jiangxi, S China
Shan-hsi see Shaanxi, China
Shan-hsi see Shanxi, China
Shannon 67 A6 Ir. An tSionainn. river W Ireland
Shan Plateau 114 B3 plateau E Myanmar (Burma)
Shansi see Shanxi
Shantar Islands see Shantarskiye Ostrova
Shantarskiye Ostrova 93 G3 Eng. Shantar Islands. island group E Russian Federation
Shantou 106 D6 var. Shan-t'ou, Swatow. Guangdong, S China
Shan-t'ou see Shantou
Shantung see Shandong
Shanxi 106 C4 var. Jin, Shan-hsi, Shansi, Shanxi Sheng. province C China
Shan Xian see Sanmenxia
Shanxi Sheng see Shanxi
Shaoguan 106 C6 var. Shao-kuan, Cant. Kukong; prev. Ch'u-chiang. Guangdong, S China
Shao-kuan see Shaoguan
Shaqrā' 98 B4 Ar Riyāḑ, C Saudi Arabia
Shaqrā see Shuqrah
Shar 92 D5 var. Charsk. Vostochnyy Kazakhstan, E Kazakhstan
Shari 108 D2 Hokkaidō, NE Japan
Shari see Chari
Sharjah see Ash Shāriqah
Shark Bay 125 A5 bay Western Australia
Sharqī, Al Jabal ash/Sharqi, Jebel esh see Anti-Lebanon
Shashe 56 D3 var. Shashi. river Botswana/ Zimbabwe
Shashi see Shashe
Shatsky Rise 103 G1 undersea rise N Pacific Ocean
Shawnee 27 G1 Oklahoma, C USA
Shaykh, Jabal ash see Hermon, Mount
Shchadryn 85 D7 Rus. Shchedrin. Homyel'skaya Voblasts', SE Belarus
Shchedrin see Shchadryn
Shcheglovsk see Kemerovo
Shchëkino 89 B5 Tul'skaya Oblast', W Russian Federation
Shchors 87 E1 Chernihivs'ka Oblast', N Ukraine
Shchuchin see Shchuchyn
Shchuchinsk 92 C4 prev. Shchuchye. Akmola, N Kazakhstan
Shchuchye see Shchuchinsk
Shchuchyn 85 B5 Pol. Szczuczyn Nowogródzki, Rus. Shchuchin. Hrodzyenskaya Voblasts', W Belarus
Shebekino 89 A6 Belgorodskaya Oblast', W Russian Federation
Shebelē Wenz, Wabē see Shebeli
Shebeli 51 D5 Amh. Wabē Shebelē Wenz, It. Scebeli, Som. Webi Shabeelle. river Ethiopia/ Somalia
Sheberghān 101 E3 var. Shibarghān, Shiberghan, Shiberghān. Jowzjān, N Afghanistan
Sheboygan 18 B2 Wisconsin, N USA
Shebshi Mountains 54 A4 var. Schebschi Mountains. mountain range E Nigeria
Shechem see Nablus
Shedadi see Ash Shadādah
Sheffield 67 D5 N England, United Kingdom
Shekhem see Nablus
Sheki see Şäki
Shelby 22 B1 Montana, NW USA
Sheldon 23 F3 Iowa, C USA
Shelekhov Gulf 93 G2 Eng. Shelekhov Gulf. gulf E Russian Federation
Shelekhov Gulf see Shelikhova, Zaliv
Shendi 50 C4 var. Shandī. River Nile, NE Sudan
Shengking see Liaoning
Shenking see Liaoning
Shenshi/Shensi see Shaanxi
Shenyang 106 D3 Chin. Shen-yang, Eng. Moukden, Mukden; prev. Fengtien. province capital Liaoning, NE China
Shen-yang see Shenyang
Shepetivka 86 D2 Rus. Shepetovka. Khmel'nyts'ka Oblast', NW Ukraine
Shepetovka see Shepetivka
Shepparton 127 C7 Victoria, SE Australia
Sherbrooke 17 E4 Québec, SE Canada
Shereik 50 C3 River Nile, N Sudan
Sheridan 22 C2 Wyoming, C USA
Sherman 27 G2 Texas, SW USA
's-Hertogenbosch 64 C4 Fr. Bois-le-Duc, Ger. Herzogenbusch. Noord-Brabant, S Netherlands
Shetland Islands 66 D1 island group NE Scotland, United Kingdom
Shevchenko see Aktau
Shibarghān see Sheberghān
Shiberghan/Shiberghān see Sheberghān
Shibetsu 108 D2 var. Sibetu. Hokkaidō, NE Japan
Shibh Jazīrat Sīnā' see Sinai
Shibushi-wan 109 B8 bay SW Japan
Shigatse see Xigazê
Shih-chia-chuang/Shihmen see Shijiazhuang
Shihezi 104 C2 Xinjiang Uygur Zizhiqu, NW China
Shiichi see Shyichy
Shijiazhuang 106 C4 var. Shih-chia-chuang; prev. Shihmen. province capital Hebei, E China
Shikārpur 112 B3 Sind, S Pakistan
Shikoku 109 C7 var. Sikoku. island SW Japan
Shikoku Basin 103 F2 var. Sikoku Basin. undersea basin N Philippine Sea
Shikotan, Ostrov 108 E2 Jap. Shikotan-tō. island NE Russian Federation
Shikotan-tō see Shikotan, Ostrov
Shilabo 51 D5 Sumalē, E Ethiopia
Shiliguri 113 F3 prev. Siliguri. West Bengal, NE India
Shilka 93 F4 river S Russian Federation
Shillong 113 G3 state capital Meghālaya, NE India
Shimanto see Nakamura
Shimbir Berris see Shimbiris
Shimbiris 50 E4 var. Shimbir Berris. mountain N Somalia
Shimoga 110 C2 Karnātaka, W India
Shimonoseki 109 A7 var. Simonoseki, hist. Akamagaseki, Bakan. Yamaguchi, Honshū, SW Japan
Shinano-gawa 109 C5 var. Sinano Gawa. river Honshū, C Japan
Shīndand 100 D4 Herāt, W Afghanistan
Shingū 109 C6 var. Singû. Wakayama, Honshū, SW Japan
Shinjō 108 D4 var. Sinzyô. Yamagata, Honshū, C Japan
Shinyanga 51 C7 Shinyanga, NW Tanzania
Shiprock 26 C1 New Mexico, SW USA
Shīrāz 98 D4 var. Shīrāz. Fārs, S Iran
Shishchitsy see Shyshchytsy
Shivpuri 112 D3 Madhya Pradesh, C India
Shizugawa 108 D4 Miyagi, Honshū, NE Japan
Shizuoka 109 D6 var. Sizuoka. Shizuoka, Honshū, S Japan
Shklov see Shklow
Shklow 85 D6 Rus. Shklov. Mahilyowskaya Voblasts', E Belarus
Shkodër 79 C5 var. Shkodra, It. Scutari, SCr. Skadar. Shkodër, NW Albania
Shkodra see Shkodër
Shkodrës, Liqeni i see Scutari, Lake
Shkumbinit, Lumi i 79 C6 var. Shkumbî, Shkumbin. river C Albania
Shkumbî/Shkumbin see Shkumbinit, Lumi i
Sholāpur see Solāpur
Shostka 87 F1 Sums'ka Oblast', NE Ukraine
Show Low 26 B2 Arizona, SW USA
Show Me State see Missouri
Shpola 87 E3 Cherkas'ka Oblast', N Ukraine
Shqipëria/Shqipërisë, Republika e see Albania
Shreveport 20 A2 Louisiana, S USA
Shrewsbury 67 D6 hist. Scrobesbyrig'. W England, United Kingdom
Shu 92 C5 Kaz. Shū. Zhambyl, SE Kazakhstan
Shuang-liao see Liaoyuan
Shū, Kazakhstan see Shu
Shumagin Islands 14 B3 island group Alaska, USA
Shumen 82 D2 Shumen, NE Bulgaria
Shumilina 85 E5 Rus. Shumilino. Vitsyebskaya Voblasts', NE Belarus
Shumilino see Shumilina
Shunsen see Ch'unch'ŏn
Shuqrah 99 B7 var. Shaqrā. SW Yemen
Shwebo 114 B3 Sagaing, C Myanmar (Burma)
Shyichy 85 C7 Rus. Shiichi. Homyel'skaya Voblasts', SE Belarus
Shymkent 92 B5 prev. Chimkent. Yuzhnyy Kazakhstan, S Kazakhstan
Shyshchytsy 85 C6 Rus. Shishchitsy. Minskaya Voblasts', C Belarus
Siam see Thailand
Siam, Gulf of see Thailand, Gulf of
Sian see Xi'an
Siang see Brahmaputra
Siangtan see Xiangtan
Šiauliai 84 B4 Ger. Schaulen. Šiauliai, N Lithuania
Siazan' see Siyäzän
Sibay 89 D6 Respublika Bashkortostan, W Russian Federation
Šibenik 78 B4 It. Sebenico. Šibenik-Knin, S Croatia
Siberia 93 E3 var. Siberia. physical region NE Russian Federation
Siberia see Sibir'
Siberoet see Siberut, Pulau
Siberut, Pulau 116 A4 prev. Siberoet. island Kepulauan Mentawai, W Indonesia
Sibi 112 B2 Baluchistān, SW Pakistan
Sibiti 55 B6 Lékoumou, S Congo
Sibiu 86 B4 Ger. Hermannstadt, Hung. Nagyszeben. Sibiu, C Romania
Sibolga 116 B3 Sumatera, W Indonesia
Sibu 116 D3 Sarawak, East Malaysia
Sibut 54 C4 prev. Fort-Sibut. Kémo, S Central African Republic
Sibuyan Sea 117 E2 sea W Pacific Ocean
Sichon 115 C6 var. Ban Sichon, Si Chon. Nakhon Si Thammarat, SW Thailand
Si Chon see Sichon
Sichuan 106 B5 var. Chuan, Sichuan Sheng, Ssu-ch'uan, Szechuan, Szechwan. province C China
Sichuan Pendi 106 B5 basin C China
Sichuan Sheng see Sichuan
Sicilian Channel see Sicily, Strait of
Sicily 75 C7 Eng. Sicily; anc. Trinacria. island Italy, C Mediterranean Sea
Sicily, Strait of 75 B7 var. Sicilian Channel. strait C Mediterranean Sea
Sicuani 39 E4 Cusco, S Peru
Sidári 82 A4 Kérkyra, Iónia Nisiá, Greece, C Mediterranean Sea
Sidas 116 C4 Borneo, C Indonesia
Siderno 75 D7 Calabria, SW Italy
Sidhirókastron see Sidirókastro
Sidi Barrâni 50 A1 NW Egypt
Sidi Bel Abbès 48 D2 var. Sidi bel Abbès, Sidi-Bel-Abbès. NW Algeria
Sidirókastro 82 C3 prev. Sidhirókastron. Kentrikí Makedonía, NE Greece
Sidley, Mount 132 B4 mountain Antarctica
Sidney 22 D1 Montana, NW USA
Sidney 22 D4 Nebraska, C USA
Sidney 18 C4 Ohio, N USA
Sidon see Saïda
Sidra see Surt
Sidra/Sidra, Gulf of see Surt, Khalij, N Libya
Siebenbürgen see Transylvania
Siedlce 76 E3 Ger. Sedlez, Rus. Sesdlets. Mazowieckie, C Poland
Siegen 72 B4 Nordrhein-Westfalen, W Germany
Siemiatycze 76 E3 Podlaskie, NE Poland
Siena 74 B3 Fr. Sienne; anc. Saena Julia. Toscana, C Italy
Sienne see Siena
Sieradz 76 C4 Sieradz, C Poland
Sierpc 76 D3 Mazowieckie, C Poland
Sierra Leone 52 C4 off. Republic of Sierra Leone. country W Africa
Sierra Leone Basin 44 C4 undersea basin E Atlantic Ocean
Sierra Leone, Republic of see Sierra Leone
Sierra Leone Ridge see Sierra Leone Rise
Sierra Leone Rise 44 C4 var. Sierra Leone Ridge, Sierra Leone Schwelle. undersea rise E Atlantic Ocean
Sierra Leone Schwelle see Sierra Leone Rise
Sierra Madre 30 B2 var. Sierra de Soconusco. mountain range Guatemala/Mexico
Sierra Nevada 70 D5 mountain range S Spain
Sierra Nevada 25 C6 mountain range W USA
Sierra Vieja 26 D3 mountain range Texas, SW USA
Sierra Vista 26 B3 Arizona, SW USA
Sífnos 83 C6 anc. Siphnos. island Kykládes, Greece, Aegean Sea
Sigli 116 A3 Sumatera, W Indonesia
Siglufjördhur 61 E4 Nordhurland Vestra, N Iceland
Signal Peak 26 A2 mountain Arizona, SW USA
Signan see Xi'an
Signy 132 A2 UK research station South Orkney Islands, Antarctica
Siguatepeque 30 C2 Comayagua, W Honduras
Siguiri 52 D4 NE Guinea
Sihanoukville see Kâmpóng Saôm
Siilinjärvi 62 E4 Itä-Suomi, C Finland
Siirt 95 F4 var. Sert; anc. Tigranocerta. Siirt, SE Turkey
Sikandarabad see Secunderābād
Sikasso 52 D4 Sikasso, S Mali
Sikeston 23 H5 Missouri, C USA
Sikhote-Alin', Khrebet 93 G4 mountain range SE Russian Federation
Siking see Xi'an
Siklós 77 C7 Baranya, SW Hungary
Sikoku see Shikoku
Sikoku Basin see Shikoku Basin
Šilalė 84 B4 Tauragė, W Lithuania
Silchar 113 G3 Assam, NE India
Silesia 76 B4 physical region SW Poland
Silifke 94 C4 anc. Seleucia. İçel, S Turkey
Siliguri see Shiliguri
Siling Co 104 C5 lake W China
Silinhot see Xilinhot
Silistra 82 E1 var. Silistria; anc. Durostorum. Silistra, NE Bulgaria
Silistria see Silistra
Sillamäe 84 E2 Ger. Sillamäggi. Ida-Virumaa, NE Estonia
Sillamäggi see Sillamäe
Sillein see Žilina
Šilutė 84 B4 Ger. Heydekrug. Klaipėda, W Lithuania
Silvan 95 E4 Dıyarbakır, SE Turkey
Silva Porto see Kuito
Silver State see Colorado
Silver State see Nevada
Simanichy 85 C7 Rus. Simonichi. Homyel'skaya Voblasts', SE Belarus
Simav 94 B3 Kütahya, W Turkey
Simav Çayı 94 A3 river NW Turkey
Simbirsk see Ul'yanovsk
Simeto 75 C7 river Sicilia, Italy, C Mediterranean Sea
Simeulue, Pulau 116 A3 island NW Indonesia
Simferopol' 87 F5 Respublika Krym, S Ukraine
Simitla 82 C3 Blagoevgrad, SW Bulgaria
Şimlăul Silvaniei/Şimleul Silvaniei see Şimleu Silvaniei
Şimleu Silvaniei 86 B3 Hung. Szilágysomlyó; prev. Şimlăul Silvaniei, Şimleul Silvaniei. Sălaj, NW Romania
Simonichi see Simanichy
Simonoseki see Shimonoseki
Simpelveld 65 D6 Limburg, SE Netherlands
Simplon Pass 73 B8 pass S Switzerland
Simpson see Fort Simpson
Simpson Desert 126 B4 desert Northern Territory/ South Australia
Sinai 50 C2 var. Sinai Peninsula, Ar. Shibh Jazīrat Sīnā', Sīnā. physical region NE Egypt
Sinaia 86 C4 Prahova, SE Romania
Sinano Gawa see Shinano-gawa
Sīnā/Sinai Peninsula see Sinai
Sincelejo 36 B2 Sucre, NW Colombia
Sind 112 B3 var. Sindh. province SE Pakistan
Sindelfingen 73 B6 Baden-Württemberg, SW Germany
Sindh see Sind
Sindi 84 D2 Ger. Zintenhof. Pärnumaa, SW Estonia
Sines 70 B4 Setúbal, S Portugal
Singan see Xi'an
Singapore 116 B3 country capital S Singapore
Singapore 116 A1 off. Republic of Singapore. country SE Asia
Singapore, Republic of see Singapore
Singen 73 B6 Baden-Württemberg, S Germany
Singida 51 C7 Singida, C Tanzania
Singkang 117 E4 Sulawesi, C Indonesia
Singkawang 116 C3 Borneo, C Indonesia
Singora see Songkhla
Singû see Shingū
Sining see Xining
Siniscola 75 A5 Sardegna, Italy, C Mediterranean Sea
Sinj 78 B4 Split-Dalmacija, SE Croatia
Sinkiang/Sinkiang Uighur Autonomous Region see Xinjiang Uygur Zizhiqu
Sinnamarie see Sinnamary
Sinnamary 37 H3 var. Sinnamarie. N French Guiana
Sinneh see Sanandaj
Sînnicolau Mare see Sânnicolau Mare
Sinoie, Lacul see Sinoie, Lacul
Sinoie, Lacul 86 D5 prev. Lacul Sinoe. lagoon SE Romania
Sinop 94 D2 anc. Sinope. Sinop, N Turkey
Sinope see Sinop
Sinsheim 73 B6 Baden-Württemberg, SW Germany
Sint Maarten 33 G3 Eng. Saint Martin. island N Netherlands Antilles
Sint-Michielsgestel 64 C4 Noord-Brabant, S Netherlands
Sîn-Miclăuş see Gheorgheni
Sint-Niklaas 65 B5 Fr. Saint-Nicolas. Oost-Vlaanderen, N Belgium
Sint-Pieters-Leeuw 65 B6 Vlaams Brabant, C Belgium
Sintra 70 B3 prev. Cintra. Lisboa, W Portugal
Sinujiif 51 E5 Nugaal, NE Somalia
Sinus Aelaniticus see Aqaba, Gulf of
Sinus Gallicus see Lion, Golfe du
Sinyang see Xinyang
Sinzyô see Shinjō
Sion 73 A7 Ger. Sitten; anc. Sedunum. Valais, SW Switzerland
Sioux City 23 F3 Iowa, C USA
Sioux Falls 23 F3 South Dakota, N USA
Sioux State see North Dakota
Siphnos see Sífnos
Siping 106 D3 var. Ssu-p'ing, Szeping; prev. Ssu-p'ing-chieh. Jilin, NE China
Siple, Mount 132 A4 mountain Siple Island, Antarctica
Siquirres 31 E4 Limón, E Costa Rica
Siracusa 75 D7 Eng. Syracuse. Sicilia, Italy, C Mediterranean Sea
Sir Edward Pellew Group 126 B2 island group Northern Territory, NE Australia
Siret 86 C3 var. Siretul, Ger. Sereth, Rus. Seret. river Romania/Ukraine
Siretul see Siret
Siria see Syria
Sirikit Reservoir 114 C4 lake N Thailand
Sīrjān 98 D4 prev. Sa'īdābād. Kermān, S Iran
Sirna see Sýrna
Şırnak 95 F4 Şırnak, SE Turkey
Síros see Sýros
Sirte see Surt
Sirte, Gulf of 49 F2 Eng. Gulf of Sidra, Gulf of Sirti, Sidra. gulf N Libya
Sirti, Gulf of see Surt, Khalij
Sisak 78 B3 var. Siscia, Ger. Sissek, Hung. Sziszek; anc. Segestica. Sisak-Moslavina, C Croatia
Siscia see Sisak
Sisimiut 60 C3 var. Holsteinborg, Holsteinsborg, Holstenborg, Holstensborg. Kitaa, S Greenland
Sissek see Sisak
Sīstān, Daryācheh-ye see Şāberi, Hāmūn-e
Sitaş Cristuru see Cristuru Secuiesc
Siteía 83 D8 var. Sitía. Kríti, Greece, E Mediterranean Sea
Sitges 71 G2 Cataluña, NE Spain
Sitía see Siteía
Sittang see Sittoung
Sittard 65 D5 Limburg, SE Netherlands
Sitten see Sion
Sittoung 114 B4 var. Sittang. river S Myanmar (Burma)
Sittwe 114 A3 var. Akyab. Rakhine State, W Myanmar (Burma)
Siuna 30 D3 Región Autónoma Atlántico Norte, NE Nicaragua
Siut see Asyūţ
Sivas 94 D3 anc. Sebastia, Sebaste. Sivas, C Turkey
Siverek 95 E4 Şanlıurfa, S Turkey
Siwa see Sīwah
Sīwah 50 A2 var. Siwa. NW Egypt
Six Counties, The see Northern Ireland
Six-Fours-les-Plages 69 D6 Var, SE France
Siyäzän 95 H2 Rus. Siazan'. NE Azerbaijan
Sjar see Sääre
Sjenica 79 D5 Turk. Seniça. Serbia, SW Serbia
Skadar see Shkodër
Skadarsko Jezero see Scutari, Lake
Skagerak see Skagerrak
Skagerrak 63 A6 var. Skagerak. channel N Europe
Skagit River 24 B1 river Washington, NW USA
Skalka 62 C3 lake N Sweden
Skarżysko-Kamienna 76 D4 Świętokrzyskie, C Poland
Skaudvilė 84 B4 Tauragė, SW Lithuania
Skegness 67 E6 E England, United Kingdom
Skellefteå 62 D4 Västerbotten, N Sweden
Skellefteälven 62 C4 river N Sweden
Ski 63 B6 Akershus, S Norway
Skíathos 83 C5 Skíathos, Vóreies Sporádes, Greece, Aegean Sea
Skidal' 85 B5 Rus. Skidel'. Hrodzyenskaya Voblasts', W Belarus
Skidel' see Skidal'
Skiermûntseach see Schiermonnikoog
Skierniewice 76 D3 Łódzkie, C Poland
Skiftet 84 C1 strait Finland Atlantic Ocean Baltic Sea Gulf of Bothnia/Gulf of Finland
Skíros see Skýros
Skópelos 83 C5 Skópelos, Vóreies Sporádes, Greece, Aegean Sea
Skopje 79 D6 var. Üsküb, Turk. Üsküp, prev. Skoplje; anc. Scupi. country capital N FYR Macedonia
Skoplje see Skopje
Skovorodino 93 F4 Amurskaya Oblast', SE Russian Federation
Skuodas 84 B3 Ger. Schoden, Pol. Szkudy. Klaipėda, NW Lithuania
Skye, Isle of 66 B3 island NW Scotland, United Kingdom
Skylge see Terschelling
Skýros 83 C5 var. Skiros. Skńyros, Vóreies Sporádes, Greece, Aegean Sea
Skýros 83 C5 var. Skíros; anc. Scyros. island Vóreies Sporádes, Greece, Aegean Sea
Slagelse 63 B7 Vestsjælland, E Denmark
Slatina 78 C3 Hung. Szlatina; prev. Podravska Slatina. Virovitica-Podravina, NE Croatia
Slatina 86 B5 Olt, S Romania
Slavgorod see Slawharad
Slavonska Požega see Požega
Slavonski Brod 78 C3 Ger. Brod, Hung. Bród; prev. Brod, Brod na Savi. Brod-Posavina, NE Croatia
Slavuta 86 C2 Khmel'nyts'ka Oblast', NW Ukraine
Slavyansk see Slov"yans'k
Slawharad 85 E7 Rus. Slavgorod. Mahilyowskaya Voblasts', E Belarus
Sławno 76 C2 Zachodnio-pomorskie, NW Poland
Slēmānī see As Sulaymānīyah
Sliema 80 B5 N Malta
Sligo 67 A5 Ir. Sligeach. Sligo, NW Ireland
Sliven 82 D2 var. Slivno. Sliven, C Bulgaria
Slivnitsa 82 B2 Sofiya, W Bulgaria
Slivno see Sliven
Slobozia 86 C5 Ialomiţa, SE Romania
Slonim 85 B6 Pol. Słonim. Hrodzyenskaya Voblasts', W Belarus
Słonim see Slonim
Slovakia 77 C6 off. Slovenská Republika, Ger. Slowakei, Hung. Szlovákia, Slvk. Slovensko. country C Europe
Slovak Ore Mountains see Slovenské rudohorie
Slovenia 73 D8 off. Republic of Slovenia, Ger. Slowenien, Slvn. Slovenija. country SE Europe
Slovenia, Republic of see Slovenia
Slovenija see Slovenia
Slovenská Republika see Slovakia
Slovenské rudohorie 77 D6 Eng. Slovak Ore Mountains, Ger. Slowakisches Erzgebirge, Ungarisches Erzgebirge. mountain range C Slovakia
Slovensko see Slovakia
Slov"yans'k 87 G3 Rus. Slavyansk. Donets'ka Oblast', E Ukraine
Slowakei see Slovakia
Slowakisches Erzgebirge see Slovenské rudohorie
Slowenien see Slovenia
Słubice 76 B3 Ger. Frankfurt. Lubuskie, W Poland
Sluch 86 D1 river NW Ukraine
Słupsk 76 C2 Ger. Stolp. Pomorskie, N Poland
Slutsk 85 C6 Minskaya Voblasts', S Belarus
Smallwood Reservoir 17 F2 lake Newfoundland and Labrador, S Canada
Smara 48 B3 var. Es Semara. N Western Sahara
Smarhon' 85 C5 Pol. Smorgonie, Rus. Smorgon'. Hrodzyenskaya Voblasts', W Belarus
Smederevo 78 D4 Ger. Semendria. Serbia, N Serbia
Smederevska Palanka 78 D4 Serbia, C Serbia
Smela see Smila
Smila 87 E2 Rus. Smela. Cherkas'ka Oblast', C Ukraine
Smilten see Smiltene
Smiltene 84 D3 Ger. Smilten. Valka, N Latvia
Smøla 62 A4 island W Norway
Smolensk 89 A5 Smolenskaya Oblast', W Russian Federation
Smorgon'/Smorgonie see Smarhon'
Smyrna see İzmir
Snake 12 B4 river Yukon Territory, NW Canada
Snake River 24 C3 river NW USA
Snake River Plain 24 D4 plain Idaho, NW USA
Sneek 64 D2 Friesland, N Netherlands
Sneeuw-gebergte see Maoke, Pegunungan
Sněžka 76 B4 Ger. Schneekoppe, Pol. Śnieżka. mountain N Czech Republic/Poland
Śniardwy, Jezioro 76 D2 Ger. Spirdingsee. lake NE Poland
Sniečkus see Visaginas
Śnieżka see Sněžka
Snina 77 E5 Hung. Szinna. Prešovský Kraj, E Slovakia
Snowdonia 67 C6 mountain range NW Wales, United Kingdom
Snowdrift see Łutselk'e
Snow Mountains see Maoke, Pegunungan
Snyder 27 F3 Texas, SW USA
Sobradinho, Barragem de see Sobradinho, Represa de
Sobradinho, Represa de 41 F2 var. Barragem de Sobradinho. reservoir E Brazil
Sochi 89 A7 Krasnodarskiy Kray, SW Russian Federation
Société, Îles de la/Society Islands see Société, Archipel de la
Society Islands 123 G4 var. Archipel de Tahiti, Îles de la Société, Eng. Society Islands. island group W French Polynesia
Soconusco, Sierra de see Sierra Madre
Socorro 26 D2 New Mexico, SW USA
Socorro, Isla 28 B5 island W Mexico
Socotra 99 C7 var. Sokotra, Eng. Socotra. island SE Yemen
Socotra see Suquţrā
Soc Trăng 115 D6 var. Khanh Hung. Soc Trăng, S Vietnam
Socuéllamos 71 E3 Castilla-La Mancha, C Spain
Sodankylä 62 D3 Lappi, N Finland
Sodari see Sodiri
Söderhamn 63 C5 Gävleborg, C Sweden
Södertälje 63 C6 Stockholm, C Sweden
Sodiri 50 B4 var. Sawdirī, Sodari. Northern Kordofan, C Sudan
Soekaboemi see Sukabumi
Soemba see Sumba, Pulau
Soengaipenoeh see Sungaipenuh
Soerabaja see Surabaya
Soerakarta see Surakarta
Sofia see Sofiya
Sofiya 82 C2 var. Sophia, Eng. Sofia, Lat. Serdica. country capital Sofiya-Grad, W Bulgaria
Sogamoso 36 B3 Boyacá, C Colombia
Sognefjorden 63 A5 fjord NE North Sea
Sohâg see Sawhāj
Sohar see Şuḩār
Sohm Plain 44 B3 abyssal plain NW Atlantic Ocean
Sohrau see Żory
Sokal' 86 C2 Rus. Sokal. L'vivs'ka Oblast', NW Ukraine
Söke 94 A4 Aydın, SW Turkey
Sokhumi 95 E1 Rus. Sukhumi. NW Georgia
Sokodé 53 F4 C Togo
Sokol 88 C4 Vologodskaya Oblast', NW Russian Federation
Sokółka 76 E3 Podlaskie, NE Poland
Sokolov 77 A5 Ger. Falkenau an der Eger; prev. Falknov nad Ohří. Karlovarský Kraj, W Czech Republic
Sokone 52 B3 W Senegal
Sokoto 53 F3 Sokoto, NW Nigeria
Sokoto 53 F4 river NW Nigeria
Sokotra see Suquţrā
Solāpur 102 B3 var. Sholāpur. Mahārāshtra, W India
Solca 86 C3 Ger. Solka. Suceava, N Romania
Sol, Costa del 70 D5 coastal region S Spain
Soldeu 69 B7 NE Andorra Europe
Solec Kujawski 76 C3 Kujawsko-pomorskie, C Poland
Soledad 36 B1 Atlántico, N Colombia
Isla Soledad see East Falkland
Soligorsk see Salihorsk
Solikamsk 92 C3 Permskaya Oblast', NW Russian Federation
Sol'-Iletsk 89 D6 Orenburgskaya Oblast', W Russian Federation
Solingen 72 A4 Nordrhein-Westfalen, W Germany
Solka see Solca
Sollentuna 63 C6 Stockholm, C Sweden
Solo see Surakarta
Solok 116 B4 Sumatera, W Indonesia
Solomon Islands 122 C3 prev. British Solomon Islands Protectorate. country W Solomon Islands N Melanesia W Pacific Ocean
Solomon Islands 122 C3 island group Papua New Guinea/Solomon Islands
Solomon Sea 122 B3 sea W Pacific Ocean
Soltau 72 B3 Niedersachsen, NW Germany

Sol'tsy – Sydney

Sol'tsy *88 A4* Novgorodskaya Oblast', W Russian Federation
Solun *see* Thessaloníki
Solwezi *56 D2* North Western, NW Zambia
Sōma *108 D4* Fukushima, Honshū, C Japan
Somalia *51 D5 off.* Somali Democratic Republic, *Som.* Jamuuriyada Demuqraadiga Soomaaliyeed, Soomaaliya; *prev.* Italian Somaliland, Somaliland Protectorate. *country* E Africa
Somali Basin *47 E5 undersea basin* W Indian Ocean
Somali Democratic Republic *see* Somalia
Somaliland *51 D5 disputed territory* N Somalia
Somaliland Protectorate *see* Somalia
Sombor *78 C3 Hung.* Zombor. Vojvodina, NW Serbia
Someren *65 D5* Noord-Brabant, SE Netherlands
Somerset *20 A5 var.* Somerset Village. W Bermuda
Somerset *18 C5* Kentucky, S USA
Somerset Island *20 A5 island* W Bermuda
Somerset Island *15 F2 island* Queen Elizabeth Islands, Nunavut, NW Canada
Somerset Village *see* Somerset
Somers Islands *see* Bermuda
Somerton *26 A2* Arizona, SW USA
Someş *86 B3 river* Hungary/Romania Europe
Somme *68 C2 river* N France
Sommerfeld *see* Lubsko
Somotillo *30 C3* Chinandega, NW Nicaragua
Somoto *30 D3* Madriz, NW Nicaragua
Songea *51 C8* Ruvuma, S Tanzania
Songjin *see* Kimch'aek
Songkhla *115 C7 var.* Songkla, *Mal.* Singora. Songkhla, SW Thailand
Songkla *see* Songkhla
Sonoran Desert *26 A3 var.* Desierto de Altar. *desert* Mexico/USA
Sonsonate *30 B3* Sonsonate, W El Salvador
Soochow *see* Suzhou
Soomaaliya/Soomaaliyeed, Jamuuriyada Demuqraadiga *see* Somalia
Soome Laht *see* Finland, Gulf of
Sop Hao *114 D3* Houaphan, N Laos
Sophia *see* Sofiya
Sopianae *see* Pécs
Sopot *76 C2 Ger.* Zoppot. Pomorskie, N Poland
Sopron *77 B6 Ger.* Ödenburg. Győr-Moson-Sopron, NW Hungary
Sorau/Sorau in der Niederlausitz *see* Żary
Sorgues *69 D6* Vaucluse, SE France
Sorgun *94 D3* Yozgat, C Turkey
Soria *71 E2* Castilla-León, N Spain
Soroca *86 D3 Rus.* Soroki. N Moldova
Sorochino *see* Sarochyna
Soroki *see* Soroca
Sorong *117 F4* Papua, E Indonesia
Sørøy *see* Sørøya
Sørøya *62 C2 var.* Sørøy, *Lapp.* Sállan. *island* N Norway
Sortavala *88 B3 prev.* Serdobol'. Respublika Kareliya, NW Russian Federation
Sotavento, Ilhas de *52 A3 var.* Leeward Islands. *island group* S Cape Verde
Sotkamo *62 E4* Oulu, C Finland
Souanké *55 B5* Sangha, NW Congo
Soueida *see* As Suwaydā'
Souflí *82 D3 prev.* Souflíon. Anatolikí Makedonía kai Thráki, NE Greece
Souflíon *see* Souflí
Soufrière *33 F2* W Saint Lucia
Soukhné *see* As Sukhnah
Sŏul *107 E4 off.* Sŏul-t'ŭkpyŏlsi, *Eng.* Seoul, *Jap.* Keijō; *prev.* Kyŏngsŏng. *country capital* NW South Korea
Sŏul-t'ŭkpyŏlsi *see* Sŏul
Soûr *97 A5 var.* Şūr; *anc.* Tyre. SW Lebanon
Souris River *23 E1 var.* Mouse River. *river* Canada/USA
Soúrpi *83 B5* Thessalía, C Greece
Sousse *49 F2 var.* Sūsah. NE Tunisia
South Africa *56 C4 off.* Republic of South Africa, *Afr.* Suid-Afrika. *country* S Africa
South Africa, Republic of *see* South Africa
South America *34 continent*
Southampton *67 D7 hist.* Hamwih, *Lat.* Clausentum. S England, United Kingdom
Southampton Island *15 G3 island* Nunavut, NE Canada
South Andaman *111 F2 island* Andaman Islands, India, NE Indian Ocean
South Australia *127 A5 state* S Australia
South Australian Basin *120 B5 undersea basin* SW Indian Ocean
South Bend *18 C3* Indiana, N USA
South Beveland *see* Zuid-Beveland
South Bruny Island *127 C8 island* Tasmania, SE Australia
South Carolina *21 E2 off.* State of South Carolina, *also known as* The Palmetto State. *state* SE USA
South Carpathians *see* Carpaţii Meridionali
South China Basin *103 E4 undersea basin* SE South China Sea
South China Sea *103 E4 Chin.* Nan Hai, *Ind.* Laut Cina Selatan, *Vtn.* Biên Đông. *sea* SE Asia
South Dakota *22 D2 off.* State of South Dakota, *also known as* The Coyote State, Sunshine State. *state* N USA
Southeast Indian Ridge *119 D7 undersea ridge* Indian Ocean/Pacific Ocean
Southeast Pacific Basin *131 E5 var.* Belling Hausen Mulde. *undersea basin* SE Pacific Ocean
South East Point *127 C7 headland* Victoria, S Australia
Southend-on-Sea *67 E6* E England, United Kingdom
Southern Alps *129 B6 mountain range* South Island, New Zealand
Southern Cook Islands *123 F4 island group* S Cook Islands
Southern Cross *125 B6* Western Australia
Southern Indian Lake *15 F4 lake* Manitoba, C Canada
Southern Ocean *45 B7 ocean* Atlantic Ocean/ Indian Ocean/Pacific Ocean
Southern Uplands *66 C4 mountain range* S Scotland, United Kingdom
South Fiji Basin *120 D4 undersea basin* S Pacific Ocean
South Geomagnetic Pole *132 B3 pole* Antarctica
South Georgia *35 D8 island* South Georgia and the South Sandwich Islands, SW Atlantic Ocean
South Goulburn Island *124 E2 island* Northern Territory, N Australia
South Huvadhu Atoll *110 A5 atoll* S Maldives
South Indian Basin *119 D7 undersea basin* Indian Ocean/Pacific Ocean
South Island *129 C6 island* S New Zealand
South Korea *107 E4 off.* Republic of Korea, *Kor.* Taehan Min'guk. *country* E Asia
South Lake Tahoe *25 C5* California, W USA
South Orkney Islands *132 A2 island group* Antarctica
South Ossetia *95 F2 former autonomous region* SW Georgia
South Pacific Basin *see* Southwest Pacific Basin
South Platte River *22 D4 river* Colorado/ Nebraska, C USA
South Pole *132 B3 pole* Antarctica
South Sandwich Islands *35 D8 island group* SW Atlantic Ocean
South Sandwich Trench *35 E8 trench* SW Atlantic Ocean
South Shetland Islands *132 A2 island group* Antarctica
South Shields *66 D4* NE England, United Kingdom
South Sioux City *23 F3* Nebraska, C USA
South Taranaki Bight *128 C4 bight* SE Tasman Sea
South Tasmania Plateau *see* Tasman Plateau
South Uist *66 B3 island* NW Scotland, United Kingdom
South-West Africa/South West Africa *see* Namibia
South West Cape *129 A8 headland* Stewart Island, New Zealand
Southwest Indian Ocean Ridge *see* Southwest Indian Ridge
Southwest Indian Ridge *119 B6 var.* Southwest Indian Ocean Ridge. *undersea ridge* SW Indian Ocean
Southwest Pacific Basin *121 E4 var.* South Pacific Basin. *undersea basin* SE Pacific Ocean
Sovereign Base Area *80 C5 uk military installation* S Cyprus
Soweto *56 D4* Gauteng, NE South Africa
Sōya-kaikyō *see* La Perouse Strait
Spain *70 D3 off.* Kingdom of Spain, *Sp.* España; *anc.* Hispania, Iberia, *Lat.* Hispana. *country* SW Europe
Spain, Kingdom of *see* Spain
Spalato *see* Split
Spanish Town *32 B5 hist.* St.Iago de la Vega. C Jamaica
Sparks *25 C5* Nevada, W USA
Sparta *see* Spárti
Spartanburg *21 E1* South Carolina, SE USA
Spárti *83 B6 Eng.* Sparta. Pelopónnisos, S Greece
Spearfish *22 D2* South Dakota, N USA
Speightstown *33 G1* NW Barbados
Spencer *23 F3* Iowa, C USA
Spencer Gulf *127 B6 gulf* South Australia
Spey *66 C3 river* NE Scotland, United Kingdom
Spice Islands *see* Maluku
Spiess Seamount *45 C7 seamount* S Atlantic Ocean
Spijkenisse *64 B4* Zuid-Holland, SW Netherlands
Spíli *83 C8* Kríti, Greece, E Mediterranean Sea
Spin Būldak *101 E5* Kandahār, S Afghanistan
Spirdingsee *see* Śniardwy, Jezioro
Spitsbergen *61 F2 island* NW Svalbard
Split *78 B4 It.* Spalato. Split-Dalmacija, S Croatia
Špoģi *84 D4* Daugvapils, SE Latvia
Spokane *24 C2* Washington, NW USA
Spratly Islands *116 B2 Chin.* Nansha Qundao. *disputed territory* SE Asia
Spree *72 D4 river* E Germany
Springfield *18 B4 state capital* Illinois, N USA
Springfield *19 G3* Massachusetts, NE USA
Springfield *23 G5* Missouri, C USA
Springfield *18 C4* Ohio, N USA
Springfield *24 B3* Oregon, NW USA
Spring Garden *37 F2* NE Guyana
Spring Hill *21 E4* Florida, SE USA
Springs Junction *129 C5* West Coast, South Island, New Zealand
Springsure *126 D4* Queensland, E Australia
Sprottau *see* Szprotawa
Spruce Knob *19 E4 mountain* West Virginia, NE USA
Srbinje *see* Foča
Srbobran *78 D3 var.* Bácsszenttamás, *Hung.* Szenttamás. Vojvodina, N Serbia
Srebrenica *78 C4* Republika Srpska, E Bosnia and Herzegovina
Sredets *82 D2 prev.* Syulemeshlii. Stara Zagora, C Bulgaria
Sredets *82 E2 prev.* Grudovo. Burgas, E Bulgaria
Sremska Mitrovica *78 C3 prev.* Mitrovica, *Ger.* Mitrowitz. Vojvodina, NW Serbia
Srepok, Sông *see* Srêpôk, Tônle
Srêpôk, Tônle *115 E5 var.* Sông Srepok. *river* Cambodia/Vietnam
Sri Aman *116 C3* Sarawak, East Malaysia
Sri Jayawardanapura *see* Sri Jayewardanapura Kotte
Sri Jayewardanapura Kotte *110 D3 var.* Sri Jayawardanapura. Western Province, W Sri Lanka
Srīkākulam *113 F5* Andhra Pradesh, E India
Sri Lanka *110 D3 off.* Democratic Socialist Republic of Sri Lanka; *prev.* Ceylon. *country* S Asia
Sri Lanka, Democratic Socialist Republic of *see* Sri Lanka
Srinagarind Reservoir *115 C5 lake* W Thailand
Srpska, Republika *78 B3 republic* Bosnia and Herzegovina
Ssu-ch'uan *see* Sichuan
Ssu-p'ing/Ssu-p'ing-chieh *see* Siping
Stabroek *65 B5* Antwerpen, N Belgium
Stade *72 B3* Niedersachsen, NW Germany
Stadskanaal *64 E2* Groningen, NE Netherlands
Stafford *67 D6* C England, United Kingdom
Staicele *84 D3* Limbaži, N Latvia
Štaierdorf-Anina *see* Anina
Stájerlakanina *see* Anina
Stakhanov *87 H3* Luhans'ka Oblast', E Ukraine
Stalin *see* Varna
Stalinabad *see* Dushanbe
Stalingrad *see* Volgograd
Staliniri *see* Tskhinvali
Stalino *see* Donets'k
Stalinobod *see* Dushanbe
Stalinsk *see* Novokuznetsk
Stalinski Zaliv *see* Varnenski Zaliv
Stalin, Yazovir *see* Iskŭr, Yazovir
Stalowa Wola *76 E4* Podkarpackie, SE Poland
Stamford *19 F3* Connecticut, NE USA
Stampalia *see* Astypálaia
Stanislau *see* Ivano-Frankivs'k
Stanislav *see* Ivano-Frankivs'k
Stanisławów *see* Ivano-Frankivs'k
Stanke Dimitrov *see* Dupnitsa
Stanley *43 D7 var.* Port Stanley, Puerto Argentino. *dependent territory capital* East Falkland, Falkland Islands
Stanleyville *see* Kisangani
Stann Creek *see* Dangriga
Stanovoy Khrebet *91 E3 mountain range* SE Russian Federation
Stanthorpe *127 D5* Queensland, E Australia
Staphorst *64 D2* Overijssel, E Netherlands
Starachowice *76 D4* Świętokrzyskie, C Poland
Stara Kanjiža *see* Kanjiža
Stara Pazova *78 D3 Ger.* Altpasua, *Hung.* Ópazova. Vojvodina, N Serbia
Stara Planina *see* Balkan Mountains
Stara Zagora *82 D2 Lat.* Augusta Trajana. Stara Zagora, C Bulgaria
Starbuck Island *123 G3 prev.* Volunteer Island. *island* E Kiribati
Stargard in Pommern *see* Stargard Szczeciński
Stargard Szczeciński *76 B3 Ger.* Stargard in Pommern. Zachodnio-pomorskie, NW Poland
Stari Bečej *see* Bečej
Starobel'sk *see* Starobil's'k
Starobil's'k *87 H2 Rus.* Starobel'sk. Luhans'ka Oblast', E Ukraine
Starobin *85 C7 var.* Starobyn. Minskaya Voblasts', S Belarus
Starobyn *see* Starobin
Starogard Gdański *76 C2 Ger.* Preussisch-Stargard. Pomorskie, N Poland
Starokonstantinov *see* Starokostyantyniv
Starokostyantyniv *86 D2 Rus.* Starokonstantinov. Khmel'nyts'ka Oblast', NW Ukraine
Starominskaya *89 A7* Krasnodarskiy Kray, SW Russian Federation
Staryya Darohi *85 C6 Rus.* Staryye Dorogi. Minskaya Voblasts', S Belarus
Staryye Dorogi *see* Staryya Darohi
Staryy Oskol *89 B6* Belgorodskaya Oblast', W Russian Federation
State College *19 E4* Pennsylvania, NE USA
Staten Island *see* Estados, Isla de los
Statesboro *21 E2* Georgia, SE USA
States, The *see* United States of America
Staunton *19 E5* Virginia, NE USA
Stavanger *63 A6* Rogaland, S Norway
Stavers Island *see* Vostok Island
Stavropol' *89 B7 prev.* Voroshilovsk. Stavropol'skiy Kray, SW Russian Federation
Stavropol' *see* Tol'yatti
Steamboat Springs *22 C4* Colorado, C USA
Steenwijk *64 D2* Overijssel, N Netherlands
Steier *see* Steyr
Steierdorf/Steierdorf-Anina *see* Anina
Steinamanger *see* Szombathely
Steinkjer *62 B4* Nord-Trøndelag, C Norway
Stejarul *see* Karapelit
Stendal *72 C3* Sachsen-Anhalt, C Germany
Stepanakert *see* Xankǝndi
Stephenville *27 F3* Texas, SW USA
Sterling *22 D4* Colorado, C USA
Sterling *18 B3* Illinois, N USA
Sterlitamak *92 B3* Respublika Bashkortostan, W Russian Federation
Stettin *see* Szczecin
Stettiner Haff *see* Szczeciński, Zalew
Stevenage *67 E6* E England, United Kingdom
Stevens Point *18 B2* Wisconsin, N USA
Stewart Island *129 A8 island* S New Zealand
Steyerlak-Anina *see* Anina
Steyr *73 D6 var.* Steier. Oberösterreich, N Austria
Stif *see* Sétif
Stillwater *27 G1* Oklahoma, C USA
Štip *79 E6* E FYR Macedonia
Stirling *66 C4* C Scotland, United Kingdom
Stjørdalshalsen *62 B4* Nord-Trøndelag, C Norway
Stockach *73 B6* Baden-Württemberg, S Germany
Stockholm *63 C6 country capital* Stockholm, C Sweden
Stockmannshof *see* Pļaviņas
Stockton *25 B6* California, W USA
Stockton Plateau *27 E4 plain* Texas, SW USA
Stœng Trêng *115 D5 prev.* Stung Treng. Stœng Trêng, NE Cambodia
Stoke *see* Stoke-on-Trent
Stoke-on-Trent *67 D6 var.* Stoke. C England, United Kingdom
Stolbce *see* Stowbtsy
Stolbtsy *see* Stowbtsy
Stolp *see* Słupsk
Stolpmünde *see* Ustka
Stómio *82 B4* Thessalía, C Greece
Store Bælt *see* Storebælt
Storebelt *see* Storebælt
Støren *63 B5* Sør-Trøndelag, S Norway
Storfjorden *61 G2 fjord* S Norway
Storhammer *see* Hamar
Stornoway *66 B2* NW Scotland, United Kingdom
Storsjön *63 B5 lake* C Sweden
Storuman *62 C4* Västerbotten, N Sweden
Storuman *62 C4 lake* N Sweden
Stowbtsy *85 C6 Pol.* Stolbce, *Rus.* Stolbtsy. Minskaya Voblasts', C Belarus
Strabane *67 B5 Ir.* An Srath Bán. W Northern Ireland, United Kingdom
Strakonice *77 A5 Ger.* Strakonitz. Jihočeský Kraj, S Czech Republic
Strakonitz *see* Strakonice
Stralsund *72 D2* Mecklenburg-Vorpommern, NE Germany
Stranraer *67 C5* S Scotland, United Kingdom
Strasbourg *68 E3 Ger.* Strassburg; *anc.* Argentoratum. Bas-Rhin, NE France
Străşeni *86 D3 var.* Strasheny. C Moldova
Strasheny *see* Străşeni
Strassburg *see* Strasbourg, France
Strassburg *see* Aiud, Romania
Stratford *128 D4* Taranaki, North Island, New Zealand
Strathfield *126 E2* New South Wales, E Australia
Straubing *73 C6* Bayern, SE Germany
Strehaia *86 B5* Mehedinţi, SW Romania
Strelka *92 D4* Krasnoyarskiy Kray, C Russian Federation
Strigonium *see* Esztergom
Strofilia *see* Strofyliá
Strofyliá *83 C5 var.* Strofilia. Évvoia, C Greece
Stromboli *75 D6 island* Isole Eolie, S Italy
Stromeferry *66 C3* N Scotland, United Kingdom
Strömstad *63 B6* Västra Götaland, S Sweden
Strömsund *62 C4* Jämtland, C Sweden
Struga *79 D6* SW FYR Macedonia
Struma *see* Strymónas
Strumica *79 E6* E FYR Macedonia
Strumyani *82 C3* Blagoevgrad, SW Bulgaria
Strymónas *82 C3 Bul.* Struma. *river* Bulgaria/ Greece
Stryy *86 B2* L'vivs'ka Oblast', NW Ukraine
Studholme *129 B6* Canterbury, South Island, New Zealand
Stuhlweissenberg *see* Székesfehérvár
Stung Treng *see* Stœng Trêng
Sturgis *22 D3* South Dakota, N USA
Stuttgart *73 B6* Baden-Württemberg, SW Germany
Stykkishólmur *61 E4* Vesturland, W Iceland
Styr *86 C1 Rus.* Styr'. *river* Belarus/Ukraine
Su *see* Jiangsu
Suakin *50 C3 var.* Sawakin. Red Sea, NE Sudan
Subačius *84 C4* Panevėžys, NE Lithuania
Subaykhān *96 E3* Dayr az Zawr, E Syria
Subotica *78 D2 Ger.* Maria-Theresiopel, *Hung.* Szabadka. Vojvodina, N Serbia
Suceava *86 C3 Ger.* Suczawa, *Hung.* Szucsava. Suceava, NE Romania
Su-chou *see* Suzhou
Suchow *see* Xuzhou, Jiangsu, China
Suchow *see* Suzhou, Jiangsu, China
Sucker State *see* Illinois
Sucre *39 F4 hist.* Chuquisaca, La Plata. *country capital* Chuquisaca, S Bolivia
Suczawa *see* Suceava
Sudan *50 A4 off.* Republic of Sudan, *Ar.* Jumhuriyat as-Sudan; *prev.* Anglo-Egyptian Sudan. *country* N Africa
Sudanese Republic *see* Mali
Sudan, Jumhuriyat as- *see* Sudan
Sudan, Republic of *see* Sudan
Sudbury *16 C4* Ontario, S Canada
Sudd *51 B5 swamp region* S Sudan
Sudeten *76 B4 var.* Sudetes, Sudetic Mountains, *Cz./Pol.* Sudety. *mountain range* Czech Republic/ Poland
Sudetes/Sudetic Mountains/Sudety *see* Sudeten
Südkarpaten *see* Carpaţii Meridionali
Südliche Morava *see* Južna Morava
Sudong, Pulau *116 A2 island* SW Singapore Asia
Sudostroy *see* Severodvinsk
Sue *51 B5 river* S Sudan
Sueca *71 F3* País Valenciano, E Spain
Sue Wood Bay *20 B5 bay* W Bermuda North America W Atlantic Ocean
Suez *50 B1 Ar.* As Suways, El Suweis. NE Egypt
Suez Canal *50 B1 Ar.* Qanāt as Suways. *canal* NE Egypt
Suez, Gulf of *see* Khalīj as Suways
Suğla Gölü *94 C4 lake* SW Turkey
Şuḩār *99 D5 var.* Sohar. N Oman
Sühbaatar *105 E1* Selenge, N Mongolia
Suhl *73 C5* Thüringen, C Germany
Suicheng *see* Suixi
Suid-Afrika *see* South Africa
Suidwes-Afrika *see* Namibia
Suixi *106 C6 var.* Suicheng. Guangdong, S China
Sujāwal *112 B3* Sind, SE Pakistan
Sukabumi *116 C5 prev.* Soekaboemi. Jawa, C Indonesia
Sukagawa *109 D5* Fukushima, Honshū, C Japan
Sukarnapura *see* Jayapura
Sukarno, Puntjak *see* Jaya, Puncak
Sukhne *see* As Sukhnah
Sukhona *88 C4 var.* Tot'ma. *river* NW Russian Federation
Sukhumi *see* Sokhumi
Sukkertoppen *see* Maniitsoq
Sukkur *112 B3* Sind, SE Pakistan
Sukumo *109 B7* Kōchi, Shikoku, SW Japan
Sulaimaniya *see* As Sulaymānīyah
Sulaiman Range *112 C2 mountain range* C Pakistan
Sula, Kepulauan *117 E4 island group* C Indonesia
Sulawesi, Laut *see* Celebes Sea
Sulechów *76 B3 Ger.* Züllichau. Lubuskie, W Poland
Suliag *see* Sawhāj
Sullana *38 B2* Piura, NW Peru
Sullivan Island *see* Lanbi Kyun
Sulphur Springs *27 G2* Texas, SW USA
Sultānābād *see* Arāk
Sulu Archipelago *117 E3 island group* SW Philippines
Sülüktü *see* Sulyukta
Sulu, Laut *see* Sulu Sea
Sulu Sea *117 E2 var.* Laut Sulu. *sea* SW Philippines
Sulyukta *101 E2 Kir.* Sülüktü. Batkenskaya Oblast', SW Kyrgyzstan
Sumatera *115 B8 Eng.* Sumatra. *island* W Indonesia
Sumatra *see* Sumatera
Šumava *see* Bohemian Forest
Sumba, Pulau *117 E5 Eng.* Sandalwood Island; *prev.* Soemba. *island* Nusa Tenggara, C Indonesia
Sumba, Selat *117 E5 strait* Nusa Tenggara, S Indonesia
Sumbawanga *51 B7* Rukwa, W Tanzania
Sumbe *56 B2 var.* N'Gunza, *Port.* Novo Redondo. Cuanza Sul, W Angola
Sumeih *51 B5* Southern Darfur, S Sudan
Sumgait *see* Sumqayıt, Azerbaijan
Summer Lake *24 B4 lake* Oregon, NW USA
Summit *71 H5* Alaska, USA
Sumqayıt *95 H2 Rus.* Sumgait. E Azerbaijan
Sumy *87 F2* Sums'ka Oblast', NE Ukraine
Sunbury *127 C7* Victoria, SE Australia
Sunda Islands *see* Greater Sunda Islands
Sunda, Selat *116 B5 strait* Jawa/Sumatera, SW Indonesia
Sunda Trench *see* Java Trench
Sunderland *66 D4 var.* Wearmouth. NE England, United Kingdom
Sundsvall *63 C5* Västernorrland, C Sweden
Sunflower State *see* Kansas
Sungaipenuh *116 B4 prev.* Soengaipenoeh. Sumatera, W Indonesia
Sunnyvale *25 A6* California, W USA
Sunset State *see* Oregon
Sunshine State *see* Florida
Sunshine State *see* New Mexico
Sunshine State *see* South Dakota
Suntar *93 F3* Respublika Sakha (Yakutiya), NE Russian Federation
Sunyani *53 E5* W Ghana
Suoločielgi *see* Saariselkä
Suomenlahti *see* Finland, Gulf of
Suomen Tasavalta/Suomi *see* Finland
Suomussalmi *62 E4* Oulu, E Finland
Suŏng *115 D6* Kâmpóng Cham, C Cambodia
Suoyarvi *88 B3* Respublika Kareliya, NW Russian Federation
Supe *38 C3* Lima, W Peru
Supérieur, Lac *see* Superior, Lake
Superior *18 A1* Wisconsin, N USA
Superior, Lake *18 B1 Fr.* Lac Supérieur. *lake* Canada/USA
Suqrah *see* Şawqirah
Şūr *99 E5* NE Oman
Şūr *see* Soûr
Surabaja *see* Surabaya
Surabaya *116 D5 prev.* Surabaja, Soerabaja. Jawa, C Indonesia
Surakarta *116 C5 Eng.* Solo; *prev.* Soerakarta. Jawa, S Indonesia
Šurany *77 C6 Hung.* Nagysurány. Nitriansky Kraj, SW Slovakia
Sūrat *112 C4* Gujarāt, W India
Suratdhani *see* Surat Thani
Surat Thani *115 C6 var.* Suratdhani. Surat Thani, SW Thailand
Surazh *85 E5* Vitsyebskaya Voblasts', NE Belarus
Surdulica *79 E5* Serbia, SE Serbia
Sûre *65 D7 var.* Sauer. *river* W Europe
Surendranagar *112 C4* Gujarāt, W India
Surfers Paradise *127 E5* Queensland, E Australia
Surgut *92 D3* Khanty-Mansiyskiy Avtonomnyy Okrug-Yugra, C Russian Federation
Surin *115 D5* Surin, E Thailand
Surinam *see* Suriname
Suriname *37 G3 off.* Republic of Suriname, *var.* Surinam; *prev.* Dutch Guiana, Netherlands Guiana. *country* N South America
Suriname, Republic of *see* Suriname
Sūrīya/Sūrīyah, Al-Jumhūrīyah al-'Arabīyah as- *see* Syria
Surkhab, Darya-i- *see* Kahmard, Daryā-ye
Surkhob *101 F3 river* C Tajikistan
Surt *49 G2 var.* Sidra, Sirte. N Libya
Surtsey *61 E5 island* S Iceland
Suruga-wan *109 D6 bay* SE Japan
Susa *74 A2* Piemonte, NE Italy
Sūsah *see* Sousse
Susanville *25 B5* California, W USA
Susitna *14 C3* Alaska, USA
Susteren *65 D5* Limburg, SE Netherlands
Susuman *93 G3* Magadanskaya Oblast', E Russian Federation
Sutlej *112 C2 river* India/Pakistan
Suur Munamägi *84 D3 var.* Munamägi, *Ger.* Eier-Berg. *mountain* SE Estonia
Suur Väin *84 C2 Ger.* Grosser Sund. *strait* W Estonia
Suva *123 E4 country capital* Viti Levu, W Fiji
Suvalkai/Suvalki *see* Suwałki
Suwałki *76 E2 Lith.* Suvalkai, *Rus.* Suvalki. Podlaskie, NE Poland
Şuwār *see* Aş Şuwār
Suways, Qanāt as *see* Suez Canal
Suweida *see* As Suwaydā'
Suzhou *106 D5 var.* Soochow, Su-chou, Suchow; *prev.* Wuhsien. Jiangsu, E China
Svalbard *61 E1 Norwegian dependency* Arctic Ocean
Svartisen *62 C3 glacier* C Norway
Svay Riĕng *115 D6* Svay Riĕng, S Cambodia
Sveg *63 B5* Jämtland, C Sweden
Svenstavik *63 C5* Jämtland, C Sweden
Sverdlovsk *see* Yekaterinburg
Sverige *see* Sweden
Sveti Vrach *see* Sandanski
Svetlogorsk *see* Svyetlahorsk
Svetlograd *89 B7* Stavropol'skiy Kray, SW Russian Federation
Svetlovodsk *see* Svitlovods'k
Svetozarevo *see* Jagodina
Svilengrad *82 D3 prev.* Mustafa-Pasha. Khaskovo, S Bulgaria
Svitlovods'k *87 F3 Rus.* Svetlovodsk. Kirovohrads'ka Oblast', C Ukraine
Svizzera *see* Switzerland
Svobodnyy *93 G4* Amurskaya Oblast', SE Russian Federation
Svyataya Anna Trough *133 C4 var.* Saint Anna Trough. *trough* N Kara Sea
Svyetlahorsk *85 D7 Rus.* Svetlogorsk. Homyel'skaya Voblasts', SE Belarus
Swabian Jura *see* Schwäbische Alb
Swakopmund *56 B3* Erongo, W Namibia
Swan Islands *31 E1 island group* NE Honduras North America
Swansea *67 C7 Wel.* Abertawe. S Wales, United Kingdom
Swarzędz *76 C3* Poznań, W Poland
Swatow *see* Shantou
Swaziland *56 D4 off.* Kingdom of Swaziland. *country* S Africa
Swaziland, Kingdom of *see* Swaziland
Sweden *62 B4 off.* Kingdom of Sweden, *Swe.* Sverige. *country* N Europe
Sweden, Kingdom of *see* Sweden
Sweetwater *27 F3* Texas, SW USA
Świdnica *76 B4 Ger.* Schweidnitz. Wałbrzych, SW Poland
Świdwin *76 B2 Ger.* Schivelbein. Zachodnio-pomorskie, NW Poland
Świebodzice *76 B4 Ger.* Freiburg in Schlesien, Swiebodzice. Walbrzych, SW Poland
Świebodzin *76 B3 Ger.* Schwiebus. Lubuskie, W Poland
Świecie *76 C3 Ger.* Schwertberg. Kujawsko-pomorskie, C Poland
Swindon *67 D7* S England, United Kingdom
Swinemünde *see* Świnoujście
Świnoujście *76 B2 Ger.* Swinemünde. Zachodnio-pomorskie, NW Poland
Swiss Confederation *see* Switzerland
Switzerland *73 A7 off.* Swiss Confederation, *Fr.* La Suisse, *Ger.* Schweiz, *It.* Svizzera; *anc.* Helvetia. *country* C Europe
Sycaminum *see* Hefa
Sydenham Island *see* Nonouti
Sydney *126 D1 state capital* New South Wales, SE Australia

Sydney – Therezina

Sydney 17 G4 Cape Breton Island, Nova Scotia, SE Canada
Sydney Island see Manra
Syedpur see Saidpur
Syemyezhava 85 C6 Rus. Semezhevo. Minskaya Voblasts', C Belarus
Syene see Aswân
Syeverodonets'k 87 H3 Rus. Severodonetsk. Luhans'ka Oblast', E Ukraine
Syktyvkar 88 D4 prev. Ust'-Sysol'sk. Respublika Komi, NW Russian Federation
Sylhet 113 G3 Sylhet, NE Bangladesh
Synel'nykove 87 G3 Dnipropetrovs'ka Oblast', E Ukraine
Syowa 132 C2 Japanese research station Antarctica
Syracuse 19 E3 New York, NE USA
Syracuse see Siracusa
Syrdar'ya 92 B4 Sirdaryo Viloyati, E Uzbekistan
Syria 96 B3 off. Syrian Arab Republic, var. Siria, Syrie, Ar. Al-Jumhūrīyah al-'Arabīyah as-Sūrīyah, Sūrīya. country SW Asia
Syrian Arab Republic see Syria
Syrian Desert 97 D5 Ar. Al Hamad, Bādiyat ash Shām. desert SW Asia
Syrie see Syria
Sýrna 83 E7 var. Sirna. island Kykládes, Greece, Aegean Sea
Sýros 83 C6 var. Síros. island Kykládes, Greece, Aegean Sea
Syulemeshlii see Sredets
Syvash, Zaliv see Syvash, Zatoka
Syvash, Zatoka 87 F4 Rus. Zaliv Syvash. inlet S Ukraine
Syzran' 89 C6 Samarskaya Oblast', W Russian Federation
Szabadka see Subotica
Szamotuły 76 B3 Poznań, W Poland
Szászrégen see Reghin
Szatmárrnémeti see Satu Mare
Száva see Sava
Szczecin 76 B3 Eng./Ger. Stettin. Zachodnio-pomorskie, NW Poland
Szczecinek 76 B2 Ger. Neustettin. Zachodnio-pomorskie, NW Poland
Szczeciński, Zalew 76 A2 var. Stettiner Haff, Ger. Oderhaff. bay Germany/Poland
Szczuczyn Nowogródzki see Shchuchyn
Szczytno 76 D3 Ger. Ortelsburg. Warmińsko-Mazurskie, NE Poland
Szechuan/Szechwan see Sichuan
Szeged 77 D7 Ger. Szegedin, Rom. Seghedin. Csongrád, SE Hungary
Szegedin see Szeged
Székelykeresztúr see Cristuru Secuiesc
Székesfehérvár 77 C6 Ger. Stuhlweissenberg; anc. Alba Regia. Fejér, W Hungary
Szeklerburg see Miercurea-Ciuc
Szekler Neumarkt see Târgu Secuiesc
Szekszárd 77 C7 Tolna, S Hungary
Szempcz/Szenc see Senec
Szenice see Senica
Szenttamás see Srbobran
Szeping see Siping
Szilágysomlyó see Şimleu Silvaniei
Szinna see Snina
Sziszek see Sisak
Szitás-Keresztúr see Cristuru Secuiesc
Szkudy see Skuodas
Szlatina see Slatina
Szlovákia see Slovakia
Szolnok 77 D6 Jász-Nagykun-Szolnok, C Hungary
Szombathely 77 B6 Ger. Steinamanger; anc. Sabaria, Savaria. Vas, W Hungary
Szprotawa 76 B4 Ger. Sprottau. Lubuskie, W Poland
Sztálinváros see Dunaújváros
Szucsava see Suceava

T

Tabariya, Bahrat see Tiberias, Lake
Table Rock Lake 27 G1 reservoir Arkansas/Missouri, C USA
Tábor 77 B5 Jihočeský Kraj, S Czech Republic
Tabora 51 B7 Tabora, W Tanzania
Tabrīz 98 C2 var. Tebriz; anc. Tauris. Āžarbāyjān-e Sharqī, NW Iran
Tabuaeran 123 G2 prev. Fanning Island. atoll Line Islands, E Kiribati
Tabūk 98 A4 Tabūk, NW Saudi Arabia
Täby 63 C6 Stockholm, C Sweden
Tachau see Tachov
Tachov 77 A5 Ger. Tachau. Plvenský Kraj, W Czech Republic
Tacloban 117 F2 off. Tacloban City. Leyte, C Philippines
Tacloban City see Tacloban
Tacna 39 E4 Tacna, SE Peru
Tacoma 24 B2 Washington, NW USA
Tacuarembó 42 D4 prev. San Fructuoso. Tacuarembó, C Uruguay
Tademaït, Plateau du 48 D3 plateau C Algeria
Tadmor/Tadmur see Tudmur
Tādpatri 110 C2 Andhra Pradesh, E India
Tadzhikistan see Tajikistan
Taegu 107 E4 off. Taegu-gwangyŏksi, var. Daegu, Jap. Taikyū. SE South Korea
Taegu-gwangyŏksi see Taegu
Taehan-haehyŏp see Korea Strait
Taehan Min'guk see South Korea
Taejŏn 107 E4 off. Taejŏn-gwangyŏksi, Jap. Taiden. C South Korea
Taejŏn-gwangyŏksi see Taejŏn
Tafassâsset, Ténéré du 53 G2 desert N Niger
Tafila/Ţafilah, Muḩāfaẓat aţ see Aţ Ţafilah
Taganrog 89 A7 Rostovskaya Oblast', SW Russian Federation
Taganrog, Gulf of 87 G4 Rus. Taganrogskiy Zaliv, Ukr. Tahanroz'ka Zatoka. gulf Russian Federation/Ukraine
Taganrogskiy Zaliv see Taganrog, Gulf of
Taguatinga 41 F3 Tocantins, C Brazil
Tagus 70 C3 Port. Rio Tejo, Sp. Río Tajo. river Portugal/Spain
Tagus Plain 58 A4 abyssal plain E Atlantic Ocean
Tahanroz'ka Zatoka see Taganrog, Gulf of
Tahat 49 E4 mountain SE Algeria
Tahiti 123 H4 island Îles du Vent, W French Polynesia
Tahiti, Archipel de see Société, Archipel de la
Tahlequah 27 G1 Oklahoma, C USA
Tahoe, Lake 25 B5 lake California/Nevada, W USA
Tahoua 53 F3 Tahoua, W Niger
Taichū see T'aichung
T'aichung 106 D6 Jap. Taichū; prev. Taiwan. C Taiwan
Taiden see Taejŏn
Taieri 129 B7 river South Island, New Zealand
Taihape 128 D4 Manawatu-Wanganui, North Island, New Zealand
Taihoku see T'aipei
Taikyū see Taegu
Tailem Bend 127 B7 South Australia
T'ainan 106 D6 Jap. Tainan; prev. Dainan. S Taiwan
T'aipei 106 D6 Jap. Taihoku; prev. Daihoku. country capital N Taiwan
Taiping 116 B3 Perak, Peninsular Malaysia
Taiwan 106 D6 off. Republic of China, var. Formosa, Formo'sa. country E Asia
Taiwan see T'aichung
T'aiwan Haihsia/Taiwan Haixia see Taiwan Strait
Taiwan Strait 106 D6 var. Formosa Strait, Chin. T'aiwan Haihsia, Taiwan Haixia. strait China/Taiwan
Taiyuan 106 C4 var. T'ai-yuan, T'ai-yüan; prev. Yangku. province capital Shanxi, C China
T'ai-yuan/T'ai-yüan see Taiyuan
Ta'izz 99 B7 SW Yemen
Tajikistan 101 E3 off. Republic of Tajikistan, Rus. Tadzhikistan, Taj. Jumhurii Tojikiston; prev. Tajik S.S.R. country C Asia
Tajikistan, Republic of see Tajikistan
Tajik S.S.R see Tajikistan
Tajo, Río see Tagus
Tak 114 C4 var. Rahaeng. Tak, W Thailand
Takao see Kaohsiung
Takaoka 109 C5 Toyama, Honshū, SW Japan
Takapuna 128 D2 Auckland, North Island, New Zealand
Takhiatash see Takiatosh
Takhtakupyr see Taxtako'pir
Takikawa 108 D2 Hokkaidō, NE Japan
Takla Makan Desert 104 B3 Eng. Takla Makan Desert. desert NW China
Takla Makan Desert see Taklimakan Shamo
Takow see Kaohsiung
Takutea 123 G4 island S Cook Islands
Talabriga see Aveiro, Portugal
Talabriga see Talavera de la Reina, Spain
Talachyn 85 D6 Rus. Tolochin. Vitsyebskaya Voblasts', NE Belarus
Talamanca, Cordillera de 31 E5 mountain range S Costa Rica
Talara 38 B2 Piura, NW Peru
Talas 101 F2 Talasskaya Oblast', NW Kyrgyzstan
Talaud, Kepulauan 117 F3 island group E Indonesia
Talavera de la Reina 70 D3 anc. Caesarobriga, Talabriga. Castilla-La Mancha, C Spain
Talca 42 B4 Maule, C Chile
Talcahuano 43 B5 Bío Bío, C Chile
Taldykorgan 92 C5 Kaz. Taldyqorghan; prev. Taldy-Kurgan. Taldykorgan, SE Kazakhstan
Taldy-Kurgan/Taldyqorghan see Taldykorgan
Ta-lien see Dalian
Taliq-an see Tāloqān
Tal'ka 85 C6 Minskaya Voblasts', C Belarus
Talkhof see Puurmani
Tallahassee 20 D3 prev. Muskogean. state capital Florida, SE USA
Tall al Abyaḑ see At Tall al Abyaḑ
Tallin see Tallinn
Tallinn 84 D2 Ger. Reval, Rus. Tallin; prev. Revel. country capital Harjumaa, NW Estonia
Tall Kalakh 96 B4 var. Tell Kalakh. Ḩimş, C Syria
Tallulah 20 B2 Louisiana, S USA
Talnakh 92 D3 Taymyrskiy (Dolgano-Nenetskiy) Avtonomnyy Okrug, N Russian Federation
Tal'ne 87 E3 Rus. Tal'noye. Cherkas'ka Oblast', C Ukraine
Tal'noye see Tal'ne
Taloga 27 F1 Oklahoma, C USA
Tāloqān 101 E3 var. Taliq-an. Takhār, NE Afghanistan
Talsen see Talsi
Talsi 84 C3 Ger. Talsen. Talsi, NW Latvia
Taltal 42 B2 Antofagasta, N Chile
Talvik 62 D2 Finnmark, N Norway
Tamabo, Banjaran 116 D3 mountain range East Malaysia
Tamale 53 E4 C Ghana
Tamana 123 E3 prev. Rotcher Island. atoll Tungaru, W Kiribati
Tamanrasset 49 E4 var. Tamenghest. S Algeria
Tamar 67 C7 river SW England, United Kingdom
Tamar see Tudmur
Tamatave see Toamasina
Tamazunchale 29 E4 San Luis Potosí, C Mexico
Tambacounda 52 C3 SE Senegal
Tambov 89 B6 Tambovskaya Oblast', W Russian Federation
Tambura 51 B5 Western Equatoria, SW Sudan
Tâmchaket see Tâmchekeţ
Tâmchekeţ 52 C3 var. Tamchaket. Hodh el Gharbi, S Mauritania
Tamenghest see Tamanrasset
Tamiahua, Laguna de 29 F4 lagoon Veracruz-Llave, Mexico
Tamil Nādu 110 C3 prev. Madras. cultural region SE India
Tam Ky 115 E5 Quang Nam-fa Năng, C Vietnam
Tammerfors see Tampere
Tampa 21 E4 Florida, SE USA
Tampa Bay 21 E4 bay Florida, SE USA
Tampere 63 D5 Swe. Tammerfors. Länsi-Suomi, W Finland
Tampico 29 E3 Tamaulipas, C Mexico
Tamworth 127 D6 New South Wales, SE Australia
Tanabe 109 C7 Wakayama, Honshū, SW Japan
Tana Bru 62 D2 Finnmark, N Norway
Tanais see Don
Lake Tana 50 C4 var. Lake Tana. lake NW Ethiopia
Tana, Lake see T'ana Hāyk'
Tanami Desert 124 D3 desert Northern Territory, N Australia
Tananarive see Antananarivo
Ţăndărei 86 D5 Ialomiţa, SE Romania
Tandil 43 D5 Buenos Aires, E Argentina
Tandjoengkarang see Bandar Lampung
Tanega-shima 109 B8 island Nansei-shotō, SW Japan
Tanen Taunggyi see Tane Range
Tane Range 114 B4 Bur. Tanen Taunggyi. mountain range W Thailand
Tanezrouft 48 D4 desert Algeria/Mali
Ţanf, Jabal aţ 96 D4 mountain SE Syria
Tanga 51 C7 Tanga, E Tanzania
Tanganyika and Zanzibar see Tanzania
Tanganyika, Lake 51 B7 lake E Africa
Tanger 48 C2 var. Tangiers, Tangier, Fr./Ger. Tangerk, Sp. Tánger; anc. Tingis. NW Morocco
Tangerk see Tanger
Tanggula Shan 104 C4 mountain W China
Tangier see Tanger
Tangiers see Tanger
Tangra Yumco 104 B5 var. Tangro Tso. lake W China
Tangro Tso see Tangra Yumco
Tangshan 106 D3 var. T'ang-shan. Hebei, E China
T'ang-shan see Tangshan
Tanimbar, Kepulauan 117 F5 island group Maluku, E Indonesia
Tanjungkarang/Tanjungkarang-Telukbetung see Bandar Lampung
Tanna 122 D4 island S Vanuatu
Tannenhof see Krynica
Tan-Tan 48 B3 SW Morocco
Tan-tung see Dandong
Tanzania 51 C7 off. United Republic of Tanzania, Swa. Jamhuri ya Muungano wa Tanzania; prev. German East Africa, Tanganyika and Zanzibar. country E Africa
Tanzania, Jamhuri ya Muungano wa see Tanzania
Tanzania, United Republic of see Tanzania
Taoudenit see Taoudenni
Taoudenni 53 E2 var. Taoudenit. Tombouctou, N Mali
Tapa 84 E2 Ger. Taps. Lääne-Virumaa, NE Estonia
Tapachula 29 G5 Chiapas, SE Mexico
Tapaiu see Gvardeysk
Tapajós, Rio 41 E2 var. Tapajóz. river NW Brazil
Tapajóz see Tapajós, Rio
Taps see Tapa
Ţarābulus 49 F2 var. Ţarābulus al Gharb, Eng. Tripoli. country capital NW Libya
Ţarābulus al Gharb see Ţarābulus
Tarābulus/Ţarābulus ash Shām see Tripoli
Taraclia 86 D4 Rus. Tarakilya. S Moldova
Tarakilya see Taraclia
Mount Taranaki 128 C4 var. Egmont. volcano North Island, New Zealand
Tarancón 71 E3 Castilla-La Mancha, C Spain
Taranto 75 E5 var. Tarentum. Puglia, SE Italy
Taranto, Gulf of 75 E6 Eng. Gulf of Taranto. gulf S Italy
Taranto, Gulf of see Taranto, Golfo di
Tarapoto 38 C2 San Martín, N Peru
Tarare 69 D5 Rhône, E France
Tarascon 69 D6 Bouches-du-Rhône, SE France
Tarawa 122 D2 atoll Tungaru, W Kiribati
Taraz 92 C5 prev. Aulie Ata, Auliye-Ata, Dzhambul, Zhambyl. Zhambyl, S Kazakhstan
Tarazona 71 E2 Aragón, NE Spain
Tarbes 69 B6 anc. Bigorra. Hautes-Pyrénées, S France
Tarcoola 127 A6 South Australia
Taree 127 D6 New South Wales, SE Australia
Tarentum see Taranto
Târgovişte 86 C5 prev. Tîrgovişte. Dâmboviţa, S Romania
Targu Jiu 86 B4 prev. Tîrgu Jiu. Gorj, W Romania
Târgul-Neamţ see Târgu-Neamţ
Târgul-Săcuiesc see Târgu Secuiesc
Târgu Mureş 86 B4 prev. Oşorhei, Tîrgu Mures, Ger. Neumarkt, Hung. Marosvásárhely. Mureş, C Romania
Târgu-Neamţ 86 C3 var. Târgul-Neamţ; prev. Tîrgu-Neamţ. Neamţ, NE Romania
Târgu Ocna 86 C4 Hung. Aknavásár; prev. Tîrgu Ocna. Bacău, E Romania
Târgu Secuiesc 86 C4 Ger. Neumarkt, Szekler Neumarkt, Hung. Kezdivásárhely; prev. Chezdi-Oşorheiu, Târgul-Săcuiesc, Tîrgu Secuiesc. Covasna, E Romania
Tar Heel State see North Carolina
Tarija 39 G5 Tarija, S Bolivia
Tarim 99 C6 C Yemen
Tarim Basin 102 C2 Eng. Tarim Basin. basin NW China
Tarim Basin see Tarim Pendi
Tarim He 104 B3 river NW China
Tarma 38 C3 Junín, C Peru
Tarn 69 C6 cultural region S France
Tarn 69 C6 river S France
Tarnobrzeg 76 D4 Podkarpackie, SE Poland
Tarnopol see Ternopil'
Tarnów 77 D5 Małopolskie, S Poland
Tarraco see Tarragona
Tarragona 71 G2 anc. Tarraco. Cataluña, E Spain
Tarrasa see Terrassa
Tàrrega 71 F2 var. Tarrega. Cataluña, NE Spain
Tarsatica see Rijeka
Tarsus 94 C4 İçel, S Turkey
Tartous/Tartouss see Ţarţūs
Tartu 84 D3 Ger. Dorpat; prev. Rus. Yurev, Yury'ev. Tartumaa, SE Estonia
Ţarţūs 96 A3 off. Muḩāfaẓat Ţarţūs, var. Tartous, Tartus. governorate W Syria
Ţarţūs, Muḩāfaẓat see Ţarţūs
Ta Ru Tao, Ko 115 B7 island S Thailand Asia
Tarvisio 74 D2 Friuli-Venezia Giulia, NE Italy
Tarvisium see Treviso
Tashauz see Daşoguz
Tashi Chho Dzong see Thimphu
Tashkent see Toshkent
Tash-Kömür see Tash-Kumyr
Tash-Kumyr 101 F2 Kir. Tash-Kömür. Dzhalal-Abadskaya Oblast', W Kyrgyzstan
Tashqurghan see Kholm
Tasikmalaja see Tasikmalaya
Tasikmalaya 116 C5 prev. Tasikmalaja. Jawa, C Indonesia
Tasman Basin 120 C5 var. East Australian Basin. undersea basin S Tasman Sea
Tasman Bay 129 C5 inlet South Island, New Zealand
Tasmania 127 B8 prev. Van Diemen's Land. state SE Australia
Tasmania 130 B4 island SE Australia
Tasman Plateau 120 C5 var. South Tasmania Plateau. undersea plateau SW Tasman Sea
Tasman Sea 120 C5 sea SW Pacific Ocean
Tassili-n-Ajjer 49 E4 plateau E Algeria
Tatabánya 77 C6 Komárom-Esztergom, NW Hungary
Tatar Pazardzhik see Pazardzhik
Tathlīth 99 B5 'Asīr, S Saudi Arabia
Tatra Mountains 77 D5 Ger. Tatra, Hung. Tátra, Pol./Slvk. Tatry. mountain range Poland/Slovakia
Tatra/Tátra see Tatra Mountains
Tatry see Tatra Mountains
Ta-t'ung/Tatung see Datong
Tatvan 95 F3 Bitlis, SE Turkey
Ta'ū 123 F4 var. Tau. island Manua Islands, E American Samoa
Taukum, Peski 101 G1 desert SE Kazakhstan
Taumarunui 128 D4 Manawatu-Wanganui, North Island, New Zealand
Taungdwingyi 114 B3 Magway, C Myanmar (Burma)
Taunggyi 114 B3 Shan State, C Myanmar (Burma)
Taungoo 114 B4 Bago, C Myanmar (Burma)
Taunton 67 C7 SW England, United Kingdom
Taupo 128 D3 Waikato, North Island, New Zealand
Taupo, Lake 128 D3 lake North Island, New Zealand
Tauragė 84 B4 Ger. Tauroggen. Tauragė, SW Lithuania
Tauranga 128 D3 Bay of Plenty, North Island, New Zealand
Tauris see Tabrīz
Tauroggen see Tauragė
Taurus Mountains 94 C4 Eng. Taurus Mountains. mountain range S Turkey
Taurus Mountains see Toros Dağları
Tavas 94 B4 Denizli, SW Turkey
Tavastehus see Hämeenlinna
Tavira 70 C5 Faro, S Portugal
Tavoy see Dawei
Tavoy Island see Mali Kyun
Ta Waewae Bay 129 A7 bay South Island, New Zealand
Tawakoni, Lake 27 G2 reservoir Texas, SW USA
Tawau 116 D3 Sabah, East Malaysia
Ţawkar see Tokar
Tawzar see Tozeur
Taxco 29 E4 var. Taxco de Alarcón. Guerrero, S Mexico
Taxco de Alarcón see Taxco
Takiatosh 100 C2 Rus. Takhiatash. Qoraqalpog'iston Respublikasi, W Uzbekistan
Taxtako'pir 100 D1 Rus. Takhtakupyr. Qoraqalpog'iston Respublikasi, NW Uzbekistan
Tay 66 C3 river C Scotland, United Kingdom
Taylor 27 G3 Texas, SW USA
Taymā' 98 A4 Tabūk, NW Saudi Arabia
Taymyr, Ozero 93 E2 lake N Russian Federation
Taymyr, Poluostrov 93 E2 peninsula N Russian Federation
Taz 92 D3 river N Russian Federation
T'bilisi 95 G2 Eng. Tiflis. country capital SE Georgia
Tchad see Chad
Tchad, Lac see Chad, Lake
Tchien see Zwedru
Tchongking see Chongqing
Tczew 76 C2 Ger. Dirschau. Pomorskie, N Poland
Te Anau 129 A7 Southland, South Island, New Zealand
Te Anau, Lake 129 A7 lake South Island, New Zealand
Teapa 29 G4 Tabasco, SE Mexico
Teate see Chieti
Tebingtinggi 116 B3 Sumatera, N Indonesia
Tebriz see Tabrīz
Techirghiol 86 D5 Constanţa, SE Romania
Tecomán 28 D4 Colima, SW Mexico
Tecpan 29 E5 var. Tecpan de Galeana. Guerrero, S Mexico
Tecpan de Galeana see Tecpan
Tecuci 86 C4 Galaţi, E Romania
Tedzhen see Harīrūd/Tejen
Tedzhen see Tejen
Tees 67 D5 river N England, United Kingdom
Tefé 40 D2 Amazonas, N Brazil
Tegal 116 C4 Jawa, C Indonesia
Tegelen 65 D5 Limburg, SE Netherlands
Tegucigalpa 30 C3 country capital Francisco Morazán, SW Honduras
Teheran see Tehrān
Tehrān 98 C3 var. Teheran. country capital Tehrān, N Iran
Tehuacán 29 F4 Puebla, S Mexico
Tehuantepec 29 F5 var. Santo Domingo Tehuantepec. Oaxaca, SE Mexico
Gulf of Tehuantepec 29 F5 var. Gulf of Tehuantepec. gulf S Mexico
Tehuantepec, Gulf of see Tehuantepec, Golfo de
Isthmus of Tehuantepec 29 F5 var. Isthmus of Tehuantepec. isthmus SE Mexico
Tehuantepec, Isthmus of see Tehuantepec, Istmo de
Tejen 100 C3 Rus. Tedzhen. Ahal Welaýaty, S Turkmenistan
Tejen see Harīrūd
Tejo, Rio see Tagus
Te Kao 128 C1 Northland, North Island, New Zealand
Tekax 29 H4 var. Tekax de Álvaro Obregón. Yucatán, SE Mexico
Tekax de Álvaro Obregón see Tekax
Tekeli 92 C5 Almaty, SE Kazakhstan
Tekirdağ 94 A2 It. Rodosto; anc. Bisanthe, Raidestos, Rhaedestus. Tekirdağ, NW Turkey
Te Kuiti 128 D3 Waikato, North Island, New Zealand
Tela 30 C2 Atlántida, NW Honduras
Telanaipura see Jambi
Tel Aviv-Jaffa see Tel Aviv-Yafo
Tel Aviv-Yafo 97 A6 var. Tel Aviv-Jaffa. Tel Aviv, C Israel
Teles Pirés see São Manuel, Rio
Telish 82 C2 prev. Azizie. Pleven, N Bulgaria
Tell Abiad/Tell Abyad see At Tall al Abyaḑ
Tell Kalakh see Tall Kalakh
Tell Shedadi see Ash Shadādah
Tel'man/Tel'mansk see Gubadag
Teloekbetoeng see Bandar Lampung
Telo Martius see Toulon
Telschen see Telšiai
Telšiai 84 B3 Ger. Telschen. Telšiai, NW Lithuania
Telukbetung see Bandar Lampung
Temerin 78 D3 Vojvodina, N Serbia
Temeschburg/Temeschwar see Timişoara
Temesvár/Temeswar see Timişoara
Temirtau 92 C4 prev. Samarkandski, Samarkandskoye. Karaganda, C Kazakhstan
Tempio Pausania 75 A5 Sardegna, Italy, C Mediterranean Sea
Temple 27 G3 Texas, SW USA
Temuco 43 B5 Araucanía, C Chile
Temuka 129 B6 Canterbury, South Island, New Zealand
Tenasserim 115 B6 Tanintharyi, S Myanmar (Burma)
Ténenkou 52 D3 Mopti, C Mali
Ténéré 53 G3 physical region C Niger
Tenerife 48 A3 island Islas Canarias, Spain, NE Atlantic Ocean
Tengger Shamo 105 E3 desert N China
Tengréla 52 D4 var. Tingréla. N Ivory Coast
Tenkodogo 53 E4 S Burkina
Tennant Creek 126 A3 Northern Territory, C Australia
Tennessee 20 C1 off. State of Tennessee, also known as The Volunteer State. state SE USA
Tennessee River 20 C1 river S USA
Tenos see Tínos
Tepelena see Tepelenë
Tepelenë 79 C7 var. Tepelena, It. Tepeleni. Gjirokastër, S Albania
Tepeleni see Tepelenë
Tepic 28 D4 Nayarit, C Mexico
Teplice 76 A4 Ger. Teplitz; prev. Teplice-Šanov, Teplitz-Schönau. Ustecký Kraj, NW Czech Republic
Teplice-Šanov/Teplitz/Teplitz-Schönau see Teplice
Tequila 28 D4 Jalisco, SW Mexico
Teraina 123 G2 prev. Washington Island. atoll Line Islands, E Kiribati
Teramo 74 C4 anc. Interamna. Abruzzi, C Italy
Tercan 95 E3 Erzincan, NE Turkey
Terceira 70 A5 var. Ilha Terceira. island Azores, Portugal, NE Atlantic Ocean
Terceira, Ilha see Terceira
Terekhovka see Tsyerakhowka
Teresina 41 F2 var. Therezina. state capital Piauí, NE Brazil
Termez see Termiz
Termia see Kýthnos
Términos, Laguna de 29 G4 lagoon SE Mexico
Termiz 101 E3 Rus. Termez. Surkhondaryo Viloyati, S Uzbekistan
Termoli 74 D4 Molise, C Italy
Terneuzen 65 B5 var. Neuzen. Zeeland, SW Netherlands
Terni 74 C4 anc. Interamna Nahars. Umbria, C Italy
Ternopil' 86 C2 Pol. Tarnopol, Rus. Ternopol'. Ternopil's'ka Oblast', W Ukraine
Ternopol' see Ternopil'
Terracina 75 C5 Lazio, C Italy
Terranova di Sicilia see Gela
Terranova Pausania see Olbia
Terrassa 71 G2 Cast. Tarrasa. Cataluña, E Spain
Terre Adélie 132 C4 physical region Antarctica
Terre Haute 18 B4 Indiana, N USA
Terre Neuve see Newfoundland and Labrador
Terschelling 64 C1 Fris. Skylge. island Waddeneilanden, N Netherlands
Teruel 71 F3 anc. Turba. Aragón, E Spain
Tervel 82 E1 prev. Kurtbunar, Rom. Curtbunar. Dobrich, NE Bulgaria
Tervueren see Tervuren
Tervuren 65 C6 var. Tervueren. Vlaams Brabant, C Belgium
Teseney 50 C4 var. Tessenei. W Eritrea
Tessalit 53 E2 Kidal, NE Mali
Tessaoua 53 G3 Maradi, S Niger
Tessenderlo 65 C5 Limburg, NE Belgium
Tessenei see Teseney
Testigos, Islas los 37 E1 island group N Venezuela
Tete 57 E2 Tete, NW Mozambique
Teterow 72 C3 Mecklenburg-Vorpommern, NE Germany
Tétouan 48 C2 var. Tetouan, Tetuán. N Morocco
Tetovo 79 D5 Razgrad, N Bulgaria
Tetschen see Děčín
Tetuán see Tétouan
Teverya see Tverya
Te Waewae Bay 129 A7 bay South Island, New Zealand
Texarkana 20 A2 Arkansas, C USA
Texarkana 27 H2 Texas, SW USA
Texas 27 F3 off. State of Texas, also known as Lone Star State. state S USA
Texas City 27 H4 Texas, SW USA
Texel 64 C2 island Waddeneilanden, NW Netherlands
Texoma, Lake 27 G2 reservoir Oklahoma/Texas, C USA
Teziutlán 29 F4 Puebla, S Mexico
Thaa Atoll see Kolhumadulu
Thai, Ao see Thailand, Gulf of
Thai Binh 114 D3 Thai Binh, N Vietnam
Thailand 115 C5 off. Kingdom of Thailand, Th. Prathet Thai; prev. Siam. country SE Asia
Thailand, Gulf of 115 C6 var. Gulf of Siam, Th. Ao Thai, Vtn. Vinh Thai Lan. gulf SE Asia
Thailand, Kingdom of see Thailand
Thai Lan, Vinh see Thailand, Gulf of
Thai Nguyên 114 D3 Bắc Thai, N Vietnam
Thakhèk 114 D4 var. Muang Khammouan. Khammouan, C Laos
Thamarid see Thamarīt
Thamarīt 99 D6 var. Thamarīd, Thumrayt. SW Oman
Thames 128 D3 Waikato, North Island, New Zealand
Thames 67 B8 river S England, United Kingdom
Thandwe 114 A4 var. Sandoway. Rakhine State, W Myanmar (Burma)
Thanh Hoa 114 D3 Thanh Hoa, N Vietnam
Thanintari Taungdan see Bilauktaung Range
Thanlwin see Salween
Thar Desert 112 C3 var. Great Indian Desert, Indian Desert. desert India/Pakistan
Tharthār, Buḩayrat ath 98 B3 lake C Iraq
Thásos 82 C4 Thásos, E Greece
Thásos 82 C4 island E Greece
Thaton 114 B4 Mon State, S Myanmar (Burma)
Thayetmyo 114 A4 Magway, C Myanmar (Burma)
The Crane 33 H2 var. Crane. S Barbados
The Dalles 24 B3 Oregon, NW USA
The Flatts Village see Flatts Village
The Hague see 's-Gravenhage
Theodosia see Feodosiya
The Pas 15 F5 Manitoba, C Canada
Therezina see Teresina

Thérma – Ţubruq

Thérma 83 D6 Ikaría, Dodekánisa, Greece, Aegean Sea
Thermaic Gulf 82 B4 Eng. Thermaic Gulf; anc. Thermaicus Sinus. gulf N Greece
Thermaic Gulf/Thermaicus Sinus see Thermaïkós Kólpos
Thermiá see Kýthnos
Thérmo 83 B5 Dytikí Ellás, C Greece
The Rock 71 H4 New South Wales, SE Australia
The Sooner State see Oklahoma
Thessaloníki 82 C3 Eng. Salonica, Salonika, SCr. Solun, Turk. Selânik. Kentrikí Makedonía, N Greece
The Valley 33 G3 dependent territory capital E Anguilla
The Village 27 G1 Oklahoma, C USA
The Volunteer State see Tennessee
Thiamis see Kalamás
Thian Shan see Tien Shan
Thibet see Xizang Zizhiqu
Thief River Falls 23 F1 Minnesota, N USA
Thienen see Tienen
Thiers 69 C5 Puy-de-Dôme, C France
Thiès 52 B3 W Senegal
Thikombia see Cikobia
Thimbu see Thimphu
Thimphu 113 G3 var. Thimbu; prev. Tashi Chho Dzong. country capital W Bhutan
Thionville 68 D3 Ger. Diedenhofen. Moselle, NE France
Thíra 83 D7 Santorini, Kykládes, Greece, Aegean Sea
Thíra 83 D7 Santorini, Kykládes, Greece, Aegean Sea
Thíra 83 D7 Santorini, Kykládes, Greece, Aegean Sea
Thitu Island 106 C8 island NW Spratly Islands
Tholen 64 B4 island SW Netherlands
Thomasville 20 D3 Georgia, SE USA
Thompson 15 F4 Manitoba, C Canada
Thonon-les-Bains 69 D5 Haute-Savoie, E France
Thorenburg see Turda
Thorlákshöfn 61 E5 Sudhurland, SW Iceland
Thorn see Toruń
Thornton Island see Millennium Island
Thorshavn see Tórshavn
Thospitis see Van Gölü
Thouars 68 B4 Deux-Sèvres, W France
Thoune see Thun
Thracian Sea 82 D4 Gk. Thrakikó Pélagos; anc. Thracium Mare. sea Greece/Turkey
Thracium Mare/Thrakikó Pélagos see Thracian Sea
Three Kings Islands 128 C1 island group N New Zealand
Thuin 65 B7 Hainaut, S Belgium
Thule see Qaanaaq
Thumrayt see Thamarīt
Thun 73 A7 Fr. Thoune. Bern, W Switzerland
Thunder Bay 16 B4 Ontario, S Canada
Thuner See 73 A7 lake C Switzerland
Thung Song 115 C7 var. Cha Mai. Nakhon Si Thammarat, SW Thailand
Thurso 66 C2 N Scotland, United Kingdom
Thýamis see Kalamás
Tianjin 106 D4 var. Tientsin. Tianjin Shi, E China
Tianjin see Tianjin Shi
Tianjin Shi 106 D4 var. Jin, Tianjin, T'ien-ching, Tientsin. municipality E China
Tian Shan see Tien Shan
Tianshui 106 B4 Gansu, C China
Tiba see Chiba
Tiber 74 C4 Eng. Tiber. river C Italy
Tiber see Tevere, Italy
Tiber see Tivoli, Italy
Tiberias see Tverya
Tiberias, Lake 97 B5 var. Chinnereth, Sea of Bahr Tabariya, Sea of Galilee, Ar. Bahrat Tabariya, Heb. Yam Kinneret. lake N Israel
Tibesti 54 C2 var. Tibesti Massif, Ar. Tibistī. mountain range N Africa
Tibesti Massif see Tibesti
Tibet see Xizang Zizhiqu
Tibetan Autonomous Region see Xizang Zizhiqu
Tibet, Plateau of 104 B4 var. Xizang Gaoyuan, Eng. Plateau of Tibet. plateau W China
Tibet, Plateau of see Qingzang Gaoyuan
Tibisti see Tibesti
Tibnī see At Tibnī
Tiburón, Isla 28 B2 var. Isla del Tiburón. island NW Mexico
Tiburón, Isla del see Tiburón, Isla
Tichau see Tychy
Tîchît 52 D2 var. Tichitt. Tagant, C Mauritania
Tichitt see Tîchît
Ticinum see Pavia
Ticul 29 H3 Yucatán, SE Mexico
Tidjikdja see Tidjikja
Tidjikja 52 C2 var. Tidjikdja; prev. Fort-Cappolani. Tagant, C Mauritania
T'ien-ching see Tianjin Shi
Tienen 65 C6 var. Thienen, Fr. Tirlemont. Vlaams Brabant, C Belgium
Tiên Giang, Sông see Mekong
Tien Shan 104 B3 Chin. Thian Shan, Tian Shan, T'ien Shan, Rus. Tyan'-Shan'. mountain range C Asia
Tientsin see Tianjin
Tierp 63 C6 Uppsala, C Sweden
Tierra del Fuego 43 B8 island Argentina/Chile
Tiflis see T'bilisi
Tifton 20 D3 Georgia, SE USA
Tifu 117 F4 Pulau Buru, E Indonesia
Tighina 86 D4 Rus. Bendery; prev. Bender. E Moldova
Tigranocerta see Siirt
Tigris 98 B2 Ar. Dijlah, Turk. Dicle. river Iraq/Turkey
Tiguentourine 49 E3 E Algeria
Ti-hua/Tihwa see Ürümqi
Tijuana 28 A1 Baja California, NW Mexico
Tikhoretsk 89 A7 Krasnodarskiy Kray, SW Russian Federation
Tikhvin 88 B4 Leningradskaya Oblast', NW Russian Federation
Tiki Basin 121 G3 undersea basin S Pacific Ocean
Tiksi 93 F2 Respublika Sakha (Yakutiya), NE Russian Federation
Tilburg 64 C4 Noord-Brabant, S Netherlands
Tilimsen see Tlemcen
Tilio Martius see Toulon
Tillabéri 53 F3 var. Tillabéry. Tillabéri, W Niger
Tillabéry see Tillabéri
Tílos 83 E7 island Dodekánisa, Greece, Aegean Sea
Timan Ridge 88 D3 Eng. Timan Ridge. ridge NW Russian Federation
Timan Ridge see Timanskiy Kryazh
Timaru 129 B6 Canterbury, South Island, New Zealand
Timbaki/Timbákion see Tympáki
Timbedgha 52 D3 var. Timbédra. Hodh ech Chargui, SE Mauritania
Timbédra see Timbedgha
Timbuktu see Tombouctou
Timiş 86 A4 county SW Romania
Timişoara 86 A4 Ger. Temeschwar, Temeswar, Hung. Temesvár; prev. Temeschburg. Timiş, W Romania
Timmins 16 C4 Ontario, S Canada
Timor 103 F5 island Nusa Tenggara, C Indonesia
Timor Sea 103 F5 sea E Indian Ocean
Timor Timur see East Timor
Timor Trench see Timor Trough
Timor Trough 103 F5 var. Timor Trench. trough NE Timor Sea
Timrå 63 C5 Västernorrland, C Sweden
Tindouf 48 C3 W Algeria
Tineo 70 C1 Asturias, N Spain
Tingis see Tanger
Tingo María 38 C3 Huánuco, C Peru
Tingréla see Tengréla
Tinhosa Grande 54 E2 island N Sao Tome and Principe, Africa, E Atlantic Ocean
Tinhosa Pequena 54 E1 island N Sao Tome and Principe, Africa, E Atlantic Ocean
Tinian 122 B1 island S Northern Mariana Islands
Tínos 83 D6 Tínos, Kykládes, Greece, Aegean Sea
Tínos 83 D6 anc. Tenos. island Kykládes, Greece, Aegean Sea
Tip 79 E6 Papua, E Indonesia
Tipitapa 30 D3 Managua, W Nicaragua
Tip Top Mountain 16 C4 mountain Ontario, S Canada
Tirana see Tiranë
Tiranë 79 C6 var. Tirana. country capital Tiranë, C Albania
Tiraspol 86 D4 Rus. Tiraspol'. E Moldova
Tiraspol' see Tiraspol
Tiree 66 B3 island W Scotland, United Kingdom
Tîrgovişte see Târgovişte
Tîrgu Jiu see Târgu Jiu
Tîrgu Mures see Târgu Mureş
Tîrgu-Neamţ see Târgu-Neamţ
Tîrgu Ocna see Târgu Ocna
Tîrgu Secuiesc see Târgu Secuiesc
Tirlemont see Tienen
Tírnavos see Týrnavos
Tirnovo see Veliko Tŭrnovo
Tirol 73 C7 off. Land Tirol, var. Tyrol, It. Tirolo. state W Austria
Tirol, Land see Tirol
Tirolo see Tirol
Tirreno, Mare see Tyrrhenian Sea
Tiruchchirāppalli 110 C3 prev. Trichinopoly. Tamil Nādu, SE India
Tiruppattūr 110 C2 Tamil Nādu, SE India
Tiruvantapuram Thiruvanathapuram/Trivandrum
Tisa 81 F1 Ger. Theiss, Rom./Slvn./SCr. Tisa, Rus. Tissa, Ukr. Tysa. river SE Europe
Tisa see Tisza
Tiszakécske 77 D7 Bács-Kiskun, C Hungary
Titano, Monte 74 E1 mountain C San Marino
Titicaca, Lake 39 E4 lake Bolivia/Peru
Titograd see Podgorica
Titose see Chitose
Titova Mitrovica see Mitrovicë
Titovo Užice see Užice
Titu 86 C5 Dâmboviţa, S Romania
Titule 55 D5 Orientale, N Dem. Rep. Congo
Tiverton 67 C7 SW England, United Kingdom
Tivoli 74 C4 anc. Tiber. Lazio, C Italy
Tizimín 29 H3 Yucatán, SE Mexico
Tizi Ouzou 49 E1 var. Tizi-Ouzou. N Algeria
Tizi-Ouzou see Tizi Ouzou
Tiznit 48 B3 SW Morocco
Tjilatjap see Cilacap
Tjirebon see Cirebon
Tlaquepaque 28 D4 Jalisco, C Mexico
Tlascala see Tlaxcala
Tlaxcala 29 F4 var. Tlascala, Tlaxcala de Xicohténcatl. Tlaxcala, C Mexico
Tlaxcala de Xicohténcatl see Tlaxcala
Tlemcen 48 D2 var. Tilimsen, Tlemsen. NW Algeria
Tlemsen see Tlemcen
Toamasina 57 G3 var. Tamatave. Toamasina, E Madagascar
Toba, Danau 116 B3 lake Sumatera, W Indonesia
Tobago 33 H5 island NE Trinidad and Tobago
Toba Kakar Range 112 B2 mountain range NW Pakistan
Tobol 92 C4 Kaz. Tobyl. river Kazakhstan/Russian Federation
Tobol'sk 92 C3 Tyumenskaya Oblast', C Russian Federation
Tobruch/Tobruk see Ţubruq
Tobyl see Tobol
Tocantins 41 E3 off. Estado do Tocantins. state C Brazil
Tocantins 41 E3 off. Estado do Tocantins. region C Brazil
Tocantins, Estado do see Tocantins
Tocantins, Rio 41 F2 river N Brazil
Tocoa 30 D2 Colón, N Honduras
Tocopilla 42 B2 Antofagasta, N Chile
Todi 74 C4 Umbria, C Italy
Todos os Santos, Baía de 41 G3 bay E Brazil
Toetoes Bay 129 B8 bay South Island, New Zealand
Tofua 123 E4 island Ha'apai Group, C Tonga
Togo 53 E4 off. Togolese Republic; prev. French Togoland. country W Africa
Togolese Republic see Togo
Tojikiston, Jumhurii see Tajikistan
Tokanui 129 B7 Southland, South Island, New Zealand
Tokar 50 C3 var. Ţawkar. Red Sea, NE Sudan
Tokat 94 D3 Tokat, N Turkey
Tokelau 123 E3 NZ overseas territory W Polynesia
Tőketerebes see Trebišov
Tokio see Tōkyō
Tokmak 101 G2 Kir. Tokmok. Chuyskaya Oblast', N Kyrgyzstan
Tokmak 87 G4 var. Velykyy Tokmak. Zaporiz'ka Oblast', SE Ukraine
Tokmok see Tokmak
Tokoroa 128 D3 Waikato, North Island, New Zealand
Tokounou 52 C4 C Guinea
Tokushima 109 C6 var. Tokusima. Tokushima, Shikoku, SW Japan
Tōkyō 108 A1 var. Tokio. country capital Tōkyō, Honshū, S Japan
Tōkyō-wan 108 A2 bay S Japan
Tolbukhin see Dobrich
Toledo 70 D3 anc. Toletum. Castilla-La Mancha, C Spain
Toledo 18 D3 Ohio, N USA
Toledo Bend Reservoir 27 G3 reservoir Louisiana/Texas, SW USA
Toletum see Toledo
Toliara 57 F4 var. Toliary; prev. Tuléar. Toliara, SW Madagascar
Toliary see Toliara
Tolmein see Tolmin
Tolmin 73 D7 Ger. Tolmein, It. Tolmino. W Slovenia
Tolmino see Tolmin
Tolna 77 C7 Ger. Tolnau. Tolna, S Hungary
Tolnau see Tolna
Tolochin see Talachyn
Tolosa 71 E1 País Vasco, N Spain
Tolosa see Toulouse
Toluca 29 E4 var. Toluca de Lerdo. México, S Mexico
Toluca de Lerdo see Toluca
Tol'yatti 89 C6 prev. Stavropol'. Samarskaya Oblast', W Russian Federation
Tomah 18 B2 Wisconsin, N USA
Tomakomai 108 D2 Hokkaidō, NE Japan
Tomar 70 B3 Santarém, W Portugal
Tomaschow see Tomaszów Mazowiecki
Tomaschow see Tomaszów Lubelski
Tomaszów see Tomaszów Mazowiecki
Tomaszów Lubelski 76 E4 Ger. Tomaschow. Lubelskie, E Poland
Tomaszów Mazowiecka see Tomaszów Mazowiecki
Tomaszów Mazowiecki 76 D4 var. Tomaszów Mazowiecka; prev. Tomaszów, Ger. Tomaschow. Łódzkie, C Poland
Tombigbee River 20 C3 river Alabama/Mississippi, S USA
Tombouctou 53 E3 Eng. Timbuktu. Tombouctou, N Mali
Tombua 56 A2 Port. Porto Alexandre. Namibe, SW Angola
Tomelloso 71 E3 Castilla-La Mancha, C Spain
Tomini, Gulf of 117 E4 var. Teluk Tomini; prev. Teluk Gorontalo. bay Sulawesi, C Indonesia
Tomini, Teluk see Tomini, Gulf of
Tomsk 92 D4 Tomskaya Oblast', C Russian Federation
Tomür Feng see Pobedy, Pik
Tonezh see Tonyezh
Tonga 123 E4 off. Kingdom of Tonga, var. Friendly Islands. country SW Pacific Ocean
Tonga, Kingdom of see Tonga
Tongatapu 123 E5 island Tongatapu Group, S Tonga
Tongatapu Group 123 E5 island group S Tonga
Tonga Trench 121 E3 trench S Pacific Ocean
Tongchuan 106 C4 Shaanxi, C China
Tongeren 65 D6 Fr. Tongres. Limburg, NE Belgium
Tongking, Gulf of 106 B7 Chin. Beibu Wan, Vtn. Vinh Bắc Bô. gulf China/Vietnam
Tongliao 105 G2 Nei Mongol Zizhiqu, N China
Tongres see Tongeren
Tongshan see Xuzhou, Jiangsu, China
Tongtian He 104 C4 river C China
Tonj 51 B5 Warab, SW Sudan
Tônlé Sap 115 D5 Eng. Great Lake. lake W Cambodia
Tonopah 25 C6 Nevada, W USA
Tonyezh 85 C7 Rus. Tonezh. Homyel'skaya Voblasts', SE Belarus
Tooele 22 B4 Utah, W USA
Toowoomba 127 E5 Queensland, E Australia
Topeka 23 F4 state capital Kansas, C USA
Toplicza see Topliţa
Topliţa 86 C3 Ger. Töplitz, Hung. Marosheviz; prev. Topliţa Română, Hung. Oláh-Toplicza, Toplicza. Harghita, C Romania
Topliţa Română/Töplitz see Topliţa
Topoľčany 77 C6 Hung. Nagytapolcsány. Nitriansky Kraj, W Slovakia
Topolovgrad 82 D3 prev. Kavakli. Khaskovo, S Bulgaria
Topolya see Bačka Topola
Top Springs Roadhouse 124 E3 Northern Territory, N Australia
Torda see Turda
Torez 87 H3 Donets'ka Oblast', SE Ukraine
Torgau 72 D4 Sachsen, E Germany
Torhout 65 A5 West-Vlaanderen, W Belgium
Torino 74 A2 Eng. Turin. Piemonte, NW Italy
Tornacum see Tournai
Torneå see Tornio
Torneträsk 62 C3 lake N Sweden
Tornio 62 D4 Swe. Torneå. Lappi, NW Finland
Tornionjoki 62 D3 river Finland/Sweden
Torniojoki 62 D3 river Finland/Sweden
Toro 70 D2 Castilla-León, N Spain
Toronto 16 D5 province capital Ontario, S Canada
Torquay 67 C7 SW England, United Kingdom
Torrance 24 D2 California, W USA
Torre, Alto da 70 B3 mountain C Portugal
Torre del Greco 75 D5 Campania, S Italy
Torrejón de Ardoz 71 E3 Madrid, C Spain
Torrelavega 70 D1 Cantabria, N Spain
Torrens, Lake 127 A6 salt lake South Australia
Torrent 71 F3 Cas. Torrente, var. Torrent de l'Horta. País Valenciano, E Spain
Torrent de l'Horta/Torrente see Torrent
Torreón 28 D3 Coahuila de Zaragoza, NE Mexico
Torres Strait 126 C1 strait Australia/Papua New Guinea
Torres Vedras 70 B3 Lisboa, C Portugal
Torrington 22 D3 Wyoming, C USA
Tórshavn 61 F5 Dan. Thorshavn. Dependent territory capital Faeroe Islands
To'rtkok'l 100 D2 var. Türtkül, Rus. Turtkul'; prev. Petroaleksandrovsk. Qoraqalpog'iston Respublikasi, W Uzbekistan
Tortoise Islands see Colón, Archipiélago de
Tortosa 71 F2 anc. Dertosa. Cataluña, E Spain
Tortue, Montagne 37 H3 mountain range C French Guiana
Tortuga, Isla see La Tortuga, Isla
Toruń 76 C3 Ger. Thorn. Toruń, Kujawsko-pomorskie, C Poland
Tõrva 84 D3 Ger. Törwa. Valgamaa, S Estonia
Törwa see Tõrva
Torzhok 88 B4 Tverskaya Oblast', W Russian Federation
Tosa-wan 109 B7 bay SW Japan
Toscana 74 B3 Eng. Tuscany. region C Italy
Toscano, Arcipelago 74 B4 Eng. Tuscan Archipelago. island group C Italy
Toshkent 101 E2 Eng./Rus. Tashkent. country capital Toshkent Viloyati, E Uzbekistan
Totana 71 E4 Murcia, SE Spain
Tot'ma see Sukhona
Totness 37 G3 Coronie, N Suriname
Tottori 109 B6 Tottori, Honshū, SW Japan
Touâjîl 52 C2 Tiris Zemmour, N Mauritania
Touggourt 49 E2 NE Algeria
Toukoto 52 C3 Kayes, W Mali
Toul 68 D3 Meurthe-et-Moselle, NE France
Toulon 69 D6 anc. Telo Martius, Tilio Martius. Var, SE France
Toulouse 69 B6 anc. Tolosa. Haute-Garonne, S France
Toungoo see Taungoo
Touraine 68 B4 cultural region C France
Tourane see Đà Nẵng
Tourcoing 68 C2 Nord, N France
Tournai 65 A6 var. Tournay, Dut. Doornik; anc. Tornacum. Hainaut, SW Belgium
Tournay see Tournai
Tours 68 B4 anc. Caesarodunum, Turoni. Indre-et-Loire, C France
Tovarkovskiy 89 B5 Tul'skaya Oblast', W Russian Federation
Tower Island see Genovesa, Isla
Townsville 126 D3 Queensland, NE Australia
Towoeti Meer see Towuti, Danau
Towraghoudi 100 D4 Herāt, NW Afghanistan
Towson 19 F4 Maryland, NE USA
Towuti, Danau 117 E4 Dut. Towoeti Meer. lake Sulawesi, C Indonesia
Toyama 109 C5 Toyama, Honshū, SW Japan
Toyama-wan 109 B5 bay W Japan
Toyohara see Yuzhno-Sakhalinsk
Toyota 109 C6 Aichi, Honshū, SW Japan
Tozeur 49 E2 var. Tawzar. W Tunisia
Trâblous see Tripoli
Trabzon 95 E2 Eng. Trebizond; anc. Trapezus. Trabzon, NE Turkey
Traiectum ad Mosam/Traiectum Tungorum see Maastricht
Traiskirchen 73 E6 Niederösterreich, NE Austria
Trajani Portus see Civitavecchia
Trajectum ad Rhenum see Utrecht
Trakai 85 C5 Ger. Traken, Pol. Troki. Vilnius, SE Lithuania
Traken see Trakai
Tralee 67 A6 Ir. Trá Lí. SW Ireland
Trá Lí see Tralee
Tralles Aydin see Aydın
Trang 115 C7 Trang, S Thailand
Transantarctic Mountains 132 B3 mountain range Antarctica
Transilvania see Transylvania
Transilvaniei, Alpi see Carpaţii Meridionali
Transjordan see Jordan
Transsylvanische Alpen/Transylvanian Alps see Carpaţii Meridionali
Transylvania 86 B4 Eng. Ardeal, Transilvania, Ger. Siebenbürgen, Hung. Erdély. cultural region NW Romania
Transylvanian Alps 86 B4 var. Alpi Transilvaniei, Carpaţii Sudici, Eng. South Carpathians, Transylvanian Alps, Ger. Südkarpaten, Transsylvanische Alpen, Hung. Déli-Kárpátok, Erdélyi-Havasok. mountain range C Romania
Trapani 75 B7 anc. Drepanum. Sicilia, Italy, C Mediterranean Sea
Trâpeăng Vêng 115 D5 Kâmpóng Thum, C Cambodia
Trapezus see Trabzon
Traralgon 127 C7 Victoria, SE Australia
Trasimenischersee see Trasimeno, Lago
Trasimeno, Lago 74 C4 Eng. Lake of Perugia, Ger. Trasimenischersee. lake C Italy
Traù see Trogir
Traverse City 18 C2 Michigan, N USA
Tra Vinh 115 D6 var. Phu Vinh. Tra Vinh, S Vietnam
Travis, Lake 27 F3 reservoir Texas, SW USA
Travnik 78 C4 Federacija Bosna I Hercegovina, C Bosnia and Herzegovina
Trbovlje 73 E7 Ger. Trifail. C Slovenia
Treasure State see Montana
Třebíč 77 B5 Ger. Trebitsch. Vysočina, C Czech Republic
Trebinje 79 C5 Republika Srpska, S Bosnia and Herzegovina
Trebišov 77 D6 Hung. Tőketerebes. Košický Kraj, E Slovakia
Trebitsch see Třebíč
Trebnitz see Trzebnica
Tree Planters State see Nebraska
Trélazé 68 B4 Maine-et-Loire, NW France
Trelew 43 C6 Chubut, SE Argentina
Tremelo 65 C5 Vlaams Brabant, C Belgium
Trenčín 77 C5 Ger. Trentschin, Hung. Trencsén. Trenčiansky Kraj, W Slovakia
Trencsén see Trenčín
Trengganu, Kuala see Kuala Terengganu
Trenque Lauquen 42 C4 Buenos Aires, E Argentina
Trent see Trento
Trento 74 C2 Eng. Trent, Ger. Trient; anc. Tridentum. Trentino-Alto Adige, N Italy
Trenton 19 F4 state capital New Jersey, NE USA
Trentschin see Trenčín
Tres Arroyos 43 D5 Buenos Aires, E Argentina
Treskavica 78 C4 mountain range SE Bosnia and Herzegovina
Tres Tabernae see Saverne
Treves/Trèves see Trier
Treviso 74 C2 anc. Tarvisium. Veneto, NE Italy
Trichinopoly see Tiruchchirāppalli
Trichūr 110 C3 var. Thrissur. Kerala, SW India
Tridentum/Trient see Trento
Trier 73 A5 Eng. Treves, Fr. Trèves; anc. Augusta Treverorum. Rheinland-Pfalz, SW Germany
Triesen 72 E2 SW Liechtenstein Europe
Triesenberg 72 E2 SW Liechtenstein
Trieste 74 D2 Slvn. Trst. Friuli-Venezia Giulia, NE Italy
Trifail see Trbovlje
Tríkala 82 B4 prev. Trikkala. Thessalía, C Greece
Trikkala see Tríkala
Trimontium see Plovdiv
Trinacria see Sicilia
Trincomalee 110 D3 var. Trinkomali. Eastern Province, NE Sri Lanka
Trindade, Ilha da 45 C5 island Brazil, W Atlantic Ocean
Trinidad 39 F3 Beni, N Bolivia
Trinidad 42 D4 Flores, S Uruguay
Trinidad 22 D5 Colorado, C USA
Trinidad 33 H5 island C Trinidad and Tobago
Trinidad and Tobago 33 H5 off. Republic of Trinidad and Tobago. country SE West Indies
Trinidad and Tobago, Republic of see Trinidad and Tobago
Trinité, Montagnes de la 37 H3 mountain range C French Guiana
Trinity River 27 G3 river Texas, SW USA
Trinkomali see Trincomalee
Trípoli 83 B6 prev. Trípolis. Pelopónnisos, S Greece
Tripoli 96 B4 var. Tarābulus, Ţarābulus ash Shām, Trâblous; anc. Tripolis. N Lebanon
Tripoli see Ţarābulus
Trípolis see Trípoli, Greece
Tripolis see Tripoli, Lebanon
Tristan da Cunha 47 B7 dependency of Saint Helena SE Atlantic Ocean
Triton Island 106 B7 island S Paracel Islands
Trivandrum 110 C3 var. Thiruvanathapuram, Tiruvantapuram. state capital Kerala, SW India
Trnava 77 C6 Ger. Tyrnau, Hung. Nagyszombat. Trnavský Kraj, W Slovakia
Trnovo see Veliko Tŭrnovo
Trogir 78 B4 It. Traù. Split-Dalmacija, S Croatia
Troglav 78 B4 mountain Bosnia and Herzegovina/Croatia
Trois-Rivières 17 E4 Québec, SE Canada
Troki see Trakai
Trollhättan 63 B6 Västra Götaland, S Sweden
Tromsø 62 C2 Fin. Tromssa. Troms, N Norway
Tromssa see Tromsø
Trondheim 62 B4 Ger. Drontheim; prev. Nidaros, Trondhjem. Sør-Trøndelag, S Norway
Trondheimsfjorden 62 B4 fjord S Norway
Trondhjem see Trondheim
Troódos 80 C5 var. Troodos Mountains. mountain range C Cyprus
Troodos Mountains see Troódos
Troppau see Opava
Troy 20 D3 Alabama, S USA
Troy 19 F3 New York, NE USA
Troyan 82 C2 Lovech, N Bulgaria
Troyes 68 D3 anc. Augustobona Tricassium. Aube, N France
Trst see Trieste
Trstenik 78 E4 Serbia, C Serbia
Trucial States see United Arab Emirates
Trujillo 30 D2 Colón, NE Honduras
Trujillo 38 B3 La Libertad, NW Peru
Trujillo 70 C3 Extremadura, W Spain
Truk Islands see Chuuk Islands
Trŭn 82 B2 Pernik, W Bulgaria
Truro 17 F4 Nova Scotia, SE Canada
Truro 67 C7 SW England, United Kingdom
Trzcianka 76 B3 Ger. Schönlanke. Pila, Wielkopolskie, C Poland
Trzebnica 76 C4 Ger. Trebnitz. Dolnośląskie, SW Poland
Tsalka 95 F2 S Georgia Asia
Tsamkong see Zhanjiang
Tsangpo see Brahmaputra
Tsarevo 82 E2 prev. Michurin. Burgas, E Bulgaria
Tsarigrad see İstanbul
Tsaritsyn see Volgograd
Tschakathurn see Čakovec
Tschaslau see Čáslav
Tschenstochau see Częstochowa
Tsefat 97 B5 var. Safed, Ar. Safad; prev. Zefat. Northern, N Israel
Tselinograd see Astana
Tsetsen Khan see Öndörhaan
Tsetserleg 104 D2 Arhangay, C Mongolia
Tshela 55 B6 Bas-Congo, W Dem. Rep. Congo
Tshikapa 55 C7 Kasai-Occidental, SW Dem. Rep. Congo
Tshuapa 55 D6 river C Dem. Rep. Congo
Tshwane 56 D4 var. Epitoli; prev. Pretoria. country capital Gauteng, NE South Africa
Tsinan see Jinan
Tsing Hai see Qinghai Hu, China
Tsinghai see Qinghai, China
Tsingtao/Tsingtau see Qingdao
Tsinkiang see Quanzhou
Tsintao see Qingdao
Tsitsihar see Qiqihar
Tsu 109 C6 var. Tu. Mie, Honshū, SW Japan
Tsugaru-kaikyo 108 C3 strait N Japan
Tsumeb 56 B3 Otjikoto, N Namibia
Tsuruga 109 C6 var. Turuga. Fukui, Honshū, SW Japan
Tsuruoka 108 D4 var. Turuoka. Yamagata, Honshū, C Japan
Tsushima 109 A7 var. Tsushima-tō, Tusima. island group SW Japan
Tsushima-tō see Tsushima
Tsyerakhowka 85 D8 Rus. Terekhovka. Homyel'skaya Voblasts', SE Belarus
Tsyurupinsk see Tsyurupyns'k
Tsyurupyns'k 87 E4 Rus. Tsyurupinsk. Khersons'ka Oblast', S Ukraine
Tu see Tsu
Tuamotu, Archipel des see Tuamotu, Îles
Tuamotu Fracture Zone 121 H3 fracture zone E Pacific Ocean
Tuamotu Islands 123 H4 var. Archipel des Tuamotu, Dangerous Archipelago, Tuamotu Islands. island group N French Polynesia
Tuamotu Islands see Tuamotu, Îles
Tuapi 31 E2 Región Autónoma Atlántico Norte, NE Nicaragua
Tuapse 89 A7 Krasnodarskiy Kray, SW Russian Federation
Tuba City 26 B1 Arizona, SW USA
Tubbergen 64 E3 Overijssel, E Netherlands
Tubeke see Tubize
Tubize 65 B6 Dut. Tubeke. Walloon Brabant, C Belgium
Tubmanburg 52 C5 NW Liberia
Ţubruq 49 H2 Eng. Tobruk, It. Tobruch. NE Libya

Tubuai, Îles/Tubuai Islands – Vatican City

Tubuai, Îles/Tubuai Islands see Australes, Îles
Tucker's Town 20 B5 E Bermuda
Tuckum see Tukums
Tucson 26 B3 Arizona, SW USA
Tucumán see San Miguel de Tucumán
Tucumcari 27 E2 New Mexico, SW USA
Tucupita 37 E2 Delta Amacuro, NE Venezuela
Tucuruí, Represa de 41 F2 reservoir NE Brazil
Tudela 71 E2 Basq. Tutera; anc. Tutela. Navarra, N Spain
Tudmur 96 C3 var. Tadmur, Tamar, Gk. Palmyra, Bibl. Tadmor. Ḥimṣ, C Syria
Tuguegarao 117 E1 Luzon, N Philippines
Tuktoyaktuk 15 E3 Northwest Territories, NW Canada
Tukums 84 C3 Ger. Tuckum. Tukums, W Latvia
Tula 89 B5 Tul'skaya Oblast', W Russian Federation
Tulancingo 29 E4 Hidalgo, C Mexico
Tulare Lake Bed 25 C7 salt flat California, W USA
Tulcán 38 B1 Carchi, N Ecuador
Tulcea 86 D5 Tulcea, E Romania
Tul'chin see Tul'chyn
Tul'chyn 86 D3 Rus. Tul'chin. Vinnyts'ka Oblast', C Ukraine
Tuléar see Toliara
Tulia 27 E2 Texas, SW USA
Tūlkarm 97 D7 West Bank, Israel
Tulle 69 C5 anc. Tutela. Corrèze, C France
Tulln 73 E6 var. Oberhollabrunn. Niederösterreich, NE Austria
Tully 126 D3 Queensland, NE Australia
Tulsa 27 G1 Oklahoma, C USA
Tuluá 36 B3 Valle del Cauca, W Colombia
Tulun 93 E4 Irkutskaya Oblast', S Russian Federation
Tumaco 36 A4 Nariño, SW Colombia
Tumba, Lac see Ntomba, Lac
Tumbes 38 A2 Tumbes, NW Peru
Tumkūr 110 C2 Karnātaka, W India
Tumuc-Humac Mountains 41 E1 var. Serra Tumucumaque. mountain range N South America
Tumucumaque, Serra see Tumuc-Humac Mountains
Tunca Nehri see Tundzha
Tunduru 51 C8 Ruvuma, S Tanzania
Tundzha 82 D3 Turk. Tunca Nehri. river Bulgaria/Turkey
Tungabhadra Reservoir 110 C2 lake S India
Tungaru 123 E2 prev. Gilbert Islands. island group W Kiribati
T'ung-shan see Xuzhou
Tungsten 14 D4 Northwest Territories, W Canada
Tung-t'ing Hu see Dongting Hu
Tunis 49 E1 var. Tūnis. country capital NE Tunisia
Tunis, Golfe de 80 D3 Ar. Khalīj Tūnis. gulf NE Tunisia
Tunisia 49 F2 off. Tunisian Republic, Ar. Al Jumhūrīyah at Tūnisīyah, Fr. République Tunisienne. country N Africa
Tunisian Republic see Tunisia
Tunisienne, République see Tunisia
Tūnisīyah, Al Jumhūrīyah at see Tunisia
Tūnis, Khalīj see Tunis, Golfe de
Tunja 36 B3 Boyacá, C Colombia
Tuong Buong see Tương Đương
Tương Đương 114 D4 var. Tuong Buong. Nghê An, N Vietnam
Tüp see Tyup
Tupelo 20 C2 Mississippi, S USA
Tupiza 39 G5 Potosí, S Bolivia
Turabah 99 B5 Makkah, W Saudi Arabia
Turangi 128 D4 Waikato, North Island, New Zealand
Turan Lowland 100 C2 var. Turan Plain, Kaz. Turan Oypaty, Rus. Turanskaya Nizmennost', Turk. Turan Pesligi, Uzb. Turan Pasttekisligi. plain C Asia
Turan Oypaty/Turan Pesligi/Turan Plain/Turanskaya Nizmennost' see Turan Lowland
Turan Pasttekisligi see Turan Lowland
Ţurayf 98 A3 Al Ḥudūd ash Shamālīyah, NW Saudi Arabia
Turba see Teruel
Turbat 112 A3 Baluchistān, SW Pakistan
Turčianský Svätý Martin see Martin
Turda 86 B4 Ger. Thorenburg, Hung. Torda. Cluj, NW Romania
Turek 76 C3 Wielkopolskie, C Poland
Turfan see Turpan
Turin see Torino
Turkana, Lake 51 C6 var. Lake Rudolf. lake N Kenya
Turkestan 92 B5 Kaz. Türkistan. Yuzhnyy Kazakhstan, S Kazakhstan
Turkey 94 B3 off. Republic of Turkey, Turk. Türkiye Cumhuriyeti. country SW Asia
Turkey, Republic of see Turkey
Turkish Republic of Northern Cyprus 80 D5 disputed territory Cyprus
Türkistan see Turkestan
Türkiye Cumhuriyeti see Turkey
Türkmenabat 100 D3 prev. Rus. Chardzhev, Chardzhou, Chardzhui, Lenin-Turkmenski, Turkm. Chärjew. Lebap Welaýaty, E Turkmenistan
Türkmen Aylagy 100 B2 Rus. Turkmenskiy Zaliv. lake gulf W Turkmenistan
Turkmenbashi see Türkmenbaşy
Türkmenbaşy 100 B2 Rus. Turkmenbashi; prev. Krasnovodsk. Balkan Welaýaty, W Turkmenistan
Türkmenbasy Aylagy 100 A2 prev. Rus. Krasnovodskiy Zaliv, Turkm. Krasnowodsk Aylagy. lake Gulf W Turkmenistan
Turkmenistan 100 B2 ; prev. Turkmenskaya Soviet Socialist Republic. country C Asia
Turkmenskaya Soviet Socialist Republic see Turkmenistan
Turkmenskiy Zaliv see Türkmen Aylagy
Turks and Caicos Islands 33 E2 UK dependent territory N West Indies
Turku 63 D6 Swe. Åbo. Länsi-Suomi, SW Finland
Turlock 25 B6 California, W USA
Turnagain, Cape 128 D4 headland North Island, New Zealand
Turnau see Turnov
Turnhout 65 C5 Antwerpen, N Belgium
Turnov 76 B4 Ger. Turnau. Liberecký Kraj, N Czech Republic
Tŭrnovo see Veliko Tŭrnovo
Turnu Măgurele 86 B5 var. Turnu-Măgurele. Teleorman, S Romania
Turnu Severin see Drobeta-Turnu Severin
Turócszentmárton see Martin
Turoni see Tours
Turpan 104 C3 var. Turfan. Xinjiang Uygur Zizhiqu, NW China
Turpan Depression see Turpan Pendi
Turpan Pendi 104 C3 Eng. Turpan Depression. depression NW China
Turpentine State see North Carolina
Türtkül/Turtkul' see To'rtko'l
Turuga see Tsuruga
Turuoka see Tsuruoka
Tuscaloosa 20 C2 Alabama, S USA
Tuscan Archipelago see Toscano, Arcipelago
Tuscany see Toscana
Tusima see Tsushima
Tutela see Tulle, France
Tutela see Tudela, Spain
Tutera see Tudela
Tuticorin 110 C3 Tamil Nādu, SE India
Tutrakan 82 D1 Silistra, NE Bulgaria
Tutuila 123 F4 island W American Samoa
Tuvalu 123 E3 prev. Ellice Islands. country SW Pacific Ocean
Tuwayq, Jabal 99 C5 mountain range C Saudi Arabia
Tuxpan 28 D4 Jalisco, C Mexico
Tuxpan 28 D4 Nayarit, C Mexico
Tuxpán 29 F4 var. Tuxpán de Rodríguez Cano. Veracruz-Llave, E Mexico
Tuxpán de Rodríguez Cano see Tuxpán
Tuxtepec 29 F4 var. San Juan Bautista Tuxtepec. Oaxaca, S Mexico
Tuxtla 29 G5 var. Tuxtla Gutiérrez. Chiapas, SE Mexico
Tuxtla see San Andrés Tuxtla
Tuxtla Gutiérrez see Tuxtla
Tuy Hoa 115 E5 Phu Yên, S Vietnam
Tuz, Lake 94 C3 lake C Turkey
Tver' 88 B4 prev. Kalinin. Tverskaya Oblast', W Russian Federation
Tverya 97 B5 var. Tiberias; prev. Teverya. Northern, N Israel
Twin Falls 24 D4 Idaho, NW USA
Tyan'-Shan' see Tien Shan
Tychy 77 D5 Ger. Tichau. Śląskie, S Poland
Tyler 27 G3 Texas, SW USA
Tylos see Bahrain
Tympáki 83 C8 var. Timbaki; prev. Timbákion. Kríti, Greece, E Mediterranean Sea
Tynda 93 F4 Amurskaya Oblast', SE Russian Federation
Tyne 66 D4 river N England, United Kingdom
Tyôsi see Chōshi
Tyras see Dniester
Tyre see Soûr
Tyrnau see Trnava
Týrnavos 82 B4 var. Tírnavos. Thessalía, C Greece
Tyrol see Tirol
Tyros see Bahrain
Tyrrhenian Sea 75 B6 It. Mare Tirreno. sea N Mediterranean Sea
Tyumen' 92 C3 Tyumenskaya Oblast', C Russian Federation
Tyup 101 G2 Kir. Tüp. Issyk-Kul'skaya Oblast', NE Kyrgyzstan
Tywyn 67 C6 W Wales, United Kingdom
Tzekung see Zigong
Tziá 83 C6 prev. Kéa, Kéos; anc. Ceos. island Kykládes, Greece, Aegean Sea

U

UAE see United Arab Emirates
Uanle Uen see Wanlaweyn
Uaupés, Rio see Vaupés, Río
Ubangi-Shari see Central African Republic
Ube 109 B7 Yamaguchi, Honshū, SW Japan
Úbeda 71 E4 Andalucía, S Spain
Uberaba 41 F4 Minas Gerais, SE Brazil
Uberlândia 41 F4 Minas Gerais, SE Brazil
Ubol Rajadhani/Ubol Ratchathani see Ubon Ratchathani
Ubon Ratchathani 115 D5 var. Muang Ubon, Ubol Rajadhani, Ubol Ratchathani, Udon Ratchathani. Ubon Ratchathani, E Thailand
Ubrique 70 D5 Andalucía, S Spain
Ubsu-Nur, Ozero see Uvs Nuur
Ucayali, Río 38 D3 river C Peru
Uchiura-wan 108 D3 bay NW Pacific Ocean
Uchkuduk see Uchquduq
Uchquduq 100 D2 Rus. Uchkuduk. Navoiy Viloyati, N Uzbekistan
Uchtagan Gumy/Uchtagan, Peski see Uçtagan Gumy
Uçtagan Gumy 100 C2 var. Uchtagan Gumy, Rus. Peski Uchtagan. desert NW Turkmenistan
Udaipur 112 C3 prev. Oodeypore. Rājasthān, N India
Uddevalla 63 B6 Västra Götaland, S Sweden
Udine 74 D2 anc. Utina. Friuli-Venezia Giulia, NE Italy
Udintsev Fracture Zone 132 A5 tectonic feature S Pacific Ocean
Udipi see Udupi
Udon Ratchathani see Ubon Ratchathani
Udon Thani 114 C4 var. Ban Mak Khaeng, Udorndhani. Udon Thani, N Thailand
Udorndhani see Udon Thani
Udupi 110 B2 var. Udipi. Karnātaka, SW India
Uele 55 D5 var. Welle. river NE Dem. Rep. Congo
Uelzen 72 C3 Niedersachsen, N Germany
Ufa 89 D6 Respublika Bashkortostan, W Russian Federation
Ugāle 84 C2 Ventspils, NW Latvia
Uganda 51 B6 off. Republic of Uganda. country E Africa
Uganda, Republic of see Uganda
Uhorshchyna see Hungary
Uhuru Peak see Kilimanjaro
Uíge 56 B1 Port. Carmona, Vila Marechal Carmona. Uíge, NW Angola
Uinta Mountains 22 B4 mountain range Utah, W USA
Uitenhage 56 C5 Eastern Cape, S South Africa
Uithoorn 64 C3 Noord-Holland, C Netherlands
Ujda see Oujda
Ujelang Atoll 122 C1 var. Wujlān. atoll Ralik Chain, W Marshall Islands
Újgradiska see Nova Gradiška
Újmoldova see Moldova Nouă
Ujungpandang see Makassar
Ujung Salang see Phuket
Újvidék see Novi Sad
UK see United Kingdom
Ukhta 92 C3 Respublika Komi, NW Russian Federation
Ukiah 25 B5 California, W USA
Ukmergė 84 C4 Pol. Wiłkomierz. Vilnius, C Lithuania
Ukraina see Ukraine
Ukraine 86 C2 off. Ukraine, Rus. Ukraina, Ukr. Ukrayina; prev. Ukrainian Soviet Socialist Republic, Ukrainskay S.S.R. country SE Europe
Ukraine see Ukraine
Ukrainian Soviet Socialist Republic see Ukraine
Ukrainskay S.S.R/Ukrayina see Ukraine
Ulaanbaatar 105 E2 Eng. Ulan Bator; prev. Urga. country capital Töv, C Mongolia
Ulaangom 104 C2 Uvs, NW Mongolia
Ulan Bator see Ulaanbaatar
Ulanhad see Chifeng
Ulan-Ude 93 E4 prev. Verkhneudinsk. Respublika Buryatiya, S Russian Federation
Uleälv see Oulujoki
Uleträsk see Oulujärvi
Ulft 64 E4 Gelderland, E Netherlands
Ullapool 66 C3 N Scotland, United Kingdom
Ulm 73 B6 Baden-Württemberg, S Germany
Ulsan 107 E4 Jap. Urusan. SE South Korea
Ulster 67 B5 province Northern Ireland, United Kingdom/Ireland
Ulungur Hu 104 B2 lake NW China
Uluru 125 D5 var. Ayers Rock. monolith Northern Territory, C Australia
Ulyanivka 87 E3 Rus. Ul'yanovka. Kirovohrads'ka Oblast', C Ukraine
Ul'yanovka see Ulyanivka
Ul'yanovsk 89 C5 prev. Simbirsk. Ul'yanovskaya Oblast', W Russian Federation
Umán 29 H3 Yucatán, SE Mexico
Uman' 87 E3 Rus. Uman. Cherkas'ka Oblast', C Ukraine
Uman see Uman'
Umanak/Umanaq see Uummannaq
'Umān, Khalīj see Oman, Gulf of
'Umān, Salṭanat see Oman
Umbrian-Machigian Mountains see Umbro-Marchigiano, Appennino
Umbro-Marchigiano, Appennino 74 C3 Eng. Umbrian-Machigian Mountains. mountain range C Italy
Umeå 62 C4 Västerbotten, N Sweden
Umeälven 62 C4 river N Sweden
Umiat 14 D2 Alaska, USA
Umm Buru 50 A4 Western Darfur, W Sudan
Umm Durmān see Omdurman
Umm Ruwaba 50 C4 var. Umm Ruwābah, Um Ruwāba. Northern Kordofan, C Sudan
Umm Ruwābah see Umm Ruwaba
Umnak Island 14 A3 island Aleutian Islands, Alaska, USA
Um Ruwāba see Umm Ruwaba
Umtali see Mutare
Umtata 56 D5 Eastern Cape, SE South Africa
Una 78 B3 river Bosnia and Herzegovina/Croatia
Unac 78 B3 river W Bosnia and Herzegovina
Unalaska Island 14 A3 island Aleutian Islands, Alaska, USA
'Unayzah 98 B4 var. Anaiza. Al Qaşīm, C Saudi Arabia
Unci see Almería
Uncía 39 F4 Potosí, C Bolivia
Uncompahgre Peak 22 B5 mountain Colorado, C USA
Undur Khan see Öndörhaan
Ungaria see Hungary
Ungarisches Erzgebirge see Slovenské rudohorie
Ungarn see Hungary
Ungava Bay 17 E1 bay Québec, E Canada
Ungava Peninsula 16 D1 peninsula Québec, SE Canada
Ungeny see Ungheni
Ungheni 86 D3 Rus. Ungeny. W Moldova
Unguja see Zanzibar
Üngüz Angyrsyndaky Garagum 100 C2 Rus. Zaunguzskiye Garagumy. desert N Turkmenistan
Ungvár see Uzhhorod
Unimak Island 14 B3 island Aleutian Islands, Alaska, USA
Union 21 E1 South Carolina, SE USA
Union City 20 C1 Tennessee, S USA
Union of Myanmar see Burma
United Arab Emirates 99 C5 Ar. Al Imārāt al 'Arabīyah al Muttaḥidah, abbrev. UAE; prev. Trucial States. country SW Asia
United Arab Republic see Egypt
United Kingdom 67 B5 off. United Kingdom of Great Britain and Northern Ireland, abbrev. UK. country NW Europe
United Kingdom of Great Britain and Northern Ireland see United Kingdom
United Mexican States see Mexico
United Provinces see Uttar Pradesh
United States of America 13 B5 off. United States of America, var. America, The States, abbrev. U.S., USA. country North America
United States of America see United States of America
Unst 66 D1 island NE Scotland, United Kingdom
Ünye 94 D2 Ordu, W Turkey
Upala 30 D4 Alajuela, NW Costa Rica
Upata 37 E2 Bolívar, E Venezuela
Upemba, Lac 55 D7 lake SE Dem. Rep. Congo
Upernavik 60 C2 var. Upernivik. Kitaa, C Greenland
Upernivik see Upernavik
Upington 56 C4 Northern Cape, W South Africa
'Upolu 123 F4 island SE Samoa
Upper Klamath Lake 24 A4 lake Oregon, NW USA
Upper Lough Erne 67 A5 lake SW Northern Ireland, United Kingdom
Upper Red Lake 23 F1 lake Minnesota, N USA
Upper Volta see Burkina
Uppsala 63 C6 Uppsala, C Sweden
Uqsuqtuuq see Gjoa Haven
Ural 90 B3 Kaz. Zayyq. river Kazakhstan/Russian Federation
Ural Mountains 92 C3 var. Ural'skiy Khrebet, Eng. Ural Mountains. mountain range Kazakhstan/Russian Federation
Ural Mountains see Ural'skiye Gory
Ural'sk 92 B3 Kaz. Oral. Zapadnyy Kazakhstan, NW Kazakhstan
Ural'skiy Khrebet see Ural'skiye Gory
Uraricoera 40 D1 Roraima, N Brazil
Ura-Tyube see Üroteppa
Urbandale 23 F3 Iowa, C USA
Urdunn see Jordan
Uren' 89 C5 Nizhegorodskaya Oblast', W Russian Federation
Urga see Ulaanbaatar
Urganch 100 D2 Rus. Urgench; prev. Novo-Urgench. Xorazm Viloyati, W Uzbekistan
Urgench see Urganch
Urgut 101 E3 Samarqand Viloyati, C Uzbekistan
Lake Urmia 99 C2 var. Matianus, Sha Hi, Urumi Yeh, Eng. Lake Urmia; prev. Daryācheh-ye Reẓā'īyeh. lake NW Iran
Urmia, Lake see Orūmīyeh, Daryācheh-ye
Uroševac see Ferizaj
Üroteppa 101 E2 Rus. Ura-Tyube. NW Tajikistan
Uruapan 29 E4 var. Uruapan del Progreso. Michoacán de Ocampo, SW Mexico
Uruapan del Progreso see Uruapan
Uruguai, Rio see Uruguay
Uruguay 42 D4 off. Oriental Republic of Uruguay; prev. La Banda Oriental. country E South America
Uruguay 42 D3 var. Rio Uruguai, Río Uruguay. river E South America
Uruguay, Oriental Republic of see Uruguay
Uruguay, Río see Uruguay
Urumchi see Ürümqi
Urumi Yeh see Orūmīyeh, Daryācheh-ye
Ürümqi 104 C3 var. Tihwa, Urumchi, Urumqi, Urumtsi, Wu-lu-k'o-mu-shi, Wu-lu-mu-ch'i; prev. Ti-hua. Xinjiang Uygur Zizhiqu, NW China
Urumtsi see Ürümqi
Urundi see Burundi
Urup, Ostrov 93 H4 island Kuril'skiye Ostrova, SE Russian Federation
Urusan see Ulsan
Urziceni 86 C5 Ialomiţa, SE Romania
Usa 88 E3 river NW Russian Federation
Uşak 94 B3 prev. Ushak. Uşak, W Turkey
Ushak see Uşak
Ushant see Ouessant, Île d'
Ushuaia 43 B8 Tierra del Fuego, S Argentina
Usinsk 88 E3 Respublika Komi, NW Russian Federation
Üsküb/Üsküp see Skopje
Usmas Ezers 84 B3 lake NW Latvia
Usol'ye-Sibirskoye 93 E4 Irkutskaya Oblast', C Russian Federation
Ussel 69 C5 Corrèze, C France
Ussuriysk 93 G5 prev. Nikol'sk, Nikol'sk-Ussuriyskiy, Voroshilov. Primorskiy Kray, SE Russian Federation
Ustica 75 B6 island S Italy
Ust'-Ilimsk 93 E4 Irkutskaya Oblast', C Russian Federation
Ústí nad Labem 76 A4 Ger. Aussig. Ústecký Kraj, NW Czech Republic
Ustinov see Izhevsk
Ustka 76 C2 Ger. Stolpmünde. Pomorskie, N Poland
Ust'-Kamchatsk 93 H2 Kamchatskaya Oblast', E Russian Federation
Ust'-Kamenogorsk 92 D5 Kaz. Öskemen. Vostochnyy Kazakhstan, E Kazakhstan
Ust'-Kut 93 E4 Irkutskaya Oblast', C Russian Federation
Ust'-Olenëk 93 E3 Respublika Sakha (Yakutiya), NE Russian Federation
Ustrzyki Dolne 77 E5 Podkarpackie, SE Poland
Ust'-Sysol'sk see Syktyvkar
Ust Urt see Ustyurt Plateau
Ustyurt Plateau 100 B1 var. Ust Urt, Uzb. Ustyurt Platosi. plateau Kazakhstan/Uzbekistan
Ustyurt Platosi see Ustyurt Plateau
Usulután 30 C3 Usulután, SE El Salvador
Usumacinta, Río 30 B1 river Guatemala/Mexico
Usumbura see Bujumbura
U.S./USA see United States of America
Utah 22 B4 off. State of Utah, also known as Beehive State, Mormon State. state W USA
Utah Lake 22 B4 lake Utah, W USA
Utena 84 C4 Utena, E Lithuania
Utica 19 F3 New York, NE USA
Utina see Udine
Utrecht 64 C4 Lat. Trajectum ad Rhenum. Utrecht, C Netherlands
Utsunomiya 109 D5 var. Utunomiya. Tochigi, Honshū, S Japan
Uttarakhand 113 E2 cultural region N India
Uttar Pradesh 113 E3 prev. United Provinces, United Provinces of Agra and Oudh. cultural region N India
Utunomiya see Utsunomiya
Uulu 84 D2 Pärnumaa, SW Estonia
Uummannaq 60 C3 var. Umanak, Umanaq. Kitaa, C Greenland
Uummannarsuaq see Nunap Isua
Uvalde 27 F4 Texas, SW USA
Uvaravichy 85 D7 Rus. Uvarovichi. Homyel'skaya Voblasts', SE Belarus
Uvarovichi see Uvaravichy
Uvea, Île 123 E4 island N Wallis and Futuna
Uvs Nuur 104 C1 var. Ozero Ubsu-Nur. lake Mongolia/Russian Federation
'Uwaynāt, Jabal al 66 A3 var. Jebel Uweinat. mountain Libya/Sudan
Uweinat, Jebel see 'Uwaynāt, Jabal al
Uyo 53 G5 Akwa Ibom, S Nigeria
Uyuni 39 F5 Potosí, W Bolivia
Uzbekistan 100 D2 off. Republic of Uzbekistan. country C Asia
Uzbekistan, Republic of see Uzbekistan
Uzhgorod see Uzhhorod
Uzhhorod 86 B2 Rus. Uzhgorod; prev. Ungvár. Zakarpats'ka Oblast', W Ukraine
Užice 78 D4 prev. Titovo Užice. Serbia, W Serbia

V

Vaal 56 D4 river C South Africa
Vaals 65 D6 Limburg, SE Netherlands
Vaasa 63 D5 Swe. Vasa; prev. Nikolainkaupunki. Länsi-Suomi, W Finland
Vaassen 64 D3 Gelderland, E Netherlands
Vác 77 C6 Ger. Waitzen. Pest, N Hungary
Vadodara 112 C4 prev. Baroda. Gujarāt, W India
Vaduz 72 E2 country capital W Liechtenstein
Vág see Váh
Vágbeszterce see Považská Bystrica
Váh 77 C5 Ger. Waag, Hung. Vág. river W Slovakia
Vähtjer see Gällivare
Väinameri 84 C2 prev. Muhu Väin, Ger. Moon-Sund. sea E Baltic Sea
Vajdahunyad see Hunedoara
Valachia see Wallachia
Valday 88 B4 Novgorodskaya Oblast', W Russian Federation
Valdecañas, Embalse de 70 D3 reservoir W Spain
Valdepeñas 71 E4 Castilla-La Mancha, C Spain
Valdés, Península 43 C6 peninsula SE Argentina
Valdez 14 C3 Alaska, USA
Valdia see Weldiya
Valdivia 43 B5 Los Lagos, C Chile
Val-d'Or 16 D4 Québec, SE Canada
Valdosta 21 E3 Georgia, SE USA
Valence 69 D5 anc. Valentia, Valentia Julia, Ventia. Drôme, E France
Valencia 71 F3 País Valenciano, E Spain
Valencia 24 D1 California, USA
Valencia 36 D1 Carabobo, N Venezuela
Valencia, Gulf of 71 F3 var. Gulf of Valencia. gulf E Spain
Valencia, Gulf of see Valencia, Golfo de
Valencia/València see País Valenciano
Valenciennes 68 D2 Nord, N France
Valentia see Valence, France
Valentia see País Valenciano
Valentia Julia see Valence
Valentine State see Oregon
Valera 36 C2 Trujillo, NW Venezuela
Valetta see Valletta
Valga 84 D3 Ger. Walk, Latv. Valka. Valgamaa, S Estonia
Valira 69 A8 river Andorra/Spain Europe
Valjevo 78 C4 Serbia, W Serbia
Valjok see Válljohka
Valka 84 D3 Ger. Walk. Valka, N Latvia
Valka see Valga
Valkenswaard 65 D5 Noord-Brabant, S Netherlands
Valladolid 29 H3 Yucatán, SE Mexico
Valladolid 70 D2 Castilla-León, NW Spain
Vall D'Uxó see La Vall D'Uixó
Valle de La Pascua 36 D2 Guárico, N Venezuela
Valledupar 36 B1 Cesar, N Colombia
Vallejo 25 B6 California, W USA
Vallenar 42 B3 Atacama, N Chile
Valletta 75 C8 prev. Valetta. country capital E Malta
Valley City 23 E2 North Dakota, N USA
Válljohka 62 D2 var. Valjok. Finnmark, N Norway
Valls 71 G2 Cataluña, NE Spain
Valmiera 84 D3 Est. Volmari, Ger. Wolmar. Valmiera, N Latvia
Valona see Vlorë
Valozhyn 85 C5 Pol. Wołożyn, Rus. Volozhin. Minskaya Voblasts', C Belarus
Valparaíso 42 B4 Valparaíso, C Chile
Valparaiso 18 C3 Indiana, N USA
Valverde del Camino 70 C4 Andalucía, S Spain
Van 95 F3 Van, E Turkey
Vanadzor 95 F2 prev. Kirovakan. N Armenia
Vancouver 14 D5 British Columbia, SW Canada
Vancouver 24 B3 Washington, NW USA
Vancouver Island 14 D5 island British Columbia, SW Canada
Vanda see Vantaa
Van Diemen Gulf 124 D2 gulf Northern Territory, N Australia
Van Diemen's Land see Tasmania
Vaner, Lake see Vänern
Vänern 63 B6 Eng. Lake Vaner; prev. Lake Vener. lake S Sweden
Vangaindrano 57 G4 Fianarantsoa, SE Madagascar
Van Horn 26 D3 Texas, SW USA
Lake Van 95 F3 Eng. Lake Van; anc. Thospitis. salt lake E Turkey
Van, Lake see Van Gölü
Vannes 68 A3 anc. Dariorigum. Morbihan, NW France
Vantaa 63 D6 Swe. Vanda. Etelä-Suomi, S Finland
Vanua Levu 123 E4 island N Fiji
Vanuatu 122 C4 off. Republic of Vanuatu; prev. New Hebrides. country SW Pacific Ocean
Vanuatu, Republic of see Vanuatu
Van Wert 18 C4 Ohio, N USA
Vapincum see Gap
Varakļāni 84 D4 Madona, C Latvia
Vārānasi 113 E3 prev. Banaras, Benares, hist. Kasi. Uttar Pradesh, N India
Varangerfjorden 62 E2 Lapp. Várjjatvuotna. fjord N Norway
Varangerhalvøya 62 D2 Lapp. Várnjárga. peninsula N Norway
Varannó see Vranov nad Topl'ou
Varasd see Varaždin
Varaždin 78 B2 Ger. Warasdin, Hung. Varasd. Varaždin, N Croatia
Varberg 63 B7 Halland, S Sweden
Vardar 79 E6 Gk. Axiós. river FYR Macedonia/Greece
Varde 63 A7 Ribe, W Denmark
Vareia see Logroño
Varėna 85 B5 Pol. Orany. Alytus, S Lithuania
Varese 74 B2 Lombardia, N Italy
Vârful Moldoveanu 86 B4 var. Moldoveanul; prev. Vîrful Moldoveanu. mountain C Romania
Várjjatvuotna see Varangerfjorden
Varkaus 63 E5 Itä-Suomi, C Finland
Varna 82 E2 prev. Stalin; anc. Odessus. Varna, E Bulgaria
Varnenski Zaliv 82 E2 prev. Stalinski Zaliv. bay E Bulgaria
Várnjárga see Varangerhalvøya
Varshava see Warszawa
Vasa see Vaasa
Vasilikí 83 A5 Lefkáda, Iónia Nisiá, Greece, C Mediterranean Sea
Vasilishki 85 B5 Pol. Wasiliszki. Hrodzyenskaya Voblasts', W Belarus
Vasil'kov see Vasyl'kiv
Vaslui 86 D4 Vaslui, C Romania
Västerås 63 C6 Västmanland, C Sweden
Vasyl'kiv 87 E2 var. Vasil'kov. Kyyivs'ka Oblast', N Ukraine
Vaté see Éfaté
Vatican City 75 A7 off. Vatican City. country S Europe
Vatican City see Vatican City

Vatnajökull – Watertown

Vatnajökull 61 E5 *glacier* SE Iceland
Vatter, Lake *see* Vättern
Vättern 63 B6 *Eng.* Lake Vatter; *prev.* Lake Vetter. *lake* S Sweden
Vaughn 26 D2 New Mexico, SW USA
Vaupés, Río 36 C4 *var.* Rio Uaupés. *river* Brazil/Colombia
Vava'u Group 123 E4 *island group* N Tonga
Vavuniya 110 D3 Northern Province, N Sri Lanka
Vawkavysk 85 B6 *Pol.* Wołkowysk, *Rus.* Volkovysk. Hrodzyenskaya Voblasts', W Belarus
Växjö 63 C7 *var.* Vexiö. Kronoberg, S Sweden
Vaygach, Ostrov 88 E2 *island* NW Russian Federation
Veendam 64 E2 Groningen, NE Netherlands
Veenendaal 64 D4 Utrecht, C Netherlands
Vega 62 B4 *island* C Norway
Veglia *see* Krk
Veisiejai 85 B5 Alytus, S Lithuania
Vejer de la Frontera 70 C5 Andalucía, S Spain
Veldhoven 65 D5 Noord-Brabant, S Netherlands
Velebit 78 A3 *mountain range* C Croatia
Velenje 73 E7 *Ger.* Wöllan. N Slovenia
Veles 79 E6 *Turk.* Köprülü. C FYR Macedonia
Velho *see* Porto Velho
Velika Kikinda *see* Kikinda
Velika Morava 78 D4 *var.* Glavn'a Morava, Morava, *Ger.* Grosse Morava. *river* C Serbia
Velikaya 91 G2 *river* NE Russian Federation
Veliki Bečkerek *see* Zrenjanin
Velikiye Luki 88 A4 Pskovskaya Oblast', W Russian Federation
Velikiy Novgorod 88 B4 *prev.* Novgorod. Novgorodskaya Oblast', W Russian Federation
Veliko Tŭrnovo 82 D2 *prev.* Tirnovo, Trnovo, Tŭrnovo. Veliko Tŭrnovo, N Bulgaria
Velingrad 82 C3 Pazardzhik, C Bulgaria
Veľký Krtíš 77 D6 Banskobystrický Kraj, C Slovakia
Vellore 110 C2 Tamil Nādu, SE India
Velobriga *see* Viana do Castelo
Velsen *see* Velsen-Noord
Velsen-Noord 64 C3 *var.* Velsen. Noord-Holland, W Netherlands
Vel'sk 88 C4 *var.* Velsk. Arkhangel'skaya Oblast', NW Russian Federation
Velykyy Tokmak *see* Tokmak
Vendôme 68 C4 Loir-et-Cher, C France
Venedig *see* Venezia
Vener, Lake *see* Vänern
Venetia *see* Venezia
Venezia 74 C2 *Eng.* Venice, *Fr.* Venise, *Ger.* Venedig; *anc.* Venetia. Veneto, NE Italy
Venezia, Golfo di *see* Venice, Gulf of
Venezuela 36 D2 *off.* Republic of Venezuela; *prev.* Estados Unidos de Venezuela, United States of Venezuela. *country* N South America
Venezuela, Estados Unidos de *see* Venezuela
Venezuela, Gulf of 36 C1 *Eng.* Gulf of Maracaibo, Gulf of Venezuela. *gulf* NW Venezuela
Venezuela, Gulf of *see* Venezuela, Golfo de
Venezuelan Basin 34 B1 *undersea basin* E Caribbean Sea
Venezuela, Republic of *see* Venezuela
Venezuela, United States of *see* Venezuela
Venice 20 C4 Louisiana, S USA
Venice *see* Venezia
Venice, Gulf of 74 C2 *It.* Golfo di Venezia, *Slvn.* Beneški Zaliv. *gulf* N Adriatic Sea
Venise *see* Venezia
Venlo 65 D5 *prev.* Venloo. Limburg, SE Netherlands
Venloo *see* Venlo
Venta 84 B3 *Ger.* Windau. *river* Latvia/Lithuania
Venta Belgarum *see* Winchester
Ventia *see* Valence
Ventimiglia 74 A3 Liguria, NW Italy
Ventspils 84 B2 *Ger.* Windau. Ventspils, NW Latvia
Vera 42 D3 Santa Fe, C Argentina
Veracruz 29 F4 *var.* Veracruz Llave. Veracruz-Llave, E Mexico
Veracruz Llave *see* Veracruz
Vercellae *see* Vercelli
Vercelli 74 A2 *anc.* Vercellae. Piemonte, NW Italy
Verdal *see* Verdalsøra
Verdalsøra 62 B4 *var.* Verdal. Nord-Trøndelag, C Norway
Verde, Cabo *see* Cape Verde
Verde, Costa 70 D1 *coastal region* N Spain
Verden 72 B3 Niedersachsen, NW Germany
Veria *see* Véroia
Verkhnedvinsk *see* Vyerkhnyadzvinsk
Verkhneudinsk *see* Ulan-Ude
Verkhoyanskiy Khrebet 93 F3 *mountain range* NE Russian Federation
Vermillion 23 F3 South Dakota, N USA
Vermont 19 F2 *off.* State of Vermont, *also known as* Green Mountain State. *state* NE USA
Vernal 22 B4 Utah, W USA
Vernon 27 F2 Texas, SW USA
Verőcze *see* Virovitica
Véroia 82 B4 *var.* Veria, Vérroia, *Turk.* Karaferiye. Kentrikí Makedonía, N Greece
Verona 74 C2 Veneto, NE Italy
Vérroia *see* Véroia
Versailles 68 D1 Yvelines, N France
Versecz *see* Vršac
Verulamium *see* St Albans
Verviers 65 D6 Liège, E Belgium
Vesdre 65 D6 *river* E Belgium
Veselinovo 82 D2 Shumen, NE Bulgaria
Vesontio *see* Besançon
Vesoul 68 D4 *anc.* Vesulium, Vesulum. Haute-Saône, E France
Vesterålen 62 B2 *island group* N Norway
Vestfjorden 62 C3 *fjord* C Norway
Vestmannaeyjar 61 E5 Sudhurland, S Iceland
Vesulium/Vesulum *see* Vesoul
Vesuna *see* Périgueux
Vesuvius 75 D5 *Eng.* Vesuvius. *volcano* S Italy
Vesuvius *see* Vesuvio
Veszprém 77 C7 *Ger.* Veszprim. Veszprém, W Hungary
Veszprim *see* Veszprém
Vetrino 82 E2 Varna, E Bulgaria
Vetrino *see* Vyetryna
Vetter, Lake *see* Vättern
Veurne 65 A5 *var.* Furnes. West-Vlaanderen, W Belgium
Vexiö *see* Växjö
Viacha 39 F4 La Paz, W Bolivia
Viana de Castelo *see* Viana do Castelo
Viana do Castelo 70 B2 *var.* Viana de Castelo; *anc.* Velobriga. Viana do Castelo, NW Portugal
Vianen 64 C4 Utrecht, C Netherlands
Viangchan 114 C4 *Eng./Fr.* Vientiane. *country capital* C Laos
Viangphoukha 114 C3 *var.* Vieng Pou Kha. Louang Namtha, N Laos
Viareggio 74 B3 Toscana, C Italy
Viborg 63 A7 Viborg, NW Denmark
Vic 71 G2 *var.* Vich; *anc.* Ausa, Vicus Ausonensis. Cataluña, NE Spain
Vicentia *see* Vicenza
Vicenza 74 C2 *anc.* Vicentia. Veneto, NE Italy
Vich *see* Vic
Vichy 69 C5 Allier, C France
Vicksburg 20 B2 Mississippi, S USA
Victoria 57 H1 *country capital* Mahé, SW Seychelles
Victoria 14 D5 *province capital* Vancouver Island, British Columbia, SW Canada
Victoria 80 A5 *var.* Rabat. Gozo, NW Malta
Victoria 27 G4 Texas, SW USA
Victoria 127 C7 *state* SE Australia
Victoria *see* Masvingo, Zimbabwe
Victoria Bank *see* Vitória Seamount
Victoria de Durango *see* Durango
Victoria de las Tunas *see* Las Tunas
Victoria Falls 56 C3 Matabeleland North, W Zimbabwe
Victoria Falls 56 C2 *waterfall* Zambia/Zimbabwe
Victoria Falls *see* Iguaçu, Salto do
Victoria Island 15 F3 *island* Northwest Territories/Nunavut, NW Canada
Victoria, Lake 51 B6 *var.* Victoria Nyanza. *lake* E Africa
Victoria Land 132 C4 *physical region* Antarctica
Victoria Nyanza *see* Victoria, Lake
Victoria River 124 D3 *river* Northern Territory, N Australia
Victorville 25 C7 California, W USA
Vicus Ausonensis *see* Vic
Vicus Elbii *see* Viterbo
Vidalia 21 E2 Georgia, SE USA
Videm-Krško *see* Krško
Vídeň *see* Wien
Vidin 82 B1 *anc.* Bononia. Vidin, NW Bulgaria
Vidzy 85 C5 Vitsyebskaya Voblasts', NW Belarus
Viedma 43 C5 Río Negro, E Argentina
Vieng Pou Kha *see* Viangphoukha
Vienna *see* Wien, Austria
Vienna *see* Vienne, France
Vienne 69 D5 *anc.* Vienna. Isère, E France
Vienne 68 B4 *river* W France
Vientiane *see* Viangchan
Vientos, Paso de los *see* Windward Passage
Vierzon 68 C4 Cher, C France
Viesīte 84 C4 *Ger.* Eckengraf. Jēkabpils, S Latvia
Vietnam 114 D4 *off.* Socialist Republic of Vietnam, *Vtn.* Công Hoa Xa Hôi Chu Nghia Việt Nam. *country* SE Asia
Vietnam, Socialist Republic of *see* Vietnam
Vietri *see* Viêt Tri
Viêt Tri 114 D3 *var.* Vietri. Vinh Phu, N Vietnam
Vieux Fort 33 F2 S Saint Lucia
Vigo 70 B2 Galicia, NW Spain
Viipuri *see* Vyborg
Vijayawāda 110 D1 *prev.* Bezwada. Andhra Pradesh, SE India
Vila *see* Port-Vila
Vila Artur de Paiva *see* Cubango
Vila da Ponte *see* Cubango
Vila de João Belo *see* Xai-Xai
Vila de Mocímboa da Praia *see* Mocímboa da Praia
Vila do Conde 70 B2 Porto, NW Portugal
Vila do Zumbo 56 D2 *prev.* Vila do Zumbu, Zumbo. Tete, NW Mozambique
Vila do Zumbu *see* Vila do Zumbo
Vilafranca del Penedès 71 G2 *var.* Villafranca del Panadés. Cataluña, NE Spain
Vila General Machado *see* Camacupa
Vila Henrique de Carvalho *see* Saurimo
Viļaka 84 D4 *Ger.* Marienhausen. Balvi, NE Latvia
Vilalba 70 C1 Galicia, NW Spain
Vila Marechal Carmona *see* Uíge
Vila Nova de Gaia 70 B2 Porto, NW Portugal
Vila Nova de Portimão *see* Portimão
Vila Pereira de Eça *see* N'Giva
Vila Real 70 C2 *var.* Vila Rial. Vila Real, N Portugal
Vila Rial *see* Vila Real
Vila Robert Williams *see* Caála
Vila Salazar *see* N'Dalatando
Vila Serpa Pinto *see* Menongue
Vileyka *see* Vilyeyka
Vilhelmina 62 C4 Västerbotten, N Sweden
Vilhena 40 D3 Rondônia, W Brazil
Vília 83 C5 Attikí, C Greece
Viliya 85 C5 *Lith.* Neris. *river* W Belarus
Viliya *see* Neris
Viljandi 84 D2 *Ger.* Fellin. Viljandimaa, S Estonia
Vilkaviškis 84 B4 *Pol.* Wyłkowyszki. Marijampolė, SW Lithuania
Villa Acuña 28 D2 *var.* Ciudad Acuña. Coahuila de Zaragoza, NE Mexico
Villa Bella 39 F2 Beni, N Bolivia
Villacarrillo 71 E4 Andalucía, S Spain
Villa Cecilia *see* Ciudad Madero
Villach 73 D7 *Slvn.* Beljak. Kärnten, S Austria
Villacidro 75 A5 Sardegna, Italy, C Mediterranean Sea
Villa Concepción *see* Concepción
Villa del Pilar *see* Pilar
Villafranca de los Barros 70 C4 Extremadura, W Spain
Villafranca del Panadés *see* Vilafranca del Penedès
Villahermosa 29 G4 *prev.* San Juan Bautista. Tabasco, SE Mexico
Villajoyosa 71 F4 *Cat.* La Vila Joiosa. País Valenciano, E Spain
Villa María 42 C4 Córdoba, C Argentina
Villa Martín 39 F5 Potosí, SW Bolivia
Villa Mercedes 42 C4 San Juan, Argentina
Villanueva 28 D3 Zacatecas, C Mexico
Villanueva de la Serena 70 C3 Extremadura, W Spain
Villanueva de los Infantes 71 E4 Castilla-La Mancha, C Spain
Villarrica 42 D2 Guairá, SE Paraguay
Villavicencio 36 B3 Meta, C Colombia
Villaviciosa 70 D1 Asturias, N Spain
Villazón 39 G5 Potosí, S Bolivia
Villena 71 F4 País Valenciano, E Spain
Villeurbanne 69 D5 Rhône, E France
Villingen-Schwenningen 73 B6 Baden-Württemberg, S Germany
Villmanstrand *see* Lappeenranta
Vilna *see* Vilnius
Vilnius 85 C5 *Pol.* Wilno, *Ger.* Wilna; *prev. Rus.* Vilna. *country capital* Vilnius, SE Lithuania
Vil'shanka 87 E3 *Rus.* Ol'shanka. Kirovohrads'ka Oblast', C Ukraine
Vilvoorde 65 C6 *Fr.* Vilvorde. Vlaams Brabant, C Belgium
Vilvorde *see* Vilvoorde
Vilyeyka 85 C5 *Pol.* Wilejka, *Rus.* Vileyka. Minskaya Voblasts', NW Belarus
Vilyuy 93 F3 *river* NE Russian Federation
Viña del Mar 42 B4 Valparaíso, C Chile
Vinaròs 71 F3 País Valenciano, E Spain
Vincennes 18 B4 Indiana, N USA
Vindhya Mountains *see* Vindhya Range
Vindhya Range 112 D4 *var.* Vindhya Mountains. *mountain range* N India
Vindobona *see* Wien
Vineland 19 F4 New Jersey, NE USA
Vinh 114 D4 Nghê An, N Vietnam
Vinh Loi *see* Bac Liêu
Vinishte 82 C2 Montana, NW Bulgaria
Vinita 27 G1 Oklahoma, C USA
Vinkovci 78 C3 *Ger.* Winkowitz, *Hung.* Vinkovcze. Vukovar-Srijem, E Croatia
Vinkovcze *see* Vinkovci
Vinnitsa *see* Vinnytsya
Vinnytsya 86 D2 *Rus.* Vinnitsa. Vinnyts'ka Oblast', C Ukraine
Vinogradov *see* Vynohradiv
Vinson Massif 132 A3 *mountain* Antarctica
Viranşehir 95 E4 Şanlıurfa, SE Turkey
Vîrful Moldoveanu *see* Vârful Moldoveanu
Virginia 23 G1 Minnesota, N USA
Virginia 19 E5 *off.* Commonwealth of Virginia, *also known as* Mother of Presidents, Mother of States, Old Dominion. *state* NE USA
Virginia Beach 19 F5 Virginia, NE USA
Virgin Islands *see* British Virgin Islands
Virgin Islands (US) 33 F3 *var.* Virgin Islands of the United States; *prev.* Danish West Indies. *US unincorporated territory* E West Indies
Virgin Islands of the United States *see* Virgin Islands (US)
Virôchey 115 E5 Rôtânôkiri, NE Cambodia
Virovitica 78 C2 *Ger.* Virovititz, *Hung.* Verőcze; *prev. Ger.* Werowitz. Virovitica-Podravina, NE Croatia
Virovititz *see* Virovitica
Virton 65 D8 Luxembourg, SE Belgium
Virtsu 84 D2 *Ger.* Werder. Läänemaa, W Estonia
Vis 78 B4 *It.* Lissa; *anc.* Issa. *island* S Croatia
Vis *see* Fish
Visaginas 84 C4 *prev.* Sniečkus. Utena, E Lithuania
Visākhapatnam 113 E5 *var.* Vishakhapatnam. Andhra Pradesh, SE India
Visalia 25 C6 California, W USA
Visby 63 C7 *Ger.* Wisby. Gotland, SE Sweden
Viscount Melville Sound 15 F2 *prev.* Melville Sound. *sound* Northwest Territories, N Canada
Visé 65 D6 Liège, E Belgium
Viseu 70 C2 *prev.* Vizeu. Viseu, N Portugal
Vishakhapatnam *see* Visākhapatnam
Vislinskiy Zaliv *see* Vistula Lagoon
Visoko 78 C4 Federacija Bosna I Hercegovina, C Bosnia and Herzegovina
Visttasjohka 62 D3 *river* N Sweden
Vistula 76 C2 *Eng.* Vistula, *Ger.* Weichsel. *river* C Poland
Vistula *see* Wisła
Vistula Lagoon 76 C2 *Ger.* Frisches Haff, *Pol.* Zalew Wiślany, *Rus.* Vislinskiy Zaliv. *lagoon* Poland/Russian Federation
Vitebsk *see* Vitsyebsk
Viterbo 74 C4 *anc.* Vicus Elbii. Lazio, C Italy
Viti *see* Fiji
Viti Levu 123 E4 *island* W Fiji
Vitim 93 F4 *river* C Russian Federation
Vitória 41 F4 *state capital* Espírito Santo, SE Brazil
Vitoria *see* Vitoria-Gasteiz
Vitoria Bank *see* Vitória Seamount
Vitória da Conquista 41 F3 Bahia, E Brazil
Vitoria-Gasteiz 71 E1 *var.* Vitoria, *Eng.* Vittoria. País Vasco, N Spain
Vitória Seamount 45 B5 *var.* Victoria Bank, Vitoria Bank. *seamount* C Atlantic Ocean
Vitré 68 B3 Ille-et-Vilaine, NW France
Vitsyebsk 85 E5 *Rus.* Vitebsk. Vitsyebskaya Voblasts', NE Belarus
Vittoria 75 C7 Sicilia, Italy, C Mediterranean Sea
Vittoria *see* Vitoria-Gasteiz
Vizcaya, Golfo de *see* Biscay, Bay of
Vizianagaram 113 E5 *var.* Vizianagram. Andhra Pradesh, E India
Vizianagram *see* Vizianagaram
Vjosës, Lumi i 79 C7 *var.* Vijosa, Vijosë, *Gk.* Aóos. *river* Albania/Greece
Vlaanderen *see* Flanders
Vlaardingen 64 B4 Zuid-Holland, SW Netherlands
Vladikavkaz 89 B8 *prev.* Dzaudzhikau, Ordzhonikidze. Respublika Severnaya Osetiya, SW Russian Federation
Vladimir 89 B5 Vladimirskaya Oblast', W Russian Federation
Vladimirovka *see* Yuzhno-Sakhalinsk
Vladimir-Volynskiy *see* Volodymyr-Volyns'kyy
Vladivostok 93 G5 Primorskiy Kray, SE Russian Federation
Vlagtwedde 64 E2 Groningen, NE Netherlands
Vlasotince 79 E5 Serbia, SE Serbia
Vlieland 64 C1 *Fris.* Flylân. *island* Waddeneilanden, N Netherlands
Vlijmen 64 C4 Noord-Brabant, S Netherlands
Vlissingen 65 B5 *Eng.* Flushing, *Fr.* Flessingue. Zeeland, SW Netherlands
Vlodava *see* Włodawa
Vlonë/Vlora *see* Vlorë
Vlorë 79 C7 *prev.* Vlonë, *It.* Valona, Vlora. Vlorë, SW Albania
Vlotslavsk *see* Włocławek
Vöcklabruck 73 D6 Oberösterreich, NW Austria
Vogelkop *see* Doberai, Jazirah
Vohimena, Tanjona 57 F4 *Fr.* Cap Sainte Marie. *headland* S Madagascar
Voiron 69 D5 Isère, E France
Vojvodina 78 D3 *Ger.* Wojwodina. Vojvodina, N Serbia
Volga 89 B7 *river* NW Russian Federation
Volga Uplands 59 G3 *var.* Volga Uplands. *mountain range* W Russian Federation
Volga Uplands *see* Privolzhskaya Vozvyshennost'
Volgodonsk 89 B7 Rostovskaya Oblast', SW Russian Federation
Volgograd 89 B7 *prev.* Stalingrad, Tsaritsyn. Volgogradskaya Oblast', SW Russian Federation
Volkhov 88 B4 Leningradskaya Oblast', NW Russian Federation
Volkovysk *see* Vawkavysk
Volmari *see* Valmiera
Volnovakha 87 G3 Donets'ka Oblast', SE Ukraine
Volodymyr-Volyns'kyy 86 C1 *Pol.* Włodzimierz, *Rus.* Vladimir-Volynskiy. Volyns'ka Oblast', NW Ukraine
Vologda 88 B4 Vologodskaya Oblast', W Russian Federation
Vólos 83 B5 Thessalía, C Greece
Volozhin *see* Valozhyn
Vol'sk 89 C6 Saratovskaya Oblast', W Russian Federation
Volta 53 E5 *river* SE Ghana
Volta Blanche *see* White Volta
Volta, Lake 53 E5 *reservoir* SE Ghana
Volta Noire *see* Black Volta
Volturno 75 D5 *river* S Italy
Volunteer Island *see* Starbuck Island
Volzhskiy 89 B6 Volgogradskaya Oblast', SW Russian Federation
Võnnu 84 E3 *Ger.* Wendau. Tartumaa, SE Estonia
Voorst 64 D3 Gelderland, E Netherlands
Voranava 85 C5 *Pol.* Werenów, *Rus.* Voronovo. Hrodzyenskaya Voblasts', W Belarus
Vorderrhein 73 B7 *river* SE Switzerland
Vóreioi Sporádes *see* Vóreies Sporádes
Vórioi Sporádhes *see* Vóreies Sporádes
Vorkuta 92 C2 Respublika Komi, NW Russian Federation
Vormsi 84 C2 *var.* Vormsi Saar, *Ger.* Worms, *Swed.* Ormsö. *island* W Estonia
Vormsi Saar *see* Vormsi
Voronezh 89 B6 Voronezhskaya Oblast', W Russian Federation
Voronovo *see* Voranava
Voroshilov *see* Ussuriysk
Voroshilovgrad *see* Luhans'k, Ukraine
Voroshilovsk *see* Stavropol', Russian Federation
Võru 84 D3 *Ger.* Werro. Võrumaa, SE Estonia
Vosges 68 E4 *mountain range* NE France
Vostochnyy Sayan *see* Eastern Sayans
Vostock Island *see* Vostok Island
Vostok 132 C3 *Russian research station* Antarctica
Vostok Island 123 G3 *var.* Vostock Island; *prev.* Stavers Island. *island* Line Islands, SE Kiribati
Voznesens'k 87 E3 *Rus.* Voznesensk. Mykolayivs'ka Oblast', S Ukraine
Vranje 79 E5 Serbia, SE Serbia
Vranov *see* Vranov nad Topl'ou
Vranov nad Topľou 77 D5 *var.* Vranov, *Hung.* Varannó. Prešovský Kraj, E Slovakia
Vratsa 82 C2 Vratsa, NW Bulgaria
Vrbas 78 C3 Vojvodina, NW Serbia
Vrbas 78 C3 *river* N Bosnia and Herzegovina
Vršac 78 E3 *Ger.* Werschetz, *Hung.* Versecz. Vojvodina, NE Serbia
Vsetín 77 C5 *Ger.* Wsetin. Zlínský Kraj, E Czech Republic
Vučitrn *see* Vushtrri
Vukovar 78 C3 *Hung.* Vukovár. Vukovar-Srijem, E Croatia
Vulcano, Isola 75 C7 *island* Isole Eolie, S Italy
Vung Tau 115 E6 *prev. Fr.* Cape Saint Jacques, Cap Saint-Jacques. Ba Ria-Vung Tau, S Vietnam
Vushtrri 79 D5 *Serb.* Vučitrn. N Kosovo
Vyatka 89 C5 *river* NW Russian Federation
Vyatka *see* Kirov
Vyborg 88 B3 *Fin.* Viipuri. Leningradskaya Oblast', NW Russian Federation
Vyerkhnyadzvinsk 85 D5 *Rus.* Verkhnedvinsk. Vitsyebskaya Voblasts', N Belarus
Vyetryna 85 D5 *Rus.* Vetrino. Vitsyebskaya Voblasts', N Belarus
Vynohradiv 86 B3 *Cz.* Sevluš, *Hung.* Nagyszöllös, *Rus.* Vinogradov; *prev.* Sevlyush. Zakarpats'ka Oblast', W Ukraine

W

Wa 53 E4 NW Ghana
Waag *see* Váh
Waagbistritz *see* Považská Bystrica
Waal 64 C4 *river* S Netherlands
Wabash 18 C4 Indiana, N USA
Wabash River 18 B5 *river* N USA
Waco 27 G3 Texas, SW USA
Wad Al-Hajarah *see* Guadalajara
Waddān 49 F3 NW Libya
Waddenzee 64 C1 *var.* Wadden Zee. *sea* SE North Sea
Wadden Zee *see* Waddenzee
Waddington, Mount 14 D5 *mountain* British Columbia, SW Canada
Wādī as Sīr 97 B6 *var.* Wadi es Sir. 'Ammān, NW Jordan
Wadi es Sir *see* Wādī as Sīr
Wadi Halfa 50 B3 *var.* Wādī Ḥalfā'. Northern, N Sudan
Wādī Mūsā 97 B7 *var.* Petra. Ma'ān, S Jordan
Wad Madanī *see* Wad Medani
Wad Medani 50 C4 *var.* Wad Madanī. Gezira, C Sudan
Waflia 117 F4 Pulau Buru, E Indonesia
Wagadugu *see* Ouagadougou
Wagga Wagga 127 C7 New South Wales, SE Australia
Wagin 125 B7 Western Australia
Wāh 112 C1 Punjab, NE Pakistan
Wahai 117 F4 Pulau Seram, E Indonesia
Wahaybah, Ramlat Al *see* Wahībah, Ramlat Āl
Wahiawā 25 A8 *var.* Wahiawa. O'ahu, Hawaii, USA, C Pacific Ocean
Wahībah, Ramlat Ahl *see* Wahībah, Ramlat Āl
Wahībah Sands 99 E5 *var.* Ramlat Ahl Wahībah, Ramlat Al Wahaybah, *Eng.* Wahibah Sands. *desert* N Oman
Wahībah Sands *see* Wahībah, Ramlat Āl
Wahpeton 23 F2 North Dakota, N USA
Wahran *see* Oran
Waiau 129 A7 *river* South Island, New Zealand
Waigeo, Pulau 117 G4 *island* Maluku, E Indonesia
Waikaremoana, Lake 128 E4 *lake* North Island, New Zealand
Wailuku 25 B8 Maui, Hawaii, USA, C Pacific Ocean
Waimate 129 B6 Canterbury, South Island, New Zealand
Waiouru 128 D4 Manawatu-Wanganui, North Island, New Zealand
Waipara 129 C6 Canterbury, South Island, New Zealand
Waipawa 128 E4 Hawke's Bay, North Island, New Zealand
Waipukurau 128 D4 Hawke's Bay, North Island, New Zealand
Wairau 129 C5 *river* South Island, New Zealand
Wairoa 128 E4 Hawke's Bay, North Island, New Zealand
Wairoa 128 D2 *river* North Island, New Zealand
Waitaki 129 B6 *river* South Island, New Zealand
Waitara 128 D4 Taranaki, North Island, New Zealand
Waitzen *see* Vác
Waiuku 128 D3 Auckland, North Island, New Zealand
Wakasa-wan 109 C6 *bay* C Japan
Wakatipu, Lake 129 A7 *lake* South Island, New Zealand
Wakayama 109 C6 Wakayama, Honshū, SW Japan
Wake Island 130 C2 *US unincorporated territory* NW Pacific Ocean
Wake Island 120 D1 *atoll* NW Pacific Ocean
Wakkanai 108 C1 Hokkaidō, NE Japan
Walachei/Walachia *see* Wallachia
Wałbrzych 76 B4 *Ger.* Waldenburg, Waldenburg in Schlesien. Dolnośląskie, SW Poland
Walcourt 65 C7 Namur, S Belgium
Wałcz 76 B3 *Ger.* Deutsch Krone. Zachodnio-pomorskie, NW Poland
Waldenburg/Waldenburg in Schlesien *see* Wałbrzych
Waldia *see* Weldiya
Wales 14 C2 Alaska, USA
Wales 67 C6 *Wel.* Cymru. *cultural region* Wales, United Kingdom
Walgett 127 D5 New South Wales, SE Australia
Walk *see* Valga, Estonia
Walk *see* Valka, Latvia
Walker Lake 25 C5 *lake* Nevada, W USA
Wallachia 86 B5 *var.* Walachia, *Ger.* Walachei, *Rom.* Valachia. *cultural region* S Romania
Walla Walla 24 C2 Washington, NW USA
Wallenthal *see* Haţeg
Wallis and Futuna 123 E4 *Fr.* Territoire de Wallis et Futuna. *French overseas territory* C Pacific Ocean
Wallis et Futuna, Territoire de *see* Wallis and Futuna
Walnut Ridge 20 B1 Arkansas, C USA
Waltenberg *see* Zalău
Walthamstow 67 B7 Waltham Forest, SE England, United Kingdom
Walvisbaai *see* Walvis Bay
Walvis Bay 56 A4 *Afr.* Walvisbaai. Erongo, NW Namibia
Walvish Ridge *see* Walvis Ridge
Walvis Ridge 47 B7 *var.* Walvish Ridge. *undersea ridge* E Atlantic Ocean
Wan *see* Anhui
Wanaka 129 B6 Otago, South Island, New Zealand
Wanaka, Lake 129 A6 *lake* South Island, New Zealand
Wanchuan *see* Zhangjiakou
Wandel Sea 61 E1 *sea* Arctic Ocean
Wandsworth 67 A8 Wandsworth, SE England, United Kingdom
Wanganui 128 D4 Manawatu-Wanganui, North Island, New Zealand
Wangaratta 127 C7 Victoria, SE Australia
Wankie *see* Hwange
Wanki, Río *see* Coco, Río
Wanlaweyn 51 D6 *var.* Wanle Weyn, *It.* Uanle Uen. Shabeellaha Hoose, SW Somalia
Wanle Weyn *see* Wanlaweyn
Wanxian *see* Wanzhou
Wanzhou 106 B5 *var.* Wanxian. Chongqing Shi, C China
Warangal 113 E5 Andhra Pradesh, C India
Warasdin *see* Varaždin
Warburg 72 B4 Nordrhein-Westfalen, W Germany
Ware 15 E4 British Columbia, W Canada
Waremme 65 C6 Liège, E Belgium
Waren 72 C3 Mecklenburg-Vorpommern, NE Germany
Wargla *see* Ouargla
Warkworth 128 D2 Auckland, North Island, New Zealand
Warnemünde 72 C2 Mecklenburg-Vorpommern, NE Germany
Warner 27 G1 Oklahoma, C USA
Warnes 39 G4 Santa Cruz, C Bolivia
Warrego River 127 C5 *seasonal river* New South Wales/Queensland, E Australia
Warren 18 D3 Michigan, N USA
Warren 18 D3 Ohio, N USA
Warren 19 E3 Pennsylvania, NE USA
Warri 53 F5 Delta, S Nigeria
Warrnambool 127 B7 Victoria, SE Australia
Warsaw/Warschau *see* Warszawa
Warszawa 76 D3 *Eng.* Warsaw, *Ger.* Warschau, *Rus.* Varshava. *country capital* Mazowieckie, C Poland
Warta 76 B3 *Ger.* Warthe. *river* W Poland
Wartberg *see* Senec
Warthe *see* Warta
Warwick 127 E5 Queensland, E Australia
Washington 22 A2 NE England, United Kingdom
Washington DC 19 E4 *country capital* District of Columbia, NE USA
Washington Island *see* Teraina
Washington, Mount 19 G2 *mountain* New Hampshire, NE USA
Wash, The 67 E6 *inlet* E England, United Kingdom
Wasiliszki *see* Vasilishki
Waspam 31 E2 *var.* Waspán. Región Autónoma Atlántico Norte, NE Nicaragua
Waspán *see* Waspam
Watampone 117 E4 *var.* Bone. Sulawesi, C Indonesia
Watenstedt-Salzgitter *see* Salzgitter
Waterbury 19 F3 Connecticut, NE USA
Waterford 67 B6 *Ir.* Port Láirge. Waterford, S Ireland
Waterloo 23 G3 Iowa, C USA
Watertown 19 F2 New York, NE USA
Watertown 23 F2 South Dakota, N USA